South India
& Kerala

Maharashtra
p82

◉
**Mumbai
(Bombay)**
p42

**Telangana &
Andhra Pradesh**
p226

Goa
p118

**Karnataka &
Bengaluru**
p170

**Andaman
Islands**
p408

Kerala
p262

**Tamil Nadu &
Chennai**
p324

THIS EDITION WRITTEN AND RESEARCHED BY
John Noble
Abigail Blasi, Paul Harding, Trent Holden, Isabella Noble, Iain Stewart

THALI P464

DAULATABAD P92

DECORATIONS FOR PONGAL
FESTIVAL, TAMIL NADU P327

GRAHAM CROUCH / GETTY IMAGES ©

KEREN SU / GETTY IMAGES ©

RELIGIOUS IMAGES/UIG / GETTY IMAGES ©

Contents

Welcome to South India & Kerala

Like a giant wedge plunging into the Indian Ocean, South India is the subcontinent's steamy heartland - a lush contrast to the peaks and plains of the North.

A Fabulous Heritage

Wherever you go in the south you'll be bumping into the magnificent relics of the splendid civilisations that have inhabited this land over two millennia – the amazing rock-cut shrines carved out by Buddhists, Hindus and Jains at Ajanta and Ellora; the palaces, tombs, forts and mosques of Muslim dynasties on the Deccan; Tamil Nadu's inspired Pallava sculptures and towering Chola temples; the magical ruins of the Vijayanagar capital at Hampi... and a whole lot more. It's a diverse cultural treasure trove with few parallels.

Luscious Landscapes

South India's thousands of kilometres of coastline frame fertile plains and rolling hills – a landscape that changes constantly as you travel and is kept glisteningly green by the double-barrelled monsoon. The palm-strung strands and inland waterways of the west give way to spice gardens, tea plantations, tropical forests and cool hill-station retreats in the Western Ghats. The drier Deccan 'plateau' is far from flat, being crossed by numerous hilly ranges and spattered with dramatic outcrops often topped by picturesque old forts. And across the region, wild forests are preserved as parks and sanctuaries, where you can seek out wildlife from elephants and tigers to monkeys and sloth bears.

City Spice

South India's vibrant cities are the pulse of a country that is fast-forwarding through the 21st century while also at times seemingly stuck in the Middle Ages. From in-yer-face Mumbai (Bombay) or increasingly sophisticated Chennai (Madras) to historic Hyderabad, IT capital Bengaluru (Bangalore) and the colonial-era quaintness of Kochi (Cochin) and Puducherry (Pondicherry), southern cities are great for browsing teeming markets and colourful boutiques. And, of course, for indulging in a smorgasbord of their cuisines, whether you fancy simple southern favourites such as *idlis* (spongy rice cakes) and dosas (savoury crêpes), spicy west-coast seafood curries, Mughal-influenced biryanis or inventive fusion creations in chic city dining haunts.

Soul Stirring

Spirituality weaves its way throughout the vast and complex tapestry that is contemporary India. The multitude of sacred sites, spectacular festivals and time-honoured rituals are testament to a long, colourful, sometimes tumultuous religious history. Soak it all up at massed Hindu pilgrimage temples or tranquil hilltop shrines, and feel the centuries of tradition at ancient Buddhist caves or big city mosques. And if you like, become part of it all with some meditation or yoga in the land of yoga's birth.

Why I Love South India

By John Noble, Writer

When I wake of a morning in South India, there's only one certainty about the day ahead: it will never, ever be dull. Extremes of poverty and wealth may confront, and the crush of humanity and traffic exasperate, but in between times I'll be experiencing people, scenery, colour, buildings, *life* – the like of which I won't encounter in any other country in the world. The biggest risk of travelling here, whether in Tamil Nadu's heaving temple towns, Kerala's lazy backwaters or Mumbai's frenzied bazaars, is that the rest of the world can seem so sadly routine afterwards.

For more about our writers, see page 544

Above: Fishermen, Kovalam (p270), Kerala

South India & Kerala

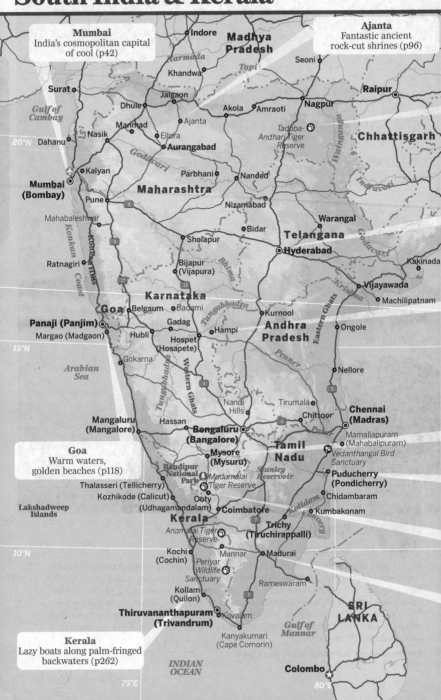

Mumbai
India's cosmopolitan capital of cool (p42)

Ajanta
Fantastic ancient rock-cut shrines (p96)

Goa
Warm waters, golden beaches (p118)

Kerala
Lazy boats along palm-fringed backwaters (p262)

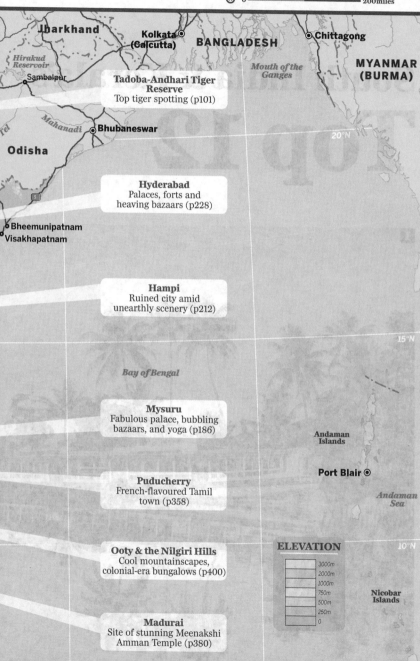

Jharkhand

Kolkata ◉
(Calcutta)

BANGLADESH

◉ Chittagong

Hirakud Reservoir

Sambalpur

Mouth of the Ganges

MYANMAR (BURMA)

Mahanadi

Tadoba-Andhari Tiger Reserve
Top tiger spotting (p101)

Tel

Bhubaneswar ◉

20°N

Odisha

Hyderabad
Palaces, forts and
heaving bazaars (p228)

◉ Bheemunipatnam
Visakhapatnam

Hampi
Ruined city amid
unearthly scenery (p212)

15°N

Bay of Bengal

Mysuru
Fabulous palace, bubbling
bazaars, and yoga (p186)

Andaman Islands

Puducherry
French-flavoured Tamil
town (p358)

Port Blair ◉

Andaman Sea

Ooty & the Nilgiri Hills
Cool mountainscapes,
colonial-era bungalows (p400)

10°N

ELEVATION

	3000m
	2000m
	1000m
	750m
	500m
	250m
	0

Nicobar Islands

Madurai
Site of stunning Meenakshi
Amman Temple (p380)

85°E

90°E

South India & Kerala's
Top 12

Kerala's Beautiful Backwaters

1 It's not every day you come across a place as sublime as Kerala's backwaters (p258): 900km of interconnected rivers, lakes and glassy lagoons lined with lush tropical flora. And if you do, it's unlikely there will be a way to experience it that's quite as serene and intimate as a few days on a teak-and-palm-thatch houseboat. Float along the water – as the sun sinks behind whispering palms, while you nibble on seafood so fresh it's almost wriggling – and forget about life on land for a while.

Go Goa

2 Silken sand, gently crashing waves, thick coconut groves, hot pink sunsets...yes, if there's one place that effortlessly fulfils every beach paradise cliché, it's Goa (p118). With a few exceptions, Goa's beaches are a riot of activity, with a constant cavalcade of roaming sarong vendors, stacks of ramshackle beachside eateries and countless oiled bodies slowly baking on row after row of sun lounges. Goa is also known for its inland spice plantations and lovely heritage buildings, most notably its handsome Portuguese cathedrals. Agonda (p156)

FELIX HUG / GETTY IMAGES ©

ALAN LAGADU / GETTY IMAGES ©

Maharashtra's Magnificent Cave Shrines

3 The 2nd-century-BC Buddhist monks who created the Ajanta caves (p96) had an eye for the dramatic. The 30 rock-cut forest shrines and monasteries punctuate a horseshoe-shaped cliff. Centuries afterwards, monks added exquisite carvings and paintings depicting Buddha. Along an escarpment at Ellora, less than 150km away, Hindus, Jains and Buddhists spent five centuries carving out another 34 cave shrines and monasteries – plus the Kailasa Temple, the world's biggest monolithic structure. Ajanta Caves (p96)

Enigmatic Hampi

4 Today's surreal boulderscape of Hampi (p212) was once the glorious Vijayanagar, capital of a powerful Hindu empire. Still glorious in ruin, its temples and royal structures combine with the terrain in mystical ways: giant rocks balance on skinny pedestals near ancient elephant stables, temples tuck into crevices between boulders, and round coracle boats float by rice paddies and bathing buffalo near a gargantuan bathtub for a queen. Watching the sunset cast a rosy glow over the extraordinary landscape, you might just forget what planet you're on. Lotus Mahal (p213)

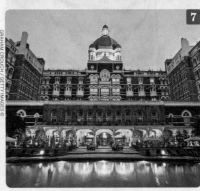

Historic Hyderabad

5 If you're a history buff, you'll get your fill in Hyderabad (p228). The city has a fascinating story and oodles of historic attractions, including massive Golconda fort, the graceful Charminar mosque-cum-monument, and the magnificent tombs and palaces of bygone rulers. But it's also a city of buzzing bazaars (fabrics, pearls, scented oils, billions of bangles...) and a feast for the tummy. Acclaimed for its traditional Mughal-style spicy kebabs and biryani (steamed rice with meat and/or vegetables), Hyderabadi fare gets a hearty round of applause for its inventive preparations.
Charminar (p229)

Puducherry Savoir Faire

6 A little pocket of France in Tamil Nadu? *Pourquoi pas?* In this former French colony, mustard-coloured houses line cobblestone rues (streets), austere cathedrals are adorned with architectural frou-frou, and the croissants are the real deal. But Puducherry (Pondicherry; p358) is also a classic Tamil town – with all the history and hubbub that go along with that – and a classic retreat town, too, with the Sri Aurobindo Ashram at its heart. Turns out that yoga, *pain au chocolat*, Hindu deities and colonial-era architecture make for a *très* atmospheric mix.

Mumbai's Architectural Gems

7 Mumbai (Bombay; p42) has long embraced its globetrotting influences and inventively made them its own. The result is an architectural melange of buildings with a raft of design influences. Art deco and modern towers lend the city its cool, but it's the eclectic Victorian-era structures – Indo-Saracenic, Venetian Gothic and other old flourishes – that have made Mumbai the flamboyant beauty she is. All those slender spires, curvaceous arches and onion domes, offset by lofty palms and leafy banyans, are apt embellishments for this movie-star city. Taj Mahal Palace Hotel, Mumbai (p45)

Out in the Wild

8 Getting out into the wild jungles, bush and hills of South India is always a thrilling experience, and dozens of parks and protected areas are waiting for adventurers. Tadoba-Andhari Tiger Reserve (p101) has some of India's best tiger-spotting chances, and Nagarhole National Park and Wayanad Wildlife Sanctuary are top spots for wild elephants. In almost any park you can expect to see a range of deer, antelope and primates, and plenty of birds; and the landscapes themselves are always stunning. Tiger, Maharashtra

Mesmerising Markets

9 Wriggling through South India's jam-packed bazaar streets puts your finger on the pulse of the place like nothing else. All walks of Indian life are here, whether hawking kerbside shoe repairs, standing behind a counter of glittering jewellery, or dressed up to go browsing with friends. Incense and snack-stall aromas mingle with the blare of music and traffic to assault your senses to the full. Every town has its bazaars, but try not to miss Mumbai's seething bazaar district (p77), or the multifarious markets around Hyderabad's Charminar. Pomegranates, Crawford Market, (p77), Mumbai

Majestic Mysuru

10 Welcome to Mysuru (Mysore; p186) – a city whose name describes the spot where a brave goddess conquered a ferocious demon. Apart from taking in its formidable history and flamboyant palaces, this is also a place for a wander through bazaars filled with the aroma of sandalwood and fresh flowers. Mysuru is also an international yoga centre and is known for its energetic festivals. Dussehra, celebrating the triumph of good over evil, is one of the most spectacular occasions, with merry street parades and the dazzling lighting-up of the enormous maharaja's palace. Mysore Palace (p187)

Tamil Nadu Hill Stations

11 The palm-fringed beaches, flat plains and cultural cities are all well and good, but it can get mighty hot down there! India's princes and British colonials long retreated to mountain towns such as Ooty (Udhagamandalam; p400), Kodaikanal and Coonoor for cool respite from the relentless lowland heat. Today the hill stations still have plenty of crisp mountain air, shady forests, sprawling tea plantations and quirky echoes-of-the-British Raj charm. Curl up by the fireside with a steaming cup of local tea, peer over the misty hills at the mountain birds swooping by and experience India's chilled-out side. Ooty (p400)

Madurai's Meenakshi Amman Temple

12 Madurai's joyful Meenakshi Amman Temple (p381) is surrounded by 12 tall *gopurams* (gate towers) encrusted with deities, demons and heroes – the high point of southern temple architecture. Dedicated to Sundareswarar (a form of Shiva) and his consort, Meenakshi (a triple-breasted incarnation of the goddess Parvati), the complex is a feast of deftly crafted pillars, sculptures and friezes and murals. Try to be there to see the evening procession carrying an icon of Sundareswarar to spend the night with Meenakshi at her shrine.

Need to Know

For more information, see Survival Guide (p489)

Currency
Indian rupee (₹)

Languages
Hindi, English and regional languages

Visas
Some nationalities can obtain a 30-day visa on arrival. For longer trips, most people get a six-month tourist visa, valid from the date of issue, not the date you arrive in India.

Money
ATMs in most large towns; carry cash or travellers cheques as backup. MasterCard and Visa are the most widely accepted credit cards.

Mobile Phones
Roaming connections are good in cities, poor in the countryside. Local SIMs are available in most areas; they involve paperwork and up to 24 hours' wait for activation.

Time
Indian Standard Time (GMT/UTC plus 5½ hours). No daylight saving.

When to Go

Mumbai
GO Nov–Feb

Hyderabad
GO Nov–Mar

Panaji
GO Nov–Mar

Chennai
GO Dec–Apr

Thiruvananthapuram
GO Nov–Mar

- Desert, dry climate
- Tropical climate, rain year-round
- Tropical climate, wet & dry seasons
- Warm to hot summers, mild winters

Low Season
(Apr–Jun)

➡ April is hot; May and June are scorching. Competitive hotel prices.

➡ From June, the monsoon sweeps from south to north, bringing draining humidity.

➡ Beat the heat (but not the crowds) in the cool hills.

Shoulder Season
(Jul–Nov)

➡ Monsoon rain-showers persist through to September.

➡ The eastern coast and southern Kerala see heavy rain and sometimes cyclones from October to early December.

High Season
(Dec–Mar)

➡ Pleasant weather with warm days, reasonably cool nights. Peak tourists. Peak prices.

➡ December and January bring chilly nights further north.

➡ Temperatures climb steadily from February.

PLAN YOUR TRIP NEED TO KNOW

Useful Websites

Lonely Planet (www.lonely planet.com/india) Destination information, the Thorn Tree travel forum and more.

Incredible India (www. incredibleindia.org) Official India tourism site.

The Alternative (www.thealter native.in) A green and socially conscious take on travel and Indian life.

Templenet (www.templenet. com) Temple talk.

Rediff News (www.rediff.com/ news) Portal for India-wide news.

Important Numbers

From outside India, dial your international access code, then India's country code, then the number (minus the initial '0').

Country code	91
International access code	00
Ambulance	102
Fire	101
Police	100

Exchange Rates

Australia	A$1	₹50
Canada	C$1	₹52
Euro zone	€1	₹70
Japan	¥100	₹53
New Zealand	NZ$1	₹47
UK	UK£1	₹98
US	US$1	₹64

For current exchange rates see www.xe.com

Daily Costs

**Budget:
Less than ₹2000**

➡ Double room in a budget hotel: ₹500–₹1000

➡ All-you-can-eat thali (plate meal): ₹60–₹250

➡ Transport: ₹100–₹500

**Midrange:
₹2000–7000**

➡ Double hotel room: ₹1200–₹4000

➡ Meal in midrange restaurant: ₹250–₹1000

➡ Admission to historic sights and museums: ₹100–₹800

**Top End:
More than ₹7000**

➡ Deluxe hotel room: ₹5000–₹20,000

➡ Meal in superior restaurant: ₹1000–₹4000

➡ First-class train travel: ₹500–₹2000

➡ Renting a car and driver: ₹1500–₹4000 per day

Opening Hours

Banks 10am to 4pm Monday to Friday, to 1pm Saturday

Restaurants 8am or 9am to 10pm or 11pm (some midrange and top-end restaurants may not open till lunchtime)

Bars noon to midnight

Shops 10am or 11am to 8pm or 9pm (some close Sunday)

Markets 7am to 8pm, but very variable

Arriving in South India

Chhatrapati Shivaji International Airport (Mumbai; p79) Prepaid taxis to Colaba and Fort cost ₹700 (₹800 with AC). Suburban trains to the Fort area (₹9) run from Andheri train station, a ₹60 autorickshaw ride from the airport.

Chennai International Airport (p342) Prepaid taxis cost ₹480 (₹580 with AC) to Egmore, and ₹400/500 to T Nagar. Suburban trains to central Chennai (₹5) run from Tirusulam station, about 10 minutes' walk from the terminal. A new Metro Rail rapid transit system, expected to start operating in 2016, will make everything much easier.

Getting Around

Air Most larger cities have flights to other Indian cities with a variety of airlines including several budget carriers. Well worth considering for long hops.

Train Railways criss-cross almost every part of the country, with frequent services on most routes; inexpensive tickets available even in sleeping carriages.

Bus Buses go everywhere, at similar speed to trains. Air-con services, especially Volvo services, are generaly the most comfortable and most expensive. Some routes are served 24 hours but others may have just one or two buses a day.

Car and driver The most convenient option for multistop trips or trips to out-of-the-way places. Easily arranged through travel agencies and many hotels.

For much more on **getting around**, see p508.

If You Like...

Forts & Palaces

South India's history is a colourful tapestry of wrangling dynasties interwoven with influxes of seafaring traders and conquerors. Their legacy lives on in a remarkable collection of palaces and forts.

Mysore Palace One of India's grandest, most spectacular royal buildings; a confection of rare artworks, stained glass, mosaics and carved wood. (p187)

Maharashtra The land of Shivaji is thick with defensive masterpieces, like hilltop **Daulatabad** (p92) and the island fortress **Janjira** (p102).

Hyderabad Golconda Fort complements the opulent palaces and ethereal royal tombs of the city of pearls. (p231)

Bidar Fort So weathered and peaceful, it's hard to believe this complex was once capital of a powerful sultanate. (p225)

Beaches

South India has the country's most breathtaking stretches of coastline.

Kerala backed by dramatic cliffs and with a busy backpacker scene, **Varkala** (p274) and the more deserted **Thottada** (p320), shaded by nodding palms, are absolute visions.

Goa Even when overrun with crowds, Goa's beaches are still somehow lovely: **Palolem** (p157) and **Mandrem** (p147) are among the prettiest, as is **Gokarna** (p208), close by in Karnataka.

Mumbai (Bombay) Hit Chowpatty beach at dusk to snack on local delicacies, people-watch and see just how hot-pink the sunset can get. (p53)

Andaman Islands Pristine tropical beaches far away from everything on **Havelock** (p417), **Neil** (p420) and **Little Andaman** (p425) islands.

Grand Temples & Ancient Ruins

Nowhere does grand temples like the subcontinent. From Tamil Nadu's psychedelic Hindu towers to the faded splendour of the Buddhist caves of Ajanta and Ellora, the range is as vast as it is sublime.

Tamil Nadu Hundreds of fantastical structures, like Madurai's Meenakshi Amman Temple, soar skyward in riotous rainbows of masterfully sculpted deities. (p381)

Ajanta & Ellora The magnificent old rock-cut shrines of **Ajanta** (p96) and **Ellora** (p93) are revered for their spiritual significance as well as their architectural prowess.

Hampi The rosy-hued temples and crumbling palaces of mighty Vijayanagar are strewn among other-worldly-looking boulders and hills. (p212)

Mamallapuram (Mahabalipuram) Sublime relief carvings and free-standing and rock-cut temples sculpted by medieval Pallava artisans dot this easygoing seaside town. (p346)

Bazaars

Megamalls may be popping up like monsoon frogs in the cities, but the traditional outdoor bazaars – with their tangled lanes lined by shops selling everything from freshly ground spices and floral garlands to kitchen utensils and colourful saris – can't be beat.

Goa Flea markets at **Anjuna** (p142) and **Baga** (p139) have become huge attractions, while bazaars at **Margao** (p152) and **Panaji (Panjim)** (p127) make for atmospheric wandering.

Mumbai Among modern malls, this megalopolis has wonderful old markets conveniently dedicated to themes: Mangaldas (fabric), Zaveri (jewellery), Crawford (food) and Chor (antiques). (p77)

Mysuru (Mysore) Iconic Devaraja Market is about 125 years old and filled with about 125 million flowers, fruits and spices. (p188)

Hyderabad Bazaars of the historic Charminar area hawk everything from pearls and lac bangles to livestock and wedding outfits. (p241)

City Sophistication

It's true that most Indians live in villages, but India's cities have vibrant arts scenes, terrific multicuisine restaurants and oodles of style.

Mumbai Fashion, film, art, dining and bubbling nightlife, on an elaborate stage of fanciful architecture and scenic water views. (p42)

Hyderabad The architecture of extraordinarily wealthy bygone dynasties sits just across town from a refined restaurant, nightlife and arts scene. (p228)

Bengaluru (Bangalore) The southern face of progressive, modern India, Bengaluru is the hub of India's IT industry and a great place for drinking, dining and shopping. (p172)

Puducherry (Pondicherry) A lively coastal town known for its quaintly faded French flavour, Puducherry is India at its eclectic best. (p358)

Chennai (Madras) This long-standing cultural and commercial hub has added an increasingly sophisticated layer of luxury hotels and bright, contemporary eateries, boutiques and nightspots. (p327)

Nature

South India offers plenty of opportunities to search for wild things in wild places.

Wayanad Wildlife Sanctuary Remote, beautiful, unspoiled Keralan sanctuary with good chances of spotting wild elephants. (p317)

Top: Vagator (p143), Goa
Bottom: Meenakshi Amman Temple (p381), Madurai

Nagarhole National Park Little-visited park with jungle and rivers; good for elephant sightings and you might just be lucky enough to glimpse a tiger. (p199)

Tadoba-Andhari Tiger Reserve One of India's best chances to see tigers, with around 120 counted here, plus gaur (bison), chital deer, nilgai antelope, sloth bears and leopards. (p101)

Periyar Wildlife Sanctuary Kerala sanctuary with gaur, sambar deer, around 1000 elephants and a few tigers. (p290)

Hill Stations

The colonial-era tradition of heading for the cool elevations of the Western Ghats, when the plains get too hot, is alive and well among honeymooners, families and pretty much everyone else.

Ooty (Udhagamandalam) The 'Queen of Hill Stations', Ooty combines typical Indian bustle with green parks and British Raj-era bungalows, amid the verdant Nilgiri hills. (p400)

Kodaikanal A smaller, quirkier, more scenic alternative to Ooty, centred on a pretty lake. (p390)

Matheran This weekend retreat for Mumbaikars is not only scenic and car free, it's also reached by toy train. (p106)

Munnar Base yourself in a beautiful out-of-town resort and trek through the emerald-green plantations of South India's major tea-growing area. (p294)

Boat Tours

Seeing South India from the water offers a whole new angle on its attractions.

Kerala Languorous houseboat drifting on the backwaters around **Alappuzha** (Alleppey;

p282), canoe tours from **Kollam** (Quilon; p279) and bamboo-raft tours in **Periyar Wildlife Sanctuary** (p290).

Goa Dolphin- and croc-spotting tours on the Mandovi River. (p133)

Andaman Islands See mangroves, rainforest and reefs with 50 types of coral at Mahatma Gandhi Marine National Park. (p416)

Malvan Take a trip along Maharashtra's beautiful Karli River backwaters. (p105)

Meditation & Yoga

The art of wellbeing has long been ardently cultivated in the south. Numerous courses and treatments strive to heal mind, body and spirit, with meditation and yoga especially abundant.

Mysuru The home of Ashtanga yoga, Mysuru (Mysore) rivals Rishikesh as one of India's most popular places to practise and get certified. (p193)

Goa Multifarious yoga, meditation and other spiritual-health pursuits are taught and practised in Goa, chiefly between October and April. (p120)

Vipassana International Academy This centre at Igatpuri, Maharashtra, conducts intensive meditation courses in the Theravada Buddhist tradition. (p88)

Sri Aurobindo Ashram This Puducherry ashram, founded by the renowned Sri Aurobindo, seeks to synthesise yoga and modern science. (p359)

Isha Yoga Residential yoga courses and retreats at Poondi, near Coimbatore. (p397)

Traveller Enclaves

Sometimes you just want to stop moving for a bit and chill with fellow travellers:

swap travel tales, read, take afternoon naps, play cards or drink beer...

Hampi The stunning beauty of Hampi's landscape and architecture makes everyone want to stay for a while, which has led to a well-developed traveller community. (p212)

Arambol Goa is one big traveller enclave, but Palolem and the cheaper Arambol are its current epicentres. (p148)

Gokarna Originally a Goa overflow destination, Gokarna's beaches are cosy, beautiful, relaxed and part of a sacred ancient village. (p208)

Mamallapuram Cheap accommodation, exquisite ancient architecture, and surfing on one of the nicest stretches of Tamil Nadu's coast. (p346)

Water Sports

Diving, snorkelling and surfing all are growing rapidly along South Indian coasts.

Andaman Islands World-class diving and snorkelling in crystal-clear waters with deep corals and masses of marine life – 1370km from mainland India. (p408)

Malvan Diving is becoming a big draw here with coral reefs, sea caves, abundant marine life and a recently opened top-class scuba school. (p105)

Surfing Soaring in popularity along the southern coast, with schools at **Kovalam** (p270), which has probably the best waves, Goa, Mamallapuram and Puducherry.

Lakshadweep These pristine lagoons and unspoiled coral reefs 300km off Kerala have wonderful diving and snorkelling, but are only accessible on package trips. (p323)

Month By Month

January

Post-monsoon cool lingers, although it never gets truly cool in the most southerly states. Pleasant weather and several festivals make it a popular time to travel (book ahead!).

✰ Free India

Republic Day commemorates the founding of the Republic of India on 26 January 1950.

✰ Kite Festival

Sankranti, the Hindu festival marking the sun's passage into Capricorn and the end of the harvest, is celebrated in many ways across India, but it's the mass kite-flying in Maharashtra, Telangana and Andhra Pradesh (among other states) that steals the show.

✰ Pongal

In Tamil Nadu the festival of Pongal marks the end of the harvest season. Families prepare pots of *pongal* (a mixture of rice, sugar, dhal and milk), symbolic of prosperity and abundance, then feed them to decorated cows. (p327)

✰ Celebrating Saraswati

On Vasant Panchami, the 'fifth day of spring', Hindus dress in yellow and place books, musical instruments and other educational objects in front of idols of Saraswati, the goddess of learning, to receive her blessing. The festival may fall in February.

February

The weather is comfortable in most areas, with summer heat starting to percolate in the south. It's still peak travel season.

✰ Shivaratri

This day of Hindu fasting recalls the *tandava* (cosmic victory dance) of Lord Shiva. Temple processions are followed by the chanting of mantras and anointing of linga (phallic images of Shiva). Shivaratri can also fall in March.

✰ Carnival in Goa

The four-day party kicking off Lent is big in Goa, especially Panaji (Panjim). Sabado Gordo (Fat Saturday), starts it off with parades, and the revelry continues with street parties, concerts and general merrymaking. Can also fall in March.

March

The last month of the travel season, March is full-on hot in most of India.

✰ Holi

More celebrated in North India but still embraced by many southerners, Holi is an ecstatic festival; Hindus celebrate the beginning of spring according to the lunar calendar, in February or March, by throwing coloured water and *gulal* (powder) at anyone within range. Bonfires the night before symbolise the demise of demoness Holika.

✰ Rama's Birthday

During Ramanavami, which lasts anywhere from one to nine days, Hindus celebrate Rama's birth with processions, fasting and feasting, enactments of scenes from the Ramayana and, at some temples, weddings of Rama and Sita idols.

April

The hot has well and truly arrived in South India, and with the rise in temperature also comes a rise in competitive travel deals and a drop in tourist traffic. In the national parks and reserves, wildlife becomes easier to spot as animals come out to find water.

✨ Mahavir's Birthday

In April or late March, Mahavir Jayanti commemorates the birth of Jainism's 24th and most important *tirthankar* (teacher and enlightened being). Temples are decorated and visited, Mahavir statues are given ritual baths, processions are held and offerings are given to the poor.

May

In most of the country it's hot. Really hot. Which makes it high season in Ooty (Udhagamandalam), Kodaikanal and the south's other hill stations. Festivals slow down as humidity builds up in anticipation of the rain.

June

The monsoon begins in most areas, and where it doesn't you've got pre-monsoon extreme heat, so June's not a popular travel month in South India.

Top: Diwali – the 'Festival of Lights
Bottom: Celebrating with *gulal* during the Holi festival

✱ Ramadan (Ramazan)

Thirty days of dawn-to-dusk fasting mark the ninth month of the Islamic calendar. Muslims traditionally turn their attention to God, with a focus on prayer and purification. Ramadan begins around 7 June 2016 and 27 May 2017.

July

It's really raining almost everywhere, with many remote roads being washed out. Consider doing a rainy-season meditation retreat, an ancient Indian tradition.

✱ Eid al-Fitr

Muslims celebrate the end of Ramadan with three days of festivities. Prayers, shopping and gift-giving may all be part of the celebrations. Around 5 July 2016 and 25 June 2017.

✱ Brothers & Sisters

On Raksha Bandhan (Narial Purnima), girls fix amulets known as *rakhis* to the wrists of brothers and close male friends to protect them in the coming year. Brothers reciprocate with gifts and promises to take care of their sisters.

August

It's still high monsoon season: wet wet wet. Some folks swear by visiting tropical areas like Kerala or Goa at this time of year: the jungles are lush, bright green and glistening in the rain.

✱ Snake Festival

The Hindu festival Naag Panchami, particularly vibrant in Pune and Kolhapur, Maharashtra, is dedicated to Ananta, the serpent upon whose coils Vishnu rested between universes. Women return to family homes and fast, while serpents are venerated as totems against flooding and other evils. Dates: 7 August 2016 and 27 July 2017.

✱ Independence Day

This public holiday on 15 August marks the anniversary of India's independence from Britain in 1947. Celebrations include flag-hoisting ceremonies, parades and patriotic cultural programs.

✱ Krishna's Birthday

Janmastami celebrations range from fasting to *puja* (prayers) and offering sweets, to drawing elaborate *rangoli* (rice-paste designs) outside homes. Held around 25 August 2016 and 15 August 2017.

✱ Parsi New Year

Parsis celebrate Pateti, the Zoroastrian new year, especially in Mumbai (Bombay). Houses are cleaned and decorated with flowers and *rangoli,* the family dresses up and eats special fish dishes and sweets, and offerings are made at the Fire Temple.

September

The rain begins to ease up somewhat, but with temperatures still relatively high throughout southern India the moisture-filled air can create a fatiguing steam-bath-like environment.

✱ Ganesh Chaturthi

Hindus celebrate Ganesh Chaturthi, the birth of the elephant-headed god, by setting up decorative statues of him on many streets then parading them around town before ceremonially depositing them in rivers, lakes, reservoirs or the sea. Particularly riotous in Mumbai (Bombay), but also big in Hyderabad, Chennai (Madras) and elsewhere (5 to 15 September 2016, 25 August to 5 September 2017).

✱ Eid al-Adha

Muslims commemorate Ibrahim's readiness to sacrifice his son to God by slaughtering a goat or sheep and sharing it with family, the community and the poor. Around 11 September 2016 and 1 September 2017.

October

Though the southeast coast (and southern Kerala) can still be rainy, this is when India starts to get its travel mojo on. October brings festivals, reasonably comfy temperatures and post-monsoon lushness.

✱ Gandhi's Birthday

The national holiday of Gandhi Jayanti (2 October) is a solemn celebration of Mohandas Gandhi's birth, with prayer meetings at his cremation site in Delhi, and no alcohol on sale countrywide.

Navratri

The Hindu 'Festival of Nine Nights' leading up to Dussehra celebrates the goddess Durga in all her incarnations. Festivities, in September or October, are particularly vibrant in Maharashtra.

Dussehra

Colourful Dussehra celebrates the victory of the Hindu god Rama over the demon-king Ravana and the triumph of good over evil. Dussehra is big in Mysuru (Mysore), which hosts one of India's grandest parades. Falls around 11 October 2016 and 30 September 2017. (p194)

Muharram

During this Islamic month of grieving and remembrance, Shiite Muslims commemorate the martyrdom of the Prophet Mohammed's grandson Imam Hussain, an event known as Ashura, with beautiful processions on the 10th day, including a particularly huge one in Hyderabad. Ashura falls on 23 October 2015, 11 October 2016 and 1 October 2017.

Diwali

In the lunar month of Kartika, Hindus celebrate Diwali for five days, giving gifts, lighting fireworks, and burning butter and oil lamps (or hanging lanterns) to lead Lord Rama home from exile. One of India's prettiest and noisiest festivals. Begins around 11 November 2015, 30 October 2016 and 18 October 2017.

November

The northeast monsoon is sweeping Tamil Nadu and Kerala, but it's a good time to be anywhere low altitude, as the temperatures are generally pleasant.

Guru Nanak's Birthday

Nanak Jayanti, birthday of Guru Nanak, founder of Sikhism, is celebrated with prayer, *kirtan* (devotional singing) and processions for three days. Around 25 November 2015 and 14 November 2016.

International Film Festival of India

The International Film Festival of India (www.iffi.nic.in), the country's biggest movie jamboree, attracts Bollywood's finest to Panaji, Goa, for premieres, parties and screenings.

Karthikai Deepam

Celebrating Shiva's restoration of light to the world, this festival is especially massive at Tiruvannamalai, where Shiva appeared atop Mt Arunachala as a lingam of fire. Hundreds of thousands of pilgrims converge on the town for the full-moon night (25 November 2015 and 12 December 2016). (p357)

December

December is peak tourist season for a reason: the weather's glorious (except for the chilly mountains), the humidity is lower than usual, the mood is festive and the beach is sublime.

The Prophet's Birthday

The Islamic festival of Eid-Milad-un-Nabi celebrates the birth of the Prophet Mohammed with prayers and processions. Around 24 December 2015 and 12 December 2016.

Weddings

Marriage season peaks in December, and you may see a *baraat* (bridegroom's procession), complete with white horse and fireworks, on your travels. Across the country, loud music and spectacular parties are the way they roll, with brides in *mehndi* (henna) and pure gold.

Christmas Day

Christians celebrate the birth of Jesus Christ on 25 December. The festivities are especially big in Goa and Kerala, with musical events, elaborate decorations and special Masses, while Mumbai's Catholic neighbourhoods become festivals of lights.

Itineraries

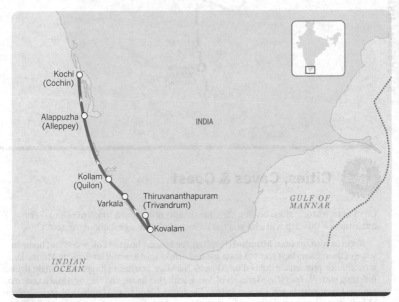

 Classic Kerala

With its coconut-palm-fringed beaches and lazy backwater boat rides, Kerala can justly claim to be India's most laid-back state. But there's plenty of colour and fun to spice up your tropical idyll: elephant festivals and snake-boat races, Kathakali dance-dramas, quaint colonial quarters and a famously flavoursome cuisine.

Spend a day visiting the zoological gardens and museums in the capital, **Thiru-vananthapuram** (Trivandrum), before making the half-hour hop to the beach resort of **Kovalam**. Then shift down another gear at **Varkala**, a holy town with a dizzying clifftop guesthouse-and-restaurant enclave, where you can chill out with some yoga or surfing. Continue north to **Kollam** (Quilon) and take the tourist cruise along the canals to Alappuzha (Alleppey) with an overnight stop at the Matha Amrithanandamayi Mission, the pink ashram of 'The Hugging Mother'. Reaching **Alappuzha** (Alleppey), you're at houseboat central. Scout for a houseboat or canoe operator and discover what the sublime backwaters are all about. Continuing north by train to **Kochi** (Cochin), take the short ferry ride to the old colonial outpost of Fort Cochin. Aromatic seafood barbecues, welcoming homestays, colonial-era mansions, Kathakali shows and the intriguing Jewish quarter at Mattancherry make this a fascinating place to while away a few days.

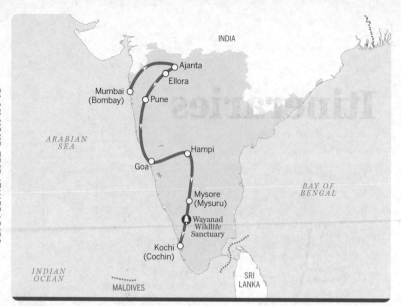

Cities, Caves & Coast

4 WEEKS

City lights, historic sites, beachy bliss, jungle adventure and a touch of colonial-era quaintness – this trip will give you the flavour of all that's best about the south.

Begin in cosmopolitan **Mumbai** (Bombay), the beating heart of Bollywood and home to some of the nation's best spots to shop, eat and drink. Take a sunset stroll along Marine Dr, an oceanside promenade dubbed the 'Queen's Necklace' because of its sparkling night lights, finishing with *bhelpuri* (fried rounds of dough with rice, lentils and chutney) and a neck massage on Chowpatty Beach. Catch a ferry to Elephanta Island from Mumbai's historic Gateway of India to explore its stunning rock-cut temples and the triple-faced sculpture of Lord Shiva.

Next, head northeast to explore the ancient cave art at **Ajanta** and **Ellora**, situated within 150km of each other near Aurangabad. The incredible frescoed Buddhist caves of Ajanta are clustered along a horseshoe-shaped gorge, while the rock-cut caves of Ellora – containing a mix of Hindu, Jain and Buddhist shrines – are set on a 2km escarpment. After soaking up cave culture, journey southwest to **Pune**, Maharashtra's IT hub, with excellent museums and bars and the infamous Osho International Meditation Resort. Next stop: the tropical beach haven of **Goa** for some soul-reviving sandcastle therapy. Wander through a lush spice plantation, visit Portuguese-era cathedrals at Old Goa, shop at Anjuna's colourful flea market and take your pick from dozens of fabulous beach spots, before travelling east to the traveller hotspot of **Hampi** in neighbouring Karnataka. Ramble around Hampi's enigmatic boulder-strewn landscape and imagine what life here was like when it was a centre of the mighty Vijayanagar empire. Make the long trip down to **Mysuru** (Mysore) to explore the Maharaja's Palace, one of India's grandest royal buildings, and shop for silk and sandalwood in its colourful markets. From Mysuru it's an exciting bus ride across the Western Ghats into Kerala and the **Wayanad Wildlife Sanctuary**, a pristine forest and jungle reserve and one of the best places in the south to spot wild elephants. Finally, take the hair-raising road down to the coast and make your way to **Kochi**, Kerala's intriguing colonial city where a blend of Portuguese, Dutch and English history combines with wonderful homestays and a buzzing traveller scene.

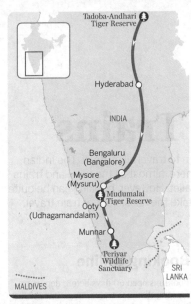

3 WEEKS — Cities, Hill Stations & Sanctuaries

An offbeat trip through the cities, wildlife parks and hill stations of the Deccan and Western Ghats will give you a true taste of the fascinating variety of inland South India.

Start with a venture to Maharashtra's **Tadoba-Andhari Tiger Reserve**, offering some of India's best prospects of sighting wild tigers, then journey south to the old princely capital **Hyderabad**, with its Islamic monuments and labyrinthine bazaars. Continue south to the culinary and shopping delights of India's 21st-century IT capital, **Bengaluru** (Bangalore), and glimpse a royal past at its Bangalore Palace. Next stop: the royal city of **Mysuru** (Mysore). Gawp at the Maharaja's Palace, a grand complex topped with red and white domes. Head south to **Mudumalai Tiger Reserve**, where you can spot wild elephants and take a jeep safari through jungle, and on to the cool hill town of **Ooty** (Udhagamandalam), one of India's most-loved holiday retreats. Take the toy train down to Coimbatore, then cross into Kerala and the tea-covered hills of **Munnar**, with fine hiking and secluded forest accommodation. Finish with some jungle trekking and more chances of a tiger sighting at pretty **Periyar Wildlife Sanctuary**.

12 DAYS — Tamil Nadu's Temples

A journey through Tamil Nadu is a trip into South India's spiritual soul: Tamils are among India's most fervent in their Hindu faith, and their temples are the 3D expression of devotion.

Delve into the history of **Chennai** (Madras) with a wander around the Government Museum before visiting the Kapaleeshwarar and Parthasarathy Temples. Travel south to beachside **Mamallapuram** (Mahabalipuram) and its rock-cut shrines. Move inland to **Tiruvannamalai** where the Arunachaleswar Temple is one of India's largest sacred complexes, below a hill where Shiva appeared as a lingam of fire. Take a break from temple towns in the old French seaside colony of **Puducherry** (Pondicherry), then head inland to the World Heritage–listed medieval temples of **Kumbakonam** and **Thanjavur**. Continue to **Trichy** (Tiruchirappalli), home to the Rock Fort Temple and the Sri Ranganathaswamy Temple, probably India's biggest temple. Then head south to **Madurai** and the Meenakshi Amman Temple, widely reckoned the pinnacle of South Indian temple architecture. Wind down at **Kanyakumari**, the southern tip of India, with its temple to the sea goddess Kumari.

Plan Your Trip
Booking Trains

In India, riding the rails is a reason to travel all by itself. The Indian rail network goes almost everywhere, almost all the time, and trains have seats to suit every size of wallet. However, booking can be quite an undertaking – book online to take the hassle out of train travel.

Train Classes

Air-Conditioned 1st Class (1AC)
The most expensive class, with two- or four-berth compartments with locking doors and meals included.

Air-Conditioned 2-Tier (2AC)
Two-tier berths arranged in groups of four and two in an open-plan carriage. Bunks convert to seats by day and there are curtains, offering some privacy.

Air-Conditioned 3-Tier (3AC)
Three-tier berths arranged in groups of six in an open-plan carriage with no curtains; popular with Indian families.

AC Executive Chair
Comfortable, reclining chairs and plenty of space; usually on Shatabdi express trains.

AC Chair
Similar to the Executive Chair carriage but with less-fancy seating.

Sleeper Class
Open-plan carriages with three-tier bunks and no AC; the open windows afford great views.

Unreserved/reserved 2nd Class (II/SS or 2S)
Wooden or plastic seats and a lot of people – but cheap!

Booking Online

Bookings open 60 days before departure for long-distance trains, sometimes earlier for short-haul trips. Seats fill up quickly – reserve at least a week ahead where possible, though shorter journeys are usually easier to obtain.

Express and mail trains form the mainstay of Indian rail travel. Not all classes are available on every train service, but most long-distance services have general (2nd-class) compartments with unreserved seating and more comfortable reserved compartments, usually with the option of sleeper berths for overnight journeys. Sleeper trains offer the chance to travel huge distances for not much more cost than the price of a midrange hotel room.

Shatabdi express trains are same-day services with seating only; Rajdhani express trains are long-distance overnight services between Delhi and state capitals with a choice of 1AC, 2AC, 3AC and 2nd class. More expensive sleeper categories provide bedding. In all classes, a padlock and a length of chain are useful for securing your luggage to the baggage racks provided. For more information on booking trains, including in person at stations, see p514.

For following websites are useful for online international bookings.

RAILWAY RAZZLE DAZZLE

You can live like a maharaja on one of South India's luxury train tours, with accommodation on board, tours, admission fees and meals included in the ticket price. A new Mumbai–Goa train is also on the cards; check online to see if this is up and running.

Deccan Odyssey (www.coxandkings.co.uk) Nine nights covering the main tourist spots of Maharashtra and Goa. Fares per person start at a decidedly upmarket UK£6090/3495 for single/double occupancy (includes flights). There are also several other shorter luxurious trips on offer.

Golden Chariot (www.coxandkings.co.uk) Tours the south in sumptuous style from October to March, starting in Bengaluru (Bangalore); 10-night trips visit Mysuru (Mysore), Hampi and Goa. Rates per person start at UK£4445 (includes flights).

Cleartrip (www.cleartrip.com) A reliable private agency and the easiest way to book; accepts international MasterCard and Visa credit cards. Can only book direct journeys. If booking from outside India before you have a local mobile number, a work-around is to enter a random number, and use email only to communicate.

IRCTC (www.irctc.co.in) Government site offering bookings for regular trains and luxury tourist trains; only American Express cards issued in UK and Australia for international ticketing, but accepts these erratically.

Make My Trip (www.makemytrip.com) Reputable private agency; accepts international cards. Again, you'll need an Indian mobile number. You'll then need to create an IRCTC User ID: choose a User ID (username), put in your name, birth date and address. For the 'Pincode' (postcode) '123456' will work. For the State choose 'Other'.

Yatra (www.yatra.com) Books flights and trains; accepts international cards.

Reservations

You must make a reservation for all chair-car, sleeper, 1AC, 2AC and 3AC carriages. No reservations are required for general unreserved (2nd-class) compartments. Book well ahead for overnight journeys or travel during holidays and festivals. Waiting until the day of travel to book is not recommended.

Train Passes

IndRail passes permit unlimited rail travel for a fixed period, ranging from one day to 90 days, but offers limited savings and you must still make reservations. Prices start at US$19/43/95 (sleeper/2AC, 3AC & chair car/1AC) for 24 hours.The easiest way to book these is through the IndRail pass agency in your home country – click on the Passenger Info/Tourist Information link on www.indianrailways.gov.in/railwayboard for details.

Plan Your Trip

Yoga, Spas & Spiritual Pursuits

Birthplace of at least three religions, India offers a profound spiritual journey for those so inclined. Even sceptical travellers can enjoy the benefits of trips to spas and yoga centres.

What to Choose

Ashrams

South India has plenty of ashrams – places of communal living established around the philosophies of a guru (a spiritual guide or teacher).

Ayurveda

Ayurveda is the ancient science of Indian herbal medicine and holistic healing, based on natural plant extracts, massage and therapies to treat body and mind.

Yoga

Yoga's roots lie firmly in India and you'll find hundreds of schools to suit all levels.

Buddhist Meditation

Various centres offer training in *vipassana* (mindfulness meditation) and Buddhist philosophy; many require a vow of silence and abstinence from tobacco, alcohol and sex.

Spa Treatments

South India's spas offer an enticing mix of international therapies and local techniques based on ancient ayurvedic traditions.

Ayurveda

Ayurveda – Indian herbal medicine – aims to restore balance in the body; see also the boxed text on p278.

Goa

Ayurvedic Massage Centre
(☑9420896843; 1/1½hr massage from ₹1000/1500; ⊙9am-8pm) Two centres in Mandrem.

Karnataka

Ayurvedagram (p177) In a garden setting in Whitefield, 25km from central Bengaluru (Bangalore).

Soukya (p177) Ayurveda and yoga at Whitefield outside Bengaluru (Bangalore).

Indus Valley Ayurvedic Centre (p192) Therapies from ancient scriptures in Lalithadripura, 16km east of Mysuru (Mysore).

Swaasthya Ayurveda Centre (p192) Retreats and therapies in Mysuru (Mysore).

Swaasthya Ayurveda Retreat Village (p201) Relaxing retreat in Coorg (Kodagu).

SwaSwara (p210) Therapies and artistic pursuits at Gokarna's Om Beach.

Kerala

Dr Franklin's Panchakarma Institute (p274) Reputable treatments at Chowara, south of Kovalam.

Eden Garden (p275) Treatments and packages near the beach at Varkala.

Santhigiri Ayurveda Centre (p279) Seven-to-21-day packages and day treatments in Kollam. Also branches at **Kovalam** (p279) and **Periyar** (p291).

Ayur Dara (p302) Treatments from one to three weeks on Vypeen Island, Kochi.

Mumbai (Bombay)

Yoga Cara (p60) Ayurveda and massage.

Tamil Nadu

Sita (p360) Ayurveda and yoga in Puducherry (Pondicherry).

Yoga

You can practise yoga almost everywhere, from beach resorts to mountain retreats. In 2014, at India's initiative, the UN adopted a resolution declaring 21 June International Yoga Day.

Andaman Islands

Flying Elephant (p419) Yoga and meditation in tropical surroundings on Havelock Island.

Goa

Himalaya Yoga Valley (p147) Popular training school in Mandrem.

Swan Yoga Retreat (p143) Retreats in a soothing jungle location in Assagao.

Himalayan Iyengar Yoga Centre (p148) Reputable courses based in Arambol.

Bamboo Yoga Retreat (p157) Beachfront yoga in Patnem.

Karnataka

Mysore was the birthplace of Ashtanga yoga, and there are centres all over the state (p193).

Kerala

Trivandrum, Varkala and Kochi are popular places for yoga.

Sivananda Yoga Vedanta Dhanwantari Ashram (p270) Renowned for extended hatha yoga courses; 35km from Trivandrum.

Maharashtra

Kaivalyadhama Yoga Hospital (p107) Yogic healing in Lonavla.

Ramamani Iyengar Memorial Yoga Institute (p112) Advanced courses in Pune.

Mumbai (Bombay)

Yoga Institute (p61) Daily and longer-term programs.

Yoga House (p60) Hatha yoga in a lovely setting.

Yoga Cara (p60) More hatha and Iyengar yoga.

Tamil Nadu

International Centre for Yoga Education & Research (p361) Has 10-day introductory courses and advanced training in Puducherry.

Krishnamacharya Yoga Mandiram (p333) Yoga courses, therapy and training in Chennai.

Meditation

Whether for an introduction or more advanced study, there are region-wide courses and retreats.

Andhra Pradesh & Telangana

Numerous Burmese-style *vipassana* courses include:

Dhamma Vijaya (p247) Near Eluru.

Dhamma Nagajjuna (p248) Nagarjuna Sagar.

Maharashtra

Vipassana International Academy (p88) Holds 10-day vipassana courses at Igatpuri.

Mumbai (Bombay)

Global Pagoda (p59) *Vipassana* courses from one to 10 days on Gorai Island.

Spa Treatments

From solo practitioners to opulent spas, there are choices nationwide. Be cautious of dodgy one-on-one massages by private (often unqualified) operators – seek recommendations and trust your instincts.

Top: Take a yoga class in India, the birthplace of yoga

Bottom: Meditate in Varkala (p274), Kerala

Goa

Nilaya Hermitage (☏0832-2269793; www.
nilaya.com; Arpora; ✳@🛜🆒) Famous celebrity
hangout in Arpora.

Karnataka

Emerge Spa (p192) Pampering Asian-
influenced treatments near Mysuru.

Kerala

Neeleshwar Hermitage (☏0467-
2287510; www.neeleshwarhermitage.com;
Ozhinhavalappu, Neeleshwar; s/d cottages from
₹13,300/15,800, seaview ₹21,000/22,800;
✳🛜🆒) Beachfront eco-resort near Bekal.

Mumbai (Bombay)

Antara Spa (p60) International treatments.

Palm Spa (p60) Renowned Colaba spa.

Ashrams

Many ashrams are headed by charismatic
gurus. Some tread a fine line between spiritual community and personality cult. Many
gurus have amassed fortunes collected from

devotees, and others have been accused of
sexually exploiting their followers. Always
check the reputation of any ashram you wish
to join.

Most ashrams offer philosophy, yoga or
meditation courses. A donation is appropriate to cover your expenses.

Kerala

Matha Amrithanandamayi Mission
(p281) Famed for its female guru Amma, 'The
Hugging Mother'.

Maharashtra

Brahmavidya Mandir Ashram (p101)
Established by Gandhi's disciple Vinoba Bhave at
Sevagram.

Sevagram Ashram (p100) Founded by
Gandhi.

Tamil Nadu

Sri Aurobindo Ashram (p359) Founded by
Sri Aurobindo in Puducherry.

Isha Yoga Center (p397) Offers intensive
all-level yoga programs in Coimbatore.

Sri Ramana Ashram (p357) Founded by Sri
Ramana Maharshi; Tiruvannamalai.

Plan Your Trip
Volunteering

For all India's beauty, rich culture and history, poverty and hardship are unavoidable facts of life. Many travellers feel motivated to help, and charities and aid organisations across the country welcome committed volunteers. Here's a guide to help you start making a difference.

How to Volunteer

Choosing an Organisation
Consider how your skills will benefit the people you are trying to help, and choose an organisation that can specifically benefit from your abilities.

Time Required
Think realistically about how much time you can devote to a project. You're more likely to be of help if you commit for at least a month, ideally more.

Money
Giving your time for free is only part of the story; most organisations expect volunteers to cover their own accommodation, food and transport.

Working nine to five
Make sure you understand what you are signing up for; many organisations expect volunteers to work full time, five days a week.

Transparency
Ensure that the organisation you choose is reputable and transparent about how it spends its money. Where possible, get feedback from former volunteers.

Aid Programs in South India

India faces considerable challenges and there are numerous opportunities for volunteers. It may be possible to find a placement after you arrive, but charities and nongovernment organisations (NGOs) generally prefer volunteers who have applied in advance and been approved for the kind of work involved. **Ethical Volunteering** (www.ethicalvolunteering.org) provides useful guidelines for choosing an ethical sending agency.

As well as international organisations, local charities and NGOs often have opportunities, though it can be harder to assess the work that these organisations are doing. For listings of local agencies, check www.ngosindia.com or contact the Delhi-based **Concern India Foundation** (☏011-26210998; www.concernindiafoundation.org; A-52 Amar Colony, Lajpat Nagar IV).

Following is a list of organisations offering volunteering opportunities. Note that Lonely Planet does not endorse any organisations that we do not work with directly, so it is essential that you do your own thorough research before agreeing to volunteer with any organisation.

Community

Many community volunteer projects work to provide health care and education to villages.

Karnataka

➡ **Kishkinda Trust** (p215) ✎ Volunteers needed to assist with sustainable community development at Anegundi, near Hampi.

Mumbai (Bombay)

➡ **Slum Aid** (www.slumaid.org) Working in Mumbai slums to improve lives; placements from two weeks to six months.

Working with Children

The following charities provide support for disadvantaged children. Note that ethical organisations should require background checks for anyone working with children.

Goa

➡ **Mango Tree Goa** (p131; Mapusa) Opportunities for volunteer nurses and teaching assistants to help impoverished children.

➡ **El Shaddai** (p131; Assagao) Placements helping impoverished and homeless children; one-month minimum commitment.

Mumbai (Bombay)

➡ **Child Rights & You** (p60) Volunteers can assist with campaigns to raise funds for projects around India; four-week minimum commitment.

➡ **Vatsalya Foundation** (p60) Long- and short-term opportunities teaching and running sports activities for street children.

Tamil Nadu

➡ **RIDE** (p353; Kanchipuram) Volunteer teachers and support staff help rural communities and children rescued from forced labour.

Environment & Conservation

The following charities focus on environmental education and sustainable development:

Andaman Islands

➡ **ANET** (Andaman & Nicobar Environmental Team; ☎03192-280081; www.anetindia. org; North Wandoor) Volunteers assist with environmental activities from field projects to general maintenance.

➡ **Reef Watch** (☎9930678367; www. reefwatchindia.org; Lacadives, Chiriya Tapu) Marine conservation NGO accepting volunteers for anything from beach clean ups and fish surveys to teaching; three-week minimum.

Karnakata

➡ **Rainforest Retreat** (p201; Coorg) ✎ Organic farming, sustainable agriculture and waste management are catchphrases at this lush hideway amid spice plantations.

AGENCIES OVERSEAS

There are so many international volunteering agencies, it can be bewildering trying to assess which ones are reputable. Agencies offering the chance to do whatever you want, wherever you want, are almost always tailoring projects to the volunteer rather than finding the right volunteer for the work that needs to be done. Look for projects that will derive real benefits from your skills. To find sending agencies in your area, read Lonely Planet's *Volunteer: A Traveller's Guide,* or try one of the following.

Indicorps (www.indicorps.org) Matches volunteers to projects across India, particularly in social development.

Voluntary Service Overseas (VSO; www.vso.org.uk) British organisation offering long-term professional placements in India and worldwide.

Workaway (www.workaway.info) Connects people with hotels, guesthouses, organic farms, restaurants and more, where they will get free accommodation and food in return for working five days a week.

Tamil Nadu

➡ **Keystone Foundation** (p399; Kotagiri)
✔ Offers occasional opportunities to help improve environmental conditions, working with indigenous communities.

Working with Animals

From stray dogs to rescued reptiles, opportunities for animal lovers are plentiful.

Goa

➡ **Animal Rescue Centre** (p154; Chapolim) Animal welfare group that also has volunteer opportunities.

➡ **GAWT** (p154; Curchorem) Goa Animal Welfare Trust operates a shelter near Margao.

➡ **International Animal Rescue** (p154; Assagao) Animal Tracks rescue in North Goa.

➡ **Primate Trust India** (www. primatetrustindia.org; Camurlim) This rehabilitation centre cares for orphaned and injured monkeys or rescued illegal pets. Volunteer placements are available for a minimum one-month stay if you book in advance and obtain the necessary visa.

Mumbai (Bombay)

➡ **Welfare of Stray Dogs** (p61) Volunteers can work with the animals, manage stores or educate kids in school programs.

Tamil Nadu

➡ **Madras Crocodile Bank** (p346) A reptile conservation centre on the East Coast Rd with openings for volunteers (minimum two weeks).

Telangana

➡ **Blue Cross of Hyderabad** (☏23544355; www.bluecrosshyd.in; Rd No 35, Jubilee Hills) A shelter in Hyderabad with over 1300 animals; volunteers help care for shelter animals or work in the office.

Heritage & Restoration

Those with architecture and building skills should look at the following.

Tamil Nadu

➡ **ArcHeS** (www.arche-s.com; Karaikkudi) Aims to preserve the architectural and cultural heritage of Chettinadu; openings for historians, geographers and architects.

Plan Your Trip
Travel with Children

Fascinating and thrilling; India can be every bit as exciting for children as it is for their wide-eyed parents. The scents, sights and sounds of India will inspire and challenge young enquiring minds, and with careful preparation and vigilance, a lifetime of vivid memories can be sown.

South India for Kids

In many respects, travel with children in India can be a delight, and warm welcomes are frequent. Locals will thrill at taking a photograph or two beside your bouncing baby. But while all this is fabulous for outgoing children it may prove tiring, or even disconcerting to younger kids and those with more retiring dispositions.

As a parent on the road in India, the key is to stay alert to your children's needs and to remain firm in fulfilling them, even if you feel you may offend a well-meaning local by doing so. The attention your children will inevitably receive is almost always good-natured; kids are the centre of life in many Indian households, and your own will be treated just the same. Hotels will almost always come up with an extra bed or two, and restaurants with a familiar meal.

Children's Highlights
Best Natural Encounters

➡ **Elephants** Kids can feed, ride, bathe and get sprayed by elephants at parks in **Kerala** (Periyar; p290) and **Goa** (p120).

➡ **Dolphins, Goa** Splash out on a dolphin-spotting boat trip from almost any Goan beach to see them cavorting among the waves (p133).

Best Regions for Kids
Goa

Palm-fringed, white-sand beaches and inexpensive exotic food make Goa an ideal choice for family holidays. If you're looking to stay for a while, you'll find apartments and homey guesthouses to suit all budgets.

Karnataka

The magical ruins of Hampi will bewitch all ages, and who won't get excited about searching for wild elephants and hoping to glimpse a tiger or leopard in Bandipur and Nagarhole National Parks? And there's beach bliss with the opportunity to take surfing lessons at Gokarna.

Kerala

Canoe and houseboat adventures, surf beaches, Arabian Sea sunsets, snake-boat races, wildlife-spotting and elephant festivals. From the Ghats down to the coast, Kerala offers action and relaxation in equal measures.

➡ **Hill Station Monkeys** Head up to Matheran (Maharashtra) for close encounters with cheeky monkeys. (p106)

Fun Forms of Transport

➡ **Autorickshaw, anywhere** Hurtle at top speed in these child-scale vehicles.

➡ **Hand-pulled rickshaw, Matheran** A narrow-gauge diesel toy train takes visitors most of the way up to this cute, monkey-infested hill station, after which your children can choose to continue to the village on horseback or in a hand-pulled rickshaw (p106).

➡ **Houseboat, Alappuzha (Alleppey)** Hop on a houseboat to luxuriously cruise Kerala's beautiful backwaters. If you happen to hit town on the second Saturday in August, take the kids along to see the spectacular Nehru Trophy boat race. (p282)

Best Beaches

➡ **Palolem, Goa** Hole up in a beachfront palm-thatched hut and watch your kids cavort at beautiful Palolem beach, featuring the shallowest, safest waters in Goa. (p157)

➡ **Patnem, Goa** Just up the leafy lane from Palolem, quieter Patnem draws scores of long-stayers with children to its nice sand beach and cool, calm, child-friendly beach restaurants. (p157)

➡ **Havelock Island** Splash about in the shallows at languid Havelock Island, part of the Andaman Island chain, where, for older children, there's spectacular diving on offer. (p417)

Planning
Before You Go

➡ Look at climate charts; choose your dates to avoid the extremes of temperature that may put younger children at risk.

➡ Visit your doctor well in advance of travel to discuss vaccinations, health advisories and other heath-related issues involving your children.

➡ For more tips on travel in India, and first-hand accounts of travels in the country, pick up Lonely Planet's *Travel with Children* or visit the Thorn Tree travel forum at lonelyplanet.com.

What to Pack

You can get some of these items in many parts of India too, but often prices are at a premium and brands may not be those you recognise:

➡ For babies or toddlers: disposable or washable nappies, nappy rash cream (Calendula cream works well against heat rash too), extra bottles, a good stock of wet wipes, infant formula and canned, bottled or rehydratable food.

➡ A fold-up baby bed or the lightest possible travel cot you can find (companies such as KidCo make excellent pop-up tent-style beds) since hotel cots may prove precarious. Don't take a stroller/pushchair, as this will be impractical to use as pavements are often scarce. A much better option is a backpack, for smaller kids, so they're lifted up and out of the daunting throng, plus with a superb view.

➡ A few less-precious toys that won't be mourned if lost or damaged.

➡ A swimming jacket, life jacket or water wings for the sea or pool.

➡ Good sturdy footwear.

➡ Audiobooks or a tablet loaded with games and music; great for whiling away long journeys.

➡ Child-friendly insect repellent, hats and sun lotion are a must.

Eating

➡ You may have to work hard to find something to satisfy sensitive childhood palates, but if you're travelling in the more family-friendly regions of India, such as Goa, Kerala or the big cities, you'll find it easier to feed your brood. Here you will find familiar Western dishes in abundance.

➡ While on the road, easy portable snacks such as bananas, samosas, *puri* (puffy dough pockets) and packaged biscuits (Parle G brand are a perennial hit) are available.

➡ Adventurous eaters and vegetarian children will delight in paneer (unfermented cheese) dishes, simple dhals (mild lentil curries), creamy kormas, buttered naans (tandoori breads), pilaus (rice dishes) and Tibetan *momos* (steamed or fried dumplings).

➡ Few children, no matter how culinarily unadventurous, can resist the finger food fun of a vast South Indian dosa (paper-thin lentil-flour pancake) served up for breakfast.

Accommodation

➡ India offers such an array of accommodation options – from beach huts to heritage boutiques to five-star fantasies – that you're bound to be able to find something that will appeal to the whole family.

➡ The swish upmarket hotels are almost always child friendly, but so are many upper-midrange hotels, whose staff will usually rustle up an extra mattress or two; some places won't mind cramming several children into a regular-sized double room along with their parents.

➡ The very best five-star hotels come equipped with kids' pools, games rooms and even kids' clubs, while an occasional night with a warm bubble bath, room service, macaroni cheese and the Disney channel will revive even the most disgruntled young traveller's spirits.

On the Road

➡ Travel in India, be it by taxi, local bus, train or air, can be arduous for the whole family. Concepts such as clean public toilets, changing rooms and safe playgrounds etc are rare in much of the country. Public transport is often extremely overcrowded so plan fun, easy days to follow longer bus or train rides.

➡ Pack plenty of diversions (iPads or laptops with a stock of movies downloaded make invaluable travel companions, as do audiobooks, plus the good old-fashioned story books, cheap toys and games available widely across India).

➡ If you are hiring a car and driver – a sensible and flexible option – and you require safety capsules, child restraints or booster seats, you will need to make this absolutely clear to the hiring company as early as possible. Don't expect to find these items readily available. And finally, don't be afraid to tell your driver to slow down and drive responsibly.

Health

➡ The availability of a decent standard of health care varies widely in India. Talk to your doctor about where you will be travelling to get advice on vaccinations and what to include in your first-aid kit.

➡ Access to health care is certainly better in traveller-frequented parts of the country where it's almost always easy to track down a doctor at short notice (most hotels will be able to recommend a reliable one).

➡ Prescriptions are quickly and cheaply filled over the counter at numerous pharmacies, often congregating near hospitals.

➡ Diarrhoea can be very serious in young children. Seek medical help if persistent or accompanied by fever; rehydration is essential. Heat rash, skin complaints such as impetigo, insect bites or stings can be treated with the help of a well-equipped first-aid kit.

Regions at a Glance

South India is made up of a wonderfully diverse patchwork of states. The vernaculars are varied, the customs are distinctive, there's a variety of culinary choices and the topography is spectacularly changeable. Whether you're a foodie, a nature lover, a temple enthusiast, an architecture buff or a beach bum (or all of those), you'll find plenty to make you happy all over the region.

For travellers, South India's remarkable diversity is most often apparent in its extraordinary wealth of architecture, landscapes, cuisine, performing arts, festivals and wildlife. And then there's the diverse spirituality – the beating heart of the entire nation – which faithfully pulsates all the way from cosmopolitan Mumbai (Bombay) to the steamy jungles of the southern plains.

Mumbai (Bombay)

Architecture
Cuisine
Nightlife

Angels in the Architecture

Thank the British (and Indian stonemasons) for Mumbai's glorious colonial-era architecture; including the Chhatrapati Shivaji Terminus, the High Court and the University of Mumbai.

Divine Dinners

Flavours from all over India mingle in Mumbai. Sample *dhansak* (curried lentil stew) in Parsi canteens, munch on *bhelpuri* on Chowpatty Beach, or sit down to a globe-trotting feast in a contemporarily stylish restaurant.

Bollywood Beats

Sharing their city with the world's most prolific film industry, Mumbaikars are party people. Keep an eye out for Bollywood stars as you dance until dawn in lounges and clubs crammed with beautiful people.

p42

Maharashtra

Caves
Beaches
Forts

Caves as Galleries

The World Heritage-listed caves at Ajanta and Ellora hide exquisite cave paintings and amazing rock sculptures created by Buddhist, Hindu and Jain artists 1000 to 2200 years ago.

Secret Sands

Strung out along Maharashtra's Konkan Coast are some of the most secluded beaches in India, perfect for romantics and adventurers, and with a burgeoning diving scene at Malvan.

Formidable Fortresses

Battleground of countless long-gone empires, Maharashtra is peppered with spectacular redoubts, from mighty rock-top Daulatabad, and Janjira, rising sheer from the sea, to Raigad (capital of local hero Shivaji), which you need a ropeway to get up to.

p82

Goa

Beaches
Cuisine
Architecture

Super Sands

So beautiful they're almost a cliché, Goa's beaches have undeniably been discovered, but with the surf breaking over your toes and palm fronds swaying overhead, it doesn't seem to matter.

Colonial Cookpot

Goa has fresh-off-the-boat seafood and cooks who blend tricks and ingredients from India and Portugal to create a fabulous interplay of flavours.

A Catholic Legacy

When the Portuguese decamped from Goa in 1961, they left behind a grand colonial legacy: mansions in Quepem and Chandor, shop-houses in Panaji (Panjim), stately basilicas in Old Goa and villas scattered along the coastline.

p118

Karnataka & Bengaluru

Architecture
Parks
Yoga

Aesthetic Extravagance

From Mysore Palace and Bijapur's exquisite mausoleums to Hampi's Virupaksha Temple and the Hoysala sculptures of Belur, Halebid and Somnathpur, Karnataka's monuments are a feast for the eyes.

Pristine Reserves

Draped in tropical greenery, the Nilgiri Biosphere Reserve boasts some of the most pristine forests in India, including Bandipur and Nagarhole National Parks, with their abundant wildlife.

Perfecting Your Poses

Mysuru (Mysore) is the birthpace of Ashtanga yoga, drawing thousands of people yearly from around the globe to learn, practise or learn to teach yoga. There are many schools and centres around the state as well.

p170

Telangana & Andhra Pradesh

Religion
Cuisine
Architecture

Soulful Sites

Hindu pilgrims flock to Tirumala's Venkateshwara Temple, while Buddhists contemplate amid the ruins of ancient monastries and Muslims mark Muharram with a procession through Hyderabad's Old City.

Brilliant Biryanis

Synonymous with Hyderabad, biryani is a local obsession. Similarly famous Hyderabadi *haleem* (mutton stew with pounded spiced wheat) has been patented so that it can't be called *haleem* unless it meets local quality standards.

Monumental Marvels

Hyderabad's Charminar is one of India's most famous structures, and Hyderabad's palaces, royal tombs and Golconda fort are testament to its past rulers' wealth.

p226

Kerala

Waterways
Cuisine
Wildlife

Serene Backwaters

Behind the beaches, the inlets and lakes of Kerala's backwaters spread far inland; exploring this waterlogged world by houseboat or canoe is one of India's most relaxing pleasures.

Fire & Spice

Delicious, delicate dishes flavoured with coconut, chilli and myriad spices – the Keralan kitchen is a melting pot of international cultural influences and local ingredients.

Wild Beasts

Kerala has been dealt a fine hand of wildlife-filled national parks, where, amid lush mountain landscapes, you can seek out wild elephants, tigers, leopards and other native Indian species.

p262

Tamil Nadu & Chennai

Temples
Hill Stations
Hotels

Towering Temples

The amazing architecture, daily rituals and colourful festivals of Tamil Nadu's Hindu temples draw pilgrims from around India. Major temples are topped by soaring, sculpture-encrusted *gopurams* (gateway towers) and intricately carved *mandapas* (pavilions).

Cool Escapes

Ooty (Udhagamandalam), Kodaikanal and other hill stations of the Westerns Ghats offer cool weather, festivals, colonial-era guesthouses and hikes to viewpoints overlooking the plains.

Heritage Hotels

Elegantly atmospheric spots to lay your head include the townhouses of Puducherry's French Quarter, palace hotels in the hills, and the Chettiar mansions of the south.

p324

Andaman Islands

Diving
Beaches
Tribes

Undersea Adventures

Explore underwater jungles of coral teeming with tropical fish in jewel-bright colours – India's prime diving destination has easy dips for first-timers and challenging drift dives for veterans.

Superior Sands

If you're searching for that picture-postcard beach or kilometres of deserted coastline, the Andamans boast some of the most unspoiled beaches in India.

Island Culture

An anthropologist's dream, the Andamans are home to dozens of fascinating tribal groups; most reside on outlying islands closed to tourists, but even the major islands offer a beguiling blend of South Asian and Southeast Asian culture.

p408

On the Road

Mumbai (Bombay)

022 / POP 21.1 MILLION

Best Places to Eat

➡ Peshawri (p71)

➡ Revival (p68)

➡ Dakshinayan (p70)

➡ Koh (p69)

➡ La Folie (p68)

Best Places to Stay

➡ Taj Mahal Palace, Mumbai (p64)

➡ Residency Hotel (p65)

➡ Abode Bombay (p64)

➡ Sea Shore Hotel (p63)

➡ Juhu Residency (p66)

Why Go?

Mumbai is big. It's full of dreamers and hard-labourers, starlets and gangsters, stray dogs and exotic birds, artists and servants, fisherfolk and *crorepatis* (millionaires) – and lots of people. It has India's most prolific film industry, some of Asia's biggest slums (as well as the world's most expensive home) and the largest tropical forest in an urban zone. Mumbai is India's financial powerhouse, fashion epicentre and a pulse point of religious tension. It's even evolved its own language, Bambaiyya Hindi, which is a mix of...everything.

If Mumbai is your introduction to India, prepare yourself. The city isn't a threatening place but its furious energy, limited public transport and punishing pollution makes it challenging for visitors. The heart of the city contains some of the grandest colonial-era architecture on the planet but explore a little more and you'll uncover unique bazaars, hidden temples, hipster enclaves and India's premier restaurants and nightlife.

When to Go
Mumbai (Bombay)

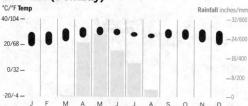

Dec & Jan The very best, least sticky weather.

Aug & Sep Mumbai goes crazy for Ganesh during its most exciting festival, Ganesh Chaturthi.

Oct–Apr There's very little rain, post-monsoon; the best time of year for festivals.

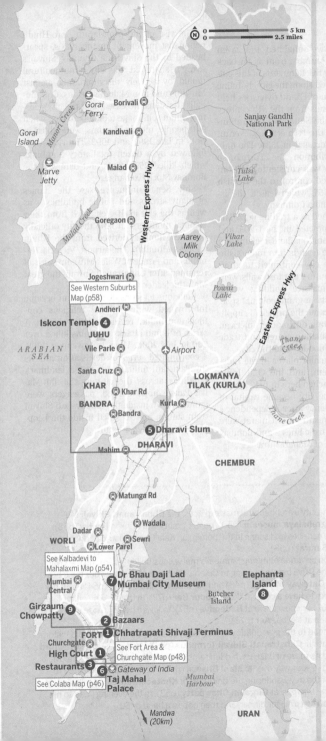

Mumbai Highlights

1 Marvelling at the magnificence of Mumbai's colonial-era architecture: **Chhatrapati Shivaji Terminus** (p47), **High Court** (p51) and **Gateway of India** (p46)

2 Investigating the labyrinthine lanes and stalls in Mumbai's ancient **bazaar district** (p77)

3 Dining like a maharaja at one of India's best restaurants such as **Indigo** (p67)

4 Feeling the love with the Krishna crowd at the unique **Iskcon Temple** (p57)

5 Exploring the self-sufficient world of Asia's largest shantytown, **Dharavi Slum** (p63)

6 Sleeping at the **Taj Mahal Palace, Mumbai** (p64), one of the world's iconic hotels, or having a drink at its bar, Mumbai's first

7 Ogling the gorgeous Renaissance revival interiors of the **Dr Bhau Daji Lad Mumbai City Museum** (p53)

8 Beholding the commanding triple-headed Shiva at **Elephanta Island** (p59)

9 Catching the city's sea breeze among playing kids, big balloons and a hot-pink sunset at **Girgaum Chowpatty** (p53)

History

Koli fisherfolk have inhabited the seven islands that form Mumbai from as far back as the 2nd century BC. Remnants of this culture remain huddled along the city shoreline today. A succession of Hindu dynasties held sway over the islands from the 6th century AD until the Muslim Sultans of Gujarat annexed the area in the 14th century, eventually ceding it to Portugal in 1534. The only memorable contribution the Portuguese made to the area was christening it Bom Bahai. They handed control to the English government in 1665, which leased the islands to the East India Company.

Bombay flourished as a trading port. The city's fort was completed in the 1720s, and a century later ambitious land reclamation projects joined the islands into today's single landmass. The city continued to grow, and in the 19th century the fort walls were dismantled and massive building works transformed the city in grand colonial style. When Bombay became the principal supplier of cotton to Britain during the American Civil War, the population soared and trade boomed as money flooded into the city.

Bombay was a major player in the Independence movement, and the Quit India campaign was launched here in 1942 by Mahatma Gandhi. The city became capital of the Bombay presidency after Independence, but in 1960 Maharashtra and Gujarat were divided along linguistic lines – and Bombay became the capital of Maharashtra.

The rise of the pro-Marathi, pro-Hindu regionalist movement in the 1980s, spearheaded by the Shiv Sena (literally 'Shivaji's Army'), shattered the city's multicultural mould by actively discriminating against Muslims and non-Maharashtrians. Communalist tensions increased, and the city's cosmopolitan self-image took a battering when 900 people, mostly Muslims, were killed in riots in late 1992 and 1993. The riots were followed by a dozen retaliatory bombings which killed 257 people and damaged the Bombay Stock Exchange.

Shiv Sena's influence saw the names of many streets and public buildings – as well as the city itself – changed from their colonial monikers. In 1996 the city officially became Mumbai (derived from the Hindu goddess Mumba). The airport, Victoria Terminus and Prince of Wales Museum were all renamed after Chhatrapati Shivaji, the great Maratha leader.

Religious tensions deepened and became intertwined with national religious conflicts and India's relations with Pakistan. A series of bomb attacks on trains killed over 200 in July 2006. Then, in November 2008, a coordinated series of devastating attacks (by Pakistani militants) targeted landmark buildings across the city, as the Taj Mahal Palace hotel burned, passengers were gunned down inside the Chhatrapati Shivaji train station and 10 killed inside the Leopold Cafe backpacker haunt.

MUMBAI IN...

Two Days

Begin at one of the city's architectural masterpieces, the **Chhatrapati Shivaji Maharaj Vastu Sangrahalaya museum** (p50), before grabbing a drink in **Pantry** (p68) and exploring the galleries and scene in the bohemian Kala Ghoda district. Lunch Gujarati-style at **Samrat** (p68).

In the afternoon continue admiring Mumbai's marvellous buildings around the Oval Maiden and Marine Drive before heading to Colaba, the heart of the city. Tour the city's iconic sights, the **Gateway of India** (p46) and **Taj Mahal Palace hotel** (p64) around sunset, and be sure to have a drink at the **Harbour Bar** (p72). In the evening either fine dine at **Indigo** (p67) or chow down at **Bademiya** (p67), followed by (for those with the stamina) a nightcap at sky bar **Aer** (p73).

The next day, head to the granddaddy of Mumbai's colonial-era giants, the old Victoria Terminus train station, **Chhatrapati Shivaji Terminus** (p47). Then investigate **Crawford Market** (p77) and its maze of bazaars, hidden temples and unique street life. Lunch at **Revival** (p68). Make your way over to **Mani Bhavan** (p53), the museum dedicated to Gandhi, and finish the day wandering the tiny lanes of **Khotachiwadi** (p53) followed by a beach sunset and bhelpuri at **Girgaum Chowpatty** (p53). In the evening head to hip nightlife hub **Bluefrog** (p74) for dinner, and then bop to a band or DJ.

TOP FESTIVALS IN MUMBAI

Mumbai Sanskruti (⊘ Jan) This free, two-day celebration of Hindustani classical music is held on the steps of the gorgeous Asiatic Society Library in the Fort area.

Kala Ghoda Festival (www.kalaghodaassociation.com; ⊘ Feb) Getting bigger and more sophisticated each year, this two-week-long art fest held in Kala Ghoda and the Fort area sees tons of performances and exhibitions.

Elephanta Festival (www.maharashtratourism.gov.in; ⊘ Mar) This classical music and dance festival takes place on the waterfront Apollo Bunder at the Gateway of India.

Nariyal Poornima (⊘ Aug) This Koli celebration in Colaba marks the start of the fishing season and the retreat of monsoon winds.

Ganesh Chaturthi (⊘ Aug/Sep) Mumbai gets totally swept up by this 10- to 12-day celebration of the Hindu god Ganesh. On the festival's first, third, fifth, seventh and 11th days, families and communities take their Ganesh statues to the seashore at Chowpatty and Juhu beaches and auspiciously submerge them.

Mumbai Film Festival (MFF; www.mumbaifilmfest.org; ⊘ Oct) New films from the sub-continent and beyond are screened at the weeklong MFF at cinemas across Mumbai.

In late 2012, when the Sena's charismatic founder Bal Thackeray died (500,000 attended his funeral), the Shiv Sena mission begin to falter, and in the 2014 assembly elections, President Modi's BJP became the largest party in Mumbai.

Despite recent troubles Mumbaikars are a resilient bunch. Increased security is very much part of everyday life today and the city's status as the engine room of the Indian economy remains unchallenged. However, the Mumbai politicians certainly have their work cut out, with the megacity's feeble public transport, gridlocked streets, pollution and housing crisis all in desperate need of attention.

⊙ Sights

Mumbai is an island connected by bridges to the mainland. The city's commercial and cultural centre is at the southern, claw-shaped end of the island known as South Mumbai. The southernmost peninsula is Colaba, traditionally the travellers' nerve centre, with many of the major attractions.

Directly north of Colaba is the busy commercial area known as Fort, where the British fort once stood. This part of the city is bordered on the west by a series of interconnected grassy areas known as maidans (pronounced may-*dahns*).

Continuing north you enter 'the suburbs' which contain the airport and many of Mumbai's best restaurants, shopping and nightspots. The upmarket districts of Bandra, Juhu and Lower Parel are key areas.

⊙ Colaba

Along the city's southernmost peninsula, Colaba is a bustling district packed with elegant art deco and colonial-era mansions, budget-to-midrange lodgings, bars and restaurants, street stalls and a fisherman's quarter. Colaba Causeway (Shahid Bhagat Singh Marg) dissects the district.

If you're here in August, look out for the Koli festival Nariyal Poornima, which is big in Colaba.

★ **Taj Mahal Palace, Mumbai**   LANDMARK
(Map p46; Apollo Bunder) Mumbai's most famous landmark, this stunning hotel is a fairy-tale blend of Islamic and Renaissance styles, and India's second-most photographed monument. It was built in 1903 by the Parsi industrialist JN Tata, supposedly after he was refused entry to one of the European hotels on account of being 'a native'. Dozens were killed inside the hotel when it was targeted during the 2008 terrorist attacks, and images of its burning facade were beamed across the world. The fully restored hotel reopened on Independence Day 2010.

Much more than an iconic building, the Taj's history is intrinsically linked with the nation: it was the first hotel in India to employ women, the first to have electricity (and fans), and it also housed freedom-fighters (for no charge) during the struggle for independence.

Colaba

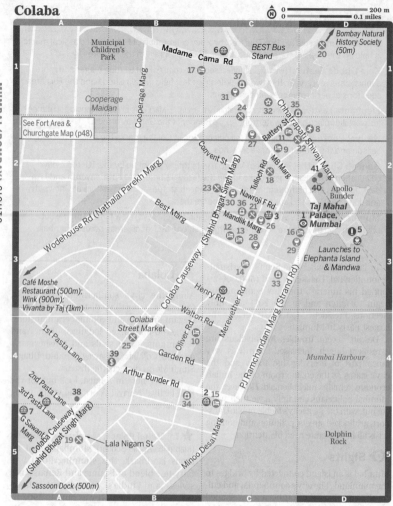

Today the Taj fronts the harbour and Gateway to India, but it was originally designed to face the city (the entrance has been changed).

Gateway of India
MONUMENT

(Map p46) This bold basalt arch of colonial-era triumph faces out to Mumbai Harbour from the tip of Apollo Bunder. Incorporating Islamic styles of 16th-century Gujarat, it was built to commemorate the 1911 royal visit of King George V, but wasn't completed until 1924. Ironically, the British builders of the gateway used it just 24 years later to parade the last British regiment as India marched towards independence. These days, the gateway is a favourite gathering spot for locals and a top place for people-watching. Giant-balloon sellers, photographers, vendors making *bhelpuri* (thin fried rounds of dough with rice, lentils, lemon juice, onion, herbs and chutney) and touts rub shoulders with locals and tourists, creating all the hubbub of a bazaar. In March, they are joined by classical dancers and musicians who perform during the Elephanta Festival (p45).

Boats depart from the gateway's wharfs for Elephanta Island.

Colaba

Sassoon Dock WATERFRONT
Sassoon Dock is a scene of intense and pungent activity at dawn (around 5am) when colourfully clad Koli fisher-folk sort the catch unloaded from fishing boats at the quay. The fish drying in the sun are *bombil*, used in the dish Bombay duck. Photography at the dock is prohibited.

◉ Fort Area & Churchgate

Lined up in a row and vying for your attention with aristocratic pomp, many of Mumbai's majestic Victorian buildings pose on the edge of Oval Maidan. This land, and the Cross and Azad Maidans immediately to the north, was on the oceanfront in those days, and this series of grandiose structures faced west directly to the Arabian Sea.
Kala Ghoda, or 'Black Horse', is a hip, atmospheric subneighbourhood of Fort just north of Colaba. It contains many of Mumbai's museums and galleries alongside a wealth of colonial-era buildings and some of the city's best restaurants and cafes.

★**Chhatrapati Shivaji Terminus** HISTORIC BUILDING
(Victoria Terminus; Map p48) Imposing, exuberant and overflowing with people, this monumental train station is the city's most extravagant Gothic building and an aphorism for colonial-ear India. It's a meringue of Victorian, Hindu and Islamic styles whipped into an imposing Daliesque structure of buttresses, domes, turrets, spires and stained-glass. As historian Christopher London put it, 'the Victoria Terminus is to the British Raj what the Taj Mahal is to the Mughal empire'.
Some of the architectural detail is incredible, with dog-faced gargoyles adorning the magnificent central tower and peacock-filled windows above the central courtyard. Designed by Frederick Stevens, it was completed in 1887, 34 years after the first train in India left this site.

Fort Area & Churchgate

Girgaum
Chowpatty
(1.5km)

Metro Big
(100m)

41

Bombay
Hospital

New Marine Lines
(Sir Vithaldas Thackersey Rd)

Enlargement

Mahatma Gandhi (MG) Rd

49

24

14

33

31

Master Rd

26

29

39

27

3

45

Dr VB Gandhi Marg

7

K Dubash Marg

46

15

Marine Dr

Maharshi Karve (MK) Rd

44

D Rd

38

C Rd

Churchgate
Train Station

CHURCHGATE

B Rd

Back Bay

28

A Rd

E Rd

Indiatourism

Western
Railways
Reservation
Office

13

Veer Nariman Rd

Brabourne
Stadium

40

Dinsha Wachha Marg

35

J Tata Rd

37

Air India

56

Maharshi Karve Rd

Oval
Maidan

8

Madame Cama Rd

19

Jet
Airways

See Colaba Map (p46)

**NARIMAN
POINT**

42

43

Barrister Rajni Patel Marg

55

36

J Bajaj Marg

Municipal
Children's
Park

Cooperage
Maidan

59

57

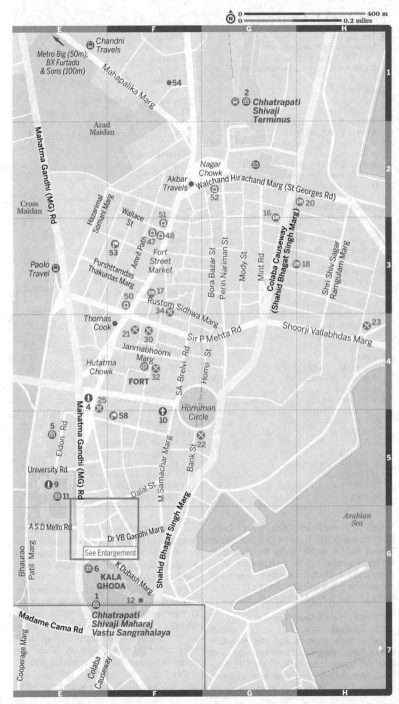

Fort Area & Churchgate

Officially renamed Chhatrapati Shivaji Terminus (CST) in 1998, it's still better known locally as VT. Sadly, its interior is far less impressive, with ugly modern additions and a neglected air – stray dogs roam around the ticket offices – despite the structure's Unesco World Heritage Site status.

★ **Chhatrapati Shivaji Maharaj Vastu Sangrahalaya** MUSEUM
(Prince of Wales Museum; Map p48; http://csmvs.in; K Dubash Marg, Kala Ghoda; Indian/foreigner ₹50/300, camera/video ₹200/1000; ⊙10.15am-6pm) Mumbai's biggest and best museum displays a mix of exhibits from across India. The domed behemoth, an intriguing hodgepodge of Islamic, Hindu and British architecture, is a flamboyant Indo-Saracenic design by George Wittet (who also designed the Gateway of India).

Its vast collection includes impressive Hindu and Buddhist sculpture, terracotta figurines from the Indus Valley, Indian miniature paintings, porcelain and some particularly vicious-looking weaponry. Good information is provided in English, and audio guides are available in seven languages.

Two of the upstairs galleries are air-conditioned, offering a welcome relief to

THE ART DISTRICT

India's contemporary art scene has exploded in recent years, and Mumbai, along with Delhi, is the centre of the action. A slew of galleries are showing incredible work in some gorgeous spaces across the city.

Kala Ghoda hosts a wonderful two-week festival (p45) each February, with some great exhibitions (as well as music, theatre, dance and literary events).

Year-round, the second Thursday of each month is 'Art Night Thursday', when galleries stay open late and the vibe is social. Gallery crawls are sometimes organised; check **Mumbai Boss** (www.mumbaiboss.com) for the latest or the free fold-up *Mumbai Art Map*, available at galleries and bookstores. To go more in depth, check out the magazine *Art India*, available at most English-language bookshops, which has news, background and criticism on work from across the country.

Or, just read nothing and go see pretty things on your own: many galleries are within walking distance of one another in Colaba and Fort. If street art is more your thing, don't miss the Great Wall of Mumbai (p57).

Chatterjee & Lal (Map p46; www.chatterjeeandlal.com; 1st fl, Kamal Mansion, Arthur Bunder Rd, Colaba; ☺11am-7pm Tue-Sat) Work by emerging artists and historical material.

Galerie Mirchandani + Steinruecke (Map p46; www.galeriems.com; 1st fl, Sunny House, 16/18 Mereweather Rd, Colaba; ☺11am-7pm Tue-Sat) Contemporary Indian art and sculpture; the gallery is just behind the Taj Mahal Palace hotel.

Gallery Maskara (Map p46; www.gallerymaskara.com; 6/7 3rd Pasta Lane, Colaba; ☺11am-7pm Tue-Sat) This Colaba gallery showcases exciting contemporary art.

Jhaveri Contemporary (www.jhavericontemporary.com; Krishna Niwas, 58A Walkeshwar Rd, Walkeshwar, Malabar Hill; ☺11am-6pm Tue-Sat) Cutting-edge photography and art from Indian and overseas artists.

Project 88 (Map p46; www.project88.in; BMP Building, NA Sawant Marg, Colaba; ☺11am-7pm Tue-Sat) Well established gallery which features leading Indian artists.

the summer heat. There's a fine cafeteria at the entrance and the museum shop is also excellent.

Marine Drive   PROMENADE
(Map p48; Netaji Subhashchandra Bose Rd) Built on reclaimed land in 1920, Marine Dr arcs along the shore of the Arabian Sea from Nariman Point past Girgaum Chowpatty and continues to the foot of Malabar Hill. Lined with flaking art deco apartments, it's one of Mumbai's most popular promenades and sunset-watching spots. Its twinkling nighttime lights earned it the nickname 'the Queen's Necklace'.

Hundreds gather on the promenade around Nariman Point in the early evening to snack and chat, when it's a good place to meet Mumbaikars.

University of Mumbai   HISTORIC BUILDING
(Bombay University; Map p48; Bhaurao Patil Marg) Looking like a 15th-century French-Gothic mansion plopped incongruously among Mumbai's palm trees, this structure was designed by Gilbert Scott of London's St Pan-

cras train station fame. There's an exquisite **University Library** and **Convocation Hall**, as well as the 80m-high **Rajabai Clock Tower** (Map p48), decorated with detailed carvings. Since the 2008 terror attacks, there's no public access to the grounds but it's still well worth admiring from the street.

High Court   HISTORIC BUILDING
(Map p48; Eldon Rd; ☺10.45am-2pm & 2.45-5pm Mon-Fri) A hive of daily activity, packed with judges, barristers and other cogs in the Indian justice system, the High Court is an elegant 1848 neo-Gothic building. The design was inspired by a German castle and was obviously intended to dispel any doubts about the authority of the justice dispensed inside.

Visitors are permitted to explore the building and attend cases. Inside it's quite a spectacle, with court officials kitted out in starched white tunics offset with red cummerbunds and scarlet berets, while robed barristers strut about with their chests puffed out.

MUMBAI (BOMBAY) SIGHTS

No photography is permitted; cameras have to be left with guards at the entrance.

Keneseth Eliyahoo Synagogue   SYNAGOGUE
(Map p48; www.jacobsassoon.org; Dr VB Gandhi Marg, Kala Ghoda; camera/video ₹100/500; ⊘11am-6pm Mon-Sat, 1-6pm Sun) Built in 1884, this unmistakable sky-blue synagogue still functions and is tenderly maintained by the city's dwindling Jewish community. It's protected by very heavy security, but the caretaker is welcoming (and will point out a photo of Madonna, who dropped by in 2008).

St Thomas' Cathedral   CHURCH
(Map p48; Veer Nariman Rd; ⊘7am-6pm) This charming cathedral, begun in 1672 and finished in 1718, is the oldest British-era building standing in Mumbai: it was once the eastern gateway of the East India Company's fort (the 'Churchgate'). The cathedral is a marriage of Byzantine and colonial-era architecture, and its airy interior is full of grandiose colonial-era memorials.

Jehangir Art Gallery   ART GALLERY
(Map p48; www.jehangirartgallery.com; 161B MG Rd, Kala Ghoda; ⊘11am-7pm) FREE Recently renovated, this excellent gallery hosts shows by local artists and the occasional big name; it's also home to Samovar Café (p69).

National Gallery of Modern Art   MUSEUM
(NGMA; Map p46; www.ngmaindia.gov.in; MG Rd; Indian/foreigner ₹10/150; ⊘11am-6pm Tue-Sun)

DHARAVI SLUM

Mumbaikars were ambivalent about the stereotypes in 2008's *Slumdog Millionaire*, but slums are very much a part of – some would say the foundation of – Mumbai city life. An astonishing 60% of Mumbai's population lives in slums, and one of the city's largest slums is Dharavi. Originally inhabited by fisher-folk when the area was still creeks, swamps and islands, it became attractive to migrant workers from South Mumbai and beyond when the swamp began to fill in due to natural and artificial causes. It now incorporates 2.2 sq km of land sandwiched between Mumbai's two major railway lines, and is home to perhaps as many as a million people.

While it may look a bit shambolic from the outside, the maze of dusty alleys and sewer-lined streets of this city-within-a-city are actually a collection of abutting settlements. Some parts of Dharavi have mixed populations, but in other parts inhabitants from different parts of India, and with different trades, have set up homes and tiny factories. Potters from Saurashtra (Gujarati) live in one area, Muslim tanners in another; embroidery workers from Uttar Pradesh work alongside metalsmiths; while other workers recycle plastics as women dry pappadams in the searing sun. Some of these thriving industries, as many as 20,000 in all, export their wares, and the annual turnover of business from Dharavi is thought to exceed US$700 million.

Up close, life in the slums is fascinating to witness. Residents pay rent, most houses have kitchens and electricity, and building materials range from flimsy corrugated-iron shacks to permanent multistorey concrete structures. Perhaps the biggest issue facing Dharavi residents is sanitation, as water supply is irregular – every household has a 200L drum for water storage. Very few dwellings have a private toilet or bathroom, so some neighbourhoods have constructed their own (to which every resident must contribute financially) while other residents are forced to use rundown public facilities.

Many families have been here for generations, and education achievements are higher than in many rural areas: around 15% of children complete a higher education and find white-collar jobs. Many choose to stay, though, in the neighbourhood they grew up in.

Slum tourism is a polarising subject, so you'll have to decide for yourself. If you opt to visit, Reality Tours & Travel (p63) does a illuminating tour, and puts a percentage of profits back into Dharavi. Some tourists opt to visit on their own, which is OK as well – just don't take photos. Take the train from Churchgate station to Mahim, exit on the west side and cross the bridge into Dharavi.

To learn more about Mumbai's slums, check out Katherine Boo's 2012 book *Behind the Beautiful Forevers*, about life in Annawadi, a slum near the airport, and *Rediscovering Dharavi*, Kalpana Sharma's sensitive and engrossing history of Dharavi's people, culture and industry.

KHOTACHIWADI

The storied *wadi* (hamlet) of **Khotachiwadi** (Map p54) is a bastion clinging onto Mumbai life as it was before high-rises. A Christian enclave of elegant two-storey wooden mansions, it's 500m northeast of Girgaum Chowpatty, lying amid Mumbai's predominantly Hindu and Muslim neighbourhoods. These winding lanes allow a wonderful glimpse into a quiet(ish) life free of rickshaws and taxis. It's not large, but you can spend a little while wandering the alleyways and admiring the old homes and, around Christmas, their decorations.

To find Khotachiwadi, aim for **St Teresa's Church** (Map p54), on the corner of Jagannath Shankarsheth Marg (JSS Marg) and Rajarammohan Roy Marg (RR Rd/Charni Rd), then head directly opposite the church on JSS Marg and duck down the second and third lanes on your left.

Well-curated shows of Indian and international artists in a bright and spacious exhibition space.

Delhi Art Gallery
ART GALLERY

(Map p48; www.delhiartgallery.com; 58 VB Gandhi Marg, Kala Ghoda; ⊙11am-7pm) **FREE** Spread over four floors of a beautifully restored cream colonial-era structure. Showcases important modern Indian art from its extensive collection and well-curated exhibitions.

◉ Kalbadevi to Mahalaxmi

★ Dr Bhau Daji Lad Mumbai City Museum
MUSEUM

(Map p54; www.bdlmuseum.org; Dr Babasaheb Ambedkar Rd; Indian/foreigner ₹10/100; ⊙10am-6pm Thu-Tue) This gorgeous museum, built in Renaissance revival style in 1872 as the Victoria & Albert Museum, contains 3500-plus objects relating to Mumbai's history – photography and maps, textiles, books and manuscripts, *bidriware*, laquerware, weaponry and exquisite pottery.

The landmark building was renovated in 2008, with its Minton tile floors, gilded ceiling mouldings, ornate columns, chandeliers and staircases all restored to their former glory. Contemporary music, dance and drama feature in the new Plaza area, where there's a cafe and shop.

The museum is located in the lush gardens of Jijamata Udyan; skip the zoo.

Mani Bhavan
MUSEUM

(Map p54; ☑23805864; www.gandhi-manibhavan.org; 19 Laburnum Rd, Gamdevi; donation appreciated; ⊙9.30am-6pm) As poignant as it is tiny, this museum is in the building where Mahatma Gandhi stayed during visits to Bombay from 1917 to 1934. The leader formulated his philosophy of satyagraha (nonviolent protest) and launched the 1932 Civil Disobedience campaign from here. Exhibitions include a photographic record of his life, along with dioramas and documents, such as letters he wrote to Adolf Hitler and Franklin D Roosevelt and tributes from Ho Chi Minh and Einstein.

Girgaum Chowpatty
BEACH

(Map p54) This city beach is a favourite evening spot for courting couples, families, political rallies and anyone out to enjoy what passes for fresh air. Evening *bhelpuri* at the throng of stalls at the beach's southern end is an essential part of the Mumbai experience. Forget about taking a dip: the water's toxic.

On the 10th day of the Ganesh Chaturthi festival (p45), in August or September, millions flock here to submerge huge Ganesh statues: it's joyful mayhem.

Mumba Devi Temple
HINDU TEMPLE

(Map p54; Bhuleshwar) Pay a visit to the city's patron goddess at this 18th-century temple, about 1km north of Chhatrapati Shivaji Terminus. Among the deities in residence is Bahuchar Maa, goddess of the transgender *hijras*, and *puja* (prayer) is held here several times a day.

Haji Ali Dargah
MOSQUE

(Map p54; www.hajialidargah.in; off V Desai Chowk) Floating like a sacred mirage off the coast, this Indo-Islamic shrine located on an offshore inlet is a striking sight. Built in the 19th century, it contains the tomb of the Muslim saint Pir Haji Ali Shah Bukhari. Legend has it that Haji Ali died while on a pilgrimage to Mecca and his casket miraculously floated back to this spot.

Kalbadevi to Mahalaxmi

N

0   0   800 m
    0.5 miles

BYCULLA

1 Dr Bhau Daji Lad Mumbai City Museum

Victoria Gardens (Veermata Jijabai Bhonsle Udyan)

Patanwala Marg

Victoria Rd

S Balwant Singh Rd

Byculla Train Station

Jijibhoy Rd

Clare Rd

Bapurao Jagtap Marg

Maulana Azad Rd

Morland Rd

12

14

Mahalaxmi Train Station

6

J Boman Behram Marg

Foras Rd

Mumbai Central Bus Terminal

National CTC

22

Mahalaxmi Racecourse

Bluefrog (1km); Aer (1.1km); Canvas Laugh (1.5km); Cathay Pacific (1.6km); Comedy Store (2km)

Mumbai Central Train Station

Falkland Rd

Willingdon Sports Club Golf Course

Tardeo Rd

Nehru Centre (200m)

Lala Lajpat Rai Rd

17

Japanese Consulate

TARDEO

Altamount Rd

21

G Deshmukh Rd (Peddar Rd)

Kemp's Corner

4

Arabian Sea

7

29

20 Vatsalabai Desai Chowk

Bhulabhai Desai Rd (Warden Rd)

CUMBALLA HILL

Breach Candy Hospital

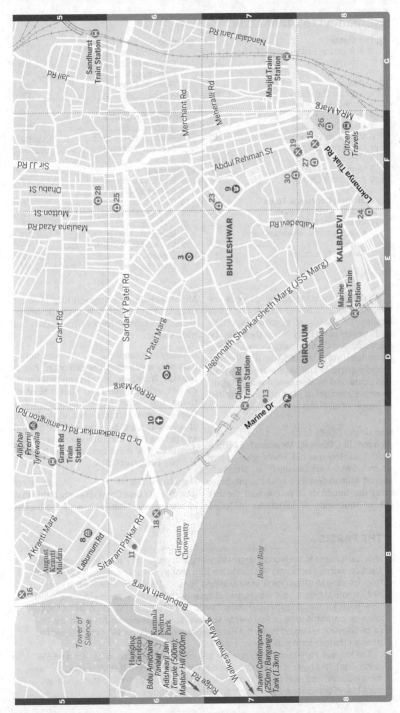

Kalbadevi to Mahalaxmi

It's only possible to visit the shrine at low tide, via a long causeway (check tide times locally). Thousands of pilgrims, especially on Thursday and Friday (when there may be *qawwali,* devotional singing), cross it daily, many donating to beggars who line the way.

Sadly parts of the shrine are in a poor state, damaged by storms and the saline air, though a renovation plan exists. It's visited by people of all faiths.

Mahalaxmi Dhobi Ghat — GHAT
(Map p54; Dr E Moses Rd, Mahalaxmi; ☉ 4.30am-dusk) This 140-year-old dhobi ghat (place where clothes are washed) is Mumbai's biggest human-powered washing machine: every day hundreds of people beat the dirt out of thousands of kilograms of soiled Mumbai clothes and linen in 1026 open-air troughs. The best view is from the bridge across the railway tracks near Mahalaxmi train station.

Bombay Panjrapole — ANIMAL SHELTER
(Map p54; www.bombaypanjrapole.org.in; Panjrapole Marg, Bhuleshwar; ☉ 11am-6pm) In the middle of bustling Bhuleshwar market is, of all things, this shelter for 300 homeless cows. Donkeys, goats, birds, dogs and ducks are also looked after. You can wander around and pet the cows and calves and, for a small donation, feed them fresh greens. It's near Madhav Baug Post Office.

Mahalaxmi Temple — HINDU TEMPLE
(Map p54; off V Desai Chowk) It's only fitting that in money-mad Mumbai one of the busiest

THE PARSIS

Mumbai is home to the world's largest surviving community of Parsis, people of the ancient Zoroastrian faith, who fled Iran in the 10th century to escape religious persecution from invading Muslims. 'Parsi' literally means Perisan. Zoroastrians believe in a single deity, Ahura Mazda, who is worshipped at *agiaries* (fire temples) across Mumbai, which non-Parsis are forbidden to enter. Parsi funeral rites are unique: the dead are laid out on open-air platforms to be picked over by vultures. The most renowned of these, the **Tower of Silence**, is located below the Hanging Gardens in Malabar Hill, yet screened by trees and hidden from public view.

The Mumbai Parsi community is extremely influential and successful, with a 98.6% literacy rate (the highest in the city). Famous Parsis include the Tata family (India's foremost industrialists), author Rohinton Mistry and Queen singer Freddie Mercury. If you want to try Parsi cuisine, head to Brittania restaurant (p69).

WORTH A TRIP

THE GREAT WALL OF MUMBAI

Starting as an initiative by artists to add colour to a suburban street in Bandra, the Wall Project (www.thewallproject.com) has introduced vibrant public art, murals and graffiti across the city. There's no official membership, and the art has been created by both amateurs and professionals.

The guidelines are that no advertising, political statements, religious content or obscene messaging should be used. Social messaging that's too preachy is not encouraged either.

Hundreds of individuals have joined the project, with most murals dealing with personal stories: their dreams, desire for change, criticisms and frustrations.

Perhaps the most spectacular stretch is a 2km canvas along Senapati Bapat Marg (Tulsi Pipe Rd), between the train stations of Mahim and Dadar on the Western Line, where the art parallels the tracks. It's a very thought-provoking and enriching experience to take in; allow an hour and a half to explore.

This particular wall had long been coveted by the Wall Project founders, but they expected firm opposition from the authorities. Instead they were actually approached by the city's Municipal Commissioner, who invited them to create something. Around 400 people contributed.

Many murals on Senapati Bapat Marg have a theme that's relevant to India and Mumbai such as the environment, pollution and pressures of metropolitan life. One mural of a Mumbai cityscape simply says 'Chaos is our Paradise'.

Bandra is another area rich in street art, where many walls and bridges have been customised: Chapel Lane is a good place to start investigating.

and most colourful temples is dedicated to Mahalaxmi, the goddess of wealth. Perched on a headland, it is the focus for Mumbai's Navratri (Festival of Nine Nights) celebrations in September/October.

Babu Amichand Panalal
Adishwarji Jain Temple   JAIN TEMPLE
(Walkeshwar Marg, Malabar Hill; ⊙5am-9pm) This temple is renowned among Jains for its beauty – given how beautiful Jain temples are, that's saying a lot. Check out the paintings and especially the ecstatically colourful zodiac dome ceiling. It's a small, actively used temple; visitors should be sensitive and dress modestly.

Nehru Centre   CULTURAL COMPLEX
(☑24964676, 24964680; www.nehru-centre. org; Dr Annie Besant Rd, Worli; Discovery of India admission free, planetarium adult/child ₹50/25; ⊙10am-6pm Tue-Sun, Discovery of India 11am-5pm, planetarium English show 3pm) The Nehru Centre is a cultural complex that includes a planetarium, theatre, gallery and an interesting history exhibition, Discovery of India. The architecture is striking: the tower looks like a giant cylindrical pineapple, the planetarium like a UFO. High-quality dance, drama and live music events are held here.

The complex is just inland from Lala Laipat Rai Rd.

Malabar Hill   AREA
(around BG Kher Marg) Mumbai's most exclusive neighbourhood, at the northern end of Back Bay, surprisingly contains one of Mumbai's most sacred oases. Concealed between apartment blocks is Banganga Tank, an enclave of serene temples, bathing pilgrims, meandering, traffic-free streets and picturesque old *dharamsalas* (pilgrims' rest houses). According to Hindu legend, Lord Ram created this tank by piercing the earth with his arrow. For some of the best views of Chowpatty, about 600m west, and the graceful arc of Marine Dr, visit Kamala Nehru Park.

◉ Western Suburbs

★Iskcon Temple   HINDU TEMPLE
(Map p58; www.iskconmumbai.com; Juhu Church Rd, Juhu; ⊙4.30am-1pm & 4-9pm) A focus for intense, celebratory worship in the sedate suburbs, this temple is a compelling place to visit. Iskcon Juhu has a key part in the Hare Krishna story, as founder AC Bhaktivedanta Swami Prabhupada spent extended periods here (you can visit his modest living

Western Suburbs

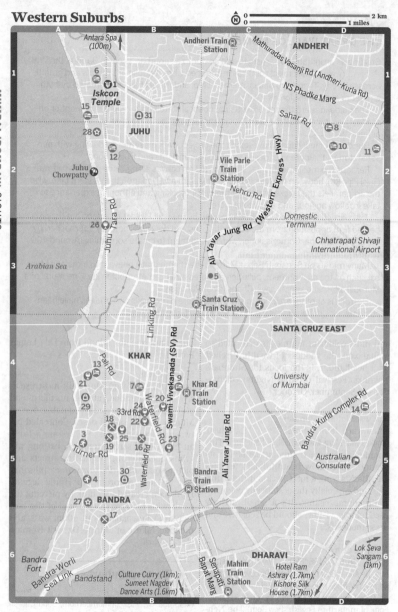

quarters in the adjacent building). The temple compound comes alive during prayer time as the faithful whip themselves into a devotional frenzy of joy, with *kirtan* dancing accompanied by crashing hand symbols and drumbeats.

Murals that are dotted around the compound detail the Hare Krishna narrative. The Iskcon (p66) hotel that is located here is also recommended, as is the canteen (meals ₹70).

Western Suburbs

👁 Gorai Island

Global Pagoda BUDDHIST TEMPLE
(www.globalpagoda.org; Gorai; ⏱ 9am-7pm, meditation classes 10am-6pm) Rising up like a mirage from polluted Gorai Creek is this breathtaking, golden 96m-high stupa modelled on Myanmar's Shwedagon Pagoda. Its dome, which houses relics of Buddha, was built entirely without supports using an ancient technique of interlocking stones, and the meditation hall beneath it seats 8000.

There's a museum dedicated to the life of the Buddha and his teaching, and 20-minute meditation classes are offered daily; an on-site meditation centre also offers 10-day courses.

To get here, take a train from Churchgate to Borivali (exit the station at the 'West' side), then take bus 294 (₹5) or an autorickshaw (₹40) to the ferry landing, where Esselworld ferries (return ₹50) depart every 30 minutes. The last ferry to the pagoda is at 5.30pm.

👁 Elephanta Island

⭐ **Elephanta Island** HINDU TEMPLE
(Gharapuri; Indian/foreigner ₹10/250; ⏱ caves 9am-5pm Tue-Sun) Northeast of the Gateway of India in Mumbai Harbour, the rock-cut temples on Gharapuri, better known as Elephanta Island, are a Unesco World Heritage Site. Created between AD 450 and 750, the labyrinth of cave temples represent some of India's most impressive temple carving. The main Shiva-dedicated temple is an intriguing latticework of courtyards, halls, pillars and shrines; its magnum opus is a 6m-tall statue of Sadhashiva, depicting a three-faced Shiva as the destroyer, creator and preserver of the universe, his eyes closed in eternal contemplation.

It was the Portuguese who dubbed the island Elephanta because of a large stone elephant near the shore (this collapsed in 1814 and was moved by the British to Mumbai's Jijamata Udyan). There's a small museum on-site, with informative pictorial panels on the origin of the caves.

Pushy, expensive guides are available – but you don't really need one as Pramod Chandra's *A Guide to the Elephanta Caves*, widely for sale, is more than sufficient.

Launches (Map p46) head to Gharapuri from the Gateway of India every half-hour from 9am to 3.30pm. Buy tickets (economy/deluxe ₹130/160) at the booths lining Apollo Bunder. The voyage takes about an hour.

The ferries dock at the end of a concrete pier, from where you can walk or take the miniature train (₹10) to the stairway (admission ₹10) leading up to the caves. It's lined with souvenir stalls and patrolled by pesky monkeys. Wear good shoes.

Activities

Mumbai has surprisingly good butterfly- and birdwatching opportunities. Sanjay Gandhi National Park is popular for woodland birds, while the mangroves of Godrej (13km east of Bandra) are rich in waders. The **Bombay Natural History Society** (BNHS; Map p48; ☑22821811; www.bnhs.org; Hornbill House, Shahid Bhagat Singh Marg; ☺9am-5.30pm Mon-Fri) runs excellent trips every weekend.

Outbound Adventure   OUTDOOR ADVENTURE
(☑26315019; www.outboundadventure.com) This outfit runs one-day rafting trips on the Ulhas River from July to early September (₹2000 per person). After a good rain, rapids can get up to Grade III+, though usually the rafting is calmer. Also organises camping (from ₹1500 per person per day) and canoeing trips.

MUMBAI FOR CHILDREN

Kidzania (www.kidzania.in; 3rd flr, R City, LBS Marg, Ghatkopar West; ☺child/adult Tue-Fri ₹950/500, Sat & Sun ₹950/700) is Mumbai's latest attraction, an educational activity centre where kids can learn all about piloting a plane, fighting fires, policing and get stuck into lots of art- and craft-making. It's on the outskirts on the city, 10km northeast of the Bandra Kurla Complex.

Little tykes with energy to burn will love the Gorai Island amusement parks, **Esselworld** (www.esselworld.in; adult/child ₹790/490; ☺11am-7pm, from 10am weekends) and **Water Kingdom** (www.waterkingdom.in; adult/child ₹690/490; ☺11am-7pm, from 10am weekends). Both have lots of rides, slides and shade. Combined tickets are ₹1190/990 (adult/child).

The free **Hanging Gardens**, in Malabar Hill, have animal topiaries, swings in the shade and coconut-wallahs. **Kamala Nehru Park**, across the street, has a two-storey 'boot house'. Bombay Natural History Society (p60) also conducts nature trips for kids.

Wild Escapes   TREKKING
(☑66635228; www.wild-escapes.com; treks from ₹780) Weekend trekking trips to forts, valleys and waterfalls around Maharashtra.

Yoga House   YOGA
(Map p58; ☑65545001; www.yogahouse.in; 53 Chimbai Rd, Bandra; class ₹700; ☺8am-10pm) A variety of yoga traditions are taught at this homey, Western-style yoga centre, housed in a Portuguese-style bungalow by the sea. There's also a charming cafe.

Yoga Cara   YOGA, MASSAGE
(Map p58; ☑022-26511464; www.yogacara.in; 1st fl, SBI Bldg, 18A New Kant Wadi Rd, Bandra; ☺yoga per class/week ₹600/1500) Classic hatha and iyengar yoga institute. Massages (from ₹1850 per hour) and treatments are excellent here; the SoHum rejuvenating massage is recommended. Ayurvedic cooking classes are also offered.

Antara Spa   SPA
(☑022-66939999; www.theclubmumbai.com; 197 DN Nagar, Andheri West; 1hr massage from ₹2450; ☺10am-10pm) Luxury spa with skilled therapists offering a range of therapies and treatments, including Swedish, Thai and hot-stone massages.

Palm Spa   SPA
(Map p46; ☑022-66349898; www.thepalmsspaindia.com; Chhatrapati Shivaji Marg, Colaba; 1hr massage from ₹3200; ☺9.30am-10.30pm) Indulge in a rub, scrub or tub at this renowned Colaba spa. The exfoliating lemongrass and green-tea scrub is ₹2500.

Child Rights & You   VOLUNTEERING
(CRY; Map p54; ☑23096845; www.cry.org; 89A Anand Estate, Sane Guruji Marg, Mahalaxmi) Raises funds for marginalised children. Volunteers can assist with campaigns (online and on the ground), research, surveys and media, as well as occasional fieldwork. A four-week commitment is required.

Lok Seva Sangam   VOLUNTEERING
(☑022-24070718; http://loksevasangam.wordpress.com; D/1, Everard Nagar Eastern Express Hwy, Sion) Works to improve lives in the city's slums. Medical staff who can speak Hindi/Marathi or those with fundraising skills are needed.

Vatsalya Foundation   VOLUNTEERING
(Map p54; ☑24962115; www.thevatsalyafoundation.org; Anand Niketan, King George V Memorial, Dr E Moses Rd, Mahalaxmi) Works with

SANJAY GANDHI NATIONAL PARK

It's hard to believe that within 1½ hours of the teeming metropolis you can be surrounded by a 104-sq-km protected tropical forest. At **Sanjay Gandhi National Park** (⏹28866449; Borivali; adult/child ₹30/15, vehicle ₹100, safari admission ₹50; ⊙7.30am-6pm Tue-Sun, last entry 4pm) bright flora, birds, butterflies and elusive wild leopards replace pollution and concrete, all surrounded by forested hills on the city's northern edge. Urban development has muscled in on the fringes, but the heart of the park is still very peaceful.

A trekking ban is in force to protect wildlife, but you can still walk in the woods if you go with Bombay Natural History Society. On your own, you can cycle (hire bikes cost ₹20 per hour, ₹200 deposit) or take the shuttle to the Shilonda Waterfall, Vihar and Tulsi Lakes (where there's boating) and the most intriguing option, the **Kanheri Caves** (Indian/foreigner ₹5/100), a set of 109 dwellings and monastic structures for Buddhist monks 6km inside the park. The caves, not all of which are accessible, were developed over 1000 years, beginning in the 1st century BC, as part of a sprawling monastic university complex. Avoid the zoo-like lion and tiger 'safari' as the animals are in cages and enclosures.

Inside the park's main northern entrance is an information centre with a small exhibition on the park's wildlife. The best time to see birds is October to April and butterflies August to November.

The nearest station is Borivali, served by trains on the Western Railway line from Churchgate station (30 minutes, frequent).

Mumbai's street children. There are long- and short-term opportunities in teaching English, computer skills and sports activities.

Welfare of Stray Dogs   VOLUNTEERING
(Map p48; ⏹64222838; www.wsdindia.org; Yeshwant Chambers, B Bharucha Rd, Kala Ghoda) Operates sterilisation and antirabies programs. Volunteers can walk dogs, treat street dogs, manage stores, educate kids in school programs or fundraise.

✍ Courses

★Yoga Institute   YOGA
(Map p58; ⏹26122185; www.theyogainstitute. org; Shri Yogendra Marg, Prabhat Colony, Santa Cruz East; per 1st/2nd month ₹650/450) At its peaceful leafy campus near Santa Cruz, the respected Yoga Institute has daily classes as well as weekend and weeklong programs, and longer residential courses including teacher training (with the seven-day course a prerequisite).

Kaivalyadhama Ishwardas Yogic Health Centre   YOGA
(Map p54; ⏹22818417; www.kdhammumbai.org; 43 Marine Dr; ⊙6am-7pm Mon-Sat) Several daily yoga classes as well as workshops; fees include a ₹800 monthly membership fee and a ₹600 admission fee.

★Bharatiya Vidya Bhavan   LANGUAGE COURSE, MUSIC
(Map p54; ⏹23871860; www.bhavans.info; 2nd fl, cnr KM Munshi Marg & Ramabai Rd, Girgaum; per hour ₹500; ⊙4-8pm) Excellent private Hindi, Marathi, Gujarati and Sanskrit language classes. Contact Professor Ghosh (a Grammy Award–winning composer and musician) for lessons in tabla, vocals, sitar or classical dance.

Sumeet Nagdev Dance Arts   DANCE
(SNDA; ⏹24366777; www.sumeetnagdevdance arts.in; Silver Cascade Bldg, SB Marg, Dadar West; 1hr class ₹450) SNDA offers tons of dance classes, from samba and ballet to 'Indian Folk Bollywood'. Classes are also held at a **Chowpatty location** (Studio Balance, Krishna Kunj, 29/30 KM Munshi Marg).

☞ Tours

Fiona Fernandez' *Ten Heritage Walks of Mumbai* (₹395) has walking tours of the city, with fascinating historical background. The Government of India tourist office can provide a list of approved multilingual guides; most charge ₹750/1000 per half-/full day.

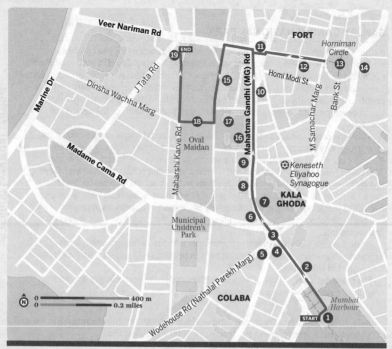

City Walk
Architectural Mumbai

START GATEWAY OF INDIA
END EROS CINEMA
LENGTH 2.5KM; 1½ HOURS

Mumbai's defining feature is its distinctive mix of colonial-era and art deco architecture. Starting from the **1 Gateway of India** (p46), walk up Chhatrapati Shivaji Marg past the art deco residential and commercial complex **2 Dhunraj Mahal**, towards **3 Regal Circle**. Walk the circle for views of the surrounding buildings – including the art deco **4 Regal cinema** (p76) and the **5 Majestic Hotel**, now the Sahakari Bhandar cooperative store. Continue up MG Rd, past the beautifully restored facade of the **6 National Gallery of Modern Art** (p52). Opposite is the landmark **7 Chhatrapati Shivaji Maharaj Vastu Sangrahalaya** (p50) built in glorious Indo-Saracenic style. Back across the road is the 'Romanesque Transitional' **8 Elphinstone College** and the **9 David Sassoon Library & Reading Room**, where members escape the afternoon heat lazing on planters'

chairs on the upper balcony. Continue north to admire the vertical art deco stylings of the **10 New India Assurance Company Building**. On an island ahead lies **11 Flora Fountain**, depicting the Roman goddess of flowers. Turn east down Veer Nariman Rd, walking towards **12 St Thomas' Cathedral** (p52). Ahead lies the stately **13 Horniman Circle**, an arcaded ring of buildings laid out in the 1860s around a beautifully kept botanical garden. It's overlooked from the east by the neoclassical **14 Town Hall**, home to the Asiatic Society library. Backtrack to Flora Fountain, continuing west and turning south onto Bhaurao Patil Marg to see the august **15 High Court** (p51) and the ornate **16 University of Mumbai** (p51). The university's 80m-high **17 Rajabai Clock Tower** (p51) is best observed from within the **18 Oval Maidan**. Turn around to compare the colonial-era edifices with the row of art deco beauties lining Maharshi Karve (MK) Rd, culminating in the wedding-cake tower of the classic **19 Eros Cinema** (p76).

A **cruise** on Mumbai Harbour is a good way to see the Gateway of India and Colaba harbourfont from the sea. Half-hour ferry rides (₹80) depart from the Gateway of India; tickets are sold on-site.

★**Reality Tours & Travel** SLUM TOUR
(Map p48; ☑9820822253; www.realitytour sandtravel.com; 1/26, Unique Business Service Centre, Akber House, Nowroji Fardonji Rd; most tours ₹750-1500) ✎ Compelling tours of the Dharavi slum, with 80% of post-tax profits going to the agency's own NGO, **Reality Gives** (www.realitygives.org). Street food, market, bicycle and Night Mumbai tours are also excellent.

Bombay Heritage Walks WALKING TOUR
(☑23690992, 9821887321; www.bombayherit agewalks.com; per 2hr tour from ₹2500, for up to 5 people) Run by two enthusiastic architects, BHW has terrific tours of heritage neighbourhoods.

Mumbai Magic Tours CITY TOUR
(☑9867707414; www.mumbaimagic.com; 2hr tour per person from ₹1750) Designed by the authors of the fabulous **Mumbai Magic blog** (www.mumbai-magic.blogspot.com), these city tours focus on food markets, traditional dance and music, and Jewish heritage, among others.

Nilambari Bus Tours BUS TOUR
(MTDC; ☑020-22845678; www.maharashtratour ism.gov.in; 1hr tour lower/upper deck ₹60/180; ⊙7pm & 8.15pm Sat & Sun) Maharashtra Tourism runs open-deck bus tours of illuminated heritage buildings on weekends. Buses depart from and can be booked at both the **MTDC booth** (Map p46) and the **MTDC office** (☑22841877; www.maharashtra tourism.gov.in; Madame Cama Rd, Nariman Point; ⊙9.45am-5.30pm Mon-Sat).

🛏 Sleeping

Mumbai has the most expensive accommodation in India, and you'll never quite feel like you're getting your money's worth. Welcome to Mumbai real estate!

Colaba is compact, has the liveliest tourist scene and many budget and midrange options. The neighbouring Fort area is convenient for the main train stations (CST and Churchgate). Most of the top-end places are dotted along Marine Dr and out in the suburbs. Note that although there are very few hotels in the cosmopolitan areas of Juhu

and Bandra, many airport hotels are only a 15-minute taxi ride away.

No matter where you stay, always book ahead.

🛏 Colaba

★**Sea Shore Hotel** GUESTHOUSE $
(Map p46; ☑22874237; 4th fl, 1-49 Kamal Mansion, Arthur Bunder Rd; s/d without bathroom ₹700/1100; 🛜) This place is really making an effort, with small but immaculately clean and inviting rooms, all with flat-screen TVs, set off a railway-carriage-style corridor. Half the rooms even have harbour views (the others don't have a window). The modish communal bathrooms are well-scrubbed and have a little gleam and sparkle. Wi-fi in the reception area only.

Carlton Hotel HOTEL $
(Map p46; ☑22020642; 1st fl, Florence House, Mereweather Rd; s/d/tr without bathroom from ₹1050/1550/2300, s/d with AC ₹2900/3200; ❄) Rooms here are a fair deal for the location, with original floor tiles, high ceilings, a contemporary touch or two, and some boasting balconies with colonial-era Colaba views; however, many lack private bathrooms. The building itself is rundown and staff could be more eager to please.

Bentley's Hotel HOTEL $
(Map p46; ☑22841474; www.bentleyshotel.com; 17 Oliver Rd; r incl breakfast ₹1740-2490; ❄🛜) A welcoming Parsi-owned place in the heart of Colaba which travellers either love or hate, depending on which of the five apartment buildings they end up in. First choice are the spacious, colonial-style rooms in the main building; avoid Henry Rd and JA Allana Marg. Air-conditioning is ₹315 extra, wi-fi is reception-only.

India Guest House GUESTHOUSE $
(Map p46; ☑22833769; 3rd fl, 1/49 Kamal Mansion, Arthur Bunder Rd; s/d without bathroom from

₹400/500; 🛜) Run by the same people as the excellent Sea Shore Hotel, this overflow place is not as attractive but its boxrooms (some with partial sea views) are cheap as chapatis and enjoy a fine location. However, the design (partition walls, shared bathrooms at one end of the corridor) means that it feels more student house than hotel.

Salvation Army Red Shield Guest House
GUESTHOUSE $

(Map p46; 📞 22841824; red_shield@vsnl.net; 30 Mereweather Rd; dm incl breakfast ₹350, d with fan/AC incl breakfast ₹1100/1500; 🌀@) A Mumbai institution popular with rupee-pinching travellers. Accommodation is very spartan (and a little grubby) but doable for a night or so. Dorms cannot be reserved in advance: come just after the 9am kickout to ensure a spot. Curfew is midnight.

★ YWCA
GUESTHOUSE $$

(Map p46; 📞 22025053; www.ywcaic.info; 18 Madame Cama Rd; s/d/tr with AC incl breakfast & dinner ₹2400/3640/5450; 🌀@🛜) Efficiently managed, and within walking distance of all the sights in Coloba and Fort, the YMCA is a good deal and justifiably popular. The spacious, well-maintained rooms boast desks and wardrobes and multichanelled TVs (though wi-fi is restricted to the lobby). Tariffs include a buffet breakfast, dinner and a daily newspaper.

Hotel Suba Palace
HOTEL $$

(Map p46; 📞 22020636, 22020639; www.hotelsubapalace.com; Battery St; s/d with AC incl breakfast ₹5520/6340; 🌀🛜) 'Palace' is pushing it a little but this modern, brilliantly located little place is certainly verging on boutique hotel territory with its contemporary decor: neutral tones are offset with zebra-print quilted headboards in the tasteful rooms. There's a good in-house restaurant and free wi-fi.

Regent Hotel
HOTEL $$

(Map p46; 📞 22021518; 8 Best Marg; s/d with AC incl breakfast ₹3920-4910; 🌀@🛜) A dependable choice where staff go the extra mile to help out guests. Located just off Coloba's main drag and has well-furnished rooms with good-quality mattresses and modern marble-floored bathrooms.

Hotel Moti
GUESTHOUSE $$

(Map p46; 📞 22025714; hotelmotiinternational@yahoo.co.in; 10 Best Marg; d/tr with AC ₹3300/4500; 🌀@🛜) A gracefully crumbling, colonial-era building in prime Colaba, where owner Raj is generous with advice about the city. Rooms are simply furnished (many have some period charm, like ornate stucco ceilings), but all could be better maintained.

★ Taj Mahal Palace, Mumbai
HERITAGE HOTEL $$$

(Map p46; 📞 66653366; www.tajhotels.com; Apollo Bunder; s/d tower from ₹15,800/17,620, palace from ₹23,530, 25,990; 🌀@🛜🏊) The grand dame of Mumbai is one of the world's most iconic hotels and has hosted a roster of presidents and royalty. Sweeping arches, staircases and domes and a glorious garden and pool ensure an unforgettable stay. Rooms in the adjacent tower lack the period details of the palace itself, but many have spectacular, full-frontal views of the Gateway to India.

With a myriad of excellent in-house eating and drinking options, plus spa and leisure facilities, it can be a wrench to leave the hotel premises. All guests are entitled to an exceptional guided tour, which provides illuminating context about the hotel's role in the city's history.

★ Abode Bombay
BOUTIQUE HOTEL $$$

(Map p46; 📞 8080234066; www.abodebombaytiquehotels.com; 1st fl, Lansdowne House, MB Marg; r with AC incl breakfast ₹5850-14,400; 🌀🛜) Terrific new hip hotel, stylishly designed using colonial-era and art deco furniture, reclaimed teak flooring and original artwork; the luxury rooms have glorious free-standing bath tubs. Staff are very switched on to travellers' needs, and breakfast is excellent with fresh juice and delicious local and international choices. A little tricky to find, it's located behind the Regal Cinema.

Vivanta by Taj
HOTEL $$$

(📞 022-66650808; www.vivantabytaj.com; 90 Cuffe Pde; s/d from ₹8050/9230; 🌀🛜🏊) In a quiet, leafy neighbourhood 1.5km south of the Gateway, this towering hotel has relatively modest rates (for Mumbai!), considering its excellent facilities which include a large pool, excellent gym, lounge bar and lots of good dining choices.

Gordon House Hotel
HOTEL $$$

(Map p46; 📞 22894400; www.ghhotel.com; 5 Battery St; r incl breakfast ₹7700; 🌀🛜) Light, airy, spacious and well-equipped rooms a stone's throw from the Gateway to India.

GROWING PAINS

Shoehorned into a narrow peninsula that juts into the Arabian Sea, Mumbai is one of the world's most congested and densely populated megacities. The numbers are startling: over 22 million live in the Mumbai conurbation and around 60% of these live in slums.

While the city is blessed with sea to the west and a large bay to the east, it's also cursed by the narrowness of the spit of land it calls home. Every day over six million commuters from the outer suburbs attempt to reach their workplaces in the south of the city via a network of antiquated suburban trains and buses. A desperately needed metro link to the heart of the city is planned (but not scheduled to be completed until at least 2020, if on time). For years the city planners invested in an ever-increasing number of flyovers, as car ownership has grown by 58% since 2000, while failing to build a single bus lane or cycle path. Gridlock is the norm and the pollution is punishing, with particulate and nitric oxide levels way above WHO danger levels.

The future of the city is in the balance. Mumbai is one of the least green cities on earth, with open spaces, parks and recreation grounds accounting for only 2.5% of its total area (Delhi has 20%, Chandigarh 35%). Yet on the eastern side of town, stretching north from the shoreline of Colaba, is a vast area of decaying docklands which has been long-slated for redevelopment. Will it be set aside for green space, parks and leisure facilities or luxury housing and concrete?

Design-wise each floor is themed: the decor ranges Mediterranean (think terracotta tiles, bold colours), Scandinavian (blond wood, clean lines) and Country (er...patchwork quilts?). There's a good Asian restaurant on the ground floor.

🛏 Fort Area & Churchgate

Traveller's Inn   HOTEL $

(Map p48; ☑22644685; 26 Adi Marzban Path; dm/d ₹630/1880, d with AC incl breakfast ₹2550; ✸@🛜) On a quiet, tree-lined street, this small hotel is a very sound choice with clean, if tiny, rooms with cable TV that represent good value. The three (fan-cooled) dorms can get Hades-hot in summer but are a steal for Mumbai – bring your own ice pack (and exorcist). The location's excellent, staff are helpful and there's free wi-fi in the lobby.

Hotel Lawrence   GUESTHOUSE $

(Map p48; ☑22843618; 3rd fl, ITTS House, 33 Sai Baba Marg, Kala Ghoda; s/d/tr without bathroom incl breakfast ₹850/950/1500) Run by kindly folk, this venerable place has been hosting shoestring travellers for years. Rooms are certainly basic but kept pretty tidy, as are the communal bathrooms. Boasts an excellent Kala Ghoda location, on a quiet little lane accessed by a ramshackle old lift.

Hotel Oasis   HOTEL $

(Map p48; ☑30227886, 30227889; www.hotel oasisindia.in; 276 Shahid Bhagat Singh Marg; r ₹1620-3050; ✸🛜) Hotel Oasis enjoys a convenient location near the CST and offers decent accommodation for the modest rates asked. Rooms are smallish, and some are low on natural light, but they have flat-screen TVs and in-room wi-fi.

★Residency Hotel   HOTEL $$

(Map p48; ☑22625525; www.residencyhotel.com; 26 Rustom Sidhwa Marg, Fort; s/d with AC incl breakfast from ₹4430/4670; ✸@🛜) The best-run midranger in Mumbai, the Residency is the kind of dependable place where you can breathe a sigh of relief after a long journey and be certain you'll be looked after well. It's fine value too, with contemporary rooms that boast mood lighting, fridges, flat-screens and hip en suite bathrooms. Its Fort location is excellent and you'll find some fascinating books to browse over breakfast in the pleasant cafe. For the best rates, always book via the hotel's own website.

Welcome Hotel   HOTEL $$

(Map p48; ☑6631488; welcomehotel@gmail.com; 257 Shahid Bhagat Singh Marg; s/d incl breakfast from ₹3280/3890, without bathroom from ₹1810/2020; ✸🛜) Service is a little hit 'n' miss but rooms here are simple and comfortable, and shared bathrooms are well kept. Top-floor executive rooms are more boutique than midrange.

Trident
HOTEL $$$

(Oberoi Hotel; Map p48; ☑66324343; www.tridenthotels.com; Marine Dr; s/d from ₹15,300/17,000; ❄@🛜🛝) This Marine Dr landmark is part of the Oberoi Hotel complex, but offers better value and a pleasing contemporary look in its restaurants, bars and pool area. Upper-floor ocean-view rooms offer truly spectacular vistas of the Queen's Necklace. Wi-fi, surprisingly, costs extra.

🛏 Western & Northern Suburbs

⭐ Juhu Residency
BOUTIQUE HOTEL $$

(Map p58; ☑67834949; www.juhuresidency.com; 148B Juhu Tara Rd, Juhu; s/d with AC incl breakfast & wi-fi from ₹5850; ❄@🛜) Essential oil aromas greet you in the lobby at this excellent boutique hotel with an inviting, relaxing atmosphere (and a fine location, five minutes' walk from Juhu beach). The chocolate-and-coffee colour scheme in the modish rooms works well, each boasting marble floors, dark woods, artful bedspreads and flat-screen TVs. There are three restaurants – good ones – for just 18 rooms.

To top it all, free airport pick-ups are included.

Hotel Oriental Aster
HOTEL $$

(Map p58; ☑022-28232323; http://theorientalaster.com; 45 Tarun Bharat Society, Dr Karanjiya Road; r with AC & breakfast from ₹4700; ❄🛜) An efficiently run airport hotel with attractive modern rooms that have space and a splash of art on show; bathrooms are small but perfectly formed. There's 24-hour room service, and free wi-fi and airport transportation.

Anand Hotel
HOTEL $$

(Map p58; ☑26203372; anandhote@yahoo.co.in; Gandhigram Rd, Juhu; s/d with AC from ₹2580/4230; ❄🛜) Yes, the decor's in 50 shades of beige but the Anand's rooms are comfortable, spacious and represent decent value, considering the prime location on a quiet street next to Juhu beach. The excellent in-house Dakshinayan restaurant (p70) scores highly for authentic, inexpensive meals too. It's a particularly good deal for solo travellers.

Hotel Regal Enclave
HOTEL $$

(Map p58; ☑67261111; www.regalenclave.com; 4th Rd, Khar West; r with AC incl breakfast from ₹6000; ❄🛜) Enjoys a stellar location in an exceedingly leafy part of Khar, right near the station (some rooms have railway views) and close to all of Bandra's best eating, drinking and shopping. Rooms are spacious and comfortable, with pleasant if unoriginal decor. Rates include airport pick-up.

Iskcon
GUESTHOUSE $$

(Map p58; ☑26206860; www.iskconmumbai.com/guest-house; Juhu Church Rd, Juhu; s/d ₹3100/3500, with AC ₹3400/4000; ❄@🛜) An intriguing place to stay inside Juhu's lively Iskcon complex. Though the hotel building is a slightly soulless concrete block, some rooms enjoy vistas over the Hare Krishna temple compound. Spartan decor is offset by the odd decorative flourish such as Gujarati *sankheda* (lacquered country wood) furniture, and staff are very welcoming.

Hotel Neelkanth
HOTEL $$

(Map p58; ☑26495566, 26495569; 354 Linking Rd, Khar West; s/d from ₹2460/3380; ❄🛜) Rooms at the friendly Neelkanth are inadvertently retro, with lots of marble and chrome-trimmed wooden furniture; check out the sublimely mod logo too. Yes, it's old-fashioned, but it's also decent value for this neighbourhood with great shopping nearby.

Hotel Suba International
BOUTIQUE HOTEL $$

(Map p58; ☑67076707; www.hotelsubainternational.com; Sahar Rd, Andheri East; r with AC incl breakfast from ₹6400; ❄🛜) A 'boutique business' hotel that's very close to the airport (free transfers are included) and boasts modish rooms with clean lines and stylish touches.

Le Sutra
BOUTIQUE HOTEL $$$

(Map p58; ☑022-66420025; www.lesutra.in; 14 Union Park, Khar West; s/d incl breakfast from ₹7900/10,450; ❄🛜) This hip hotel in the happening Khar area blends contemporary chic with traditional artefacts (textiles and hand-carved chairs) and some statement art in its lovely rooms. The in-house gallery, spa, cafe and restaurants (Out of the Blue and Olive) seal the deal. Check the website for special offers that include dinner or a spa treatment.

Sofitel Mumbai BKC
HOTEL $$$

(Map p58; ☑022-61175000; www.sofitel-mumbai-bkc.com; C-57, Bandra Kurla Complex Rd; s/d from ₹7720/8500; ❄🛜🛝) Located in Mumbai's BKC business district, which is handy for the airport and close enough to Bandra, the Sofitel offers commodious comfort levels. Rooms have a mod-Indian design and facilities are excellent, with great restaurants and one of the best breakfast buffets in the city.

ITC Maratha
HOTEL $$$

(Map p58; ☑ 28303030; www.itchotels.in; Sahar Rd, Andheri East; s/d incl breakfast from ₹16,450/19,200; ❄@🕙❄) The five-star hotel with the most luxurious Indian character, from the Rajasthani-style lattice windows around the atrium, to the rooms with their silk throw pillows and lush raspberry-and-grey colour schemes. Peshawri (p71), one of Mumbai's best restaurants, is located here.

Sun-n-Sand
HOTEL $$$

(Map p58; ☑ 66938888; www.sunnsandhotel.com; 39 Juhu Chowpatty; r with AC from ₹10,000; ❄@🕙❄) A beachfront institution with well-maintained if slightly dated rooms that are big on browns and beiges. Rates (add ₹1000 or so for a sea view) are competitive given the location in exclusive Juhu and free airport transfers. Staff are eager to please.

✖ Eating

Flavours from all over India collide with international trends and taste buds in Mumbai. Colaba is home to most of the cheap tourist haunts, while Fort and Churchgate are more upscale, a trend that continues as you head north to Mahalaxmi and the western suburbs, where you'll find Mumbai's most international and expensive restaurants.

Sample Gujarati or Keralan thalis (all-you-can-eat meals), Mughlai kebabs, Goan vindaloo and Mangalorean seafood. And don't forget, if you see Bombay duck on a menu, it's actually *bombil* (fish dried in the sun and deep-fried).

✖ Colaba

Bademiya
MUGHLAI, FAST FOOD $

(Map p46; Tulloch Rd; light meals ₹60-150; 🕙8pm-1.30am) Formerly a tiny, outrageously popular late-night street stall, Bademiya now encompasses a (dingy) seating area too. Yes, prices have risen, but it remains a key Colaba hang-out for its trademark buzz and bustle, plus its delicious meat-heavy menu. Expect spicy, fresh-grilled kebabs, mutton and chicken curries, and tikka rolls.

Olympia
INDIAN $

(Map p46; Rahim Mansion, 1 Shahid Bhagat Singh Marg; meals ₹80-140; 🕙7am-midnight) While we didn't encounter any athletes at the Olympia, its *masala kheema* (spicy minced meat; ₹40) is certainly a breakfast of champions when munched with a couple of roti. A simple place renowned for its pocket-friendly meat dishes; the seekh kebab and chicken butter fry masala (₹80) are also great.

Hotel OCH
INDIAN $

(Map p46; Shahid Bhagat Singh Marg; mains ₹50-150; 🕙7am-10.30pm) A good Colaba cheapie, with decent lunch thalis and lots of Punjabi dishes in a large, cafeteria-like setting. Popular with families and cops working next door.

Sufra
MIDDLE EASTERN $$

(Map p46; 16A Cusrow Baug, Shahid Bhagat Singh Rd; meals ₹120-250; 🕙11am-11.45pm) Serves up excellent Arab dishes such as *kibbeh* (chicken, burgul and mint bites), falafel, shwarma, kebabs and fresh juices at very reasonable rates. It's a tiny place with just a few tables so best for a hit and run or takeaway.

★Indigo
FUSION, CONTINENTAL $$$

(Map p46; ☑ 66368980; www.foodindigo.com; 4 Mandlik Marg; mains ₹780-1250; 🕙noon-3pm & 6.30pm-midnight; 🕙) This incredibly classy

---

STREET FOOD

Mumbai's street cuisine is vaster than many Western culinary traditions. Stalls tend to get started in late afternoon, when chai complements much of the fried deliciousness; items are ₹10 to ₹25.

Most street food is vegetarian. Chowpatty Beach is a great place to try Mumbai's famous *bhelpuri*. Stalls offering samosas, *pav bhaji* (spiced vegetables and bread), *vada pav* (deep-fried spiced lentil-ball sandwich), *bhurji pav* (scrambled eggs and bread) and *dabeli* (a mixture of potatoes, spices, peanuts and pomegranate, also on bread) are spread through the city.

For a meaty meal, Mohammed Ali and Merchant Rds in Kalbadevi are famous for kebabs. In Colaba, Bademiya is a late-night Mumbai rite of passage, renowned for its chicken tikka rolls.

The office workers' district on the north side of Kala Ghoda is another good hunting ground for street snacks.

Colaba institution is a colonial-era property converted into a temple of fine dining. Serves inventive, expensive European and Asian cuisine and offers a long wine list, sleek ambience and a gorgeous rooftop deck. Favourites include the pulled duck tortellini, Kochi oysters, and pork belly with maple-glazed apple. Reserve ahead.

Indigo Delicatessen
CAFE $$$

(Map p46; www.indigodeli.com; Pheroze Bldg, Chhatrapati Shivaji Marg; snacks/mains from ₹320/470; ⊙8.30am-midnight; 🐟) Bustling and fashionable cafe-restaurant with cool tunes and massive wooden tables. The menu includes all-day breakfasts (₹155 to ₹385) and international classics such as pork ribs, thin-crust pizza and inventive sandwiches. It's busy so service can be stretched.

Self-Catering

Colaba Market
MARKET

(Map p46; Lala Nigam St; ⊙7am-5pm) The Colaba market has fresh fruit and vegetables.

Saharkari Bhandar Supermarket
SUPERMARKET

(Map p46; ✎22022248; cnr Colaba Causeway & Wodehouse Rd; ⊙10am-8.30pm) Well-stocked for self-caterers.

🍴 Fort Area & Churchgate

Pradeep Gomantak Bhojanalaya
MAHARASHTRIAN $

(Map p48; Sheri House, Rustom Sidhwa Marg; mains ₹60-150; ⊙11am-4pm & 7.30-10pm) A simple but satisfying place that serves Malvani cuisine and gets very busy at lunchtime. Its *bombil* rice plate (₹70) and crab masala (₹65) are very flavoursome and prepared with real care and attention. Wash your meal down with *sol kadhi* (a soothing, spicy drink of coconut milk and kokum).

Badshah Snacks & Drinks
INDIAN $

(Map p54; Lokmanya Tilak Rd; snacks & drinks ₹40-120; ⊙7am-12.30am) Opposite Crawford Market, Badshah's been serving snacks, fruit juices and its famous *falooda* (rose-flavoured drink made with milk, cream, nuts and vermicelli) to hungry bargain-hunters for more than 100 years.

★ La Folie
CAFE $$

(Map p48; Ropewalk Lane, Kala Ghoda; croissants/cakes from ₹110/220; ⊙noon-11pm) Chocoholics and cake fetishistas look no further, this minuscule Kala Ghoda place will satisfy your cravings, and then some. Owner Sanjana Patel spent seven years in France studying the art (addiction?) of pastry- and chocolate-making, which was obviously time well spent. Try the delectable Madagascar cake (chocolate with raspberry mousse) with a latte (₹130) or the 70% cocoa Venezuelan-sourced chocolates.

Frankly, wherever you are dining in South Mumbai skip the dessert menu and head here instead.

★ Revival
INDIAN $$

(Map p54; www.revivalindianthali.com; 361 Sheikh Memon St, Kalbadevi, opp Mangaldas market; mains ₹200-360, thali from ₹350; ⊙noon-4pm & 7.30-10.30pm, lunch only Sun; ❀▱) Thali mecca near Crawford Market where waiters in silken dhoti come one after another to fill your plates with dozens of delectable (veg-only) curries, sides, chutneys, rotis and rice dishes in an all-you-can-eat gastro onslaught. The thali menu changes daily and the premises are air-conditioned.

Pantry
CAFE $$

(Map p48; www.thepantry.in; B Bharucha Rd; snacks/meals from ₹200/270; ⊙8.30am-11pm; 🐟) Pantry is a bakery-cafe that offers a choice of fine pies and pastries, soups and sandwiches plus delicious mains (such as curry leaf chicken with burgal pilaf). Breakfasts are legendary: try the tomato scrambled eggs with parmesan and rosti, or some organic-flour waffles with fruit. The elegantly restored historic premises are also perfect for a coffee and slab of cake.

Samrat
GUJARATI $$

(Map p48; ✎42135401; www.prashantcaterers.com; Prem Ct, J Tata Rd; thali ₹400, mains ₹160-290; ⊙noon-11pm; ❀) Samrat has an à la carte menu but most rightly opt for the famous Gujarati thali – a cavalcade of taste and texture, sweetness and spice that includes four curries, three chutneys, curd, rotis and other bits and pieces. Beer is available.

Oye Kake
NORTH INDIAN $$

(Map p48; 13C Cawasji Patel St; mains ₹120-180; ⊙11am-4pm & 7-11pm) Intimate all-veg Punjabi place where the daily thali (₹170) is widly popular with local office workers and renowned for its authenticity. Signature dishes include the panner tikka masala, *sarson da saag* (mustard leaf curry) and the *parathas;* lassis are excellent too. Prepare to have to wait for a table.

DABBA-WALLAHS

A small miracle of logistics, Mumbai's 5000 *dabba-wallahs* (literally 'food container person'; also called tiffin-wallahs) work tirelessly to deliver hot lunches to office workers throughout the city.

Lunch boxes are picked up each day from restaurants and homes and carried on heads, bicycles and trains to a centralised sorting station. A sophisticated system of numbers and colours (many wallahs don't read) identifies the destination of each lunch. More than 200,000 meals are delivered – always on time, come (monsoon) rain or (searing) shine. This system has been used for over a century and there's only about one mistake per six million deliveries. (In a 2002 analysis, *Forbes Magazine* found that the *dabba-wallahs* had a six-sigma, or 99.99966%, reliability rating.)

Look for these master messengers midmorning at Churchgate and CST stations.

A Taste of Kerala　　KERALAN $$
(Map p48; Prospect Chambers Annex, Pitha St, Fort; mains ₹70-170, thali from ₹110; ⊙6am-midnight) Inexpensive Keralan eatery with lots of coconut and southern goodness on the menu; try a thali (served on a banana leaf) or one of the seafood specials like the prawn pepper masala. It also serves Punjabi and meat dishes. Staff are very welcoming, and there's an air-conditioned dining room.

Café Moshe　　CAFE $$
(Map p46; www.moshes.in; Chhatrapati Shivaji Marg; light meals ₹200-380; ⊙9am-midnight; ☎) Moshe's menu has more than a nod to the Middle East, with excellent mezze, pita bread sandwiches and wraps, salads and outstanding hummus bowls (₹250 to ₹280) that have a choice of toppings. Desserts, juices and coffee also score highly.

Other outlets, all serving the same great food, include the flagship **restaurant** (7 Minoo Manor, Cuffe Pde; ⊙9am-midnight), in a heritage building, and the bookstore **cafe** (Map p54; Crossword, NS Patkar Marg) at Kemp's Corner.

Bademiya Restaurant　　NORTH INDIAN $$
(Map p48; ☎22655657; Botawala Bldg, Horniman Circle; mains ₹110-220; ⊙11am-1am) The grownup, sit-down version of Bademiya's legendary Colaba street-side stand (p67) has the classic rolls and rotis, plus biryanis, tikka masalas and dhals. Delivers.

Kala Ghoda Café　　CAFE $$
(Map p48; www.kgcafe.in; 10 Ropewalk Lane, Kala Ghoda; light meal ₹100-280, dinner ₹380-530; ⊙8.30am-11.45pm; ☎) ⊘ Tiny boho cafe with a handful of tables that's a favourite with creative types. There's usually interesting art or photography. Serves organic coffee and tea, sandwiches, salads and breakfasts.

Suzette　　FRENCH $$
(Map p48; www.suzette.in; Atlanta Bldg, Vinayak K Shah Marg, Nariman Point; meals ₹300-450; ⊙9am-11pm Mon-Sat; ☎) This relaxed Parisian-style place with delectable crêpes, croques, salads, pasta and loungy music. On the crêpe front, sweet tooths should try the jaggery and butter; for a savoury flavour, order an *italie* (with pesto, mozzarella and mushrooms). The **Bandra branch** (Map p58; St John's St, Pali Naka; ⊙9am-11pm) has outdoor seating and is open daily.

Brittania　　PARSI $$
(Map p48; Wakefield House, Ballard Estate; mains ₹150-550; ⊙noon-4pm Mon-Sat) This Parsi institution has been around since 1923 and retains a (faded) colonial-era feel. The signature dishes are the *dhansak* (meat with curried lentils and rice) and the berry *pulao* – spiced and boneless mutton or chicken, or veg or egg, buried in basmati rice and tart barberries that are imported from Iran. It's a little tricky to find. Cash only.

Samovar Café　　CAFE $$
(Map p48; Jehangir Art Gallery, MG Rd, Kala Ghoda; snacks & meals ₹90-170; ⊙11am-7pm Mon-Sat) Inside the art gallery, this cafe is perfect for a snack (try the rolls; ₹100 to ₹120) or meal (the pepper mutton chops are great). It overlooks the gardens of the Chhatrapati Shivaji Maharaj Vastu Sangrahalaya museum. Cappuccinos and beers are also on offer.

★Koh　　THAI $$$
(Map p48; ☎39879999; InterContinental, Marine Dr; mains ₹850-1850; ⊙12.30-3pm & 7.30-midnight) Destination Thai restaurant with a

real wow factor, where celeb chef Ian Kittichai works his native cuisine into an international frenzy of flavour. The massamun curry (Thai Muslim-style spiced lamb shank with cucumber relish) is his signature (and most expensive) dish, but there are lots of sublime seafood and vegetarian choices too. Well worth a splurge.

★ Mamagoto ASIAN $$$

(Map p48; ☑ 022-67495660; www.mamagoto.in; 5 Surya Mahal, B Bharucha Marg; meals ₹350-550; ☻ noon-11.30pm) Mamagoto means 'play with food' in Japanese and this zany little Kala Ghoda place is certainly fun, with a relaxed vibe, cool tunes and kooky decor (think pop and propaganda art). The menu really delivers, with punchy Pan-Asian flavours: combo meal deals (₹400 to ₹550) include a great juice, and the authentic Malay-style Penang curry is terrific.

There's also a branch in Bandra (☑ 022-26552600; www.mamagoto.in; 133 Gazebo House, Hill Rd, Bandra; ☻ noon-11.30pm).

Burma Burma ASIAN $$$

(Map p48; ☑ 022-40036600; www.burmaburma.in; Oak Lane, off MG Road; meals ₹330-500; ☻ noon-3pm & 7-10.30pm) Sleek, stylish new restaurant that marries contemporary design with a few traditional artefacts (prayer wheels line one wall) and provides a beautiful setting for the cuisine of Myanmar. The menu is well priced, intricate and ambitious with inventive salads (try the tea leaf), curries and soups: *oh no khow suey* is a glorious coconut-enriched noodle broth. No alcohol is served.

Khyber MUGHLAI, INDIAN $$$

(Map p48; ☑ 40396666; 145 MG Rd; mains ₹380-800; ☻ 12.30-4pm & 7.30-11.30pm) The much-acclaimed Khyber has a Northwest Frontier-themed design that incorporates murals featuring turbaned Mughal royalty, lots of exposed brickwork and oil lanterns – just the sort of place an Afghan warlord might feel at home. The meat-centric menu features gloriously tender kebabs, rich curries and lots of tandoori favourites roasted in Khyber's famous red masala sauce. Garlic or butter naan bread (₹95) is the perfect accompaniment.

Trishna SEAFOOD $$$

(Map p48; ☑ 22703214; www.trishna.co.in; Ropewalk Lane, Kala Ghoda; mains ₹320-1110; ☻ noon-3pm & 6.30pm-12.15am) Behind a modest entrance on a quiet Kala Ghoda lane is this often-lauded, intimate South Indian seafood restaurant. It's not a trendy place – the decor is old school, seating a little cramped and menu perhaps too long – but the cooking is superb, witness the Hyderabadi fish tikka, jumbo prawns with green pepper sauce, and outstanding crab dishes.

Mahesh Lunch Home SEAFOOD $$$

(Map p48; ☑ 22023965; www.maheshlunchhome.com; Cowasji Patel St; mains ₹280-1300; ☻ 11.30am-4pm & 7pm-midnight) A great place to try Mangalorean or Chinese-style seafood in Mumbai. It's renowned for its ladyfish, pomfret, lobster, crab (try this with butter garlic pepper sauce) and salt-and-pepper squid (₹425). There's also a Juhu branch.

✂ Kalbadevi to Mahalaxmi

New Kulfi Centre ICE CREAM $

(Map p54; cnr Chowpatty Seaface & Sardar V Patel Rd; kulfi per 100gm ₹40-70; ☻ 10am-1am) Serves the best *kulfi* (Indian firm-textured ice cream) you'll have anywhere. Killer flavours include pistachio, *malai* (cream) and mango.

Cafe Noorani NORTH INDIAN $$

(Map p54; Tardeo Rd, Haji Ali Circle; mains ₹80-300; ☻ 8am-11.30pm) Inexpensive, old-school eatery that's a requisite stop before or after visiting the Haji Ali mosque. Mughlai and Punjabi staples dominate, with kebabs chargrilled to perfection and great biriyanis; try the chicken kadai (₹200).

✂ Western Suburbs

North Mumbai is home to the city's trendiest dining, centered on Bandra West and Juhu.

Hotel Ram Ashray SOUTH INDIAN $

(Bhandarkar Rd, King's Circle, Matunga East; light meals ₹40-70; ☻ 5am-9.30pm) In the Tamil enclave of King's Circle, 80-year-old Ram Ashray is beloved by southern families for its spectacular dosas, *idli* (spongy, round, fermented rice cake) and *uttapa* (savoury rice pancake with toppings). Filter coffee is strong and flavoursome. The menu, written on a chalkboard, changes daily. It's just outside Matunga Rd train station's east exit.

★ Dakshinayan SOUTH INDIAN $$

(Map p58; Anand Hotel, Gandhigram Rd, Juhu; light meals ₹90-170; ☻ 11am-3pm & 6-11pm, from 8am Sun) With *rangoli* on the walls, servers in lungis and sari-clad women lunching (*chappals* off under the table), Dakshinayan channels Tamil Nadu. There are delicately textured dosas (₹110 to ₹165), *idli* and *uttapam,* village-fresh chutneys and perhaps the best *rasam* (tomato soup with spices and tamarind) in Mumbai. Finish off with a South Indian filter coffee – served in a stainless-steel set.

Chilli-heads should order *molagapudi idli* (₹110), a dozen *idli* coated in 'gunpowder' (potent spices).

★ Yoga House
CAFE $$

(Map p58; www.yogahouse.in; 53 Chimbai Rd, Bandra West; light meals ₹140-250; ⊗8am-10pm; ☎) This haven of pastel shades, scatter cushions and greenery in Yoga House's seaside bungalow is the perfect retreat from Mumbai's mean streets. The menu is very creative and healthy – much of it raw vegan and all of it wholesome. Signature items include its famous salads (₹195 to ₹350), soups, 10-grain bread (₹130) and hash browns (with spinach, mozzarella and peppers).

Soul Fry
GOAN, SEAFOOD $$

(Map p58; ☎022-26046892; Silver Croft, Pali Mala Rd, Pali Hill; mains ₹140-390; ⊗noon-3pm & 7.30pm-midnight; ❊) Rightly famous for its terrific seafood, this lively, scruffy-yet-atmospheric Goan place by Pali market is just the place to escape Bandra's Bollywood set. Crab curry, tamarind prawns and Goan meat dishes such as chicken *xacuti* are authentic and loaded with coastal flavour. There's an air-conditioned interior and bench seating on the terrace. Be warned: Monday night is karaoke night.

Raaj Bhog
GUJARATI $$

(Map p58; 3rd Rd, Cosmos Commercial Center, Khar West; meals ₹180-300; ⊗11am-3.30pm & 7-11pm) Modestly priced restaurants are not easy to find in this part of town so this new Gujarati place by Khar station is a welcome addition. The (unlimited) deluxe thali (₹280) is filling and varied; it's served with basmati rice and rotis.

Prithvi Cafe
CAFE $$

(Map p58; Juhu Church Rd, Juhu; light meals ₹70-165; ⊗9am-11pm) A bohemian cafe on a large, shady terrace attached to the Prithvi Theatre that's something of a cultural hub of intellectuals, artists and theatre types. The snacky food – croissants, sandwiches, *chaat* (savoury snacks) and Punjabi standards – is OK, but it's the setting that's special.

★ Peshawri
NORTH INDIAN $$$

(Map p58; ☎28303030; ITC Maratha, Sahar Rd, Andheri East; meals ₹1100-2700; ⊗12.45-2.45pm & 7-11.45pm) Make this Northwest Frontier restaurant, outside the international airport, your first or last stop in Mumbai. The buttery *dhal bukhara* (a thick black dhal cooked for a day; ₹700) is perhaps the signature dish, but its kebabs are sublime: try the *peshawri* (chargrilled lamb marinated in yoghurt and spices).

Despite the five-star surrounds (and prices) you're encouraged to eat with your hands and the seating is low.

Culture Curry
SOUTH INDIAN, SEAFOOD $$$

(www.culturecurry.com; Kataria Rd, Matunga West; mains ₹260-500; ⊗noon-3.45pm & 7pm-12.30am) Exquisite dishes from all over the south, from Andhra and Coorg to Kerala, are the speciality here. Best for vegie and seafood dishes; the *prawn hirva rassa* (with green mango and coconut; ₹379) is a symphony of South Indian flavour. From Matunga Rd train station, it's about 750m west along Kataria Rd.

Salt Water Café
CAFE, FUSION $$$

(Map p58; www.saltwatercafe.in; 87 Chapel Rd, Bandra West; breakfasts ₹180-290, mains ₹410-650; ⊗12.30-3.30pm & 7.30-11.50pm; ☎) A Bandra institution where filmi producers and expats socialise in the stylish air-conditioned dining room or buzzing terrace. Stick to the classic breakfasts, omelettes and sandwiches (₹350 to ₹410) as some of the zany fusion flavour combinations are perhaps too much of a culinary clash.

Eat Around the Corner
CAFE $$$

(Map p58; www.eataroundthecorner.in; cnr 24th & 30th Rds; light meals ₹250-400, mains ₹280-600; ⊗7am-1am; ☎) Visually it's quite a concept, its minimalist interior replete with banquette and bench seating and a long, long display counter of tempting treats (falafel, soups, salads, cakes, pastries). Prices are high, not that the young, wealthy clientelle seem bothered.

▼ Drinking & Nightlife

Forget the capital, Mumbai is a city that really knows how to enjoy itself. Whatever your tipple and whatever your taste, you'll find it here – from dive bar to sky bar. Colaba is rich in unpretentious publike joints (but also has some very classy places), while

Bandra and Juhu are home turf for the filmi and model set. Some of the most intriguing new places are opening in midtown areas such as Lower Parel.

Wednesday and Thursday are big nights at some clubs, as well as the traditional Friday and Saturday; there's usually a cover charge. Dress codes apply, so don't rock up in shorts and sandals. The trend in Mumbai is towards resto-lounges as opposed to full-on nightclubs. You're also technically supposed to have a license to drink in Maharashtra; some bars require you to buy a temporary one, for a nominal fee.

Colaba

★ Harbour Bar
BAR

(Map p46; Taj Mahal Palace, Mumbai, Apollo Bunder; ⏰11am-11.45pm) With unmatched views of the Gateway of India and harbour, this timeless bar inside the Taj is an essential visit. Drinks aren't uber-expensive (₹395/800 for a beer/cocktail) given the surrounds and the fact they come with very generous portions of nibbles (including jumbo cashews).

★ Colaba Social
BAR

(Map p46; www.socialoffline.in; ground fl, Glen Rose Bldg, BK Boman Behram Marg, Apollo Bunder; ⏰9am-1.30am; 🛜) The Social opened with

bang in late 2014, thanks to its stellar cocktail list (most are just ₹300 or so; try the Longest Island Ice Tea) and fab Colaba location. During the day it's a social-cum-workspace for laptop-toting, brunching creative types, but by 6pm the place is crammed with a raucous young crowd. Snacks (₹120 to ₹380) and espresso coffee are available.

Also hosts DJ and live-music events, art and photography exhibits and stand-up comedy acts.

Woodside Inn
PUB

(Map p46; Wodehouse Rd, Regal Circle; ⏰10am-1am) As close as you'll get to a London pub in Mumbai, this cosy place has a gregarious vibe and serves Gateway craft beers on draught (₹300); try the wheat beer. There's comfort food (mains ₹300 to ₹450) and a great daily happy hour (4pm to 8pm).

Cafe Mondegar
PUB

(Map p46; Metro House, 5A Shahid Bhagat Singh Rd; ⏰7.30pm-12.30am) Old-school bar that draws a mix of foreigners and locals who all cosy up together in the small space, bonding over the jukebox, which is cranked up to energise the crowd.

Busaba
LOUNGE

(Map p46; www.busaba.net; 4 Mandlik Marg; ⏰6.30pm-1am; 🛜) Sunken couches and contem-

---

QUEER MUMBAI

Mumbai's LGBTQ scene is still quite underground, especially for women, but it's gaining momentum. No dedicated LGBTQ bars/clubs have opened yet, but gay-friendly 'safe house' venues often host private gay parties (announced on Gay Bombay).

Humsafar Trust (Map p58; ☎022-26673800; www.humsafar.org; 3rd fl, Manthan Plaza Nehru Rd, Vakola, Santa Cruz East) Runs tons of programs and workshops; one of its support groups organises the monthly gathering 'Sunday High'. It's also closely connected to the erratically published but pioneering magazine **Bombay Dost** (www.bombaydost.co.in).

Galaxy (www.gaylaxymag.com) India's best gay e-zine; well worth consulting and has lots of Mumbai content.

Gay Bombay (www.gaybombay.org) A great place to start, with event listings including meet-ups in Bandra, GB-hosted bar and film nights, hiking trips and other info.

Kashish Mumbai International Queer Film Festival (www.mumbaiqueerfest.com) Excellent annual May event with a mix of Indian and foreign films; in 2014, 154 films from 31 countries were featured.

LABIA (Lesbian & Bisexuals in Action; labia_india@yahoo.com) Lesbian and bi support group based in Mumbai; provides a counselling service for women.

Queer Azaadi Mumbai (www.queerazaadi.wordpress.com) Organises Mumbai's Pride Parade, which is usually held in early February.

Queer Ink (www.queer-ink.com) Online publisher with excellent books, DVDs and merchandise. Also hosts a monthly arts event with speakers, workshops, poetry, comedy, music and a marketplace.

porary Buddha art give this restaurant-bar a loungey vibe. Cocktails are pricey (from ₹450) but potent and a DJ plays house on weekends. The upstairs **restaurant** (mains from ₹480) serves pan-Asian; its back room feels like a posh treehouse. Reserve ahead for dinner.

Leopold Cafe
BAR

(Map p46; www.leopoldcafe.com; cnr Colaba Causeway & Nawroji F Rd; ⊙7.30am-12.30am) Love it or hate it, most tourists end up at this clichéd Mumbai travellers' institution at one time or another. Around since 1871, Leopold's has wobbly ceiling fans, crap service and a rambunctious atmosphere conducive to swapping tales with strangers. There's also food and a cheesy DJ upstairs on weekend nights.

Wink
NIGHTCLUB

(Vivanta by Taj, 90 Cuffe Pde; ⊙6pm-1am) Saturday and Sunday are thumping here, but it's a classy place most nights with its sophisticated decor (low beige sofas, intricately carved screens), long whiskey list and famous Winktinis.

Fort Area & Churchgate

Dome
LOUNGE

(Map p48; Hotel InterContinental, 135 Marine Dr, Churchgate; ⊙5.30pm-1.30am; ☏) This white-on-white rooftop lounge has awesome views of Mumbai's crescent beach from its 8th-floor vantage. Cocktails (₹850 to ₹1200) beckon the hip young things of Mumbai each night. Indulge yourself with a Ki Garden (vodka, elderberry and cloudy apple juice) or nurse a Kingfisher (₹375).

Liv
NIGHTCLUB

(Map p48; 1st fl, 145 MG Rd, Kala Ghoda; cover per couple ₹3000; ⊙10pm-1.30am Wed-Sat) Exclusive new Kala Ghoda club that draws an up-for-it crowd of SoBo (South Bombay) pretty young things with its out-there LED lighting and intimate feel. Musically, Wednesday is hip hop, on Friday it's Bollywood Boogie, while on Saturday EDM DJs let rip.

Kalbadevi to Mahalaxmi

Haji Ali Juice Centre
JUICE BAR

(Map p54; Lala Lajpatrai Rd, Haji Ali Circle; juices & snacks ₹30-180; ⊙5am-1.30am) Serves fresh juices, milkshakes, mighty fine *falooda* and fruit salads. Strategically placed at the en-

trance to Haji Ali mosque, it's a great place to cool off after a visit.

Shiro
LOUNGE, NIGHTCLUB

(☏66511201; www.shiro.co.in; Bombay Dyeing Mills Compound, Worli; ⊙7.30pm-1.30am) Visually this place is stunning, with water pouring from the hands of a towering Japanese goddess into lotus ponds, which reflect shimmering light on the walls. It's totally over the top, but the drinks (as well as the Asian-fusion dishes) are excellent. By 10.30pm or so it morphs into more of a club, with DJs spinning some mean salsa (Wednesday), disco (Friday) and house (Saturday). It's about 3km north of the Mahalaxmi Racecourse.

Ghetto
BAR

(Map p54; ☏23538418; 30 Bhulabhai Desai Marg, opp Tirupathi Apt; ⊙7pm-1am) A grungy, graffiti-covered hang-out blaring classic and contemporary rock (Red Hot Chili Peppers, Rolling Stones) to a dedicated set of regulars. You can shoot pool here too.

Western Suburbs

★Bonobo
BAR

(Map p58; www.facebook.com/BonoboBandra; Kenilworth Mall, 33rd Rd, Bandra West, off Linking Rd; ⊙6pm-1am; ☏) The scenesters' first choice in Bandra, this bar champions underground and alternative music. DJs spin drum 'n' bass and electronica, big beats and funk tech-house, and musicians play folk and blues. There's a great rooftop terrace.

★Aer
LOUNGE

(Four Seasons Hotel, 34th fl, 114 Dr E Moses Rd, Worli; cover Fri & Sat after 8pm ₹2500; ⊙5.30pm-midnight; ☏) Boasting astounding sea, sunset and city views, Aer is Mumbai's premier sky bar. Drink prices are steep, but that's kind of the point: cocktails cost around ₹900, beers start at ₹350 and happy hour is 5.30pm to 8pm. A DJ spins house and lounge tunes nightly from 9pm.

Toto's Garage
BAR

(Map p58; ☏26005494; 30th Rd, Bandra West; ⊙6pm-1am) Highly sociable, down-to-earth local dive done up in a car mechanic theme where you can go in your dirty clothes, drink draught beer (₹200 a glass) and listen to classic rock. Check out the upended VW Beetle above the bar. Always busy and has a good mix of guys and gals.

Daily
BAR

(Map p58; SV Rd, Bandra; ⊗6pm-1.30am; 🛜) Hip and happening new Bandra bar that take its moniker from the good news stories the owners have collated (and suspended on pages from the ceiling). Attracts a lively crowd with decadent cocktails, sangria pitchers, snappy service and a cool indoor/outdoor design. Also hosts films and live music.

Trilogy
NIGHTCLUB

(Map p58; www.trilogy.in; Hotel Sea Princess, Juhu Tara Rd, Juhu; cover per couple after 11pm ₹2000; ⊗10.30pm-3am Wed-Sat) This glam, glitzy Juhu club, like its clientele, is gorgeous, with two dance floors spectacularly illuminated by LED cube lights that are synced with the epic sound system. It's hip hop on Wednesday, house on Friday and EDM on Saturday.

Hoppipola
BAR

(Map p58; 757 Ramee Guestline, MD Ali Quereshi Chowk, off SV Rd; ⊗noon-1am; 🛜) With its wacky design (including squadrons of toy planes suspended from the roof) and abundant board games, Hoppipola doesn't take itself too seriously, with decor that's more playschool than lounge bar. Get stuck into some test-tube shots or a tower of beer and it's perfect for a session of Jenga drinking games. Bar grub (from ₹200) is tasty too.

Olive Bar & Kitchen
BAR

(Map p58; ☎26058228; www.olivebarandkitchen.com; 14 Union Park, Khar West; ⊗7.30pm-1am daily, plus noon-3.30pm Sat & Sun; 🛜) The watering hole of choice for Bandra's filmi elite and aspiring starlets, Olive is a Mediterranean-style bar-restaurant whose whitewashed walls, candle-lit terraces and rooms evoke Ibiza and Mykonos. It's the perfect setting for inspired Greek and Italian food (mains ₹600 to ₹1100) and vibing DJ sounds. Thursdays and weekends are packed. There's a second branch (Map p54; ☎40859595; Gate No 8, Mahalaxmi Racecourse; ⊗noon-3.30pm & 7.30pm-1.30am) in Mahalaxmi.

Big Nasty
BAR

(Map p58; 1st fl, 12 Union Park, Khar West, above Shatranj Napoli; ⊗7pm-12.30am) The decor may be industrial, but the Nasty is fun and unpretentious. It's best known for its cheap(ish) drinks – beers from ₹220, wine from ₹350 and cocktails starting at ₹400.

Elbo Room
PUB

(Map p58; St Theresa Rd, Khar West, off 33rd Rd; ⊗11am-1am) This publike place has a very so-cial vibe and an Italian-Indian menu that's best enjoyed on the plant-filled terrace.

☆ Entertainment

Mumbai has an exciting live music scene, some terrific theatres, an emerging network of comedy clubs and, of course, cinemas and sporting action.

Consult **Mumbai Boss** (www.mumbaiboss.com), **Time Out Mumbai** (www.timeoutmumbai.net) and www.nh7.in for live-music listings. Unfortunately, Hindi films aren't shown with English subtitles. The cinemas we've listed all show English-language movies, along with some Bollywood numbers.

Mumbai has some great arts festivals, the major ones include the excellent Mumbai Film Festival (p45) in October, May's **Kashish-Mumbai International Queer Film Festival** (www.mumbaiqueerfest.com), Prithvi Theatre's November festival for excellent drama and music, and Mumbai Sanskruti (p45), which sees two days of Hindustani classical music. The National Centre for the Performing Arts hosts numerous cultural festivals throughout the year.

★ Bluefrog
LIVE MUSIC,

(☎61586158; www.bluefrog.co.in; D/2 Mathuradas Mills Compound, Senapati Bapat Marg, Lower Parel; admission ₹300-1200; ⊗6.30pm-1.30am Tue-Sat, from 11.30am Sun) Mumbai cultural mecca, a world-class venue for concerts (everything from indie to Mexican), stand-up comedy and lots of DJ-driven clubby nights (hip hop, house and techno). There's also a restaurant with space-age pod seating (book ahead for dinner) in the intimate main room. Happy hour is 6.30pm to 9pm.

National Centre for the Performing Arts
THEATRE, LIVE MUSIC

(NCPA; Map p48; ☎66223737, box office 22824567; www.ncpamumbai.com; Marine Dr & Sri V Saha Rd, Nariman Point; tickets ₹200-800; ⊗box office 9am-7pm) This vast cultural centre is the hub of Mumbai's high-brow music, theatre and dance scene. In any given week, it might host experimental plays, poetry readings, photography exhibitions, a jazz band from Chicago or Indian classical music. Many performances are free. The **box office** (Map p48) is at the end of NCPA Marg.

Prithvi Theatre
THEATRE

(Map p58; ☎26149546; www.prithvitheatre.org; Juhu Church Rd, Juhu; tickets ₹80-300) A Juhu institution that's a great place to see both

BOLLYWOOD DREAMS

Mumbai is the glittering epicentre of India's gargantuan Hindi-language film industry. From silent beginnings, with a cast of all-male actors (some in drag) in the 1913 epic *Raja Harishchandra,* and the first talkie, *Lama Ara (*1931), it now churns out more than 1000 films a year – more than Hollywood. Not surprising considering it has a captive audience of one-sixth of the world's population.

Every part of India has its regional film industry, but Bollywood continues to entrance the nation with its escapist formula in which all-singing, all-dancing lovers fight and conquer the forces keeping them apart. These days, Hollywood-inspired thrillers and action extravaganzas vie for moviegoers' attention alongside the more family-oriented saccharine formulas.

Bollywood stars can attain near godlike status in India and star-spotting is a favourite pastime in Mumbai's posher establishments. You can also see the stars' homes as well as a film/TV studio with **Bollywood Tours** (www.bollywoodtours.in; 8hr tour per person ₹6000), but you're not guaranteed to see a dance number and you may spend much of it in traffic.

Extra, Extra!

Studios sometimes want Westerners as extras to add a whiff of international flair (or provocative dress, which locals often won't wear) to a film.

If you're game, just hang around Colaba (especially the Salvation Army hostel) where studio scouts, recruiting for the following day's shooting, will find you. A day's work, which can be up to 16 hours, pays ₹500. You'll get lunch, snacks and (usually) transport. The day can be long and hot with loads of standing around the set; not everyone has a positive experience. Complaints range from lack of food and water to dangerous situations and intimidation when extras don't comply with the director's orders. Others describe the behind-the-scenes peek as a fascinating experience. Before agreeing to anything, always ask for the scout's identification and go with your gut.

Hindi- and English-language theatre or an arthouse film, and there's a cafe (p71) for drinks. Its excellent international theatre festival in November showcases contemporary Indian theatre and includes international productions.

Canvas Laugh COMEDY
(☏ 022-43485000; www.canvaslaughclub.com; 3rd fl, Palladium Mall, Phoenix Mills, Lower Parel; tickets ₹200-750) Popular comedy club that hosts around 50 shows per month, with twice-nightly programs on weekends. All comedians use English. It's 1km north of Mahalaxmi train station.

Comedy Store COMEDY
(☏ 022-39895050; www.thecomedystore.in; D2 Mathuradas Mills Compound, Senapati Bapat Marg, Lower Parel; tickets from ₹400; ⊙ 8pm-midnight Tue & Sun) Stand-up comedy (in English) featuring established and upcoming Indian comedians that's always a good night out. It's based at the Bluefrog, but the Comedy Store also pops up at other venues across town; check the website for details.

Liberty Cinema CINEMA, LIVE MUSIC
(Map p48; ☏ 9820027841; www.thelibertycinema.com; 41/42 New Marine Lines, near Bombay Hospital) Stunning art deco Liberty was once the queen of Hindi film – think red-carpet openings with Dev Anand. It fell on hard times in recent years, but is rebounding.

Mehboob Studios LIVE MUSIC, GALLERY
(Map p58; ☏ 022-26421628; 100 Hill Rd, Bandra West) As well as live music, these famous film studios also host the annual Times Litfest (in December), art exhibitions and film screenings.

Wankhede Stadium SPORTS
(Mumbai Cricket Association; Map p48; ☏ 22795500; www.mumbaicricket.com; D Rd, Churchgate; ⊙ ticket office 11.30am-7pm Mon-Sat) Test matches and one-day internationals are played a few times a year in season (October to April). Contact the Cricket Association for ticket information; for a test match you'll probably have to pay for the full five days.

D Y Patil Stadium SPORTS
(☏ 022-27731545; Yashwantrao Chavan Marg, Nerul, Navi Mumbai) A 55,000-capacity stadium

that hosts the ISL's Mumbai City FC football team, plus occasional IPL cricket matches. It's 21km east of central Mumbai. Tickets are available at the gate.

Regal Cinema
CINEMA
(Map p46; ☑22021017; Shahid Bhagat Singh Rd, Regal Circle, Colaba; tickets ₹130-180) A faded art deco masterpiece that's good for both Hollywood and Bollywood blockbusters.

Eros
CINEMA
(Map p48; ☑22822335; www.eroscinema.co.in; Maharshi Karve Rd, Churchgate; tickets ₹100-170) To experience Bollywood blockbusters in situ, the Eros is the place.

Metro Big
CINEMA
(☑39894040; www.bigcinemas.com; MG Rd, New Marine Lines, Fort; tickets ₹130-600) This grand dame of Bombay talkies was just renovated into a multiplex.

Shopping

Mumbai is India's great marketplace, with some of the best shopping in the country.

Be sure to spend a day at the markets north of CST for the classic Mumbai shopping experience. In Fort, booksellers, with surprisingly good wares (not all pirated), set up shop daily on the sidewalks around Flora Fountain. Snap up a bargain backpacking wardrobe at **Fashion Street** (MG Rd), the strip of stalls lining MG Rd between Cross and Azad Maidans. Hone your bargaining skills. Kemp's Corner has many good shops for designer threads.

Colaba

Bungalow 8
CLOTHING, ACCESSORIES
(Map p46; www.bungaloweight.com; 1st, 2nd & 3rd fls, Grants Bldg, Arthur Bunder Rd; ⊙10.30am-7.30pm) Original, high-end, artisanal clothing, jewellery, home decor and other objects of beauty, spread across three loftlike floors.

Phillips
ANTIQUES
(Map p46; www.phillipsantiques.com; Wodehouse Rd, Colaba; ⊙10am-7pm Mon-Sat) Art deco and colonial-era furniture, wooden ceremonial masks, silver, Victorian glass and also high-quality reproductions of old photos, maps and paintings.

Cottonworld Corp
CLOTHING
(Map p46; ☑22850060; www.cottonworld.net; Mandlik Marg; ⊙10.30am-8pm Mon-Sat, noon-8pm Sun) Stylish Indian-Western-hybrid

goods made from cotton, linen and natural materials (including er...paper made from rhino and elephant dung). Yes, you read that right. Only in India.

Bombay Electric
CLOTHING
(Map p46; www.bombayelectric.in; 1 Reay House, Best Marg; ⊙11am-9pm) High fashion is the calling at this trendy, slightly overhyped unisex boutique, which it sells at top rupee alongside arty accessories and a handful of fashionable antiques.

Central Cottage Industries Emporium
HANDICRAFTS, SOUVENIRS
(Map p46; ☑22027537; www.cottageemporium.in; Chhatrapati Shivaji Marg; ⊙10am-6pm) Fair-trade souvenirs including pashminas. Second branch in **Colaba** (Map p46; Kamal Mansion, Arthur Bunder Rd; ⊙11am-7pm Mon-Sat).

Fort Area & Churchgate

★Kitab Khana
BOOKS
(Map p48; www.kitabkhana.in; Somaiya Bhavan, 45/47 MG Rd, Fort; ⊙10.30am-7.30pm) This bookstore has a brilliantly curated selection of books, all of which are 20% off all the time. There's a great little **cafe** (Map p48; www.cafefoodforthought.com; light meals ₹120-180) at the back.

★Contemporary Arts & Crafts
HOMEWARES
(Map p48; www.cac.co.in; 210 Dr Dadabhai Naoroji Rd, Fort; ⊙10.30am-7.30pm) Modish, high-quality takes on traditional crafts: these are not your usual handmade souvenirs.

Artisans' Centre for Art, Craft & Design
CLOTHING, ACCESSORIES
(Map p48; ☑22673040; 1st fl, 52-56 Dr VB Gandhi Marg, Kala Ghoda; ⊙11am-7pm) Exhibits high-end handmade goods – from couture and jewellery to handicrafts and luxury *khadi* (homespun cloth).

Khadi & Village Industries Emporium
CLOTHING
(Khadi Bhavan; Map p48; 286 Dr Dadabhai Naoroji Rd, Fort; ⊙10.30am-6.30pm Mon-Sat) A dusty, 1940s time warp full of traditional Indian clothing, silk and *khadi*, and shoes.

Chimanlals
HANDICRAFTS
(Map p48; www.chimanlals.com; Wallace St, Fort; ⊙9.30am-6pm Mon-Fri, to 5pm Sat) The beautiful traditional printed papers here will make you start writing letters.

WORTH A TRIP

BAZAAR DISTRICT

Mumbai's main market district is one of Asia's most fascinating, an incredibly dense combination of humanity and commerce that's a total assault on the senses. If you've just got off a plane from the West, or a taxi from Bandra – hold on tight. This working-class district stretches north of Crawford Market up as far as Chor Bazaar, a 2.5km walk away. Such are the crowds (and narrowness of the lanes), allow yourself two to three hours to explore it thoroughly.

You can buy just about anything here, but as the stores and stalls are very much geared to local tastes, most of the fun is simply taking in the street life and investigating the souklike lanes rather than buying souvenirs. The markets merge into each other in an amoeba-like mass, but there are some key landmarks so you can orientate yourself.

Crawford Market (Mahatma Phule Market; Map p54; cnr DN & Lokmanya Tilak Rds) Crawford Market is the largest in Mumbai, and contains the last whiff of British Bombay before the tumult of the central bazaars begins. Bas-reliefs by Rudyard Kipling's father, Lockwood Kipling, adorn the Norman Gothic exterior. Fruit and vegetables, meat and fish are mainly traded, but it's also an excellent place to stock up on spices. If you're lucky to be here during alphonso mango season (May to June) be sure to indulge.

Mangaldas Market (Map p54) Mangaldas Market, traditionally home to traders from Gujarat, is a minitown, complete with lanes of fabrics. Even if you're not the type to have your clothes tailored, drop by DD Dupattawala (Map p54; Shop No 217, 4th Lane, Mangaldas Market; ☺9.30am-6.30pm) for pretty scarves and dupattas at fixed prices. Zaveri Bazaar (Map p54) for jewellery and Bhuleshwar Market (Map p54; cnr Sheikh Menon St & M Devi Marg) for fruit and veg are just north of here. Just a few metres further along Sheikh Menon Rd from Bhuleshwar is a Jain pigeon-feeding station, flower market and a religious market.

Chor Bazaar (Map p54) Chor Bazaar is known for its antiques, though nowadays much of it is reproductions; the main area of activity is Mutton St, where shops specialise in 'antiques' and miscellaneous junk. Dhabu St, to the east, is lined with fine leather goods.

Royal Music Collection MUSIC STORE
(Map p48; 192 Kitab Mahal, Dr Dadabhai Naoroji Rd, Fort; ☺11am-9pm Mon-Sat) Brilliant street stall selling vintage vinyl (from ₹250).

Fabindia CLOTHING, HOMEWEARS
(Map p48; www.fabindia.com; Jeroo Bldg, 137 MG Rd, Kala Ghoda; ☺10am-8pm) Ethically sourced cotton and silk fashions and homewares in a modern-meets-traditional Indian shop.

Chetana Book Centre BOOKS
(Map p48; www.chetana.com; K Dubash Marg, Kala Ghoda; ☺10.30am-7.30pm Mon-Sat) This great spirituality bookstore has lots of books on Hinduism and a whole section on 'Afterlife/ Death/Psychic'.

Standard Supply Co PHOTOGRAPHY
(Map p48; ☏22612468; Walchand Hirachand Marg, Fort; ☺10am-7pm Mon-Sat) Everything for digital and film photography.

Oxford Bookstore BOOKS
(Map p48; www.oxfordbookstore.com; Apeejay House, 3 Dinsha Wachha Marg, Churchgate;

☺8am-10pm) Spacious store with a good selection of travel books and a **tea bar** (teas ₹35-80; ☺10am-10pm).

Kalbadevi to Mahalaxmi

Shrujan HANDICRAFTS
(Map p54; www.shrujan.org; Sagar Villa, Bhulabhai Desai Marg, Breach Candy, opp Navroze Apts; ☺10am-7.30pm Mon-Sat) ✎ Nonprofit that sells the intricately-embroidered clothing, bags, cushions covers and shawls of 3500 women in 114 villages in Kutch, Gujarat. There's also a (hard-to-find) **Juhu branch** (Map p58; Hatkesh Society, 6th North South Rd, JVPD Scheme; ☺10am-7.30pm Mon-Sat).

Mini Market/Bollywood Bazaar ANTIQUES, SOUVENIRS
(Map p54; ☏23472427; 33/31 Mutton St; ☺11am-8pm Sat-Thu) Sells vintage Bollywood posters and other movie ephemera.

BX Furtado & Sons MUSIC STORE
(Map p54; www.furtadosonline.com; Jer Mahal, Dhobi Talao; ☺10.30am-7.30pm Mon-Sat) *The*

place in town for musical instruments: sitars, tablas, accordions and local and imported guitars.

🏠 Western Suburbs

Indian Hippy   ART
(Map p58; ☑8080822022; www.hippy.in; 17/C Sherly Rajan Rd, Bandra West, off Carter Rd; portraits from ₹10,000; ☺by appointment) Because you need to have your portrait hand-painted in the style of a vintage Bollywood poster. Bring (or email) a photo. Also sells LP clocks, vintage film posters and all manner of (frankly bizarre) Bollywood-themed products.

Play Clan   SOUVENIRS, CLOTHING
(Map p58; www.theplayclan.com; Libra Towers, Hill Rd, Bandra West; ☺11am-8.30pm) Kitschy, design-y goods that are pricey but the best in town. Check out the eye masks and cartoon Hanuman cushion covers.

Kishore Silk House   CLOTHING, HANDICRAFTS
(Bhandarkar Rd, Matunga East; ☺10am-8.30pm Tue-Sun) Handwoven saris and dhotis from Tamil Nadu and Kerala.

ℹ Information

EMERGENCY
Call the **police** (☑100) for emergencies.

INTERNET ACCESS
Anita CyberCafé (Map p48; Cowasji Patel Rd, Fort; per hour ₹30; ☺9am-10pm Mon-Sat, 2-10pm Sun) Opposite one of Mumbai's best chai stalls (open evenings).

Portasia (Map p48; Kitab Mahal, Dr Dadabhai Naoroji Rd, Fort; per hour ₹30; ☺9am-9pm Mon-Sat) Its entrance is down a little alley.

MEDIA
To find out what's going on in Mumbai, check out the highly informative **Mumbai Boss** (www.mumbaiboss.com). The *Hindustan Times* is the best paper; its *Café* insert has a good what's-on guide. **Time Out Mumbai** (www.timeoutmumbai.net) no longer publishes a Mumbai magazine but its website is worth consulting.

MEDICAL SERVICES
Bombay Hospital (Map p48; ☑22067676, ambulance 22067309; www.bombayhospital.com; 12 New Marine Lines) A private hospital with the latest medical technology and equipment.

Breach Candy Hospital (Map p54; ☑23672888, emergency 23667809; www.breachcandyhospital.org; 60 Bhulabhai Desai Marg, Breach Candy) The best in Mumbai, if not India. It's 2km northwest of Chowpatty Beach.

MONEY
ATMs are everywhere, and foreign-exchange offices changing cash are also plentiful.
Thomas Cook (Map p46; ☑66092608; Colaba Causeway; ☺9.30am-6pm) Has a branch in the Fort area also.

POST
Main post office (Map p48; Walchand Hirachand Marg; ☺10am-7pm Mon-Sat, to 4pm Sun) The main post office is an imposing building beside CST. Poste restante (☺10am-3pm Mon-Sat) is at the 'Delivery Department' Letters should be addressed c/o Poste Restante, Mumbai GPO, Mumbai 400 001. Bring your passport to collect mail. Opposite the post office are parcel-wallahs who will stitch up your parcel for ₹40.

TELEPHONE
Call ☑197 for directory assistance.

TOURIST INFORMATION
Indiatourism (Government of India Tourist Office; Map p48; ☑22074333; www.incredibleindia.com; Western Railways Reservation Complex, 123 Maharshi Karve Rd; ☺8.30am-6pm Mon-Fri, to 2pm Sat) Provides information for the entire country, as well as contacts for Mumbai guides and homestays.

Maharashtra Tourism Development Corporation Booth (MTDC; ☑22841877; Apollo Bunder; ☺8.30am-4pm Tue-Fri, to 9pm Sat & Sun) For city bus tours.

Maharashtra Tourism Development Corporation (MTDC; Map p48; ☑22044040; www.maharashtratourism.gov.in; Madame Cama Rd, Nariman Point; ☺10am-5pm Mon-Sat, closed 2nd & 4th Sat) The MTDC's head office has helpful staff and lots of pamphlets to give away.

TRAVEL AGENCIES
Akbar Travels (www.akbartravelsonline.com; ☺10am-7pm Mon-Fri, to 6pm Sat); Colaba (Map p46; ☑22823434; 30 Alipur Trust Bldg, Shahid Bhagat Singh Marg); Fort (Map p48; ☑22633434; 167/169 Dr Dadabhai Naoroji Rd) Extremely helpful and can book car/drivers and buses. Also has good exchange rates.

Thomas Cook (Map p48; ☑61603333; www.thomascook.in; 324 Dr Dadabhai Naoroji Rd, Fort; ☺9.30am-6pm Mon-Sat) Flight and hotel bookings, plus foreign exchange.

VISAS
Foreigners' Regional Registration Office (FRRO; Map p48; ☑22620446; www.immigrationindia.

nic.in; Annexe Bldg No 2, CID, Badaruddin Tyabji Marg, near Special Branch; ☺9.30am-1pm Mon-Fri) Tourist and transit visas can no longer be extended except in emergency situations; check the latest online.

ⓘ Getting There & Away

AIR

Mumbai's **Chhatrapati Shivaji International Airport** (BOM; Map p58; ☑66851010; www.csia.in), about 30km from the city centre, was nearing the end of a $2 billion modernisation program at the time of research. The impressive international terminal is complete, while its new domestic terminal should be fully operational some time in 2015, creating a fully integrated airport.

At the time of writing, the airport still comprised of one international terminal and a separate domestic terminal (also known locally as Santa Cruz airport) 5km away. A free shuttle bus runs between the two terminals every half-hour (journey time 15 minutes) for ticket-holders. Both terminals have ATMs, foreign-exchange counters and tourist-information booths.

Travel agencies and airlines' websites are usually best for booking flights. The following airlines have offices in town and/or at the airport:

Air India (Map p48; ☑27580777, airport 28318666; www.airindia.com; Air India Bldg, cnr Marine Dr & Madame Cama Rd, Nariman Point; ☺9.30am-6.30pm Mon-Fri, to 5.15pm Sat & Sun) International and domestic routes.

Jet Airways (Map p48; ☑022-39893333; www.jetairways.com; B1, Amarchand Mansion, Madam Cama Rd, Colaba; ☺9am-6pm Mon-Sat) India's second-largest domestic carrier.

Major nonstop domestic flights from Mumbai include the following:

DESTINATION	FARE (₹)	DURATION (HR)
Bengaluru	3700	1½
Chennai	5800	2
Delhi	5900	2
Goa	3300	1
Hyderabad	4200	1½
Jaipur	4300	1¾
Kochi	5700	2
Kolkata	6100	2¾
Nagpur	4200	1½

BUS

Numerous private operators and state governments run long-distance buses to and from Mumbai.

Long-distance government-run buses depart from the **Mumbai Central bus terminal** (Map p54;

ⓘ AIRPORT ARRIVAL

Many international flights arrive after midnight. Beat the daytime traffic by heading straight to your hotel, and carry detailed landmark directions: many airport taxi drivers don't speak English and may not use official street names.

☑enquiry 23024075; Jehangir Boman Behram Rd) right by Mumbai Central train station. They're cheaper and more frequent than private services, but standards are usually lower. The **MSRTC** (Maharashtra State Road Transport Corporation; ☑1800221250; www.msrtc.gov.in) website theoretically has schedules and is supposed to permit online booking, though in practice it's next to useless.

Private buses are usually more comfortable and simpler to book (if a bit more costly). Most depart from Dr Anadrao Nair Rd near Mumbai Central train station, but many buses to southern destinations depart from Paltan Rd, near Crawford Market. Check departure times and prices with **Citizen Travels** (Map p54; ☑23459695; www.citizenbus.com; D Block, Sitaram Bldg, Paltan Rd) or **National CTC** (Map p54; ☑23015652; Dr Anadrao Nair Rd). Fares to popular destinations (such as Goa) are up to 75% higher during holiday periods.

Private buses to Goa vary in price from ₹350 (bad choice) to ₹2600. Many leave from way out in the suburbs but **Chandni Travels** (Map p48; ☑22713901, 22676840) has six daily from in front of Azad Maidan and **Paolo Travel** (Map p48; ☑0832-6637777; www.paolotravels.com), with an 8pm daily departure from Fashion St, are convenient to the centre.

TRAIN

Three train systems operate out of Mumbai, but the most important services for travellers are Central Railways and Western Railways. Tickets for either system can be bought from any station that has computerised ticketing.

Central Railways (☑139), handling services to the east, south, plus a few trains to the north, operates from CST (also known as 'VT'). Foreign-tourist–quota tickets and Indrail passes can be bought at Counter 52.

Some Central Railways trains depart from Dadar (D), a few stations north of CST, or Lokmanya Tilak (LTT), 16km north of CST.

Western Railways (☑139) has services to the north from Mumbai Central train station, usually called Bombay Central (BCT). The **reservation centre** (Map p48; ☺8am-8pm Mon-Sat, to 2pm Sun), opposite Churchgate station, has foreign-tourist–quota tickets.

ℹ Getting Around

TO/FROM THE AIRPORTS

International

Prepaid Taxi Taxis with set fares cost ₹700/800 (non-AC/AC) to Colaba and Fort and ₹450/550 to Bandra. The journey to Colaba takes about an hour at night (via the Sealink) and 1½ to two hours during the day.

Autorickshaws Available but they only go as far south as Bandra (daytime/night around ₹180/240).

Train If you arrive during the day (but not during 'rush hour' – 6am to 11am) and are not weighed down with luggage, consider the train: take an autorickshaw (around ₹60) to Andheri train station and then the Churchgate or CST train (₹9, 45 minutes).

Taxi From South Mumbai to the international airport should be around ₹500. Allow two hours for the trip if you travel between 4pm and 8pm.

Domestic

There's a prepaid taxi counter in the arrivals hall. A non-AC/AC taxi costs ₹600/700 to Colaba or Fort and ₹370/480 to Bandra.

Alternatively, if it's not rush hour, catch an autorickshaw (around ₹45) to Vile Parle station, where you can get a train to Churchgate (₹8, 45 minutes).

BOAT

PNP (📞 22885220) and **Maldar Catamarans** (📞 22829695) run regular ferries to Mandwa (one way ₹125 to ₹155), useful for access to Murud-Janjira and other parts of the Konkan Coast, avoiding the long bus trip out of Mumbai. Buy **tickets** (Map p46) near the Gateway of India.

BUS

Few travellers bother with city buses but **BEST** (www.bestundertaking.com) has a useful search facility for hardcore shoestringers and masochists – you'll also need to read the buses'

Devanagiri numerals and beware of pickpockets. Fares start at ₹5.

CAR

Cars with driver can be hired for moderate rates. Air-conditioned cars start at ₹1550/1800 for half/full-day rental of around 80km.

Clear Car Rental (📞 0888-8855220; www. clearcarrental.com)

Metro

The first section of Line 1, Mumbai's new **metro** (www.mumbaimetroone.com) opened in 2014. Initially it only connected seven stations in the far northern suburbs, well away from anywhere of interest to visitors. However Line 1 is scheduled to be extended south as far as Jacob Circle (5km north of Chhatrapati Shivaji Terminus) sometime in 2015, bringing it past Lower Parel.

Single fares cost between ₹10 and ₹20, with monthly Trip Passes (from ₹600) also available. Access to stations is by escalator, carriages are air-conditioned, and there are seats reserved for women and the disabled. Line 3 (a 33km underground line connecting Cuffe Pde south of Colaba, all the main railway terminals, Bandra and the airport) will be the next line to be constructed. It's been approved but won't open for many years.

MOTORCYCLE

Allibhai Premji Tyrewalla (Map p54; 📞 23099313, 23099417; www.premjis. com; 205 Dr D Bhadkamkar (Lamington) Rd; ⏰ 10am-7pm Mon-Sat) Sells new and used motorcycles with a guaranteed buy-back option. Long-term rental schemes (two months or more) start at around ₹25,000, with a buy-back price of around 60% after three months.

TAXI & AUTORICKSHAW

Mumbai's black-and-yellow taxis are inexpensive and the most convenient way to get around southern Mumbai; drivers *almost* always use the meter without prompting. The minimum fare is ₹21 (for up to 1.6km), a 5km trip costs about ₹50.

MAJOR LONG-DISTANCE BUS ROUTES

DESTINATION	PRIVATE NON-AC/AC SLEEPER (₹)	GOVERNMENT NON-AC (₹)	DURATION (HR)
Ahmedabad	400-650/500-2300	N/A	7-12
Aurangabad	400/550-900	472 (five daily)	9-11
Hyderabad	800-2500 (all AC)	N/A	16
Mahabaleshwar	400-2100 (all AC)	335 (three daily)	7-8
Panaji (Panjim)	600-750/700-2700	2400	14-16
Pune	250-735 (all AC)	224 (half-hourly)	3-5
Udaipur	800-1200/1500-2050	N/A	13-16

Consult www.makemytrip.com for latest schedules and prices

MAJOR TRAINS FROM MUMBAI

DESTINATION	TRAIN NO & NAME	SAMPLE FARE (₹)	DURATION (HR)	DEPARTURE
Agra	12137 Punjab Mail	580/1515/2195/3760 (A)	22	7.40pm CST
Ahmedabad	12901 Gujarat Mail	315/805/1135/1915 (A)	9	10pm BCT
	12009 Shatabdi Exp	960/1870 (C)	7	6.25am BCT
Aurangabad	11401 Nandigram Exp	235/620/885 (B)	7	4.35pm CST
	17617 Tapovan Exp	140/500 (C)	7	6.15am CST
Bengaluru	16529 Udyan Exp	505/1355/1975/3375 (A)	25	8.05am CST
Chennai	12163 Chennai Exp	570/1485/2145/3670 (A)	23½	8.30pm CST
Delhi	12951 Rajdhani Exp	2030/2810/4680 (D)	16	4.35pm BCT
Hyderabad	12701 Hussain-sagar Exp	425/1115/1590/2695 (A)	14½	9.50pm CST
Indore	12961 Avantika Exp	440/1150/1640/2780 (A)	14	7.05pm BCT
Jaipur	12955 Jaipur Exp	535/1405/2025/3455 (A)	18	6.50pm BCT
Kochi	16345 Netravati Exp	615/1635/2400 (B)	25½	11.40am LTT
Madgaon (Goa)	10103 Mandovi Exp	390/1055/1520/2575 (A)	12	7.10am CST
	12133 Mangalore Exp	420/1100/1570 (B)	9	10pm CST
Pune	11301 Udyan Exp	485/690/1150 (D)	3½	8.05am CST

Station abbreviations: CST (Chhatrapati Shivaji Terminus); BCT (Mumbai Central); LTT (Lokmanya Tilak); D (Dadar). Fares: (A) sleeper/3AC/2AC/1AC, (B) sleeper/3AC/2AC, (C) sleeper/CC, (D) 3AC/2AC/1AC

Autorickshaws are the name of the game north of Bandra. The minimum fare is ₹17, up to 1.6km, a 3km trip is about ₹30.

Both taxis and autorickshaws tack 25% onto the fare between midnight and 5am.

Tip: Mumbaikars tend to navigate by landmarks, not street names (especially new names), so have some details before heading out.

TRAIN

Mumbai's suburban train network is one of the world's busiest; forget travelling during rush hours. Trains run from 4am to 1am and there are three main lines:

Western Line The most useful; operates out of Churchgate north to Charni Rd (for Girgaum Chowpatty), Mumbai Central, Mahalaxmi (for the Dhobi Ghat), Bandra, Vile Parle (for the domestic airport), Andheri (for the international airport) and Borivali (for Sanjay Gandhi National Park), among others.

Central Line Runs from CST to Byculla (for Veermata Jijabai Bhonsle Udyan, formerly Victoria Gardens), Dadar and as far as Neral (for Matheran).

From Churchgate, 2nd-/1st-class fares are ₹5/48 to Mumbai Central, ₹8/85 to Vile Parle, and ₹9/116 to Borivali.

To avoid the queues, buy a **coupon book** (₹50), good for use on either train line, then 'validate' the coupons at the machines before boarding.

'Tourist tickets' permit unlimited travel in 2nd/1st class for one (₹75/225), three (₹115/415) or five (₹135/485) days.

Watch your valuables, and gals, stick to the ladies-only carriages except late at night, when it's more important to avoid empty cars.

Maharashtra

Best Places to Eat

➡ Malaka Spice (p113)

➡ Chaitanya (p105)

➡ Dario's (p113)

➡ Bhoj (p91)

➡ Little Italy (p117)

Best Places to Stay

➡ Hotel Sunderban (p112)

➡ Verandah in the Forest (p107)

➡ Beyond (p85)

➡ Hotel Panchavati (p89)

➡ Hotel Plaza (p99)

Why Go?

India's third-largest state, Maharashtra showcases many of India's iconic attractions. There are lazy, palm-fringed beaches, lofty, cool-green mountains, World Heritage Sites and bustling cosmopolitan cities. In the far east of the state are some of the nation's most impressive national parks, including the Tadoba-Andhari Tiger Reserve.

Inland lie the extraordinary cave temples of Ellora and Ajanta, undoubtedly Maharashtra's greatest monuments, hewn by hand from solid rock. Matheran, a colonial-era hill station served by a toy train, has a certain allure. Pilgrims and inquisitive souls are drawn to cosmopolitan Pune, a city famous for its 'sex guru' and alternative spiritualism. And westwards, the romantic Konkan Coast fringing the Arabian Sea is lined with spectacular, crumbling forts and sandy beaches, some of the best around the pretty resort of Malvan, which is fast becoming one of India's premier diving centres.

When to Go
Nasik

°C/°F Temp   Rainfall inches/mm

Jan It's party time at Nasik's wineries, marked by grape harvesting and crushing galas.

Sep The frenzied, energetic Ganesh Chaturthi celebrations reach fever pitch.

Dec Clear skies, mild temperatures; the secluded beaches of Murud, Ganpatipule and Tarkali are lovely.

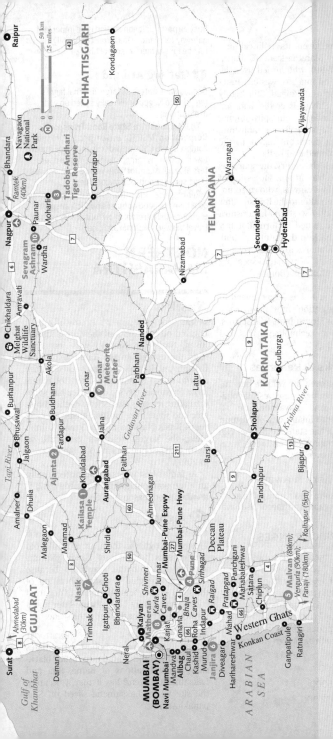

Maharashtra Highlights

1 Being amazed by the intricate beauty of the **Kailasa Temple** (p94) at Ellora

2 Wandering through ancient cave galleries at **Ajanta** (p96)

3 Searching for big cats inside **Tadoba-Andhari Tiger Reserve** (p101)

4 Delving into new-age spiritualism and modern Indian cuisine in diverse, progressive **Pune** (p109)

5 Diving or snorkelling in the big blue off **Malvan** (p105)

6 Wondering at the might of a lost civilisation at the colossal fort of **Janjira** (p102)

7 Sipping in the wine country around **Nasik** (p87)

8 Exploring the spectacular viewpoints at the hill station of **Matheran** (p106)

9 Contemplating the power of nature at the primordial **Lonar Meteorite Crater** (p101)

10 Learning about the Gandhian way of life at the **Sevagram Ashram** (p100)

History

Maharashtra was given its political and ethnic identity by Maratha leader Chhatrapati Shivaji (1627–80), who lorded over the Deccan plateau and much of western India from his stronghold at Raigad. Still highly respected today, Shivaji is credited for instilling a strong, independent spirit among the region's people, as well as establishing Maharashtra as a dominant player in the power relations of medieval India.

From the early 18th century, the state was under the administration of a succession of ministers called the Peshwas, who ruled until 1819, ceding thereafter to the British. After Independence in 1947, western Maharashtra and Gujarat were joined to form Bombay state. But it was back to the future in 1960, when modern Maharashtra was formed with the exclusion of Gujarati-speaking areas and with Mumbai (Bombay) as its capital.

Since then the state has forged ahead to become one of the nation's most prosperous, with one of India's largest industrial sectors, partly thanks to its technology parks and software exports.

National Parks & Reserves

Maharashtra has over 30 wildlife sanctuaries, including six tiger reserves: Tadoba-Andhari, Pench and Navagaon are all grouped around the inland city of Nagpur. In the far south of the state the Malvan National Marine Park protects coral reefs, islets and coastal mangroves.

ⓘ Getting There & Away

Mumbai is Maharashtra's main transport hub, though Pune, Aurangabad and Nagpur also have

---

SLEEPING PRICE RANGES

In Maharashtra, hotel rooms above ₹1000 attract a 7.42% Service Tax, plus a 'Luxury Tax' of 4% (for tariffs of ₹750 to ₹1200) or 10% (tariffs over ₹1200). Many hotels will negotiate one or both of the taxes away in quiet times.

The following price ranges refer to a double room with bathroom and are inclusive of tax:

$ less than ₹2000

$$ ₹2000 to ₹5000

$$$ more than ₹5000

---

busy airports. Jalgaon station is an important gateway for Ajanta. Goa airport is handily placed for the far southern resort of Malvan.

ⓘ Getting Around

Because the state is so large, internal flights (eg Pune to Nagpur) will really speed up your explorations.

The **Maharashtra State Road Transport Corporation** (MSRTC; www.msrtc.gov.in) runs a comprehensive bus network spanning all major towns and many remote places. Private operators also have comfortable Volvo and Mercedes Benz services between major cities.

Renting a car and driver to explore the Konkan coastline is a good option as public transport is poor on this stretch: allow four or five days to travel between Mumbai and Goa.

NORTHERN MAHARASHTRA

Nasik

📞 0253 / POP 1.57 MILLION / ELEV 565M

Located on the banks of the holy Godavari River, Nasik (or Nashik) gets its name from the episode in the Ramayana where Lakshmana, Rama's brother, hacked off the *nasika* (nose) of Ravana's sister. Today this large provincial city's old quarter has some intriguing temples that reference the Hindu epic and some huge bathing ghats. Every 12 years, Nasik plays host to the grand Kumbh Mela, the largest religious gathering on Earth (the last one was in 2015, the next one in 2027).

As India's best wines are produced locally, an afternoon touring the vineyards (p87) is another good reason to drop by.

⊙ Sights

Ramkund   GHAT

This bathing ghat in the heart of Nasik's old quarter sees hundreds of Hindu pilgrims arriving daily to bathe, pray and – because the waters provide *moksha* (liberation of the soul) – to immerse the ashes of departed friends and family. It's a shame litter and a scruffy adjacent market taint the scene.

Kala Rama Temple   HINDU TEMPLE

(⊙6am-10pm) The city's holiest shrine dates back to 1794 and contains unusual blackstone representations of Rama, Sita and Lakshmana. Legend has it that it occupies the site where Lakshmana sliced off Surpanakha's nose.

Gumpha Panchavati
HINDU TEMPLE

(☉6am-9.30pm) Sita is said to have hid in this cavelike temple while being assailed by the evil Ravana. You'll have to stoop and shuffle into the cave as the entrance is very narrow.

🛏 Sleeping

Hotel Samrat
HOTEL $

(☎2577211; www.hotelsamratnasik.com; Old Agra Rd; s/d from ₹950/1330, with AC ₹1580/1820; ❄🤶) Offering good value, with comfortable rooms that have large windows and pine furniture; the budget options have garish colour schemes, the upmarket rooms are more restrained. Located right next to the bus stand, its spick-and-span vegetarian restaurant is open 24 hours, making it popular as a refuelling stop.

Hotel Abhishek
HOTEL $

(☎2514201; www.hotelabhishek.com; Panchavati Karanja; s/d from ₹370/490, with AC ₹770/830; ❄🤶) Found just off the Panchavati Karanja roundabout, this decent budget place offers clean if ageing rooms, hot showers (mornings only) and appetising vegetarian food. Service varies a bit according to who is on reception duty.

Hotel Panchavati
HOTEL $

(☎2575771; www.panchavatihotels.com; 430 Chandak Wadi, Vakil Wadi Rd; s/d incl breakfast ₹1300/1500, with AC from ₹1500/1900; ❄🤶) This hotel in a sprawling complex contains a multitude of different room categories, two good restaurants and a bar. Rooms are perhaps a little dated (expect uniquely Indian mismatched decor) but spacious, kept clean and pretty well maintained. Wi-fi access is only in the lobby.

Ibis
HOTEL $$

(☎0253-6635555; www.ibis.com; Trimback Rd; s/d ₹2580/2760; ❄🤶) Sleek, modern, well-equipped, smallish rooms that boast fine-quality beds and linen; wi-fi is fast and reliable. With a good restaurant, gym and 24-hour room service, it all adds up to a great package. Located 4km west of the centre.

Ginger
HOTEL $$

(☎0253-6616333; www.gingerhotels.com; Plot P20, Satpur MIDC, Trimbak Rd; s/d ₹3060/3670; ❄🤶) Primarily a business hotel, it features DIY service, but there are luxe features and conveniences aplenty, and rooms have blonde wood, high cleanliness standards and swish ensuites, and are fresh and in-

---

TOP STATE FESTIVALS

Naag Panchami (☉Jul/Aug) A traditional snake-worshipping festival, held in Pune and Kolhapur.

Ganesh Chaturthi (☉Aug/Sep) Celebrated with fervour all across Maharashtra; Pune goes particularly hysteric in honour of the elephant-headed deity.

Dussehra (☉Sep & Oct) A Hindu festival, but it also marks the Buddhist celebration of the anniversary of the famous humanist and Dalit leader BR Ambedkar's conversion to Buddhism.

Ellora Ajanta Aurangabad Festival (☉Nov) Aurangabad's cultural festival brings together the best classical and folk performers from across the region, while promoting a number of artistic traditions and handicrafts on the side.

Kalidas Festival (☉Nov) Commemorates the literary genius of legendary poet Kalidas through spirited music, dance and theatre in Nagpur.

Sawai Gandharva Sangeet Mahotsav (☉Dec) An extravaganza of unforgettable performances by some of the heftiest names in Indian classical music in Pune.

---

viting. It's around 4km west of the central district.

★ Beyond
RESORT $$$

(☎09970090010; www.sulawines.com; Gangapur-Savargaon Rd; d/ste incl breakfast from ₹7750; ❄❄) Sula Vineyards' luxury resort is set by a lake and bordered by rolling hills, where you can roam the landscape on bicycles, go kayaking on the still waters or laze the hours away at the spa or games room. Its 32 beautifully designed, contemporary rooms are pricey but very tasteful and the in-house dining options are great.

🍴 Eating

Shilpa's Food Lounge
INDIAN, MULTICUISINE $

(Vakil Wadi Rd; meals ₹60-150; ☉8.30am-11pm; 🤶) A clean, modern and welcoming new place in the heart of town with good selection of Indian, continental and Chinese food, plus air-con. The *misal pav* (₹45), an unusual Maharashtrian breakfast prepared

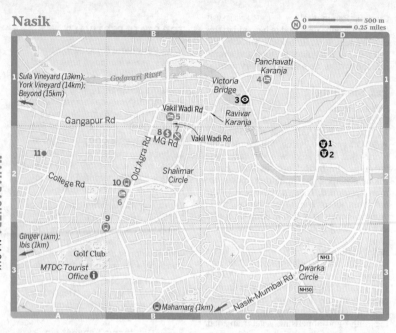

with bean sprouts and served with bread, is the best in town.

Khyber　　　　MUGHLAI, MULTICUISINE $$
(Hotel Panchavati, 430 Chandak Wadi, Vakil Wadi Rd; mains ₹180-300; ⊘11.30am-11.30pm) At the Hotel Panchavati, this restaurant is known for its delectable Afghani-style dishes, including *murgh shaan-e-khyber* (chicken marinated with herbs and cooked in a creamy gravy).

Soleil by La Plage　　　　FRENCH, INDIAN $$$
(☑7722020927; Sula Vineyards, Gangapur-Savargaon Rd; meals ₹600-1100; ⊘12.30-3.30pm & 7.30-10.30pm) Spectacular new restaurant on the Sula estate, created by the French owners of a famous Goan establishment. The design is urban and bohemian, with hip seating and lots of space for a serious gastronomic feast. Stick to Gallic classics like the *coq au vin*, though Indian and international dishes are also available (as are Sula wines, of course).

ℹ Information

Cyber Café (Vakil Wadi Rd; per hour ₹20; ⊘10am-10pm) Staff are friendly and helpful.
MTDC Tourist Office (☑2570059; www.maharashtratourism.gov.in; T/I; Golf Club, Old Agra Rd; ⊘10.30am-5.30pm Mon-Sat) About 1km south of the Old Central bus stand; helpful staff.

ℹ Getting There & Around

BUS

The **New Central bus stand** has services to Aurangabad (semideluxe ₹292, 4½ hours) and Pune (semideluxe/deluxe ₹308/570, 4½ hours). Nasik's **Old Central bus stand** (CBS; ☑0253-

2309310) has buses to Trimbak (₹35, 45 minutes). South of town, the **Mahamarg bus stand** has services to Mumbai Central (semi deluxe ₹278, four hours) and Shirdi (₹114, 2½ hours). Private bus agents based near the CBS run buses to Pune, Mumbai, Aurangabad and Ahmedabad. Most buses depart from Old Agra Rd, and most Mumbai-bound buses terminate at Dadar in Mumbai.

TRAIN

The Nasik Rd train station is 8km southeast of the town centre, but a useful **railway reservation office** (1st fl, Commissioner's Office, Canada Corner; ◷ 8am-8pm Mon-Sat) is 500m west of the Old Central bus stand. There are around 15 daily trains to Mumbai so you won't have to wait long; these include the daily Pushpak Express (1st/2nd/3rd class ₹1230/735/535, 4½ hours, 3.15pm). There are four daily departures to Aurangabad; try the Tapovan Express (2nd class/chair ₹85/320, 3½ hours, 9.50am). An autorickshaw to the station costs about ₹125.

Around Nasik

Bhandardara

The picturesque village of Bhandardara is nestled deep in the folds of the Sahyadris, about 70km from Nasik. A little-visited place surrounded by craggy mountains, it is one of Maharashtra's best escapes from the bustle of urban India.

Most of Bhandardara's habitation is thrown around **Arthur Lake**, a horseshoe-shaped reservoir fed by the waters of the Pravara River. The lake is barraged on one side by the imposing **Wilson Dam**, a colonial-era structure dating back to 1910. If you like walking, consider a hike to the summit of **Mt Kalsubai**, which at 1646m was once used as an observation point by the Marathas. Alternatively, you could hike to the ruins of the **Ratangad Fort**, another of Shivaji's erstwhile strongholds, which has wonderful views of the surrounding ranges.

The charming **Anandvan Resort** (☎9920311221; www.anandvanresorts.com; d from ₹7350; ❄) a hilltop hotel with a choice of comfy cottages and villas overlooking Arthur Lake, allows you to sleep in style, while the **MTDC Holiday Resort** (☎0242-4257032; budget/deluxe r from ₹1100/4000; ❄), further down the hill, has both renovated comfortable rooms and reasonable budget options.

Bhandardara can be accessed by taking a local bus from Nasik's Mahamarg bus stand

GRAPES OF NASIK

From wimpy raisins to full-bodied wines, the grapes of Nasik have come a long way. The surrounding region had been producing table grapes since ancient times. However, it was only in the early 1990s that a couple of entrepreneurs realised that Nasik, with its fertile soils and temperate climate, boasted good conditions for wine cultivation. In 1997 industry pioneer Sula Vineyards fearlessly invested in a crop of sauvignon blanc and chenin blanc, and the first batch of domestic wines hit the shelves in 2000. Nasik hasn't looked back.

These days, the wine list in most of Nasik's wineries has stretched to include shiraz, merlot, cabernet, semillon and zinfandel as well as a few sparkling wines, and most of these drops can be sampled first-hand by visiting one of the estates.

During harvest season (January to March), some wineries also organise grape-crushing festivals, marked by unbridled revelry. Events are usually advertised on the wineries' websites.

Sula Vineyards (☎09970090010; www.sulawines.com; Gangapur-Savargaon Rd, Govardhan; ◷11am-10pm) Sula Vineyards, 15km west of Nasik, offers a slick, professional tour (around 45 minutes) of its impressive estate and high-tech facilities. This is rounded off with a wine-tasting session (four/six wines ₹150/250) that features its best drops and offers excellent tasting tips. The cafe here has commanding views of the countryside (though only snacks are sold and it does get very busy); for meals the neighbouring French restaurant Soleil by La Plage is recommended.

York Winery (☎0253-2230700; www.yorkwinery.com; Gangapur-Savargaon Rd, Gangavarhe; ◷noon-10pm, tours 12.30-6pm) A further kilometre from Sula Vineyards, York Winery offers tours and wine-tasting sessions (₹100) in a top-floor room that has scenic views of the lake and surrounding hills. Five reds, a rosé and chenin blanc are produced. There's a large garden where continental snacks (olives, cheeses) are offered.

to Ghoti (₹38, one hour), from where an auto-rickshaw ride costs ₹90. A taxi from Nasik can also drop you at your resort for about ₹1500.

Igatpuri

Heard of *vipassana*, haven't you? Well head to Igatpuri to see where (and how) it all happens. Located about 44km south of Nasik, this village is home to the headquarters of the world's largest *vipassana* meditation institution, the **Vipassana International Academy** (📷 02553-244076; www.dhamma.org; donations accepted), which institutionalises this strict form of meditation first taught by Gautama Buddha in the 6th century BC and reintroduced to India by teacher SN Goenka in the 1960s. Ten-day residential courses (advance bookings compulsory) are held throughout the year, though teachers warn that it requires rigorous discipline. Basic accommodation, food and meditation instruction are provided free of charge, but donations upon completion are accepted. Consult the academy website for detailed transport information; options from Nasik include share taxi and state bus links (both leave from the New Central bus stand).

Trimbak

Trimbakeshwar Temple　　HINDU TEMPLE
(entrance ₹200 to avoid queue; ⊙ 5.30am-9pm) The moody Trimbakeshwar Temple stands in the centre of Trimbak, 33km west of Nasik. It's one of India's most sacred temples, containing a *jyoti linga,* one of the

TOP YOGA & MEDITATION CENTRES

The Vipassana International Academy in Igatpuri has long been a destination for those wishing to put mind over matter through an austere form of Buddhist meditation. The boundaries of yoga, on the other hand, are constantly pushed at the Ramamani Iyengar Memorial Yoga Institute (p112) in Pune and the Kaivalyadhama Yoga Hospital (p107) in Lonavla. For a more lavish and indulgent form of spiritual engagement, there's the superluxurious Osho International Meditation Resort (p111) in Pune, where one can meditate in style, while flexing a few muscles in the unique game of zennis (Zen tennis).

12 most important shrines to Shiva. Only Hindus are allowed in, but non-Hindus can peek into the courtyard. Nearby, the waters of the Godavari River flow into the **Gangadwar bathing tank**, where all are welcome to wash away their sins. Regular buses run from the Old Central bus stand in Nasik to Trimbak (₹30, 45 minutes).

Aurangabad

📷 0240 / POP 1.28 MILLION / ELEV 515M

Aurangabad lay low through most of the tumultuous history of medieval India and only hit the spotlight when the last Mughal emperor, Aurangzeb, made the city his capital from 1653 to 1707. With the emperor's death came the city's rapid decline, but the brief period of glory saw the building of some fascinating monuments, including a Taj Mahal replica (Bibi-qa-Maqbara), and these continue to draw a steady trickle of visitors. Alongside other historic relics, such as a group of ancient Buddhist caves, these Mughal relics make Aurangabad a good choice for a weekend excursion from Mumbai. But the real reason for traipsing here is because the town is an excellent base for exploring the World Heritage Sites of Ellora and Ajanta.

Silk fabrics were once Aurangabad's chief revenue generator, and the town is still known across the world for its hand-woven Himroo and Paithani saris.

The train station, cheap hotels and restaurants are clumped together in the south of the town along Station Rd East and Station Rd West. The MSRTC bus stand is 1.5km to the north of the train station. Northeast of the bus stand is the buzzing old town, with its narrow streets and Muslim quarter.

⊙ Sights

★**Bibi-qa-Maqbara**　　MONUMENT
(Indian/foreigner ₹5/100; ⊙ dawn-10pm) Built by Aurangzeb's son Azam Khan in 1679 as a mausoleum for his mother Rabia-ud-Daurani, Bibi-qa-Maqbara is widely known as the poor man's Taj. With its four minarets flanking a central onion-domed mausoleum, the white structure certainly does bear a striking resemblance to Agra's Taj Mahal. It is much less grand, however, and apart from having a few marble adornments, namely the plinth and dome, much of the structure is finished in lime mortar.

Apparently the prince conceived the entire mausoleum in white marble, but was thwarted by his frugal father who opposed his extravagant idea of draining state coffers for the purpose. However, despite the use of cheaper material and the obvious weathering, it's a sight far more impressive than the average gravestone.

The Bibi's formal gardens are a delight to explore, with the Deccan hills providing a scenic backdrop.

Aurangabad Caves
CAVES

(Indian/foreigner ₹5/100; ☉ dawn-dusk) Architecturally speaking, the Aurangabad Caves aren't a patch on Ellora or Ajanta, but they do throw some light on early Buddhist architecture and, above all, make for a quiet and peaceful outing. Carved out of the hillside in the 6th or 7th century AD, the 10 caves, comprising two groups 1km apart (retain your ticket for entry into both sets), are all Buddhist. Cave 7, with its sculptures of scantily clad lovers in suggestive positions, is a perennial favourite.

The caves are about 2km north of Bibi-qa-Maqbara. A return autorickshaw from the mausoleum shouldn't cost more than ₹180 including waiting time.

Panchakki
GARDENS

(Indian/foreigner ₹5/20; ☉ 6.15am-9.15pm) The garden complex of Panchakki, literally meaning 'water wheel', takes its name from the ancient hydromill which, in its day, was considered a marvel of engineering. It's still in working condition but is today really only of minor interest (unless you're a hydro-engineer perhaps).

Baba Shah Muzaffar, a Sufi saint and spiritual guide to Aurangzeb, is buried here. His memorial garden, flanked by a series of fish-filled tanks, is at the rear of the complex.

Shivaji Museum
MUSEUM

(Dr Ambedkar Rd; admission ₹5; ☉ 10.30am-6pm Fri-Wed) This simple museum is dedicated to the life of the Maratha hero Shivaji. Its collection includes a 500-year-old chain-mail suit and a copy of the Quran, handwritten by Aurangzeb.

☞ Tours

Classic Tours (☑ 2337788; www.classictours. info; MTDC Holiday Resort, Station Rd East) and the **Indian Tourism Development Corporation** (ITDC; ☑ 2331143; MTDC Holiday Resort, Station Rd East) both run daily bus tours to the Ajanta and Ellora Caves. Be aware that these are mass-market tours popular with domestic tourists and designed to cover as much ground as possible in a short period of time. The trip to Ajanta Caves costs ₹450 and the tour to Ellora Caves, ₹325; prices include a guide but don't cover admission fees. The Ellora tour also includes all the other major Aurangabad sites along with Daulatabad Fort and Aurangzeb's tomb in Khuldabad, which is a lot to swallow in a day. All tours start and end at the MTDC Holiday Resort.

Ashoka Tours & Travels
TOURS

(☑ 2359102, 9890340816; www.touristaurangabad. com; Hotel Panchavati, Station Rd West; ☉ 8am-8pm) The stand-out Aurangabad agency, with excellent city and regional tours and decent car hire at fair rates. Prices for an aircon car and up to four people are ₹2400 for Ellora and ₹1400 for Ajanta. Run by Ashok T Kadam, a knowledgeable former autorickshaw driver.

☐ Sleeping

★ Hotel Panchavati
HOTEL $

(☑ 2328755; www.hotelpanchavati.com; Station Rd West; s/d ₹1000/1130, with AC ₹1150/1250; ❄ @ ☎) The best budget hotel in town, the Panchavati is run by ever-helpful, switched-on managers who understand travellers' needs. Rooms are compact but thoughtfully appointed, with comfortable beds that have paisley-style bedspreads and 24-hour hot water (and room service). There are two restaurants and a bar, and it's a great place to hook up with other traveller.

Also home to the ever-reliable Ashoka Tours & Travels, which offers trips to Ellora and Ajanta.

Hotel Oberoi
HOTEL $

(☑ 2323841; www.hoteloberoi.in; Osmanpura Circle, Station Rd East; s/d ₹900/1000, with AC ₹1260/1380; ❄ ☎) Cheekily named, and nothing to do with the five-star chain, this renovated hotel is owned by the same people behind Hotel Panchavati so there's good service and helpful staff. The spacious rooms are modern with flat-screen TVs and comfy beds, and the attractive bathrooms are in good shape. Call for a free pick-up from the train or bus stations.

Hotel Regal Plaza
HOTEL $

(☑ 0240-2329322; www.hotelregalplaza.com; Station Rd West; s/d ₹870/990, with AC ₹1110/1200; ❄ ☎) Its mirror facade is a bit bling but staff here take care of guests and the light, airy rooms are in good shape and all have

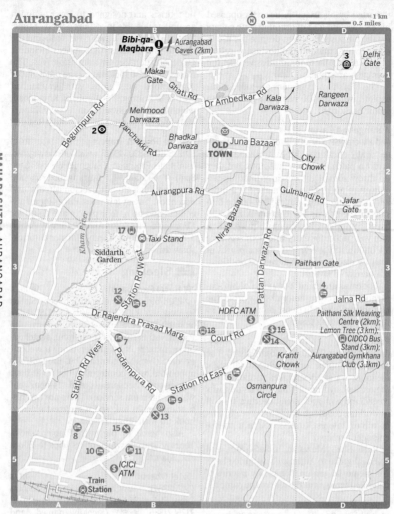

cable TV. Pick-ups and drop-offs from bus and train stations are complimentary and value-for-money tours are offered. There's a dining room for Indian and Chinese meals.

MTDC Holiday Resort HOTEL **$**
(☏ 2331513; Station Rd East; d from ₹1420, with AC from ₹1980; ❄) Very close to the train station, this curiously disorganised state-owned hotel has rooms that vary quite a bit: all are spacious but maintenance is an issue so take a look at a few. There's a well-stocked bar, a restaurant and a couple of travel agencies (for Ellora and Ajanta tours) on-site.

Keys Hotel HOTEL **$$**
(☏ 0240-6654000; www.keyshotels.com; Padampura Circle; r/ste from ₹3160/4560; ❄ ☎) A modern, inviting hotel a kilometre from the train station where the rooms have a contemporary look, featuring laminate flooring, attractive wooden desks and wardrobes, and good beds with luxury linen. There's a gym (with free weights) and the in-house restaurant is a good bet for a bite.

Aurangabad Gymkhana Club HOTEL **$$**
(☏ 0240-2476501; Mukunwadi Circle, Airport Rd; s/d from ₹2560/2860; ❄ ☎ ⛱) Near the airport, this large hotel is perfect for exercise

Aurangabad

junkies with a 40m pool and one of the best gyms in the city. Its design is a little odd, with rooms around a covered courtyard but all are very spacious (the renovated ones are modern and worth the extra rupees). In-house dining is very tasty and good value. Service is a little chaotic but well-meaning.

Hotel Green Olive
HOTEL $$

(☎ 0240-2329490; www.dasilvascoffee.com; 13/3 Bhagya Nagar, off Station Rd West; r from ₹3700; ❄ 🛜) Impressive newcomer with a boutique-ish feel thanks to its stylish, well-equipped and well-maintained rooms. The staff here look after guests well and can organise transport and tours.

Hotel Amarpreet
HOTEL $$

(☎ 6621133; www.amarpreethotel.com; Jalna Rd; s/d from ₹3880/5170; ❄ @ 🛜 🏊) Dated though spacious rooms, but the all-smiles management makes up for it with polite service, excellent housekeeping and a great selection of food and booze. Located on a busy road, so ask for a room away from the traffic.

VITS
HOTEL $$

(☎ 2350701; www.vitshotelaurangabad.com; Station Rd East; r/ste incl breakfast ₹4680/8190; ❄ @ 🛜 🏊) Handy to the train station, this city-centre landmark is now looking dated but its location is still a winner. Rooms are well-equipped and decent value, but the dining situation and complimentary breakfast is poor (a renovation of the cafe is planned, management says). There's a small gym.

★ Lemon Tree
HOTEL $$$

(☎ 6603030; www.lemontreehotels.com; R7/2 Chikalthana, Airport Rd; r incl breakfast from ₹5590; ❄ @ 🛜 🏊) The Lemon Tree offers elegance and class, looking more like a billionaire's luxury whitewashed Mediterranean villa than an Indian hotel. It's well designed too: all rooms face inwards, overlooking perhaps the best pool on the Deccan plateau, all 50m of it. The standard rooms, though not large, are brightened by vivid tropical tones offset against snow-white walls. Located near the airport, 6km from the centre.

✕ Eating

Swad Veg Restaurant
INDIAN $

(Kanchan Chamber, Station Rd East; mains ₹70-130) Swad offers a great range of Indian snacks and staples, such as dosas, plus a few pizzas, ice creams and shakes. Try the Gujarati thali (₹170), an endless train of dishes that diners gobble up under the benevolent gaze of patron saint swami Yogiraj Hanstirth.

Kailash
INDIAN $

(Station Rd East; mains ₹85-120; ⊙ 8am-11pm) This busy pure-veg restaurant looks and feels vaguely like an Indian take on an American diner, with big portions in familial surrounds. There's lots of Punjabi and South Indian food, as well as rice and noodle dishes, and an air-conditioned section.

★ Bhoj
INDIAN $$

(Station Rd West; thalis ₹180; ⊙ 11am-3pm & 7-11pm) Rightly famous for its delicious unlimited Rajasthani and Gujarati thalis, Bhoj is a wonderful place to refuel and relax after a hard day on the road (or rail). It's on the 1st floor of a somewhat scruffy little shopping arcade, but the decor, ambience, service and presentation are all first rate.

MAHARASHTRA AURANGABAD

Hotel Panchavati
MULTICUISINE **$$**

(Station Rd West; mains ₹60-280; ⊘7am-10pm; 🛜) This budget hotel's restaurant has Chinese and Korean food in addition to an extensive Indian menu and cold beer. Ambience isn't a selling point here, but it's air-conditioned and staff are friendly.

Tandoor
NORTH INDIAN **$$**

(Shyam Chambers, Station Rd East; mains ₹160-290) Offers fine tandoori dishes and flavoursome North Indian veg and nonveg options in a weirdly Pharaonic atmosphere. Try the wonderful sizzler kebabs. A few Chinese dishes are also on offer, but patrons clearly prefer the dishes coming out of the tandoor.

🛍 Shopping

Himroo material is a traditional Aurangabad speciality made from cotton, silk and silver threads. Most of today's Himroo shawls and saris are produced using power looms, but some showrooms still stock hand-loomed cloth.

Himroo saris start at around ₹1200, for a cotton and silk blend. Paithani saris, which are of a superior quality, range from ₹5000 to ₹300,000 – but some of them take more than a year to make. Make sure you get authentic Himroo, not 'Aurangabad silk'.

Paithani Silk Weaving Centre
TEXTILES

(www.paithanisilk.com; 54, P-1, Town Center, Lokmat Nagar; ⊘11.30am-8pm) One of the best places to come and watch weavers at work is the Paithani Silk Weaving Centre where you'll find good-quality items for sale. It's about 6km east of Kranti Chowk (behind the Air India office), so take a taxi.

ℹ Information

MTDC Office (☑2331513; MTDC Holiday Resort, Station Rd East; ⊘10am-5.30pm Mon-Sat) Quite helpful and has a stock of brochures.
Post Office (Juna Bazaar; ⊘10am-6pm Mon-Sat)
Sai Internet Café (Station Rd East; per hour ₹15; ⊘8am-10pm) Has reliable connections; one of several on this block.
State Bank of India (Kranti Chowk; ⊘11am-5pm Mon-Fri, to 1pm Sat) Handles foreign exchange.

ℹ Getting There & Away

AIR
The airport is 10km east of town. Daily direct flights go to Delhi (around ₹8500) and Mumbai (around ₹4500) with both Air India and Jet Airways.

BUS
Buses leave about every half-hour from the **MSRTC bus stand** (Station Rd West) to Pune (semideluxe/deluxe ₹330/620, five hours) and roughly hourly to Nasik (semideluxe ₹290, 4½ hours) between 8am and 10pm. Private bus agents are clustered on Dr Rajendra Prasad Marg and Court Rd; a few sit closer to the bus stand. Deluxe overnight bus destinations include Mumbai (with/without AC from ₹550/350, sleeper ₹900 to ₹1500, 7½ to 9½ hours), Ahmedabad (seat ₹400, sleeper ₹800 to ₹1050, 13 to 15 hours) and Nagpur (sleeper with AC ₹600, without AC ₹700 to ₹1050, 8½ to 10 hours).

Ordinary buses head to Ellora from the MSRTC bus stand every half-hour (₹30, one hour) and hourly to Jalgaon (₹155, four hours) via Fardapur (₹95, 2½ hours), which is the drop-off point for Ajanta.

From the **CIDCO bus stand** (Airport Rd), by the Lemon Tree hotel junction, ordinary buses leave for the Lonar meteorite crater (every two hours, 4½ hours, ₹172).

TRAIN
Aurangabad's **train station** (Station Rd East) is not on a main line, but it has four daily direct trains to/from Mumbai. The Tapovan Express (2nd class/chair ₹140/500, 7½ hours) departs Aurangabad at 2.35pm; the Janshatabdi Express (2nd class/chair ₹172/575, 6½ hours) departs Aurangabad at 6am. For Hyderabad, trains include the Ajanta express (sleeper/2nd class/1st class ₹805/1150/1925, 10 hours, 10.45pm). To reach northern or eastern India, take a bus to Jalgaon and board a train there.

ℹ Getting Around

Autorickshaws are common here. The taxi stand is next to the MSRTC bus stand; shared 4WDs also depart from here for Ellora and Daulatabad but are usually very packed. Renting a car and driver is a much better option.

Ashoka Tours & Travels (p89) rates for return trip with a car/driver to Ellora is ₹1250/1400 in a car/AC car; to Ajanta it's ₹2080/2400.

Around Aurangabad

Daulatabad

This one's straight out of a Tolkien fantasy. A most beguiling structure, the 12th-century hilltop fortress of Daulatabad is located about 15km north of Aurangabad, en route to Ellora. Now in ruins, the citadel was originally conceived as an impregnable fort by the Yadava kings. Its most infamous high point came in 1328, when it was named

Daulatabad (City of Fortune) by eccentric Delhi sultan Mohammed Tughlaq and made the capital – he even marched the entire population of Delhi 1100km south to populate it. Ironically, Daulatabad – despite being better positioned strategically than Delhi – soon proved untenable as a capital due to an acute water crisis, and Tughlaq forced the weary inhabitants all the way back to Delhi, which had by then been reduced to a ghost town.

Daulatabad's central bastion sits atop a 200m-high craggy outcrop known as Devagiri (Hill of the Gods), surrounded by a 5km fort (Indian/foreigner ₹10/100; ☉6am-6pm). The climb to the summit takes about an hour, and leads past an ingenious series of defences, including multiple doorways designed with odd angles and spike-studded doors to prevent elephant charges. A tower of victory, known as the Chand Minar (Tower of the Moon), built in 1435, soars 60m above the ground to the right; it's closed to visitors. Higher up, you can walk into the Chini Mahal, where Abul Hasan Tana Shah, king of Golconda, was held captive for 12 years before his death in 1699. Nearby, there's a 6m cannon, cast from five different metals and engraved with Aurangzeb's name.

Part of the ascent goes through a pitch-black, bat-infested, water-seeping, spiralling tunnel. Guides (₹500) are available near the ticket counter to show you around, and their torch-bearing assistants will lead you through the dark passageway for a small tip. On the way down you'll be left to your own devices, so carry a torch.

As the fort is in ruins (with crumbling staircases and sheer drops) and involves a steep ascent, the elderly, children and those suffering from vertigo or claustrophobia will find it a tough challenge. Allow 2½ hours to explore the structure, and bring water.

Khuldabad

Time permitting, take a pit stop in the scruffy-walled settlement of Khuldabad (Heavenly Abode), a quaint little Muslim pilgrimage village just 3km from Ellora. Buried deep in the pages of history, Khuldabad is where a number of historic figures lie interred, including emperor Aurangzeb, the last of the Mughal greats. Despite matching the legendary King Solomon in terms of state riches, Aurangzeb was an ascetic in his personal life, and insisted that

he be buried in a simple tomb, which you'll find in the courtyard of the **Alamgir Dargah** (☉7am-8pm).

Generally a calm place, Khuldabad is swamped with pilgrims every April when a robe said to have been worn by the Prophet Mohammed, and kept within the dargah (shrine), is shown to the public. Across the road from the Alamgir Dargah, another shrine is said to contain strands of the Prophet's beard.

Ellora

☐ 02437

Give a man a hammer and chisel, and he'll create art for posterity. Come to the World Heritage **Ellora cave temples** (Indian/foreigner ₹10/250; ☉dawn-dusk Wed-Mon), 30km northwest of Aurangabad, and you'll know exactly what we mean. The epitome of ancient Indian rock-cut architecture, these caves were chipped out laboriously over five centuries by generations of Buddhist, Hindu and Jain monks. Monasteries, chapels, temples – the caves served every purpose, and they were stylishly embellished with a profusion of remarkably detailed sculptures. Unlike the caves at Ajanta, which are carved into a sheer rock face, the Ellora caves line a 2km-long escarpment, the gentle slope of which allowed architects to build elaborate courtyards in front of the shrines, and render them with sculptures of a surreal quality.

Ellora has 34 caves in all: 12 Buddhist (AD 600–800), 17 Hindu (AD 600–900) and five Jain (AD 800–1000) – though the exact timescales of these caves' construction is the subject of academic debate. Undoubtedly the grandest is the awesome Kailasa Temple (Cave 16), the world's largest monolithic sculpture, hewn top to bottom against a rocky slope by 7000 labourers over a period of 150 years. Dedicated to Lord Shiva, it is clearly among the best that ancient Indian architecture has to offer.

The established academic theory is that the site represents the renaissance of Hinduism under the Chalukya and Rashtrakuta dynasties, the subsequent decline of Indian Buddhism and a brief resurgence of Jainism under official patronage. However, due to the absence of inscriptional evidence, it's been impossible to accurately date most of Ellora's monuments. Some scholars argue that some Hindu temples predate those in

Ellora Caves

N
0 ———— 100 m
0 ———— 0.05 miles

30–34
Jain Group

Parasnath

33

34 32

31

30

29

28

27

26

24 25

23

22 21

20

19

18

17

Hotel
Kailas

Ticket
Office

Visitor
Centre
(500m)

MTDC Ellora
Restaurant &
Beer Bar

Kailasa
Temple 16

13–29
Hindu Group

15

14

13

12

11

10
9
8
7
6
5
4
1 2 3

Daulatabad
(15km);
Aurangabad
(30km)

1–12
Buddhist Group

the Buddhist group. What is certain is that their coexistence at one site indicates a lengthy period of religious tolerance.

Official guides can be hired at the ticket office in front of the Kailasa Temple for ₹1070 (up to five people). Guides have an extensive knowledge of cave architecture so are worth the investment. If your tight itinerary forces you to choose between Ellora or Ajanta, Ellora wins hands down in terms of architecture (though Ajanta's setting is more beautiful and more of a pleasure to explore).

Ellora is very popular with domestic tourists; if you can visit on a weekday, it's far less crowded. The whole complex is in desperate need of reorganising: currently the car park is far too close to the temples so expect plenty of background honking and beeping as you tour the caves.

◉ Sights

★ **Kailasa Temple**   HINDU TEMPLE
One of Incredible India's greatest monuments, this astonishing temple, carved from solid rock, was built by King Krishna I in AD 760 to represent Mt Kailasa (Kailash), Shiva's Himalayan abode. To say that the assignment was daring would be an understatement. Three huge trenches were bored into the sheer cliff face, a process that entailed removing 200,000 tonnes of rock by hammer and chisel, before the temple could begin to take shape, and its remarkable sculptural decoration added.

Covering twice the area of the Parthenon in Athens and being half as high again, Kailasa is an engineering marvel that was executed straight from the head with zero margin for error. Modern draughtsmen might have a lesson or two to learn here.

The temple houses several intricately carved panels, depicting scenes from the Ramayana, the Mahabharata and the adventures of Krishna. Also worth admiring are the immense monolithic pillars that stand in the courtyard, flanking the entrance on both sides, and the southeastern gallery that has 10 giant and fabulous panels depicting the different avatars of Lord Vishnu.

After you're done with the main enclosure, bypass the hordes of snack-munching day trippers to explore the temple's many dank, bat-urine–soaked corners with their numerous forgotten carvings. Afterwards, hike up a foot trail to the south of the complex that takes you to the top perimeter of the 'cave', from where you can get a bird's-eye view of the entire temple complex.

Buddhist Caves

Calm and contemplation infuse the 12 Buddhist caves, which stretch to the south of Kailasa. All are Buddhist *viharas* (monasteries) used for study and worship, but the multi-storeyed structures also included cooking, living and sleeping areas.

The one exception is Cave 10, which is a *chaitya* (assembly hall). While the earliest caves are simple, Caves 11 and 12 are more ambitious; both have three stories and are on par with the more impressive Hindu temples.

Cave 1, the simplest *vihara*, may have been a granary. Cave 2 is notable for its ornate pillars and the imposing seated Buddha, which faces the setting sun. Cave 3 and Cave 4 are unfinished and not well preserved.

Cave 5 is the largest *vihara* in this group, at 18m wide and 36m long; the rows of stone benches hint that it may once have been an assembly hall.

Cave 6 is an ornate *vihara* with wonderful images of Tara, consort of the Bodhisattva Avalokiteshvara, and of the Buddhist goddess of learning, Mahamayuri, looking remarkably similar to Saraswati, her Hindu equivalent. Cave 7 is an unadorned hall, but from here you can pass through a doorway to Cave 8, the first cave in which the sanctum is detached from the rear wall. Cave 9 is notable for its wonderfully carved fascia.

Cave 10 is the only *chaitya* in the Buddhist group and one of the finest in India. Its ceiling features ribs carved into the stonework; the grooves were once fitted with wooden panels. The balcony and upper gallery offer a closer view of the ceiling and a frieze depicting amorous couples. A decorative window gently illuminates an enormous figure of the teaching Buddha.

Cave 11, the Do Thal (Two Storey) Cave, is entered through its third basement level, not discovered until 1876. Like Cave 12, it possibly owes its size to competition with Hindu caves of the same period.

Cave 12, the huge Tin Thal (Three Storey) Cave, is entered through a courtyard. The locked shrine on the top floor contains a large Buddha figure flanked by his seven previous incarnations. The walls are carved with relief pictures.

Hindu Caves

Drama and excitement characterise the Hindu group (Caves 13 to 29). In terms of scale, creative vision and skill of execution, these caves are in a league of their own.

All these temples were cut from the top down, so it was never necessary to use scaffolding – the builders began with the roof and moved down to the floor. Highlights include caves 14, 15, 16, 21 and 29.

Cave 13 is a simple cave, most likely a granary. Cave 14, the Ravana-ki-Khai, is a Buddhist *vihara* converted to a temple dedicated to Shiva sometime in the 7th century.

Cave 15, the Das Avatara (Ten Incarnations of Vishnu) Cave, is one of the finest at Ellora. The two-storey temple contains a mesmerising Shiva Nataraja, and Shiva emerging from a lingam (phallic image) while Vishnu and Brahma pay homage.

Caves 17 to 20 and caves 22 to 28 are simple monasteries.

Cave 21, known as the Ramesvara Cave, features interesting interpretations of familiar Shaivite scenes depicted in the earlier temples. The figure of the goddess Ganga, standing on her Makara (mythical sea creature), is particularly notable.

The large Cave 29, the Dumar Lena, is thought to be a transitional model between the simpler hollowed-out caves and the fully developed temples exemplified by the Kailasa. It has views over a nearby waterfall.

Jain Caves

The five Jain caves, the last created at Ellora, may lack the ambitious size of the best Hindu temples, but they are exceptionally detailed, with some remarkable paintings and carvings.

The caves are 1km north of the last Hindu temple (Cave 29) at the end of the bitumen road; autorickshaws run here from the main car park.

Cave 30, the Chhota Kailasa (Little Kailasa), is a poor imitation of the great Kailasa Temple and stands by itself some distance from the other Jain temples.

In contrast, Cave 32, the Indra Sabha (Assembly Hall of Indra), is the finest of the Jain temples. Its ground-floor plan is similar to that of the Kailasa, but the upstairs area is as ornate and richly decorated as the downstairs is plain. There are images of the Jain *tirthankars* (great teachers) Parasnath and Gomateshvara, the latter surrounded by wildlife. Inside the shrine is a seated figure of Mahavira, the last *tirthankar* and founder of the Jain religion.

Cave 31 is really an extension of Cave 32. Cave 33, the Jagannath Sabha, is similar in plan to 32 and has some well-preserved sculptures. The final temple, the small **Cave 34**, also has interesting sculptures. On the hilltop over the Jain temples, a 5m-high image of Parasnath looks down on Ellora.

🛏 Sleeping & Eating

Hotel Kailas
HOTEL **$$**

(☑ 244446; www.hotelkailas.com; r ₹2110, with AC from ₹3510; ❄) The sole decent hotel near the site, with attractive cottages set in leafy grounds. The restaurant (mains ₹110 to ₹250) is excellent, with a menu chalked up on a blackboard that includes sandwiches, breakfasts, curries and tandoori favourites.

MTDC Ellora Restaurant & Beer Bar
INDIAN **$**

(mains/thalis from ₹90/110; ⊘ 8am-5pm) Located within the temple complex, this is a good place for lunch.

ⓘ Information

Ellora Visitor Centre (⊘ 9am-5.30pm Wed-Mon) Ellora's impressive new visitor centre, 750m west of the site, is worth dropping by to put the caves in historical context. It features modern displays and information panels, a 15-minute video presentation, and two galleries: one on the Kailasa Temple (with a diorama of the temple) and other dedicated to the site itself. A cafe, craft centre and restaurant are planned.

ⓘ Getting There & Away

Note that the temples are closed on Tuesday. Buses regularly ply the road between Aurangabad and Ellora (₹30, one hour); the last bus departs from Ellora at 8pm. Share 4WDs are also an option, but get packed; they leave when full and stop outside the bus stand in Aurangabad (₹70). A full-day tour to Ellora, with stops en route, costs ₹1400 in an AC car; try Ashoka Tours & Travels (p89). Autorickshaws ask for ₹700.

Ajanta

☑ 02438

Superbly set in a remote river valley 105km northeast of Aurangabad, the remarkable cave temples of Ajanta are this region's second World Heritage Site. Much older than Ellora, these secluded caves date from around the 2nd century BC to the 6th century AD and were among the earliest monastic institutions to be constructed in the country. Ironically, it was Ellora's rise that brought about Ajanta's downfall, and historians believe the site was abandoned once the focus had shifted to Ellora.

Ajanta was deserted for about a millenium, as the Deccan forest claimed and shielded the caves, with roots and shoots choking the sculptures, until 1819, when a British hunting party led by officer John Smith stumbled upon them purely by chance.

One of the primary reasons to visit Ajanta is to admire its renowned 'frescoes', actually temperas, which adorn many of the caves' interiors. With few other examples from ancient times matching their artistic excellence and fine execution, these paintings are of unfathomable heritage value. It's believed that the natural pigments for these paintings were mixed with animal glue and vegetable gum, to bind them to the dry surface. Many caves have small, craterlike holes in their floors, which acted as palettes during paint jobs. Despite their age, the paintings in most caves remain finely preserved today, and many attribute it to their relative isolation from humanity for centuries. However, it would be a tad optimistic to say that decay hasn't set in.

◉ Sights

★ Ajanta Caves
CAVE

(Indian/foreigner ₹10/250, video ₹25, authorised guide ₹750; ⊘ 9am-5.30pm Tue-Sun) Ajanta's caves line a steep face of a horseshoe-shaped gorge bordering the Waghore River. Five of the caves are *chaityas* (prayer halls) while others are *viharas* (monasteries). Caves 8, 9, 10, 12, 13 and part of 15 are early Buddhist caves, while the others date from around the 5th century AD (Mahayana period). In the austere early Buddhist school, the Buddha was never represented directly but always alluded to by a symbol such as the footprint or wheel of law.

During busy periods, viewers are allotted 15 minutes within the caves, many of which have to be entered barefoot (socks or shoe covers allowed). Caves 3, 5, 8, 22, 28, 29 and 30 remain either closed or inaccessible.

Cave 1
CAVE

Cave 1, a Mahayana *vihara,* was one of the last to be excavated and is the most beautifully decorated. This is where you'll find a rendition of the Bodhisattva Padmapani, the most famous and iconic of the Ajanta artworks. A verandah in front leads to a large congregation hall, housing sculptures and narrative murals known for their splendid perspective and elaborate detailing of dress,

Ajanta Caves

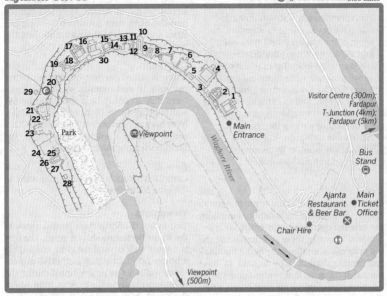

daily life and facial expressions. The colours in the paintings were created from local minerals, with the exception of the vibrant blue made from Central Asian lapis lazuli. Look up to the ceiling to see the carving of four deer sharing a common head.

Cave 2 CAVE

Cave 2 is a late Mahayana *vihara* with deliriously ornamented columns and capitals, and some fine paintings. The ceiling is decorated with geometric and floral patterns. The murals depict scenes from the Jataka tales, including Buddha's mother's dream of a six-tusked elephant, which heralded his conception.

Cave 4 CAVE

Cave 4 is the largest *vihara* at Ajanta and is supported by 28 pillars. Although never completed, the cave has some impressive sculptures: four statues surround a huge central Buddha, and there are scenes of people fleeing from the 'eight great dangers' to the protection of Avalokitesvara.

Cave 6 CAVE

Cave 6 is the only two-storey *vihara* at Ajanta, but parts of the lower storey have collapsed. Inside is a seated Buddha figure and an intricately carved door to the shrine.

Upstairs the hall is surrounded by cells with fine paintings on the doorways.

Cave 7 CAVE

Cave 7 has an atypical design, with porches before the verandah leading directly to the four cells and the elaborately sculptured shrine.

Cave 9 CAVE

Cave 9 is one of the earliest *chaityas* at Ajanta. Although it dates from the early Buddhist period, the two figures flanking the entrance door were probably later Mahayana additions. Columns run down both sides of the cave and around the 3m-high dagoba at the far end.

Cave 10 CAVE

Cave 10 is thought to be the oldest cave (200 BC) and was the first one to be spotted by the British hunting party. Similar in design to cave 9, it is the largest *chaitya*. The facade has collapsed and the paintings inside have been damaged, in some cases by graffiti dating from soon after their rediscovery. One of the pillars to the right bears the engraved name of Smith, who left his mark here for posterity.

❶ AJANTA ETIQUETTE

Flash photography is strictly prohibited within the caves, due to its adverse effect on natural dyes used in the paintings. Authorities have installed rows of tiny pigment-friendly lights, which cast a faint glow within the caves, but additional lighting is required for glimpsing minute details, and you'll have to rely on long exposures for photographs.

Most buses ferrying tour groups don't arrive until noon. To avoid the crowds stay locally in Fardapur or make an early start from Aurangabad.

Cave 16   CAVE
Cave 16, a *vihara,* contains some of Ajanta's finest paintings and is thought to have been the original entrance to the entire complex. The best known of these paintings is the 'dying princess' – Sundari, wife of the Buddha's half-brother Nanda, who is said to have fainted at the news that her husband was renouncing the material life (and her) in order to become a monk. Carved figures appear to support the ceiling, and there's a statue of the Buddha seated on a lion throne teaching the Noble Eightfold Path.

Cave 17   CAVE
With carved dwarfs supporting the pillars, cave 17 has Ajanta's best-preserved and most varied paintings. Famous images include a princess applying make-up, a seductive prince using the old trick of plying his lover with wine, and the Buddha returning home from his enlightenment to beg from his wife and astonished son. A detailed panel tells of Prince Simhala's expedition to Sri Lanka: with 500 companions he is shipwrecked on an island where ogresses appear as enchanting women, only to seize and devour their victims. Simhala escapes on a flying horse and returns to conquer the island.

Cave 19   CAVE
Cave 19, a magnificent *chaitya,* has a remarkably detailed facade; its dominant feature is an impressive horseshoe-shaped window. Two fine, standing Buddha figures flank the entrance. Inside is a three-tiered dagoba with a figure of the Buddha on the front. Outside the cave, to the west, sits a striking image of the Naga king with seven cobra hoods around his head. His wife, hooded by a single cobra, sits by his side.

Cave 24   CAVE
Had it been finished, cave 24 would be the largest *vihara* at Ajanta. Here you can see how the caves were constructed – long galleries were cut into the rock and then the rock between them was broken through.

Cave 26   CAVE
A largely ruined *chaitya,* cave 26 is now dramatically lit and contains some fine sculptures that shouldn't be missed. On the left wall is a huge figure of the reclining Buddha, lying back in preparation for nirvana. Other scenes include a lengthy depiction of the Buddha's temptation by Maya.

Cave 27   CAVE
Cave 27 is virtually a *vihara* connected to the cave 26 *chaitya.*

Viewpoints
Two lookouts offer picture-perfect views of the whole horseshoe-shaped gorge. The first is a short walk beyond the river, crossed via a bridge below cave 8. A further 40-minute uphill walk (not to be attempted during the monsoons) leads to the lookout from where the British party first spotted the caves.

🛏 Sleeping & Eating

Accommodation options close to the caves are quite limited. Aurangabad (or even Jalgaon) has far more choice, while Fardapur is the closest option and most convenient for arriving at the caves early morning.

MTDC Holiday Resort Fardapur   HOTEL **$$**
(☑ 244230; Aurangabad-Jalgaon Rd, Fardapur; d ₹1480, with AC ₹1860; ❄) Recently renovated, this government hotel is now a good option set amid lawns in a peaceful location off the main road in Fardapur, 5km from the caves. Rooms are in good shape and well-equipped; there's a bar garden and restaurant (order ahead for your meal).

MTDC Ajanta Tourist Complex   HOTEL **$$**
(☑ 09422204325; Fardapur T-junction; cottage ₹2320; ❄) Located just behind the shopping 'plaza' and the bus stand, these five cottages nestled amid grassy lawns have some charm, though maintenance could be better. There's no restaurant here.

Ajanta Restaurant & Beer Bar   FAST FOOD **$**
(mains ₹90-150, thalis from ₹130; ⊙ 9am-5.30pm Tue-Sun) This cafe-restaurant right by the main ticket office at the caves serves a decent vegetarian thali and cold drinks, including beer.

ℹ️ Information

A cloakroom is available at the Fardapur T-junction (but not at the caves), where you can leave gear (₹10 per item for four hours).

Ajanta Visitor Centre (🕙9am-5.30pm Tue-Sun) This state-of-the-art new facility is one of India's very best, with highly impressive replicas of four caves (1, 2, 16 and 17) in real scale, audio guides available in many languages, excellent painting and sculpture galleries, story of Buddhism in India, an audio-visual arena and large cafe.

ℹ️ Getting There & Away

Note that the caves are closed on Monday. Buses from Aurangabad or Jalgaon will drop you at the Fardapur T-junction (where the highway meets the road to the caves), 4km from the site. From here, after paying an 'amenities' fee (₹10), walk to the departure point for the buses (with/without AC ₹20/15), which zoom up to the caves. Buses return half-hourly to the T-junction; the last bus is at 5pm.

All MSRTC buses passing through Fardapur stop at the T-junction. After the caves close you can board buses to either Aurangabad or Jalgaon outside the MTDC Holiday Resort in Fardapur, 1km down the main road towards Jalgaon. Taxis are available in Fardapur; ₹1300/1600 should get you to Jalgaon/Aurangabad.

Jalgaon

📞 0257 / POP 468,300 / ELEV 208M

Apart from being a handy base for exploring Ajanta 60km away, the industrial city of Jalgaon is really nothing more than a convenient transit town. It has rail connections to all major cities across India.

🛏️ Sleeping & Eating

⭐ **Hotel Plaza**   HOTEL **$**
(📞9370027354, 2227354; hotelplaza_jal@yahoo.com; Station Rd; dm ₹250, s/d from ₹550/750, r with AC from ₹1300; ❄️@🛜) Offering brilliant value, this extremely well-managed and presented hotel is only a short hop from the station. Rooms vary in size and layout, but with whitewashed walls, a minimalist feel and almost Swiss-clean bathrooms, they're a steal at this price. The effusive owner is a mine of useful information and can assist with train reservations, car hire and recommendations.

Hotel Royal Palace   HOTEL **$$**
(📞2233555; www.hotelroyalpalace.in; Mahabal Rd, Jai Nagar; s/d incl breakfast from ₹2520/2680; ❄️🛜) Rooms here don't quite reach the heights promised by the chintzy lobby

but they're decent value and comfortable enough, particularly if you like beige-on-beige colour schemes. The in-house restaurant is a pure-veg affair with North Indian, coastal, Chinese and Continental food. Free pick-ups are offered from the train station.

Hotel Arya   INDIAN **$**
(Navi Peth; mains ₹50-100; 🕗8.30am-10.50pm) Delicious vegetarian food, particularly Punjabi cuisine, though a few Chinese and South Indian dishes are also offered. It's a short walk south down Station Rd, left at MG Rd, and left at the clock tower. You may have to queue for a table at lunchtime.

ℹ️ Information

Banks, ATMs and internet cafes are on Nehru Rd, which runs along the top of Station Rd.

ℹ️ Getting There & Around

Several express trains connecting Mumbai (sleeper/2AC ₹280/1000, eight hours), Delhi (sleeper/2AC ₹530/1970, 18 hours), Ahmedabad (sleeper/2AC ₹345/1322, 14 hours) and Varanasi (sleeper/2AC ₹515/1950, 20 hours) stop at Jalgaon train station. Eight daily trains head for Nagpur (sleeper/2AC ₹290/1090, seven to nine hours).

Buses to Fardapur (₹60, 1½ hours) depart half-hourly from the bus stand starting at 6am, continuing to Aurangabad (₹155, four hours).

Jalgaon's train station and bus stand are about 2km apart (₹25 by autorickshaw). Private bus companies on Station Rd offer services to Aurangabad (₹170 to ₹200, 3½ hours) and Mumbai (₹450 to ₹650, 9½ hours).

Nagpur

📞 0712 / POP 2.43 MILLION / ELEV 305M

Way off the main tourist routes, the isolated city of Nagpur lacks must-see sites but is an important gateway to several reserves and parks including Tadoba-Andhari Tiger Reserve and Pench National Park. It's also close to the temples of Ramtek and the ashrams of Sevagram. Summer is the best time to taste the city's famous oranges.

🛏️ Sleeping & Eating

Nagpur's hotels are not great value and cater primarily to business travellers. Central Ave is noisy but close to the train station.

Hotel Blue Moon   HOTEL **$**
(📞0712 2726061; Central Ave; s/d from ₹650/850, with AC ₹1100/1350; ❄️) Large, plain rooms that don't win any awards for imagination

but are one of the better budget options in this pricey city. It's one of the closest hotels to the train station. Staff are helpful.

Legend Inn — HOTEL $$

(☏ 6658666; www.thelegendinn.com; 15 Modern Society, Wardha Rd; s/d from ₹3300/3700; ❋ �🖭) On the main highway for the Tadoba-Andhari Tiger Reserve, this is an efficiently run hotel with well-appointed and -presented rooms, a good restaurant and smiley staff. Free pick-ups are included from the airport, 1km away. The 'gym' is two running machines in the basement. Rates drop by 10% in summer.

Peanut Hotel — HOTEL $$

(☏ 0712-3250320; www.peanuthotels.com; Bharti House, 43 Kachipura Garden, New Ramdaspeth; s/d from ₹2790/2960, with AC from ₹3090/3260; ❋ ᐤ) Located on a leafy residential street, this new hotel's modern, whitewashed rooms have a contemporary look and are kept spick and span; all are no smoking. It's 2km southeast of the train station.

Krishnum — SOUTH INDIAN $

(Central Ave; mains ₹50-80; ⊘11.30am-10pm) This popular place dishes out South Indian snacks and generous thalis, as well as freshly squeezed fruit juices. There are branches in other parts of town.

Picadilly Checkers — FAST FOOD $

(VCA Complex, Civil Lines; mains ₹60-80; ⊘11am-10pm) A favourite eating joint for Nagpur's college brigade, with a good range of vegetarian quick bites on offer.

ℹ Information

Numerous ATMs line Central Ave.

Computrek (18 Central Ave; per hour ₹20; ⊘10am-10pm) Internet access on the main drag.

MTDC (☏ 2533325; near MLA Hostel, Civil Lines; ⊘10am-5.45pm Mon-Sat) Staff here can help with getting to national parks near Nagpur.

ℹ Getting There & Around

AIR

The airport is 7km southwest of the centre. Domestic airlines, including Air India, Indigo and Jet Airways, fly daily to Delhi (from ₹5500, 1½ hours), Mumbai (from ₹4400, 1½ hours) and Kolkata (from ₹7500, 1½ hours), as well as Ahmedabad, Bengaluru, Chennai, Jaipur and Pune. Taxis/autorickshaws from the airport to the city centre cost ₹380/200.

BUS

The main MSRTC bus stand is 2km south of the train station. Ordinary buses head for Wardha (₹88, three hours) and Ramtek (₹45, 1½ hours). There are two buses to Jalgaon (₹650, 10 hours) and four daily to Pune (₹1070, 16 hours).

TRAIN

From Mumbai's CST, the Duronto Express runs daily to Nagpur (sleeper/2AC ₹470/1830, 10 hours, 9.15pm). From Nagpur, it departs at 8.50pm and arrives at 7.50am the following morning. Heading north to Kolkata is the Gitanjali Express (sleeper/2AC ₹480/1920, 17½ hours, 7.05pm). Several expresses bound for Delhi and Mumbai stop at Jalgaon (sleeper/2AC ₹280/1020, eight hours), for Ajanta caves.

Around Nagpur

Ramtek

About 40km northeast of Nagpur, Ramtek is believed to be the place where Lord Rama, of the epic Ramayana, spent some time during his exile with his wife Sita and brother Lakshmana. The place is marked by a cluster of **temples** (⊘6am-9pm) about 600 years old, which sit atop the Hill of Rama and have their own population of resident monkeys. Autorickshaws will cart you the 5km from the bus stand to the temple complex for ₹80. You can return to town via the 700 steps at the back of the complex. On the road to the temples you'll pass the delightful **Ambala Tank**, lined with small shrines. Boat rides around the lake are available.

Buses run half-hourly between Ramtek and the MSRTC bus stand in Nagpur (₹52, 1½ hours). The last bus to Nagpur is at 7pm.

Sevagram

☏ 07152

About 85km from Nagpur, Sevagram (Village of Service) was chosen by Mahatma Gandhi as his base during the Indian Independence Movement. Throughout the freedom struggle, the village played host to several nationalist leaders, who would regularly come to visit the Mahatma at his **Sevagram Ashram** (☏ 07152-284753; www. gandhiashramsevagram.org; ⊘9am-noon & 2-6pm). The overseers of this peaceful ashram, built on 40 hectares of farmland, have carefully restored the original huts where Gandhi lived and worked, and which now house some of his personal effects.

LONAR METEORITE CRATER

If you like off-beat adventures, travel to Lonar to explore a prehistoric natural wonder. About 50,000 years ago, a meteorite slammed into the earth here, leaving behind a massive crater, 2km across and 170m deep. In scientific jargon, it's the only hypervelocity natural-impact crater in basaltic rock in the world. In lay terms, it's as tranquil and relaxing a spot as you could hope to find, with a shallow green lake at its base and wilderness all around. The lake water is supposedly alkaline and excellent for the skin. Scientists think that the meteorite is still embedded about 600m below the southeastern rim of the crater.

crater's edge is home to several Hindu temples as well as wildlife, including langurs, peacocks, deer and numerous birds.

The **MTDC Tourist Complex** (☑ 07260221602; d ₹1300, with AC ₹2590; ❄) has a prime location just across the road from the crater, and offers newly renovated deluxe rooms that are in excellent shape, with stylish ensuite bathrooms. There are regular buses between Lonar and the CIDCO bus stand in Aurangabad (p92).

Very basic lodging is available in the **Yatri Nivas** (☑ 284753; d ₹100), across the road from the entry gate; advance booking is recommended. Simple vegetarian meals can be served in the ashram's dining hall with prior notice.

Just 3km from Sevagram, Paunar village is home to the **Brahmavidya Mandir Ashram** (☑ 07152-288388; ◷ 6am-noon & 2-8pm). Founded by Vinoba Bhave, a nationalist and disciple of Gandhi, the ashram is run almost entirely by women. Modelled on *swaraj* (self-sufficiency), it's operated on a social system of consensus, with no central management.

Sevagram can be reached by taking a Wardha-bound bus from Nagpur (₹85, three hours).

Tadoba-Andhari Tiger Reserve

One of the best places to see tigers in India, the seldom-visited **Tadoba-Andhari Tiger Reserve** (◷ dawn-dusk Wed-Mon), 150km south of Nagpur, is now much more accessible thanks to the upgrading of state highways. Seeing fewer visitors than most other forest reserves in India, this is a place where you can get up close with wildlife without having to jostle past truckloads of shutter-happy tourists. Mammals in the reserve include gaurs, chitals, nilgais, sloth bears and leopards as well as very healthy tiger numbers (estimated at around 120, with 24 cubs born in 2014). Of the 280 bird species logged in the park, there's a raptor population that includes crested serpent eagles, oriental honey buzzards and rare species of owls. The park also remains open throughout the year, unlike many in India.

Walking safaris (₹850) in the buffer zone allow you to look for tracks, observe birds and insects at close quarters, and catch the scents and sounds of wild India. Guides from the Gond tribe accompany you through the forest.

Guided canoe trips (₹1200 per person) on the Irai and Tadoba lakes allow you the chance explore inlets, islands and bays, with a chance of seeing crocodiles and magnificent birdlife, including the grey-headed fish eagle, ospreys and storks. Electric pontoon boats (₹800 per person) also operate.

Four state buses ply the road between Nagpur and Chandrapur (₹138, 3½ hours).

The nearest train station of Wardha (connected by trains from Hyderabad and Nagpur) is 40km from the reserve.

🛏 Sleeping & Eating

Tiger Trails Jungle Lodge   LODGE $$$
(☑ 0712-6541327; www.tigertrails.in; Khutwanda Gate; s/d incl all meals ₹9500/15,000; ❄☃) The Tiger Trails Jungle Lodge is owned by passionate enthusiasts who have spent decades studying tigers inside the national park. A special lodge, it's located in the wildlife-rich buffer zone. Accommodation is spacious and divided between rooms in an older block (with big roof terrace) and more modern, better-appointed options. Camera traps around the property regularly 'catch' tigers. All safari tours (from ₹4500) are with expert guides, accommodation is spacious and comfortable, and meals generous and tasty.

THE LEGEND OF BABA AMTE

The legend of Murlidhar Devidas 'Baba' Amte (1914–2008) is oft-repeated in humanitarian circles around the world. Hailing from an upper-class Brahmin family in Wardha, Amte was snugly ensconced in material riches and on his way to becoming a successful lawyer when he witnessed a leper die unattended in the streets one night. It was an incident that changed him forever.

Soon after, Amte renounced worldly comforts, embracing an austere life through which he actively worked for the benefit of leprosy patients and those belonging to marginalised communities. In the primitive forested backyards of eastern Maharashtra, he set up his ashram called **Anandwan** (Forest of Joy; ☑ 07176-282034; www.anandwan. in). A true Gandhian, Amte believed in self-sufficiency, and his lifelong efforts saw several awards being conferred upon him, including the Ramon Magsaysay Award in 1985.

Amte's work has been continued by his sons Vikas and Prakash and their wives – the latter couple also won the Magsaysay Award in 2008. The family now runs many ashrams in these remote parts to care for the needy, both humans and animals. Over 2500 people are currently cared for, including 1500 leprosy patients. Animals in the 'orphanage' include otters, eagles, crocodiles, monkeys, wild boars, deer, hyenas, snakes, leopards and lions. There's also a school for tribal people.

Volunteering opportunities are available and donations welcome (via website).

Svasara LODGE $$$
(☑ 9370 008008; www.svasararesorts.com; Kolara Gate; d incl all meals ₹14,000; ❄) Svasara is a beautifully designed new luxury lodge where the gorgeous suites and facilities really take the jungle out of the location. The food is great and safaris are well organised and lead by enthusiastic staff.

MTDC Resort HOTEL $
(☑ 02168-260318; Bombay Point Rd; d from ₹1645) The MTDC Resort has recently been renovated and now has comfortable, well-furnished rooms and cottages, some overlooking the Irai lake, and good dining facilities. Staff are helpful and arrange good jungle safaris in 4WDs (₹2700 per vehicle, plus ₹300 for a mandatory guide). Bookings and packages can be made at the MTDC's Nagpur office.

SOUTHERN MAHARASHTRA

Konkan Coast

A little-developed shoreline running south from Mumbai all the way to Goa, this picturesque strip of coast is peppered with postcard beaches, fishing villages and magnificent ruined forts. Travelling through this tropical backwater can be sheer bliss. However, remember that accommodation is scant and transport limited and a little unreliable. The best option, if you've the funds, is to rent a car in Mumbai and drift slowly down the coast to Goa. What you'll get in return is an experience that money can't buy.

Murud

☑ 02144 / POP 13,100
The sleepy fishing hamlet of Murud – 165km from Mumbai – should be on any itinerary of the Konkan Coast. The relaxed pace of life, fresh seafood, stupendous offshore Janjira fort (and the chance to feel the warm surf rush past your feet) makes the trip here well worthwhile.

Murud's beach is fun for a run or game of cricket with locals. Peer through the gates of the off-limits Ahmedganj Palace, estate of the Siddi Nawab of Murud, or scramble around the decaying mosque and tombs on the south side of town.

⊙ Sights

★ Janjira FORT
(⊙ 7am-dusk) The commanding, brooding fortress of Janjira, built on an island 500m offshore, is the most magnificent of the string of forts which line the Konkan coastline. This citadel was completed in 1571 by the Siddis, descendants of slaves from the Horn of Africa, and was the capital of a princely state.

Over the centuries Siddi alignment with Mughals provoked conflict with local kings, including Shivaji and his son Sambhaji, who attempted to tunnel to it. However, no outsider (including British, French and Portuguese colonists) ever made it past the fort's 12m-high granite walls which, when seen during high tide, seem to rise straight from the sea. Unconquered through history, the fort is finally falling to forces of nature as its mighty walls slowly crumble and wilderness reclaims its innards.

Still, there's a lot to see today, including the remarkable close-fitting stonework that's protected the citadel against centuries of attack by storms, colonists and gunpowder. You approach the fort via a brooding grey-stone gateway, and then can explore its ramparts (complete with giant cannons) and 19 bastions, large parts of which are intact. Its inner keep, palaces and mosque are in ruins, though the fort's huge twin reservoirs remain. As many of the surviving walls and structures are in poor shape, tread carefully as you explore the site, which is unfortunately littered with trash.

The only way to reach Janjira is by boat (₹20 return, 20 minutes) from Rajpuri port. Boats depart from 7am to 4.45pm daily and allow you 45 minutes to explore the fort. To get to Rajpuri from Murud, take an autorickshaw (₹75) or hire a bicycle.

🛏 Sleeping & Eating

Devakinandan Lodge
GUESTHOUSE **$**
(📞9273524061; r ₹1000-1200) This simple little guesthouse has clean, basic rooms with TV and attached bathrooms with hot water. You'll find a few hammocks scattered in its beach-facing garden. The family owners are friendly but speak very little English.

Sea Shell Resort
HOTEL **$$**
(📞274306; www.seashellmurud.com; Darbar Rd; r with/without AC from ₹2500/2000; ❄ 🌊) Set back from the beachside road, this cheery place has neat, spacious breezy sea-facing rooms with hot-water bathrooms and a multi-cuisine restaurant. Staff can be a bit vacant on reception but dolphin safaris can be arranged. The pool is tiny.

Golden Swan Beach Resort
HOTEL **$$**
(📞274078; www.goldenswan.com; Darbar Rd; s/d incl breakfast from ₹3800; ❄ 🌊) Rates are a little steep (particularly the cheaper options), but these seafront cottages and rooms occupy a fine spot on a great stretch of beach, with distant views of Ahmedganj Palace and Kasa Fort. There are also rooms in a charming old bungalow a short walk away. The in-house restaurant is superb, try the Szechwan chicken. Rates increase on weekends.

New Sea Rock Restaurant
INDIAN **$**
(Rajpuri; mains ₹50-180; ⊙7am-8pm) Perched on a cliff overlooking the beach at Rajpuri, this joint has an awesome view of Janjira. A perfect place to steal a million-dollar sunset for the price of a chai (₹10), though you will probably be tempted to try the Indian or Chinese mains.

Hotel Vinayak
INDIAN **$**
(Darbar Rd; mains ₹70-150; ⊙8am-10pm) Its sea-facing terrace is the perfect place to tuck into a delicious and fiery Malvani thali (₹80 to ₹180), served with pink kokam syrup to smother the spices. Fresh fish (₹100 to ₹250), prawn dishes and good breakfasts are also available.

❶ Getting There & Around

Ferries and catamarans (₹95 to ₹160, one hour) from the Gateway of India in Mumbai cruise to Mandva pier between 6am and 7pm. The ticket includes a free shuttle bus to Alibag (30 minutes). Rickety local buses from Alibag head down the coast to Murud (₹52, two hours). Alternatively, hourly buses from Mumbai Central bus stand take almost six hours to Murud (ordinary/semideluxe ₹158/212).

The nearest railhead is at Roha, two hours away and poorly connected.

Bicycles (₹75 per hour) and cars (from ₹1500 per day) can be hired at the Golden Swan Beach Resort.

Around Murud

RAIGAD FORT

Alone on a high and remote hilltop, 24km off Hwy 66, the enthralling **Raigad Fort** (Indian/foreigner ₹5/100; ⊙8am-5.30pm) served as Shivaji's capital from 1648 until his death in 1680. The fort was later sacked by the British, and some colonial structures added, but monuments such as the royal court, plinths of royal chambers, the main marketplace and Shivaji's tomb still remain, and it's worth an excursion.

You can hike a crazy 1475 steps to the top. But for a more 'levitating' experience, take the vertigo-inducing **ropeway** (www.raigadropeway.com; return ₹200; ⊙8.30am-5.30pm) – actually a cable car – which climbs up the cliff and offers a bird's-eye view of the deep gorges below. Be warned this is a very popular attraction with domestic tourists and you may have to wait up to an hour for a ride during holiday times. Guides (₹200) are available within the fort complex. **Sarja Restaurant** (snacks ₹30-100), adjoining the

THE ROAD TO RUINS

A scenic coastal road parallels the shoreline north of Murud, skirting headlands, beaches and rocky shores. Just a couple of kilometres from town, the clifftop **Nawab's Palace** is an extraordinary Victorian Gothic-Mughal structure that's been abandoned for years but would make a perfect heritage hotel. You can peek through its gates (complete with coat of arms) from the roadside for a glimpse of the palace.

Sixteen kilometres north of Murud, **Kashid Beach** is a beautiful sandy cove where you can take a dip and sip on tender coconuts. It's a peaceful spot, though expect a smattering of camel-ride-wallahs and banana boats on weekends. The road continues north, gripping the contours of the exposed shoreline, affording superb oceanic views until you reach the tiny traditional fishing village of **Korlai**, 31km from Murud. Perched on the rocky headland above the village are the ruined remains of **Korlai Fort**, which once guarded the giant Kundaliker river estuary and still affords panoramic vistas.

Share autorickshaws (₹100) run as far as Kashid Beach. Cars and bicycles can be hired at the Golden Swan Beach Resort in Murud.

ropeway's base terminal, is a good place for lunch or snacks.

Autorickshaws (₹180, 45 minutes) shuttle up to Raigad from the town of Mahad on Hwy 66 (look out for the 'Raigad Ropeway' sign). Mahad is located 158km south of Mumbai and 88km from Murud. The Mahad–Raigad road is paved and in good condition. Taxis charge ₹2000 for a day trip here from Murud.

Ganpatipule

[☑] 02357

The tiny beach resort of Ganpatipule has been luring a steady stream of sea-lovers over the years with its warm waters and wonderful stretches of sand. Located about 375km from Mumbai, it's a village that snoozes through much of the year, except during holidays such as Diwali or Ganesh Chaturthi. These are times when hordes of boisterous tourists turn up to visit the seaside **Ganesha Temple** (⊙6am-9pm) housing a monolithic orange Ganesh.

Activities on and off the beach at Ganpatipule include camel and boat rides (dolphins are sometimes encountered in the morning). Away from a small crowded section near the temple, you'll find the beach is perfect for a long walk along the sand.

🛏 Sleeping & Eating

There are plenty of guesthouses in Ganpatipule but at the time of research we couldn't find one that would rent out rooms to foreigners. We were told this is because Mumbai bomb plotter David Healey spent time in the town.

MTDC Resort   HOTEL $$
([☑] 235248; d from ₹2250, with AC ₹2550; ❋🕾) Spread over prime beachfront, this huge operation is something of a holiday camp for Mumbaiker families. Its concrete rooms and cottages would benefit from a little updating, but all boast magnificent full-frontal ocean views. It also packs in a decent restaurant that serves cold beer.

Bhau Joshi Bhojnalay   INDIAN $
(mains ₹50-80; ⊙11am-10.30pm) A clean, orderly restaurant inland from the beach that offers delicious Maharashtrian food including *baingan masala* (eggplant curry; ₹80) and okra and tomato dishes.

ℹ Information

There are several ATMs in Ganpatipule including one about 400m inland from the MTDC Resort.

ℹ Getting There & Around

Ganpatipule has limited transport links. Ratnagiri, 40km to the south, is the nearest major town. Hourly buses (₹50, 1½ hours) connect the two places; autorickshaws/taxis cost ₹400/750.

Several buses leave Ganpatipule for Mumbai (₹400 to ₹650, 10 hours) between 6.30pm and 10pm; there are also three daily buses to both Pune (₹350) and Kolhapur (₹145).

Ratnagiri train station is on the Konkan Railway line. From Ratnagiri, the Mandovi Express goes daily to Mumbai (2nd class/1st class ₹160/1670, 7½ hours, 2.10pm). The return train heading for Goa (2nd class/1st class ₹120/1400, 5½ hours) is at 1.10pm. From Ratnagiri's old bus stand, buses leave for Goa (semideluxe ₹270, six hours) and Kolhapur (₹160, four hours).

Malvan

☎ 02365

A government tourism promo parades the emerging Malvan region as comparable to Tahiti, which is a tad ambitious, but it does boast near-white sands, sparkling seas and jungle-fringed backwaters. Offshore there are coral reefs, sea caves and vibrant marine life – diving is becoming a huge draw with the opening of a new world-class diving school.

Malvan town is one of the prettiest on the Konkan Coast. It's a mellow place with a good stock of old wooden buildings and a busy little harbour and bazaar. Stretching directly south of the centre is lovely Tarkali beach, home to many hotels and guesthouses.

◉ Sights & Activities

There are several dodgy dive shops operating in Malvan, which allow unqualified diving; if you want to dive, stick with a registered operator.

The southern end of Tarkali beach is bordered by the broad, beautiful Karli river. Several boat operators (you'll find them moored on the northern bank) offer multi-stop boat trips along this backwater, to Seagull Island, Golden Rock, Dolphin Point and cove beaches. A three-hour trip with a maximum of six people costs ₹1800 per boat.

Sindhudurg Fort   FORT

Built by Shivaji and dating from 1664, this monstrous fort lies on an offshore island and can be reached by frequent ferries (9am to 5.30pm, ₹50) from Malvan's harbour. It's not as impressive as Janjira up the coast, and today lies mostly in ruins, but it remains a powerful presence. You can explore its ramparts and the coastal views are impressive. Boatmen allow you one hour on the island.

Tarkali Beach   BEACH

A golden arc south of Marvan, this crescent-shaped sandy beach is a vision of tropical India, fringed by coconut palms and casuarina trees, plus the odd cow. At dusk (between October and February) fishermen work together to haul in huge, kilometre-long nets that are packed with sardines.

★ **IISDA**   DIVING

(Indian Institute of Scuba Diving & Aquasports; ☑ 02365-248790; www.iisda.gov.in; Tarkali Beach; per dive ₹3000, PADI Open Water ₹22,000) This state-of-the-art new PADI diving cen-

tre is India's finest, run by marine biologist and all-round diving pro Dr Sarang Kulkarni. It offers professional instruction, a 20m-long and 8m-deep pool for training, air-conditioned classrooms and comfortable sleeping quarters for students. IISDA is also a marine conservation centre and there's even a restaurant, bar and tennis court. Located 7km south of Malvan.

🛏 Sleeping & Eating

MTDC Holiday Resort   BUNGALOW $$

(☑ 252390; Tarkali Beach; bungalow/boathouse from ₹3110/5400; ❄ 🛜) The MTDC Holiday Resort enjoys a wonderful location on a lovely stretch of clean sand 5km south of Malvan town. Its concrete bungalows and boathouses (actually boat-shaped wooden cabins with huge front decks) are a little tired, but spacious. There's a restaurant for seafood, local and Chinese grub. No beer, and wi-fi limited to the reception area only.

★ **Chaitanya**   MALVANI, INDIAN $$

(☑ 02365-252172; 502 Dr Vallabh Marg; mains ₹70-250; ⊙11am-11pm) On Malvan's main drag, this great, family-run place specialises in Konkan cuisine including *bangda tikhale* (fish in thick coconut sauce), prawns malvani and very flavoursome crab masala; staff will keep topping up the *sol kadhi* (coconut and fruit digestive) bowl as you eat. Its vegetarian dishes are excellent. It's always packed with locals and has an air-con section.

Athithi Bamboo   INDIAN $$

(Church St; mains ₹60-240; ⊙noon-3.30pm & 8-10.30pm) On the north side of the harbour, this large casual place offers excellent thalis (from ₹60) and lots of fresh fish. There's no

---

KONKAN SPECIALITIES

Often called Malvani cuisine, this coastal region has many special dishes and snacks you should try.

dhondas – cucumber cakes made from cucumber and palm sugar

kaju chi aamti – spicy cashew-nut curry

kombdi vade – spicy chicken prepared with lime and coconut

mori masala – shark curry

sol kadhi – pink-coloured, slightly sour digestive made from coconut milk and kokum fruit; accompanies many meals

MALVAN NATIONAL MARINE PARK

The shoreline around Malvan is incredibly diverse, with rich wetlands, sandy and rocky beaches, mangroves and river estuaries. But underwater it's arguably even more compelling, with coral and caves that shelter abundant marine life and extensive forests of *sargassum* seaweed which acts as a nursery for juvenile fish. Rocky offshore islands attract schools of snapper and large grouper, butterfly fish, yellow-striped fusiliers and lobster. Pods of dolphins are regularly seen between November and February. And the world's largest fish, the whale shark, even puts in an appearance every now and then.

Presently only a small section is protected as the **Malvan National Marine Park**, which encompasses the Sindhudurg Fort, yet such is its rich diversity that marine biologists, including IISDA's director Dr Sarang Kulkarni, feel it's essential that the boundaries are extended. The reef extends for 16km offshore and has been described as India's Great Barrier Reef. A submerged plateau, the **Angria Bank** is 40km long and 20km wide, with healthy coral and an abundance of sealife: nurse sharks are seen on almost every dive. IISDA has plans to operate day trips and liveaboard excursions to Angria; consult its website for information.

sign in English and you sit under a tin roof (so it gets very hot during the day), but the seafood is surf-fresh and cooking is Konkan-authentic.

❶ Information

There are numerous ATMs in Malvan.

Bank of India ATM (Dr Vallabh Marg)

Scorpion Cyber (Dr Vallabh Marg; ⊙10am-10pm) Several terminals for internet access.

❶ Getting There & Away

The closest train station is Kudal, 38km away. Frequent buses (₹30, one hour) cover the route from Malvan bus stand, or an autorickshaw is about ₹500. Malvan has ordinary buses to:

Kolhapur ₹170, five hours, seven daily

Mumbai ₹500, 12 hours, one daily

Panaji ₹110, 3½ hours, four daily

Ratnagiri ₹165, five hours, three daily

Malvan is only 80km from northern Goa; taxis charge ₹1200 for the two-hour trip.

Matheran

📞 02148 / POP 5750 / ELEV 803M

Matheran, literally 'Jungle Above', is a tiny patch of peace and quiet capping a craggy Sahyadri summit within spitting distance of Mumbai's heat and grime. Endowed with shady forests criss-crossed with foot trails and breathtaking lookouts, it still retains an elegance and colonial-era ambience, though creeping commercialism and illegal construction are marring its appeal.

Getting to Matheran is really half the fun. While speedier options are available by road, nothing beats arriving in town on the narrow-gauge toy train that chugs up to the heart of the settlement. Motor vehicles are banned within Matheran, making it an ideal place to give your ears and lungs a rest and your feet some exercise.

◉ Sights & Activities

You can walk along shady forest paths to most of Matheran's viewpoints in a matter of hours; it's a place well suited to stress-free ambling. To catch the sunrise, head to **Panorama Point**, while **Porcupine Point** (also known as Sunset Point) is the most popular (read: packed) as the sun drops. **Louisa Point** and **Little Chouk Point** also have stunning views of the Sahyadris.

If you're here on a weekend or public holiday you might want to avoid the most crowded section around **Echo Point**, **Charlotte Lake** and **Honeymoon Point**, which get rammed with day trippers.

You can reach the valley below One Tree Hill down the path known as **Shivaji's Ladder**, supposedly trod upon by the Maratha leader himself. Horse-wallahs will hustle you constantly for rides (about ₹300 per hour).

🛏 Sleeping & Eating

Hotels in Matheran are generally overpriced and many places have a minimum two-night stay. Checkout times vary wildly (as early as 7am), as do high- and low-season rates. Matheran shuts shop during the monsoons.

Hope Hall Hotel   HOTEL $

(📞 230253; www.hopehallmatheran.com; MG Rd; d Mon-Fri ₹1370, Sat & Sun ₹1710) Run by a very hospitable family, this long-running place has been hosting happy travellers for years; the house dates back to 1875. Spacious rooms with high ceilings and arty touches are in two blocks at the rear of the leafy garden. Good breakfasts and drinks are available. Ask Maria to show you her amazing mineral and crystal collection. Rates double during peak holiday periods.

MTDC Resort　　　　　LODGE $$
(☏02148-230277; d ₹1580, with AC ₹5050; ❄) This government-run place offers functional, economy rooms, disappointing family rooms, and modern, very attractive air-conditioned rooms in the Shruti villa. The downside is it's located next to the Dasturi car park, so you're away from the midtown action. There's a good restaurant.

★ **Verandah in the Forest**　HERITAGE HOTEL $$$
(☏230296; www.neemranahotels.com; Barr House; d incl breakfast from ₹5880) This deliciously preserved 19th-century bungalow thrives on undiluted nostalgia, with quaintly luxurious rooms. Find yourself reminiscing about bygone times in the company of ornate candelabras, oriental rugs, antique teak furniture, Victorian canvases and grandfather clocks. The verandah has a lovely aspect over Matheran's wooded hillsides, and the in-house restaurant offers fine Indian food and a terrific four-course c ontinental dinner (₹600).

Hotel Woodlands　　　　HOTEL $$$
(☏230271; www.woodlandsmatheran.com; Chinoy Rd; r from ₹5540) A venerable old homestead with historic charm and enough modern comforts thrown in to keep the most fussy guest satisfied. The forested setting is very relaxing and the playground should keep the kids occupied. But it's the verandah that steals the show; a great place to kick back.

Shabbir Bhai　　　　　INDIAN $
(Merry Rd; mains ₹70-120; ⊙10am-10pm) Known locally as the 'Byrianiwala', this funky joint has a full North Indian menu, but it's all about the spicy biryanis: chicken, mutton and veg. To find it, take the footpath uphill beside the Jama Masjid on MG Rd.

ⓘ Information

Entry to Matheran costs ₹40 (₹20 for children), which you pay on arrival at the train station or the Dasturi car park.
Union Bank of India (MG Rd; ⊙10am-2pm Mon-Fri, to noon Sat) Has an ATM.

ⓘ Getting There & Away

TAXI
Buses (₹25) and shared taxis (₹75) run from Neral to Matheran's Dasturi car park (30 minutes). Horses (₹300) and hand-pulled rickshaws (₹400) wait here to whisk you (relatively speaking) to Matheran's main bazaar. You can also walk this stretch in a little under an hour (around 3.5km uphill) and your luggage can be hauled for around ₹220.

TRAIN
The toy train (2nd class/1st class ₹35/225) chugs between Matheran and Neral Junction five times daily. The service is suspended during monsoons.

From Mumbai's CST station there are two daily express trains to Neral Junction at 7am and 8.40am (2nd class/1st class ₹45/205, 1½ hours). Other expresses from Mumbai stop at Karjat, down the line from Neral, from where you can backtrack on a local train or catch a bus to Matheran (₹30). From Pune, there are at least 13 daily departures to Karjat. Note: trains from Pune don't stop at Neral Junction.

ⓘ Getting Around

Apart from hand-pulled rickshaws and horses, walking is the only other transport option in Matheran.

Lonavla

☏02114 / POP 57,400 / ELEV 625M
Lonavla is an overdeveloped (and overpriced) resort town about 106km southeast of Mumbai. It's far from attractive, with its main drag consisting almost exclusively of garishly lit shops flogging *chikki*, the rock-hard, brittle sweet made in the area.

The main reason to come here is to visit the nearby Karla and Bhaja caves which, after those at Ellora and Ajanta, are the best in Maharashtra.

Hotels, restaurants and the main road to the caves lie north of the train station. Most of the Lonavla township and its markets are located south of the station.

🏃 Activities

Kaivalyadhama Yoga Hospital　　YOGA
(☏273039; www.kdham.com; 2-week course incl full board US$800) This progressive yoga centre is located in neatly kept grounds about 2km from Lonavla, en route to the Karla and Bhaja Caves. Founded in 1924 by Swami Kuvalayanandji, it combines yoga courses with

MAHARASHTRA LONAVLA

naturopathic therapies. Courses cover full board, yoga classes, programs and lectures.

Nirvana Adventures PARAGLIDING
(☑ 022-26053724; www.flynirvana.com) Mumbai-based Nirvana Adventures offers paragliding courses (two-day learner course ₹8500 per person including full board) and short tandem flights (from ₹2500) in a charming rural setting near the town of Kamshet, 25km from Lonavla.

🛏 Sleeping & Eating

Lonavla's hotels tend to have inflated prices, low standards and early checkouts.

★ Ferreira Resort HOTEL $
(☑ 272689; www.ferreiraresortlonavala.blogspot.co.uk; DT Shahani Rd; s/d Sun-Thu ₹1350/1500, Fri & Sat ₹1600/1800 ; ❋ 🐀) It's certainly not a resort, but it is something of a rarity in Lonavla: a family-run, well-priced place in a quiet residential location that's close to the train station. All the 16 clean, well presented air-con rooms have a balcony and there's a little lawned garden and small restaurant. The owners are helpful and informative about the region.

Citrus HOTEL $$$
(☑ 398100; www.citrushotels.com; DT Shahani Rd; r from ₹6380; ❋ 🐀 ⛱) The design and decor of the rooms here don't quite reach the hip hotel target market, but are spacious and well presented and have a modish feel. The garden area has a generously sized pool and loungers. It's a little overpriced, but that's Lonavla.

Biso ITALIAN $$
(Citrus Hotel, DT Shahani Rd; mains ₹230-340; ⊙ noon-3.30pm & 7-10.30pm; 🐀) This could be a delightfully redeeming feature of your Lonavla trip. A top-class alfresco restaurant with an excellent selection of pastas, wood-fired pizzas and desserts.

ℹ Information

There are numerous ATMs in town.
Balaji Cyber Café (1st fl, Khandelwal Bldg, New Bazaar; per hour ₹15; ⊙ 12.30-10.30pm) Has internet access. Located immediately south of the train station.

ℹ Getting There & Away

Lonavla is serviced by MSRTC buses departing from the bus stand to Dadar in Mumbai (ordinary/semideluxe ₹76/118, two hours) and Pune (ordinary/semideluxe ₹66/105, two hours). Luxury AC buses (₹200 to ₹330) also travel to both cities.

All express trains from Mumbai's CST to Pune stop at Lonavla (2nd class ₹75 to ₹90, chair ₹255 to ₹305, 2½ to three hours).

Karla & Bhaja Caves

While they pale in comparison to Ajanta or Ellora, the Karla and Bhaja rock-cut caves, which date from around the 2nd century BC, are among the better examples of Buddhist cave architecture in India. They are also low on commercial tourism, making them ideal places for a quiet excursion. Karla has the most impressive single cave, but Bhaja is a quieter site to explore.

◎ Sights

Karla Cave CAVE
(Indian/foreigner ₹5/100; ⊙ 9am-5pm) Karla Cave, the largest early *chaitya* (Buddhist temple) in India, is reached by a 20-minute climb from a mini-bazaar at the base of a hill. Completed in 80 BC, the *chaitya* is around 40m long and 15m high, and sports a vaulted interior and intricately executed sculptures of Buddha, human and animal figures. Excluding Ellora's Kailasa Temple, this is probably the most impressive cave temple in the state.

A semicircular 'sun window' filters light in towards a dagoba or stupa (the cave's representation of the Buddha), protected by a carved wooden umbrella, the only remaining example of its kind. The cave's roof also retains ancient teak buttresses. The 37 pillars forming the aisles are topped by kneeling elephants. The carved elephant heads on the sides of the vestibule once had ivory tusks. There's a **Hindu temple** in front of the cave, thronged by pilgrims whose presence adds colour to the scene.

Bhaja Caves CAVE
(Indian/foreigner ₹5/100; ⊙ 9am-6pm) It's a 3km jaunt from the main road, on the other side of the expressway, to the Bhaja Caves, where the setting is lusher, greener and quieter than at Karla Cave. Thought to date from around 200 BC, 10 of the 18 caves here are *viharas* (Buddhist monasteries), while Cave 12 is an open *chaitya* (Buddhist temple), earlier than that at Karla, containing a simple dagoba. Beyond this is a strange huddle of 14 stupas, five inside and nine outside a smaller cave.

🛏 Sleeping & Eating

MTDC Karla Resort HOTEL $$
(☑ 02114-282230; d ₹1740, with AC from ₹2090;
❄) Set off the highway, close to the Karla–
Bhaja access point, this large resort in a ru-
ral location attracts weekending Mumbai
families thanks to its water park (closed in
winter) and play facilities. It's much more
peaceful during the week. There's a wide
choice of rooms and cottages, from economy
to smart, and a restaurant.

❶ Getting There & Around

Karla is 11km east of Lonavla, and Bhaja 9km.
Both can be visited on a local bus (₹16, 30 min-
utes) to the access point, from where it's about
a 6km return walk on each side to the two sites.
But that would be exhausting and hot. Autorick-
shaws charge around ₹500 from Lonavla for the
tour, including waiting time.

Pune

☑ 020 / POP 5.14 MILLION / ELEV 535M

A thriving, vibrant metropolis, Pune is a
centre of academia and business that epit-
omises 'New India' with its baffling mix of
capitalism, spiritualism, ancient and mod-
ern. It's also globally famous, or notorious,
for an ashram, the Osho International Med-
itation Resort, founded by the late guru
Bhagwan Shree Rajneesh.

Pune was initially given pride of place by
Shivaji and the ruling Peshwas, who made it
their capital. The British took the city in 1817
and, thanks to its cool and dry climate, soon
made it the Bombay Presidency's monsoon
capital. Globalisation knocked on Pune's
doors in the 1990s, following which it went
in for an image overhaul. However, some
colonial-era charm was retained in a few
old buildings and residential areas, bringing
about a pleasant coexistence of the old and
new, which (despite the pollution and traffic)
makes Pune a worthwhile place to explore.

In August/September Ganesh Chaturthi
(p85) brings on a tide of festivities across
the city, and provides a fantastic window for
exploring the city's cultural side. On a more
sombre note, the fatal 2010 terrorist attack
on the German Bakery, a once favourite
haunt for travellers and ashramites, remains
a painful memory in this peace-loving city.

The city sits at the confluence of the Mu-
tha and Mula rivers. Mahatma Gandhi (MG)
Rd, about 1km south of Pune train station,
is the main commercial street. The leafy

upmarket suburb of Koregaon Park, north-
east of the train station, is home to numer-
ous hotels, restaurants, coffee shops and, of
course, the Osho ashram.

◉ Sights & Activities

Aga Khan Palace PALACE
(Ahmednagar Rd; Indian/foreigner ₹5/100; ◷ 9am-
5.30pm) The grand Aga Khan Palace is set in
a peaceful wooded 6.5-hectare plot north-
east of the centre. Built in 1892 by Sultan Aga
Khan III, this graceful building was where
Mahatma Gandhi and other prominent na-
tionalist leaders were interned by the British
following Gandhi's Quit India campaign in
1942. The main palace now houses the **Gan-
dhi National Memorial** where you can peek
into the room where the Mahatma used to
stay. Photos and paintings exhibit moments
in his extraordinary life.

Both Kasturba Gandhi, the Mahatma's
wife, and Mahadeobhai Desai, his secretary
for 35 years, died here in confinement. You'll
find their shrines (containing their ashes) in
a quiet garden to the rear.

Raja Dinkar Kelkar Museum MUSEUM
(www.rajakelkarmuseum.com; Bajirao Rd, 1377-1378
Natu Baug; Indian/foreigner ₹50/200; ◷ 10am-
5.30pm) An oddball of a museum that's
one of Pune's true delights, housing only a
fraction of the 20,000-odd objects of Indian
daily life painstakingly collected by Dinkar
Kelkar (who died in 1990). The quirky
pan-Indian collection includes hundreds of
hookah pipes, writing instruments, lamps,
textiles, toys, entire doors and windows,
kitchen utensils, furniture, puppets, jewel-
lery, betel-nut cutters and an amazing gal-
lery of musical instruments.

Tribal Cultural Museum MUSEUM
(28 Queen's Garden; Indian/foreigner ₹10/200;
◷ 10.30am-5.30pm Mon-Sat) This small
museum showcases artefacts (jewellery,
utensils, musical instruments, even black-
magic accessories) from remote tribal belts.
Highlights include some demonic-looking
papier-mâché festival masks and superb
monochrome Warli paintings.

Shaniwar Wada FORT
(Shivaji Rd; Indian/foreigner ₹5/100; ◷ 8am-6pm)
The remains of this fortressed palace of the
Peshwa rulers are located in the old part of
the city. Built in 1732, Shaniwar Wada was
destroyed in a fire in 1828, but the massive
walls and ramparts remain, as does a mighty
fortified gateway. In the evenings, there's a

MAHARASHTRA PUNE

Pune

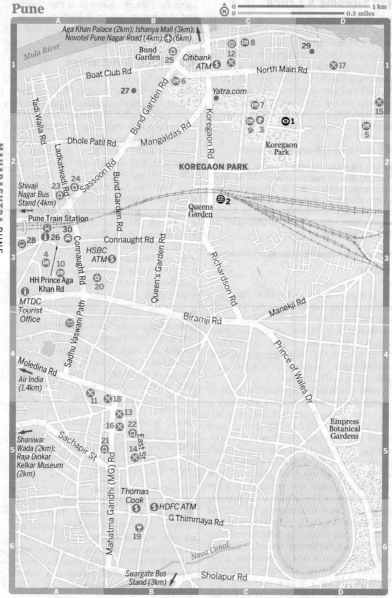

Aga Khan Palace (2km); Ishanya Mall (3km);
Novotel Pune Nagar Road (4km); ✈(6km)

Mula River

Boat Club Rd

Bund Garden Rd

Dhole Patil Rd

Mangaldas Rd

Tadi Walla Rd

Ladkatvadi Rd

Sassoon Rd

Bund Garden Rd

Shivaji Nagar Bus Stand (4km)

Pune Train Station

Connaught Rd

Queen's Garden Rd

Richardson Rd

Sadhu Vaswani Path

HH Prince Aga Khan Rd

MTDC Tourist Office

Moledina Rd

Air India (1.4km)

Biramji Rd

Manekji Rd

Prince of Wales Dr

Shaniwar Wada (2km); Raja Dinkar Kelkar Museum (2km)

Sachapir St

Mahatma Gandhi (MG) Rd

East St

Thomas Cook

HDFC ATM

G Thimmaya Rd

Empress Botanical Gardens

Nava Canal

Swargate Bus Stand (3km)

Sholapur Rd

Bund Garden

Citibank ATM

North Main Rd

Yatra.com

Koregaon Rd

KOREGAON PARK

Koregaon Park

Queens Garden

HSBC ATM

45-minute sound-and-light show (in English at 8.30pm; ₹25) though a minimum of 10 people is needed for the show to commence.

Pataleshvara Cave Temple   HINDU TEMPLE
(Jangali Maharaj Rd; ⏰6am-9.30pm) Set across the river is the curious rock-cut Patalesh-

vara Cave Temple, a small and unfinished (though actively used) 8th-century temple, similar in style to the grander caves at Elephanta Island. Adjacent is the **Jangali Maharaj Temple** (⏰6am-9.30pm), dedicated to a Hindu ascetic who died here in 1818.

Pune

Osho Teerth Gardens GARDENS
(⊙ 6-9am & 3-6pm) The 5-hectare Osho Teerth gardens are a verdant escape from urban living with giant bamboo, jogging trails, a gurgling brook and smooching couples. You don't have to be an Osho member as they're accessible to all.

**Osho International
Meditation Resort** MEDITATION
(☏ 66019999; www.osho.com; 17 Koregaon Park) Indelibly linked with Pune's identity, this iconic ashram-resort, located in a leafy, up-scale northern suburb, has been drawing thousands of *sanyasins* (seekers) since the death of Osho in 1990. With its swimming pool, sauna and spa, 'zennis' and boutique guesthouse, it is, to some, the ultimate place to indulge in some luxe meditation. Alternately, detractors point fingers at the blatant commercialisation and high cost and accuse it of marketing a warped version of the mystic East to rich, gullible Westerners.

To make up your own mind you'll have to cough up the (steep) registration and daily meditation fees. Tours of the facilities are no longer permitted – the only way to access Osho is to pay an initial ₹1400, which covers registration (passport required) and a mandatory on-the-spot HIV test (sterile needles used). You'll also need two robes (one ma-

roon and one white, ₹500 to ₹700 per robe) and attend a welcome session (daily at 9am). Note that the rules and regulations are very strict, even pedantic: swimmers are only allowed to wear, and have to pay for, Osho maroon swimwear and there are mandatory (Osho maroon) clothes for the gym. Indian nationals are also lectured about behaviour (eg not hassling foreign women) in special etiquette classes.

Once you've got all this out the way, you can then pay for a meditation pass (₹760/1560 per day Indian/foreigner, with discounts for longer stays). Oh, that's apart from the fee to enter the Basho Spa (where the pool, Jacuzzi, gym, saunas and tennis courts are all located), which will be a further ₹280.

The main centre for meditation and the nightly white-robed spiritual dance in the Osho Auditorium (no coughing or sneezing, please). The Osho Samadhi, where the guru's ashes are kept, is also open for meditation. The commune's 'Multiversity' runs a plethora of courses in meditation and other esoteric techniques. In the evenings, as well as meditation sessions, there's a 'nightlife' program, with parties, cinema and theatre and 'creativity nights'. Photography is not permitted anywhere in the ashram.

Ramamani Iyengar Memorial Yoga Institute
YOGA

(☑25656134; www.bksiyengar.com; 1107 B/1 Hare Krishna Mandir Rd, Model Colony) To attend classes at this famous institute, 7km northwest of the train station, you need to have been practising yoga for at least eight years.

🛏 Sleeping

Pune's main accommodation hubs are around the train station, where budget places proliferate, and leafy Koregaon Park, where you'll find good midrange options. Many upmarket places are on the road to the airport, 6km or so from the centre.

Hotel Homeland
HOTEL $

(☑26123203; www.hotelhomeland.net; 18 Wilson Garden; s/d ₹1040/1250, with AC from ₹1410/1620; ❄) A landmark art deco building that's very convenient to the train station, yet tucked away from the associated din. Rooms are in good shape with freshly painted walls, and there's a coffee shop and restaurant. Be sure to book ahead.

Hotel Surya Villa
HOTEL $

(☑26124501; www.hotelsuryavilla.com; 294/2 Koregaon Park; s/d from ₹1340/1670, with AC ₹1670/2350; ❄🛜) The Surya's functional, tiled rooms are well kept and generously proportioned, and though a little Spartan, they do have bathrooms with hot water, wi-fi and cable TV. It enjoys a good location on a quiet street in Koregaon Park, close to popular cafes.

★Hotel Sunderban
HOTEL $$

(☑26124949; www.tghotels.com; 19 Koregaon Park; s/d incl breakfast from ₹3300/3850; ❄🛜) Set around a manicured lawn right next to the Osho Resort, this renovated art deco bungalow effortlessly combines colonial-era class with boutique appeal. Deluxe rooms in the main building sport antique furniture, while even the cheapest options are beautifully presented (though lack a private bathroom). The priciest rooms are across the lawns, in a sleek, glass-fronted building.

An additional draw is the in-house fine-dining restaurant, Dario's.

Novotel Pune Nagar Road
HOTEL $$

(☑67056000; www.novotel.com; Weikfield IT City Infopark, Pune-Nagar Rd; s/d from ₹4330/4650; ❄🛜🏊) Around 5km northeast of the centre, handily placed for the airport and tech parks, this contemporary-chic hotel gets everything right, with an excellent restaurant-cafe, a rooftop pool big enough for laps, good gym, superb service and commodious rooms. It's fine value.

OSHO: GURU OF SEX

Ever tried mixing spirituality with primal instincts, and garnishing with oodles of expensive trinkets? Well, Bhagwan Shree Rajneesh (1931–90) certainly did. Osho, as he preferred to be called, was one of India's most flamboyant 'export gurus' to market the mystic East to the world, and undoubtedly the most controversial.

Initially based in Pune, he followed no particular religion or philosophy, and outraged many across the world with his advocacy of sex as a path to enlightenment. A darling of the international media, he quickly earned himself the epithet 'sex guru'. In 1981, Rajneesh took his curious blend of Californian pop psychology and Indian mysticism to the USA, where he set up an agricultural commune in Oregon. There, his ashram's notoriety, as well as its fleet of (material and thus valueless!) Rolls-Royces grew, until raging local opposition following a bizarre, infamous food poisoning incident (designed to manipulate local elections) moved the authorities to charge Osho with immigration fraud. He was fined US$400,000 and deported.

An epic journey then began, during which Osho and his followers, in their search for a new base, were either deported from or denied entry into 21 countries. By 1987, he was back at his Pune ashram, where thousands of foreigners soon flocked for his nightly discourses and meditation sessions.

They still come from across the globe. Such is the demand for the resort's facilities that prices are continually on the rise, with luxury being redefined every day. Interestingly, despite Osho's comments on how nobody should be poor, no money generated by the resort goes into helping the disadvantaged.

In recent years the Osho institute has embraced the digital age, with its iOsho portal offering iMeditate programs, Osho radio and Osho library; subscriptions are required.

Hotel Lotus
HOTEL $$

(📞 26139701; www.hotelsuryavilla.com; Lane 5, Koregaon Park; s/d ₹1640/2230, with AC ₹2230/2820; ✻ 🛜) Hotel Lotus is good value for the quiet, Koregaon Park location, and though the rooms are not that spacious, they are light and airy, most with balconies. There's no restaurant, though they offer room service and there are plenty of good eating options close by.

Samrat Hotel
HOTEL $$

(📞 26137964; thesamrathotel@vsnl.net; 17 Wilson Garden; s/d from ₹2110/2530, with AC from ₹2930/3390; ✻ 🛜) It's not quite as grand as its fancy lobby would indicate, but with a central location just a few steps from the train station and spacious, well-maintained rooms, the Samrat represents decent value. Complimentary airport pick-up.

Hotel Srimaan
HOTEL $$

(📞 26136565; srimaan@vsnl.com; 361/5 Bund Garden Rd; s/d ₹3120/3600; ✻ @ 🛜) With a good location opposite the Pune Central shopping mall, free wi-fi and a well-regarded Italian restaurant, this business hotel is a solid choice. Rooms are compact but quite luxurious for the price.

Osho Meditation Resort Guesthouse
GUESTHOUSE $$$

(📞 66019900; www.osho.com; Koregaon Park; s/d ₹6930/7510; ✻ 🛜) This uberchic place will only allow you in if you come to meditate at the Osho International Meditation Resort. The rooms and common spaces are an exercise in modern minimalist aesthetics with several ultra-luxe features – including purified fresh air supplied in all rooms!

✖ Eating

Kayani Bakery
BAKERY $

(6 East St; cakes & biscuits per kg from ₹200; ⊙7.30am-1pm & 3.30-8pm) A Raj-era institution that seems to be stuck in a time warp, where those in the know queue (in the loose sense of the word) for Shrewsbury biscuits (₹320 per kilogram), bread, Madeira (₹100) and sponge cakes (₹40).

Juice World
CAFE $

(2436/B East St; snacks ₹60-80; ⊙11am-11.30pm) This casual cafe with outdoor seating serves wholesome snacks such as *pav bhaji* (spiced vegetables and bread) and delicious fresh fruit juices and shakes. On a hot day it's impossible to walk past its fruit displays and not drop in for a drink.

Coffee House
CAFE $

(2A Moledina Rd; mains ₹60-140; ⊙8am-11.30pm) A calm and clean, coffee-coloured, almost art deco retreat with a huge menu and satisfying filter coffee. Dishes include dosas and other excellent South Indian menu items, plus North Indian curries and Chinese.

German Bakery
BAKERY $$

(North Main Rd; cakes ₹40-170, mains ₹160-190; ⊙6.30am-11.30pm; 🛜) A Pune institution famous for its traveller-geared grub, including omelettes, breakfasts, Greek salad, cappuccinos and lots of sweet treats (try the mango cheesecake). Located on a very busy traffic-plagued corner, it's running again after the fatal terrorist attack here in 2010.

Prem's
MULTICUISINE $$

(North Main Rd, Koregaon Park; mains ₹140-340; ⊙8am-11.30pm; 🛜) In a quiet, tree-canopied courtyard, Prem's is perfect for a lazy, beery daytime drinking session, with lots of imported beers to try, perhaps with one of its famous sizzlers. The morning after? Well, Prem's is the logical choice again, with the city's best breakfast selection: eggs Benedict with smoked salmon (₹160), cereals, pancakes and detox shots.

Mayur
INDIAN $$

(www.mayurthali.com; 2434 East St; dishes/thalis from ₹60/300; ⊙8am-11pm) Famous throughout Pune for its sweet, spicy and unlimited Gujarati-style thalis, which are lovingly prepared, as well as good lassis and juices!

★ Malaka Spice
ASIAN FUSION $$$

(www.malakaspice.com; Lane 5, Koregaon Park, North Main Rd; mains ₹280-730; ⊙11.30am-11.30pm; 🛜) Mouth-watering Southeast Asian fare that's been given a creative tweak or two by star chefs. Choose from the classic or street menu, both strong on seafood, vegetarian, chicken, duck and mutton offerings. Eat alfresco or in the air-con room (which doubles as an art gallery).

★ Dario's
ITALIAN $$$

(www.darios.in; Hotel Sunderban, 19 Koregaon Park; mains ₹310-380; ⊙11.30am-3pm & 7-11pm; 🛜) At the rear of Hotel Sunderban, this Italian place is perhaps the most elegant dining experience in Pune, with fine art in the stunning air-con dining room and a gorgeous courtyard for alfresco meals. Expensive but worth a splurge with homemade pasta, milanesas, fish and fine salads: try a Bosco (₹450) with milanesas and mushrooms.

MAHARASHTRA PUNE

The Place: Touche the Sizzler
MULTICUISINE **$$$**

(7 Moledina Rd; mains ₹330-480; ⊙11.30am-3.30pm & 7-10.45pm) The perfect old-school eating option where the menu evokes the days of the Raj, Queen Victoria and all that old chap: shrimp cocktails, Russian salads, steak cordon bleu and a few options from the tandoor. The smoking sizzlers (veg, seafood, beef, chicken) can't be beat.

 Drinking & Entertainment

1000 Oaks
NIGHTCLUB

(2417 East St; ⊙7pm-late) An old favourite with a cosy pub-style bar, a compact dance floor and a charming terrace for those who prefer it quieter. Pitchers (₹700 to ₹750) of Long Island iced tea and sangria are very popular. There's live music on Sunday.

Hoppipola – All Day Bar & Bonhomie
BAR

(ITI Park, Aundh; ⊙noon-11pm Tue-Sun, 5-11pm Mon; 🐾) Hip new bar in the university zone that attracts a young arty, studenty crowd with its zany decor, chillout garden, wine and cocktail selection and good bar food: try the rasta chicken. There's a relaxed vibe dur-ing the week, but it gets rammed on weekends. It's around 6km west of the centre.

★ **Bluefrog**
NIGHTCLUB, LIVE MUSIC

(☑020-40054001; www.bluefrog.co.in; Ishan-ya Mall, off Airport Rd, Yerwada; ⊙6pm-12.30am Tue-Fri, 1pm Sat & Sun) This new Pune branch of Mumbai's famous Bluefrog has really shaken up the city's nightlife, with exciting electronic DJs, live music from all over the world, theatre and stand-up comedy, de-pending on the night. The seriously stylish venue has hip semicircular seating pods, a sweeping bar, full range of cocktails (₹450) and good grub (₹300 to ₹700)

Inox
CINEMA

(www.inoxmovies.com; Bund Garden Rd) A multi-plex where you can take in the latest block-buster from Hollywood or Mumbai.

 Shopping

Bombay Store
SOUVENIRS

(www.thebombaystore.com; 322 MG Rd; ⊙10.30am-8.30pm Mon-Sat) Stocks quality handicrafts, souvenirs, quirky bags, hip ac-cessories and contemporary furnishings.

Ishanya Mall
MALL

(www.ishanya.com; off Airport Rd, Yerwada; ⊙11am-10pm) Huge new mall that's richly endowed with interior design and fashion stores. Shop till you drop then head to the food court (or Bluefrog, which is also located here).

Fabindia
CLOTHING

(www.fabindia.com; Sakar 10, Sassoon Rd; ⊙10am-8pm) For Indian saris, silks and cottons, as well as linen shirts for men and diverse ac-cessories including bags and jewellery.

Crossword
BOOKS

(www.crossword.in; 1st fl, Sohrab Hall, Ladkatwadi Rd; ⊙10.30am-9pm) An excellent collection of fiction, nonfiction and magazines. There's a smaller branch on East St.

Pune Central
MALL

(Bund Garden Rd, Koregaon Park; ⊙10am-10pm) This centrally located mall is full of global labels and premium Indian tags.

❶ Information

You'll find several internet cafes along Pune's main thoroughfares and there are dozens of ATMs spread through the city and at the train station.

Main Post Office (Sadhu Vaswani Path; ⊙10am-6pm Mon-Sat)

MTDC Tourist Office (☑26126867; I Block, Central Bldg, Dr Annie Besant Rd; ⊙10am-

---

MAHABALESHWAR

Once a summer capital under the Brit-ish, today the hill station of Mahabalesh-war (1327m) is an over-developed mess, tainted by an ugly building boom and traffic chaos as tourists attempt a mad dash to tick off its viewpoints. There's no massive reason to visit, though the town can be used as a base to visit the impressive Pratapgad fort (p116) an hour or so away. Don't even consider dropping by during the monsoon when the whole town virtually shuts down (and a staggering 6m of rain falls).

From Mahabaleshwar bus stand, state buses leave roughly hourly for Pune (semideluxe ₹240, 3 ½ hours). Luxury buses can be booked via agents in the bazaar for Goa (₹1300 to ₹1780, 12 hours, some with a changeover in Surur); Mumbai (₹525 to ₹800, 7½ hours) and Pune (₹630 to ₹790, 3½ hours).

For the Pratapgad fort, a state bus (₹130 return, one hour, 9.15am) does a daily round-trip, with a waiting time of around one hour; taxi drivers charge a fixed ₹1000 return.

MAJOR TRAINS FROM PUNE

DESTINATION	TRAIN NO & NAME	FARE (₹)	DURATION (HR)	DEPARTURE
Bengaluru	16529 Udyan Express	455/1765	21	11.45am
Chennai	12163 Chennai Express	515/1950	19½	12.10am
Delhi	11077 Jhelum Express	615/2400	27½	5.20pm
Hyderabad	17031 Hyderabad Express	330/1280	13½	4.35pm
Mumbai CST	12124 Deccan Queen	105/370	3½	7.15am

Express fares are sleeper/2AC; Deccan Queen fares are 2nd class/chair

5.30pm Mon-Sat, closed 2nd & 4th Sat) Buried in a government complex south of the train station. There's also an MTDC desk (◷10am-5.30pm Mon-Sat) at the train station.

Shivam Computers (Koregaon Park; per hour ₹20; ◷10am-10pm) Quick connections and helpful staff.

Thomas Cook (☑66007903; 2418 G Thimmaya Rd; ◷9.30am-6pm Mon-Sat) Cashes travellers cheques and exchanges foreign currency.

Yatra.com (☑020-65006748; www.yatra.com; Koregaon Park Rd; ◷10am-8pm Mon-Sat) The city office of the internet ticketing company.

ℹ Getting There & Away

AIR

Airlines listed below fly daily from Pune to Mumbai (from ₹5400, 45 minutes), Delhi (from ₹5800, two hours), Jaipur (from ₹3800, 1½ hours), Bengaluru (from ₹2100, 1½ hours), Nagpur (from ₹2400, 1½ hours), Goa (from ₹2500, one hour) and Chennai (from ₹3700, 1½ hours).

Air India (☑26052147; www.airindia.in; 39 Dr B Ambedkar Rd)

GoAir (☑9223222111; www.goair.in)

IndiGo (☑9910383838; www.goindigo.in)

Jet Airways (☑022-39893333; www.jetairways.com; 243 Century Arcade, Narangi Baug Rd)

BUS

Buses leave the **Pune train station stand** (☑020-26126218) for Mumbai, Goa, Belgaum, Kolhapur (₹350, five hours, hourly), Mahabaleshwar and Lonavla (₹170, 2½ hours, hourly). Deluxe buses shuttle from here to Dadar (Mumbai; ₹330, 3½ hours) every hour. From the **Shivaji Nagar bus stand** (☑020-25536970) buses go to Aurangabad (from ₹270, five to six hours, every 45 minutes), Ahmedabad and Nasik, while buses for Sinhagad, Bengaluru and Mangalore leave from the **Swargate bus stand** (☑020-24441591).

Private buses head to Panaji in Goa (ordinary from ₹300, AC sleeper ₹700 to ₹1200, 11 hours), Nasik (semideluxe/deluxe ₹270/550, 5½

hours) and Aurangabad (₹250/550, 5½ hours). Pune has three bus stands.

TAXI

Shared taxis (up to four passengers) link Pune with Mumbai airport around the clock. They leave from the **taxi stand** (☑02026121090) in front of Pune train station (₹475 per seat, 2½ hours). To rent a car and driver try **Simran Travels** (☑26153222; North Main Rd, Koregaon Park).

TRAIN

Pune train station (sometimes called Pune Junction) is in the heart of the city, on HH Prince Aga Khan Rd. There are very regular, roughly hourly, services to Mumbai, and good links to cities including Delhi, Chennai and Hyderabad.

ℹ Getting Around

The modern airport is 8km northeast of the city. From the centre of town, an autorickshaw costs about ₹120 and a taxi ₹280.

Autorickshaws can be found everywhere; a trip from the train station to Koregaon Park costs about ₹40 (more at night).

Around Pune

Sinhagad

The ruined **Sinhagad** (Lion Fort; ◷dawn-dusk) **FREE**, situated about 24km southwest of Pune, was wrested by Maratha leader Shivaji from the Bijapur kings in 1670. In the epic battle (where he lost his son Sambhaji, Shivaji is said to have used monitor lizards yoked with ropes to scale the fort's craggy walls. Today, it's in a poor state, but worth visiting for the sweeping views and opportunity to hike in the hills. From Sinhagad village, shared 4WDs (₹50) can cart you 10km to the base of the summit. Bus 50 runs frequently to Sinhagad village from Swargate (₹27, 45 minutes).

PRATAPGAD FORT

The spectacular **Pratapgad Fort** (Indian/foreigner ₹10/100; ⊙9am-dusk), built by Shivaji in 1656 (and still owned by his descendents), straddles a high mountain ridge 24km northwest of the town of Mahabaleshwar. In 1659, Shivaji agreed to meet Bijapuri general Afzal Khan here, in an attempt to end a stalemate. Despite a no-arms agreement, Shivaji, upon greeting Khan, disembowelled his enemy with a set of iron *baghnakh* (tiger's claws). Khan's tomb marks the site of this painful encounter at the base of the fort. Pratapgad is reached by a 500-step climb that affords brilliant views. For ₹200 a guide will take you to 20 points of interest, taking nearly two hours.

From the bus stand in Mahabaleshwar, 120km south of Pune, a state bus (₹130 return, one hour, 9.15am) does a daily shuttle to the fort, with a waiting time of around one hour. Taxi drivers in Mahabaleshwar charge a fixed ₹1000 return.

Shivneri

Situated 90km northwest of Pune, above the village of Junnar, **Shivneri Fort** (⊙dawn-dusk) **FREE** holds the distinction of being the birthplace of Shivaji. Within the ramparts of this ruined fort are the old royal stables, a mosque dating back to the Mughal era and several rock-cut reservoirs. The most important structure is Shivkunj, the pavilion in which Shivaji was born.

About 4km from Shivneri, on the other side of Junnar, is an interesting group of Hinayana Buddhist caves called **Lenyadri** (Indian/foreigner ₹5/100; ⊙dawn-dusk). Of the 30-odd caves, cave 7 is the most impressive, and interestingly houses an image of the Hindu god Ganesh.

Hourly buses (₹85, two hours) connect Pune's Shivaji Nagar terminus with Junnar. A cab from Pune is about ₹2600.

Kolhapur

📞 0231 / POP 561,300 / ELEV 550M

A little-visited city, Kolhapur is the perfect place to get intimate with the flamboyant side of India. Only a few hours from Goa, this historic settlement boasts an intensely fascinating temple complex. In August, Kolhapur is at its vibrant best, when **Naag Panchami** (⊙Jul/Aug), a snake-worshipping festival, is held in tandem with one at Pune. Gastronomes take note: the town is also the birthplace of the famed, spicy Kolhapuri cuisine, especially chicken and mutton dishes.

The old town around the Mahalaxmi Temple is 3km southwest of the bus and train stations, while the 'new' palace is a similar distance to the north. Rankala Lake, a popular spot for evening strolls, is 5km southwest of the stations.

⊙ Sights

The atmospheric old town quarter around the Mahalaxmi Temple and Old Palace has a huge (traffic-free) plaza and is accessed by a monumental gateway.

★ **Mahalaxmi Temple**   HINDU TEMPLE

(⊙5am-10.30pm) One of Maharashtra's most important and vibrant places of worship, the Mahalaxmi Temple is dedicated to Amba Bai (Mother Goddess). The temple's origins date back to AD 10, but much of the present structure is from the 18th century. It draws an unceasing tide of humanity, as pilgrims press to enter the holy inner sanctuary and bands of musicians and worshippers chant devotions. Non-Hindus are welcome and it's a fantastic place for people-watching.

★ **Shree Chhatrapati Shahu Museum**   MUSEUM

(Indian/foreigner incl coffee ₹20/75; ⊙9.30am-5.30pm) 'Bizarre' takes on a whole new meaning at this 'new' palace, an Indo-Saracenic behemoth designed by British architect 'Mad' Charles Mant for the Kolhapur kings in 1884. The madcap museum features countless trophies from the kings' trigger-happy jungle safaris, including walking sticks made from leopard vertebrae and ashtrays fashioned out of tiger skulls and rhino feet. The armoury houses enough weapons to stage a mini-coup. The horror-house effect is brought full circle by the taxidermy section. Don't miss the highly ornate Durbar Hall, where the rulers held court sessions, and dotted around the palace you'll find dozens of portraits of the portly maharajas to admire. Photography is prohibited inside. There's a little cafe by the entrance for snacks (and where foreigners may claim their complimentary coffee). A rickshaw from the train station will cost ₹35.

Old Palace
HISTORIC BUILDING

In the heart of the old town this palace was once the ruling Chatrapati's main residence, and is still occupied by some in the family. You can enter the building's front courtyard but there's little to see today except a temple dedicated to the deity Bhavani Mata.

Motibag Thalim
COURTYARD

Kolhapur is famed for the calibre of its Kushti wrestlers, and at the Motibag Thalim, young athletes train in an earthen pit. The *akhara* (training ground) is reached through a low doorway and passage beside the entrance to Bhavani Mandap (ask for directions). You are free to walk in and watch, as long as you don't mind the sight of sweaty, semi-naked men and the stench of urine emanating from the loos.

Kasbagh Maidan
SPORTS ARENA

Professional wrestling bouts are held between June and December in this red-earth arena a short walk south of Motibag Thalim.

🛏 Sleeping & Eating

Hotel Pavillion
HOTEL $

(☎ 2652751; www.hotelpavillion.co.in; 392 Assembly Rd; s/d incl breakfast ₹1460/1730, with AC from ₹1920/2240; ✸ @) Located at the far end of a leafy park-cum-office-area, this hotel guarantees a peaceful stay. Its large, well-equipped rooms are perhaps a little dated but many have windows that open out to delightful views of seasonal blossoms.

Hotel Panchshil
HOTEL $$

(☎ 2537517; www.hotelpanchshilkolhapur.com; 517 A2 Shivaji Park; s/d ₹3400/3740; ✸ 🕾) The age-ing lobby and location on a busy road are a little off-putting but the rooms have been given the full makeover treatment and are very inviting, comfortable and stylish. The Little Italy restaurant downstairs is another excellent reason to check in.

Hotel K Tree
HOTEL $$

(☎ 0231-2526990; www.hotelktree.com; 65 E, Shivaji Park; s/d incl breakfast from ₹3230/3880; ✸ 🕾) With high service standards and very inviting modish rooms, this new hotel is fine value. It's located on a quiet side street, so there's little traffic noise and the multicusine restaurant has an extensive menu.

Surabhi
INDIAN $

(Hotel Sahyadri Bldg; mains ₹70-100; ⊙ 10am-10pm) A great place to savour Kolhapur's legendary snacks such as spicy *misal* (puffed rice tossed with fried rounds of dough, lentils, onions, herbs and chutneys), thalis and lassi. It's close to the bustling bus stand.

⭐ Little Italy
ITALIAN $$

(☎ 0231-2537133; www.littleitaly.in; 517 A2 Shivaji Park; mains ₹250-450) If you've been clocking up some hard yards on India's roads, this authentic, professionally run restaurant is just the place to head to sustain you for the next trip. All the flavours are to savour, with a delicious, veg-only menu of antipasta, thin-crust pizzas (from a wood-fired oven), *al dente* pasta and a great wine list (by the glass available).

ℹ Information

Axis Bank ATM Near the Mahalaxmi Temple.

Internet Zone (Kedar Complex, Station Rd; per hour ₹20; ⊙ 8am-11pm)

MTDC Tourist Office (☎ 2652935; Assembly Rd; ⊙ 10am-5.30pm Mon-Sat) Located opposite the Collector's Office.

State Bank of India (Udyamnagar; ⊙ 10am-2pm Mon-Sat) A short autorickshaw ride southwest of the train station near Hutatma Park. Handles foreign exchange and has an ATM.

ℹ Getting There & Around

From the bus stand, services head regularly to Pune (semideluxe/deluxe ₹280/500, five hours), Ratnagiri (ordinary/semideluxe ₹120/154, four hours) and ordinary-only buses to Malvan (₹170, five hours). Most private bus agents are on the western side of the square at Mahalaxmi Chambers, across from the bus stand. There are over a dozen daily dozen services to Panaji (semideluxe ₹400, AC sleeper ₹800 to ₹1050, 5½ hours). Overnight AC services head to Mumbai (seat ₹450, sleeper ₹600 to ₹1250, nine hours).

The train station, known as Chattrapati Shahu Maharaj Terminus, is 10 minutes' walk west of the bus stand. Three daily expresses, including the 10.50pm Sahyadri Express, go to Mumbai (sleeper/2AC ₹305/1165, 13 hours) via Pune (₹210/805, eight hours). The Rani Chennama Express makes the long voyage to Bengaluru (sleeper/2AC ₹4000/1555, 17½ hours, 2.20pm). There are no direct trains to Goa.

Autorickshaws are abundant in Kolhapur and many drivers carry conversion charts to calculate fares from the outdated meters.

Kolhapur airport was not operational at the time of research.

Goa

⏼ 0832 / POP 1.46 MILLION

Why Go?

Goa is like no other state in India. It could be the Portuguese colonial influence, the endless beaches, the glorious whitewashed churches or the relaxed culture of *susegad* – a uniquely Goan term that translates as 'laid-backness' and is evident in all aspects of daily life and in the Goan people themselves.

But Goa is far more than its old-school reputation as a hippie haven or its contemporary status as a beach getaway. Goa is as naturally and culturally rich as it is compact; you can go birdwatching in a butterfly-filled forest, marvel at centuries-old cathedrals, trek out to milky waterfalls and aromatic spice farms or meander the capital's charming alleyways. Add a dash of Portuguese-influenced food and architecture, infuse with a colourful blend of religious traditions, pepper with parties and beach shacks, and you've got a recipe that makes Goa easy to enjoy and extremely hard to leave.

Best Places to Eat

➡ Ruta's World Cafe (p151)

➡ Go With the Flow (p138)

➡ Black Sheep Bistro (p126)

➡ Bomra's (p134)

➡ Ourem 88 (p161)

Best Beaches

➡ Palolem (p157)

➡ Mandrem (p147)

➡ Cola & Khancola (p156)

➡ Anjuna (p139)

➡ Arambol (p148)

When to Go

Goa (Panaji)

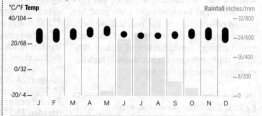

°C/°F Temp — 40/104, 20/68, 0/32, -20/-4 — J F M A M J J A S O N D

Rainfall inches/mm — 32/800, 24/600, 16/400, 8/200, 0

Sep–Nov
Post-monsoon, some shacks are up but crowds are still down

Dec–Feb Festivals, Christmas and great weather; peak prices and crowds from mid-Dec to early Jan.

Mar–Apr
Carnival and Easter celebrations as the season winds down.

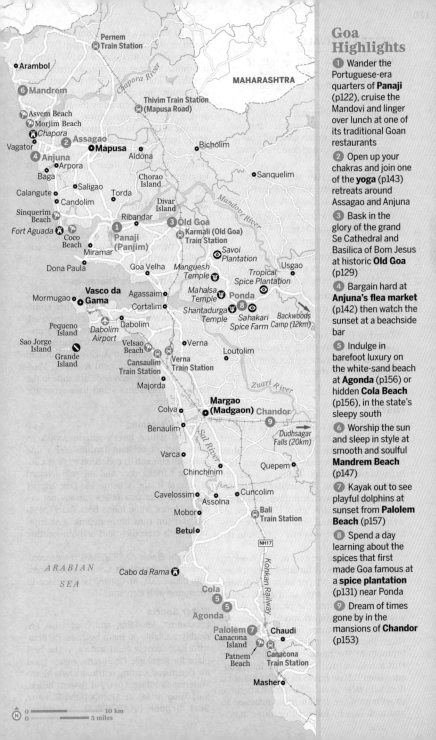

Goa Highlights

1 Wander the Portuguese-era quarters of **Panaji** (p122), cruise the Mandovi and linger over lunch at one of its traditional Goan restaurants

2 Open up your chakras and join one of the **yoga** (p143) retreats around Assagao and Anjuna

3 Bask in the glory of the grand Se Cathedral and Basilica of Bom Jesus at historic **Old Goa** (p129)

4 Bargain hard at **Anjuna's flea market** (p142) then watch the sunset at a beachside bar

5 Indulge in barefoot luxury on the white-sand beach at **Agonda** (p156) or hidden **Cola Beach** (p156), in the state's sleepy south

6 Worship the sun and sleep in style at smooth and soulful **Mandrem Beach** (p147)

7 Kayak out to see playful dolphins at sunset from **Palolem Beach** (p157)

8 Spend a day learning about the spices that first made Goa famous at a **spice plantation** (p131) near Ponda

9 Dream of times gone by in the mansions of **Chandor** (p153)

GOA ACTIVITIES

Feast of the Three Kings (p153; 6 Jan, Chandor & Reis Magos) Boys re-enact the story of the three kings bearing gifts for Christ.

Shigmotsav (Shigmo) of Holi (Feb/Mar; statewide) Goa's version of the Hindu festival Holi sees coloured powders thrown about and parades in most towns.

Sabado Gordo (Feb/Mar; Panaji) A procession of floats and street parties on the Saturday before Lent.

Carnival (p123; Mar; statewide) A four-day festival kicking off Lent; the party's particularly jubilant in Panaji.

Fama de Menino Jesus (2nd Mon in Oct; Colva) Statue of the baby Jesus is paraded through the streets of Colva.

Feast of St Francis Xavier (p129; 3 Dec; Old Goa) A 10-day celebration of Goa's patron saint

Feast of Our Lady of the Immaculate Conception (p123; 8 Dec; Margao, Panaji) Fairs and concerts around Panaji's famous church.

History

Goa went through a dizzying array of rulers from Ashoka's Mauryan empire in the 3rd century BC to the long-ruling Kadambas. Subsequent conflict saw the Muslim Delhi sultanate and then Bahmani sultanate fighting the Hindu Vijayanagar empire for control; these were violent times, and in addition to many deaths, lots of Hindu temples were razed. The Adil Shahs of Bijapur created the capital we now call Old Goa in the 15th century.

The Portuguese arrived in 1510, seeking control of the region's lucrative spice routes. They defeated the Bijapur kings and steadily pushed their power from their grand capital at Old Goa out into the provinces. Portuguese rule and religion spread throughout the state – sometimes by force – and the Goan Inquisition brought repression and brutality in the name of Christianity. The Portuguese resisted India's 1947 Independence from Britain but in 1961, after almost a decade in talks to encourage the Portuguese to withdraw, the Indian Army marched in and took Goa by force within three days –

virtually without a fight – ending almost five centuries of Portuguese occupation.

Today Goa enjoys one of India's highest per-capita incomes and comparatively high health and literacy rates, with tourism, iron-ore mining (though this is mired in controversy and was suspended by the High Court during 2013–14), agriculture and fishing forming the basis of its economy. The legacy of the Portuguese can still be found almost everywhere, in the state's scores of old mansions, its cuisine, churches and even in its language.

Activities

In season Goa has a whole host of options for yoga and alternative therapies, water sports, paragliding, cooking classes and wildlife-watching.

Yoga & Alternative Therapies

Every imaginable form of yoga, meditation, reiki, ayurvedic massage and other spiritually orientated health regime is practised, taught and relished in Goa, though they usually operate only in the winter season (October or November to April). Palolem and Patnem, in the south, and Arambol, Mandrem, Anjuna, Assagao and Calangute in the north, all offer courses and have reputable yoga retreats.

Wildlife-Watching

Goa is a nature lover's paradise, with an abundance of brilliant birdlife and a fine (but well concealed) collection of fauna, including barking deer and the odd leopard in several inland sanctuaries. Day Tripper (p135) in Calangute offers various nature-related tours, while John's Boat Tours (p133) in Candolim runs birdwatching boat trips, along with crocodile- and dolphin-spotting rides.

Jungle Book (☑ 9822121431; www.goaeco-tourism.com; Bazar Wada, Colem; elephant rides/wash from ₹700), in Colem, is the place to commune with elephants.

Water Sports

Parasailing, jet-skiing and boat trips are readily available on main beaches. Palolem, with its relatively calm waters, is the best place for kayaking. Goa's tame surf is good for beginners: surfing outfits include Vaayu Waterman's Village (p147) at Aswem Beach, Surf Wala (p148) at Arambol and **Banana Surf School** (☑ 7057998120; www.goasurf.

com; Utorda Beach; lessons €45-250; ⊘ 7.30am-12.30pm Oct-Mar) at Utorda.

Goa has four scuba diving outfits where you can gain PADI certification and go on dive trips to Grande Island and further afield. Goa Aquatics (p135), Barracuda Diving (p135) and Goa Diving (☑ 9049442647; www.goadiving.com; courses from ₹11,000, one-/two-tank dive ₹3000/5000) are recommended.

ⓘ Information

The Goa Tourism Development Corporation (p128) provides maps and information, operates hotels throughout the state and runs a host of one-day and multiday tours.

ⓘ Getting There & Away

AIR

Goa's only airport, Dabolim, is served directly by domestic flights, a handful of international flights from the Middle East; and seasonal package-holiday charters, mostly from Russia, Europe and Britain.

Unless you're on a charter you'll generally have to fly in to a major Indian city and change to a domestic flight with Jet Airways, Air India, SpiceJet or IndiGo.

BUS

Plenty of long-distance interstate buses – both state-run and private – operate to and from Panaji, Margao, Mapusa and Chaudi, near Palolem. Fares for private operators are only slightly higher than for Kadamba government buses, and they fluctuate throughout the year. Long-distance buses may be standard, air-conditioned (AC), Volvo (the most comfortable seater buses) and sleeper. For fares, timetables and online booking see www.goakadamba.com.

TRAIN

The **Konkan Railway**, the main train line running through Goa, connects Mumbai and Mangalore, though the rail line continues all the way south to Trivandrum. The biggest station in Goa is Margao's Madgaon station. See the Margao section (p152) for useful trains. Other smaller stations on the line include Pernem for Arambol, Thivim for Mapusa and the northern beaches, Karmali (Old Goa) for Panaji, and Canacona for Palolem.

ⓘ Getting Around

TO/FROM THE AIRPORT

Dabolim's prepaid taxi counter in the arrivals hall makes arriving easy; buy your ticket here and you'll be ushered to a cab. Real budgeteers without much luggage can try walking out to the main road and waving down one of the frequent buses heading east from Vasco da Gama to Margao and catch onward transport from there.

BUS

Goa's extensive network of local buses run frequently and fares range from ₹5 to ₹40. Travelling between north, central and south Goa you'll need to change buses at either Panaji or Margao.

CAR & MOTORCYCLE

It's easy in Goa to organise a private car with a driver for long-distance day trips. Expect to pay from ₹2000 for a full day out on the road (usually defined as eight hours and 80km). It's also possible, if you have the nerves and the need to feel independent, to procure a self-drive car. A

SLEEPING PRICES IN GOA

Accommodation prices in Goa vary considerably depending on the season and demand. High-season prices run from November to late February, but prices climb higher to a peak rate during the crowded Christmas and New Year period (around 22 December to 3 January). Mid-season is October and March to April, and low season is the monsoon (May to September). These seasonal dates can vary a little depending on the monsoon and the granting of shack licences, which are renewed every couple of years. As well as hotels, seasonal beach huts and guesthouses, throughout Goa's coastal belt are private rooms and whole houses to let, generally for stays of a week or more.

All accommodation rates listed are for the high season – but not the peak Christmas period, when you'll almost certainly have to book ahead anyway. Always call ahead for rates and ask about discounts. Most accommodation places have an 11am or noon checkout. To compare or book beach huts in South Goa, check out www.beachhutbooking.com.

Accommodation price ranges used in this chapter are as follows:

$ below ₹1200

$$ ₹1200 to ₹5000

$$$ above ₹5000

small Maruti will cost from ₹900 to ₹1200 per day and a large jeep around ₹2000, excluding petrol and usually with a kilometre limit. Your best bet for rental is online at sites such as www.goa2u.com and www.mygoatour.com.

You'll rarely go far on a Goan road without seeing a tourist whizzing by on a scooter or motorbike, and renting one is a breeze. You'll likely pay from ₹200 to ₹300 per day for a scooter, ₹400 for a smaller Yamaha motorbike, and ₹500 for a Royal Enfield Bullet. These prices can drop considerably if you're renting for more than a few days or if it's an off-peak period – it's all supply and demand, so bargain if there are lots of machines around.

Bear in mind that Goan roads – while better than many Indian roads – can be tricky, filled with human, bovine, canine, feline, mechanical and avian obstacles, as well as potholes, speed-breakers and hairpin bends. Take it slowly, avoid riding at night (when black cows and drunk tourists can prove dangerous), don't attempt a north–south day trip on a 50cc scooter, and ask for a helmet – in theory, compulsory, though the law is still routinely ignored by Goans and tourists alike.

TAXI & AUTORICKSHAW

Taxis are widely available for town-hopping, but the local union cartel means prices are high, especially at night. A new initiative by Goa Tourism is the **Women Taxi Service** (☎ 0832-2437437), with female drivers, phone-only bookings and only females, couples or families accepted as passengers. The vehicles are fitted with GPS monitoring, martial-arts trained drivers and accurate meters. Fares can even by paid with a credit card.

Unlike elsewhere in India, autorickshaws are not much cheaper than taxis and are not as common, but they're still good for short trips if you can find one. Motorcycle taxis, known as 'pilots', are also a licensed form of taxi in Goa, identified by a yellow front mudguard. They're only really common around major taxi stands and beach resorts and cost half the price of a taxi.

DRUGS

Acid, ecstasy, cocaine, charas (hashish), marijuana and most other forms of drugs are illegal in India (though still available in Goa), and purchasing or carrying drugs is fraught with danger. Goa's Fort Aguada jail is filled with prisoners, including some foreigners, serving lengthy sentences for drug offences. Being caught in possession of even a small quantity of illegal substances can mean a 10-year stretch.

CENTRAL GOA

Panaji (Panjim)

POP 115,000

One of India's most relaxed state capitals, Panaji (Panjim) overlooks the mouth of the broad Mandovi River, where party boats and floating casinos cast neon reflections in the night. A glorious whitewashed church lords over the city centre, a broad tree-lined boulevard skirts the river and grand colonial-era buildings rub shoulders with arty boutiques, old-school bookshops and backstreet bars.

But it's the tangle of narrow streets in the old quarter of Fontainhas that really steal the show. Nowhere is the Portuguese influence felt more strongly than here, where the late afternoon sun lights up yellow houses with purple doors, and around each corner you'll find crumbling ochre-coloured mansions with wrought-iron balconies, terracotta-tiled roofs and oyster-shell windows. Panjim is a place for walking, enjoying the peace of the afternoon siesta, eating well and meeting real Goans. A day or two in the capital really is an essential part of your Goan experience.

⊙ Sights & Activities

One of the great pleasures of Panaji is long, leisurely strolls through the sleepy Portuguese-era districts of Sao Tomé, Fontainhas and Altinho. Riverside Campal Gardens, west of the centre, and Miramar Beach, 2km further on, are also popular spots.

★ **Church of Our Lady of the Immaculate Conception** CHURCH
(cnr Emilio Gracia & Jose Falcao Rds; ⊙ 10am-12.30pm & 3-5.30pm Mon-Sat, 11am-12.30pm & 3.30-5pm Sun, English Mass 8am) Panaji's spiritual, as well as geographical, centre is this elevated, pearly white church, built in 1619 over an older, smaller 1540 chapel and stacked like a fancy white wedding cake. When Panaji was little more than a sleepy fishing village, this church was the first port of call for sailors from Lisbon, who would give thanks for a safe crossing, before continuing to Ela (Old Goa) further east up the river. The church is beautifully illuminated at night.

Goa State Museum MUSEUM
(☎ 0832-2438006; www.goamusem.gov.in; EDC Complex, Patto; ⊙ 9.30am-5.30pm Mon-Sat)

FREE This spacious museum east of town houses an eclectic, if not extensive, collection of items tracing aspects of Goan history. As well as some beautiful Hindu and Jain sculptures and bronzes, there are nice examples of Portuguese-era furniture, coins, an intricately carved chariot and a pair of quirky antique rotary lottery machines.

Goa State Central Library   LIBRARY
(Sanskruti Bhavan, Patto; ⊙9am-7.30pm Mon-Fri, 9.30am-5.45pm Sat & Sun) **FREE** Panaji's ultra-modern new state library, near the state museum, has six floors of reading material, a bookshop and gallery. The 2nd floor features a children's book section and internet browsing (free, but technically only for academic research). The 4th floor has Goan history books and the 6th a large collection of Portuguese books.

Houses of Goa Museum   MUSEUM
(☑0832-2410711; www.archgoa.org; near Nisha's Play School, Torda; adult/child ₹100/25; ⊙10am-7.30pm Tue-Sun) This multilevel museum was created by a well-known local architect, Gerard da Cunha, to illuminate the history of Goan architecture. Interesting displays on building practices and European and local design will change the way you see those old Goan homes. The triangular building is an architectural oddity in itself, and the museum traces Goan architectural traditions, building materials and styles in an indepth but accessible style. From Panaji, a taxi or rickshaw will cost you about ₹400 one-way.

☞ Tours

Goa Tourism and several private companies offer cruises on the Mandovi River from Santa Monica Jetty. With bars and DJs playing loud music, these can get rowdy on weekends but are an entertaining perspective on the capital.

Heritage walking tours (☑9823025748; per person ₹500, per person for five or more ₹250), covering the old Portuguese quarter, are conducted by experienced local guides on demand.

Mandovi River Cruises   CRUISE
(sunset cruise ₹200, dinner cruise ₹650, backwater cruise ₹900; ⊙sunset cruise 6pm, sundown cruise 7.15pm, dinner cruise 8.45pm Wed & Sat, backwater cruise 9.30am-4pm Tue & Fri) Goa Tourism operates a range of entertaining hour-long cruises along the Mandovi River aboard the *Santa Monica* or *Shantadurga*. All include

ⓘ EMERGENCIES
Dialling ☑108 will connect you to the police, fire brigade or medical services.

a live band and usually performances of Goan folk songs and dances. There are also twice-weekly, two-hour dinner cruises and a twice-weekly, all-day backwater cruise, which takes you down the Mandovi to Old Goa, stopping for lunch at a spice plantation and then heading back past Divar and Chorao Islands. All cruises depart from the Santa Monica Jetty next to the Mandovi Bridge, where you can purchase tickets.

✯ Festivals & Events

International Film Festival of India   FILM FESTIVAL
(www.iffi.nic.in; Panaji; ⊙Nov) Film screenings and Bollywood glitterati everywhere.

Feast of Our Lady of the Immaculate Conception   RELIGIOUS
(Margao, Panaji; ⊙8 Dec) Fairs and concerts are held, as is a beautiful church service at Panaji's Church of Our Lady of the Immaculate Conception.

Carnival   RELIGIOUS
(statewide; ⊙Mar) A four-day festival kicking off Lent; the party's particularly jubilant in Panaji.

⌅ Sleeping

As in the rest of Goa, prices vary in Panaji depending on supply and demand.

★Old Quarter Hostel   HOSTEL $
(☑0832-6517606; www.thehostelcrowd.com; 31st Jan Rd, Fontainhas; dm ₹450, d with AC from ₹2000; �***) Backpackers rejoice! This cool new hostel in an old Portuguese-style house in historic Fontainhas offers slick four-bed dorms with lockers and two comfortable doubles upstairs, along with a cafe, arty murals, good wi-fi and bikes. Noon checkout.

Pousada Guest House   GUESTHOUSE $
(☑9850998213, 0832-2422618; sabrinateles@yahoo.com; Luis de Menezes Rd; s/d from ₹800/1050, d with AC ₹1575; �***) The five rooms in this bright-yellow place are simple but clean and come with comfy spring-mattress beds and TV. Owner Sabrina is friendly and no-nonsense, and it's one of Panaji's better budget guesthouses.

Panaji (Panjim)

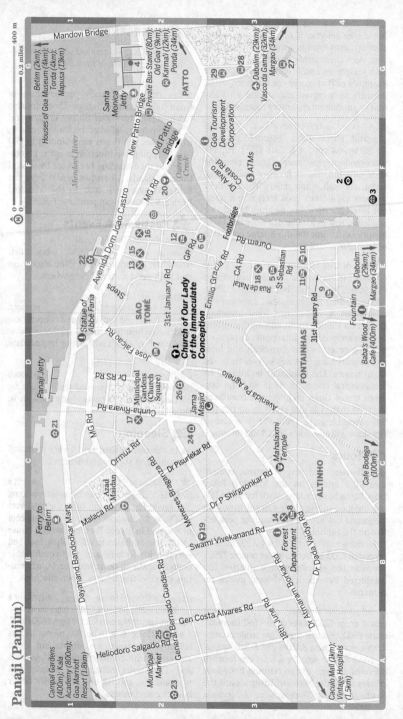

Campal Gardens (400m); Kala Academy (800m); Goa Marriott Resort (1.8km)

Ferry to Betim

Panaji Jetty

Mandovi Bridge

Betim (2km); Houses of Goa Museum (4km); Torda (4km); Mapusa (13km)

Santa Monica Jetty

New Patto Bridge

Old Patto Bridge

Private Bus Stand (80m); Old Goa (9km); Karmali (12km); Ponda (34km)

PATTO

Dabolim (29km); Vasco da Gama (32km); Margao (34km)

Mandovi River

Ourem Creek

Goa Tourism Development Corporation

MG Rd

Dr Alvaro Costa Rd

ATMs

Footbridge

Ourem Rd

Statue of Abbé Faria

Steps

Avenida Dom Jcao Castro

Jose Falcao Rd

SAO TOMÉ

31st January Rd

Church of Our Lady of the Immaculate Conception

Emilio Gracia Rd

GP Rd

CA Rd

Rua de Natal

St Sebastian Rd

FONTAINHAS

31st January Rd

Fountain

Baba's Wood Cafe (400m)

Dabolim (29km); Margao (34km)

Municipal Gardens (Church Square)

DR RS Rd

Cunha-Rivara Rd

Jama Masjid

Avenida Pe Agnelo

Ormuz Rd

Dr Pisurlekar Rd

Mahalaxmi Temple

ALTINHO

Cafe Bodega (100m)

Azad Maidan

Malaca Rd

Menezes Braganza Rd

Dr P Shirgaonkar Rd

Swami Vivekanand Rd

Forest Department

Dr Dada Vaidya Rd

Dr Atmaram Borkar Rd

Dayanand Bandodkar Marg

18th June Rd

Gen Costa Alvares Rd

General Bernado Guedes Rd

Heliodoro Salgado Rd

Municipal Market

Caculo Mall (2km); Vintage Hospitals (1.5km)

400 m
0.2 miles

Panaji (Panjim)

GOA PANAJI (PANJIM)

★ **Panjim Inn** HERITAGE HOTEL **$$**
(☏ 0832-2226523, 9823025748; www.panjiminn.
com; 31st Jan Rd; s ₹3400-6000, d ₹3900-6500,
ste ₹5950; ❋ ⎙) One of the original herit-
age hotels in Fontainhas, the Panjim Inn
has been a long-standing favourite for its
character and charm, friendly owners and
helpful staff. This beautiful 19th-century
mansion has 12 charismatic rooms in
the original house, along with 12 newer
rooms with modern touches, but all have
four-poster beds, colonial-era furniture and
artworks. Buffet breakfast is included, and
the restaurant serves excellent Goan food.

Panjim Pousada GUESTHOUSE **$$**
(☏ 0832-2226523; www.panjiminn.com; 31st Jan
Rd; s ₹3400-4400, d ₹3900-4900; ❋ ⎙) In an
old Hindu mansion, the nine divine rooms
at Panjim Pousada are set off by a stunning
central courtyard, with antique furnishings
and lovely art on the walls. Various doorways and staircases lead to the rooms; those
on the upper level are the best.

Afonso Guesthouse GUESTHOUSE **$$**
(☏ 9764300165, 0832-2222359; www.afonsoguest-
house.com; St Sebastian Rd; d ₹1800-3000; ❋ ⎙)

Run by the friendly Jeanette, this pretty
Portuguese-style townhouse offers spacious,
well-kept rooms with timber ceilings. The
rooftop terrace makes for sunny breakfast-
ing (extra) with Fontainhas views. Add ₹200
for air-con. It's a simple, serene stay in the
heart of the most atmospheric part of town.
Checkout is 9am and bookings are accepted
online but not by phone.

Casa Paradiso HOTEL **$$**
(☏ 0832-3290180; www.casaparadisogoa.com;
Jose Falcao Rd; d/tr with AC ₹1911/2200; ❋) A
neat and welcoming little stay in the heart
of the city. Up a small flight of stairs, the
simple but clean rooms come with TV, hot
water and noon checkout.

Mayfair Hotel HOTEL **$$**
(☏ 0832-2223317; manishafernz@yahoo.com; Dr
Dada Vaidya Rd; s/d from ₹1105/1330, d with AC
₹1690; ❋ ⎙) The oyster-shell windows and
mosaic tiling in the lobby of this popular
corner hotel are promising but the rooms
are not quite as bright. Ask to see a few as
there are new and old wings with rooms
of varying quality, some overlooking a po-
tentially nice back garden. Friendly family

owners have been sheltering travellers for many years. Noon checkout.

Casa Nova
GUESTHOUSE $$

(☎ 9423889181; www.goaholidayaccommodation.com; Gomes Pereira Rd; ste ₹4300; ❄ 🕸) In a gorgeous Portuguese-style house (c 1831) in Fontainhas, Casa Nova comprises just one stylish, exceptionally comfy apartment, accessed via a little alley and complete with arched windows, wood-beam ceilings, and mod-cons such as a kitchenette and wi-fi.

Goa Marriott Resort
INTERNATIONAL $$$

(☎ 0832-2463333; www.marriott.com; Miramar Beach; d ₹7000-15,000; ❄ 🕸 ❄) Miramar's plush Goa Marriot Resort is the best in the Panaji area. Fve-star treatment begins in the lobby and extends to the rooms-with-a-view. The 24-hour Waterfront Terrace & Bar is a great place for a sundowner overlooking the pool, while its Simply Grills restaurant is a favourite with well-heeled Panjimites.

Eating

You'll never go hungry in Panaji, where food is enjoyed fully and frequently. A stroll down 18th June or 31st January Rds will turn up a number of cheap canteen-style options, as will a circuit of the Municipal Gardens.

★ Viva Panjim
GOAN $

(☎ 0832-2422405; 31st Jan Rd; mains ₹100-170; ⊙ 11.30am-3.30pm & 7-11pm Mon-Sat, 7-11pm Sun) Well known to tourists, this little side-street eatery, in an old Portuguese-style house

---

---

and with a few tables out on the laneway, still delivers tasty Goan classics at reasonable prices. There's a whole page devoted to pork dishes, along with tasty *xacuti* and *cafrial*-style dishes, seafood such as kingfish vindaloo and crab *xec xec,* and desserts such as *bebinca* (richly layered Goan dessert made from egg yolk and coconut).

Hotel Vihar
VEGAN $

(MG Rd; mains ₹40-100; ⊙ 7.30am-10pm) A vast menu of 'pure veg' food, great big thalis and a plethora of fresh juices make this clean, simple canteen a popular place for locals and visitors alike.

Anandashram
INDIAN, GOAN $

(31st Jan Rd; thalis ₹80-130, seafood ₹200-350; ⊙ noon-3.30pm & 7.30-10.30pm Mon-Sat) This little place is renowned locally for seafood, serving up simple but tasty fish curries, as well as veg and nonveg thalis for lunch and dinner.

Hotel Venite
GOAN $$

(31st Jan Rd; mains ₹210-260; ⊙ 9am-10.30pm) With its cute rickety balconies overhanging the cobbled street, Venite has long been among the most atmospheric of Panaji's old-school Goan restaurants. The menu is traditional, with spicy sausages, fish curry rice, pepper steak and *bebinca* featuring, but Venite is popular with tourists and prices are consequently rather inflated. It's not to be missed though.

★ Cafe Bodega
CAFE $$

(☎ 0832-2421315; Altinho; mains ₹120-320; ⊙ 10am-7pm Mon-Sat, to 4pm Sun; 🕸) It's well worth a trip up to Altinho Hill for this serene cafe-gallery in a lavender-and-white Portuguese-style mansion in the grounds of Sunaparanta Centre for the Arts. Enjoy good coffee, juices and fresh-baked cakes around the inner courtyard or lunch on super pizzas and sandwiches.

Verandah
GOAN $$

(☎ 0832-2226523; 31st Jan Rd; mains ₹180-360; ⊙ 11am-11pm) The breezy 1st-floor restaurant at Panjim Inn is indeed on the balcony, with just a handful of finely carved tables and fine Fontainhas street views. Goan cuisine is the speciality, but there's also a range of Indian and continental dishes and local wines.

★ Black Sheep Bistro
EUROPEAN, TAPAS $$$

(☎ 0832-2222901; www.blacksheepbistro.in; Swami Vivekanand Rd; tapas ₹180-225, mains

₹320-450) One of the new breed of Panaji boutique restaurants, Black Sheep's impressive pale-yellow facade gives way to a sexy dark-wood bar and loungy dining room. The tapas dishes are light, fresh and expertly prepared in keeping with their farm-to-table philosophy. Salads, pasta, local seafood and dishes like lamb osso bucco also grace the menu, while an internationally trained sommelier matches food to wine.

Baba's Wood Cafe
ITALIAN $$$

(☑ 0832-3256213; 49 Mala, Fontainhas; pizza & pasta ₹300-500; ⊙ noon-3pm & 7-11.30pm) Sharing an interesting premises with a wood-craft gallery, this upmarket Italian restaurant in a quiet street near the Maruti Temple has a lovely little alfresco dining area and a menu featuring more than 20 different pasta dishes from ravioli to carbonara. Pizzas are wood-fired and the pasta is homemade, while desserts include tiramisu and chocolate fondue. Good for a splurge.

Upper House
GOAN $$$

(☑ 0832-2426475; www.theupperhousegoa.com; Cunha-Rivara Rd; mains ₹220-440; ⊙ 11am-10pm) Climbing the stairs to the Upper House is like stepping into a cool European restaurant, with a modern but elegant dining space overlooking the Municipal Gardens, a chic neon-lit cocktail bar and a more formal restaurant at the back. The food is very much Goan though, with regional specialities such as crab *xec xec,* fish curry rice and pork vindaloo prepared to a high standard at relatively high prices.

🍷 Drinking & Nightlife

Panaji's simple little bars with a few plastic tables and chairs are a great way to get chatting with locals over a glass of feni.

Cafe Mojo
BAR

(www.cafemojo.in; Menezes Braganza Rd; ⊙ 10am-4am Mon-Thu, to 6am Fri-Sun) The decor is cosy English pub, the clientele young and up for a party, and the hook is the e-beer system. Each table has it's own beer tap and LCD screen: you buy a card (₹1000), swipe it at your table and start pouring – it automatically deducts what you drink (you can also use the card for spirits, cocktails or food). Wednesday night is ladies night, Thursday karaoke and the weekends go till late.

Riverfront & Down the Road
BAR

(cnr MG & Ourem Rds; ⊙ 11am-1am) This restaurant's balcony overlooking the creek and Old Patto Bridge makes for a cosy beer or cocktail spot with carved barrels for furniture. The ground-floor bar (from 6pm) is the only real nightspot on the Old Quarter side of town, with occasional live music.

⭐ Entertainment

Several casino boats sit moored on the Mandovi, offering a surprisingly entertaining night out.

Kala Academy
CULTURAL CENTRE

(☑ 0832-2420452; http://kalaacademygoa.org; Dayanand Bandodkar Marg) On the west side of the city, in Campal, is Goa's premier cultural centre, which features a program of dance, theatre, music and art exhibitions throughout the year. Many shows are in Konkani, but there are occasional English-language productions. The website has an up-to-date calendar of events.

INOX Cinema
CINEMA

(☑ 0832-2420900; www.inoxmovies.com; Old GMC Heritage Precinct; tickets ₹180-200) This comfortable, plush multiplex cinema shows Hollywood and Bollywood blockbusters. Book online to choose your seats in advance.

Deltin Royale
CASINO

(☑ 8698599999; www.deltingroup.com/deltin-royale; Noah's Ark, RND Jetty, Dayanand Bandodkar Marg; weekday/weekend ₹2500/3000, premium weekend ₹4000-4500; ⊙ 24hr, entertainment 9pm-1am) Goa's biggest luxury floating casino, Deltin Royal has 123 tables, the Vegas Restaurant, a Whisky Bar and a creche. Entry includes gaming chips worth ₹1500/2000 weekday/weekend and to the full value of your ticket with the premium package. Unlimited food and drinks included.

Casino Pride
CASINO

(☑ 0832-6516666; www.bestgoacasino.com; Dayanand Bandodkar Marg; weekday/weekend ₹1500/2000; ⊙ 24hr, entertainment 9-11pm) These two casino boats are loosely modelled on Mississippi-style paddle boats. *Pride I* has 40 gaming tables, kids' play room and an outdoor party deck. Admission includes ₹1000 coupon for gaming. Unlimited dinner buffet is included, as well as free drinks if you're playing a table. *Pride II* is the same deal but smaller.

🔒 Shopping

Panaji's covered **municipal market** (Heljogordo Salgado Rd; ⊙ from 7.30am) is a great place for people-watching and buying necessities.

Caculo Mall
MALL

(☑0832-2222068; 16 Shanta, St Inez; ⊙8am-11pm) Goa's biggest mall is four levels of air-conditioned family shopping heaven with brand-name stores, food court, kids' toys, Time Zone arcade games and a movie theatre.

Singbal's Book House
BOOKS

(Church Sq; ⊙9.30am-1pm & 3.30-7.30pm Mon-Sat) On the corner opposite Panaji's main church, Singbal's has an excellent selection of international magazines and newspapers, and lots of books on Goa and travel.

Marcou Artifacts
CRAFTS

(☑0832-2220204; www.marcouartifacts.com; 31st Jan Rd; ⊙9am-8pm) This small shop showcases one-off painted tiles, fish figurines and hand-crafted Portuguese and Goan ceramics at reasonable prices. Also showrooms at the Hotel Delmon and Margao's market.

Khadi Gramodyog Bhavan
HANDICRAFTS

(Dr Atmaram Borkar Rd; ⊙9am-noon & 3-7pm Mon-Sat) 🖋 Goa's only outpost of the government's Khadi & Village Industries Commission has an excellent range of hand-woven cottons, oils, soaps, spices and other handmade products that come straight from (and directly benefit) regional villages.

ⓘ Information

Goa Tourism Development Corporation
(Goa Tourism, GTDC; ☑0832-2437132; www.goa-tourism.com; Paryatan Bhavan, Dr Alvaro Costa Rd; ⊙9.30am-5.45pm Mon-Sat) Better known as Goa Tourism, the GTDC office is in the slick new Paryatan Bhavan building across the Ourem Creek and near the bus stand. However, it's more corporate office than tourist office and is of little use to casual visitors, unless you want to book one of GTDC's host of tours.

Government of India Tourist Office (☑0832-2223412; www.incredibleindia.com; Communidade Bldg, Church Sq; ⊙9.30am-1.30pm & 2.30-6pm Mon-Fri, 10am-1pm Sat) The staff at this central tourist office can be helpful, especially for information outside Goa. This office is expected to move to the same building as Goa Tourism by the time you read this.

Main Post Office (MG Rd; ⊙9.30am-5.30pm Mon-Sat) Offers swift parcel services and Western Union money transfers.

Vintage Hospitals (☑0832-6644401, ambulance 9764442220; www.vintagehospitals.com; Caculo Enclave, St Inez; ⊙24hr) Central Panaji's best hospital in an emergency; it's just west of the centre near Caculo Mall.

ⓘ Getting There & Away

A taxi from Panaji to Dabolim Airport takes about an hour, and costs ₹670 (₹770 for AC).

BUS

All government buses depart from the huge and busy **Kadamba bus stand** (☑interstate enquiries 0832-2438035, local enquiries 0832-2438034; www.goakadamba.com; ⊙reservations 8am-8pm), with local services heading out every few minutes. To get to south Goan beaches, take an express bus to Margao and change there; for far northern beaches, change at Mapusa. Kadamba station has an ATM, internet cafe, food outlets and even a Ganesh temple. Destinations include:

Calangute (₹20, 45 minutes)

Candolim (₹15, 35 minutes)

Mapusa (₹15, 30 minutes)

Margao (express shuttle; ₹30, 35 minutes)

Old Goa (₹10, 15 minutes)

Private operators have booths outside Kadamba, but the buses depart from the private interstate bus stand next to New Patto Bridge. One reliable company is **Paulo Travels** (☑0832-2438531; www.phmgoa.com; G1, Kardozo Bldg). Some high-season government and private long-distance fares include the following:

Bengaluru (₹600 to ₹1200, 14 to 15 hours, around 30 daily)

Hampi (private sleeper; ₹900 to ₹1100, 10 to 11 hours, 2-3 daily)

Mumbai (₹350 to ₹1100, 12 to 14 hours, frequent)

Pune (₹325 to ₹1000, 11 hours, frequent)

TRAIN

Panaji's closest train station is Karmali (Old Goa), 12km to the east, where many long-distance services stop (check timetables). A taxi there costs ₹350. Panaji's **Konkan Railway reservation office** (☑0832-2712940; www.konkanrailway.com; ⊙8am-8pm Mon-Sat) is on the 1st floor of the Kadamba bus stand. See the Margao section (p152) for major trains.

ⓘ Getting Around

Panaji is generally a pleasure to explore on foot. Frequent buses run between Kadamba and the municipal market and on to Miramar and Dona Paula.

To Old Goa, an autorickshaw/taxi should cost around ₹300/350.

Scooters and motorbikes can easily be hired from around the post office from around ₹200/300 per day.

A useful shortcut across the river to the northern beaches is the free vehicle **ferry** (⊙every 20 min 6am-10pm) to Betim.

Old Goa

From the 16th to the 18th centuries, when Old Goa's population exceeded that of Lisbon or London, Goa's former capital was considered the 'Rome of the East'. You can still sense that grandeur as you wander what's left of the city, with its towering churches and cathedrals and majestic convents. Its rise under the Portuguese, from 1510, was meteoric, but cholera and malaria outbreaks forced the abandonment of the city in the 1600s. In 1843 the capital was officially shifted to Panaji.

Some of the most imposing churches and cathedrals are still in use and are remarkably well preserved, while other historical buildings have become museums or ruined sites. It's a fascinating day trip, but it can get crowded: consider visiting on a weekday morning, when you can take in Mass at Sé Cathedral or the Basilica of Bom Jesus (remember to cover shoulders and legs in the churches; no beachwear).

The major event of the year is the 10 day Novena leading up to the **Feast of St Francis Xavier** on 3 December. Once every decade on this date, the Exposition sees the casket containing St Francis' body carried through Old Goa's streets; the next one is 2024.

Sights

Basilica of Bom Jesus CHURCH

(⊙7.30am-6.30pm) Famous throughout the Roman Catholic world, the imposing Basilica of Bom Jesus contains the tomb and mortal remains of St Francis Xavier, the so-called Apostle of the Indies. St Francis Xavier's missionary voyages throughout the East became legendary. His 'incorrupt' body is in the mausoleum to the right, in a glass-sided coffin amid a shower of gilt stars.

Construction on the basilica began in 1594 and was completed in 1605, to create an elaborate late-Renaissance structure, fronted by a facade combining elements of Doric, Ionic and Corinthian design.

Sé Cathedral CATHEDRAL

(⊙9am-6pm; Mass 7am & 6pm Mon-Sat, 7.15am, 10am & 4pm Sun) At over 76m long and

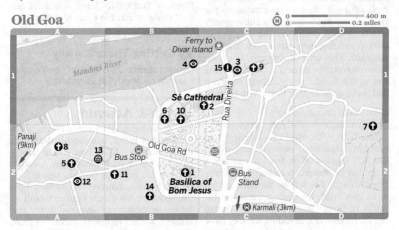

Old Goa

55m wide, the cavenerous Sé Cathedral is the largest church in Asia. Building work commenced in 1562, on the orders of King Dom Sebastiao of Portugal, and the finishing touches where finally made some 90 years later. The exterior of the cathedral is notable for its plain style, in the Tuscan tradition. Also of note is its rather lopsided look resulting from the loss of one of its bell towers, which collapsed in 1776 after being struck by lightning. The remaining tower houses the famous **Sino de Ouro** (Golden Bell), the largest in Asia and renowned for its rich tone, which once tolled to accompany the Inquisition's notoriously cruel *autos-da-fé* (trials of faith), held out the front of the cathedral on what was then the market square.

Church of St Francis of Assisi   CHURCH

West of the Sé Cathedral, the Church of St Francis of Assisi is no longer in use for worship, and consequently exudes a more mournful air than its neighbours.

The church started life as a small chapel, built on this site by eight Franciscan friars on their arrival in 1517. In 1521 it was replaced by a church consecrated to the Holy Ghost, which was then subsequently rebuilt in 1661, with only the doorway of the old building incorporated into the new structure. This original doorway, in ornate Manueline style, contrasts strongly with the rest of the facade, the plainness of which had become the fashion by the 17th century.

Museum of Christian Art   MUSEUM

(www.museumofchristianart.com; admission ₹50, camera ₹100; ☺9am-6pm) This excellent museum, in a stunningly restored space within the 1627 Convent of St Monica, contains a collection of statues, paintings and sculptures, though the setting warrants a visit in its own right. Interestingly, many of the works of Goan Christian art made during the Portuguese era, including some of those on display here, were produced by local Hindu artists.

Church of St Cajetan   CHURCH

(☺9am-5.30pm) Modelled on the original design of St Peter's in Rome, the Church of St Cajetan was built by Italian friars of the Order of Theatines, who were sent by Pope Urban III to preach Christianity in the kingdom of Golconda (near Hyderabad). The friars were not permitted to work in Golconda, so settled at Old Goa in 1640. The construction of the church began in 1655.

Church of Our Lady of the Mount   CHURCH

This church is often overlooked due to its location on a wooded hilltop, some 2km east of the central area. A sealed road leads to an overgrown flight of steps (don't walk it solo) and the hill on which the church stands commands an excellent view of Old Goa, with the church spires seemingly rising out a sea of palms.

Monastery of St Augustine   HISTORIC SITE

The melancholy, evocative ruins of this once vast and impressive Augustinian monastery are all that remain of a huge structure founded in 1572 and abandoned in 1835. The building's facade came tumbling down in 1942; all that remains, amid piles of rubble, is the towering skeletal belfry, though the bell itself was rescued and now hangs in Panaji's Church of Our Lady of the Immaculate Conception.

Other Sights

There are plenty of other monuments in Old Goa to explore, including the Viceroy's Arch, Adil Shah Palace Gateway, Chapel of St Anthony, Chapel of St Catherine, Albuquerque's Steps, the Convent & Church of St John, Sisters' Convent and the Church of Our Lady of the Rosary.

❶ Getting There & Away

Frequent buses to Old Goa depart from Panaji's Kadamba bus stand (₹10, 25 minutes).

Ponda & Around

The workaday inland town of Ponda, 29km southeast of Panaji, has two big drawcards in the vicinity – Goa's best Hindu temple complexes and spice plantations – and is well worth a day away from the beach. Temple aficionados, however, might be a little disappointed; most were built or rebuilt after the originals were destroyed by the Portuguese, so they're not as ancient as those elsewhere in India.

The 18th-century hilltop **Mangueshi Temple** at Priol, 5km northwest of Ponda, is dedicated to Manguesh, a god known only in Goa, while 1km away at Mardol is the **Mahalsa Temple**, also dedicated to a specifically Goan deity. The 1738 **Shantadurga Temple**, meanwhile, just west of Ponda, is dedicated to Shantadurga, the goddess of peace, and is one of the most famous shrines in Goa.

There are regular buses to Ponda from Panaji (₹20, 1½ hours) and Margao (₹18, one

SPICE UP YOUR LIFE

The Ponda region is the centre of commercial spice farms, producing vanilla, pepper, cardamom, nutmeg, chilli and tumeric, along with crops such as cashew, betel nut, coconut, pineapple and papaya. Farms offer a guided tour of the plantation, buffet thali-style lunch, and in some cases elephant rides and cultural shows.

Savoi Plantation (☏0832-2340272, 9822133309; adult/child ₹600/300; ☉9am-4.30pm) This 200-year-old plantation is the least touristy farm, where you'll find a warm welcome from knowledgeable guides keen to walk you through the 40-hectare plantation at your own pace.

Sahakari Spice Farm (☏0832-2312394; www.sahakarifarms.com; admission incl lunch ₹400; ☉8am-4.30pm) Well-touristed farm 2km from Ponda; good place for elephant rides and bathing (₹700 each) in the small river.

Pascoal Organic Spice Village (☏0832-2344268; www.pascoalfarm.com; farm tour & lunch adult/child ₹400/200; ☉9am-4pm) About 7km from Ponda, Pascoal offers bamboo river-rafting, elephant rides and cultural shows, along with farm tours and lunch.

Tropical Spice Plantation (☏0832-2340329; www.tropicalspiceplantation.com; Keri; admission incl lunch ₹400; ☉9am-4pm) One of the busiest farms frequented by tour groups, 5km north of Ponda. Feed the elephants and enjoy a banana-leaf buffet lunch.

Butterfly Conservatory of Goa (☏0832-2985174; www.bcogoa.org; Priol; admission ₹100; ☉9am-4.30pm) Near the spice farms, this small butterfly sanctuary, 5km north of Ponda, houses more than 100 species of free-flying butterflies.

hour), after which you'll need to arrange a taxi to visit the temples or spice farms. Taxis from Panaji charge ₹1500 for a day trip to the area (up to eight hours and 80km).

NORTH GOA

Mapusa

POP 40,100

The pleasantly bustling market town of Mapusa (pronounced 'Mapsa') is the largest in northern Goa and a transport hub for local and interstate buses. The main reason for travellers to visit is for the busy **Mapusa Market** (☉8am-6.30pm Mon-Sat), which attracts scores of buyers and sellers from neighbouring towns and villages. It's a good place to pick up the usual embroidered bedsheets and the like at prices lower than in the beach resorts. The market operates daily, but Friday is the biggest day.

Mapusa is also home to the rewarding little **Other India Bookstore** (☏0832-2263306; www.otherindiabookstore.com; Mapusa Clinic Rd; ☉9am-5pm Mon-Fri, to 1pm Sat), specialising in 'dissenting wisdom' and alternative press – a small but spectacular selection of books on nature, environment, politics, education and natural health.

Volunteering

If you're interested in volunteering while in Goa, there are a couple of well-established charity organisations around Mapusa.

El Shaddai   VOLUNTEERING
(☏0832-2461068, 0832-6513286; www.childrescue.net; El Shaddai House, Socol Vaddo, Assagao) El Shaddai is a British-founded charity that aids impoverished and homeless children throughout Goa. Volunteers able to commit to more than four weeks' work with El Shaddai can apply through the website. There's a rigorous vetting process, so start well in advance. Volunteers are also welcome to visit one of the Assagao schools between 4.30pm and 6.30pm (call ahead). For more information, there's a stall at the Anjuna flea market.

Mango Tree Goa   VOLUNTEERING
(☏9881261886; www.mangotreegoa.org; 'The Mango House', near Vrundavan Hospital, Karaswada, Mapusa) Offers placements for volunteers providing support for disadvantaged children around Mapusa.

🛏 Sleeping & Eating

There's little reason to stay the night in Mapusa when the beaches of the north coast are so close and most long-distance transport departs in the evening.

Hotel Vilena
HOTEL $

(☑ 0832-2263115; Feira Baixa Rd; d with/without bathroom ₹840/630, with AC ₹1575; ☀) Mapusa's best budget choice, with 14 plain double rooms, is not much to look at, but staff are welcoming.

Hotel Vrundavan
INDIAN $

(thalis from ₹75; ☺ 7am-10pm Wed-Mon) This all-veg place bordering the Municipal Gardens is a great place for a hot chai, *pau bhaji* (bread with spicy veg) or a quick breakfast.

Ruta's World Cafe
INTERNATIONAL $$

(☑ 0832-2250757; www.caferuta.com; St Xavier's College Rd, opp Ashirwad Bldg; mains ₹110-270; ☺ 10am-8pm Mon-Sat) The second branch of Ruta's excellent brand of fresh and tasty American-inspired cuisine has given travellers a good culinary reason to visit Mapusa. Sandwiches, salads and comfort foods such as jambalaya. It's north of the centre, in the same Portuguese-style house as Fabindia.

Pub
PUB

(near the market; mains from ₹100; ☺ 10am-4pm & 7-11pm Mon-Sat) Don't be put off by the dingy entrance or stairwell: once you're upstairs, this breezy place opposite the market is great for watching the milling crowds over a cold beer or feni. Eclectic daily specials make it a good spot for lunch.

ⓘ Getting There & Away

If you're coming to Goa by bus from Mumbai, Mapusa's **Kadamba bus stand** (☑ 0832-2232161) is the jumping-off point for the northern beaches. Local services run every few minutes; for buses to the southern beaches, take a bus to Panaji, then Margao, and change there.

Local services include the following:

Anjuna (₹15, 20 minutes)
Arambol (₹27, 1½ hours)
Calangute/Candolim (₹10/12, 20/35 minutes)
Panjim (₹15, 20 minutes)
Thivim (₹15, 20 minutes)

Interstate services run out of the same lot, but private operators have their offices next to the bus stand. There's generally little difference in price between private services and the Kadamba buses, but shop around as there are various standards of bus. Long-distance services include the following:

Bengaluru (private; AC or sleeper ₹1400, 13-14hr)
Mumbai (private; non-AC ₹700, AC ₹1200, 12-15hr)
Pune (private; non-AC from ₹650, AC ₹1200, sleeper ₹1000, 11-13hr)

There's a prepaid taxi stand outside the bus terminal where you can catch taxis to Anjuna

---

GREEN GOA

Goa's environment has suffered from an onslaught of tourism over the last 40 years, but also from the effects of logging, mining and local customs (rare turtle eggs have traditionally been considered a delicacy). Construction proceeds regardless of what the local infrastructure or ecosystem can sustain, while plastic bottles pile up in vast mountains. There are, however, a few easy ways to minimise your impact on Goa's environment:

➡ Take a bag when shopping and refill water bottles with filtered water where possible.

➡ Rent a bicycle instead of a scooter, for short trips at least; bicycle rentals are declining as a result of our scooter infatuation and the bikes are poor quality, but they'll bounce back if the demand is there.

➡ Goa Tourism now employs cleaners to comb the beaches each morning picking up litter but do your part by disposing of cigarette butts, litter and plastic bottles.

Turtles are protected by the **Forest Department** (www.forest.goa.gov.in), which operates information huts on beaches such as Agonda, Galgibag and Morjim, where turtles arrive to lay eggs. Also doing good work over many years is the **Goa Foundation** (☑ 0832-2256479; www.goafoundation.org; St Britto's Apts, G-8 Feira Alta, Mapusa), the state's main environmental pressure group based in Mapusa. It has spearheaded a number of conservation projects since its inauguration in 1986, including pressure to stop illegal mining, and its website is a great place to learn more about Goan environmental issues. The group's excellent *Fish Curry & Rice* (₹600), a sourcebook on Goa's environment and lifestyle, is sold at Mapusa's Other India Bookstore. The Foundation occasionally runs volunteer projects.

(₹300), Calangute (₹300), Arambol (₹500) and Panaji (₹500); autorickshaws typically charge ₹50 less than taxis.

Thivim, about 12km northeast of town, is the nearest train station on the Konkan Railway. Local buses meet trains; an autorickshaw into Mapusa from Thivim costs around ₹200.

Candolim, Sinquerim & Fort Aguada

POP 8600

Candolim's long and languid beach, which curves round as far as smaller Sinquerim beach in the south, is largely the preserve of mature, slow-roasting tourists from the UK, Russia and Scandinavia (and elsewhere in India), and is fringed with seasonal beach shacks, all offering sun beds and shade in exchange for your custom.

Back from the beach, busy Fort Aguada Rd is among one of the best resort strips in Goa for shops and services, and is home to dozens of restaurants, bars and hotels, but it lacks the personality of many other beach towns and independent travellers might find it a bit soulless.

◉ Sights & Activities

Fort Aguada FORT
(☉8.30am-5.30pm) FREE Standing on the headland overlooking the mouth of the Mandovi River, Fort Aguada occupies a magnificent and successful position, confirmed by the fact it was never taken by force. A highly popular spot to watch the sunset, with uninterrupted views both north and south, the fort was built in 1612, following the increasing threat to Goa's Portuguese overlords by the Dutch, among others.

John's Boat Tours TOUR
(☏0832-6520190, 9822182814; www.johnboat tours.com; Fort Aguada Rd, Candolim; ☉9am-9pm) A respected and well-organised Candolim-based operator offering a wide variety of boat and jeep excursions, as well as overnight houseboat cruises (₹5500 per person including meals). Choose from dolphin-watching cruises (₹1000), a return boat trip to the Wednesday Anjuna flea market (₹800), or the renowned 'Crocodile Dundee' river trip, to catch a glimpse of the Mandovi's mugger crocodile.

Sinquerim Dolphin Trips BOAT TOUR
(per person ₹300; ☉8.30am-5pm) The boatmen on the Nerul River below Fort Aguada

have banded together, so trips are now fixed price. A one-hour dolphin-spotting and sightseeing trip costs ₹300 per person with a minimum of 10 passengers. Trips pass Nerul (Coco) Beach, Fort Aguada Jail, the fort, and 'Jimmy Millionaire's House.'

🛏 Sleeping

Candolim has a good range of accommodation; the southern end is dominated by the five-star Taj hotels, while the best budget and midrange choices are in the lush laneways back from the northern beach.

Dona Florina HOTEL $
(☏9923049076, 0832-2489051; www.donaflorina. co.in; Monteiro's Rd, Escrivao Vaddo; r ₹1000-2000; ※ �🖥) Friendly Dona Florina is a good value, spotless guesthouse in a pleasant tangle of laneways and family-run hotels just back from the beach. Front-facing upper-floor rooms have sea views, there's daily yoga on the roof terrace, and the lack of vehicle access ensures a peaceful experience.

Zostel HOSTEL $
(☏917726864942; www.zostel.com; Candolim; dm ₹450-550, d ₹1800; ※ �🖥) The first Goan addition to this funky Indian hostel chain has popped up on the Candolim–Calangute border, bringing budget dorm beds to package-tour central. There are six- and eight-bed dorms with aircon, a 10-bed dorm and a female-only dorm, all in a whitewashed two-storey house set back from Fort Aguada Rd. Facilities include a kitchen, free wi-fi, common room and lockers. There's just one double room.

★Bougainvillea Guest House GUESTHOUSE $$
(☏0832-2479842, 9822151969; www.bougainvil-leagoa.com; Sinquerim; r ₹2500, penthouse ₹6000; ※ �🖥) A lush, plant-filled garden leads the way to this gorgeous family-run guesthouse, located off Fort Aguada Rd. The eight light-filled suite rooms are spacious and spotless, with fridge, flat-screen TV and either balcony or private sit-out; the top-floor penthouse has its own rooftop terrace. This is the kind of place guests come back to year after year. Book ahead.

D'Mello's Sea View Home HOTEL $$
(☏0832-2489650; www.dmellos.com; Monteiro's Rd, Escrivao Vaddo; d ₹1200-1700; ※ @ �🖥) D'Mello's has grown up from small beginnings but is still family-run and occupies four buildings around a lovely garden. The front building has the sea view rooms

so check out a few, but all are clean and well-maintained. Add ₹500 if you want aircon. Wi-fi is available in the central area.

★ **Marbella Guest House** BOUTIQUE HOTEL $$$
(☑0832-2479551, 9822100811; www.marbella-goa.com; Sinquerim; r ₹3400-4200, ste ₹4900-6400; ❋🖭🛜) This stunning Portuguese-era villa, filled with antiques and enveloped in a peaceful courtyard garden, is a romantic and sophisticated old-world remnant. Rooms are individually themed, including Moghul, Rajasthani and Bouganvillea. The penthouse suite is a dream of polished tiles, four-poster bed with separate living room, dining room and terrace. Its kitchen serves up some imaginative dishes. Located off Fort Aguada Rd. No kids under 12.

✖ Eating & Drinking

Candolim's plentiful beach shacks are always popular places to eat or relax with a beer, and there are some excellent restaurants along Fort Aguada Rd.

Viva Goa! GOAN, SEAFOOD $
(Fort Aguada Rd; mains ₹90-180; ⊙11am-midnight) This inexpensive, locals-oriented little place, also popular with in-the-know tourists, serves fresh fish and Goan seafood specialities such as a spicy mussel fry. Check market price of seafood before ordering.

Zappa's CAFE $
(☑9767019410; Candolim; mains ₹40-120; ⊙8am-2pm) A tiny cafe sandwiched between the beach and busy Fort Aguada Rd, Zappa's serves up tasty breakfast and brunch dishes and some of the freshest pasta dishes in town. The owner has spent many years living and cooking in Europe. Zappa's beach shack is directly west.

★ **Café Chocolatti** CAFE, BAKERY $$
(409A Fort Aguada Rd; sweets ₹50-200, mains ₹270-420; ⊙9am-5.30pm) The lovely garden tearoom at Café Chocolatti may be on the main Fort Aguada Rd but it's a divine and peaceful retreat where chocolate brownies, waffles and banoffee pie with a strong cup of coffee or organic green tea seem like heaven. Also a great range of salads, paninis, crepes and quiches for lunch. Take away a bag of chocolate truffles, homemade by the in-house chocolatier.

Stone House STEAKHOUSE, SEAFOOD $$
(Fort Aguada Rd; mains ₹150-500; ⊙11am-3pm & 7pm-midnight) Surf 'n' turf's the thing at this venerable old Candolim venue, inhabiting a stone house and its leafy front courtyard, with the improbable-sounding 'Swedish Lobster' topping the list. It's also a popular blues bar with live music most nights of the week in season.

★ **Bomra's** BURMESE $$$
(☑9767591056; www.bomras.com; 247 Fort Aguada Rd; mains from ₹300; ⊙noon-2pm & 7-11pm) Wonderfully unusual food is on offer at this sleek little place serving interesting modern Burmese cuisine with a fusion twist. Aromatic curries include straw mushroom, lychee, water-chestnut, spinach, and coconut curry and duck curry with sweet tamarind and groundnut shoot. Decor is palm-thatch style huts in a lovely courtyard garden.

Tuscany Gardens ITALIAN $$$
(☑0832-6454026; www.tuscanygardens.in; Fort Aguada Rd; mains ₹240-410; ⊙1-11pm) You can easily be transported to Tuscany at Candolim's cosy, romantic Italian restaurant, where perfect antipasti, pasta, pizza and risotto are the order of the day. Try the chicken breast stuffed with gorgonzola and ham, the seafood pizza or buffalo mozzarella salad.

Bob's Inn BAR
(Fort Aguada Rd, Candolim; ⊙noon-4pm & 7pm-midnight) The African wall hangings, palm-thatch, communal tables and terracotta sculptures are a nice backdrop to the *rava* (semolina) fried mussels or the prawns 'chilly fry' with potatoes, but this Candolim institution is really just a great place to drop in for a drink.

LPK Waterfront CLUB
(www.lpkwaterfront.com; couples ₹1500; ⊙9.30pm-4am) The initials stand for Love, Peace and Karma: welcome to North Goa's biggest new club, the whimsical, sculpted waterfront LPK. It's actually across the Nerul River from Candolim (so technically in Nerul) but its club nights attract party-goers from all over with huge indoor and outdoor dance areas.

🔒 Shopping

Newton's SUPERMARKET
(Fort Aguada Rd; ⊙9am-midnight) If you're desperately missing Edam cheese or Pot Noodles, or just want to do some self-catering, Newton's is Goa's biggest supermarket. There's a good line in toiletries,

wines, children's toys and luxury food items. The downside is that it's usually packed and security guards won't allow bags inside.

ℹ Getting There & Away

Buses run frequently to Panaji (₹15, 35 minutes) and Mapusa (₹12, 35 minutes) and stop at the turn-off near John's Boat Tours. Calangute buses (₹5, 15 minutes) start at the Fort Aguada bus stop and can be flagged down on Fort Aguada Rd.

Calangute & Baga

POP 15,800

Love it or loathe it, Calangute and Baga are Goa's most popular beaches – at least with the cashed-up domestic tour crowd and European package tourists. Once a refuge of wealthy Goans, and later a 1960s hot spot for naked, revelling hippies, Calangute has adapted its scant charms to extended Indian families, groups of Indian bachelors and partying foreigners. This is Goa's most crowded beach stretch – from the traffic-clogged streets to the Arabian Sea, which fills up with people, boats and jet skis – though the southern beach is more relaxed. Baga, to the north, is notorious for drinking and dancing, while Northern Baga, across the Baga River, is surprisingly tranquil, with a few budget guesthouses and some top-notch restaurants.

🏃 Activities

Water Sports

You'll find numerous jet-ski and parasailing operators on Calangute and Baga beaches. Parasailing costs around ₹800 per ride, jet-skiing costs ₹1500 per 15 minutes.

Two local scuba diving operators are recommended: **Goa Aquatics** (Map p136; ☑9822685025; www.goaaquatics.com; 136/1 Gaura Vaddo; dive trip from ₹5000, dive course ₹14,000-25,000) in Calangute and **Barracuda Diving** (Map p136; ☑9822182402, 0832-2279409; www.barracudadiving.com; Sun Village Resort; dive trip/course from ₹4500/6000) in Baga.

👉 Tours

Day Tripper TOUR
(Map p136; ☑0832-2276726; www.daytrippergoa.com; Gaura Vaddo, Calangute; ⊗9am-5.30pm Mon-Sat Nov-Apr) Calangute-based Day Tripper is one of Goa's biggest and most reliable tour agencies. It runs a wide variety of minibus and boat trips around Goa, in-

cluding two-hour dolphin trips (₹500 per person), trips to Dudhsagar Falls (₹1530), a houseboat stay (₹5300 per person) and also interstate tours to Hampi and the Kali River (for rafting and birdwatching trips) in Karnataka.

GTDC Tours TOUR
(Goa Tourism Development Corporation; Map p136; ☑0832-2276024; ⊗www.goa-tourism.com) Goa Tourism's tours can be booked online or at the refurbished GTDC Calangute Residency hotel beside the beach. The full-day North Goa tour (₹225, 9.30am to 6pm daily) departs from Calangute or Mapusa and takes in the Mandovi estuary, Candolim, Calangute, Anjuna and inland to Mayem Lake.

🛏 Sleeping

Calangute and Baga's sleeping options are plentiful, lining the main roads and laneways down to the beach for several kilometres. Generally, the quietest hotels are in south Calangute, and across the bridge north of Baga.

🛏 Calangute

★**Ospy's Shelter** GUESTHOUSE $
(Map p136; ☑7798100981, 0832-2279505; ospeys.shelter@gmail.com; d ₹800-900) Tucked away between the beach and St Anthony's Chapel, in a quiet, lush little area full of palms and sandy paths, Ospey's is a traveller favourite

BACKWOODS CAMP

In a forest near Bhagwan Mahaveer Sanctuary, full of butterflies and birds, **Backwoods Camp** (☑9822139859; www.backwoodsgoa.com; Matkan, Tambdi Surla; 1-/2-/3-day ₹4500/7500/11,000) is a magical, serene spot. The resort is about 1km from Tambdi Surla temple in the state's far east, and for birdwatching enthusiasts it offers one of Goa's richest sources birding, with everything from Ceylon frogmouths and Asian fairy bluebirds to puff-throated babblers and Indian pittas putting in a regular appearance. Accommodation is in comfortable tents on raised platforms, bungalows and farmhouse rooms. Rates include three guided birdwatching walks daily.

N

0 — 1 km
0 — 0.5 miles

1

25

Club Cubana (500m);
Saturday Nite
Market (650m);
Mukti Kitchen (1km);
Splashdown
Water Park (1.3km)
Arpora (2km);
Anjuna (4km)

See Anjuna Map (p140)

Baga River Rd
Baga River

8

13

19

Baga Bus
Stand

16

6

BAGA

5

*Beach
Shacks*

Calangute - Baga Rd

18

22

Baga
Beach

Tito's Lane

*Baga
Market*

23

11

Calangute - Baga Rd

Calangute - Anjuna Rd

12

Saõ João
Batista
Church

20

Temple

Calangute
Bus Stand

4

21

17

Market

7

ARABIAN
SEA

Dr Afonso Rd

Calangute-Anjuna Rd

Saligao
(2.5km)

St Anthony's
Chapel

14

9

Bob's Inn (200m); Zostel
(200m); Viva Goa! (600m);
2 Dona Florina (850m);
● D'Mello's Sea View
Home (850m); Candolim
(1km); Zappa's (1.2km);
Newton's (1.5km);
John's Boat Tours (2km)

Holiday St

15

10

3

24

Calangute & Baga

and only a two-minute walk from the beach. Spotless upstairs rooms have fridges and balconies and the whole place has a cosy family feel. Take the road directly west of the chapel – but it's tough to find, so call ahead.

Johnny's Hotel
HOTEL $

(Map p136; ☑ 0832-2277458; www.johnnyshotel. com; s ₹400-600, d ₹700-900, with AC ₹1000-1200; ❋❂) The 15 simple rooms at this backpacker-popular place make for a sociable stay, with a downstairs restaurant-bar and regular yoga and reiki classes. A range of apartments and houses are available for longer stays. It's down a lane lined with unremarkable midrange hotels and is just a short walk to the beach.

Coco Banana
GUESTHOUSE $

(Map p136; ☑ 0832-2279068; www.cocobananagoa. com; d ₹950, with AC ₹1500; ❋❂) Among the palms south of the main entrance to Calangute Beach, colourful Coco Banana has been

providing a soothing retreat for travellers for many years. Run by the friendly Walter, rooms are spacious and spotless and the vibe mellow. For families or groups, ask about the self-contained apartments at nearby Casa Leyla.

Hotel Golden Eye
HOTEL $$

(Map p136; ☑ 9822132850, 0832-2277308; www. hotelgoldeneye.com; Holiday St; d ₹2000, with AC ₹2500, sea-facing rooms from ₹4500, apt ₹5000-8000; ❋❂) This popular beachfront hotel at the end of 'Holiday St' has a fine range of rooms and apartments, from tidy ones at the back to the boutique sea-facing rooms with modern decor, air-con and cable TV. Unlike some midrangers it's welcoming to independent walk-in travellers, though you'll need to book ahead in season. The Flying Dolphin beach shack is out front.

Hotel Seagull
HOTEL $$

(Map p136; ☑ 0832-2179969; Holiday St; d with AC ₹2500; ❋❂❂) Bright, friendly and welcoming, the Seagull's rooms, set in a cheerful blue-and-white house in south Calangute, are light and airy with air-con and a small pool out back. Downstairs is the fine Blue Mariposa bar-restaurant, serving Goan, Indian and continental dishes.

⌂ Baga

★ Indian Kitchen
GUESTHOUSE $

(Map p136; ☑ 9822149615, 0832-2277555; www.indiankitchen-goa.com; s/d/chalet ₹770/990/1500; ❋@❂❂) If a colourful budget stay is what you're after, look no further than this family-run guesthouse, which offers a range of rooms from basic to more spacious, comfy apartments, but all with lots of effort at individual charm. There's a neat central courtyard and, surprisingly for a budget place, a sparklingly clean pool out the back. Each room has its own terrace or sit-out.

Melissa Guest House
GUESTHOUSE $

(Map p136; ☑ 9822180095, 0832-2279583; Baga River Rd; d ₹800) Across the Baga River, Melissa Guest House has just four neat little rooms, all with attached bathrooms and hot-water showers, in a tatty garden. Good value for the location.

Divine Guest House
GUESTHOUSE $$

(Map p136; ☑ 0832-2279546, 9370273464; www. indivinehome.com; Baga River Rd; s ₹600, d ₹1200-1300, with AC ₹1650-3000; ❋@❂) Not the

GOA CALANGUTE & BAGA

bargain it once was, Divine still sits pretty on the relatively quiet headland north of the Baga River. The 'Praise the Lord' gatepost offers a little gentle proselytising from the friendly family, while the rooms are homey and bright with the odd individual touches. Wi-fi is prepaid.

Alidia Beach Cottages   GUESTHOUSE $$

(Map p136; ☑0832-2279014; Calungute-Baga Rd, Saunta Waddo; d ₹2000, with AC from ₹3300; ❋ ♠ ☀) Set back behind a whitewashed church off busy Baga Rd, this convivial but quiet place has well kept Mediterranean-style rooms orbiting a gorgeous pool. The cheaper, non-air-con rooms at the back are not as good, but all are in reasonably good condition, staff are eager to please, and there's a path leading directly to Baga Beach.

Cavala Seaside Resort   HOTEL $$

(Map p136; ☑0832-2276090; www.cavala. com; Calangute-Baga Rd; s/d incl breakfast from ₹1500/3000, d & ste with AC ₹3500-5500; ❋ ♠ ☀) Idiosyncratic, ivy-clad Cavala has been harbouring Baga-bound travellers for over 25 years and is often full. Perhaps as a result service is indifferent, but there's a big range of rooms, pool and a bar-restaurant with frequent live music.

✗ Eating

Calangute and Baga boast probably the greatest concentration of dining options anywhere in Goa, with everything from the simplest street food to the finest filet steak. The beach shacks are an obvious go-to, but there are some interesting gems along the 'Strip' and some excellent upmarket offerings on the north side of the Baga River.

✗ Calangute

Plantain Leaf   INDIAN $

(Map p136; ☑0832-2279860; veg thali ₹100, mains ₹90-270; ❂8am-11pm) In the heart of Calangute's busy market area, 1st-floor Plantain Leaf has consistently been the area's best veg restaurant for many years. It's gone through a change though, dumping the classic South Indian banana leaf thalis, adding nonveg (meat) to the menu and expanding its repertoire to more North Indian flavours. It's still a good place for a thali, along with seafood (fish thali ₹150), kebabs and biriyani, and just sneaks in to the budget category.

Cafe Sussegado Souza   GOAN $$

(Map p136; ☑8652839651; Calangute-Anjuna Rd; mains ₹160-280; ❂noon-midnight) In a little yellow Portuguese-style house just south of the Calangute market area, Cafe Sussegado is the place to come for Goan food such as fish curry rice, chicken *xacuti* and pork *sorpotel* (a vinegary stew made from liver, heart and kidneys), with a shot of feni to be going on with. Authentic, busy and good atmosphere.

Infantaria   BAKERY, ITALIAN $$

(Map p136; Calangute-Baga Rd; pastries ₹50-200, mains ₹160-440; ❂7.30am-midnight) Infanteria began life as Calangute's best bakery but has developed into an extremely popular Italian-cum-Indian restaurant. The bakery roots are still there, though, with homemade cakes, croissants, little flaky pastries and real coffee. Get in early for breakfast before the good stuff runs out. For lunch and dinner it's Goan and Italian specialities and a full bar. Regular live music in season.

A Reverie   INTERNATIONAL $$$

(Map p136; ☑9823505550; www.areverie.com; Holiday St; mains ₹475-700; ❂7pm-late) A gorgeous award-winning lounge bar, all armchairs, cool jazz and whimsical outdoor space, this is the place to spoil yourself, with the likes of Serrano ham, grilled asparagus, French wines and Italian cheeses. Although fine dining, A Reverie likes to style itself as 'fun dining' and doesn't take itself too seriously. On the snack list, check out the Indian taco truck (₹275), wasabi prawns or barbecue pulled-pork rolls.

✗ Baga

Britto's   MULTICUISINE, BAR $$

(Map p136; ☑0832-2277331; Baga Beach; mains ₹180-460; ❂8.30am-midnight) Long-running Britto's is an arena-sized Baga institution at the north end of the beachfront, with a sandy floor if you've forgotten you're on the beach. It's a good spot for breakfast and gets busy for lunch and dinner. The drinks list is longer than the food menu and young Indian tourists are fond of ordering the iced Kingfisher mini-kegs. All good fun and live music most nights in season.

★ Go With the Flow   INTERNATIONAL, BRAZILIAN $$$

(Map p136; ☑7507771556; www.gowiththeflow goa.com; Baga River Rd; mains ₹200-650; ❂from 6pm Mon-Sat) Stepping into the fantasy neon-lit garden of illuminated white-wicker furniture is wow factor enough, but the food is equally out of this world. With a global menu leaning towards European and South American flavours, Brazilian chef Guto brings a wealth of experience and culinary imagination to the table. Try some of the small bites (ask about a tasting plate) or go straight for the pork belly or duck ravioli.

★ Fiesta CONTINENTAL $$$
(Map p136; ☑ 0832-2279894; www.fiestagoa.in; Tito's Lane; mains ₹250-600; ☺ 7pm-late) Follow the lamplights off happening Tito's Lane: there's something magical about stepping into Fiesta's candlelit split-level tropical garden. Soft music and exotic furnishings add to an upmarket Mediterranean-style dining experience that starts with homemade pizza and pasta and extends to French-influenced seafood dishes and some of the finest desserts around. Worth a splurge.

🍷 Drinking & Nightlife

Baga's boisterous club scene – centred on Tito's Lane – has long been well known among the tourist crowd looking for a late night out. Some find the scene a little sleazy here and the bar staff indifferent. Solo women are welcomed into clubs (usually free) but should exercise care and take taxis to and from venues.

Club Cubana CLUB
(☑ 9823539000; www.clubcubanagoa.com; Arpora; ☺ 9.30pm-4am) Billing itself as the 'nightclub in the sky,' this hilltop place in Arpora (a few kilometres north of Baga) has been providing a late-night pool party scene for more than a decade. As with most clubs it's couples or ladies only (though solo males can usually pay a premium to get in) and, depending on the night, it's open bar with a cover charge of ₹1000 to ₹2000. Wednesday is ladies night.

Café Mambo CLUB
(Map p136; ☑ 7507333003; www.cafemambogoa.com; Tito's Lane, Baga; cover charge couples ₹500; ☺ 10.30pm-3am) Part of the Tito's empire, Mambo is one of Baga's most happening clubs with an indoor/outdoor beachfront location and nightly DJs pumping out house, hip-hop and Latino tunes. Couples or females only.

🛍 Shopping

Both **Mackie's Saturday Nite Bazaar** (Map p136; www.mackiesnitebazaar.com; ☺ from 6pm Sat Nov-Apr), in Baga, and the larger **Saturday Nite Market** (www.snmgoa.com; Arpora; ☺ from 6pm Sat Nov-Mar), in Arpora, about 2km northeast of Baga, set up in season and are fun alternatives to Anjuna's Wednesday market, with food stalls, entertainment and the usual souvenir stalls. They have been cancelled from time to time in recent years for reasons unclear. Ask around to see when they're on.

Karma Collection SOUVENIRS
(Map p136; www.karmacollectiongoa.com; Calangute-Arpora Rd; ☺ 9.30am-10.30pm) Beautiful home furnishings, textiles, ornaments, bags and other enticing stuff – some of it antique – has been sourced from across India, Pakistan and Afghanistan and gathered at Karma Collection, which makes for a mouth-watering browse. Fixed prices, though it's not cheap.

Literati Bookshop & Cafe BOOKS
(Map p136; ☑ 0832-2277740; www.literati-goa.com; Calangute; ☺ 10am-6.30pm Mon-Sat) A refreshingly different bookstore, in the owners' South Calangute home, and a very pleasant Italian-style garden cafe. Come for a fine espresso and browse the range of books by Goan and Indian authors as well as antiquarium literature. Check the website for readings and other events.

ℹ Information

Currency exchange offices, ATMs, pharmacies and internet cafes cluster around Calangute's main market and bus stand area, and along the Baga and Candolim roads.

ℹ Getting There & Around

Frequent buses to Panaji (₹20, 45 minutes) and Mapusa (₹10) depart from the Baga and Calangute bus stands, and a local bus (₹5) runs between the Baga and Calangute stands every few minutes; catch it anywhere along the way. Taxis charge an extortionate ₹100 between Calangute and Baga. A prepaid taxi from Dabolim Airport to Calangute costs ₹750.

Anjuna

Good old Anjuna. The stalwart of India's hippy scene still drags out the sarongs and sandalwood each Wednesday for its famous, and once infamous, flea market. With its raggedy beach, rice paddies and cheap guesthouses huddled in relatively peaceful pockets, it continues to pull in backpackers and long-term hippies, while midrange tourists are also increasingly making their way here. The village itself might be a bit frayed around the edges – if your only introduction is the tatty cliff-tops around the bus stand you may be unimpressed. But look further and you may come to appreciate Anjuna's haphazard charm, and see why it remains a favourite of both long-stayers and first-timers.

◉ Sights & Activities

Anjuna's charismatic little **beach** runs for almost 2km from the northern village area to the flea market. The northern end is mostly cliffs lined with cheap cafes and basic guesthouses, but the beach proper is a nice stretch of sand (when the tide is out) with a bunch of multistorey beach bars at the southern end.

There's lots of yoga, reiki and ayurvedic massage offered around Anjuna and nearby Assagao; look for notices at Artjuna Cafe and the German Bakery. Drop-in classes are organised by **Brahmani Yoga** (☑ 9545620578; www.brahmaniyoga.com; Tito's White House, Aguada-Siolim Rd; classes ₹600, 10-class pass ₹4500), at Tito's White House.

Splashdown Water Park   SWIMMING
(☑ 0832-2273008; www.splashdowngoa.com; Anjuna-Baga Rd, Arpora; weekdays/weekends ₹380/420, spectators ₹260/300; ☺ 10.30am-6pm) This fabulous collection of pools, fountains and waterslides will keep kids (and adults) happy all day long. A nice cafe and bar overlook over the action. It's in Arpora, roughly halfway between Anjuna and Baga.

Mukti Kitchen   COOKING
(☑ 08007359170; www.muktikitchen.com; Anjuna-Baga Rd, Arpora; veg/nonveg ₹1500/1800; ☺ 11am-2pm & 5-8pm) Mukti shares her cooking skills twice daily at these recommended classes on

Anjuna

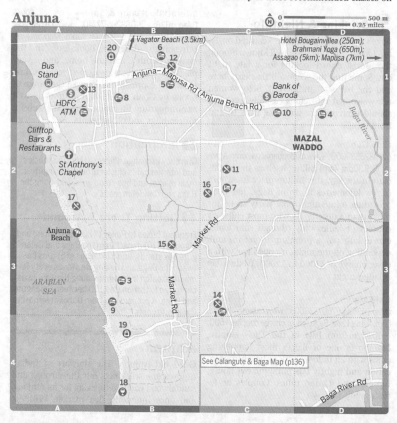

the Anjuna Rd in Arpora. Courses include five dishes which can be tailored – veg or nonveg, Goan, Indian or ayurvedic. Minimum four people, maximum six; book one day ahead.

🛏 Sleeping

Most accommodation and other useful services are sprinkled along the beach cliffs, on the Anjuna-Mapusa Rd leading to the bus stand or down shady inland lanes.

Prison Hostel
HOSTEL **$**

(☏0832-2273745; www.thehostelcrowd.com; 940 Market Rd; dm ₹350-400, with AC ₹450, d ₹1400; ❄ ☎) Cell-like rooms are not uncommon in India but this quirky new backpacker hostel on Anjuna's Market Rd goes a step further and is themed like a jail. Apart from the bars on the windows and B&W decor, there's no sense of incarceration here, however. Clean four- to 10-bed dorms have individual lockers and bed-lights, there's a good kitchen, and breakfast and wi-fi are included. Expect loud music and partying guests.

Red Door Hostel
HOSTEL **$**

(☏0832-2274423; reddoorhostels@gmail.com; dm without/with AC ₹500/600, d without/with AC ₹1600/2000; ❄ ☎) A recent addition to North Goa's hostel scene, Red Door is a welcoming place close to Anjuna's central crossroads. Clean four- and six-bed dorms plus a few private rooms. Facilities include lockers, free wi-fi, garden and good communal areas, including a well-equipped kitchen. Laidback vibe and resident pet dogs.

Vilanova
GUESTHOUSE **$**

(☏0832-6450389, 9225904244; mendonca90@rediffmail.com; Anjuna Beach Rd; d ₹600-700, with AC ₹1200; ❄) Big, clean rooms have a fridge, TV, 24-hour hot water and window screens and are set in three Portuguese-style bungalows in a cute little compound. Good vibes and a comfortable family atmosphere, with friendly staff and a good restaurant.

Florinda's
GUESTHOUSE **$**

(☏9890216520; s/d ₹500/700, with AC ₹1500; ❄ ☎) One of the better budget places near the beach, Florinda's has clean rooms, with 24-hour hot water, window screens and mosquito nets, set around a pretty garden. The few air-con rooms fill up fast.

Paradise
GUESTHOUSE **$**

(☏9922541714; janet_965@hotmail.com; Anjuna-Mapusa Rd; d ₹800-1000, with AC ₹2000; ❄ @ ☎) This friendly place is fronted by an old Portuguese home and offers neat, clean rooms with well-decorated options in the newer annexe. The better rooms have TV, fridge and hammocks on the balcony. Friendly owner Janet and family also run the pharmacy, general store, restaurant, internet cafe, Connexions travel agency and money exchange!

Peace Land
GUESTHOUSE **$**

(San Miguel's; ☏9822685255, 0832-2273700; s/d from ₹600/800, with AC ₹1200-1500; ❄ ☎) A good budget deal with small but tidy rooms arranged around a tranquil courtyard garden back from the main Anjuna road. It's run by a friendly family and there's a pool table, chillout area, hammocks and a decent restaurant.

Sea Horse
HUT **$$**

(☏9764465078; www.vistapraiaanjuna.com; ☺ hut without/with AC ₹1500/1800; ❄ ☎) A line-up of timber cabins behind the beach restaurant of the same name, Sea Horse is decent value for the location. The huts are small and have modern bathrooms but get a little hot – go for the air-con rooms if it's humid. Staff are friendly and accommodating. The same owners have a pricier beachfront set-up called Praia Anjuna.

GOA ANJUNA

Banyan Soul
BOUTIQUE HOTEL $$

(☑ 9820707283; www.thebanyansoul.com; d ₹2200; ✳ ⑅) A slinky 12-room option, tucked down the lane off Market Rd, and lovingly conceived and run by Sumit, a young Mumbai escapee. Rooms are chic and well equipped with air-con and TV, and there's a lovely library and shady seating area beneath a banyan tree.

Palacete Rodrigues
HERITAGE HOTEL $$

(☑ 0832-2273358; www.palacetegoa.com; Mazal Vaddo; d & ste ₹3000-6000; ✳ ⑅ ☷) This lovely family-run mansion, filled with antiques and ornate furniture, is as quirky as you'll find in Anjuna – perhaps too over-the-top for some. Some of the 14 rooms and suites are themed and decorated along ethnic cultural lines: French, Chinese, Japanese and Goan.

Casa Anjuna
HERITAGE HOTEL $$$

(☑ 0832-2274123-5; www.casaboutiquehotels. com; D'Mello Vaddo 66; r from ₹7700; ✳ ⑅ ☷) This heritage hotel is enclosed in lovely plant-filled gardens around an inviting pool, managing to shield itself from the hype of central Anjuna. All rooms have antique furnishings and period touches; like many upmarket places it's better value out of season when rates halve.

✕ Eating & Drinking

The southern end of Anjuna beach boasts a string of super-sized semipermanent beach shacks serving all day food and drinks and partying late into the night – good ones include Cafe Lilliput, Curlies, Shiva Garden and Janet & John's. Oxford Arcade (Anjuna-Vagator Rd; ☉ 8.30am-9pm) is an excellent, modern supermarket where you can stock up on imported goods and cheap booze.

★ Artjuna Cafe
CAFE $

(☑ 0832-2274794; www.artjuna.com; Market Rd; mains ₹80-290; ☉ 8am-10.30pm) Artjuna is right up there with our favourite cafes in Anjuna. Along with all-day breakfast, outstanding espresso coffee, salads, sandwiches and Middle Eastern surprises such as baba ganoush, tahini and felafel, this sweet garden cafe has an excellent craft and lifestyle shop, yoga classes and one of Anjuna's best noticeboards. Great meeting place.

Burger Factory
BURGERS $$

(Anjuna-Mapusa Rd; burgers ₹250-450; ☉ noon-11pm) There's no mistaking what's on offer at this little alfresco diner/kitchen. The straightforward menu is chalked up on a blackboard at the side, and though the burgers aren't cheap, they are interesting and expertly crafted. Choose between beef or chicken burgers and toppings such as cheddar, wasabi and mayo or beetroot and aioli.

Om Made Cafe
MEDITERRANEAN $$

(D'Mello Vaddo; dishes ₹120-250; ☉ 9am-sunset) A highlight on Anjuna's same-same clifftop strip, this cheery little place offers striped deckchairs from which to enjoy the views and the super breakfasts, sandwiches and salads. The food is fresh and organic.

Dhum Biryani & Kebabs
INDIAN $$

(Anjuna-Mapusa Rd; mains ₹180-350; ☉ 9am-1am) Loved by visitors and locals alike, Dhum Biryani serves up consistently good kebabs as well as biryani and other usual suspects.

Martha's Breakfast Home
CAFE $$

(meals ₹60-300; ☉ 7.30am-1.30pm) As the name suggests, welcoming Martha's speciality is breakfast, served up in a quiet garden on the way down to the flea-market site. Omelettes, fresh juice and cereal are *de rigueur,* but the stars of the show are the waffles with maple syrup and strawberries (in season). There are some nice rooms (₹700) here and a two-bedroom house to rent (₹10,000 per week). Located off Market Rd.

ANJUNA'S FLEA MARKET EXPERIENCE

Anjuna's Wednesday flea market (☉ 8am-late Wed Nov-late Mar) is as much part of the Goan experience as a day on the beach. More than three decades ago it was the sole preserve of hippies smoking jumbo joints and convening to compare experiences on the heady Indian circuit. Nowadays, things are far more mainstream with stalls carrying crafts from Kashmir and Karnataka, mirrored textiles from Rajasthan, spices from Kerala and Tibetan trinkets. There are a couple of bars with live music and cold beer.

The market is still good fun and shows no sign of waning in popularity, so dive in and enjoy the ride. The best time to visit is early (from 8am) or late afternoon (around 4pm till close just after sunset).

YOGA RETREATS

The Anjuna/Vagator/Assagao area has a number of yoga retreats where you can immerse yourself in courses, classes and a zen vibe during the October-March season.

Purple Valley Yoga Retreat (☑0832-2268363; www.yogagoa.com; 142 Bairo Alto, Assagao; dm/s one week from £600/750, two weeks £980/1200; ☎) Popular yoga resort in Assagao offering one- and two-week residential and nonresidential Ashtanga courses.

Swan Yoga Retreat (☑0832-2268024, 8007360677; www.swan-yoga-goa.com; Assagao; per person one week from ₹17,500) In a peaceful jungle corner of Assagao, Swan Retreat is a very zen yoga experience. Minimum week-long yoga retreats start every Saturday and include eco-accommodation, ayurvedic veg meals, meditation, daily classes and an optional afternoon 'masterclass'.

Yoga Magic (☑0832-6523796; www.yogamagic.net; Anjuna; s/d lodge ₹6750/9000, ste ₹9000/12,000; ☎) ✔ Solar lighting, vegetable farming and compost toilets are just some of the worthy initiatives practised in this luxurious yoga resort. The lodge features dramatic Rajasthani tents under a thatched shelter.

German Bakery   MULTICUISINE **$$**
(www.german-bakery.in; bread & pastries ₹50-90, mains ₹100-450; ⊙8.30am-11pm; ☎) Leafy and filled with prayer flags, occasional live music and garden lights, German Bakery is a long-standing favourite for hearty and healthy breakfast, fresh-baked bread and organic food, but these days the menu runs to pasta, burgers and pricey seafood. Prices are up and service is down though. Healthy juices (think wheatgrass) and espresso coffee.

Heidi's Beer Garden   GERMAN **$$**
(☑9886376922; Market Rd; mains ₹100-400; ⊙11am-11pm) It may well be Goa's first German-style beer garden and restaurant, which is reason enough to call into Heidi's. Another is the range of some 40 international beers from Germany, Belgium, Mexico, Japan, Portugal and more. The imported beers are relatively expensive, but you can still order local beers, including a Goan draught. The food is mostly German and European, including bratwurst sausages and the acclaimed German thali (₹400).

Curlies   BAR
(www.curliesgoa.com; ⊙9am-3am) At the southern end of Anjuna Beach, Curlies mixes laid-back beach-bar vibe with sophisticated night spot – the party nights here are notorious. There's a parachute silk-covered rooftop lounge bar and an enclosed late-night dance club. on Thursday and Saturday.

ℹ Information

Anjuna has three ATMs, clustered together on the main road to the beach, and another down near the bus stand. Free wi-fi is common in guesthouses and cafes.

ℹ Getting There & Away

Buses to Mapusa (₹15) depart every half-hour or so from the main **bus stand** near the beach; some from Mapusa continue on to Vagator and Chapora. Two daily buses to Calangute depart from the main crossroads. Taxis and autos gather at both stops, and you can hire scooters and motorcycles easily from the crossroads.

Vagator & Chapora

Vagator's twin beaches are small by Goan standards but the dramatic red-stone cliffs, rolling green hills, patches of forest and a crumbling 17th-century Portuguese **fort** provide Vagator and its diminutive neighbour Chapora with one of the prettiest settings on the north Goan coast. Once known for wild trance parties and heady, hippy lifestyle, Vagator has slowed down, but it's still the place of choice for many backpackers and partygoers, and tiny Chapora – reminiscent of *Star Wars'* Mos Eisley Cantina – remains a fave for longstayers and charas smokers.

🛏 Sleeping

🛏 Vagator

You'll see lots of signs for 'Rooms to Let' in private homes and guesthouses.

★**Jungle Hostel**   HOSTEL **$**
(☑0832-2273006; www.thehostelcrowd.com; Vagator Beach Rd; dm ₹450, with AC ₹500, s/d

Vagator & Chapora

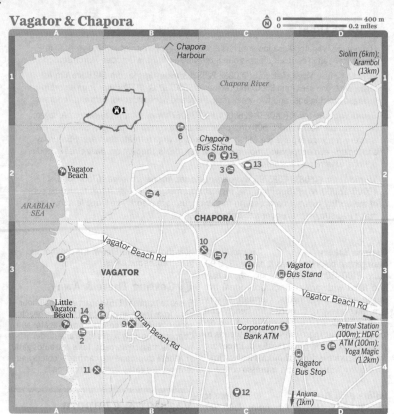

Vagator & Chapora

◎ Sights
1 Chapora Fort	B1

🛏 Sleeping
2 Alcove Resort	A4
3 Baba	C2
4 Baba Place	B2
5 Bean Me Up	D4
6 Casa de Olga	B2
7 Jungle Hostel	C3
8 Shalom	A3

✕ Eating
Bean Me Up Soya Station	(see 5)
9 Bluebird	B4

10 Mango Tree Bar & Cafe	C3
11 Thalassa	A4

🍸 Drinking & Nightlife
12 Hilltop	C4
13 Jai Ganesh Fruit Juice Centre	C2
14 Nine Bar	A4
15 Paulo's Antique Bar	C2
Scarlet Cold Drinks	(see 13)

🛍 Shopping
16 Rainbow Bookshop	C3

₹900/1400; ✳@🛜) True backpacker hostels are on the rise in Goa, but this was one of the originals, bringing the dorm experience and an international vibe to Vagator. The six-bed dorms are clean and bright and things like

lockers, wi-fi, breakfast, communal kitchen and travel advice are free.

Bean Me Up　　　　　　　　　GUESTHOUSE $
(Enterprise Guest House; ☎7769095356; www. beanmeup.in; 1639/2 Deulvaddo; d ₹1200, without

bathroom ₹900; 🛜) Set around a leafy, para-chute-silky courtyard that's home to Vaga-tor's best vegan restaurant (p145), rooms at the Enterprise Guest House look simple but are themed with individual exotic decor, earthy shades, mosquito nets and shared verandahs. The mellow yoga-friendly vibe matches the clientele.

Shalom GUESTHOUSE $
(📞919881578459, 0832-2273166; www.shalom guesthousegoa.com; d ₹800-1400, with AC ₹1800; ❈@🛜) Arranged around a placid gar-den not far from the path down to Little Vagator Beach, this established place run by a friendly family (whose home is ons-ite) offers a variety of extremely well-kept rooms and a two-bedroom apartment for long-stayers.

Alcove Resort HOTEL $$
(📞0832-2274491; www.alcovegoa.com; Little Vagator Beach; d ₹3300, with AC ₹3850, cottage ₹4400/4950; ❈@🛜🏊) The location over-looking Little Vagator Beach is hard to beat at this price. Attractively furnished rooms, slightly larger cottages and four suites sur-rounding a decent central pool, restaurant and bar, make this a good place for those who want a touch of affordable luxury.

🛏 Chapora

Head down the road to the harbour and you'll find lots of rooms – and whole homes – for rent.

Casa de Olga GUESTHOUSE $
(📞0832-2274355, 9822157145; eadsouza@yahoo. co.in; r ₹600-1200, without bathroom from ₹300) This welcoming family-run homestay, set around a nice garden on the way to Chapo-ra harbour, offers spotless rooms of varying sizes in a three-storey building. The best are the brand-new top-floor rooms with swanky bathrooms, TV and balcony. Budget travel-lers will be happy with the compact ground-floor rooms with shared bathroom.

Baba GUESTHOUSE $
(📞0832-2273339; babavilla11@yahoo.in; d ₹500, without bathroom ₹250) At this price, and with its laid-back Chapora location, Baba is often full with long-stayers but you might be lucky as a walk-in. The 14 rooms are clean and simple but serviceable. Lo-cated behind the Baba Restaurant on the main street.

Baba Place GUESTHOUSE $
(📞9822156511; babaplace11@yahoo.com; Chapo-ra Fort Rd; d without/with AC ₹800/1200; ❈🛜) Brand new at the time of research, Baba Place features a rooftop terrace with views of Chapora Fort, immaculate, decent-sized rooms with verandah, and a nice, quiet Chapora location.

🍴 Eating

🍴 Vagator

★Bean Me Up Soya Station VEGAN $$
(www.beanmeup.in; 1639/2 Deulvaddo; mains ₹180-350; ⊘8am-11pm; 🛜) Bean Me Up has gone all vegan, but even nonveg travellers will be blown away by the taste, variety and filling plates on offer in this relaxed garden restaurant. The extensive menu includes ve-gan pizzas, ice creams and innovative salads. Ingredients are as diverse as coconut, cash-ew milk and cashew cheese, quinoa, tofu and lentil dhal.

Bluebird GOAN $$
(www.bluebirdgoa.com; Ozran Beach Rd; mains ₹250-370; ⊘8.30am-11pm) Bluebird specialis-es in Goan cuisine, with genuine vindaloos, chicken *cafrial*, fish curry rice and Goan sausages among the temptations, as well as some delicately spiced seafood dishes. Dine in the lovely open garden cafe. The attached guesthouse has some nice rooms.

Mango Tree Bar & Cafe MULTICUISINE $$
(Vagator Beach Rd; mains ₹120-550; ⊘24hr) With loud reggae, crappy service, dark-wood fur-niture, a sometimes rambunctious bar scene, ancient expats leaning over the bar, draught beer and an overall great vibe, the Mango Tree is a classic Vagator meeting place. It's open late (24 hours if it's busy enough), the food is pretty good – from Goan to Euro-pean, pizza, Thai and Mexican – and films or sports are sometimes shown on the big screen.

★Thalassa GREEK $$$
(📞9850033537; www.thalassagoa.com; mains ₹300-750; ⊘4pm-midnight) Authentic and ri-diculously good Greek food is served alfres-co on a breezy terrace to the sound of the sea just below. Kebabs, souvlaki and thoughtful seafood dishes are the speciality, but vegie dishes are also excellent; the *spanakorizo*

WHERE'S THE PARTY?

Goa was long legendary among Western visitors for its all-night, open-air trance parties, until a central government 'noise pollution' ban on loud music in open spaces between 10pm and 6am largely curbed its often notorious, drug-laden party scene (late nights are still allowed in sound-proof interior spaces). If you're looking for the remainder of the real party scene, though, you'll need to keep your ear close to the ground, and wait out for word in Vagator or Anjuna. Authorities tend to turn a blind eye to parties during the peak Christmas–New Year period.

(spinach and rice cooked with Greek olive oil and herbs and topped with feta) is outstanding. Wash it all down with a jug of sangria. It's very popular around sunset – book ahead for a beachside table.

✗ Chapora

Tiny Chapora's eating scene is not as evolved as Vagator's. **Scarlet Cold Drinks** (juices & snacks ₹30-80; ⊙8.30am-midnight) and **Jai Ganesh Fruit Juice Centre** (Chapora; juices ₹40-80; ⊙8.30am-midnight) are both popular meeting places side by side in close proximity to the thickest gusts of charas (hasish) smoke. Scarlet has an exceptionally good noticeboard, while Jai Ganesh has cold coffee and avocado lassis.

♟ Drinking & Entertainment

Vagator's party scene is hanging on, especially over the peak Christmas/New Year period. The Russians, having taken the party crown away from the Israelis, seem to create nightlife in various spots around town.

Paulo's Antique Bar BAR
(Chapora; ⊙11.30am-11pm) In season this hole-in-the-wall bar on Chapora's main street overflows with good music and cold beer at night. Even during the afternoon the few tables on the verandah are a good spot to watch the world go by.

Nine Bar BAR
(⊙6pm-4am) Once the hallowed epicentre of Goa's trance scene, the open-air Nine Bar, on the clifftop overlooking Little Vagator Beach, has now moved into an indoor space so the parties can still go all night. Look out for flyers and local advice to see when the big party nights are on.

Hilltop CLUB
(☑0832-2273665; ⊙sunset-late) Hilltop is a long-serving Vagator trance and party ven-

ue that's deserted by day but comes alive from sunset. Its edge-of-town neon-lit coconut grove location allows it, on occasion, to bypass the 10pm noise regulations to host concerts, parties and the occasional international DJ. Sunday sessions (5pm to 10pm) are legendary here, and in season there's usually an evening market and techno party on Friday night.

🛍 Shopping

Rainbow Bookshop BOOKS
(Vagator Beach Rd; ⊙10am-2pm & 3-7pm) Long-running shop stocking a good range of secondhand and new books.

ℹ Information

Vagator's closest ATM is the HDFC at the petrol station on the back road to Anjuna and Mapusa. Plenty of internet places are scattered around town and lots of accommodation places offer wi-fi.

ℹ Getting There & Away

Frequent buses run from Chapora, through Vagator, to Mapusa (₹10) throughout the day, many via Anjuna. The buses start in Chapora village, but there are a couple of other stops in Chapora and Vagator. Scooters/motorbikes can easily be hired for around ₹200/300 per day in high season.

Morjim & Aswem

Morjim and Aswem, a peaceful strip of uncrowded sand stretching north from the Chapora river mouth, are two North Goan beaches where sunbathing doesn't attract hordes of hawkers, dogs and onlookers. The water, though, does suffer from a bit of river run-off pollution and the sand is more black than golden. Rare olive ridley turtles nest at Morjim's southern end from November to February, so this is a protected area, but it's developing rapidly due mainly to a heavy influx of Russian visitors.

🏃 Activities

Vaayu Waterman's Village
SURFING

(🖉 9850050403; www.vaayuvision.org; Aswem; surfboard hire per hr ₹500, lessons ₹2700) Goa's only surf shop is also an activity and art centre where you can arrange lessons and hire equipment for surfing, kiteboarding, stand up paddleboarding, kayaking and wakeboarding. Enthusiastic young owners also run an art gallery, cafe and funky accommodation across the road from Aswem beach.

🛏 Sleeping & Eating

★ Wanderers Hostel
HOSTEL $

(🖉 9619235302; www.wanderershostel.com; Morjim; dm incl breakfast ₹500, luxury tent d ₹2000; ❄ 🗐 ➿) This relatively new hostel about five minutes' walk back from Morjim Beach is a real find. The main building, decorated with original travellers murals, has 40 beds in spotless air-con dorms with lockers, bed lights and free wi-fi, full kitchen, clean bathrooms, cosy communal areas and a pool table. In the garden next door is a tent village with swimming pool and yoga retreat centre (classes free to guests).

Goan Café & Resort
RESORT $$

(🖉 0832-2244394; www.goancafe.com; apt & cottage from ₹1800, with AC ₹2200, treehouse without/with bathroom from ₹1200/1700; ❄ 🗐) Fronting Morijm Beach, this excellent family-run resort has a fine array of beachfront stilted 'treehouse' huts and more solid rooms (some with AC) at the back. The Friends Corner restaurant is good; it's not licensed but you're welcome to BYO.

Meems' Beach Resort
RESORT $$

(🖉 0832-2247015; www.meemsbeachresort. com; r ₹2000, with AC ₹2500, f ₹4000; ❄ 🗐) A solid guesthouse with 11 very clean rooms, Meems' is just across the road from the beach. A feature here is the atmospheric garden restaurant with low tables and floor cushions, specialising in Kashmiri cuisine and Vietnamese barbecue.

Yab Yum
HUTS $$$

(🖉 0832-6510392; www.yabyumresorts.com; hut from ₹5800; 🗐) 🏄 This top-notch choice has unusual, stylish, dome-shaped huts – some look like giant hairy coconuts – made of a combination of all-natural local materials,

including mud, stone and mango wood. A whole host of yoga and massage options are available, and it's all set in one of the most secluded beachfront jungle gardens you'll find in Goa.

La Plage
MEDITERRANEAN $$

(mains ₹210-400; ⏱ 9am-10pm Nov-Mar) Rnowned in these parts, La Plage takes beach shack to the next level with its inspired gourmet French-Mediterranean food. Along with excellent salads, seafood and fabulous desserts (try the chocolate thali), La Plage stocks great wines. It's usually open from late November to April.

ℹ Getting There & Around

Although local buses run between Siolim and Morjim, unless you have your own transport it's easiest to take a taxi from Arambol, Mapusa or Anjuna.

Mandrem

Mellow Mandrem has developed in recent years from an in-the-know piece of beach heaven for those seeking a change from the traveller scenes of Arambol and Anjuna to a fairly mainstream but still incredibly lovely hangout. An unusual feature of Mandrem is the narrow river inlet separating the white-sand beach from most of the accommodation strip and road – rickety bamboo bridges connect you to the beach, where seasonal shack restaurants set up. Development here is still low-key compared to most resorts in Goa and the beaches are largely free of hawkers and tourist crowds. There's plenty of yoga, meditation and ayurveda on offer, good dining and space to lay down with a good book. Many travellers believe there's no better place in North Goa.

🏃 Activities

Himalaya Yoga Valley
YOGA

(🖉 9960657852; www.yogagoaindia.com; Mandrem Beach) The winter home of a popular Dharamsala outfit, HYV specialises in hatha and ashtanga residential teacher-training courses, but also has daily drop-in classes (₹400; 1½ hours; 8am, 10am and 3pm daily) and 10-day yoga refresher courses.

Oceanic Yoga
YOGA

(🖉 9049247422; www.oceanicyoga.com; Junas Waddo, Mandrem; drop-in class ₹300-400) Oceanic officers drop-in classes, seven-day yoga and meditation retreats, reiki and yoga teacher-training courses.

🛏 Sleeping & Eating

⭐ **Dunes Holiday Village**   BEACH HUT **$**

(☑ 0832-2247219; www.dunesgoa.com; r & hut ₹900-1100; @ 🛜) The pretty huts here are peppered around a palm-filled lane leading to the beach; at night, globe lamps light up the place like a palm-tree dreamland. Huts range from basic to more sturdy 'treehouses' (huts on stilts). It's a friendly, good-value place with a decent beach restaurant, massage, yoga classes and a marked absence of trance.

⭐ **Mandala**   RESORT **$$**

(☑ 9158266093, www.themandalagoa.com; r & hut ₹1600-5500; ❋ 🛜) Mandala is a very shanti and beautifully designed eco-village with a range of huts and a couple of quirky air-con rooms in the 'Art House.' Pride of place goes to the barn-sized two-storey villas inspired by the design of a Keralan houseboat. There are no beach views or even direct beach access but the location, overlooking the tidal lagoon, is serene with a large garden, daily yoga sessions and an organic restaurant.

Beach Street   RESORT **$$**

(Lazy Dog; ☑ 0832-3223911; Mandrem Beach; r & hut ₹3300-4400; 🛜 ❋) This large and relatively new beachfront villa has neat and tidy rooms, while the seasonal beachfront huts are spacious and well designed. The pool is a nice touch but it's only a short walk over the bamboo bridge to the beach.

ℹ Getting There & Around

It's a nightmare trying to get anywhere in a hurry on public transport. Most travellers taxi to their chosen accommodation, then either hire a scooter/motorbike or use taxis from there.

Arambol (Harmal)

With its craggy cliffs, sweeping beach and remote northerly location, Arambol first emerged in the 1960s as a mellow paradise for long-haired long-stayers, and ever since travellers have been drifting up to this blissed-out corner of Goa. As a result, in high season the beach and the road leading down to it (known as Glastonbury St) can get pretty crowded – with huts, people and nonstop stalls selling the usual tourist stuff.

Further north around the headland is the near-deserted Querim (Keri) beach where the Terekhol River meets the coast.

🏃 Activities

Follow the cliff path north of Arambol Beach to pretty Kalacha Beach, which meets the small 'sweetwater' lake, a great spot for swimming.

Arambol Paragliding   PARAGLIDING

(10min flight ₹1500; ⊘ noon-6pm) The headland above Kalacha Beach (Sweetwater Lake) is an ideal launching point for paragliding. There are a number of independent operators: ask around at the shack restaurants on the beach, arrange a pilot, then make the short hike to the top of the headland. Most flights are around 10 minutes, but if conditions are right you can stay up much longer.

Himalayan Iyengar Yoga Centre   YOGA

(www.hiyogacentre.com; Madhlo Vaddo; 5-day yoga course ₹4000; ⊘ 9am-6pm Tue-Sun Nov-Mar) Arambol's reputable Himalayan Iyengar Yoga Centre, which runs five-day courses in hatha yoga from mid-November to mid-March, is the winter centre of the iyengar yoga school in Dharamkot, near Dharamsala in north India. First-time students must take the introductory five-day course, then can continue with more advanced five-day courses at a reduced rate.

Surf Wala   SURFING

(www.surfwala.com; Surf Club; 1½hr lesson from ₹2000, 3-/5-day course ₹5000/8000) If you're a beginner looking to get up on a board, join the international team of surfers based at Arambol's Surf Club. Prices include board hire, wax and rashie. Check the website for instructor contact details – between them they speak English, Russian, Hindi, Konkani and Japanese! Board-only rental is ₹500.

🛏 Sleeping

Arambol is known for its sea-facing, cliff-hugging budget huts – trawl the cliffside to the north of Arambol's main beach for the best hut options. It's almost impossible to book in advance: simply turn up early in the day to check who's checking out. The beach stretch is also lined with shack restaurants with hut accommodation at the back, much like Palolem.

Chilli's   HOTEL **$**

(☑ 9921882424; d ₹600, apt with AC ₹1000; ⊘ year-round; ❋) Near the beach entrance on Glastonbury St, this clean and friendly canary-yellow place is one of Arambol's better non-beachfront bargains. Chilli's offers 10 decent, no-frills rooms, all with attached bathroom, fan and a hot-water shower. The top-floor apartment with AC and TV is great value. Owner Derek hires out motorbikes and scooters and free advice.

Shree Sai Cottages HUT $
(☑0832-3262823, 9420767358; shreesai_cottages @yahoo.com; hut without bathroom ₹400-600) A good example of what's on offer along the cliffs, Shree Sai has simple, cute, sea-facing huts on the cliffs overlooking Kalacha Beach.

Om Ganesh BEACH HUT $
(☑9404436447; r & hut ₹400-800) Popular seasonal huts along the cliff path and a good restaurant, Om Ganesh has been around for a while and also has solid rooms in a building on the hillside.

Arambol Plaza Beach Resort HOTEL $$
(☑9545550731, 0832-2242052; Arambol Beach Rd; r & cottage ₹1800-2500; ✳🛜❄) On the road between the upper village and the beach, Arambol Plaza is a reasonable mid-range choice with cute timber cottages around a decent pool. All rooms are air-con but avoid the poorly maintained rooms in the building at the side.

Surf Club GUESTHOUSE $$
(www.surfclubgoa.com; d ₹1200-1600; 🛜) In its own space at the end of a lane, on the very southern end of Arambol Beach, the Surf Club is one of those cool little hang-outs that offer a bit of everything: simple but clean rooms, a funky bar with live music, surf lessons and a seasonal kindergarten.

🍴 Eating & Drinking

Beach shacks with chairs and tables on the sand and parachute-silk canopies line the beach at Arambol. There are more restaurants and cafes lining the main road from the village to the beach. For simpler fare, head up to Arambol village, by the bus stop, where small local joints will whip you up a thali and a chai for less than ₹50.

Shimon MIDDLE EASTERN $
(meals ₹100-160; ⊙9am-11pm) Just back from the beach, and understandably popular with Israeli backpackers, Shimon is the place to fill up on exceptional felafel. For something more unusual go for *sabich,* crisp slices of eggplant stuffed into pita bread along with boiled egg, boiled potato and salad. The East-meets-Middle-East thali (₹360) comprises a little bit of almost everything on the menu.

Dylan's Toasted & Roasted CAFE $
(☑9604780316; www.dylanscoffee.com; coffee & desserts from ₹60; ⊙9am-11pm late Nov-Apr) The Goa (winter) incarnation of a Manali institution, Dylan's is a fine place for an espresso, a chocolate chip cookies and old-school dessert. A nice hang-out just back from the southern beach entrance.

Fellini ITALIAN $$
(mains ₹180-350; ⊙from 6.30pm) On the left-hand side just before the beach, this unsignposted but long-standing Italian joint is perfect if you're craving a carbonara or calzone. More than 20 wood-fired, thin-crust pizza varieties are on the menu, but save space for a very decent rendition of tiramisu.

Double Dutch MULTICUISINE $$
(mains ₹110-390, steaks ₹420-470; ⊙7am-10pm) In a peaceful garden set back from the main road to the Glastonbury St beach entrance, Double Dutch has long been popular for its steaks, salads, Thai and Indonesian dishes, and famous apple pies. It's a very relaxed meeting place with secondhand books, newspapers and a useful noticeboard for current Arambolic affairs.

ℹ Information
The nearest ATM is in Arambol village near the bus stop.

ℹ Getting There & Around
Buses to Mapusa (₹30, one hour) depart from Arambol village every half-hour. A taxi to Mapusa or Anjuna should cost around ₹600. If you're heading north to Mumbai, travel agents can book bus tickets and you can board at a stop on the highway in the main village.

Lots of places in Arambol rent scooters and motorbikes, for ₹250 and ₹350, respectively, per day.

SOUTH GOA

Margao (Madgaon)
POP 94,400
Margao (also called Madgaon) is the capital of south Goa and for travellers is chiefly a transport hub, with the state's major train

Margao (Madgaon)

0   200 m
0   0.1 miles

Panaji (33km)

Fatorda Stadium
(200m)

Market

Chandor
(15km);
Ponda
(17km)

Kadamba
Bus Stand

Colva
(6km)

LARGO
DE IGREJA

MONTE
HILL

Damodar
Temple

7
Paulo Travels
3

Abade Faria Rd

Padre Miranda Rd

Bank

9

5
2

Valaulikar Rd

Municipal
Gardens

Bank

Miguel LF Rd

Central
Bus Stand

Isidoro Baptista Rd

6
1
Luis Miranda Rd

8

Rue F de Loiola

Erasmo Carvalho Rd

4

10

Station Rd

(2km);
Palolem (37km)

Margao (Madgaon)

and bus stations. Although lacking much of Panaji's charm, it's a bustling market town of a manageable size for getting things done, or for simply enjoying the busy energy of urban India without big-city hassles.

◎ Sights

It's worth a walk around the **Largo de Igreja** district, home to lots of atmospherically crumbling and restored old Portuguese-era homes, and the richly decorated 17th-century **Church of the Holy Spirit**, particularly impressive when a Sunday morning service is taking place.

The city's business district orbits the rectangular **Municipal Gardens**, a mini-oasis of lawns, flowers and paths. At the southern end the Municipal Building is home to the **Municipal Library** (Abade Faria Rd; ⊙8am-8pm Mon-Fri, 9am-noon & 4-7pm Sat & Sun), which has some great books on Goa and a retro reading room where locals gather to read the daily paper.

🛏 Sleeping

Hotel Tanish HOTEL $
(☎0832-2735858; www.hoteltanishgoa.com; Reliance Trade Centre, Valaulikar Rd; s/d ₹900/1200, s/d/ste with AC ₹1100/1500/2000; ✱) Oddly situated inside a modern mall, this top-floor hotel offers good views of the surrounding countryside, with stylish, well-equipped rooms. Suites come with a bathtub, a big TV and a view all the way to Colva; just make sure you get an outside-facing room, as some overlook the mall interior.

Om Shiv Hotel HOTEL $$
(☎0832-2710294; www.omshivhotel.com; Cine Lata Rd; d ₹2750-3850, ste ₹5000; ✱@⌢) In a bright-yellow building tucked away behind the Bank of India, Om Shiv does a decent line in fading 'executive' rooms, all of which have air-con and balcony. The suites have good views, there's a gym and the 7th-floor **Rockon Pub**.

Nanutel Margao HOTEL $$
(☎0832-6722222; Padre Miranda Rd; s/d incl breakfast ₹3780/4100, ste ₹4750-5300; ✱⌢✱) Margao's best business class hotel by some margin, Nanutel is modern and slick with a lovely pool, good restaurant, bar and coffee shop, and clean air-con rooms. The location, between the Municipal Gardens and Largo de Igreja district, is convenient for everything.

✕ Eating

Swad INDIAN $
(New Market; ₹50-10; ⊙7.30am-8pm) Some of Margao's best veg food is dished up at the family-friendly, lunch-break favourite Swad, across from Lotus Inn. The thalis, South Indian tiffins and other mains are all reliably tasty.

Café Tato INDIAN $
(Valaulikar Rd; thalis ₹90; ⊙7am-10pm Mon-Sat) A favourite local lunch spot: tasty vegetarian fare in a bustling backstreet canteen, and delicious all-you-can-eat thalis.

★Ruta's World Cafè AMERICAN, INTERNATIONAL $$
(☎0832-2710757; www.caferuta.com; Fr Miranda Rd; mains ₹150-350; ⊙10am-7pm Mon-Sat) Ruta's is a quality addition to Margao's otherwise average dining scene and an excellent reason to get off the beach. After years working as an award-winning cook, teacher and recipe book author on the San Francisco scene, chef Ruta Kahate has brought some of her culinary magic to Goa (there's another restaurant in Mapusa; p132).

★Longhuino's GOAN, MULTICUISINE $$
(Luis Miranda Rd; mains ₹95-205; ⊙8.30am-10pm) A local institution since 1950, quaint old Longhuino's has been serving up tasty Indian, Goan and Chinese dishes, popular with locals and tourists alike. Go for a Goan dish such as *ambot tik*, and leave room for the retro desserts like rum balls and tiramasu. Service is as languid as the slowly

whirring ceiling fans but it's a great place to watch the world go by over a coffee or beer.

Shopping

MMC New Market
MARKET

(☉ 8.30am-9pm Mon-Sat) Margao's crowded, covered canopy of colourful stalls is a fun place to wander around, sniffing spices, sampling soaps and browsing the household merchandise.

Golden Heart Emporium
BOOKS

(Confidant House, Abade Faria Rd; ☉ 10am-1.30pm & 4-7pm Mon-Sat) One of Goa's best bookshops, Golden Heart is crammed from floor to ceiling with fiction, nonfiction, children's books, and illustrated volumes on the state's food, architecture and history. It also stocks otherwise hard-to-get titles by local Goan authors. It's situated down a little lane off Abade Faria Rd, on the right-hand side as you're heading north.

ℹ Information

Banks offering currency exchange and 24-hour ATMs are all around town, especially near the municipal gardens and along Luis Miranda Rd. There's a handy HDFC ATM and an internet cafe in the Caro Centre near Longuinhos.

ℹ Getting There & Around

BUS

Long-distance buses depart from Kadamba bus stand and a private stand, both about 2km north of the Municipal Gardens. Shuttle buses (₹30, 35 minutes) run to Panaji every few minutes. For North Goa destinations head to Panaji and change there. Local buses to Benaulim (₹10, 20 minutes), Colva (₹10, 20 minutes) and Palolem (₹40, one

MAJOR TRAINS FROM MARGAO (MADGAON)

DESTINATION	TRAIN	FARE (₹)	DURATION (HR)	DEPARTURES
Bangalore	02779 Vasco da Gama-SBC Link (D)	360/970	15	3.50pm
Chennai (Madras; via Yesvantpur)	17312 Vasco-da-Gama-Chennai Express (C)	475/1275/1850	21	3.20pm Thu
Delhi	12431 Rajdhani Express (A)	2110/3050	27	10.10am Wed, Fri, Sat
Ernakulam	12618 Lakshadweep Express (C)	445/1165/1665	14½	7.20pm
	16345 Netravati Express (C)	415/1120/1620	15	11.10pm
Hubli	02779 Vasco-da-Gama-SBC Link (D)	160/485	6½	3.50pm
Mangalore	12133 Mangalore Express (C)	290/735/1035	5½	7.10am
Mumbai (Bombay)	10112 Konkan Kanya Express (C)	390/1055/1250	12	6pm
	10104 Mandovi Express (C)	390/1055/1520	12	9.15am
Pune	12779 Goa Express (C)	335/930/1315	12	3.50pm
Thiruvananthapuram	12432 Rajdhani Express (A)	1775/2420	19	12.45pm Mon, Wed, Thu
	16345 Netravati Express (C)	480/1290/1875	19½	11.10pm

Fares: (A) 3AC/2AC, (B) 2S/CC, (C) sleeper/3AC/2AC, (D) sleeper/3AC

hour) stop at the bus stop on the east side of the Municipal Gardens every 15 minutes or so.

Private buses ply interstate routes several times daily, most departing between 5.30pm and 7.30pm, and can be booked at offices around town; try **Paulo Travel.** (✆0832-2702405; ww.phmgoa.com; Hotel Nanutel, Padre Miranda Rd)

TAXI

Taxis go to Palolem (₹900), Panaji (₹800), Dabolim airport (₹600), Calangute (₹1000) and Anjuna (₹1200). Except for the train station, where there's a prepaid booth, you'll have to negotiate the fare with the driver.

TRAIN

Margao's well-organised train station, about 2km south of town, serves the Konkan Railway and other routes. Its **reservation hall** (✆PNR enquiry 0832-2700730, information 0832-2712790; ☺8am-2pm & 2.15-8pm Mon-Sat, 8am-2pm Sun) is on the 1st floor. A taxi or autorickshaw to or from the town centre should cost around ₹100.

Chandor

The lush village of Chandor, 15km east of Margao, makes a perfect day away from the beaches, and it's here more than anywhere else in the state that the once opulent lifestyles of Goa's former landowners, who found favour with the Portuguese aristocracy, are still visible in its quietly decaying colonial-era mansions. Chandor hosts the colourful **Feast of the Three Kings** on the 6 January, during which local boys re-enact the arrival of the three kings from the Christmas story.

Braganza House, built in the 17th century, is possibly the best example of what Goa's scores of once grand and glorious mansions have today become. Built on land granted by the King of Portugal, the house was divided from the outset into two wings, to house two sides of the same family. The **West Wing** (✆0832-2784201; donation ₹150; ☺9am-5pm) belongs to one set of the family's descendants, the Menezes-Bragança, and is filled with gorgeous chandeliers, Italian marble floors, rosewood furniture, and antique treasures from Macau, Portugal, China and Europe. Despite the passing of the elderly Mrs Aida Menezes-Bragança in 2012, the grand old home, which requires considerable upkeep, remains open to the public. Next door, the **East Wing** (✆0832-2784227;

WORTH A TRIP

HAMPI

The surreal ruins of the Vijayanagar empire at Hampi (p896), in Karanakata, are a popular detour or overnight trip from Goa. Hampi can be reached by train from Margao to Hospet on the VSG Howrah Express which departs at 7.10am Tuesday, Thursday, Friday and Saturday (sleeper/3AC/2AC ₹235/620/885, eight hours). More convenient are the overnight sleeper buses direct to Hampi from Margao and Panaji operated by Paulo Travel (₹900 to ₹1100, 10 to 11 hours, 2-3 daily).

donation ₹100; ☺10am-6pm) is owned by the Braganza-Pereiras, descendants of the other half of the family. It's nowhere near as grand, but it's beautiful in its own lived-in way, and has a small but striking family chapel that contains a carefully hidden fingernail of St Francis Xavier – a relic that's understandably a source of great pride. Both homes are open daily, and there's almost always someone around to let you in. Donations are requested and expected.

About 1km east of Chandor's church, the original building of the **Fernandes House** (✆0832-2784245; donation ₹200; ☺9am-6pm), also known as Casa Grande, dates back more than 500 years, while the Portuguese section was tacked on by the Fernandes family in 1821. The secret basement hideaway, full of gun holes and with an escape tunnel to the river, was used by the family to flee attackers.

Colva & Benaulim

POP 12,000

Colva and Benaulim boast broad, open beaches, but are no longer the first place backpackers head in south Goa – most tourists here are of the domestic or ageing European varieties. There's no party scene as in north Goa and they lack the beauty and traveller vibe of Palolem. Still, these are the closest beaches to the major transport hubs of Margao and Dabolim airport. Benaulim has the greater charm, with only a small strip of shops and a village vibe, though out of high season it sometimes has the melancholy feel of a deserted seaside town.

◉ Sights & Activities

The beach entrance at Colva, and to a lesser extent Benaulim, throng with operators keen to sell you **parasailing** (per ride ₹800), **jet-skiing** (per 15 minutes s/d ₹300/500), and one-hour **dolphin-watching trips** (per person from ₹300).

★ Goa Chitra   MUSEUM
(☎0832-6570877; www.goachitra.com; St John the Baptist Rd, Mondo Vaddo, Benaulim; admission ₹200; ⊙9am-6pm Tue-Sun) Artist and restorer Victor Hugo Gomes first noticed the slow extinction of traditional objects – from farming tools to kitchen utensils to altarpieces – as a child in Benaulim. He created this ethnographic museum from the more than 4000 cast-off objects that he collected from across the state over 20 years (he often had to find elderly people to explain their uses). Admission to this fascinating museum is via a one-hour guided tour, held on the hour. Goa Chitra is 3km east of Maria Hall – ask locally for directions.

🛏 Sleeping

🛏 Colva

Colva still has a few basic budget guesthouses among the palm groves back from the beach; ask around locally.

Sam's Guesthouse   HOTEL $
(☎0832-2788753; r ₹650; 🛜) Away from the fray, north of Colva's main drag on the road running parallel to the beach, Sam's is a big, cheerful place with friendly owners and spacious rooms that are a steal at this price. Rooms are around a pleasant garden courtyard and there's a good restaurant and a whacky bar.

Colmar Beach Resort   RESORT $
(☎022-67354666 in Mumbai; www.colmarbeachresort.net; d ₹700, with AC from ₹1100, poolside cottage ₹1500; ❄🛜🏊) Colmar Beach Resort is the closest budget place to Colva's beach and, provided you're not expecting too much, it can make a reasonable stay. The cottages around the small pool are the pick, while the ageing rooms at the back are cheaper and a bit grimy. The beach is right in front and the restaurant-bar is quite good.

La Ben   HOTEL $
(☎0832-2788040; www.laben.net; Colva Beach Rd; r ₹1100, with AC ₹1400; ❄🛜) Neat, clean and not entirely devoid of atmosphere. If you're not desperately seeking anything with character, La Ben has decent, good-value rooms and has been around for ages. A great addition is the Garden Restaurant.

Skylark Resort   HOTEL $$
(☎0832-2788052; www.skylarkresortgoa.com; d ₹2885-3639, f ₹4270; ❄🛜🏊) A serious step up from the budget places, Skylark's clean, fresh rooms are graced with bits and pieces of locally made teak furniture and block-print bedspreads, while the lovely pool makes a pleasant place to lounge. The best (and more expensive) rooms are those facing the pool.

🛏 Benaulim

There are lots of homes around town advertising simple rooms to let. This, combined with a couple of decent budget options, make Benaulim a better (and quieter) bet for backpackers than Colva.

Rosario's Inn   GUESTHOUSE $
(☎0832-2770636; r ₹450, with AC ₹450 800; ❄) Across a football field flitting with young players and dragonflies, family-run Rosario's

---

PUPPY LOVE

International Animal Rescue (Animal Tracks; ☎0832-2268272; www.internationalanimalrescuegoa.org.in; Madungo Vaddo, Assagao; ⊙9am-4pm) runs the Animal Tracks rescue facility in Assagao, North Goa. At Colva's **Goa Animal Welfare Trust Shop** (☎0832-2653677; www.gawt.org; ⊙9.30am-1pm & 4-7pm Mon-Sat), next to Skylark Resort, you can pick up some gifts, donate clothes and other stuff you don't want, and borrow books from the lending library. You can also learn more about the work of **GAWT** (☎0832-2653677; www.gawt.org; Old Police Station, Curchorem; ⊙9am-5.30pm Mon-Sat, 10am-1pm Sun), which operates a shelter in Curchorem (near Margao). At Chapolim, a few kilometres northeast of Palolem, the **Animal Rescue Centre** (☎0832-2644171; Chapolim; ⊙10am-1pm & 2.30-5pm Mon-Sat) also takes in sick, injured or stray animals. Volunteers are welcome at the shelters, even for a few hours, to walk or play with the dogs.

is a large establishment with very clean, simple rooms and a restaurant. Excellent value.

D'Souza Guest House
GUESTHOUSE $

(☏ 0832-277 0583; d ₹600) With just three rooms, this blue-painted house in the back lanes is run by a local Goan family and comes with bundles of homey atmosphere and a lovely garden. It's often full so book ahead.

Palm Grove Cottages
HOTEL $$

(☏ 0832-2770059; www.palmgrovegoa.com; Vaswado; d incl breakfast ₹2020-3700; ❄ 🅰) Old-fashioned, secluded charm and Benaulim's leafiest garden wecomes you at Palm Grove Cottages, a great midrange choice. The quiet AC rooms, some with a balcony, all have a nice feel but the best are the spacious deluxe rooms in a separate Portuguese-style building. The Palm Garden Restaurant here is exceptionally good.

Anthy's Guesthouse
GUESTHOUSE $$

(☏ 0832-2771680; anthysguesthouse@rediffmail.com; Sernabatim Beach; d ₹1300, with AC ₹1700; ❄) One of a handful of places lining Sernabatim Beach itself, Anthy's is a firm favourite with travellers for its good restaurant, book exchange, and its well-kept chalet-style rooms, which stretch back from the beach surrounded by a garden.

Blue Corner
BEACH HUTS $$

(☏ 9850455770; www.bluecornergoa.com; huts ₹1600) Behind the beach shack restaurant a short walk north of the main beach entrance is this group of sturdy cocohuts – not so common around here – with fan and verandah. The restaurant gets good reviews.

✖ Eating & Drinking

✖ Colva

Colva's beach has a string of shacks offering the standard fare and fresh seafood.

Sagar Kinara
INDIAN $

(Colva Beach Rd; mains ₹60-180; ⊙7am-10.30pm) A pure-veg restaurant upstairs (nonveg is separate, downstairs) with tastes to please even committed carnivores, this place is clean, efficient and offers cheap and delicious North and South Indian cuisine all day.

Leda Lounge & Restaurant
BAR

(⊙7.30am-midnight) Part sports bar, part music venue, part cocktail bar, Leda is Colva's best nightspot by a long shot. There's live music from Thursday to Sunday, fancy

DUDHSAGAR FALLS

On the eastern border with Karnataka, Dudhsagar Falls (603m) are Goa's most impressive waterfalls, and the second highest in India, best seen as soon as possible after the rains. The main access is the village of Colem, from where jeeps (₹400 per person for six passengers) make the bumpy but scenic 40-minute drive to the car park from where it's a short scramble to the falls

A nice way to get here is the 8.15am train to Kulem (Colem) from Margao (check return times), then pick up a jeep. An easier option (especially if coming from your beach resort rather than Margao) is to take a taxi, book with a travel agent, or take a full-day GTDC tour from Panaji, Mapusa or Calangute (₹1200, Wed & Sun).

drinks (Mojitos, Long Island iced teas) and good food (mains ₹270 to ₹600).

✖ Benaulim

Pedro's Bar & Restaurant
GOAN, MULTICUISINE $$

(Vasvaddo Beach Rd; mains ₹110-350; ⊙7am-midnight) Set amid a large, shady garden on the beachfront and popular with local and international travellers, Pedro's offers standard Indian, Chinese and Italian dishes, as well as Goan choices and 'sizzlers.'

Johncy Restaurant
GOAN, MULTICUISINE $$

(Vasvaddo Beach Rd; mains ₹110-350; ⊙7am-midnight) Unlike most beach shacks, Johncy has been around forever, dispensing standard Goan, Indian and Western favourites from its location just back from the sand.

Club Zoya
CLUB

(☏ 9822661388; www.clubzoya.com; ⊙from 8pm) The party scene has hit sleepy little Benaulim in the form of barn-sized Club Zoya, with international DJs, big light shows and a cocktail bar featuring speciality flavoured and infused vodka drinks. Something's on most nights here in season but check the website for upcoming events and DJs.

❶ Information

Colva has several ATMs strung along the east–west Colva Beach Rd. Benaulim has a HDFC ATM on the back road to Colva.

ⓘ Getting There & Around

Scooters can be rented at Colva and Benaulim for around ₹250.

COLVA

Buses run from Colva to Margao every few minutes (₹10, 20 minutes) until around 7pm. An autorickshaw/taxi to Margao costs ₹200/250.

BENAULIM

Buses from Benaulim to Margao are also frequent (₹10, 20 minutes); they stop at the Maria Hall crossroads, 1.2km east of the beach. Some from Margao continue south to Varca and Cavelossim.

Benaulim to Agonda

Immediately south of Benaulim are the beach resorts of Varca and Cavelossim, with wide, pristine sands and a line of flashy five-star hotels set amid landscaped private grounds fronting the beach. About 3km south of Cavelossim, at the end of the peninsula, **Mobor** and its beach is one of the prettiest spots along this stretch of coast, with simple beach shacks serving good food. The pick here is **Blue Whale** (mains ₹100-350).

Cross the Sal River from Cavelossim to Assolna on the huge new bridge and continue south to the rustic but charming fishing village of **Betul**.

From Betul the road winds over gorgeous, undulating hills thick with palm groves. It's worth detouring to the bleak old Portuguese fort of **Cabo da Rama**, which has a small church within the fort walls, stupendous views and several old buildings rapidly becoming one with the trees.

Back on the main road to Agonda, look out for the turn-off to the right (west) to **Cola Beach**, one of south Goa's most gorgeous hidden beach gems complete with emerald-green lagoon. It's reached via a rough 2km dirt road from the highway, but it's not totally deserted – a couple of busy hut villages and a tent resort set up in season. About 500m north of the Cola turn-off is another jungle-strewn path to **Khancola** (or Kakolem) beach, with steep steps leading to a secluded beach and just a handful of huts.

Agonda is another 2.5km south of the Cola Beach turnoff.

Agonda

Agonda Beach is a fine 2km stretch of white sand framed between two forested headlands. Travellers have been drifting here for

years and seasonal hut villages – some very luxurious – now occupy almost all available beachfront space, but it's still much more low-key than Palolem and a good choice if you're after some relaxation. Rare Olive Ridley turtles nest at the northern end, which is protected by the Forest Department.

There's lots of yoga and ayurveda in Agonda and a community feel among the shops and cafes in the street running parallel to the beach. There's a HDFC ATM near the church crossroads.

🛏 Sleeping & Eating

Some of Goa's most sophisticated and luxurious beach huts, along with beachfront restaurants and bars, set up along the foreshore from November to May, and there are a few more permanent places on the sideroad running parallel to the beach.

Fatima Guesthouse   GUESTHOUSE $
(☑0832-2647477; d ₹600-700, with AC ₹800; ☀️🛜) An ever-popular two-storey guesthouse with clean rooms, a good restaurant and highly obliging staff, on the southern stretch of Agonda's beach road. The rooftop yoga classes and extended courses (and the budget price) mean it's often full.

Abba's Gloryland   GUESTHOUSE $
(☑9404312232, 0832-2647822; www.abbasgloryland.com; hut/r ₹1000/1200; 🛜) Set back from the road at the northern end of the beach, this friendly, family-run place offers cool, tiled rooms in a pink building, and neat bamboo huts with slate floors. A good budget option with no sea views but only a short walk from the beach.

Agonda White Sand   BEACH HUTS $$
(☑9823548277; www.agondawhitesand.com; Agonda Beach; hut from ₹3800; 🛜) Beautifully designed and constructed cottages with open-air bathrooms and spring mattresses surround a central bar and restaurant at this stylish beachfront place. Less than 100m away the same owners have a pair of amazing five-star sea-facing villas (₹7000 to ₹9000) with enormous beds and cavernous bathrooms large enough to contain a garden and fish pond!

★**H2O Agonda**   BEACH HUTS $$$
(☑9423836994; www.h2oagonda.com; d incl breakfast ₹4500-6500; ☀️🛜) With its purple and mauve muslin curtains and Arabian nights ambience, H2O is among the most

impressive of Agonda's luxury cottage set-ups. From the hotel-style reception, walk through a leafy garden to the spacious cottages with air-con, TV and enormous open-air bathrooms. The more expensive sea-facing cottages, with zebra print spreads on king-size beds, are worth paying extra for.

Fatima Thali Shop   SOUTH INDIAN $
(veg/fish thali ₹80/100) Beloved by locals and visitors, tiny Fatima, with just four tables, is an Agonda institution, with filling South Indian thalis whipped up inside its improbably small kitchen. It's also a cosy spot for breakfast, salads and chai.

Palolem & Around

Palolem is undoubtedly one of Goa's most postcard-perfect beaches: a gentle curve of palm-fringed sand facing a calm bay. But in season it's bursting at the seams.

If you want to see what Palolem looked like 10 or 15 years ago, turn up in September or early October, before the beach huts start to go up. Once the hammering and sawing starts, the beachfront is transformed into a toy-town of colourful and increasingly sophisticated timber and bamboo huts fronted by palm-thatch restaurants. It's still a great place to be and is popular with backpackers, long-stayers and families. Aside from being one of the safest swimming and kayaking beaches in Goa, Palolem is a great place to learn to cook, drop in to yoga classes or hire a motorbike and cruise to surrounding beaches, waterfalls and wildlife parks. At night you can listen to live rock or reggae as the sun sets or dance in silence at a head-phone party.

Further south is the small rocky cove of **Colomb Bay**, with several basic places to stay, and then peaceful and pretty **Patnem Beach**, a more relaxed version of Palolem with just a dozen or so beach hut villages and shack restaurants.

🏃 Activities

Yoga
There are courses and classes on offer at numerous places in Palolem and Patnem. Bhakti Kutir (p159) and Space Goa (p160) offer daily drop-in yoga classes, while Butterfly Book Shop (p161) arranges daily yoga (₹300) and cooking classes (₹1200).

In Patnem, **Bamboo Yoga Retreat** (☑9765379887; www.bamboo-yoga-retreat.com; Patnam Beach; s/d from ₹5300/7400; 🛜) is recommended but exclusive to guests. About 4km further south Shamana Retreat is a new outfit with an attractively remote jungle location.

Beach Activities
Kayaks are available for rent on Palolem beaches (₹150 per hour), as well as a few stand-up paddleboards (₹500). Fishermen and other boat operators hanging around the beach offer dolphin-spotting trips or rides to tiny **Butterfly Beach**, north of Palolem, for around ₹1200 for two people.

Trekking
Cotigao Wildlife Sanctuary   NATURE RESERVE
(☑0832-2965601; adult/child ₹20/10, camera/video ₹30/150; ⊙7am-5.30pm) About 9km

GOA PALOLEM & AROUND

WORTH A TRIP

DAYTRIPPING DOWN SOUTH

Goa's far south is tailor-made for daytripping. Hire a motorbike or charter a taxi and try these road trips from Palolem, Patnem or Agonda.

➡ **Tanshikar Spice Farm** (☑0832-2608358, 9421184114; www.tanshikarspicefarm.com; Netravali; spice tour incl lunch ₹450; ecohuts inc meals ₹1500 per person; ⊙10am-4pm) About 35km inland from Palolem via forest and farms is this excellent spice plantation, along with jungle treks to waterfalls and the enigmatic 'bubble lake'.

➡ **Talpona & Galgibag** These two near-deserted beach gems are scenically framed (naturally) by the Talpona and Galgibag rivers. Olive Ridley turtles nest on Galgibag and there are a couple of excellent shack restaurants and huts. The winding country drive here is half the fun.

➡ **Polem Beach** Goa's most southerly beach, 25km south of Palolem, has just one set of beach huts and a real castaway feel. A trip here should be combined with the detour to Talpona and Galgibag.

Palolem

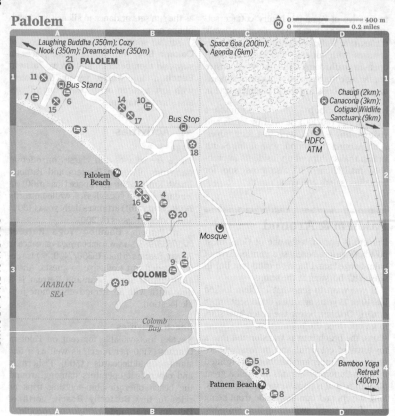

southeast of Palolem, and a good day trip, is the beautiful, remote-feeling Cotigao Wildlife Sanctuary, Goa's second-largest sanctuary and easily its most accessible, if you have your own transport. Don't expect to bump into its more exotic residents (including gaurs, sambars, leopards and spotted deer), but frogs, snakes, monkeys, insects and blazingly plumed birds are in no short supply.

Goa Jungle Adventure　　　OUTDOORS
(📞 9850485641; www.goajungle.com; trekking & canyoning trips ₹1890-3590) This adventure company, run by an experienced French guide, will take you out for thrilling trekking and canyoning trips in the Netravali area at the base of the Western Ghats, where you climb, jump and abseil into remote waterfilled plunges. Trips run from a half-day to several days, and extended rafting trips into Karnataka are also sometimes offered.

🛏 Sleeping

🛏 Palolem

Most of Palolem's accommodation is of the seasonal beach-hut variety, though there are plenty of old-fashioned guesthouses or family homes to be found back from the beach with decent rooms from ₹600. It's still possible to find a basic palm-thatch hut without bathroom somewhere near the beach for ₹700, but most of the huts these days are made of plywood or timber and come with attached bathrooms and multiple levels. The very best seafacing rooms feature aircon, flat-screen TVs and balconies and command more than ₹5000! Since the huts are dismantled and rebuilt each year, standards and ownership can vary – the places listed here are either permanent guesthouses or well-established hut operations.

pond are top-notch. The sea-view cottages are the more expensive and there are some air-con rooms – including a Jacuzzi room. There's a popular multicuisine restaurant, tapas restaurant and quality spa centre.

Art Resort
HUT $$
(☏9665982344; www.art-resort-goa.com; Ourem Rd; hut ₹1500-2500; ☎) The nicely designed cottages behind an excellent beachfront restaurant have a Bedouin camp feel with screened sit-outs and modern art works sprinkled around. The resort hosts art exhibitions and has regular live music.

Cozy Nook
HUT $$
(☏0832-2643550, 9822584760; www.cozynook goa.com; hut ₹2500-3500) This long-running operation at the northern end of the beach has well-designed cottages, including some treehouses, and a funky bar.

Dreamcatcher
HUT $$
(☏0832-2644873; www.dreamcatcher.in; hut ₹1750-2500) Probably the largest resort in Palolem, Dreamcatcher's 60 sturdy huts are nevertheless secluded, set in a coconut grove just back from the far northern end of the beach. One of the highlights here is the riverside restaurant and cocktail bar, and the wide range of holistic treatments, massage and yoga on offer, with daily drop-in yoga and reiki courses available. Access it from the back road running parallel to the beach.

Kate's Cottages
GUESTHOUSE $$
(☏9822165261; www.katescottagesgoa.com; Ourem Rd; d ₹3000-5000; ☀☎) The two stunning rooms above Fern's restaurant are beautifully designed with heavy timber finishes, huge four-poster beds, TV, modern bathrooms and views to the ocean from the balcony. There are also a couple of cheaper ground-floor cottages.

Village Guesthouse
GUESTHOUSE $$
(☏9960487627, 0832-2645767; www.village guesthousegoa.com; d incl breakfast ₹3400-4300; ☀☎) The Village is a lovely expat-run boutique hotel with eight spotless and spacious air-con rooms that are a cut above most Palolem hotels. Nicely furnished with sparkling bathrooms, four-poster beds, TV and homely touches, it makes a good base if you value peace more than being on the beach. Breakfast is served in the rear garden.

Bhakti Kutir
COTTAGE $$
(☏0832-2643469, 9823627258; www.bhakti kutir.com; Colomb Bay; cottage ₹2200-3300; ☎)

My Soulmate
GUESTHOUSE $
(☏9823785250; mysolmte@gmail.com; d ₹1000, with AC ₹1500; ☀) This friendly and spotless two-storey guesthouse in a good location just off the main Palolem Beach road is a good nonbeach bet. Neat rooms come with TV and hot water and the newer ones have sexy circular beds. Good cafe, nice staff.

Sevas
HUT $
(☏9422065437; www.sevaspalolemgoa.com; s/d hut ₹600/800, family cottage ₹1600; @☎) Hidden in the jungle on the Colomb Bay side of Palolem, Sevas has a range of simple palm-thatch huts with open-air bathrooms, larger family huts and rooms set in a lovely shaded garden area. Wi-fi is ₹100 per day.

★Ciaran's
HUT $$
(☏0832-2643477; www.ciarans.com; hut incl breakfast ₹3000-4000, r with AC ₹4500; ☀☎) Ciaran's has some of the most impressive huts on the beachfront. Affable owner John has worked hard over the years to maintain a high standard and his beautifully designed cottages around a plant-filled garden and

GOA PALOLEM & AROUND

Ensconced in a thick wooded grove in the Colomb Bay area south of Palolem, Bhakti's well-equipped rustic cottages are a little worn and you might find yourself sharing with local wildlife but this is still a popular eco and spiritual retreat with an ayurvedic massage centre and daily drop-in yoga classes.

Palolem Beach Resort RESORT $$
(☎0832-2645775, 9764442778; www.cubagoa.com/palolem; r ₹3000, with AC ₹4000, cottages ₹3000; ※☎) You can't beat the location, on the beachfront at the main road entrance to the beach, but Palolem Beach Resort has lifted its prices in keeping with most places in Palolem. It's good value in the fringe seasons when it's one of the only beachfront places open. There are average permanent rooms (air-con ones are better), seasonal huts at the front and a friendly beachfront restaurant.

Patnem

Long-stayers will love Patnem's choice of village homes and apartments available for rent. A very basic house can cost ₹10,000 per month, while a fully equipped apartment can run up to ₹40,000.

Mickys HUT $
(☎9850484884; www.mickyhuts.com; Patnem Beach; r & hut ₹800-1500, without bathroom hut ₹400; ☎) If you don't mind huts so basic they don't even have electricity, you can sleep cheap here. Fear not: there are also better huts with power and attached bath; rooms are available most of the year (closed only August and September). It's run by a friendly family at the northern end of the beach.

Mickys Naughty Corner is a cruisy beach-front cafe in front of the accommodation.

Papaya's HUT $$
(☎9923079447; www.papayasgoa.com; hut ₹3000, with AC ₹4000; ※☎) Solid huts constructed with natural materials head back into the palm grove from Papaya's popular restaurant, which does great versions of all the beachfront classics. Each hut is lovingly built, with lots of wood, four-poster beds and floating muslin.

✖ Eating

With limited beach space, restaurant shacks are banned from the sand at Palolem and Patnem, but there are plenty of beach-facing restaurants on the periphery, all offering all-day dining and fresh seafood. Palolem also has some interesting dining choices back along the main road to the beach.

Little World Cafe CAFE $
(chai ₹10, snacks ₹70-120; ⊙8am-6pm) This shanti little cafe serves up Palolem's best masala chai, along with healthy juices.

Shiv Sai INDIAN $
(thalis ₹70-90, mains ₹60-150; ⊙9am-11pm) A thoroughly local lunch joint on the parallel beach road, Shiv Sai serves tasty thalis of the vegie, fish and Gujarati kinds.

★ Space Goa CAFE $$
(☎80063283333; www.thespacegoa.com; mains ₹90-250; ⊙8.30am-5pm) On the Agonda road, Space Goa combines an excellent organic whole-food cafe with a gourmet deli, craft shop and a wellness centre offering reiki and reflexology. The food is fresh and delicious,

---

SILENT PARTIES

Considerately sidestepping the statewide ban on loud music after 10pm, Palolem is the home of popular silent rave parties where guests don a pair of headphones and dance the night away in inward bliss but outward quiet. You get the choice of two or three channels featuring inhouse Goan and international DJs playing hip hop, house, electro and funk. The concept came from British expats (now operating at Alpha Bar) but others jumped on the bandwagon and at last count there were four events, all operating on different nights:

Silent Noise @ Alpha Bar (www.silentnoise.in; cover charge ₹500; ⊙9pm-4am Thu Nov-Apr) The original headphone party organisers.

Deafbeat (Cleopatra's, Palolem Beach Rd; ₹500, before 11pm free; ⊙from 9pm Wed)

Laughing Buddha (cover charge ₹400; ⊙from 10pm Tue)

Neptune Point (www.neptunepoint.com; Neptune's Point, Colomb Bay; cover charge ₹600; ⊙9am-4am Sat Nov-Apr) South of Palolem at Colomb Bay

with fabulous salads, paninis and meze, and the desserts – such as chocolate beetroot cake – are divine. Drop-in morning yoga classes are ₹500.

★ Café Inn
CAFE $$

(Palolem Beach Rd; meals ₹150-550; ⊙10am-11pm; ☎) If you're craving a cappuccino, semi-open-air Café Inn, which grinds its own blend of beans to perfection, is one of Palolem's favourite hang-outs – and it's not even on the beach. Its breakfasts are immense, and comfort-food burgers and panini sandwiches hit the spot. From 6pm there's an excellent barbecue. Free wi-fi.

German Bakery
BAKERY, MULTICUISINE $$

(Ourem Rd; pastries ₹25-80, mains ₹80-210; ⊙7am-10pm) Tasty baked treats are the stars at the Nepali-run German Bakery, but there is also an excellent range of set breakfasts and croissants with yak cheese. It's set in a peaceful garden festooned with flags.

Fern's By Kate's
GOAN $$

(☑9822165261; mains ₹200-450; ⊙8.30am-10.30pm; ☎) Back from the beach, this solid timber place with a vague nautical feel serves up excellent authentic Goan food such as local sausages, fish curry rice and shark *amok tik*.

★ Home
CONTINENTAL $$

(☑0832-2643916; www.homeispatnem.com; Patnem Beach; mains ₹180-290; ⊙8.30am-9.30pm; ☎) Standing out from the beach shacks like a beacon, this bright white, relaxed vegetarian restaurant is run by a British couple and serves up Patnem's best breakfasts, pastas, risotto and salads, continental-style. A highlight here is the dessert menu – awesome chocolate brownies, apple tart and cheesecake. Home also rents out eight nicely decorated, light rooms (from ₹1500).

Magic Italy
ITALIAN $$

(☑88057 67705; Palolem Beach Rd; mains ₹180-460; ⊙5pm-midnight) On the main beach road, Magic Italy has been around for a while and the quality of its pizza and pasta remains high, with imported Italian ingredients like ham, salami, cheese and olive oil, imaginative wood-fired pizzas and homemade pasta. Sit at tables, or Arabian-style on floor cushions. Busy but chilled.

★ Ourem 88
FUSION $$$

(☑8698827679; mains ₹440-650; ⊙6-10pm Tue-Sat) Big things come in small packages at British-run Ourem 88, a gastro sensation with just a handful of tables and a small but masterful menu. Try tender calamari stuffed with Goan sausage, slow-roasted pork belly, fluffy souffle or fillet steak with Béarnaise sauce. Worth a splurge.

🍷 Drinking & Nightlife

Leopard Valley
CLUB

(www.leopardvalley.com; Palolem-Agonda Rd; admission from ₹600; ⊙9pm-4.30am Fri) South Goa's biggest new outdoor dance club is a sight (and sound) to behold, with 3D laser light shows, pyrotechnics and state-of-the-art sound systems blasting local and international DJs. It's in an isolated but easily reached location between Palolem and Agonda, but given noise restrictions we don't know if it will endure. Friday night at time of research but possibly Sunday too.

🛍 Shopping

Butterfly Book Shop
BOOKS

(☑9341738801; ⊙9am-10.30pm) The best of several good bookshops in town, this cute and cosy place stocks best sellers, classics, and a good range of books on yoga, meditation and spirituality. This is also the base for yoga classes and cooking courses.

ℹ Information

Palolem's main road is lined with travel agencies, internet places and money changers. The nearest ATM is about 1.5km away, where the main highway meets Palolem Beach Rd, or head to nearby Chaudi.

ℹ Getting There & Around

Frequent buses run to nearby Chaudi (₹7) from the bus stop on the corner of the road down to the beach. There are hourly buses to Margao (₹40, one hour) from the same place. From Chaudi you can also pick up regular buses to Margao, from where you can change for Panaji, or south to Polem Beach and Karwar (Karnataka). Local buses run regularly to Agonda (₹10).

The closest train station is Canacona, 2km from Palolem's beach entrance, which is useful for trains south to Gokarna and Mangalore.

An autorickshaw from Palolem to Patnem should cost ₹80, to Chaudi ₹120 and to Agonda ₹250. A taxi to Dabolim Airport is around ₹1200.

Scooters and motorbikes can easily be hired along the main road leading to the beach from ₹200. Mountain bikes (₹100 per day) can be hired from Seema Bike Hire on Ourem Rd.

Above Mountain-top temple, near Hampi (p212).

Ancient & Historic Sites

South India has a remarkable assortment of monuments and ruins that testify to the splendour of the many cultures that have strutted across its broad canvas. From serene places of worship to remnants of grandiose empires, the opportunities to marvel at the genius of long-gone civilisations are manifold.

Golgumbaz mausoleum (p222), Bijapur

Palaces & Tombs

The rulers of South India's bygone kingdoms and sultanates not only proclaimed their pomp while alive by erecting opulent palaces, many of them were also buried in opulent tombs – some of which rank among the region's most exquisite architecture.

Southern Palaces

First prize among South India's flamboyant royal residences goes to the fabulous Mysore Palace, but Mysore's rival princely state of Hyderabad put up a stern challenge with the chandelier-bedecked Chowmahalla Palace; the Purani Haveli, with its 54m-long wardrobe; and the hilltop Falaknuma Palace on the city's outskirts, a splendiferous neoclassical construction that is now a super-luxury hotel.

Tombs of Bijapur

Bijapur ruled one of the five Deccan sultanates that dominated the plateau lands in the 16th and 17th centuries. Its delicately graceful Ibrahim Rouza is a sort of southern Taj Mahal in that it was built by a sultan as a mausoleum for his wife (and its minarets are said to have inspired those of the Taj itself), while the massive Golgumbaz, another royal mausoleum, boasts what was said to be once the world's second-biggest dome (with incredible acoustics).

Qutb Shahi Tombs

The final resting place of the builders of Golconda fort and their kin, these 21 magnificent domed tombs stand within sight of the fort on the edge of Hyderabad. The domes are mounted on cubical bases with beautiful colonnades and delicate stucco ornamentation.

1. Meenakshi Amman Temple (p381), Madurai 2. Temple in Hampi (p212) 3. Shore Temple (p347), Mamallapuram

Hindu Sacred Sites

South India is home to some of the most spectacular devotional architecture in this Hindu-majority country: soaring *gopurams* (gateway towers), exquisite *mandapas* (pavilions) and some of the most intricately chiselled deity sculptures you'll ever see.

Madurai

In Madurai, one of India's oldest cities, the Meenakshi Amman Temple, abode of the triple-breasted goddess Meenakshi, is rated by many as the epitome of classic South Indian temple architecture. The temple, with an amazing 12 tall *gopurams*, predominantly dates from the 17th century, but its origins are believed to reach back 2000 years to when Madurai was the capital of the ancient Pandyan kingdom.

Hampi

Now a rather sleepy hamlet, from 1336 to 1565 Hampi was the thriving centre of the powerful Vijayanagar empire. Its World Heritage–listed ruins are strewn amid boulders of all shapes and sizes, the result of hundreds of millions of years of volcanic activity and erosion. Especially fine examples of temple art can be seen at the 15th-century Virupaksha Temple and 16th-century Vittala Temple.

Mamallapuram

The exquisite sculptures dotting the seaside town of Mamallapuram (Mahabalipuram) were carved by artisans of the Pallava dynasty in the 7th and 8th centuries. They range from the beautifully sculpted free-standing Shore Temple to the Five Rathas – temples carved from living rock with wonderful animal figures beside them – and the giant relief carving Arjuna's Penance, bursting with scenes from Hindu myth.

Thanjavur

The multitiered *vimana* tower soaring above Thanjavur's Brihadishwara Temple is the ultimate expression of the power and creativity of the medieval Chola dynasty. This 11th-century temple, still a living place of worship, is also adorned with graceful sculptures of Hindu deities.

1. Buddha statues adorn a cave entrance, Ajanta (p96)
2. Cave mural, Ajanta (p96) 3. Caves at Ellora (p93)

Buddhist, Hindu & Jain Caves

The World Heritage–listed caves of Ajanta and Ellora, situated within 100km of each other, are stunning galleries of ancient cave art replete with historic sculptures, rock-cut shrines and natural-dye paintings. These are just the most spectacular of the many cave or rock-cut shrines from the time before South Indians started building free-standing stone structures.

Ajanta

The 30 Buddhist caves of Ajanta, with origins in the 2nd century BC, are clustered along a horseshoe-shaped gorge above the Waghore River. One of their most renowned features is the natural-dye tempera paintings (similar to frescoes) decorating many of the caves' interiors. Some of these murals are even coloured with crushed semiprecious stones such as lapis lazuli. Don't miss Cave 1, with some particularly superb artwork including a wonderful rendition of Buddhism's Bodhisattva Padmapani, or Cave 17, with wonderfully preserved images including a princess applying make-up.

Ellora

The Ellora caves – a collection of Hindu, Jain and Buddhist shrines constructed between AD 600 and 1000 – are situated on a 2km-long escarpment. There are 34 in all: 17 Hindu, 12 Buddhist and five Jain. Most famed is Cave 16, the Kailasa Temple (in honour of the Hindu god Shiva), which is the biggest monolithic sculpture in the world and was skilfully carved into the cliff face by thousands of labourers over a period of 150 years.

Guntupalli

One of more than 100 ancient Buddhist sites in rural Andhra Pradesh, the 2nd-century-BC monastery at Guntupalli sits high on a hilltop overlooking an expanse of forest and rice fields. Monks' dwellings line the cliffside, with lovely arched stone facades sculpted to look like wood.

VISAGE / GETTY IMAGES ©

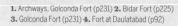

1. Archways, Golconda Fort (p231) 2. Bidar Fort (p225)
3. Golconda Fort (p231) 4. Fort at Daulatabad (p92)

SAURABH / GETTY IMAGES ©

Forts

Battleground of many a rival empire in centuries gone by, South India is dotted with forts that have survived the vagaries of time, with many of them sprawled across strategic hilltops and wrapped within sturdy walls protecting a treasure trove of monuments.

Golconda

Hyderabad's 16th-century sultans mounted Golconda fort on a 120m-high granite hill, with two rings of ramparts, one 11km in circumference. Mughal emperor Aurangzeb had to resort to bribing a defending general to reduce the fort in 1687, after a fruitless year-long siege. Golconda is a feast of crenellated walls, cannon-mounted bastions and imposing gates studded with ominous iron spikes to repel raiding war elephants.

Daulatabad

The central bastion of the crumbling Daulatabad fortress, crowning a 200m-high outcrop called Devagiri (Hill of the Gods), is reached by an hour's climb via spiralling tunnels, multiple doorways and spiked gates. The eccentric Delhi sultan Mohammed Tughlaq conceived a grand plan to make Daulatabad his capital, and marched the entire population of Delhi 1100km here in 1328 – but his dream was swiftly cut short by a dire water shortage.

Bidar

South India's now-neglected biggest fort was once the bustling capital of much of the region. Although largely in a state of deteriorating disrepair, there are still noteworthy remnants of its glory days, including the Rangin Mahal (Painted Palace), with elaborate tilework, teak pillars and inlaid panels, and the Sixteen-Pillared Mosque, with ancient inscriptions.

Janjira

The brooding fortress of Janjira looms sheer out of the sea 500m off the Maharashtrian coast. Built in the 16th century by descendants of African slaves, Janjira was never conquered by an enemy. Only nature is succeeding in reclaiming the now-abandoned fort.

Karnataka & Bengaluru

Best Places to Eat

➜ Karavalli (p180)

➜ Koshy's Bar &
Restaurant (p180)

➜ Sapphire (p194)

➜ Lalith Bar &
Restaurant (p206)

Best Places to Stay

➜ Casa Piccola Cottage
(p178)

➜ Green Hotel (p192)

➜ Golden Mist (p201)

➜ Dhole's Den (p198)

➜ Waterwoods Lodge (p199)

Why Go?

Blessed with a a diverse makeup conforming to all the romance of quintessential India, Karnataka delivers with its winning blend of palaces, tiger reserves, megacities, ancient ruins, beaches and legendary hang-outs.

At its nerve centre is the silicon-capital Bengaluru (Bangalore), overfed with the good life. Scattered around the epicurean city are rolling hills dotted with spice and coffee plantations, the regal splendour of Mysuru (Mysore), and jungles teeming with monkeys, tigers and Asia's biggest population of elephants.

If that all sounds too mainstream, head to the countercultural enclave of tranquil Hampi with hammocks, psychedelic sunsets and boulder-strewn ruins. Or the blissful beaches of Gokarna, a beach haven minus the doof doof. Otherwise leave the tourist trail behind entirely, and take a journey to the stunning Islamic ruins of northern Karnataka.

When to Go
Bengaluru

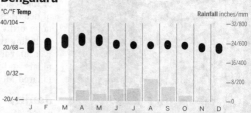

Mar–May The best season to watch tigers and elephants in Karnataka's pristine national parks.

Oct Mysuru's Dussehra (Dasara) carnival brings night-long celebrations and a jumbo parade.

Dec & Jan The coolest time to explore the northern districts' forts, palaces, caves and temples.

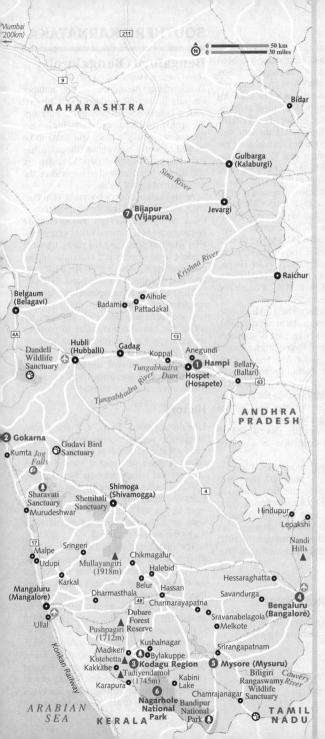

Karnataka & Bengaluru Highlights

❶ Marvelling at the gravity-defying boulders, and wandering among the melancholic ruins of **Hampi** (p212)

❷ Hitting **Gokarna** (p209) for its beautiful beaches and legendary chilled-out atmosphere minus the resorts

❸ Savouring aromatic coffee while recharging your soul in the cool highlands of the **Kodagu Region** (p199)

❹ Drinking yourself under the table, or tucking into top-notch global cuisine in **Bengaluru** (p179)

❺ Being bowled over by the grandiose **royal palace** (p187) in Mysuru

❻ Spying on lazy tuskers in the forests bordering serene Kabini Lake at **Nagarhole National Park** (p199)

❼ Strolling in the peaceful manicured grounds of exquisite 16th-century Islamic monuments in **Bijapur** (p222)

History

A rambling playing field of religions, cultures and kingdoms, Karnataka has been ruled by a string of charismatic rulers through history. India's first great emperor, Chandragupta Maurya, made the state his retreat when he embraced Jainism at Sravanabelagola in the 3rd century BC. From the 6th to the 14th centuries AD, the land was under a series of dynasties such as the Chalukyas, Cholas, Gangas and Hoysalas, who left a lasting mark in the form of stunning cave shrines and temples across the state.

In 1327 Mohammed Tughlaq's army sacked Halebid. In 1347 Hasan Gangu, a Persian general in Tughlaq's army, led a rebellion to establish the Bahmani kingdom, which was later subdivided into five Deccan sultanates. Meanwhile, the Hindu kingdom of Vijayanagar, with its capital in Hampi, rose to prominence. Having peaked in the early 1550s, it fell in 1565 to a combined effort of the sultanates.

In subsequent years the Hindu Wodeyars of Mysore grew in stature and extended their rule over a large part of southern India. They remained largely unchallenged until 1761, when Hyder Ali (one of their generals) deposed them. Backed by the French, Hyder Ali and his son Tipu Sultan set up capital in Srirangapatnam and consolidated their rule. However, in 1799 the British defeated Tipu Sultan and reinstated the Wodeyars. Historically, this flagged off British territorial expansion in southern India.

Mysore remained under the Wodeyars until Independence – post-1947, the reigning maharaja became the first governor. The state boundaries were redrawn along linguistic lines in 1956 and the extended Kannada-speaking state of Mysore was born. It was renamed Karnataka in 1972, with Bangalore (now Bengaluru) as the capital.

SLEEPING PRICE RANGES

The following price ranges are for a double room with bathroom and are inclusive of tax:

$ less than ₹800

$$ ₹800 to ₹2500

$$$ more than ₹2500

SOUTHERN KARNATAKA

Bengaluru (Bangalore)

080 / POP 10.2 MILLION / ELEV 920M

Cosmopolitan Bengaluru is the number one city in the Indian deep south, blessed with a benevolent climate and a burgeoning drinking, dining and shopping scene. It's not necessarily a place you come to be wowed by world-class sights (though it has some lovely parks and striking Victorian-era architecture), but instead to experience the new modern face of India.

As the hub of India's booming IT industry, it vies with Mumbai (Bombay) as the nation's most progressive city, and its creature comforts can be a godsend to the weary traveller who has done the hard yards. It's a big student town where you'll encounter hip locals chatting in English while drinking craft beer and wearing '80s metal band T-shirts.

The past decade has seen a mad surge of development, coupled with traffic congestion and rising pollution levels. However, it's a city that has also taken care to preserve its green space and its colonial-era heritage. So while urbanisation continually pushes its boundaries outward, the central district (dating back to the British Raj years) remains more or less unchanged.

History

Literally meaning 'Town of Boiled Beans', Bengaluru supposedly derived its name from an ancient incident involving an old village woman who served cooked pulses to a lost and hungry Hoysala king. Kempegowda, a feudal lord, was the first person to mark out Bengaluru's extents by building a mud fort in 1537. The town remained obscure until 1759, when it was gifted to Hyder Ali by the Mysore maharaja.

The British arrived in 1809 and made it their regional administrative base in 1831, renaming it Bangalore. During the Raj era the city played host to many a British officer, including Winston Churchill, who enjoyed life here during his greener years and famously left a debt (still on the books) of ₹13 at the Bangalore Club.

Now home to countless software, electronics and business-outsourcing firms, Bengaluru's knack for technology developed early. In 1905 it was the first Indian city to have electric street lighting. Since the 1940s it has been home to Hindustan Aeronautics

Ltd (HAL), India's largest aerospace company. And if you can't do without email, you owe it all to a Bangalorean – Sabeer Bhatia, the inventor of Hotmail, grew up here.

The city's name was changed back to Bengaluru in November 2006, though few care to use it in practice.

ℹ Orientation

Finding your way around Bengaluru can be difficult at times. In certain areas, roads are named after their widths (eg 80ft Rd). The city also follows a system of mains and crosses: 3rd Cross, 5th Main, Residency Rd, for example, refers to the third lane on the fifth street branching off Residency Rd. New affluent pockets are springing up across the city, including the ritzy suburbs of Indirangar, JP Nagar, Koramangala and Whitefield – all with Western-style malls, nightlife and restaurants.

◉ Sights

★ National Gallery of Modern Art
ART GALLERY

(NGMA; ☑080-22342338; www.ngmaindia.gov.in/ngma_bangaluru.asp; 49 Palace Rd; Indian/foreigner ₹10/150; ☺10am-5pm Tue-Sun) Housed in a century-year-old mansion – the former vacation home of the Raja of Mysore – this world-class art museum showcases an impressive permanent collection as well as changing exhibitions. The Old Wing exhibits works from pre-Independence, including paintings by Raja Ravi Varma and Abanindranath Tagore (nephew of Rabindranath Tagore, and founder of the avant-garde Bengal School art movement). Interconnected by a walk bridge, the sleek New Wing focuses on contemporary post-Independence works.

Lalbagh Botanical Gardens
GARDENS

(☑9888947670; www.horticulture.kar.nic.in/lalbagh.htm; Lalbagh Rd; admission ₹10; ☺6am-7pm) Spread over 97 hectares of landscaped terrain, the expansive Lalbagh Botanical Gardens were laid out in 1760 by the famous Mysore ruler Hyder Ali. As well as amazing centuries-old trees it claims to have the world's most diverse species of plants. Bangalore Walks (p177) has guided tours.

Cubbon Park
GARDENS

(www.horticulture.kar.nic.in/cubbon.htm; Kasturba Rd) In the heart of Bengaluru's business district is Cubbon Park, a sprawling 120-hectare garden where Bengaluru's residents converge to steal a moment from the rat race that rages outside.

It's surrounded by wonderful colonial-era architecture, including the red-painted Gothic-style **State Central Library** (Cubbon Park); the colossal neo-Dravidian-style **Vidhana Soudha** (Dr Ambedkar Rd), built in 1954 and which serves as the legislative chambers of the state government; and neoclassical **Attara Kacheri** (High Court; Cubbon Park) built in 1864 and housing the High Court. The latter two are closed to the public.

Karnataka Chitrakala Parishath ART GALLERY (www.karnatakachitrakalaparishath.com; Kumarakrupa Rd; admission ₹50; ☺10am-5.30pm Mon-Sat) A superb gallery with a wide range of Indian and international contemporary art on show, as well as permanent displays of Mysore-style paintings and folk and tribal art from across Asia. A section is devoted to Russian master Nicholas Roerich, known for his vivid paintings of the Himalaya.

Government Museum MUSEUM (Kasturba Rd; admission ₹4; ☺10am-5pm Tue-Sun, closed every 2nd Sat) In a beautiful red colonial-era building dating from 1877, you'll find a dusty collection of 12th-century stone carvings and artefacts excavated from Halebid, Hampi and Attriampakham. Your ticket also gets you into the **Venkatappa Art Gallery** (Kasturba Rd; ☺10am-5pm Tue-Sun) **FREE** next door, where you can see works and personal memorabilia of K Venkatappa (1887–1962), court painter to the Wodeyars.

Bangalore Palace PALACE (Palace Rd; Indian/foreigner ₹225/450, camera/video ₹675/1405; ☺10am-5.30pm) The private residence of the Wodeyars, erstwhile maharajas of the state, Bangalore Palace preserves a slice of bygone royal splendour. Still the residence of the current maharaja, an audio guide provides a detailed explanation of the building, vaguely designed to resemble Windsor Castle, and you can marvel at the lavish interiors and galleries featuring grisly hunting memorabilia, family photos and a collection of nude portraits.

Visvesvaraya Industrial & Technical Museum MUSEUM (www.vismuseum.gov.in; Kasturba Rd; adult/child ₹40/free; ☺10.30am-5pm) One mainly for kids, this hands-on science museum makes you feel a bit like you're on a school excursion, but there are some cool electrical and engineering displays, plus kitschy fun-house

Bengaluru (Bangalore)

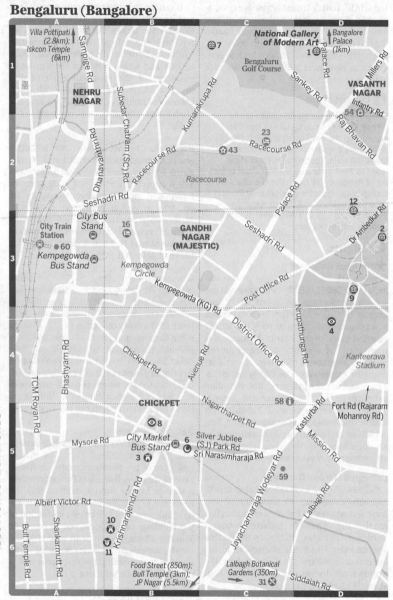

mirrors and a walk-on piano. There's also a replica of the Wright brothers' 1903 flyer.

Tipu Sultan's Palace
PALACE

(Albert Victor Rd; Indian/foreigner ₹5/100, video ₹25; ⊙ 8.30am-5.30pm) Situated close to the vibrant Krishnarajendra Market is the elegant palace of Tipu Sultan, which is notable for its teak pillars and ornamental frescoes. Though it is not as beautiful (or as well maintained) as Tipu's summer palace in Srirangapatnam, near to Mysuru, it's an in-

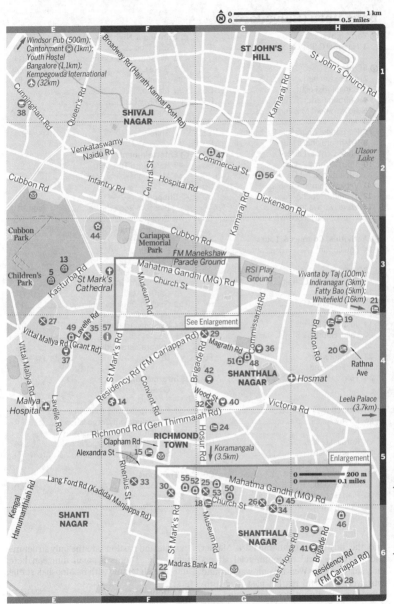

teresting monument, and worth an outing when combined with other nearby sights such as the ornate 17th-century **Venkataraman Temple** (Krishnarajendra Rd; ⊙8.30am-6pm) that is located next door, and the

massive **Jamia Masjid** (SJ Park Rd), as well as the fort and market.

Krishnarajendra Market　　MARKET
(City Market; Silver Jubilee Park Rd; ⊙6am-10pm)
For a taste of traditional urban India, dive

Bengaluru (Bangalore)

into the bustling Krishnarajendra Market and the dense grid of commercial streets that surround it. Weave your way around this lively colourful market past fresh produce, piles of vibrant dyes, spices and copperware. The colourful **flower market** in the centre is the highlight.

Bangalore Fort   FORT
(KR Rd) The remnants of this 1761 fort is a peaceful escape from the chaotic city surrounds, with its manicured lawn and stone pink walls. The fort remained in use until its destruction by the British in 1791, and today

the gate and bastions are the only structures remaining. There's a small dungeon here, and Ganesh temple with its Mooshak statue.

Bull Temple   HINDU TEMPLE
(Bull Temple Rd, Basavangudi; ⊙7am-8.30pm) Built by Kempegowda in the 16th-century Dravidian style, the Bull Temple contains a huge granite monolith of Nandi (Shiva's bull) and is one of Bengaluru's most atmospheric. Nearby is the **Swee Dodda Ganapathi Temple** (Bull Temple Rd; ⊙7am-8.30pm), with an equally enormous Ganesh idol. The temples are 1km south of Tipu Sultan's Palace.

Iskcon Temple   HINDU TEMPLE
(www.iskconbangalore.org; Chord Rd, Hare Krishna Hill; ⊙7.30am-1pm & 4.15-8.30pm Mon-Fri, to 1pm Sat, to 2pm Sun) Built by the International Society of Krishna Consciousness (Iskcon), also referred to as the Hare Krishnas, this shiny temple, inaugurated in 1997, is lavishly decorated in a mix of ultracontemporary and traditional styles. There are many food stalls here so bring an appetite. It's around 10km northwest from the centre of town.

 Activities

Ayurvedagram   AYURVEDA, YOGA
(☑080-65651090;   www.ayurvedagram.com; Hemmandanhalli, Whitefield; 1-day package from ₹4000) Set over three hectares of tranquil gardens with heritage homes transplanted from Kerala, this centre specialises in specifically tailored ayurvedic treatments, yoga and rejuvenation programs. It's in the outer suburb of Whitefield, around 25km from central Bengaluru.

Soukya   YOGA
(☑080-28017000; www.soukya.com; Soukya Rd, Samethanahalli, Whitefield; 7-day package per day incl treatments, meals & accommodation from ₹8800; ⊙6am-8.30pm) Internationally renowned retreat on a picture-perfect 12-hectare organic farm running long-term programs in ayurvedic therapy and yoga, as well as medical and therapeutic skin treatments (₹3300 per hour).

Equilibrium   ROCK CLIMBING
(www.facebook.com/EquilibriumClimbingStation; 6th fl, Devatha Plaza, 606 Residency Rd; from ₹150; ⊙6am-11pm) India's first indoor climbing centre is more indoor bouldering, which will suit those en route to Hampi, a world-renowned climbing destination. It also arranges weekend climbing excursions.

 Tours

In a city lacking in blockbuster sights, there are a couple of companies offering fantastic grassroots tours to get under Bengaluru's skin.

★**Bangalore Walks**   WALKING TOUR
(☑9845523660; www.bangalorewalks.com; adult/child ₹500/300; ⊙7-10am Sat & Sun) Highly recommended tours with the choice of a walk through Lalbagh Gardens, a medieval Old City history walk or 19th-century Victorian walk. There's a delicious breakfast en route. Book in advance.

Bus Tours   SIGHTSEEING
(www.karnatakaholidays.net; half-day non AC/AC ₹230/255, full day non AC/AC ₹385/485) The government tourism department runs city bus tours, all of which begin at Badami House. The basic half-day city tour runs twice daily

---

TOP STATE FESTIVALS

Udupi Paryaya (⊙Jan/Feb) Held even-numbered years, with a procession and ritual marking the handover of swamis at Udupi's Krishna Temple in January.

Classical Dance Festival (⊙Jan/Feb) Some of India's best classical dance performances take place in Pattadakal.

Vijaya Utsav (p215) A three-day extravaganza of culture, heritage and the arts in Hampi.

Tibetan New Year (⊙Jan/Feb) Lamas in Tibetan refugee settlements in Bylakuppe take shifts leading nonstop prayers that span the weeklong celebrations.

Vairamudi Festival (⊙Mar/Apr) Lord Vishnu is adorned with jewels at Cheluvanarayana Temple in Melkote, including a diamond-studded crown belonging to Mysuru's former maharajas, attracting 400,000 pilgrims.

Ganesh Chaturthi (p208) Families march their Ganesh idols to the sea in Gokarna at sunset in September.

Dussehra (p194) Mysore Palace is lit up in the evenings and a vibrant procession hits town to the delight of thousands.

Lakshadeepotsava (p207) Thousands and thousands of lamps light up the Jain pilgrimage town of Dharmasthala in November, offering spectacular photo ops.

Huthri (Madikeri; Nov/Dec) The Kodava community in Madikeri celebrates the start of the harvesting season with ceremony, music, traditional dances and feasting for a week.

at 7.30am and 2pm, while the full-day tour departs at 7.15am Wednesday to Sunday.

The day trips around Bengaluru are worth considering, particularly the daily departure to the hard-to-get-to Belur, Halebid and Sravanabelagola (non AC/AC ₹800/850) departing 6.30am and returning 10pm.

🛏 Sleeping

Decent budget rooms are in short supply but a stack of dive lodges line Subedar Chatram (SC) Rd, east of the bus stands and around the train station.

🛏 MG Road Area

Hotel Ajantha   HOTEL $$
(☑ 080-25584321; www.hotelajantha.in; 22A MG Rd, s/d incl breakfast with fan ₹1450/1990, with AC ₹2200/2630; ✱ 🛜) An old budget favourite Ajantha is no longer the steal it once was, but it's still affordable for the MG Rd area with a range of par-for-the-course rooms in a compound.

St Mark's Inn   HOTEL $$
(☑ 080-41122783; www.stmarkshotels.com; St Marks Rd; s/d incl breakfast ₹2500/2800; ✱ 🛜) A top-value designer hotel with immaculate rooms decked out with modern decor, big comfy beds, in-room safe and sparkling stainless-steel bathroom fittings, plus free wi-fi and buffet breakfast.

Hotel Empire International   HOTEL $$
(☑ 080-42678888; www.hotelempire.in; 36 Church St; s/d incl breakfast from ₹1780/2140; ✱) The slightly shabby Hotel Empire remains excellent value for its handy central location in happening Church St. Rooms vary in size and decency so ask to check out a few before committing, but they are generally spacious

with speedy wi-fi. Its hotel in up-and-coming **Kormangala** (☑ 080-40222777; www.hotelempire.in; 103 Industrial Area; s/d ₹2135/2570) is another good choice.

Tom's Hotel   HOTEL $$
(☑ 080-25575875; www.hoteltoms.com; 1/5 Hosur Rd; s/d incl breakfast with fan ₹1900/2080, with AC ₹2310/2560; ✱ 🛜 ✱) Long favoured for its low tariffs, bright and cheerful Tom's allows you to stay in a central location in spacious clean rooms with friendly staff.

★ Casa Piccola Cottage   HERITAGE HOTEL $$$
(☑ 080-22990337; www.casacottage.com; 2 Clapham Rd; r incl breakfast from ₹4300; ✱ 🛜) Within a beautifully renovated heritage building, Casa Piccola's atmospheric rooms offer a tranquil sanctuary from the city madness. Its personalised brand of hospitality has garnered it a solid reputation and rooms come with tiled floors, spotless bathrooms and traditional bedspreads, and garden surrounds of papaya and avocado trees. Also offers furnished apartments.

Oberoi   HOTEL $$$
(☑ 080-41358222; www.oberoihotels.com; 39 MG Rd; s/d from ₹12,000/13,000; ✱ @ 🛜 ✱) Staking its claim as one of Bengaluru's most luxurious hotels, the colossal Oberoi is set over more than a hectare of lush gardens around an enchanting 120-year-old tree. It mixes colonial-era ambience with modern touches, from tablet-controlled devices to TVs in bathrooms.

Laika Boutique Stay   B&B $$$
(☑ 9482806630; www.laikabangalore.in; Rathna Rd; r incl breakfast ₹4780; ✱ 🛜) Hidden down a leafy side street, this homely guesthouse is a wonderful choice for those seeking a more local experience combined with style and comfort.

TOURING KARNATAKA

There are some unique ways of getting around Karnataka.

Golden Chariot (☑ 11-42866600; www.thegoldenchariot.co.in; s/d 7 nights incl full board & activities US$5278/7630; 🛜) Beginning in Bengaluru, this luxurious train journey takes you through the romance of Karnataka, visiting palaces, temples, ancient ruins and wildlife. Its AC cabins are equipped with mod cons, plus several bars and restaurants.

goMowgli (☑ 9008730975; www.gomowgli.in; per day from ₹1700) Set up by a bunch of local travellers, this hop-on-hop-off bus journeys across Karnataka aiming to provide more enriching cultural experiences.

Art of Bicycle (☑ 8129945707; www.artofbicycletrips.com; per person from ₹2250) Cycling tours in the countryside around Bengaluru and beyond, including to Nandi Hills or 10-day journeys to Gokarna.

Vivanta by Taj
HOTEL $$$

(☎ 080-66604444; www.vivantabytaj.com; 41/3, MG Rd; s/d from ₹10,000/12,000; ❀@✿❋) Mixing boutique chic with five-star standards, Vivanta has an appealing casualness without skimping on professionalism. The pick of the rooms have rooftop views and a grassy lawn area. Its luxurious pool is perfect for those wanting to lounge around.

Jüsta MG Rd
BOUTIQUE HOTEL $$$

(☎ 080-41135555; www.justahotels.com/mg-road-bangalore; 21/14 Craig Park Layout, MG Rd; s/d incl breakfast ₹3980/4670; ❀✿) A wonderful alternative to Bengaluru's plethora of generic business hotels, this intimate art hotel has slick and spacious rooms with Japanese-inspired motifs throughout.

🛏 Other Areas

Hotel Adora
HOTEL $

(☎ 080-22200024; 47 SC Rd; s/d ₹600/832, with AC ₹990/1560; ❀) A largish budget option with unfussy rooms near the train and Kempegowda bus stations. Downstairs is a good veg restaurant.

Youth Hostel Bangalore
HOSTEL $

(☎ 080-25924040; www.youthhostelbangalore.com; 65/2 Millers Rd; dm/d ₹150/650, d with AC ₹850; ❀✿) Strictly for those on a tight budget, this *very* basic hostel is popular with Indian students, and allows you to opt for extras such as bucket hot water (₹15), wi-fi (per hour ₹20) and downstairs security lockers (per day ₹20). Discounts for YHA members. It's close to Cantonment train station, north of the city.

Mass Residency
GUESTHOUSE $$

(☎ 9945091735; massresidency@yahoo.com; 18, 2nd Main Rd, 11th Cross, JP Nagar; r incl breakfast with fan/AC ₹1600/2000; ❀✿) In a laid-back neighbourhood away from the city centre, this welcoming guesthouse is run by two brothers who are world travellers themselves. It has comfortable enough rooms, but wins rave reviews for its warm hospitality and free neighbourhood walking tours.

★Villa Pottipati
HERITAGE GUESTHOUSE $$$

(☎ 080-41144725; www.villa-pottipati.neemrana-hotels.com; 142 8th Cross, 4th Main, Malleswaram; s/d incl breakfast from ₹3300/4400; ❀@✿❋) On the city's outskirts, this heritage building was once the garden home of the wealthy ex-pat Andhra family. Needless to say, it's flooded with memories and quaintness such as antique furniture, knick-knacks and arched doorways. Its garden is full of ancient trees and a dunk-sized pool.

★Leela Palace
HOTEL $$$

(☎ 080-25211234; www.theleela.com; 23 HAL Airport Rd; s/d from ₹19,000/20,500) Modelled on Mysore Palace, the astonishing Leela isn't actually a palace (it was built in 2003), but it certainly feels fit for royalty. Gleaming marble, thick luxuriant carpets, regal balconies and period features are done superbly, as are its stately grounds with beautiful gardens, waterfalls, classy restaurants, bars and boutique galleries. It's within the Leela Galleria complex, 5km east of MG Rd.

Taj West End
HERITAGE HOTEL $$$

(☎ 080-66605660; www.tajhotels.com; Racecourse Rd; s/d incl breakfast from ₹24,000/25,500; ❀✿❋) The West End saga flashbacks to 1887, when it was incepted by a British family as a 10-room hostel for passing army officers. Since then, nostalgia has been a permanent resident at this lovely property which – spread over eight hectares of tropical gardens – has evolved as a definitive icon of Indian luxury hospitality.

🍴 Eating

Bengaluru's adventurous dining scene keeps pace with the whims and rising standards of its hungry, moneyed locals and IT expats. You'll find high-end dining, gastropubs and cheap local favourites.

🍴 MG Road Area

Khan Saheb
INDIAN $

(www.khansaheb.co; 9A Block, Brigade Rd; rolls from ₹60; ⊙ noon-11.30pm) A tasty cheap eat famous for its rolls filled with anything from charcoal-grilled meats and tandoori prawns to paneer and mushroom tikka.

★Koshy's Bar & Restaurant
INDIAN $$

(39 St Mark's Rd; mains ₹160-350; ⊙ 9am-11pm) They say half of Bengaluru's court cases are argued around Koshy's tables, and many hard-hitting newspaper articles written over its steaming coffees. Serving the city's intelligentsia for decades, this buzzy and joyful resto-pub is where you can put away tasty North Indian dishes in between fervent discussions and mugs of beer.

Queen's Restaurant
INDIAN $$

(7 Church St; mains ₹140-240; ⊘12.30-3.30pm & 7-10.30pm Tue-Sun) Intimate and atmospheric, reputed Queen's interior is rustic village-style, with painted motifs adorning earthy walls. It serves quick and tasty Indian dishes such as a range of vegetable and dhal preparations, to go with fluffy, hot chapati.

Church St Social
GASTROPUB $$

(46/1 Church St; mains ₹150-350; ⊘9am-11pm Mon-Thu, to 1am Fri & Sat) Bringing hipsterism to Bengaluru, this industrial warehouse-style space serves cocktails in beakers to go with a menu of all-day breakfasts, jalapeño mac 'n' cheese, southern fried chicken burgers and inventive Indian classics.

★ Karavalli
SEAFOOD $$$

(☑080-66604545; Gateway Hotel, 66 Residency Rd; mains ₹500-1500; ⊘12.30-3pm & 6.30-11pm) The Arabian Sea may be 400km away, but you'll have to come only as far as this classy spot to savour South India's finest coastal cuisines. The decor is a stylish mash of traditional thatched roof, vintage woodwork and beaten brassware. In the garden seating enjoy superb fiery Mangalorean fish dishes or its signature lobster *balchao* (₹1495).

Sunny's
ITALIAN $$$

(☑080-41329366; www.sunnysbangalore.in; 50 Lavelle Rd; mains ₹380-730; ⊘12.30-3pm & 7-11pm; 🛜) A well-established fixture on Bengaluru's restaurant scene, classy Sunny's is all about authentic charcoal thin-crust pizzas, homemade pastas, imported cheese and some of the best desserts in the city.

DON'T MISS

FOOD STREET

For a local eating experience, head to VV Puram, aka **Food Street** (Sajjan Rao Circle, VW Puram; ⊘from 5pm), with its strip of hole-in-the-wall eateries cooking up classic street-food dishes. Things kick off in the early evening when the stalls fire up and people stand around watching rotis being handmade and spun in the air or *bhaji* (vegetable fritters) dunked into hot oil before being dished up on paper plates, where you can eat standing in the street.

It's all-vegetarian with a range of dosas (lentil-flour pancake), curries, roti and deep-fried goodies.

Ebony
MULTICUISINE $$$

(☑41783333; www.ebonywithaview.com; 13th fl, Barton Centre, 84 MG Rd; mains ₹300-500; ⊘12.30-3pm & 7-11pm) While there's a delectable menu of Indian, Thai and European dishes, here it's all about the romantic views from its luxurious rooftop, making it a good spot to treat yourself for a night out.

Fava
MEDITERRANEAN $$$

(www.fava.in; UB City, 24 Vittal Mallya Rd; mains ₹350-850; ⊘11am-11pm) Dine alfresco on Fava's canopy-covered decking, feasting on large plates of mezze, fish kebabs, zatar sausages or something from the organic menu.

★ Olive Beach
MEDITERRANEAN $$$

(☑080-41128400; www.oliveharandkitchen.com; 16 Wood St, Ashoknagar; mains ₹530-800; ⊘noon-11.30pm) A white-washed villa straight from the coast of Santorini, Olive Beach does a menu that evokes wistful memories of sunny Mediterranean getaways. Things change seasonally, but expect Moroccan lamb tagines, caramelised pork belly and savoury tarts, as well as fantastic cocktails.

🍴 Other Areas

★ Mavalli Tiffin Rooms
SOUTH INDIAN $

(MTR; www.mavallitiffinrooms.com; Lalbagh Rd; dosa from ₹50, meals from ₹130; ⊘6.30-11am, 12.30-2.45pm, 3.30-7.30pm & 8-9.30pm) A legendary name in South Indian comfort food, this super-popular eatery has had Bengaluru eating out of its hands since 1924. Head to the dining room upstairs, queue for a table, and then admire the dated images of southern beauties etched on smoky glass as waiters bring you savoury local fare, capped by frothing filter coffee served in silverware. It's a definitive Bengaluru experience.

Gramin
INDIAN $

(☑080-41104104; 20, 7th Block Raheja Arcade, Koramangala; mains ₹90-180; ⊘12.30-3.30pm & 7-11pm) Translating to 'from the village', Gramin offers a wide choice of flavourful rural North Indian fare at this cosy, eclectic all-veg place popular with locals. Try the excellent range of lentils and curries best had with oven-fresh rotis, accompanied by sweet rose-flavoured lassi served in a copper vessel.

Windsor Pub
INDIAN $$

(7 Kodava Samaja Bldg, 1st Main Vasanthnagar; mains ₹250-350; ⊘11.30am-3pm & 6-11pm) Its dark pub interior may not inspire, but it has a fantastic menu of regional favourites

such as flavoursome Mangalorean fish, or the tangy *pandhi* (pork) masala from Kodagu's hills. It also does draught beer and a soundtrack of blues, jazz and '70s rock. It's near Bangalore Palace.

⭐**Fatty Bao** ASIAN $$$
(www.facebook.com/thefattybao; 610 12th Main Rd, Indiranagar; mains ₹380-650; ⊘11am-3.30pm & 7-11pm) This hip rooftop restaurant serves up Asian hawker food to a crowd of fashionable, young Bangalorean foodies in a vibrant setting with colourful chairs and wooden bench tables. There's ramen, Thai curries and Malaysian street food, as well as Asian-inspired cocktails such as lemongrass mojitos. There's a branch of Monkey Bar is downstairs..

 Drinking & Nightlife

Bars & Lounges

Bengaluru's rock-steady reputation and wide choice of chic watering holes makes it the place to indulge in a spirited session of pub-hopping in what's the original beer town of India. Many microbreweries have sprung up in the past few years, producing quality locally made ales. All serve food too.

The trendiest nightclubs will typically charge a cover of around ₹1000 per couple, but it's often redeemable against drinks or food.

Monkey Bar PUB
(www.monkeybarindia.com; 14/1 Wood St, Ashoknagar; ⊘noon-11pm) From the owners of Olive Beach comes this vintage gastropub that draws a mixed, jovial crowd to knock back drinks around the bar or at wooden booth seating. Otherwise head down to the basement to join the 'party' crew shooting pool, playing foosball and rocking out to bangin' tunes. There's also a branch in **Indiranagar** (925 12th Main Rd, Indiranagar).

Plan B PUB
(20 Castle St, Ashoknagar; ⊘11am-11.30pm Sun-Thu, to 1am Fri & Sat) It may not have fancy craft beer on tap, but this popular student hang-out instead has 3.5L beer towers and 15 different burgers. It also runs the industrial chic **Plan B Loaded** (13 Rhenius St, Richmond Town) gastropub.

Pecos BAR
(Rest House Rd; ⊘10.30am-11pm) Hendrix, The Grateful Dead and Frank Zappa posters adorn the walls of this divey, narrow tri-level

bar. It's a throwback to simpler times where cassettes line the shelves behind the bar, sport is on the TV and the only thing to quench your thirst is one choice of cheap beer on tap. No wonder it's an all-time favourite with students. There are now several branches in the immediate area.

Shiro BAR
(www.shiro.co.in; UB City, 24 Vittal Mallya Rd; ⊘12.30-11.30pm Sun-Thu, to 1am Fri & Sat) A sophisticated lounge for getting sloshed in style, Shiro has elegant interiors complemented by the monumental Buddha busts and Apsara figurines or outdoor seating.

13th Floor BAR
(13th fl, Barton Centre, 84 MG Rd; ⊘5-11pm Sun-Thu, to 1am Fri & Sat) Forget your superstitions and head up to 13th Floor's terrace, with all of Bengaluru glittering at your feet. Happy hour is 5pm to 7pm.

Microbreweries

Biere Club MICROBREWERY
(www.thebiereclub.com; 20/2 Vittal Mallya Rd; ⊘11am-11.30pm Sun-Thu, to 1am Fri & Sat) Beer lovers rejoice as South India's first microbrewery serves up handcrafted beers on tap, six of which are brewed on-site. Large copper boilers sit behind the bar.

Arbor Brewing Company MICROBREWERY
(www.arborbrewing.com; 8 Magrath; noon-11.30pm Sun-Thu, to 1am Fri & Sat) This classic brewpub

with roots in Michigian, USA, was one of the first microbreweries to get the ball rolling in Bengaluru with its eight beers brewed on-site including IPA, pilsner and Belgian beers.

Toit Brewpub
MICROBREWERY

(www.toit.in; 298 100ft Rd, Indiranagar; ⊙noon-11.30pm Sun-Thu, to 1am Fri & Sat) A brick-walled gastropub split over three levels where lively punters sample its quality beers brewed on-site, including two seasonals and an Irish red ale on tap.

Brewski
MICROBREWERY

(www.brewsky.in; 4th & 5th Fl Goenka Chambers, 19th Main Rd, JP Nagar; ⊙ noon-11.30pm Mon-Thu, to 1am Fri & Sat) This rooftop brewery is a cool new spot with city views and a funky restaurant with vintage decor. It brews six beers including a golden ale, wheat beer and stout.

Barleyz
MICROBREWERY

(www.barleyz.com; 100ft Rd, Koramangala; ⊙11am-11.30pm Sun-Thu, to 1am Fri & Sat) A suave rooftop beer garden with potted plants, Astroturf and tables with built-in BBQ grills. Offers free tastings of its six beers, and does growlers for takeaway. There's also excellent wood-fired pizza.

Big Pitcher
MICROBREWERY, CLUB

(www.bigpitcher.in; 4121 HAL Airport Rd; ⊙noon-11.30pm Sun-Thu, to 1am Fri & Sat) More nightclub than pub, with six floors, but its Brazilian brewer does six beers. Head up to its glamorous rooftop for wonderful views.

Vapour
MICROBREWERY, BAR

(www.vapour.in; 773 100ft Rd, Indiranagar) Multilevel complex divided into several bars and restaurants, though its highlight is the rooftop with big screen to enjoy its six microbrews, including a rice beer and guest ale.

Cafes

Dyu Art Cafe
CAFE

(www.dyuartcafe.yolasite.com; 23 MIG, KHB Colony, Koramangala; ⊙10am-10.30pm; 🕾) An atmospheric cafe-gallery in a leafy neighbourhood with a peaceful courtyard reminiscent of a Zen temple. It has coffee beans from Kerala and does good filtered, espresso and iced coffee, to go with homemade cakes.

Matteo
CAFE

(www.matteocoffea.com; Church St; ⊙9am-11pm; 🕾) The coolest rendezvous in the city centre where arty locals lounge on retro couches sipping first-rate brews while chatting, plugged into free wi-fi, or browsing a great selection of newspapers and mags.

Infinitea
CAFE

(www.infinitea.in; 2 Shah Sultan Complex, Cunningham Rd; pot of tea from ₹100; ⊙11am-11pm; 🕾) This smart yet homely cafe has an impressive menu of steaming cuppas, including orthodox teas from the best estates, and a few selections such as blooming flowers. Order your pot and team it with a delectable sweet or light lunch. Sells loose tea by the gram.

☆ Entertainment

Live Music

Humming Tree
LIVE MUSIC

(www.facebook.com/thehummingtree; 12th Main Rd, Indiranagar; ⊙11am-11.30pm Sun-Thu, to 1am Fri & Sat) One of Bengaluru's premier live-music venues, this warehouse-style venue has bands (starting around 9pm), DJs and a rooftop bar. Cover charge is anything from free to ₹300.

B Flat
LIVE MUSIC

(⊘8041739250; www.facebook.com/thebflat bar; 776 100ft Rd, Indiranagar; cover charge ₹300; ⊙6.30-11.30pm Sun-Thu, to 1am Fri & Sat) A pub and live-music venue that features some of India's best blues and jazz bands.

Sport

M Chinnaswamy Stadium
SPORTS

(www.ksca.co.in; MG Rd) For a taste of India's sporting passion, attend one of the regular cricket matches at M Chinnaswamy Stadium. Check online for the upcoming schedule of Tests, one-dayers and Twenty20s.

Bangalore Turf Club
HORSE RACING

(www.bangaloreraces.com; Racecourse Rd) Horse racing is big in Bengaluru and can make for a fun day out. Races are generally held on Friday and Saturday afternoons.

Theatre

Ranga Shankara
THEATRE

(⊘26592777; www.rangashankara.org; 36/2 8th Cross, JP Nagar) Interesting theatre (in a variety of languages and genres) and dance are held at this cultural centre.

🔒 Shopping

Bengaluru's shopping options are abundant, ranging from teeming bazaars to glitzy malls. Some good shopping areas include Commercial St, Vittal Mallya Rd and the MG Rd area.

Mysore Saree Udyog CLOTHING
(www.mysoresareeudyog.com; 1st fl, 316 Kamaraj Rd; ⊕10.30am-11pm) A great choice for top-quality silk saris and men's shirts, this busy store has been in business for over 70 years and has something to suit all budgets. Most garments are made with Mysore silk; also stocks 100% *pashmina* (wool shawls).

Cauvery Arts & Crafts Emporium SOUVENIRS
(49 MG Rd; ⊕10am-9pm) Large government-run emporium famous for it expansive collection of quality sandalwood and rosewood products as well as textiles.

Kynkyny Art Gallery ART
(www.kynkyny.com; Embassy Sq, 148 Infantry Rd; ⊕10am-7pm Mon-Sat) This sophisticated commercial gallery inside a stunning colonial-era building sells works by contemporary Indian artists, priced suitably for all budgets. Also sells designer furniture.

Forest Essentials COSMETICS
(www.forestessentialsindia.com; 4/1 Lavelle Junction Bldg, Vittal Mallya Rd; ⊕10am-9pm) Smell the lemongrass as you browse the shelves at this tranquil store selling all-organic ayurvedic essential oils and beauty products.

Fabindia CLOTHING, HOMEWARES
(www.fabindia.com; 54 17th Main, Koramangala; ⊕10am-8pm) Commercial St (152 Commercial St; ⊕10am-8.30pm); Garuda Mall (Garuda Mall, McGrath Rd; ⊕10am-8pm); MG Rd (1 MG Rd; ⊕10am-8pm) Hugely successful chain with a range of traditional clothing, homewares and accessories in traditional cotton prints and silks. Quality skincare products too.

UB City MALL
(www.ubcitybangalore.in; 24 Vittal Mallya Rd; ⊕11am-9pm) Global haute couture (Louis Vuitton, Jimmy Choo, Burberry) and Indian high fashion come to roost at this towering mall in the central district.

Garuda Mall MALL
(McGrath Rd) A modern mall with all the usual food and clothing chains.

Forum MALL
(www.theforumexperience.com/forumbangalore. htm; Hosur Rd, Koramangala; ⊕10am-11pm) Shiny mall complex in Koramangala.

Leela Galleria MALL
(23 Airport Rd, Kodihalli) A glamorous mall with high end shops. It's nearby to the ritzy suburb of Indiranagar.

Indiana Crockery HOMEWARES
(97/1 MG Rd; ⊕10.30am-9pm) Good spot to buy thali trays, brass utensils and chai cups for that dinner party back home.

Goobe's Book Republic BOOKS
(www.goobes.wordpress.com; 11 Church St; ⊕10.30am-9pm Mon-Sat, noon-9pm Sun) Great little bookstore selling new and secondhand, cult and mainstream books and comics.

Gangarams Book Bureau BOOKS
(2nd fl, 48 Church St; ⊕10am-8pm Mon-Sat) Excellent selection of Indian titles, guidebooks and Penguin classics.

Bookworm BOOKS
(Shrungar Shopping Complex, MG Rd; ⊕10am-9pm) Great secondhand bookstore filled with contemporary and classic literature as well as travel guidebooks.

Blossom Book House BOOKS
(www.blossombookhouse.com; 84/6 Church St; ⊕10.30am-9.30pm) Great deals on new and secondhand books.

Magazines BOOKS
(41/1 Rayan Tower, Church St; ⊕10am-10pm) Huge collection of international magazines.

ℹ **Information**

INTERNET ACCESS
Being an IT city, internet cafes are plentiful in Bengaluru, as is wi-fi access in hotels.

LEFT LUGGAGE
The City train station and Kempegowda bus stand have 24-hour cloakrooms (per day ₹10).

MAPS
The tourist offices give out decent city maps and you can find maps at most major bookstores.

MEDIA
Time Out Bengaluru (www.timeout.com/bangalore), *What's Up Bangalore* (www.whatsupguides.com) and *Explocity* (www.bangalore.explocity.com) cover all the latest events, nightlife, dining and shopping in the city; magazines are available in major bookshops.

MEDICAL SERVICES
Hosmat (⊠25593796; www.hosmatnet.com) For critical injuries and general illnesses.
Mallya Hospital (⊠22277979; www.mallyahospital.net; 2 Vittal Mallya Rd) Emergency services and 24-hour pharmacy.

MONEY
ATMs are everywhere, as are moneychangers around MG Rd.

POST

Main post office (Cubbon Rd; ⊙10am-7pm Mon-Sat, to 1pm Sun)

TOURIST INFORMATION

Government of India tourist office (GITO; ☑25585417; 2nd level, 48 Church St; ⊙9.30am-6pm Mon-Fri, 9am-1pm Sat) Very helpful for Bengaluru and beyond.

Karnataka State Tourism Development Corporation (KSTDC) Badami House (☑080-43344334; www.karnatakaholidays.net; Kasturba Rd; ⊙10am-7pm Mon-Sat); Karnataka Tourism House (☑41329211; 8 Papanna Lane, St Mark's Rd; ⊙10am-7pm Mon-Sat) Mainly for booking tours and government-run accommodation around Karnataka, but also has a useful website.

TRAVEL AGENCIES

Skyway (☑22111401; www.skywaytour.com; 8 Papanna Lane, St Mark's Rd; ⊙9am-6pm Mon-Sat) Thoroughly professional and reliable outfit for booking long-distance taxis and air tickets.

ⓘ Getting There & Away

AIR

International flights arrive at Bengaluru's **Kempegowda International Airport** (www.bengaluruairport.com). Domestic flights also leave here with daily flights to major cities across India, including Chennai (₹2600, two hours), Mumbai (₹4000, two hours), Hyderabad (₹3000, one hour), Delhi (₹6100, 2½ hours) and Goa (₹2500, one hour).

AirAsia (☑1860-5008000; www.airasia.com)

Air India (☑22978427; www.airindia.com; Unity Bldg, JC Rd)

GoAir (☑47406091; www.goair.in)

IndiGo (☑9910383838; www.goindigo.in)

Jet Airways (☑39893333; www.jetairways.com; Unity Bldg, JC Rd)

SpiceJet (☑18001803333; www.spicejet.com)

BUS

Bengaluru's huge, well-organised **Kempegowda bus stand** (Gubbi Thotadappa Rd), also commonly known as either the Central or Majestic, is directly in front of the City train station.

Karnataka State Road Transport Corporation (KSRTC; ☑44554422; www.ksrtc.in) buses run from here throughout Karnataka.

The KSRTC website lists current schedules and fares. At the time of research booking online wasn't possible using an international credit card, but check if things have changed. Otherwise KSRTC has convenient booking counters around town, or computerised advance booking at the station. It's wise to book long-distance journeys in advance.

Private bus operators line the street facing Kempegowda bus stand, or you can book through a travel agency.

Interstate bus operators also run from Kempegowda bus stand.

TRAIN

Bengaluru's **City train station** (www.bangalorecityrailwaystation.in; Gubbi Thotadappa Rd) is the main train hub. There's also **Cantonment train station** (Station Rd), a sensible spot to disembark if you're arriving and headed for the MG Rd area, while **Yeshvantpur train station** (Rahman Khan Rd), 8km northwest of downtown, is the starting point for trains to Goa.

If you have a local phone number, tickets can be booked online at www.irctc.co.in. If a train is booked out, foreign travellers can use the foreign-tourist quota. The computerised **reservation office** (☑139; ⊙8am-8pm Mon-Sat, to 2pm Sun), on the left facing the station, has separate counters for credit-card purchase, women and foreigners. Luggage can be left at the 24-hour cloakroom on Platform 1 at the City train station.

ⓘ Getting Around

TO/FROM THE AIRPORT

The swish Kempegowda International Airport is in Hebbal, about 40km north from the MG Rd area. Metered AC taxis from the airport to the city centre cost between ₹750 and ₹1000.

Flybus KSRTC runs the Flybus to Mysuru (₹750, four hours) departing the airport at 10.30am and 9pm.

Vayu Vajra (☑18004251663; www.mybmtc.com) Vayu Vajra's airport shuttle service has an AC bus to Kempegowda (Central Majestic) bus stand or MG Rd (₹210), departing hourly from 6.10am to 10.25pm.

AUTORICKSHAW

The city's autorickshaw drivers are legally required to use their meters; few comply. After 10pm, 50% is added to the metered rate. Flag fall is ₹25 for the first 2km and then ₹13 for each extra kilometre.

BUS

Bengaluru has a thorough local bus network, operated by the **Bangalore Metropolitan Transport Corporation** (BMTC; www.mybmtc.com), with a useful website for timetable and fares. Red AC Vajra buses criss-cross the city, while green Big10 deluxe buses connect the suburbs.

Ordinary buses run from the City bus stand, next to Kempegowda (Central Majestic) bus stand; a few operate from the City Market bus stand.

To get from the City train station to the MG Rd area, catch any bus from Platform 17 or 18 at the City bus stand. For the City Market bus stand, take bus 31, 31E, 35 or 49 from Platform 8.

TAXI

Standard rates for a long-haul Tata Indica cab are ₹8.5 per kilometre for a minimum of 250km, plus a daily allowance of ₹200 for the driver. An eight-hour day rental is around ₹2000.

Olacabs (🖰 33553355; www.olacabs.com) Professional, efficient company with modern air-con cars. Online and phone bookings.

Meru Cabs (🖰44224422; www.merucabs.com)

METRO

Bengaluru's shiny new AC metro service, known as Namma Metro, is still very much a work in progress, but it does have a few lines up and running. The most relevant to tourists is Line 1 from MG Rd to Indiranagar (₹13), running every 15 minutes, 6am to 10pm. For the latest updates on the service, log on to www.bmrc.co.in.

TRANSPORT FROM BENGALURU

Major Bus Services from Bengaluru

DESTINATION	FARE (₹)	DURATION (HR)	FREQUENCY
Chennai	390 (R)/690 (V)/757 (S)	7-8	hourly, 5.35am-11.45pm
Ernakulam	587 (R)/1012 (V)/1062 (S)	10-12	7 daily, 4-9.45pm
Hampi	546 (R)	8½	1 daily, 11pm
Hospet	326 (R)/566 (V)/695 (S)	8	14 buses, 4.30-11pm, hourly
Hyderabad	672 (R)/812 (V)/1012 (S)	9½-11	23 daily, 7.30am-10.30pm
Mumbai	1690 (V)	17½-19	4 daily, 3-9pm
Mysuru	190 (R)/270 (V)	3	Every 10min, 24hr
Ooty	256 (R)/490 (V)	8	9 daily, 6.15am-11.15pm
Panaji	1190 (V)	13	4 daily, 6.20-8pm
Gorkana	562 (R)	12	2 daily, from 9pm

Fares: (R) Rajahamsa Semideluxe, (V) Airavath AC Volvo, (S) AC Sleeper

Major Trains from Bengaluru

DESTINATION	TRAIN NO & NAME	FARE (₹)	DURATION (HR)	DEPARTURES
Chennai	12658 Chennai Mail	260/920	6½	10.40pm
	12028 Shatabdi	785/1510	5	6am & 4.25pm Wed-Mon
Delhi	12627 Karnataka Exp	815/3110	39	7.20pm
	12649 Sampark Kranti Exp	795/3030	35	10.10pm Mon, Wed, Fri, Sat & Sun
Hospet	16592 Hampi Exp	255/970	9½	10pm
Hubli	16589 Rani Chennamma Exp	270/1040	8½	9.15pm
Kolkata	12864 YPR Howrah Exp	740/2820	34½	7.35pm
Mumbai	11302 Udyan Exp	505/1975	23½	8.30pm
Mysuru	12007 Shatabdi	435/825	2	11am Thu-Tue
	12614 Tippu Exp	90/305	2½	3pm
Trivandrum	16526 Kanyakumari Exp	420/1630	16½	8pm

Fares: Shatabdi fares are AC chair/AC executive; Express (Exp/Mail) fares are 2nd-class/AC chair for day trains and sleeper/2AC for night trains.

Around Bengaluru

If Bengaluru's mayhem and traffic jams are doing your head in, then head to the hills for some fresh air, rural culture and lovely scenery.

Nandi Hills

Rising to 1455m, **Nandi Hills** (admission ₹10, car ₹150; ☺6am-6pm), 60km north of Bengaluru, were once the summer retreat of Tipu Sultan (his palace is still here). Today it's the Bengaluru techie's favourite weekend getaway, and is predictably congested on Saturday and Sunday; aim to visit midweek. Nonetheless, it's a good place for a leisurely hike, panoramic views of sweeping plains and two notable **Chola temples**. It's a 2km hike to the top from the entrance gate for those without a vehicle. Macaques run amok, so avoid carrying food.

At the top of Nandi Hills, **Hotel Mayura Pine Top** (☎8970650019; mains ₹80-160; ☺10.30am-8pm) does good Indian dishes which can be enjoyed with excellent views from it's glassed-in restaurant. Its **rooms** (fan/AC ₹1500/3000) also feature stellar views.

Around Nandi Hills is one of India's premier wine-growing regions.

Buses head to Nandi Hills (₹65, two hours) from Bengaluru's Kempegowda (Central Majestic) bus stand.

KARNATAKA CITY NAME CHANGES

From 1 November 2014 the Karnataka government officially announced the name changes of 12 cities across the state, returning to their precolonial titles. The following are most relevant to tourists:

➡ Bangalore to Bengaluru

➡ Mysore to Mysuru

➡ Mangalore to Mangaluru

➡ Hospet to Hosapete

➡ Hubli to Hubballi

➡ Bijapur to Vijapura

➡ Gulbarga to Kalaburgi

➡ Shimoga to Shivamogga

Hessaraghatta

Located 30km northwest of Bengaluru, Hessaraghatta is home to **Nrityagram** (☎080-28466313; www.nrityagram.org; self-guided tour ₹50; ☺10am-2pm Tue-Sun), a leading dance academy established in 1990 to revive and popularise Indian classical dance. The brainchild and living legacy of celebrated dancer Protima Gauri Bedi (1948–98), the complex was designed like a village by Goa-based architect Gerard da Cunha. You can take a self-guided tour, or book a tour, lecture and demonstration and vegetarian meal (₹1500 to ₹2000, minimum 10 people). Note the early 2pm closure.

From Bengaluru's City Market, buses 266, 253, 253D and 253E run to Hessaraghatta (₹25, one hour), with bus 266 continuing on to Nrityagram. From Hessaraghatta an autorickshaw will cost ₹70.

🛏 Sleeping

Taj Kuteeram   HOTEL **$$$**
(☎080-28466326; www.tajhotels.com; d from ₹4800; ❄@☎) Opposite Nrityagram dance village, Kuteeram isn't as luxurious as other Taj Group hotel offerings, but it's still very nice with a balance of comfort and rustic charm, and designs by renowned architect Gerard da Cunha. It also offers ayurveda and yoga sessions.

Janapada Loka Folk Arts Museum

Janapada Loka Folk Arts Museum   MUSEUM (Bangaluru-Mysuru Rd; Indian/foreigner ₹20/100; ☺9am-5.30pm) A worthwhile stopover between Bengaluru and Mysuru, this museum is dedicated to the preservation of rural local culture. It has a wonderful collection of folk-art objects, including 500-year-old shadow puppets, festival costumes, musical instruments and a superb temple chariot and a replica of a traditional village. It's situated 53km south of Bengaluru, 3km from Ramnagar; any Mysuru–Bengaluru bus can drop you here.

Mysuru (Mysore)

☎0821 / POP 895,000 / ELEV 707M
One of South India's most famous tourist destinations, Mysuru (which recently changed its name from Mysore) is known for its glittering royal heritage and magnif-

WHISKEY & WINE

In a country not known for being a big exponent of fine wines and liquors (anyone who has stepped foot into one of India's ubiquitous 'wine shops' can attest to this), Bengaluru (Bangalore) is very much an exception to the rule. It's a city that's not only gained a thirst for craft beer (p181), but has on its doorstep one of India's premier wine-growing regions in Nandi Hills. While an emerging industry, it's fast gaining a reputation internationally with some 18 wineries in the area. Also a few clicks out of town is India's first single-malt whiskey distillery, where you're also able to sample the goods.

Grover Wineries (☑9379627188; www.groverzampa.in; 1½hr tour Mon-Fri ₹850, Sat & Sun ₹1000) Highly recommended tours of Grover Wineries where you'll learn about India's wine industry that produces quality white and red varietals. Prices include tastings of five wines in the cellar rooms accompanied by cheese and crackers, followed by lunch. From February to May you'll also see grape crushing and visit its vineyards. It's located on the approach to Nandi Hills, around 40km north of Bengaluru; you'll need to hire a car to get here.

Amrut (☑080-23100402; www.amrutdistilleries.com; Mysuru Rd; tour free) Established in 1948, India's first producer of single malt whiskey, Amrut offers free distillery tours run by knowledgeable guides. You get taken through the entire process before tasting its world-class single malts and blends. It's 20km outside Bangaluru on the road to Mysuru; pre-bookings essential.

---

icent monuments and buildings. Its World Heritage–listed palace may be what brings most travellers here, but it's also a thriving centre for the production of premium silk, sandalwood and incense. These days ashtanga yoga is another drawcard, attracting visitors worldwide with its reputation as one of India's best places to practise yoga.

History

Mysuru owes its name to the mythical Mahisuru, a place where the demon Mahisasura was slain by the goddess Chamundi. Its regal history began in 1399, when the Wodeyar dynasty of Mysuru was founded, though they remained in service of the Vijayanagar empire until the mid-16th century. With the fall of Vijayanagar in 1565, the Wodeyars declared their sovereignty, which – save a brief period of Hyder Ali and Tipu Sultan's supremacy in the late 18th century – remained unscathed until Independence in 1947.

⊙ Sights

Mysuru isn't known as the City of Palaces for nothing, being home to a total of seven and an abundance of majestic heritage architecture dating from the Wodeyars dynasty and British rule. The majority of grand buildings are owned by the state, and used as anything from hospitals, colleges and government buildings to heritage hotels. Visit www.karnatakatourism.org/Mysore/en for list of notable buildings.

★ **Mysore Palace**   PALACE
(Maharaja's Palace; www.mysorepalace.gov.in; Indian/foreigner incl audio guide ₹40/200, child under 10yr free; ⊙10am-5.30pm) Among the grandest of India's royal buildings, this fantastic palace was the former seat of the Wodeyar maharajas. The old palace was gutted by fire in 1897; the one you see now was completed in 1912 by English architect Henry Irwin at a cost of ₹4.5 million. The interior of this Indo-Saracenic marvel – a kaleidoscope of stained glass, mirrors and gaudy colours – is lavish and undoubtedly over the top. The decor is further embellished by carved wooden doors, mosaic floors and a series of paintings depicting life in Mysore during the Edwardian Raj era.

The way into the palace takes you past a fine collection of sculptures and artefacts. Don't forget to check out the armoury, with an intriguing collection of 700-plus weapons.

Every Sunday and national holiday, from 7pm to 7.45pm, the palace is illuminated by nearly 100,000 light bulbs that accent its majestic profile against the night.

Entrance to the palace grounds is at the **South Gate** on Purandara Dasa Rd. While you are allowed to snap the palace's exterior, photography within is strictly prohibited.

Mysuru (Mysore)

Cameras must be deposited in lockers at the palace entrance. See illustrated highlight (p190) for more detail.

Devaraja Market
MARKET

(Sayyaji Rao Rd; ⊙6am-8.30pm) Dating from Tipu Sultan's reign, this lively bazaar has local traders selling traditional items such as flower garlands, spices and conical piles of *kumkum* (coloured powder used for bindi dots), all of which makes for some great photo ops. Refresh your bargaining skills before shopping.

Chamundi Hill
VIEWPOINT

At a height of 1062m, on the summit of Chamundi Hill, stands the **Sri Chamundeswari Temple** (⊙7am-2pm, 3.30-6pm & 7.30-9pm), dominated by a towering 40m-high *gopuram* (gateway tower). It's a fine half-day excursion, offering spectacular views of the city below. Queues are long at weekends, so visit during the week. From Central bus

stand take bus 100 (₹17, 25 minutes) or 201 (₹28, AC) that rumbles up the narrow road to the summit. A return autorickshaw trip will cost about ₹400.

Alternatively, you can take the foot trail comprising 1000-plus steps that Hindu pilgrims use to visit the temple. One-third of the way down is a 5m-high statue of **Nandi** (Shiva's bull) that was carved out of solid rock in 1659.

Jaganmohan Palace
PALACE

(Jaganmohan Palace Rd; adult/child ₹120/60; ⊙8.30am-5pm) Built in 1861 as the royal auditorium, this stunning palace just west of the Mysore Palace, houses the **Jayachamarajendra Art Gallery**. Set over three floors it has a huge collection of Indian paintings, including works by noted artist Raja Ravi Varma and traditional Japanese art. There's also regal memorabilia from the Mysore royal family, weapons and rare musical instruments.

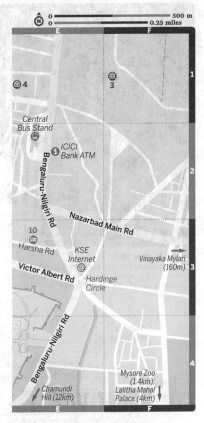

KARNATAKA & BENGALURU MYSURU (MYSORE)

Indira Gandhi Rashtriya Manav
Sangrahalaya MUSEUM
(National Museum of Mankind; ☑2526531; www.igrms.com; Wellington Lodge, Irwin Rd; ⊙10am-5.30pm Tue-Sun) FREE Lovely arts and cultural centre that presents rotating exhibitions showcasing arts from rural India.

Government House HISTORIC BUILDING
(Irwin Rd) Dating from 1805, Government House, formerly the British Residency, is a Tuscan Doric building set in 20 hectares of gardens.

Jayalakshmi Vilas Mansion
Museum Complex MUSEUM
(Mysore University Campus; ⊙10.15am-5pm Mon-Sat) FREE Housed in a grand mansion, on the university campus west of town, this museum specialises in folklore, with artefacts, stone tablets and sculptures, including rural costumes and a wooden puppet of the 10-headed demon king Ravana.

St Philomena's Cathedral CHURCH
(St Philomena St; ⊙8am-5pm) The beauty of towering St Philomena's Cathedral, built between 1933 and 1941 in neo-Gothic style, is emphasised by lovely stained-glass windows. It's on the northern outskirts of town.

Rail Museum MUSEUM
(KRS Rd; adult/child ₹15/10, camera/video ₹20/30; ⊙9.30am-6.30pm Tue-Sun) Behind the train station, this open-air museum's main exhibit is the Mysore maharani's saloon, a wood-panelled beauty dating from 1899 that provides an insight into the way in which the royals once rode the railways. A **toy train** (₹10) rides the track around the museum.

Mysore Zoo ZOO
(Indiranagar; adult/child ₹50/20, camera ₹20; ⊙8.30am-5.30pm Wed-Mon) Unlike many other pitiful zoos in India, Mysore Zoo conforms to much higher standards, set in pretty gardens that date from 1892. Highlights include white tigers, lowland gorillas and rhinos. It's situated around 2km southeast of Mysore Palace.

(Continued on p192)

Mysore Palace

The interior of Mysore Palace houses opulent halls, royal paintings, intricate decorative details, as well as sculptures and ceremonial objects. There is a lot of hidden detail and much to take in, so be sure to allow yourself at least a few hours for the experience. A guide can also be invaluable.

After entering the palace the first exhibit is the **Doll's Pavilion** ❶, which showcases the maharaja's fine collection of traditional dolls and sculptures acquired from around the world. Opposite the **Elephant Gate** ❷ you'll see the seven cannons that were used for special occasions, such as the birthdays of the maharajas. Today the cannons are still fired as part of Dasara festivities.

At the end of the Doll's Pavilion you'll find the **Golden Howdah** ❸. Note the fly whisks on either side; the bristles are made from fine ivory.

Make sure you check out the paintings depicting the Dasara procession in the halls on your way to the **Marriage Pavilion** ❹ and look into the courtyard to see what was once the wrestling arena. It's now used during Dasara only. In the Marriage Pavilion, take a few minutes to scan the entire space. You can see the influence of three religions in the design of the hall: the glass ceiling represents Christianity, stone carvings along the hallway ceilings are Hindu design and the top-floor balcony roof (the traditional ladies' gallery) has Islamic-style arches.

When you move through to the **Private Durbar Hall** ❺, take note of the intricate ivory inlay motifs depicting Krishna in the rosewood doors. The **Public Durbar Hall** ❻ is usually the last stop where you can admire the panoramic views of the gardens through the Islamic arches.

Private Durbar Hall
Rosewood doors lead into this hall, which is richly decorated with stained-glass ceilings, steel grill work and chandeliers. It houses the Golden Throne, only on display to the public during Dasara.

Entry to the Palace

Doll's Pavilion
The first exhibit, the Doll's Pavilion, displays the gift collection of 19th- and early-20th-century dolls, statues and Hindu idols that were given to the maharaja by dignitaries from around the world.

Public Durbar Hall
The open-air hall contains a priceless collection of paintings by Raja Ravi Varma and opens into an expansive balcony supported by massive pillars with an ornate painted ceiling of 10 incarnations of Vishnu.

Marriage Pavilion
This lavish hall used for royal weddings features themes of Christianity, Hindu and Islam in its design. The highlight is the octagonal painted glass ceiling featuring peacock motifs, the bronze chandelier and the colonnaded turquoise pillars.

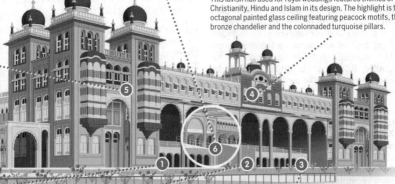

Elephant Gate
Next to the Doll's Pavilion, this brass gate has four bronze elephants inlaid at the bottom, an intricate double-headed eagle up the top and a hybrid lion-elephant creature (the state emblem of Karnataka) in the centre.

Golden Howdah
At the far end of the Doll's Pavilion, a wooden elephant howdah decorated with 80kg of gold was used to carry the maharaja in the Dasara festival. It now carries the idol of goddess Chamundeswari.

(Continued from p189)

Karanji Lake Nature Park
PARK,
(Indiranagar; admission ₹25, camera ₹20; ☻8.30am-5.30pm) Next to the zoo, this nature park is the place to spy on various bird species, including herons, rose-ringed parakeets, painted storks and butterflies.

🏃 Activities

Emerge Spa
AYURVEDA
(☑2522500; www.thewindflower.com; Windflower Spa & Resort, Maharanapratap Rd, Nazarbad; Abhayanga massage ₹2150; ☻7am-9pm) Slick, out-of-town resort offering pampering ayurvedic sessions. Try the one-hour Abhayanga massage, which involves two therapists. It's located 3km southeast of Mysore Palace; rates include pick up and drop-off.

Indus Valley Ayurvedic Centre
AYURVEDA
(☑2473263; www.ayurindus.com; Lalithadripura) Set on 10 hectares of gardens, 16km east of town, this classy centre derives its therapies from ancient scriptures and prescriptions. The overnight package (single/double including full board US$180/320) includes one session each of ayurveda, yoga and beauty therapy.

Swaasthya Ayurveda Centre
AYURVEDA
(☑9845913471, 6557557; www.swaasthya.com; 726/B, 6th Cross, opp Yoganarsimhaswamy Temple; treatments from ₹250) Situated around 15km north of Mysuru, Swaasthya Ayurveda Centre has professional ayurveda therapists providing traditional treatments and all-inclusive packages that include accommodation and food. Also a retreat in (Kodagu) Coorg.

🎓 Courses

Shruthi Musical Works
MUSIC
(☑9845249518; 1189 3rd Cross, Irwin Rd; per hour ₹400; ☻10.30am-9pm Mon-Sat, to 2pm Sun) Music teacher Jayashankar gets good reviews for his tabla instruction.

👉 Tours

KSTDC Transport Office
BUS TOUR
(city tour ₹210) KSTDC runs a daily Mysuru city tour, taking in city sights (excluding the palace), Chamundi Hill, Srirangapatnam and Brindavan Gardens. It starts daily at 8.30am, ends at 8.30pm and is likely to leave you breathless! Other tours go to Belur, Halebid and Sravanabelagola (₹550) on Tuesday and Thursday from 7.30am to 9pm.

All tours leave from the KSTDC transport office (p195) next to Hotel Mayura Hoysala,

from where bookings are made, or at travel agencies around town.

Royal Mysore Walks
WALKING
(☑9632044188; www.royalmysorewalks.com; 2hr walk ₹600-1500) An excellent way to familiarise yourself with Mysuru's epic history and heritage, these weekend walks offer a range of themes from royal history to food walks.

🛏 Sleeping

Mysuru attracts tourists throughout the year and can fill up very quickly during Dussehra (p194). Booking early is recommended.

Hotel Maurya
HOTEL $
(☑2426677; 9/5 Hanumantha Rao St; s/d from ₹180/330; ⊛📶) Maurya is your classic cheap Indian hotel with large, unremarkable rooms but it's still a good budget choice. It offers TV and AC too.

Mysore Youth Hostel
HOSTEL $
(☑2544704; www.yhmysore.com; Gangothri Layout; dm ₹130) On a patch of green lawn 3km west of town, this hostel has clean, well-maintained male and female dorms. OK, there's a 10.30pm curfew, no alcohol allowed, bucket hot water and no towels, but you can't go past these prices. Discounts are available for students. Take a city bus to Maruthi Temple, from where it's a short walk; an autorickshaw costs ₹60.

⭐ Parklane Hotel
HOTEL $$
(☑4003500; www.parklanemysore.com; 2720 Harsha Rd; r from ₹2000; ⊛@📶⊛) Travellers' central on Mysuru's tourist circuit, the Parklane is over-the-top kitsch but it's hard to dislike with its massive and immaculate rooms, ultracomfortable and thoughtfully outfitted with mobile-chargers and considerate toiletry kits. Its lively open-air restaurant is always buzzing, and it has a small rooftop pool too.

Hotel Mayura Hoysala
HOTEL $$
(☑2426160; www.karnatakaholidays.net; 2 Jhansi Lakshmi Bai Rd; s/d incl breakfast with fan ₹1350/1500, with AC ₹2480/2750; ⊛) The potential of this beautiful historic building remains unrealised as this government-owned hotel continues to offer its blend of mothballed heritage. It's still worthy of consideration, especially at these rates. The bar here is popular with Mysuru's tipplers.

⭐ Green Hotel
HERITAGE GUESTHOUSE $$$
(☑4255000; www.greenhotelindia.com; 2270 Vinoba Rd, Jayalakshmipuram; s/d incl breakfast

from ₹3880/4480; ☎) ✆ The character-filled Green Hotel has unndergone several fascinating reincarnations over the years. It was originally built as the Chittaranjan Palace in the 1920s by the marajah for his three daughters, before becoming a major film studio from the 1950s to 1987. Today its 31-rooms, set among charming gardens, are all run on solar power and those in the Palace building include themes such as a Writers room or kitschy Bollywood decor.

Dinner in the evenings is also wonderfully atmospheric with candle-lit tables set up on the lawn. Best of all, the profits are

MYSURU (MYSORE) ASHTANGA YOGA

What Rishikesh is to North India, Mysuru is to the South. This world-famous centre for yoga attracts thousands of international students each year to learn, practise or become certified in teaching ashtanga.

For the most part students are required to be austerely committed to the art, and will need at least a month. While in more recent times there's a growing trend for drop-in classes or week-long courses, for long-term students you'll need to register far in advance, as courses are often booked out.

Yoga Centres

Ashtanga Yoga Research Institute (AYRI; ☑9880185500; www.kpjayi.org; 235 8th Cross, 3rd Stage, Gokulam; 1st/2nd month ₹33,700/22,500) Founded by the renowned ashtanga teacher K Pattabhi Jois, who taught Madonna her yoga moves. He has since passed away and the reigns have been handed over to his son, who is proving very popular. You need to register two months in advance.

IndeaYoga (Ānanda Yoga India; ☑2416779; www.indeayoga.com; 144E 7th Main, Gokulam; 4/8 weeks US$1200/1600) Very popular school offering hatha and ashtanga yoga with a young guru, Bharath Shetty, who practised under the late BKS Iyengar from Pune. Also does drop-in classes.

Mystic School (☑4288490; www.mysoreyoga.in; 100 3rd A Main Rd, Gokulam) Gets good feedback for its diverse program covering hatha and asthanga, meditation and lectures. Suitable for short- and long-term students at all levels. Offers accommodation too.

Atma Vikasa Centre (☑2341978; www.atmavikasayoga.com; 18, 80ft Rd, Ramakrishnanagar) Backbending expert Yogacharya Venkatesh offers courses in yoga, Sanskrit and meditation. It's located in a peaceful suburb 5km southwest of the palace.

Sleeping & Eating

Most foreign yoga students congregate in the upmarket residential suburb of Gokulam. Few yoga centres offer accommodation, so you'll need to make your own arrangements; check out Facebook groups, **Ashtanga Community in Mysore** and **Mysore Yoga Community Group** for accommodation rentals. Expect to pay ₹12,000 to ₹15,000 per month for a private apartment.

Mystic School & Om Cafe (☑4288490; www.mysoreyoga.in; 100 3rd Main Rd, Gokulam; r with/without kitchen per month ₹25,000/18,000; ❋⛄✦) This is the most stylish accommodation in Gokulam offering squeaky-clean studios with kitchenettes, as well as an atmospheric rooftop cafe (8am to 8.30pm), Finnish sauna and plunge pool.

Urban Oasis (☑2410713; www.urbanoasis.co.in; 7 Contour Rd, 3rd Stage, Gokulam; r from ₹1800, monthly from ₹30,000; ❋⛄) More of a business hotel, but popular with students for its clean, modern rooms.

Anokhi Garden Guest House (☑9620793762; www.anokhigarden.com; 408 Contour Rd, 3rd Stage, Gokulam; s/d from ₹2000/3000; ⏲cafe 8am-12.30pm Thu-Sun; ⛄) French-run boutique guesthouse in a leafy property, with a lovely cafe that does vegetarian and vegan meals.

Anu's Bamboo Hut (☑9900909428; anugan@gmail.com; 365, 2nd Main, 3rd Stage, Gokulam; lunch buffet ₹250; ⏲1-3pm & 5-7pm Fri-Wed) Rooftop shack cafe catering to yoga students with healthy vegetarian lunch buffets and evening smoothies. A great source of info; also offers cooking classes (₹450).

distributed to charity and environmental projects across India. It's 3km west of town.

★ **Lalitha Mahal Palace** HERITAGE HOTEL $$$

(☎2526100; www.lalithamahalpalace.in; r incl breakfast ₹4830-12,080; ❋@☎) A former maharaja's guesthouse built in 1921, this majestic heritage building has been operating as a hotel since 1974. Old-world charm comes in bucket loads from the 1920s birdcage elevator to mosaic tiled floors. The heritage classic rooms are where you'll feel the history. Spacious four-poster beds sit next to antique furniture, claw-foot baths sit on marble bathroom floors, and shuttered windows look out to stately landscaped gardens. It's around 5km from the centre of town.

Royal Orchid Metropole HERITAGE HOTEL $$$

(☎4255566; www.royalorchidhotels.com; 5 Jhansi Lakshmi Bai Rd; s/d incl breakfast from ₹7170/8540; ❋☎≋) Originally built by the Wodeyars to serve as the residence of the maharaja's British guests, this is undoubtedly one of Mysuru's leading heritage hotels. The charming colonial-era structure has 30 rooms oozing historical character, and there are magic shows and snake-charming performances when tour groups pass through.

✖ Eating & Drinking

Malgudi Café CAFE $

(Green Hotel; 2270 Vinoba Rd, Jayalakshmipuram; cakes from ₹40, sandwiches ₹60; ☺10am-7pm; ☎) ✐ Set around an inner courtyard within the Green Hotel, this ambient cafe brews excellent coffees and Himalayan teas to be enjoyed with tasty cakes and sandwiches. Staff come from underprivileged backgrounds and are mostly women, and profits assist with disadvantaged communities, so you can do your bit by ordering a second cuppa.

Hotel RRR SOUTH INDIAN $

(Gandhi Sq; mains ₹90-130; ☺11.30am-4.30pm & 7-11pm) Classic Andhra-style food is ladled out at this ever-busy eatery, and you may have to queue for a table during lunch. One item to try is the piping-hot veg thali (₹90) served on banana leaves.

Vinayaka Mylari SOUTH INDIAN $

(769 Nazarbad Main Rd; mains ₹30-50; ☺6.30am-1.30pm & 4-8pm) Local foodies say this is one of the best eateries in town to try South Indian classics of *masala dosa* (curried vegetables in a crisp pancake) and *idlis* (South Indian spongy, round, fermented rice cakes). There's a similar branch up the road, Hotel Mylari, run by the owner's brother, and both are as good as each other.

Cafe Aramane SOUTH INDIAN $

(Sayyaji Rao Rd; mains ₹90-110; ☺7am-10.30pm) ✐ In a character-filled heritage building, this typically busy South Indian eatery rolls out steaming breakfast platters for Mysuru's office-goers, and welcomes them back in the evenings with aromatic filter coffee and a convoy of delicious snacks, including speciality *dosas* each day of the week.

★ **Sapphire** INDIAN $$

(Lalitha Mahal Palace; mains ₹250-1000; ☺12.30-7.45pm & 8-11pm) Dine in absolute royal Indian-style in the grand ballroom of the Lalitha Mahal Palace hotel. And grand it is, with high stained-glass ceilings, lace tablecloths and polished teak floors. Order the royal Mysore silver thali (₹485) which gets you an assortment of vegetables, breads and

---

DUSSEHRA JAMBOREE

Mysuru is at its carnivalesque best during the 10-day **Dussehra** (Dasara ; ☺Sep/Oct) festival held September or October. During this time the Mysore Palace is dramatically lit up every evening, while the town is transformed into a gigantic fairground, with concerts, dance performances, sporting demonstrations and cultural events.

On the last day the celebrations are capped off in grand style. A dazzling procession of richly costumed elephants, garlanded idols, liveried retainers and cavalry, marches through the streets to the rhythms of clanging brass bands.

Mysuru is choc-a-bloc with tourists during the festival, especially on the final day. To bypass suffocating crowds, consider buying a **Dasara VIP Gold Card** (₹7500 for two adults). Though expensive, it assures you good seats at the final day gala and helps you beat the entry queues at other events and performances, while providing discounts on accommodation, dining and shopping. It's also possible to buy tickets (₹250 to ₹1000) just for entering the palace and Bannimantap for the final day's parades. Contact the the **Dasara Information Centre** (☎0821-2423800; www.mysoredasara.gov.in) for more details.

sweets served on lavish brassware. Weekends are buffet menu only. The nonguest ₹1000 entrance fee is refundable if you're here to eat.

Parklane Hotel   MULTICUISINE **$$**
(2720 Harsha Rd, Parklane Hotel; mains ₹100-140) Mysuru's most social restaurant with outdoor tables, lit up moodily by countless lanterns. The menu does delicious regional dishes from across India accompanied by live traditional music.

Tiger Trail   INDIAN **$$$**
(Royal Orchid Metropole, 5 Jhansi Lakshmi Bai Rd; mains ₹250-750; ⊙7.30am-11.30pm) This sophisticated restaurant works up delectable Indian dishes in a courtyard that twinkles with torches and fairy lights at night and a menu comprising jungle recipes collected from different tiger reserves across India. Also has a lunch buffet from ₹450.

Pelican Pub   PUB
(Hunsur Rd; mains ₹100-190; ⊙11am-11pm) A popular watering hole located on the fringes of upmarket Gokulam, this laid-back joint serves beer for ₹65 a mug in the indoor classic pub or alfresco-style garden setting out back. There's live music Wednesday.

🛍 Shopping

Mysuru is a great place to shop for its famed sandalwood products, silk saris and wooden toys. It is also one of India's major incense-manufacturing centres.

Look for the butterfly-esque 'Silk Mark'; it's an endorsement for quality silk.

Government Silk Weaving Factory   CLOTHING
(☑8025586550; www.ksicsilk.com; Mananthody Rd, Ashokapuram; ⊙8.30am-4pm Mon-Sat, outlet 10.30am-7pm daily) Given that Mysuru's prized silk is made under its very sheds, this government-run outlet is the best and cheapest place to shop for the exclusive textile. Behind the showroom is the factory, where you can drop by to see how the fabric is made. It's around 2km south of town.

Sandalwood Oil Factory   SOUVENIRS
(Mananthody Rd, Ashokapuram; ⊙outlet 9.30am-6.30pm, factory closed Sun) A quality-assured place for sandalwood products including incense, soap, cosmetics and the prohibitively expensive pure sandalwood oil (if in stock). Guided tours are available to show you around the factory.

Cauvery Arts & Crafts Emporium   CRAFTS, SOUVENIRS
(Sayyaji Rao Rd; ⊙10.30am-8pm) Not the cheapest place, but the selection at this government emporium is extensive and there's no pressure to buy.

Sumangali Silks   CLOTHING
(off Gandhi Sq; ⊙10.30am-8.30pm) Exceptionally popular with Indian ladies, this multi-level store stocks silk saris, with quality of varying degrees depending on how much you want to spend.

Sri Sharada Grand Musical Works   MUSIC STORE
(2006 Seebaiah Rd) Sells a variety of traditional musical instruments including tabla sets and assorted percussion instruments.

ℹ Information

Most hotels have wi-fi access, otherwise internet cafes charge around ₹50 per hour.

The City bus stand's left-luggage cloakroom is open from 6am to 11pm and costs ₹10 per bag for 12 hours.

Government Hospital (☑4269806; Dhanvanthri Rd) Has a 24-hour pharmacy.

Karnataka Tourism (☑2422096; www.karnatakatourism.org; 1st fl, Hotel Mayura Hoysala, 2 Jhansi Lakshmi Bai Rd; ⊙10am-5.30pm Mon-Sat) Extremely helpful and has plenty of brochures.

KSTDC Transport Office (☑2423652; www.karnatakaholidays.net; Yatri Navas Bldg, 2 Jhansi Lakshmi Bai Rd; ⊙8.30am-8.30pm) Offers general tourist information and provides a useful map. Has counters at the train station and Central bus stand, as well as this main office.

Main Post Office (cnr Irwin & Ashoka Rds; ⊙10am-6pm Mon-Sat)

Thomas Cook (☑2420090; Silver Tower, 9/2 Ashoka Rd; ⊙9.30am-6pm Mon-Sat) Foreign currency.

ℹ Getting There & Away

BUS

The **Central bus stand** (Bengaluru-Nilgiri Rd) handles all KSRTC long-distance buses. The **City bus stand** (Sayyaji Rao Rd) is for city, Srirangapatnam and Chamundi Hill buses.

TRAIN

Train tickets can be bought from Mysuru's **railway reservation office** (☑131; ⊙8am-8pm Mon-Sat, to 2pm Sun).

ℹ️ Getting Around

Agencies at hotels and around town rent cabs from ₹8 per kilometre, with a minimum of 250km per day, plus a daily allowance of ₹200 for the driver.

Count on around ₹800 for a day's sightseeing in an autorickshaw.

Around Mysuru (Mysore)

Consider one of KSTDC's tours (p192) for visiting sights around Mysuru.

Srirangapatnam

📞 08236

Steeped in bloody history, the fort town of Srirangapatnam, 16km from Mysuru, is built on an island straddling the Cauvery River. The seat of Hyder Ali and Tipu Sultan's power, this town was the de facto capital of much of southern India during the 18th century. Srirangapatnam's glory days ended when the British waged an epic war against Tipu Sultan in 1799, when he was defeated and killed. His sword and the ring he wore in battle are now displayed in the British Museum in London. The ramparts, battlements and some of the gates of the fort still stand, as do a clutch of monuments. The island is now linked to the mainland by bridge.

👁 Sights

Daria Daulat Bagh   PALACE

(Summer Palace; Indian/foreigner ₹20/100; ⊙9am-5pm) Set within lovely manicured grounds, Srirangapatnam's star attraction is

Tipu's summer palace, 1km east of the fort. Built largely out of teak, the palace may not look like much from the outside, but the lavish decoration that covers every inch of its interiors is impressive. The ceilings are embellished with floral designs, while the walls bear murals depicting courtly life and Tipu's campaigns against the British. There's a small museum within displaying artefacts and interesting paintings.

Gumbaz   MAUSOLEUM

(⊙8am-6.30pm) **FREE** Located within a serene garden, the historically significant Gumbaz is the resting place of the legendary Tipu Sultan, his equally famed father, Hyder Ali, and his wife. The interior of the onion-dome mausoleum is painted in tiger-like motif as a tribute to the sultan. Across from the tomb is the **Masjid-E-Aska** tomb.

Sri Ranganathaswamy Temple   HINDU TEMPLE

(⊙7.30am-1pm & 4-8pm) Constructed in 894 AD, this attractive Vaishnavite temple has a mix of Hoysala and Vijayanagar design. Within are cavernous walkways, pillars and the centerpiece 4.5m-long reclining statue of Ranganatha, a manifestation of Vishnu.

Jamia Masjid   MOSQUE

This cream-coloured mosque with two minarets was built by the sultan in 1787 and features an interesting blend of Islamic and Hindu architecture. Climb the stairs at the back for panoramic views of the site.

Colonel Bailey's Dungeon   HISTORIC SITE

FREE North of the island, on the banks of the Cauvery, is this well-preserved 18th-century

KSRTC BUSES FROM MYSURU (MYSORE)

DESTINATION	FARE (₹)	DURATION (HR)	FREQUENCY
Bandipur	78 (O)/200 (V)	2	via Ooty every 30min 6.30am-3.30pm
Bengaluru	133 (O)/190 (R)/270 (V)	3	every 20min
Channarayapatna	84 (O)	2	hourly
Chennai	586 (R)/916 (R)	10-12	5 daily from 5pm
Ernakulam	620-820 (V)	9-11	4 daily from 5pm
Gokarna	481 (O)	12	1 daily
Hassan	114 (O)	3	hourly
Hospet	386 (O)/551 (R)	10-12	6 daily
Mangaluru	249 (O)/391 (R)/502 (V)	6	hourly
Ooty	131 (O)/193 (R)/351 (V)	4-5	12 daily

Fares: (O) Ordinary, (R) Rajahamsa Semideluxe, (V) Airavath AC Volvo

MAJOR TRAINS FROM MYSURU (MYSORE)

DESTINATION	TRAIN NO & NAME	FARE (₹)	DURATION (HR)	DEPARTURE TIME
Bengaluru	16215 Chamundi Express	2nd class/AC 75/255	2½	6.45am
Bengaluru	12613 Tippu Express	2nd class/AC chair 90/305	2½	11.15am
Bengaluru	12008 Shatabdi Express	AC chair/AC executive chair 370/765	2	2.15pm daily Thu-Tue
Chennai	12008 Shatabdi Express	AC chair/AC executive chair 935/1830	7	2.15pm daily Thu-Tue
Hosapete (for Hampi)	16592 Hampi Express	3AC/2AC sleeper 1000/1440	11½	6.40pm
Hubli	17301 Mysore Dharwad Express	sleeper/2AC 275/1055	9½	10.30pm

white-walled dungeon used to hold British prisoners of war, including Colonel Bailey who died here in 1780. Jutting out from the walls are stone fixtures used to chain prisoners. East along the river from here is **Thomas Inman's Dungeon**, hidden away beneath undulating terrain, with a more undiscovered feel that's fun to explore.

🛏 Sleeping & Eating

Mayura River View HOTEL $$
(🕿0823-6252114; d with fan/AC from ₹2000/2500; ❋) There's not much atmosphere here, but these government bungalows have a nice location on a quiet patch of riverbank. Day-trippers can pop in for lunch (mains ₹150 to ₹120) to gaze at the river while guzzling beer.

ℹ Getting There & Away

Take buses 313 or 313A (₹25 to ₹30, 45 minutes) that depart every hour from Mysuru's City bus stand. Passenger trains travelling from Mysuru to Bengaluru (₹2, 20 minutes) also stop here. Bus 307 (₹18, 30 minutes) heading to Brindavan Gardens is just across from Srirangapatnam's main bus stand. A return autorickshaw will cost from Mysuru ₹700, and a taxi around ₹1000.

ℹ Getting Around

The sights are spread out, so hiring an autorickshaw (₹300 for three hours) is the best option for getting around.

Melkote

Life in the devout Hindu town of Melkote (also called Melukote), about 50km north of Mysuru, revolves around the atmospheric 12th-century **Cheluvanarayana Temple** (Raja St; ⊗8am-1pm & 5-8pm), with its rose-coloured *gopuram* (gateway tower) and ornately carved pillars. Get a workout on the hike up to the hilltop **Yoganarasimha Temple**, which offers fine views of the surrounding hills.

Three KSRTC buses shuttle daily between Mysuru and Melkote (₹100, 1½ hours).

Somnathpur

The astonishingly beautiful **Keshava Temple** (Indian/foreigner ₹5/100; ⊗8.30am-5.30pm) is one of the finest examples of Hoysala architecture, on par with the masterpieces of Belur and Halebid. Built in AD 1268, this star-shaped temple, 33km from Mysuru, is adorned with superb stone sculptures depicting various scenes from the Ramayana, Mahabharata and Bhagavad Gita, and the life and times of the Hoysala kings.

Somnathpur is 12km south of Bannur and 10km north of Tirumakudal Narsipur. Take a half-hourly bus from Mysuru to either village (₹40, 30 minutes) and change there.

Bandipur National Park

📞 08229
Part of the Nilgiri Biosphere Reserve, **Bandipur National Park** (Indian/foreigner ₹75/1000, video ₹1000; ⊗6am-9.30am & 4-6pm) is one of South India's most famous wilderness areas. Covering 880 sq km, it was once the Mysore maharajas' private wildlife reserve, and is now a protected zone for over 100 species of mammals, including tigers, elephants, leopards, gaur (Indian bison), chital (spotted deer), sambars, sloth bears, dhole (wild dogs), mongoose and langurs. It's also home to an impressive 350 species of birds.

Only 80km south of Mysuru on the Ooty road, it's easily accessible from Bengaluru and Mysuru.

🏃 Activities

Only government vehicles are permitted to run safaris within the park.

Bandipur Safari Lodge   JEEP SAFARI
(☑ 08229-236043; 2hr safari per person ₹2500; ☺ 6.30am & 4.30pm) Easily the best option is with Bandipur Safari Lodge who have open-air 4WDs and minibuses, accompanied by knowledgeable guides.

Forest Department Safari   JEEP SAFARI
(☑ 08229-236051; 1hr safari per person incl permit ₹1100; ☺ hourly departures 6am-9.30am & 3.30-6.30pm) The forest department has rushed, impersonal bus drives arranged at the park headquarters. Avoid crowded weekends.

🛏 Sleeping & Eating

Forest Department
Bungalows   GUESTHOUSE $$
(☑ 08229-236051; www.bandipurtigerreserve.in; 9-/20-bed dm ₹680/1000, bungalow foreigner from ₹3000; ☎) Basic lodging at the park HQ is convenient for location and atmosphere, but the downside is foreigners have to pay an additional ₹1000 per night for park entry fees. Dorms are rented out in the entirety, so you won't need to share with strangers. You can book online.

Tiger Ranch   LODGE $$
(☑ 8095408505; www.tigerranch.net; Mangala Village; cottage incl full board ₹1510) The only place in Bandipur offering a genuine wilderness experience, Tiger Ranch has a reputation as somewhere you either love or hate (many find it a bit too rustic). Either way you're guaranteed a memorable stay in basic but attractive cottages that blend wonderfully into nature. It has an atmospheric thatched-roof dining hall, and evenings can be enjoyed around the bonfire. Animals visit occasionally, so you should be vigilant at night, and be warned monkeys and rodents can be serious a nuisance, so do not leave food (or any of your valuables!) lying around your room. There's no alcohol here, so bring your own. It's located 10km from the park; call ahead to arrange a pick-up (₹300).

MC Resort   HOTEL $$
(☑ 9019954162; www.mcresort.in; Bangaluru-Ooty Rd, Melukamanahally; r incl full board ₹2500; ☎ 🏊) Slightly tacky but low-key resort with reasonable rooms, swimming pool, wi-fi and convenient location near the park. Rates are inclusive of meals making it a good deal.

Hotel Bandipur Plaza   HOTEL $$
(☑ 08229-233200; Ooty-Mysuru Hwy; r ₹1500) Its highway location may not be what you hope for when visiting a national park, but its rooms are functional and more affordable in an otherwise pricey destination. It's nearby Bandipur Safari Lodge, so convenient for safaris into the park.

★Dhole's Den   LODGE $$$
(☑ 08229-236062; www.dholesden.com; Kaniyanapura Village; camping/s/d incl full board from ₹3000/9000/10,000; ☎) 🍃 With a boutique design that's lifted straight from the pages of an architectural magazine, Dhole's effectively mixes comfort with lovely pastoral surrounds. Stylish rooms are decked out with art and colourful fabrics, plus couches and deck chairs. The bungalows are worth the upgrade for extra space and privacy. It's environmentally conscious with solar power, tank water and organic vegies. Camping is available for those on a budget. It's a 20-minute drive from the park headquarters.

Serai   RESORT, LODGE $$$
(☑ 08229-236075; www.theserai.in; Kaniyanapura Village; r incl full board from ₹20,000; 🎔 ☎ 🏊) Backing on to the park, this luxurious resort has Mediterrean-inspired villas spread over 15 hectares of landscaped property that's in harmony with the natural surrounds. Thatched-roof rooms feature elegant touches such as stone-wall showers and wildlife photography on the walls. Its glassed-in restaurant and infinity pool both maximise outlooks to Nilgiri Hills.

Bandipur Safari Lodge   COTTAGES $$$
(☑ 08229-233001; www.junglelodges.com; Mysuru-Ooty Rd; r incl full board & safari Indian/foreigner ₹6420/8700; 🎔) This sprawling government-owned camp has well-maintained, comfortable cottages, but it lacks character and 'safari' atmosphere.

ℹ Getting There & Away

Buses between Mysore and Ooty can drop you at Bandipur (₹78, 2½ hours), an 88km journey. Skyway (p184) can arrange an taxi from Mysuru for about ₹2000.

Nagarhole National Park & Around

Blessed with rich wildlife, attractive jungle and a scenic lake, **Nagarhole National Park** (Rajiv Gandhi National Park; Indian/foreigner ₹200/1000, video ₹1000; ⊙6am-6pm), pronounced 'nag-ar-hole-eh', is one of Karnataka's best wildlife getaways. Adjoining **Kabini Lake**, it forms an important animal corridor that runs through neighbouring Bandipur National Park – making up a part of the Nilgiri Bioshpere Reserve. Despite sharing the same wildlife, it sees much fewer visitors than Bandipur, making it all the more appealing. Set over 643 sq km, Nagarhole features a good blend of dense jungle and open sightlines along the river bank, which makes for fantastic wildlife-watching. Its lush forests are home to tigers, leopards, elephants, gaur, barking deer, dhole, bonnet macaques and common langurs, plus 270 species of birds. The park can remain closed for long stretches between July and October, when rains transform the forests into a slush-pit.

The traditional inhabitants of the land, the hunter-gatherer Jenu Kuruba people, still live in the park, despite government efforts to relocate them.

The best time to view wildlife is during summer (April to May), though winter (November to February) is more comfortable.

Government-run **4WD safaris** (Kabini River Lodge; 2½hr 4WD safari ₹2000) and **boat trips** (Kabini River Lodge; per person ₹2000) are conducted from Kabini River Lodge between 6.30am and 9.30am and 3.15pm and 6.15pm, which are good ways to see animals.

🛏 Sleeping & Eating

Many places screen wildlife docos in the evening.

Karapur Hotel
GUESTHOUSE $$
(📱9945904840; Karapura roundabout; r ₹1000) The only cheapish option close to Kabini is this simple lodge with a few rooms above a shop in Karapura, 3km from the park.

★ Waterwoods Lodge
GUESTHOUSE $$$
(📱082-28264421; www.waterwoods.in; s/d incl full board ₹6500/8500; 🅰🛜🏊) Situated on a grassy embankment overlooking scenic Kabini Lake, Waterwoods has undergone extensive renovations to evolve from intimate guesthouse to stunning boutique lodge. Most rooms have balconies with views, swing chairs, hardwood floors and designer flair. It's kid-friendly with trampoline, infinity pool, free canoe hire and wood-fired pizzas.

Bison Resort
LODGE $$$
(📱080-41278708; www.thebisonresort.com; Gundathur Village; s/d incl full board from US$315/350, camping per person from ₹2500; 🏊) Inspired by the luxury safari lodges in Africa, Bison succeeds in replicating the classic wilderness experience with a stunning waterfront location and choice between canvas-walled cottages, stilted bungalows or bush camping. Adding to the experience is the wooden-decked swimming pool sundowners, nightly bonfires, bush dinners and expert naturalists.

KAAV Safari Lodge
LODGE $$$
(📱08228-264492; www.kaav.com; Mallali Cross, Kabini; s/d incl full board ₹13,000/16,000; 🅰🛜🏊) A swish designer hotel, KAAV has open-plan rooms with polished concrete floors, modern bathrooms, king-sized beds and spacious balconies that open directly to the national park. Otherwise head up to the viewing tower to lounge on plush day beds, or take a dip in its infinity pool.

Kabini River Lodge
LODGE $$$
(📱08228-264405; www.junglelodges.co; per person India/foreigner incl full board & activities from ₹6280/11,420; 🏊) Located in the serene, tree-lined grounds of the former Mysore maharaja's hunting lodge, these now government-run bungalows have a prime location beside the lake with a choice between large tented cottages and bungalows. It has an atmospheric colonial-style bar.

ℹ Getting There & Away

The park's main entrance is 93km southwest of Mysuru. A few buses depart daily from Mysore to Karapuram (₹65, 2½ hours), around 3km from Kabini Lake.

Kodagu (Coorg) Region

Nestled amid ageless hills that line the southernmost edge of Karnataka is the luscious Kodagu (Coorg) region, gifted with emerald landscapes and acres of plantations. A major centre for coffee and spice production, this rural expanse is also home to the unique Kodava race, believed to have descended from migrating Persians and Kurds, or perhaps even

Greeks left behind from Alexander the Great's armies. The uneven terrain and cool climate make it a fantastic area for trekking, birdwatching or lazily ambling down little-trodden paths winding around carpeted hills. All in all, Kodagu is rejuvenation guaranteed.

Kodagu was a state in its own right until 1956, when it merged with Karnataka. The region's chief town and transport hub is Madikeri, but for an authentic Kodagu experience, you have to venture into the plantations. Avoid weekends, when places can quickly get filled up.

🏃 Activities

Exploring the region by foot is a highlight for many visitors. Treks are part cultural experience, part nature encounter, involving hill climbs, plantation visits, forest walks and homestays.

The best season for trekking is October to March; there are no treks during monsoon. The most popular peaks are the seven-day trek to Tadiyendamol (1745m), and to Pushpagiri (1712m) and Kotebetta (1620m). As well as good walking shoes you'll need insect repellant. A trekking guide is essential for navigating the labyrinth of forest tracks.

V-Track
TREKKING

(☑ 08272-229102, 08272-229974; v_track@rediffmail.com; College Rd, Madekeri, opp Corporation Bank; ⊙ 10am-2pm & 4.30-8pm Mon-Sat) Veteran guides Raja Shekhar and Ganesh can arrange one- to weeklong treks, which include guide, accommodation and food. Rates are ₹950 to ₹1150 per person per day, depending upon group size.

Coorg Trails
TREKKING

(☑ 08272-220491, 9886665459; www.coorgtrails.com; Main Rd; ⊙ 9am-8.30pm) Another recommended outfit, Coorg Trails can arrange day treks around Madikeri for ₹450 per person, and a 16km trek to Kotebetta, including an overnight stay in a village (from ₹850).

Madikeri (Mercara)

☑ 08272 / POP 32,500 / ELEV 1525M

Also known as Mercara, this congested market town is spread out along a series of ridges. The only reason for coming here is to organise treks or sort out the practicalities of travel.

◉ Sights & Activities

Madikeri Fort
HISTORIC SITE

Originally Tipu Sultan's fort in the 16th century, before Raja Lingarajendra II took over in 1812, today it's the less glamorous site of the municipal headquarters. Within the fort's walls are the hexagonal palace (now the dusty district commissioner's office) and colonial-era church, which houses a quirky museum (⊙ 10am-5.30pm Sun-Fri) FREE displaying eclectic exhibits.

Raja's Seat
VIEWPOINT

(MG Rd; entry ₹5; ⊙ 5.30am-7.30pm) The place to come to watch the sunset, as the raja himself did, with fantastic outlooks to rolling hills and endless valleys.

Raja's Tombs
HISTORIC BUILDING

(Gaddige) FREE The quietly beautiful Raja's Tombs are built in Indo-Sarcenic style with domed tombs that serve as the resting place for Kodava royalty and dignitaries. Located 7km from town, an autorickshaw costs ₹200 return.

Abbi Falls
WATERFALL

A spectacular sight after the rainy season, these 21.3m-high falls can pack a punch. It's ₹250 for a return autorickshaw, including stop off at Raja's Tombs.

Coorg Sky Adventures
SCENIC FLIGHT

(☑ 9448954384; www.coorgskyadventures.com; 10-/30min ₹2500/4850) Head up into the skies via a microlight flight for tremendous views of Coorg's lush scenery.

Ayurjeevan
AYURVEDA

(☑ 944974779; www.ayurjeevancoorg.com; Kohinoor Rd, Madikeri; 1hr from ₹1200; ⊙ 7am-7pm) An ayurvedic 'hospital' that offers a range of intriguing and rejuvenating techniques. It's a short walk from the State Bank India.

🛏 Sleeping & Eating

With fantastic guesthouses in the surrounding plantations, there's no reason to stay in Madikeri, though you may have to a spend a night if you arrive late.

Hotel Chitra
HOTEL $

(☑ 08272-225372; www.hotelchitra.co.in; School Rd; dm ₹250, d from ₹750, with AC ₹1620; ❄) A short walk off Madikeri's main traffic intersection is this austere hotel, providing low-cost, no-frills rooms. Friendly service coupled with spacious rooms and dorms make it a good budget option.

Hotel Mayura Valley View
HOTEL $$
(☑228387; d incl breakfast from ₹2400; ❄) On the hilltop past Raja's Seat, this government hotel is one of Madikeri's best, with large bright rooms and fantastic valley views. Its restaurant-bar with terrace overlooking the valley is a great spot for a beer.

★ Coorg Cuisine
INDIAN $$
(Main Rd; mains ₹100-120; ◷noon-4pm & 7-10pm) Finally a place that makes an effort to serve regional dishes, cooking up unique Kodava specialities such as *pandhi barthadh* (pork dry fry) and *kadambuttu* (rice dumplings), and some tasty veg options too. It's above a shop on the 1st floor on the main road.

ℹ Information
State Bank of India (☑229959; College Rd) and **HDFC Bank** (Racecourse Rd) have ATMs.
Cyber Inn (Kohinoor Rd; per hour ₹20; ◷9am-9pm)
Travel Coorg (☑08272-321009; www.travel coorg.in; ◷24hr) Provides a good overview of things to do, as well as arranging homestays, trekking guides and other activities. It's outside the KSRTC bus stand.

ℹ Getting There & Away
Regular buses depart from the KSRTC bus stand for Bengaluru (fan/AC ₹400/485, six hours), stopping in Mysuru (₹200/250, 3½ hours) en route. Deluxe buses go to Mangaluru (₹200/280, four hours, three daily), while frequent ordinary buses head to Hassan (₹120, four hours).

Around Madikeri
Spread around Madikeri are Kodagu's enchanting and leafy spice and coffee plantations. Numerous estates here offer 'homestays', which are actually more like B&Bs (and normally closed during monsoon). Some seriously luxurious high-end resorts have opened up too.

♣ Activities
★ Jiva Spa
AYURVEDA
(☑0827-2665800; www.tajhotels.com/jivaspas/index.html; Vivanta, Galibeedu) Surrounded by rainforest, Jiva Spa at the stunning Vivanta hotel (p202) is *the* place to treat yourself with a range of rejuvenating treatments amid lavish atmosphere. Appointments essential.

Swaasthya Ayurveda Retreat Village
AYURVEDA
(www.swaasthya.com; Bekkesodlur Village; s/d incl full board & yoga class ₹2500/4000; ☎) For an exceptionally peaceful and refreshing ayurvedic vacation, head to south Coorg to soothe your soul among the lush greenery on 1.6 hectares of coffee and spice plantations.

🛏 Sleeping
★ Golden Mist
HOMESTAY $$
(☑9448903670, 08272-265629; www.golden-mist. net; Galibeedu; s/d incl full board ₹2500/4000; @☎) One of Coorg's finest plantation stays, the friendly Indian-German-managed Golden Mist has character-filled loft-style cottages on its lovely property of rice paddies and tea-, coffee- and spice-plantations. Meals are tasty rustic dishes made from the farm's organic produce, including homemade cheese and bread. Rates include highly recommended walks and plantation tours. A rickshaw costs ₹170 from Madikeri.

Rainforest Retreat
GUESTHOUSE $$
(☑08272-265638, 08272-265639; www.rainfores tours.com; Galibeedu; dm incl breakfast ₹1000, s/d tent ₹1500/2000, cottage from ₹2500/4000) 🌿 A nature-soaked refuge immersed within forest and plantations, Rainforest Retreat is supported by an NGO that devotes

---

ℹ SPICE OF LIFE

If you have space in your bag, pick up some local spices and natural produce from Madikeri's main market. Here you'll find coffee beans, vanilla, nutmeg, lemongrass, pepper and cardamom, which all come in from the plantations. Sickly sweet 'wines' are also widely available.

Several chocolatiers also try their hand at handmade truffles using spices such as cardamom, pepper and coffee. Don't expect Belgian quality, but there are some interesting varieites such as betel-nut chocolate from **Choci Coorg** (www.chocicoorg.com; opp bus stand, Madikeri; ◷9am-9.30pm) or fiery birdseye chilli chocolate from **Chocotila** (Green Acres; ☑08272-238525; Yavakopadi Village, Kabbinakad).

itself to exploring organic and ecofriendly ways of life. Accommodation is lazy camping (pre-pitched tents with beds), cottages with solar power or private dorms. Rates include plantation tours, birdwatching and treks. Check the website for volunteering opportunities. An autorickshaw from Madkeri is ₹200.

★ **Vivanta**   HOTEL **$$$**
(☑ 08272-665800; www.vivantabytaj.com; Galibeedu; r from ₹13,000; @ 🛜 ≋) Another stunner by the Taj Group, built across 73 hectares of misty rainforest. Its stylish design incorporates principles of space and minimalism, and effectively blends itself into its environment. Old cattle tracks lead to rooms, with pricier ones featuring private indoor pools, fireplaces and butlers. Meanwhile the 9000 sq ft presidential suite, costing a cool lakh (₹100,000), is the size of a small village.

Other highlights are its stunning views from the lobby and infinity pool, the outdoor ampitheatre surrounded by water, ayurvedic spa and game console room.

Kakkabe

☑ 08272

About 40km from Madikeri, the village of Kakkabe is an ideal base to plan an assault on Kodagu's highest peak, Tadiyendamol.

At the bottom of the summit, 3km from Kakkabe, is the picturesque **Nalakunad Palace** (🕙 9am-5pm) `FREE`, the restored hunting lodge of a Kodagu king dating from 1794. The caretaker will happily show you around.

Regular buses run to Kabbinakad from Madikeri (₹50, 1½ hours) or it's around ₹500 for an autorickshaw.

🛏 Sleeping & Eating

Honey Valley Estate   GUESTHOUSE **$**
(☑ 08272-238339;   www.honeyvalleyindia.in;   r with/without bathroom from ₹800/550) Located 3km from Kakkabe this wonderful trekking guesthouse sits at 1250m above sea level, transporting you into a lovely cool, fresh climate with plenty of birdlife. The owners' friendliness, ecomindedness and local knowledge of 18 trekking routes is a plus. It's accessible by jeep (inclusive of rates) or by a one-hour uphill walk.

BYLAKUPPE

Tiny Bylakuppe was among the first refugee camps set up in South India to house thousands of Tibetans who fled following the 1959 Chinese invasion. Over 10,000 Tibetans live here (including some 3300 monks), making it South India's largest Tibetan settlement.

The area's highlight is the atmospheric **Namdroling Monastery** (www.palyul.org), home to the spectacular **Golden Temple** (Padmasambhava Buddhist Vihara; 🕙 7am-8pm), presided over by three 18m-high gold-plated Buddha statues. The temple is at its dramatic best when prayers are in session and it rings out with gongs, drums and the drone of hundreds of young monks chanting. You're welcome to sit and meditate; look for the small blue guest cushions lying around. The **Zangdogpalri Temple** (🕙 7am-8pm), a similarly ornate affair, is next door.

Foreigners are not allowed to stay overnight in Bylakuppe without a Protected Area Permit (PAP) from the Ministry of Home Affairs in Delhi, which can take up to five months to process. Contact the **Tibet Bureau Office** (☑ 11-26479737; www.tibetbureau.in; New Delhi) for details. Day-trippers are welcome to visit, however.

If you have a permit, the simple **Paljor Dhargey Ling Guest House** (☑ 8223-258686; pdguesthouse@yahoo.com; d ₹500) is opposite the Golden Temple. For delicious *momos* (Tibetan dumplings) or *thukpa* (noodle soup), pop into the Tibetan-run **Malaya Restaurant** (opp Golden Temple; momos ₹60-90; 🕙 7am-9pm). Otherwise there are many hotels in nearby Kushnalagar, including **Ice Berg** (☑ 9880260544; Main Rd; s/d from ₹600/800), with clean functional rooms.

Autorickshaws (shared/solo ₹15/40) run to Bylakuppe from Kushalnagar, 6km away. Buses frequently run 34km to Kushalnagar from Madikeri (₹40, 45 minutes) and Hassan (₹78, 2½ hours). Most buses on the Mysuru–Madikeri route stop at Kushalnagar (₹85 to ₹180, two hours).

Chingaara GUESTHOUSE $$
(☎08272-204488; www.chingaara.com; Kabbini-akad; r incl half board ₹1800-2900) Run by the same family as Honey Valley Estate (from which it's just up the hill), this delightful farmhouse has roaming donkeys and is surrounded by verdant coffee plantations. Attractive rooms are spacious, and most have good views – room 9 especially. It's 2.5km up a steep hill; call ahead to get Chingaara's jeep to pick you up from Kabbinakad junction.

★ **Tamara Resort** RESORT $$$
(☎0827-2238000; www.thetamara.com; Yavaka-padi Village; r incl meals & activities from ₹21,500; ✳ ☎) Immersed within 70 hectares of coffee plantations, this romantic nature resort has stilted cottages that soar above the lush green surrounds. Luxurious rooms all have teak floorboards, balconies, king-sized beds, chessboard coffee tables and French-press plungers with Coorg coffee. Its memorable restaurant is raised above the plantations with a glass-bottom floor to look down upon.

Additional highlights are its spa, yoga classes and coffee cupping sessions. It's popular with honeymooners.

Belur & Halebid

☑ 08177 / ELEV 968M
The Hoysala temples at Halebid (also known as Halebeedu) and Belur (also called Beluru) are the apex of one of the most artistically exuberant periods of ancient Hindu cultural development. Architecturally, they are South India's answer to Khajuraho in Madhya Pradesh and Konark near Puri in Odisha.

Only 16km lie between Belur and Halebid; they are connected by frequent buses from 6.30am to 7pm (₹25, 40 minutes).

To get here you'll need to pass through the busy transport hub of Hassan – easily accessible from Mysuru and Bengaluru, with buses departing regularly to Mysore (₹115, three hours), Bengaluru (semideluxe/deluxe ₹195/392, 3½ hours) and Mangaluru (₹166/380, 3½ hours). From Hassan's well-organised train station, several passenger trains head to Mysuru daily (2nd class ₹140, 2½hours). For Bengaluru, there's the red-eye 2.50am 16518 Bangalore Express (sleeper ₹180, 5½ hours). It's also possible to visit on day trip from Bengaluru or Mysuru with a KSTDC tour (p177).

Belur

The **Channakeshava Temple** (Temple Rd; ⊙7.30am-7.30pm) was commissioned in AD 1116 to commemorate the Hoysalas' victory over the neighbouring Cholas. It took more than a century to build, and is currently the only one among the three major Hoysala sites still in daily use – try to be there for the ritual *puja* (prayer) ceremonies at around 8.45am and 6.45pm. Some parts of the temple, such as the exterior lower friezes, were not sculpted to completion and are thus less elaborate than those of the other Hoysala temples. However, the work higher up is unsurpassed in detail and artistry, and is a glowing tribute to human skill. Particularly intriguing are the angled bracket figures depicting women in ritual dancing poses. While the front of the temple is reserved for images depicting erotic sections from the Kamasutra, the back is strictly for gods. The roof of the inner sanctum is held up by rows of exquisitely sculpted pillars, no two of which are identical in design.

Scattered around the temple complex are other smaller temples, a marriage hall which is still used, and the seven-storey *gopuram*, which has sensual sculptures explicitly portraying the activities of dancing girls. Guides can be hired for ₹250.

Hotel Mayura Velapuri (☎0817-7222209; Kempegowda Rd; d with fan/AC from ₹1000/1350; ✳), a state-run hotel gleaming with post-renovation glory, is located on the way to the temple. Its restaurant-bar serves a variety of Indian dishes (from ₹80) to go with beer. The cheaper **Sumukha Residency** (☎08177-222181; Temple Rd; s/d ₹350/730) is another option.

There's an Axis ATM on the road leading to the temple.

There are frequent buses to/from Hassan (₹40 to ₹90, 45 minutes), 38km away.

Halebid

Construction of the stunning **Hoysaleswara Temple** (⊙dawn-dusk), Halebid's claim to fame, began around AD 1121 and went on for more than 190 years. It was never completed, but nonetheless stands today as a masterpiece of Hoysala architecture. The interior of its inner sanctum, chiselled out of black stone, is marvellous. On the outside, the temple's richly sculpted walls are covered with a flurry of Hindu deities, sages, stylised animals and friezes depicting the life of the Hoysala rulers. Two statues of

KARNATAKA & BENGALURU BELUR & HALEBID

Nandi (Shiva's bull) sit to the left of the main temple, facing the inner sanctum. Guides are available for ₹250.

The temple is in large gardens, adjacent to which is a small **museum** (admission ₹5; ⊙9am-5pm Sat-Thu) with a collection of beautiful sculptures from around Halebid.

Take some time out to visit the nearby, smaller **Kedareswara Temple**, or a little-visited enclosure containing three **Jain temples** about 500m away.

Hotel Mayura Shanthala (⌨0817-7273224; d incl breakfast with AC from ₹1500; ❋❄☎), set in a leafy garden opposite the temple complex, is the best sleeping option.

Regular buses depart for Hassan (₹35, one hour), 33km away, while buses to Belur are ₹25 for the 15km journey.

Sravanabelagola

⌨ 08176

Atop the bald rock of Vindhyagiri Hill, the 17.5m-high statue of the Jain deity Gomateshvara (Bahubali) is visible long before you reach the pilgrimage town of Sravanabelagola. Viewing the statue close up is the main reason for heading to this sedate town, whose name means 'Monk of the White Pond'.

⊙ Sights

Gomateshvara Statue   JAIN MONUMENT
(Bahubali; ⊙6.30am-6.30pm) A steep climb up 614 steps takes you to the top of Vindhyagiri Hill, the summit of which is lorded over by the towering naked statue of the Jain deity Gomateshvara (Bahubali). Commissioned by a military commander in the service of the Ganga king Rachamalla and carved out of a single piece of granite by the sculptor Aristenemi in AD 98, it is said to be the world's tallest monolithic statue. Leave your shoes at the foot of the hill.

Bahubali was the son of emperor Vrishabhadeva, who later became the first Jain *tirthankar* (revered teacher) Adinath. Embroiled in fierce competition with his brother Bharatha to succeed his father, Bahubali realised the futility of material gains and renounced his kingdom. As a recluse, he meditated in complete stillness in the forest until he attained enlightenment. His lengthy meditative spell is denoted by vines curling around his legs and an ant hill at his feet.

Every 12 years, millions flock here to attend the **Mastakabhisheka** (⊙Feb; 2018) ceremony, when the statue is dowsed in holy waters, pastes, powders, precious metals and stones.

Jain Temples

Apart from the Bahubali statue, there are several interesting Jain temples in town. The **Chandragupta Basti** (Chandragupta Community; ⊙6am-6pm), on Chandragiri Hill opposite Vindhyagiri, is believed to have been built by Emperor Ashoka. The **Bhandari Basti** (Bhandari Community; ⊙6am-6pm), in the southeast corner of town, is Sravanabelagola's largest temple. Nearby, **Chandranatha Basti** (Chandranatha Community; ⊙6am-6pm) has well-preserved paintings depicting Jain tales.

🛏 Sleeping & Eating

The local Jain organisation **SDJMI** (⌨08176-257258) handles bookings for its 15 guesthouses (double/triple ₹250/310). The office is behind the Vidyananda Nilaya Dharamsala, past the post office.

Hotel Raghu   HOTEL $
(⌨08176-257238; s/d from ₹400/500, d with AC ₹900; ❋) Basic but clean rooms with a popular vegetarian restaurant downstairs, which works up an awesome veg thali (₹80).

ℹ Getting There & Away

There are no direct buses from Sravanabelagola to Hassan or Belur – you must go to Channarayapatna (₹43, 20 minutes) and catch an onward connection there. Three daily buses run direct to Bengaluru (₹156, 3½ hours) and Mysuru (₹85, 2½ hours).

KARNATAKA COAST

Mangaluru (Mangalore)

⌨ 0824 / POP 484,785

Alternating from relaxed coastal town to hectic nightmare, Mangaluru (more commonly known as Mangalore) has a Jekyll and Hyde thing going, but it's a pleasant enough place to break up your trip. While there's not a lot to do here, it has an appealing off-the-beaten-path feel, and the spicy seafood dishes are sensational.

It sits at the estuaries of the picturesque Netravathi and Gurupur Rivers on the Arabian Sea coast and has been a major pit stop on international trade routes since the 6th century AD. It was ruled by the Portuguese during the 16th and 17th centuries, before the British took over a century later.

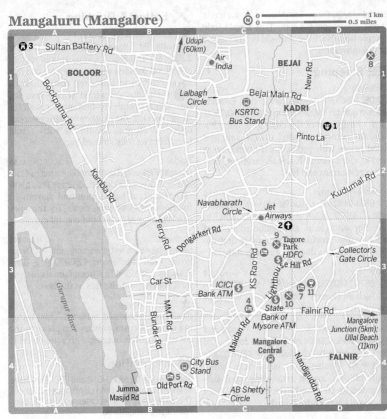

Mangaluru (Mangalore)

◉ Sights

Ullal Beach   BEACH
While it's no Om Beach, this stretch of golden sand is a good place to escape the city heat. It's about an hour's drive south of town. An autorickshaw is ₹200 one way, or catch the frequent bus 44A or 44C (₹10) from the City bus stand.

St Aloysius College Chapel   CHURCH
(Lighthouse Hill; ⊙9am-6pm) Catholicism's roots in Mangaluru date back to the arrival of the Portuguese in the early 1500s, and one of the most impressive legacies is the 1880 Sistine Chapel-like St Aloysius chapel, with its walls and ceilings painted with brilliant frescoes.

Sultan's Battery   FORT
(Sultan Battery Rd; ⊙6am-6pm) The only remnant of Tipu Sultan's fort is this small lookout with views over scenic backwaters. It's 4km from the city centre on the headland of the old port; bus 16 will get you there.

KARNATAKA & BENGALURU MANGALURU (MANGALORE)

Kadri Manjunatha Temple
HINDU TEMPLE

(Kadri; ⊙6am-1pm & 4-8pm) This Kerala-style temple houses a 1000-year-old bronze statue of Lokeshwara.

🛏 Sleeping

Hotel Roopa
HOTEL $

(☑0824-2421272; www.roopahotel.com; Balmatta Rd; s/d with fan ₹400/1000, with AC ₹1250/1500; ❄☎) Easily one of the city's best value hotels, the centrally located Roopa combines good prices with professional management and modern rooms. It has an excellent basement restaurant and bar.

Hotel Manorama
HOTEL $

(☑0824-2440306; KS Rao Rd; s/d from ₹600/630, with AC ₹1070; ❄) A decent budget hotel in the city with clean, good-value rooms and a lobby that provides a memorable first impression with its display of Hindu statues.

Adarsh Hotel
HOTEL $

(☑0824-2440878; Market Rd; s/d ₹310/460) Old-school cheapie with divey but well-kept rooms. It's often booked out.

Gateway Hotel
HOTEL $$$

(☑0824-6660420; www.tajhotels.com; Old Port Rd; s/d incl breakfast from ₹7170/8060; ❄@☎≋) Plasma TVs, large beds laden with pillows, and a swimming pool surrounded by lawn and deck chairs, it's high standards across the board.

Summer Sands Beach Resort
HOTEL $$$

(☑8861373737; www.summersands.in; Ullal Beach; d incl half board ₹6780; ❄@≋) Set amid palm groves on a remote patch along Ullal Beach, Summer Sands offers kitschy bungalows in a tropical-resort-style set-up. Its restaurant has a great seafood selection.

🍴 Eating & Drinking

★ Lalith Bar & Restaurant
SEAFOOD $$

(Balmatta Rd; mains ₹150-400; ⊙11.30am-3.30pm & 6.30-11.30pm) Specialising in regional seafood delights such as spicy masala fish fry smothered in saucy red coconut curry, or scrumptious deep-fried prawn rava fry, this scruffy upstairs restaurant is a must for those seeking out authentic Mangalorean dishes. It all goes beautifully with a cold beer, from its fully stocked bar.

Kadal
SOUTH INDIAN $$

(Nalapad Residency, Lighthouse Hill Rd; mains ₹150-220; ⊙11.30am-3.30pm & 6.30-11pm) This high-rise restaurant has elegant and warmly lit interiors with sweeping views. Try the spicy chicken *uruval* (a coconut coastal curry).

Gajalee
SEAFOOD $$$

(www.gajalee.com/rest_mangalore.html; Circuit House, Kadri Hills; mains ₹150-1200; ⊙11am-3.30pm & 6.30-11pm) In a town famous for seafood, locals often cite this as the best.

★ Liquid Lounge
PUB

(☑4255175; Balmatta Rd; ⊙11am-11.30pm) Bringing a slice of cosmopolitan Bangalore to the coast, this pub is buzzing with young locals.

ℹ Information

State Bank of Mysore, HDFC and ICICI Bank have ATMs on Balmatta Rd and Lighthouse Hill Rd. There are cheap internet cafes, costing ₹15 per hour, along Balmatta Rd.

ℹ Getting There & Away

AIR

The **airport** (☑0824-2254252; www.mangaloreairport.com) is precariously perched atop a plateau in Bajpe, about 20km northeast of town.

MAJOR TRAINS FROM MANGALORE CENTRAL

DESTINATION	TRAIN NO & NAME	FARE (₹)	DURATION (HR)	DEPARTURE TIME
Bengaluru	16524 Bangalore Express	sleeper/2AC 300/1150	11½	8.55pm
Chennai	12686 Chennai Express	sleeper/2AC 460/1715	15½	4.20pm
Gokarna	16523 Karwar Express	sleeper/2AC 205/770	4½	8.20am
Gokarna	56640 Madgaon Passenger	2nd-class 75	4	5.50am
Thiruvanantha-puram	16630 Malabar Express	sleeper/2AC 345/1335	15	6.20pm

There are daily flights to Mumbai, Bengaluru, Hyderabad and Chennai.

Air India (☑ 2451046; Hathill Rd)
Jet Airways (☑ 2441181; Ram Bhavan Complex, KS Rao Rd)
SpiceJet (☑ 1800-1803333)

BUS

The **KSRTC bus stand** (☑ 0824-2211243; Bejai Main Rd) is 3km from the city centre. Deluxe buses depart half-hourly to Bengaluru (₹370 to ₹720, eight to nine hours), via Madikeri (₹140 to ₹300, five hours) and Mysuru (₹260 to ₹500, seven hours).

Dharmasthala ₹72, 2½ hours, 2.20pm daily
Ernakulam ₹793, nine hours, night bus
Gokarna ₹234, 5½ hours, 12.45pm daily
Hassan ₹65 to ₹356, five hours, 10 daily
Panaji ₹352 to ₹580, 8½ hours, twice daily

For Udupi (₹55, 1½ hours) head to the **City bus stand** (State Bank stand).

TRAIN

The main train station Mangalore Central is south of the city centre.

Mangalore Junction (aka Kankanadi), 5km east of Mangaluru, has the 1.55pm 12134 Mumbai Express, stopping at Margao in Goa (sleeper/2AC ₹290/1035, five hours), continuing to Mumbai (sleeper/2AC ₹540/2045, 14½ hours).

ⓘ Getting Around

To get to the airport, take buses 47B or 47C from the City bus stand, or catch a taxi (₹500).

An autorickshaw to Mangalore Junction (Kankanadi) train station costs around ₹80, or take bus 9 or 11B.

Dharmasthala

Inland from Mangaluru are a string of Jain temple towns, such as Venur, Mudabidri and Karkal. The most interesting among them is Dharmasthala, 75km east of Mangaluru by the Netravathi River. Some 10,000 pilgrims pass through this town every day. During holidays and major festivals such as the five-day pilgrim festival of **Lakshadeepotsava** (☺ Nov), the footfall can go up tenfold.

The **Manjunatha Temple** (☺ 6.30am-2pm & 5-9pm) is Dharmasthala's main shrine, devoted to Shiva. Men have to enter bare-chested with legs covered. Simple free meals are available in the temple's **kitchen** (☺ 11.30am-2.15pm & 7.30-10pm), attached to a hall that can seat up to 3000.

Associated sights in town include the 12m-high **statue of Bahubali** at Ratnagiri

Hill, and the **Manjusha Museum** (admission ₹5; ☺ 9am-1pm & 4.30-9pm), which houses an eclectic collection of everything from artefacts to quirky collections of vintage cameras, telephones and typewriters. Don't forget to visit the fantastic **Car Museum** (admission ₹3; ☺ 8.30am-1pm & 2-7pm), home to 48 vintage autos, including a 1903 Renault and 1920s Studebaker President used by Mahatma Gandhi.

Should you wish to stay, contact the helpful **temple office** (☑ 0825-6277121; www.shridharmasthala.org) for accommodation in pilgrim lodges (per person ₹50).

There are frequent buses to Dharmasthala from Mangaluru (₹72, 2½ hours).

Udupi (Udipi)

☑ 0820

Udupi is a buzzing yet relaxed pilgrim town that's home to the atmospheric 13th-century **Krishna Temple** (Car St; ☺ 3.30am-10pm), which draws thousands of Hindu pilgrims throughout the year. Surrounded by eight maths (monasteries), it's a hive of ritual activity, with temple musicians playing at the entrance, elephants on hand for *puja*, and pilgrims constantly passing through. Non-Hindus are welcome inside the temple; men must enter bare-chested. Come late afternoon for the best atmosphere.

Udupi is famed for its vegetarian food, and recognised across India for its sumptuous thali and as the birthplace of the humble dosa.

ICICI (Car St) has an ATM near the temple.

⭢ Sleeping & Eating

Shri Vidyasamuda Choultry   HOTEL $
(☑ 2520820; Car St; r ₹150-300) There are several pilgrim hotels near the temple, but this simple offering is the best with views looking over the ghat.

Hotel Sriram Residency   HOTEL $$
(☑ 2530761; www.hotelsriramresidency.com; r with fan/AC from ₹940/1680; ❄) Udupi's most modern hotel is set over numerous floors, along with multiple restaurants and bars. It's a short walk from the temple complex.

Woodlands   INDIAN $
(Dr UR Rao Complex; dosas from ₹60, thalis from ₹90; ☺ 8am-3.15pm & 5.30-10.30pm) In the town that's famous for its vegetarian fare, Woodlands is regarded as one of the best places to sample the goods. It's a short walk south of Krishna Temple.

ⓘ Getting There & Away

Udupi is 58km north of Mangaluru along the coast; regular buses ply the route (₹56, 1½ hours). Buses also head to Gokarna (₹180, six hours) and Bengaluru (₹410 to ₹870, 10 hours). Regular buses head to Malpe (₹8, 30 minutes).

Malpe

☑ 0820

A fishing harbour on the west coast 4km from Udupi, Malpe has nice beaches ideal for flopping about in the surf. The **Paradise Isle Beach Resort** (☑0820-2538777; www.theparadiseisle.com; r with fan/AC from ₹2000/4750; ❄@🌐📶) has decent rooms; ask for one with a sea view. It can also organise **housebriat cruises** (per couple ₹4000; ☉Oct-Mar) on backwaters that are similarly scenic to Kerala's, yet all a bit undeveloped.

From Malpe pier you can take a government ferry (₹100 return, 45 minutes, departing when full from 9am to 5.30pm) or charter a private ferry from Malpe Beach to tiny **St Mary's Island**. It's known for where Portuguese explorer Vasco da Gama supposedly landed in 1498, and for curious hexagonal basalt formations No boats run from June to mid-October. Buses to Udupi are ₹8, and an autorickshaw ₹80.

Jog Falls

☑ 08186

Nominally the highest waterfalls in India, Jog Falls only come to life during the monsoon. The tallest of the four falls is the Raja, which drops 293m. For a good view of the falls, bypass the area close to the bus stand and hike to the foot of the falls down a 1200-plus-step path. Watch out for leeches during the wet season.

Hotel Mayura Gerusoppa (☑08186-244732; d with fan/AC from ₹1800/2200; ❄), near the car park, has a few enormous, musty double rooms. Stalls near the bus stand serve thalis and noodle dishes.

Jog Falls isn't the easiest place to reach without a car, so most people hire a taxi; a return trip from Gokarna costs around ₹2000. Otherwise you can get a string of buses which head via Kumta and turn off at Honavar (₹66); or Shimoga (Shivamogga) if coming via Bengaluru (₹468, nine hours).

Gokarna

☑ 08386

A regular nominee among travellers' favourite beaches in India, Gokarna is a more laid-back and less-commercialised version of Goa. It attracts a crowd for a low-key, chilled-out beach holiday and not for full-scale parties. Most accommodation is in thatched bamboo huts along its several stretches of blissful coast.

There are two Gokarnas; adjacent to the beaches is the sacred Hindu pilgrim town of Gokarna, full of ancient temples that come to life during festivals such as **Shivaratri** (☉Feb/Mar) and **Ganesh Chaturthi** (☉Sep). While its lively bazaar is an interesting place to visit, most foreign tourists don't hang

---

RANI ABBAKKA THE WARRIOR QUEEN

The legendary exploits of Rani Abbakka, one of India's first freedom fighters – who happened to be a female – is one that gets surprisingly little attention outside the Mangaluru region. An Indian Joan of Arc, her inspiring story is just waiting to be picked up by a Bollywood/Hollywood screenwriter.

As the Portuguese consolidated power along India's western coastline in the 16th century, seizing towns across Goa and down to Mangalore, their attempts to take Ullal proved more of a challenge. This was thanks to its 'fearless queen' who proved to be a major thorn in their grand plans to control the lucrative spice trade. Her efforts to continually repel their advances is the stuff of local legend.

Well trained in the art of war, both in strategy and combat, she knew how to brandish a sword. And while she was eventually defeated, it was a result of her treacherous ex-husband, who conspired against her in leaking intelligence to the enemy.

Her efforts to rally her people to defeat the powerful Portuguese is not forgotten by locals: she's immortalised in a bronze statue on horseback at the roundabout on the road to Ullal beach, and has an annual festival dedicated to her.

The shore temple that looks over the beautiful Someshwara beach a few kilometres south from Ullal was the former site of her fort, but only sections of its wall remains intact.

SURFING SWAMIS

While there has always been a spiritual bond between surfer and Mother ocean, the-Surfing Ashram (Mantra Surf Club; ☑ 9880659130; www.surfingindia.net; 6-64 Kolachikambla, Mulki; s/d incl full board from ₹3000/4500; ☎) at Mulki, 30km north of Mangaluru, takes things to a whole new plane. At this Hare Krishna ashram, which was established by its American guru who's been surfing since 1963 (and living in India for four decades), devotees follow a daily ritual of *puja* (prayers), chanting, mediation and vegetarian diet in between catching barrels.

There's surf year-round, but the best waves are May to June and September to October. The swamis can also assist with information on surfing across India. Board hire is ₹700 per day (also bodyboards and stand-up paddleboards) and lessons are ₹2500 per day.

Accommodation is pricey, but it has a homely beach-house feel, and rates include meals.

All are welcome to visit, but it's important to be aware that it's strictly a place of worship and there are guidelines to abide by, including abstinence from meat, alcohol, tobacco and sex during your stay. See the website for more details.

around overnight, instead making a bee-line straight to the adjoining beaches.

Note that bag searches and passport checks by the police are common upon arrival.

◉ Sights & Activities

Temples

Foreigners and non-Hindus are not allowed inside Gokarna's temples. However, there are plenty of colourful rituals to be witnessed around town. At the western end of Car St is the **Mahabaleshwara Temple**, home to a revered lingam. Nearby is the **Ganapati Temple**, while at the other end of the street is the **Venkataraman Temple**. About 100m further south is **Koorti Teertha**, the large temple tank where locals, pilgrims and immaculately dressed Brahmins perform their ablutions.

Beaches & Surfing

The best beaches are due south of Gokarna town, with Om Beach and Kudle Beach being the most popular. Don't walk around the paths after dark, and not alone at any time – it's easy to slip or get lost, and muggings have occurred.

Om Beach   BEACH

Gokarna's most famous beach twists and turns over several kilometres in a way that's said to resemble the outline of an Om symbol. It's a great mix of lovely long beach and smaller shady patches of sand, perfect for sunbathing and swimming. It's a 20-minute walk to Kudle Beach; an autorickshaw to Gokarna town is about ₹150.

Kudle Beach   BEACH

Lined with rows of restaurants and guesthouses, Kudle Beach has emerged as a popular alternative to Om Beach. It's one of Gokarna's longest beaches, with plenty of room to stretch out on its attractive sands.

It's a 20-minute hike from both Gokarna town or Om Beach along a path that heads atop along the barren headland with expansive sea views. Otherwise it's a ₹60 autorickshaw ride to town.

Gokarna Beach   BEACH

While Gokarna's main town beach isn't meant for casual bathing, and is more popular with domestic tourists, walk up a bit and you'll find a long stretch of pristine sand that seems to go forever – perfect for those seeking isolation.

Cocopelli Surf School   SURFING

(☑ 8105764969; www.cocopelli.org; Gokarna Beach; lesson per person ₹2000, board rental per 2hr ₹750; ☺Oct-May) Offers lessons by internationally certified instructors and rents boards. Has accommodation along here too.

Half Moon & Paradise Beach   BEACH

Well hidden away south of Om Beach lie the small sandy coves of Half Moon Beach and Paradise Beach. **Half Moon** is the more attractive, with a lovely sweep of powdery sand and basic hut accommodation. **Paradise Beach** is a mix of sand and rocks, and a haven with the long-term 'turn-on-tune-in-drop-out' crowd; unfortunately the government routinely destroys all the huts out this way, leaving it in a ramshackle state – hence it's BYO everything here.

From Om Beach, these beaches are a 30-minute and one-hour walk, respectively. Watch out for snakes and don't walk it after dark. A fishing boat from Om Beach will cost around ₹700, which can fit 10 people. For Paradise Beach you can also grab a bus to Velikom from Gokarna (₹12, 20 minutes), from where it's a 15-minute walk.

🛏 Sleeping & Eating

With a few exceptions, the choice here is basic, but perfectly comfortable, beach shacks. Most close from May to August.

🏖 Om Beach

Om Shree Ganesh   BUNGALOW $
(🖉 8386-257310; www.omshreeganesh.com; hut ₹500, without bathroom ₹300) A winning combination of cheap bungalows, friendly management and beachside location makes this place justifiably popular. Its atmospheric double-storey restaurant rocks at night and does tasty dishes such as tandoori prawns, mushroom tikka and *momos*.

Sangham   BUNGALOW $
(🖉 9448101099; r with/without bathroom ₹500/300) A blissful spot overlooking the water with a sandy path leading to the bungalows out back among banana trees; life's definitely a beach at Sangham.

Moksha Cafe   BUNGALOW $
(🖉 9741358997; Om Beach; r with/without bathroom ₹600/300) In the middle of Om Beach, these graffiti-splashed bungalows are as good as any with private porches, hammocks and sandy garden full of coconut palms.

Dolphin Bay Cafe   BUNGALOW $
(🖉 9742440708; r from ₹200; ⊙ 8am-10pm) Literally plonked on the beach, Dolphin Bay is your classic chilled-out shack **restaurant** (mains ₹80-180) that makes Gokarna so great. It has a choice of sandy-floor huts or sturdier concrete rooms.

Dolphin Shanti   GUESTHOUSE $
(🖉 9740930133; r from ₹200) Occupying the last plot of land on Om Beach (heading towards Half Moon beach), this mellow guesthouse sits perched upon the rocks with fantastic ocean views, and lives up to its name with dolphins often spotted. Rooms are ultra basic yet appealing.

Nirvana Café   GUESTHOUSE $
(🖉 329851; d ₹250, cottage ₹400-600; @) Towards the southern end of Om, Nirvana has popular el cheapo huts and spacious cottages set among a shady landscaped garden. Internet costs ₹60 per hour and hammocks are for sale if you need one.

Namaste Café   GUESTHOUSE $
(🖉 08386-257141; www.namastegokarna.com; Om Beach; r with fan/AC from ₹800/1500; ✳🤶) At the beginning of Om, this long-standing guesthouse has a very different vibe to the others, with a proper resort feel. It's an excellent choice, especially if you're after the comforts of AC, wi-fi, hot water, cold beer and romantic open-air restaurant with dreamy sea views. These days it's more popular with domestic travellers.

SwaSwara   HOTEL $$$
(🖉 08386-257132; www.swaswara.com; Om Beach; s/d 5 nights €1730/2300; ✳@🤶🏊) One of South India's finest retreats, this health resort offers a holiday based around yoga and ayurveda. No short stays are possible, but once you've set eyes upon its elegant private villas – some with forest views, others with

FORMULA BUFFALO

Call it an indigenous take on the Grand Prix, Kambla, or traditional buffalo racing, is a hugely popular pastime among villagers along the southern Karnataka coast. Popularised in the early 20th century and born out of local farmers habitually racing their buffaloes home after a day in the fields, the races have now hit the big time. Thousands of spectators attend each edition, and racing buffaloes are pampered and prepared like thoroughbreds.

Kambla events are held between November and March, usually on weekends. Parallel tracks are laid out in a paddy field, along which buffaloes hurtle towards the finish line. In most cases the man rides on a board fixed to a ploughshare, literally surfing his way down the track behind the beasts. The faster creatures can cover the 120m-odd distance through water and mud in around 14 seconds!

river – you'll be happy to stay put. All have small garden courtyards full of basil and lemongrass, open-air showers and sitting areas.

Kudle Beach

Sea Rock Cafe GUESTHOUSE $
(☏7829486382; Kudle Beach; r from ₹300) Yet more chilled-out bungalows, with an option of more-comfortable rooms and a beachside restaurant where the good times roll.

Ganga View GUESTHOUSE $
(☏9591978042; Kudle Beach; r from ₹250; 🛜) At the end of Kudle, relaxed Ganga is a perennial favourite. Also has rooms up the hill with soaring views. Wi-fi costs ₹50 per hour.

Goutami Prasad GUESTHOUSE $
(☏9972382302; Kudle Beach; hut from ₹200, r from ₹500) Relaxed, family-run guesthouse with a prime spot in the centre of Kudle Beach. Choose between basic huts with sandy floors or more comfortable, spotless rooms.

Uma Garden GUESTHOUSE $
(☏9916720728; Kudle Beach; r without bathroom ₹250) Tucked around the corner at the beginning of Kudle, this bucolic guesthouse has a laid-back owner and sea-facing vegetarian restaurant.

Strawberry Farmhouse GUESTHOUSE $$
(☏7829367584; Kudle Beach; r from ₹700; ❄) A kitschy guesthouse at the northern section of Kudle with over-the-top bright cottages (some with AC) and prime position looking out to the water.

Half Moon Beach

Half Moon Garden Cafe BUNGALOW $
(☏9743615820; Half Moon Beach; hut ₹200) A throwback to the hippie days, this hideaway has a blissful beach and bare-bones huts without electricity.

Gokarna Beach

This seemingly endless stretch of beach is the place for a more isolated relaxed beachside hang-out.

Hema Shree Garden BUNGALOW $
(☏9845983223; Gokarna Beach; r from ₹250) A superchilled beach guesthouse that's a 20-minute walk along Gokarna Beach with a variety of rooms around its tropical garden, plus some bungalows looking directly to the ocean.

OFF THE BEATEN TRACK

MURUDESHWAR

A worthwhile stopover for those taking the coastal route from Gokarna to Mangaluru, is Murudeshwar, a beachside pilgrimage town. It's most notable for its colossal seashore statue of **Lord Shiva** (Murudeshwar), which sits directly on the shore overlooking the Arabian Sea, making for spectacular photo-ops. For the best views, take the lift 20 stories to the top of the skyscraper-like **Shri Murudeshwar Temple** (lift ₹10; ⏰ lift 7.45am-12.30pm & 3.15-6.45pm).

It's 3km off the main highway, accessed by train or bus passing up and down the coast. If you want to stay the night, **Hotel Kawari's Palm Grove** (☏08385-260178; r with fan/AC from ₹500/1000; ❄) has decent enough rooms 500m from the action.

Namaste Garden BUNGALOW $
(☏9448906436; Gokarna Beach; r ₹500) Delightfully simple huts with hammocks, beachside tables and umbrellas. It's in the middle of Gokarna Beach, 10 minutes from town.

Gokarna Town

Shree Shakti Hotel HOTEL $
(☏9036043088; Gokarna Beach Rd; s/d ₹300/600) On Gokarna's main strip, this friendly hotel is excellent value with immaculate lime-green rooms above a restaurant which does excellent food, including homemade ice cream.

Greenland Guesthouse GUESHTOUSE $
(☏9019651420; www.gokarnagreenland.in; Gokarna Town; r from ₹200) Hidden down a jungle path outside town, this mellow family-run guesthouse has clean rooms in vibrant colours. Will suit those not wanting a beach shack, but somewhere with character.

Hotel Gokarna International HOTEL $
(☏9739629390; Main Rd; r with fan/AC from ₹450/1000; @) This typical institutional Indian hotel is worth a look if you want large AC rooms with TV and balcony.

🛍 Shopping

Shree Radhakrishna Bookstore BOOKS
(Car St, Gokarna Town; ⏰10am-6pm) Secondhand novels, postcards and maps.

ℹ Information

Axis Bank (Main St, Gokarna Town)

SBI (Main St, Gokarna Town)

Shama Internet Centre (Car St, Gokarna Town; per hour ₹40; ⊙10am-11pm)

Sub post office (1st fl, cnr Car & Main Sts, Gokarna Town; ⊙10am-4pm Mon-Sat)

ℹ Getting There & Away

BUS

A mix of local and private buses depart daily to Bengaluru (₹509, 12 hours) and Mysuru (from ₹550, 12 hours), as well as Mangaluru (₹240, 6½ hours) and Hubli (₹190, four hours), mostly transferring at Kumta (₹34, one hour), or Honnavar (₹55, two hours) for Jog Falls.

For Hampi, **Paolo Travels** (⌀0832-6637777; www.plimgoa.com) is a popular choice which heads via Hospet (fan/AC ₹1100/1600, seven hours). Note if you're coming from Hampi, you'll be dropped at Ankola from where there's a free transfer for the 26km journey to Gokarna.

There are also regular buses to Panaji (₹116, four hours) and Mumbai (₹900, 12 hours).

TRAIN

Many express trains stop at Gokarna Road station, 9km from town; however, double check your ticket as some stop at Ankola, 26km away. Many of the hotels and small travel agencies in Gokarna can book tickets.

The 3am 12619 Matsyagandha Express goes to Mangaluru (sleeper ₹235, 4½ hours); the return train leaves Kumta around 6.30pm for Margao (Madgaon; sleeper ₹170, 2½ hours) and Mumbai (sleeper/2AC, ₹465/1735, 12 hours).

Autorickshaws charge ₹200 to go to Gokarna Road station (or ₹500 to Ankola); a bus from Gokarna charges ₹40, every 30 minutes.

CENTRAL KARNATAKA

Hampi

⌀08394

Unreal and bewitching, the forlorn ruins of Hampi dot an unearthly landscape that will leave you spellbound the moment you cast your eyes on it. Heaps of giant boulders perch precariously over miles of undulating terrain, their rusty hues offset by jade-green palm groves, banana plantations and paddy fields. While it's possible to see the ancient ruins and temples of this World Heritage Site in a day or two, this goes against Hampi's relaxed grain. Plan on lingering for a while.

The main travellers' ghetto has traditionally been Hampi Bazaar, a village crammed with budget lodges, shops and restaurants, and towered over by the majestic Virupaksha Temple. However, recent demolitions have seen tranquil Virupapur Gaddi across the river become the new hang-out. Both offer different experiences, and it's recommended to spend a few nights at each.

Hampi is generally a safe, peaceful place, but don't wander around the ruins after dark or alone, as it can be dangerous terrain to get lost in, especially at night.

History

Hampi and its neighbouring areas find mention in the Hindu epic Ramayana as Kishkinda, the realm of the monkey gods. In 1336 Telugu prince Harihararaya chose Hampi as the site for his new capital Vijayanagar, which – over the next couple of centuries – grew into one of the largest Hindu empires in Indian history. By the 16th century it was a thriving metropolis of about 500,000 people, its busy bazaars dabbling in international commerce, brimming with precious stones and merchants from faraway lands. All this, however, ended in a stroke in 1565, when a confederacy of Deccan sultanates razed Vijayanagar to the ground, striking it a death blow from which it never recovered.

◉ Sights

Set over 36 sq km, there are some 3700 monuments to explore in Hampi, and it would take months if you were to do it justice. The ruins are divided into two main areas: the **Sacred Centre**, around Hampi Bazaar with its temples, and the **Royal Centre**, towards Kamalapuram, where the Vijayanagara royalty lived and governed.

Sacred Centre

★**Virupaksha Temple**   HINDU TEMPLE
(Map p217; admission ₹2, camera ₹50; ⊙dawn-dusk) The focal point of Hampi Bazaar is the Virupaksha Temple, one of the city's oldest structures, and Hampi's only remaining working temple. The main *gopuram* (gateway tower), almost 50m high, was built in 1442, with a smaller one added in 1510. The main shrine is dedicated to Virupaksha, an incarnation of Shiva.

If Lakshmi, the **temple elephant**, and her attendant are around, she'll smooch (bless) you for a coin; she gets her morning bath at 8am down by the river ghats.

To the south, overlooking Virupaksha Temple, **Hemakuta Hill** has a few early ruins, including monolithic sculptures of

Narasimha (Vishnu in his man-lion incarnation) and Ganesha. At the east end of the recently abandonded Hampi Bazaar is a monolithic **Nandi statue**, around which stand colonnaded blocks of the ancient marketplace. Overlooking the site is Matanga Hill, whose summit affords dramatic views of the terrain at sunrise.

Within the now-derelict bazaar is the **Hampi Heritage Gallery** (Map p217; ☺10am-1pm & 3-6pm Tue-Sun) `FREE`, exhibiting interesting historical photos of the ruins.

★**Vittala Temple**   HINDU TEMPLE
(Map p214; Indian/foreigner ₹10/250, child under 15 free; ☺8.30am-5.30pm) The undisputed highlight of the Hampi ruins, the 16th-century Vittala Temple stands amid the boulders 2km from Hampi Bazaar. Work possibly started on the temple during the reign of Krishnadevaraya (r 1509–29). It was never finished or consecrated, yet the temple's incredible sculptural work remains the pinnacle of Vijayanagar art.

The ornate **stone chariot** that stands in the courtyard is the temple's showpiece and represents Vishnu's vehicle with an image of Garuda within. Its wheels were once capable of turning. The outer 'musical' pillars reverberate when tapped. They were supposedly designed to replicate 81 different Indian instruments, but authorities have placed them out of tourists' bounds for fear of further damage, so no more do-re-mi.

As well as the main temple, whose sanctum was illuminated using a design of reflective waters, you'll find the marriage hall and prayer hall, the structures to the left and right upon entry, respectively.

Lakshimi Narasmiha   HINDU TEMPLE
(Map p214) An interesting stop off along the road to the Virupaksha Temple is the 6.7m monolithic statue of the bulging-eyed Lakshimi Narasmiha in a cross-legged lotus position and topped by a hood of seven snakes.

Krishna Temple   HINDU TEMPLE
(Map p214) Built in 1513, the Krisha Temple is fronted by a D-cupped *apsara* and 10 incarnations of Vishnu. It's on the road to the Virupaksha Temple.

Sule Bazaar   HISTORIC SITE
(Map p214) Halfway along the path from Hampi Bazaar to Vittala Temple, a track to the right leads over the rocks to deserted Sule Bazaar, one of ancient Hampi's principle centres of commerce and reputedly its red-light district. At the southern end of this area is the beautiful 16th-century **Achyutaraya Temple** (Map p214).

Royal Centre & Around

While it can be accessed by a 2km foot trail from the Achyutaraya Temple, the **Royal Centre** is best reached via the Hampi–Kamalapuram road. A number of Hampi's major sites stand here.

Mahanavami-diiba   RUIN
(Map p214) The Mahanavami-diiba is a 12m-high three-tiered platform with intricate carvings and panoramic vistas of the walled complex of ruined temples, stepped tanks and the King's audience hall. The platform was used as a Royal viewing area for the Dasara festivities, religious ceremonies and processions.

Hazarama Temple   HINDU TEMPLE
(Map p214) Hazarama Temple features exquisitive carvings that depict scenes from the Ramayana, and polished black granite pillars.

Zenana Enclosure   RUIN
(Map p214; Indian/foreigner ₹10/250; ☺8.30am-5.30pm) Northeast of the Royal Centre within the walled ladies' quarters is the Zenana Enclosure. Its peaceful grounds and manicured lawns feel like an oasis amid the arid surrounds. Here is the **Lotus Mahal** (Map p214), a delicately designed pavilion which was supposedly the queen's recreational mansion. It overlooks the 11 grand **Elephant Stables** (Map p214; ☺8.30am-5.30pm) with arched entrances and domed chambers. There's also a small museum and army barracks within the high-walled enclosure.

Queen's Bath   RUIN
(Map p214; ☺8.30am-5.30pm) South of the Royal Centre you'll find various temples and elaborate waterworks, including the Queen's Bath, deceptively plain on the outside but amazing within, with its Indo-Islamic architecture.

Archaeological Museum   MUSEUM
(Map p214; Kamalapuram; ☺10am-5pm Sat-Thu) Worth popping in for its quality collection of sculptures from local ruins, plus neolithic tools, fascinating coins, 16th-century weaponry and a large floor model of the Vijayanagar ruins.

Hampi & Anegundi

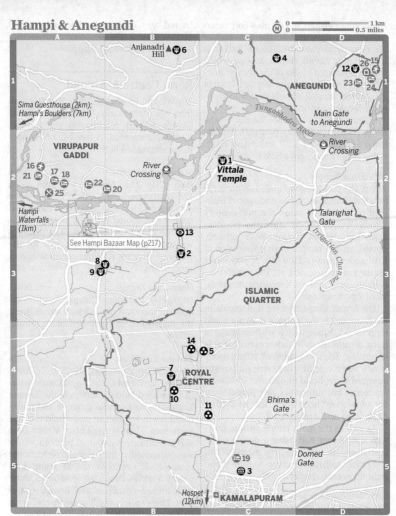

🏃 Activities

Hampi Waterfalls
WATERFALL

About a 2km walk west of Hampi Bazaar, past banana plantations, you can scramble over boulders to reach the attractive Hampi 'waterfalls,' a series of small whirlpools among the rocks amid superb scenery.

Bouldering & Rock Climbing

Hampi is the undisputed bouldering capital of India. The entire landscape is a climber's adventure playground made of granite crags and boulders, some bearing the marks of ancient stonemasons. *Golden Boulders* (2013) by Gerald Krug and Christiane Hupe has information about bouldering in Hampi.

Tom & Jerry
BOULDERING

(☎ 8277792588, 9482746697; luckykoushik1@ gmail.com; Virupapur Gaddi; 2½hr class ₹500) Two local lads who are doing great work in catering to climbers' needs, providing quality mats, shoes and local knowledge. They also organise climbing trips upcountry to Badami.

Thimmaclimb
BOULDERING

(Map p214; ☎ 8762776498; www.thimmaclimb.wix. com/hampi-bouldering; Shiva Guesthouse, Virupapur

Hampi & Anegundi

Gaddi; class from ₹350-500) A small operation run by local pro Thimma, who guides, runs lessons and stocks professional equipment for hire and sale.

Birdwatching

Get in touch with **Kishkinda Trust** (TKT; ☑ 08533-267777; www.thekishkindatrust.org) in Anegundi for info on birdwatching in the area, which has over 230 species, including the greater flamingo. *The Birds of Hampi* (2014) by Samad Kottur is the definitive guide.

🎉 Festivals & Events

Vijaya Utsav   RELIGIOUS
(Hampi Festival; ☉ Jan) Hampi's three-day extravaganza of culture, heritage and the arts in January.

Virupaksha Car Festival   RELIGIOUS FESTIVAL
(☉ Mar/Apr) The Virupaksha Car Festival in March/April is a big event, with a colourful procession characterised by a giant wooden chariot (the temple car from Virupaksha Temple) being pulled along the main strip of Hampi bazaar.

🛌 Sleeping

Most guesthouses are cosy family-run digs, perfect for the budget traveller. A handful of places also have larger, more-comfortable rooms with air-con and TV.

🛏 Hampi Bazaar

⭐**Padma Guest House**   GUESTHOUSE $
(Map p217; ☑ 08394-241331; padmaguest house@gmail.com; d from ₹800; ❄ 🛜) In a quiet corner of Hampi Bazaar, this amiable guesthouse feels more like a homestay, with basic, squeaky-clean rooms, many of which have views of Virupaksha Temple.

Archana Guest House   GUESTHOUSE $
(Map p217; ☑ 08394-241547; addihampi@yahoo. com; d from ₹600; 🛜) On the riverfront, quiet and cheerful Archana is one of the few places in the bazaar with a view. It's set over two houses opposite each other, with rooms painted in vivid purple and green, and has an open-air restaurant overlooking the river.

Pushpa Guest House   GUESTHOUSE $
(Map p217; ☑ 9448795120; pushpaguest house99@yahoo.in; d from ₹850, with AC from ₹1200; ❄ 🛜) The highly recommendable Pushpa is a top all-rounder that gets you a comfortable, attractive and spotless room.

> ### ⓘ HAMPI RUINS TICKET
>
> The ₹250 ticket for Vittala Temple entitles you to same-day admission into most of the paid sites across the ruins (including around the Royal Centre and the Archaeological Museum), so don't lose your ticket.

It has a lovely sit-out on the 1st floor, and reliable travel agency.

Vicky's
GUESTHOUSE $

(Map p217; ☑9480561010; vickyhampi@yahoo.co.in; r ₹600; ☎) An old faithful done up in pop purple and green, with decent rooms and friendly owner.

Netra Guesthouse
GUESTHOUSE $

(Map p217; ☑9480569326; r with/without bathroom from ₹400/250) Basic but relaxed rooms for shoestringers, with ambient restaurant.

Ganesh Guesthouse
GUESTHOUSE $

(Map p217; vishnuhampi@gmail.com; r ₹400-800, with AC ₹1200-2000; ✻☎) The small family-run Ganesh has been around for 20 years, yet only has downstairs rooms, giving it an appealing intimacy. Also has a nice rooftop restaurant.

Kiran Guest House
GUESTHOUSE $

(Map p217; ☑9448143906; kiranhampi2012@gmail.com; r ₹400-600; ☎) Chilled-out guesthouse on the riverfront and banana groves.

Ranjana Guest House
GUESTHOUSE $$

(Map p217; ☑08394-241696; ranjanaguesthouse@gmail.com; r from ₹1000; ✻) Run by a tight-knit family, Ranjana prides itself on well-appointed rooms and killer temple views from its sunny rooftop terrace.

Gopi Guest House
GUESTHOUSE $$

(Map p217; ☑08394-241695; www.gopiguesthouse.com; r with AC ₹1200; ✻@☎) Split over two properties on the same street, long-standing Gopi offers quality rooms that are almost upscale for Hampi's standards. Its rooftop cafe is a nice place to hang out.

🛌 Virupapur Gaddi

Many travellers prefer the tranquility of Virupapur Gaddi, across the river from Hampi Bazaar.

Hema Guest House
GUESTHOUSE $

(Map p214; ☑8762395470; rockyhampi@gmail.com; Virupapur Gaddi; d ₹350; ☎) Rows of cute and comfy colourful cottages situated in a shady grove, all with hammocks, and perpetually full restaurant.

Sunny Guesthouse
GUESTHOUSE $

(Map p214; ☑9448566368; www.sunnyguesthouse.com; r ₹200-750; @☎) Sunny both in name and disposition, this popular guesthouse is a hit among backpackers for its cheap rooms, tropical garden, hammocks and chilled-out restaurant.

Gopi Guesthouse
GUESTHOUSE $

(Map p214; ☑9481871816; www.hampiisland.com; Virupapura Gaddi; r ₹300-1200; ☎) A classic Hampi set-up with basic huts and hammocks in its garden as well as a chilled-out restaurant. Also has plush rooms with tiled floors and hot water.

Shanthi
GUESTHOUSE $

(Map p214; ☑9449260162; shanthi.hampi@gmail.com; cottage ₹800-1500; @) A more upmarket choice, Shanthi's earth-themed, thatched cottages have rice-field, river and sunset views, with couch swings dangling in their front porches.

Manju's Place
GUESTHOUSE $

(Map p214; ☑9449247712; r ₹300, without bathroom from ₹100) The place for those who like

---

DEMOLITION OF HAMPI BAZAAR

While in 1865 it was the Deccan sultanates who levelled Vijayanagar, today a different battle rages in Hampi, between conservationists bent on protecting Hampi's architectural heritage and the locals who have settled there.

In mid-2012 the government's master plan that had been in the works since the mid-2000s, and which aims to classify all of Hampi's ruins as protected monuments, was dramatically and forcefully put into action. Overnight shops, hotels and homes in Hampi Bazaar were bulldozed, reducing the atmospheric main strip to rubble overnight, as villagers who'd made the site a living monument were evicted.

While villagers were compensated with a small plot of land in Kaddirampur, 4km from the bazaar (where there is talk of new guesthouses eventually opening up), many locals remain displaced years later as they await their pay out.

While at the time of research, rubble from the demolished buildings remained, iconic hang-outs had been destroyed (including riverside restaurants such as the Mango Tree) and the main temple road resembled a bombed-out town; guesthouses and restaurants on the fringes of the bazaar remain intact.

Hampi Bazaar

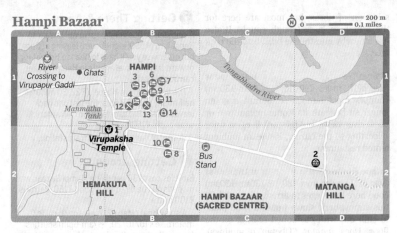

Hampi Bazaar

things quiet, with attractive mud-brick huts in a bucolic setting among rice fields.

Sima Guesthouse　　　　　GUESTHOUSE $
(☏9481664504; r with shared bathroom ₹200-300) A quirky guesthouse that is situated away from the crowds, low-key Sima has *very* basic but memorable rooms incorporated into boulder faces. Unexpectedly has a tiny skate ramp, along with a couple of boards.

Hampi's Boulders　　　　　LODGE $$$
(☏9448034202; www.hampisboulders.com; Narayanpet; r incl full board from ₹7000; ❈🛜❄) The only luxury option in these parts, this 'eco-wilderness' resort sits amid leafy gardens 7km west of Virupapur Gaddi. There's a choice of themed rooms, but by far the best are the chic cottages with elegant furnishing, river views and outdoor showers. Rates include guided walks and transfer from Hampi.

🛏 Kamalapuram

Hotel Mayura Bhuvaneshwari　　HOTEL $$
(Map p214; ☏08394-241574, 8970650025; s/d from ₹1620/1800; ❈🛜) This tidy government operation, which is located about 3km south of the Royal Centre, has well-appointed but dated rooms, a lovely big garden, much-appreciated bar, and good multicuisine restaurant.

🍴 Eating

Due to Hampi's religious significance, meat is strictly off the menu in all restaurants, and alcohol is banned (though some restaurants can order it for you).

Ravi's Rose　　　　　MULTICUISINE $
(Map p217; mains from ₹100; ⊗8am-10pm) This slightly sketchy rooftop-restaurant is the bazaar's most social hang-out, with a good

selection of dosas, but most are here for the, erm, tasty lassis (cough, cough). It also has a nearby guesthouse built into the rock face.

Mango Tree   MULTICUISINE $$
(Map p217; mains ₹90-310; ⊙7.30am-9.30pm) Hampi's most famous restaurant may no longer sit beneath its iconic mango tree or boast river views, but its spirit lives on since relocating to the bazaar, inside an ambient tented restaurant.

Prince Restaurant   MULTICUISINE $$
(Map p217; mains from ₹80; ⊙7.30am-9.30pm) Food here takes ages to arrive, so thankfully this atmospheric shady hut is a good place to chill out with cushioned seating on the floor. Does *momos* (Tibetan dumplings), pizzas etc.

★Laughing Buddha   MULTICUISINE $
(Map p214; mains from ₹80; ⊙8am-10pm; 🛜) Now that Hampi's famous riverside restaurants have closed on the other side, Laughing Buddha has taken over as the most atmospheric place to eat, with serene river views that span beyond to the temples and ruins. Its menu is curries, burgers, pizzas, you know the drill...

🛍 Shopping

Akash Art Gallery & Bookstore   BOOKS
(Map p217; Hampi Bazaar; ⊙6am-9pm) This gallery and bookstore has an excellent selection of books on Hampi and India, plus a range of secondhand fiction. Pick up the free map it offers.

ⓘ Information

There's no ATM in Hampi; the closest is 3km away in Kamalapuram – an autorickshaw costs ₹100 for a return trip.

Internet (per hour ₹40) is ubiquitous in Hampi Bazaar, though most guesthouses have free wi-fi these days. A good tourist resource for Hampi is www.hampi.in.

Tourist office (Map p217; 🗐241339; ⊙10am-5.30pm Sat-Thu) This dingy office inside Virupaksha Temple has brochures but is more useful for arranging cycling tours (per person ₹400 including bike and guide), walking guides (half-/full day ₹600/1000) and bus tours (₹350, seven hours), all of which head to the ruins.

ⓘ Getting There & Away

A semideluxe bus connects Hampi Bazaar to Bengaluru (₹550, eight hours) leaving at 8pm, but otherwise you'll have to head to Hospet for onward travel. Travel agents in Hampi Bazaar can book tickets.

The first bus from Hospet (₹22, 30 minutes, half-hourly) is at 5.45am; the last one back leaves Hampi Bazaar at 7.30pm. An autorickshaw costs ₹150 to ₹200.

Hospet is Hampi's nearest train station.

ⓘ Getting Around

Bicycles cost ₹30 per day in Hampi Bazaar, while mopeds can be hired for around ₹150. Petrol is ₹100 a litre.

A small **boat** (Map p217; person/bicycle/motorbike ₹10/10/20; ⊙7am-6pm) shuttles frequently across the river to Virupapur Gaddi. A large backpack will cost ₹10 extra, while a special trip after 6pm is ₹50 to ₹100 per person depending on how late you cross.

Walking the ruins is possible, but expect to cover at least 7km just to see the major sites. Autorickshaws and taxis are available for sightseeing. Hiring an autorickshaw for the day costs ₹750.

Around Hampi

Anegundi

Across the Tungabhadra River, about 5km northeast of Hampi Bazaar, sits Anegundi, an ancient fortified village that's part of the Hampi World Heritage Site but predates Hampi by way of human habitation. Gifted with a landscape similar to Hampi, Anegundi has been spared the blight of commercialisation, and thus continues to preserve the local atmosphere minus the touristy vibe.

◉ Sights & Activities

Mythically referred to as Kishkinda, the kingdom of the monkey gods, Anegundi retains many of its historic monuments, such as sections of its defensive wall and gates, and the Ranganatha Temple (Map p214; ⊙dawn-dusk) devoted to Rama. Also worth visiting is the Durga Temple (Map p214; ⊙dawn-dusk), an ancient shrine closer to the village.

Hanuman Temple   HINDU TEMPLE
(Map p214; ⊙dawn-dusk) The whitewashed Hanuman Temple, accessible by a 570-step

climb up the Anjanadri Hill, has fine views of the rugged terrain around. Many believe this is the birthplace of Hanuman, the Hindu monkey god who was Rama's devotee and helped him in his mission against Ravana. The hike up is pleasant, though you'll be courted by impish monkeys, and within the temple you'll find a large group of chillum-puffing sadhus.

Kishkinda Trust CULTURAL PROGRAMS, OUTDOOR ADVENTURE
(TKT; Map p214; ☑08533-267777; www.tktkish kinda.org; Main Rd, Anegundi) For cultural events, activities and volunteering opportunities, get in touch with Kishkinda Trust, an NGO based in Anegundi that works with local people.

🛏 Sleeping & Eating

A great place to escape the hippies in Hampi, Anegundi has fantastic homestays in restored heritage buildings. Most guesthouses in Anegundi are managed by **Uramma Heritage Homes** (☑9449972230; www.urammaheritagehomes.com; Anegundi).

Peshagar Guest House GUESTHOUSE $
(Map p214; ☑09449972230; www.urammaherit agehomes.com; s/d ₹450/850) Six simple rooms done up in rural motifs open around a pleasant common area in this heritage house with courtyard garden and basic rooftop.

⭐**Uramma Cottage** COTTAGE $$
(Map p214; ☑08533-267792; www.urammaher itagehomes.com; s/d from ₹2000/2500; ❋🐕) Delightful thatched-roof cottages with rustic farmhouse charm that are both comfortable and attractive and set in a relaxed landscaped garden setting.

Uramma House GUESTHOUSE $$
(Map p214; ☑09449972230; www.urammaher itagehomes.com; s/d ₹2000/3500, house for 4 people ₹7000; 🐕) This 4th-century heritage house is a gem, with traditional-style rooms featuring boutique touches.

Hoova Craft Shop & Café CAFE $
(Map p214; mains ₹60-100; ⊙8.30am-9.30pm) A lovely place for an unhurried local meal.

🛍 Shopping

Banana Fibre Craft Workshop HANDICRAFTS
(Map p214; ⊙10am-1pm & 2-5pm Mon-Sat) Watch on at this small workshop as workers ply their trade making a range of handicrafts and accessories using the bark of a banana tree, and recycled materials. Of course they sell it all too.

ℹ Getting There & Away

Anegundi is 7km from Hampi, and reached by crossing the river on a coracle (₹10) from the pier east of the Vittala Temple. By far the most convenient way is to hire a moped or bicycle (if you're feeling energetic) from Virupapur Gaddi. An autorickshaw costs ₹200.

Hospet (Hosapete)

☑08394 / POP 164,200
A hectic, dusty regional centre, Hospet (renamed as Hosapete in 2014) is certainly nothing to write home about, and notable only as a transport hub for Hampi.

🛏 Sleeping & Eating

Hotel Malligi HOTEL $$
(☑08394-228101; www.malligihotels.com; Jabunatha Rd; r ₹990-5000; ❋@🐕❄) Hotel Malligi has built a reputation around clean and well-serviced rooms, aquamarine swimming pool and a good multicuisine restaurant.

Udupi Sri Krishna Bhavan SOUTH INDIAN $
(Bus Stand; thali ₹45, mains ₹50-70; ⊙6.30am-10.30pm) Opposite the bus stand, this clean spot dishes out Indian vegie fare, including thalis.

DAROJI SLOTH BEAR SANCTUARY

About 30km south of Hampi, amid a scrubby undulated terrain, lies the **Daroji Sloth Bear Sanctuary** (₹25; ⊙9.30am-6pm), which nurses a population of around 150 free-ranging sloth bears in an area of 83 sq km. You have a very good chance of spotting them, as honey is slathered on the rocks to coincide with the arrival of visitors. However, you can only see them from afar at the viewing platform. Bring binoculars, or there's no point turning up. Generally 4pm to 6pm is the best time to visit.

The sanctuary is also home to leopards, wild boars, hyenas, jackals and others animals, but you're unlikely to see anything other than peacocks. You'll need to arrange transport to get here, which should cost around ₹600 for an autorickshaw and ₹1000 for a car.

ℹ Information

You'll find ATMs along the main drag and Shanbagh Circle. Internet joints (₹40 per hour) are common.

ℹ Getting There & Away

BUS

Hospet's bus stand has services to Hampi from Bay 10 every half-hour (₹22, 30 minutes). Overnight private sleeper buses ply to/from Goa (10 hours) and Gokarna (eight hours) for ₹850 to ₹1150, and to Bengaluru (₹340 to ₹700, 6½ hours) and Mysuru (₹380 to ₹605, 8½ hours).

TRAIN

Hospet's train station is a ₹20 autorickshaw ride from town. The 18047 Amaravathi Express and KCG YPR Express head to Margao (Magdaon), Goa (sleeper/2AC ₹225/855, 7½ hours) at 6.30am on Monday, Wednesday, Thursday and Saturday. The 16591 Hampi Express departs nightly at 9pm for Bengaluru (3AC/2AC/1AC ₹680/970/1635, nine hours) and Mysore (₹860/1240/2075, 12½ hours)

Hubli (Hubballi)

📞 0836 / POP 943,857

Prosperous Hubli (recently renamed as Hubballi) is a hub for rail routes for Mumbai, Bengaluru, Goa and northern Karnataka. The train station is a 15-minute walk from the old bus stand. Most hotels sit along this stretch.

🛏 Sleeping & Eating

Hotel Ajanta   HOTEL $

(📞 0836-2362216; Jayachamaraj Nagar; s/d from ₹390/510) This well-run place near the train station has basic, functional rooms. Its popular ground-floor restaurant serves delicious regional-style thalis for ₹55.

Ananth Residency   HOTEL $$

(📞 0836-2262251; ananthresidencyhubli@yahoo.co.uk; Jayachamaraj Nagar; d from ₹1600; ❄) A comfortable option that sports a sleek business-hotel look, and cheerful restaurant with chilled beer.

ℹ Information

There's an ATM opposite the bus stand. On the same stretch are several internet cafes, charging ₹30 per hour.

ℹ Getting There & Away

AIR

The airport is around 5km from the centre of town. SpiceJet has daily flights to Bengaluru.

BUS

There are frequent morning semideluxe servies to Bengaluru (semideluxe/AC Volvo/sleeper ₹434/650/690, 8½ hours) until around 9.30am, Bijapur (₹165 to ₹250, seven hours) and Hospet (₹144 to ₹237, four hours). There's an 8am bus to Gokarna (₹161, four hours) and regular connections to Mangaluru (₹356 to ₹600, 9½ hours), Mumbai (semideluxe/sleeper ₹700/1100, 11 hours), Mysuru (₹450, 10 hours) and Panaji (₹171 to ₹304, seven hours).

TRAIN

From the train station, plenty of expresses head to Hospet (sleeper/2AC class ₹140/690, 2½ hours, six daily), Bengaluru (sleeper/2AC ₹300/1085, eight hours, four daily) and Mumbai (sleeper/2AC ₹380/1480, 15½ hours). The 11pm 06948 Hubli-Vasco Link Express goes to Goa (sleeper/3AC ₹160/485, 6½ hours).

NORTHERN KARNATAKA

Badami

📞 08357 / POP 26,000

Once the capital of the mighty Chalukya empire, today Badami is famous for its magnificent rock-cut cave temples, and red sandstone cliffs that resemble the Wild West. While the dusty main road is an eyesore that will have you wanting to get the hell out of there, its backstreets are a lovely area to explore with old houses, carved wooden doorways and the occasional Chalukyan ruin.

History

From about AD 540 to 757, Badami was the capital of an enormous kingdom stretching from Kanchipuram in Tamil Nadu to the Narmada River in Gujarat. It eventually fell to the Rashtrakutas, and changed hands several times thereafter, with each dynasty sculpturally embellishing Badami in their own way.

The sculptural legacy left by the Chalukyan artisans in Badami includes some of the earliest and finest examples of Dravidian temples and rock-cut caves.

⊙ Sights & Activities

The bluffs and horseshoe-shaped red sandstone cliff of Badami offer some great low-altitude climbing. For more information, visit www.indiaclimb.com.

Badami's caves overlook the 5th-century **Agastyatirtha Tank** and the waterside **Bhutanatha temples**. On the other side of the tank is an **archaeological museum** (admission ₹5; ⊙9am-5pm Sat-Thu), which houses superb examples of local sculpture, including a remarkably explicit Lajja-Gauri image of a fertility cult that once flourished in the area. The stairway behind the museum climbs through a sandstone chasm and fortified gateways to reach the ruins of the **North Fort**.

Cave Temples   CAVE
(Indian/foreigner ₹5/100, video camera ₹25, tour guide ₹300; ⊙6am-6pm) Badami's highlights are its beautiful cave temples. **Cave One**, just above the entrance to the complex, is dedicated to Shiva. It's the oldest of the four caves, probably carved in the latter half of the 6th century. On the wall to the right of the porch is a captivating image of Nataraja striking 81 dance moves in the one pose. On the right of the porch area is a huge figure of Ardhanarishvara. On the opposite wall is a large image of Harihara, half Shiva and half Vishnu.

Dedicated to Vishnu, **Cave Two** is simpler in design. As with caves one and three, the front edge of the platform is decorated with images of pot-bellied dwarfs in various poses. Four pillars support the verandah, their tops carved with a bracket in the shape of a *yali* (mythical lion creature). On the left wall of the porch is the bull-headed figure of Varaha, the emblem of the Chalukya empire. To his left is Naga, a snake with a human face. On the right wall is a large sculpture of Trivikrama, another incarnation of Vishnu.

Between the second and third caves are two sets of steps to the right. The first leads to a natural cave with a small image of Padmapani (an incarnation of the Buddha). The second set of steps – sadly, barred by a gate – leads to the hilltop South Fort.

Cave Three, carved in AD 578, is the largest and most impressive. On the left wall is a carving of Vishnu, to whom the cave is dedicated, sitting on a snake. Nearby is an image of Varaha with four hands. The pillars have carved brackets in the shape of *yalis*.

The ceiling panels contain images, including Indra riding an elephant, Shiva on a bull and Brahma on a swan. Keep an eye out for the image of drunken revellers, in particular one lady being propped up by her husband. There's also original colour on the ceiling; the divots on the floor at the cave's entrance were used as paint palettes.

Dedicated to Jainism, **Cave Four** is the smallest of the set and dates between the 7th and 8th centuries. The right wall has an image of Suparshvanatha (the seventh Jain *tirthankar*) surrounded by 24 Jain *tirthankars*. The inner sanctum contains an image of Adinath, the first Jain *tirthankar*.

⏰ Sleeping & Eating

Mookambika Deluxe   HOTEL $
(☏08357-220067; hotelmookambika@yahoo.com; Station Rd; d with fan/AC from ₹850/1750; ✴) A friendly hotel with comfy rooms done up in matt orange and green. Staff are a good source of travel info.

Hotel Mayura Chalukya   HOTEL $$
(☏08357-220046; Ramdurg Rd; d with fan/AC from ₹1000/1500; ✴) Away from the bustle, this stock-standard government hotel has large, clean rooms with an OK restaurant serving Indian staples.

Krishna Heritage   HOTEL $$$
(☏08357-221300; www.krishnaheritagebadami. com; Ramdurg Rd; r incl breakfast from ₹3500) An upmarket resort 2km from town set on sprawling grounds with a distinct African feel; including a roaming flock of guinea fowl. Rooms are massive with open-air showers and balconies.

Golden Caves Cuisine   MULTICUISINE $
(Station Rd; mains ₹60-120; ⊙8.30am-11.30pm) Produces good North and South Indian fare, with a pleasant outdoor area that's perfect for beers on a balmy evening.

ⓘ Information

There are ATMs on the main road.
Hotel Rajsangam (Station Rd; per hour ₹20) Internet is available at Hotel Rajsangam in the town centre.
KSTDC tourist office (☏220414; Ramdurg Rd; ⊙10am-5.30pm Mon-Sat) The KSTDC tourist office, adjoining Hotel Mayura Chalukya, has brochures on Badami, but otherwise isn't useful.

KARNATAKA & BENGALURU BADAMI

❶ Getting There & Away

Buses regularly shuffle off from Badami's bus stand on Station Rd to Kerur (₹25, 45 minutes), which has connections to Bijapur and Hubli. Buses to Hospet (₹180, six hours) also leave from here.

Several trains run to Bijapur including the 11424 Solapur Express (₹70, 3½ hours, 5.30pm), while the Hubli Express goes to Hubli (2nd class ₹75, 3½ hours, 11am). For Bengaluru, take the 16536 Gol Gumbaz Express (2nd class ₹330, 13 hours, 7.15pm).

❶ Getting Around

Theoretically you can visit Aihole and Pattadakal in a day from Badami if you get moving early. It's much easier and less stressful to arrange an autorickshaw or taxi for the day; it costs around ₹900/1500 for a day trip to Pattadakal, Aihole and nearby Mahakuta.

Start with Aihole (₹40, one hour), then move to Pattadakal (₹23, 30 minutes), and finally return to Badami (₹23, one hour). The last bus from Pattadakal to Badami is at 4pm.

Around Badami

There's no accommodation or restaurants at either Pattadakal or Aihole.

Pattadakal

A secondary capital of the Badami Chalukyas, Pattadakal is known for its temples, which are collectively a World Heritage Site.

Pattadakal is 20km from Badami, with buses (₹23) departing every 30 minutes until about 5pm. There's a morning and afternoon bus to Aiole (₹20), 13km away.

Barring a few that date back to the 3rd century AD, most of Pattadakal's temples (Indian/foreigner ₹10/250, video camera ₹25; ☉6am-6pm) were built during the 7th and 8th centuries AD. Historians believe Pattadakal served as an important trial ground for the development of South Indian temple architecture. A guide here costs about ₹250.

The main Virupaksha Temple is a massive structure, its columns covered with intricate carvings depicting episodes from the Ramayana and Mahabharata. A giant stone sculpture of Nandi (Shiva's bull) sits to the temple's east. The Mallikarjuna Temple, next to the Virupaksha Temple, is almost identical in design. About 500m south of the main enclosure is the Jain Papanatha Temple, its entrance flanked by elephant sculptures.

Aihole

Some 100 temples, built between the 4th and 6th centuries AD, speck the ancient Chalukyan regional capital of Aihole (ay-ho-leh). Most, however, are either in ruins or engulfed by the modern village. Aihole documents the embryonic stage of South Indian Hindu architecture, from the earliest simple shrines, such as the most ancient Ladkhan Temple, to the later and more complex buildings, such as the Meguti Temple.

Aihole is about 40km from Badami and 13km from Pattadakal.

The most impressive of all the temples in Aihole is the 7th-century Durga Temple (Indian/foreigner ₹5/100, camera ₹25; ☉8am-6pm), notable for its semicircular apse (inspired by Buddhist architecture) and the remains of the curvilinear *sikhara* (temple spire). The interiors house intricate stone carvings. The small museum (admission ₹5; ☉9am-5pm Sat-Thu) behind the temple contains further examples of Chalukyan sculpture.

To the south of the Durga Temple are several other temple clusters, including early examples. About 600m to the southeast, on a low hillock, is the Jain Meguti Temple. Watch out for snakes if you're venturing up.

Bijapur (Vijapura)

📞 08352 / POP 326,360 / ELEV 593M

A fascinating open-air museum dating back to the Deccan's Islamic era, dusty Bijapur (renamed Vijapura in 2014) tells a glorious tale dating back some 600 years. Blessed with a heap of mosques, mausoleums, palaces and fortifications, it was the capital of the Adil Shahi kings from 1489 to 1686, and one of the five splinter states formed after the Islamic Bahmani kingdom broke up in 1482. Despite its strong Islamic character, Bijapur is also a centre for the Lingayat brand of Shaivism, which emphasises a single personalised god. The Lingayat Siddeshwara Festival runs for eight days in January/February.

◉ Sights

★ Golgumbaz   MONUMENT
(Indian/foreigner ₹5/100, camera ₹25; ☉6am-6pm) Set in tranquil gardens, the magnificent Golgumbaz mausoleum houses the tombs of emperor Mohammed Adil Shah (r 1627–56), his two wives, his mistress (Rambha), one of his daughters and a grandson.

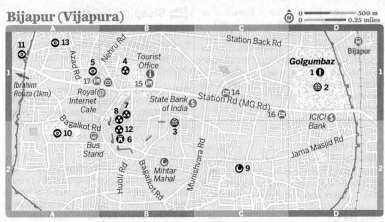

Bijapur (Vijapura)

KARNATAKA & BENGALURU BIJAPUR (VIJAPURA)

Octagonal seven-storey towers stand at each corner of the monument, which is capped by an enormous dome. An astounding 38m in diameter, it's said to be the largest dome in the world after St Peter's Basilica in Rome.

Climb the steep, narrow stairs up one of the towers to reach the 'whispering gallery' within the dome. An engineering marvel, its acoustics are such that if you whisper into the wall, a person on the opposite side of the gallery can hear you clearly. Unfortunately people like to test this out by hollering (its unnerving acoustics have the nightmarish effect of a bad acid trip).

The **archaeological museum** (admission ₹5; ◷10am-5pm Sat-Thu) has an excellent collection of Persian carpets, weapons and scrolls dating back to Bijapur's heyday.

★ **Ibrahim Rouza**   MONUMENT
(Indian/foreigner ₹5/100, video ₹25; ◷6am-6pm) The beautiful Ibrahim Rouza is among the most elegant and finely proportioned Islamic

monuments in India. Its 24m-high minarets are said to have inspired those of the Taj Mahal, and its tale is similarly poignant: built by emperor Ibrahim Adil Shah II (r 1580–1627) as a future mausoleum for his queen, Taj Sultana. Ironically, he died before her, and was thus the first person to be rested there. Also interred here with Ibrahim Adil Shah are his queen, children and mother.

For a tip (₹150 is fine), caretakers can show you around the monument, including the dark labyrinth around the catacomb where the actual graves are located.

Citadel   FORT
Surrounded by fortified walls and a wide moat, the citadel once contained the palaces, pleasure gardens and durbar (royal court) of the Adil Shahi kings. Now mainly in ruins, the most impressive of the remaining fragments is the colossal archway of **Gagan Mahal**, built by Ali Adil Shah I around 1561 as a dual-purpose royal residency and durbar

hall. The gates here are locked, but someone will be on hand to let you in.

The ruins of Mohammed Adil Shah's seven-storey palace, the **Sat Manzil**, are nearby. Across the road stands the delicate **Jala Manzil**, once a water pavilion surrounded by secluded courts and gardens. On the other side of Station Rd (MG Rd) are the graceful arches of **Bara Kaman**, the ruined mausoleum of Ali Roza.

Central Market
MARKET

(Station Rd; ☺9am-9pm) A refreshing change in pace from historic ruins, this lively market is an explosion of colour and scents with flowers, spices and fresh produce on sale.

Jama Masjid
MOSQUE

(Jama Masjid Rd; ☺9am-5.30pm) Constructed by Ali Adil Shah I (r 1557–80), the finely proportioned Jama Masjid has graceful arches, a fine dome and a vast inner courtyard with room for more than 2200 worshippers. Women should cover their heads and not wear revealing clothing.

Asar Mahal
HISTORIC BUILDING

FREE Built by Mohammed Adil Shah in about 1646 to serve as a Hall of Justice, the Asar Mahal once housed two hairs from Prophet Mohammed's beard. The rooms on the upper storey are decorated with frescoes and a square tank graces the front. It's out of bounds for women.

Upli Buruj
HISTORIC SITE

Upli Buruj is a 16th-century, 24m-high watchtower near the western walls of the city. An external flight of stairs leads to the top, where you'll find two hefty cannons and good views of other monuments.

Malik-e-Maidan
HISTORIC SITE

(Monarch of the Plains) Perched upon a platform is this beast of a cannon – over 4m long, almost 1.5m in diameter and estimated to weigh 55 tonnes. Cast in 1549, it was supposedly brought to Bijapur as a war trophy thanks to the efforts of 10 elephants, 400 oxen and hundreds of men!

Jod Gumbad
HISTORIC SITE

In the southwest of the city, off Bagalkot Rd, stand the twin Jod Gumbad tombs with handsome bulbous domes. An Adil Shahi general and his spiritual adviser, Abdul Razzaq Qadiri, are buried here.

🛏 Sleeping & Eating

Hotel Tourist
HOTEL $

(☑08352-250655; Station Rd; s/d ₹180/350) A dive bang in the middle of the bazaar, with scrawny (but clean) rooms.

Hotel Mayura Adil Shahi Annexe
HOTEL $

(☑08352-250401; Station Rd; s/d from ₹540/600, with AC ₹990; ❄) One of the better government hotels with massive rooms, balconies and a garden. Prices rise on weekends.

Hotel Pearl
HOTEL $$

(☑08352-256002; www.hotelpearlbijapur.com; Station Rd; d with fan/AC from ₹940/1300; ❄) Decent midrange hotel with clean motel-style rooms that are arranged around a central atrium, and conveniently located to Golgumbaz.

Hotel Madhuvan International
HOTEL $$

(☑08352-255571; Station Rd; d with fan/AC ₹1000/1400; ❄🖥) Hidden down a lane off Station Rd, this pleasant hotel boasts lime-green walls, tinted windows and a lovely garden **restaurant** (mains ₹60-80; ☺9am-11am, noon-4pm & 7-11pm).

ⓘ Information

You'll find ATMs about town, including **State Bank of India** (Station Rd) and **ICICI Bank** (Station Rd).

Royal Internet Cafe (Station Rd, below Hotel Pearl; per hour ₹30; ☺9.30am-9.30pm)

Tourist office (☑08352-250359; Hotel Mayura Adil Shahi Annexe, Station Rd; ☺10am-5.30pm Mon-Sat) Has a good brochure on Bijapur with useful map.

ⓘ Getting There & Away

BUS

The following services leave from the **bus stand** (☑08352-251344):

Bengaluru Ordinary/sleeper ₹577/692, 12 hours

Bidar ₹270, seven hours, three evening buses

Gubarga (Kalaburgi) ₹155 to ₹240, four hours

Hospet ₹240 to ₹340, five hours

Hubli ₹163, six hours

Hyderabad ₹367 to ₹604, eight to 10 hours, four daily

Mumbai ₹610, 12 hours, five daily, via Pune (₹380 to ₹430, 10 hours)

TRAIN

Trains from Bijapur station:

Badami 17320 Hubli-Secunderabad Express, sleeper/2AC ₹140/690, 3½ hours, several daily night trains

Bengaluru 16536 Golgumbaz Express, sleeper/2AC ₹375/1455, 15½ hours, 5pm

Hyderabad 17319 Secunderabad Express, sleeper/2AC ₹250/955, 9½ hours, 2am

Mumbai 51030 BJP BB Fast Passenger, sleeper ₹215, 13 hours, four weekly

ℹ Getting Around

Given the amount to see and the distance to cover, ₹500 is a fair price to hire an autorickshaw for a day of sightseeing. Expect to pay ₹40 to get from the train station to the town centre, and ₹50 between Golgumbaz and Ibrahim Rouza.

Bidar

☑ 08482 / POP 211,944 / ELEV 664M

Despite being home to amazing ruins and monuments, Bidar, hidden away in Karnataka's far northeastern corner, gets very little tourist traffic – which of course makes it all the more appealing. It's a city drenched in history, with the old-walled town being the first capital of Bahmani kingdom (1428–87) and later the capital of the Barid Shahi dynasty.

◉ Sights

Bidar Fort FORT

(⊙9am-5pm) Keep aside a few hours for peacefully wandering around the remnants of this magnificent 15th-century fort, the largest in South India – and once the administrative capital of much of the region. Surrounded by a triple moat hewn out of solid red rock and 5.5km of defensive walls (the second longest in India), the fort has a fairytale entrance that twists in an elaborate chicane through three gateways.

Guides from the archaeological office have the keys to unlock the most interesting ruins within the fort. These include the **Rangin Mahal** (Painted Palace), with elaborate tilework, teak pillars and panels with mother-of-pearl inlay, **Solah Khamba Mosque** (Sixteen-Pillared Mosque), and **Tarkash Mahal** with exquisitive Islamic inscriptions and wonderful rooftop views. There's a small **museum** in the former royal bath with local artefacts.

Bahmani Tombs HISTORIC SITE

(⊙dawn-dusk) FREE The huge domed tombs of the Bahmani kings in Ashtur, 3km east of Bidar, were built to house the remains of the sultans, of which the painted interior of Ahmad Shah Bahman's tomb is the most impressive.

Choukhandi HISTORIC BUILDING

(⊙dawn-dusk) FREE Located 500m from the Badami Tombs is the serene mausoleum of Sufi saint Syed Kirmani Baba, who travelled here from Persia during the golden age of the Bahmani empire. An uncanny air of calm hangs within the monument, and its polygonal courtyard houses rows of medieval graves.

Khwaja Mahmud Gawan Madrasa RUIN, HISTORIC SITE

(⊙dawn-dusk) FREE Dominating the heart of the old town are the ruins of Khwaja Mahmud Gawan Madrasa, a college for advanced learning built in 1472. To get an idea of its former grandeur, check out the remnants of coloured tiles on the front gate and one of the minarets which still stands intact.

🛏 Sleeping & Eating

Hotel Mayura HOTEL $

(☑08482-228142; Udgir Rd; d with fan/AC from ₹900/2000; ❄) Smart and friendly, with cheerful and well-appointed rooms, bar and restaurant, this is the best hotel to camp at in Bidar. It's bang opposite the central bus stand. Look out for its NBC-peacock symbol.

Hotel Mayura Barid Shahi HOTEL $

(☑08482-221740; Udgir Rd; s/d ₹500/600, r with AC ₹1000; ❄) Otherwise featureless with simple, institutional rooms, this place scores due to its central location and garden bar-restaurant.

★ **Jyothi Fort** INDIAN $

(Bidar Fort; mains ₹70-110; ⊙9am-5pm) A peaceful setting at the fort's entry with tables set up on the grass under sprawling tamarind trees. It has delicious vegetarian meals.

ℹ Information

You can find **ATMs** (Udgir Rd) and **internet** (per hour ₹ 20; ⊙9am-9pm) on the main road and opposite Hotel Mayura Barid Shahi.

ℹ Getting There & Away

From the bus stand, frequent buses run to Gulbarga (₹115, three hours) and two evening buses to Bijapur (₹280, seven hours). There are also buses to Hyderabad (₹143, four hours, 6.30pm) and Bengaluru (semideluxe/AC ₹700/900, 12 hours, six daily).

Trains head to Hyderabad (sleeper ₹120, five hours, three daily) and Bengaluru (sleeper ₹722 to ₹1012, 13 to 17 hours, twice daily).

ℹ Getting Around

You can arrange a day tour in an autorickshaw for around ₹400.

Telangana & Andhra Pradesh

Best Places to Eat

➜ Southern Spice (p238)

➜ Hotel Shadab (p238)

➜ SO (p238)

➜ Shah Ghouse Cafe (p238)

➜ Sea Inn (p249)

Best Off the Beaten Track

➜ Guntupalli (p249)

➜ Sankaram (p251)

➜ Moula Ali Dargah (p233)

➜ Bhongir Fort (p244)

Why Go?

Hyderabad, the fascinating capital of Telangana, is reason enough on its own to visit this region. Its old quarter of colourful markets, teahouses, biryani restaurants and narrow lanes is studded with the monuments and palaces of bygone dynasties. On the city's fringes rise the fabled Golconda fort and magnificent tombs of departed royalty. Meanwhile Hyderabad's newer districts are lit up by the classy restaurants, hotels, boutiques and bars of IT-fuelled economic advance.

The other attractions of these two states (which were one state until they split in 2014) are less brazen, but dig around and you will unearth gems – like the wonderful medieval temple sculptures of Palampet, the beauty of ancient Buddhist sites such as Sankaram and Guntupalli hidden in deep countryside, the cheery coastal holiday vibe of Visakhapatnam, and the positive vibrations emanating from the vast pilgrim crowds at Tirumala Temple.

When to Go
Hyderabad

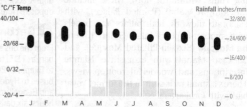

May–Jun Join locals digging into *haleem*, a Ramadan (Ramzan) favourite.

Nov–Feb Explore Hyderabad's sights in perfect 20-25°C weather.

Dec–Apr Best time to enjoy Vizag's coastal attractions – little rain, not *too* hot.

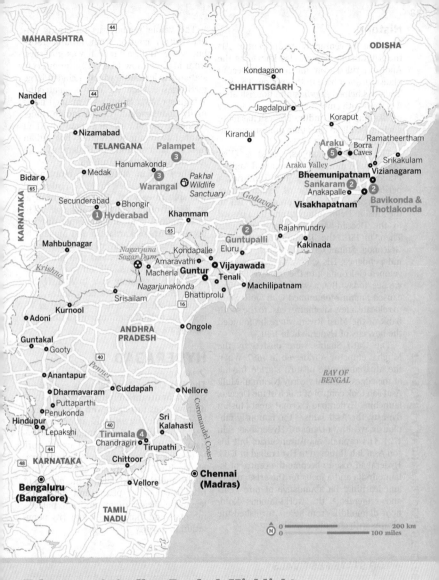

Telangana & Andhra Pradesh Highlights

1 Exploring the markets, feasting on the food and gazing on the architectural marvels of historical and contemporary **Hyderabad** (p228)

2 Absorbing the meditative vibrations of monks past at beautiful **Sankaram** (p251), **Bavikonda** (p251),

Thotlakonda (p251), and **Guntupalli** (p249), destinations on a 2300-year-old monastic trail

3 Enjoying the genius of Kakatiya sculptors at **Palampet** (p245) and **Warangal** (p244)

4 Finding devotion you didn't know you had alongside thousands of Hindu pilgrims at **Tirumala** (p252)

5 Enjoying the lush green forests and wide green valleys as your train chugs through the spectacular Eastern Ghats up to **Araku** (p251)

History

From the 3rd century BC to 3rd century AD the Satavahana empire, also known as the Andhras, ruled over much of the Deccan plateau from a base in this region. The Satavahanas helped Buddhism to flourish after it arrived with emperor Ashoka's missionary monks, and today Andhra Pradesh has more ancient Buddhist sites than almost any other Indian state.

The Hindu Kakatiyas, based at Warangal, ruled most of Telangana and Andhra Pradesh from the 12th to 14th centuries, a period that saw the rise of Telugu culture and language. Warangal eventually fell to the Muslim Delhi Sultanate and then passed to the Deccan-based Bahmani Sultanate. Then, in 1518, the Bahmanis' governor at Golconda, Sultan Quli Qutb Shah, claimed independence. His Qutb Shahi dynasty developed Golconda into the massive fortress we see today. But a water shortage there caused Sultan Mohammed Quli Qutb Shah to relocate a few kilometres east to the south bank of the Musi River, where he founded the new city of Hyderabad in 1591.

The Qutb Shahis were ousted by the Mughal emperor Aurangzeb in 1687. When the Mughal empire in turn started fraying at the edges, its local viceroy Nizam ul-Mulk Asaf Jah took control of much of the Deccan, launching Hyderabad's second great Muslim dynasty, the Asaf Jahis – the famously fabulously wealthy nizams of Hyderabad – in 1724. His capital was Aurangabad, but his son Asaf Jah II moved to Hyderabad in 1763. Hyderabad rose to become the centre of Islamic India and a focus for the arts, culture and learning. Its abundance of rare gems and minerals – the world-famous Kohinoor diamond is from here – furnished the nizams with enormous wealth.

The whole region was effectively under British control from around 1800, but while Andhra Pradesh was governed from Madras (now Chennai), the princely state of Hyderabad – which included large territories outside the city populated by Telugu-speaking Hindus – remained nominally independent. Come Indian Independence in 1947, nizam Osman Ali Khan wanted to retain sovereignty, but Indian military intervention saw Hyderabad state join the Indian union in 1948.

When Indian states were reorganised along linguistic lines in 1956, Hyderabad was split three ways. What's now Telangana joined other Telugu-speaking areas to form Andhra Pradesh state; other districts became parts of Karnataka and Maharashtra. Telangana was never completely happy with this arrangement, and after prolonged campaigning, it was split off from Andhra Pradesh as a separate state in 2014. Hyderabad remains capital of both states until Andhra Pradesh gets its new capital at Vijayawada up and running, with a time limit of 10 years.

HYDERABAD

🎵 040 / POP 6.81 MILLION

The Old City of Hyderabad is everything you might dream an Indian old city to be – narrow lanes thronged with markets, chai shops, wandering animals, autorickshaws, a whirl of noise, colour, languages and religions dotted with stately old architecture in varying states of repair. Two unbelievably wealthy Muslim royal houses, the Qutb Shahs and the Asaf Jahs, came and went from this city of pearls and diamonds, leaving a legacy of magnificent palaces, mosques and tombs and a majority population in poverty.

TOP STATE FESTIVALS

Sankranti (p235; ☉ Jan) This important Telugu festival marks the end of harvest season. Kite-flying abounds, doorsteps are decorated with colourful *kolams* (rice-flour designs) and men adorn cattle with bells and fresh horn paint.

Brahmotsavam (Venkateshwara Temple, Tirumala; ☉ Sep/Oct) This nine-day festival sees the Venkateshwara temple at Tirumala (p252) awash in vast crowds of worshippers. Special *pujas* and chariot processions are held, and it's an auspicious time for *darshan* (deity-viewing).

Muharram (Hyderabad; ☉ Sep/Oct) Commemorates the martyrdom of Mohammed's grandson Hussain. A huge procession throngs the Old City in Hyderabad (p235).

Hyderabad's other pole is far younger – its Hi-Tech City, or 'Cyberabad', out west, which since the 1990s has propelled the city into the modern world with its accoutrements of glittery malls, multiplexes, clubs, pubs and sleek restaurants to sit alongside the traditional biryani joints and teahouses.

Between the old and the new lie, in both material and geographical terms, dense inner city areas like Abids, north of the Old City, and leafy middle-class areas like Banjara Hills and Jubilee Hills. In the northeast, site of one of Hyderabad's three main train stations, is Secunderabad, the former British military cantonment still referred to as Hyderabad's 'twin city', though they are effectively one now.

One thing you have to accept wherever you are in Hyderabad: the traffic is appalling. Happily a new Metro Rail rapid transit system, coming on stream as we speak, should ease things.

Hyderabad's Muslim population (Urdu-speaking) is concentrated mostly in the Old City and nearby areas north of the Musi River. The majority of the population are Telugu-speaking Hindus and there's also a growing number of migrants from other parts of India attracted by the IT boom.

◉ Sights

◉ Old City

★**Charminar**   MONUMENT
(Map p236; Indian/foreigner ₹5/100; ⊙9am-5.30pm) Hyderabad's principal landmark and city symbol was built by Mohammed Quli Qutb Shah in 1591 to commemorate the founding of Hyderabad and the end of epidemics caused by Golconda's water shortage. The beautiful four-column, 56m-high structure has four arches facing the cardinal points, with minarets atop each column (hence the name Charminar, 'four minarets'). It stands at the heart of Hyderabad's most atmospheric area (also known as Charminar), a labyrinth of lanes crowded with shops, stalls, markets and shoppers.

The Charminar's second floor, home to Hyderabad's oldest mosque, and the upper columns, are not open to the public. The structure is illuminated from 7pm to 9pm.

★**Chowmahalla Palace**   PALACE
(Map p236; www.chowmahalla.com; Indian/foreigner ₹40/150, camera ₹50; ⊙10am-5pm Sat-Thu)

This opulent 18th- and 19th-century palace, the main residence of several nizams, comprises four garden courtyards in a line from north to south. Most dazzling is the Khilwat Mubarak at the end of the first courtyard, a magnificent durbar hall where nizams held ceremonies under 19 enormous chandeliers of Belgian crystal. Its side rooms today house photos and historical exhibits extolling the nizams' virtues. Its balcony once served as seating for the royal women, who attended durbars in purdah.

Several other halls contain interesting exhibits of nizams' personal possessions, arts, crafts and costumes, and in the southernmost courtyard you'll find a 1911 yellow Rolls-Royce which was preserved for very special occasions and has travelled only 356 miles in more than a century.

Salar Jung Museum   MUSEUM
(Map p236; www.salarjungmuseum.in; Salar Jung Rd; Indian/foreigner ₹10/150, camera ₹50; ⊙10am-5pm Sat-Thu) This vast and varied collection was put together by Mir Yousuf Ali Khan (Salar Jung III), who was briefly grand vizier to the seventh nizam, Osman Ali Khan (r 1911–48), before devoting his large fortune to amassing Asian and European art and craftworks. The 40-plus galleries include early South Indian bronzes and wood and stone sculptures, Indian miniature paintings, European fine art, historic manuscripts, a room of jade and another room of very fancy walking sticks.

A special highlight is the remarkable *Veiled Rebecca* by 19th-century Italian sculptor Benzoni. The museum is very popular, and can be bedlam on Sundays.

HEH The Nizam's Museum   MUSEUM
(Purani Haveli; Map p236; off Dur-e-Sharwah Hospital Rd; adult/child ₹80/15, camera ₹150; ⊙10am-5pm Sat-Thu) The Purani Haveli was a home of the sixth nizam, Mahbub Ali Khan (r 1869–1911). He was rumoured to have never worn the same thing twice: hence the 54m-long, two-storey Burmese teak

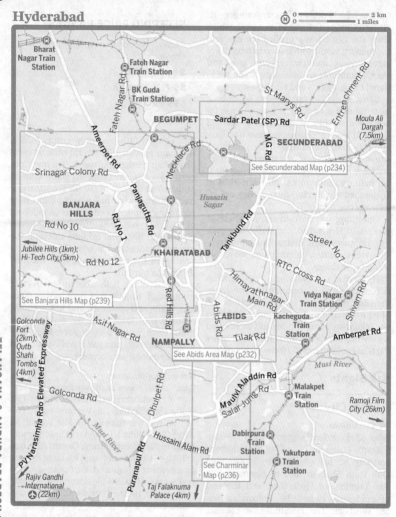

wardrobe. Much of the museum, occupying just one wing of the long palace compound, is devoted to personal effects of the seventh nizam, Osman Ali Khan, including his silver cradle, gold-burnished throne and lavish Silver Jubilee gifts.

Mecca Masjid
MOSQUE

(Map p236; Shah Ali Banda Rd, Charminar; ⏰4.30am-9pm) This mosque is one of the world's largest, with 10,000 men praying here at major Muslim festivals, and also one of Hyderabad's oldest buildings, begun in 1617 by the city's founder Mohammed Quli Qutb Shah. Women are not allowed inside the main prayer hall, and male tourists are unlikely to be let in either (they can look through the railings). Female tourists, even with headscarves, may not even be allowed into the vast courtyard if their clothing is judged too skimpy or tight.

Several bricks embedded above the prayer hall's central arch are made with soil from Mecca, hence the mosque's name. An enclosure alongside the courtyard contains the tombs of several Hyderabad nizams.

Badshahi Ashurkhana
MUSLIM SACRED SITE

(Map p236; High Court Rd) The 1594 Badshahi Ashurkhana (literally 'royal house of mourning') was one of the first structures built by the Qutb Shahs in their new city of Hyderabad. In a courtyard set back from the road, its walls are practically glowing with intricate, brightly coloured tile mosaics. The Ashurkhana is packed during Muharram, as well as on Thursdays, when local Shiites gather to commemorate the martyrdom of Hussain Ibn Ali. Visitors should remove shoes and dress modestly (including a headscarf for women).

⊙ Abids Area

State Museum
MUSEUM

(Map p232; Public Gardens Rd, Nampally; admission ₹10, camera/video ₹100/500; ⊘10.30am-4.30pm Sat-Thu, closed 2nd Sat of month) This sprawling museum, in a fanciful 1920 building constructed by the seventh nizam as a playhouse for one of his daughters, hosts a collection of important archaeological finds as well as an exhibit on the region's Buddhist history, with relics of the Buddha himself. There's also an interesting decorative-arts gallery, where you can learn about Bidriware inlaid metalwork and *kalamkari* textile painting, plus a bronze sculpture gallery and a 4500-year-old Egyptian mummy

British Residency
HISTORIC BUILDING

(Koti Women's College; Koti) This palatial Palladian residence, built in 1803-06 by James Achilles Kirkpatrick, the British Resident (official East India Company representative) in Hyderabad, features in William Dalrymple's brilliant historical love story *White Mughals*. It's sadly dilapidated today, though long-mooted restoration plans may at last be coming to fruition. If you enter the grounds a caretaker will probably offer to open up the grand original building (tip ₹50 to ₹100 when you've finished).

Kirkpatrick became enchanted by Hyderabad courtly culture, converted to Islam and married Khair-un-Nissa, a teenage relative of the Hyderabad prime minister. The Residency and its extensive gardens became the Osmania University College for Women, known as Koti Women's College, in 1949. Inside the grand classical portico, you can admire the Durbar Hall, with Islamic geometric designs on its high ceiling above the chandeliers and classical columns, and the elaborate curving staircase behind. In the overgrown gardens to the southwest you'll find a British cemetery and, if you're lucky, the surviving entrance to the Residency's zenana (women's quarters) and a model of the Residency building made by Kirkpatrick for Khair-un-Nissa – though our guide refused to venture beyond the cemetery for fear of snakes! Detours (p234) does fascinating White Mughals tours which include the Residency.

Birla Mandir
HINDU TEMPLE

(Map p232; ⊘7am-noon & 2-9pm) The ethereal Birla Mandir, constructed of white Rajasthani marble in 1976, graces Kalabahad (Black Mountain), one of two rocky hills overlooking Hussain Sagar. Dedicated to Venkateshwara, it's a popular Hindu worship centre, with a relaxed atmosphere, and affords magnificent views over the city, especially at sunset.

Birla Modern Art Gallery
MUSEUM

(Map p232; www.birlasciencecentre.org; Naubat Pahad Lane, Adarsh Nagar; admission ₹50; ⊘10.30am-6pm) This skilfully curated collection of modern and contemporary art is the best of its kind in South India. Look for paintings by superstars Jogen Chowdhury, Tyeb Mehta and Arpita Singh. Also here is the fun Birla Science Centre (Map p232; museum/planetarium ₹50/50; ⊘10.30am-8pm, planetarium shows 11.30am, 4pm & 6pm), comprising a museum of science, dolls and archaeology, and a planetarium.

⊙ Other Areas

★ Golconda Fort
FORT

(Indian/foreigner ₹5/100, sound-and-light show adult ₹70-130; ⊘9am-5pm, English-language sound-and-light show 6.30pm Nov-Feb, 7pm Mar-Oct) It was the Qutb Shahs in the 16th century who made Golconda into the massive fortress whose substantial ruins we see today. The mighty citadel is built on a 120m-high granite hill, surrounded by crenellated ramparts of large masonry blocks, with another ring of crenellated ramparts, 11km in perimeter, outside it. Morning visits are best for relative peace and quiet.

By the time of the Qutb Shahs, Golconda fort had already existed for at least three centuries under the Kakatiyas and Bahmani sultanate, and was already famed for its diamonds, which were mostly mined in

TELANGANA & ANDHRA PRADESH HYDERABAD

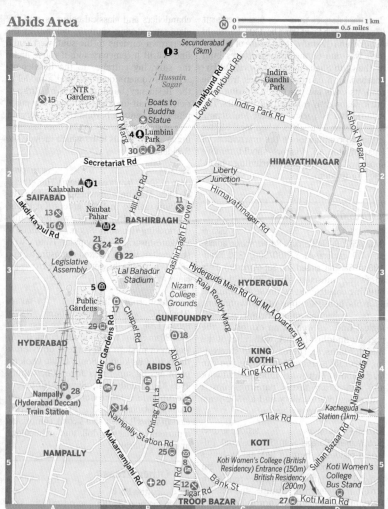

the Krishna River valley, but cut and traded here. The Qutb Shahs moved to their new city of Hyderabad in 1591, but maintained Golconda as a citadel until the Mughal emperor Aurangzeb took it in 1687 after a year-long siege, ending Qutb Shahi rule.

Golconda's massive gates were studded with iron spikes to obstruct war elephants. Within the fort, a series of concealed glazed earthenware pipes ensured a reliable water supply, while the ingenious acoustics guaranteed that even the smallest sound from the entrance would echo across the fort complex.

Guides charge at least ₹600 per 90-minute tour. Small ₹20 guide booklets are also available. Inside the citadel gate, an anticlockwise circuit leads through gardens and up past mostly minor buildings to the top of the hill, where you'll find the functioning Hindu Jagadamba Mahakali Temple and the three-storey durbar hall, with fine panoramas. You then descend to the old palace buildings in the southeastern part of the fort and return to the entrance passing the elegant three-arched Taramati Mosque.

Golconda is about 10km west from Abids or the Charminar: autorickshaws charge

Abids Area

around ₹400 return, including waiting. Buses 65G and 66G run from Charminar bus stop to Golconda via GPO Abids hourly; the journey takes about an hour. Bus 142K goes from Koti bus stop via GPO Abids about every 90 minutes.

★ **Qutb Shahi Tombs**　　　　　HISTORIC SITE
(Tolichowki; adult/child ₹10/5, camera/video ₹20/100; ☉9.30am-5.30pm Sat-Thu) These 21 magnificent domed granite tombs, with almost as many mosques, sit serenely in landscaped gardens about 2km northwest of Golconda Fort, where many of their occupants spent large parts of their lives. Seven of the eight Qutb Shahi rulers were buried here, as well as family members and a few physicians, courtesans and other favourites. An exhibition near the entrance provides helpful explanatory information.

The tombs' great domes are mounted on cubical bases, many of which have beautiful colonnades and delicate lime stucco ornamentation. You could easily spend half a day taking photos and wandering in and out of the mausoleums. Among the finest is that of Mohammed Quli, the founder of Hyderabad, standing 42m tall on a platform near the edge of the complex, with views back towards Golconda.

The tombs are an easy walk from Golconda, or about ₹30 by autorickshaw. Infrequent buses 80S and 142K also link the two places.

Paigah Tombs　　　　　　　HISTORIC SITE
(Santoshnagar; ☉9.30am-5pm) FREE The aristocratic Paigah family, purportedly descendents of the second Caliph of Islam, were fierce loyalists of the nizams, serving as statespeople, philanthropists and generals under and alongside them. The Paigahs' necropolis, in a quiet neighbourhood 4km southeast of Charminar, is a small compound of exquisite mausoleums made of marble and lime stucco. It's signposted down a small lane opposite Owaisi Hospital on the Inner Ring Rd.

The complex contains 27 carved-marble tombs in enclosures with delicately carved walls and pillars, stunning geometrically patterned filigree screens and, overhead, tall, graceful turrets. At the western end a handsome mosque is reflected in its large ablutions pool.

Moula Ali Dargah　　　MUSLIM SACRED SITE
Out on the city's northeastern fringes, the dramatic rock mound of Moula Ali hill is a wonderful change of pace, with distant views, cool breezes and at the top, up 500 steps, a dargah (shrine to a Sufi saint) containing what's believed to be a handprint of Ali, the son-in-law of the Prophet Mohammed. The dargah's reputed healing properties make it a pilgrimage site for the sick.

Secunderabad

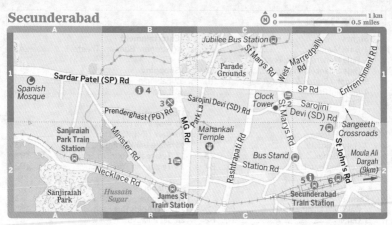

Secunderabad

Sleeping
1 Raj Classic Inn B2
2 YMCA International Guest
  House C1

Eating
3 Paradise B1

Information
4 Telangana Tourism B1
5 Telangana Tourism sec D2

Transport
6 Rathifile Bus Stand D2
7 Secunderabad Bus Stop
  (Pushpak) D2
  Secunderabad Junction
  Bus Stop .... (see 5)
  Secunderabad Reservation
  Complex .... (see 6)

Visitors are normally allowed inside the dargah, which is covered in thousands of tiny mirrors, only during the three-day Moula Ali *urs* festival during Muharram, but you can admire them it outside at other times.

Moula Ali hill is 9km northeast of Secunderabad – around ₹110 one-way by autorickshaw, or take bus 16A or 16C from Rathifile bus stand to ECIL bus stand, and an autorickshaw 2km from there.

Buddha Statue & Hussain Sagar MONUMENT
(Map p232; boats adult/child ₹55/35) Set picturesquely on a plinth in the Hussain Sagar, a lake created by the Qutb Shahs, is one of the world's largest free-standing stone Buddha statues (18m tall). It's an especially magnificent sight when illuminated at night.

Frequent boats make the 30-minute return trip to the statue from both **Eat Street** (Map p239; ◔launches 3-8pm) and popular **Lumbini Park** (Map p232; admission ₹10; ◔9am-9pm). The Tankbund Rd promenade, on the eastern shore of Hussain Sagar, has great views of the statue.

Tours

Detours
CULTURE, FOOD
(☑9000850505; www.detoursindia.com; per person 3hr walk ₹2500, half-/full day tour incl transport & admissions from ₹3500/5500) Fascinating and entertaining individual and small-group tours led by the enthusiastic, knowledgeable Jonty Rajagopalan and her small team. Options cover off-the-beaten-track corners of Hyderabad and original angles on the classic sights, plus markets, food (with cooking lessons and eating included), wedding culture, religion and crafts.

Telangana Tourism
SIGHTSEEING
(☑1800-42546464; www.telanganatourism.gov. in) On weekends Telangana Tourism does an afternoon-and-evening tour to Chowmahalla Palace, Falaknuma Palace and the Golconda sound-and-light show for ₹3100/2000 with/without high tea at Falaknuma. It also offers daily bus tours of city sights (from ₹350 plus admission tickets) and Ramoji Film City (₹1250/1100 AC/non-AC), evening Golconda sound-and-light trips, and out-of-town trips. Book at any Telangana Tourism office (p241).

Heritage Walks
WALKING TOUR

(Map p236; ☑9849728841; www.aptdc.in/her-itage_walks; per person ₹50; ⊙7.30-9am Sun) These Sunday-morning walks from the Charminar were designed and are some-times led by architect Madhu Vottery, whose *Guide to Heritage of Hyderabad* is part of a movement to foster Hyderabad's rich archi-tectural heritage.

✦ Festivals & Events

Sankranti
HINDU

(regionwide; ⊙ Jan) Hyderabad's skies fill with kites during this important Telugu harvest festival.

Muharram
MUSLIM

(⊙Sep/Oct) Muharram is the first month of the Islamic year and commemorates the martyrdom of Mohammed's grandson Hussain with mass mourning and all-night sermons. Black-clad Shiite throngs gather at Badshahi Ashurkhana, and a massive Old City procession on the 10th day draws crowds from around the region.

🛏 Sleeping

The inner-city Abids area is convenient for Nampally station and the Old City. For more space and greenery head to middle-class Banjara Hills, about 4km northwest of Abids. At top-end hotels good discounts are often available from the rack rates quoted here.

Golden Glory Guesthouse
GUESTHOUSE $

(Map p239; ☑040-23554765; www.goldenglory-guesthouse.com; off Rd No 3, Banjara Hills; s/d incl breakfast ₹900/1240, with AC ₹1240/1690; ❊🛜) This well-run place has a nice location on a leafy residential street in Banjara Hills. The 22 rooms are modest, but clean and homey, and some have balconies. There's free wi-fi

throughout, and several moderately priced eateries are nearby.

Hotel Rajmata
HOTEL $

(Map p232; ☑040-66665555; royalrajmata@gmail.com; Public Gardens Rd; s/d ₹900/1020, AC ₹2030/2250; ❊🛜) The Rajmata, popular with families, is only 250m from Nampally station, but set back from the busy main road, which keeps things quiet. Standard quarters are aged but roomy; air-con rooms are overpriced but fresh.

Hotel Suhail
HOTEL $

(Map p232; ☑040-24610299; www.hotelsuhail.in; Troop Bazar; s/d/tr from ₹600/800/1100, air-con ₹1100/1365/1600; ❊@🛜) Better than most comparable places in Abids, the Suhail has friendly staff and large, quiet rooms with balconies and hot water. It's tucked away on a lane off Bank St.

YMCA International Guest House
HOSTEL $

(Map p234; ☑040-27801190; secunderabadymca@yahoo.co.in; St Mary's Rd, Secunderabad; dm ₹125, s/d ₹500/600, without bathroom ₹350/450, r with AC ₹950; ❊) This friendly hostel in a quiet spot in Secunderabad has basic rooms, some with balconies. The sheets are cleaner than the walls, and the shared bathrooms are fine.

Taj Mahal Hotel
HOTEL $$

(Map p232; ☑040-24758250; www.hoteltajma-halindia.com; Abids Rd; incl breakfast s ₹1690-3150, d ₹2420-3150; ❊🛜) The original 1924 building houses the reception and a few bedrooms ('heritage' rooms have some character, others are plain); the majority of rooms are in a modern block at the side and reasonably attractive in simple contem-porary greys and reds. It adds up to good value, with helpful reception, free wi-fi and air-con in all rooms.

KITSCHABAD

Along with Hyderabad's world-class sights are some attractions that err on the quirky side.

Ramoji Film City (www.ramojifilmcity.com; adult/child from ₹800/700; ⊙8.30am-10pm) The Telangana/Andhra Pradesh film industry, 'Tollywood', is massive, and so is the 6.7-sq-km Film City, where films and TV shows in Telugu, Tamil and Hindi, among others, are made. The day-visit ticket includes a bus tour, funfair rides and shows. Take bus 206 or 209 from Koti Women's College (1½ hours, 30km) or a Telangana Tourism (p234) tour.

Sudha Cars Museum (www.sudhacars.com; Bahadurpura; Indian/foreigner ₹50/200, camera ₹50; ⊙9.30am-6.30pm) The eccentric creations of auto-enthusiast K Sudhakar include cars in the shape of a cricket bat, hamburger and snooker table, among other wacky designs. And they all work. The museum is 3km west of Charminar.

Charminar

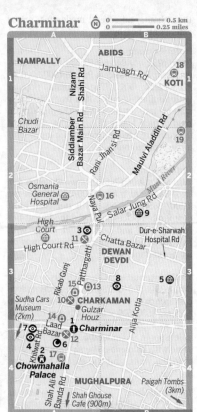

painstakingly mending such nizam-esque indulgences as embossed-leather wallpaper and 24-carat-gold ceiling trim. The rooms are stunning, and it's astoundingly opulent.

Non-guests can come for lunch/dinner (from ₹2420/3025) or 'high tea' (₹2240), served from 3.30pm to 5pm on the Jade Room terrace. Guests (including those just there to eat) get a free palace tour at 5pm. Book meals two days ahead, or you won't get past the outer gate of the 1.2km driveway.

The Taj group also runs three of Hyderabad's other best hotels, in Banjara Hills: the opulent **Taj Krishna** (Map p239; ☏040-66662323; www.tajhotels.com; Rd No 1; s/d from ₹44,970; ❇@⊙☀), stylish **Taj Deccan** (Map p239; ☏040-66669999; www.tajhotels.com; Rd No 1; s/d from ₹12,930/14,060; ❇@⊙☀) and lakeside **Taj Banjara** (Map p239; ☏040-66669999; www.tajhotels.com; Rd No 1; s/d from ₹9560/10,680; ❇@⊙☀).

Hotel Harsha
HOTEL $$

(Map p232; ☏040-23201188; www.hotelharsha.net; Public Gardens Rd; s/d incl breakfast from ₹2020/2240; ❇❄⊙) Rooms don't have tons of character and can be noisy but they're big, clean, comfy and in good shape. Nampally station is close, check-out is 24 hours and staff are all smiles. One of the city's best deals. Wi-fi is ₹110 per hour.

Raj Classic Inn
HOTEL $$

(Map p234; ☏040-27815291; rajclassicinn@gmail.com; 50 MG Rd, Secunderabad; s/d incl breakfast from ₹1580/1920; ❇⊙) Clean, spacious rooms a short ride from Secunderabad.

★ Taj Falaknuma Palace
HERITAGE HOTEL $$$

(☏040-66298585; www.tajhotels.com; Engine Bowli, Falaknuma; s/d from ₹41,600/43,290; ❇@⊙) The Taj group took more than a decade to restore the former residence of the sixth nizam, an 1884 neoclassical palace on a panoramic hilltop south of the city,

Fortune Park Vallabha
HOTEL $$$

(Map p239; ☏040-39884444; www.fortunehotels.in; Rd No 12, Banjara Hills; s/d incl breakfast from ₹5060/6190; ❇@⊙) Fortune Park provides large, comfy, contemporary rooms with stained-glass panels, tea/coffee makers and a good array of toiletries, plus a terrific breakfast buffet and free morning yoga sessions. It's a pleasure to stay in, except for the hard-to-fathom wi-fi charging system!

Royalton Hotel
HOTEL $$$

(Map p232; ☑040-67122000; www.royaltonhotel. in; Fateh Sultan Lane, Abids; s/d incl breakfast from ₹5060/5650; ❄️🛜) In a relatively quiet part of Abids, Royalton's gargantuan black lobby chandelier and mirrored lifts give off a slight Manhattan vibe. Rooms have tasteful textiles, glass showers and tea/coffee makers. The hotel is vegetarian, and alcohol-free.

Marigold
HOTEL $$$

(Map p239; ☑040-67363636; www.marigoldhotels. com; Ameerpet Rd, Greenlands; s/d incl breakfast from ₹6750/7870; ❄️@🛜🏊) The Marigold is as practical as it is stylish. Rooms are smart but not try-hard, with golds, neutrals and fresh flowers, while the lobby has vanishing-edge fountains and artful chandeliers. The rooftop pool is a great feature.

The **GreenPark** (Map p239; ☑040-66515151; www.hotelgreenpark.com; Ameerpet Rd, Greenlands; s/d incl breakfast from ₹5630/6750; ❄️@🛜), under the same ownership next door, is a notch lower in style and comfort but still a worthy alternative.

✕ Eating

In the early evenings, look out for *mirchi bhajji* (chilli fritters), served at street stalls with tea. The Hyderabadi style is famous: chillis are stripped of their seeds, stuffed with tamarind, sesame and spices, dipped in chickpea batter and fried.

Per local usage, we use the term 'meal' instead of 'thali'.

✕ Old City & Abids Area

Govind Dosa
STREET FOOD $

(Map p236; Charkaman; snacks ₹30-60; ⊗6am-noon) Probably the city's most famous breakfast cook, cheery Govind's street-corner stand is permanently surrounded by happy Hyderabadis savouring his delicious dosas and *idlis* (spongy fermented rice cakes), including unusual dosas with *upma* (a seasoned semolina porridge) and *tawa idlis* topped with chilli powder and spices.

Kamat Andhra Meals
ANDHRA $

(Map p232; Troop Bazar; meals ₹90; ⊗11am-4pm & 7-11pm) This small, simple restaurant does authentic and delicious veg Andhra meals on banana leaves, topped up till your tongue falls off from the heat. In the same compound, the Maharashtrian **Kamat Jowar Bhakri** (Map p232; meals ₹130-180; ⊗noon-4pm & 7-11pm) and the South and North Indian **Kamat Restaurant** (Map p232; meals & mains ₹75-180; ⊗7am-10.30pm) are also good. No relation to Kamat Hotel.

Nimrah
CAFE $

(Map p236; Charminar; baked goods ₹2-10; ⊗5.30am-11pm) Irani cafes – old-fashioned teahouses founded by 19th-century Persian immigrants and serving super-thick, super-sweet Irani chai – are an endangered breed in India these days, but Hyderabad still has a goodly number. Nimrah, almost underneath the Charminar's arches, has a particularly tasty range of Irani baked goods to accompany your chai pick-me-up.

The classic dunk is Osmania biscuits (melt-in-the-mouth shortbreads). Nimrah also offers *dil khush* ('happy heart') and *dil pasand,* types of pie/pastry with sweet coconut-y fillings, and more.

HYDERABAD CUISINE

Hyderabad has a food culture all its own and Hyderabadis take great pride and pleasure in it. It was the Mughals who brought the tasty biryanis, skewer kebabs and *haleem* (a thick Ramadan soup of pounded, spiced wheat with goat, chicken or beef, and lentils). Mutton (goat or lamb) is the classic biryani base, though chicken, egg and vegetable biryanis are plentiful too. Biryanis come in vast quantity and one serve may satisfy two people.

If you're in Hyderabad during Ramadan (known locally as Ramzan), look out for the clay ovens called *bhattis*. You'll probably hear them before you see them. Men gather around, taking turns to vigorously pound *haleem* inside purpose-built structures. Come nightfall, the serious business of eating begins. The taste is worth the wait.

Andhra cuisine, found in Telangana as well as Andhra Pradesh, is more curry- and pilau-based, often with coconut and/or cashew flavours, and famous across India for its delicious spicy hotness. Vegetarians are well catered for, but you'll find plenty of fish, seafood and meat dishes too.

★Hotel Shadab HYDERABADI $$
(Map p236; High Court Rd, Charminar; mains ₹140-300; ⊗noon-11.30pm) This hopping restaurant, packed with Old City families and good vibes, is the capital of biryani, kebabs and mutton and, during Ramadan, *haleem* (thick soup of spiced wheat with goat, chicken or beef). Head upstairs to the air-con room.

★Shah Ghouse Cafe HYDERABADI $$
(Shah Ali Banda Rd; mains ₹100-190; ⊗noon-2am) During Ramadan, Hyderabadis line up for Shah Ghouse's famous *haleem*, and at any time of year the biryani is near-perfect. Don't expect ambience: just good, hard-working, traditional food, in a no-frills upstairs dining hall.

Dakshina Mandapa SOUTH INDIAN $$
(Map p232; Taj Mahal Hotel, Abids Rd; mains & meals ₹160-195; ⊗7am-10.30pm) A beloved spot for South Indian vegetarian meals. You may have to wait for a lunch table, but order the South Indian thali and you'll be brought heap after heap of rice and refills of exquisite, burn-your-tongue-off veg dishes. The air-con room upstairs does a very good ₹300 lunch buffet (noon to 3pm).

Kamat Hotel SOUTH INDIAN $$
(Map p232; Secretariat Rd, Saifabad; meals ₹95-170, mains ₹150-200; ⊗8am-10pm) Each Kamat is slightly different, but they're all good for South Indian fare. There's another **branch** (Map p232; Nampally Station Rd; meals & mains ₹70-165; ⊗7am-10pm) near Nampally station.

Gufaa NORTH INDIAN $$$
(Map p232; Ohri's Cuisine Court, Bashirbagh Rd; mains ₹250-600; ⊗11am-3.30pm & 7-11.30pm) Gufaa ('Cave') has faux-rock walls, zebra-striped furniture and a Bollywood oldies soundtrack. And it serves Peshawari food (good veg and nonveg kebabs and curries). Somehow it all works, and even the dhal here is special. A good drinks menu too.

✗ Banjara Hills & Jubilee Hills

★Southern Spice SOUTH INDIAN $$
(Map p239; Rd No 3; mains ₹170-500, thalis ₹210-320; ⊗noon-3.30pm & 7-10.30pm) Southern Spice does a fine Andhra meal as well as specialities from all over the south, in several cosy, warm-toned rooms. It's a good place to sample typical Andhra dishes such as *natu kodi iguru* ('country chicken') or *chapa pulusu*, a tasty, spicy fish dish.

Chutneys SOUTH INDIAN $$
(Map p239; Shilpa Arcade, Rd No 3; mains & meals ₹240-300; ⊗7am-11pm) Chutneys is famous for its South Indian meals and all-day dosas, *idlis* and *uttapams*. Its dishes are low on chilli, so you can get the full 'Andhra meals' experience without the pain. It's a bustling place with teams of purple-shirted waiters.

★SO ASIAN, MEDITERRANEAN $$$
(☑040-23558004; www.notjustso.com; Aryan's, Rd No 92, near Apollo Hospital, Jubilee Hills; mains ₹375-625; ⊗noon-11pm; 🐾) On a quiet Jubilee Hills rooftop, with candles, loungy playlists and sugarcane and banana plants, SO is one of the most atmospheric eating spots in town. And the pan-Asian and Mediterranean dishes are exquisite. Downstairs are the highly popular **Little Italy** (☑23558001; www.littleitaly.in; mains ₹350-600; ⊗noon-3pm & 7-11pm) and MOB (p240). It's on a side-road off the south side of KBR National Park, 4km west of Banjara Hills' Rd No 1.

Fusion 9 CONTINENTAL $$$
(Map p239; ☑040-65577722; www.fusion9.in; Rd No 1; mains ₹550-975; ⊗12.30-3.30pm & 7-11.30pm) Soft lighting and cosy decor set off oven-roasted seabass or Moroccan veg tagine with lemon couscous. One of the best international menus in town. Downstairs, **Deli 9** (Map p239; snacks ₹40-230; ⊗9.30am-10.30pm; 🐾) has quiches, cakes, crepes and free wi-fi.

Firdaus INDIAN $$$
(Map p239; ☑040-66662323; Taj Krishna, Rd No 1; mains ₹500-1100; ⊗12.30-3pm & 7.30-11.45pm) For a refined evening of top-class Hyderabadi and other dishes to the strains of live *ghazals* (classical Urdu love songs, accompanied by harmonium and tabla), book a table at elegant Firdaus. It even serves *haleem* outside Ramadan.

Barbeque Nation INDIAN $$$
(Map p239; ☑040-64566692; www.barbeque-nation.com; ANR Centre, Rd No 1; veg/nonveg lunch ₹620/745, dinner ₹940/1060; ⊗noon-3.30pm & 6.30-10.30pm) All-you-can-eat kebabs, curries, salads and desserts in unpretentious surrounds, with many veg and nonveg options. A great-value place to come when you're hungry! Prices go up ₹150 for Sunday lunch, and down ₹240 for Monday and Tuesday dinner and before 7pm any night.

Banjara Hills

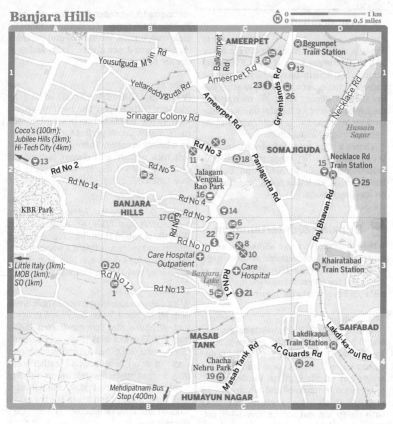

Banjara Hills

✕ Secunderabad

Paradise
HYDERABADI $$

(Persis; Map p234; www.paradisefoodcourt.com; cnr SD & MG Rds; biryani ₹220-285; ⊙11.30am-11pm) Paradise is synonymous with biryani in these parts. The main, Secunderabad location has five different dining areas. No need to pay the 20% surcharge for the air-con rooms: the 1st-floor 'roof garden' is bright, airy and attractive, with whirring fans.

There's a large, modern **branch** (Map p232; ☑040-66661188; NTR Gardens; mains ₹240-500; ⊙11am-11pm) closer to Abids and Banjara Hills, though we found the biryani there a bit less flavoursome.

🍷 Drinking & Entertainment

Where nightspots charge admission, a percentage is usually redeemable against drinks or food. The *Deccan Chronicle*, *Times of India* and the entertaining www.fullhyderabad.com have 'what's on' information.

★ Lamakaan
CAFE, THEATRE

(Map p239; ☑9642731329; www.lamakaan.com; next to JVR Park, Banjara Hills; ⊙10am-10.30pm Tue-Sun; 🛜) This non-commercial 'inclusive cultural space' is an open centre where artists put on plays, films, music, exhibitions, organic markets and whatever else inspires. It also has a great Irani cafe, with cheap tea and snacks, free wi-fi, artsy types collaborating on the leafy patio and a bulletin board of Hyderabad's most interesting possibilities.

★ MOB
BAR

(www.facebook.com/itismob; Aryan's, Rd No 92, near Apollo Hospital, Jubilee Hills; ⊙noon-11.30pm; 🛜) A refreshingly mixed-gender, mixed-age crowd flocks to this pub-like space for the simple pleasures of conversation, terrific Belgian beer (tap or bottled) and tasty finger food. You can dine at SO (p238) or Little Italy (p238) in the same building. Packed on Friday and Saturday evenings. It's on a side-road off the south side of KBR National Park, 4km west of Banjara Hills' Rd No 1.

Kismet
CLUB

(Map p239; ☑040-23456789; www.theparkhotels.com/hyderabad; The Park, Somajiguda; admission per couple ₹500-2000; ⊙9pm-midnight or later Wed-Sun) *The* happening nightclub, glamorous Kismet is all curves, with loungey booth seating and a big dance floor. Men won't get past the three ranks of bouncers without female companions. Wednesday and Saturday are electronic dance nights; Friday and Sunday are Bollywood.

Coco's
BAR

(Map p239; ☑040-23540600; 217 Rd No 2, Jubilee Hills; ⊙11am-11pm) The rooftop setting, with rustic bamboo couches and thatch roofs, makes Coco's perfect for a cold drink on a balmy evening. There's live blues and soft rock nightly, and decent Indian and Continental food. Enter down a lane beside Café Coffee Day.

Hard Rock Cafe
BAR

(Map p239; GVK One Mall, Rd No 1, Banjara Hills; beer/cocktails from ₹210/370; ⊙noon-11.30pm) With the standard Hard Rock recipe of stars' guitars and pub grub, this is a warm and relaxed place for a drink and bite. There's usually a live band at 9pm Thursdays.

10 Downing Street
BAR

(Map p239; www.10downingstreetindia.com; Greenlands Rd, My Home Tycoon department store rear yard; admission after 9pm men/women ₹1200/free; ⊙11.30am-midnight) Lively and perennially popular, 10DS has 'typical English pub' decor of wood panelling and leather sofas, plus a small space for dancing to different music nightly – retro Friday, club Saturday, Bollywood Sunday, and so on. The bar is well stocked and does satisfactory pub and Continental food.

Ravindra Bharathi Theatre
THEATRE

(Map p232; ☑040-23233672; www.ravindrabharathi.org; Ladki-ka-pul Rd, Saifabad) Regular music, dance and drama performances.

🛍 Shopping

Charminar (p241) is the most exciting place to shop: you'll find exquisite pearls, slippers, gold and fabrics alongside billions of bangles.

Malkha
CLOTHING

(Map p239; www.malkha.in; Khadi Bhavan, Masab Tank Rd, opposite NMDC bus stop, Humayun Nagar; ⊙10am-7pm Mon-Sat) ✎ Unlike industrial cotton, Malkha cloth is made near the cotton fields, by hand and with natural dyes, reducing strain to the cotton and the environment and putting primary producers in control. The result is gorgeous; pick up shawls or fabric at reasonable prices.

Himalaya Book World BOOKS
(Map p239; Panjagutta Circle, Banjara Hills;
⊕10.30am-10pm) A fine selection of English-
language fiction and nonfiction by Indian
and international authors.

Fabindia CLOTHING
(Map p239; www.fabindia.com; Rd No 9, Banjara
Hills; ⊕11am-8.30pm Tue-Sun) 🥭 Lovely wom-
en's and some men's clothes in artisanal fabrics with contemporary prints and colours,
at fair prices. Has a **branch** (Map p232; Fateh
Maidan; ⊕10.30am-8.30pm) in Bashirbagh.

Lepakshi HANDICRAFTS
(Map p232; www.lepakshihandicrafts.gov.in; Abids
Rd, Gunfoundry; ⊕10am-8pm Mon-Sat) Big selec-
tion of Telangana, Andhra and other crafts.

Suvasa CLOTHING
(Map p239; www.suvasa.in; Rd No 12, Banjara Hills;
⊕11am-7.30pm) Suvasa's block-printed kurtas
(long shirts with a short or no collar), baggy
salwar pants and dupattas (scarves) are a
step up in cut and prints from most mainstream boutiques. A Suvasa kurta plus some
churidhars (leggings) equals your new favourite travel outfit.

Hyderabad Perfumers PERFUME
(Map p236; Patthargatti; ⊕10am-8.30pm Mon-
Sat) This fourth-generation family business
can whip something up for you on the spot.

ℹ️ Information

INTERNET ACCESS
Aloe Vera Home (Map p232; Chirag Ali Lane;
per hour ₹20; ⊕6am-10pm) Small room in a
side lane.

MEDICAL SERVICES
Care Hospital (☑emergency 105711; www.care-
hospitals.com) A reputable private hospital with
several branches, including 24-hour pharmacies, in Banjara Hills (Map p239; ☑30418888;
Rd No 1); Banjara Hills Outpatient (Map p239;
☑39310444; 4th Lane, Rd No 10); Nampally
(Map p232; ☑30417777; Mukarramjahi Rd).

MONEY
Citibank ATM (Map p239; Prashanthi Mansion,
Rd No 1, Banjara Hills) Citibank ATMs allow
withdrawals up to ₹40,000, saving on bank
charges. Also at City Center Mall (Map p239;
Rd No 1, Banjara Hills) and GVK One Mall (Map
p239; Rd No 1, Banjara Hills).
State Bank of India (Map p232; HACA Bhavan,
Saifabad; ⊕10.30am-4pm Mon-Fri) Currency
exchange.

POST
General Post Office (Map p232; Abids Circle;
⊕8am-7.30pm Mon-Sat, 10am-1pm Sun)

TOURIST INFORMATION
Indiatourism (Map p239; ☑040-23409199;
www.incredibleindia.org; Tourism Plaza, Green-
lands Rd; ⊕9.30am-6pm Mon-Fri, 9.30am-1pm
Sat) Very helpful, with information on Hydera-
bad, Telangana and beyond.
Telangana Tourism (☑1800 42546464; www.
telanganatourism.gov.in) Tourist informa-
tion and bookings for state-government-run
tours and hotels in Telangana. Branches at
Bashirbagh (Map p232; ☑66745986; Shakar
Bhavan; ⊕6.30am-8.30pm), Tankbund Rd
(Map p232; ☑65581555; ⊕6.30am-8.30pm),
Greenlands Rd (Map p239; ☑040-23414334;
Tourism Plaza; ⊕7am-8pm), Hyderabad airport
(☑040-24253215), Secunderabad (Map p234;

CHARMINAR MARKETS

Hyderabadis and visitors of every stripe flock to the Charminar area's labyrinthine lanes
to browse, buy and wander. Patthargatti, the broad avenue leading in from the Musi
River, is lined with shops selling clothes (especially wedding outfits), perfumes and Hyderabad's famous pearls. **Laad Bazar** (Map p236), running west from the Charminar, is
famed for its sparkling bangle shops: lac bangles, made from a resinous insect secretion
and encrusted with colourful beads or stones, are a Hyderabad speciality. In Laad Bazar
you'll also find perfumers, wedding goods and fabrics.

Laad Bazar opens into **Mehboob Chowk** (Map p236), a square with a 19th-century
clock tower and mosque, shops selling antiquarian books and antiques, a livestock market
on its south side, and a market in exotic birds, **Chiddi Bazar** (Map p236), just southwest.

A short distance north, the **Patel Market** (Map p236), selling cloth fabrics, cranks into
action from around 11am in the back lanes between Patthargatti and Rikab Gunj. Further
north again and on the other side of Patthargatti, the wholesale vegetable market **Mir
Alam Mandi** (Map p236) trades in all kinds of fresh stuff from 6.30am to 6.30pm daily.

☑ 040-27893100; Yatri Nivas Hotel, SP Rd; ⊙ 6.30am-8.30pm) and Secunderabad station (Map p234; ☑ 27801614; ⊙ 10am-8pm). The Andhra Pradesh Tourism Development Corporation (APTDC; ☑ 1800 42545454; www.aptdc. gov.in), with the same functions for Andhra Pradesh state, shares the same offices, for the moment at least.

ℹ Getting There & Away

AIR

Hyderabad's massive, modern, efficient **Rajiv Gandhi International Airport** (☑ 040-66546370; www.hyderabad.aero; Shamshabad) is 25km southwest of the city center. It has direct daily flights to 19 Indian cities (on Air Costa, Air India, IndiGo, Jet Airways or Spice-Jet), Chicago, London and several Southeast Asian and Gulf destinations. Only two domestic airlines have city airline offices:

Air India (Map p232; ☑ 040-23389711; HACA Bhavan, Saifabad; ⊙ 9.45am-1.15pm & 2-5pm Mon-Sat)

Jet Airways (Map p232; ☑ 040-39893333; Summit Apts, Hill Fort Rd)

BUS

The main terminal is the 74-platform **Mahatma Gandhi bus station** (MGBS, Imlibun Bus Station; Map p236; ☑ 040-24614406; ⊙ advance booking offices 8am-10.30pm) near Abids. Air-con services by the TSRTC (www.tsrtcbus. in) are quite good; for Karnataka, go with KSRTC near platform 30. Many long-distance services depart in the evening. When booking ahead, women should request seats up front as these are reserved for women.

Secunderabad's **Jubilee bus station** (Map p234; ☑ 040-27802203) is smaller; frequent city buses run here from St Mary's Rd near

Secunderabad station. Useful routes from here include:

Bengaluru (ordinary/Volvo AC/sleeper ₹610/1000/1600, 10 to 12 hours, seven daily)

Vijayawada (non-AC/AC ₹310/450, five to seven hours, 11 daily)

Mumbai ('express' ₹600, 14 hours, 2pm)

TRAIN

Secunderabad, **Nampally** (officially called Hyderabad Deccan), and **Kacheguda** are Hyderabad's three major train stations. Most through trains stop at Kacheguda.

The reservation complexes at **Nampally** (Map p232; ☑ 040-27829999; ⊙ 8am-8pm Mon-Sat, 8am-2pm Sun) and **Secunderabad** (Rathifile; Map p234; St John's Rd; ⊙ 8am-8pm Mon-Sat, 8am-2pm Sun), both in separate buildings away from the stations, have foreign-tourist-quota counters (bring passport and visa photocopies, along with originals). For inquiries and PNR status, phone ☑ 139.

There are around 20 trains a day each to Warangal (sleeper/3AC/2AC ₹170/535/735, 2½ hours) and Vijayawada (₹190/495/720, six hours), mostly from Secunderabad.

ℹ Getting Around

TO/FROM THE AIRPORT

Bus

The TSRTC's Pushpak air-conditioned bus service runs between about 4am and 11pm to and from various stops in the city, including **AC Guards** (Map p239; ₹200, two or three buses hourly) and **Secretariat** (Map p232; ₹200, about hourly), both about 1.5km from Abids, **Paryatak Bhavan** (Map p239) on Greenlands Rd (₹250, about hourly), and **Secunderabad** (Map p234; ₹250, twice hourly). The trip takes about one hour. Contact **TSRTC** (Telangana State

BUSES FROM MAHATMA GANDHI BUS STATION

DESTINATION	FARE (₹)	DURATION (HR)	FREQUENCY
Bengaluru	720-1010	9-11	21 buses 5-10.30pm
Bidar	150	4½	hourly 5am-10pm
Chennai	700-1200	12-14	4 buses 6.30-9pm
Hospet	355-850	8-11	9 daily
Mumbai	1100 (AC)	14	6.30pm Thu & Sun
Mysore	1130-1210	12 14	4 buses 5-7.45pm
Tirupati	700-1000	12	half-hourly 1.30-10pm
Vijayawada	350-480	6	half-hourly
Visakhapatnam	730-1100	13	hourly 2-10pm
Warangal	155-195	4	half-hourly

MAJOR TRAINS FROM HYDERABAD & SECUNDERABAD

DESTINATION	TRAIN NO & NAME	FARE (₹)	DURATION (HR)	DEPARTURE TIME & STATION
Bengaluru	22692 or 22694 Rajdhani	1815/1330 (B)	12	6.50pm Secunderabad
	12785 Bangalore Exp	370/970/1370 (A)	11½	7.05pm Kacheguda
Chennai	12604 Hyderabad–Chennai Exp	405/1055/1500 (A)	13	5.20pm Nampally
	12760 Charminar Exp	425/1115/1590 (A)	14	6.30pm Nampally
Delhi	12723 AP Exp	670/1745/2545 (A)	27	6.25am Nampally
	22691 or 22693 Rajdhani	2360/3245 (B)	22	7.50am Secunderabad
Kolkata	12704 Falaknuma Exp	630/1650/2395 (A)	26	4pm Secunderabad
Mumbai	12702 Hussainsagar Exp	425/1115/1590 (A)	14½	2.45pm Nampally
	17032 Mumbai Exp	395/1070/1545 (A)	16½	8.40pm Nampally
Tirupati	12734 Narayanadri Exp	385/1005/1430 (A)	12	6.05pm Secunderabad
	12797 Venkatadri Exp	375/980/1385 (A)	11½	8.05pm Kacheguda
Visakhapatnam	12728 Godavari Exp	405/1055/1500 (A)	12½	5.15pm Nampally

Fares: (A) sleeper/3AC/2AC, (B) 3AC/2AC

Road Transport Corporation; ☑1800 2004599; http://tsrtcbus.in) or check http://hyderabad.aero for timings.

Taxi

The prepaid taxi booth is on the lowest level of the terminal; ignore touts on the way down. Fares to Abids or Banjara Hills are ₹600 to ₹700. **Meru Cabs** (☑040-44224422) and **Sky Cabs** (☑040-49494949) 'radio taxis', with counters in the arrivals area, charge ₹21 per kilometre (₹26 at night), which works out much the same. Meru and Sky also provide reliable service for trips within the city.

AUTORICKSHAW

Official fares are ₹20 for the first 1.6km, then ₹11 for each additional kilometre, with a 50% surcharge between 11pm and 5am. But most drivers won't use their meters so you must negotiate and will probably end up paying ₹20 to ₹25 per kilometre (more after dark).

BUS

City buses (₹6 to ₹12 for most rides) run everywhere but you'll usually need local help in finding the right stop and right bus; www.hyderabadbusroutes.com gives routes with some stops mapped, but can be inaccurate.

CAR

Arrange car hire through your hotel. The going rate for a small AC car such as an Indica, with a driver, is ₹1000 to ₹1200 per day for city sightseeing (eight hours/80km maximum), and ₹2800 to ₹3200 per day for out-of-town trips (up to 300km).

METRO RAIL

Hyderabad Metro Rail (www.hmr.gov.in), a 72km rapid transit network being phased into operation between 2015 and 2017, will make getting around the city a whole lot easier! Trains will run on elevated tracks above Hyderabad's streets, with 66 stations on three lines.

TELANGANA & ANDHRA PRADESH HYDERABAD

SELECTED HYDERABAD CITY BUS ROUTES

65G, 66G	Charminar–Golconda Fort, via Afzalgunj, GPO Abids; both about hourly
49M	Secunderabad Junction–Mehdipatnam via Rd No 1 (Banjara Hills); frequent
8A	Charminar–Secunderabad Junction via Afzalgunj, GPO Abids; frequent
40, 86	Secunderabad Junction–Koti Bus Stop; both frequent
127K	Koti Bus Stop–Jubilee Hills via GPO Abids, Public Gardens, Rd Nos 1 & 12 (Banjara Hills); frequent

TRAIN

MMTS suburban trains (www.mmtstraintimings.in; fares ₹5-11) are convenient for the three main stations, but infrequent (every 30 to 45 minutes). There are two routes: Hyderabad (Nampally) to Lingampalli (northwest of Banjara Hills) stops at Necklace Rd, Begumpet and Hi-Tech City; Falaknuma (south of Old City) to Lingampalli stops at Kacheguda and Secunderabad stations and joins the Hyderabad–Lingampalli line at Begumpet.

TELANGANA

The most interesting spots to visit in the newly created state of Telangana, outside its capital Hyderabad, lie in and around the state's second city, Warangal.

Bhongir

Most Hyderabad–Warangal buses and trains stop at Bhongir, 60km from Hyderabad. It's worth stopping to climb the fantastical-looking 12th-century Chalukyan **hill fort** (admission ₹3, camera ₹10; ⊙10am-5pm), sitting on what resembles a gargantuan stone egg right above the bus station. You can leave backpacks at the ticket office.

Warangal

☑ 0870 / POP 620,000

Warangal was the capital of the Kakatiya kingdom, which ruled most of present-day Telangana and Andhra Pradesh from the 12th to early 14th centuries. **Telangana Tourism** (☑ 0870-2571339; opposite Indian Oil, Nakkalgutta, Hanumakonda; ⊙10.30am-5pm Mon-Sat) is helpful.

⊙ Sights

Fort   FORT
Warangal's fort, on the southern edge of town, was a massive construction with three circles of walls (the outermost 7km around). Most of it is now either fields or buildings, but at the centre is a huge, reassembled Shaivite **Svayambhu Temple** (Indian/foreigner ₹5/100; ⊙9am-6pm), with handsome, large *torana* gateways at its cardinal points. An autorickshaw from Warangal station costs around ₹300 return.

The ticket also covers the Kush Mahal (Shitab Khan Mahal), a 16th-century royal hall 400m west. Almost opposite the Svayambhu entrance is a **park** (admission ₹10; ⊙7am-7pm) containing the high rock Ekashila Gutta, topped by another Kakatiya temple overlooking a small lake.

1000-Pillared Temple   HINDU TEMPLE
(⊙6am-6pm) Six kilometres northwest of Warangal station in the adjoining town of Hanumakonda (Hanamkonda), the 1000-Pillared Temple, constructed in 1163, is a fine example of Kakatiya architecture and sculpture, in a leafy setting. Unusually, the cross-shaped building has shrines to the sun god Surya (to the right as you enter), Vishnu (centre) and Shiva (left). Despite the name, it certainly does not have 1000 pillars. Behind rises Hanumakonda Hill, site of the original Kakatiya capital.

Other ancient temples in Hanumakonda include the lakeside Bhadrakali Temple, 2km southeast of the 1000-Pillared Temple, whose idol of the mother goddess Kali sits with a weapon in each of her eight hands, and the small Siddeshwara Temple on the south side of Hanumakonda Hill.

🛏 Sleeping & Eating

Vijaya Lodge   HOTEL $
(☑ 0870-2501222; Station Rd; s ₹260, d ₹450-700)
About 350m from Warangal's train and bus stations, the Vijaya is well organised, with helpful staff. Rooms are borderline dreary, with showers by bucket, but workable. The upper floors are better.

Hotel Ashoka   HOTEL $$
(☑ 0870-2578491; hotelashoka_wgl@yahoo.co.in; Main Rd, Hanumakonda; r ₹1580-2250; ✳@)
Straightforward, well-kept, air-con rooms at a busy, well-run hotel near the Hanumakonda bus stand and 1000-Pillared Temple. Also here are the good veg restaurant **Kanishka**

(meals ₹110; ☺ 6.30am-10.30pm) plus a nonveg restaurant, a pub and a bar-restaurant.

Hotel Landmark — HOTEL $$
(☑ 0870-2546333; Nakkalagutta; r ₹1800; ❇ 🛜) A decent alternative, 2km out of town along the Hyderabad road.

Sri Geetha Bhavan — ANDHRA $
(Market Rd, Hanumakonda; mains ₹80-95; ☺ 6am-11pm) Really good South Indian meals (₹80) in pleasant air-con surroundings.

❶ Getting There & Around

Buses to Hyderabad (₹130 to ₹195, four hours) leave about three times hourly from **Hanumakonda bus stand** (☑ 9959226056; New Bus Stand Rd) and hourly from **Warangal bus stand** (☑ 2565595; Station Rd), opposite the train station.

From Warangal several trains daily run to the Hyderabad (sleeper/3AC/2AC ₹170/535/735, three hours), Vijayawada (₹190/535/735, three hours) and Chennai (₹375/980/1385, 11½ hours).

Shared autorickshaws (₹15) ply fixed routes around Warangal and Hanumakonda.

Palampet

In lovely green countryside 65km northeast of Warangal, the stunning **Ramappa Temple** (camera ₹25; ☺ 6am-6pm) FREE, built in 1213, is the outstanding gem of Kakatiya architecture, covered in wonderfully detailed carvings of animals, lovers, wrestlers, musicians, dancers, deities and Hindu legends. Brackets on its external pillars support superb black-basalt carvings of mythical creatures and sinuous women twined with snakes. The large temple tank, **Ramappa Cheruvu**, 1km south, is popular with migrating birds.

The easiest way to get here is by taxi (around ₹1800 return from Warangal), but buses also run half-hourly from Hanumakonda to Mulugu (₹50, one hour), then a further 13km to Palampet (₹20).

ANDHRA PRADESH

The recently reduced state of Andhra Pradesh stretches 850km along the Bay of Bengal between Tamil Nadu and Odisha, and inland up into the picturesque Eastern Ghats. It's the proud standard-bearer of a long tradition of Telugu language and culture, and is one of India's wealthiest states.

Explorers will discover one of India's most visited temples (at Tirumala), some fascinating and remote ancient sites from the earliest days of South Indian Buddhism, and one of the nicest stretches of India's east coast, north of Visakhapatnam – and you'll be able to enjoy the spicily delicious Andhra cuisine everywhere. Andhra's tourism websites are www.aptourism.gov.in and www.aptdc.gov.in.

Vijayawada

☑ 0866 / POP 1.05 MILLION

Centrally located in the new Andhra Pradesh, the commercial and industrial city of Vijayawada, on the north bank of the Krishna River, is to be Andhra's new capital. The state government has ambitious plans to construct a showpiece capital complex encompassing 17 existing villages on the south side of the river, at a cost of over 1 trillion rupees (US$16 billion).

Vijayawada is a good base for visiting some fascinating old Buddhist sites in the lush and green surrounding area. The city is considered by many to be the heart of Andhra culture and language, and its 12th-century **Kanaka Durga Temple** (Durga Temple Ghat Rd, Indrakeeladri Hill) draws many pilgrims. The 1.3km-long Prakasam Barrage across the Krishna here feeds three irrigation canals which run through the city.

◎ Sights

★ **Undavalli Cave Temples** — HINDU TEMPLE
(Indian/foreigner ₹5/100; ☺ 9am-5pm) Just 6km southwest of downtown Vijayawada, on the south side of the Krishna River, this stunning four-storey cave temple was probably originally carved out of the hillside for Buddhist monks in the 2nd century AD, then converted to Hindu use in the 7th century. The shrines are now empty except those on the third level, one of which houses a huge reclining Vishnu. Three gnome-like stone Vasihnavite gurus or preachers gaze out over the rice paddies from the terrace. Bus 301 (₹20, 20 minutes) runs here every 20 minutes from Vijayawada bus station; autorickshaws ask ₹250 return.

🛏 Sleeping & Eating

Hotel Sripada — HOTEL $
(☑ 0866-6644222; hotelsripada@rediffmail.com; Gandhi Nagar; s ₹900-1460, d ₹1010-1690; ❇) One of the few cheaper hotels in Vijayawada

authorised to accept foreign guests, the Sripada has small but bright rooms in reasonable condition, a decent restaurant and helpful staff. Near the train station.

Hotel Southern Grand   HOTEL $$
(☎0866-6677777; www.hotelsoutherngrand.com; Papaiah St, Gandhi Nagar; incl breakfast s ₹1910-2360, d ₹2250-2700; ❇☎) Rates here are very reasonable for such neat, spotless and contemporary rooms. Just 600m from the train station, the hotel also has an excellent veg restaurant, Arya Bhavan (Hotel Southern Grand, Papaiah St, Gandhi Nagar; mains ₹120-165, thalis ₹105-160; ☺7am-11pm), a useful travel desk, Southern Travels (☎0870-6677777; Hotel Southern Grand, Papaiah St, Gandhi Nagar), and offers free airport and station transfers.

Gateway Hotel   HOTEL $$$
(☎0866-6644444; www.thegatewayhotels.com; MG Rd; s/d from ₹5060/5900; ❇☎☀) This classy Taj group hotel has six floors of well-equipped, contemporary rooms around its high atrium lobby, plus two stylish restaurants, a bar and Vijayawada's only hotel pool. Check the website for discounts. It's 3km southeast of the train station.

★Minerva Coffee Shop   INDIAN $$
(Museum Rd; mains ₹180-220, meals ₹140-220; ☺7am-11pm) Round the corner from the large Big Bazaar shop, this outpost of the excellent Minerva chain does great North and South Indian veg cuisine in bright, spotless surroundings, with good, friendly service. Meals (thalis) are only available from 11.30am to 3.30pm but top-notch dosas, idlis and uttapams (₹35 to ₹70) are served all day. There's another branch (MG Rd; meals ₹185-220; ☺7am-11pm) with similarly excellent food in airy surrounds on MG Rd.

ℹ Information

Department of Tourism (☎0866-2578880; train station; ☺10am-5pm)

ℹ Getting There & Around

The train and bus stations have prepaid auto-rickshaw stands.

BUS

Services from the large **Pandit Nehru Bus Station** (Arjuna St) include:

Chennai (non-AC/AC ₹450/750, eight to 10 hours, seven daily)

STATE OF GOOD KARMA

Lying at a nexus of major Indian land routes and sea routes across the Bay of Bengal, Andhra Pradesh played an important role in the early history of Buddhism. Andhra and Telangana have about 150 known Buddhist stupas, monasteries, caves and other sites. They speak of a time when Andhra Pradesh, or 'Andhradesa', was a hotbed of Buddhist activity, when Indian monks set off for Sri Lanka and Southeast Asia to spread the Buddha's teachings, and monks came from far and wide to learn from renowned Buddhist teachers.

Andhradesa's Buddhist culture lasted around 1500 years from the Buddha's own lifetime in the 6th century BC. The dharma really took off in the 3rd century BC under the Mauryan emperor Ashoka, who dispatched monks across his empire to teach and construct stupas enshrining relics of the Buddha. (Being near these was thought to help progress on the path to enlightenment.)

After Ashoka's death in 232 BC, succeeding rulers of central Andhra Pradesh, the Satavahanas and then the Ikshvakus, continued to support Buddhism. At their capital Amaravathi, the Satavahanas adorned Ashoka's stupa with elegant decoration. They built monasteries across the Krishna Valley and exported the dharma through their sophisticated maritime network. It was under Satavahana rule that Nagarjuna, considered the progenitor of Mahayana Buddhism, is believed to have lived, in the 2nd or 3rd centuries AD. The monk, equal parts logician, philosopher and meditator, wrote several ground-breaking works that shaped Buddhist thought.

Today, even in ruins, you can get a sense of how large some of the stupas were, how expansive the monastic complexes, and of how the monks lived, sleeping in caves and fetching rainwater from stone-cut cisterns. Many of the sites have stunning views across seascapes or countryside. The complexes at Nagarjunakonda (p247) and Amaravathi (p247) have good infrastructure and helpful museums on-site. For a bit more adventure, head out from Vijayawada to Guntupalli (p249) or Bhattiprolu, or from Visakhapatnam to Thotlakonda (p251), Bavikonda (p251) and Sankaram (p251).

Eluru (₹45, 1½ hours, half-hourly)

Hyderabad (non-AC/AC ₹310/450, five to seven hours, half-hourly)

Tirupati (non-AC/AC ₹420/570, nine hours, half-hourly)

Visakhapatnam (non-AC/AC ₹415/550, eight hours, half-hourly)

TRAIN

Vijayawada Junction station is on the main Chennai–Kolkata and Chennai–Delhi railway lines. The 12841/12842 Coromandel Express between Chennai and Kolkata is quick for journeys up and down the coast. Typical journey times and sleeper/3AC/2AC fares:

Chennai (₹290/735/1035, seven hours, 13 daily)

Hyderabad (₹190/495/720, 6½ hours, 20 daily)

Tirupati (₹235/635/905, seven hours, 12 daily)

Warangal (₹190/535/735, three hours, 24 daily)

Around Vijayawada

Amaravathi

Amaravathi, 43km west of Vijayawada, was the earliest centre of Buddhism in the southern half of India. India's biggest stupa (Indian/foreigner ₹5/100; ⊘7am-7pm), 27m high and 49m across, was constructed here in the 3rd century BC. Amaravathi flourished as a capital of the Satavahana kingdom which ruled from Andhra across the Deccan for four or five centuries, becoming the fountainhead of Buddhist art in South India. All that remains of the stupa now are its circular base and a few parts of the surrounding stone railing. The great hemispherical dome is gone – but the next-door museum (admission ₹5; ⊘9am-5pm Sat-Thu) has a model of the stupa and some of the intricate marble carvings depicting the Buddha's life with which the Satavahanas covered and surrounded it. A section of reconstructed stone railing gives you an idea of the stupa's massive scale.

About 1km away, on the edge of town, is the 20m-high Dhyana Buddha statue, erected on the site where the Dalai Lama spoke in 2006.

Bus 301 from Vijayawada bus station runs to Amaravathi (₹60, two hours) every 20 minutes, via Unduvalli, through some lovely countryside.

Eluru

The city of Eluru, 60km east of Vijayawada on the road and railway to Visakhapatnam, is the jumping-off point for the remote old Buddhist site of Guntupalli (p249) and the Dhamma Vijaya meditation centre at Vijayarai. Buses depart Eluru for Vijayarai (₹15, 20 minutes) half-hourly.

Dhamma Vijaya　　　　　　MEDITATION
(✆9441449044; www.dhamma.org; Eluru-Chinta lapudi Rd, Vijayarai) Monthly intensive 10-day *vipassana* silent meditation courses are offered in lush palm- and cocoa-forested grounds; apply in advance. Payment is by donation.

Nagarjunakonda

A road trip of about 180km west from Vijayawada or 170km southeast from Hyderabad, followed by a 45-minute boat trip over Nagarjuna Sagar reservoir, brings you to the unique island of Nagarjunakonda, peppered with ancient Buddhist structures. Until 1960, when the big Nagarjunasagar Dam was built on the Krishna River, the island was the top of a hill in the Krishna valley. The Ikshvaku Dynasty had its capital here in the 3rd and 4th centuries AD, when the area was probably the most important Buddhist centre in South India, with some 30 monasteries nearby. Excavations in the 1950s, in anticipation of the dam, unearthed stupas, *viharas* (monasteries), *chaitya-grihas* (prayer halls with stupas), *mandapas* (pillared pavilions) and many outstanding white-marble sculptures. The finds were reassembled on Nagarjunakonda.

◉ Sights & Activities

Nagarjunakonda Museum　　　　MUSEUM
(incl monuments Indian/foreigner ₹10/105; ⊘9am-4pm Sat-Thu) The thoughtfully laid-out Nagarjunakonda Museum has Buddha statues and some superbly detailed carvings depicting the Buddha's lives and local contemporary life. The reassembled remains of several buildings, including stupa bases, walls of monastery complexes and pits for horse sacrifice, are arranged along a 1km path running along the island. The largest stupa, in the Chamtasri Chaitya Griha group, contained a bone fragment thought to be from the Buddha himself.

Sri Parvata Arama
MUSEUM

(Buddhavanam) 8km north of the dam is this Buddhism theme park, featuring a recreation of the huge Amaravathi stupa. It has been under construction by the state tourism authorities for several years and was scheduled to open in late 2015. Coming by bus from Hyderabad, alight at Buddha Park.

Dhamma Nagajjuna
MEDITATION

(☑9440139329, 9348456780; www.nagajjuna. dhamma.org; Hill Colony) Keeping the Buddha's teachings alive in the region, Dhamma Nagajjuna, 8km north of the dam, offers 10-day *vipassana* silent meditation courses in charming flower-filled grounds overlooking Nagarjuna Sagar. Apply in advance; payment is by donation. Coming by bus from Hyderabad, alight at Buddha Park.

🛏 Sleeping & Eating

Nagarjuna Resort
HOTEL $

(☑08642-242471; Vijayapuri South; r ₹800 with AC ₹1500; ❄) The most convenient place to stay, across the road from the boat launch, has spacious, slightly shabby rooms with geysers and balconies with good views.

Haritha Vijaya Vihar
HOTEL $$

(☑08680-277362/3; r with AC incl breakfast Mon-Thu ₹1350-1690, Fri-Sun ₹2480-2810; ❄🏊) Six kilometres north of the dam is Telangana Tourism's Haritha Vijaya Vihar, with decent rooms, nice gardens and lovely lake views.

Hotel Siddhartha
INDIAN $$

(Buddhavanam, Hill Colony; mains ₹110-210; ❀6am-11pm) The best food in the Nagarjuna area is at Hotel Siddhartha, where curries, biryanis, fish dishes and lots of snacks are served in an airy pavilion.

❶ Getting There & Away

The easiest way to visit Nagarjunakonda, other than with a private vehicle, is a bus tour from Hyderabad with Telangana Tourism (p234) (₹550), running on weekends only.

Public buses from Hyderabad's Mahatma Gandhi Bus Station run hourly to Hill Colony/Nagarjuna Sagar (₹200, four hours): alight at Pylon and catch an autorickshaw (₹15/100 shared/private) 8km to Vijayapuri South.

Boats (₹100 return) depart for the island from Vijayapuri South, 7km south of the dam, theoretically at 9.30am, 11.30am and 1.30pm, and stay for one or two hours. The first two boats may not go if not enough people turn up, but the 1.30pm boat goes every day and starts back from the island at 4.30pm.

Visakhapatnam
☑0891 / POP 1.73 MILLION

Visit Visakhapatnam – also called Vizag (*vie*-zag) – during the December-to-February holiday season and you'll see domestic tourism in rare form: balloons, fairy floss (cotton candy) and, of course, weddings! This is where Andhra Pradesh comes to have fun by the sea, and the crowds only enhance the area's kitschy atmosphere. The pedestrian promenade along Ramakrishna Beach has appeal, nearby Rushikonda beach is Andhra's best, and the surrounding area contains one of Andhra's most important Hindu temples, several ancient Buddhist sites, and the rural Araku Valley.

The beach-resort vibe exists despite the fact that Vizag is Andhra Pradesh's largest city, famous for steel and its big port.

If you visit in mid-January you may coincide with **Visakha Utsav**, an annual festival with food stalls on Ramakrishna Beach, exhibitions and cultural events.

◎ Sights & Activities

Ramakrishna Beach
BEACH

Ramakrishna (RK) Beach stretches 4km up the coast from the large port area in the south of town, overlooking the Bay of Bengal with its mammoth ships and brightly painted fishing boats.

Submarine Museum
MUSEUM

(Beach Rd; adult/child ₹40/20, camera ₹50; ❀2-8.30pm Tue-Sat, 10am-12.30pm & 2-8.30pm Sun) Towards the north end of the RK Beach promenade you'll find the 91m-long, Soviet-built, Indian navy submarine *Kursura,* now a facinating museum.

Kailasagiri Hill
PARK

(admission ₹5, cable car round-trip adult/child ₹75/40; ❀11am-8pm) Kailasagiri Hill, rising above Beach Rd in the north of town, has a cable car with panoramic views, attractive gardens, a sculpture park, playgrounds, a toy train, a marble Shiva and Parvati and several cafes. Bus 10K runs there from the RTC Complex and Ramakrishna Beach.

Rushikonda
BEACH

Rushikonda, 10km north of town, is one of the nicest stretches of India's east coast, and the best beach for swimming. To avoid unwanted attention, women should go for modest swimming attire (T-shirts

GUNTUPALLI

Getting here is a very scenic adventure. The former Buddhist **monastic compound** (Indian/foreigner ₹5/100; ⊙10am-5pm), high on a hilltop overlooking a vast expanse of forest and paddy fields, is specially noteworthy for its circular rock-cut *chaitya-griha* shrine. The cave's domed ceiling is carved with 'wooden beams' designed to look like those in a hut. The *chaitya-griha* has a well-preserved stupa and, like the monks' dwellings lining the same cliff, a gorgeous arched facade also designed to look like wood. Check out the stone 'beds' in the monks' cells, and the compound's 60-plus votive stupas. The monastery was active from the 2nd century BC to 3rd century AD.

From Eluru, on the Vijayawada–Visakhapatnam road and railway, take a bus 35km north to Kamavarapukota (₹35, one hour, half-hourly), then a local bus or autorickshaw 10km west to Guntupalli. A taxi from Eluru costs around ₹1500 return.

and shorts). Weekends are busy and festive. Surfers and kayakers can rent decent boards and kayaks from local surf pioneer **Melville Smythe** (☑9848561052; per hr surfboard ₹400-600, 2-person kayak ₹300, surf tuition ₹200), by the jet-ski hire.

You can reach Rushikonda by bus 900K from the train station or RTC Complex, or a shared autorickshaw up Beach Rd.

Simhachalam Temple   HINDU TEMPLE

(⊙7-11.30am, 12.30-2.30pm, 3.30-7pm) Andhra's second most visited temple (after Tirumala) is a 16km drive northwest of town. Large but tranquil and orderly, it's dedicated to Varahalakshmi Narasimha, a combination of Vishnu's boar and lion-man avatars. A ₹100 ticket will get you to the deity (and a sip of holy water) much quicker than a ₹20 one. Buses 6A and 28 go here from the RTC Complex and train station.

The temple's architecture bears much Odishan influence, including the 13th-century main shrine with its carved stone panels (the lion-man can be seen disembowelling a demon on the rear wall).

🛏 Sleeping

Beach Rd is the place to stay, but it's low on inexpensive hotels.

SKML Beach Guest House   GUESTHOUSE $

(☑9848355131; ramkisg.1074@gmail.com; Beach Rd, Varun Beach; r ₹1000-1200, with AC ₹1600-2000) SKML is towards the less select southern end of Ramakrishna Beach but its 12 rooms are clean and decent. Best are the two top-floor 'suites' with sea views, a terrace and a bit of art.

Hotel Morya   HOTEL $

(☑0891-2731112; www.hotelmorya.com; Bowdara Rd; s/d from ₹480/620, r with AC ₹1570; ❋) A reasonable cheapie 600m south of the train station. Standard rooms are small and lack ventilation, but the others are good-sized, and check-out is 24 hours. You can't miss its bright neon sign at night.

Haritha Beach Resort   HOTEL $$

(☑0891-2788826; www.aptdc.gov.in; Rushikonda; r with AC incl breakfast ₹1920-2810; ❋) Rooms at this state-run hotel are bare if clean, but the executive and luxury categories are large, with balconies overlooking its prime asset – the hillside location facing Rushikonda Beach. Just below, and with beach access, **Vihar** (Rushikonda; mains ₹100-240; ⊙11am-10.30pm) is great for a beer or meal.

★ Park   HOTEL $$$

(☑0891-3045678; www.theparkhotels.com; Beach Rd; s/d incl breakfast from ₹8150/10,480; ❋@🛜📶) Vizag's best hotel is elegant and tasteful, but also warm and inviting. The large and lovely beachfront gardens contain a fine pool and three of the hotel's four restaurants. Rooms are cosy and sophisticated.

Ambica Sea Green   HOTEL $$$

(☑0891-2821818; www.ambicaseagreen.com; Beach Rd; r incl breakfast from ₹5060; ❋📶) The very comfy, well-equipped rooms here all have sea views and are much less pricey than other top-end Beach Rd hotels. There's reliable free wi-fi and breakfast is a big buffet.

🍴 Eating

★ Sea Inn   ANDHRA $$

(Beach Rd, Rushikonda; mains ₹90-180; ⊙noon-4pm) The chef here cooks Andhra-style curries the way her mum did, with fish, seafood, chicken or veg, and serves them up in a simple, semi-open-air dining room with bench seating, about 300m north of the Haritha Resort turn-off.

Dharani
INDIAN $$

(Daspalla Hotel, Suryabagh; thalis & mains ₹170-220; ☻noon-3.30pm & 7-10.30pm) Words don't do justice to the super-deliciousness of the meals at this family veg restaurant. Be sure to try the Daspalla special filter coffee: you'll die. The fabulous Daspalla Hotel has several other restaurants too, including Andhra nonveg and North Indian veg options.

Little Italy
ITALIAN $$

(1st fl, South Wing, ATR Towers, Vutagedda Rd, Paandurangapuram; mains ₹230-400; ☻noon-3pm & 7-11pm) This all-veg spot 500m back from Ramakrishna Beach does fine thin-crust pizza and reasonable salads in a neat, tranquil ambience. No alcohol, but good mocktails.

Vista
MULTICUISINE $$$

(The Park, Beach Rd; mains ₹350-900; ☻dinner 7.30-11pm) Of the Park's four restaurants, the indoor Vista is our overall pick for its long, truly global menu and excellent all-you-can-eat dinner buffet (₹900). If you prefer alfresco dining, Bamboo Bay (The Park, Beach Rd; mains ₹450-970; ☻7.30-11pm) does good Andhra, Chettinad and Mughlai food.

ⓘ Information

The RTC Complex has several internet cafes (per hour ₹20).

APTDC (☑0891-2788820; www.aptdc.gov. in; RTC Complex; ☻6.30am-9.30pm) Tours, hotel bookings, tourist information. Has a train station office (p250) too.

ⓘ Getting There & Away

AIR

Direct flights by **Air India** (☑0891-2746501; www.airindia.com; LIC Building Complex, Jeevan Prakash Marg), **Air Costa** (www.aircosta.in), **Indigo** (www.goindigo.in) or **SpiceJet** (www.spicejet.com) go daily to Bengaluru, Bhubaneswar, Chennai, Delhi, Hyderabad, Kolkata and Mumbai.

BOAT

Boats depart roughly twice-monthly for Port Blair in the Andaman Islands. See www.and.nic. in for expected schedules. Tickets for the 56-hour journey (₹2268 to ₹8841) go on sale two or three days before departure at **AV Bhanojirow, Garuda Pattabhiramayya & Co** (☑0891-

2565597; ops@avbgpr.com; Harbour Approach Rd, Next to NMDC, Port Area; ☻9am-5pm). Bring your passport, two photocopies, and two photos.

BUS

Services from Vizag's well-organised **RTC Complex** (☑2746400) include the following:

Vijayawada (general/superluxury'/AC ₹356/425/610, eight hours, hourly 5am to midnight)

Hyderabad (non-AC/AC ₹727/1120, 13 hours, about hourly 2.30pm to 9pm)

Jagdalpur (₹227, eight hours, two daily)

CAR

Genial, English-speaking **Srinivasa 'Srinu' Rao** (☑7382468137) is a good driver for out-of-town trips. He charges around ₹3000 for an Araku Valley day trip and ₹1400 to Sankaram and back.

Reliable **Guide Tours & Travels** (☑9848265559, 0891-2754477; Shop 15, Sudarshan Plaza; ☻7am-10pm), opposite the RTC Complex, charges around ₹3200 plus tolls for a day trip up to 300km.

TRAIN

Visakhapatnam station, on the western edge of town, is on the main Kolkata–Chennai line. The 12841/12842 Coromandel Express is fastest in both directions – 12½ hours to Chennai (sleeper/3AC/2AC ₹425/1115/1590) and 14 hours to Kolkata (₹460/1200/1715). Over 20 daily trains run to Vijayawada (₹255/645/900, seven hours) and about 10 to Bhubaneswar (₹290/750/1050, seven hours). The daily 58538 Visakhapatnam-Koraput Passenger and the 18512 Visakhapatnam–Koraput Intercity Express (Monday and Friday only) head near Chatikona, Onkadelli and Chandoori Sai in Odisha. The **reservation centre** (☻8am-10pm Mon-Sat, to 2pm Sun) is 300m south of the main building.

ⓘ Getting Around

To Visakahapatnam airport, 12km west of downtown, take an autorickshaw (₹250), taxi (₹400), or bus 38 from the RTC Complex (₹15, 30 minutes). The arrivals hall has a prepaid taxi booth.

The train station has a prepaid autorickshaw booth but otherwise you have to negotiate fares. Rides to Ramakrishna Beach should cost ₹60 from the train station and ₹50 from the RTC Complex. Shared autorickshaws run right along Beach Rd from the port at the south end of town to Rushikonda, 10km north of Vizag, and Bheemunipatnam, 25km north, charging between ₹5 (for a 1km hop) and ₹40 (Vizag to Bheemunipatnam): flag down any autorickshaw.

Around Visakhapatnam

Sankaram

Forty kilometres southwest of Vizag, this stunning Buddhist complex (⊙8am-5pm) FREE, also known by the names of its two parts, Bojjannakonda and Lingalakonda, occupies a rocky outcrop about 300m long. Used by monks from the 2nd to 9th centuries AD, the outcrop is covered with rock-cut caves, stupas, ruins of monastery structures and reliefs of the Buddha. Bojjannakonda, the eastern part, has a pair of rock-cut shrines with several gorgeous carvings of the Buddha inside and outside. Above sit the ruins of a huge stupa and a monastery. Lingalakonda, at the western end, is piled with tiers of rock-cut stupas, some of them enormous. Both parts afford fabulous views over the surrounding rice paddies.

A car from Vizag costs ₹1400. Or take a bus (₹42, 1½ hours, every half-hour from the RTC Complex) or train (₹35, one hour) to Anakapalle, 3km away, and then an autorickshaw (₹120 return including waiting).

Bavikonda & Thotlakonda

Bavikonda (⊙9am-5pm) FREE and Thotlakonda (pedestrian/car ₹5/30; ⊙8am-5.30pm) were Buddhist monasteries on scenic hilltop sites north of Vizag that each hosted up to 150 monks, with the help of massive rainwater tanks. The site was excavated in the 1980s and 90s.

The monasteries flourished from around the 3rd century BC to the 3rd century AD, and had votive stupas, congregation halls, *chaitya-grihas, viharas* and refectories. Thotlakonda has sea views, and Bavikonda has special importance because a relic vessel found in its Mahachaitya stupa contained a piece of bone believed to be from the Buddha himself.

Bavikonda and Thotlakonda are reached from turnoffs 14km and 15km, respectively, from Vizag on Bheemunipatnam road: Bavikonda is 3km off the main road and Thotlakonda 1.25km. Vizag autorickshaw drivers charge around ₹600 return to see both: you can also reach the turnoffs by shared autorickshaw or bus 900K. An autorickshaw from the main road to Bavikonda and back costs ₹100 to ₹150.

Bheemunipatnam

This former Dutch settlement, 25km north of Vizag, is the oldest municipality in mainland India, with bizarre sculptures on the beach, an 1861 lighthouse, an interesting Dutch cemetery, and Bheemli Beach, where local grommets surf not-very-clean waters on crude homemade boards. From Vizag, catch bus 900K or a shared autorickshaw.

Araku Valley

☑ 08936 / ELEV 975M

Andhra's best train ride is through the beautiful, lushly forested Eastern Ghats to the Araku Valley, centred on Araku town, 115km north of Vizag. The area is home to isolated tribal communities and known for its tasty organic coffee and lovely green countryside. The 58501 Visakhapatnam Kirandul Passenger train (₹30, four hours) leaves Vizag at 6.50am; train 58502 returns from Araku at 2.50pm. Hourly buses from Vizag (₹70 to ₹105) take 4½ hours, and a taxi day trip costs between ₹3000 to ₹4000. The APTDC runs a variety of tours that all include a tribal dance performance and a visit to the million-year-old limestone Borra Caves (adult/child ₹60/45, camera ₹100; ⊙10am-1pm & 2-5pm), 38km before Araku.

At Araku town, the Museum of Habitat (admission ₹10; ⊙8am-1.30pm & 2.30-8pm), next to the bus station and 2km east of the train station, has extensive exhibits on eastern Andhra Pradesh's tribal peoples, including mock-ups of hunting, ceremonial and other scenes. Next door, you can sample and buy local coffee and chocolate-covered coffee beans at Araku Valley Coffee House (coffee ₹25-95; ⊙8.30am-9pm), and browse tribal crafts at Araku Aadiwasi Arts & Crafts (⊙8am-8pm). On Fridays villagers crowd into Araku for the weekly market.

The oddly unfriendly Hotel Rajadhani (☑08936-249580; www.hotelrajadhani.com; r ₹800, with AC ₹1200; ❄), halfway between the train and bus stations, has clean, reasonably-sized rooms and the Vasundhara Restaurant (⊙6am-11pm), serving good Indian meals. The APTDC has two decent hotels: Hill Resort Mayuri (Mayuri; ☑08936-249204; incl breakfast cottage ₹893, r ₹1349-2361; ❄) just behind the museum, and Valley Resort (☑08936-249202; r incl breakfast ₹1130-2030, with AC ₹2250; ❄), 1km east, which is favoured by Tollywood film crews.

Tirumala & Tirupati

POP 287,000 (TIRUPATI), 7700 (TIRUMALA)

The holy hill of Tirumala is, on any given day, thronged with tens of thousands of blissed-out devotees, many of whom have made long journeys to see the powerful Lord Venkateshwara here, at his home. Around 60,000 pilgrims come each day, and *darshan* runs 24/7. The efficient **Tirumala Tirupati Devasthanams** (TTD; ☑ 0877-2277777, 0877-2233333; www.tirumala.org) (TTD) brilliantly administers the multitudes, employing 20,000 people to do so. Despite the crowds, a sense of order, serenity and ease mostly prevails, and a trip to the Holy Hill can be fulfilling, even if you're not a pilgrim.

'It is believed that Lord Sri Venkateshwara enjoys festivals', according to the TTD. And so do his devotees: *darshan* queues during the annual nine-day **Brahmotsavam festival** (⊙ late Sep/early Oct) can run up to several kilometres.

Tirupati, the town at the bottom of the hill, has many hotels and restaurants and is the main transport nexus for Tirumala. You'll find most of your worldly needs around the Tirupati bus station (TP Area) and, 700m west, the train station.

◉ Sights

Venkateshwara Temple   HINDU TEMPLE
Devotees flock to Tirumala to see Venkateshwara, an avatar of Vishnu. 'Ordinary *darshan'* requires a wait of anywhere from two to eight hours in claustrophobic metal cages ringing the temple. Special-entry *darshan* tickets (₹300) will get you through the queue faster, though you'll still have to brave the cages, which is part of the fun, kind of... Head to the Seeghra Darshan counters at Vaikuntam Queue Complex 1 for these.

There are different hours for special-entry *darshan* each day: check the website. Upon entry, you'll have to sign a form declaring your faith in Lord Venkateshwara.

Among the many powers attributed to Venkateshwara is the granting of any wish made before the idol at Tirumala. Legends about the hill itself and the surrounding area appear in the *Puranas,* and the temple's history may date back 2000 years. The main temple is an atmospheric place, though you'll be pressed between hundreds of devotees when you see it. Venkateshwara inspires bliss and love among his visitors from the back of the dark and magical inner sanctum; it smells of incense, resonates with chanting and may make you religious. You'll have a moment to say a prayer and then you'll be shoved out again. Don't forget to collect your delicious *ladoo* from the counter: Tirumala *ladoos* (sweet balls made with chickpea flour, cardamom and dried fruits) are famous across India.

Many pilgrims donate their hair to the deity – in gratitude for a wish fulfilled, or to renounce ego – so hundreds of barbers attend to devotees. Tirumala and Tirupati are filled with tonsured men, women and children.

🛏 Sleeping & Eating

The TTD runs vast **dormitories** (beds free) and **guesthouses** (r ₹50 3000) near the temple in Tirumala, intended for pilgrims. To stay, check in at the Central Reception Office. Huge **dining halls** (meals free) on the hill feed thousands of pilgrims daily; veg restaurants also serve meals for ₹25.

Hotel Annapurna   HOTEL $
(☑ 0877-2250666; 349 G Car St, Tirupati; r ₹1240 with AC ₹1920; ☀) Rooms at the Annapurna are clean, simple and pink. Since it's on a corner across from the train station, the front rooms can be noisy. Its veg **restaurant** (mains ₹110-210; ⊙ 5.30am-11pm) has fresh juices and excellent food.

Hotel Mamata Residency   HOTEL $
(☑ 0877-2225873; 1st fl, 170 TP Area, Tirupati; s/d/tr/q ₹400/600/800/1000, AC ₹750/999/1249/1499; ☀) A spick-and-span cheapie between the train and bus stations, but you may find all the AC rooms are full.

Hotel Regalia   HOTEL $$
(☑ 0877-2238699; Ramanuja Circle, Tirupati; r incl breakfast ₹2360; ☀🛜) On the east side of town, 1.5km from the train station (₹30 by autorickshaw), the Regalia provides attractive, spotless, contemporary rooms, and the included breakfast is a big buffet.

★ **Minerva Grand**   HOTEL $$
(☑ 0877-6688888; http://minervahotels.in; Renigunta Rd, Tirupati; s/d with AC from ₹3150/3830; ⊙ restaurants 7am-11.30pm; ☀🛜) The Minerva has the best rooms in town – comfy business-style abodes with desks, plump pillows and good mattresses. Its two restaurants, both with icy AC, are tops too: the veg-only **Minerva Coffee Shop** (Minerva Grand, Renigunta Rd; thalis ₹185-220; ⊙ 7am-11.30pm) does superb thalis and dynamite

filter coffee, while the **Blue Fox** (Minerva Grand, Renigunta Rd; mains ₹205-370; ⊘7am-11.30pm) does veg and nonveg dishes and serves alcohol.

Maya   INDIAN $$
(⌨ 0877-2225521; bhimasdeluxe@rediffmail.com; Bhimas Deluxe Hotel, 34-38 G Car St, Tirupati; meals & mains ₹130-190; ⊘6am-10pm) Great veg meals in the basement of the Bhimas Deluxe, near the train station.

ⓘ Getting There & Away

It's possible to visit Tirumala on a (very) long day trip from Chennai. The APSRTC runs 51 daily buses direct to Tirumala (₹165 to ₹219, five hours) from Chennai's CMBT bus station.

AIR

Tirupati Airport (www.tirupatiairport.com) is at Renigunta, 14km east of town. **Air India** (⌨ 0877-2283981, airport 0877-2283992; www.airindia.in; Srinivasam Pilgrim Amenities Complex, Tirumala By-Pass Road,Tirumala Bypass Rd; ⊘9.30am-5.30pm), **SpiceJet** (⌨ 9871803333; www.spicejet.com) and **Air Costa** (⌨ 9949852229; www.aircosta.in) all fly to Hyderabad daily.

BUS

Tirupati's **bus station** (⌨ 0877-2289900) is a wonder of logistics. Useful services, all once or twice hourly, include the following:
Bengaluru (express/Volvo/night Volvo ₹230/400/450, four to six hours)
Chennai (express/Volvo ₹121/222, four hours)
Hyderabad (superluxury/Volvo ₹610/950, 10 to 12 hours)
Vijayawada (express/superluxury ₹350/460, nine hours)

TRAIN

There are numerous daily departures to main destinations; the **reservation office** (⊘8am-8pm Mon-Sat, 8am-2pm Sun) is opposite the station's east end. Typical journey times and fares for sleeper/3AC/2AC:
Bengaluru (₹250/635/885, seven hours)
Chennai (₹140/485/690, three to four hours)
Hyderabad (₹380/1030/1480, 13 hours)
Vijayawada (₹235/635/905, seven hours)

ⓘ Getting Around

There's a prepaid taxi booth outside the east end of the train station.

BUS

There's a stand for buses to Tirumala opposite the train station, with departures every few

minutes. The scenic one-hour trip costs ₹45/82 one-way/return.

WALKING

The TTD has constructed probably the best foot-path in India for pilgrims to walk up to Tirumala. It's about 12km from the start of the path at Alipiri on the north side of Tirupati (₹50 by autorick-shaw), and takes three to six hours. You can leave your luggage at Alipiri and it will be transported free to the reception centre. There are rest points along the way, and a few canteens.

Around Tirumala & Tirupati

Chandragiri Fort

This fort 15km west of Tirupati dates back 1000 years, but its heyday came in the late 16th century when the rulers of the declining Vijayanagar Empire, having fled from Hampi, made it their capital. At the heart of a 1.5km-long stout-walled enclosure beneath a rocky hill, the **palace area** (Indian/foreigner ₹10/100; ⊘9am-5pm Sat-Thu) contains nice gardens and the Raja Mahal, a heavily restored Vijayanagar palace reminiscent of Hampi buildings, with an interesting museum of bronze and stone sculptures. The upper fort on the hillside is frustratingly out of bounds. Buses for Chandragiri (₹10) leave Tirupati hourly. Prepaid taxis are ₹500 return.

Sri Kalahasti

Sri Kalahasti, 37km east of Tirupati, is known for its important Sri Kalahasteeswara Temple and for being, along with Machilipatnam near Vijayawada, a centre for the ancient textile-painting art of *kalamkari*. Cotton cloth is primed with *myrabalam* (resin) and cow's milk; figures are drawn with a pointed bamboo stick dipped in fermented jaggery and water; and the dyes are made from cow dung, ground seeds, plants and flowers. You can see artists at work, and buy some of their products, in the Agraharam neighbourhood, 2.5km from the bus stand. **Sri Vijayalakshmi Fine Kalamkari Arts** (⌨ 9441138380; Door No 15-890; ⊘daily) is a 40-year-old family business employing over 60 artists. *Dupatta* scarves start around ₹1500.

Buses leave Tirupati for Sri Kalahasti every 10 minutes (₹35, one hour); a prepaid taxi is ₹900 return.

TELANGANA & ANDHRA PRADESH AROUND TIRUMALA & TIRUPATI

Kerala

Serene Kerala is a state shaped by its wonderful natural landscape: a long, luxurious coastline; wandering backwaters; lush palms and spice plantations; and cool mountain escapes. Add the kaleidoscope of culture best experienced in the unique performing arts and you'll understand why Kerala is a destination not to be missed.

Above Backwater canals near Kumarakom (p289)

Tea plantation near Top Station (p297)

Hill Stations & Sanctuaries

Kerala's hill country in the Western Ghats is a sumptuous natural spectacle where narrow roads wind up through jungle-thick vegetation and provide dizzying views over peacock green tea plantations. A cooling altitude helps to make the towns soothing places to escape from the cares of the world, while the wildlife sanctuaries are unspoiled wildernesses offering the chance to spot exciting wild animals.

Munnar

Best known of the hill stations is Munnar, with contoured green fields carpeting the hills as far as the eye can see. This is South India's tea-growing heartland, but also a great place to trek to viewpoints across epic mountain scenery. Some wonderfully remote lodgings are hidden in the hills, tucked deep into spice and flower gardens or cardamom and coffee plantations.

Wayanad & Periyar

The northern area around Wayanad Wildlife Sanctuary has shimmering green rice paddies and plantations of coffee, cardamom, ginger and pepper everywhere you look. The rolling hills are fragrant with wild herbs and punctuated by mammoth clumps of bamboo. It's one of the best places to spot wild elephants and there are plenty of opportunities for trekking, including up the area's highest mountain, Chembra Peak (2100m).

At Periyar Wildlife Sanctuary, a tiger reserve since 1978 and Kerala's most-visited wildlife sanctuary, you can cruise on Periyar Lake, stay in an island palace, or embark on a jungle trek with a trained tribal guide.

Beaches

Goa might pull in the package-holiday crowds, but Kerala's coastline – almost 600km of it – boasts a stunning string of golden-sand beaches, fringed by palms and washed by the Arabian Sea. The southern beaches are the busiest. Less-discovered, wilder choices await in the north.

Southern Beaches

Most established of the resorts along the coast is Kovalam, only a short hop from the capital, Thiruvananthapuram (Trivandrum). Once a quiet fishing village, Kovalam has two sheltered crescents of beach perfect for paddling, overlooked by a town that's almost entirely made up of hotels. If you're looking for something less built up, some lovely beaches and resorts cluster south of Kovalam in the area around Pulinkudi and Chowara, where ayurvedic treatments are popular.

North of Trivandrum is Varkala, which straggles along its dramatic, russet-and-gold-streaked cliffs. Although a holy town popular with Hindu pilgrims, Varkala has also developed into Kerala's backpacker bolthole and the cliffs are lined with guesthouses, open-front restaurants and bars all moving to a reggae, rock and trance soundtrack. For a quieter scene, travellers are drifting north to Odayam and Kappil beaches.

Even further north, Alappuzha (Alleppey) is best known for its backwaters, but also has a decent beach, while Kochi (Cochin) has Cherai Beach on Vypeen Island, a lovely stretch of white sand, with miles of lazy lagoons and backwaters only a few hundred metres from the seafront.

1. Papanasham beach (p275), Varkala
2. Keralan coastline
3. Beach at sunset, Kovalam (p270)

Far North & Islands

Fewer travellers make it to Kerala's far north, which means there are some beautifully deserted pockets of beach, where resorts are replaced by more traditional village life. Among the best are the peaceful white-sand beaches south of Kannur, or further north around the Valiyaparamba backwaters between Kannur and Bekal.

Even more far flung are the Lakshadweep Islands, a palm-fringed archipelago 300km west of Kerala. As well as pristine beaches, the islands boast some of India's best scuba diving and snorkelling.

Best Beach Towns

Varkala The beautiful cliff-edged coastline of Varkala is a Hindu holy place as well as a lively backpacker-focused resort. Good base for yoga, surfing or just chilling out.

Kovalam Kerala's most commercial beach resort, but still fun and scenic despite the crowds and hawkers. Resorts here and further south have a strong focus on ayurvedic treatments.

Kannur While Kannur itself is not particularly appealing, head 8km south to Thottada for gorgeous beaches and seafront homestays in local villages. Kannur town's 4km-long Payyambalam Beach is popular with locals.

Backwaters

Kerala's 900km of waterways spread watery tendrils through a lusciously green landscape. Palm-shaded, winding canals are lined by back-in-time villages, many of which are accessible only by boat. It's an environment unique to Kerala and an unforgettable South India experience.

Houseboats

To glide along the canals in a punted canoe, or sleep under a firmament of stars in a traditional houseboat, is pure enchantment. The distinctive houseboats that cluster around the main hubs of Alappuzah (Alleppey) and Kollam (Quilon) are designed like traditional rice barges or *kettuvallam* ('boats with knots', so-called because the curvaceous structure is held together by knotted coir).

There are several ways to explore the backwaters. The most popular is to rent a houseboat for a night or two; these sleep anywhere from two to 14 or more people. They vary wildly in luxury and amenities. The hire includes staff (at least a driver and cook, but usually additional kitchen staff and crew), so catering is included, and you'll eat traditional Keralan meals of fish and vegetables cooked in coconut milk. However, the popularity of these tours can mean that the main waterways get very busy – even gridlocked – in peak season. A one-night houseboat trip won't get you far through the backwaters.

Which Houseboat?

The choice of houseboats – especially at Alleppey – is mind-boggling and your selection of boat and operator can make or break the experience.

1. Houseboats cruising on Kerala's backwaters
2. Backwaters around Alappuzha (p282)
3. Fishermen in Kollam (p279)

➡ Avoid booking a houseboat until you arrive at the backwaters; inspect a few boats before committing.

➡ Ask to see the operators' certification: those houseboat owners who have a 'Green Palm' or 'Gold Star' certificate have met requirements such as solar panels, sanitary tanks and low-emission engines. Punt-powered boats are even better.

➡ Visit the houseboat dock in Alleppey, talk to returning travellers or guesthouse owners, and search online to gauge costs and quality.

➡ Avoid peak season (mid-December to mid-January) when prices peak and the waterways are clogged.

Ferries & Canoes

The cheapest means of seeing the waterways is to take a public ferry. You can take trips from town to town, though you won't see much of the smaller canals, where it is really tranquil. Two of the most popular trips are the all-day tourist cruise between Kollam and Alleppey, a scenic but slow trip, and the 2½-hour ferry from Alleppey to Kottayam.

The best way to explore deep into the network and escape the bigger boats is on a canoe tour, which allows you to travel along the narrower canals and see village life in a way that's impossible on a houseboat or ferry. Village tours with a knowledgeable guide are another tranquil way to explore the region and understand some of the local culture.

Performing Arts

Kerala has an intensely rich culture of performing arts – living art forms are passed on to new generations in specialised schools and arts centres.

Kathakali

Kathakali, with its elaborate ritualised gestures, heavy masklike make-up, and dramatic stories of love, lust and power struggles based on the Ramayana, the Mahabharata and the Puranas, stems in part from 2nd-century temple rituals, though its current form developed around the 16th century. The actors tell the stories through precise *mudras* (hand gestures) and facial expressions. Traditionally performances start in temple grounds at around 8pm and go on all night, though versions for those with shorter attention spans are performed in many tourist centres, to give you a taste of the art.

Theyyam

Theyyam is believed to be older than Hinduism, having developed from harvest folk dances. It's performed in *kavus* (sacred groves) in northern Kerala. The word refers to the ritual itself, and to the shape of the deity or hero portrayed, of whom there are around 450. The costumes are magnificent, with face paint, armour, garlands and huge headdresses. The performance consists of frenzied dancing to a wild drumbeat, creating a trancelike atmosphere.

Kalarippayat

Taking its moves from both Kathakali and *theyyam* is the martial art of *kalarippayat,* a ritualistic discipline taught throughout

MITCHELL KANASHKEVICH / GETTY IMAGES ©

CHRISTOPHER PILLITZ / GETTY IMAGES ©

NEIL MCALLISTER / GETTY IMAGES ©

1. Artists applying makeup before a Kathakali performance **2.** *Kalarippayat* martial artists **3.** *Theyyam* ritual

Kerala. It's taught and displayed in an arena called a *kalari,* which combines gymnasium, school and temple.

Places to See Performing Arts

In the spring there are numerous festivals offering the chance to see Kathakali, with Thirunakkara in Kottayam in March and the Pooram festival in Kollam in April. The easiest places for travellers to see performances are at cultural centres such as **Kerala Kathakali Centre** (p308), **See India Foundation** (p308) and **Greenix Village** (p308) in Kochi; **Mudra** (p293) in Kumily; and **Punarjani** (p296) and **Thirumeny** (p296) in Munnar. In Kovalam and Varkala there are short versions of the art in season.

If you're interested in learning more about the art of Kathakali, **Kerala**

Kalamandalam (p315) near Thrissur and **Margi Kathakali** (p265) in Trivandrum offer courses for serious students, or you can attend these schools to see performances and practice sessions.

Both the Kochi and Kumily centres have shows of *kalarippayat,* or you can visit the martial-arts training centres of **CVN Kalari Sangham** (p265) in Trivandrum and **Ens Kalari** (p308) in Nettoor, close to Ernakulam.

The best areas to see *theyyam* performances are around Kannur, Payyanur and Valiyaparamba, in the northern backwater area, where there are more than 500 *kavus.* The season is from October to May. For advice on finding performances, contact the **Tourist Desk** (p310) in Kochi or homestays at Thottada Beach.

Kerala

Best Wildlife-Watching

➡ Wayanad Wildlife Sanctuary (p317)

➡ Periyar Wildlife Sanctuary (p290)

➡ Thattekkad Bird Sanctuary (p297)

➡ Parambikulam Wildlife Sanctuary (p298)

Best Homestays

➡ Green Woods Bethlehem (p303)

➡ Varnam Homestay (p318)

➡ Tranquil (p319)

➡ Graceful Homestay (p267)

➡ Reds Residency (p303)

Why Go?

A sliver of a coastal state in India's deep south, Kerala is shaped by its layered landscape: almost 600km of glorious Arabian Sea coast and beaches; a languid network of glistening backwaters; and the spice- and tea-covered hills of the Western Ghats. Just setting foot on this swathe of soul-quenching, palm-shaded green will slow your subcontinental stride to a blissed-out amble. Kerala is a world away from the frenzy of elsewhere, as if India had passed through the Looking Glass and become an altogether more laid-back place.

Besides its famous backwaters, elegant houseboats, ayurvedic treatments and delicately spiced, taste-bud-tingling cuisine, Kerala is home to wild elephants, exotic birds and the odd tiger, while vibrant traditions such as Kathakali plays, temple festivals and snake-boat races frequently bring even the smallest villages to life. It's hard to deny Kerala's liberal use of the slogan 'God's Own Country'.

When to Go
Thiruvananthapuram

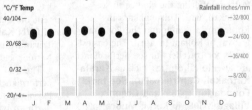

| **Dec–Feb** Perfect beach and backwater weather. Ernakulathappan Utsavam festival in Kochi. | **Apr** Kathakali at Kottayam and Kollam festivals, and the elephant procession in Thrissur. | **Aug–Oct** End of the monsoon period: Onam festival, snake-boat races. |

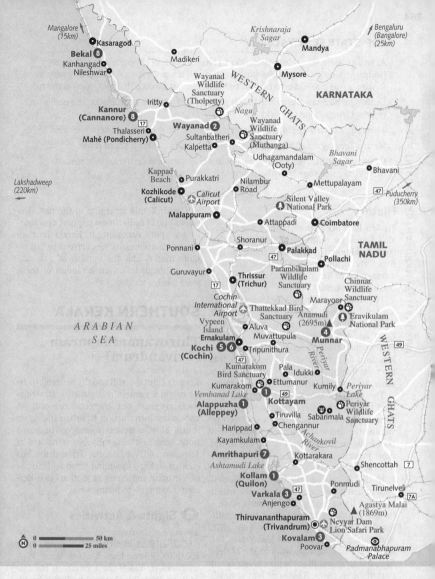

Kerala Highlights

1 Cruising in a houseboat or punted canoe through slippery **backwaters** (p288) from Alappuzha, Kollam or Kottayam

2 Spotting wild elephants at **Wayanad** (p317) amid mountain scenery and epic forest treks

3 Watching days slip away at the clifftop beach resort of **Varkala** (p274) or having some laid-back beach fun in **Kovalam** (p270)

4 Bedding down in a remote resort and trekking through emerald tea plantations around **Munnar** (p294)

5 Feeling the history and relaxing in a homestay in calm **Fort Cochin** (p298)

6 Experience a performance of **Kathakali** (p309) or the martial arts **kalarippayat** (p309) in Kochi

7 Calling in for a cuddle at the **ashram** (p281) of 'The Hugging Mother' in Amrithapuri

8 Exploring unspoilt beaches and **theyyam** rituals at **Kannur** (p320) and **Bekal** (p322)

TOP STATE FESTIVALS

As well as the major state festivals, Kerala has hundreds of temple festivals, *theyyams* (trance-induced rituals), snake-boat regattas and street parades. *A Hundred Festivals for You,* a free publication produced by Kochi's Tourist Desk (p310), lists many of them.

Ernakulathappan Utsavam (p303) Eight days of festivities culminating in a parade of elephants, music and fireworks.

Thrissur Pooram (p314) The elephant procession to end all elephant processions.

Nehru Trophy Boat Race (p282) The most popular of Kerala's boat races.

Onam (⊙ Aug/Sep) Kerala's biggest cultural celebration, when the entire state celebrates the golden age of mythical King Mahabali for 10 days.

History

Traders have been drawn to the scent of Kerala's spices for more than 3000 years. The coast was known to the Phoenicians, the Romans, the Arabs and the Chinese, and was a transit point for spices from the Moluccas (eastern Indonesia).

The kingdom of Cheras ruled much of Kerala until the early Middle Ages, competing with kingdoms and small fiefdoms for territory and trade. Vasco da Gama's arrival in 1498 opened the floodgates to European colonialism as Portuguese, Dutch and English interests fought Arab traders, and then each other, for control of the lucrative spice trade.

The present-day state of Kerala was created in 1956 from the former states of Travancore, Kochi and Malabar. A tradition of valuing the arts and education resulted in a post-Independence state that is one of the most progressive in India, with the nation's highest literacy rate.

In 1957 Kerala had the first freely elected communist government in the world, which has gone on to hold power regularly since – though the Congress-led United Democratic Front (UDF) has been in power since 2011. Many Malayalis (speakers of Malayalam, the state's official language) work in the Middle East and their remittances play a significant part in the economy. A big hope for the state's future is the relatively recent boom in tourism, with Kerala emerging in the past decade as one of India's most popular new tourist hot spots. According to Kerala Tourism almost 12 million visitors arrived in 2013 – more than double the number of a decade ago – though less than a million of these were foreign tourists.

SOUTHERN KERALA

Thiruvananthapuram (Trivandrum)

☑ 0471 / POP 958,000

Kerala's capital – still usually referred to by its colonial name, Trivandrum – is a relatively compact but energetic city and an easy-going introduction to urban life down south. Most travellers merely springboard from here to the nearby beach resorts of Kovalam and Varkala, but Trivandrum has enough sights – including a zoo and cluster of Victorian museums in glorious neo-Keralan buildings – to justify a stay.

◉ Sights & Activities

Zoological Gardens   ZOO
(☑ 0471-2115122; adult/child ₹20/5, camera/video ₹50/100; ⊙ 9am-5.15pm Tue-Sun) Yann Martel famously based the animals in his *Life of Pi* on those he observed in Trivandrum's zoological gardens. Shaded paths meander through woodland, lakes and native forest, where tigers, macaques and hippos gather in reasonably large open enclosures.

★ **Napier Museum**   MUSEUM
(adult/child ₹10/5; ⊙ 10am-5pm Tue & Thu-Sun, 1-5pm Wed) Housed in an 1880 wooden building designed by Robert Chisholm, a British architect whose Fair Isle–style version of the Keralan vernacular shows his enthusiasm

SLEEPING PRICE RANGES

Accommodation price ranges for this chapter are:

$ less than ₹1200

$$ ₹1200 to ₹5000

$$$ more than ₹5000

for local craft, this museum has an eclectic display of bronzes, Buddhist sculptures, temple carts and ivory carvings. The carnivalesque interior is stunning and worth a look in its own right.

Natural History Museum MUSEUM
(adult/child ₹20/5; ☺10am-4.45pm Tue & Thu-Sun, 1-4.45pm Wed) In the zoological park complex, the Natural History Museum has hundreds of stuffed animals and birds, and a fine skeleton collection.

Shri Chitra Art Gallery ART GALLERY
(adult/child ₹20/5; ☺10am-4.45pm Tue-Sun) Inside the grounds of the zoo itself, this gallery has paintings by the Rajput, Mughal and Tanjore schools, and portraits by renowned artist Ravi Varma (1848–1906).

★ Museum of History & Heritage MUSEUM
(☏9567019037; www.museumkeralam.org; Park View; adult/child Indian ₹20/10, foreigner ₹200/50, camera ₹25; ☺10am-5.30pm Tue-Sun) In a lovely heritage building within the Kerala Tourism complex, this beautifully presented museum traces Keralan history and culture through superb static displays and interactive audiovisual presentations. Exhibits range from Iron Age implements to bronze and terracotta sculptures, murals, *dhulichitra* (floor paintings) to recreations of traditional Keralan homes.

Shri Padmanabhaswamy Temple HINDU TEMPLE
(☺inner sanctum 3.30am-7.30pm; Hindus only) Trivandrum's spiritual heart is this 260-year-old temple in the Fort area. The main entrance is the 30m-tall, seven-tier eastern *gopuram* (gateway tower). In the inner sanctum (Hindus only), the deity Padmanabha reclines on the sacred serpent and is made from over 10,000 *salagramam* (sacred stones) that were purportedly transported from Nepal by elephant.

The path around to the right of the gate offers good views of the *gopuram*.

Puthe Maliga Palace Museum MUSEUM
(Fort; Indian/foreigner ₹15/50, camera/video ₹30/250; ☺9.30am-12.45pm & 3-4.45pm Tue-Sun) The 200-year-old palace of the Travancore maharajas has carved wooden ceilings, marble sculptures and imported Belgian glass. Inside you'll find Kathakali images, an armoury, portraits of maharajas, ornate thrones and other artefacts. Admission includes an informative one-hour guided tour,

though you can just visit the outside of the palace grounds (free), where you'll also find the Chitrali Museum (admission ₹50) containing loads of historical memorabilia, photographs and portraits from the Travancore dynasty.

🍴 Courses

Ayushmanbhava Ayurvedic Centre AYURVEDA, YOGA
(☏0471-2556060; www.ayushmanbhava.com; Pothujanam; massage from ₹800; ☺yoga classes 6.30am) This centre, 5km west of MG Rd, offers massage, daily therapeutic-yoga classes, as well as longer ayurvedic treatments. Also accommodation and a herbal garden.

Margi Kathakali School CULTURAL PROGRAM
(☏0471-2478806; www.margitheatre.org; Fort) Conducts courses in Kathakali and Kootiattam (traditional Sanskrit drama) for beginner and advanced students. Fees average ₹300 per two-hour class. Visitors can peek at uncostumed practice sessions held from 10am to noon Monday to Friday. It's in an unmarked building behind the Fort School, 200m west of the fort.

CVN Kalari Sangham MARTIAL ARTS
(☏0471-2474182; www.cvnkalari.in; South Rd; 15-day/1-month course ₹1000/2000) Long-term courses in *kalarippayat* for serious students (aged under 30) with some experience in martial arts. Training sessions are held Monday to Saturday from 7am to 8.30am.

THE INDIAN COFFEE HOUSE STORY

The Indian Coffee House is a place stuck in time. Its India-wide branches feature old-India prices and waiters dressed in starched white with peacock-style headdresses. It was started by the Coffee Board in the early 1940s, during British rule. In the 1950s the Board began to close down cafes across India, making employees redundant. At this point, the Keralan-born communist leader Ayillyath Kuttiari Gopalan Nambiar began to support the workers and founded with them the India Coffee Board Worker's Co-operative Society. The Coffee House has remained ever since, always atmospheric, and always offering bargain snacks and drinks such as Indian filter coffee, rose milk and *idlis*. It's still run by its employees, all of whom share ownership.

Thiruvananthapuram (Trivandrum)

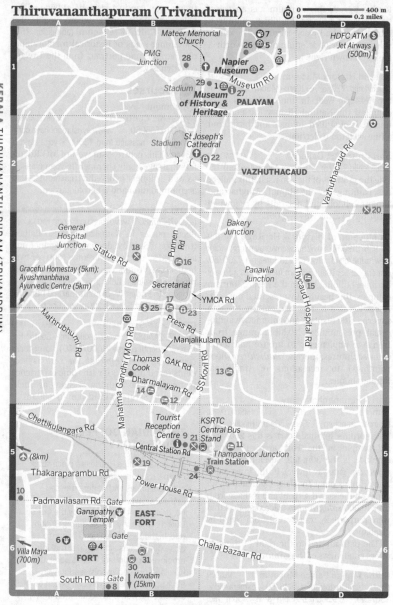

Tours

KTDC Tours
BUS TOUR
(☎0471-2330031; www.ktdc.com) The KTDC runs several tours, all leaving from the Tourist Reception Centre at the Hotel Chaithram on Central Station Rd. The City Tour (₹300) includes the zoo, museums and other local sights; the Kanyakumari Day Tour (₹700) visits Padmanabhapuram Palace, Kanyakumari in Tamil Nadu and the nearby Suchindram Temple. Other trips include Neyyar Dam (₹400) and Kovalam (₹200).

Thiruvananthapuram (Trivandrum)

🛏 Sleeping

There are several decent budget and mid-range hotels along Manjalikulam Rd, north of Central Station Rd.

Princess Inn HOTEL $
(☑0471-2339150; princess_inn@yahoo.com; Manjalikulam Rd; s/d from ₹450/550, with AC from ₹950/1130; ❉🕾) In a glass-fronted building, the Princess Inn promises a relatively quiet sleep in a central side-street location. It's comfortable, with satellite TV and immaculate bathrooms; it's worth paying a little more for the spacious 'deluxe' rooms.

YMCA International Guesthouse HOSTEL $
(☑0471-2330059; www.ymcatvm.org; YMCA Rd; s/d ₹790/1130, with AC ₹1270/1690; ❉) Centrally located, this is a good budget deal, although prices have crept up and it's often full with groups. Rooms are spacious and clean with tiled bathrooms and TV. Both men and women accepted.

Hotel Regency HOTEL $
(☑0471-2330377; www.hotelregency.com; Manjalikulam Cross Rd; s/d ₹620/1000, with AC ₹1180/1500; ❉🕾) This tidy, welcoming place offers small but spotless rooms with satellite TVs; the deluxe rooms are larger and there's wi-fi available in the lobby.

Greenland Lodge HOTEL $
(☑0471-2328114; Thampanoor Junction; s/d ₹430/680, with AC ₹900/1130; ❉) Close to the muted mayhem of the train station and bus stand, pastel-coloured Greenland is an acceptable budget option for the location. Rooms are cleanish but variable so ask to see a few. Officious staff demand a hefty two-night advance deposit.

★**Graceful Homestay** HOMESTAY $$
(☑9847249556, 0417-2444358; www.graceful-homestay.com; Pothujanam Rd, Philip's Hill; incl breakfast downstairs s/d ₹1450/1650, upstairs & ste s/d ₹2200/2750; @🕾) In Trivandrum's leafy western suburbs, this lovely, serene house set in a couple of hectares of garden is owned by Sylvia and run by her brother Giles. The four rooms are all neatly furnished with individual character and access to kitchen, living areas and balconies. The pick of the rooms has an amazing covered terrace with views overlooking a sea of palms. It's around 6km from the train station and 5km from the airport; call ahead for directions.

★**Varikatt Heritage** HOMESTAY $$
(☑9895239055, 0417-2336057; www.varikat theritage.com; Punnen Rd; r/ste incl breakfast ₹4000/5000; 🕾) Trivandrum's most charismatic place to stay is the 250-year-old home of Colonel Roy Kuncheria. It's a wonderful Indo-Saracenic bungalow with four rooms

flanked by verandahs facing a pretty garden. Every antique – and the home itself – has a family story attached. Lunch and dinner available (₹500).

Vivanta by Taj HOTEL $$$
(☏ 0417-6612345; www.vivantabytaj.com; Thycaud Hospital Rd; s/d incl breakfast from ₹9000/11,800; ✳@🛜🏊) The lobby here is bigger than most hotels in town, so the Taj doesn't disappoint with the wow factor. Rooms are sufficiently plush, the lawn and pool area is well-maintained, and there's a spa, 24-hour gym and several good restaurants, including Smoke on the Water poolside grill.

Hyacinth by Sparsa HOTEL $$$
(☏ 0471-2552999; Manorama Rd; d incl breakfast ₹4800-7200, ste ₹10,800; ✳🛜🏊) A white, modern luxury hotel close to the city centre, Hyacinth is more boutique chic than five-star flash. It features functional, well-appointed rooms, a rooftop pool, a fitness centre and several good restaurants.

🍴 Eating

★ **Indian Coffee House** INDIAN $
(Maveli Cafe; Central Station Rd; snacks ₹10-60; ☺7am-10.30pm) This branch of Indian Coffee House serves its strong coffee and snacks in a crazy red-brick tower that looks like a cross between a lighthouse and a pigeon coop, and has a spiralling interior lined with concrete benches and tables. You have to admire the hard-working waiters.

Ariya Nivaas INDIAN $
(Manorama Rd; mains ₹30-140, thalis ₹100; ☺6.45am-10pm, lunch 11.30am-3pm) Trivandrum's best all-you-can-eat South Indian veg thalis

mean Ariya Nivaas is always busy at lunchtime, but service is snappy and the food fresh.

Ananda Bhavan SOUTH INDIAN $
(☏ 0417-2477646; MG Rd; dishes ₹12-40; ☺lunch & dinner) Classic cheap veg place specialising in tiffin snacks and dosas.

Azad Restaurant INDIAN $
(MG Rd; dishes ₹50-200; ☺11am-11.30pm) Busy family favourite serving up authentic Keralan fish dishes, like fish *molee,* and excellent biryanis and tandoori. There's another branch in Press Rd.

Cherries & Berries CAFE $$
(☏ 0471-2735433; www.cherriesandberries.in; Carmel Towers, Cotton Hill; dishes ₹100-200; ☺10am-10pm; 🛜) For serious comfort food, icy air-con and free wi-fi that really works, take a trip east of the centre to Cherries & Berries. The menu includes waffles, mini-pizzas, hot dogs, toasties, good coffee and indulgent chocolate-bar milkshakes – try the Kit Kat shake (₹150).

★ **Villa Maya** KERALAN $$$
(☏ 0471-2578901; www.villamaya.in; 120 Airport Rd, Injakkal; starters ₹350-600, mains ₹450-1050; ☺11am-11pm) Villa Maya is more an experience than a restaurant. Dining is either in the magnificent 18th-century Dutch mansion or in private curtained niches in the tranquil courtyard garden, where you'll be lulled by lily ponds and trickling fountains. The Keralan cuisine itself is expertly crafted, delicately spiced and beautifully presented. Seafood is a speciality, with dishes like stuffed crab with lobster butter, but there

BUSES FROM TRIVANDRUM (KSRTC BUS STAND)

DESTINATION	FARE (₹)	DURATION (HR)	FREQUENCY
Alleppey	120, AC 211	3½	every 15min
Chennai	595	17	10 daily
Ernakulam (Kochi)	167, AC 281	5½	every 20min
Kanyakumari	67-81	2	6 daily
Kollam	60	1½	every 15min
Kumily (for Periyar)	231	8	2 daily
Munnar	235	8	3 daily
Neyyar Dam	34	1½	every 40min
Thrissur	225	7½	every 30min
Udhagamandalam (Ooty)	510	14	1 daily
Varkala	60	1¼	hourly

MAJOR TRAINS FROM TRIVANDRUM

DESTINATION	TRAIN NO & NAME	FARE (₹)	DURATION (HR)	DEPARTURE
Bengaluru	16525 Bangalore Express	420/1120/1630	18	12.45pm
Chennai	12696 Chennai Express	470/1230/1760	16½	5.20pm
Coimbatore	17229 Sabari Express	255/680/970	9¼	7.15am
Mumbai	16346 Netravathi Express	670/1785/2625	31	9.50am
Mangalore	16604 Maveli Express	340/910/1310	12½	7.30pm

Fares: sleeper/3AC/2AC

are some tantalising veg dishes too. Between lunch and dinner (3pm to 7pm) you can order snacks like sandwiches, pizzas and calzones. Ask the friendly staff for a free tour of the historic manor.

🛍 Shopping

Connemara Market　　　　　MARKET
(MG Rd; ⊙from 7am) Vendors sell vegetables, fish, live goats, fabric, clothes, spices and more at this busy market.

SMSM Institute　　　　HANDICRAFTS
(www.keralahandicrafts.in; YMCA Rd; ⊙9am-8pm Mon-Sat) Kerala Government–run handicraft emporium with an Aladdin's cave of fix-priced goodies.

ℹ Information

ABC Internet (MG Rd, Capital Centre; per 30min ₹20; ⊙9am-9pm) One of several good internet places in this small mall.

KIMS (Kerala Institute of Medical Sciences; ☑ 0471-3041000, emergency 0471-3041144; www.kimskerala.com; Kumarapuram; ⊙24hr) Best choice for medical problems; about 7km northwest of Trivandrum railway station.

Main Post Office (☑ 0471-2473071; MG Rd) Trivandrum's central post office.

Tourist Facilitation Centre (☑ 0471-2321132; Museum Rd; ⊙24hr) Near the zoo; supplies maps and brochures.

Tourist Reception Centre (KTDC Hotel Chaithram; ☑ 0471-2330031; Central Station Rd; ⊙7am-9pm) Arranges KTDC-run tours.

ℹ Getting There & Away

AIR

Trivandrum's airport serves international destinations with direct flights to/from Colombo in Sri Lanka, Male in the Maldives and major Gulf regions such as Dubai, Sharjah, Muscat, Bahrain and Kuwait.

Within India, **Air India** (☑ 2317341; Mascot Sq), **Jet Airways** (☑ 2728864; Sasthamangalam Junction), **IndiGo** (www.goindigo.in) and **SpiceJet** (☑ 09871803333; www.spicejet.com; Trivandrum airport) fly between Trivandrum and Mumbai (Bombay), Kochi, Bengaluru (Bangalore), Chennai (Madras) and Delhi.

All airline bookings can be made at the efficient **Airtravel Enterprises** (☑ 3011300; www.ate.travel; MG Rd, New Corporation Bldg).

BUS

State-run and private buses use Trivandrum's giant new concave **KSRTC Central Bus Stand** (☑ 0471-2462290; www.keralatc.com; Central Station Rd, Thampanoor), opposite the train station.

Buses leave for Kovalam beach (₹15, 30 minutes, every 20 minutes) between 6am and 9pm from the southern end of the East Fort bus stand on MG Rd.

TRAIN

Trains are often heavily booked, so it's worth visiting the **reservation office** (☑ 139; ⊙8am-8pm Mon-Sat, to 2pm Sun) at the main train station or booking online. While most major trains arrive at **Trivandrum Central Station** close to the city centre, some express services terminate at **Vikram Sarabhai Station** (Kochuveli), about 7km north of the city – check in advance.

Within Kerala there are frequent express trains to Varkala (2nd/sleeper/3AC ₹45/140/485, one hour), Kollam (₹55/170/535, 1¼ hour) and Ernakulam (₹95/195/535, 4½ hours), with trains passing through either Alleppey (₹80/170/535, three hours) or Kottayam (₹80/140/485, 3½ hours). There are also numerous daily services to Kanyakumari (2nd/sleeper/3AC ₹80/140/485, three hours).

ℹ️ Getting Around

The **airport** (📞 2501424) is 10km from the city and 15km from Kovalam; take local bus 14 from the East Fort and City Bus stand (₹9). Prepaid taxi vouchers from the airport cost ₹350 to the city and ₹500 to Kovalam.

Autorickshaws are the easiest way to get around, with short hops costing ₹30 to ₹50.

Around Trivandrum

Neyyar Wildlife Sanctuary

Surrounding an idyllic lake created by the 1964 Neyyar Dam 35km north of Trivandrum, the main attraction at this sanctuary is the **Lion Safari Park** (📞0471-2272182, 9714347582; Indian/foreigner ₹200/300; ⏰9am-4pm Tue-Sun). Admission includes a boat ride across the lake, a lion safari and a visit to a **deer park** and **Crocodile Production Centre** (named for Australian legend Steve Irwin). The fertile forest lining the shore is home to gaurs, sambar deer, sloth, elephants, lion-tailed macaques and the odd tiger.

Get here from Trivandrum's KSRTC bus stand by frequent bus (₹34, 1½ hours). A taxi is about ₹1000 return (with two hours' waiting time) from Trivandrum, or ₹1400 from Kovalam. The KTDC office in Trivandrum also runs tours to Neyyar Dam (₹400).

Sivananda Yoga Vedanta Dhanwantari Ashram

Just before Neyyar Dam, the superbly located **Sivananda Yoga Vedanta Dhanwantari Ashram** (📞0471-2273093; www.sivananda.org.in/neyyardam; dm & tent ₹750, tw ₹950-1200, with AC ₹1700), established in 1978, is renowned for its hatha yoga courses. Courses start on the 1st and 16th of each month, run for a minimum of two weeks and include various levels of accommodation and vegetarian meals. Low season (May to September) rates are ₹100 less. There's an exacting schedule (5.30am to 10pm) of yoga practice, meditation and chanting. Bookings essential. Month-long yoga-teacher training and ayurvedic massage courses are also available.

Kovalam

📞 0471

Once a calm fishing village clustered around its crescent beaches, Kovalam today is Kerala's most developed resort. The main stretch, **Lighthouse Beach**, is touristy with hotels and restaurants built up along the shore, while **Hawah Beach** to the north is usually crowded with day trippers heading straight from the taxi stand to the sand. Neither beach is particularly clean, but at less than 15km from the capital it's a convenient place to have some fun by the sea, there's some promising surf, and it makes a good base for ayurvedic treatments and yoga courses.

About 2km further north, **Samudra Beach** has several upmarket resorts, restaurants and a peaceful but steep beach.

ℹ️ Dangers & Annoyances

There are strong rips at both ends of Lighthouse Beach that carry away several swimmers every year. Swim only between the flags in the area patrolled by lifeguards and avoid swimming during the monsoon.

🔘 Sights & Activities

Vizhinjam Lighthouse LIGHTHOUSE
(Indian/foreigner ₹10/25, camera/video ₹20/25; ⏰10am-5pm) Kovalam's most distinguishing feature is the working candy-striped lighthouse at the southern end of the beach. Climb the spiral staircase for vertigo-inducing views up and down the coast.

Kovalam Surf Club SURFING
(📞9847347367; www.kovalamsurfclub.com; Lighthouse Beach; 1½ hr lessons ₹1000, board rental half-/full day ₹500/1000) This surf shop and club on Lighthouse Beach offers lessons (from introductory to performance), board rental and a community focus.

Santhigiri AYURVEDA
(📞0471-2482800; www.santhigiriashram.org; Lighthouse Beach Rd; from ₹1100; ⏰9am-8pm) Recommended massages and ayurvedic treatments.

🛏️ Sleeping

Kovalam is packed with hotels and guesthouses, though true budget places are becoming a dying breed in high season. Beachfront properties are the most expensive and sought-after, but look out for smaller places tucked away in the labyrinth of sandy paths behind the beach among the palm groves and rice paddies; they're usually much better value. All places offer big discounts outside the December–January high season; book ahead in peak times.

Kovalam

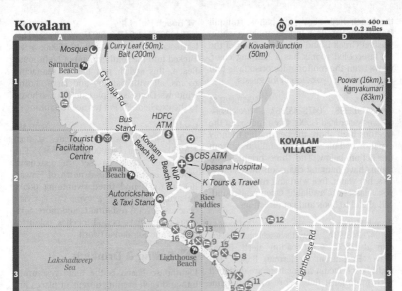

Kovalam

Green Valley Cottages   GUESTHOUSE $
(☑ 0471-2480636; indira_ravi@hotmail.com; r ₹700-1000) Back amongst the palm trees and overlooking a lily pond, this serene complex feels a little faded but it's quiet and good value. The 22 rooms are simple, but the upper rooms have good views from the front terraces.

Hotel Greenland   GUESTHOUSE $
(☑ 0471-2486442; hotelgreenlandin@yahoo.com; r ₹500-1400) This friendly family-run place has refurbished rooms in a multilevel com-

plex just back from the beach. It's not flash but rooms have lots of natural light and the larger upstairs rooms have balconies.

Dwaraka Lodge   GUESTHOUSE $
(☑ 0471-2480411; d ₹500) With regular licks of paint helping to cover up the war wounds of this tired old-timer attached to Rock Cafe, friendly Dwaraka is the cheapest oceanside property.

Paradesh Inn   GUESTHOUSE $$
(☑ 9995362952; inn.paradesh@yahoo.com; Avaduthura; d incl breakfast from ₹1800; @) Back from

the beach high above the palms, tranquil Italian-run Paradesh Inn resembles a white-washed Greek island hideaway. Each of the six fan-cooled rooms has a hanging chair, views from the rooftop, nice breakfasts and *satya* cooking ('yoga food') for guests.

Treetops
GUESTHOUSE $$

(🗹9847912398, 0471-2481363; treetopsofk-ovalam@yahoo.in; d ₹1500; @🛜) Indeed in the treetops high above the beach, this friendly expat-owned place is a peaceful retreat from the action below. The three bright, clean rooms have hanging chairs on the terraces, TVs, hot water, free wi-fi and rooftop views; yoga classes are available. Open year-round; call ahead to book and get directions.

Beach Hotel
GUESTHOUSE $$

(🗹0471-2481937; www.thebeachhotel-kovalam. com; d ₹2850; 🛜) Location alert! Below Waves Restaurant & German Bakery, the eight beach-facing rooms here are designed with minimalist flair, ochre tones and finished with smart, arty touches.

Maharaju Palace
GUESTHOUSE $$

(🗹9946854270; www.maharajupalace.com; s/d incl breakfast ₹2600/3300, cottage ₹4200/5300; ❄🛜) More of a peaceful retreat than a palace, this quirky Dutch-owned place in a lane just back from the beach has more character than most, with timber furnishings, including the odd four-poster bed, and a separate cottage in the garden. The lovely breakfast terrace is hung with chintzy chandeliers.

Jeevan Ayurvedic Beach Resort
RESORT $$

(🗹9846898498, 0471-2480662; www.jeevanre-sort.net; d ₹1800-4200, with AC ₹2400-12,000; ❄❄) Beachfront Jeevan is an inviting sort of place with one of the only seafront pools on this strip. Expect decent-sized rooms with bathtubs. All but the cheapest ground-floor rooms have sea views and balconies.

Wilson Ayurvedic Resort
HOTEL $$

(🗹0471-2480051; Lighthouse Beach; d ₹750-1250, with AC ₹2000-3500; ❄🛜❄) Wilson has clean and reasonably well-maintained rooms orbiting a pool just back from Lighthouse Beach. It has a leafy holiday-resort vibe and offers ayurvedic treatments.

Sea Flower
HOTEL $$

(🗹0471 2480554; www.seaflowerkovalam.com; d ₹2300; 🛜) At the southern end of Lighthouse Beach, this friendly little place is handy for Lighthouse Rd and is reasonably priced for the beachfront location. Rooms are simple but fresh, with balconies and sea views.

★ Beach Hotel II
HOTEL $$$

(🗹9400031243, 0471-2481937; www.thebeachho-tel-kovalam.com; d ₹4500, with AC ₹5600; ❄🛜) Tucked into the southern end of Lighthouse Beach, this stylish pad has 10 sea-facing rooms, all with balcony and large sliding windows. Decor is simple chic. It's also home to the excellent Fusion terrace restaurant.

Leela
HOTEL $$$

(🗹0471-2480101; www.theleela.com; d from ₹16,200, ste from ₹40,000; ❄@❄❄) The sumptuous Leela is set in extensive grounds on the headland north of Hawah Beach. You'll find three swimming pools, an ayurvedic centre, a gym, two 'private beaches', several restaurants and more. Spacious rooms have period touches, colourful textiles and Keralan artwork.

🍴 Eating & Drinking

Lighthouse Beach is the main restaurant hub and each evening dozens of places lining the beach promenade display the catch of the day – just pick a fish or lobster, settle on a price and decide how you want it prepared. Market price varies enormously depending on the day's catch, but at the time of research it was around ₹350 per fish fillet, ₹900 per half kilo of tiger prawns, and ₹3500 per kilo of lobster. Unlicensed places might serve alcohol in mugs, or with the bottles hidden discreetly out of sight (or not, depending on current government rules).

Samudra Beach, to the north, is quieter but also has some restaurants worth seeking out. For a romantic dining splurge, the restaurants at Leela and Vivanta by Taj are pricey but top class.

Suprabhatham
KERALAN $

(meals ₹80-230; 🕖7am-10pm) This little veg place hidden back from the beach doesn't look like much, but it dishes up excellent, inexpensive Keralan cooking, vegetarian thalis and fresh fruit juices in a rustic setting.

Varsha Restaurant
SOUTH INDIAN $

(mains ₹100-175; 🕖8am-10pm) This little restaurant just back from Lighthouse Beach serves some of Kovalam's best vegetarian food at budget prices. Dishes are fresh and carefully prepared. A great spot for breakfast and lunch in particular.

Waves Restaurant & German Bakery
MULTICUISINE $$

(Beach Hotel; breakfast ₹80-450, mains ₹250-450; 🕖7.30am-11pm; 🛜) With its broad, burnt-

KERALA GOING DRY?

In an effort to curb high per capita alcohol consumption and perceived associated social problems (including India's highest suicide rate), the Keralan government is going dry. In 2014, the government announced a 10-year plan to move towards full prohibition by gradually closing down bars (except those in five-star hotels) and state-run liquor outlets. At the time of writing, almost 700 bars had been closed, mostly in three- and four-star hotels, though many government-run liquour outlets were still dispensing bottles of IMFL rum and brandy to long queues. The plan is to close 10% of these outlets each year over 10 years.

It remains to be seen how this ban might affect the tourism industry or how far the government will take it. The general consensus is that while hard liquour bars will remain closed, 'beer parlours' would open in their place and that a Kingfisher will still be available at tourist places. It's also likely that the black market will boom.

orange balcony, ambient soundtrack and wide-roaming menu, Waves is usually busy with foreigners. It morphs into the German Bakery, a great spot for breakfast with fresh bread, croissants, pastries and decent coffee, while dinner turns up Thai curries, German sausages, pizza and seafood. There's a small bookshop attached. Wi-fi is ₹40.

Swiss Cafe   CAFE $$
(mains ₹110-490; ⊘7.15am-10pm) Swiss Cafe stands out for tasty Euro dishes like rosti, schnitzel, pasta and pizza, unusual dishes like roast lamb in whisky sauce as well as the usual fresh seafood and Indian staples. The balcony, with its wicker chairs, is a good place to take in the action.

Malabar Cafe   INDIAN $$
(mains ₹110-450; ⊘8am-11pm) The busy tables tell a story: with candlelight at night and views through pot plants to the crashing waves, Malabar offers tasty food and good service.

Fusion   MULTICUISINE $$
(mains ₹150-450; ⊘7.30am-10.30pm; 🛜) The terrace restaurant at Beach Hotel II is one of the best dining experiences on Lighthouse Beach with an inventive East-meets-West menu – a range of Continental dishes, Asian fusion, and interesting seafood numbers like lobster steamed in vodka. Also serves French press coffee and herbal teas.

Curry Leaf   MULTICUISINE $$
(Samudra Beach; mains ₹100-350; ⊘8am-8.30pm) On a small hilltop overlooking Samudra Beach, this new two-storey restaurant boasts enviable ocean and sunset views, eager staff and good food ranging from fresh seafood and tandoori to continental dishes. It requires a bit of a walk along paths or up

hill from the beach, but the uncrowded location is part of the charm.

Bait   SEAFOOD $$$
(Vivanta by Taj; mains ₹300-750; ⊘12.30-3pm & 6-10.30pm) The seafood restaurant at the Taj off Samudra Beach is designed as an upmarket alfresco beach shack. Watch the chefs at work in the open kitchen; the seafood and spicy preparations are top-notch.

ⓘ Information

About 500m uphill from Lighthouse Beach are HDFC and Axis ATMs, and there are Federal Bank and ICICI ATMs at Kovalam Junction. There are several small internet cafes charging around ₹30 per hour.

Global Internet (Leo Restaurant; internet/wi-fi per hour ₹40/30; ⊘9am-9pm; 🛜) Check your email on the terminals or hook up to the wi-fi in the restaurant.

Post Office (Kovalam Beach Rd; ⊘9am-1pm Mon-Sat) Near Leela Hotel.

Tourist Facilitation Centre (☏0471-2480085; Kovalam Beach Rd; ⊘9.30am-5pm) Helpful; in the entrance to Government Guesthouse near the bus stand.

Upasana Hospital (☏0471-2480632) Has English-speaking doctors who can take care of minor injuries.

ⓘ Getting There & Around

BUS

Buses start and finish at an unofficial stand on the main road outside the entrance to Leela resort and all buses pass through Kovalam Junction, about 1.5km north of Lighthouse Beach. Buses connect Kovalam and Trivandrum every 20 minutes between 5.30am and 10pm (₹15, 30 minutes). For northbound onward travel it's easiest to take any bus to Trivandrum and change there, but there are two buses daily to Ernakulam (₹210, 5½ hours), stopping at Kallambalam (for Varkala, ₹750, 1½ hours), Kollam (₹85, 2½ hours) and Alleppey (₹125, four hours). There are also a couple of buses for Kanyakumari (₹80, two hours).

TAXI

A taxi between Trivandrum and Kovalam beach is around ₹400; an autorickshaw should cost ₹300. From the bus stand to the north end of Lighthouse Beach costs around ₹50.

MOTORCYCLE

K Tours & Travel (☏ 8089493376, 0471-2127003; scooters/Enfields per day from ₹400/600) next door to Devi Garden Restaurant just above Hawa Beach, rents out scooters and Enfields.

Around Kovalam

Poovar

About 16km southeast of Kovalam, almost at the Tamil Nadu border, Poovar is the gateway to a region of beaches, estuaries, villages and upmarket resorts that comprise the 'mini backwaters' of Kerala's far south.

Boat operators along the Neyyar River will take you on 1½- to two-hour cruises through the waterways visiting the beach, bird-filled mangrove swamps and forested Poovar Island for around ₹2500 for two people. Travel agents in Kovalam can also arrange these trips.

Poovar Island Resort   RESORT $$$
(☏ 0471-2212068, 9895799044; www.poovarislandresorts.com; s/d cottage from ₹9600/10,800, floating cottage from ₹15,000/16,200; 🌀🌐🏊) Accessible only by boat, this resort is popular for its romantic 'floating' cottages moored on the water's edge – though most of the rooms are on land and designed in Keralan architectural style. It's a soothing, peaceful and very well-appointed place to retreat from the mainland or beach resorts.

Varkala

☏ 0470 / POP 42,270

Perched almost perilously along the edge of 15m-high red laterite cliffs, the resort of Varkala has a naturally beautiful setting and the cliff-top stretch has steadily grown into

---

AYURVEDIC RESORTS

Between Kovalam and Poovar, amid seemingly endless swaying palms, laid-back village life and some empty golden-sand beaches, are a string of upmarket ayurvedic resorts that are worth a look if you're serious about immersing yourself in ayurvedic treatments. They're all between 6km and 10km southeast of Kovalam.

Dr Franklin's Panchakarma Institute (☏ 0471-2480870; www.dr-franklin.com; Chowara; s/d hut €23/30, r from €28/37, with AC €41/60; @🌐🏊) For those serious about ayurvedic treatment, this is a reputable and less expensive alternative to the flashier resorts. Daily treatment with full meal plan costs €70. Accommodation is comfortable but not resort style.

Niraamaya Surya Samudra (☏ 0471-2480413; www.niraamaya.in; Pulinkudi; r incl breakfast ₹18,000-32,000; 🌀🌐🏊) The latest incarnation of Surya Samudra offers A-list-style seclusion. The 22 transplanted traditional Keralan homes come with four-poster beds and open-air bathrooms, set in a palm grove above sparkling seas. There's an infinity pool carved out of a single block of granite, renowned Niraamaya Spa, ayurvedic treatments, gym and spectacular outdoor yoga platforms.

Bethsaida Hermitage (☏ 0471-2267554; www.bethsaidahermitage.com; Pulinkudi; s €90-150, d €150-165; 🌀🌐🏊) This charitable organisation helps support two nearby orphanages and several other worthy causes. As a bonus, it's also a luxurious and remote beachside escape, with sculpted gardens, seductively slung hammocks, putting-green-perfect lawns, palms galore and professional ayurvedic treatments and yoga classes.

Thapovan Heritage Home (☏ 0471-2480453; www.thapovan.com; s/d hillside from ₹3200/4000, cottages ₹5300/6700, beachfront s/d cottage ₹5600/7000; 🌀🌐) Two properties only 100m apart – one consists of beachfront cottages in Keralan style, and the other is the gorgeous hilltop location where Keralan teak cottages are filled with handcrafted furniture and set among perfectly manicured grounds with wonderful views to the ocean and swaying palm groves. Ayurvedic treatments range from one-hour massages to 28-day treatment marathons, as well as yoga and meditation sessions.

Kerala's most popular backpacker hang-out. A small strand of beach nuzzles Varkala's cliff edge, where restaurants play innocuous trance music and stalls sell T-shirts, baggy trousers and silver jewellery. It's touristy and the sales pitch can be tiring, but Varkala is still a great place to watch the days slowly turn into weeks, and it's not hard to escape the crowds further north or south where the beaches are cleaner and quieter.

Despite its backpacker vibe, Varkala is essentially a temple town, and the main Papanasham beach is a holy place where Hindus come to make offerings for passed loved ones, assisted by priests who set up shop beneath the Hindustan Hotel.

ℹ Dangers & Annoyances

The beaches at Varkala have strong currents; even experienced swimmers have been swept away. During the monsoon the beach all but disappears and the cliffs themselves are slowly being eroded. Take care walking on the cliff path, especially at night – much of it is unfenced and it can be slippery in parts.

If women wear bikinis or even swimsuits on the beach at Varkala, they are likely to feel uncomfortably exposed to stares. Wearing a sarong when out of the water will help avoid offending local sensibilities. Dress conservatively if going into Varkala town.

⊙ Sights

Janardhana Temple   HINDU TEMPLE
Varkala is a temple town and Janardhana Temple is the main event – its technicolour Hindu spectacle sits hovering above Beach Rd. It's closed to non-Hindus, but you may be invited in the temple grounds where there is a huge banyan tree and shrines to Ayyappan, Hanuman and other deities.

Sivagiri Mutt   ASHRAM
(☑0470-2602807; www.sivagirimutt.org) Sivagiri Mutt is the headquarters of the Shri Narayana Dharma Sanghom Trust, the ashram devoted to Shri Narayana Guru (1855–1928), Kerala's most prominent guru. This is a popular pilgrimage site and the resident swami is happy to talk to visitors.

Ponnumthuruthu Island   ISLAND
(boat ride ₹250 per person) About 10km south of Varkala, this island in the middle of a backwater lake is home to the Shiva-Parvati Hindu Temple, also known as the Golden Temple. The main reason to venture down here is the scenic punt-powered boat ride to and around the island.

Kappil Beach   BEACH
About 9km north of Varkala by road, Kappil Beach is a prettty and, as yet, undeveloped stretch of sand. It's also the start of a mini network of backwaters. The Kappil Lake Boat Club, near the bridge, hires out boats for short trips on the lake.

🏃 Activities

The gently undulating path from the northern clifftop continues for a photogenic 7km to Kappil Beach, passing a subtley changing beach landscape, including Odayam Beach and the fishing village of Edava. The walk is best done early in the morning.

Yoga (per session ₹300 to ₹400) is offered at several guesthouses, and boogie boards (₹100) can be hired from places along the beach; be wary of strong currents. Many of the resorts and hotels along the north cliff offer ayurvedic treatments and massage.

Laksmi's   BEAUTY & MASSAGE
(☑9895948080; Clafouti Beach Resort; manicure/pedicure ₹600-1000, henna ₹500, massage ₹1200; ⊙9am-7pm) This tiny place offers quality ladies-only treatments such as threading and waxing, manicures and massage.

Haridas Yoga   YOGA
(www.pranayogavidya.com; Hotel Green Palace; classes ₹300; ⊙8am & 4.30pm Aug-May) Recommended drop-in 1½-hour hatha yoga classes with experienced teachers.

Eden Garden   MASSAGE
(☑0470-2603910; www.edengarden.in; massages from ₹1000) Offers a more upmarket ayurvedic experience, including single treatments and packages.

Soul & Surf   SURFING, YOGA
(☑9895580106; www.soulandsurf.com; South Cliff; surf lessons ₹2300, surf guides ₹1150; ⊙Oct-May) This UK outfit organises surfing trips and yoga retreats in season, with accommodation at their South Cliff pad. They also run the Papanasam Surf School for beginners, with 1½-hour lessons. If you already surf and there's space, join one of the regular surf tours (₹1150). Board rental is ₹850/1600 for a half/full day.

🛌 Sleeping

Most places to stay are crammed in along the north cliff where backpackers tend to congregate, but there are some nice

Varkala

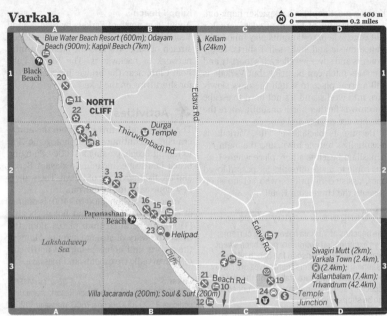

Varkala

◉ **Sights**
1 Janardhana Temple...............................C3

◉ **Activities, Courses & Tours**
2 Eden Garden...C3
3 Haridas Yoga B2
4 Laksmi's..A2

◉ **Sleeping**
Eden Garden....................................(see 2)
5 Gateway Hotel Janardhanapuram C3
6 Jicky's..B2
7 Kaiya House..C3
8 Kerala Bamboo House A2
9 Krishnatheeram.......................................A1
10 Omsam Guesthouse C3
11 Puthooram...A1
12 Sea Pearl Chalets..................................C3

◉ **Eating**
13 Café del Mar...B2
14 Cafe Italiano A2
15 Coffee Temple..B2
16 God's Own Country Kitchen.................B2
17 Juice Shack...B2
18 Oottupura Vegetarian Restaurant.......B3
19 Sreepadman C3
20 Trattorias A1
21 Wait n Watch...C3

◉ **Entertainment**
22 Rock n Roll Cafe.....................................A1

◉ **Transport**
23 Autorickshaw Stand..............................B3
24 Autorickshaw Stand..............................C3

places down by the southern cliffs. Less-developed Odayam Beach, about 1km further north of Varkala's Black Beach, is a tranquil alternative.

Practically all accommodation places can be reached by taxi or autorickshaw via the network of lanes leading to the cliffs, but the commission racket is alive and well – make sure your driver takes you to the place you've asked for.

★ **Jicky's**　　　　　　　　　　　GUESTHOUSE $
(☑9846179325, 0470-2606994; www.jickys.com; s ₹500, d ₹800-1200, AC cottage ₹3000; ✳🅰) In the palm groves just back from the cliffs and taxi stand, family-run Jicky's remains as friendly as they come and has blossomed into several buildings offering plenty of choice for travellers. The rooms in the main whitewashed building are fresh, and nearby are two charming octagonal double cottages,

and some larger air-con rooms. Offers good off-season discounts.

★ Kaiya House
GUESTHOUSE $$

(☑ 9746126909, 9995187913; www.kaiyahouse.com; d incl breakfast ₹2750, d with AC ₹3300; ❀ 🛜) What Kaiya House lacks in sea views it makes up for with charm, welcoming owners and sheer relaxation. Each of the five rooms is thoughtfully furnished and themed (African, Indian, Chinese, Japanese and English) with four-poster beds and artworks on the walls. There's a lovely rooftop terrace and rear courtyard with calming vibe. Expat owner Debra will welcome you with tea, advice and free walking tours. The clifftop is a 10-minute walk away.

Eden Garden
RESORT $$

(☑ 0470-2603910; www.edengarden.in; cottages ₹1500-2000, deluxe ₹4500; 🛜) Stylish rooms come with high wooden ceilings and attractive furniture, set around a lush lily pond. There are also bamboo cottages and deluxe organically-shaped cottages like white space-mushrooms with intricate paintwork, round beds, and mosaic circular baths. Ayurvedic packages from three to 30 days.

Kerala Bamboo House
RESORT $$

(☑ 9895270993; www.keralabamboohouse.com; huts d ₹2500-3500, r with AC ₹5000; ❀ 🛜) For that simple bamboo-hut experience, this popular place squishes together dozens of pretty Balinese-style huts and a neatly maintained garden about half-way along the North Cliff walk. Ayurvedic treatments, yoga and cooking classes (₹600 per person, minimum two people) are on offer.

Puthooram
RESORT $$

(☑ 9895675805, 0470-3202007; www.puthooram.com; r ₹400-1350, with AC ₹1650-3300; ❀ @) Puthooram's wood-lined bungalows are set around a charming little garden of pot plants. Room prices and standards vary so check out a few; rooms with sea view are pricier.

Omsam Guesthouse
GUESTHOUSE $$

(☑ 0470-2604455; www.omsamguesthome.com; South Cliff; d ₹2500-3500, d with AC ₹4500; ❀ 🛜) The seven rooms in this beautiful Keralan-style guesthouse are a delight, with heavy timber stylings and furniture. Good location south of the main beach.

Sea Pearl Chalets
RESORT $$

(☑ 0470-2660105; www.seapearlchalets.com; d ₹2030) Perched on Varkala's quieter southern cliff, these basic, pod-like huts have unbeatable views and are surrounded by prim lawns. Worth checking out before they tumble into the ocean.

Krishnatheeram
RESORT $$$

(Ayur Holy Beach Resort; ☑ 0470-2601305; www.krishnatheeram.com; r ₹5000, with AC ₹6000; ❀ 🛜 🏊) Overlooking Black Beach and one of the few northern beachfront resorts with a pool, this neat ayurvedic resort specialises in yoga therapy, with daily classes and professional ayurvedic treatments.

Villa Jacaranda
GUESTHOUSE $$$

(☑ 0470-2610296; www.villa-jacaranda.biz; d incl breakfast ₹5200-7000; 🛜) The ultimate in understated luxury, this romantic retreat back from the southern beach has just four spacious, bright rooms in a large two-storey house, each with a balcony and decorated with a chic blend of minimalist modern and period touches. The top-floor room has its own rooftop garden with sea views.

Blue Water Beach Resort
COTTAGES $$$

(☑ 0470-2664422, 9446848534; www.bluewaterstay.com; Odayam Beach; cottages ₹5000, with AC ₹7500; ❀ 🛜) At quiet Odayam Beach, north of Varkala, Blue Water has sturdy individual timber cottages with tiled roofs arranged in a pleasant lawn area sloping to the beach.

Gateway Hotel Janardhanapuram
HOTEL $$$

(☑ 0470-6673300; www.thegatewayhotels.com; d incl breakfast from ₹9000, ste ₹12,500; ❀ @ 🛜 🏊) Varkala's flashiest hotel, the rebadged Gateway, is looking hot with gleaming linen and mocha cushions in rooms overlooking the garden, while the more expensive rooms have sea views and balconies. There's a fantastic pool with bar (nonguests ₹500), tennis court and the well-regarded GAD restaurant.

✖ Eating & Drinking

Most restaurants in Varkala offer the same traveller menu of Indian, Asian and continental fare to a soundtrack of easy-listening trance and Bob Marley, but the quality of the cliffside 'shacks' has improved out of sight over the years and most offer free wi-fi. Join in the nightly Varkala saunter till you find a place that suits.

Sreepadman
SOUTH INDIAN $

(thalis ₹75; ⊙ 5am-10pm) For cheap and authentic Keralan fare – think dosas and thalis – where you can rub shoulders with rickshaw drivers and pilgrims rather than tourists, pull up a seat at hole-in-the-wall Sreepadman, opposite the Janardhana Temple and overlooking the large bathing tank.

Oottupura Vegetarian Restaurant INDIAN $
(mains ₹45-100) Near the taxi stand, this budget eatery has a respectable range of cheap veg dishes, including breakfast *puttu* (flour with milk, bananas and honey).

Coffee Temple CAFE $
(coffee ₹70-100, mains ₹80-250; ☺6am-7pm; 🖰) For your early-morning coffee fix it's hard to beat this English-run place, where the beans are freshly ground, there's fresh bread and a daily paper. The menu has also expanded into crêpes and Mexican burritos, fajitas and tacos – and it's no worse for that.

Juice Shack CAFE $
(juices from ₹70, snacks ₹80-250; ☺6am-8.30pm; 🖰) It certainly looks a bit 'shack-like' next to the fancy neighbours, but this funky little health-juice bar still turns out great juices, smoothies and snacks such as Mexican wraps.

Cafe Italiano ITALIAN $$
(mains ₹200-400; ☺7am-11pm; 🖰) As well as good pizza, pasta and crêpes, two-storey Italiano is worth a visit for its library and book exchange and for the tree growing through the upper deck.

Café del Mar MULTICUISINE $$
(dishes ₹120-450; ☺9am-10pm; 🖰) It doesn't have the big balcony of some of its neighbours, but Café del Mar is usually busy thanks to efficient service, good coffee and consistently good food.

God's Own Country Kitchen MULTICUISINE $$
(North Cliff; mains ₹80-400; ☺8.30am-10pm; 🖰) This fun place doesn't really need to play on Kerala Tourism's tagline – the food is good, there's a great little upper-floor deck and there's live music some nights in season.

Trattorias MULTICUISINE $$
(meals ₹100-400; ☺8.30am-11pm) Trattorias aims to specialise in Italian with a decent range of pasta and pizza but also offers Japanese – including sushi – and Thai dishes. This was one of the original places with an Italian coffee machine, and the wicker chairs and sea-facing terrace are cosy.

Wait n Watch INDIAN $$
(Hindustan Beach Retreat; mains ₹120-280; ☺11am-10pm; 🖰) The top-floor restaurant and cocktail bar at this ugly beachfront hotel block offers tasty-enough Indian fare and seafood, but the main reason to take the elevator is for the view from the balcony (with just a couple of tables) over the action of the beach. There's another alfresco restaurant by the pool.

AYURVEDA

With its roots in Sanskrit, the word ayurveda comes from *ayu* (life) and *veda* (knowledge); the knowledge or science of life. Principles of ayurvedic medicine were first documented in the Vedas some 2000 years ago, but may have been practised centuries earlier.

Ayurveda sees the world as having an intrinsic order and balance. It argues that we possess three *doshas* (humours): *vata* (wind or air); *pitta* (fire); and *kapha* (water/earth), known together as the *tridoshas*. Deficiency or excess in any of them can result in disease: an excess of *vata* may result in dizziness and debility; an increase in *pitta* may lead to fever, inflammation and infection. *Kapha* is essential for hydration.

Ayurvedic treatment aims to restore the balance, and hence good health, principally through two methods: panchakarma (internal purification), and herbal massage. Panchakarma is used to treat serious ailments, and is an intense detox regime, a combination of five types of therapies to rid the body of built-up endotoxins. These include: *vaman* (therapeutic vomiting); *virechan* (purgation); *vasti* (enemas); *nasya* (elimination of toxins through the nose); and *raktamoksha* (detoxification of the blood). Before panchakarma begins, the body is first prepared over several days with a special diet, oil massages (*snehana*) and herbal steam baths (*swedana*). Although it may sound pretty grim, panchakarma purification might only use a few of these treatments at a time, with therapies like bloodletting and leeches only used in rare cases. Still, this is no spa holiday. The herbs used in ayurveda grow in abundance in Kerala's humid climate – the monsoon is thought to be the best time of year for treatment, when there is less dust in the air, the pores are open and the body is most receptive to treatment – and every village has its own ayurvedic pharmacy.

☆ Entertainment

Kathakali performances are organised during high season – look out for notices locally.

Rock n Roll Cafe LIVE MUSIC
(☑ 8136858684; ⊙ 24hr) Music is the thing at this otherwise unremarkable restaurant-bar. There's live music, DJs or movies on most nights in season, as well as tabla lessons. There's also cold beer, a good cocktail list and food is available from 6pm.

ℹ Information

A 24-hour ATM at Temple Junction takes Visa cards, and there are several more ATMs in Varkala town. Many of the travel agents lining the cliff do cash advances on credit cards and change travellers cheques. Most restaurants and cafes offer free wi-fi.

ℹ Getting There & Away

There are frequent local and express trains to Trivandrum (2nd/sleeper/3AC ₹45/140/485, one hour) and Kollam (2nd/sleeper/3AC ₹45/140/485, 40 minutes), as well as seven daily services to Alleppey (2nd/sleeper/3AC ₹95/140/485, two hours). From Temple Junction, three daily buses pass by on their way to Trivandrum (₹60, 1½ to two hours), with one heading to Kollam (₹40, one hour).

ℹ Getting Around

It's about 2.5km from the train station to Varkala Beach, with autorickshaws going to Temple Junction for ₹80 and North Cliff for ₹100. Local buses also travel regularly between the train station and Temple Junction (₹5).

A few places along the cliff hire out scooters/motorbikes for ₹350/450 per day.

Kollam (Quilon)

☑ 0474 / POP 349,000

Kollam (Quilon) is the southern approach to Kerala's backwaters and one end of the popular backwater ferry trip to Alleppey. One of the oldest ports in the Arabian Sea, it was once a major commercial hub that saw Roman, Arab, Chinese and later Portuguese, Dutch and British traders jostle into port – eager to get their hands on spices and the region's cashew crops. The centre of town is reasonably hectic, but surrounding it are the calm waterways of Ashtamudi Lake, fringed with coconut palms, cashew plantations and traditional villages – a great place to get a feel for the backwaters without the crowds.

◉ Sights & Activities

The best thing to do from Kollam is explore the backwaters around **Munroe Island** by canoe, via a network of canals off Ashtamudi Lake about 15km north of Kollam.

There's a rowdy **fishing harbour** at Kollam Beach where customers and fisherfolk alike pontificate on the value of the day's catch; there's also an evening fish market from 5pm to 9pm. There's an average **beach** 2km south of town, marked at the northern end by the **Thangassery Lighthouse**.

★ Canal Cruise BOATING
(www.dtpckollam.com; tours per person ₹500; ⊙ 9am-1.30pm & 2-6.30pm) Excellent tours through the canals of Munroe Island are organised by the DTPC and a few private operators. After a 25km drive to the starting point, you take a three-hour trip via punted canoe to observe daily village life, see *kettuvallam* (rice barge) construction, toddy (palm beer) tapping, coir-making (coconut fibre), prawn and fish farming, and do some birdwatching on spice-garden visits.

Houseboat Cruises BOATING
(www.dtpckollam.com; overnight cruise ₹5000-9200, Kollam to Alappuzha cruise ₹14,000) Kollam has far fewer houseboats than Alleppey, which can mean a less touristy experience. The DTPC organises houseboat cruise packages, both locally and to Alleppey and Kochi.

Santhigiri Ayurveda Centre AYURVEDA
(☑ 9287242407, 0474-2763014; www.santhigiriashram.com; Asramam Rd, Kadappakada; massage from ₹1200) An ayurvedic centre with more of an institutional than a spa vibe, popular for its seven- to 21-day treatment packages.

★ Festivals & Events

The Kollam region hosts many festivals and boat regattas – in November and December there are temple festivals somewhere in the region virtually every day.

Kollam Pooram RELIGIOUS
(Apr) Colourful annual temple festival featuring elephants and mock sword fights.

President's Trophy Boat Race BOAT RACE
(⊙ 1 Nov) On Ashtamudi Lake, this is the most prestigious regatta in Kollam region.

Kottamkulangara Chamaya Vilakku RELIGIOUS
(⊙ Mar/Apr) Local men dress as women and carry lamps to the temple at Chavara, 15km north of Kollam.

Kollam (Quilon)

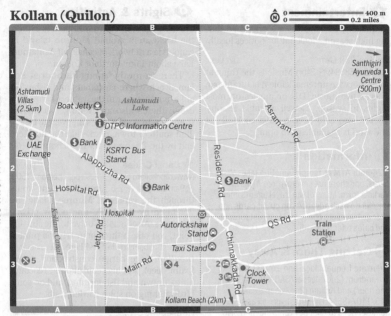

Kollam (Quilon)

🛏 Sleeping

The DTPC office keeps a list of homestays in and around Kollam.

Munroe Island
Backwaters Homestay
HOMESTAY $

(☎ 9048176186; Munroe Island; cottage ₹1200) The three colourful cottages built in Keralan style and hidden away in the backwaters of Munroe Island about 25km north (by road) of Kollam allow travellers to delve into the village experience. The friendly family can arrange canoe tours and meals..

Karuna Residency
GUESTHOUSE $

(☎ 0474-2760066; Main Rd; dm ₹150; s/d ₹400/600) This little budgeteer is starting to show its age and is very basic, but it's still in reasonable condition and the owner is accustomed to travellers.

⭐ Ashtamudi Villas
GUESTHOUSE $$

(☎ 9847132449, 0474-2706090; www.ashtamudivillas.com; near Kadavoor Church, Mathilil; d ₹1500-2000; 🖥) These charming brick cottages on the water's edge are easily the best choice for a relaxing, affordable stay in Kollam. Ebullient host Prabhath Joseph offers a warm welcome and pulls out all the stops with thoughtful architectural design, colourful decor, gleaming bathrooms, hammocks swinging between palm trees by the lake and a library of books on Kerala. Access is by road or boat – call ahead for directions.

Nani Hotel
HOTEL $$

(☎ 0474-2751141; www.hotelnani.com; Chinnakada Rd; d incl breakfast ₹1460, with AC ₹2250-3650; ❄@🖥) This boutique business hotel is a surprise in Kollam's busy centre, and very good value. Built by a cashew magnate, its beautifully designed architecture mixes traditional Keralan elements and modern lines for a sleek look. Even the cheaper rooms have flat-screen TVs, feathery pillows and sumptuous bathrooms.

Eating

Hotel Guru Prasad INDIAN $
(Main Rd; meals ₹10-45; ⊘11am-3pm) In a neat colonial building, this busy lunch place draws (mostly male) punters with cheap thalis.

Wok & Grill MULTICUISINE $$
(☑0474-2753400; mains ₹120-290; ⊘11am-3pm & 6-10pm) The combination of Thai, Chinese, Arabic and North Indian cuisines offers some tasty, meaty dishes at this modern, clean restaurant. Choose from Kung Pao chicken, green curry, ginger garlic prawns and shwarma rolls.

Prasadam MULTICUISINE $$
(☑0474-2751141; Nani Hotel, Chinnakada Rd; mains ₹160-250, lunch thalis ₹125; ⊘8am-10pm) The restaurant at the Nani Hotel has a slightly formal feel with high-backed chairs amid intricate copper-relief artwork depicting Kollam history. Meals, including Keralan dishes such as Travancore egg masala, as well as tandoori and Chinese, are beautifully prepared, and the tasty thalis are excellent value at lunchtime.

ⓘ Information

DTPC Information Centre (☑0474-2745625; www.dtpckollam.com; ⊘8am-7pm) Helpful and can organise backwater trips; near the KSRTC bus stand and boat jetty.

ⓘ Getting There & Away

BOAT

Many travellers take the canal boat to or from Alleppey (₹400; eight hours; 10.30am) as part of the classic backwaters tour (p288). From the main boat jetty there are frequent public ferry services across Ashtamudi Lake to Guhanandapuram (one hour). Fares are around ₹10 return, or ₹3 for a short hop.

BUS

Kollam is on the Trivandrum–Kollam–Alleppey–Ernakulam bus route, with buses departing every 10 or 20 minutes to Trivandrum (₹70, two hours), Alleppey (₹80, 2½ hours), Kumily (₹125, five hours, 7.50am) and Ernakulam (Kochi, ₹150, 3½ hours). Buses depart from the **KSRTC bus stand** (☑0474-2752008), conveniently near the boat jetty.

TRAIN

There are frequent trains to Ernakulam (sleeper/3AC ₹140/485, 3½ hours, six daily), Trivandrum (₹140/485, one hour) via Varkala (₹36/165, 30 minutes), and Alappuzha (Alleppey; ₹170/535, 1½ hours).

Around Kollam

Krishnapuram Palace Museum MUSEUM
(☑0479-2441133; admission ₹10, camera/video ₹25/250; ⊘9.30am-4.30pm Tue-Sun) Two kilometres south of Kayamkulam (between

---

MATHA AMRITHANANDAMAYI MISSION

The incongruously pink **Matha Amrithanandamayi Mission** (☑04762897578; www.amritapuri.org; Amrithapuri) is the famous ashram of one of India's few female gurus, Amrithanandamayi, also known as Amma (Mother) or 'The Hugging Mother' because of the *darshan* (audience) she offers, often hugging thousands of people in marathon all-night sessions.

The ashram runs official tours at 4pm and 5pm daily. It's a huge complex, with about 3000 people living there permanently – monks, nuns, students and families, both Indian and foreign. It offers food, ayurvedic treatments, yoga and meditation. Amma travels around for much of the year, so you might be out of luck if in need of a cuddle. A busy time of year at the ashram is around Amma's birthday on 27 September.

Visitors should dress conservatively and there is a strict code of behaviour. With prior arrangement – register online – you can stay at the ashram in a triple room for ₹250 per person, or ₹500 for a single (including simple vegetarian meals).

Since the ashram is on the main canal between Kollam and Alleppey, many travellers break the ferry ride by getting off here, staying a day or two, then picking up another cruise. Alternatively, cross to the other side of the canal and grab a rickshaw 10km south to Karunagappally or 12km north to Kayankulam (around ₹200), from where you can catch onward buses or trains.

If you're not taking the cruise, catch a train to either Karunagappally or Kayankulam and take an autorickshaw (around ₹200) to Vallickavu and cross the pedestrian bridge from there. If you intend to stay a while, you can book online for an ashram taxi – they pick up from as far away as Kochi or Trivandrum.

Kollam and Alleppey), this restored palace is a fine example of grand Keralan architecture. Inside are paintings, antique furniture, sculptures and a renowned 3m-high mural depicting the Gajendra Moksha (liberation of Gajendra, chief of the elephants) as told in the Mahabharata.

Buses (₹26, one hour) leave Kollam every few minutes for Kayamkulam. Get off at the bus stand near the temple gate, 2km before the palace.

Alappuzha (Alleppey)

☑ 0477 / POP 74,200

Alappuzha – still better known as Alleppey – is the hub of Kerala's backwaters, home to a vast network of waterways and more than a thousand houseboats. Wandering around the small but chaotic city centre, with its modest grid of canals, you'd be hard-pressed to agree with the 'Venice of the East' tag. But step out of this mini-mayhem – west to the beach or in practically any other direction towards the backwaters – and Alleppey is graceful and greenery-fringed, disappearing into a watery world of villages, punted canoes, toddy shops and, of course, houseboats. Float along and gaze over paddy fields of succulent green, curvaceous rice barges and village life along the banks. This is one of Kerala's most mesmerisingly beautiful and relaxing experiences.

◉ Sights & Activities

Alleppey Beach   BEACH
Alleppey's main beach is about 2km west of the city centre; there's no shelter at the beach itself and swimming is fraught due to strong currents, but the sunsets are good and there are a few places to stop for a drink or snack, including a good coffee shop. The beach stretches up and down the coast.

RKK Memorial Museum   MUSEUM
(☑ 0477-2242923; www.rkkmuseum.com; NH47, near Powerhouse Bridge; Indian/foreigner ₹150/350; ☺ 9am-5pm Tue-Sun) The Revi Karuna Karan (RKK) Memorial Museum, in a grand building fronted by Greco-Roman columns, contains a lavish collection of crystal, porcelain, ivory, Keralan antiques, furniture and artworks from the personal collection of wealthy businessman Revi Karuna Karan. The museum was created as a memorial after he passed away in 2003.

Kerala Kayaking   KAYAKING
(☑ 0477-2245001, 9846585674; www.keralakayaking.com; 4/7/10hr per person ₹1500/3000/4500) The original kayaking outfit in Alleppey. The young crew here offer excellent guided kayaking trips through narrow backwater canals. Paddles in single or double kayaks include a support boat and motorboat transport to your starting point. There are four-hour morning and afternoon trips, seven- or 10-hour day trips, and multiday village tours can also be arranged.

Shree Krishna Ayurveda
Panchkarma Centre   AYURVEDA
(☑ 09847119060; www.krishnayurveda.com; 3/5/7-day treatments from €275/420/590) For ayurvedic treatments; one-hour rejuvenation massages are ₹1000, but it specialises in three-, five- and seven-night packages with accommodation and yoga classes. Rates are cheaper with two people sharing accommodation. It's near the Nehru race finishing point.

Elephant Camp   ELEPHANTS
(☑ 9249905525; 30/60min program ₹400/1000; ☺ 8am-5.30pm) This small elephant camp near the north end of Punnamada Lake offers elephant experiences from 30 minutes to two hours. Longer sessions include feeding, bathing and a trunk shower.

☞ Tours

Any guesthouse, hotel, travel agent or the DTPC can arrange canoe or houseboat tours of the backwaters (see p288).

Kashmiri-style *shikaras* (covered boats) gather along the North Canal on the road to the houseboat dock. They charge ₹300 to ₹400 per hour for motorised canal and backwater trips. Punt-powered dugout canoes are slower but more ecofriendly. They charge from ₹250 per hour and most tours require four to five hours with village visits, walks and a visit to a toddy bar.

✯ Festivals & Events

Nehru Trophy Boat Race   BOAT RACE
(www.nehrutrophy.nic.in; tickets ₹50-2000; ☺ 2nd Sat in Aug) This is the most popular and fiercely contested of Kerala's boat race regattas. Thousands of people, many aboard houseboats, gather around the starting and finishing points on Alleppey's Punnamada Lake to watch snakeboats with up to 100 rowers battle it out.

🛏 Sleeping

Even if you're not planning on boarding a houseboat, Alleppey has some of the most charming and best-value accommodation in Kerala, from heritage homes and resorts to family-run homestays with backwater views.

The rickshaw-commission racketeers are at work here, particularly at the train and bus stations; ask to be dropped off at a landmark close to your destination, or if you're booked in, call ahead to say you're on the way.

Matthews Residency
GUESTHOUSE $

(☑9447667888, 0477-2235938; www.palmyresidency.com; off Finishing Point Rd; r ₹450-750; @🛜) One of the better budget deals, this place has six spotless rooms with Italian marble floors, three with garden-facing verandahs. It's north of the canal five minutes' walk from the bus stand but set well back from the road amid lush greenery.

⭐ Mandala Beach House
GUESTHOUSE $

(☑8589868589; www.mandalabeachhouse.com; Alleppey Beach; d ₹600-900, cottages ₹750, ste ₹2000; 🛜) Beachfront accommodation on a budget doesn't get much better than this in Alleppey. Super laid-back Mandala sits on the edge of the sand and has a range of simple rooms – the best being the glass-fronted 'penthouse' with unbeatable sunset views. Impromptu parties are known to crank up here in season, and there's a quieter nearby annexe.

Johnson's
GUESTHOUSE $

(☑9846466399, 0477-2245825; www.johnsons-kerala.com; d ₹500-850; @🛜) This backpacker favourite in a tumbledown mansion is as quirky as its owner, the gregarious Johnson Gilbert. It's a rambling residence with themed rooms filled with funky furniture, loads of plants outside and a canoe-shaped fish tank for a table. Johnson also hires out his eco-houseboat (www.ecohouseboat.com; ₹7000-13,000) and has a secluded riverside guesthouse in the backwaters.

Nanni Beach Residence
GUESTHOUSE $

(☑9895039767; www.nannitours.com; Cullan Rd; d ₹250-600) A very good deal, this easy-going guesthouse is a short walk from the beach and 1.5km north of the train station. Rooms are simple and the upstairs ones are spacious. Young owner Shibu is a good source of local information and works hard making the place homely.

Palmy Lake Resort
HOMESTAY $

(☑9447667888, 0477-2235938; www.palmyresorts.com; Punnamada Rd East; cottages d ₹1000) With six individual cottages, there's some lakeside charm, swinging hammocks and a sense of calm at this welcoming family homestay with homecooked meals.

Paradise Inn
GUESTHOUSE $

(dm ₹250, d from ₹600, with AC ₹1250; ❄🛜) This double-storey guesthouse north of the main canal offers daily yoga classes (₹300) in its rooftop shala, budget dorms and a restaurant. Owner Antony organises tours.

Vedanta Wake Up!
HOSTEL $

(☑0477-2231133; www.vedantawakeup.com; Punnamuda Rd; dm ₹700, d with AC ₹2000; ❄🛜) In a good location just north of the houseboat dock, this new hostel has neat and clean air-con dorms, cosy common areas, a cafe and the usual extras like lockers and wi-fi. It's a good place to meet other travellers, especially if you're looking to get a houseboat group together.

Cherukara Nest
HOMESTAY $$

(☑9947059628, 0477-2251509; www.cherukaranest.com; d/tr incl breakfast ₹900/1100, with AC ₹1500, AC cottages ₹1500; ❄@🛜) Set in well-tended gardens, with a pigeon coop at the back, this lovely heritage home has the sort of welcoming family atmosphere that makes you want to stay. In the main house there are four large characterful rooms, with high ceilings, lots of polished wood touches and antediluvian doors with ornate locks – check out the spacious split-level air-con room. Owner Tony also has a good-value houseboat (2/4-people ₹6000/8000) – one of the few that still uses punting power.

Gowri Residence
GUESTHOUSE $$

(☑9847055371, 0477-2236371; www.gowriresidence.com; Mullackal Rd; d ₹600-1200, AC cottages ₹1500-2000; ❄🛜) This rambling complex about 800m north of North Canal has an array of rooms and cottages in a large garden: traditional wood-panelled rooms in the main house, and several types of bungalows made from either stone, wood, bamboo or thatch – the best have cathedral ceilings, air-con and flat-screen TVs. Overall the place is looking a little faded.

Tharavad
HOMESTAY $$

(☑0477-242044; www.tharavadheritageresort.com; d ₹2500-3500; ❄) In a quiet canalside location between the town centre and beach, this

Alappuzha (Alleppey)

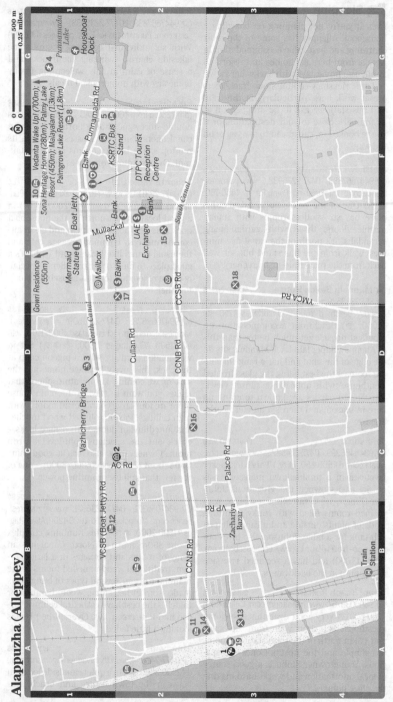

Puṇṇamada Lake

Houseboat Dock

Vedanta Wake Up! (700m); Palmy Lake Resort (450m); Malayalam (13km); Palmgrove Lake Resort (1.8km)

Sona Heritage Home (280m);

Gowri Residence (550m)

Puṇṇamada Rd

KSRTC Bus Stand

DTPC Tourist Reception Centre

Bank

Bank

Boat Jetty

Mullackal Rd

Mermaid Statue

UAE Exchange Bank

Bank

Mailbox

South Canal

North Canal

CCSB Rd

YMCA Rd

Vazhicherry Bridge

Cullan Rd

CCNB Rd

AC Rd

Palace Rd

VCSB (Boat Jetty) Rd

CCNB Rd

VP Rd

Zachariya Bazar

Train Station

Alappuzha (Alleppey)

charming ancestral home has lots of glossy teak and antiques, shuttered windows, five characterful rooms and well-maintained gardens.

Sona Heritage Home   GUESTHOUSE $$
(☑0477-2235211; www.sonahome.com; Lakeside, Finishing Point; r ₹800-900, with AC ₹1400-1500; ❄❋) Run by the affable Joseph, this beautiful old heritage home has high-ceilinged rooms with faded flowered curtains, Christian motifs and four-poster beds overlooking a well-kept garden.

Malayalam   RESORT $$
(☑9496829424, 0477-2234591; malayalamresorts @yahoo.com; Punnamada; r ₹1600-2500; ❋) This little family-run pad has four cute bamboo cottages and a pair of spacious two-storey four-room houses facing the lake near the Nehru Trophy starting point. Views from the upstairs rooms with balcony are sweet. Walk past the Keraleeyam resort reception and along the canal bank.

Palmgrove Lake Resort   RESORT $$
(☑0477-2235004; www.palmgrovelakeresort.com; Punnamada; cottages d ₹2800-3300, ste ₹4000; ❄❋) Close to the starting point of the Neh-

ru Trophy Snake Boat Race on Punnamada Lake, the stylish but ageing individual double cottages here are set in a palm-filled garden with lake views. They're all air-con and the owners are planning on building some new ones.

Punnamada Homestay   HOMESTAY $$
(☑9847044688, 0484-2371761; d incl meals ₹3000; ❋) This attractive heritage-style family home is about 8km north of Alleppey in a peaceful location close to Punnamada Lake. The two rooms are neat, well-furnished and have private balconies, while the home-cooking is first-rate.

★**Raheem Residency**   HOTEL $$$
(☑0477-2239767; www.raheemresidency.com; Beach Rd; d €120-150; ❄❋❄) This thoughtfully renovated 1860s heritage home is a joy to visit, let alone stay in. The 10 rooms have been restored to their former glory and have bathtubs, antique furniture and period fixtures. The common areas are airy and comfortable, and there are pretty indoor courtyards, a well-stocked library, a great little pool and an excellent restaurant. Creative types should enquire about Raheem's writers' retreats.

✖ Eating & Drinking

★**Mushroom**   ARABIAN, INDIAN $
(mains ₹70-140; ⊙ noon-midnight) Breezy open-air restaurant with wrought-iron chairs specialising in cheap, tasty and spicy halal meals like chicken kali mirch, fish tandoori and chilli mushrooms. Lots of locals and travellers give it a good vibe. It's near the South Police Station.

Kream Korner Art Cafe   MULTICUISINE $
(☑0477-2252781; www.kreamkornerartcafe.com; Mullackal Rd; dishes ₹40-250; ⊙ 9am-10pm) The most colourful dining space in town, this food-meets-art restaurant greets you with brightly painted tables and contemporary local art on the walls. It's a relaxed, airy place popular with Indian and foreign families for its inexpensive and tasty menu of Indian and Chinese dishes.

Thaff   INDIAN $
(YMCA Rd; meals ₹45-120; ⊙ 9am-9pm Sun-Thu, 9am-10pm Sat & Sun) This popular restaurant serves tasty South Indian bites, with some North Indian and Chinese flavours mixed in. It does succulent spit-roasted-chicken, biryanis and brain-freezing ice-cream shakes.

There's another busy hole-in-wall location on Punnamada Rd.

Le Coffee Time
CAFE

(Alleppey Beach; coffee & snacks ₹70-150; ⊙8.30am-5pm; ☎) Friendly beachfront place with a genuine Italian espresso machine, some shady tables and free wi-fi.

Dreamers
MULTICUISINE $$

(☑8086752586; www.dreamersrestaurant.com; Alleppey Beach; mains ₹130-450; ⊙11am-10.30pm) Designed to vaguely resemble a *kettuvallam* (rice barge), Dreamers, across from Alleppey Beach, is a rustic but cool little restaurant with an upper deck, serving a wide variety of dishes from Tibetan momos and Thai curries to seafood and pizzas.

Harbour Restaurant
MULTICUISINE $$

(☑0484-2230767; Beach Rd; meals ₹120-300; ⊙10am-10pm) This enjoyable beachside place is run by the nearby Raheem Residency. It's more casual and budget-conscious than the hotel's restaurant, but promises a range of well-prepared Indian, Chinese and continental dishes, and some of the coldest beer in town.

Royale Park Hotel
INDIAN $$

(YMCA Rd; meals ₹120-250; ⊙7am-10.30pm, bar from 10.30am; ☎) There's an extensive menu at this air-con hotel restaurant, and the food, including veg and fish thalis, is consistently good. You can order from the same menu in the surprisingly nice upstairs bar and wash down your meal with a cold Kingfisher.

Chakara Restaurant
MULTICUISINE $$$

(☑0477-2230767; Beach Rd; mini Kerala meal ₹500, mains from ₹450; ⊙12.30-3pm & 7-10pm) The restaurant at Raheem Residency is Alleppey's finest, with seating on a bijou open rooftop, reached via a spiral staircase, with views over to the beach. The menu creatively combines traditional Keralan and European cuisine, specialising in locally caught fish.

ℹ Information

DTPC Tourist Reception Centre (☑0477-2253308; www.dtpcalappuzha.com; Boat Jetty Rd; ⊙9am-5pm) Close to the bus stand and boat jetty. Staff are helpful and can advise on homestays and houseboats.

Tourist Police (☑0477-2251161; ⊙24hr) Next door to the DTPC.

UAE Exchange (cnr Cullan & Mullackal Rds; ⊙9.30am-6pm Mon-Fri, to 4pm Sat, to 1pm Sun) Changes cash and travellers cheques.

ℹ Getting There & Away

BOAT
Ferries run to Kottayam (₹10) from the boat jetty on VCSB (Boat Jetty) Rd.

BUS
From the KSRTC bus stand, frequent buses head to Trivandrum (₹122, 3½ hours, every 20 minutes), Kollam (₹70, 2½ hours) and Ernakulam (Kochi, ₹52, 1½ hours). Buses to Kottayam (₹43, 1¼ hours, every 30 minutes) are much faster than the ferry. One bus daily leaves for Kumily at 6.40am (₹120, 5½ hours). The Varkala bus (₹89, 3½ hours) leaves at 9am and 10.40am daily.

TRAIN
There are numerous daily trains to Ernakulam (2nd-class/sleeper/3AC ₹50/170/535, 1½ hours) and Trivandrum (₹80/140/485, three hours) via Kollam (₹66/140/485, 1½ hours). Six trains a day stop at Varkala (2nd-class/AC chair ₹65/255, two hours). The train station is 4km west of town.

ℹ Getting Around

An autorickshaw from the train station to the boat jetty and KSRTC bus stand is around ₹60. Several guesthouses around town hire out scooters for ₹300 per day.

Around Alleppey

Kattoor & Marari Beaches

The beaches at Kattoor and Marari, 10km and 14km north of Alleppey respectively, are a popular beachside alternative to the backwaters. Marari is the flashier of the two, with some exclusive five-star beachfront accommodation, while Kattoor, sometimes known as 'Secret Beach', is more of a fishing village, where development is at a minimum and sandy back lanes lead down to near-deserted sands.

🛏 Sleeping

★ Secret Beach Inn
HOMESTAY $

(☑9447786931; www.secretbeach.in; Kattoor Beach; r ₹350-1000; ☎) It almost seems a shame to mention this special little homestay, but with just two rooms it will never feel crowded. The location is sublime, with a small lagoon separating the property from a near-deserted piece of Kattoor Beach; get there by floating mat or walk through the village. Home-cooked meals are available and the talented and welcoming

WORTH A TRIP

GREEN PALM HOMES

Green Palm Homes (✆9495557675, 0477-2724497; www.greenpalmhomes.com; Chennam-kary; r without bathroom incl full board ₹2250, with bathroom ₹3250-4000; ❄) Just 12km from Alleppey on a backwater island, Green Palm Homes is a series of homestays that seem a universe away, set in a picturesque village, where you sleep in simple rooms in villagers' homes among rice paddies (though 'premium' rooms with attached bathroom and air-con are available). It's splendidly quiet, there are no roads in sight and you can take a guided walk, hire bicycles (₹50 per hour) and canoes (₹100 per hour), or take cooking classes with your hosts (₹150).

To get here, call ahead and catch one of the hourly ferries from Alleppey to Chennamkary (₹10, 1¼ hours).

young owner Vimal is an accredited yoga and kalarippayat instructor.

A Beach Symphony   BOUTIQUE COTTAGES **$$$**
(✆9744297123; www.abeachsymphony.com; cottages ₹13,000-16,500; ❄🏊🌐) With just four individually designed cottages, this is one of Marari's most exclusive beachfront resorts. The Keralan-style cottages are plush and private – Violin Cottage even has its own plunge pool in a private garden.

Kottayam

✆0481 / POP 335,000

Conveniently placed between the Western Ghats and the backwaters, Kottayam is renowned for being the centre of Kerala's spice and rubber trade, rather than for its aesthetic appeal. For most travellers it's a hub town, well connected to both the mountains and the backwaters, with many travellers taking the public c anal cruise to or from Alleppey before heading east to Kumily or north to Kochi. The city itself has a crazy, traffic-clogged centre, but you don't have to go far to be in the villages and waterways.

The **Thirunakkara Utsavam festival** is held in March at the Thirunakkara Shiva Temple.

🛏 Sleeping

There's enough accommodation in Kottayam to justify a stay if you're coming off the Alleppey ferry but there are better lakeside stays (at a price) at Kumarakom.

Homestead Hotel   HOTEL **$**
(✆0481-2560467; KK Rd; s/d from ₹500/860, d with AC ₹1690; ❄) In a little compound back from busy KK Rd, Homestead has reasonably well-maintained budget rooms – though some are a little musty and come with eye-watering green decor.

Ambassador Hotel   HOTEL **$**
(✆0481-2563293; ambassadorhotelktm@yahoo. in; KK Rd; s/d from ₹400/560, with AC from ₹950; ❄) This old-school place is one of the better budget hotels in the town centre. Rooms with TV are spartan but fairly clean, spacious and quiet for this price. It has a bar, an adequate restaurant, a pastry counter and a boat-shaped fish tank in the lobby.

**Windsor Castle &
Lake Village Resort**   HOTEL **$$$**
(✆0481-2363637; www.thewindsorcastle.net; MC Rd; s/d from ₹3600/5200, Lake Village cottages ₹7200; ❄🌐🏊) This grandiose white box has some of Kottayam's best hotel rooms, but the more interesting accommodation is in the Lake Village behind the hotel. Deluxe cottages, strewn around the private backwaters and manicured gardens, are top-notch. There's a pleasant restaurant overlooking landscaped waterways.

🍴 Eating

Thali   SOUTH INDIAN **$**
(1st fl, KK Rd; meals ₹40-140; ⏱8am-8pm) A lovely, spotlessly kept 1st-floor dining room with slatted blinds, Thali is a swankier version of the typical Keralan set-meal place. The food here is great, including Malabar fish curry and thalis.

Meenachil   MULTICUISINE **$**
(2nd fl, KK Rd; dishes ₹60-170; ⏱noon-3pm & 6-9.30pm) A favourite place in Kottayam to fill up on Indian and Chinese fare. The family atmosphere is friendly, the dining room modern and tidy, and the menu expansive.

★Nalekattu   SOUTH INDIAN **$$$**
(Windsor Castle Hotel; MC Rd, dishes ₹190-500; ⏱noon-3pm & 7-10pm) The traditional Keralan restaurant at the Windsor Castle overlooks

KERALA'S BACKWATERS

The undisputed highlight of a trip to Kerala is travelling through the 900km network of waterways that fringe the coast and trickle inland. Long before the advent of roads, these waters were the slippery highways of Kerala, and many villagers still use paddle-power as their main form of transport. Trips through the backwaters traverse palm-fringed lakes studded with cantilevered Chinese fishing nets, and wind their way along narrow, shady canals where coir (coconut fibre), copra (dried coconut kernels) and cashews are loaded onto boats. Along the way are isolated villages where farming life continues as it has for eons.

Tourist Cruises

The popular tourist cruise between Kollam and Alleppey (₹400) departs from either end at 10.30am, arriving at 6.30pm, daily from July to March and every second day at other times. Generally, there's a 1pm lunch stop and a brief afternoon chai stop. Bring drinks, snacks, sunscreen and a hat. It's a scenic and leisurely way – the journey takes eight hours – to get between the two towns, but the boat travels along only the major canals – you won't have many close-up views of the village life that makes the backwaters so magical. Another option is to take the trip halfway (₹200) and get off at the Matha Amrithanandamayi Mission (p281).

Houseboats

If the stars align, renting a houseboat designed like a *kettuvallam* (rice barge) could well be one of the highlights of your trip to India. It can be an expensive experience (depending on your budget) but for a couple on a romantic overnight jaunt or split between a group of travellers, it's usually worth every rupee. Drifting through quiet canals lined with coconut palms, eating delicious Keralan food, meeting local villagers and sleeping on the water – it's a world away from the usual clamour of India.

Houseboats cater for couples (one or two double bedrooms) and groups (up to seven bedrooms!). Food (and an onboard chef to cook it) is generally included in the quoted cost, as is a driver/captain. Houseboats can be chartered through a multitude of private operators in Alleppey, Kollam and Kottayam. This is the biggest business in Kerala and the quality of boats varies widely, from rust buckets to floating palaces of varying cleanliness – try to inspect the boat before agreeing on a price. Travel-agency reps will be pushing you to book a boat as soon as you set foot in Kerala, but it's better to wait till you reach a backwater hub: choice is greater in Alleppey (an extraordinary 1000-plus boats), and you're much more likely to be able to bargain down a price if you turn up and see what's on offer. Most guesthouses and homestays can also book you on a houseboat.

---

some picturesque backwaters and serves tasty Keralan specialities like *chemeen* (prawn curry).

ⓘ Information

DTPC Office (☑ 0481-2560479; www.dtpckottayam.com; ◷ 10am-5pm Mon-Sat) At the boat jetty. Offers daily backwater trips to Allepey and Kumarakom for ₹350. Private operators nearby offer similar trips.

ⓘ Getting There & Away

BOAT
Daily ferries run to Alleppey from the jetty (₹10).

BUS
The **KSRTC bus stand** has buses to Trivandrum (₹120, four hours, every 20 minutes), Alleppey (₹43, 1¼ hours, hourly) and Ernakulam (Kochi, ₹56, two hours, every 20 minutes). There are

also frequent buses to nearby Kumarakom (₹15, 30 minutes, every 15 minutes), to Thrissur (₹105, four hours, hourly), Calicut (₹190, seven hours, 13 daily), Kumily for Periyar Wildlife Sanctuary (₹93, four hours, every 30 minutes) and Munnar (₹119, five hours, five daily). There are also buses to Kollam (₹75, three hours, four daily), where you can change for Varkala.

TRAIN
Kottayam is well served by frequent trains running between Trivandrum (2nd-class/sleeper/3AC ₹80/140/485, 3½ hours) and Ernakulam (₹55/140/485, 1½ hours).

ⓘ Getting Around

The KSRTC bus stand is 1km south of the centre; the boat jetty is a further 2km (at Kodimatha). An autorickshaw from the jetty to the KSRTC bus stand is around ₹50, and from the bus stand to the train station about ₹40.

In the busy high season, when prices peak, you're likely to get caught in backwater-gridlock – some travellers are disappointed by the number of boats on the water. It's possible to travel by houseboat between Alleppey and Kollam and part way to Kochi – though these trips spend more time on open lakes and large canals than true backwaters and take longer than most travellers expect. Expect a boat for two people for 24 hours to cost about ₹6000 to ₹8000 at the budget level; for four people, ₹10,000 to ₹12,000; for larger boats or for air-conditioning expect to pay from ₹15,000 to ₹30,000. Shop around to negotiate a bargain – though this will be harder in the peak season. Prices triple from around 20 December to 5 January.

Village Tours & Canoe Boats

More and more travellers are opting for village tours or canal-boat trips. Village tours usually involve small groups of five to six people, a knowledgeable guide and an open canoe or covered *kettuvallam*. The tours (from Kochi, Kollam or Alleppey) last from 2½ to six hours and cost from around ₹400 to ₹800 per person. They include visits to villages to watch coir-making, boat building, toddy (palm beer) tapping and fish farming. The Munroe Island trip from Kollam (p955) is an excellent tour of this type; the Tourist Desk in Ernakulam also organises recommended tours.

Public Ferries

If you want the local backwater transport experience for just a few rupees, there are State Water Transport (www.swtd.gov.in) boats between Alleppey and Kottayam (₹19, 2½ hours) five times daily starting from Alleppey at 7.30am. The trip crosses Vembanad Lake and has a more varied landscape than the Kollam–Alleppey cruise.

Environmental Issues

Pollution from houseboat motors is becoming a major problem as boat numbers increase. The Keralan authorities have introduced an ecofriendly accreditation system for houseboat operators. Among the criteria an operator must meet before being issued with the 'Green Palm Certificate' are the installation of solar panels and sanitary tanks for the disposal of waste – ask operators whether they have the requisite certification. Consider choosing one of the few remaining punting, rather than motorised, boats if possible, though these can only operate in shallow water.

Around Kottayam

Kumarakom

☑ 0481

Kumarakom, 16km west of Kottayam and on the shore of vast Vembanad Lake – Kerala's largest lake – is an unhurried backwater village with a smattering of dazzling top-end sleeping options and a renowned bird sanctuary. You can arrange houseboats on Kumarakom's less-crowded canals, but expect to pay considerably more than in Alleppey.

☉ Sights

Kumarakom Bird Sanctuary NATURE RESERVE (Indian/foreigner ₹50/150; ☉6am-5pm) This reserve on the 5-hectare site of a former rubber plantation is the haunt of a variety of domestic and migratory birds. October to February is the time for travelling birds like the garganey teal, osprey, marsh harrier and steppey eagle; May to July is the breeding season for local species such as the Indian shag, pond herons, egrets and darters. Early morning is the best viewing time. A guide costs ₹300 for a two-hour tour (₹400 from 6am to 8am).

🛏 Sleeping

Cruise 'N Lake RESORT $$ (☑9846036375, 0481-2525804; www.kumarakom.com/cruiselake; Puthenpura Tourist Enclave, Cheepunkal; d ₹1500, with AC ₹2000; ❋) Location, location. Surrounded by backwaters on one side and a lawn of rice paddies on the other, this is the ideal affordable Kumarakom getaway. The rooms in two separate buildings are plain but all have verandahs facing the water. Go a couple of kilometres past the sanctuary to Cheepunkal and take a left; it's then 2km down a rugged dirt road. Management can arrange pick-ups from Kottayam, and houseboats and all meals are available from here.

Tharavadu Heritage Home   GUESTHOUSE $$
(☑ 0481-2525230; www.tharavaduheritage.com; d from ₹1150, bamboo cottage ₹1680, d with AC ₹2650-3000; ❉ @) Rooms are either in the superbly restored 1870s teak family mansion or in equally comfortable individual creek-side bamboo cottages. All are excellently crafted and come with arty touches. It's 4km before the bird sanctuary.

Sree Vallabha Temple

Devotees make offerings at this temple, 2km from Tiruvilla, in the form of traditional, regular all-night **Kathakali** performances that are open to all. Around 10km east of here, the **Aranmula Boat Race**, one of Kerala's biggest snake-boat races, is held during Onam in August/September.

THE WESTERN GHATS

Periyar Wildlife Sanctuary

☑ 04869

South India's most popular wildlife sanctuary, **Periyar** (☑ 04869-224571; www.periyar tigerreserve.org; Indian/foreigner ₹25/450; ❉ 6am-6pm; last entry 5pm) encompasses 777 sq km and a 26-sq-km artificial lake created by the British in 1895. The vast region is home to bison, sambar, wild boar, langur, 900 to 1000 elephants and 35 to 40 hard-to-spot tigers. Firmly established on both the Indian and foreigner tourist trails, the place can sometimes feel a bit like Disneyland-in-the-Ghats, but its mountain scenery and jungle walks make for an enjoyable visit.

Kumily is the closest town and home to a growing strip of hotels, homestays, spice shops, chocolate shops and Kashmiri emporiums. Thekkady, 4km from Kumily, is the sanctuary centre with the KTDC hotels and boat jetty. Confusingly, when people refer to the sanctuary they tend to use Thekkady, Kumily and Periyar interchangeably.

👁 Sights & Activities

Various tours and trips access Periyar Wildlife Sanctuary, all arranged through the Ec-

otourism Centre. Most hotels and agencies around town can arrange all-day jeep **jungle safaris** (per person ₹1600-2000; ❉ 5am-6.30pm) which cover over 40km of trails in jungle bordering the park, though many travellers complain that at least 30km of the trip is on sealed roads.

Cooking classes (₹300-450) are offered by local homestays. There are recommended four-hour classes at **Bar-B-Que** (☑ 04869-320705; KK Rd; ₹500), about 1km from the bazaar on the road to Kottayam.

Several spice plantations are open to visitors and most hotels can arrange tours (₹450/750 by autorickshaw/taxi).

Periyar Lake Cruise   BOATING
(adult/child ₹150/50; ❉ departures 7.30am, 9.30am, 11.15am, 1.45pm & 3.30pm) These 1½-hour boat trips around the lake are the main way to tour the sanctuary without taking a guided walk. You might see deer, boar and birdlife but it's generally more of a cruise – often a rowdy one – than a wildlife-spotting experience. Boats are operated by the forest department and the KTDC – the ticket counters are together in the main building above the boat jetty, and you must buy a ticket before boarding the boat. In high season get to the ticket office 1½ hours before each trip to buy tickets. The first and last departures offer the best prospects for wildlife spotting, and October to March are generally the best time to see animals.

Ecotourism Centre   OUTDOOR ADVENTURE
(☑ 8547603066, 04869-224571; www.periyartiger-reserve.org; Thekkady Rd; ❉ 9am-1pm & 2-5pm) The main operator of explorations into the park is the Ecotourism Centre, run by the Forest Department. These include border hikes (₹1500), 2½-hour nature walks (₹300), half-/full day bamboo rafting (₹1500/200) and 'jungle patrols' (₹1000), which cover 4km to 5km and are the best way to experience the park close up, accompanied by a trained tribal guide. Rates are per person and trips usually require a minimum of four. There are also overnight 'tiger trail' treks (₹5000 per person) run by former poachers retrained as guides, covering 20km to 30km.

Gavi Ecotourism   OUTDOOR ADVENTURE
(☑ 04869-223270, 994792399; www.kfdcecotour-ism.com; treks per person from ₹1000; ❉ 9am-8pm) This Forest Department venture offers jeep safaris, treks and boating to Gavi, a cardamom plantation and jungle area bordering the sanctuary about 45km from Kumily. Hotels can help organise similar jeep trips.

Connemara Tea Factory TEA FACTORY
(Vandiperiyar; tours ₹100; ☺tours hourly 9am-4pm) About 13km from Kumily, this 75-year-old working tea factory and plantation offers interesting guided tours of the tea-making process and tea garden and ends with some tea-tastings. Regular buses from Kumily pass by the entrance.

Abraham's Spice Garden SPICE GARDEN
(☑04869-222919; www.abrahamspice.com; Spring Valley; tours ₹100; ☺7am-6.30pm) Abraham's Spice Garden is a family-run farm operating for more than 50 years. It's 3km from Kumily on the Kottayam Rd.

Highrange Spices SPICE GARDEN
(☑04869-222117; tours ₹100; ☺7am-6pm) Highrange Spices, 3km from Kumily, has 4 hectares of spice garden where you can see ayurvedic herbs and vegetables growing.

Spice Walk SPICE PLANTATION
(☑04869-222449; www.spicewalk.com; Churakulam Coffee Estate; tours ₹150; ☺8.45am-5.30pm) Part of Churakulam Coffee Estate, Spice Walk is a 44-hectare plantation surrounding a small lake. Informative walks take around one hour and include explanations of coffee and cardamom processing, but there's also fishing and boating and a small cafe at the front. It's only 2km from Kumily.

Elephant Junction ELEPHANT RIDES
(₹400-5000; ☺8.30am-6pm) In a lovely 16-hectare patch of forest about 2km from Kumily, you can wash, feed and ride elephants. Programs start from a half-hour ride (₹400) up to full day that includes elephant bathing, plantation tours, breakfast and lunch. This is a better option for interacting with elephants than the touristy operation in Kumily village.

Santhigiri Ayurveda AYURVEDA
(☑8113018007, 04869-223979; www.santhigiri-ashram.org; Munnar Rd, Vandanmedu Junction; ☺8am-8pm) An authentic place for the ayurvedic experience, offering top-notch massage (₹900 to ₹1800) and long-term treatments lasting seven to 14 days.

Kumily & Periyar Wildlife Sanctuary

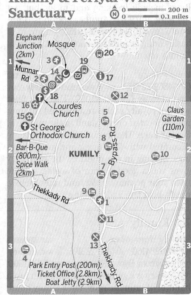

Kumily & Periyar Wildlife Sanctuary

Activities, Courses & Tours
1 Ecotourism Centre B3
2 Gavi Ecotourism A1
3 Santhigiri Ayurveda A1

Sleeping
4 Bamboo Grove A3
5 Chrissie's Hotel B2
6 El-Paradiso B2
7 Green View Homestay B2
8 Mickey Homestay B2
9 Spice Village A2
10 Tranquilou... B2

Eating
11 Ambadi Restaurant B3
Chrissie's Cafe ....(see 5)
12 Ebony's Cafe.. B1
13 French Restaurant & Bakery A3
14 Shri Krishna... A1

Entertainment
15 Kadathanadan Kalari Centre A2
16 Mudra Cultural Centre........................... A2

Information
17 DTPC Office... B1
Ecotourism Centre ....(see 1)
18 Federal Bank ATM................................... A1

Transport
19 Kumily Bus Stand.................................... A1
20 Tamil Nadu Bus Station......................... A1

🛏 Sleeping

🛏 Inside the Sanctuary

The KTDC runs three steeply priced hotels in the park, including Periyar House, Aranya Nivas and the grand Lake Palace. Note that there's effectively a curfew at these places – guests are not permitted to roam the sanctuary after 6pm.

The Ecotourism Centre can arrange tented accommodation inside the park at the **Jungle Camp** (per person incl meals ₹2000). Rates include trekking and meals but not the park entry fee. Another option is **Bamboo Grove** (d incl breakfast ₹1500), a group of basic cottages and tree houses not far from Kumily town.

Lake Palace   HOTEL $$$
(✆04869-223887; www.lakepalacethekkady.com; r incl all meals ₹24,000-30,000) There's a faint whiff of royalty at this restored old summer palace, located on an island in the middle of Periyar Lake. The six charismatic rooms are decorated with flair using antique furnishings. Staying in the midst of the sanctuary gives you a good chance of seeing wildlife from your private terrace, and rates include meals, boat trip and trekking.

🛏 Kumily

Mickey Homestay   GUESTHOUSE $
(✆9447284160, 04869-223196; www.mickey-homestay.com; Bypass Rd; r & cottages ₹700-1000; 🛜) Mickey is a genuine homestay with just a handful of intimate rooms in a family house and a rear cottage, all with homely touches that make them some of the cosiest in town. Balconies have rattan furniture and hanging bamboo seats, and the whole place is surrounded by greenery.

★ Green View Homestay   HOMESTAY $$
(✆9447432008, 04869-224617; www.sureshgreenview.com; Bypass Rd; r incl breakfast ₹500-1750; 🛜) It has grown from its humble homestay origins but Green View is a lovely place that manages to retain its personal and friendly family welcome from owners Suresh and Sulekha. The two buildings house several classes of well-maintained rooms with private balconies – the best are the upper-floor rooms overlooking a lovely rear spice garden. Excellent vegetarian meals and cooking lessons (veg/nonveg ₹350/450) are available.

El-Paradiso   HOMESTAY $$
(✆9447431950, 04869-222350; www.goelparadiso.com; Bypass Rd; d ₹950-1850, q ₹2500; @🛜) This immaculate family homestay has fresh rooms with balconies and hanging chairs, or opening onto a terrace overlooking greenery at the back. Cooking classes (₹400) are a speciality here.

Tranquilou   HOMESTAY $$
(✆04869-223269; www.tranquilouhomestay.com; off Bypass Rd; r incl breakfast ₹1200-2800; @🛜) Another of Kumily's friendly family homestays in a peaceful location. Neatly furnished rooms surround a pleasant garden; the two doubles that adjoin a shared sitting room are a good family option.

Claus Garden   HOMESTAY $$
(✆9567862421, 04869-222320; www.homestay.in; Thekkumkadu; d/tr/f ₹1600/1800/2000; 🛜) Set well away from the hustle and bustle and up a steep hill with good views, this German-run place has gently curving balconies, spotless rooms and a rooftop overlooking a lush green garden. The family option is two rooms sharing a bathroom. Organic breakfast with fresh-baked bread is available for ₹250.

Chrissie's Hotel   GUESTHOUSE $$
(✆9447601304, 04869-224155; www.chrissies.in; Bypass Rd; r ₹1920-2400, f ₹3840; 🛜) This four-storey building behind the popular expat-run restaurant of the same name somehow manages to blend in with the forest-green surrounds. The chic rooms are spacious and bright, with cheery furnishings, lamps and colourful pillows. Yoga, shiatsu and reiki classes can be arranged. Wi-fi in lobby only.

Spice Village   HOTEL $$$
(✆0484-3011711; www.cghearth.com; Thekkady Rd; villas ₹18,700-24,000; 🛜🏊) ✦ This CGH Earth place takes its green credentials very seriously and has captivating, spacious cottages that are smart yet cosily rustic, in pristinely kept grounds. Its restaurant does lavish lunch and dinner buffets (₹1400 to ₹1800), there's a colonial-style bar and you can find the **Wildlife Interpretation Centre** (✆04869-222028; ⊙6am-6pm) here, which has a resident naturalist showing slides and answering questions about the park. Good value out of high season when rates halve.

Eating

There are a few good cheap veg restaurants in Kumily's busy bazaar area, and some decent traveller-oriented restaurants on the road to the wildlife sanctuary. Most homestays will offer home-cooked meals on request.

Shri Krishna
INDIAN $

(KK Rd; meals ₹70-130; ⏰lunch & dinner) A local favourite in the bazaar, serving up spicy pure veg meals including several takes on the lunchtime thali.

Chrissie's Cafe
MULTICUISINE $$

(www.chrissies.in; Bypass Rd; meals ₹150-350; ⏰8am-10pm) A perennially popular traveller haunt, this clean, airy 1st-floor and rooftop cafe satisfies with cakes and snacks, excellent coffee, well-prepared Western faves like pizza and pasta, and even a Middle Eastern platter (₹275).

Ebony's Cafe
MULTICUISINE $$

(Bypass Rd; meals ₹90-200; ⏰8.30am-9.30pm) This fading rooftop joint with lots of pot plants, check tablecloths and traveller-friendly tunes serves up a simple assortment of Indian and continental food from mashed potato to basic pasta.

French Restaurant & Bakery
CAFE, BAKERY $$

(meals ₹90-200; ⏰8am-9.30pm) This family-run shack set back from the main road is a good spot for breakfast or lunch, mainly for the fluffy tuna or cheese baguettes baked on site, but also pasta and noodle dishes.

Ambadi Restaurant
INDIAN $$

(dishes ₹100-250; ⏰7.30am-9.30pm) At the English manor-style hotel of the same name, Ambadi has a more formal feel than most with an almost church-like decor, but the broad menu of North and South Indian dishes is very reasonably priced and the food is good.

⭐ Entertainment

Mudra Cultural Centre
CULTURAL SHOWS

(☑9446072901; www.mudraculturalcentre.com; Lake Rd; admission ₹200, video ₹200; ⏰Kathakali 5pm & 7pm; kalari 6pm & 7.15pm) Kathakali shows at this cultural centre are highly entertaining. Make-up and costume starts 30 minutes before each show; use of still cameras is free and welcome. Arrive early for a good seat. There also two *kalarippayat* (martial arts) performances nightly.

Kadathanadan Kalari Centre
CULTURAL PROGRAM

(www.kalaripayattu.co.in; Thekkady Rd; tickets ₹200; ⏰shows 6-7pm) Hour-long demonstrations of the exciting Keralan martial art of *kalarippayat* are staged here every evening. Tickets are available from the box office throughout the day.

ℹ Information

There's a Federal Bank ATM accepting international cards at the junction with the road to Kottayam, and several internet cafes in the bazaar area.

DTPC Office (☑04869-222620; ⏰10am-5pm Mon-Sat) Behind the bus stand; you can pick up a map but that's about it.

Ecotourism Centre (☑8547603066, 04869-224571; www.periyartigerreserve.org; ⏰9am-1pm & 2-5pm) For park tours, information and guided walks.

Mt Sinai Cyber Cafe (☑04869-222170; Thekkady Junction; per hour ₹20; ⏰9am-10pm) Reliable internet cafe upstairs in Kumily's main bazaar.

ℹ Getting There & Away

Kumily's KSRTC bus stand is at the eastern edge of town.

Eleven buses daily operate between Ernakulam (Kochi) and Kumily (₹145, five hours). Buses leave every 30 minutes for Kottayam (₹84, four hours), with two direct buses to Trivandrum at 8.45am and 11am (₹210, eight hours) and one daily bus to Alleppey at 1.10pm (₹120, 5½ hours). Private buses to Munnar (₹80, four to five hours) also leave from the bus stand at 6am, 9.45am and noon.

SABARIMALA

Deep in the Western Ghats, about 20km west of Gavi and some 50km from the town of Erumeli, is a place called Sabarimala, home to the Ayyappan temple. It's said to be one of the world's most visited pilgrimage centres, with anywhere between 40 and 60 million Hindu devotees trekking here each year. Followers believe the god Ayyappan meditated at this spot. Non-Hindus can join the pilgrimage but strict rules apply, and women aged 12 to 50 are only allowed as far as the Pampa checkpoint. For information see www.sabarimala.kerala.gov.in or www.sabarimala.org.

Tamil Nadu buses leave every 30 minutes to Madurai (₹90, four hours) from the Tamil Nadu bus stand just over the border.

ℹ Getting Around

It's only about 1.5km from Kumily bus stand to the main park entrance, but it's another 3km from there to Periyar Lake; you might catch a bus (almost as rare as the tigers), but will more likely take an autorickshaw from the entry post (₹70) or set off on foot – but bear in mind there's no walking path so you'll have to dodge traffic on the road. Autorickshaws will take you on short hops around town for ₹30.

Kumily town is small enough to explore on foot but some guesthouses hire bicycles (₹200) and most can arrange scooter hire (₹500) if you want to explore further afield.

Munnar

📞 04865 / POP 68,200 / ELEV 1524M

The rolling hills around Munnar, South India's largest tea-growing region, are carpeted in emerald-green tea plantations, contoured, clipped and sculpted like ornamental hedges. The low mountain scenery is magnificent – you're often up above the clouds watching veils of mist clinging to the mountaintops. Munnar town itself is a scruffy administration centre, not unlike a North Indian hill station, but wander just a few kilometres out of town and you'll be engulfed in a sea of a thousand shades of green.

Once known as the High Range of Travancore, today Munnar is the commercial centre of some of the world's highest tea-growing estates. The majority of the plantations are operated by corporate giant Tata, with some in the hands of local co-operative Kannan Devan Hills Plantation Company (KDHP).

◉ Sights & Activities

The main reason to visit Munnar is to explore the lush, tea-filled hillocks that surround it. Hotels, homestays, travel agencies, autorickshaw drivers and practically every passerby will want to organise a day of sightseeing for you: shop around, though rates are fairly standard. The best way to experience the hills is on a guided trek, which can range from a half-day 'soft trekking' around tea plantations (from ₹600 per person) to more arduous full-day mountain treks (from ₹800), which open up some stupendous views. Trekking guides can easily be organised through hotels and guesthouses or the DTPC.

Bear in mind that the tea plantations are private property and trekking around without a licensed guide is trespassing.

Tea Museum MUSEUM
(📞 04865-230561; adult/child ₹80/35, camera ₹20; ⊙ 9am-4pm Tue-Sun) About 1.5km northwest of town, this museum is as close as you'll get to a working tea factory around Munnar. It's a demo model of the real thing, but it still shows the basic process. A collection of old bits and pieces from the colonial era, including photographs and a 1905 tea-roller, are also kept here. A 30-minute video explaining the history of Munnar, its tea estates and the programs put in place for its workers screens hourly. The walk to or from town follows the busy road with views of tea plantations; an autorickshaw charges ₹25 from the bazaar.

Nimi's Lip Smacking Classes COOKING
(📞 9745513373, 9447330773; www.nimisrecipes.com; classes ₹1500; ⊙ 5pm Mon-Fri, 2pm Sat & Sun) Nimi Sunilkumar has earned a solid reputation for Keralan cooking, publishing her own cookbook, website and blog, and now offers daily cooking classes in Munnar. You'll learn traditional Keralan recipes and the cost includes a copy of her book *Lip Smacking Dishes of Kerala*. She's based in an unassuming building next to the DTPC.

☞ Tours

The DTPC (p297) runs three fairly rushed but inexpensive full-day tours to points around Munnar. The **Sandal Valley Tour** (per person ₹400; ⊙ tour 9am-6pm) visits Chinnar Wildlife Sanctuary, several viewpoints, waterfalls, plantations, a sandalwood forest and villages. The **Tea Valley tour** (per person ₹400; ⊙ tour 10am-6pm) visits Echo Point, Top Station and Rajamalai (for Eravikulam National Park), among other places. The **Village Sightseeing Tour** (per person ₹400; ⊙ 9.30am-6pm) covers Devikulam, Anayirankal Dam, Ponmudy and a farm tour among others. You can hire a taxi to visit the main local sights for around ₹1300.

🛏 Sleeping

Munnar has plenty of accommodation but it seems a shame to stay in Munnar town when the views and peace are out in the hills and valleys. There are some good budget options just south of the town centre; if you really want to feel the serenity and are willing to pay a bit more, head for the hills.

🛏 Around Town

⭐ JJ Cottage
HOMESTAY $

(📞 9447228599, 04865-230104; jjcottagemunnar@gmail.com; d ₹350-800; @ 🛜) The sweet family at this little purple place 2km south of town (but easy walking distance from the main bus stand) will go out of its way to make sure your stay is comfortable. The varied and uncomplicated rooms are ruthlessly clean, bright and good value, and have TV and hot water. The one deluxe room on the top floor has a separate sitting room and sweeping views.

Green View
GUESTHOUSE $

(📞 9447825447, 04865-230940; www.greenviewmunnar.com; d ₹500-800; @ 🛜) This tidy guesthouse has 10 fresh budget rooms, a friendly welcome and reliable tours and treks. The best rooms are on the upper floor and there's a super rooftop garden where you can sample 15 kinds of tea. The young owner organises trekking trips (www.munnartrekking.com) and also runs **Green Woods Anachal** (📞 04865-230189; Anachal; d incl breakfast ₹750), a four-room budget house out in the spice plantations, 10km outside of Munnar.

Zina Cottages
GUESTHOUSE $

(📞 04865-230349; r ₹700-1000) On the outskirts of town but immersed in lush tea plantations and with some fine views, this fading 50-year-old house offers an interesting location with good walks from your doorstep but slightly run-down rooms. They offer pickup from town.

Kaippallil Inn
GUESTHOUSE $

(📞 9495029259; kaippallilinn@gmail.com; r ₹350-800) A stiff walk uphill from the bazaar, Kaippallil is a reasonable budget bet in the town centre, thanks mainly to the serene Benoy, who offers free yoga, reiki and meditation sessions and plenty of tea. It looks a little tatty from the outside but the rooms are clean enough and the top ones have little corner balconies with city views.

Royal Retreat
HOTEL $$

(📞 8281611100, 04865-230240; www.royalretreat.co.in; d ₹3000-3600, ste ₹4400; @ 🛜) Away from the bustle just south of the main bus stand, Royal Retreat is an average but reliable midranger with neat ground-level rooms facing a pretty garden and others with tea plantation views.

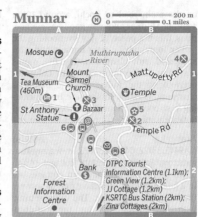

Munnar

🛏 Sleeping
1 Kaippallil Inn A1

🍴 Eating
2 Eastend B1
3 Rapsy Restaurant A1
4 Sree Mahaveer Bhojanalaya B1

🎭 Entertainment
5 Thirumeny Cultural Centre B1

ℹ Transport
Autorickshaw Stand .... (see 9)
6 Buses to Coimbatore A2
7 Buses to Ernakulam, Kottayam & Trtivandrum A2
8 Buses to Kumily & Madurai B2
9 Buses to Top Station A2

🛏 Munnar Hills

⭐ Green Valley Vista
GUESTHOUSE $$

(📞 9447432008, 04865-263261; www.greenvalleyvista.com; Chithirapuram; d incl breakfast ₹1500-2000; 🛜) The valley views are superb, facilities top-notch and the welcome warm at this new guesthouse. There are three levels but all rooms face the valley and have private balconies with dreamy greenery views, as well as flat-screen TVs and modern bathrooms with hot water. Staff can organise trekking, jeep safaris and village tours. It's about 11km south of Munnar.

⭐ Rose Gardens
HOMESTAY $$

(📞 9447378524, 04864-278243; www.munnarhomestays.com; NH49 Rd, Karadipara; r incl breakfast ₹4500; @ 🛜) Despite its handy location on the main road to Kochi, around 10km south of Munnar and with good bus connections, this is a peaceful spot overlooking the owner Tomy's idyllic plant nursery and mini spice and fruit plantation. The five rooms are large and comfortable with balconies overlooking the valley, and the family is charming. Cooking lessons are free, including fresh coconut pancakes for breakfast and delicately spiced Keralan dishes for dinner.

Aranyaka
RESORT $$
(☑ 9443133722, 04865-230023; www.aranyakaresorts.com; Pallivasal Tea Estate; cottages ₹4800-6000; ☎) These neat modern cottages set in a landscaped garden have fine views over the Pallivasal Tea Estate. The valley setting, with views of waterfalls and the Muthirappuzhayar River, feels remote but is only 8km from Munnar town.

Dew Drops
GUESTHOUSE $$
(☑ 04842-216455; wilsonhomes2003@yahoo.co.in; Kallar; r incl breakfast ₹2800-3150) Set in thick forest around 20km south of Munnar, this remote-feeling place lies on 97 hectares of spice plantation and farmland (not tea plantations). There are eight bright, simple rooms each with a verandah. The peace here is zen but some find it a little isolated

Bracknell Forest
GUESTHOUSE $$$
(☑ 9446951963; www.bracknellforestmunnar.com; Bison Valley Rd, Ottamaram; r incl breakfast ₹5000-6000; @☎) A remote-feeling 9.5km southeast of Munnar, this place houses 11 neat rooms with balconies and views of a lush valley and cardamom plantation. It's surrounded by deep forest on all sides. The small restaurant has wraparound views. A transfer from Munnar costs around ₹400 but call ahead for directions.

Windermere Estate
RESORT $$$
(☑ 0484-2425237; www.windermeremunnar.com; Pothamedu; s/d incl breakfast from ₹8300/9600, villa ₹18,300/21,600; ❄@☎) Windermere is a charming boutique-meets-country-retreat 4km southeast of Munnar. There are supremely spacious garden and valley view rooms, but the best are the suite-like 'Plantation Villas' with spectacular views, surrounded by 26 hectares of cardamom and coffee plantations. There's a cosy library above the country-style restaurant.

✗ Eating

Early-morning food stalls in the bazaar serve breakfast snacks and cheap meals, but some of the best food is served up at the homestays and resorts.

Rapsy Restaurant
INDIAN $
(Bazaar; dishes ₹50-140; ☺8am-9pm) This spotless glass-fronted sanctuary from the bazaar is packed at lunchtime, with locals lining up for Rapsy's famous *paratha* (flaky fried bread) or biryani. It also makes a decent stab at fancy international dishes like Spanish omelette, Israeli *shakshuka* (eggs with tomatoes and spices) and Mexican salsa.

SN Restaurant
INDIAN $
(AM Rd; meals ₹50-110; ☺7.30am-10pm) Just south of the DTPC office, SN is a cheery place with a warm orange interior; it appears to be perpetually packed with people digging into thalis, *masala dosas* (thin pancake stuffed with curried vegetables) and other Indian veg and nonveg dishes.

Sree Mahaveer Bhojanalaya
NORTH INDIAN $$
(Mattupetty Rd; meals ₹100-250; ☺8.30am-10.30pm) This pure veg restaurant attached to SN Annex Hotel has a nice deep-orange look with slatted blinds at the windows. It's madly popular with families for its great range of thalis: take your pick from Rajasthani, Gujarati, Punjabi and more, plus a dazzling array of veg dishes.

Eastend
INDIAN $$
(Temple Rd; dishes ₹110-250; ☺7.30am-10.30am, noon-3.30pm & 6.30-10.30pm) In the slightly fancy hotel of the same name, this brightly lit, smartish place serves Chinese, North and South Indian and Kerala specialities, including occasional lunch and dinner buffets.

☆ Entertainment

Punarjani Traditional Village
CULTURAL SHOWS
(☑ 04865-216161; www.punarjanimunnar.org; 2nd Mile, Pallivasal; tickets ₹200-300; ☺shows 5pm & 6pm) Touristy but entertaining daily performances of Kathakali (5pm) and kalari (6pm). Arrive at 4pm if you want to see the ritual Kathakali make-up session. Tickets are available on the day but for the best seats consider booking a day in advance. It's about 8km south of Munnar town.

Thirumeny Cultural Centre
CULTURAL PROGRAM
(☑ 9447827696; Temple Rd; shows ₹200; ☺Kathakali shows 5-6pm & 7-8pm; kalari 6-7pm & 8-9pm) On the road behind the East End Hotel, this small theatre stages one-hour Kathakali shows and *kalari* (martial arts) demonstrations twice nightly.

ℹ Information

There are ATMs near the bridge, south of the bazaar.

DTPC Tourist Information Office (📞 04865-231516; keralatourismmunnardtpc@gmail.com; Alway-Munnar Rd; ⊘ 8.30am-6.30pm) Marginally helpful; operates a number of tours and can arrange trekking guides.

Forest Information Centre (📞 04865-231587; enpmunnar@gmail.com; ⊘ 10am-5pm) Wildlife Warden's Office, for accommodation bookings in Chinnar Wildlife Sanctuary.

Olivia Communications (per hour ₹35; ⊘ 9am-9pm) Cramped but surprisingly fast internet cafe in the bazaar.

ℹ Getting There & Away

Roads around Munnar are in poor condition and can be affected by monsoon rains. The main **KSRTC bus station** (AM Rd) is south of town, but it's best to catch buses from stands in Munnar town (where more frequent private buses also depart). The main stand is in the bazaar.

There are around 13 daily buses to Ernakulam (Kochi, ₹114, 5½ hours), two direct buses to Alleppey (₹158, five hours) at 6.20am and 1.10pm, and four to Trivandrum (₹231, nine hours).

Private buses go to Kumily (₹80, four hours) at 11.25am, 12.20pm and 2.25pm.

A taxi to Ernakulam costs around ₹3000, and to Kumily ₹2500.

ℹ Getting Around

Gokulam Bike Hire (📞 9447237165; per day ₹300-350; ⊘ 7.30am-7.30pm), in the former bus stand south of town, has motorbikes and scooters for hire. Call ahead.

Autorickshaws ply the hills around Munnar with bone-shuddering efficiency; they charge up to ₹800 for a day's sightseeing.

Around Munnar

Top Station

High above Kerala's border with Tamil Nadu, Top Station is popular for its spectacular views over the Western Ghats. From Munnar, four daily buses (₹40, from 7.30am, 1½ hours) make the steep 32km climb in around an hour, or book a return taxi (₹1000).

Eravikulam National Park

Eravikulam National Park   NATIONAL PARK
(📞 04865-231587; www.eravikulam.org; Indian/foreigner ₹75/250, camera/video ₹25/2000; ⊘ 8am-5pm Mar-Dec) Eravikulam National Park, 16km from Munnar, is home to the endangered, but almost tame, Nilgiri tahr (a type of mountain goat). From Munnar, an autorickshaw/taxi costs around ₹300/400 return; a government bus takes you the final 4km from the checkpoint (₹40).

Chinnar Wildlife Sanctuary

Chinnar Wildlife Sanctuary   NATURE RESERVE
(www.chinnar.org;   Indian/foreigner   ₹100/150, camera/video ₹25/150; ⊘ 7am-6pm) About 60km northeast of Munnar, this wildlife sanctuary hosts deer, leopards, elephants and the endangered grizzled giant squirrel. Trekking and tree house or hut accommodation within the sanctuary are available, as well as ecotour programs like river-trekking, cultural visits (two tribal groups inhabit the sanctuary) and waterfall treks (around ₹600 per person). For details contact the Forest Information Centre in Munnar. Buses from Munnar can drop you off at Chinnar (₹40, 1½ hours), or taxi hire for the day will cost around ₹1500.

Thattekkad Bird Sanctuary

Thattekkad Bird Sanctuary   NATURE RESERVE
(📞 04852588302;   Indian/foreigner   ₹25/165, camera/video ₹25/150; ⊘ 6.30am-6pm) , cut through by two rivers and two streams, Thattekkad Bird Sanctuary is home to over 320 fluttering species – unusual in that they are mostly forest, rather than water birds – including Malabar grey hornbills, Ripley owls, jungle nightjars, grey drongos, darters and rarer species like the Sri Lankan frogmouth. There are kingfishers, flycatchers, warblers, sunbirds and flower peckers.

Thattekkad is on the Ernakulam–Munnar road. Take a direct bus from either Ernakulam (₹35, two hours) or Munnar (₹60, three hours) to Kothamangalam, from where a Thattekkad bus travels the final 12km (₹8, 25 minutes), or catch an autorickshaw for around ₹250.

🛏 Sleeping

Jungle Bird Homestay   HOMESTAY **$$**
(📞 0485-2588143, 9947506188; www.junglebird-homestay.blogspot.com.au; per person incl meals ₹1300) A good budget option is this homestay inside the park, run by the enthusiastic Ms Sudah and son Gireesh, who

PARAMBIKULAM WILDLIFE SANCTUARY

Parambikulam Wildlife Sanctuary (☑ 04253-245025, 9442201690; www.parambikulam. org; Indian/foreigner ₹10/150, camera/video ₹25/150; ⏲ 7am-6pm; last entry 4pm) Possibly the most protected environment in South India – nestled behind three dams in a valley surrounded by Keralan and Tamil Nadu sanctuaries – Parambikulam Wildlife Sanctuary constitutes 285 sq km of Kipling-storybook scenery and wildlife-spotting goodness. Far less touristed than Periyar, it's home to elephants, bison, gaur, sloths, sambar, crocodiles, tigers, panthers and some of the largest teak trees in Asia. The sanctuary is best avoided during monsoon (June to August) and it sometimes closes in March and April.

Contact the Information Centre in Anappady to arrange tours of the park, hikes (one-/ two-day trek from ₹3000/6000, shorter treks from ₹600) and accommodation in tree-top huts (₹3000 to ₹5000) or niche tents (₹6000).

You have to enter the park from Pollachi (40km from Coimbatore and 49km from Palakkad) in Tamil Nadu. There are two buses in either direction between Pollachi and Parambikulam via Annamalai daily (₹19, 1½ hours).

will meet guests at the gate. They also offer expert guided birdwatching trips (₹750 for three hours).

Soma Birds Lagoon
RESORT $$$

(☑ 0471-2268101; www.somabirdslagoon.com; Palamatton, Thattekkad; s/d incl breakfast €75/85, with AC from €97/113; ❄ ☲) For accommodation with a little more style, the lovely Soma Birds Lagoon, set deep in the villages near Thattekkad, is a low-key resort on a seasonal lake among spacious and manicured grounds. The basic rooms and cottages here are roomy, with lots of wood trim and lamp lighting. Popular with visiting ornithologists, it's 16km from Kothamangalam.

Hornbill Camp
TENTED CAMP $$$

(☑ 0484-2092280; www.thehornbillcamp.com; d full board US$100) About 8km by road from Thattekkad Bird Sanctuary, the tented Hornbill Camp has accommodation in large permanent tents, in a sublimely peaceful location facing the Periyar River. Kayaking, cycling and a spice-garden tour, as well as all meals, are included in the price. Birdwatching guides cost ₹1500.

CENTRAL KERALA

Kochi (Cochin)

☑ 0484 / POP 601,600

Serene Kochi has been drawing traders and explorers to its shores for over 600 years. Nowhere else in India could you find such an intriguing mix: giant fishing nets from China, a 400-year-old synagogue, ancient mosques, Portuguese houses and the crumbling remains of the British Raj. The result is an unlikely blend of medieval Portugal, Holland and an English village grafted onto the tropical Malabar Coast. It's a delightful place to spend some time and nap in some of India's finest homestays and heritage accommodation. Kochi is also a centre for Keralan arts and one of the best places to see Kathakali and *kalarippayat* (p309).

Mainland Ernakulam is the hectic transport and cosmopolitan hub of Kochi, while the historical towns of Fort Cochin and Mattancherry, though well-touristed, remain wonderfully atmospheric – thick with the smell of the past. Other islands, including Willingdon and Vypeen, are linked by a network of ferries and bridges.

◎ Sights

◎ Fort Cochin

Fort Cochin has a couple of small, sandy beaches which are only really good for people-watching in the evening and gazing out at the incoming tankers. A popular promenade winds around from Mahatma Gandhi Beach to the Chinese fishing nets and fish market. This part of Fort Cochin's foreshore is rubbish-strewn and grubby but locals are working towards cleaning it up.

Look out along the shore for the scant remains of Fort Immanuel, the 16th-century Portuguese fort from which the area takes its name.

Kochi (Cochin)

Chinese Fishing Nets   LANDMARK

(Map p300) The unofficial emblems of Kerala's backwaters, and perhaps the most photographed, are the half-dozen or so giant cantilevered Chinese fishing nets on Fort Cochin's northeastern shore. A legacy of traders from the AD 1400 court of Kublai Khan, these enormous, spiderlike contraptions require at least four people to operate their counterweights at high tide. Modern fishing techniques are making these labour-intensive methods less and less profitable, but they still supply the fresh seafood you'll see for sale. Smaller fishing nets are dotted around the shores of Vembanad Lake.

Indo-Portuguese Museum   MUSEUM

(Map p300; ☎0484-2215400; Indian/foreigner ₹10/25; ☺9am-1pm & 2-6pm Tue-Sun) This museum in the garden of the Bishop's House preserves the heritage of one of India's earliest Catholic communities, including vestments, silver processional crosses and altarpieces from the Cochin diocese. The basement contains remnants of the Portuguese Fort Immanuel.

Maritime Museum   MUSEUM

(Beach Rd; adult/child ₹40/20, camera/video ₹100/150; ☺9.30am-12.30pm & 2.30-5.30pm Tue-Sun) In a pair of former bomb shelters, this museum traces the history of the Indian navy, as well as maritime trade dating back to the Portuguese and Dutch, through a series of rather dry relief murals and information panels. There's plenty of naval memorabilia, including a couple of model battleships outside in the garden.

St Francis Church   CHURCH

(Map p300; Church Rd; ☺8.30am-5pm) Constructed in 1503 by Portuguese Franciscan friars, this is believed to be India's oldest European-built church. The edifice that stands here today was built in the mid-16th century to replace the original wooden structure. Explorer Vasco da Gama, who died in Cochin in 1524, was buried in this spot for 14 years before his remains were taken to Lisbon – you can still visit his tombstone in the church.

Santa Cruz Basilica   CHURCH

(Map p300; cnr Bastion St & KB Jacob Rd; ☺7am-8.30pm) The imposing Catholic basilica was originally built on this site in 1506, though the current building dates to 1902. Inside are artefacts from the different eras in Kochi and a striking pastel-coloured interior.

Dutch Cemetery   HISTORIC SITE

(Map p300; Beach Rd) Consecrated in 1724, this cemetery near Kochi beach contains

Fort Cochin

200 m
0.1 miles

Customs Jetty

✕ 24

🏠 13
🏠 30

Bazaar (Boat Jetty) Rd

27

Mattancherry (2km)

Coast Guard

River (Calvathy) Rd

New Rd

Kunnumpuram Junction

🔵 40

🔵 37

Amravathi Rd

19 🏠 22

Jolies Homestay (150m);
Costa Gama Home Stay (530m)

Ferry to Vypeen Island

Fort Cochin Bus Stand

Dispensary Rd

🏠 15

St Peter & Paul Church

Amravathi Rd

36 🔵

Fort Nagar

Fosse St

Residale Branch Rd

Vypeen Island (300m)

Tourist Taxi Stand

🏠 9

Rampath Rd

🏠 38

Tower Rd

Outdoor Cafes

Burgher St

🏛 4

29 🏠

🏠 39

KB Jacob Rd

31 ✕

KB Jacob Rd

11 🏠

Tourist Desk
Information Counter

🏠 17

Princess St

🏠 20

🏠 23

🏠 21

Bastion St

🏠 5

Peter Celli St

34 🏠

KL Bernard Rd

Green Woods (700m);
Bethlehem (700m);
Reds Residency (960m)

🏠 16

Rose St

🏠 1 ◉

🏠 26

7

🏠 28

🏠 35

🏠 32

8 🏠 18

Quiros St

🏠 10

12

🏠 6

Church Rd

Parade Grounds

Post Office Rd

Dutch Cemetery Rd

Mahatma Gandhi Beach

Vembanad Lake

Parade Ground Rd

Parade St

Napier St

Lily St

🏠 25

🏠 14

🏛 33

Elphinstone St

🏛 3

Maritime Museum (600m)

🏠 2

FORT COCHIN

Fort Cochin

KERALA KOCHI (COCHIN)

the worn and dilapidated graves of Dutch traders and soldiers. Its gates are normally locked but a caretaker might let you in, or ask at St Francis Church.

Kashi Art Gallery ART GALLERY
(Map p300; ☎0484-2215769; www.kashiartgallery. com; Burgher St; ⊙8.30am-7.30pm) The pioneer of Fort Cochin's art revival, Kashi displays changing exhibitions of local artists; most travellers come for the good cafe.

⊙ Mattancherry & Jew Town

About 3km southeast of Fort Cochin, Mattancherry is the old bazaar district and centre of the spice trade. These days it's packed with spice shops and pricey Kashmiri-run emporiums that autorickshaw drivers will fall over backwards to take you to for a healthy commission – any offer of a cheap tour of the district will inevitably lead to a few shops. In the midst of this, Jew Town is a bustling port area with a fine synagogue. Scores of small firms huddle together in dilapidated old buildings and the air is filled with the biting aromas of ginger, cardamom, cumin, turmeric and cloves, though the lanes around the Dutch Palace and synagogue are packed with antique and tourist-curio shops rather than spices.

★**Mattancherry Palace** MUSEUM
(Dutch Palace; Map p302; ☎0484-2226085; Palace Rd; adult/child ₹5/free; ⊙9am-5pm Sat-Thu) Mattancherry Palace was a generous gift presented to the Raja of Kochi, Veera Kerala Varma (1537–61), as a gesture of goodwill by the Portuguese in 1555. The Dutch renovated the palace in 1663, hence its alternative name, the Dutch Palace. The star attractions here are the astonishingly preserved Hindu murals, depicting scenes from the Ramayana, Mahabharata and Puranic legends in intricate detail.

★**Pardesi Synagogue** SYNAGOGUE
(Map p302; admission ₹5; ⊙10am-1pm & 3-5pm Sun-Thu, closed Jewish holidays) Originally built in 1568, this synagogue was partially destroyed by the Portuguese in 1662, and rebuilt two years later when the Dutch took Kochi. It features an ornate gold pulpit and elaborate hand-painted, willow-pattern floor tiles from Canton, China, which were added in 1762. It's magnificently illuminated by Belgian chandeliers and coloured-glass lamps. The graceful clock tower was built in 1760.

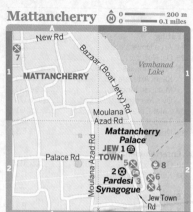

Mattancherry

MATTANCHERRY

Vembanad Lake

New Rd

Bazaar (Boat Jetty) Rd

Moulana Azad Rd

Mattancherry Palace

JEW 1
TOWN 5
2 3
Pardesi Synagogue

Palace Rd

Moulana Azad Rd

Jew Town Rd

8
6
4

There is an upstairs balcony for women, who worshipped separately according to Orthodox rites. Note that shorts, sleeveless tops, bags and cameras are not allowed inside.

◉ Ernakulam

Kerala Folklore Museum
MUSEUM

(☏0484-2665452; www.keralafolkloremuseum.org; Folklore Junction, Thevara; Indian/foreigner ₹100/200, camera ₹100; ⊙9.30am-6pm) Created in Keralan style from ancient temples and beautiful old houses collected by its owner, an antique dealer, the museum includes over 4000 artefacts and covers three architectural styles: Malabar on the ground-floor, Kochi on the 1st, Travancore on the 2nd. Upstairs is a beautiful wood-lined theatre with a 17th-century wooden ceiling. It's about 6km south of Ernakulam Junction

train station. A rickshaw from Ernakulam should cost ₹90, or you can take any bus to Thivara from where it's a ₹25 rickshaw ride. An autorickshaw from Fort Cochin should cost ₹200.

☆ Activities

Ayur Dara
AYURVEDA

(☏0484-2502362, 9447721041; www.ayurdara.com; Murikkumpadam, Vypeen Island; ⊙9am-5.30pm) Run by third-generation ayurvedic practitioner Dr Subhash, this delightful waterside treatment centre specialises in treatments of one to three weeks (₹1500 per day). By appointment only. It's 3km from the Vypeen Island ferry.

SVM Ayurveda Centre
AYURVEDA

(Kerala Ayurveda Pharmacy Ltd; Map p300; ☏9847371667; www.svmayurveda.com; Quieros St; massage from ₹900, rejuvenation from ₹1200; ⊙9.30am-7pm) A small Fort Cochin centre, offering relaxing massages and Hatha yoga daily. Longer rejuvenation packages are also available.

☆ Courses

The Kerala Kathakali Centre (p308) has lessons in classical Kathakali dance, music and make-up (short and long-term courses from ₹350 per hour).

For a crash course in the martial art of *kalarippayat*, Ens Kalari (p308) is a famed training centre which offers short intensive courses from one week to one month.

Cook & Eat
COOKING

(Map p300; ☏0484-2215377; www.leelahomestay.com; Quiros St; classes ₹700; ⊙11am & 6pm) Mrs Leelu Roy runs popular two-hour cooking classes in her big family kitchen at Leelu Homestay, teaching five dishes and her homemade garam masala to classes of five to 10 people.

☆ Tours

Tourist Desk Information Counter
TOURS

(Map p304; ☏9847044688, 0484-2371761; www.touristdesk.in; Ernakulam Boat Jetty & Tower Rd, Fort Cochin) This excellent private tour agency runs the popular full-day Water Valley Tour (₹850, departs 8am) by houseboat through local backwater canals and lagoons. A canoe trip through smaller canals and villages is included, as is lunch and hotel pick-ups. It also offers a sunset dinner cruise (₹750) by canoe from Narakkal Village on Vypeen Island, with the option of an overnight stay at a beach bungalow, and an overnight **Munnar Hill Station Tour** (₹3000) with transport, accommodation and meals. Staff here are a good source of information on local temple festivals.

KTDC   BOAT TOUR
(Map p300; ☑ 0484-2353234; Marine Dr, Kochi; ☺ 10am-5pm Mon-Sat) The KTDC has half-day **backwater tours** (₹600) at 8.30am and 2pm, and full-day **houseboat backwater trips** (₹700) visiting local weaving factories, spice gardens and toddy tappers.

Elephant Training Camp   ELEPHANT RIDE
(Kodanadu; ☺ 7am-6pm) Most hotels and tourist offices can arrange the day trip out to the elephant training camp at Kodanadu, 50km from Kochi. Here you can go for a ride (₹200), or help out with washing the gentle beasts if you arrive by 8am. Entry is free, though the elephant trainers will expect a small tip. A return trip out here in a taxi should cost around ₹1200.

Art of Bicycle Trips   BICYCLE TOUR
(Map p300; ☑ 9656703909; www.artofbicycletrips.com; Bastion St; tours ₹1450-4200; ☺ 9am-6pm) Guided bicycle tours on quality mountain bikes include a morning tour of the historic Fort area (₹1450), a half-day ride towards the backwaters (₹2450) and a full-day trip south towards Alleppey with backwater canoeing (₹4200). A great way to see the area at a slow place.

Kerala Bike Tours   BICYCLE TOUR
(☑ 04842356652, 9388476817; www.keralabiketours.com; Kirushupaly Rd, Ravipuram) Organises motorcycle tours around Kerala and the Western Ghats and hires out touring-quality Enfield Bullets (from US$155 per week) with unlimited mileage, full insurance and free recovery/maintenance options.

✦ Festivals & Events

Ernakulathappan Utsavam   FESTIVAL
(Shiva Temple, Ernakulam, Kochi; ☺ Jan/Feb) Eight days of festivities culminating in a parade of 15 splendidly decorated elephants, plus music and fireworks.

Cochin Carnival   FESTIVAL
(www.cochincarnival.org; ☺ 21 Dec) The Cochin Carnival is Fort Cochin's biggest bash, a 10-day festival culminating on New Year's Eve. Street parades, colourful costumes, embellished elephants, music, folk dancing and lots of fun.

🛏 Sleeping

Fort Cochin can feel a bit touristy and crowded in season but, with some of Kerala's finest accommodation, it's a great place to escape the noise and chaos of the mainland. This is India's homestay capital, with dozens of family houses offering clean budget rooms, home-cooked meals and a hearty welcome.

Ernakulam is cheaper and more convenient for onward travel, but the ambience and accommodation choices are less inspiring. Regardless of where you stay, book ahead during December and January. At other times you may be able to bargain for a discount. Go on line at www.fortcochinhomestays.com to check out a few places.

🛏 Fort Cochin

★ Green Woods Bethlehem   HOMESTAY $
(☑ 9846014924, 0484-3247791; greenwoodsbethlehem1@vsnl.net; d incl breakfast ₹1000-1200, with AC ₹1500; ❈ 🕸) With a smile that brightens weary travellers, welcoming owner Sheeba looks ready to sign your adoption papers the minute you walk through her front door. Down a quiet laneway and with a walled garden thick with plants and palms, this is one of Kochi's most serene homestays. The rooms are humble but cosy; breakfast is served in the fantastic, leafy rooftop cafe, where cooking classes and demonstrations are often held.

Princess Inn   GUESTHOUSE $
(Map p300; ☑ 0484-2217073; princessinnfortkochi@gmail.com; Princess St; s/d/tr ₹400/600/1000) Sticking to its budget guns, the friendly Princess Inn spruces up its otherwise dull, tiny rooms with cheery bright colours. The communal spaces are welcoming, and the three large, front-facing rooms are good value for this location.

Costa Gama Home Stay   HOMESTAY $
(☑ 0484-2216122; www.stayincochin.com; Thamaraparambu Rd; r ₹800, with AC ₹1200; ❈ 🕸) With just three rooms, this cosy little place gets good reviews. Across the road are another three rooms in a heritage-style building with a nice terrace.

★ Reds Residency   HOMESTAY $$
(☑ 9388643747, 0484-3204060; www.redsresidency.in; 11/372 A, KJ Herschel Rd; d incl breakfast ₹900-1200, with AC from ₹1200, AC rooftop cottage ₹1500; ❈ @ 🕸) Reds is a lovely homestay with hotel-quality rooms but a true family

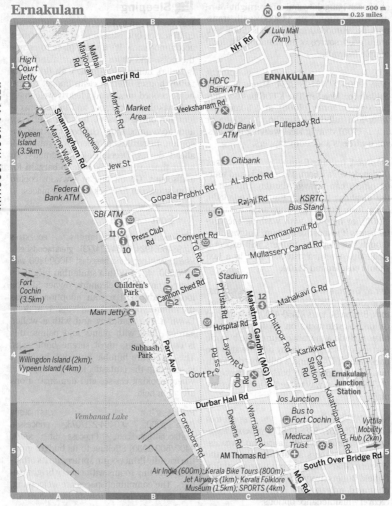

welcome from knowledgeable hosts Philip and Maryann. The seven rooms – including a triple and four-bed family room – are modern and immaculate, and there's a brilliant self-contained 'penthouse' cottage with kitchen on the rooftop. It's in a peaceful location south of the centre.

Walton's Homestay GUESTHOUSE **$$**
(Map p300; ☑ 9249721935, 0484-2215309; www.waltonshomestay.com; Princess St; r incl breakfast ₹1600-3000; ✳ 🛜) The fastidious Mr Walton offers big wood-furnished rooms in his lovely old house that's painted a nautical white with blue trim and buried behind a bookstore. Downstairs rooms open onto a lush garden while upstairs rooms have balcony, and there's a communal breakfast room.

Jojies Homestay HOMESTAY **$$**
(☑ 9567045544; 1/1276 Chirattapallam, off KB Jacob Road; d ₹1500-2500; 🛜) Clean, friendly and welcoming homestay popular with travellers thanks to helpful owners and big breakfasts.

Raintree Lodge GUESTHOUSE **$$**
(Map p300; ☑ 9847029000, 0484-3251489; www.fortcochin.com; Peter Celli St; r ₹2800; ✳ 🛜) The intimate and elegant rooms at this historic place flirt with boutique-hotel status. Each of the five rooms has a great blend of contemporary style and heritage carved-wood furniture and the front upstairs rooms have gorgeous vine-covered Romeo-and-Juliet balconies. Good value.

Delight Home Stay GUESTHOUSE **$$**
(Map p300; ☑ 9846121421, 0484-2217658; www.delightfulhomestay.com; Post Office Rd; r incl breakfast ₹1600-1800, with AC ₹2500; ✳ 🛜) And delightful it is. This grand house's exterior is adorned with frilly white woodwork, and the six rooms are spacious and polished. There's a charming little garden, elegant breakfast room and an imposing sitting room covered in wall-to-wall teak. Good food is served and cooking classes are offered in the open kitchen.

Daffodil GUESTHOUSE **$$**
(Map p300; ☑ 9895262296, 0484-2218686; www.daffodilhomestay.com; Njaliparambu Junction; d incl breakfast ₹1600, with AC ₹2500; ✳ @ 🛜) Run by a welcoming local couple, Daffodil has eight big and brightly painted modern rooms with a sense of privacy, but the best feature is the carved-wood Keralan balcony upstairs.

Saj Homestay HOMESTAY **$$**
(Map p300; ☑ 9847002182; www.sajhome.com; Amravathi Rd, near Kunnumpuram Junction; d incl breakfast from ₹900, with AC ₹2200; ✳ 🛜) There are six upstairs rooms at this welcoming homestay run by helpful Saj. It can be a bit street-noisy at the front but the rooms are clean and travellers rave about the breakfast.

Noah's Ark HOMESTAY **$$**
(Map p300; ☑ 9745365260, 0484-2215481; www.noahsarkcochin.com; 1/508 Fort Cochin Hospital Rd; r ₹2800-3500; ✳ @ 🛜) This large modern family home, with a sweeping spiral staircase from the reception room and four immaculate, upmarket rooms – two with a balcony – comes with a friendly welcome but plenty of privacy.

Sonnetta Residency GUESTHOUSE **$$**
(Map p300; ☑ 9895543555, 0484-2215744; www.sonnettaresidency.com; 1/387 Princess St; d/f ₹1575/2250, with AC ₹2250/2800; ✳ 🛜) Right in the thick of the Fort Cochin action, the six rooms at this friendly Portuguese-era place are immaculately kept and well-presented, with nice, chintzy touches like curtains, colourful bedspreads and indoor plants. Every room has air-con but you can choose not to use it at the cheaper rate.

★**Malabar House** HOTEL **$$$**
(Map p300; ☑ 0484-2216666; www.malabarhouse.com; Parade Ground Rd; r €240, ste incl breakfast €330-380; ✳ @ 🛏) What may just be one of the fanciest boutique hotels in Kerala, Malabar flaunts its uber-hip blend of modern colours and period fittings like it's not even trying. While the suites are huge and lavishly appointed, the standard rooms are more snug. The award-winning restaurant and wine bar are top-notch.

★**Brunton Boatyard** HOTEL **$$$**
(☑ 0484-2215461; bruntonboatyard@cghearth.com; River Rd; r/ste ₹26,000/34,000; ✳ @ 🛜 🛏) This imposing hotel faithfully reproduces 16th- and 17th-century Dutch and Portuguese architecture in its grand complex. All of the rooms look out over the harbour, and have bathtubs and balconies with a refreshing sea breeze that beats air-con any day. The hotel is also home to the excellent History Restaurant and Armoury Bar, along with a couple of open-air cafes.

Spice Fort BOUTIQUE HOTEL **$$$**
(Map p300; ☑ 9364455440; www.duneecogroup.com; Princess St; r ₹8500-11,000; ✳ 🛜 🛏) The

chic red-and-white spice-themed rooms here have TVs built into the bed heads, cool tones and immaculate bathrooms. They all orbit an inviting pool in a heritage courtyard shielded from busy Princess St. Great location, excellent restaurant, friendly staff.

Tea Bungalow · HOTEL $$$

(Map p300; ☑ 0484-3019200; www.teabungalow.in; 1/1901 Kunumpuram; r ₹15,000-18,000; ❈@🛜🛋) This mustard-coloured colonial building was built in 1912 as headquarters of a UK spice trading company before being taken over by Brooke Bond tea. The 10 graceful boutique rooms – all named after sea ports – are decorated with flashes of strong colour and carved colonial-era wooden furniture, and have Bassetta-tiled bathrooms. Off-season rates drop by 60%.

Old Harbour Hotel · HOTEL $$$

(Map p300; ☑ 0484-2218006; www.oldharbourhotel.com; 1/328 Tower Rd; r/ste ₹10,200/17,600; ❈@🛋) Set around an idyllic garden with lily ponds and a small pool, the dignified Old Harbour is housed in a 300-year-old Dutch/ Portuguese-era heritage building. The elegant mix of period and modern styles lend it a more intimate feel than some of the more grandiose competition. There are 13 rooms and suites, some facing directly onto the garden, and some with open-air bathrooms.

Fort House Hotel · HOTEL $$$

(Map p300; ☑ 0484-2217103; www.hotelforthouse.com; 2/6A Calvathy Rd; r incl breakfast ₹5500; ❈@) Close to the ferry point, this is one of the few truly waterfront hotels, though the 16 smart air-con rooms are set back in a lush garden, with the restaurant taking prime waterside position.

🛏 Mattancherry & Jew Town

Caza Maria · HOMESTAY $$

(Map p302; ☑ 9846050901; cazamaria@rediffmail.com; Jew Town Rd; r incl breakfast ₹4500; ❈) Right in the heart of Jew Town, this unique place has just two large heritage rooms overlooking the bazaar. Fit for a maharaja, the rooms feature an idiosyncratic style, with each high-ceilinged room painted in bright colours, filled to the brim with antiques.

🛏 Ernakulam

John's Residency · HOTEL $

(Map p304; ☑ 0484-2355395; TD Rd; s/d from ₹550/650, with AC ₹1600; ❈) John's is a genuine backpacker place with helpful staff, local

information and a quiet location that's still a short walk from the boat jetty. Rooms are small (deluxe rooms are bigger) but decorated with flashes of colour that give them a welcoming funky feel in this price bracket.

Boat Jetty Bungalow · HOTEL $

(Map p304; ☑ 0484-2373211; www.boatjettybungalow.com; Cannon Shed Rd; s/d ₹430/735, with AC ₹960/1465; ❈) This 140-year-old former jettty manager's house has been refurbished and opened in 2014 as a very good value hotel with 22 compact and clean rooms with TV. It's a short walk to the boat jetty to Fort Cochin.

Saas Tower · HOTEL $$

(Map p304; ☑ 0484-2365319, www.saastower.com; Cannon Shed Rd; s/d ₹1200/1800, with AC from ₹2100/2400, ste from ₹3600; ❈@) The flashy lobby is more promising than the rooms in this midrange business hotel but if you're after a step up from the budget hotels near the jetty, it isn't a bad option. Clean rooms filled with wooden furniture, a restaurant, business centre and a day spa with ayurvedic treatments.

Grand Hotel · HOTEL $$

(Map p304; ☑ 9895721014, 0484-2382061; www.grandhotelkerala.com; MG Rd; s/d incl breakfast from ₹3250/4000, ste ₹6000; ❈@🛜) This 1960s hotel, with its polished original art deco fittings, exudes the sort of retro cool that modern hotels would love to recreate. The spacious rooms have gleaming parquet floors and large modern bathrooms, and there's a good restaurant and Ernakulam's most sophisticated bar.

🛏 Around Kochi

Kallancherry Retreat · HOMESTAY $

(☑ 0484-2240564, 9847446683; www.kallancherryretreat.com; Kumbalanghi Village; r without/with AC ₹800/1000, cottage without/with AC ₹1000/1500; ❈🛜) Escape the Kochi tourist crowds to this serene budget waterfront homestay and expansive garden in the village of Kumbalanghi, about 15km south of Fort Cochin. Rooms are either in the family home or in a sublime lakefront cottage. Offers Chinese fishing nets on your doorstep, boat trips, village tours and home-cooked meals.

★ Olavipe · HOMESTAY $$$

(☑ 0478-2522255; www.olavipe.com; Olavipe; s/d incl meals ₹5100/8500) This gorgeous 1890s traditional Syrian-Christian home is on a

16-hectare farm surrounded by backwaters, 28km south of Kochi. A restored mansion of rosewood and glistening teak, it has several large and breezy rooms beautifully decorated in original period decor.

✕ Eating & Drinking

Some of Fort Cochin's best dining can be found in the homestays, but there are lots of good restaurants and cafes.

✕ Fort Cochin

Behind the Chinese fishing nets are **fishmongers** (Map p300; seafood per kilo ₹200-1000) from whom you can buy the day's catch – fresh fish, prawns, crab and lobster – then take your selection to one of the row of simple but popular restaurants on nearby Tower Rd where they will cook it and serve it to you for an additional charge. Market price varies but you'll easily get a feel for prices if you wander along and bargain.

Teapot CAFE $
(Map p300; Peter Celli St; mains ₹70-140; ☺8.30am-8.30pm) This atmospheric cafe is the perfect venue for 'high tea', with 16 types of tea, sandwiches, cakes and a few meals served in chic, airy rooms. Witty tea-themed accents include loads of antique teapots, tea chests for tables and a tea-tree-based table.

Solar Cafe CAFE $
(Map p300; Bazaar Rd; meals ₹80-130; ☺8am-8pm) This arty upstairs cafe serves organic breakfasts and lunches, cinnamon coffee and fresh juice, in a lime-bright, book-lined setting opposite the Customs Jetty.

Oy's Restaurant MULTICUISINE $
(Map p300; www.oys.co.in; Burgher St; mains ₹50-200; ☺8.30am-10pm; 🕿) Oy's has made a name for itself among travellers with loungy decor, chill-out soundtrack, cafe comfort food and Asian–focused dishes.

★ Dal Roti INDIAN $$
(Map p300; ☑9746459244; 1/293 Lily St; meals ₹100-230; ☺noon-3.30pm & 6.30-10.30pm Wed-Mon) There's a lot to like about busy Dal Roti. Friendly and knowledgeable owner Ramesh will hold your hand through his expansive North Indian menu, which even sports its own glossary, and help you dive into his delicious range of vegetarian, egg-etarian and nonvegetarian options. From *kati* rolls (flatbrad rolled with stuffing) to seven types of thali, you won't go hungry. No alcohol.

Kashi Art Cafe CAFE $$
(Map p300; Burgher St; breakfast & snacks ₹90-250; ☺8.30am-10pm) An institution in Fort Cochin, this natural-light-filled place has a zen-but-casual vibe and solid wood tables that spread out into a semi-courtyard space. The coffee is as strong as it should be and the daily continental breakfast and lunch specials are excellent. A small gallery shows off local artists.

Arca Nova SEAFOOD $$
(Map p300; 2/6A Calvathy Rd; mains ₹190-650; ☺7.30am-10.30pm) The waterside restaurant at the Fort House Hotel is a prime choice for a leisurely lunch. It specialises in fish dishes and you can sit out at tables overlooking the water or in the serenely spacious covered garden area.

Upstairs Italian ITALIAN $$$
(Map p300; ☑9745682608; Bastion St; mains ₹250-600; ☺10am-11pm) For authentic Italian fare – Gorgonzola, prosciutto, olive oil, Parmesan cheese – head upstairs to this cosy little place serving Kochi's best pizza, pasta and antipasto. Pricey but worth a splurge.

★ Malabar Junction INTERNATIONAL $$$
(Map p300; ☑0484-2216666; Parade Ground Rd; mains ₹360-680, 5-course degustation ₹2000; ☺lunch & dinner) Set in an open-sided pavilion, the restaurant at Malabar House is movie-star cool, with white-tableclothed tables in a courtyard close to the small pool. There's a seafood-based, European-style menu – the signature dish is the impressive seafood platter with grilled vegetables. Upstairs, the wine bar serves upmarket tapas-style snacks and fine wine by the glass.

✕ Mattancherry & Jew Town

Ramathula Hotel INDIAN $
(Kaylkka's; Map p302; Kayees Junction, Mattancherry; biryani ₹40-60; ☺lunch & dinner) This place is legendary for its chicken and mutton biryanis – get here early or miss out. It's better known by the chef's name, Kayikka's.

Caza Maria MULTICUISINE $$
(Map p302; Bazaar Rd; mains ₹210-700; ☺9am-8pm) This enchanting 1st-floor place is a bright-blue, antique-filled heritage space with soft music and a changing daily menu of North Indian, South Indian and French dishes.

Café Jew Town
CAFE $$

(Map p302; Bazaar Rd; snacks ₹120-200; ⊙9am-6pm) Walk through chic antique shops and galleries to reach this sweet Swiss-owned cafe; the few tables proffer good cakes, snacks and Italian coffee.

Cafe Crafters
CAFE $$

(Map p302; Jew Town Rd; mains ₹100-280; ⊙9.30am-6.30pm) In the heart of Mattancherry's Jewish Quarter, this charming little 1st-floor restaurant cooks up Keralan seafood and continental efforts like sandwiches and burgers. Prime position is the small balcony overlooking the street.

★ Ginger House
INDIAN $$$

(Map p302; Bazaar Rd; mains ₹190-700; ⊙8.30am-6pm) Hidden behind a massive antique-filled godown (warehouse) is this fantastic waterfront restaurant, where you can feast on Indian dishes and snacks – ginger prawns, ginger ice cream, ginger lassi … you get the picture. To get to the restaurant, walk through the astonishing Heritage Arts showroom with amazing sculptures and antiques – check out the giant snake-boat canoe. If you ask, the owner might show you the rest of the collection upstairs.

✕ Ernakulam

Ernakulam's mega shopping malls provide food-court dining. Another interesting development is the leafy Panampilly Ave, in a residential area south of the main train station, which is lined with modern fine-dining and fast-food restaurants.

Frys Village Restaurant
KERALAN $

(Map p304; Chittoor Rd; mains ₹80-150; ⊙noon-3.30pm & 7-10.30pm) This brightly decorated and breezy place with an arched ceiling is a great family restaurant with authentic Keralan food, especially seafood like *pollichathu* or crab roast. Fish and veg thalis are available for lunch.

Chillies
INDIAN $$

(Map p304; Layam Rd; meals ₹130-280, thali ₹140; ⊙11.30am-3.30pm & 7.30-11pm) A dark, buzzing 1st-floor place, serving Kochi's best spicy Andhra cuisine on banana leaves. Try a thali for all-you-can-eat joy.

Grand Pavilion
INDIAN $$$

(Map p304; MG Rd; meals ₹250-370) The restaurant at the Grand Hotel is as elegant and retro-stylish as the hotel itself, with cream-coloured furniture and stiff tablecloths. It serves a tome of a menu that covers dishes from most of the Asian continent.

☆ Entertainment

There are several places in Kochi where you can view Kathakali. The performances are designed for tourists, but they're a good introduction to this intriguing art form. The standard program starts with the intricate make-up application and costume-fitting, followed by a demonstration and commentary on the dance and then the performance – usually two hours in all. The fast-paced traditional martial art of *kalarippayat* can also be easily seen, often at the same theatres.

☆ Fort Cochin

Kerala Kathakali Centre
CULTURAL PROGRAM

(Map p300; ✆0484-2217552; www.kathakalicentre.com; KB Jacob Rd; shows ₹250-300; ⊙make-up from 5pm, show 6-7.30pm) In an intimate, wood-lined theatre, this recommended place provides a useful introduction to Kathakali, complete with handy translations of the night's story. The centre also hosts performances of *kalarippayat* at 4pm to 5pm daily, traditional music at 8pm to 9pm Sunday to Friday and classical dance at 8pm to 9pm Saturday.

Greenix Village
CULTURAL PROGRAM

(Map p300; ✆9349372050, 0484-2217000; www.greenix.in; Kalvathy Rd; shows ₹300-500; ⊙10am-6pm, shows from 5pm) This touristy 'cultural village' seeks to put the full gamut of Keralan music and arts under one roof with a small cultural museum, yoga classes (₹450), performances of Kathakali and *kalarippayat* (₹300) and other cultural shows in an impressive complex.

☆ Ernakulam

See India Foundation
CULTURAL PROGRAM

(Map p304; ✆0484-2376471; devankathakali@yahoo.com; Kalathiparambil Lane; admission ₹300; ⊙make-up 6pm, show 7-8pm) One of the oldest Kathakali theatres in Kerala, it has small-scale shows with an emphasis on the religious and philosophical roots of Kathakali.

Ens Kalari
CULTURAL PROGRAM

(✆0484-2700810; www.enskalari.org.in; Nettoor; admission by donation; ⊙demonstrations 7.15-8.15pm) If you want to see real professionals have a go at *kalarippayat,* it's best to travel out to this renowned *kalarippayat* learning centre, 8km southeast of Ernakulam. There are one-hour demonstrations daily (one day's notice required).

🔒 Shopping

Broadway in Ernakulam is good for local shopping, spice shops and clothing. On Jew Town Rd in Mattancherry you'll find a plethora of Gujarati-run shops selling genuine antiques mingled with knock-offs and copies. Most of the shops in Fort Cochin are identikit Kashmiri-run shops selling a mixed bag of North Indian crafts. Many shops around Fort Cochin and Mattancherry operate lucrative commission rackets, with autorickshaw drivers getting huge kickbacks for dropping tourists at their door.

Lulu Mall　　　　　　　　　　　MALL

(☑0484-2727777; www.lulu.in; NH47, Edapally; ⊙9am-11pm; 🛜) India's largest shopping mall, Lulu is an attraction in its own right with people coming from all over to shop here, hang out in the food courts or cinema, and go ice-skating or ten-pin bowling. Sprawling over seven hectares, the state-of-the-art aircon mall has more than 215 brand outlets from Calvin Klein to KFC. It's in Edapally, about 9km from the boat jetty.

Niraamaya　　　　　　　　　　CLOTHING

(Map p300; Quiros St, Fort Cochin; ⊙10am-5.30pm Mon-Sat) Popular throughout Kerala, Niraamaya sells 'ayurvedic' clothing and fabrics – all made of organic cotton, coloured with natural herb dyes or infused with ayurvedic oils. There's another branch in Mattancherry.

Centre Square Mall　　　　　　　　MALL

(Map p304; ☑0484-4041888; MG Rd, Ernakulam; ⊙10am-11pm) In central Ernakulam, this flashy new mall is smaller than Lulu but still has five floors of shopping, including a top-floor food court and bowling alley, as well as a cinema.

Idiom Bookshop　　　　　　　　　BOOKS

(Map p300; Bastion St; ⊙10.30am-9pm Mon-Sat) Huge range of quality new and used books in Fort Cochin.

TRADITIONAL KERALAN ARTS

Kathakali

The art form of Kathakali crystallised at around the same time as Shakespeare was scribbling his plays. The Kathakali performance is the dramatised presentation of a play, usually based on the Hindu epics the Ramayana, the Mahabharata and the Puranas. All the great themes are covered – righteousness and evil, frailty and courage, poverty and prosperity, war and peace.

Drummers and singers accompany the actors, who tell the story through their precise movements, particularly *mudras* (hand gestures) and facial expressions.

Preparation for the performance is lengthy and disciplined. Paint, fantastic costumes, ornamental headpieces and meditation transform the actors both physically and mentally into the gods, heroes and demons they are about to play. Dancers even stain their eyes red with seeds from the *chundanga* plant to maximise the drama.

Traditional performances can last for many hours, but you can see cut-down performances in tourist hot spots all over the state, and there are Kathakali schools in Trivandrum (p265) and near Thrissur that encourage visitors.

Kalarippayat

Kalarippayat (or *kalari*) is an ancient tradition of martial arts training and discipline, still taught throughout Kerala. Some believe it is the forerunner of all martial arts, with roots tracing back to the 12th-century skirmishes among Kerala's feudal principalities.

Masters of *kalarippayat,* called Gurukkal, teach their craft inside a special arena called a *kalari.* You can see often *kalarippayat* performances at the same venues as Kathakali.

The three main schools of *kalarippayat* can be divided into northern and central, both practised in northern Kerala and Malabar region, and southern *kalarippayat.* As well as open hand combat and grappling, demonstrations of the martial art are often associated with the use of weapons, including sword and shield *(valum parichayum)*, short stick *(kurunthadi)* and long stick *(neduvadi)..*

Fabindia
CLOTHING, HOMEWARES

(Map p300; ☑0484-2217077; www.fabindia.com; Napier St, Fort Cochin; ⊙10.30am-8.30pm) Fine Indian textiles, fabrics, clothes and household linen from this renowned brand.

Cinnamon
CLOTHING

(Map p300; Post Office Rd, Fort Cochin; ⊙10am-7pm Mon-Sat) Cinnamon sells gorgeous Indian-designed clothing, jewellery and homewares in an ultrachic white retail space.

Tribes India
HANDICRAFTS

(Map p300; ☑0484-2215077; Post Office Rd, Head Post Office, Fort Cochin; ⊙10am-6.30pm Mon-Sat) Tucked behind the post office, this TRIFED (Ministry of Tribal Affairs) enterprise sells tribal artefacts, paintings, shawls, figurines etc, at reasonable fixed prices and the profits go towards supporting the artisans.

ℹ️ Information

INTERNET ACCESS

There are several internet cafes around Princess St in Fort Cochin charging ₹40 per hour; many homestays and hotels offer free wi-fi.

MEDICAL SERVICES

Lakeshore Hospital (☑0484-2701032; www. lakeshorehospital.com; NH Bypass, Marudu) Modern hospital 8km southeast of Ernakulam.

Medical Trust (Map p304; ☑0484-2358001; www.medicaltrusthospital.com; MG Rd) Central hospital.

MONEY

UAE Exchange (⊙9.30am-6pm Mon-Fri, to 2pm Sat) Ernakulam (Map p304; ☑2383317; MG Rd, Perumpillil Bldg); Ernakulam (☑3067008; Chettupuzha Towers, PT Usha Rd Junction); Fort Cochin (Map p300; ☑2216231; Amravathi Rd) Foreign exchange and travellers cheques.

POST

College Post Office (Map p304; ☑0484-2369302; Convent Rd, Ernakulam; ⊙9am-5pm Mon-Sat)

Ernakulam Post Office (Map p304; ☑0484-2355467; Hospital Rd; ⊙9am-8pm Mon-Sat, 10am-5pm Sun) Also branches on MG Rd and Broadway.

Main Post Office (Map p300; Post Office Rd, Fort Cochin; ⊙9am-5pm Mon-Fri, to 3pm Sat).

TOURIST INFORMATION

There's a tourist information counter at the airport. Many places distribute a free brochure that includes a map and walking tour entitled *Historical Places in Fort Cochin*.

KTDC Tourist Reception Centre (Map p304; ☑0484-2353234; Shanmugham Rd, Ernakulam; ⊙8am-7pm) Also organises tours. There's another office at the jetty at Fort Cochin.

Tourist Desk Information Counter (www. touristdesk.in) Ernakulam (Map p304; ☑9847044688, 0484-2371761; Boat Jetty;

MAJOR BUSES FROM ERNAKULAM

The following bus services operate from the KSRTC bus stand and Vyttila Mobility Hub.

DESTINATION	FARE (₹)	DURATION (HR)	FREQUENCY
Alleppey	52	1½	every 10min
Bengaluru	4600-1100	14	4 daily
Calicut	170	5	hourly
Chennai	590	16	1 daily, 2pm
Coimbatore	150	4½	hourly
Kannur	220-250	8	5 daily
Kanyakumari	230	8	2 daily
Kollam	114	3½	every 30min
Kothamangalam	40	2	every 10min
Kottayam	57	2	every 30min
Kumily (for Periyar)	130	5	8 daily
Mangalore	335	12	6.30pm & 9.30pm
Munnar	100	4½	every 30min
Thrissur	55	2	every 10min
Trivandrum	170	5	every 30min

MAJOR TRAINS FROM ERNAKULAM

DESTINATION	TRAIN NO & NAME	FARE (₹)	DURATION (HR)	DEPARTURE
Bengaluru	16525 Bangalore Express (A)	345/930/1335	13	5.35pm
Chennai	12624 Chennai Mail (A)	395/1035/1470	12	7.30pm
Delhi	12625 Kerala Express (B)	885/2275/3375	46	3.45pm
Goa (Madgaon)	16346 Netravathi Express (B)	415/1120/1620	15	2.10pm
Mumbai	16346 Netravathi Express (B)	615/1635/2400	27	2.10pm

Fares: sleeper/3AC/2AC; (A) departs from Ernakulam Town (B) departs Ernakulam Junction

⊘8am-6pm); Fort Cochin (Map p300; ☑ 0484-2216129; Tower Rd, Fort Cochin; ⊘8am-7pm) At this private tour agency, with offices at Ernakalum's ferry terminal and in Fort Cochin, the staff are extremely knowledgeable and helpful about Kochi and beyond. They run several popular and recommended tours, including a festival tour, and publish information on festivals and cultural events.

Tourist Police Ernakulam (Map p304; ☑ 0484-2353234; Shanmugham Rd; ⊘8am-6pm); Fort Cochin (Map p300; ☑ 0484-2215055; ⊘24hr)

❶ Getting There & Away

AIR

Kochi International Airport is a popular hub, with international flights to/from the Gulf States, Sri Lanka, the Maldives, Malaysia and Singapore.

On domestic routes, Jet Airways, Air India, Indigo and Spicejet fly direct daily to Chennai, Mumbai, Bengalaru, Hyderabad, Delhi and Trivandrum (but not Goa). Air India flies to Delhi daily and to Agatti in the Lakshadweep islands six times a week.

BUS

All long-distance services operate from Ernakulam. The **KSRTC bus stand** (Map p304; ☑ 2372033; ⊘reservations 6am-10pm) still has a few services but most state-run and private buses pull into the massive new **Vyttila Mobility Hub** (☑ 2306611; www.vyttilamobilityhub.com; ⊘24hr), a state-of-the-art transport terminal about 2km east of Ernakulam Junction train station. Numerous private bus companies have super-deluxe, air-con, video and Volvo buses to long-distance destinations such as Bengaluru, Chennai, Mangalore, Trivandrum and Coimbatore; prices vary depending on the standard but the best buses are about 50% higher than government buses. Agents in Ernakulam and

Fort Cochin sell tickets. Private buses also use the Kaloor bus stand, 1km north of the city.

A prepaid autorickshaw from Vyttila costs ₹73 to the boat jetty, ₹190 to Fort Cochin and ₹370 to the airport.

TRAIN

Ernakulam has two train stations, Ernakulam Town and Ernakulam Junction. Reservations for both are made at the Ernakulam Junction **reservations office** (☑ 132; ⊘8am-8pm Mon-Sat, 8am-2pm Sun).

There are local and express trains to Trivandrum (2nd-class/sleeper/3AC ₹95/195/535, 4½ hours), via either Alleppey (₹50/170/535, 1½ hours) or Kottayam (₹55/140/485, 1½ hours). Trains also run to Thrissur (2nd/AC chair ₹60/255, 1½ hours), Calicut (sleeper/3AC/2AC ₹140/485/690, 4½ hours) and Kannur (₹220/535/735, 6½ hours).

❶ Getting Around

An above-ground **metro** (www.kochmetro.org) is under construction in Ernakalum, which will connect the airport with the city when completed. The first phase is due in 2016.

TO/FROM THE AIRPORT

Kochi International Airport (☑ 2610125; www. cochinairport.com) is at Nedumbassery, 30km northeast of Ernakulam. Air-con buses run between the airport and Fort Cochin (₹80, one hour, eight daily), some going via Ernakulam. Taxis to/from Ernakulam cost around ₹850, and to/from Fort Cochin around ₹1200, depending on the time of night.

BOAT

Ferries are the fastest and most enjoyable form of transport between Fort Cochin and the mainland. The jetty on the eastern side of Willingdon Island is called Embarkation; the west one, opposite Mattancherry, is Terminus; and the main stop at Fort Cochin is Customs, with another stop at the Mattancherry Jetty near the synagogue. One-way fares are ₹4 (₹6 between Ernakulam and Mattancherry).

Ernakulam

There are services to both Fort Cochin jetties (Customs and Mattancherry) every 25 to 50 minutes from Ernakulam's main jetty between 4.40am and 9.10pm.

Ferries also run every 20 minutes or so to Willingdon and Vypeen Islands.

Fort Cochin

Ferries run from Customs Jetty to Ernakulam regularly between 5am and 9.50pm. Ferries also hop between Customs Jetty and Willingdon Island 18 times a day.

Car and passenger ferries cross to Vypeen Island from Fort Cochin virtually nonstop.

LOCAL TRANSPORT

There are no regular bus services between Fort Cochin and Mattancherry Palace, but it's an enjoyable 30-minute walk through the busy warehouse area along Bazaar Rd. Autorickshaws should cost around ₹70, much less if you promise to look in a shop. Most short autorickshaw trips around Ernakulam shouldn't cost more than ₹50.

To get to Fort Cochin after ferries (and buses) stop running you'll need to catch a taxi or autorickshaw – Ernakulam Town train station to Fort Cochin should cost around ₹400; prepaid autorickshaws during the day cost ₹250.

Scooters (₹300 per day) and Enfields (₹400 to ₹600) can be hired from agents in Fort Cochin.

Around Kochi

Cherai Beach

On Vypeen Island and 25km from Fort Cochin, Cherai Beach makes a nice day trip or getaway from Kochi, especially if you hire a scooter or motorbike in Fort Cochin. The main beach entrance can get busy at times but with miles of lazy backwaters just a few hundred metres from the seafront, it's a pleasant place to explore.

To get here from Fort Cochin, catch the vehicle-ferry to Vypeen Island (₹3) and either hire an autorickshaw from the jetty (around ₹400) or catch one of the frequent buses (₹15, one hour) and get off at Cherai village, 1km from the beach. Buses also go here direct from Ernakulam via the Vallarpadam bridge.

🛏 Sleeping & Eating

Brighton Beach House GUESTHOUSE $$
(☑ 9946565555; www.brightonbeachhouse.org; d ₹2000-2500) Brighton Beach House has five basic rooms in a small building right near the shore. The beach is rocky here, but the place is filled with hammocks to loll in, and has a neat, elevated stilt-restaurant that serves perfect sunset views with dinner.

Cherai Beach Resort RESORT $$
(☑ 0484-2416949; www.cheraibeachresorts.com; villas from ₹3500, with AC from ₹4500; ❄@) This collection of distinctive cottages scattered around a meandering lagoon has the beach on one side and backwaters on the other. Bungalows are individually designed using natural materials, with either curving walls or split-levels or lookouts onto the backwaters. There's even a tree growing inside one room.

Les 3 Elephants RESORT $$$
(☑ 0484-2480005, 9349174341; www.3elephants. in; Convent St; cottages ₹5000-10,000; ❄🛜) Hidden back from the beach but with the backwaters on your doorstep, Les 3 Elephants is a superb French-run ecoresort. The 11 beautifully designed boutique cottages are all different but have private sit-outs, thoughtful personal touches and lovely backwater views out to Chinese fishing nets. The restaurant serves home-cooked French-Indian fare. Worth the trip.

Chilliout Cafe CAFE $$
(mains ₹160-320; ☉9am-late Oct-May) For continental-style comfort food by the beach (think burgers, pizzas and barbecue) Chilliout Cafe is a cool hang-out with sea breezes and a relaxed vibe.

Tripunithura

At Tripunithura, 16km southeast of Ernakulam, **Hill Palace Museum** (☑ 0484-2781113; admission ₹20; ☉9am-12.30pm & 2-4.30pm Tue-Sun) was formerly the residence of the Kochi royal family and is an impressive 49-building palace complex. It now houses the collections of the royal families, as well as 19th-century oil paintings, old coins, sculptures and paintings, and temple models. From Ernakulam catch the bus to Tripunithura from MG Rd or Shanmugham Rd, behind the Tourist Reception Centre (₹5 to ₹10, 45 minutes); an autorickshaw should cost around ₹300 return with one-hour waiting time.

Parur & Chennamangalam

Nowhere is the tightly woven religious cloth that is India more apparent than in Parur, 35km north of Kochi. Here, one of the oldest synagogues (admission ₹5; ⊙9am-5pm Tue-Sun) in Kerala, at Chennamangalam, 8km from Parur, has been fastidiously renovated. Inside you can see door and ceiling wood reliefs in dazzling colours, while just outside lies one of the oldest tombstones in India, inscribed with the Hebrew date corresponding to 1269. The Jesuits first arrived in Chennamangalam in 1577 and there's a Jesuit church and the ruins of a Jesuit college nearby. Aloso here is a Hindu temple on a hill overlooking the Periyar River, a 16th-century mosque, and Muslim and Jewish burial grounds.

In Parur town, you'll find the agraharam (place of Brahmins) – a small street of closely packed and brightly coloured houses originally settled by Tamil Brahmins.

Parur is compact, but Chennamangalam is best visited with a guide. Travel agencies in Fort Cochin can organise tours.

Thrissur (Trichur)

☏0487 / POP 315,600

While the rest of Kerala has its fair share of celebrations, untouristy, slightly chaotic Thrissur is the cultural cherry on the festival cake. With a list of energetic festivals as long as a temple elephant's trunk, the region supports several institutions that nurse the dying classical Keralan performing arts back to health. Centred on a large park (known as the 'Round') and temple complex, Thrissur is home to a Nestorian Christian community whose denomination dates to the 3rd century AD.

◉ Sights & Activities

Thrissur is renowned for its central temple, as well as for its numerous impressive churches, including the massive Our Lady of Lourdes Cathedral, towering, whitewashed Puttanpalli (New) Church and the Chaldian (Nestorian) Church.

Vadakkunathan
Kshetram Temple   HINDU TEMPLE
Finished in classic Keralan architecture and one of the oldest Hindu temples in the

Thrissur (Trichur)

◉ Sights
1 Archaeology Museum B1
2 Vadakkunathan Kshetram Temple B2

◉ Sleeping
3 Hotel Luciya Palace A3
4 Pathans Hotel.....................................A3
5 YMCA International Guesthouse........B2

◉ Eating
6 India Gate...B1
7 Navaratna Restaurant.........................A2
Pathans Restaurant....................(see 4)

◉ Transport
8 KSRTC Bus Stand...............................A4
9 Priyadarshini (North) Bus Stand........B1
10 Sakthan Thampuran Bus Stand.........B4

state, Vadakkunathan Kshetram Temple crowns the hill at the epicentre of Thrissur.

Only Hindus are allowed inside, though the mound surrounding the temple has sweeping views and the surroudning park is a popular spot to linger.

Archaeology Museum MUSEUM
(adult/child ₹20/5, camera/video ₹50/250; ☺9.30am-1pm & 2-4.30pm Tue-Sun) The refurbished Archaeology Museum is housed in the wonderful 200-year-old Sakthan Thampuran Palace. Its mix of artefacts include 12th-century Keralan bronze sculptures, giant earthenware pots, weaponry, coins and a lovely carved chessboard. To the side is a shady heritage garden.

⚜️ Festivals & Events

In a state where festivals are a way of life, Thrissur stands out for temple revelry.

Thypooya Maholsavam FESTIVAL
(☺Jan/Feb) The festival stars a *kavadiyattam* (a form of ritualistic dance) procession in which dancers carry tall, ornate structures called *kavadis*.

Uthralikavu Pooram FESTIVAL
(☺Mar/Apr) The climactic day of this event sees 20 elephants circling the shrine.

Thrissur Pooram FESTIVAL
(☺Apr/May) At Vadakkumnathan Kshetram Temple, this is the largest and most colourful and biggest of Kerala's temple festivals with wonderful processions of caparisoned elephants.

🛏️ Sleeping

Pathans Hotel HOTEL $
(☎0487-2425620; www.pathansresidentialhotel.in; Round South; ☺s/d from ₹587/784, with AC ₹1045/1450; ❄) No-frills rooms at no-frills prices and the location is unbeatable across from the central park. The basic, cleanish and secure rooms are on the 5th and 6th floors (served by a painfully slow lift) and have TVs and occasional hot water.

YMCA International Guesthouse GUESTHOUSE $
(☎0487-2331190; www.ymcathrissur.org; Palace Rd; d ₹700, with AC ₹1050) Clean, comfortable and secure. A good budget choice when it's not full with school groups.

Hotel Luciya Palace HOTEL $$
(☎0487-2424731; www.hotelluciyapalace.com; Marar Rd; s/d with AC ₹2250/3100, ste ₹5625; ❄) In a cream, colonial-themed building, this is

one of the few places in town that has some character and the spacious, modern air-con rooms are good value. It's in a quiet cul-de-sac but close to the temple and town centre action, and has a neat lawn garden, a decent restaurant and a busy bar.

🍴 Eating & Drinking

India Gate INDIAN $
(Palace Rd; dishes ₹80-130; ☺8am-10pm) In the Kalliyath Royal Square building, this bright, pure-veg place has a vintage feel and an extraordinary range of dosas, including jam, cheese and cashew versions. In the same complex is a Chinese restaurant (China Gate) and a fast-food joint (Celebrations)

Pathans Restaurant INDIAN $
(1st fl, Round South; dishes ₹30-80; ☺6.30am-9.30pm) On the 1st floor of the Pathans Hotel building, this easy-going place opens early for a cheap breakfast and is popular with families for lunch (thalis ₹50).

Navaratna Restaurant MULTICUISINE $$
(Round West; dishes ₹100-180; ☺noon-9.30pm) Cool, dark and intimate, this is one of the classiest dining experiences in town, with seating on raised platforms. Downstairs is veg and upstairs is nonveg, with lots of North Indian specialities, Chinese and a few Keralan dishes.

ℹ️ Information

There are several ATMs and internet cafes around town.
DTPC Office (☎0487-2320800; Palace Rd; ☺10am-5pm Mon-Sat) You might be able to pick up some local brochures from this tourist office.

ℹ️ Getting There & Away

BUS

State buses leave around every 30 minutes from the KSRTC bus stand bound for Trivandrum (₹214, 7½ hours), Ernakulam (Kochi, ₹65, two hours), Calicut (₹102, 3½ hours), Palakkad (₹57, 1½ hours) and Kottayam (₹105, four hours). Hourly buses go to Coimbatore (₹94, three hours).

Regular services also chug along to Guruvayur (₹26, one hour), Irinjalakuda (₹25, one hour) and Cheruthuruthy (₹28, 1½ hours). Two private bus stands (Sakthan Thampuran and Priyadarshini) have more frequent buses to these destinations, though the chaos involved in navigating each station hardly makes using them worthwhile.

TRAIN

Services run regularly to Ernakulam (2nd-class/AC chair ₹60/255, 1½ hours), Calicut (₹70/255, three hours) and Coimbatore (₹90/305, three hours).

Around Thrissur

Kerala Kalamandalam   CULTURAL PROGRAM

(☑ 04884262418; www.kalamandalam.org; courses per month ₹2500; ☺ Jun-Mar) Using an ancient Gurukula system of learning, students undergo intensive study in Kathakali, *mohiniyattam* (dance of the enchantress), Kootiattam, percussion, voice and violin. A Day with the Masters (₹1000, including lunch) is a morning program allowing visitors to tour the theatre and classes and see various art and cultural presentations. Email to book in advance. It's 26km north of Thrissur.

Natana Kairali Research & Performing Centre for Traditional Arts   CULTURAL PROGRAM

(☑ 0480-2825559; www.natanakairali.org) This school, 20km south of Thrissur near Irinjalakuda, offers training in traditional arts, including rare forms of puppetry and dance..

🛏 Sleeping

River Retreat   GUESTHOUSE $$

(☑ 0488-4262244; www.riverretreat.in; Palace Rd, Cheruthuruthy; d from ₹3480-6540, ste ₹7800, cottage ₹8580; ❋ 🛜 ☁) River Retreat is an excellent hotel and ayurvedic resort in the former summer palace of the Maharajas of Cochin. Along with ayurvedic treatments, facilities include a pool, gym and business centre. It's about 30km north of Thrissur.

NORTHERN KERALA

Kozhikode (Calicut)

☑ 0495 / POP 432,100

Northern Kerala's largest city, Calicut was always a prosperous trading town and was once the capital of the formidable Zamorin dynasty. Vasco da Gama first landed near here in 1498, on his way to snatch a share of the subcontinent for king and country (Portugal that is). These days, trade depends mostly on exporting Indian labour to the Middle East, while agriculture and the timber industry are economic mainstays. For travellers it's mainly a jumping-off point for Wayanad or for the long trip over the ghats to Mysuru (Mysore) or Bengaluru (Bangalore.)

◉ Sights

Mananchira Square, a large central park, was the former courtyard of the Zamorins and preserves the original spring-fed tank. South of the centre, the 650-year-old **Kuttichira Mosque** is in an attractive wooden four-storey building that is supported by impressive wooden pillars and painted brilliant aquamarine, blue and white. The central **Church of South India** was established by Swiss missionaries in 1842 and has unique Euro-Keralan architecture.

About 1km west of Mananchira Square is Kozhikode Beach – not much for swimming but good enough for a sunset promenade.

🛏 Sleeping

Alakapuri   HOTEL $

(☑ 0495-2723451; MM Ali Rd; s/d from ₹700/1300, with AC from ₹1600; ❋) Built motel-style around a green lawn (complete with fountain!) this place is set back from a busy market area. Various rooms are a little scuffed and dingy, but reasonable value.

Beach Hotel   HOTEL $$

(☑ 9745062055, 0495-2762055; www.beachheritage.com; Beach Rd; r with seaview or AC inc breakfast ₹3500; ❋ @) Built in 1890 to house the Malabar British Club, this is a slightly worn but charming 10-room hotel. Some have bathtubs and secluded sea-facing verandahs; others have original polished wooden floors and private balconies. All are tastefully furnished and drip with character.

Hyson Heritage   HOTEL $$

(☑ 0495-4081000; www.hysonheritage.com; Bank Rd; s/d inc breakfast from ₹2700/3600; ❋ 🛜) You get a bit of swank for your rupee at this central business hotel. Rooms are spick and span and shielded from the main road. There's a good restaurant and a gym.

★ Harivihar   BOUTIQUE HOMESTAY $$$

(☑ 9388676054, 0495-2765865; www.harivihar.com; Bilathikulam; s/d incl meals €110/140; 🛜) In northern Calicut, the ancestral home of the Kadathanadu royal family is as serene as it gets, a traditional Keralan family compound with pristine lawns. The seven rooms are large and beautifully furnished with dark-wood antiques. There's an ayurvedic

Kozhikode (Calicut)

Kozhikode (Calicut)

and yoga centre, with packages available. The pure veg food is delicious and cooking classes are available. It's hard to find (taxi drivers are largely baffled), so call ahead.

✗ Eating & Drinking

Paragon Restaurant   INDIAN $$
(Kannur Rd; dishes ₹125-340; ⊗8am-midnight, lunch from noon) You might struggle to find a seat at this always-packed restaurant, founded in 1939. The overwhelming menu is famous for fish dishes such as fish in tamarind sauce, and its legendary chicken biryani.

Salkaram & Hut   INDIAN $$
(Beach Rd; mains ₹110-290; ⊗7am-10.30pm) At the back of the Beach Hotel are two restaurants with the same menu: the air-con Salkaram, and the cool open-sided bamboo 'hut' restaurant-bar serving a big range of fish and chicken dishes and Malabari cuisine. It's a breezy place for a cold beer..

Indian Coffee House   CAFE
(GH Rd; ₹10-60; ⊗8am-9pm) For tasty snacks and good coffee.

ℹ Information

There are HDFC and State Bank of India ATMs in town, and several internet cafes.

ℹ Getting There & Away

AIR
Calicut airport is about 25km south of the city in Karipur. It serves major domestic routes as well as international flights to the Gulf.

Spicejet has the best domestic connections with direct flights to Mumbai, Bangalore and Chennai. **Air India** (✆2771974; 5/2521 Bank Rd, Eroth Centre) flies to Kochi and Coimbatore. **Jet Airways** (✆271 2375; Calicut Airport) has one daily flight to Mumbai. Flights to Goa go via Bangalore or Mumbai.

BUS
The new KSRTC **bus stand** (Mavoor Rd) has government buses to Bengaluru (Bangalore, via Mysore, ₹335-500, eight hours, 10 daily), Mangalore (₹300, seven hours, three daily) and to Ooty (₹130, 5½ hours, 5am & 6.45am). There are frequent buses to Thrissur (₹100, 3½ hours) and Kochi (₹180, four hours, eight daily). For Wayanad district, buses leave every 15 minutes heading to Sultanbatheri (₹75, three hours) via Kalpetta (₹60, two hours). Private buses for various long-distance locations also use this stand.

TRAIN
The train station is 1km south of Mananchira Sq. There are frequent trains to Kannur (2nd-class/

sleeper/3AC ₹60/140/485, two hours), Mangalore (sleeper/3AC/2AC ₹195/535/735, five hours), Ernakulam (₹165/485/690, 4½ hours) via Thrissur (₹200/535/735, three hours), and all the way to Trivandrum (₹275/705/985, 11 hours).

Heading southeast, trains go to Coimbatore (sleeper/3AC/2AC ₹170/535/735, 4½ hours), via Palakkad (₹140/485/690, 3½ hours).

❶ Getting Around

Calicut has a glut of autorickshaws and most are happy to use the meter. It costs about ₹40 from the station to the KSRTC bus stand or most hotels. An autorickshaw/taxi to the airport costs around ₹400/600.

Wayanad Wildlife Sanctuary

♪ 04936 / POP 816,500

Many Keralans rate the Wayanad region as the most beautiful part of their state. Encompassing part of a remote forest reserve that spills into Tamil Nadu and Karnataka, Wayanad's landscape combines epic mountain scenery, rice paddies of ludicrous green, skinny betel nut trees, bamboo, red earth, spiky ginger fields, and rubber, cardamom and coffee plantations. Foreign travellers are making it here in increasing numbers, partly because it provides easy access between Mysuru (Mysore) or Bengaluru (Bangalore) and Kerala, but it's still fantastically unspoilt and satisfyingly remote. It's also an excellent place to spot wild elephants.

The 345-sq-km sanctuary has two separate pockets – Muthanga in the east bordering Tamil Nadu, and Tholpetty in the north bordering Karnataka. Three main towns in Wayanad district make good bases and transport hubs for exploring the sanctuary – Kalpetta in the south, Sultanbatheri (Sultan Battery) in the east and Mananthavadi in the northwest – though the best of the accommodation is scattered throughout the region. Most hotels and homestays can arrange guided jeep tours to various parts of Wayanad.

◉ Sights & Activities

★ **Wayanad Wildlife Sanctuary**   NATURE RESERVE

(www.wayanadsanctuary.org; admission to each part Indian/foreigner ₹115/300, camera/video ₹40/225; ⊙7-10am & 3-5pm) Entry to both parts of the sanctuary is only permitted as part of a jeep safari, which can be arranged at the sanctuary entrances. At the time of research there was no trekking in the park for safety reasons. Both Tholpetty and Muthanga close during the June to August monsoon period.

At **Tholpetty** (♪04935-250853; jeep tours ₹500; ⊙7-10am & 3-5pm), the two-hour **jeep tours** can be rough going but are a great way to spot wildlife. Similar tours are available at **Muthanga** (♪0493-6271010; jeep tours ₹500). At both locations arrive at least an hour before the morning or afternoon openings to register and secure a vehicle, as there are a limited number of guides and jeeps permitted in the park at one time.

Thirunelly Temple   HINDU TEMPLE

(⊙dawn-dusk) Thought to be one of the oldest on the subcontinent, Thirunelly Temple is 10km from Tholpetty. Non-Hindus cannot enter, but it's worth visiting for the otherworldly cocktail of ancient and intricate pillars. Follow the path behind the temple to the stream known as **Papanasini**, where Hindus believe you can wash away all your sins.

Edakal Caves   CAVES

(adult/child ₹20/10, camera ₹30; ⊙9am-4pm Tue-Sun) The highlight of these remote hilltop 'caves' – more accurately a small series of caverns – is the ancient collection of petroglyphs in the top cave, thought to date back over 3000 years. From the car park near Ambalavayal it's a steep 20-minute walk up a winding road to the ticket window, then another steep climb up to the light-filled top chamber. On a clear day there are exceptional views out over the Wayanad district. The caves get crowded on weekends and are closed Monday.

Wayanad Heritage Museum   MUSEUM

(Ambalavayal; admission ₹20; ⊙9am-5pm) In the small village of Ambalavayal, about 5km from Edva Caves, this museum exhibits headgear, weapons, pottery, carved stone and other artefacts dating back to the 15th century that shed light on Wayanad's significant Adivasi population.

Uravu   HANDICRAFTS CENTRE

(♪0493-6231400; www.uravu.net; Thrikkaippetta; ⊙8.30am-5pm Mon-Sat) 🌿 Around 6km southeast of Kalpetta a collective of workers create all sorts of artefacts from bamboo. You can visit the artists' workshops, where they work on looms, paintings and carvings, and support their work by buying vases, lampshades, bangles and baskets.

Kannur Ayurvedic Centre
AYURVEDA

(☑0436203001; www.ayurvedawayanad.com; Kalpetta; massage from ₹1200, yoga & meditation ₹1200; ☺yoga classes 6-7am) For rejuvenation and curative ayurvedic treatments, visit this small, government-certified and family-run clinic, in the backstreets of Kalpetta. Accommodation and yoga classes available.

Trekking

There are some top opportunities for independent trekking around the district (though not in the wildlife sanctuary itself). Top treks include **Chembra Peak** (2100m), the area's tallest summit; **Vellarimala**, with great views and lots of wildlife-spotting opportunities; and **Pakshipathalam**, a seven-hour return mountain trek in the northern Brahmagiri Hills that takes you to a formation of large boulders high in the forest. Permits and guides are mandatory and can be arranged at forest offices in South or North Wayanad or through your accommodation. The standard cost for permit and guide is ₹2500 for up to five people – try to arrange a group in advance. The **DTPC office** in Kalpetta also organises trekking guides and transport.

🛏 Sleeping & Eating

There's plenty of accommodation in Wayanad's towns, but the isolated homestays or resort accommodation scattered throughout the region are better choices.

🛏 Kalpetta

PPS Residency
HOTEL $

(☑04936-203431; www.ppstouristhome.com; Kalpetta; s/d ₹400/500, d with AC ₹1500; ❄) This friendly budget place in the middle of Kalpetta has a variety of reasonably clean rooms in a motel-like compound as well as a multicuisine restaurant. Helpful management can arrange trips around Wayanad.

Haritagiri
HOTEL $$

(☑04936-203145; www.hotelharitagiri.com; Kalpetta; s/d incl breakfast from ₹1450/1850, with AC from ₹1850/2500; ❄🛜🏊) Set back from Kalpetta's busy main streets, this is a comfortable midrange option, and some of the rooms have balconies. There are two restaurants, a gym and an ayurvedic 'village' on-site.

🛏 Sultanbatheri

Mint Flower Residency
HOTEL $$

(☑04936-222206, 9745222206; www.mintflowerresidency.com; Sultan Batheri; s/d ₹830/1375, with AC ₹1075/1670) The new budget annexe of Mint Flower Hotel is in great condition. It's no-frills but rooms are spotless and come with hot water and TV.

Issac's Hotel Regency
HOTEL $$

(☑04936-220512; www.issacsregency.com; Sultanbatheri; s/d/tr from ₹1150/1600/1800, with AC from ₹1550/2000/2250; ❄@🏊) This quiet and no-nonsense place near the local bus stand has routine, large and relatively tidy rooms in a U-shaped building.

🛏 Around Wayanad

★Varnam Homestay
HOMESTAY $$

(☑9745745860, 04935-215666; www.varnamhomestay.com; Kadungamalayil House, Payyampally; s/d incl meals ₹1500/2400, villa ₹1800/3000; ❄🛜) This oasis of peace and calm is a lovely place to stay only a few kilometres from Karikulum in northern Wayanad. Varghese and Beena will look after you with Wayanad stories, local information and delicious home-cooking with organic farm-fresh ingredients. Rooms are in a traditional family home or a newer elevated 'tree house' villa, and the property is surrounded by jungle and spice plantations. Forest drives and trekking to tribal villages can be arranged.

Greenex Farms
RESORT $$

(☑9645091512; www.greenexfarms.com; Chundale Estate Rd, Moovatty; r ₹2250-4500) Greenex Farms is a wonderfully remote-feeling place surrounded by spice and tea plantations about 8km southwest of Kalpetta. Each of the private cottages is individually designed with separate lounge, bathroom, balconies and superb views.

Pachyderm Palace
GUESTHOUSE $$

(☑9847044688, reservations 0484-2371761; www.touristdesk.in/pachydermpalace.htm; Tholpetty; s/d incl meals ₹2000/4000, tree house ₹4000) This fine old Keralan house lies just outside the gate of Tholpetty Wildlife Sanctuary – handy for early-morning treks, tours and wildlife viewing. The varied rooms include two secluded stilt-bungalow 'tree houses' surrounded by forest and another private cottage. Venu is a stupendous cook, and his son Dilip is a great guide who can organise village and mountain treks.

Wayanad District

Ente Veedu HOMESTAY $$

(☎9446834834, 0493-5220008; www.enteveedu.co.in; Panamaram; r incl breakfast ₹2500-3500, with AC ₹3500-4000; @🛜) Isolated and set in a lovely location overlooking sprawling banana plantations and rice paddies, this homestay halfway between Kalpetta and Mananthavady is definitely worth seeking out. There are several large rooms, two bamboo-lined rooms with private balconies, hammocks and wicker lounges to enjoy the sensational views. Lunch and dinner are available for ₹250/350 veg/nonveg.

⭐**Tranquil** HOMESTAY $$$

(☎04936220244; www.tranquilresort.com; Kuppamudi Estate, Kolagapara; full board s/d from ₹14,400/13,750, tree house ₹17,750/24,600, tree villa ₹18,300/26,400; 🛜☒) This wonderfully serene and exclusive homestay is in the middle of an incredibly lush 160 hectares of pepper, coffee, vanilla and cardamom plantations. The elegant house has sweeping verandahs filled with plants and handsome furniture, and there are two tree houses that may be the finest in the state. A network of marked walking trails meander around the plantation.

🛈 Information

The **DTPC office** (☎04936202134; www.dtpc-wayanad.com; Kalpetta; ☉10am-5pm Mon-Sat) at Kalpetta can help organise tours, permits and trekking. There are UAE Exchange offices in Kalpetta and Sultanbatheri, and ATMs can be found in each of the three main towns.

🛈 Getting There & Away

Although remote, Wayanad is easily accessible by bus from Calicut and Kannur in Kerala, and from Mysore (Karnataka) and Ooty (Tamil Nadu). Buses brave the winding roads – including nine spectacular hairpin bends – between Calicut and Kalpetta (₹60 to ₹76, two hours) every 15 minutes, with some continuing on to Sultanbatheri (₹80, three hours) and others to Mananthavadi (₹87, three hours). Hourly buses run between Kannur and Mananthavadi (₹70, 2½ hours).

From Sultanbatheri, an 8am bus heads out for Ooty (₹100, four hours), with a second one passing through town at around 12.45pm. Buses run from Kalpetta to Mysore (₹130 to ₹160, four hours, hourly), via Sultanbatheri, but note that the border gate is closed between 7pm and 6am. There are four daily buses to Mysore (₹144, three hours) on the northern route from Mananthavadi, where the border is open 24 hours.

❶ Getting Around

The Wayanad district is quite spread out but plenty of private buses connect the main towns of Mananthavadi, Kalpetta and Sultanbatheri every 10 to 20 minutes during daylight hours (₹15 to ₹25, 45 minutes to one hour). From Mananthavadi, regular buses also head to Tholpetty (₹15, one hour). You can hire jeeps or taxis to get between towns for ₹600 to ₹800 each way, or hire a vehicle to tour the region for around ₹2000 per day.

There are plenty of autorickshaws and taxis for short hops within the towns.

Kannur & Around

☎ 0497 / POP 1.2 MILLION

Kerala's northern coast is far less tourist-ed than the south, which for many is an attraction in its own right. The main draw in this part of coastal Kerala are the beautiful, undeveloped beaches and the enthralling *theyyam* possession rituals.

Under the Kolathiri rajas, Kannur (Can-nanore) was a major port bristling with international trade – explorer Marco Polo christened it a 'great emporium of spice trade'. Since then, the usual colonial sus-pects, including the Portuguese, Dutch and British, have had a go at exerting their influ-ence on the region. Today it is an unexciting, though agreeable, town known mostly for its weaving industry and cashew trade.

This is a predominantly Muslim area, so local sensibilities should be kept in mind: wear a sarong over your bikini on the beach.

◉ Sights & Activities

Kannur's main town beach is the 4km-long **Payyambalam Beach** (beach park ₹5, camera ₹25), which starts about 1.5km east of the train station, just past the military can-tonment. The beach park gets busy in the evening when families and couples come down to watch the sunset and picnic.

**Loknath Weavers'
Co-operative**   HANDICRAFTS WORKSHOP
(☎0497-2726330; ⊗8.30am-5.30pm Mon-Sat) **FREE** Established in 1955, this is one of the oldest cooperatives in Kannur and occu-pies a large building busily clicking with the sound of looms. You can stop by for a quick (free) tour; the shop here displays the fruits of the workers' labours (with the obligatory sales pitch). It's 4km south of Kannur town.

**Kerala Dinesh
Beedi Co-Operative**   HANDICRAFTS WORKSHOP
(☎0497-2835280; www.keraladinesh.com; ⊗8am-6pm Tue-Sat) **FREE** The Kannur region is known for the manufacture of *beedis,* those tiny Indian cigarettes deftly rolled inside green leaves. This is one of the largest and purportedly best manufacturers, with a fac-tory at Thottada, 7km south of Kannur and about 4km from Thottada Beach. A skilled individual can roll up to 1000 a day! Visi-tors are welcome to look around; an auto-rickshaw should cost around ₹120 return from Kannur town.

🛏 Sleeping & Eating

Although there are plenty of hotels in Kannur town, the best places to stay are homestays near the beach at Thottada (8km south) and towards Thalassery.

🛏 Kannur Town

Hotel Meridian Palace   HOTEL **$**
(☎9995999547, 0497-2701676; www.hotelmeridi-anpalace.com; Bellard Rd; s/d from ₹400/550, de-luxe ₹850/1000, with AC ₹1400-1700; ❀) In the market area opposite the main train station, this is hardly palatial but it's friendly enough and offers a cornucopia of clean budget rooms and a Punjabi restaurant.

Mascot Beach Resort   HOTEL **$$**
(☎0497-2708445; www.mascotresort.com; d ₹2400, with AC from ₹3600, ste ₹7200; ❀@🛈🖳) All rooms are sea-facing at this compact, slightly faded midrange hotel looking over the small, rocky Baby Beach. Facilities are good, including a pool with a view and the seaside Mermaid restaurant.

Hotel Odhen's   MALABAR **$**
(Onden Rd; meals ₹30-60; ⊗8.30am-5pm) This popular local restaurant in Kannur's mar-ket area is usually packed at lunchtime. The speciality is Malabar cuisine, including tasty seafood curries and banana-leaf thalis.

🛏 Thottada Beach & Around

★Blue Mermaid Homestay   HOMESTAY **$$**
(☎9497300234; www.bluemermaid.in; Thottada Beach; s/d inc breakfast & dinner ₹2000/3000, d with AC ₹3600; ❀🛈) With a prime location among the palms facing Thottada Beach, Blue Mermaid is a charming and immacu-late guesthouse with rooms in a tradition-al home, bright air-con rooms in a newer building and a whimsical stilted 'honey-moon cottage'. Friendly young owners cook

up fine Keralan meals, with breakfast and dinner included.

Waves Beach Resort HOMESTAY $$
(☎9495050850; www.wavesbeachresort.co.in; Adikadalayai, Thottada Beach; s/d incl meals ₹2000/3000; ☎) Crashing waves will lull you to sleep at this very cute pair of hexagonal laterite brick huts overlooking a semi-private little crescent beach. There are four rooms here (two up, two down). The welcoming owners, Seema and Arun, also have rooms in two other nearby properties, including cheaper rooms in an old Keralan house.

Costa Malabari GUESTHOUSE $$
(☎09447775691, reservations 0484-2371761; www.touristdesk.in/costamalabari; Thottada Beach; s/d incl meals ₹3000-3500; ❄☎) Surrounded by lush greenery on a hill back from the beach, Costa Malabari pioneered tourism in this area. There are spacious rooms in an old hand-loom factory, and extra rooms are offered in two other nearby bungalows. The home-cooked Keralan food is plentiful. Manager Kurien is an expert on the *theyyam* ritual and can help arrange a visit.

Kannur Beach House HOMESTAY $$
(☎0497-2708360, 9847184535; www.kannurbeachhouse.com; Thottada Beach; s/d ₹2400/3400) The original beachfront homestay is a traditional Keralan building with handsome wooden shutters, but the rooms are looking a little worn. Still, you can enjoy sensational ocean sunset views from your porch or balcony. A small lagoon separates the house from the beach. Breakfast and dinner included.

Ezhara Beach House HOMESTAY $$
(☎0497-2835022; www.ezharabeachhouse.com; 7/347 Ezhara Kadappuram; s/d incl meals ₹1250/2500; ☎) Fronting the unspoilt Kizhunna Ezhara beach, midway between Kannur and Thalassery railway stations (11km from each) the blue Ezhara Beach House is run by no-nonsense Hyacinth. The five rooms are simple but the house has character.

❶ Getting There & Away

BUS
Kannur has several bus stands: the enormous central bus stand – is the place to catch private and some government buses, but most long-distance buses still use the KSRTC bus stand near the Caltex junction, 1km northeast of the train station.

There are daily buses to Mysore (₹200, eight hours, six daily), Madikeri (₹80, 2½ hours, 11am) and Ooty (via Wayanad, ₹225, nine hours, 7.30am & 10pm). For the Wayanad region, buses leave every hour from the central bus stand to Mananthavadi (₹80, 2½ hours).

For Thottada Beach, take bus No 29 (₹8) from Plaza Junction opposite the train station and get off at Adikatalayi village.

THEYYAM

Kerala's most popular ritualistic art form, *theyyam* is believed to pre-date Hinduism, originating from folk dances performed during harvest celebrations. An intensely local ritual, it's often performed in *kavus* (sacred groves) throughout northern Kerala.

Theyyam refers both to the shape of the deity/hero portrayed, and to the actual ritual. There are around 450 different *theyyams*, each with a distinct costume, made up of face paint, bracelets, breastplates, skirts, garlands and exuberant, intricately crafted headdresses that can be up to 6m or 7m tall. During performances, each protagonist loses his physical identity and speaks, moves and blesses the devotees as if he were that deity. Frenzied dancing and wild drumming create an atmosphere in which a deity indeed might, if it so desired, manifest itself in human form.

During October to May there are annual rituals at each of the hundreds of *kavus*. *Theyyams* are often held to bring good fortune to important events such as marriages and housewarmings. The best place for visitors to see *theyyam* is in village temples in the Kannur region of northern Kerala (most frequently between late November and mid-April). In peak times (December to February) there should be a *theyyam* ritual happening somewhere almost every night.

Although tourists are welcome to attend, this is not a dance performance but a religious ritual, and the usual rules of temple behaviour apply: dress appropriately, avoid disturbing participants and villagers; refrain from displays of public affection. Photography is permitted, but avoid using a flash. For details on where and when, ask at your guesthouse or contact Kurien at Costa Malabari in Thottada Beach..

TRAIN

There are frequent daily trains to Calicut (2nd-class/AC chair ₹60/255, 1½ hours), Ernakulam (sleeper/3AC/2AC ₹₹220/535/735, 6½ hours) and Alleppey (₹245/625/870). Heading north there are express trains to Mangalore (sleeper/3AC/2AC ₹140/485/690, three hours) and up to Goa (sleeper/3AC/2AC ₹350/910/1285, eight hours).

Bekal & Around

📞 0467

Bekal and nearby Palakunnu and Udma, in Kerala's far north, have some long white-sand beaches begging for DIY exploration. The area is gradually being colonised by glitzy five-star resorts catering to fresh-from-the-Gulf millionaires, but it's still worth the trip for off-the-beaten-track adventurers.

The laterite-brick **Bekal Fort** (Indian/foreigner ₹5/100; ⊙8am-5pm), built between 1645 and 1660, sits on Bekal's rocky headland and houses a small Hindu temple and plenty of goats. Next door, **Bekal Beach** (admission ₹5) encompasses a grassy park and a long, beautiful stretch of sand that turns into a circus on weekends and holidays when local families descend here for rambunctious leisure time. Isolated **Kappil Beach**, 6km north of Bekal, is a beautiful, lonely stretch of fine sand and calm water, but beware of shifting sandbars.

Apart from the five-star Vivanta by Taj and Lalit hotels in Bekal, there are lots of cheap, poor-quality hotels scattered between Kanhangad (12km south) and Kasaragod (10km north), with a few notable exceptions.

Nirvana@Bekal   COTTAGES $$

(📞9446463088, 0467-2272900; www.nirvanabekal.com; Bekal Fort Rd; d incl breakfast ₹1800-4700; 🅰) Right below the walls of Bekal Fort, these laterite brick cottages in a beachfront palm-filled garden are the best value in town. There's a restaurant, ayurvedic treatments and even a cricket bowling machine!

⭐ Neeleshwar Hermitage   RESORT $$$

(📞0467-2287510; www.neeleshwarhermitage.com; Ozhinhavalappu, Neeleshwar; s/d cottages from ₹13,300/15,800, seaview ₹21,000/22,800; 🅰🅰🅰) This spectacular beachfront ecoresort consists of 16 beautifully designed thatch-roof cottages modelled on Keralan fisherman's huts but with modern comforts like iPod docks and a five-star price tag. Built according to the principles of Kerala Vastu, the resort has an infinity pool, nearly 5 hectares of lush gardens fragrant with frangipani, superb organic food and yoga programs.

ⓘ Getting There & Around

A couple of local trains stop at Fort Bekal station, right on Bekal Beach. Kanhangad, 12km south, and Kasaragod, 10km to the north, are major train stops. Frequent buses run from Bekal to both Kanhangad and Kasaragod (around ₹12, 20 minutes), from where you can pick up major trains to Mangalore, Goa or south to Kochi. An autorickshaw from Bekal Junction to Kappil Beach is around ₹60.

OFF THE BEATEN TRACK

VALIYAPARAMBA BACKWATERS

Kerala's 'northern backwaters' offer an intriguing alternative to better-known waterways down south. This large body of water is fed by five rivers and fringed by ludicrously green groves of nodding palms. One of the nearest towns is **Payyanur**, 50km north of Kannur. It's possible to catch the ferry from Kotti, from where KSWTD operates local ferries to the surrounding islands. The 2½-hour trip (₹10) from Kotti takes you to the Ayitti Jetty, 8km from Payyanur, from where you can also catch the return ferry.

You can stay at the peaceful **Valiyaparamba Retreat** (📞0484-2371761; www.touristdesk.in/valiyaparambaretreat.htm; d incl meals ₹3000), a secluded place 15km north of Payyanur and 3km from Ayitti Jetty. It has two simple rooms and two stilted bungalows, fronted by an empty golden-sand beach. Kochi's Tourist Desk (p310) also runs **day trips** on a traditional houseboat around the Valiyaparamba Backwaters.

Around 22km south of Bekal, **Bekal Boat Stay** (📞0467-2282633, 9447469747; www.bekalboatstay.com; Kottappuram, Nileshwar) offers overnight houseboat trips (₹6000 to ₹8000) around the Valiyaparamba backwaters. Day cruises (₹4000 for up to six people) are also available. It's about 2km from Nileshwar – get off any bus between Kannur and Bekal and take an autorickshaw from there (₹30).

LAKSHADWEEP

POP 64,500

Comprising a string of 36 palm-covered, white-sand-skirted coral islands 300km off the coast of Kerala, Lakshadweep is as stunning as it is isolated. Only 10 of these islands are inhabited, mostly by Sunni Muslim fishermen, and foreigners are only allowed to stay on a few of these. With fishing and coir production the main sources of income, local life on the islands remains highly traditional, and a caste system divides the islanders between Koya (land owners), Malmi (sailors) and Melachery (farmers).

The real attraction of the islands lies under the water: the 4200 sq km of pristine archipelago lagoons, unspoiled coral reefs and warm tropical waters.

Lakshadweep can only be visited on a prearranged package trip. At the time of research, resorts on **Kadmat, Minicoy, Kavaratti, Agatti** and **Bangaram** islands were open to tourists – though most visits to the islands are boat-based packages which include a cruise from Kochi, island visits, watersports, and nights spent on board. Packages include permits and meals, and can be arranged though SPORTS.

🛏 Sleeping

Kadmat Beach Resort　　　　RESORT $$$
(☑ 0484-4011134; www.kadmat.com; 3/4 night d from €605/693; ❄) Kadmat Beach Resort has 28 modern air-con cottages facing the beach. The island can be reached by overnight boat from Kochi, or by boat transfer from Agatti airport on Tuesday and Saturday.

Minicoy Island Resort　　　　RESORT $$$
(☑ 0484-2668387; www.lakshadweeptourism.com; s/d with AC from ₹5000/6000; ❄) The remote island of Minicoy, the second-largest island in Lakshadweep and the closest geographically to the Maldives, offers acommodation in modern cottages or a 20-room guesthouse. Booking is via SPORTS – check out the Swaying Palms and Coral Reef packages.

ℹ Information

SPORTS (Society for the Promotion of Recreational Tourism & Sports; ☑ 9495984001,

DIVING

Lakshadweep is a scuba diver's dream, with excellent visibility and amazing marine life living on undisturbed coral reefs. The best time to dive is between November and mid-May when seas are calm and visibility is 20m to 40m. There are dive centres on Kadmat, Kavaratti, Minicoy and Agatti islands, and SPORTS can organise dive packages or courses.

Based on Agatti Island, **Dive Lakshadweep** (☑ 9446055972; www.divelakshadweep.com; Agatti Island; s dive ₹3000, PADI open water course ₹24,000) offers a variety of PADI courses and dive packages, including Discover Scuba (₹1700) dives for beginners.

0484-2668387; www.lakshadweeptourism. com; IG Rd, Willingdon Island; ☉10am-5pm Mon-Sat) SPORTS is the main organisation for tourist information and booking package tours.

PERMITS

At the time of writing, foreigners were allowed to stay at the government resorts on Kadmat and Minicoy islands, Agatti (which has a private resort and the only airport), Kavaratti and Bangaram (tent resort); enquire at SPORTS. Visits require a special permit (one month's notice) which can be organised by tour operators or SPORTS in Kochi.

ℹ Getting There & Away

Air India flies between Kochi and Agatti Island (from ₹7000 return) daily except Sunday. Boat transport between Agatti and Kadmat or Kavaratti is included in the package tours available.

Six passenger ships – MV *Kavaratti*, MV *Arabian Sea*, MV *Lakshadweep Sea*, MV *Bharat Seema*, MV *Amindivi* and MV *Minicoy* operate between Kochi and Lakshadweep, taking 14 to 20 hours.

Cruise packages start from a weekend package (adult/child ₹6185/7216) to a five-day three-island cruise from ₹17,000/24,000.

See the package section of www.lakshadweeptourism.com for more details.

Tamil Nadu & Chennai

Best Temples

➜ Meenakshi Amman
Temple (p381)

➜ Brihadishwara Temple
(p371)

➜ Arunachaleshwar Temple
(p356)

➜ Sri Ranganathaswamy
Temple (p375)

➜ Nataraja Temple (p367)

Best Places to Stay

➜ Visalam (p380)

➜ Les Hibiscus (p362)

➜ Bungalow on the Beach
(p367)

➜ Sinna Dorai's Bungalow
(p398)

➜ 180° McIver (p398)

Why Go?

Tamil Nadu is the homeland of one of humanity's living classical civilisations, stretching back uninterrupted for two millennia and very much alive today in the Tamils' language, dance, poetry and Hindu religion.

But this state, with its age-old trading vocation, is as dynamic as it is immersed in tradition. Fire-worshipping devotees who smear tikka on their brows in the famously spectacular Tamil temples might rush off to IT offices to develop new software applications – and then unwind at a swanky night-time haunt in rapidly modernising Chennai (Madras). When the heat and noise of Tamil Nadu's temple towns overwhelm, escape to the very end of India where three seas mingle, or up to the cool, forest-clad, wild-life-prowled Western Ghats. It's all packed into a state that remains proudly distinct from the rest of India, while at the same time being among the most welcoming.

When to Go

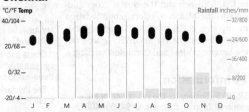

Chennai

Jan Pongal (harvest) celebrations spill into the streets and the weather is at its (relative) coolest.

Jul–Sep Hit the hill stations after the crowded 'season' but while the weather is still good.

Nov–Dec The full-moon festival of lights.

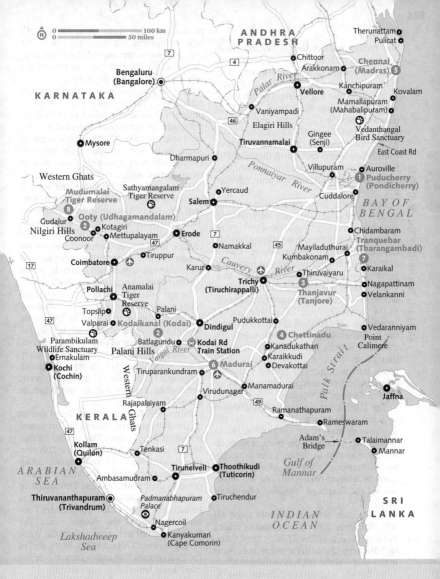

Tamil Nadu Highlights

1 Soaking up the unique Franco-Indian flair and yoga scene of **Puducherry** (Pondicherry; p358)

2 Climbing into the cool, misty forests of the Western Ghats at **Kodaikanal** (p390) or **Ooty** (p400)

3 Admiring the magnificence of Chola architecture at Thanjavur's **Brihadishwara Temple** (p371)

4 Spending the night in an opulent mansion in **Chettinadu** (p378)

5 Exploring the countless faces of the traditional but cosmopolitan capital **Chennai** (Madras; p327)

6 Getting lost in the colour of Madurai's **Meenakshi Amman Temple** (p381)

7 Relaxing at tranquil **Tranquebar** (p367), a quirky old Danish colony

8 Tracking down rare, exotic wildlife at **Mudumalai Tiger Reserve** (p406)

History

The Tamils consider themselves the standard bearers of Dravidian – pre-Aryan Indian – civilisation. Dravidians are defined as speakers of languages of the Dravidian family, the four most important of which are all rooted in South India – Tamil, Malayalam (Kerala), Telugu (Telangana and Andhra Pradesh) and Kannada (Karnataka). South Indian cultures and history are distinct from Aryan North India, and Tamils' ability to trace their identity back in an unbroken line to classical antiquity is a source of considerable pride.

Despite the Dravidians' long-standing southern location, elements of Dravidian culture – including a meditating god seated in the lotus position, possibly the world's first depiction of the yogi archetype – existed in the early Indus civilisations of northwest India some 4000 years ago. Whether Dravidian culture was widespread around India before Aryan cultures appeared in the north in the 2nd millennium BC, or whether the Dravidians only reached the south because the Aryans drove them from the north, is a matter of debate. But there is no question that the cushion of distance has allowed South Indian cultures to develop with little interruption from northern influences or invasions for over 2000 years.

The Tamil language was well established in Tamil Nadu by the 3rd century BC, the approximate start of the Sangam Age, when Tamil poets produced the body of classical literature known as Sangam literature. Romantic versions of the era have the region ruled by feuding poet-kings; one visitor described the Tamils as favouring rose petals over gold.

The Sangam period lasted until about AD 300, with three main Tamil dynasties arising in different parts of Tamil Nadu ('Tamil Country'): the early Cholas in the centre, the Cheras in the west and the Pandyas in the south.

By the 7th century the Pallavas, also Tamil, established an empire based at Kanchipuram extending from Tamil Nadu north into Andhra Pradesh. They take credit for the great stone carvings of Mamallapuram (Mahabalipuram) and also constructed the region's first free-standing temples.

Next up were the medieval Cholas (whose connection with the early Cholas is hazy). Based in the Cauvery valley of central Tamil Nadu, at their peak the Cholas ruled Sri Lanka and the Maldives plus much of South India, and extended their influence to Southeast Asia, spreading Tamil ideas of reincarnation, karma and yogic practice.

The Cholas raised Dravidian architecture to new levels with the magnificent towered temples of Thanjavur and Gangaikondacholapuram, and carried the art of bronze image casting to its peak, especially in their images of Shiva as Nataraja, the cosmic dancer. *Gopurams*, the tall temple gate towers characteristic of Tamil Nadu today, make their appearance in late Chola times.

By the late 14th century much of Tamil Nadu was under the sway of the Vijayanagar empire based at Hampi in Karnataka. As the Vijayanagar state weakened in the 16th century, some of their local governors, the Nayaks, set up strong independent kingdoms, notably at Madurai and Thanjavur. Vijayanagar and Nayak sculptors carved wonderfully detailed statues and reliefs at many Tamil temples.

Europeans first landed on Tamil shores in the 16th century, when the Portuguese settled at San Thome. The Dutch, British, French and Danes followed in the 17th century, striking deals with local rulers to set up coastal trading colonies. Eventually it came down to the British, based at Chennai (then called Madras), against the French, based at Puducherry (then called Pondicherry), for supremacy among the colonial rivals. The British won out in the three Carnatic Wars, fought between 1744 and 1763. By the end of the 18th century British dominance over the majority of Tamil lands was assured.

The area governed by the British from Madras, the Madras Presidency, included parts of Andhra Pradesh, Kerala and Karnataka, an arrangement that continued after Indian ndependence in 1947, until Kerala, Karnataka, Andhra Pradesh and present-day Tamil Nadu (130,058 sq km) were created on linguistic lines in the 1950s. It wasn't until 1968 that the current state (population 72.1 million) was officially named Tamil Nadu.

SLEEPING PRICES

Accommodation price ranges for this chapter are as follows:

$ below ₹1100

$$ ₹1100 to ₹5000

$$$ above ₹5000

TOP STATE FESTIVALS

Pongal (statewide; ⊙mid-Jan) marks the end of the harvest season and is one of Tamil Nadu's most important festivals, named after a rice-and-lentil dish cooked at this time in new clay pots. Animals, especially cows, are honoured for their contributions.

Other important festivals include:

International Yoga Festival (p362; ⊙4–7 Jan) Shows, workshops and competitions in Puducherry.

Thyagaraja Aradhana (p373; ⊙Jan) Carnatic music in Thiruvaiyaru.

Teppam (Float) Festival (p382; ⊙Jan/Feb) Meenakshi temple deities are paraded around Madurai.

Natyanjali Dance Festival (p368; ⊙Feb/Mar) Five days of professional classical dance in Chidambaram.

Chithirai Festival (p383; ⊙Apr/May) Two-week event in Madurai celebrating the marriage of Meenakshi to Sundareswarar (Shiva).

Karthikai Deepam Festival (p357; statewide; ⊙Nov/Dec) Festival of lights.

Chennai Festival of Music & Dance (p333; ⊙mid-Dec–mid-Jan) A huge celebration of South Indian music and dance in the state capital.

Mamallapuram Dance Festival (p349; ⊙Dec–Jan) Four weekends of classical and folk dance from across India on open-air stages in Mamallapuram.

CHENNAI (MADRAS)

♪ 044 / POP 8.7 MILLION

With its withering southern heat, roaring traffic and scarcity of outstanding sights, the 'capital of the south' has always been the rather dowdy sibling among India's four biggest cities. But if you have time to explore Chennai's diverse neighbourhoods and role as keeper of South Indian artistic and religious traditions, the odds are this 400-sq-km conglomerate of urban villages will sneak its way into your heart.

Among Chennai's greatest assets are its people, who are infectiously enthusiastic about their hometown; they won't hit you with a lot of hustle and hassle. Recent years have added a new layer of cosmopolitan glamour, in the shape of luxury hotels, sparkling boutiques, classy contemporary restaurants and a sprinkling of swanky bars and clubs open well into the night.

Even if you're just caught here between connections, it's well worth poking around the museums, exploring the temples or taking a sunset saunter along Marina Beach.

The old British Fort St George and the jumble of narrow streets and bazaars that is George Town constitute the historic hub of the city. The two main train stations, Egmore and Central, sit inland from the fort. Much of the best eating, drinking, shopping and accommodation lies in the leafier southern and southwestern suburbs such as Nungambakkam, T Nagar (Thyagaraya Nagar), Alwarpet and, increasingly, Velachery and Guindy. The major thoroughfare linking northern with southern Chennai is Anna Salai (Mount Rd).

History

The southern neighbourhood of Mylapore existed long before the rest of Chennai and there is evidence that it traded with Roman and even Chinese and Greek merchants. The Portuguese established their San Thome settlement on the coast nearby in 1523. Another century passed before Francis Day and the British East India Company rocked up in 1639, searching for a good southeast Indian trading base, and struck a deal with the local Vijayanagar ruler to build a fort-cum–trading-post at Madraspatnam fishing village. This was Fort St George, erected between 1640 and 1653.

The three Carnatic Wars between 1744 and 1763 saw Britain and its colonialist rival France allying with competing South Indian princes in their efforts to get the upper hand over the locals – and each other. The French occupied Fort St George from 1746 to 1749 but the British eventually won out, and the French withdrew to Pondicherry.

As capital of the Madras Presidency, one of the four major divisions of British India,

Chennai (Madras)

TAMIL NADU & CHENNAI

Royal Enfield Factory (1km)

Andaman Shipping Office Ticketing Counter (200m)

Rajaji Salai (North Beach Rd)

Beach Train Station

Parry's Corner

GEORGE TOWN

Esplanade Rd

NSC Bose Rd

Rattan Bazaar Rd

Mint St

Elephant Gate

VOC Rd (Wall Tax Rd)

GH Rd

Fort Entrance

Rajaji Salai

Fort St George

Fort Train Station

Park Town Train Station

Island Grounds

Kuvam River

Swami Sivananda Salai

Chintadripet Train Station

CHEPAUK

Chepauk Train Station

Chepauk Stadium

Wallajah Rd

Anna Sq

Central Train Station

Park Train Station

Nehru Stadium

Sydenham's Rd

VEPERY

Vepery High Rd

EVK Sampath Salai

Egmore Train Station

EGMORE

Poonamallee High Rd (EVR Periyar Salai)

West Kuvam River Rd

Langs Garden Rd

Adinathar Rd

Rajarathinam Stadium

Pantheon Rd

Halls Rd

Ellis Rd

Triplicane High Rd (Quaide-Millath Rd)

Triplicane Train Station

Bharathi Salai (Pycroft's Rd)

Perambur Barracks Rd

Ritherdon Rd

Purusavakkam High Rd

Nehru Park

Casa Major Rd

College Rd

Anderson Rd

Greams Rd

Ethiraj Salai

PUDUPET

THOUSAND LIGHTS

Haddows Rd

NUNGAMBAKKAM

Khader Nawaz Khan Rd

Binny Rd

Anna Salai (Mount Rd)

See Anna Salai, Egmore & Triplicane Map (p334)

Chetpet Train Station

Valluvar Kottam High Rd

CHETPET

Harrington Rd

Sterling Rd

Tank Bund Rd

New Avadi Rd

Kilpauk Garden Rd

CMBT (3km); Omni Bus Stand (3.5km)

Nelson Manickam Rd

Nungambakkam Train Station

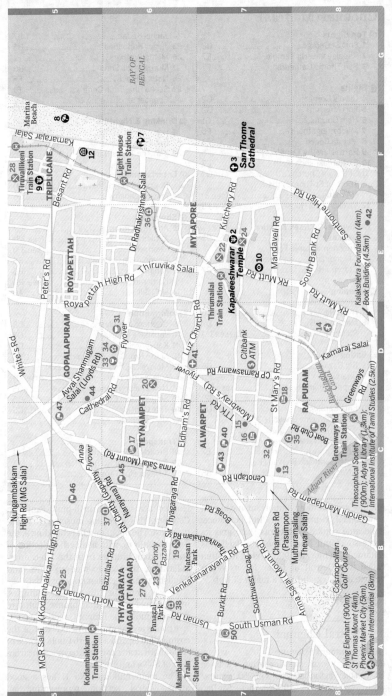

TAMIL NADU & CHENNAI

BAY OF BENGAL

Marina Beach
Kamarajar Salai

8

7

San Thome Cathedral

3

TRIPLICANE
Tiruvallikeni Train Station
28
9

Light House Train Station
12

Besant Rd

Kutchery Rd

Santhome High Rd

Dr Radhakrishnan Salai

MYLAPORE
36

22
Kapaleeshwarar Temple **2** **24**

10

Mandaveli Rd

RK Mutt Rd

South Bank Rd

ROYAPETTAH
Peter's Rd
Royapettah High Rd

Thiruvika Salai

Thirumailai Train Station

Kalakshetra Foundation (4km);
Book Building (4.5km)
42

GOPALAPURAM
Roya pettah High Rd

Luz Church Rd

Citibank ATM

Kamaraj Salai

White's Rd

31
Flyover

33 34
Ayya Shanmugam Salai (Lloyds Rd)

CP Ramaswamy Rd

41

St Mary's Rd

14

RK Mutt Rd

RA PURAM

Buckingham Canal

Greenways

Flyover

20

47
Cathedral Rd

44

TEYNAMPET

Eldham's Rd

TTK Rd (Mowbray's Rd)

18

Greenways Rd

Boat Club Rd
39

Theosophical Society
(900m); Adyar Library (1.3km);
International Institute of Tamil Studies (2.5km)

Nungambakkam
High Rd (MG Salai)

46

Anna Flyover

17

Anna Salai (Mount Rd)

45

ALWARPET

15
40

16

43

32

35

Cenotaph Rd

13

Adyar River

Gandhi Mandapam Rd

MGR Salai (Kodambakkam High Rd)

37
GN Chetty Rd (Gopathy Narayana Chetty Rd)

Anna Flyover

Sir Thyagaraya Rd

Boag Rd

Thanikachalam Rd

Chamiers Rd
(Pasumpon Muthuramaling Thevar Salai)

Anna Salai (Mount Rd)

Flying Elephant (900m);
St Thomas Mount (4km);
Phoenix Market City (5km);
Chennai International (8km)

North Usman Rd

25

Bazullah Rd

THYAGARAYA
NAGAR (T NAGAR)

23
Pondy Bazaar
19

Natesan Park

Venkatanarayana Rd

Burkit Rd

Southwest Boag Rd

Cosmopolitan
Golf Course

Kodambakkam
Train Station

27

Panagal Park
38

Usman Rd

South Usman Rd

50

Mambalam
Train Station

Chennai (Madras)

Madras grew into an important naval and commercial centre. After Independence, it became capital of Madras state and its successor Tamil Nadu. The city itself was renamed Chennai in 1996. Today, it's often called 'the Detroit of India' for its boom vehicle industry, and it is a major IT hub.

◎ Sights

◎ Central Chennai

★ **Government Museum**   MUSEUM
(Map p334; www.chennaimuseum.org; Pantheon Rd, Egmore; Indian/foreigner ₹15/250, camera/video ₹200/500; ◎9.30am-5pm Sat-Thu)

Housed across the British-built Pantheon Complex, this excellent museum is Chennai's best. The big highlight is building 3, the **Bronze Gallery**, with a superb collection of South Indian bronzes from the 7th-century Pallava era through to modern times, and English-language explanatory material.

It was from the 9th to 11th centuries, in the Chola period, that bronze sculpture peaked. Among the Bronze Gallery's impressive pieces are many of Shiva as Nataraja, the cosmic dancer, and a superb Chola bronze of Ardhanarishvara, the androgynous incarnation of Shiva and Parvati.

The main building (No 1) has a good archaeological section representing all the major South Indian periods from 2nd-century-BC Buddhist sculptures to 16th-century- Vijayanagar work, with special rooms devoted to Hindu, Buddhist and Jain sculpture. Building 2, the **Anthropology Galleries**, traces South Indian human history back to prehistoric times, displaying tribal artefacts from across the region.

The museum also includes the **National Art Gallery**, **Contemporary Art Gallery** and **Children's Museum**, on the same ticket. You may find some sections temporarily closed for renovation.

High Court
NOTABLE BUILDING

(Map p328; Parry's Corner) Completed in 1892, this imposing red Indo-Saracenic structure is said to be the largest judicial building in the world after the Courts of London. Depending on current regulations, you may or may not be allowed to wander the grounds on Sundays until 1pm. If you fancy trying, take your passport.

★ Fort St George
FORT

(Map p328; Rajaji Salai; ⊙9am-5pm) Finished in 1653 by the British East India Company, the fort has undergone many facelifts over the years. Inside the vast perimeter walls is now a precinct housing Tamil Nadu's Legislative Assembly & Secretariat, and a smattering of older buildings. One of these, the **Fort Museum** (Map p328; Indian/foreigner ₹5/100; ⊙9am-5pm Sat-Thu), has displays on Chennai's origins and the fort itself, and interesting military memorabilia and artwork from colonial times. The 1st-floor portrait gallery of colonial-era VIPs includes a very assured-looking Robert Clive (Clive of India).

Also within the fort is **St Mary's Church** (Map p328; ⊙10am-5pm Mon-Sat), completed

in 1680, and India's oldest surviving British church. To its right is the former Admiralty House (Clive's House). **Clive's Corner** (Map p328; ⊙9am-6pm) `FREE`, at the end of the building, houses a quirky memorial museum to Robert Clive.

Marina Beach
BEACH

(Map p328) Take an early-morning or evening stroll (you really don't want to roast here at any other time) along the 3km-long main stretch of Marina Beach and you'll pass cricket matches, flying kites, fortune-tellers, fish markets, corn-roasters and families enjoying the sea breeze. Don't swim: strong rips make it dangerous. At its southern end, the newly reopened, ridiculously popular **Madras Lighthouse** (Map p328; Marina Beach; Indian/foreigner ₹20/50, camera ₹25; ⊙10am-1pm & 3-5pm Tue-Sun) is India's only lighthouse with a lift; the panoramic city and beach views are fabulous.

Parthasarathy Temple
HINDU TEMPLE

(Map p328; Singarachari St, Triplicane; ⊙6am-noon & 4-9pm) Built under the 8th-century Pallavas and unusually dedicated to Krishna (a form of Vishnu) as the charioteer Parthasarathy, this is one of Chennai's oldest temples. Most of its elaborate carvings, however, date from its 16th-century Vijayanagar expansion, including the fine colonnade fronting the main entrance. It's special for its shrines dedicated to five of the incarnations of Vishnu.

Vivekananda House
MUSEUM

(Vivekanandar Illam, Ice House; Map p328; www.vivekanandahouse.org; Kamarajar Salai; adult/child ₹10/5; ⊙10am-12.15pm & 3-7.15pm Thu-Tue) The marshmallow-pink Vivekananda House is

TAMIL NADU & CHENNAI (MADRAS)

DRAVIDIAN PRIDE

Since before Indian Independence in 1947, Tamil politicians have railed against caste (which they see as favouring light-skinned Brahmins) and the Hindi language (seen as North Indian cultural imperialism). The pre-Independence 'Self Respect' movement and Justice Party, influenced by Marxism, mixed South Indian communal values with class-war rhetoric, and spawned Tamil political parties that remain the major powers in Tamil Nadu today. In the early post-Independence decades there was even a movement for an independent Dravida Nadu nation comprising the four main South Indian peoples, but there was little solidarity between different groups. Today Dravidian politics is largely restricted to Tamil Nadu, where parties are often led by former film stars.

During the conflict in nearby Sri Lanka, many Indian Tamil politicians loudly defended the Tamil Tigers, the organisation that assassinated Rajiv Gandhi in a village near Chennai (Madras) in 1991. There is still considerable prejudice among the generally tolerant Tamils towards anything Sinhalese. The most obvious sign of Tamil pride that you'll see today is the white shirt and white *mundu* (sarong), worn by any Tamil public figure worth their salt.

interesting not only for its displays on the famous 'wandering monk', Swami Vivekananda, but also for its semicircular form, built in 1842 to store ice imported from the USA. Vivekananda stayed here briefly in 1897 and preached his ascetic Hindu philosophy to adoring crowds. The displays include a photo exhibition on the swami's life and the room where Vivekananda stayed, now used for meditation. Free weekly one-hour meditation classes may be available.

◎ Southern Chennai

★ Kapaleeshwarar Temple   HINDU TEMPLE
(Map p328; Ponnambala Vathiar St, Mylapore; ☺5.30am-12.15pm & 4-9.30pm) The Mylapore neighbourhood is one of Chennai's most characterful and traditional; it predated colonial Madras by several centuries. The Kapaleeshwarar Temple is Chennai's most active and impressive temple, believed to have been built after the Portuguese destroyed the seaside original in 1566. It displays the main architectural elements of many a Tamil Nadu temple – a rainbow-coloured *gopuram* (gateway tower), pillared *mandapas* (pillared pavilions), and a huge tank – and is dedicated to the state's most popular deity, Shiva.

Legend tells that in an angry fit Shiva turned his consort Parvati into a peacock, and commanded her to worship him here to regain her normal form. Parvati supposedly did so at a spot just outside the northeast corner of the temple's central block, where a shrine commemorates the event. Hence the name Mylapore, or 'town of peacocks'.

The temple's colourful Brahmotsavam festival (in March/April) sees the deities paraded around Mylapore's streets.

★ San Thome Cathedral   CHURCH
(Map p328; www.santhomechurch.com; Santhome High Rd; ☺6am-7.30pm) This soaring Roman Catholic cathedral, a stone's throw from the beach, was founded by the Portuguese in the 16th century, then rebuilt in neo-Gothic style in 1896, and is said to mark the final resting place of St Thomas the Apostle. It's believed 'Doubting Thomas' brought Christianity to the subcontinent in AD 52 and was killed at St Thomas Mount, Chennai, in AD 72. Behind the cathedral is the entrance to the tomb of St Thomas (Map p328; admission free; ☺6am-8pm).

Although most of St Thomas' mortal remains are apparently now in Italy, a small cross on the tomb wall contains a tiny bone fragment marked 'Relic of St Thomas'. The museum above displays Thomas-related artefacts including the lancehead believed to have killed him.

St Thomas' Pole, at the beach end of the street on the cathedral's south side, is said to have miraculously saved the cathedral from the 2004 tsunami.

Sri Ramakrishna Math   RELIGIOUS COMPLEX
(Map p328; www.chennaimath.org; 31 RK Mutt Rd; ☺Universal Temple 4.30-11.45am & 3-9pm, evening prayers 6.30-7.30pm) The tranquil, flowery grounds of the Ramakrishna Math are a world away from the chaos outside. Orange-robed monks glide around and there's a reverential feel. The Math is a monastic order following the teachings of the 19th-century sage Sri Ramakrishna, who preached the essential unity of all religions. The Universal Temple here is a handsome modern building incorporating architectural elements from several different religions. It's open to all, to worship, pray or meditate.

Theosophical Society   GARDEN
(www.ts-adyar.org; south end of Thiru Vi Ka Bridge, Adyar; ☺grounds 8.30-10am & 2-4pm Mon-Sat) **FREE** Between the Adyar River and the coast, the 100-hectare grounds of the Theosophical Society provide a peaceful, green, vehicle-free retreat from the city. A lovely spot just to wander, they contain a church, mosque, Buddhist shrine, Zoroastrian temple and Hindu temple as well as a huge variety of native and introduced flora, including the offshoots of a 400-year-old banyan tree torn down by a storm in the 1980s.

The Adyar Library (1yr reader's card ₹50, deposit ₹250; ☺9am-5pm Tue-Sun) here has a huge collection of religion and philosophy books (some on display), from 1000-year-old Buddhist scrolls to handmade 19th-century Bibles.

Kalakshetra Foundation   ARTS SCHOOL
(☎044-24521169; www.kalakshetra.in; Muthulakshmi St, Thiruvanmiyur; Indian/foreigner incl craft centre ₹100/500; ☺campus 9-11.30am Mon-Fri Jul-Feb, craft centre 9am-1pm & 2-5pm Mon-Sat, all closed 2nd & 4th Sat of month) Founded in 1936, Kalakshetra is a leading serious school of Tamil classical dance and music (sponsoring many students from disadvantaged backgrounds), set in beautiful, shady grounds in far south Chennai During morning class times visitors can (quietly) wander the grounds, and visit the Rukmini

Devi Museum. Across the road is the **Kalakshetra Craft Centre** where you can see Kanchipuram-style hand-loom weaving, textile block-printing and the fascinating, rare art of *kalamkari* (hand-painting on textiles with vegetable dyes).

The Thiruvanmiyur bus stand, terminus of many city bus routes, is 500m west of the Kalakshetra entrance.

While here it's also worth visiting the **Book Building** (📞044-24426696; www.tarabooks.com; Plot 9, CGE Colony, Kuppam Beach Rd, Thiruvanmiyur; ⏰10am-7.30pm Mon-Sat), 700m south of Kalakshetra, where Tara Books stages free exhibitions, talks and workshops, as well as displaying its own highly original handmade books. With prior notice, you can visit the book-making workshop (10 minutes' drive away).

St Thomas Mount
SACRED SITE

(Parangi Malai; off Lawrence Rd; camera ₹10; ⏰6am-8pm) The reputed site of St Thomas' martyrdom in AD 72 rises in the southwest of the city, 2.5km north of St Thomas Mount train station. The Church of Our Lady of Expectation, built atop the 'mount' by the Portuguese in 1523, contains what are supposedly a fragment of Thomas' finger bone and a cross he carved; the city views are wonderful.

🏃 Activities

Krishnamacharya Yoga Mandiram
YOGA, MEDITATION

(Map p328; 📞044-24952900; www.kym.org; 31 4th Cross St, RK Nagar; class US$30; ⏰8am-7pm) Highly regarded, serious two-week and month-long yoga and yoga therapy courses, and teacher training.

🎓 Courses

International Institute of Tamil Studies
LANGUAGE

(📞044-22542781; www.ulakaththamizh.org; CIT Campus, 2nd Main Rd, Tharamani) Runs intensive three-month and six-month courses in Tamil.

Kalakshetra Foundation
TEXTILE PAINTING

(📞044-24521169; www.kalakshetra.in; Muthulakshmi St, Thiruvanmiyur; per week ₹2500) Kalakshetra's crafts centre offers one-week to one-month courses in the fascinating old art of *kalamkari* – hand-painting of textiles using vegetable inks – which survives in only a handful of places. Courses run from 10am to 1pm Monday to Friday.

🧭 Tours

The Tamil Nadu Tourism Development Corporation (p342) conducts half-day city tours (non-AC/AC ₹300/370) and day trips to Mamallapuram (₹450/550). Book ahead for weekends and holidays; be ready for cancellations on quiet weekdays. Every full moon there's an overnight pilgrimage trip to Tiruvannamalai (₹600/780).

★ Detours
WALKING TOURS

(Map p328; 📞9000850505, 9840060393; www.detoursindia.com; RM Towers, 108 Chamiers Rd, Alwarpet) A fantastic way to explore Chennai is with Detours' off-beat, in-depth history, faith, and food tours, run by local experts. Four-hour early-morning food walks cost ₹5000 to ₹6000 per person.

Storytrails
WALKING TOURS

(Map p328; 📞9962201244, 044-45010202; www.storytrails.in; 21/2 1st Cross St, TTK Rd, Alwarpet; 3hr tour for up to 4 people ₹3500) Entertaining neighbourhood walking tours on themes such as dance, temples, jewellery and bazaars.

Royal Enfield Factory
FACTORY TOUR

(📞044-42230400; www.royalenfield.com; Tiruvottiyur High Rd, Tiruvottiyur; per person ₹600) The classic Enfield Bullet motorcycle has been manufactured since 1955 in far northern Chennai. Two-hour tours run on the second and fourth Saturdays of each month at 10.30am. Bookings essential.

🎊 Festivals & Events

Chennai Festival of Music & Dance
MUSIC, DANCE

(Madras Music & Dance Season; ⏰mid-Dec–mid-Jan) One of the largest of its type in the

---

TRADITIONAL TRADERS

Even as Chennai expands relentlessly to the south, west and north, George Town, the local settlement that grew up near the British Fort St George, remains the city's wholesale centre. Many of its narrow streets are entirely devoted to selling one particular product, as they have for hundreds of years – flowers in Badrian St, paper goods in Anderson St, jewellery on NSC Bose Rd. Even if you aren't buying, wander the mazelike streets to see Indian life flowing seamlessly from the past into the present.

TAMIL NADU & CHENNAI CHENNAI (MADRAS)

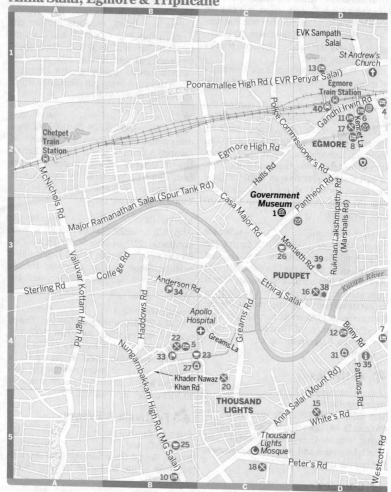

world, this festival celebrates South Indian music and dance.

🛏 Sleeping

Hotels in Chennai are pricier than in the rest of Tamil Nadu and don't, as a rule, offer much bang for your buck. The Triplicane High Rd area is best for budget accommodation. There are some cheapies in Egmore, along with a few good midrange options. The number of top-end hotels has risen dramatically over the past couple of years, mostly in the more middle-class southern areas.

Many hotels in Chennai fill up by noon, so call ahead. The most expensive hotels have good discounts online.

🛏 Egmore & Around

New Lakshmi Lodge   HOTEL $
(Map p334; ☑ 044-42148725, 044-28194576; www.
nll.co.in; 16 Kennet Lane; s/d ₹500/880, r with AC
₹1400-1500; ﹡) With small and bare but spotless, pastel-walled rooms spread over four floors around a central parking courtyard, this huge block is not a bad budget

❄ 🛜) Spread across two residential buildings engulfed by greenery in upmarket Wallace Garden, Hanu Reddy is exactly the kind of peaceful homey hideaway that central Chennai needs. The eight cosy, unpretentious rooms come with air-con, free wi-fi, tea/coffee sets, and splashes of colourful artwork; the teensy terraces have bamboo lounging chairs. Service hits the perfect personal-yet-professional balance.

YWCA International
Guest House
GUESTHOUSE **$$**

(Map p334; ☑ 044-25324234; igh@ywcamadras.org; 1086 Poonamallee High Rd; incl breakfast s ₹1500-1980, d ₹1800-2400, s/d without AC ₹900/1350; ❄ @ 🛜) The YWCA guesthouse, set in shady grounds, offers very good value along with a calm atmosphere. Efficiently run by helpful staff, it has good-sized, brilliantly clean rooms, spacious common areas and solid-value meals (₹175/275 for veg/nonveg lunch or dinner). Wi-fi (in the lobby) costs ₹100 per day. Renovations were underway at the time of research.

Hotel Chandra Park
HOTEL **$$**

(Map p334; ☑ 044-40506060; www.hotelchandrapark.com; 9 Gandhi Irwin Rd; incl breakfast s ₹1320-2280, d ₹1500-2580; ❄ 🛜) Chandra Park's prices remain mysteriously lower than most similar establishments. Standard rooms are small but have air-con, clean towels and tight, white sheets. Throw in a decent (if male-dominated) bar, a hearty buffet breakfast, and free wi-fi, and this is excellent value by Chennai standards.

Fortel
HOTEL **$$$**

(Map p334; ☑ 044-30242424; www.fortelhotels.com; 3 Gandhi Irwin Rd; incl breakfast s ₹4200-6600, d ₹4800-7200; ❄ 🛜) Conveniently close to Egmore train station, the Fortel is cool and stylish in a wood, mirrors and white walls way, with cushion-laden beds, free wi-fi and a good restaurant, Madras Masala. Most station-facing rooms have views of St Andrew's Church rising through trees. It's worth asking about discounts.

🏨 Triplicane & Around

Paradise Guest House
HOTEL **$**

(Map p334; ☑ 044-28594252; paradisegh@hotmail.com; 17 Vallabha Agraharam St; r ₹500, with AC ₹800-1000; ❄ 🛜) Paradise offers some of Triplicane's best-value digs – simple rooms with clean tiles, a breezy rooftop, friendly staff and hot water by the steaming bucket. Wi-fi costs ₹50 per hour.

choice. Book ahead, as it's often full. Go for the upper floors for more privacy.

Raj Residency
HOTEL **$**

(Map p334; ☑ 044-28192219; www.rajresidencyhotel.com; 2/22 Kennet Lane; s ₹840-1020, d ₹1020-1180, with AC s ₹1180-1310, d ₹1310-1550; ❄ 🛜) The non-AC rooms here are reasonable value, a bit dingy and worn but clean enough, in shades of brown.

★ Hanu Reddy Residences
B&B **$$**

(Map p334; ☑ 044-45038413; www.hanureddyresidences.com; 6A/24 3rd St, Wallace Garden, Nungambakkam; r incl breakfast ₹3600-4200;

Anna Salai, Egmore & Triplicane

Broad Lands Lodge GUESTHOUSE $
(Map p334; ☎044-28545573; broadlandshotel@yahoo.com; 18 Vallabha Agraharam St; s ₹400-450, d ₹500-1000; ❋☞) In business since 1951, Broad Lands was a hippie-era stalwart and probably hasn't had a fresh coat of pale-blue paint since. But this laid-back colonial-era mansion, with leafy courtyards and rooms up rambling staircases, still has its devotees, who don't seem to mind the barebone, idiosyncratic rooms, dank bathrooms, or high-volume muezzins of Wallajah Big Mosque. Reception-only wi-fi (a 21st-century concession) is free.

Cristal Guest House HOTEL $
(Map p334; ☎044-28513011; 34 CNK Rd; r ₹400, with AC ₹750; ❋) The clean, pink abodes in this modern building aren't quite the cheapest rooms in Chennai, but they're only about

₹10 more expensive than many others nearby – which means the hotel is more likely to have vacancies.

La Woods HOTEL $$
(Map p334; ☎044-28608040; www.lawoodshotel.com; 1 Woods Rd; r incl breakfast ₹3500; ❋☞) Wonderfully erratic colour schemes throw fresh whites against lime-greens and turquoises at this friendly modern hotel, new in 2013. The shiny, well-kept, contemporary rooms are perfectly comfy, with free wi-fi and mountains of pillows, as well as kettles, hairdryers, and 'global' plug sockets.

Vivanta by Taj – Connemara HERITAGE HOTEL $$$
(Map p334; ☎044-66000000; www.vivantabytaj.com; Binny Rd; r incl breakfast ₹11,990-14,390; ❋@☞❋) The top-end Taj Group has four

hotels in and around Chennai, but this is the only one with historical ambience, built in the 1850s as the British governor's residence. There's a beautiful pool in tropical gardens, and even the smallest, cream-coloured rooms are very comfy and airy, with all mod cons. Chettinadu Raintree restaurant is one of Chennai's best.

Southern Chennai

⭐ Footprint B&B
B&B $$
(Map p328; ☑ 9840037483; www.chennaibe dandbreakfast.com; Gayatri Apts, 16 South St, Alwarpet (behind Sheraton Park Hotel); r incl breakfast ₹4500; ❈@🛜) This is a beautifully comfortable, relaxed base for your Chennai explorations, spread over four apartments on a quiet street in a leafy neighbourhood. Bowls of wild roses and old-Madras photos set the scene for 12 cosy, spotless rooms, with king-size or wide twin beds. Breakfasts (Western or Indian) are generous, wi-fi is free and the welcoming owners are full of Tamil Nadu tips. Book ahead.

Madras B&B
B&B $$
(Map p328; ☑ 9677135753; madrasbnb@gmail. com; Flat 1/3, Nandini Apts, 72/45 1st Main Rd, RA Puram; r incl breakfast ₹3000; ❈🛜) Like a cosy self-service lodge, this friendly little place has just three (soon to be seven) good-sized, straightforward but comfy and stylish rooms in a peaceful, private apartment, which makes it popular with yoga students. Help yourself to the fully equipped kitchen, free wi-fi, library, and relaxed communal lounge with flower bowls. Bookings recommended.

⭐ Park Hotel
BOUTIQUE HOTEL $$$
(Map p334; ☑ 044-42676000; www.thepark hotels.com; 601 Anna Salai; s ₹12,590-14,990, d ₹13,790-16,190, ste from ₹19,190; ❈@🛜☒) We love this superchic boutique hotel, which flaunts design everywhere you look, from the towering lobby's bamboo, steel and gold cushions to the posters from classic South Indian movies shot in Gemini Studios, the site's previous incarnation. Rooms have lovely lush bedding and stylish touches such as feathered lamps and glass-walled bathrooms. There are three restaurants, a rooftop pool, a luxury spa, and three packed-out nightspots too!

Hyatt Regency
HOTEL $$$
(Map p328; ☑ 044-61001234; www.chennai.re gency.hyatt.com; 365 Anna Salai; incl breakfast s ₹10,190-11,990, d ₹11,390-13,190; ❈@🛜☒)

Smart, swish, and bang up to date, this towering, triangular beauty of a hotel is the most central of Chennai's top-end newbies. Contemporary art surrounds the sun-flooded atrium, local chefs head up three good restaurants and a popular bar, and glossy all-modern rooms have walk-through bathrooms and fabulous sea/city panoramas through massive picture windows. The pool is fringed by flowery gardens.

Raintree
HOTEL $$$
(Map p328; ☑ 044-42252525; www.raintree hotels.com; 120 St Mary's Rd, Alwarpet; s/d ₹9590/10,790; ❈@🛜☒) At this 'ecosensitive' hotel, floors are bamboo or rubber, water and electricity conservation hold pride of place, and the AC-generated heat warms the bathroom water. The sleek, minimalist rooms are comfy and stylish, with free wi-fi; freshly revamped rooms should be ready for 2015. The rooftop supports a sea-view infinity pool (doubling as insulation) along with a restaurant.

🍴 Eating

Chennai is packed with inexpensive 'meals' joints ('messes'), serving thalis for lunch and dinner, and tiffin (snacks) such as *idlis* (spongy, round fermented rice cakes), *vadas* (deep-fried lentil-flour doughnuts) and dosas. It's perfectly possible to eat every meal at Chennai's 24 Saravana Bhavan restaurants, where you can count on quality vegetarian food. In the Muslim area around

TYPICALLY TAMIL FOOD

Tamil Nadu's favourite foods are overwhelmingly vegetarian, full of coconut and chilli. You'll find dosas, *idlis* (spongy, round fermented rice cakes) and *vadas* (deep-fried lentil-flour doughnuts), all served with coconut chutney and *sambar* (lentil broth). Almost as ubiquitous is the *uttapam*, a thick, savoury rice pancake with finely chopped onions, green chillies and coriander. South Indian 'meals' – thalis based around rice, lentil dishes, *rasam* (hot and sour tamarind soup) and chutneys, often served on banana leaves – are also good. The main local exception to the all-veg diet is Chettinad food, from the Chettinad region south of Trichy. For a tea-growing state, Tamil Nadu adores its filter coffee, with milk, sugar, and a dash of chicory.

TAMIL NADU & CHENNAI CHENNAI (MADRAS)

Triplicane High Rd you'll find great biryani stops every few steps.

Classier Indian restaurants are on the rise, and international cuisines have really taken off in Chennai, so there's plenty of up-market dining, especially at top-end hotels.

Useful, well-stocked supermarkets include **Spencer's** (Map p328; 15 EVK Sampath Salai, Vepery; ⊙7.30am-9.30pm), not too far from Egmore and Central stations; Big Bazaar at **T Nagar** (Map p328; 34 Sir Thyagaraya Rd; ⊙10.30am-9.30pm) and **Express Avenue Mall** (Express Avenue, White's Rd; ⊙10am-9pm); and **Nilgiri's** (Map p334; 25 Shafee Mohammed Rd, Thousand Lights West; ⊙8.30am-9.30pm) off Nungambakkam's Khader Nawaz Khan Rd.

✕ Egmore

★ Hotel Saravana Bhavan
INDIAN $

(Map p334; www.saravanabhavan.com; 21 Kennet Lane; mains ₹75-140; ⊙6am-10pm) Dependably delish, South Indian thali 'meals' at this famous Chennai vegetarian chain run around ₹80 to ₹100. It's also excellent for South Indian breakfasts (*idlis* and *vadas* from ₹33), filter coffee and other Indian vegetarian fare. Branches include **George Town** (Map p328; 209 NSC Bose Rd; ⊙6am-10pm), **Triplicane** (Map p334; Shanthi Theatre Complex, 44 Anna Salai; ⊙7am-11pm), **Thousand Lights** (Map p334; 293 Peter's Rd; mains ₹115-175; ⊙7.30am-11pm), **Mylapore** (Map p328; 70 North Mada St; ⊙6am-10pm) and **T Nagar** (Map p328; 102 Sir Thyagaraya Rd; ⊙7am-10.30pm), along with London, Paris, and New York!

The Thousand Lights branch, more upscale, does a ₹300 lunch and dinner buffet.

Annalakshmi
INDIAN $$

(Map p334; ☑044-28525109; www.annalakshmichennai.co.in; 1st fl, Sigapi Achi Bldg, 18/3 Rukmani Lakshmipathy Rd; mains ₹180-280, set/buffet lunch ₹750/400; ⊙noon-2.30pm & 7-9pm Tue-Sun) Very fine South and North Indian vegetarian fare in a beautiful dining room decorated with carvings and paintings, inside a high-rise behind the Air India building. The buffet lunch is served in another part of the same block. Annalakshmi is run and staffed by devotees of Swami Shanthanand Saraswathi, and proceeds support medical programs for the poor.

Madras Masala
MULTICUISINE $$

(Map p334; Fortel, 3 Gandhi Irwin Rd; mains ₹188-375; ⊙7am-11pm) Reincarnated from its former Continental-focused life, this restaurant at the Fortel hotel has an impressive range of Indian veg and nonveg dishes, including great biryanis. It's tranquil, tasteful and friendly, with red crushed-velvet booths and local-life paintings.

✕ Triplicane & Around

Ratna Café
SOUTH INDIAN $

(Map p334; 255 Triplicane High Rd; dishes ₹50-110; ⊙6am-10.45pm) Though often crowded and cramped, Ratna is famous for its scrumptious *idlis* and the hearty doses of its signature *sambar* (lentil broth) that go with them – people have been sitting down to this ₹30 dish at all hours since 1948. There's a new AC room out the back.

A2B
SOUTH INDIAN $

(Map p334; 47/23 Bharathi Salai; mains ₹90-130; ⊙7am-11pm) Tuck into South Indian classics or veg biryani in the clean AC hall upstairs, or go for the sweets downstairs. Nearby **Natural Fresh** (Map p328; 35 Bharathi Salai; scoop ₹53; ⊙11am-11pm) does excellent ice cream.

★ Amethyst
MULTICUISINE, CAFE $$$

(Map p334; ☑044-45991633; www.amethystchennai.com; White's Rd, Royapettah; mains ₹240-450; ⊙10am-11pm; ☎) Set in an exquisitely converted warehouse with a wraparound verandah from which tables spill out into lush gardens, Amethyst is a nostalgically posh haven that's outrageously popular with expats and well-off Chennaiites. Top-notch, European-flavoured treats range over quiches, pasta, crepes, creative salads (watermelon and feta), and even afternoon tea. Fight for your table, then check out the stunning Indian couture boutique.

✕ Nungambakkam & Around

Tuscana Pizzeria
ITALIAN $$$

(Map p334; ☑044-45038008; www.tuscanakryptos.in; 19, 3rd St, Wallace Garden; pizzas & pasta ₹480-780; ⊙noon-11pm) This, my pizza-loving friends, is the real deal, and Chennai has well and truly embraced it. Tuscana turns out authentic thin-crust pizzas with toppings such as prosciutto and mozzarella, as well as creative takes such as spiced paneer masala pizza, and tasty pastas. It even has whole-wheat and gluten-free options. Best to book ahead.

Raintree
CHETTINADU $$$

(Map p334; www.vivantabytaj.com; Vivanta by Taj – Connemara, Binny Rd; mains ₹500-1000; ⊙12.30-

CHENNAI STREET FOOD

Chennai may not have the same killer street food reputation as Delhi or Mumbai (Bombay), but there are some sensational streetside delicacies around, especially in Mylapore, George Town, Egmore and T Nagar (Thyagaraya Nagar).

Jannal Kadai (Map p328; Ponnambala Vathiar St, Mylapore; bajjis ₹20; ⏰ 7.30-10am & 5.30-8.45pm Mon-Sat, 7.30-10am Sun) You take what you're given from the chap in the 'window shop', a fast and furious hole-in-the-wall famous for its hot crispy *bajjis* (vegetable fritters), *bondas* (mashed potato patty) and *vadas* (deep-fried lentil-flour doughnuts). Look for the navy-blue windows opposite Pixel Service.

Seena Bhai Tiffin Centre (Map p328; 11/1 NSC Bose Rd; idlis & uttapams ₹40; ⏰ 6pm-midnight) Nothing but deliciously griddled, ghee-coated *idlis* and *uttapams* (thick, savoury rice pancakes with onions, chillies and coriander) at this 35-year-old eatery in the thick of George Town.

Mehta Brothers (Map p328; 310 Mint St; dishes ₹15-25; ⏰ 4-9pm Mon-Sat) This tiny spot pulls in the crowds with the deep-fried delights of its signature Maharashtrian *vada pavs*, spiced potato fritters in buns, doused in garlicky chutney.

2.45pm & 7.30-11.45pm) This 25-year-old wood-ceilinged restaurant is probably the best place in Chennai to savour the delicious flavours of Tamil Nadu's Chettinadu region. Chettinad cuisine is famously meat-heavy and superbly spicy without being chilli-laden, but veg dishes are good too. When the weather behaves, you can dine outside in the leafy garden with water lilies.

✕ Southern Chennai

Murugan Idli Shop SOUTH INDIAN $
(Map p328; 77 GN Chetty Rd, T Nagar; dishes ₹50-85; ⏰ 7am-11.30pm) Those in the know generally agree this particular branch of the small Madurai-born chain serves some of the best *idlis* and South Indian meals in town. We heartily agree.

Chamiers MULTICUISINE, CAFE $$
(Map p328; 106 Chamiers Rd, RA Puram; mains ₹295-380, breakfasts ₹195-335; ⏰ 8am-11.30pm; 🛜) This 1st-floor cafe feels a continent away from Chennai, except that Chennaiites love it too. Flowery wallpaper, leaves through the windows, wicker chairs, wi-fi (per hour ₹100), wonderful carrot cake and cappuccino, English breakfasts, American pancakes, pasta, quiches, quesadillas, salads...

Junior Kuppanna SOUTH INDIAN $$
(Map p328; 4 Kannaiya St, North Usman Rd, T Nagar; mains ₹130-190, thalis veg/nonveg ₹160/190; ⏰ noon-4pm & 7-11pm) From an impeccably clean kitchen (which you can tour if you like), come limitless, flavour-packed lunchtime thalis, dished up traditional-style on banana leaves. This typical, frenzied Chennai 'mess' also has a full menu, and carnivores tiring of the pure-veg lifestyle can seek solace in specialities like mutton brains and pan-fried seer fish. Arrive early: it's popular.

Enté Keralam KERALAN $$
(Map p328; ☎ 044-32216591; http://entekeralam.in; 1 Kasturi Estate 1st St, Poes Garden; mains ₹215-450; ⏰ noon-3pm & 7-11pm) A calm ambience seeps through the four orange-toned rooms of this Keralan restaurant, holding just three or four tables each. Try the lightly spiced *pachakkari* vegetable stew with light, fluffy *appam* (rice pancake) or *kozhi porichatu* (deep-fried marinated chicken) and wind up with tender coconut ice cream or *paal ada payasam*, a kind of sweet rice pudding.

★**Dakshin** SOUTH INDIAN $$$
(Map p328; ☎ 044-24994101; Sheraton Park Hotel, 132 TTK Rd, Alwarpet; mains ₹690-1670; ⏰ 12.30-2.45pm & 7-11.15pm) Widely considered Chennai's finest South Indian restaurant, Dakshin specialises in the cuisines of Kerala, Tamil Nadu, Andhra Pradesh and Karnataka. Traditional sculptures and mirrored pillars set the temple-inspired scene, and flute and tabla musicians play nightly except Monday. Food suggestion: the Andhra Pradesh fish curry – and perhaps a little something from the impressive whiskey and wine list.

★**Copper Chimney** NORTH INDIAN $$$
(Map p328; ☎ 044-28115770; 74 Cathedral Rd, Gopalapuram; mains ₹290-700; ⏰ noon-3pm & 7-11pm) Meat-eaters will drool over the yummy North Indian tandoori dishes served

here in stylishly minimalist surroundings, but the veg food is fantastic too (even some Jain specialities). The *machchi* tikka – skewers of tandoori-baked fish – is superb, as is the spiced paneer kebab.

Drinking & Nightlife

Chennai nightlife is on the up, but you'll need a full wallet for a night out here. Chennai has possibly the most liberal licensing laws in India – for five-star hotels. Bars and clubs in these hotels serve alcohol 24 hours a day, seven days a week, so that's where most of the after-dark fun happens. Solo guys ('stags') can be turned away. Dress codes are strict: no shorts and sandals.

Other hotel bars, mostly male-dominated, generally close at midnight. If you're buying your own alcohol, look for 'premium' TASMAC government liquor stores inside malls. For listings see www.timescity.com/chennai.

Zara the Tapas Bar
BAR
(Map p328; ☑ 044-28111462; zaratapasbar.in; 71 Cathedral Rd; cocktails ₹430-550, tapas ₹230-380; ☺ 12.30pm-midnight) Where else in the world can you find DJs playing club music beneath bullfighting posters next to TVs showing cricket? Zara is packed with a young, fashionable crowd most nights, and it's a good idea to book a table. And the tapas? The *jamón serrano* is sacrilegiously minced into a paste, but the *tortilla española* is authentically good. Live bands on Tuesdays.

Pasha
NIGHTCLUB
(Map p334; Park Hotel, 601 Anna Salai; per couple ₹2000 incl ₹1500 drink voucher, women free; ☺ 8.30pm-2.30am) A stylish, early-20s bunch packs into this glitzy, two-level, Persian-themed club, where popular Bollywood night takes over on Wednesdays and Saturdays. See big-name international DJs take to the decks. Dress code: smart casual.

Flying Elephant
BAR, RESTAURANT
(☑ 044-71771234; Park Hyatt, 39 Velachery Rd, Guindy; per couple ₹3000 incl ₹2000 drink voucher, women free; ☺ 11pm-3am Sat, restaurant 7-11pm

daily) Slickly contemporary and favoured by the elite, the Park Hyatt's high-energy, restaurant morphs into Chennai's hottest new party pad from 11pm on Saturday. Drinks are pricey (by any standards) but it's all very glam, with a sunken bar. The world fusion food (mains ₹650 to ₹1670), whipped up in five live kitchens, is good too. Head to the Guindy area, towards the airport.

Brew Room
CAFE
(Map p328; Savera Hotel, Dr Radhakrishnan Salai; coffees ₹100-175, dishes ₹250-350; ☺ 8am-10pm; ☎) The trendy home-brew cafe has hit Chennai, and Chennai loves it. Decked out in neorustic style, Brew Room does coffee like you've never had here, from double espresso and Italian cappuccino to French press and Americano. The contemporary Continental menu includes great vegetarian and vegan choices – even tofu!

Leather Bar
BAR
(Map p334; Park Hotel, 601 Anna Salai; ☺ 24hr) 'Leather' refers to furniture, floor and wall coverings rather than anything kinky. This tiny, chic pad has mixologists dishing up fancy drinks and DJs spinning dance tunes from around 9pm.

Dublin
PUB, NIGHTCLUB
(Map p328; Sheraton Park Hotel, 132 TTK Rd, Alwarpet; per couple ₹2000 incl ₹1000 drink voucher; ☺ from 8pm Wed-Sat) Belting out beats from hip-hop to Bollywood, this long-running, three-floor party place is an Irish pub until 10pm, then it becomes a packed-out club that goes to 3am on Friday and Saturday. No unaccompanied men (stags).

Café Coffee Day
CAFE
(Map p334; www.cafecoffeeday.com; Ispahani Centre, 123 Nungambakkam High Rd; ☺ 10am-10.30pm; ☎) Reliably good hot and cold coffees and teas for ₹60 to ₹120. Also at **Egmore** (Map p334; Alsa Mall, Montieth Rd; ☺ 11am-9pm), **Nungambakkam** (Map p334; Khader Nawaz Khan Rd, Nungambakkam; ☺ 9am-11pm) and **Express Avenue Mall** (Map p334; 3rd fl, Express Avenue Mall, White's Rd; ☺ 9.30am-10pm).

☆ Entertainment

There's *bharatanatyam* (Tamil classical dance) and/or a Carnatic music concert going on somewhere in Chennai almost every evening. Check listings in the *Hindu* or *Times of India*, or on www.timescity.com/chennai. The **Music Academy** (Map p328;

☑044-28112231; www.musicacademymadras.in; 168 (old 306) TTK Rd, Royapettah) is the most popular venue; the Kalakshetra Foundation (p332) and **Bharatiya Vidya Bhavan** (Map p328; ☑044-24643420; www.bhavanchennai.org; East Mada St, Mylapore) also stage many events.

🔒 Shopping

T Nagar has great shopping, especially at Pondy Bazaar and in the Panagal Park area. Many of the finest Kanchipuram silks turn up in Chennai, and the streets around Panagal Park are filled with silk shops; if you're lucky enough to be attending an Indian wedding, this is where you buy your sari.

Nungambakkam's Khader Nawaz Khan Rd is a lovely lane of increasingly upmarket designer boutiques, cafes and galleries.

Chennai's shopping malls are full of major international and Indian apparel chains. The best include **Express Avenue** (White's Rd, Royapettah; ☺10am-9pm), **Chennai Citi Centre** (Map p328; 10 Dr Radhakrishnan Salai, Mylapore; ☺10am-11.30pm), **Spencer Plaza** (Map p334; Anna Salai; ☺10.30am-9pm), and the new **Phoenix Market City** (142 Velachery Main Rd, Velachery; ☺11am-10pm). Spencer Plaza is a bit downmarket from the others, with smaller craft and souvenir shops.

🔒 Central Chennai

★**Higginbothams**   BOOKS
(Map p334; higginbothams@vsnl.com; 116 Anna Salai; ☺9am-8pm) Open since 1844, this grand white building is reckoned to be India's oldest bookshop. It has a brilliant English-language selection, including Lonely Planet books, and a good range of maps.

Naturally Auroville   HANDICRAFTS
(Map p334; 8 Khader Nawaz Khan Rd, Nungambakkam; ☺10.30am-9pm) Colourful handicrafts and home-decor trinkets, including bedspreads, incense, scented candles, and handmade-paper notebooks, all from Auroville, near Puducherry.

Starmark   BOOKS
(www.starmark.in; 2nd fl, Express Avenue, White's Rd; ☺10.30am-9.30pm) Smart new bookshop with an excellent collection of English, Indian and Tamil fiction and nonfiction, India travel books and Lonely Planet guides.

Evoluzione   CLOTHING
(Map p334; www.evoluzionestyle.com; 3 Khader Nawaz Khan Rd, Nungambakkam; ☺10.30-7.30pm

ℹ HOLIDAY TRANSPORT

All kinds of transport in, to and from Tamil Nadu get booked up weeks in advance for periods around major celebrations, including Pongal, Karthikai Deepam, Gandhi Jayanti and Diwali. Plan ahead.

Mon-Sat, noon-6pm Sun) This high-end boutique showcases neotraditional creations by cutting-edge Indian designers. Great for browsing, even if your budget won't allow the fabulously glittery wedding gowns!

Poompuhar   HANDICRAFTS
(Map p334; 108 Anna Salai; ☺10am-8pm Mon-Sat, 11am-7pm Sun) This large branch of the fixed-price state-government handicrafts chain is good for everything from cheap technicolour plaster deities to a ₹200,000, metre-high bronze Nataraja.

🔒 Southern Chennai

★**Nalli Silks**   TEXTILES
(Map p328; www.nallisilks.com; 9 Nageswaran Rd, T Nagar; ☺9am-9pm) Set up in 1928, the huge supercolourful granddaddy of Chennai silk shops sparkles with wedding saris and all kinds of Kanchipuram silks, as well as silk dhotis (long loincloths) for the boys. There's a jewellery branch next door.

Fabindia   CLOTHING, HANDICRAFTS
(www.fabindia.com; 35 TTK Rd, Mylapore; ☺10.30am-8.30pm) This fair-trade, nationwide chain sells stylishly contemporary village-made clothes and crafts. Perfect for picking up a kurta (long shirt with short/no collar) to throw over leggings. This branch also has incense, ceramics, table and bed linen, and natural beauty products. Also at **Woods Rd** (Map p334; 3 Woods Rd; ☺10.30am-8.30pm), **Express Avenue** (Map p334; 1st fl, Express Avenue Mall, White's Rd; ☺11am-9pm) and **T Nagar** (Map p328; 44 GN Chetty Rd, T Nagar; ☺10.30am-8.30pm).

Chamiers   CLOTHING, HANDICRAFTS
(Map p328; 106 Chamiers Rd, RA Puram; ☺10am-8pm) On the ground floor of this popular cafe-cum-boutique-complex, **Anokhi** has wonderful, East-meets-West block-printed clothes, bedding and accesories in light fabrics, at decent prices. Elegant **Amethyst Room** next door takes things upmarket with beautiful Indian-design couture.

NONSTOP DOMESTIC FLIGHTS FROM CHENNAI

DESTINATION	AIRLINES	FARE FROM (₹, ONE WAY)	DURATION (HR)	FREQUENCY (DAILY)
Bengaluru	AI, I8, SG, S2, 6E, 9W	990	1	17
Delhi	AI, SG, 6E, 9W	3776	2¾	24
Goa	AI, SG, 6E	1577	1¼-2	3-4
Hyderabad	AI, SG, 6E, 9W	1576	1-1½	13
Kochi	AI, SG, 6E, 9W	1576	1-1½	7
Kolkata	AI, SG, 6E	2777	2-2¾	9
Mumbai	AI, G8, SG, 6E, 9W	2775	2	22
Port Blair	AI, G8, SG, 9W	6684	2-2¼	4
Trivandrum	AI, SG, 6E	2172	1½	4

Airline codes; AI - Air India, G8 – Go Air, I8 – AirAsia India, SG – SpiceJet, 6E – IndiGo, 9W – Jet Airways

Kumaran Silks TEXTILES
(Map p328; www.kumaransilksonline.com; 12 Nageswaran Rd, T Nagar; ⊙9am-9pm) Saris, saris (including 'budget saris') and plenty of Kanchipuram silk.

ℹ️ Information

INTERNET ACCESS

'Browsing centres' are dotted all over town. Plenty of cafes have wi-fi.

Internet (Map p334; 6 Gandhi Irwin Rd, Egmore; per hour ₹30; ⊙8am-10pm) In the Hotel Imperial yard.

Studio (Map p334; Theetharappan St, Triplicane; per hour ₹15; ⊙9.30am-10.30pm) You'll need your passport.

LEFT LUGGAGE

Egmore and Central train stations have left-luggage offices (signed 'Cloakroom') for people with journey tickets. The airport also has left-luggage facilities.

MEDICAL SERVICES

Apollo Hospital (Map p334; ☎044-28296569, emergency 044-28293333; www.apollohospitals.com; 21 Greams Lane) State-of-the-art, expensive hospital, popular with 'medical tourists'.

Kauvery Hospital (Map p328; ☎044-40006000; www.kauveryhospital.com; 199 Luz Church Rd, Mylapore) Good, private, general hospital.

MONEY

ATMs are everywhere, including at Central train station, the airport and the main bus station.

Thomas Cook (Map p334; Phase I, Spencer Plaza, Anna Salai; ⊙9.30am-6.30pm) Changes foreign cash and American Express travellers cheques.

POST

DHL (Map p334; ☎044-42148886; www.dhl.co.in; 85 VVV Sq, Pantheon Rd, Egmore; ⊙9am-10pm Mon-Sat) Secure international parcel delivery; several branches around town.

Main post office (Map p328; Rajaji Salai, George Town; ⊙8am-8.30pm Mon-Sat, 10am-6pm Sun)

TOURIST INFORMATION

Indiatourism (Map p334; ☎044-28460285; www.incredibleindia.org; 154 Anna Salai; ⊙9am-6pm Mon-Fri) Helpful on all of India, as well as Chennai.

Tamil Nadu Tourism Development Corporation (TTDC; Map p334; ☎044-25383333; www.tamilnadutourism.org; Tamil Nadu Tourism Complex, 2 Wallajah Rd, Triplicane; ⊙10am-6pm) The state tourism body's main office takes bookings for its own bus tours, answers questions and hands out leaflets. In the same building are state tourist offices from all over India, mostly open 10am to 6pm. The TTDC has counters at Central and Egmore stations.

TRAVEL AGENCIES

Milesworth Travel (Map p328; ☎044-24320522; http://milesworth.com; RM Towers, 108 Chamiers Rd, Alwarpet; ⊙9.30am-6pm Mon-Sat) A very professional, welcoming agency that will help with all your travel needs.

ℹ️ Getting There & Away

AIR

Chennai International Airport is situated at Tirusulam in the far southwest of the city. The international terminal is about 500m west of the domestic terminal; the two are linked by a raised walkway.

There are direct flights to cities all over India, including Trichy (Tiruchirappalli), Madurai, Coimbatore and Thoothikudi (Tuticorin) within Tamil Nadu. Internationally, Chennai has plenty of direct flights to/from Colombo, Singapore, Kuala Lumpur and the Gulf states. The best fares from Europe are often on Jet Airways (via Mumbai or Delhi), Qatar Airways (via Doha) or Emirates (via Dubai). Cathay Pacific flies to Hong Kong, and Maldivian to Male.

Airline Offices

Air Asia (Map p334; ✆ 044-33008000; www.airasia.com; Ispahani Centre, 123 Nungambakkam High Rd; ⊕ 9.30am-6pm Mon-Sat)

Air India (Map p334; ✆ 044-23453375; www.airindia.com; 19 Rukmani Lakshmipathy Rd, Egmore; ⊕ 9.45am-1pm & 1.45-5.15pm Mon-Sat)

Air India Express (Map p334; ✆ 044-23453375; www.airindiaexpress.in; 19 Rukmani Lakshmipathy Rd, Egmore; ⊕ 9.45am-1pm & 1.45-5.15pm Mon-Sat)

Jet Airways (Map p334; ✆ 044-39893333; www.jetairways.com; 43/44 Montieth Rd, Egmore; ⊕ 10am-6pm Mon-Fri)

BOAT

Passenger ships sail from George Town harbour direct to Port Blair in the Andaman Islands (once weekly. The **Andaman Shipping Office Ticketing Counter** (✆ 044-25226873; www.and.nic.in; 2nd fl, Shipping Corporation of India, Jawahar Bldg, 17 Rajaji Salai, George Town; ⊕ 10am-1pm & 2-4pm Mon-Fri, 10am-12.30pm Sat) sells tickets (₹2270 to ₹8850) for the 60-hour trip. Book several days ahead, and take

three copies each of your passport data page and Indian visa along with the original. It can be a long process.

BUS

Most government buses operate from the large but surprisingly orderly **CMBT** (Chennai Mofussil Bus Terminus; Jawaharlal Nehru Rd, Koyambedu), 6km west of the centre. The most comfortable and expensive are the AC buses (and best of these are the Volvo AC services), followed by the UD (Ultra Deluxe), and these can generally be reserved in advance. There's a computerised reservation centre at the left end of the main hall, where you can book up to 60 days ahead.

The **T Nagar Bus Terminus** (Map p328; South Usman Rd) is handy for bus 599 to Mamallapuram (₹27, 1½ hours, every 30 minutes).

Private buses generally offer greater comfort than non-AC government buses to many destinations, at up to double the price. Service information is available at www.redbus.in, and tickets can be booked through many travel agencies. Their main terminal is the **Omni bus stand** (off Kaliamman Koil St, Koyambedu), 500m west of the CMBT, but some companies also pick up and drop off elsewhere in the city. Parveen Travels, for example, runs services to Bengaluru, Ernakulam (Kochi), Kodaikanal, Madurai, Ooty, Puducherry, Trichy and Thiruvananthapuram (Trivandrum) departing from its **Egmore office** (Map p334; ✆ 044-28192577; www.parveentravels.com; 11/5 Kennet Lane, Egmore).

TAMIL NADU & CHENNAI CHENNAI (MADRAS)

GOVERNMENT BUSES FROM CMBT

DESTINATION	FARE (₹)	DURATION (HR)	FREQUENCY
Bengaluru	360-700	8	60 daily
Coimbatore	405	11	16 daily
Ernakulam (Kochi)	590	16	3pm
Hyderabad	730-1200	12	5 daily 6.30pm
Kodaikanal	390	13	5pm
Kumbakonom	190-275	7	every 30min 4am-midnight
Madurai	355-430	10	every 15min 4am-midnight
Mamallapuram	80	2	every 30min 4am-midnight
Mysuru	630-1050	10	6 daily
Ooty	415	13	4.30pm, 5.45pm, 7.15pm
Puducherry	95-200	4	every 30min 4am-midnight
Rameswaram	420-445	13	5pm, 5.30pm, 5.45pm
Thanjavur	220-325	8½	every 30min 5am-11pm
Tirupathi	162-232	4	21 daily
Trichy	190-285	7	every 15min 2am-midnight
Trivandrum	565	15	12 daily

CAR

Renting a car with a driver is the easiest way of getting anywhere and is easily arranged through most travel agents, midrange or top-end hotels, or the airport's prepaid taxi desks. Sample rates for non-AC/AC cars are ₹700/800 for up to five hours and 50km, and ₹1400/1600 for up to 10 hours and 100km.

TRAIN

Interstate trains and those heading west generally depart from Central station, while trains heading south mostly leave from Egmore. The **advance reservations office** (Map p334; 1st fl, Chennai Central local station; ⊘ 8am-8pm Mon-Sat, 8am-2pm Sun), with its incredibly helpful Foreign Tourist Cell, is on the 1st floor in a separate 11-storey building just west of the main Central station building. Egmore station has its own **Passenger Reservation Office** (Map p334; Chennai Egmore station; ⊘ 8am-8pm Mon-Sat, 8am-2pm Sun).

ⓘ Getting Around

TO/FROM THE AIRPORT

The Chennai Metro Rail system, expected to open in late 2015, will provide a cheap, easy link between the airport and city. Meanwhile, the cheapest option is a suburban train to/from Tirusulam station opposite the parking areas of the domestic terminal, accessed by a pedestrian subway under the highway. Trains run every 10 to 20 minutes from 4am to midnight to/from Chennai Beach station (₹5, 42 minutes) with stops including Kodambakkam, Egmore, Chennai Park and Chennai Fort.

Prepaid taxi kiosks outside the airport's international terminal charge ₹480/580 for a non-AC/AC cab to Egmore, and ₹400/500 to T Nagar. Rates are slightly lower at prepaid taxi kiosks outside the domestic terminal.

From the CMBT, city buses 70 and 170 to Tambaram stop on the highway across from the airport.

MAJOR TRAINS FROM CHENNAI

DESTINATION	TRAIN NO & NAME	FARE (₹)	DURATION (HR)	DEPARTURE
Bengaluru	12007 Shatabdi Express*	529/1155 (A)	5	6am CC
	12609 Chennai-Bangalore Express	110/535 (B)	6½	1.35pm CC
Coimbatore	12675 Kovai Express	180/655 (B)	7½	6.15am CC
	12671 Nilgiri Express	315/805/1135 (C)	7¾	9.15pm CC
Delhi	12621 Tamil Nadu Express	780/2020/2970 (C)	33	10pm CC
Goa	17311 Vasco Express (Friday only)	475/1275/1850 (C)	22	1.50pm CC
Hyderabad	12759 Charminar Express	425/1115/1590 (C)	13½	6.10pm CC
Kochi	16041 Alleppey Express	395/1035/1470 (C)	11½	8.45pm CC
Kolkata	12842 Coromandel Express	665/1730/2520 (C)	27	8.45am CC
Madurai	12635 Vaigai Express	180/655 (B)	8	1.20pm CE
	12637 Pandyan Express	315/805/1135 (C)	9	9.20pm CE
Mumbai	11042 Mumbai Express	540/1440/2100 (C)	26	11.55am CC
Mysore	12007 Shatabdi Express*	915/1805 (A)	7	6am CC
	16021 Kaveri Express	285/755/1085 (C)	10	9pm CC
Tirupathi	16053 Tirupathi Express	80/285 (B)	3½	2.10pm CC
Trichy	12635 Vaigai Express	145/510 (B)	5	1.20pm CE
Trivandrum	12695 Trivandrum Mail	470/1230/1760 (C)	16	3.25pm CC

Departure Codes: CC – Chennai Central, CE – Chennai Egmore

*Daily except Wednesday

Fares: (A) chair/executive; (B) 2nd/chair; (C) sleeper/3AC/2AC

CHENNAI BUS ROUTES

BUS NO	ROUTE
A1	Central–Anna Salai–RK Mutt Rd (Mylapore)–Theosophical Society–Thiruvanmiyur
1B	Parry's–Central–Anna Salai–Airport
10A	Parry's–Central–Egmore (S)–Pantheon Rd–T Nagar
11	Rattan–Central–Anna Salai–T Nagar
12	T Nagar–Pondy Bazaar–Eldham's Rd–Dr Radhakrishnan Salai–Vivekananda House
15B & 15F	Broadway–Central–CMBT
21H	Broadway–Fort St George–Kamarajar Salai–San Thome Cathedral–Theosophical Society
M27	CMBT–T Nagar
27B	CMBT–Egmore (S)–Bharathi Salai (Triplicane)
27D	Egmore (S)–Anna Salai–Cathedral Rd–Dr Radhakrishnan Salai–San Thome Cathedral
32 & 32A	Central–Vivekananda House

Routes operate in both directions.

Broadway – Broadway Bus Terminus, George Town

Central – Central Station

Egmore (S) – Egmore station (south side)

Parry's – Parry's Corner

AUTORICKSHAW

Fixed autorickshaw fares are ₹25 for the first 1.8km (minimum charge), then ₹12 per kilometre. Some drivers still refuse to use their meters and quote astronomical fares, while others take unnecessarily long routes or ask for 'meter plus extra', but most will go by the meter if you insist. Avoid paying upfront, and always establish the meter is on before getting into a rickshaw. Rates rise by up to 50% from 11pm to 5am.

There are prepaid autorickshaw booths outside the CMBT (₹125 to Egmore) and Central station, and 24-hour prepaid stands with fare charts outside the north and south exits of Egmore station.

Tempting offers of ₹50 'city tours' by autorickshaw drivers sound too good to be true. They are. You'll spend the day being dragged from one shop or emporium to another.

BUS

Chennai's city bus system is worth getting to know, although buses get packed to overflowing at busy times. Fares are between ₹3 and ₹14 (up to double for express and deluxe services, and multiplied by five for Volvo AC services). Route information is online at http://busroutes.in/chennai.

METRO RAIL

Chennai Metro Rail, a new, part-underground rapid transit system, is expected to open in late 2015 and should make moving around the city much easier. Line 1 goes from the airport to Teynampet, Thousand Lights, Central train station, the High Court and Washermanpet in northern Chennai, running beneath Anna Salai for several kilometres. Line 2 goes from Central train station west to Egmore and the CMBT then south to St Thomas Mount.

TAXI

Both airport terminals have prepaid taxi kiosks. There's a **prepaid taxi stand** (Map p334; Egmore Station; ⊘ 4am-1pm) outside the south side of Egmore station; a ride of 7km, such as to Alwarpet, costs about ₹240.

Relatively reliable **Fast Track** (☑ 6000 6000) taxis charge ₹100 for up to 4km, then ₹18 per kilometre (with a 25% hike in rates between 11pm and 5am); bookings are taken by phone.

TRAIN

Efficient, cheap suburban trains run from Beach station to Fort, Park (near Central station), Egmore, Chetpet, Nungambakkam, Kodambakkam, Mambalam, Saidapet, Guindy, St Thomas Mount, Tirusulam (for the airport), and on down to Tambaram. At Egmore station, the suburban platforms (10 and 11) and ticket office are on the north side of the station. A second line branches south after Fort to Park Town, Chepauk, Tiruvallikeni (for Marina Beach), Light House and Thirumailai (near Kapaleeshwarar Temple). Trains run from 4am to midnight, several times hourly; rides cost ₹5 to ₹10.

NORTHERN TAMIL NADU

Chennai to Mamallapuram

Chennai's sprawl peters out after an hour or so heading south on the East Coast Road (ECR), at which point Tamil Nadu becomes red dirt, blue skies, palm trees, and green fields, sprinkled with towns and villages (or, if you take the 'IT Expressway' inland, huge new buildings).

Swimming along the coast is dangerous due to strong currents.

◉ Sights & Activities

Cholamandal Artists' Village
ARTIST COLONY, MUSEUM

(☑044-24490092; www.cholamandalartistsvillage.in; Injambakkam; museum ₹20; ☺museum 9.30am-6.30pm) There's a tropical bohemian groove floating around Injambakkam village, site of the Cholamandal Artists' Village, 10km south of the Adyar River. This 3-hectare artists' cooperative – founded in 1966 by artists of the Madras Movement, pioneers of modern art in South India – is a serene muse away from the world, and the art in its museum is very much worth lingering over. Look especially for work by KCS Paniker, SG Vasudev, M Senathipathi and S Nandagopal.

DakshinaChitra Museum
ARTS & CRAFTS CENTRE

(☑044-27472603; www.dakshinachitra.net; East Coast Rd, Muttukadu; Indian adult/student ₹100/50, foreign ₹250/70; ☺10am-6pm Wed-Mon) DakshinaChitra, 22km south of the Adyar River, offers a fantastic insight into South India's traditional arts and crafts. Like a treasure chest of local art and architecture, this jumble of open-air museum, preserved village, artisan workshops (pottery, silk weaving, basket making), and a new tribal art gallery is set among an exquisite collection of traditional South Indian homes.

Covelong Point
SURFING

(☑9840975916; www.covelongpoint.com) The fishing village of Kovalam, 20km north of Mamallapuram, has recently sprung into the spotlight for having probably the best surfing waves on the Tamil Nadu coast. For classes or surf companionship, head to 'social surfing school' Covelong Point, run by Kovalam's original local surf pioneer Murthy. Kovalam also hosts the hugely popular Covelong Point Surf & Music Festival (www.covelongpoint.com; ☺Sep), now into its second year.

Madras Crocodile Bank
ZOO

(☑044-27472447; www.madrascrocodilebank.org; Vadanemmeli; adult/child ₹35/10, camera/video ₹20/100; ☺8.30am-5.30pm Tue-Sun) ◢ Madras Crocodile Bank, 6km south down the ECR from Kovalam, is a fascinating peek into the reptile world, and an incredible conservation and research trust. Founded by croc/snake-man Romulus Whitaker, the Bank has thousands of reptiles, including 18 of the world's 23 species of crocodilian (crocodiles and similar creatures), and does crucial work in maintaining genetic reserves of these animals, several of which are endangered.

Tiger Cave
SACRED HINDU SITE

(Saluvankuppam; admission free; ☺6am-6pm) Just 5km north of Mamallapuram, the Tiger Cave is an unfinished but impressive rock-cut shrine, probably dating from the 7th century and dedicated to Durga (a form of Devi, Shiva's wife). What's special is the 'necklace' of 11 monstrous tigerlike heads framing its central shrine-cavity. At the north end of the parklike complex is a rock-cut Shiva shrine from the same era. Beyond the fence lies the more recently excavated Subrahmanya Temple, comprising an 8th-century granite shrine built over a Sangam-era brick temple dedicated to Murugan, which is one of the oldest known temples in Tamil Nadu.

ⓘ Getting There & Away

To reach these places, take any bus heading south from Chennai to Mamallapuram and ask to be let off at the appropriate point(s). The TTDC's Chennai–Mamallapuram round-trip bus tour (₹450 to ₹550, 10 hours) visits several of the sites and Mamallapuram itself. A full-day taxi tour from Chennai costs around ₹3000.

Mamallapuram (Mahabalipuram)

☑044 / POP 15,172

Mamallapuram was the major seaport of the ancient Pallava kingdom based at Kanchipuram, and a wander round the town's magnificent, World Heritage–listed temples and carvings inflames the imagination, especially at sunset.

And then, in addition to ancient archaeological wonders and coastal beauty, there's the traveller ghetto of Othavadai and Oulhavadai Cross Sts. Restaurants serve pasta, pizza and pancakes, shops sell hand sanitiser and things from Tibet, and you know you have landed, once again, in the great Kingdom of Backpackistan.

'Mahabs', as most call it, is under two hours by bus from Chennai, and many travellers make a beeline straight here. The town is small and laid-back, and its sights can be explored on foot or by bicycle.

◎ Sights

You can easily spend a full day exploring Mamallapuram's marvellous temples and rock carvings. Most of them were carved from the rock during the 7th-century reign of Pallava king Narasimhavarman I, whose nickname Mamalla (Great Wrestler) gave the town its name. Apart from the Shore Temple and the Five Rathas, admission is free. Official Archaeological Survey of India guides can be hired at sites for around ₹100.

★**Shore Temple**   HINDU TEMPLE
(combined 1-day ticket with Five Rathas Indian/ foreigner ₹10/250, video ₹25; ⊘6am-6pm) Standing like a magnificent fist of rock-cut elegance overlooking the sea, the two-towered Shore Temple symbolises the heights of Pallava architecture and the maritime ambitions of the Pallava kings. Its small size belies its excellent proportion and the supreme quality of the carvings, many of which have been eroded into vaguely Impressionist embellishments. Built under Narasimhavarman II in the 8th century, it's the earliest significant free-standing stone temple in Tamil Nadu.

The two towers rise above shrines to Shiva and their original linga (phallic symbols of Shiva) captured the sunrise and sunset. Between the Shiva shrines is one to Vishnu, shown sleeping. Rows of Nandi (Shiva's vehicle) statues frame the temple courtyard.

★**Five Rathas**   HINDU TEMPLE
(Pancha Ratha; Five Rathas Rd; combined 1-day ticket with Shore Temple Indian/foreigner ₹10/250, video ₹25; ⊘6am-6pm) Huddled together at the southern end of Mamallapuram, the Five Rathas look like buildings, but they were, astonishingly, all carved from single large rocks. Each of these 7th-century temples was dedicated to a Hindu god and is now named after one or more of the Pandavas, the five hero-brothers of the epic Mahabharata, or their common wife, Draupadi. The *rathas* were hidden in the sand until excavated by the British 200 years ago.

Ratha is Sanskrit for chariot, and may refer to the temples' form or to their function as vehicles for the gods. It's thought they didn't originally serve as places of worship, but were created as architectural models.

The first *ratha* on the left after you enter the gate is the **Draupadi Ratha**, in the form of a stylised South Indian hut. It's dedicated to the demon-fighting goddess Durga, who looks out from inside, standing on a lotus. A huge sculpted lion, Durga's mount, stands guard outside.

Next, on the same plinth, is the 'chariot' of the most important Pandava, the **Arjuna Ratha**, dedicated to Shiva. Its pilasters, miniature roof shrines, and small octagonal dome make it a precursor of many later temples in South India. A huge Nandi, Shiva's vehicle, stands behind. Shiva and other gods are depicted on the temple's outer walls.

The barrel-roofed **Bhima Ratha** was never completed, as is evidenced by the missing colonnade on its north side. Inside is a shrine to Vishnu. The **Dharmaraja Ratha**, tallest of the temples, is similar in form to the Arjuna Ratha but one storey higher. The carvings on its outer walls mostly represent gods, including the androgynous Ardhanarishvara (half Shiva, half Parvati) on the east side. King Narasimhavarman I appears at the west end of the south side.

The **Nakula-Sahadeva Ratha** (named after two twin Pandavas) stands aside from the other four and is dedicated to Indra. The life-size stone elephant beside it is one of the most perfectly sculpted elephants in India. Approaching from the gate to the north you see its back end first, hence its nickname Gajaprishthakara (elephant's backside).

★**Arjuna's Penance**   HINDU, MONUMENT
(West Raja St) The crowning masterpiece of Mamallapuram's stonework, this giant relief carving is one of India's greatest ancient art works. Inscribed on two huge, adjacent boulders, the Penance bursts with scenes of Hindu myth and everyday vignettes of South Indian life. In the centre *nagas* (snake-beings), descend a once water-filled cleft, representing the Ganges. To the left Arjuna (hero of the Mahabharata) performs self-mortification (fasting on one leg), so that the four-armed Shiva will grant him his most powerful weapon, the god-slaying Pasupata.

TAMIL NADU & CHENNAI MAMALLAPURAM (MAHABALIPURAM)

Mamallapuram (Mahabalipuram)

Some scholars believe the carving shows not Arjuna but the sage Bagiratha, who did severe penance to obtain Shiva's help in bringing the Ganges to earth. Shiva is attended by dwarves, and celestial beings fly across the upper parts of the carving. Below Arjuna/Bagiratha is a temple to Vishnu, mythical ancestor of the Pallava kings. The many wonderfully carved animals include a herd of elephants and – humour amid the holy – a cat mimicking Arjuna's penance to a crowd of mice.

South along the road from Arjuna's Penance are the unfinished **Panch Pandava Mandapa** (⊙6.30am-6pm) cave temple; the **Krishna Mandapa** (⊙6.30am-6pm), which famously depicts Krishna lifting Govardhana Hill to protect cows and villagers from a storm sent by Indra; an **unfinished relief carving** of similar size to Arjuna's Penance; and the **Dharmaraja Cave Temple** (⊙6.30am-6pm).

🏃 Activities

Beaches

The beach fronting the village isn't exactly pristine, but south of the Shore Temple it clears into finer sand. You'll also be further away from the leers of men who spend their days gawking at tourists. Like most of Tamil Nadu's coast, these beaches aren't great for swimming, due to dangerous rips.

Surfing

Mumu Surf School SURFING
(☎9789844191; http://mumusurfer.wix.com; 42 Fishermen's Colony; 90min group/private class ₹750/1000; ⊙7.30am-6pm) Popular, well-organised school for all levels and board rental (per hour ₹150 to ₹300).

Therapies

Numerous places in town offer massage, reiki, yoga and ayurveda, at similar rates. Ask fellow travellers, question the therapist care-

Mamallapuram (Mahabalipuram)

fully and if you have any misgivings, don't proceed.

Sri Durga   AYURVEDA, YOGA
(☑ 9840288280; www.sridurgaayurveda.com; 35 Othavadai St; 45min massage ₹750, 1hr yoga ₹200) Recommended massages and ayurvedic treatments (male therapists for men, female for women), and yoga at 7am and 6pm.

👉 Tours

Travel XS   CYCLING, BIRDWATCHING
(☑ 044-27443360; www.travel-xs.com; 123 East Raja St; bicycle tours ₹450-500; ☺9.30am-6pm Mon-Fri, 9.30am-2pm Sat) Runs half-day bicycle tours to nearby villages, visiting local potters and observing activities such as *kolam* drawing (the 'welcome' patterns outside doorways, also called *rangoli*), and organises day trips to places including Kanchipuram and Vedanthangal Bird Sanctuary.

✦✦ Festivals & Events

Mamallapuram Dance Festival   DANCE
(☺late Dec-late Jan) A four-week, weekend-only dance festival showcasing classical and folk dances from all over India, with many performances on an open-air stage against the imposing backdrop of Arjuna's Penance.

Dances include *bharatanatyam* (from Tamil Nadu), Kuchipudi (Andhra Pradesh) tribal dance, and Kathakali (Kerala).

🛏 Sleeping

Hotel Daphne   HOTEL $
(☑ 9894282876; www.moonrakersrestaurants.com; 24 Othavadai Cross St; r ₹500-1500; ⊛☺) Most rooms here are perfectly acceptable if nothing fancy, but the top-floor AC rooms 13 and 14 are great value, with four-poster beds, balconies and cane swing chairs. The courtyard and free wi-fi are other drawcards.

Tina Blue View Lodge & Restaurant   GUESTHOUSE $
(☑ 9840727270, 044-27442319; 48 Othavadai St; s/d/tr ₹500/600/900) Frayed and faded Tina is one of Mamallapuram's originals and kind of looks it, but remains deservedly popular for its whitewashed walls, blue flourishes and tropical garden, as well as tireless original owner Xavier.

Sri Harul Guest House   GUESTHOUSE $
(Sea View Guest House; ☑ 9384620173; sriharul@gmail.com; 181 Bajanai Koil St, Fishermen's Colony; r ₹800-900) Surf crashes onto the rocks right below your balcony if you land one of the half-dozen sea-view rooms at Sri Harul, one

of the better seafront budget deals. Rooms are basic, medium-sized and quite clean, and you can hang out at the rooftop cafe.

Greenwoods Beach Resort
GUESTHOUSE $

(☑ 044-27442212; greenwoods_resort@yahoo.com; 7 Othavadai Cross St; r ₹500-800, with AC ₹1200; ❀ 🛜) Perhaps the most characterful of the Othavadai Cross St cheapies and definitely not on the beach, Greenwoods is run by an enthusiastic family who put up backpackers in plain, clean-ish rooms up staircases around a pretty leafy courtyard.

Butterball Bed 'n Breakfast
B&B $$

(☑ 9094792525; 9/26 East Raja St; s/d incl breakfast ₹1700/2000; ❀ 🛜) There's a great view of the eponymous giant rock from the roof terrace, and a lovely lawn. The smallish but clean, pleasant rooms have old English prints, writing desks and blue-tiled bathrooms, and breakfast is served in its Burger Shack (9/26 East Raja St; mains ₹120-300; ⏰10am-10pm) restaurant out the front.

Hotel Mahabs
HOTEL $$

(☑ 044-27442645; www.hotelmahabs.com; 68 East Raja St; r ₹2140-2930; ❀ @ 🛜 ❄) Friendly Mahabs is centred on a pretty mural-lined pool (₹300 for nonguests) surrounded by tropical greenery. Boring brown is the room theme, but they're very clean and comfy. There's a decent in-house restaurant.

Hotel Mamalla Heritage
HOTEL $$

(☑ 044-27442060; www.hotelmamallaheritage.com; 104 East Raja St; incl breakfast s ₹2400-2640, d ₹2640-2880; ❀ 🛜 ❄) King of tour group packages, the Mamalla has big, comfortable, forgettable rooms rising around a nice pool, and a quality rooftop veg restaurant.

★ Radisson Blu Resort Temple Bay
RESORT $$$

(☑ 044-27443636; www.radissonblu.com/hotel-mamallapuram; 57 Kovalam Rd; r incl breakfast from ₹9880; ❀ @ 🛜 ❄) The Radisson's 144 luxurious chalets, villas and bungalows are strewn across manicured gardens stretching 500m to the beach. Somewhere in the midst is India's longest swimming pool, all 220m of it. Rooms range from large to enormous; the most expensive have private pools. The Radisson also offers Mamallapuram's finest (and priciest) dining and a top-notch ayurvedic spa. Best rates online.

MAMALLAPURAM HILL

Many interesting monuments are scattered across the rock-strewn hill on the west side of town. It takes about an hour to walk round the main ones. The hill area is open from 6am to 6pm and has two entrances: a northern one on West Raja St, and a southern one just off Five Rathas Rd.

Straight ahead inside the northern entrance you can't miss the huge boulder with the inspired name of Krishna's Butterball, immovable but apparently balancing precariously. Pass between the rocks north of here to the Trimurti Cave Temple, honouring the Hindu 'trinity': Brahma (left), Shiva (centre) and Vishnu (right). On the back of the same rock is a beautiful group of carved elephants.

Back south of Krishna's Butterball you reach the Ganesh Ratha, carved from a single rock with lion-shaped pillar bases. Once a Shiva temple, it became a shrine to Ganesh (Shiva's elephant-headed son) after the original lingam was removed. Southwest of here, the Varaha Mandapa houses some of Mamallapuram's finest carvings. The left panel shows Vishnu's boar avatar, Varaha, lifting the earth out of the oceans. The outward-facing panels show Vishnu's consort Lakshmi (washed by elephants) and Durga, while the right-hand panel has Vishnu in his eight-armed giant form, Trivikrama, overcoming the demon king Bali.

A little further south, then up to the left, is the 16th-century Raya Gopura (Olakkanatha Temple), probably an unfinished gopuram (gateway tower). West just up the hill is the finely carved Lion Throne. The main path continues south to the Ramanuja Mandapa and up to Mamallapuram's lighthouse (Indian/foreigner ₹10/25, camera ₹20; ⏰10am-1pm & 2-5.30pm). Just southwest of the lighthouse is the Mahishamardini Mandapa, carved from the rock with excellent scenes from the Puranas (Sanskrit stories from the 5th century AD). The left-side panel shows Vishnu sleeping on the coils of a snake; on the right, Durga bestrides her lion vehicle while killing the demon-buffalo Mahisha. Inside the central shrine, Murugan is depicted sitting between his parents Shiva and Parvati.

Ideal Beach Resort
RESORT $$$

(☎044-27442240; www.idealresort.com; East Coast Rd; s/d from ₹6000/6600; ❄@🛜☷) With a landscaped garden setting and its own stretch of (pretty nice) beach, this laid-back resort, 3km north of town, is popular with weekending families and couples. It's quiet and secluded, there's a lovely pool-side restaurant, and some rooms come with open-air showers. Nonguests can get pool/beach day passes for ₹400.

✖ Eating

Eateries on Othavadai and Othavadai Cross Sts provide semi-open-air settings, decent Western mains and bland Indian curries. Most will serve you a beer. For Indian food, there are cheap veg places near the bus stand.

Le Yogi
MULTICUISINE $$

(19 Othavadai St; mains ₹100-200; ⊙7.30am-11pm) This is some of the best Western food in town; the pasta, pizza, sizzlers and crepes are genuine and tasty (if small), service is good, and the chilled-out setting, with bamboo posts and pretty lamps dangling from a thatched roof, has a touch of the romantic.

Gecko Restaurant
MULTICUISINE $$

(www.gecko-web.com; 37 Othavadai St; mains ₹150-270; ⊙9am-10pm; 🛜) Two friendly brothers run this cute blue-and-yellow-walled spot sprinkled with colourful artwork and wood carvings. The offerings and prices aren't that different from other tourist-oriented spots, but there's more love put into the cooking here and it's tastier.

Freshly 'n Hot
CAFE $$

(Othavadai Cross St; mains ₹70-200; ⊙7am-9pm) Yes, the name makes no sense, but this tiny place is relaxed, fresh and friendly. A comparatively small menu of perfectly OK pizza, pasta, sandwiches and crepes accompanies a long list of coffees. The iced coffees are great.

Moonrakers
MULTICUISINE $$

(34 Othavadai St; mains ₹100-180; ⊙10am-10pm; 🛜) You'll probably end up here at some point; it's the kind of place that's dominated the backpacker-ghetto streetscape forever. The food won't win any prizes but it's fine, and the three floors of tables keep busy (probably partly thanks to the free wi-fi).

Water's Edge Cafe
MULTICUISINE $$$

(Radisson Blu Resort Temple Bay, 57 Kovalam Rd; mains ₹480-900; ⊙24hr) The Radisson's pool-side 'cafe' offers everything from American pancakes to grilled tofu, Indian veg dishes, and a fantastic breakfast buffet (₹970). Also here is **The Wharf** (mains ₹550-1600; ⊙noon-3pm & 7-11pm), which looks like a beach shack but is actually a gourmet seaside restaurant.

🛍 Shopping

The roar of electric stone-grinders has just about replaced the tink-tink of chisels in Mamallapuram's stone-carving workshops, enabling them to turn out ever more granite sculptures of varying quality, from ₹100 pendants to a ₹400,000 Ganesh that needs to be lifted with a crane. There are also some decent art galleries, tailors and antique shops.

Southern Arts & Crafts
ANTIQUES, HANDICRAFTS

(☎044-27443675; www.southernarts.in; 72 East Raja St; ⊙9am-7.30pm) Expensive but beautiful curios acquired from local homes, along with quality new sculptures.

Apollo Books
BOOKS

(150 Fishermen's Colony; ⊙9am-9.30pm) Good collection of books in several languages, to sell and swap.

ℹ Information

Head to East Raja St for ATMs.

AM Communications (East Raja St; per hour ₹30; ⊙11am-9pm)

Ruby Forex (East Raja St; ⊙9.30am-7pm Mon-Sat) Currency exchange.

Suradeep Hospital (☎044-27442448; 15 Thirukula St; ⊙24hr) Recommended by travellers.

Tourist office (☎044-27442232; Kovalam Rd; ⊙10am-5.45pm Mon-Fri)

ℹ Getting There & Away

From the **bus stand** (East Raja St), bus 599 heads to Chennai's T Nagar Bus Terminus (₹27, 1½ hours) every 30 minutes from 7am to 8.30pm, and AC bus 568C (588C on weekends) runs to Chennai's CMBT (₹85, two hours) every two hours, 6am to 8pm. For Chennai airport take bus 515 to Tambaram (₹40, 1½ hours, every 30 minutes), then a taxi, autorickshaw or suburban train. There are also nine daily buses to Kanchipuram (₹40, two hours). Buses to Puducherry (₹60, two hours) stop about every 30 minutes at the junction of Kovalam Rd and the Mamallapuram bypass, 1km north of the town centre.

Taxis are available from the bus stand, travel agents and hotels. It's about ₹1500 to Chennai or the airport, or ₹2000 to Puducherry.

You can make train reservations at the **Southern Railway Reservation Centre** (1st fl, 32 East Raja St; ⊙10am-1pm & 2.30-5pm Mon-Sat, 8am-1pm Sun).

ⓘ Getting Around

The easiest way to get around is by walking, though on a hot day it's a hike to see all the monuments. You can hire bicycles at some guesthouses and rental stalls for about ₹80 per day.

Kanchipuram

📞 044 / POP 164,384

Kanchipuram, 80km southwest of Chennai, was capital of the Pallava dynasty during the 6th to 8th centuries, when the Pallavas created the great stone monuments of Mamallapuram. Today a typically hectic modern Indian town, it's famed for its numerous important and vibrant temples, some dating from Pallava, Chola or Vijayanagar times, and also for its high-quality silk saris, woven on hand looms by thousands of families in the city and nearby villages. Silk and sari shops are strung along Gandhi Rd, southeast of the centre, though their wares are generally no cheaper than at Chennai silk shops. Kanchi is easily visited in a day trip from Mamallapuram or Chennai.

◉ Sights

All temples have free admission, though you may have to pay small amounts for shoe-keeping and/or cameras. Ignore claims that there's an entrance fee for non-Hindus.

Kailasanatha Temple   HINDU TEMPLE
(⊙ 6am-noon & 4-8pm) Kanchi's oldest temple is its most impressive, not for its size but for its weight of historical presence and the intricacy of its stonework. As much monument as living temple, Kailasanatha is quieter than other temples in town, and has seen a lot of restoration. Dedicated to Shiva, it was built in the 8th century by the Pallava king Narasimhavarman II, who also gave us Mamallapuram's Shore Temple.

The low-slung sandstone compound has fascinating carvings, including many of the half-animal deities in vogue in early Dravidian architecture. Note the rearing lions on the outer walls. The inner sanctum is centred on a large 16-sided lingam, which non-Hindus can view from about 8m away. The tower rising above it is a precursor of the great *vimanas* of later Chola temples. An autorickshaw from the centre costs ₹40, but walking is nice.

Ekambareshwara Temple   HINDU TEMPLE
(Ekambaranathar Temple; phone-camera/camera/video ₹10/20/100; ⊙ 6am-12.30pm & 4-8.30pm) Of the five South Indian Shiva temples associated with the five elements, this 12-hectare precinct is the shrine of earth. You enter beneath the 59m-high, unpainted south *gopuram,* whose lively carvings were chiselled in 1509 under Vijayanagar rule. Inside, a columned hall leads left into the central compound, which Nandi faces from the right. The inner sanctum (Hindus only) contains a lingam made of earth and a mirror chamber whose central Shiva image is reflected in endless repetition.

According to legend, the goddess Kamakshi (She Whose Eyes Awaken Desire; a form of Parvati, Shiva's consort) worshipped

VEDANTHANGAL BIRD SANCTUARY

Vedanthangal Bird Sanctuary (admission ₹10, camera/video ₹100/250; ⊙ 6am-6pm), 55km southwest of Mamallapuram, is a spectacular 30-hectare breeding ground for many kinds of water birds, which migrate here from November to February. Some years as many as 100,000 birds mass at Vedanthangal Lake and its marshy surrounds. The top viewing times are dawn and late afternoon.

The lushly shaded, 4.5-hectare lodge of **Karadi Malai Camp** (📞 8012033087; www.draco-india.com; Pambukudivanam, Chengalpattu; r incl breakfast ₹5000; 🐾) borders the Vallam Reserve Forest, 30km northeast of Vedanthangal on the Chengalpattu–Tirupporur road, and makes the perfect Vedanthangal base. Owned by snake-man Rom Whitaker and writer Janaki Lenin, it's packed with wildlife (you can help track the local leopard), and has three simple, comfy bamboo huts on stilts.

Some visitors make a taxi day trip to Vedanthangal from Mamallapuram, for around ₹2200. On public transport, first go to Chengalpattu, an hour's bus ride from Mamallapuram en route to Kanchipuram, then take a bus to Vedanthangal via Padalam (possibly changing buses again). Most Vedanthangal buses go to the sanctuary entrance, but some stop at the village bus station, 1km away.

Shiva under a mango tree here. In a courtyard behind the inner sanctum you can see a mango tree said to be 2500 years old, with four branches representing the four Vedas (sacred Hindu texts).

Tamil Nadu is home to three more of South India's five elemental Shiva temples: Arunachaleshwar Temple in Tiruvannamalai (fire), Nataraja Temple in Chidambaram (space) and Sri Jambukeshwara Temple in Trichy (water). The fifth is Sri Kalahasteeswara Temple (air), in Andhra Pradesh.

Kamakshi Amman Temple   HINDU TEMPLE

(◉5.30am-noon & 4-8pm) This imposing temple, dedicated to Kamakshi/Parvati, is one of India's most important places of *shakti* (female energy/deities) worship, said to mark the spot where Parvati's midriff fell to earth. It's thought to have been founded by the Pallavas. The entire main building inside is off-limits to non-Hindus, but the small, square marriage hall, to the right inside the temple's southeast entrance, has wonderfully ornate pillars. You might catch the temple elephant giving blessings just inside this entrance.

Each February/March carriages bearing the temple deities are hauled around Kanchipuram.

Varadaraja Perumal Temple   HINDU TEMPLE

(Devarajaswami Temple; 100-pillared hall ₹1, camera/video ₹5/100; ◉7.30am-noon & 3.30-8pm) The enormous 11th-century Chola-built Varadaraja Perumal Temple in southeast Kanchi is dedicated to Vishnu. Non-Hindus cannot enter the central compound, but the artistic highlight is the 16th-century '100-pillared' marriage hall, just inside the western entrance. Its pillars (actually 96) are superbly carved with animals and monsters; at its corners hang four stone chains, each carved from a single ro ck.

Every 40 years the waters of the temple tank are drained, revealing a huge wooden statue of Vishnu that is worshipped for 48 days. Next viewing: 2019.

Volunteering

RIDE   VOLUNTEERING

(Rural Institute for Development Education; ☏044-27268223; www.rideindia.org; 48 Periyar Nagar, Little Kanchipuram) Kanchipuram's famous silk-weaving industry has traditionally depended heavily on child labour. The NGO RIDE has been a leader in reducing the industry's child labour numbers from over 40,000 in 1997 to less than 1000 by 2010 (by its own estimates), and empowering the rural poor. It welcomes volunteers (one week minimum); pay between ₹3500 and ₹7000 per week for food and accommodation.

Tours

RIDE offers fascinating, original **tours** (per person incl lunch half/full day ₹600/900) covering diverse themes from silk weaving and

Kanchipuram

0 — 400 m
0 — 0.2 miles

Kanchipuram

◉ **Sights**
1 Ekambareshwara Temple.................... A1
2 Kamakshi Amman Temple A1

◉ **Sleeping**
3 GRT Regency... B3
4 Sree Sakthi Residency B2

◉ **Eating**
Dakshin .... (see 3)
Sangeetha Restaurant .... (see 4)
5 Saravana Bhavan A2

◉ **Information**
6 Axis Bank ATM B3
7 State Bank of India ATM B2

temples to Indian cookery classes with market visits.

🛏 Sleeping & Eating

RIDE   GUESTHOUSE $
(Rural Institute for Development Education; ☑ 044-27268223; www.rideindia.org; 48 Periyar Nagar, Little Kanchipuram; per person ₹750; ❉) This NGO has simple, clean rooms for travellers at its base in a residential area 5km southeast of Kanchipuram centre (signposted from the main road 1km past Varadaraja Perumal Temple). If it's quiet, the friendly owners put you up in their own colourful home next door. Home-cooked lunch and dinner are available (₹250). Book a day ahead.

GRT Regency   HOTEL $$
(☑ 044-27225250; www.grthotels.com; 487 Gandhi Rd; s/d incl breakfast ₹3420/4200; ❉ 🖥) The GRT has the cleanest and comfiest rooms you'll find in Kanchi, boasting marble floors and tea/coffee makers. The hotel's Dakshin (mains ₹190-400; ⊙7am-11pm) restaurant is a tad overpriced but offers a big multicuisine menu including breakfast omelettes, good seafood and tasty tandoori.

Sree Sakthi Residency   HOTEL $$
(☑ 044-27233799; www.sreesakthiresidency.com; 71 Nellukara St; s ₹1560-1800, d ₹1920-2160; ❉ 🖥) Simple blonde-wood furniture and coloured walls make the clean rooms fairly modern; the 'premiums' were new in 2014. The ground-floor Sangeetha Restaurant (71 Nellukara St; mains ₹85-135; ⊙6am-10.30pm) does good vegetarian food.

Saravana Bhavan   SOUTH INDIAN $$
(66 Nellukara St; mains ₹80-200, meals ₹80-110; ⊙6am-10.30pm) A reliable veg restaurant with a welcome AC hall, and thalis on the 1st floor.

ℹ Information

Web Space (Ulagalandhar Mada Veedhi; per hour ₹30; ⊙10am-10pm)

ℹ Getting There & Away

Suburban trains to Kanchipuram (₹25, 2½ hours) leave Chennai's Egmore station (platform 10) six to eight times daily. A full-day taxi from Mamallapuram costs around ₹1800.

The busy bus stand is in the centre of town. Departures include:

Chennai (₹47, two hours, every five minutes 4am to 10pm)

Mamallapuram (₹41, two hours, eight daily)

Puducherry (₹75, three hours, 15 daily)

Tiruvannamalai (₹65, three hours, hourly 5am to 8.30pm)

Vellore (₹41, two hours, every five minutes 4am to 10.30pm)

ℹ Getting Around

Bicycle hire (per hour ₹5) is available at stalls around the bus stand. An autorickshaw for a half-day tour of the five main temples (₹400 to ₹500) will inevitably involve stopping at a silk shop.

Vellore

☑ 0416 / POP 185,803

For a dusty bazaar town, Vellore feels a bit cosmopolitan, thanks to a couple of tertiary institutions and the American-founded Christian Medical College (CMC), one of India's finest hospitals, attracting both medical students and patients from across the country. On the main Chennai–Bengaluru road, Vellore is worth a stop mainly for its massive Vijayanagar fort. Many Indians come to visit the golden Sripuram Temple 10km south of town.

Central Vellore is bounded on the north by Ida Scudder Rd (Arcot Rd), home to the hospital and cheap hotels and eateries; and on the west by Officer's Line (Anna Salai), with Vellore Fort on its west side.

◎ Sights

Vellore Fort   FORT
A circuit of the moat-surrounded ramparts (nearly 2km) of Vellore's splendid fort is the most peaceful experience in town. The fort was built in the 16th century and passed through Maratha and Mughal hands before the British occupied it in 1760. These days it houses, among other things, the magnificent Vijayanagar-era Jalakantesvara Temple, two museums, two parade grounds, a church, government offices, and a police recruiting school.

Inside, the Jalakantesvara Temple (⊙6.30am-1pm & 3-8.30pm), a gem of late Vijayanagar architecture, dates from around 1566, and was once occupied as a garrison. Check out the small, detailed sculptures – especially the *yali* (mythical lion creatures) – on the walls and columns of the marriage hall in the southwest corner. The dusty exhibits in the Government Museum (Indian/foreigner ₹5/100; ⊙9.30am-5pm Sat-Thu) have seen better days, but the Archaeological Survey Museum (⊙9am-5pm Sat-Thu) FREE has a good collection of Pallava, Chola and Nayak stone sculptures, plus displays on the 1806 Vellore Mutiny, the earliest anti-British uprising by Indian troops. Next door, pretty **St John's Church** (1846) opens only for Sunday services.

🛏 Sleeping & Eating

Vellore's cheap hotels are concentrated along Ida Scudder Rd and in the busy, narrow streets just south. The cheapest are pretty grim; the better ones fill up fast.

Hotel Solai HOTEL $

(☑0416-2222996; hotelsolai@gmail.com; 26 Babu Rao St; s/d ₹380/660, with AC ₹715/1056; ❄) If you can get a room, this newish hotel near the hospital is probably the best value, with

clean rooms, reasonably airy walkways, enthusiastic staff, and a back-up generator.

GRT Regency Sameera HOTEL $$

(☑0416-2206466; www.grthotels.com; 145 Green Circle, New Bypass Rd; incl breakfast s ₹3600-5700, d ₹4440-5700; ❄🛜) Mirrored cupboards, in-room tea/coffee sets, and splashes of colour make the GRT's smart modern rooms pretty characterful, for Vellore. The free wi-fi, two restaurants, and 24-hour cafe are extra bonuses. It's 1.5km north of central Vellore, near the Chennai–Bengaluru road (surprisingly not too noisy).

Darling Residency HOTEL $$

(☑0416-2213001; www.darlingresidency.com; 11/8 Officer's Line; incl breakfast s ₹2400-2640, d ₹2760-3000; ❄@🛜) It's not five-star, but

TAMIL NADU & CHENNAI VELLORE

TAMIL NADU TEMPLES

Tamil Nadu is a gold mine for anyone wanting to explore Indian temple culture. Not only does it have some of the country's most spectacular temple architecture and sculpture, but few parts of India are as fervent in their worship of the Hindu gods as Tamil Nadu. Its 5000-odd temples are constantly abuzz with worshippers flocking in for *puja* (offering or prayer), and colourful temple festivals abound. Among the plethora of Hindu deities, Shiva probably has most Tamil temples dedicated to him, in a multitude of forms including Nataraja, the cosmic dancer, who dances in a ring of fire with two of his four hands holding the flame of destruction and the drum of creation, while the third makes the *abhaya mudra* (fear not) gesture and the fourth points to the dwarf of ignorance being trampled beneath Shiva's foot. Tamils also have a soft spot for Shiva's peacock-riding son Murugan (also Kartikeya or Skanda), who is intricately associated with their cultural identity.

The special significance of many Tamil temples makes them goals of countless Hindu pilgrims from all over India. The Pancha Sabhai Sthalangal are the five temples where Shiva is believed to have performed his cosmic dance (chief among them Chidambaram). Then there's the Pancha Bootha Sthalangal, the five temples where Shiva is worshipped as one of the five elements – land, water, sky/space, fire and air (this last in Andhra Pradesh). Each of the nine Navagraha temples in the Kumbakonam area is the abode of one of the nine celestial bodies of Hindu astronomy – key sites given the importance of astrology in Hindu faith.

Typical Tamil temple design features tall layered entrance towers called *gopurams*, encrusted with often colourfully painted sculptures of gods and demons; halls of richly carved columns called *mandapas;* a sacred water tank; and a series of compounds *(prakarams),* one within the next, with the innermost containing the central sanctum where the temple's main deity resides. The earliest Tamil temples were small rock-cut shrines; the first free-standing temples were built in the 8th century AD; *gopurams* first appeared around the 12th century.

Admission to most temples is free, but non-Hindus are often not allowed inside inner sanctums, which can be disappointing for travellers. At other temples priests may invite you in and in no time you are doing *puja,* having an auspicious *tilak* mark daubed on your forehead and being asked for a donation.

Temple touts can be a nuisance, but there are also many excellent guides who deserve both your time and rupees; use your judgement, talk to other travellers and be on the lookout for badge-wearing official guides.

A South Indian Journey by Michael Wood is a great read if you're interested in Tamil culture. **TempleNet** (www.templenet.com) is one of the best online resources.

rooms are clean and comfortable if forgettable (those at the back are quieter), reception is friendly and the hotel's four restaurants include the cool, breezy **Aaranya Roof Garden Restaurant** (mains ₹150-250; ☺11.30am-11pm). It's 1.5km south of Vellore Fort entrance.

Hotel Arthy   INDIAN **$**
(Ida Scudder Rd; dishes ₹50-70, meals ₹70-85; ☺6am-10.30pm) Cheap veg restaurants line Ida Scudder Rd, but this is one of the cleanest and most popular, with tasty North and South Indian favourites including good thalis, cheap, yummy biryani, and enough dosas to last you a lifetime.

❶ Information

Canara Bank ATM (Officer's Line) Opposite Vellore Fort entrance.

Sri Apollo (Ida Scudder Rd; internet per hour ₹30; ☺8.30am-9pm)

State Bank of India ATM (Officer's Line) About 700m south of Vellore Fort entrance.

❶ Getting There & Away

BUS

Buses use the New bus stand, 1.5km north of central Vellore. Departures include:

Bengaluru (₹138, five hours, every 30 minutes)

Chennai (AC Volvo buses ₹160, 2½ hours, hourly; other buses ₹81, three hours, every 10 minutes)

Kanchipuram (₹47, two hours, every 10 minutes)

Tiruvannamalai (₹50, two hours, every 10 minutes)

TRAIN

Vellore's main station is 5km north at Katpadi. There are at least 20 daily superfast or express trains to/from Chennai Central (2nd class/AC chair ₹90/305, 1½ to 2¼ hours) and 10 to/from Bengaluru's Bangalore City station (₹115/415, three to five hours). Buses 1 and 2 shuttle between the station and town.

Tiruvannamalai

📞 04175 / POP 145,278

There are temple towns, there are mountain towns, and then there are temple-mountain towns where God appears as a phallus of fire. Welcome to Tiruvannamalai, one of Tamil Nadu's holiest destinations. Set below boulder-strewn Mt Arunachala, this is one of South India's five 'elemental' cities of Shiva; here the god is worshipped in his fire

incarnation as Arunachaleshwar. At every full moon 'Tiru' swells with thousands of pilgrims who come to circumnavigate the base of Arunachala in a purifying ritual known as Girivalam, but at any time you'll see Shaivite priests, sadhus (spiritual men) and devotees gathered around the Arunachaleshwar Temple. Tiru's reputation for strong spiritual energies has produced numerous ashrams, and it now attracts ever-growing numbers of spiritual-minded travellers. Around the main cluster of ashrams, on and near Chengam Rd about 2km southwest of the centre, you'll find a few chilled-out cafes and the better sleeping options.

◉ Sights & Activities

⭐**Arunachaleshwar Temple**   HINDU TEMPLE
(Annamalaiyar Temple; www.arunachaleswarar.com; ☺5.30am-12.30pm & 4-9pm) This 10-hectare temple is one of the largest in India. Its oldest parts date back to the 9th century and the site was a place of worship long before that. Four huge, unpainted white *gopurams* mark the entrances, with the main, eastern one rising 13 storeys and an astonishing 66m. During festivals the Arunachaleshwar is awash in golden flames and the roasting scent of burning ghee, as befits the fire incarnation of the Destroyer of the Universe.

Inside the complex are five more *gopurams,* a 1000-pillared hall with impressive carvings, two tanks and a profusion of sub-temples and shrines. There's a helpful temple model inside the second *gopuram* from the east, where the temple elephant gives blessings. To reach the innermost sanctum, with its huge lingam, worshippers must pass through five surrounding *prakarams* (compounds).

Mt Arunachala   MOUNTAIN
This 800m-high extinct volcano dominates Tiruvannamalai and local conceptions of the element of fire, which supposedly finds its sacred abode in Arunachala's heart. Devout barefoot pilgrims, especially on full-moon and festival days, make the 14km circumambulation of the mountain, stopping at eight famous linga along the route. The inner path was closed at research time, but it's still possible to circle around on the main road, or climb the hill past two caves where Sri Ramana Maharshi lived and meditated from 1899 to 1922.

The hot ascent to the top opens up superb views of Tiruvannamalai, and takes five or six hours round-trip: start early and take water.

An unsigned path across the road from the northwest corner of Arunachaleshwar Temple leads the way up past homes and the two caves, Virupaksha (about 20 minutes up) and Skandasramam (30 minutes). Women are advised not to do the hike alone.

If you aren't that devoted, buy a Giripradakshina map (₹15) from the bookshop at Sri Ramana Ashram (p357), hire a bicycle on the roadside nearby (per day ₹40), and ride your way around. Or make an autorickshaw circuit for about ₹250 (up to double at busy times).

Sri Ramana Ashram
ASHRAM

(Sri Ramanasramam; ☎9244937292; www.sriramanamaharshi.org; Chengam Rd; ⊙office 7.30am-12.30pm & 2-6.30pm) This tranquil ashram, 2km southwest of the centre in green grounds filled with peacocks, draws devotees of Sri Ramana Maharshi, one of the first Hindu gurus to gain an international following, who died here in 1950 after half a century in contemplation. Visitors can meditate or attend daily *pujas* (prayers) and chantings, mostly in the samadhi hall where the guru's body is enshrined.

A limited amount of free accommodation (donations accepted; three to four weeks) is available for devotees only: write or email a month ahead.

Sri Seshadri Swamigal Ashram
ASHRAM

(☎04175-236999; www.tiruvarunaimahan.org; Chengam Rd; ⊙office 9am-1pm & 4-8.30pm) Dedicated to a contemporary and helper of Sri Ramana, with meditation platforms and some accommodation. It's in the southwest of town next to Sri Ramana Ashram.

Sri Anantha Niketan
ASHRAM

(☎09003480013; www.sriananthaniketan.com; Periya Paliyapattu Village; admission by donation) A place for organised retreats rather than a permanent community, Sri Anantha Niketan has tree-shaded grounds, wonderful Arunachala views, homey rooms and weekend chanting in an attractive meditation hall. It's just off the Krishnagiri road, 7km west of town. Book well ahead for November to February.

🛏 Sleeping & Eating

Most visitors stay in the less hectic Chengam Rd area, but there are also typical temple-town options near the Arunachaleshwar Temple. During Karthikai Deepam (November/December) prices can multiply several times. Hotels get heavily booked at full moon.

Hill View Residency
HOTEL $

(☎9442712441; hillviewresidency@gmail.com; 120 Seshatri Mada St; r from ₹400, with AC from ₹800) Extremely good value, Hill View has large, clean, cool, marble-floored rooms around two small garden patios, up a lane off Chengam Rd, but limited English is spoken (so booking ahead is tricky). Upstairs under a big palm roof, Tasty Café (dishes ₹70-170; ⊙8am-10pm) does well-prepared Indian and Continental food.

Arunachala Ramana Home
HOTEL $

(☎9486722892; www.arunachalaramanahome.co.in; 70 Ramana Nagar; s/d ₹500/600, with AC d ₹1200; ❄) Basic, clean and friendly, this popular place is down a lane off Chengam Rd.

Sunshine Guest House
GUESTHOUSE $$

(☎04175-235335; http://sunshineguesthouseindia.com; 5 Annamalai Nagar, Perumbakkam Rd; s/d ₹500/700, with AC ₹1400/1970; ❄🛜) In a blissfully quiet spot 1km southwest of the main ashram area, this colourful new-build fronted by pretty gardens offers excellent value. Simple but tasteful, spotless rooms, each done up after a different Hindu god, feel like walking into an Indian trinkets shop: print-design sheets, sequined fabrics,

---

THE LINGAM OF FIRE

Legend has it Shiva appeared as the original lingam of fire on Mt Arunachala to restore light to the world after his consort Parvati playfully plunged everything into darkness by closing his eyes. The Karthikai Deepam Festival (statewide; ⊙Nov/Dec) celebrates this legend throughout India but becomes particularly significant at Tiruvannamalai. The lighting of a huge fire atop Mt Arunachala on the full moon night, from a 30m wick immersed in 3 tonnes of ghee, culminates a 10-day festival for which hundreds of thousands of people converge on Tiruvannamalai. Huge crowds scale the mountain or circumnavigate its base, chanting Shiva's name. The sun is relentless, the rocks are jagged and the journey is barefoot – none of which deters the thousands of pilgrims who joyfully make their way to the top and the abode of their deity.

dangling cane chairs, and in-room water filters. Fresh breakfasts cost ₹150.

Hotel Arunachala   HOTEL **$$**
(Arunachala Inn; ☑04175-228300; www.hotelarun achala.in; 5 Vada Sannathi St; s/d ₹500/990, with AC ₹1125/1690, deluxe d ₹2250; 🕸) This place right next to the Arunachaleshwar Temple's east entrance is clean and fine with pretentions to luxury in the marblesque floors, ugly furniture, and keen management. Best are the recently revamped 'deluxe' rooms. Pure-veg **Hotel Sri Arul Jothi** (dishes ₹40-80; ☺5.30am-10.30pm) downstairs has good South Indian dishes, including thalis (₹80 to ₹100).

★ **Dreaming Tree**   CAFE, ORGANIC **$$**
(☑8870057753; www.dreamingtree.in; Ramana Nagar; mains ₹150-250; ☺9am-4.30pm Mon-Sat) 🍃 Superchilled Dreaming Tree dishes out huge portions of exquisite, health-focused veg fare, prepped with mostly organic ingredients, on a breezy hut-like rooftop with hammocks. Fabulous 'hippie salads' and grilled paneer-veg baguettes, good breakfasts, and all kinds of cakes, juices, lassis and organic coffees. Signs lead the way (about 500m) across the road from Sri Ramana Ashram.

Shanti Café   CAFE **$$**
(www.shanticafe.com; 115A Chengam Rd; dishes ₹60-200, drinks ₹30-70; ☺8.30am-8.30pm) This popular and relaxed cafe with floor-cushion seating, up a lane off Chengam Rd, serves wonderful croissants, cakes, baguettes, pancakes, juices, coffees and breakfasts. There's an **internet cafe** (per hour ₹25; ☺8.30am-1.30pm & 3-7pm Mon-Sat) downstairs.

🔒 Shopping

Shantimalai Handicrafts Development Society   HANDICRAFTS
(www.smhds.org; 83/1 Chengam Rd; ☺9am-7pm Mon-Sat) Beautiful bedspreads, incense, oils, bangles, scarves and cards, all made by local village women.

ⓘ Getting There & Around

A taxi to Puducherry with a two- to three-hour stop at Gingee costs around ₹2800.

The bus stand is 800m north of the Arunachaleshwar Temple, and a ₹50 to ₹60 autorickshaw ride from the main ashram area.

Chennai (₹110, four hours, every 15 minutes)
Puducherry (₹63, three hours, about hourly)
Trichy (₹125, six hours, about hourly)
Vellore (₹50, two hours, every 15 minutes)

Gingee (Senji)

With three separate hilltop citadels and a 6km perimeter of cliffs and thick walls, the ruins of enormous **Gingee Fort** (☑04145-222072; Indian/foreigner ₹5/100; ☺8am-5pm) rise out of the Tamil plain, 37km east of Tiruvannamalai, like something misplaced from *The Lord of the Rings*. The fort was constructed mainly in the 16th century by the Vijayanagars and later occupied by the Marathas, Mughals, French and the British before being abandoned in the 19th century.

Today, few foreigners make it here, but Gingee is popular with domestic tourists for its starring role in various films. The main road from Tiruvannamalai towards Puducherry slices through the fort, just before Gingee town. The easiest citadel to reach, **Krishnagiri**, lies north of the road. To the south are the highest of the three, **Rajagiri**, and the most distant and least interesting, **Chakklidurg**. Ticket offices are at the foot of Krishnagiri and Rajagiri.

Remains of numerous buildings stand in the site's lower parts, especially at the bottom of Rajagiri, where the main landmark of the old palace area is the white, restored, seven-storey **Kalyana Mahal** (Marriage Hall). Just east of the palace area is an 18th-century **mosque**; southeast of that is the abandoned 16th-century **Venkataramana Temple**.

It's a good hike to the top of Krishnagiri and even more so to the top of more popular Rajagiri (over 150m above the plain), and you need at least half a day to cover both hills. Start early and bring water; hill-climbing entry ends at 2.30pm.

Gingee is on the Tiruvannamalai–Puducherry bus route, with buses from Tiruvannamalai (₹23, one hour) about every 15 minutes. Get off at the fort to save a trip back out from Gingee town.

Puducherry (Pondicherry)

☑0413 / POP 244,377

Puducherry (formerly called Pondicherry and generally referred to as 'Pondy') was under French rule until 1954 and some people here still speak French (and English with French accents). Hotels, restaurants and 'lifestyle' shops sell a seductive vision of the French-subcontinental aesthetic, enhanced by Gallic creative types whose presence has in turn attracted Indian artists and designers. Thus Pondy's vibe: less faded colonial-era *ville,* more a bohemian-chic, New Age-cum–Old World hang-out on the international travel trail.

If you've come from Chennai or some of Tamil Nadu's inland cities, Pondy may well seem a sea of tranquility. The older part of this former French colony (where you'll probably spend most of your time) is full of quiet, clean, shady cobbled streets, lined with bougainvillea-draped colonial-era townhouses numbered in an almost logical manner. The newer side of town is typically, hectically South Indian.

Part of the vibe stems from the presence of the internationally famous Sri Aurobindo Ashram and its offshoot just out of town, Auroville, which draw large numbers of spiritually minded visitors.

Enjoy the shopping, the French food (hello steak!), the beer (*au revoir* Tamil Nadu alcohol taxes – Pondy is a Union Territory), the sea air and plenty of yoga and meditation.

Puducherry is split from north to south by a partially covered canal. The 'French' part of town is on the east side (towards the sea). Nehru (JN) St and Lal Bahadur Shastri St (Rue Bussy) are the main east–west streets; Mahatma Gandhi (MG) Rd and Mission St (Cathedral St) are the chief north–south thoroughfares. Many streets change names as they go along and often have English, French and Tamil names simultaneously.

⊙ Sights

★ **French Quarter**   NEIGHBOURHOOD

Pocketed away just behind the seafront is a series of cobbled streets, white-and-mustard buildings in various states of romantic dishevelment, and a slight sense of Gallic glory gone by, otherwise known as the French Quarter. A do-it-yourself heritage walk could start at the **French Consulate** (☑0413-2231000; 2 Marine St) near the north end of seafront Goubert Ave, then gradually head south.

Turn inland south of the French Consulate to shady **Bharathi Park**, with the neoclassical governor's residence, **Raj Nivas**, facing its north side. Return to the seafront at the **Gandhi Memorial**, pass the **Hôtel de Ville** (City Hall) and then potter south through the 'white town' – Dumas, Romain Rolland, Suffren and Labourdonnais Sts. Towards the southern end of Dumas St, wander into the beautiful **École Française D'Extrême-Orient**. A lot of restoration has been going on in this area: if you're interested in Pondy's architectural heritage check out **Intach Pondicherry** (www.intachpondicherry.org).

Seafront   PROMENADE

(Goubert Ave) Pondy is a seaside town, but that doesn't make it a beach destination; the city's sand is a thin strip of dirty brown that slurps into a seawall of jagged rocks. But Goubert Ave (Beach Rd) is a killer stroll, especially at dawn and dusk when half the town takes a romantic wander there. In a stroke of genius the city council has banned traffic here from 6pm to 7.30am.

There are a few sandy beaches north and south of town, but they aren't good for sunbathing due to crowds of men, and possible undertow or rip tides make swimming risky.

Sri Aurobindo Ashram   ASHRAM

(www.sriaurobindoashram.org; Marine St; ⊗general visits 8am-noon & 2-6pm) Founded in 1926 by Sri Aurobindo and a French-born woman known as 'the Mother', this spiritual community now has about 1200 members working in its many departments. Aurobindo's teachings focus on an 'integral yoga' as the path towards a 'supramental consciousness which will divinise human nature'; devotees work in the world, rather than retreating from it. General visits to the main ashram building are cursory – you just see the flower-festooned samadhi of Aurobindo and the Mother, then the bookshop, then you leave.

Ashram accommodation guests can access other areas and activities. Evening meditation around the samadhi is open to people with passes – which you can only get if you're staying at an ashram guesthouse or from the ashram's **Bureau Central** (☑0413-2233604; bureaucentral@sriaurobindoashram.org; Ambour Salai; ⊗6-7.30am, 9am-noon & 3-7pm), where there are also interesting exhibitions on Sri Aurobindo and the Mother.

Sri Manakula
Vinayagar Temple   HINDU TEMPLE

(Manakula Vinayagar Koil St; ⊗5.45am-12.30pm & 4-9pm) Pondy may have more churches than most towns, but this is still India, and the Hindu faith reigns supreme. Don't miss the chance to watch tourists, pilgrims and the curious get a head pat from the temple elephant at this temple dedicated to Ganesh, which also contains over 40 painted friezes.

Puducherry Museum   MUSEUM

(St Louis St; Indian/foreigner ₹10/50; ⊗10am-1pm & 2-5pm Tue-Sun) God knows how this cute

Puducherry (Pondicherry)

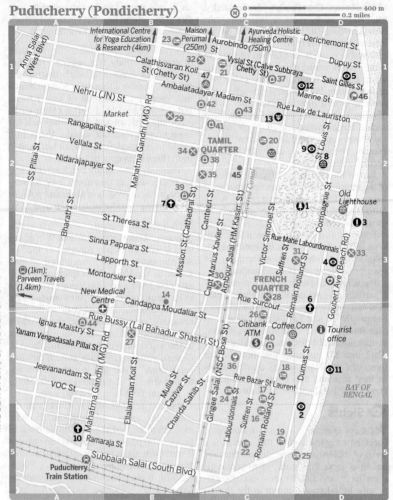

little museum keeps its artefacts from disintegrating, considering there's a whole floor of French-era furniture sitting in the South Indian humidity. On the ground floor look especially for the Chola, Vijayanagar and Nayak bronzes, and the pieces of ancient Greek and Spanish pottery and amphorae (storage vessels) excavated from Arikamedu, a once-major trading port just south of Puducherry. Upstairs is Governor Dupleix' bed.

Institut Français de Pondichéry LIBRARY
(☏ 0413-2231609; www.ifpindia.org; 11 St Louis St; ☺ 9am-1pm & 2-5.30pm Mon-Fri) This grand

neoclassical colonial-era building is also a flourishing research institution devoted to Indian culture, history and ecology. Visitors can browse books in the beach-facing library.

Activities

Sita ARTS, COOKING
(☏ 0413-4200718; www.pondicherry-arts.com; 22 Candappa Moudaliar St; classes ₹300-1000) This energetic Franco-Indian cultural centre runs a host of activities, which visitors can join (even for just a single session): Indian or

Puducherry (Pondicherry)

French cooking, *bharatanatyam* or Bollywood dance, Tamil language, *kolam* making, *mehndi* (henna 'tattoos'), yoga, pilates, ayurveda and more.

Kallialay Surf School SURFING
(☏ 9442992874; www.surfschoolindia.com; Serenity Beach, Tandriankuppam; 1hr private class ₹1400, board rental per 90min ₹400-600) Surfing is soaring in popularity along Tamil Nadu's coast, and this long-standing, well-equipped, Spanish-run school, 5km north of Puducherry, offers everything from beginner sessions to intensive 'surf camps'.

Yoga & Ayurveda
You can practise (and study) yoga at Sri Aurobindo Ashram (p359) and Auroville. Sita offers yoga, ayurvedic massages, and courses in practising ayurveda.

International Centre for Yoga Education & Research YOGA
(Ananda Ashram; ☏ 0413-2241561; www.icyer.com; 16A Mettu St, Chinnamudaliarchavady, Kottukuppam) Annual six-month yoga-teacher-training and 10-lesson, one-to-one introductory courses (₹8000).

ⓕ Tours
A wonderful way to see Pondy is with Sita's popular early-morning guided **bicycle tours** (per person from ₹1200), which include breakfast.

Shanti Travel (p365) offers recommended two-hour **walking tours** (per person ₹500) of Puducherry that are available with either English- or French-speaking guides.

PUDUCHERRY'S CATHEDRALS

Pondy has one of the best collections of over-the-top cathedrals in India. *Merci*, French missionaries. **Our Lady of Immaculate Conception Cathedral** (Mission St; ☉7-11am & 4-8.30pm), completed in 1791, is a robin's-egg-blue-and-cloud-white typically Jesuit edifice in a Goa-like Portuguese style, while the brown-and-white grandiosity of the **Sacred Heart Basilica** (Subbayah Salai; ☉7-11am & 4-8.30pm) is set off by stained glass and a Gothic sense of proportion. The twin towers and dome of the mellow-pink-and-cream **Notre Dame des Anges** (Dumas St; ☉6-10am & 4-7pm), built in the 1850s, look sublime in the late-afternoon light. The smooth limestone interior was made using eggshell plaster.

⚡ Festivals & Events

International Yoga Festival   YOGA
(☉4-7 Jan) Puducherry's ashrams and yoga culture are put on show with workshops, demonstrations and competitions, attracting experts from all over India and beyond.

Bastille Day   PARADE
(☉14 Jul) Street parades and a bit of French pomp and ceremony are part of the fun at this celebration.

🛏 Sleeping

If you've been saving for a splurge, this is the place for it: Puducherry's lodgings are as good as South India gets. Local heritage houses combine colonial-era romanticism with comfort and, dare we say, French playfulness. Most of these rooms would cost five times as much back in Europe. Book ahead for weekends.

Sri Aurobindo Ashram (p359) runs several simple but clean guesthouses. They're primarily intended for ashram guests, but many accept other travellers willing to follow their rules: 10.30pm curfew and no smoking, alcohol or drugs. The ashram's Bureau Central (p359) has a list.

Kailash Guest House   GUESTHOUSE $
(☎0413-2224485; http://kailashguesthouse.in; 43 Vysial St; s/d ₹800/1000, with AC d ₹1250; ☀) The best value for money in this price range, Kailash has simple, superclean rooms with well

mosquito-proofed windows, friendly management, and superb city views from the top floors. It's geared to traveller needs, with loungey communal areas, clothes-drying facilities, and a bar on the way.

Park Guest House   ASHRAM GUESTHOUSE $
(☎0413-2233644; parkgh@sriaurobindoashram.org; 1 Goubert Ave; r ₹800, with AC ₹900; ☀) The most sought-after ashram guesthouse in town thanks to its wonderful seafront position. All front rooms face the sea and have a porch or balcony, and there's a garden for yoga or meditation. The best-value AC rooms around, but no advance bookings.

International Guest House   ASHRAM GUESTHOUSE $
(☎0413-2336699; ingh@aurosociety.org; 47 NSC Bose St; s/d ₹500/650, with AC ₹700/1050; ☀) The sparse, clean rooms here, adorned with a single photo of the Mother, make for good-value ashram lodgings. Predictably it's very popular: book three weeks ahead.

★ Les Hibiscus   GUESTHOUSE $$
(☎9442066763, 0413-2227480; www.leshibiscus.in; 49 Suffren St; s/d incl breakfast ₹2400/2700; ☀@☎) A strong contender for our favourite Tamil Nadu hotel, Hibiscus has just four pristine, high-ceilinged rooms with gorgeous antique beds, coffee-makers and a mix of quaint Indian art and old-Pondy photos, at incredibly reasonable prices. The whole place is immaculately tasteful, breakfast is fabulous, internet is free and management is genuinely friendly and helpful. Make sure you book ahead.

Gratitude   GUESTHOUSE $$
(☎0413-2225029; www.gratitudeheritage.in; 52 Romain Rolland St; s ₹3375-5510, d ₹4240-6470, all incl breakfast; ☀☎) A wonderfully tranquil 19th-century house (no TVs, no children) with welcoming staff, sun-yellow Gratitude has been painstakingly restored to a state probably even more charming than the original. The nine spotless, individually styled rooms are spread over two floors around a tropically shaded courtyard. There's a lovely roof terrace for yoga and massages.

Maison Tamoule   HERITAGE HOTEL $$
(☎0413-2223738; www.neemranahotels.com; 44 Vysial St; r incl breakfast ₹3220-5370; ☀☎) The old Tamil Quarter has almost as many mansions as the French Quarter but is off most tourists' radars. Reincarnated under efficient new management, this excellent

heritage choice, on a quiet, tree-shaded street, mixes a soaring sense of space with a sunken teak-columned atrium, gorgeous Chettinad-tiled floors, and 10 elegantly styled rooms featuring big bath tubs (though single beds are a tad small).

Hotel de Pondichéry HERITAGE HOTEL $$
(☎0413-2227409; www.hoteldepondicherry.com; 38 Dumas St; incl breakfast s ₹2000, d ₹3000-5000; ❋🛜) A colourful heritage spot with 14 comfy, quiet, high-ceilinged, colonial-style rooms and a dash of original modern art. Their excellent restaurant, Le Club, takes up the pretty front courtyard. Staff are lovely and there's free wi-fi in the lobby.

**Coloniale Heritage
Guest House** GUESTHOUSE $$
(☎0413-2224720; www.colonialeheritage.com; 54 Romain Rolland St; r incl breakfast ₹2000-3300; ❋🛜) This colonial-era home with six comfy rooms (some up steep stairs) is chock-full of character thanks to the owner's amazing collection of gem-studded Tanjore paintings, Ravi Varma lithographs and other 19th- and 20th-century South Indian art. One room even has a swing. Breakfast is served in a sunken patio beside the leafy garden.

Nilla Guesthouse GUESTHOUSE $$
(☎9994653006; www.nillaguesthouse.com; 18 Labourdonnais St; r ₹1500-2100; ❋🛜) A simple but brilliantly characterful and well-kept home run by a welcoming host, with just five fresh, colourful, heritage-style rooms, handy communal kitchens, and free wi-fi in the loungey terrace area.

★Villa Shanti HERITAGE HOTEL $$$
(☎0413-4200028; www.lavillashanti.com; 14 Suffren St; r incl breakfast ₹7870-10,117; ❋🛜) Set in a 100-year-old building revamped by two French architects, Villa Shanti puts an exquisitely contemporary twist on the traditional Pondy heritage hotel. Beautiful fresh rooms combine super-chic design with typically Tamil materials and colonial-style elegance: four-poster beds, Chettinadu tiles, Tamil murals. The courtyard houses a popular restaurant and cocktail bar, so book upper-floor beds for early snoozing.

Maison Perumal HERITAGE HOTEL $$$
(☎0413-2227519; www.cghearth.com; 44 Perumal Koil St; r incl breakfast ₹8360-10,450; ❋🛜) Cool peaceful rooms with colourful flourishes sit above two pillared patios in this renovated 130-year-old building lined with photos of old Chettiar families and pocketed away in Pondy's less touristic Tamil Quarter. The excellent Tamil/French restaurant (dinner ₹990, lunch mains ₹275-400; ⏱12.30-2pm & 7.30-10.30pm) cooks everything from market-fresh ingredients, and staff are delightful. From March to October rates dip by 30%.

Hotel De L'Orient HERITAGE HOTEL $$$
(☎0413-2343067; www.neemranahotels.com; 17 Romain Rolland St; r incl breakfast ₹3760-8060; ❋🛜) This grand restored 18th-century mansion has breezy verandahs, keen staff, and charming rooms in all shapes and sizes, kitted out with antique furniture; some are cosy attics, others palatial. A place to get that old Pondy feel while enjoying polished service and French, Italian or creole (French-Indian) food in the courtyard Carte Blanche Restaurant (mains ₹300-580; ⏱7.30-10.30am, noon-3pm & 7-9.30pm).

✕ Eating

Puducherry is a culinary highlight of Tamil Nadu; you get great South Indian cooking plus well-prepped French and Italian cuisine. If you've been missing cheese or have a craving for pâté, you're in luck, and *everyone* in the French Quarter does good brewed coffee and crepes.

Baker Street CAFE $
(123 Rue Bussy; items ₹40-130; ⏱7am-9pm; 🛜) A popular upmarket, French-style bakery with delectable cakes, croissants and biscuits. Baguettes, brownies and quiches aren't bad either. Eat in or take away.

Indian Coffee House SOUTH INDIAN $
(125 Nehru St; dishes ₹30-60; ⏱6.30am-10pm) Snack to your heart's content on cheap, South Indian favourites – dosas, *vadas, uttapams* and ₹15 filter coffee – at this Pondy institution. It's also, incidentally, where Yann Martel's novel *Life of Pi* begins.

Surguru SOUTH INDIAN $
(235 (old 99) Mission St; mains ₹70-120; ⏱7am-10.30pm) Simple South Indian in a relatively posh setting. Surguru is the fix for thali (lunchtime only) and dosa addicts who like their veg with good strong AC.

★La Pasta ITALIAN $$
(☎9994670282; http://lapastapondy.blogspot.com; 55 Vysial St; mains ₹230-350; ⏱noon-2pm & 5-9pm Tue-Sat) Pasta lovers should make a pilgrimage to this little spot with just four

check-cloth tables, where an Italian whips up her own authentically yummy sauces and concocts her own perfect pasta in an open-plan kitchen as big as the dining area. No alcohol: it's all about the food.

Café des Arts CAFE $$
(10 Suffren St; dishes ₹130-230; ⊙8.30am-7pm Wed-Mon; 🛜) This bohemian, vintage-style cafe would look perfectly at home in Europe, but this is Pondy, so there's a cycle-rickshaw in the garden. Refreshingly light dishes range from crisp salads, baguettes and toasties to crepes, and the coffees and fresh juices are great. The old-townhouse setting is lovely, with low tables and lounge chairs spilling out in front of a quirky boutique.

Kasha Ki Aasha CAFE $$
(23 Rue Surcouf; mains ₹150-250; ⊙10am-8pm Mon-Sat) You'll get a great pancake breakfast, good lunches and delicious cakes on the low-key rooftop of this colonial-era-house-cum-craft-shop-cum-cafe run by an all-female team. Fusion food includes chips with chutney, 'European-style thali' and 'Indian enchilada', and the pretty fabrics and leather sandals downstairs come direct from their makers.

Le Café CAFE $$
(Goubert Ave; dishes ₹50-225; ⊙24hr) This seafront spot is good for baguettes, croissants, salads, cakes and organic South Indian coffee (hot or iced), plus welcome fresh breezes from the Bay of Bengal. It's popular, so you often have to wait for, or share, a table. But hey, it's all about the location.

Le Club CONTINENTAL, INDIAN $$$
(📞 0413-2339745; 38 Dumas St; mains ₹300-500; ⊙noon-3.30pm & 7-11pm Tue-Sun) The steaks (with sauces like blue cheese or Béarnaise), pizzas and crepes are all top-class at this popular romantically lit garden restaurant. Tempting local options include creole prawn curry, veg-paneer kebabs, and Malabar-style fish, and there are plenty of wines, mojitos and margaritas to wash it all down.

Villa Shanti CONTINENTAL, INDIAN $$$
(📞 0413-4200028; 14 Suffren St; mains ₹225-495; ⊙12.30-2.30pm & 7-10.30pm) Smart candle-lit tables in a palm-dotted pillared courtyard attached to a colourful bar create a casually fancy vibe at this stylish, packed-out hotel restaurant. The building's contemporary Franco-Indian flair runs right through the North Indian/European menu and, while

portions are small, flavours are superb and there are some deliciously creative veg dishes. Good cocktails too. Reserve for weekends.

Self-Catering

Nilgiri's SUPERMARKET
(23 Rangapillai St; ⊙9.30am-9pm) Well-stocked AC shop for groceries and toiletries.

🍷 Drinking & Nightlife

Although Pondy is one of the better places in Tamil Nadu to knock back a beer, closing time is a strictly enforced 11pm. Despite low taxes on alcohol, you'll really only find cheap beer in 'liquor shops' and their attached darkened bars. Hotel restaurants and bars make good drinking spots.

L'e-Space BAR, CAFE
(2 Labourdonnais St; cocktails ₹200; ⊙5-11pm) A quirky little semi-open-air upstairs bar-cafe-lounge that's friendly and sociable, and does good cocktails (assuming that the barman hasn't disappeared).

🔒 Shopping

With all the yoga yuppies congregating here, Pondy specialises in the boutique-chic-meets-Indian-bazaar school of fashion and souvenirs, and there's some beautiful and original stuff, a lot of it produced by Sri Aurobindo Ashram or Auroville. Nehru St and MG Rd are the shopping hotspots.

⭐ **Kalki** CLOTHING, ACCESSORIES
(134 Mission St; ⊙9.30am-8.30pm) Gorgeous, jewel-coloured silk and cotton fashions, as well as accessories, incense, essential oils, handmade-paper trinkets and more, mostly made at Auroville, where there's another branch (Visitors Centre; ⊙9.30am-6pm).

Fabindia CLOTHING, TEXTILES
(www.fabindia.com; 223 Mission St; ⊙10.30am-8.30pm) Going strong since 1960, the Fabindia chain stocks stunning handmade products predominantly made by villagers using traditional craft techniques, and promotes rural employment. This branch has a wonderful collection of cotton and silk garments in contemporary Indian style, along with quality fabrics, tablecloths, oils, beauty products, and even furniture.

La Maison Rose CLOTHING, HOMEWARES
(www.lamaisonrosepondicherry.com; 8 Romain Rolland St; ⊙10am-7.30pm) This restored

baby-pink mansion houses three luxurious boutiques packed with exquisite East-meets-West fashion, fabrics, jewellery, homewares and furniture. Flop over fresh juices and French-inspired dishes under the mango tree in the fairy-light-flooded courtyard **cafe-restaurant** (8 Romain Rolland St; mains ₹300-470; ⊙ noon-3pm, 7-10pm).

Auroshikha
INCENSE
(www.auroshikha.com; 28 Marine St; ⊙ 9am-1pm & 3-7pm Tue-Sun) An endless array of incense, perfumed candles and essential oils, made by Sri Aurobindo Ashram.

La Boutique d'Auroville
HANDICRAFTS
(38 Nehru St; ⊙ 9.30am-8pm) It's fun browsing through the crafts here, including jewellery, clothes, shawls, handmade cards and pretty wooden trays.

Hidesign
LEATHER GOODS
(www.hidesign.com; 69 Nehru St; ⊙ 9am-10pm) Established in Pondy in the 1970s, Hidesign sells beautifully made designer leather bags, briefcases, purses and belts in all kinds of colours, at very reasonable prices, and now has outlets across the world. The top-floor cafe, **Le Hidesign** (69 Nehru St; mains ₹120-180; ⊙ 9am-9.30pm; 🛜), serves delicious tapas and excellent coffee.

Geethanjali
ANTIQUES
(www.geethanjaliartifacts.com; 20 Rue Bussy; ⊙ 10.30am-8.30pm) The kind of place where Indiana Jones gets the sweats, this antique and curio shop sells sculptures, carved doors, wooden chests, paintings and furniture culled from Puducherry's colonial and even precolonial history. It ships to Europe for ₹20,000 per cubic metre – make sure to check that your purchases aren't subject to export restrictions.

Focus
BOOKS
(204 Mission St; ⊙ 9.30am-1.30pm & 3.30-9pm Mon-Sat) A great collection of India-related

and other English-language books (including Lonely Planet guides).

Librairie Kailash
BOOKS
(169 Rue Bussy; ⊙ 9am-1pm & 3-7.30pm Mon-Sat) Good selection of India and Asia titles in French.

ⓘ Information

ATMs are everywhere and there are numerous currency-exchange offices on Mission St near the corner of Nehru St.

Rue Bussy between Bharathi St and MG Rd is packed with clinics and pharmacies.

Coffee.Com (11A Romain Rolland St; per hour ₹80; ⊙ 10.30am-10pm) A genuine internet cafe, with good coffee and light food (₹60 to ₹300).

New Medical Centre (☏ 0413-2225287; www.nmcpondy.com; 470 MG Rd; ⊙ 24hr) Recommended private clinic and hospital.

Shanti Travel (☏ 0413-4210401; www.shantitravel.com; 13 Romain Rolland St; ⊙ 10am-1.30pm & 2.30-7pm) Professional agency offering transport tickets, walking tours, day trips and Chennai airport pick-ups.

Tourist office (☏ 0413-2339497; http://tourism.puducherry.gov.in; 40 Goubert Ave; ⊙ 9am-1pm & 2-7pm)

ⓘ Getting There & Away

BUS

The **bus stand** (Maraimalai Adigal Salai) is in the west of town, 2km from the French Quarter. For Kumbakonam, change at Chidambaram. Further services run from Villupuram (₹18, one hour, every 10 minutes), 38km west of Puducherry. Private bus companies, operating mostly overnight to various destinations, have offices along Maraimalai Adigal Salai west of the bus stand. **Parveen Travels** (☏ 0413-2201919; www.parveentravels.com; 288 Maraimalai Adigal Salai) runs an 11pm semisleeper service to Kodaikanal (₹610, eight hours).

BUSES FROM PUDUCHERRY (PONDICHERRY) BUS STAND

DESTINATION	FARE (₹)	DURATION (HR)	FREQUENCY (DAILY)
Bengaluru	310	7	8pm & 10pm
Chennai	97 (Volvo AC 190)	4	every 30min (6 Volvo AC 6.30am-6pm)
Chidambaram	60	2	48
Mamallapuram	80	2	36
Tiruvannamalai	47-62	3	11
Trichy	112	5	4.40am, 10am, 8pm, 10pm

TRAIN

Puducherry station has just a few services. Two daily trains go to Chennai Egmore, with unreserved seating only (₹45 to ₹75, four to five hours). You can connect at Villupuram for many more services north and south. The station has a computerised booking office for trains throughout India.

❶ Getting Around

Pondy's flat streets are great for getting around on foot. Autorickshaws are plentiful. Official metered fares are ₹40 for up to 2km and then ₹15 per kilometre, but most drivers refuse to use their meters. A trip from the bus stand to the French Quarter costs around ₹60.

A good way to explore Pondy and around is by rented bicycle or motorbike from various outlets (per day bicyle/scooter/motorbike ₹50/200/250) on northern Mission St, between Nehru and Chetty Sts.

Auroville

📞 0413 / POP 2345

Auroville, 'the City of Dawn', is one of those ideas that anyone with idealistic leanings will love: an international community dedicated to peace, harmony, sustainable living, and 'divine consciousness', where people from across the globe, ignoring creed, colour and nationality, work together to build a universal, cash-free, nonreligious township and realise good old human unity.

Outside opinions of Auroville's inhabitants range from admiration to accusations of self-indulgent escapism. Imagine over 100 small settlements scattered across the Tamil countryside, with 2300-odd residents of 43 nationalities. Nearly 60% of Aurovillians are foreign, and most new members require more funds than most Indians are ever likely to have. But the vibe you'll receive on a visit will probably be positive, and the energy driving the place is palpable.

Some 12km northwest of Puducherry, Auroville was founded in 1968 on the inspiration of 'the Mother', co-founder of Puducherry's Sri Aurobindo Ashram, and her philosophy still guides it. Aurovillians run a huge variety of projects ranging from schools and IT to organic farming, renewable energy and handicrafts production, employing 4000 to 5000 people from nearby villages.

The Auroville website (www.auroville. org) is an encyclopedic resource.

◉ Sights & Activities

Auroville isn't really geared for tourism – most inhabitants are just busy getting on with their lives – but it does have a good **visitors centre** (📞0413-2622239; ⊙9am-1pm & 1.30-5pm) with information services, exhibitions and Auroville products. You can buy a handbook and map (₹20), and watch a 10-minute video. Free passes for external viewing of the **Matrimandir** (⊙passes issued 9.30am-4.45pm Mon-Sat, 9.30am-12.45pm Sun), Auroville's 'soul', a 1km walk away through the woodlands, are also handed out here.

The large, golden, almost spherical Matrimandir is often said to resemble a golf ball, on a bed of lotus petals. You might equally feel that its grand simplicity, surrounded by pristine green parkland, does indeed evoke the divine consciousness it's supposed to represent. The orb's main inner chamber, lined with white marble, houses a large glass crystal that suffuses a beam of sunlight around the chamber. It's a place for individual silent concentration and if, after viewing the Matrimandir from the gardens, you want to meditate inside, you must book in person at least one day ahead at the **Matrimandir access office** (📞0413-2622204; Visitors Centre; ⊙10-11am & 2-3pm Wed-Mon).

Visitors are perfectly free to wander round Auroville's 10-sq-km network of roads and tracks. With two million trees planted since Auroville's foundation, it's a lovely shaded area.

If you're interested in getting to know Auroville, residents recommend you stay at least 10 days and join one of their introduction and orientation programs. To get seriously involved, you normally need to come as a volunteer for two to 12 months. Contact the **Auroville Guest Service** (📞0413-2622675; www.aurovilleguestservice. org; Solar Kitchen Bldg, 2km east of Visitors Centre; ⊙9.30am-1pm Mon-Sat) for advice on active participation.

🛏 Sleeping & Eating

Auroville has over 50 **guesthouses** (per person ₹250-4500) of hugely varied comfort levels, offering from two to 50 beds. The **Guest Accommodation Service** (📞0413-2622704; www.aurovilleguesthouses.org; Visitors Centre; ⊙9.30am-12.30pm & 2-5pm) can advise you, but bookings are done directly with individual guesthouses. For the peak seasons, December to March and August and September, reservations three or four months ahead are recommended.

The **Right Path Cafe** (Visitors Centre; mains ₹175-295; 8am-8.30pm Tue-Sun, 8am-4.45pm Mon), open to all, serves decent Indian and Continental food.

ℹ Getting There & Away

The main turning to Auroville from the East Coast Rd is at Periyar Mudaliarchavadi village, 6km north of Puducherry. From there it's about 6km west to the visitors centre. An autorickshaw one way from Puducherry is about ₹250, or you can take a Kottukuppam bus northbound on Ambour Salai to the Auroville turnoff (₹6 to ₹20, every 10 minutes), then an autorickshaw for ₹150. Otherwise, rent a bicycle or motorcycle from outlets on northern Mission St in Puducherry.

CENTRAL TAMIL NADU

Chidambaram

04144 / POP 62,153

There's basically one reason to visit Chidambaram: the great temple complex of Nataraja, Shiva as the Dancer of the Universe. One of the holiest of all Shiva sites, this also happens to be a Dravidian architectural highlight.

Most accommodation is close to the temple or the bus stand (500m southeast of the temple). The train station is about 1km further southeast.

⊙ Sights

★**Nataraja Temple** HINDU TEMPLE
(inner compound 6am-noon & 4.30-10pm) According to legend, Shiva and Kali got into a dance-off judged by Vishnu. Shiva dropped

---

OFF THE BEATEN TRACK

TRANQUIL TRANQUEBAR (THARANGAMBADI)

South of Chidambaram the many-armed delta of the Cauvery River stretches 180km along the coast and deep into the hinterland. The Cauvery is the beating heart of Tamil agriculture and its valley was the heartland of the Chola empire. Today the delta is one of the prettiest, poorest and most traditional parts of Tamil Nadu.

The tiny coastal town of Tharangambadi, still mostly known by its old name Tranquebar, is easily the most appealing base. A great place to recharge from the hot, crowded towns inland, this former Danish colony is quiet, neat, and set right on a long sandy beach with a few fishing boats and delicious sea breezes. It's said the air here is especially ozone-rich. The old part of town inside the 1791 Landporten gate makes a brilliantly peaceful stroll, and has been significantly restored since the 2004 tsunami, which killed about 800 people here. Intach Pondicherry (www.intachpondicherry.org) has a good downloadable map. The old Danish fort, **Dansborg** (Indian/foreigner ₹5/50, camera/video ₹30/100; 10am-1pm & 2-5.30pm Sat-Thu), dates from 1624 and contains an interesting little museum. Other notable buildings include **New Jerusalem Church** (Tamil Evangelical Lutheran Church; King's St), an intriguing mix of Indian and European styles built in 1718, and the 14th-century seafront **Masilamani Nathar Temple**, now in kaleidoscopic colours.

All accommodation is run by the **Bungalow on the Beach** (04364-288065; www. neemranahotels.com; 24 King's St; r incl breakfast ₹5400-8990, budget r ₹990; ❈ 🛜 ⌘), in the former residence of the British administrator (Denmark sold Tranquebar to the British East India Company in 1845). There are 17 beautiful old-world rooms spread across the main building and two other heritage locations in town, plus five simple, clean budget rooms in the Hotel Tamil Nadu, opposite the main building; you get wonderful temple views from budget room 5, and all rooms are AC. The main building has a fantastic swimming pool and a good multicuisine **restaurant** (mains ₹150-300; 7.30-9.30am, 12.30-2.30pm & 7-9.30pm). Booking ahead is strongly recommended.

Buses in this region get incredibly crowded, but Tranquebar has regular connections with Chidambaram (₹30, two hours, hourly) and Karaikal (₹11, 30 minutes, half-hourly). From Karaikal buses go to Kumbakonam (₹36, 2¼ hours, half-hourly 4.15am to 10.15pm), Thanjavur (₹64, 3½ hours, hourly 4.15am to 10.15pm) and Puducherry (₹85, four hours, half-hourly 4.15am to midnight).

an earring and picked it up with his foot, a move that Kali could not duplicate, so Shiva won the title Nataraja (Lord of the Dance). It is in this form that he is worshipped at this great temple, which draws an endless stream of worshippers. It was built during Chola times (Chidambaram was a Chola capital), but the main shrines date back to at least the 6th century.

The high-walled 22-hectare complex has four towering *gopurams* decked out in Dravidian stone and stucco work. The main entrance is through the east (oldest) *gopuram*, off East Car St. The 108 sacred positions of classical Tamil dance are carved in its passageway. To your right through the *gopuram* are the 1000-pillared Raja Sabha (King's Hall; ⊙festival days), and the large Sivaganga tank.

You enter the central compound (no cameras) from the east. In its southern part (left from the entrance) is the 13th-century Nritta Sabha (Dance Hall), shaped like a chariot with 56 finely carved pillars. Some say this is the very spot where Shiva outdanced Kali.

North of the Nritta Sabha, through a door, you enter the inner courtyard. Right in front is the Kanaka Sabha pavilion, where many temple rituals are performed. At *puja* times devotees crowd into and around the pavilion to witness the rites performed by the temple's hereditary Brahmin priests, the Dikshithars, who shave off some of their hair but grow the rest of it long (thus representing both Shiva and Parvati) and tie it into topknots.

Behind (north of) the Kanaka Sabha is the innermost sanctum, the golden-roofed Chit Sabha (Wisdom Hall), which holds the temple's central bronze image of Nataraja – Shiva the cosmic dancer, ending one cycle of creation, beginning another and uniting all opposites.

Priests may offer to guide you around the temple complex. Since they work as a kind of cooperative to fund the temple, you may wish to support this magnificent building by hiring one (for anything between ₹30 and ₹300, depending on language skills and knowledge). Unusually for Tamil Nadu, the temple is privately funded and managed.

✨ Festivals & Events

Of the town's many festivals, the two largest are the 10-day chariot festivals (⊙ Jun-Jul & Dec-Jan).

Natyanjali Dance Festival DANCE
(⊙Feb-Mar) Chidambaram's five-day dance festival attracts 300 to 400 classical dancers from all over India to the Nataraja Temple.

🛏 Sleeping & Eating

Many cheap pilgrims' lodges are clustered around the temple, but some are pretty grim. If there's anywhere really nice to stay in Chidambaram, we haven't found it yet. There are plenty of cheap veg eats surrounding the temple, but the best places for meals are hotels.

Hotel Saradharam HOTEL $$
(☎04144-221336; www.hotelsaradharam.co.in; 19 VGP St; r incl breakfast ₹1100, with AC ₹2160; ❄@🛜) The busy, friendly Saradharam is as good as it gets, and is conveniently located opposite the bus stand. It's a bit worn but comfortable enough, and a welcome respite from the town-centre frenzy. There's free wi-fi in the lobby, and the hotel has three restaurants – two vegetarian, plus the good multicuisine, AC Anupallavi (mains ₹130-250; ⊙7-10am, noon-3pm & 6-10.45pm).

ℹ Information

ICICI Bank ATM (Hotel Saradharam, VGP St)

ℹ Getting There & Away

Three or more daily trains head to Trichy (2nd-class/3AC/2AC ₹80/485/690, 3½ hours) via Kumbakonam and Thanjavur, and six to Chennai (₹105/485/690, 5½ hours). **Universal Travels** (⊙10am-midnight), opposite the bus stand, has three daily Volvo AC buses to Chennai (₹500, five hours).

Government buses from the bus stand include:
Chennai (₹180, six hours, every 30 minutes)
Kumbakonam (₹40, three hours, every 30 minutes)
Puducherry (₹40 to ₹50, two hours, every 30 minutes)
Thanjavur (₹60, four hours, every 30 minutes)
Tranquebar (Tharangambadi; ₹30, two hours, every 30 minutes)

Kumbakonam

☑ 0435 / POP 140,156
At first glance Kumbakonam is just another Indian junction town, but then you notice the dozens of colourful *gopurams* pointing skyward from its 18 temples, a reminder that this was once a seat of medieval South Indian power. And with another two magnif-

Kumbakonam

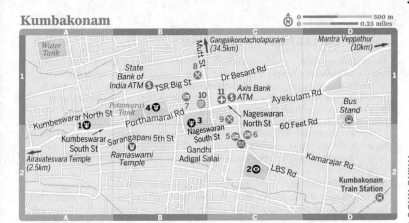

icent World Heritage–listed Chola temples (p370) nearby, it's worth staying the night.

◉ Sights

Most of the temples are dedicated to Shiva or Vishnu.

Nageshwara Temple HINDU TEMPLE

(⊗ 6.30am-noon & 4.30-8.30pm) Founded by the Cholas in 886, this is Kumbakonam's oldest temple, and is dedicated to Shiva in the guise of Nagaraja, the serpent king. On three days of the year (in April or May) the sun's rays fall on the lingam. The Nataraja shrine just to the right in front of the inner sanctum is fashioned like a horse-drawn chariot.

Sarangapani Temple HINDU TEMPLE

(⊗ 6.30am-noon & 4.30-8.30pm) Sarangapani is the largest Vishnu temple, with a 45m-high eastern *gopuram* as its main entrance (photography is not permitted inside). Past the temple cowshed (Krishna the cowherd is one of Vishnu's forms), another *gopuram* and a pillared hall, you reach the inner sanctuary, a 12th-century Chola creation styled like a chariot with big carved elephants, horses and wheels.

Kumbeshwara Temple HINDU TEMPLE

(⊗ 6.30am-noon & 4.30-8.30pm) Kumbeshwara Temple, entered via a nine-storey *gopuram* and with a long porticoed *mandapa*, is Kumbakonam's biggest Shiva temple. It dates from the 17th and 18th centuries and contains a lingam said to have been made by Shiva himself when he mixed the nectar of immortality with sand.

Mahamaham Tank WATER TANK

(⊗ 6.30am-noon & 4.30-8.30pm) Surrounded by 17 pavilions, the huge Mahamaham Tank is one of Kumbakonam's most sacred sites. It's believed that every 12 years the waters of India's holiest rivers, including the Ganges, flow into it, and at this time a festival is held; the next is due in 2016.

⌷ Sleeping & Eating

Pandian Hotel HOTEL $

(☑ 0435-2430397; 52 Sarangapani Koil Sannadhi St; s/d ₹350/660, d with AC ₹990; ▣) It's slightly institutional, but you're generally getting fair value at this clean-enough budget standby.

DON'T MISS

CHOLA TEMPLES NEAR KUMBAKONAM

Two of the three great monuments of Chola civilisation stand in villages near Kumbakonam: the Airavatesvara Temple in Darasuram and the Gangaikondacholapuram temple. Unlike the also World Heritage–listed Brihadishwara Temple at Thanjavur, today these temples receive relatively few worshippers (and visitors). They are wonderful both for their overall form (with pyramidal towers rising at the heart of rectangular walled compounds) and for the exquisite detail of their carved stone.

From Kumbakonam, frequent buses heading to nearby villages will drop you at Darasuram; buses to Gangaikondacholapuram (₹21, 1½ hours) run every half-hour. A return autorickshaw to Darasuram costs about ₹150. A half-day car trip to both temples, with Hotel Raya's is ₹1100 (₹1250 with AC).

Airavatesvara Temple (⊙6am-8pm) Only 3km west of Kumbakonam in Darasuram, this temple dedicated to Shiva was constructed by Rajaraja II (1146–63). The steps of the Rajagambhira Hall are carved with vivid elephants and horses pulling chariots. This pavilion's 108 all-different pillars have detailed carvings including dancers, acrobats and the five-in-one beast Yali (elephant's head, lion's body, goat's horns, pig's ears and a cow's backside). Inside the main shrine (⊙6am-noon & 4-8pm), you can honour the central lingam and get a *tilak* (forehead) mark for ₹10.

On the outside of the shrine are several fine carved images of Shiva. Four *mandapas* frame the corners of the courtyard complex.

Gangaikondacholapuram Temple (⊙6am-noon & 4-8pm) The temple at Gangaikondacholapuram ('City of the Chola who Conquered the Ganges'), 35km north of Kumbakonam, is dedicated to Shiva. It was built by Rajendra I in the 11th century when he moved the Chola capital here from Thanjavur, and has many similarities to the earlier Brihadishwara at Thanjavur. Its beautiful 49m-tall tower, however, has a slightly concave curve, making it the 'feminine' counterpart to the mildly convex Thanjavur one. The complex's artistic highlights are the wonderfully graceful sculptures around the tower's exterior.

A massive Nandi (Shiva's vehicle) faces the temple from the surrounding gardens. The main shrine, beneath the tower, contains a huge lingam and is approached through a long, gloomy 17th-century hall. The fine carvings on the tower's exterior include Shiva as the beggar Bhikshatana, immediately left of the southern steps; Ardhanarishvara (Shiva as half-man, half-woman) and Shiva as Nataraja, on the south side; and Shiva with Ganga, Shiva emerging from the lingam, and Vishnu with Lakshmi and Bhudevi (the first three images on the west side). Most famous of all is the striking panel of Shiva garlanding the head of his follower, Chandesvara, beside the northern steps.

Hotel Raya's HOTEL $$
(☑0435-2423170; www.hotelrayas.com; 18 Head Post Office Rd; r ₹1200, with AC ₹1440-1560; ❇) Friendly service and reliably spacious, spotless rooms make Raya's your top lodging option in town, but the new annexe (r ₹1800; ❇) has the best, brightest rooms. It runs a convenient car service for out-of-town trips, and Sathars Restaurant (mains ₹110-195; ⊙11.30am-11.30pm) here does good veg and nonveg fare in clean surroundings.

Mantra Veppathur RESORT $$$
(☑0435-2462261; www.mantraveppathur.com; 536/537A, 1 Bagavathapuram Main Rd Extension, Srisailapathipuram Village; r incl breakfast ₹8400-10,790; ❇ ⊛ ⊠) 🖉 Lost in the riverside jungle, 10km northeast of Kumbakonam, this is a welcome retreat from temple-town chaos. Comfy rustic-style rooms fronted by porches with rocking chairs have open-air showers; yoga, meditation, and ayurveda are offered; and the organic farm fuels the Indian-focused restaurant, where you can eat out on a turquoise-tiled verandah.

Hotel Sri Venkkatramana INDIAN $
(TSR Big St; thalis ₹60-100; ⊙5.30am-10.30pm Mon-Sat) Serves good fresh veg food; very popular with locals.

Taj Samudra INDIAN $$
(80 Nageswaran South St; mains ₹115-185; ⊙noon-3pm & 7-11pm) Here you can get tasty veg and

nonveg dishes from all over India, brought by friendly waiters, against an almost stylish backdrop.

ℹ Information

Speed Systems (Sarangapani Koil Sannadhi St; internet per hour ₹20; ◷ 9.30am-9.30pm) Take your passport.

ℹ Getting There & Away

Thirteen daily trains head to Thanjavur (2nd-class/3AC/2AC ₹45/485/690, 30 minutes to one hour) and eight to Trichy (₹60/485/690, two to 2½ hours). Five daily trains to/from Chennai Egmore include the overnight Mannai Express (sleeper/3AC/2AC/1AC ₹210/555/790/1315, 6½ hours) and the daytime Chennai Express/Trichy Express (₹210/555/790/1315, six to seven hours).

Government buses from the bus stand include:

Chennai (₹185 to ₹230, 6½ to eight hours, every 15 minutes)

Chidambaram (₹44, 2½ to three hours, every 20 minutes)

Karaikal (₹34, 2¼ hours, every 30 minutes)

Thanjavur (₹30, 1½ hours, every 10 minutes)

Thanjavur (Tanjore)

☏ 04362 / POP 222,943

Here are the ochre foundation blocks of perhaps the most remarkable civilisation of Dravidian history, one of the few kingdoms to expand Hinduism beyond India, a bedrock for aesthetic styles that spread from Madurai to the Mekong. A dizzying historical legacy was forged from Thanjavur, capital of the great Chola empire during its heyday. Today, this is a crowded, hectic, modern Indian town but the past is still very much present. Every day thousands of people worship at the Cholas' grand Brihadishwara Temple, and Thanjavur's labyrinthine royal palace preserves memories of other powerful dynasties from later centuries.

◉ Sights

★ Brihadishwara Temple   HINDU TEMPLE

(◷ 6am-8.30pm) Come here twice: in the morning, when the tawny granite begins to assert its dominance over the white dawn sunshine, and in the evening, when the rocks capture a hot palette of reds, oranges, yellows and pinks on the crowning glory of Chola temple architecture. The World Heritage–listed Brihadishwara Temple was

built between 1003 and 1010 by Rajaraja I (king of kings). The outer fortifications were put up by Thanjavur's later Nayak and British regimes.

You enter through a Nayak gate, followed by two original *gopurams* with elaborate stucco sculptures. You might find the temple elephant under one of the *gopurams,* dispensing good luck with a dab of his trunk to anyone who puts a rupee in it. Several shrines are dotted around the extensive grassy areas of the walled temple compound, including one of India's largest statues of Nandi (Shiva's sacred bull) facing the main temple building. Cut from a single rock, this 16th-century Nayak creation is 6m long.

A long, columned assembly hall leads to the central shrine (◷ 8.30am-12.30pm & 4-8.30pm) with its 4m-high Shiva lingam, beneath the superb 61m-high *vimana* (tower). The assembly hall's southern steps are flanked by two huge *dvarapalas* (temple guardians). Many lovely, graceful deity images stand in niches around the *vimana's* lower levels, including Shiva emerging from the lingam (beside the southern steps); Shiva as the beggar Bhikshatana (first image, south side); Harihara (half Shiva, half Vishnu) on the west wall; and Ardhanarishvara (Shiva as half-man, half-woman), leaning on Nandi, on the north side. Between the deity images are panels showing classical dance poses.

The compound also contains a helpful interpretation centre along the south wall and, in the colonnade along the west and north walls, hundreds more linga. Both west and north walls are lined with exquisite lime-plaster Chola frescoes, for years buried under later Nayak-era murals. North of the temple compound, but still within the outer fortifications, are a park (admission ₹5) containing the Sivaganga tank, and 18th-century Schwartz's Church.

★ Royal Palace   PALACE

(Indian/foreigner ₹30/150, camera ₹50/100; ◷ 9am-6pm) Thanjavur's royal palace is a mixed bag of ruin and renovation, superb art and random royal paraphernalia. The mazelike complex was constructed partly by the Nayaks who took over Thanjavur in 1535, and partly by a local Maratha dynasty that ruled from 1676 to 1855. The two don't-miss sections are the Saraswati Mahal Library Museum and the Art Gallery.

Seven different sections of the palace can be visited – and you'll need three

Thanjavur (Tanjore)

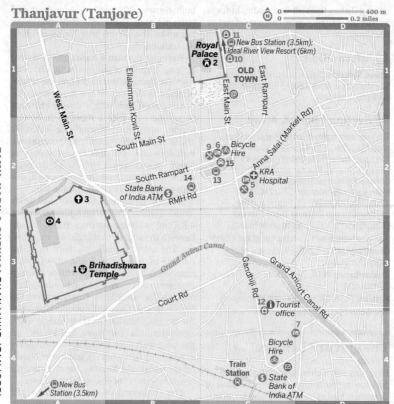

different tickets to see them all! The Art Gallery and Saraswati Mahal Library Museum are included in the 'full' ticket, along with the Mahratta Dharbar Hall, the bell tower, and the Saarjah Madi. The main entrance is from the north, via a lane off East Main St. On the way in you'll come to the main ticket office, followed by the Maratha Palace complex.

Past the ticket office, a passage to the left leads to, first, the Royal Palace Museum, a small miscellany of sculptures, weaponry, elephant bells and rajas' headgears; second, the Maharaja Serfoji Memorial Hall, commemorating the enlightened Maratha scholar-king Serfoji II (1798–1832), with a better collection overlooking a once-splendid, now crumbling courtyard; and third, the Mahratta Dharbar Hall, where Maratha rulers gave audience in a grand but faded pavilion adorned with colourful murals, including their own portraits behind the dais.

As you exit the passage, the fabulous little Sarawasti Mahal Library Museum is on your left. Perhaps Serfoji II's greatest contribution to posterity, this is testimony both to the 19th-century obsession with knowledge accumulation and to an eclectic mind that collected prints of Chinese torture methods, Audubon-style paintings of Indian flora and fauna, world atlases and rare medieval books. Serfoji amassed more than 65,000 books and 50,000 palm-leaf paper manuscripts in Indian and European languages, though most aren't displayed.

Leaving the library, turn left for the Art Gallery, set around the Nayak Palace courtyard. This contains a collection of superb, mainly Chola, bronzes and stone carvings, and one of its rooms, the 1600 Nayak Durbar Hall, has a statue of Serfoji II. From the courtyard, steps lead part of the way up a large *gopuram*-like tower to a whale skeleton said to have been washed up in Tran-

Thanjavur (Tanjore)

quebar. The renovated **Saarjah Madi** is best admired from East Main St for its ornate balconies.

✦ Festivals & Events

Thyagaraja Aradhana   MUSIC
(☉ Jan) At Thiruvaiyaru, 13km north of Thanjavur, this important five-day Carnatic music festival honours the saint and composer Thyagaraja.

▭ Sleeping

Hotel Ramnath   HOTEL $
(☏ 04362-272567; hotel_ramnath@yahoo.com; 1335 South Rampart; r ₹1000, with AC ₹1300; ❈ ☎) The best of a bunch of cheapies facing the local bus stand downtown (not quite as noisy as you'd think), the Ramnath is a decent 'upmarket budget' option with clean, smallish, pine-furnished rooms.

Hotel Valli   HOTEL $
(☏ 04362-231584; www.hotelvalli.com; 2948 MKM Rd; s/d ₹605/825, r with AC ₹1460; ❈) Near the train station, green-painted Valli offers good-value, spick-and-span rooms, friendly staff, and a basic restaurant. It's in a reasonably peaceful leafy spot beyond a bunch of greasy backstreet workshops.

Hotel Gnanam   HOTEL $$
(☏ 04362-278501; www.hotelgnanam.com; Anna Salai; s/d incl breakfast ₹2640/3000; ❈ ☎) Easily the best value in town, the Gnanam has stylish, comfy rooms (some with balconies or lovely clean bath-tubs) and ultraefficient receptionists, and is perfect for anyone needing good food, free wi-fi and other modern amenities in Thanjavur's geographic centre.

Ideal River View Resort   RESORT $$$
(☏ 04362-250533; www.idealresort.com; Vennar Bank, Palliagraharam; s/d ₹6000/6600; ☉ 7-10am, 12.30-3pm & 7.30-10pm; ❈ ☎ ⊠) Brightly furnished cottages with roomy balconies sprawling across tropical gardens on the banks of the Vennar River, 7km northwest of central Thanjavur, make this tranquil resort by far the most atmospheric sleeping spot around. You can hire bikes, do yoga, or just enjoy the pool. The semi-open-air Indian/Sri Lankan/Continental **restaurant** (mains ₹175-450) overlooks the river.

✖ Eating

Sri Venkata Lodge   SOUTH INDIAN $
(Gandhiji Rd; thalis ₹50; ☉ 5.15am-10.15pm) A friendly, popular, veg-only place near the centre of everything, that does a nice thali.

Vasanta Bhavan   INDIAN $
(1338 South Rampart; mains ₹65-85; ☉ 6am-11pm) The most popular of several veg places facing the local bus stand downtown, Vasanta Bhavan doles out biryani and North Indian curries as well as your usual southern favourites, in AC comfort.

Sahana   INDIAN $$
(Hotel Gnanam; Anna Salai; mains ₹95-160; ☉ 7am-10.30pm) This classy hotel restaurant does a very nice line in fresh, tasty, mainly Indian veg dishes, along with a decent multicuisine breakfast buffet.

Diana   MULTICUISINE $$
(Hotel Gnanam; Anna Salai; mains ₹160-400; ☉ 11am-3pm & 6.30-10.30pm) The Hotel Gnanam's smart-ish nonveg restaurant is very good, with a wide range of northern dishes and local Chettinadu fare – and even beer.

⌂ Shopping

Thanjavur is good for handicrafts shopping, especially near the palace, where outlets such as **Kandiya Heritage** (634 East Main St; ☉ 7am-7pm Mon-Sat) and **Chola Art Galerie**

(78/799 East Main St; ⊙9am-7pm) sell antiques, reproduction bronzes, brightly painted wooden horses, old European pottery, jewellery and more. For fixed prices, try state-run **Poompuhar** (Gandhiji Rd; ⊙10am-8pm Mon-Sat).

ⓘ Information

Sify iWay (927 East Main St; internet per hour ₹25; ⊙10am-9pm)

Tourist office (✆04362-230984; Gandhiji Rd; ⊙10am-5.45pm Mon-Fri) One of Tamil Nadu's more helpful offices.

ⓘ Getting There & Away

BUS

The downtown **SETC bus stand** (⊙reservation office 7.30am-8.30pm) has express buses to Chennai (₹260, eight hours) hourly from 5.30am to 12.30pm, and five times between 8pm and 10.45pm. Buses for other cities leave from the New Bus Station, 5km southwest of the centre. Many arriving buses will drop you off in the city centre on the way out there. Services from the New Bus Station include:

Chidambaram (₹90, four hours, every 30 minutes)

Kumbakonam (₹22 to ₹29, 1½ hours, every five minutes)

Madurai (₹90, four hours, every 20 minutes)

Trichy (₹24 to ₹31, 1½ hours, every 10 minutes)

TRAIN

The station is central enough, at the end of Gandhiji Rd. Five daily trains head to Chennai Egmore (seven to eight hours) including the 10.45pm Mannai Express (sleeper/3AC/2AC/1AC ₹225/600/855/1430). Seventeen trains go to Trichy (2nd-class/3AC/2AC ₹45/485/690, 1½ hours) and 12 to Kumbakonam (₹45/485/690, 30 minutes to 1¼ hours).

ⓘ Getting Around

You can hire bikes (per hour ₹6) from stalls opposite the local bus stand and train station. Bus 74 (₹6) shuttles between the New Bus Station and the local bus stand; autorickshaws cost ₹100.

Trichy (Tiruchirappalli)

✆0431 / POP 847,387

Welcome to (more or less) the geographic centre of Tamil Nadu. Tiruchirappalli, universally known as Trichy or Tiruchi, isn't just a travel junction; it also mixes up a heaving bazaar with some major must-see temples.

It's a huge, crowded, busy city, and the fact that most hotels are clumped together around the big bus station isn't exactly a plus point. But Trichy has a strong character and long history, and a sneaky way of overturning first impressions.

Trichy may have been a capital of the early Cholas in the 3rd century BC. It passed through the hands of the Pallavas, medieval Cholas, Pandyas, Delhi Sultanate and Vijayanagars before the Madurai Nayaks brought it to prominence, making it a capital in the 17th century and building its famous Rock Fort Temple.

Trichy stretches a long way from north to south, and most of what's interesting to travellers is split into three distinct areas. The Trichy Junction, or Cantonment, area in the south has most of the hotels and restaurants and the main bus and train stations. The Rock Fort Temple and main bazaar are 4km north of here; the other important temples are in Srirangam, a further 4km north, across the Cauvery River. Luckily, the whole lot is connected by a good bus service.

◉ Sights

★**Rock Fort Temple**   HINDU TEMPLE
(Map p375; admission ₹3, camera/video ₹20/100; ⊙6am-8pm) The Rock Fort Temple, perched 83m high on a massive outcrop, lords over Trichy with stony arrogance. The ancient rock was first hewn by the Pallavas and Pandyas, who cut small cave temples on its south side, but it was the war-savvy Nayaks who later made strategic use of the naturally fortified position. There are over 400 stone-cut steps to climb to the top.

From NSB Rd on the south side, you pass between small shops and cross a street before entering the temple precinct itself. Then it's 180 steps up to the Thayumanaswamy Temple, the rock's biggest temple, on the left (closed to non-Hindus). A gold-topped tower rises over its sanctum, which houses a 2m-high Shiva lingam. Further up, you pass the 6th-century Pallava cave temple on the left – it's usually railed off but if you get inside, note the famous Gangadhara panel on the left, showing Shiva restraining the waters of the Ganges with a single strand of his hair. From here it's just another 183 steps to the small Uchipillaiyar Temple at the summit, dedicated to Ganesh. The view is wonderful, with eagles wheeling beneath and Trichy sprawling all around. Back at the bottom, check out the lower rock-cut

Trichy (Tiruchirappalli)

Trichy (Tiruchirappalli)

TAMIL NADU & CHENNAI TRICHY (TIRUCHIRAPPALLI)

self-enclosed city. It has 49 separate shrines, all dedicated to Vishnu, and reaching the inner sanctum from the south, as most worshippers do, requires passing through seven *gopurams*. The first, the **Rajagopuram** (Map p375), was added in 1987, and is one of Asia's tallest temple towers at 73m high.

You pass through streets with shops, restaurants, motorbikes and cars until you reach the temple proper at the fourth *gopuram*. Inside is the ticket desk for the nearby **roof viewpoint** (ticket ₹10; ⊙6am-5pm), which gives semipanoramic views of the complex. Take no notice of would-be guides who spin all kinds of stories to get you to hire them. Non-Hindus cannot pass the sixth *gopuram* so won't see the innermost sanctum whose image shows Vishnu as Lord Ranganatha, reclining on a five-headed snake.

Turn right just before the fifth *gopuram* to the small but intriguing **Art Museum** (admission ₹5; ⊙9am-1pm & 2-6pm), with good bronzes, tusks of bygone temple elephants, and a collection of superb 17th-century Nayak ivory figurines depicting gods, demons, and kings and queens (some erotically engaged). Continue round to the left past the museum to the **Sesha Mandapa**, a 16th-century pillared hall with magnificently detailed Vijayanagar carvings of rearing horses in battle. Inside the fifth *gopuram* is the **Garuda Mandapa**, with a shrine to Vishnu's man-eagle vehicle.

cave temple, with particularly fine pillars (right past five or six houses as you exit the temple precinct, then right again down a small lane).

The stone steps get scorchingly hot in the midday sun and it's a barefoot climb, so time your visit carefully.

⭐ **Sri Ranganathaswamy Temple**   HINDU TEMPLE
(Map p375; camera/video ₹50/100; ⊙6am-9pm) All right temple-philes, here's the one you've been waiting for: quite possibly the biggest temple in India – so large, it feels like a

The temple's most important festival is the 21-day Vaikunta Ekadasi (Paradise Festival) in December/January, when the celebrated Vaishnavaite text, Tiruvaimozhi, is recited before an image of Vishnu.

Bus 1 from the Central Bus Station or the Rock Fort stops south of the Rajagopuram.

Sri Jambukeshwara Temple HINDU TEMPLE
(Tiruvanaikoil; camera/video ₹30/200; ⊙5am-9pm) If you're visiting Tamil Nadu's five elemental temples of Shiva, you need to see Sri Jambukeshwara, dedicated to Shiva, Parvati and the medium of water. The liquid theme is realised in the central shrine (closed to non-Hindus), whose Shiva lingam reputedly issues a nonstop trickle of water. If you're taking bus 1, ask for 'Tiruvanaikoil'; the temple is 350m east of the main road.

Lourdes Church CHURCH
(Map p375; College Rd; ⊙8am-8.30pm) The hush of this 19th-century neo-Gothic church makes an interesting contrast to the frenetic activity of Trichy's Hindu temples. In the cool, green campus of Jesuit St Joseph's College next door, the dusty St Joseph's College Museum (Map p375; ⊙9am-noon & 2-4pm Mon-Sat) FREE contains the creepy natural history collections of the Jesuit priests' Western Ghats excursions in the 1870s. Ask at reception as you approach the museum and someone will probably let you in.

🛏 Sleeping & Eating

Most hotels are near the Central Bus Station, a short walk north from Trichy Junction train station.

The top eateries are usually in the better hotels, but there are some decent cheaper places too.

Hotel Abbirami HOTEL $
(Map p377; ☑0431-2415001; 10 McDonald's Rd; r ₹770-990, with AC ₹1439-1919; ✳) Most appealing are the 1st- and 4th-floor renovated rooms, with light wood and colourful glass panels. Older rooms have darker wood and are a bit worn, but still well-kept. It's a busy place with friendly staff.

Hotel Mathura HOTEL $
(Map p377; ☑0431-2414737; www.hotelmathura.com; 1 Rockins Rd; r ₹700, with AC ₹1100; ✳) Rooms are very basic but tolerably clean. Many of the non-ACs are in better shape than those with AC. The 2nd floor, at least, has had a decent coat of paint.

Hotel Ramyas HOTEL $$
(Map p377; ☑0431-2414646; www.ramyas.com; 13-D/2 Williams Rd; s/d ₹990/1680, with AC s ₹2100-2700, d ₹2400-3300, all incl breakfast; ✳@🛜) Excellent rooms, service and facilities make this business-oriented hotel great value. 'Business' singles are small but it's only another ₹200-odd for a good 'executive'. Turquoise-clad Meridian (Map p377; mains ₹100-215; ⊙11.30am-3pm & 6.30-11pm) does tasty multicuisine fare, breakfast is a nice buffet, and the Chola Bar (Map p377; ⊙11am-3.30pm & 6.30-11pm) is less dingy than most hotel bars (though still male-dominated). Best is the lovely Thendral (Map p377; mains ₹100-230; ⊙7-9.30am & 6.30-11pm) roof-garden restaurant.

Grand Gardenia HOTEL $$
(☑0431-4045000; www.grandgardenia.com; 22-25 Mannarpuram Junction; s ₹3000, d ₹3600-4800, all incl breakfast; ✳🛜) Elegant modern rooms come with free wi-fi, comfy beds, and glassed-in showers at this sparkly corporate-style hotel, currently your smartest option in Trichy. Kannappa (mains ₹95-180; ⊙11.30am-11.30pm) serves up excellent Chettinadu food and the rooftop terrace hosts a good multicuisine restaurant (mains ₹115-220; ⊙7.30-10am, noon-3pm & 7-10.45pm) and a gym. Comfort and amenities outweigh the uninspiring location, near the highway 1km south of Trichy Junction station.

Femina Hotel HOTEL $$
(Map p377; ☑0431-2414501; www.feminahotel.net; 109 Williams Rd; s ₹1600-3600, d ₹2040-4200, all incl breakfast; ✳@🛜✳) It's hard to tell where the enormous Femina begins and ends. From outside it looks 1950s, but renovations have turned the interior quite contemporary. Facilities are good and staff helpful. Renovated deluxe rooms are cosy and modern, while standard rooms are a tad worn but very spacious. There's a nice outdoor pool and eateries include the Round the Clock (Map p377; mains ₹80-120; ⊙24hr) coffee-shop-cum-veg-restaurant.

Breeze Residency HOTEL $$
(Map p377; ☑0431-2414414; www.breezeresidency.com; 3/14 McDonald's Rd; s/d ₹3000/3480, ste ₹4200-6000, all incl breakfast; ✳@🛜✳) The Breeze is huge, semiluxurious and in a quiet leafy location. The best rooms are on the top floors but all are well appointed. Facilities include a gym, the Madras Restaurant (Map p377; lunch/

dinner buffet ₹400/450; ☺noon-3.30pm & 7-11pm), a 24-hour coffee shop, and a bizarre Wild West theme bar.

Hotel Royal Sathyam
HOTEL $$

(Map p375; ☑0431-4011414; http://sathyamgrouphotels.in; 42A Singarathope; s ₹1440-1920, d ₹1680-3000, all incl breakfast; ❄☏) The classiest option if you want to be close to the temple and market action. Rooms are small but smart, with extra-comfy mattresses and a fresh wood-and-whitewash theme, and it's a friendly place.

Vasanta Bhavan
INDIAN $

(Map p375; 3 NSB Rd; mains ₹60-85, thalis ₹60-120; ☺7am-10.30pm) A great spot for a meal with a view and, if you're lucky, a breeze near the Rock Fort. Tables on the outer gallery overlook the Teppakulam Tank. It's good for North Indian veg food – of the paneer and naan genre – as well as South Indian. People crowd in for the lunchtime thalis. There's another branch (Map p377; Rockins Rd; mains ₹40-85, thalis ₹80; ☺6am-11pm) in the Cantonment.

DiMora
MULTICUISINE $$

(Map p375; ☑0431-2762656; 4th fl, Ambigai City Center, Shastri Rd; mains ₹150-440; ☺noon-4pm & 7-11.30pm) Waiters in all-black take your order on mobile phones to a soundtrack of trancey lounge music that makes this smart, popular top-floor restaurant feel more Chennai than Trichy. The menu roams all over the world, but it's great for pastas, wood-fired pizzas and fresh juices, as well tandoori and other Indian dishes.

🛍 Shopping

The main bazaar, immediately south of the Rock Fort, is as chaotic and crowded as you could want.

Saratha's
CLOTHING

(Map p375; 45 NSB Rd; ☺9am-9.30pm) Bursting with clothing of every imaginable kind and colour, Saratha's claims to be (and might well be) the 'largest textile showroom in India'.

ℹ Information

Indian Panorama (☑0431-4226122; www.indianpanorama.in; 5 Annai Ave, Srirangam) Trichy-based and covering all of India, this professional, reliable travel agency/tour operator is run by an Indian–New Zealander couple.

KMC Speciality Hospital (Kauvery Hospital; Map p377; ☑0431-4077777; www.kmcspecialityhospital.in; 6 Royal Rd) Large, well-equipped, private hospital.

Tourist office (Map p377; ☑0431-2460136; McDonald's Rd; ☺10am-5.45pm Mon-Fri)

Trichy Junction Area

Trichy Junction Area

😴 Sleeping
1	Hotel Ramyas	A2
2	Breeze Residency	B2
3	Femina Hotel	A1
4	Hotel Abbirami	A2
5	Hotel Mathura	A2

🍴 Eating
	Meridian	(see 1)
	Madras Restaurant	(see 2)
	Round the Clock	(see 3)
	Thendral	(see 1)
6	Vasanta Bhavan	A2

🍷 Drinking & Nightlife
	Chola Bar	(see 1)

ℹ Information
7	State Bank of India ATM	B3
8	State Bank of India ATM	B2
9	State Bank of India ATM	A2

🚌 Transport
10	Air Asia	A1
	Femina Travels	(see 3)
11	Mihin Lanka	A1
12	Parveen Travels	A3
	SriLankan Airlines	(see 3)

GOVERNMENT BUSES FROM TRICHY (TIRUCHIRAPPALLI)

DESTINATION	FARE (₹)	DURATION (HR)	FREQUENCY
Bengaluru	350 Ultra Deluxe (UD)	9	6 UD daily
Chennai	211 regular, 260 UD, 325 AC	6-7	15 UD, 4 AC daily
Coimbatore	116 regular, 126 Deluxe (D)	5-6	every 10min, 3 D daily
Kodaikanal	126	5	6.40am, 8.40am, 11am, 11.40am, 12.40pm
Madurai	80	2½	every 15min
Ooty	260 UD	8	10.15pm UD
Rameswaram	170	6½	hourly
Thanjavur	31	1½	every 10min
Trivandrum	365	9	4 daily

🛈 Getting There & Away

AIR

Trichy's airport has four daily flights to Chennai on **Jet Airways** (www.jetairways.com) and **Air India Express** (☎ 0431-2341744; www.airindiaexpress.in).

To Colombo, **SriLankan Airlines** (Map p377; ☎ 0431-2460844; 14C Williams Rd; ⊙ 9am-5.30pm Mon-Sat) and **Mihin Lanka** (Map p377; ☎ 0431-4200070; www.mihinlanka.com; 14C Williams Rd; ⊙ 9am-5.30 Mon-Fri) each fly twice daily.

Air Asia (Map p377; ☎ 0431-4540394; www.airasia.com; 18/3-5 Ivory Plaza, Royal Rd; ⊙ 9.30am-5pm Mon-Fri, 9.30am-1pm Sat) flies to Kuala Lumpur three times daily, **Tiger Air** (www.tigerair.com) to Singapore daily, and Air India Express daily to Singapore and Dubai.

BUS

Government buses use the busy but orderly **Central Bus Station** (Map p377; Rockins Rd). The best services for longer trips are the UD (Ultra Deluxe), with the softest seats. There's a booking office for these in the southwest corner of the station. For Kodaikanal, a good option is to take one of the frequent buses to Dindigul (₹48, two hours) and change there.

Private bus companies have offices near the Central Bus Station, including **Parveen Travels** (Map p377; ☎ 0431-2419811; www.parveentravels.com; 12 Ashby Complex; ⊙ 24hr) which offers AC services to Chennai (₹560 to ₹680, six hours, seven daily) and Trivandrum (Thiruvananthapuram) (₹1100 to ₹1200, seven hours, 12.30am and 1am), plus non-AC semisleeper services to Puducherry (₹500, four hours, midnight) and Kodaikanal (₹500, 4½ hours, 2.30am).

TAXI

Travel agencies and hotels provide cars with drivers. Efficient, reasonably priced **Femina Travels** (Map p377; ☎ 0431-2418532; 109 Williams Rd; ⊙ 6am-10pm) charges ₹1900 for up to 10 hours and 100km (AC).

TRAIN

Trichy Junction station is on the main Chennai–Madurai line. Of 16 daily express services to Chennai, the best daytime option is the Vaigai Express (2nd/chair class ₹145/510, 5¾ hours) departing at 9am. The overnight Pandyan Express (sleeper/3AC/2AC/1AC ₹245/625/870/1450, 6½ hours) leaves at 11.10pm. Thirteen daily trains to Madurai include the 7.15am Tirunelveli Express (2nd/chair class ₹95/340, 2¼ hours) and the 1.15pm Guruvaya Express (2nd-class/sleeper/3AC/2AC ₹80/140/485/690, three hours). Eighteen trains head to Thanjavur (2nd-class/sleeper/3AC ₹45/140/485, 40 minutes to 1½ hours).

🛈 Getting Around

The 5km ride between the airport and Central Bus Station area costs about ₹300 by taxi and ₹150 by autorickshaw; there's a prepaid taxi stand at the airport. Or take bus K1.

Bus 1 from Rockins Rd outside the Central Bus Station goes every few minutes to Sri Ranganathaswamy Temple (₹6) and back, stopping near the Rock Fort Temple and Sri Jambukeshwara Temple en route.

SOUTHERN TAMIL NADU

Chettinadu

The Chettiars, a community of traders based in and around Karaikkudi, 95km south of Trichy, hit the big time back in the 19th century as financiers and entrepreneurs in colonial-era Sri Lanka and Southeast Asia.

They lavished their fortunes on building at least 10,000, maybe even 30,000 opulent mansions in the 75 towns and villages of their arid rural homeland, Chettinadu. No expense was spared on finding the finest materials for these palatial homes – Burmese teak, Italian marble, Indian rosewood, English steel, and art and sculpture from everywhere. In the aftermath of WWII, the Chettiars' business networks came crashing down and many families left Chettinadu. Disused mansions fell into decay and were demolished or sold off piecemeal. Awareness of their value started to revive around the turn of the 21st century, with Chettinadu making it onto Unesco's tentative World Heritage list in 2014. Several mansions have now been turned into gorgeous heritage hotels where you can enjoy authentic Chettinad cuisine, known throughout India for its brilliant use of spices.

◉ Sights & Activities

Hotels give cooking demos or classes, and provide bicycles or bullock carts for rural rambles. They can also arrange visits to sari-weavers, temples, private mansions, the Athangudi tileworkers (producing the colourful handmade tiles in most Chettiar mansions), and shrines of the popular pre-Hindu deity Ayyanar (identifiable by their large terracotta horses, Ayyanar's vehicle). The antique shops in Karaikkudi's Muneeswaran Koil St give you an idea of how much of the Chettiar heritage is still being flogged.

The nondescript town of Pudukkottai, 51km south of Trichy and 44km north of Karaikkudi, has historical significance in inverse proportion to its current obscurity: it was the capital of the only princely state in Tamil Nadu to remain officially independent throughout British rule.

Vijayalaya Cholisvaram HINDU TEMPLE
(Narthamalai) This small but stunning 8th-century temple stands on a dramatically deserted rock slope 1km southwest of Narthamalai village, about 16km north of Pudukkottai. Reminiscent of the Shore Temple at Mamallapuram, without the crowds, it was probably built in late Pallava times. The caretaker, if present, will open two rock-cut Shiva shrines in the rock face behind, one with 12 impressively large reliefs of Vishnu.

The Narthamalai turn-off is 7km south of Keeranur on the Trichy–Pudukkottai road; it's 2km west to the village.

Pudukkottai Museum MUSEUM
(Thirukokarnam, Pudukkottai; Indian/foreigner ₹5/100, camera/video ₹20/100; ⊙9.30am-5pm Sat-Thu) The relics of bygone days are on display in this wonderful museum, 4km north of Pudukkottai train station. Its eclectic collection includes musical instruments, megalithic burial artefacts, and some remarkable paintings, sculptures and miniatures.

Thirumayam Fort FORT
(Thirumayam; Indian/foreigner ₹5/100; ⊙10am-5.30pm) Simple and imposing, the renovated Thirumayam Fort, about 20km south of Pudukkottai, is worth a climb for the 360-degree views from the battlements over the surrounding countryside. There's a rock-cut Shiva shrine up some metal steps on the west side of the small hill.

Mansions

Lakshmi House HISTORIC BUILDING
(Athangudi Periya Veedu; Athangudi Rd, Athangudi; admission ₹100; ⊙9am-5pm) With perhaps the most exquisitely painted wood-carved ceilings in Chettinadu, Lakshmi House is a popular film set. Take in the especially fine materials (Belgian marble, English iron), Chettiar history panels, and curious statues of British rulers and Hindu gods above the front entrance. Athangudi is 15km northwest of Karaikkudi.

CVCT House HISTORIC BUILDING
(CVCT St, Kanadukathan; admission ₹100, camera ₹50; ⊙9am-5pm) Backed by the typical succession of pillar-lined courtyards, the impressive reception hall of this 'twin house' is shared by two branches of the same family. Don't miss the fabulous views over neighbouring mansions from the rooftop terrace. On the same street, **VVRM House** (CVCT St, Kanadukathan) is one of Chettinadu's oldest mansions, built in 1870 with distinctive egg-plaster walls, teak columns and intricate wood carvings; a ₹100 group 'donation' is expected. Kanadukathan is 9km south of Thirumayam.

PKACT House HISTORIC BUILDING
(Trichy Main Rd, Kottaiyur, opp. ICICI Bank ATM; admission ₹50; ⊙10am-5pm) Run by the Chennai-based **M.Rm.Rm. Cultural Foundation** (Map p328; mrmrmculturalfoundation.moonfruit.com), this particularly well-preserved early-1900s mansion mixes modern and traditional architecture. Unusually, you can tour the whole house; upstairs,

there's a superb collection of Ravi Varma prints. Kottaiyur is 6km north of Karaikkudi.

🛏 Sleeping & Eating

To get a feel for the palatial life, book into one of Chettinadu's top-end hotels; they're pricey but the experience is fantastic.

★ Visalam — HERITAGE HOTEL $$$

(☎ 04565-273301; www.cghearth.com; Local Fund Rd, Kanadukathan; r incl breakfast ₹6500-13,000; ❄@🛜☲) Stunningly restored and professionally run by a Malayali hotel chain, Visalam is a relatively young Chettiar mansion, done in the fashionable art-deco style of the 1930s. It's still decorated with the original owners' photos, furniture and paintings. The garden is lovely, the rooms large and full of character, and the pool setting is magical, overflowing with bougainvillea and with a low-key cafe alongside it. Kanadukathan is 9km south of Thirumayam.

★ Saratha Vilas — BOUTIQUE HOTEL $$$

(☎ 9884203175, 9884936158; www.sarathavilas.com; 832 Main Rd, Kothamangalam; r incl breakfast ₹8000-11,000; ❄@🛜) A different type of Chettiar charm inhabits this stylishly renovated, French-run mansion from 1910, 6km east of Kanadukathan. Rooms combine traditional and contemporary with distinct French panache, and the food is an exquisite mix of Chettinad and French. Most of the furnishings were personally designed by the knowledgeable architect owners, who are very active players in the preservation and promotion of Chettinadu heritage.

They're also the founders of local conservation NGO ArCHeS.

Bangala — BOUTIQUE HOTEL $$$

(☎ 04565-220221; www.thebangala.com; Devakottai Rd, Karaikkudi; r ₹6500-7000; ❄🛜☲) This lovingly restored whitewashed 'bungalow' isn't a typical mansion but has all the requisite charm, with colourful rooms, quirky decorations, antique furniture, old family photos, and a beautiful pool. It's famous for its food: the ₹1000 set meals are actually Chettiar wedding feasts worth every paisa (available to nonguests from 12.30pm to 2.30pm and 8pm to 10pm; call two hours ahead).

Chettinadu Mansion — HERITAGE HOTEL $$$

(☎ 04565-273080; www.chettinadmansion.com; 11 AR St, SARM House, Kanadukathan; s/d incl breakfast ₹5000/6400, half-board ₹5700/7800; ❄🛜☲) Slightly shabbier than other Chettiar joints, but friendly and well managed,

this colourful century-old house is still owned (and lived in) by the original family. Of its 126 rooms, just 12 are open to guests – all sizeable with free wi-fi, wacky colour schemes and private balconies looking over other mansions.

The owners also run **Chettinadu Court** (☎ 9443495598; www.deshadan.com; Raja's St, Kanadukathan; s/d incl breakfast ₹3400/4500; ❄🛜☲) a few blocks away, which has eight pleasant rooms sporting a few heritage touches. The two share an off-site pool.

ℹ Getting There & Away

Car is by far the best way to get to and around Chettinadu. Renting one with a driver from Trichy, Thanjavur or Madurai for two days costs around ₹5000. Otherwise there are buses about every five minutes from Trichy to Pudukkottai (₹25, 1½ hours) and Karaikkudi (₹85, 2½ hours); you can hop off and on along the way. From Madurai, buses run to Karaikkudi (₹37, two hours) and Pudukkottai (₹57, 2½ hours) every 10 minutes. There are also buses from Thanjavur and Rameswaram.

Madurai

☎ 0452 / POP 1.02 MILLION

Chennai may be the capital of Tamil Nadu, but Madurai claims its soul. Madurai is Tamil-born and Tamil-rooted, one of the oldest cities in India, a metropolis that traded with ancient Rome and was a great capital long before Chennai was even dreamt of.

Tourists, Indian and foreign, usually come here to see the Meenakshi Amman Temple, a labyrinthine structure ranking among the greatest temples of India. Otherwise, Madurai, perhaps appropriately given her age, captures many of India's glaring dichotomies, with a centre dominated by a medieval temple and an economy increasingly driven by IT, all overlaid with the energy and excitement of a big Indian city and slotted into a much more manageable package than Chennai's sprawl.

History

Legend has it that Shiva showered drops of nectar (*madhuram*) from his locks onto the city, giving rise to the name Madurai – 'the City of Nectar'.

Ancient documents record the existence of Madurai from the 3rd century BC. It was a trading town, especially in spices, and according to legend was the home of the third *sangam* (gathering of Tamil scholars and poets). Over the centuries Madurai came under the sway of the Cholas, Pandyas, local Muslim sultans, Hindu Vijayanagar kings, and the Nayaks, who ruled until 1736 and set out the old city in a lotus shape. Under Tirumalai Nayak (1623–59) the bulk of the Meenakshi Amman Temple was built, and Madurai became the hub of Tamil culture, playing an important role in the development of the Tamil language.

In 1840 the British East India Company razed Madurai's fort and filled in its moat. The four broad Veli streets were constructed on top and to this day define the old city's limits.

◎ Sights

★ **Meenakshi Amman Temple**   HINDU TEMPLE
(Indian/foreigner ₹5/50, phone camera ₹50; ⊙4am-12.30pm & 4-9.30pm) The abode of the triple-breasted warrior goddess Meenakshi ('fish-eyed' – an epithet for perfect eyes in classical Tamil poetry) is considered by many to be the height of South Indian temple architecture, as vital to the aesthetic heritage of this region as the Taj Mahal is to North India. It's not so much a 17th-century temple as a 6-hectare complex with 12 tall *gopurams*, encrusted with a staggering array of gods, goddesses, demons and heroes (1511 of them on the south *gopuram* alone).

According to legend, the beautiful Meenakshi (a version of Parvati) was born with three breasts and this prophecy: her superfluous breast would melt away when she met her husband. The event came to pass when she met Shiva and took her place as his consort. The existing temple was built during the 17th-century reign of Tirumalai Nayak, but its origins go back 2000 years to when Madurai was a Pandyan capital.

The four streets surrounding the temple are pedestrian-only. Dress codes and security are strict for the temple itself: no women's shoulders, or legs of either gender, may be exposed, and no cameras are allowed inside (but you *can* use phone cameras). Despite this the temple has a happier, more joyful atmosphere than some of Tamil Nadu's more solemn shrines, and is adorned with especially colourful ceiling and wall paintings. Every evening at 9pm, a frenetic, incense-clouded procession carries an icon of Sundareswarar (Shiva) to Meenakshi's shrine to spend the night; visitors are welcome to follow along.

Before entering the temple, have a look around the Pudhu Mandapa. The main temple entrance is through the eastern (oldest) gopuram. First, on the right, you'll come to the Thousand Pillared Hall, now housing an Art Museum. Moving on into the temple, you'll reach a Nandi shrine surrounded by more beautifully carved columns. Ahead is the main Shiva shrine, flanked on each side by massive *dvarapalas,* and further ahead to the left in a separate enclosure is the main Meenakshi shrine, both open only to Hindus. However , anyone wander round the Golden Lotus Tank, then leave the temple via a hall of flower sellers and the arch-ceilinged Ashta Shakti Mandapa – this is actually used as the temple entrance by most worshippers and is lined with relief carvings of the goddess's eight attributes, with perhaps the loveliest of all the temple's vibrantly painted ceilings.

➡ **Pudhu Mandapa**
(East Chitrai St) This 16th-century pillared hall stands outside the temple, opposite the eastern *gopuram*. It's filled with colourful textile and crafts stalls and tailors at sewing machines, partly hiding some of the lovely pillar sculptures, but it's easy to find the triple-breasted Meenakshi near the southeast corner, facing Sundareswarar (opposite), and their marriage, accompanied by Vishnu, just inside the western entrance. A particularly handsome light-blue Nandi (Shiva's vehicle) sits outside the *mandapa*'s eastern entrance.

➡ **Art Museum**
(Indian/foreigner ₹5/50, phone camera ₹50; ⊙6.30am-1pm & 4-9pm) Inside the temple's eastern *gopuram,* is the Nayak-period Thousand Pillar Hall (with 985 columns) on the right. This is now the Art Museum, where you can admire at your leisure a Shiva shrine with a large bronze Nataraja at the end of a corridor of superbly carved pillars, plus many other fine bronzes and colourfully painted panels. Some of the best carvings, including Krishna with his flute and Ganesh dancing with a woman on his knee, are immediately inside the museum entrance.

Gandhi Memorial Museum   MUSEUM
(Gandhi Museum Rd; camera ₹50; ⊙10am-1pm & 2-5.45pm Sat-Thu) FREE Housed in a 17th-century Nayak queen's palace, this excellent museum contains an impressively moving and comprehensive account of India's struggle for independence from 1757 to

Madurai

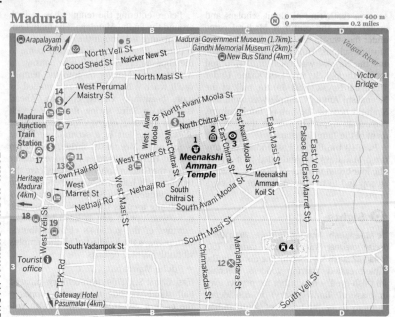

1947, and the English-language text spares no detail about British rule. Included in the exhibition is the blood-stained dhoti that Gandhi was wearing when he was assassinated in Delhi in 1948; it was here in Madurai, in 1921, that he first took up wearing the dhoti as a sign of native pride.

The small **Madurai Government Museum** (Indian/foreigner ₹5/100, camera ₹20; ⊙9.30am-5pm Sat-Thu) is next door, and the **Gandhian Literary Society Bookshop** (⊙10am-1pm & 2.30-6.30pm Mon-Sat) behind. **Yoga** (one-month unlimited membership ₹100; ⊙6am, 10.30am & 5pm Mon-Fri) takes place within the museum's grounds; no bookings needed.

Bus 75 from **Periyar Bus Stand** (West Veli St) goes to the Tamukkam bus stop on Alagarkoil Rd, 600m from the museum.

Tirumalai Nayak Palace   PALACE
(Palace Rd; Indian/foreigner ₹10/50, camera/video ₹30/100; ⊙9am-1.30pm & 2-5pm) What the Meenakshi Amman Temple is to Nayak religious architecture, Tirumalai Nayak's crumbling palace is to the secular. Although it's said to be only a quarter of its original size, its massive scale and hybrid Dravidian-Islamic style still testify to the lofty aspirations of its creator. You enter from the east – a large courtyard surrounded by tall columns topped with fancy stucco work leads through to the grand throne chamber with its 25m-high dome; two stone-carved horses frame the steps up.

☞ Tours

Foodies Day Out   FOOD TOUR
(☎9840992340; www.foodiesdayout.com; 2nd fl, 393 Anna Nagar Main Rd; per person ₹2000) For a fantastic evening exploring Madurai's culinary specialities with a local food enthusiast, contact Foodies Day Out. Minimum two people; vegetarian tours available.

Storytrails   WALKING TOUR
(☎7373675756; www.storytrails.in; 35 Krishnarayar Tank Rd; 2hr tour for up to 4 people ₹2500) This Chennai-based organisation runs highly rated story-based neighbourhood walking tours.

✿ Festivals & Events

Teppam (Float) Festival   RELIGIOUS
(⊙Jan/Feb) A popular event held on the full moon of the Tamil month of Thai, when Meenakshi temple deities are paraded around town in elaborate procession and floated in a brightly lit 'mini-temple' on the huge Mariamman Teppakkulam tank, 3km east of the old city.

Madurai

◎ **Top Sights**
1 Meenakshi Amman Temple B2

◎ **Sights**
2 Art Museum...C2
3 Pudhu Mandapa....................................C2
4 Tirumalai Nayak Palace C3

⊕ **Activities, Courses & Tours**
5 Storytrails B1

⊜ **Sleeping**
6 Hotel Park Plaza...................................A1
7 Hotel Supreme A2
8 Hotel West Tower B2
9 Madurai Residency A2
10 Royal Court...A1
11 TM Lodge A2

⊗ **Eating**
12 Murugan Idli Shop................................C3
13 Sri Sabareesh..A2
Surya ....(see 7)
Temple View ....(see 6)

ⓘ **Information**
14 Canara Bank ATM.................................A1
15 ICICI Bank ATM.....................................B1
16 State Bank of India A2
Supreme Web................................(see 7)

ⓘ **Transport**
17 Fast Track Booking Counter A2
18 Periyar Bus Stand................................A2
19 Shopping Complex Bus Stand...........A3

The evening culminates in Shiva's seduction of his wife, whereupon the icons are brought back to the temple to make love and, in so doing, regenerate the universe. Meenakshi's diamond nose stud is removed so it doesn't irritate her lover. Due to low rainfall, the 2013 and 2014 celebrations were 'dry' floats.

Chithirai Festival   RELIGIOUS
(☉ Apr/May) The highlight of Madurai's busy festival calendar is this two-week event celebrating the marriage of Meenakshi to Sundareswarar (Shiva). The deities are wheeled around the Meenakshi Amman Temple in massive chariots forming part of long, colourful processions.

🛏 Sleeping

Budget hotels in central Madurai are mostly dreary and unloved, but there is a big choice of perfectly fine, near-identical midrange places along West Perumal Maistry St, near the train station. Most have rooftop restaurants with temple and sunset views.

Hotel West Tower   HOTEL $
(☑ 0452-2349600; 42/60 West Tower St; s/d ₹500/800, with AC ₹1200/1800; ❄) The West Tower's best asset is that it's very near the temple, but it's also acceptably clean and friendly.

TM Lodge   HOTEL $
(☑ 0452-2341651; www.tmlodge.in; 50 West Perumal Maistry St; s/d ₹440/660, r with AC ₹1300; ❄) The walls are a bit grubby, but the sheets are clean. TM is efficiently run, even with a lift operator!

Madurai Residency   HOTEL $$
(☑ 0452-4380000; www.madurairesidency.com; 15 West Marret St; s ₹2380-2860, d ₹2760-3220, all incl breakfast; ❄🕸) The service is stellar and the rooms are comfy and fresh at this winner, which has one of the highest rooftop restaurants in town. It's very popular, so book at least a day ahead.

Royal Court   HOTEL $$
(☑ 0452-4356666; www.royalcourtindia.com; 4 West Veli St; s ₹3960-4910, d ₹4800-5640, all incl breakfast; ❄@🕸) The Royal Court blends a bit of white-sheeted, hardwood-floored colonial elegance with comfort, good eating options, free wi-fi and friendy yet professional service. Rooms come with tea/coffee sets. It's an excellent, central choice for someone in need of a treat.

Hotel Park Plaza   HOTEL $$
(☑ 0452-3011111; www.hotelparkplaza.net; 114 West Perumal Maistry St; s/d incl half-board ₹2880/3480; ❄🕸) The Plaza's rooms are comfortable and simply but smartly done up, with free wi-fi. Four have temple views. It also boasts a good multicuisine rooftop **Temple View** (☉ 5pm-midnight) restaurant and the (inappropriately named) **Sky High Bar** – on the 1st floor.

Hotel Supreme   HOTEL $$
(☑ 0452-2343151; www.hotelsupreme.in; 110 West Perumal Maistry St; s ₹2390-3270, d ₹2710-3470, all incl breakfast; ❄🕸) The Supreme is a well-presented, slightly faded hotel with friendly service, that's very popular with domestic tourists. There's good food at the rooftop Surya restaurant and free in-room wi-fi, and the spaceship-themed basement bar will make you wonder if someone laced your lassi last night.

Gateway Hotel Pasumalai   HOTEL $$$

(☎0452-6633000; www.thegatewayhotels.com; 40 TPK Rd, Pasumalai; s ₹6000-8390, d ₹7200-9600; @ৠ⊛⊠) A stunning escape from the city scramble, the Gateway sprawls across hilltop gardens 5km southwest of the centre. The views, outdoor pool and 45 resident peacocks are wonderful, and rooms are luxuriously comfy and equipped with glassed-in showers and do-it-yourself yoga kits. The Garden All Day restaurant is excellent.

Heritage Madurai   HERITAGE HOTEL $$$

(☎0452-3244187; www.heritagemadurai.com; 11 Melakkal Main Rd, Kochadai; s ₹5880-8820, d ₹6470-9410; ⊛ৠ⊠) This leafy haven, 4km west of central Madurai, originally housed the old Madurai Club. It's been impeccably tarted up, with intricate woodwork, a lovely sunken pool and airy, terracotta-floored 'deluxe' rooms. Best are the comfy 'villas' featuring private mini-swimming-pools. There's a good Chettinad restaurant, along with a spa, bar and 24-hour cafe.

✕ Eating

The hotel-rooftop restaurants along West Perumal Maistry St offer breezy night-time dining and temple views (don't forget the mosquito repellent); most of the hotels also have AC restaurants open for breakfast and lunch. Look out for Madurai's famous summer drink *jigarthanda* (boiled milk, almond essence, rose syrup and vanilla ice cream).

Murugan Idli Shop   SOUTH INDIAN $

(196 West Masi St; dishes ₹11-40; ⊙7am-midnight) Though it now has Chennai branches, Murugan is Madurai born and bred. Here you can put the fluffy signature *idlis* to the test, and feast on South Indian favourites such as dosas and *uttapams*.

Sri Sabareesh   INDIAN $

(49A West Perumal Maistry St; mains ₹57-85; ⊙6.30am-11.30pm) Decked with old-Madurai photos, Sri Sabareesh is a popular pure-veg spot that does decent South Indian thalis for ₹80. It's quite characterful and contemporary for a cheapie on this street.

Surya   MULTICUISINE $$

(110 West Perumal Maistry St; mains ₹80-190; ⊙4-11.30pm) The Hotel Supreme's rooftop restaurant offers excellent service, good pure-veg food and superb city and temple views, but the winner here has got to be the iced coffee, which might have been brewed by a god when you sip it on a hot, dusty day.

Garden All Day   MULTICUISINE $$$

(Gateway Hotel, 40 TPK Rd, Pasumalai; mains ₹300-525; ⊙7am-10.30pm) If you fancy splashing out, the panoramic all-day restaurant at the Gateway Hotel (5km southwest of central Madurai) does a fantastic multicuisine dinner buffet (₹800 to ₹1000). Outside in the gardens or inside in AC comfort.

GOVERNMENT BUSES FROM MADURAI

DESTINATION	FARE (₹)	DURATION (HR)	FREQUENCY
Bengaluru	440-750	9	9pm, 9.15pm, 9.30pm, 9.45pm
Chennai	325	9-10	every 30min 4am-11.30pm
Coimbatore	125	6	every 15min
Ernakulam (Kochi)	325	9	9am & 9pm
Kanyakumari	180	6	every 2hrs 6am-10pm, hourly 10pm-6am
Kodaikanal	62	4	14 buses 1.30am-2.50pm & 5.50pm
Mysuru	300-440	10	4 buses 4.30-9pm
Ooty	180	9	7.30am & 9pm
Puducherry	250	8	9pm
Rameswaram	85-110	5	every 30min 6am-midnight
Trichy	75-90	3	every 15min

🛍 Shopping

Madurai teems with cloth stalls and tailors' shops, as you might notice upon being approached by tailor touts. A great place for getting clothes made up is the Pudhu Mandapa. Here you'll find rows of tailors busily treadling away and capable of whipping up a good replica of whatever you're wearing in an hour or two. A cotton top or shirt can cost ₹350. Drivers, guides and touts will also be keen to lead you to the Kashmiri craft shops in North Chitrai St, offering to show you the temple view from the rooftop – the views are good, and so is the inevitable sales pitch.

❶ Information

State Bank of India (West Veli St) Foreign-exchange desks and ATM.

Supreme Web (110 West Perumal Maistry St; per hour ₹30; ⊙7.30am-9.30pm) Take your passport.

Tourist office (☑ 0452-2334757; 1 West Veli St; ⊙10am-5.45pm Mon-Fri)

❶ Getting There & Away

AIR

SpiceJet (www.spicejet.com) flies at least once daily to Bengaluru, Chennai, Colombo, Delhi, Dubai, Hyderabad and Mumbai (Bombay). Further Chennai flights are operated by **Jet Airways** (www.jetairways.com) three or four times daily, and **Air India** (☑ 0452-2690333; www.airindia.com) once daily.

BUS

Most government buses arrive and depart from the **New bus stand** (Melur Rd), 4km northeast of the old city. Services to Coimbatore, Kodaikanal and Ooty go from the **Arapalayam bus stand** (Puttuthoppu Main Rd), 2km northwest of the old city. Tickets for more expensive (and more comfortable) private buses are sold by agencies on the south side of the **Shopping Complex bus stand** (btwn West Veli St & TPK Rd). Most travel overnight.

TRAIN

From Madurai Junction station, 13 daily trains head north to Trichy and 10 to Chennai, the fastest being the 7am Vaigai Express (Trichy 2nd/chair class ₹93/340, two hours; Chennai ₹180/655, 7¾ hours). A good overnight train for Chennai is the 8.35pm Pandyan Express (sleeper/3AC/2AC/1AC ₹315/805/1135/1915, nine hours). To Kanyakumari the only daily train departs at 1.55am (sleeper/3AC/2AC/1AC ₹210/535/735/1230, five hours), though there's a later train some days (at varying times). Trivandrum (Thiruvananthapuram; three trains

daily), Coimbatore (three daily), Bengaluru (two daily) and Mumbai (Bombay; one daily) are other destinations.

❶ Getting Around

The airport is 12km south of town; taxis cost ₹300 to the centre. Alternatively, bus 10A runs to/from the Shopping Complex bus stand. From the New Bus Stand, bus 75 (₹11) shuttles into the city; an autorickshaw is ₹100.

Fixed-rate railway permit taxis congregate out the front of the train station. There's also a Fast Track taxi **booking counter** (☑ 0452-2888999; Madurai Junction; ⊙24hr) here; fares start at ₹75 for the first 3km, then ₹15 per kilometre.

Rameswaram

☑ 04573 / POP 44,856

Rameswaram was once the southernmost point of sacred India; to leave its boundaries was to abandon caste and fall below the status of the lowliest skinner of sacred cows. Then Rama, incarnation of Vishnu and hero of the Ramayana, led an army of monkeys and bears across a monkey-built bridge to the island of (Sri) Lanka, where he defeated the demon Ravana and rescued his wife, Sita. Afterwards, prince and princess came to this spot to offer thanks to Shiva.

If all this seems like so much folklore, it's absolute truth for millions of Hindus, who flock to the Ramanathaswamy Temple to worship where a god worshipped a god.

Apart from these pilgrims, Rameswaram is a small fishing town on a conch-shaped island, Pamban, connected to the mainland by 2km-long road and rail bridges. The town smells of drying fish and, if you aren't a pilgrim, the temple alone barely merits the journey here. But the eastern point of the island, Dhanushkodi, only 30km from Sri Lanka, has a natural magic and beauty that add considerably to Rameswaram's appeal.

Most hotels and eateries are clustered around the Ramanathaswamy Temple, which is surrounded by North, East, South and West Car Sts. Middle St heads west towards the bus stand (around 2km). The train station is 1.5km southwest of the temple.

◉ Sights

Ramanathaswamy Temple HINDU TEMPLE
(⊙5am-1pm & 3-8pm) Housing the world's most sacred sand mound (a lingam said to have been created by Rama's wife Sita, so that he could worship Shiva), this temple is

one of India's holiest shrines. Dating mainly from the 16th to 18th centuries, it's notable for its long, exquisite 1000-pillar halls and 22 *theerthams* (temple tanks), in which pilgrims bathe before visiting the deity. Attendants tip pails of water over the (often fully dressed) faithful, who then rush on to the next *theertham*.

The legend goes that, when Rama decided to worship Shiva, he figured he'd need a lingam to do the thing properly. Being a god, he sent Hanuman to find the biggest lingam around – a Himalayan mountain. But the monkey took too long, so Sita made the simple lingam of sand now enshrined in the temple's inner sanctum.

Cameras and phones are forbidden inside the temple. Only Hindus may enter the inner shrine.

🛏 Sleeping & Eating

Most hotels are geared towards pilgrims, and some cheapies (which are mostly pretty grim) refuse to take single travellers, but there's a string of reasonable midrange hotels. Book ahead before festivals. Budget travellers can try the **rooms booking office** (East Car St; ⊘24hr), opposite the main, eastern temple entrance, which often scores doubles for as low as ₹300 a night.

Inexpensive vegetarian restaurants such as **Vasantha Bhavan** (East Car St; dishes ₹30-50; ⊘7am-10pm) and **Ananda Bhavan** (West Car St; ⊘6.30am-10.30pm) serve thali lunches for ₹50 to ₹70, and evening dosas and *uttapams* for about ₹40. You might find fish in some restaurants, but no real meats.

Hotel Venkatesh　　　　　HOTEL $
(☑04573-221296; SV Koil St; r ₹495-660, with AC ₹880; ❄) Open to single travellers, the lemon-walled rooms here are tolerably clean and not bad value. It's on the westward continuation of South Car St.

Daiwik Hotels　　　　　HOTEL $$
(☑04573-223222; www.daiwikhotels.com; Madurai-Rameswaram Hwy; r ₹4330-5570; ❄@🛜) Fresh, comfy and gleaming, 'India's first four-star pilgrim hotel', 200m west of the bus station, is your swankiest choice in Rameswaram. Bright, airy rooms come smartly decked out with huge mirrors and local-life photos, and the vegetarian **Ahaan** (mains ₹140-270; ⊘7am-10pm) restaurant is very good.

Hotel Sri Saravana　　　　HOTEL $$
(☑04573-223367; www.srisaravanahotel.com; 1/9A South Car St; r ₹1400-2810; ❄) The best of the town-centre hotels, Sri Saravana is friendly and clean with decent service and spacious, colourful rooms. Those towards the top have sea views (and higher rates).

ℹ Information

Micro Net Browsing (West Car St; per hour ₹30; ⊘8.30am-8pm)
State Bank of India ATM (South Car St)

ℹ Getting There & Around

Buses run to Madurai (₹110, four hours) every 10 minutes, and to Trichy (₹180, 6½ hours) hourly. 'Ultra Deluxe' (UD) services are scheduled three times daily to Chennai (₹450, 13 hours) and once daily to Kanyakumari (₹250, eight hours), but don't always run.

WORTH A TRIP

DHANUSHKODI

The promontory stretches 22km southeast from Rameswaram, narrowing to a thin strip of sand dunes about halfway along. Near the end stands the ghost town of Dhanushkodi. Once a thriving port, Dhanushkodi was washed away by the tidal waves of a monster cyclone in 1964. The shells of its train station, church, post office and other ruins still stand among a scattering of fishers' shacks, and Adam's Bridge (or Rama's Bridge), the chain of reefs, sandbanks and islets that almost connects India with Sri Lanka, stretches away to the east. For many, this is the final stop of a long prilgrimage. Go for sunrise, when the atmosphere is at its most magical, with pilgrims performing *pujas* (prayers).

Autorickshaws charge about ₹400 round trip (including waiting time) to Moonram Chattram, a collection of fishers' huts about 14km from town. From there to Dhanushkodi it's a hot 4km beach walk, or a ₹100 two-hour round trip in a truck or minibus which goes when it fills up with 12 to 20 customers (6am to 6pm). Many hotels organise private jeeps to whizz you along to Danushkodi (around ₹1500 return). It's tempting to swim, but beware of strong rips.

The three daily trains to/from Madurai (₹35, four hours) have unreserved seating only. The Rameswaram–Chennai Express departs daily at 8pm (sleeper/3AC/2AC ₹330/890/1280, 12½ hours) via Trichy. The Rameswaram–Kanyakumari Express leaves at 8.45pm Monday, Thursday and Saturday, reaching Kanyakumari (sleeper/3AC ₹275/705) at 4.05am.

Bus 1 (₹4) shuttles between the bus stand and East Car St. Autorickshaws to the centre from the bus stand or train station cost ₹40.

Kanyakumari (Cape Comorin)

📞 04652 / POP 22,453

This is it, the end of India. There's a sense of accomplishment on making it to the tip of the subcontinent's 'V', past the final dramatic flourish of the Western Ghats and the green fields, glinting rice paddies and slow-looping wind turbines of India's deep south. Like all edges, there's a sense of the surreal here. At certain times of year you can see the sun set and the moon rise over three seas simultaneously. The Temple of the Virgin Sea Goddess, Swami Vivekananda's legacy and the 'Land's End' symbolism draw crowds of pilgrims and tourists to Kanyakumari, but it remains a small-scale, refreshing respite from the hectic Indian road.

◉ Sights & Activities

Kumari Amman Temple HINDU TEMPLE
(⊙ 4.30am-12.15pm & 4-8.15pm) The legends say the *kanya* (virgin) goddess Kumari, a manifestation of the Great Goddess Devi, single-handedly conquered demons and secured freedom for the world. At this temple at the tip of the subcontinent, pilgrims give her thanks in an intimately spaced, beautifully decorated temple, where the crash of waves from three seas can be heard behind the twilight glow of oil fires clutched in vulva-shaped votive candles (referencing the sacred femininity of the goddess).

It's believed that the sea-facing door of the temple stays locked to prevent the shimmer of the goddess's diamond nose-stud leading ships astray. You'll probably be asked for a ₹10 donation to enter the inner precinct, where men must remove their shirts, and cameras are forbidden.

The shoreline around the temple has a couple of tiny beaches, and bathing ghats where some worshippers immerse themselves before visiting the temple. The *mandapa* south of the temple is popular for

sunset-watching and daytime shade. A small souvenir-shop bazaar leads back from here to the main road.

Vivekananda Memorial MONUMENT
(admission ₹10; ⊙ 8am-4pm) Four hundred metres offshore is the rock where the famous Hindu apostle Swami Vivekananda meditated from 25 to 27 December 1892, and decided to take his moral message beyond India's shores. A two-*mandapa* memorial to Vivekananda, built in 1970, reflects temple architectural styles from across India. With all the tourist crowds this brings, Vivekananda would no doubt choose somewhere else to meditate today. Ferries shuttle out to the Vivekananda island (₹34 return) between 7.45am and 4pm.

Thiruvalluvar Statue MONUMENT
(⊙ 7.45am-4pm) FREE Looking like an Indian Colossus of Rhodes, the towering statue on the smaller island next to the Vivekananda Memorial is of the ancient Tamil poet Thiruvalluvar. The work of more than 5000 sculptors, it was erected in 2000 and honours the poet's 133-chapter work Thirukural – hence its height of exactly 133ft (40.5m). Vivekananda rock ferries (₹34 return) usually continue to Thiruvalluvar between 2pm and 4pm.

Swami Vivekananda Wandering Monk Exhibition MUSEUM
(Main Rd; admission ₹10; ⊙ 9am-12.30pm & 4-8.30pm) This excellent exhibition details Swami Vivekananda's wisdom, sayings and encounters with the mighty and the lowly during his five years as a wandering monk around India from 1888 to 1893.

Your ticket also covers the 'Awake! Awake!' Vivekananda-inspired exhibition (Vivekanandapuram; ⊙ 9am-1pm & 4-8pm Wed-Mon, 9am-1pm Tue) in Vivekanandapuram, a peaceful ashram 1km north of town, with various yoga retreats. The spiritual organisation Vivekananda Kendra (www.vivekanandakendra.org), devoted to carrying out Vivekananda's teachings, has its headquarters here.

Gandhi Memorial MONUMENT
(⊙ 7am-7pm) FREE Appropriately placed at the end of the nation that Gandhi fathered, this cream-and-blue memorial is designed in the form of an Odishan temple embellished by Hindu, Christian and Muslim architects. The central plinth was used to store some of the Mahatma's ashes before they were

immersed in the sea, and each year, on Gandhi's birthday (2 October), the sun's rays fall on the stone. Exhibits are limited to a few photos; the tower is a popular sunset-gazing spot.

Kamaraj Memorial　　　　MONUMENT
(⊘7am-6.45pm) FREE This memorial near the shoreline commemorates K Kamaraj, known as the 'Gandhi of the South'. One of the most powerful and respected politicians of post-Independence India, Kamaraj held the chief ministership of both Madras state and its successor, Tamil Nadu. The dusty photos inside have captions.

🛏 Sleeping

As befits a holiday destination, many Kanyakumari hoteliers have gone for bright, playful decor; after the bland statewide sameness of midrange hotels, it's exciting to find a huge neon-coloured tiger painted on your bedhead.

Hotel Narmadha　　　　HOTEL $
(☑04652-246365; Kovalam Rd; r ₹400-600) This long, colourful concrete block conceals friendly staff, a back-up generator and a range of cheap rooms, some of which are cleaner and have less grim bathrooms than

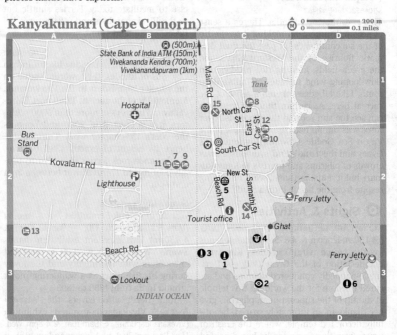

Kanyakumari (Cape Comorin)

others; the ₹600 sea-view doubles with spearmint-stripe sheets are good value.

Lakshmi Tourist Home
HOTEL $

(☑04652-246333; East Car St; r ₹750-1000, with AC ₹1350) Basic but well-kept, this relatively helpful family hotel is a decent town-centre deal. The better (and pricier) rooms come with sea views and hot water, but most are neat and clean.

Hotel Tri Sea
HOTEL $$

(☑04652-246586; www.hoteltrisea.in; Kovalam Rd; d ₹1180-2590; ❋🛜☷) You can't miss the high-rise Tri Sea, whose sea-view rooms are huge, spotless and airy, with particularly hectic colour schemes. The top-floor triples are even grander. Reception is super-efficient and the rooftop pool, sunrise and sunset viewing platforms and free in-room wifi are welcome bonuses, though the restaurant is a sad afterthought.

Hotel Sivamurugan
HOTEL $$

(☑04652-246862; www.hotelsivamurugan.com; 2/93 North Car St; r ₹1375, with AC ₹2250-2700; ❋🛜) A welcoming, well-appointed hotel, with spacious, spotless, marble-floored rooms and free wi-fi (lobby only). The 'super-deluxes' have sea glimpses past a couple of buildings. Rates stay fixed year-round (a novelty for Kanyakumari) and there's 24-hour hot water, which not all competitors can claim.

Santhi Residency
HOTEL $$

(Kovalam Rd; r ₹1000, with AC ₹1500; ❋) A smaller, older restored house with leafy courtyards, Santhi has an unusually restrained style for Kanyakumari (the only decoration in each room is a picture of Jesus). It's quiet and clean with tight-fit rooms and bathrooms.

Sparsa Resort
HOTEL $$$

(☑04652-247041; www.sparsaresorts.com; 6/112B Beach Rd; r incl breakfast ₹5400-7200; ❋🛜☷) Located away from the temple frenzy, elegant Sparsa is a good few notches above your average Kanyakumari hotel. Fresh, orange-walled rooms with low, dark-wood beds, lounge chairs and mood-lighting make for a contemporary oriental vibe and there's a lovely pool that is surrounded by palms, as well as good Indian cooking at Auroma (mains ₹150-380; ☺7-10am, noon-3pm, 7-10.30pm).

Seashore Hotel
HOTEL $$$

(☑04652-246704; http://theseashorehotel.com; East Car St; r ₹4140-7800; ❋🛜) The fanciest hotel in town centre has shiny, spacious rooms with gold curtains and cushions, glassed-in showers, free wi-fi and useful equipment including kettles and hair-dryers. It's lost some of its original sparkle, but all rooms except the cheapest have panoramic sea views, and the 7th-floor restaurant is one of Kanyakumari's best.

✖ Eating

Hotel Saravana
INDIAN $

(Sannathi St; mains ₹89-120; ☺6.30am-10pm) A clean, popular spot with plenty of North and South Indian vegetarian dishes, lunchtime thalis and crispy dosas.

Seashore Hotel
MULTICUISINE $$

(East Car St; mains ₹190-380; ☺7am-10.30pm) Amazingly, the classy 7th-floor restaurant at the Seashore Hotel is the only one in Kanyakumari with a proper sea view. There's grilled fish and plenty of pan-Indian veg and nonveg choices, plus the odd Continental creation; try the veg or seafood sizzlers. Service is spot-on and it's great for brekkie (buffet or à la carte).

Sangam Restaurant
INDIAN $$

(Main Rd; mains ₹90-280; ☺7am-11pm) It's as if the Sangam started in Kashmir, trekked the length of India, and stopped off here to offer top veg and nonveg picks from every province along the way. The food is good, the seats are soft and the joint is bustling.

ℹ Information

Tourist office (☑04652-246276; Beach Rd; ☺10am-5.45pm Mon-Fri)

Xerox, Internet, Fax (Main Rd; internet per hour ₹30; ☺9.30am-10pm Mon-Sat) Staffed by women.

ℹ Getting There & Away

BUS

The sedate **bus stand** (Kovalam Rd) is a 10-minute walk west of the centre. Ordinary buses run 11 times daily to Madurai (₹165, six hours) and at least seven times daily to Trivandrum (₹71, 2½ hours). Two daily buses, 6am and 2pm, go to Kovalam (₹80, three hours). The most comfortable buses are the 'Ultra Deluxe' (UD), which include the following:

Chennai (₹540, 12 to 14 hours, eight daily)
Kodaikanal (₹310, 10 hours, 8.15pm)
Madurai (₹220, four hours, eight daily)

TAMIL NADU & CHENNAI KANYAKUMARI (CAPE COMORIN)

PADMANABHAPURAM PALACE

With a forest's worth of intricately carved rosewood ceilings and polished-teak beams, the **Padmanabhapuram Palace** (☑ 04651-250255; Padmanabhapuram; Indian/foreigner ₹35/300, camera/video ₹50/2000; ☺ 9am-1pm & 2-4.30pm Tue-Sun), 35km northwest of Kanyakumari near the Kerala border, is considered the finest example of traditional Keralan architecture today. Asia's largest wooden palace complex, it was once the capital of Travancore, an unstable princely state taking in parts of both Tamil Nadu and Kerala. As the egos of successive rulers left their mark, it expanded into the magnificent conglomeration of 14 palaces it is today; the oldest sections date back to 1550.

Direct buses leave from Kanyakumari bus stand at 7.15am, 11am, 1pm, 1.30pm and 4.45pm (₹21, two hours); buses also run every 10 minutes between 4.30am and 10pm to Thuckalay, from where it's a short autorickshaw ride or 15-minute walk. Taxis between Kanyakumari and Kovalam (Kerala), stopping at Padmanabhapuram, cost ₹3000.

From Trivandrum (Thiruvananthapuram) take any bus towards Kanyakumari and get off at Thuckalay (₹50, 1½ hours, eight daily). The Kerala Tourist Development Corporation (KTDC; p942) runs full-day Kanyakumari tours from Trivandrum (₹700) covering Padmanabhapuram.

TAXI

Drivers ask ₹2000 to Kovalam.

TRAIN

The train station is a walkable distance north of the centre. The one daily northbound train, the Kanyakumari Express, departs at 5.20pm for Chennai (sleeper/3AC/2AC/1AC ₹415/1085/1545/2610, 13½ hours) via Madurai (₹210/535/735/1230, 4½ hours) and Trichy (₹275/705/985/1655, 7¼ hours). Two daily express trains depart at 6.50am and 10.30am for Trivandrum (Thiruvananthapuram; 2nd-class/sleeper/3AC/2AC ₹60/140/485/690, 2¼ hours), both continuing to Kollam (Quilon) and Ernakulam (Kochi). More trains go from Nagercoil Junction, 15km northwest of Kanyakumari.

For real train buffs, the Vivek Express runs all the way to Dibrugarh in Assam, 4236km and 80 hours – the longest single train ride in India. It departs from Kanyakumari at 11pm Thursday (sleeper/3AC/2AC ₹1085/2810/4235).

THE WESTERN GHATS

Welcome to the lush Western Ghats, some of the most welcome heat relief in India. Rising like an impassable bulwark of evergreen and deciduous tangle from north of Mumbai to the tip of Tamil Nadu, the World Heritage-listed Ghats (with an average elevation of 915m) contain 27% of India's flowering plants and an incredible array of endemic wildlife. In Tamil Nadu they rise to 2000m and more in the Palani Hills around Kodaikanal and the Nilgiris

around Ooty. British influence lingers a little stronger up in these hills, where the colonists built their 'hill stations' to escape the sweltering plains and covered slopes in neatly trimmed tea bushes. It's not just the air and (relative) lack of pollution that's refreshing – there's a certain acceptance of quirkiness and eccentricity here that is rarer in the lowlands. Think organic farms, handlebar-moustached trekking guides and leopard-print earmuffs.

Kodaikanal (Kodai)

☑ 04542 / POP 36,500 / ELEV 2100M

There are few more refreshing Tamil Nadu moments than boarding a bus in the heat-soaked plains and disembarking in the sharp pinch of a Kodaikanal night or morning. This misty hill station, 120km northwest of Madurai in the Palani Hills, is more relaxed and intimate than its big sister Ooty (Kodai is the 'Princess of Hill Stations', while Ooty is the 'Queen'). It's not all cold either; during the day the weather can be more like deep spring than early winter. The renowned Kodaikanal International School provides a bit of cosmopolitan flair, with students from around the globe.

Centred on a beautiful lake, Kodai rambles up and down hillsides with patches of *shola* (virgin) forest, unique to the Western Ghats in South India, and evergreen broadleaf trees such as magnolia, mahogany, myrtle and rhododendron. Another of its plant specialities is the *kurinji* shrub, whose lilac-blue blossoms appear only every 12 years: next due 2018.

Kodai is popular with honeymooners and groups, who flock to the spectacular viewpoints and waterfalls in and around town.

◉ Sights & Activities

Sacred Heart Natural Science Museum
MUSEUM

(Sacred Heart College, Law's Ghat Rd; adult/child ₹15/10, camera ₹20; ⊘9am-6pm) In the grounds of a former Jesuit seminary 4km downhill east of town, this museum has a ghoulishly intriguing miscellany of flora and fauna put together over more than 100 years by priests and trainees. Displays range over bottled snakes, human embryos (!), giant moths and stuffed animal carcasses. You can also see pressed *kurinji* flowers *(Strobilanthes kunthiana)* in case you aren't around for their flowering.

Parks & Waterfalls

Bryant Park (adult/child ₹30/15, camera/video ₹50/100; ⊘9am-6pm), landscaped and stocked by the British officer after whom it's named, is pretty, and usually busy with both tourists and canoodling couples.

Several natural beauty spots around Kodai (crowded with souvenir and snack stalls) are very popular with Indian tourists. They're best visited by taxi unless you like strolling along busy roads. Taxi drivers offer three-hour 12-stop tours for around ₹1200. On clear days, Green Valley View (6km from the centre), Pillar Rocks (7km) and less visited Moir's Point (13km), all along the same road west of town, have spectacular views to the plains far below.

To go beyond Moir's Point to forest-fringed Berijam Lake (⊘closed Tues) requires a ₹150 Forest Department permit. Taxi drivers can organise this, often the same day, and do four-hour 'forest tours' to Berijam for ₹1800.

The river that empties Kodaikanal Lake tumbles dramatically down Silver Cascade, on the Madurai road 7km from town. Compact Bear Shola Falls are in a pocket of forest on the northwest edge of town.

Walking

Assuming it's not cloaked in opaque mist, the views from paved Coaker's Walk (admission ₹10; ⊘7.30am-7pm) are beautiful, all the way down to the plains 2000m below. The stroll takes five minutes.

The 5km Kodaikanal Lake circuit is lovely in the early morning before the crowds roll in. A walk along Lower Shola Rd takes you through the Bombay Shola, the nearest surviving patch of *shola* to central Kodai.

Most serious trekking routes around Kodai require Forest Department permits which can only be obtained with time, patience and luck. Contact Kodai's District Forest Office (☑04542-240287; Muthaliarpuram; ⊘8am-5.45pm Mon-Fri, permits issued 8-10am Mon, Wed, Thu & Fri). The tourist office and guesthouses like Greenlands Youth Hostel will put you in touch with local guides, including the very experienced Vijay Kumar (☑9965524279; thenaturetrails@gmail.com), who can help with permits and offer interesting off-road routes (₹500 to ₹800 per half-day).

A good trek, if you can organise it, is the two-day Kodai–Munnar route into Kerala via Bodi and Top Station (though it involves some bus/rickshaw transport). Guides charge ₹4000 to ₹5000 per person.

Boating, Cycling & Horse Riding

If you're sappy in love like a bad Bollywood song, the thing to do in Kodai is rent a pedal boat (₹60 per half-hour for two people), rowboat (₹90 including boatman) or Kashmiri *shikara* ('honeymoon boat'; ₹350 including boatman) from the Kodaikanal Boat & Rowing Club (⊘9am-5.30pm) or Tamil Nadu Tourist Development Corporation (⊘9am-5.30pm).

Bicycle-rental (per hour/day ₹20/300) and horse-riding (per 500m/2 hours ₹50/1000) stands are dotted around the lake.

⌖ Sleeping

Some hotels hike prices by up to 100% during the 'season' (April to June). There are some lovely heritage places, and good-value midrange options if you can live without colonial-era ambience. Most hotels have a 9am or 10am checkout from April to June.

Sri Vignesh Guest House
GUESTHOUSE $

(☑9094972524; umaarkrishnan@gmail.com; Lake Rd; r ₹700-800) Up a steep driveway and surrounded by colourful, neat gardens, this simple but characterful Raj-era home is run by a friendly local couple, who welcome 'peaceful' guests (no packs of boys!). Rooms are clean and very basic, and there's hot water until noon.

Kodaikanal (Kodai)

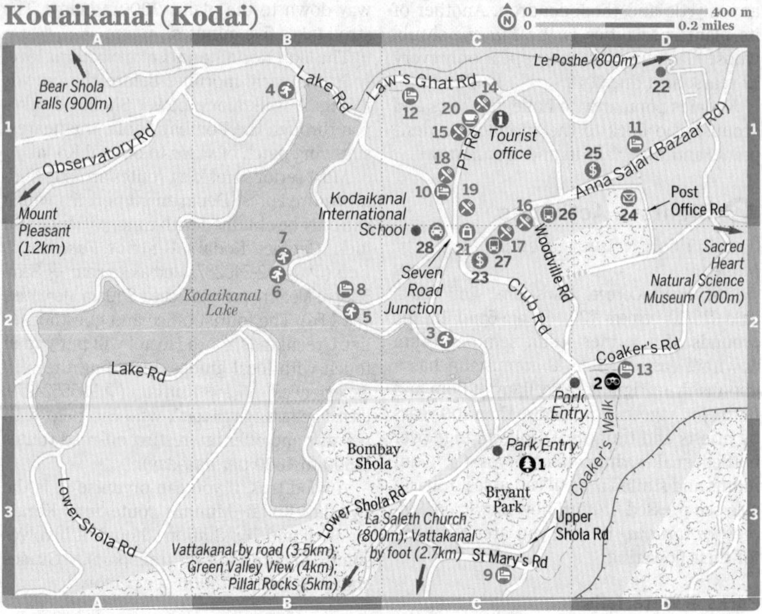

Snooze Inn HOTEL $
(☎04542-240837; www.jayarajgroup.com; Anna Salai; r ₹770-970; 📶) Rooms don't have quite as much character as the outside suggests, but this is a decent-value budget choice with clean bathrooms, free wi-fi and plenty of blankets.

Greenlands Youth Hostel HOSTEL $
(☎04542-240899; www.greenlandskodaikanal.com; St Mary's Rd; dm ₹300, d ₹600-2025; 📶) This long-running and sociable budget favourite has a pretty garden and wonderful views, but the accommodation is very bare and basic, hot water only runs from 8am to 10am, and washing in the dorms (minimum 10 people for a booking) is by buckets.

Villa Retreat HOTEL $$
(☎04542-240940; www.villaretreat.com; Club Rd; r incl breakfast ₹3480-5280; 📶) You can take in the fantastic Coaker's Walk views from your garden breakfast table at this lovely old stone-built family hotel, right next to the walk's northern end. It's a friendly place with comfy, good-sized rooms and free wi-fi in the dining room, where there's often a roaring fire on cold nights. Prices feel a tad steep, but service is incredibly attentive.

Hilltop Towers HOTEL $$
(☎04542-240413; www.hilltopgroup.in; Club Rd; r incl breakfast ₹2220-2760; 📶) Although it's bland on the outside, rustic flourishes like polished teak floors, plus keen staff, in-room tea/coffee sets and free wi-fi make the Hilltop a good midrange choice.

Mount Pleasant BOUTIQUE HOTEL $$
(☎04542-242023, 9655126023; www.kodaikanalheritage.com; 19/12-20 Observatory Rd; r incl breakfast ₹1900-3100; 📶) Despite being out on the fringe of Kodai's spaghetti-like street map, 2km west of the centre, Mount Pleasant is worth finding for its quiet setting, tasty buffet dinners, homey rooms and the welcoming Keralan owner's quirky taste – colourful wall weavings, coconut-wood beds, coir matting. Book ahead.

★**Carlton Hotel** HOTEL $$$
(☎04542-240056; www.krahejahospitality.com; Lake Rd; s/d/cottage incl half-board ₹9560/10,570/16,290; 📶) The cream of Kodai's hotels is a magnificent five-star colonial-era mansion overlooking the lake. Rooms are spacious with extra comfy beds and, for some, huge private balconies. The grounds and common areas get the old hill-station ambience spot on: open stone walls, billiards, evening bingo by the fireplace, and a bar that

Kodaikanal (Kodai)

makes you want to demand a Scotch now, dammit, from the eager staff.

Le Poshe　　　　　　　HOTEL **$$$**
(www.leposhehotel.com; 25 Sivanadi Rd; s ₹5040-7440, d ₹5400-7790, all incl breakfast; ☎) This stylish new addition to Kodai's hotel scene feels like you've stumbled into a flashy furniture showroom. Warm woods and whites give a fresh alpine-chalet-chic theme to the cosy, minimalist rooms sporting glassed-in

showers and tea/coffee makers. Staff are charming, views are lovely, and perks include a good restaurant, a spa and a gym. It's 2km north of town.

Vattakanal

Little Vattakanal village ('Vatta'), about 4.5km southwest of Kodai centre, is a great rural retreat for budget travellers. It's very popular, particularly with groups of Israeli travellers, and there's a laid-back party vibe when things gets busy. Altaf's Cafe has a few sizeable three-bed rooms for six people (sometimes more!) with private bathroom for ₹1200.

Kodai Heaven　　　　GUESTHOUSE **$**
(☎9865207207; www.kodaiheaven.com; Dolphin's Nose Rd, Vattakanal; r ₹1000-2500) Simple, hillside sharing rooms for two to six people.

Eating & Drinking

PT Rd is the best place for cheap restaurants and it's here that most travellers and students from the international school hang out.

Tava　　　　　　　　INDIAN **$**
(PT Rd; mains ₹75-110; ⊙11am-8.45pm Thu-Tue) Clean, fast and cheap, pure-veg Tava has a wide menu; try the spicy, cauliflower-stuffed *gobi paratha* or *sev puri* (crisp, puffy fried bread with potato and chutney).

Altaf's Cafe　　　　MULTICUISINE **$$**
(☎9487120846; Vattakanal; dishes ₹60-220; ⊙8.30am-9.30pm) This semi-open-air cafe whips up Italian, Indian and Middle Eastern dishes including breakfasts and *sabich* (Israeli aubergine-and-egg pita sandwiches), for the hungry travellers at Vattakanal.

Pot Luck　　　　　　CAFE **$**
(PT Rd; snacks & light meals ₹50-160; ⊙11am-7.30pm Wed-Mon) Pancakes, toasties, coffee, omelettes and quesadillas served up on a tiny, pretty terrace attached to a pottery shop.

Hotel Astoria　　　　INDIAN **$$**
(Anna Salai; mains ₹100-130; ⊙7am-10pm) This veg restaurant is always packed with locals and tourists, especially at lunchtime when it serves excellent all-you-can-eat thalis.

★ **Carlton Hotel**　　　MULTICUISINE **$$$**
(Lake Rd; buffet lunch/dinner ₹750/850; ⊙7-10am, 1-3pm & 7.30-11pm) Definitely the place to come for a splash-out buffet fill-up: a

> **WORTH A TRIP**
>
> ### VATTAKANAL WALK
>
> This is a lovely walk of about 4.5km (each way) from central Kodai, on which you might spot gaur (bison) or giant squirrels in the forested bits. From the south end of Coaker's Walk, follow St Mary's Rd west then southwest, passing La Saleth Church after 1.2km. At a fork 400m after the church, go left downhill on what quickly becomes an unpaved track passing through the Pambar Shola forest. After 450m you emerge on a bridge above some falls. Across the bridge you'll find snack stalls selling fruit, tea, coffee, bread omelettes and roasted corn with lime and masala. Follow the road 1km downhill, with panoramas opening up as you go, to Vattakanal village. Take the steep path down past Altaf's Cafe and in about 15 minutes you'll reach the Dolphin's Nose, a narrow rock lookout overhanging a precipitous drop, and a couple more snack stalls.

huge variety of excellent Indian and Continental dishes in limitless quantity.

Cloud Street
MULTICUISINE $$$
(PT Rd; mains ₹250-500; ⊙9am-9pm) Why yes, that is a real Italian-style wood-fire pizza oven. And yes, that's hummus and falafel on the menu, along with oven-baked pasta and nachos. It's all great food in a simple, relaxed setting, but it's a bit pricier than you'd expect.

Cafe Cariappa
CAFE
(PT Rd; coffees ₹70-110; ⊙6am-11pm Mon-Sat) A caffeine addict's dream, this cute, wood-panelled cafe does fantastic cappuccino, espresso, mocha, and macchiato, all infused with locally grown organic Palani Hills coffee.

Self-Catering

Pastry Corner
BAKERY $
(Anna Salai; ⊙10am-2pm & 3-6pm) Pick up yummy muffins, croissants and sandwiches at this hugely popular bakery, or squeeze onto the benches with a cuppa.

Eco Nut
ORGANIC $
(PT Rd; ⊙10.30am-6pm Mon-Sat) This tiny shop sells local organic food – wholewheat bread, muffins, muesli, spices – as well as oils, herbs and herbal remedies.

🔒 Shopping

Shops and stalls all over town sell homemade chocolate, spices, natural oils and handicrafts. Some also reflect a low-key but long-term commitment to social justice.

Re Shop
HANDICRAFTS
(www.bluemangoindia.com; Seven Rd Junction; ⊙10am-7pm Mon-Sat) Stylish jewellery, fabrics, cards and more, at reasonable prices,

made by and benefiting marginalised village women around Tamil Nadu.

Cottage Craft Shop
HANDICRAFTS
(PT Rd; ⊙10am-7pm Mon-Sat, 1.30-7pm Sun) Sells incense, embroidery, hats, bags and other goods crafted by disadvantaged groups across India, with about 80% of the purchase price returned to the makers.

ⓘ Information

Hi-Tech Internet (Seven Rd Junction; per hour ₹60; ⊙9am-8pm Mon-Sat)

Tourist office (☑ 04542-241675; PT Rd; ⊙10am-5.45pm Mon-Sat) Doesn't look too promising but they're helpful enough.

ⓘ Getting There & Away

The nearest train station is Kodai Road, down in the plains about 80km east of Kodaikanal. There are eight daily trains to/from Chennai Egmore including the overnight Pandyan Express (sleeper/3AC/2AC/1AC ₹295/760/1065/1800, eight hours), departing Chennai at 9.20pm and departing Kodai Road northbound at 9.10pm. For most closer destinations, it's quicker and easier to get a bus. Taxis to/from the station cost ₹1200. Direct buses from Kodaikanal to Kodai Road leave daily at 3pm and 4pm (₹55, three hours); there are also plenty of buses between the station and Batlagundu, on the Kodai–Madurai bus route. Kodai's post office has a **train booking desk** (Head Post Office, Post Office Rd; ⊙9am-2pm & 3-4pm Mon-Sat).

Government buses from Kodai's **bus stand** (Anna Salai) include:

Bengaluru (₹600 to ₹750, 12 hours, 5.30pm and 6pm)

Chennai (₹480, 12 hours, 6.30pm)

Coimbatore (₹120, six hours, 8.30am and 4.30pm)

Madurai (₹62, four hours, 15 daily)

Trichy (₹111, six hours, four daily)

Raja's Tours & Travels (☎ 04542-242422; Anna Salai) runs 20-seat minibuses with push-back seats to Ooty (₹400, eight hours, 7pm) and Kochi (Cochin; ₹800, 11 hours, 6pm), along with overnight AC sleeper buses to Chennai (₹1100, 12 hours) and Bengaluru (₹950, 12 hours) at 6pm.

ⓘ Getting Around

Central Kodaikanal is compact and easy to get around on foot. There are no autorickshaws (believe it or not), but plenty of taxis. Trips within town generally cost ₹150.

Around Kodaikanal

There are some fabulous country escapes in the Palani Hills below Kodaikanal.

Elephant Valley   FARMSTAY $$

(☎ 9244103418; www.duneecogroup.com; Ganesh Puram; r incl breakfast ₹3300-7200; 🛜) 🍴 Deep in the valley 22km from Kodaikanal, off the Kodai–Palani road, this ecofriendly French-run retreat sprawls across 49 hectares of mountain jungle and organic farm. Elephants, peacocks and bison wander through regularly, and comfy local-material cottages, including a treehouse, sit either side of a river. The French-Indian restaurant does wonderful meals packed with garden-fresh veg, and home-grown coffee. Wildlife spotting peaks April to July.

Coimbatore

☎ 0422 / POP 1.05 MILLION

This big business and junction city – Tamil Nadu's second largest, often known as the Manchester of India for its textile industry – is friendly enough and increasingly cosmopolitan, but the lack of interesting sights means that for most travellers it's just a stepping stone towards Ooty or Kerala. It has plenty of accommodation and eating options if you're spending the night.

🛏 Sleeping

Sree Subbu   HOTEL $

(☎ 0422-2300006; Geetha Hall Rd; s ₹370-480, d ₹660) If you don't need AC and price is the priority, Sree Subbu does a decent budget job.

Legend's Inn   HOTEL $$

(☎ 0422-4350000; www.legendsinn.com; Geetha Hall Rd; r ₹1440, s/d with AC ₹1800/2040; ❄) One of a good 10 places on this lane opposite the

train station, this is a great-value midrange choice, with spacious, clean, comfortable rooms and 24-hour checkout. It gets busy, so book ahead.

Hotel ESS Grande   HOTEL $$

(☎ 0422-2230271; www.hotelessgrande.co.in; 358-360 Nehru St; s ₹2160-2520, d ₹2520-2880, all incl breakfast; ❄@) Handy for a few of the bus stands, the friendly ESS has small but very clean, fresh rooms, all with cable internet. There are several other midrange and budget hotels on this street.

CAG Pride   HOTEL $$

(☎ 0422-4317777; www.cagpride.com; 312 Bharathiyar Rd; s ₹4080-4560, d ₹4800-5280, all incl breakfast & dinner; ❄🛜) Touches of modern art add colour to the glossy, cosy rooms here, the best of which have freshly revamped bathrooms (renovations were still underway at research time). It's smart, helpful and near the central bus stations.

Residency   HOTEL $$$

(☎ 0422-2241414; www.theresidency.com; 1076 Avinashi Rd; s/d incl breakfast from ₹6600/7080; ❄@🛜🏊) Opening through a soaring lobby, the Residency is top choice for its friendly staff, elegant and well-equipped rooms, swimming pool, free wi-fi and excellent eating and drinking options, including good-value buffet meals at the **Pavilion** (buffet breakfast/lunch/dinner ₹470/950/950; ⊙7-10am, 12.30-3pm & 7pm-midnight) restaurant. Check online for discounts.

🍴 Eating

Junior Kuppanna   SOUTH INDIAN $$

(177 Sarojini Rd; dishes ₹120-180) Your favourite South Indian thalis come piled onto banana leaves with traditional flourish, and starving carnivores will love the long menu of mostly nonveg southern specialities, all from a perfectly spotless kitchen.

Hot Chocolate   CONTINENTAL $$

(734 Avinashi Rd; mains ₹120-330; ⊙10.30am-10.30pm) Not bad at all if you're craving pasta, wraps, sandwiches or cakes.

That's Y On The Go   MULTICUISINE $$

(167 Racecourse Rd; mains ₹220-480; ⊙12.30-3pm & 7-10.30pm) Colourful, contemporary, and filled with cartoons and turquoise sofas, this is a great place for tasty global fare from Italian and Middle Eastern to Southeast Asian and North Indian.

Coimbatore

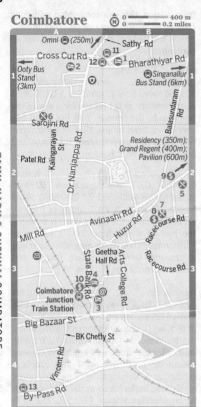

0 — 400 m
0 — 0.2 miles

Coimbatore

Sleeping
1 CAG Pride		B1
2 Hotel ESS Grande		A1
3 Legend's Inn		A3
4 Sree Subbu		A3

Eating
5 Hot Chocolate		B2
6 Junior Kuppanna		A1
7 That's Y On The Go		B2

Information
8 HSBC ATM		B2
9 State Bank of India ATM		B2
10 State Bank of India ATM		A3

Transport
11 SETC Bus Stand		B1
12 Town Bus Stand		A1
13 Ukkadam Bus Station		A4

ℹ Information

State Bank of India ATM (Coimbatore Junction) One of several ATMs outside the train station.

Travel Gate (Geetha Hall Rd; per hour ₹30; ⊙8.30am-9.30pm) Cramped internet cafe.

ℹ Getting There & Away

AIR

The airport is 10km east of town, with daily direct flights to domestic destinations including Bengaluru, Chennai, Delhi, Hyderabad and Mumbai on **Air India** (☑ 0422-2303933; www.airindia.com), **IndiGo** (www.goindigo.in), **Jet Airways** (www.jetairways.com) or **SpiceJet** (www.spicejet.com)

SilkAir (☑ 0422-4370271; www.silkair.com) flies four times weekly to/from Singapore.

BUS

From the **SETC bus stand** (Thiruvalluvar Bus Stand; Bharathiyar Rd), express or superfast government buses head to Bengaluru (₹375 to ₹750, nine hours, seven daily), Chennai (₹400, 11 hours, 10 buses 5.30pm to 10pm), Ernakulam (Kochi; ₹152 to ₹174, 5½ hours, six daily), Mysore (₹160 to ₹381, six hours, 21 daily) and Trivandrum (₹312 to ₹344, 10½ hours, six daily).

The **Ooty bus stand** (New bus stand; Mettupalayam (MTP) Rd), northwest of the centre, has services to Ooty (₹53, four hours) via Mettupalayam (₹17, one hour) and Coonoor (₹40, three hours) every 20 minutes, plus hourly buses to Kotagiri (₹32, three hours, 5.20am to 7.20pm), 16 buses daily to Mysuru (₹160 to ₹381, six hours) and six to Bengaluru (₹375 to ₹750, nine hours).

From the **Singanallur bus stand** (Kamaraj Rd), 6km east of the centre, buses go to Trichy (₹130, six hours) and Madurai (₹130, six hours) every 10 minutes. City bus 140 (₹11) shuttles between here and the **Town bus stand** (cnr Dr Nanjappa & Bharathiyar Rds).

Ukkadam bus station (NH Rd), southwest of the centre, has buses to southern destinations including Pollachi (₹23, 1¼ hours, every 5 minutes), Kodaikanal (₹120, six hours, 10am) and Munnar (₹140, 6½ hours, 8.15am), plus some services to Madurai.

Private buses to Bengaluru, Chennai, Ernakulam, Puducherry, Trichy and Trivandrum start from the **Omni bus stand** (Sathy Rd), 500m north of the Town bus stand. Agencies on Sathy Rd sell tickets.

TAXI

A taxi up the hill to Ooty (three hours) costs about ₹2100; Ooty buses often get so crowded that it's worth considering.

TRAIN

Coimbatore Junction is on the main line between Chennai and Ernakulam (Kochi, Kerala), with at least 13 daily trains in each direction. The 5.15am Nilgiri Express to Mettupalayam connects with the miniature railway departure from Mettupalayam to Ooty at 7.10am. The whole trip to Ooty takes about seven hours.

ℹ Getting Around

For the airport take bus 20 (₹11) from the Town bus stand. Many buses run between the train station and the Town bus stand. Autorickshaws charge ₹60 from the train station to the Ukkadam bus station, ₹80 to the SETC or Town Bus Stands, and ₹150 out to the Ooty bus stand.

Around Coimbatore

The Isha Yoga Center (☑0422-2515345; www.ishafoundation.org), an ashram in Poondi, 30km west of Coimbatore, is also a yoga and rejuvenation retreat and place of pilgrimage. The centrepiece is a multireligious temple housing the Dhyanalinga, believed to be unique in embodying all seven chakras of spiritual energy. Visitors are welcome to meditate or for yoga courses, which you should book in advance.

The commercial town of Mettupalayam, 40km north of Coimbatore, is the starting point for the miniature train to Ooty. If you need to stay the night before catching the 7.10am train, there's plenty of accommodation. Hotel EMS Mayura (☑04254-227936; hotelemsmayura@gmail.com; 212 Coimbatore Rd; r ₹1200, with AC ₹1800; ❋), a fine, bland mid-range hotel with a decent restaurant, is just 300m from the bus station and 1km from the train station.

Coonoor

☑0423 / POP 45,494 / ELEV 1720M

Coonoor is one of the three Nilgiri hill stations – Ooty, Kotagiri and Coonoor – that are situated high above the southern plains. Smaller and quieter than Ooty, it has some fantastic heritage hotels and guesthouses, from which you can do exactly the same kind of things as you would do from bigger, busier Ooty. From upper Coonoor, 1km to 2km above the town centre, you can look down over the sea of red-tile rooftops to the slopes beyond and soak up the peace, cool climate and beautiful scenery. But you get none of the above in central Coonoor, which is a bustling, honking mess.

◉ Sights & Activities

Sim's Park   PARK
(adult/child ₹30/15, camera/video ₹50/100; ☺8am-6.30pm) Upper Coonoor's 12-hectare Sim's Park, established in 1874, is a peaceful oasis of sloping manicured lawns with more than 1000 plant species from several continents, including magnolias, tree ferns, roses and camellias. Kotagiri-bound buses will drop you here.

Highfield Tea Estate   TEA ESTATE
(Walker's Hill Rd; ☺8am-9pm) **FREE** This 50-year-old estate (2km northeast of upper Coonoor) is one of few Nilgiri working tea factories open to visitors. Self-appointed guides jump in quickly, but you're perfectly welcome to watch the full tea-making process independently.

TAMIL NADU & CHENNAI AROUND COIMBATORE

MAJOR TRAINS FROM COIMBATORE

DESTINATION	TRAIN NO & NAME	FARE (₹)	DURATION (HR)	DEPARTURE
Bengaluru	16525 Bangalore Express	260/690/990 (B)	8½	10.55pm
Chennai Central	12676 Kovai Express	180/655 (A)	7½	2.55pm
	22640 Chennai Express	315/805/1135 (B)	7½	10.15pm
Ernakulam (Kochi)	12677 Ernakulam Express	105/385 (A)	3¾	1.10pm
Madurai	16610 Nagercoil Express	205/540 (C)	5½	8.30pm

Fares: (A) 2nd-class/AC chair; (B) sleeper/3AC/2AC; (C) sleeper/3AC

ANAMALAI TIGER RESERVE

A pristine 850-sq-km reserve of tropical jungle, *shola* forest and grassland rising to 2400m and spilling over into Kerala in the Western Ghats between Kodaikanal and Coimbatore, **Anamalai Tiger Reserve** (Indira Gandhi Wildlife Sanctuary & National Park; admission ₹20, camera/video ₹50/200; ☺ Jun-Feb) is well off most tourists' radar. Declared a tiger reserve in 2007, it's home to all kinds of exotic endemic wildlife, much of it rare and endangered – including leopards and a few elusive tigers, though you'll probably mostly spot lion-tailed macaques, peacocks, langurs, spotted deer, elephants – or crocodiles at Amaravathi Crocodile Farm.

The reserve's **Reception and Interpretation Centre** (☑ 04253-245002; Topslip; ☺ 6.30am-3.30pm) is at Topslip, 35km southwest of Pollachi. From here you can head off on **elephant rides** (per hour ₹800-1500), official one-hour **minibus jungle 'safaris'** (per person from ₹120) or **guided treks** (per 2 h ₹2000). Most people visit on day trips, but for those staying the night Topslip has **Forest Department accommodation** (r ₹500-2500) of varying comfort levels. Book several days ahead through the **District Forest Office** (☑ 04259-225356, 04259-238360; 365/1 Meenkarai Rd, Pollachi; ☺ 10am-5.45pm Mon-Fri) in Pollachi; phone reservations are accepted.

The tiny tea-plantation town of **Valparai**, on the fringes of the reserve 65km south from Pollachi and reached via a spectacular 40-hairpin-bend road, makes a beautifully peaceful Anamalai base where you're just as likely to see wildlife. Our pick of the accommodation is **Sinna Dorai's Bungalow** (☑ 9443077516; www.sinnadorai.com; Valparai; r incl full-board ₹7500; ☎). Exquisitely located on a rambling tea estate, Sinna Dorai has just six huge rooms bursting with local early-20th-century history. A cosy library, wonderful homemade meals, and charming service make you feel right at home. After-dark wildlife-spotting drives, on which you may well find elephants, bison, lion-tailed macaques, and leopards, run regularly, and experienced trekkers will lead you along local paths. It's well signposted from central Valparai.

Several daily buses connect Pollachi with Topslip (₹40, 1½ hours) and Valparai (₹42, three hours). Buses to Pollachi run from Coimbatore's Ukkadam bus station (p396), which also has four daily services to Valparai (₹65, four hours). From Kodaikanal, buses head to Pollachi (₹100, six hours) at 8.30am and 4.30pm.

Dolphin's Nose   VIEWPOINT

About 10km from town, this viewpoint exposes a vast panorama encompassing Catherine Falls across the valley. On the same road, **Lamb's Rock**, a favourite picnic spot in a pretty patch of forest, has amazing views past tea and coffee plantations to the hazy plains. The easiest way to see these sights is a rickshaw tour for around ₹600, or walk the 6km or so back into town from Lamb's Rock (mostly downhill).

🛏 Sleeping & Eating

You'll need a rickshaw, car or great legs to reach these places.

YWCA Wyoming Guesthouse   HOSTEL $

(☑ 0423-2234426; www.ywcaagooty.com; Bedford; dm/s/d ₹165/414/972) A ramshackle, 150-year-old gem, the Wyoming is draughty and creaky but oozes colonial-era character with wooden terraces and serene town views through trees. The rooms are good and clean, with geysers, and you get a friendly welcome. Meals available at two hours' notice.

★ 180° McIver   BOUTIQUE HOTEL $$

(☑ 0423-2233323; www.serendipityo.com; Orange Grove Rd; r incl breakfast ₹4200-6540; ☎) A classic 1890s British bungalow at the top of town has been turned into something special with a soupçon of French taste. The six lovely, airy rooms sport antique furniture, working fireplaces and big fresh bathrooms. On-site restaurant **La Belle Vie** (mains ₹200-450; ☺ 12.30-3.30pm & 7.30-10.30pm) attracts diners for its European-Indian food and 'tea boutique'. The panoramas from the wraparound lawn are fabulous.

Acres Wild   FARMSTAY $$

(☑ 9443232621; www.acres-wild.com; Upper Meanjee Estate, Kanni Mariamman Kovil St; r incl breakfast ₹3600-5400; ☎) 🍃 This beautifully positioned farm on the southeast edge of town is run on sustainable lines with solar heating, rainwater harvesting and cheese like you've never tasted in India from the milk of its own cows. Guests can take cheese-making courses. The five rooms, in three cottages, are large and stylish, with kitchens and fireplaces.

Your friendly Mumbaikar hosts are full of ideas for things to do away from tourist crowds. Book ahead.

Gateway Hotel HERITAGE HOTEL $$$
(☑0423-2225400; www.thegatewayhotels.com; Church Rd, Upper Coonoor; s ₹5710-9910, d ₹6310-10,520, all incl breakfast; ☎) A colonial-era priory turned gorgeous heritage hotel, the Taj-Group Gateway has homey cream-coloured rooms immersed in greenery. You get wonderful mountain views from those at the back while the good multicuisine **restaurant** (mains ₹400-600; ⊙7.30-10.30am, 12.30-3pm & 7.30-10.30pm) overlooks the gardens. Evening bonfires are lit on the lawn and there's free daily yoga along with an ayurvedic spa.

Self-Catering

Tulsi Mall SUPERMARKET
(31 Mount Pleasant Rd; ⊙10am-8.30pm Wed-Mon) Well-stocked supermarket with a good range of Western products.

🛍 Shopping

Green Shop HANDICRAFTS, FOOD
(www.lastforest.in; Jograj Bldg, Bedford Circle; ⊙9.30am-7pm Mon-Sat) ✐ Beautiful fairtrade local tribal crafts, clothes and fabrics, plus organic treats such as wild honey, nuts, chocolates and tea.

❶ Getting There & Away

Coonoor is on the miniature train line between Mettupalayam (27km) and Ooty (19km), with three daily trains just to/from Ooty as well as the daily Mettupalayam–Ooty–Mettupalayam service. Buses to and from Ooty (₹10, one hour) run every 10 minutes; buses to Kotagiri (₹11, one hour) and Coimbatore (₹45, 2½ hours) go every 20 minutes.

Kotagiri

♫ 04266 / POP 28,200 / ELEV 1800M
The oldest and smallest of the three Nilgiri hill stations, Kotagiri is a quiet, unassuming place with a forgettable town centre – its appeal is the escape to red dirt tracks in the pines, blue skies and the high green walls of the Nilgiris.

💿 Sights & Activities

You can visit **Catherine Falls**, 8km south, off the Mettupalayam road (the last 3km is on foot; the falls only flow after rain), **Elk Falls** (6km) and **Kodanad Viewpoint** (19km north), where there's a view over both the Coimbatore Plains and the Mysore Plateau. A half-day taxi tour to all three costs around ₹1000.

Sullivan Memorial MUSEUM
(☑9488771571; www.sullivanmemorial.org; Kannerimukku; adult/child ₹20/10; ⊙10am-5pm) If you're interested in the history of the Nilgiris, check out this wonderful little museum, 2km north of Kotagiri centre. The house built in 1819 by John Sullivan, founder of Ooty, has been refurbished and filled with fascinating photos, newspaper cuttings and artefacts about local tribal groups, European settlement and icons like the toy train. It also contains the **Nilgiri Documentation Centre** (www.nilgiridocumentation.org), dedicated to preserving the region's heritage.

Keystone Foundation VOLUNTEERING
(☑04266-272277; www.keystone-foundation.org; Groves Hill Rd) ✐ This Kotagiri-based NGO works to improve environmental conditions in the Nilgiris while involving, and improving living standards for, indigenous communities.

🍴 Sleeping & Eating

The Kotagiri-based Keystone Foundation's **Green Shop** (Johnstone Sq; ⊙9.30am-7pm Mon-Sat) has picnic goodies (organic chocolates, wild honey).

La Maison HERITAGE GUESTHOUSE $$$
(☑9585857732; www.lamaison.in; Hadatharai; s/d ₹7760/8890; ☎) Flower-draped, French-owned La Maison is a beautifully renovated 1890s Scottish bungalow superbly located on a hilltop surrounded by tea plantations, 5km southwest of Kotagiri. The design is quirky French-chic all the way: antique furniture, tribal handicrafts, old-Ooty paintings. Hike to waterfalls, visit tribal villages, tuck into excellent homecooked meals (₹750), or laze in the valley-facing jacuzzi.

❶ Getting There & Away

Buses run half-hourly to/from Ooty (₹15, 1½ hours), crossing one of Tamil Nadu's highest passes, and to Mettupalayam (₹16 to ₹22, 1½ hours). Buses to Coimbatore (₹30, 2½ hours) leave hourly.

Ooty (Udhagamandalam)

☎ 0423 / POP 88,430 / ELEV 2240M

Ooty may be a bit hectic for some tastes, and the town centre is an ugly mess, but it doesn't take long to get up into the quieter, greener areas where tall pines rise above what could almost be English country lanes. Ooty, 'the Queen of Hill Stations', mixes up Indian bustle and Hindu temples with lovely parks and gardens and charming Raj-era bungalows, the latter providing its most atmospheric (and most expensive) places to stay.

The town was established by the British in the early 19th century as the summer headquarters of the Madras government, and memorably nicknamed 'Snooty Ooty'. Development ploughed through a few decades ago, but somehow old Ooty survives. You just have to walk a bit further out to find it.

The journey up here on the celebrated miniature train is romantic and the scenery stunning. Even the road up from the plains is impressive. From April to June (the *very* busy 'season') Ooty is a welcome relief from the hot plains, and in the colder months (October to March) you'll need warm clothing, which you can buy cheap here, as overnight temperatures occasionally drop to 0°C.

The train and bus stations are at the west end of Ooty's racecourse, in almost the lowest part of town. To their west is the lake, while the streets of the town snake upwards all around. From the bus station it's a 20-minute walk to Ooty's commercial centre, Charing Cross. Like Kodaikanal, Ooty has an international school whose students can be seen around town.

◉ Sights

Botanical Gardens   GARDEN
(adult/child ₹30/15, camera/video ₹50/100; ☉7am-6.30pm) Established in 1848, these pretty gardens are a living gallery of the natural flora of the Nilgiris. Look out for a fossilised tree trunk believed to be 20 million years old, and on busy days, around 20 million Indian tourists.

St Stephen's Church   CHURCH
(☉10.30am-5pm, services 8am & 11am Sun) Perched above the town centre, the immaculate St Stephen's, built in 1829, is the oldest church in the Nilgiris. It has lovely stained glass, huge wooden beams hauled by elephant from the palace of Tipu Sultan 120km away, and the sometimes kitschy, sometimes touching slabs and plaques donated by colonial-era churchgoers. In the quiet, overgrown cemetery you'll find headstones commemorating many an Ooty Brit.

Nilgiri Library   LIBRARY
(☎0423-2441699; Hospital Rd; ☉10am-1pm & 2.30-6pm) This quaint little haven in a crumbling 1867 building has more than 30,000 books, including rare titles on the Nilgiris and hill tribes and 19th-century British journals. Visitors can consult books in the reading room with a temporary one-month membership (₹500). Upstairs is a portrait of Queen Victoria presented to Ooty on her 1887 Golden Jubilee.

Rose Garden   GARDEN
(Selbourne Rd; adult/child ₹30/15, camera/video ₹50/100; ☉7.30am-6.30pm) With terraced lawns and over 20,000 rose bushes of more than 2000 varieties – best between May and July – the Rose Garden is a lovely place for a stroll, and has good Ooty views from its hillside location.

Doddabetta Lookout   VIEWPOINT
(admission ₹5, camera/video ₹10/50; ☉8am-5.30pm) This is it: the highest point (2633m) of the Nilgiris and one of the best viewpoints around, assuming it's a clear day (go early for better chances of mist-free views). It's about 7km from the town centre. Kotagiri buses will drop you at the Doddabetta junction, then you have a steep-ish 3km walk or a quick jeep ride. Taxis do the round trip from Charing Cross for ₹500.

🏃 Activities

Hiking & Trekking

The best of Ooty is out in the beautiful Nilgiris. Ooty's tourist office and many accommodation places can put you in touch with local guides who do day hikes for ₹400 to ₹600 per person. You'll normally drive out of town and walk around hills, tribal villages and tea plantations.

More serious trekking in the best forest areas with plenty of wildlife – such as beyond Avalanche to the south or Parsons Valley to the west, in Mukurthi National Park, or down to Walakkad and Sairandhri in Kerala's Silent Valley National Park – requires Tamil Nadu Forest Department permits. At the time of research, the Office of the Field Director (☎0423-2444098, Mudumalai accom-

Nilgiri Hills

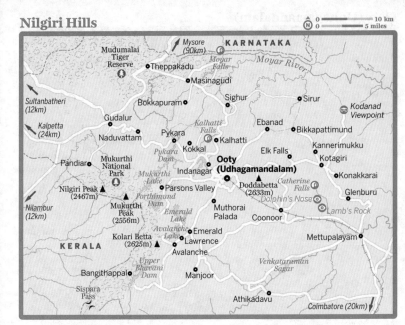

modation bookings 0423-2445971; fdmtr@tn.nic.in; Mount Stuart Hill; ⊘10am-5.45pm Mon-Fri) was not issuing permits due to rising concerns about man–animal conflict in the region; in January 2014, a tiger killed three people in the Doddabetta area, and there have been several elephant-related foreigner fatalities in recent years.

The Nilgiri Wildlife & Environment Association (☑0423-2447167; www.nwea.in; Mount Stuart Hill; ⊘10am-1pm & 2-5pm Mon-Fri, 10am-1pm Sat), the District Forest Office Nilgiris South Division (☑0423-2444083; dfosouth@sancharnet.in; Mount Stuart Hill; ⊘10am-5.45pm Mon-Fri), and the District Forest Office Nilgiris North Division (☑0423-2443968; dfonorth_ooty@yahoo.co.in; Mount Stuart Hill; ⊘10am-5.45pm Mon-Fri) can help with trekking updates and advice.

Boating

Rowboats can be rented from the Boathouse (admission ₹10, camera/video ₹20/125; ⊘9am-6pm) by Ooty's lake. Prices start from ₹120 (plus a ₹120 deposit) for a two-seater pedal boat (30 minutes).

Horse Racing

Ooty's racecourse dominates the valley between Charing Cross and the lake. Racing season runs from mid-April to mid-June, and on the two or three race days (₹10 per person) each week the town is a hive of activity. Racing happens between about 10.30am and 2.30pm.

☞ Tours

Fixed taxi tour rates are ₹800 for four hours tootling around Ooty, ₹1200 to Coonoor (four hours), or ₹1800 to Mudumalai Tiger Reserve (full-day).

🛏 Sleeping

Ooty has some gorgeous colonial-era homes at the high end and some decent backpacker crashpads, but there isn't much in the lower midrange. Be warned: it's a sellers' market during the 'season' (1 April to 15 June), when hotels hike rates and checkout time is often 9am. Book well ahead for public holidays.

YWCA Anandagiri　　　　　　HOSTEL **$**
(☑0423-2444262; www.ywcaagooty.com; Ettines Rd; dm ₹200, s ₹400-1300, d ₹800-1400) This former brewery and sprawling complex of cottages is dotted with flower gardens. A fresh coat of paint and some smartening up has increased rates, but with clean, characterful rooms and spacious common areas including a restaurant (book ahead

Ooty (Udhagamandalam)

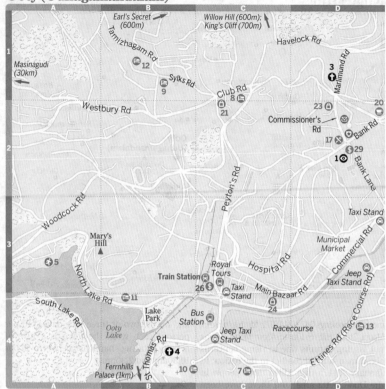

for good-value meals), you've still got some excellent budget accommodation going on. High ceilings can mean cold nights, so do ask for extra blankets.

Hotel Sweekar
HOTEL $

(☑0423-2442348; hotelsweekar@gmail.com; 236 Race View Rd; r ₹500-600) The Sweekar hosts guests in small, basic but clean rooms in a traditional Ooty cottage at the end of a flower-lined path. Hot water only runs until noon (at best), but the Sweekar is good value for its price, and incredibly popular. It's run by a very helpful and efficient Bahai manager.

Reflections Guest House
GUESTHOUSE $

(☑0423-2443834; www.reflectionsguesthouse ooty.com; 1B North Lake Rd; r ₹770-990; 🖥) A long-standing budget haunt, Reflections sits across the road from Ooty's lake, and most of its 12 clean, decent rooms have lake views. It also serves Indian and Continental food at

fair prices (₹60 to ₹180), and can organise guided day treks. Hot showers are available for two hours daily; towels on request.

★ Lymond House
HERITAGE HOTEL $$

(☑0423-2223377; http://serendipityo.com; 77 Sylks Rd; r incl breakfast ₹4800-5400; 🖥) What is it about this 1850s British bungalow that gives it the edge over its peers? The cosy cottage set-up with fresh flowers, four-poster beds, fireplaces and comfy lounges? The contemporary fittings thrown in with rich old-world style in the big rooms and bathrooms? The good food and pretty gardens? All of it, no doubt – plus an informal but wonderfully efficient management style.

Hotel Welbeck Residency
HOTEL $$

(☑0423-2223300; www.welbeck.in; Welbeck Circle, Club Rd; r ₹3240-4620; @🖥) An attractive older building that's been thoroughly spruced up with comfortable rooms, a touch of colonial-era class (a 1920 Austin saloon

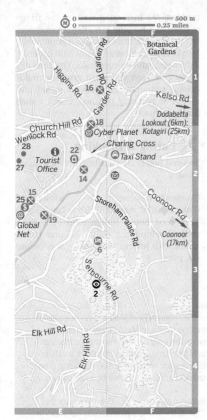

Ooty (Udhagamandalam)

at the front door!), a decent restaurant and very keen staff.

Mount View Hotel　　　　HOTEL $$
(☏ 0423-2443307; www.hotelmountviewooty.com; Ettines Rd; r ₹1970-3940; 🛜) Perched on a quiet (bumpy) driveway handy for the bus and train stations, the nine enormous, high-ceilinged, wood-lined rooms in this elegant old bungalow have been done up comfortably enough. It's just a shame they still won't use the fireplaces.

★ Savoy Hotel　　　HERITAGE HOTEL $$$
(☏ 0423-2225500; www.tajhotels.com; 77 Sylks Rd; s ₹5950-11,900, d ₹6550-12,500, all incl breakfast; @🛜) The Savoy is one of Ooty's oldest hotels, with parts dating back to 1829. Big cottages are set around a beautiful lawned garden; the pretty rooms have spacious bathrooms, log fires and bay windows. Staff are efficient and modern facilities include a bar (even cocktails), an ayurveda centre, wi-fi, and an excellent multicuisine dining room (p405). Half-board arrangements are compulsory from April to June.

Fernhills Palace　　　HERITAGE HOTEL $$$
(☏ 0423-2443911; www.fernhillspalace.co.in; Fern Hill; r incl breakfast ₹13,190-32,380; @🛜) The Maharaja of Mysore's exquisite Anglo-Indian summer palace has been lovingly restored in gorgeous, completely over-the-top princely

colonial style. If you can afford it, it's worth the splurge. All 19 rooms are big suites, with antique furnishings, teak flourishes, fireplaces and jacuzzis. Play billiards, walk in the huge, forest-fringed grounds and dine on regal fare beneath Raj-inspired murals.

King's Cliff HERITAGE HOTEL **$$$**
(☑ 0423-2452888; www.littlearth.in; Havelock Rd; r incl breakfast ₹2600-6930; 🐾) High above Ooty on Strawberry Hill is this classic colonial-era house with wood panelling, antique furnishings, a snug lounge, and good Indian/Continental cooking at the Earl's Secret (mains ₹340-600; ⊙ 8-10am, noon-3pm & 7-10pm) restaurant. The cheaper rooms don't have quite the same old-world charm as the most expensive ones.

Fortune Sullivan Court HOTEL **$$$**
(☑ 0423-2441415; www.fortunehotels.in; 123 Selbourne Rd; s ₹6000-7200, d ₹6600-7800, all incl breakfast; 🐾) In a quiet spot on the fringe of town, the Fortune is no Raj-era mansion, but twirling staircases around a grand lobby lead to comfy, colourful rooms with big beds, light woods and writing desks. The hotel has its own bar, spa and small gym, the multicuisine restaurant does decent meals, and service is perfectly polished. Check online for discounts.

🍴 Eating & Drinking

Top-end hotels are your best bet for a classy meal.

Garden Restaurant SOUTH INDIAN **$**
(Commercial Rd, mains ₹70-150; ⊙ 7am-9.30pm) Very good South Indian food in a clean setting behind the Nahar Nilgiris Hotel, along with juices, milkshakes, snacks and OK pizza.

THE NILGIRIS & THEIR TRIBES

The forest-clothed, waterfall-threaded walls of the Nilgiris (Blue Mountains) rise abruptly from the surrounding plains between the lowland towns of Mettupalayam (to the southeast) and Gudalur (to the northwest), ascended only by winding ghat roads and the famous Nilgiri Mountain Railway. The upland territory, a jumble of valleys and hills with over 20 peaks above 2000m, is a botanist's dream, with over 2300 flowering plant species, although a lot of the native *shola* forest and grasslands have been displaced by tea, eucalyptus and cattle.

The Unesco-designated Nilgiri Biosphere Reserve is a larger, 5520-sq-km area that also includes parts of Kerala and Karnataka. One of the world's biodiversity hotspots, it contains several important tiger reserves, national parks and wildlife sanctuaries.

The Nilgiris' tribal inhabitants were left pretty much to themselves in their isolated homeland until the British arrived two centuries ago. Today, the effects of colonialism and migration have reduced many tribal cultures to the point of collapse, and some have assimilated to the point of invisibility. Others, however, continue at least a semi-traditional lifestyle. Organisations such as the Keystone Foundation (p399) work to promote traditional crafts and activities.

Best known of the tribes, thanks to anthropologists' interest and their proximity to Ooty, are the Toda, who number just over 1000. Some still inhabit tiny villages (*munds*) of their traditional barrel-shaped huts made of bamboo, cane and grass. Toda women style their hair in long, shoulder-length ringlets, and are skilled embroiderers; both sexes wear distinctive black-and-red-embroidered shawls. Central to Toda life is the water buffalo, which provides milk and ghee for consumption and bartering. Traditionally, it is only at funerals that the strictly vegetarian Toda kill a buffalo, to accompany the deceased.

The 350,000-strong Badaga are thought to have migrated into the Nilgiris from Karnataka around AD 1600, and are thus not usually considered truly indigenous. Their traditional dress is of white cloth with a border of narrow coloured stripes. They worship the mother goddess Hetti Amman, to whom their December/January Hettai Habba festival is dedicated.

The Kota, traditionally cultivators, live in seven settlements in the Kotagiri area. They have adapted relatively well to modernity, with a significant number holding government jobs.

The Kurumba inhabit the thick forests of the south and are gatherers of forest products such as bamboo and wild honey, though many of them now work in agriculture.

405

Kabab Corner

NORTH INDIAN $$

(Commercial Rd; mains ₹140-360; ☺ 1-10pm) This is the place for meat-eaters who are tiring of South Indian pure-veg food. It doesn't look much from outside, but here you can tear apart perfectly grilled and spiced chunks of lamb, chicken and, if you like, paneer, sopping up the juices with pillowy triangles of naan. Also on **Club Rd** (Club Rd; mains ₹140-360; ☺ 12.30-10pm).

Shinkow's Chinese Restaurant

CHINESE $$

(38/83 Commissioner's Rd; mains ₹120-250; ☺ noon-3.45pm & 6.30-9.45pm) Shinkow's is an Ooty institution and the simple menu of chicken, pork, beef, fish, noodles and rice dishes is reliably good and quick to arrive at your check-print table.

Savoy

MULTICUISINE $$$

(✆ 0423-2225500; 77 Sylks Rd; mains ₹325-675; ☺ 12.30-3pm & 7.30-10pm) All wood walls, intimate lighting and smart red velvets, the Savoy's dining room dishes up excellent contemporary Continental, Indian and pan-Asian cuisine – including all-day breakfasts, yummy salads, pastas and kebabs, and wonderfully chocolatey desserts.

Willy's Coffee Pub

CAFE

(KCR Arcade, Walsham Rd; dishes ₹40-90; ☺ 10am-9.30pm; 🛜) Climb the stairs and join the international students for board games, wi-fi, a lending library and reasonably priced pizzas, chips, toasties, cakes and cookies.

Café Coffee Day

CAFE

(Church Hill Rd; coffee ₹60-110; ☺ 9am-11pm) Dependably good coffee, tea and cakes. There's another **branch** (Garden Rd; ☺ 9am-10.45pm) on Garden Rd.

Self-Catering

Modern Stores

SUPERMARKET

(144 Garden Rd; ☺ 9.30am-8.30pm) This mini-supermarket stocks all kinds of Western foods from muesli to marmalade, as well as Nilgiri-produced bread and cheese.

Virtue Bakes

BAKERY

(Garden Rd; ☺ 10.30am-8.30pm) Great cakes, pastries, croissants and bread to go.

🛍 Shopping

The main shopping street is Commercial Rd, where you'll find Kashmiri shops as well as outlets for Keralan crafts and *khadi* (handspun cloth). Near the botanical gardens entrance, Tibetan refugees sell jumpers and shawls, which you'll appreciate on a chilly Ooty evening.

K Mahaveer Chand

JEWELLERY

(291 Main Bazaar Rd; ☺ 10am-8pm) K Mahaveer Chand has been selling particularly beautiful Toda tribal and silver jewellery for around 40 years.

Green Shop

HANDICRAFTS, FOOD

(www.lastforest.in; Sargan Villa, off Club Rd; ☺ 10am-7pm Mon-Sat) 🌿 Run by Kotagiri's Keystone Foundation (p399), this fair-trade and organic-oriented shop sells gorgeous tribal crafts and clothes, and wild honey and other produce harvested by local indigenous farmers.

Higginbothams

BOOKS

(✆ 0423-2443736; Commercial Rd; ☺ 9am-1pm & 3.30-7.30pm) A good English-language book selection (including Lonely Planet guides), with another **branch** (✆ 0423-2442546; Commissioner's Rd; ☺ 9.30am-1pm & 2-6pm Mon-Sat) up the hill.

ℹ Information

Cyber Planet (Garden Rd; per hour ₹30; ☺ 10am-6pm)

Global Net (Commercial Rd; per hour ₹30; ☺ 10am-10pm)

Tourist office (✆ 0423-2443977; Wenlock Rd; ☺ 10am-5.45pm Mon-Fri)

ℹ Getting There & Away

The fun way to arrive in Ooty is on the miniature train from Mettupalayam. Buses also run regularly up and down the mountain from other parts of Tamil Nadu, from Kerala and from Mysuru and Bengaluru in Karnataka. Taxis cluster at several stands around town and there are fixed one-way fares to many destinations, including Coonoor (₹750), Kotagiri (₹850), Coimbatore (₹1700) and Mudumalai Tiger Reserve (₹1250).

BUS

For Kochi (Cochin, Kerala) take the 7am or 8am bus to Palakkad (₹95, six hours) and change there. **Royal Tours** (✆ 0423-2446150), opposite the train station, runs a 9am minibus to Kodaikanal (₹600, eight hours).

The Tamil Nadu and Karnataka state bus companies have reservation offices at the busy bus station. Departures include:

Bengaluru (₹391 to ₹650, eight hours, nine daily)

Chennai (₹462, 14 hours, 4.30pm & 5.45pm)

Coimbatore (₹56, four hours, every 30 minutes, 5.30am to 8.40pm)

TAMIL NADU & CHENNAI OOTY (UDHAGAMANDALAM)

Mysuru (₹136, five hours, about every 45 minutes, 6.30am to 5.45pm)

TRAIN

The miniature (or 'toy') train from Mettupalayam to Ooty – one of the Mountain Railways of India given World Heritage status by Unesco – is the best way to get here. Called the Nilgiri Mountain Railway, it requires special cog wheels on the locomotive, meshing with a third, 'toothed' rail on the ground, to manage the exceptionally steep gradients. There are wonderful forest, waterfall, mountainside and tea plantation views along the way. The section between Mettupalayam and Coonoor uses steam engines, which push, rather than pull, the train up the hill.

For the high season (April to June), book the train several weeks ahead; at other times a few days ahead is advisable (though not always essential). The train departs Mettupalayam for Ooty at 7.10am daily (1st/2nd class ₹205/30, five hours). From Ooty to Mettupalayam the train leaves at 2pm and takes 3½ hours. Departures and arrivals at Mettupalayam connect with the Nilgiri Express to/from Chennai Central. There are also three daily passenger trains each way just between Ooty and Coonoor (₹25, 1¼ hours).

Ooty is usually listed as Udhagamandalam in train timetables.

ⓘ Getting Around

There are autorickshaws and taxis everywhere. Autorickshaw fare charts are posted outside the bus station and botanical gardens and elsewhere. An autorickshaw from the train or bus station to Charing Cross costs about ₹60.

There are jeep taxi stands near the bus station and municipal market: expect to pay about 1.5 times local taxi fares.

Mudumalai Tiger Reserve

☏ 0423

In the foothills of the Nilgiris, this 321-sq-km reserve is like a classical Indian landscape painting given life: thin, spindly trees and light-slotted leaves concealing spotted chital deer and grunting wild boar. Also here are around 50 tigers, giving Mudumalai the highest tiger population density in India – though you'll be very lucky to see one. Overall the reserve is Tamil Nadu's best wildlife-spotting place. The creatures you're most likely to see include deer, peacocks, wild boar, langurs and Malabar giant squirrels. There's also a good chance of sighting wild elephants (the park has several hundred) and gaur (Indian bison).

Along with Karnataka's Bandipur and Nagarhole, Kerala's Wayanad and Tamil Nadu's newly created Sathyamangalam Tiger Reserve, Mudumalai forms part of an unbroken chain of protected areas comprising an important wildlife refuge.

Mudumalai sometimes closes for fire risk in April, May or June. Rainy July and August are the least favourable months for visiting.

The reserve's reception centre (☏ 0423-2526235; ⊙ 6-10am & 2-5.30pm), and some reserve-run accommodation, is at Theppakadu, on the main road between Ooty and Mysuru. The closest village to Theppakadu is Masinagudi, 7km east.

◉ Sights & Activities

Hiking in the reserve is not allowed and private vehicles are only permitted on the main Ooty–Gudalur–Theppakadu–Mysuru-road and the Theppakadu–Masinagudi and Masinagudi–Moyar River roads. Some wildlife can be spotted from these roads, but the best way to see the reserve is on the official 45-minute minibus tours (per person ₹135; ⊙ hourly 7-10am & 2-6pm), which make a 15km loop in camouflage-striped 15- or 26-seat buses. Book at the reception centre a couple of hours ahead.

Half-hour elephant rides (up to four people ₹860; ⊙ 7-8am & 4-5pm Sep-Jun) are also available from the reception centre; reserve 30 minutes ahead. From 8.30am to 9am and 5.30pm to 6pm you can watch the reserve's working elephants being fed at the nearby elephant camp (minibus-tour customers free, others ₹15).

Some operators may offer treks in the buffer zone around the reserve, but these are potentially dangerous and the reserve authorities advise very strongly against them; tourists have died from getting too close to wild elephants on illegal treks. Jeep safaris organised through the better resorts, with expert guides, are a safer option.

⨳ Sleeping & Eating

The reserve runs simple lodgings along a track just above the Moyar River at Theppakadu. Better accommodation is provided by numerous lodges and forest resorts outside the park's fringes, many of them welcoming family-run businesses offering high standards and breathtaking views. Most of the best cluster in Bokkapuram village, 5km from Masinagudi at the foot of the mountains.

Theppakadu

For this reserve-run accommodation you should book in advance (by phone or in person) with the Office of the Field Director (p400) in Ooty, though the reception centre accepts walk-ins if there are vacancies.

Sylvan Lodge   LODGE **$**
(d ₹780) Plain, well-scrubbed rooms, and ₹70 meals.

Theppakadu Log House   LODGE **$$**
(r ₹1360-2200) The best of the reserve-owned accommodation, with comfortable well-maintained rooms that have private bathrooms. Meals cost around ₹70.

Bokkapuram & Around

Don't wander outside your resort at night – leopards, among other wild animals, are around.

Wilds at Northernhay   LODGE **$$**
(☏9843149490; www.serendipityo.com; Singara; r incl breakfast ₹4800-5400) A wonderful lodge 8km southwest of Masinagudi, in a convert-ed coffee warehouse on a coffee plantation filled with tall trees that give it a deep-in-the-forest feel. Cosy rooms (some up in the trees) and excellent meals complement the morning and evening jeep safaris (per hour ₹3000), on which you should see a good va-riety of wildlife.

Jungle Retreat   RESORT **$$**
(☏0423-2526469; www.jungleretreat.com; Bokka-puram; dm ₹1000, r ₹4000-5400; 🛜🐾) One of the most stylish resorts around, with accom-modation in lovingly built stone cottages or a high treehouse, all spread out for maxi-mum seclusion. The bar, restaurant and common area is great for meeting travellers, and staff are knowledgeable and friendly. The pool has a stunning setting – leopards and elephants often drop by for a drink. Three daily meals cost ₹1700.

Bamboo Banks Farm   LODGE **$$**
(☏0423-2526211; www.bamboobanks.com; Masi-nagudi; full-board d ₹6140; 🛜🐾) This friendly family-owned operation has seven simple, comfy cottages tucked into its own patch of unkempt jungle, 2km south of Masinagudi. Geese waddle around, there's a peaceful grassy pool area with hammocks, meals are good South Indian buffets, and the efficient owners can organise horse riding and pri-vate safaris.

Jungle Hut   RESORT **$$$**
(☏0423-2526463; www.junglehut.in; Bokkapu-ram; full-board s ₹4400-6900, d ₹6600-9000; ❄🛜🐾) Along with ecofriendly touches and a sociable lounge, this welcoming 28-year-old resort has probably the best food in Bokkapuram (if you're visiting from another resort after dark, don't walk home alone!). Spacious rooms in cottages are scattered around large grounds, where a herd of 200-odd chital deer grazes morning and evening. Jeep safaris, treks and birdwatching can be organised.

❶ Getting There & Around

A taxi day trip to Mudumalai from Ooty costs around ₹1800. Do go at least one way by the alternative Sighur Ghat road with its spectacular 36-hairpin-bend hill. A one-way taxi from Ooty to Theppakadu should be ₹1250.

Buses between Ooty and Mysuru go via Guda-lur and stop at Theppakadu (₹37, three hours from Ooty). Smaller buses that can handle the Sighur Ghat road run from Ooty to Masinagudi (₹17, 1½ hours, 10 daily). Local buses run several times daily between Masinagudi and Theppa-kadu (₹5); shared jeeps also ply this route for ₹10 per person if there are enough passengers, or you can have one to yourself for about ₹120. Costs are similar for jeeps between Masinagudi and Bokkapuram.

Andaman Islands

Why Go?

Long fabled among travellers for its legendary beaches, world-class diving and far-flung location in the middle of nowhere, the Andaman Islands are still the ideal place to get away from it all.

Lovely opaque emerald waters are surrounded by primeval jungle and mangrove forest, and snow-white beaches that melt under flame-and-purple sunsets. The population is a friendly masala of South and Southeast Asian settlers, as well as Negrito ethnic groups whose arrival here still has anthropologists baffled. Adding to the intrigue is its remote location, some 1370km from the mainland, meaning the islands are geographically more Southeast Asia – 150km from Indonesia and 190km from Myanmar.

While the archipelago comprises some 300 islands, only a dozen or so are open to tourists, Havelock by far being the most popular for its beaches and diving. The Nicobars are strictly off limits to tourists, as are the tribal areas.

Best Beaches

➜ Radhanagar (p417)

➜ Merk Bay (p423)

➜ Ross & Smith Islands (p425)

➜ Butler Bay (p426)

➜ Lalaji Bay (p423)

Best Places to Stay

➜ Emerald Gecko (p419)

➜ Aashiaanaa Rest Home (p414)

➜ Pristine Beach Resort (p425)

➜ Blue View (p426)

➜ Blue Planet (p424)

When to Go
Port Blair

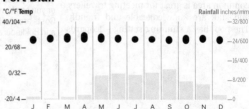

| Dec–Mar Perfect sunny days, optimal diving conditions and turtle nesting. | Oct–Dec & Mar–mid-May Weather is a mixed bag, but fewer tourists and lower costs. | Feb–Aug Pumping waves on Little Andaman for experienced surfers. |

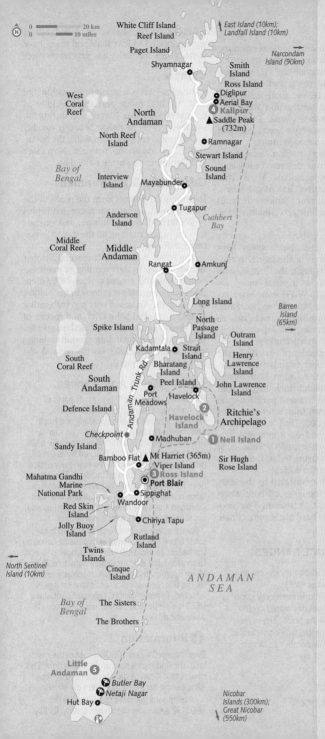

Andaman Islands Highlights

1 Disconnecting from the mainland and easing into the blissfully mellow pace of life on **Neil Island** (p420)

2 Diving, snorkelling and socialising on **Havelock Island** (p417)

3 Glimpsing Port Blair's colonial history at **Ross Island** (p414)

4 Experiencing the true wilds of Northern Andaman in **Kalipur** (p424), while island-hopping to pristine beaches and coral reefs

5 Finding Butler Bay and paradise on **Little Andaman** (p425)

Map labels:

0 —— 20 km
0 —— 10 miles
N

White Cliff Island
Reef Island
Paget Island
Shyamnagar
East Island (10km);
Landfall Island (10km)
Narcondam Island (90km)
Smith Island
Ross Island
Diglipur
Aerial Bay
West Coral Reef
4 Kalipur
Saddle Peak (732m)
North Andaman
North Reef Island
Ramnagar
Stewart Island
Sound Island
Bay of Bengal
Interview Island
Mayabunder
Cuthbert Bay
Anderson Island
Tugapur
Middle Coral Reef
Middle Andaman
Rangat
Amkunj
Long Island
Barren Island (65km)
Spike Island
North Passage Island
Outram Island
South Coral Reef
Kadamtala
Strait Island
Henry Lawrence Island
Bharatang Island
South Andaman
Peel Island
John Lawrence Island
Defence Island
Port Meadows
Havelock
2
Ritchie's Archipelago
Andaman Trunk Rd
Checkpoint
Havelock Island
Sandy Island
Madhuban
1 Neil Island
Bamboo Flat
Mt Harriet (365m)
Sir Hugh Rose Island
Viper Island
Mahatma Gandhi Marine National Park
3 Ross Island
Port Blair
Red Skin Island
Sippighat
Wandoor
Jolly Buoy Island
Chiriya Tapu
Twins Islands
Rutland Island
North Sentinel Island (10km)
Cinque Island
ANDAMAN SEA
Bay of Bengal
The Sisters
The Brothers
Little Andaman
5
Butler Bay
Netaji Nagar
Hut Bay
Nicobar Islands (300km); Great Nicobar (550km)

History

The date of initial human settlement on the Andamans and Nicobars is lost to history. Anthropologists say stone-tool crafters have lived here for 2000 years, and scholars of human migration believe local indigenous tribes have roots in Negrito and Malay ethnic groups in Southeast Asia. Otherwise, these specks in the sea have been a constant source of legend to outside visitors.

The 10th-century Persian adventurer Buzurg Ibn Shahriyar described an island chain inhabited by cannibals, Marco Polo added that the natives had dogs' heads, and tablets in Thanjavur (Tanjore) in Tamil Nadu named the archipelago Timaittivu: the Impure Islands.

None of the above was exactly tourism-brochure stuff, but visitors kept coming: the Marathas in the late 17th century and, 200 years later, the British, who used the Andamans as a penal colony for political dissidents. In WWII some islanders greeted the invading Japanese as liberators, but despite installing Indian politicians as (puppet) administrators, the Japanese military proved to be harsh occupiers.

Following Independence in 1947, the Andaman and Nicobar Islands were incorporated into the Indian Union. With migration from the mainland (including Bengali refugees fleeing the chaos of partition), the population has grown from a few thousand to more than 350,000. During this influx, tribal land rights and environmental protection were often disregarded; while some conditions are improving today, indigenous tribes remain largely in decline.

The islands were devastated by the 2004 Indian Ocean earthquake, offshore aftershocks and the resulting tsunami. The Nicobars were especially hard hit; some estimate a fifth of the population was killed, others were relocated to Port Blair and many have yet to return. Normalcy has largely returned.

Climate

Sea breezes keep temperatures within the 23°C to 31°C range and the humidity at around 80% all year. It's very wet during the southwest (wet) monsoon between roughly mid-May and early October, while the northeast (dry) monsoons between November and December also bring rainy days.

Geography & Environment

Incredibly the islands form the peaks of the Arakan Yoma, a mountain range that begins in Western Myanmar (Burma) and extends into the ocean, running all the way to Sumatra in Indonesia.

The isolation of the Andaman and Nicobar Islands has led to the evolution of many endemic plant and animal species. Of 62 identified mammals, 32 are unique to the islands, including the Andaman wild pig, crab-eating macaque, masked palm civet, and species of tree shrews and bats. Of the 250 bird species, 18 are endemic, including ground-dwelling megapodes, *hawabills* (swiftlets) and the emerald Nicobar pigeon.

ℹ Dangers & Annoyances

Crocodiles are a way of life in many parts of the Andamans, particularly Little Andaman, Wandoor, Corbyn's Cove, Baratang and North Andamans. The death of an American tourist who was attacked by a saltwater crocodile while snorkelling in Havelock in 2010 (at Neils Cove near Beach 7) was considered extremely unusual, and remains an isolated incident. There been no sightings since, but a high level of vigilance remains in place. It's important you keep informed, heed any warnings by authorities and avoid being in the water at dawn or dusk.

Sandflies are another hindrance, with these small biting insects sometimes causing havoc on the beach. To avoid infection, it's imperative not to scratch what is an incredibly itchy bite. Bring along hydrocortisone cream and calamine lotion for the bite. Seek medical assistance if it gets infected. To prevent bites, repellant containing DEET is your best bet, and avoid the beach at dawn and dusk.

ℹ Information

Even though they are 1000km east of the mainland, the Andamans still run on Indian time. This means that it can be dark by 5pm and light by 4am; people here tend to be very early risers.

All telephone numbers must include the ☑ 03192 area code, even when dialling locally.

SLEEPING PRICE RANGES

Tariffs can rise dramatically during peak season of mid-December to January – reservations are a very good idea. Camping is not permitted on the islands. The following price ranges refer to a double room with bathroom during the high season (December to March) and are inclusive of tax:

$ less than ₹800

$$ ₹800 to ₹2500

$$$ more than ₹2500

PERMITS

All foreigners need a permit to visit the Andaman Islands; it's issued free on arrival from Port Blair's airport or Haddo Jetty. The 30-day permit allows foreigners to stay in Port Blair, South and Middle Andaman (excluding tribal areas), North Andaman (Diglipur), Long Island, North Passage, Little Andaman (excluding tribal areas), and Havelock and Neil Islands. It's possible to get a 15-day extension from the **Immigration Office** (🖉 03192-237793; ⊙ 8.30am-1pm & 2-5pm Mon-Fri, to 1pm Sat) in Port Blair, or at police stations elsewhere.

Keep your permit on you at all times – you won't be able to travel without it. Police frequently ask to see it, especially when you're disembarking on other islands, and hotels will need permit details. You'll also need it to pass immigration when departing the Andamans.

The permit also allows day trips to Jolly Buoy, South Cinque, Red Skin, Ross, Narcondam, Interview and Rutland Islands, as well as the Brothers and the Sisters. For most day permits it's not the hassle but the cost. For areas such as Mahatma Gandhi Marine National Park, and Ross and Smith Islands near Diglipur, the permits cost ₹50/500 for Indians/foreigners. Students with valid ID pay minimal entry fees, so don't forget to bring your card.

The Nicobar Islands are off-limits to all except Indian nationals engaged in research, government business or trade.

ⓘ Getting There & Away

AIR

There are daily flights to Port Blair from Delhi, Kolkata and Chennai, though flights from Delhi and Kolkata are often routed through Chennai. Round-trip fares are between US$250 and US$600, depending on how early you book; some airlines offer one-way flights for as low as US$80, but these need to be booked months in advance.

Air India (🖉 03192-233108; www.airindia.com)

GoAir (🖉 03192-231540, reservations 092-23222111; www.goair.in)

Jet Airways (🖉 1800-225522, 03192-230545; www.jetairways.com)

SpiceJet (🖉 0987-1803333; www.spicejet.com)

BOAT

Depending on who you ask, the infamous boat to Port Blair is either the only *real* way to get to the Andamans or a hassle and a half. The truth lies somewhere in between. There are usually three to four sailings a month between Port Blair and Chennai (three days) and Kolkata (four to five days), plus a monthly ferry to Visakhapatnam (four days). All ferries arrive at Haddo Jetty.

Take sailing times with a large grain of salt – travellers have reported sitting on the boat at Kolkata harbour for up to 12 hours, or waiting to

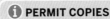

> ### ⓘ PERMIT COPIES
>
> At the time of research it was a requirement to produce a photocopy of your permit when booking ferry tickets. While you're not always asked to provide it, it's worth taking five or so copies before arriving at Port Blair's ferry office: you'll likely need them later in your trip.

dock near Port Blair for several hours. With hold-ups and variable weather and sea conditions, the trip can take a day or two extra.

Assistant Director of Shipping Services (🖉 044-25226873; 17 Rajaji Salai, Jawahar Bldg, Chennai Port; ⊙ 10am-1pm & 2-4pm Mon-Fri, to 12.30pm Sat) has boats from Chennai, **Shipping Corporation of India** (🖉 033-22543505/7, in Kolkata 033-22543400; www.shipindia.com; 13 Strand Rd, Kolkata; ⊙ 9am-1pm & 2-5pm Mon-Fri, to noon Sat) departs from Kolkata, and **Pattabhiramayya & Co** (🖉 0891-2565597; ops@avbgpr. com; Harbour Approach Rd, next to NMDC, Port Area; ⊙ 9am-5pm) from Visakhapatnam.

You can organise your return ticket at the ferry booking office (p415) at Phoenix Bay. Bring two passport photos and a photocopy of your permit. Schedules and fares can be found at www.andamans.gov.in or www.shipindia.com. Otherwise enquire at Phoenix Bay's info office.

Classes vary slightly between boats, but the cheapest is bunk (₹2270), followed by 2nd-class (six beds, ₹5817), 1st class (four beds, ₹7319) and deluxe cabins (two beds, ₹8841). Higher-end tickets cost as much as, if not more than, a plane ticket. If you go bunk, prepare for waking up to a chorus of men 'hwwaaaaching' and spitting, little privacy and toilets that tend to get...unpleasant after three days at sea. That said, it's a good way to meet locals, and one for proponents of slow, adventure travel.

Food (tiffin for breakfast, thalis for lunch and dinner) costs around ₹150/200 per day for bunk/cabin class, though bring something (fruit in particular) to supplement your diet. Some bedding is supplied, but if you're travelling bunk class bring a sleeping sheet. Many travellers take a hammock to string up on deck.

There is no ferry between Port Blair and Thailand, but private yachts can gain clearance. You can't legally get from the Andamans to Myanmar by sea. Be aware you risk imprisonment or worse from the Indian and Burmese navies if you try it.

ⓘ Getting Around

AIR

Two modes of air transport link Port Blair with the other islands. If your budget allows it, it's worth it for the views.

ℹ FERRY CANCELLATIONS

Bad weather can play havoc with your itinerary, with ferry services often cancelled if the sea is rough. Build in a few days' buffer to avoid being marooned..

Interisland Helicopter While the interisland helicopter service isn't for tourists, you can chance your luck by applying one day before at the Directorate of Civil Aviation office (📞 03192-233601; VIP Rd Port Blair Helipad) at the helipad near the airport. It runs to/from Port Blair to Little Andaman (₹2625, 35 minutes), Havelock (₹1500, 20 minutes), Diglipur (₹4125, one hour) and Mayabunder (₹3375, 45 minutes). The 5kg baggage limit precludes most tourists from using this service.

Sea Plane (📞 09531828222; andamanseaplane@gmail.com; ⊗ Mon-Sat) The amphibious Sea Plane links Port Blair with Havelock (₹4100), Little Andaman (₹7170) and Diglipur (₹10,500), landing and taking off on the water, and the runway in Port Blair. It operates January to April. Note the 5kg baggage limit.

BOAT

Most islands can only be reached by water. While this sounds romantic, ferry ticket offices can be hell: expect hot waits, slow service, queue-jumping and a rugby scrum to the ticket window. To hold your spot and advance in line, you need to be a little aggressive (but not a jerk) or be a woman; ladies' queues are a godsend for women travellers, but they really only apply in Port Blair. You can buy tickets the day you travel by arriving at the appropriate jetty an hour beforehand, but this is risky, and normally one or two days in advance is recommended. You can't pre-book ferry tickets until you've been issued your island permit (p411) upon arrival in the Andamans.

There are regular boat services to Havelock and Neil Islands (three to four per day), as well as Rangat, Mayabunder, Diglipur and Little Andaman. A schedule of interisland sailing times can be found at www.andamans.gov.in.

Two private ferry companies also run to Havelock and Neil Islands from Port Blair.

Makruzz Ferry (📞 03192-212355; www.makruzz.com)

Coastal Cruise (📞 03192-241333; www.coastalcruise.in; 13 RP Rd, Aberdeen Bazaar)

CAR & MOTORCYCLE

A car with driver costs ₹550 per 35km, or around ₹10,000 for a return trip to Diglipur from Port Blair (including stopovers along the way). Motorbikes and scooters are available for hire from Port Blair and all the islands for around ₹300 to ₹400 per day. Due to restrictions in travel within tribal areas, it's not permitted for foreigners to drive their own vehicles to North and Middle Andaman.

BUS

All roads – and ferries – lead to Port Blair, and you'll inevitably spend a night or two here booking onward travel. The main island group – South, Middle and North Andaman – is connected by road, with ferry crossings and bridges. Buses run south from Port Blair to Wandoor, and north to Baratang, Rangat, Mayabunder and Diglipur, 325km north of the capital.

Port Blair

POP 100,600

Though surrounded by attractive lush forest and rugged coastline, Port Blair is more or less your typical Indian town that serves as the provincial capital of the Andamans. It's a vibrant mix of Indian Ocean inhabitants – Bengalis, Tamils, Telugus, Nicobarese and Burmese. Most travellers don't hang around any longer than necessary (usually one or two days while waiting to book onward travel in the islands, or returning for departure), but PB's fascinating history makes for some worthwhile sightseeing.

◉ Sights

★ **Cellular Jail National Memorial** HISTORIC BUILDING
(GB Pant Rd; admission ₹10, camera/video ₹25/100, sound-and-light show adult/child ₹50/25; ⊗ 8.45am-12.30pm & 1.30-5pm) A former British prison, the evocative Cellular Jail National Memorial now serves as a shrine to the political dissidents it once jailed. Construction of the jail began in 1896 and it was completed in 1906 – the original seven wings (several of which were destroyed by the Japanese during WWII) contained 698 cells radiating from a central tower. Like many political prisons, Cellular Jail became something of a university for freedom fighters, who exchanged books, ideas and debates despite walls and wardens. Guides (₹200) are available to show you around.

There's a fairly cheesy **sound-and-light show** detailing the jail's history in English at 7.15pm on Monday, Wednesday and Friday.

Anthropological Museum MUSEUM
(MG Rd; admission ₹10, camera ₹20; ⊗ 9am-1pm & 1.30-4.30pm Tue-Sun) This museum provides a thorough and sympathetic portrait of the islands' indigenous tribal communities. The glass display cases may be old school, but they don't feel anywhere near as ancient as the simple geometric patterns etched into a

Port Blair

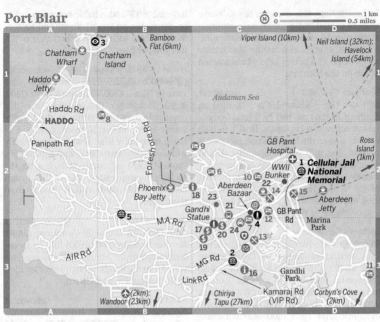

Port Blair

Jarawa chest guard, a skull left in a Sentinelese lean-to, or the totemic spirits represented by Nicobarese shamanic sculptures.

Samudrika Marine Museum MUSEUM
(Haddo Rd; adult/child ₹20/10, camera/video ₹20/50; ◷9am-1pm & 2-5pm Tue-Sun) Run by

the Indian Navy, this museum has a diverse range of exhibits with informative coverage of the islands' ecosystem, tribal communities, plants, animals and marine life. Outside is a skeleton of a young blue whale washed ashore on the Nicobars.

Chatham Saw Mill   HISTORIC SITE
(admission ₹10; ⊙ 8.30am-2.30pm) Located on Chatham Island (reached by a road bridge), the saw mill was set up by the British in 1883 and was one of the largest wood processors in Asia. The mill is still operational, and while it may not be to everyone's taste, especially conservationists, it's an interesting insight to the island's history and economy. Look out for the bomb crater, left by Japanese ordnance in WWII.

Corbyn's Cove   BEACH
No one comes to Port Blair for the beach, but if you need a break from town, Corbyn's Cove has a small curve of sand backed by palms. The coastal road here is a scenic journey, and passes several Japanese WWII bunkers along the way. Located 7km south of town, an autorickshaw costs ₹200, or rent a scooter. Crocodiles are occasionally spotted.

🛌 Sleeping

Get in touch with the tourist office (p415) for a list of homestay options in Port Blair.

⭐ Aashiaanaa Rest Home   GUESTHOUSE $
(☑ 09474217008;   shads_maria@hotmail.com; Marine Hill; r without bathroom ₹300, with AC from ₹900; ❄️ 🛜) Port Blair's most comfortable budget choice has homely rooms decked out in aquamarine and mauve, and a convenient location uphill from Phoenix Bay jetty. Most

have cable TV and reliable hot water, while pricier rooms get you a balcony and air-con. Staff can help with booking ferry tickets. Wi-fi is ₹60 per hour.

Hotel Lalaji Bay View   GUESTHOUSE $
(☑ 9476005820, 03192-236333; www.lalajibay-view.com; RP Rd; s/d ₹300/400, r with AC from ₹1200; ❄️ 🛜) Backpacker HQ in Port Blair, this popular budget hotel is run by the friendly young entrepreneur Nirman (grandson of Lalaji from Long Island) who knows exactly what makes tourists tick. Rooms are cosy, spotless and have comfy beds, but it's the sociable rooftop restaurant-bar that brings people in, with (paid) wi-fi. It's just up from the mosque.

Amina Lodge   GUESTHOUSE $
(☑ 9933258703; aminalodge@ymail.com; MA Rd, Aberdeen Bazaar; s/d ₹450/600) Run by an entertaining couple, Amina has spotless rooms with TV and a handy, though noisy, location in the bazaar. Prices are fixed.

Azad Lodge   GUESTHOUSE $
(☑ 03192-242646; MA Rd, Aberdeen Bazaar; s/d without bathroom ₹200/300, d ₹500, r with AC ₹850) An old budget favourite with basic and clean rooms.

Da Bay Inn   HOTEL $$
(☑ 9647200473; Foreshore Rd; sea-facing r incl breakfast ₹3000) Overlooking the bay, this hotel is only recommended if you get one of the sea-facing rooms. Decor is garish, but otherwise a comfortable choice.

⭐ Hotel Sinclairs Bayview   HOTEL $$$
(☑ 03192-227824; www.sinclairshotels.com/portblair; South Point; s/d incl breakfast from

---

DON'T MISS

ROSS ISLAND

Just a 20-minute boat ride from Port Blair, visiting Ross Island (not to be confused with its namesake island in North Andaman) feels like discovering a jungle-clad Lost City, à la Angkor Wat, except here the ruins are Victorian English rather than ancient Khmer. The former administrative headquarters for the British in the Andamans, Ross Island in its day was fondly called the 'Paris of the East' (along with Pondicherry, Saigon etc etc…), but the cute title, vibrant social scene and tropical gardens were all wiped out by the double whammy of a 1941 earthquake and invasion by the Japanese.

Today the old English architecture is still standing, despite an invading wave of fast-growing jungle vegetation. Landscaped paths cross the island and most of the buildings are labelled. There's a small museum with historical displays and resident spotted deer. A sound-and-light show was also on the cards at the time of research.

Ferries to Ross Island (₹100, 20 minutes) depart hourly from Aberdeen Jetty behind the aquarium in Port Blair, between 8.30am and 2pm every day except Wednesday.

₹8100/8600; ❄ 🛜 🏊) Located on the road to Corbyn's Cove, 2km outside town, Sinclairs' large modern rooms open right out to the water. It has a nice seaside garden with hammocks to lounge in, and a Japanese WWII bunker onsite. Free airport transfer.

Fortune Resort – Bay Island HOTEL **$$$**
(📞 03192-234101; www.fortunehotels.in; Marine Hill; s/d incl breakfast from ₹7090/7630; ❄ 🛜 🏊) One of PB's finest, with lovely bay views, tropical garden, and modern rooms with a polished floors; ask for one that's sea-facing.

J Hotel HOTEL **$$$**
(📞 03192-246000; www.jhotel.in; Aberdeen Bazaar; r incl breakfast from ₹4300; ❄ 🛜) A slick designer hotel in the heart of the bazaar, with modern rooms and chic rooftop restaurant. Lack of natural light is a downside until you remember the 5am sunrise!

🍴 Eating & Drinking

⭐ **Excel Restaurant** INTERNATIONAL, INDIAN **$**
(Hotel Lalaji Bay View, RP Rd; mains from ₹100; ⏱ 7am-11pm; 🛜) This alluring bamboo rooftop restaurant above Hotel Lalaji Bay View (not to be confused with the seedy downstairs bar), brings a 'Havelock' menu to the city, with grilled fish, burgers, Israeli dishes etc. Wi-fi access (₹60 per hour) and a fully stocked bar makes it *the* place to hang out.

Gagan Restaurant INDIAN **$**
(Clock Tower, Aberdeen Bazaar; mains from ₹90-200; ⏱ 7am-10pm) Popular with locals, this hole-in-the-wall Bengali restaurant serves up great food at good prices, including Nicobari fish, crab curries, coconut chicken, and dosas for breakfast.

Annapurna INDIAN **$**
(MG Rd; mains ₹100-150; ⏱ 6.30am-10.30pm) An excellent veg option that looks like a high-school cafeteria and serves delicious dosas and rich North Indian–style curries.

Lighthouse Residency SEAFOOD **$$**
(MA Rd; mains ₹80-800; ⏱ 11am-11pm) Select your meal from the display of red snapper, crab or tiger prawns to barbecue (served with rice and chips), and head to its rooftop for a cold Kingfisher beer. There's a cheaper **second branch** (Marina Park; mains ₹80-400) in an outdoor shack near the water.

Bayview MULTICUISINE **$$$**
(Hotel Sinclairs Bayview; mains ₹110-500; ⏱ 11am-11pm) Right on the water with a lovely cool sea breeze, the Bayview is a top spot to grab lunch out of town.

Nico Bar BAR
(Marine Hill; ⏱ 11am-11pm) The closest you'll get to the Nicobars, Fortune Bay Hotel's bar is the spot for sea breezes and scenic views (the picture on the ₹20 note is based on this spot). A great place to while away an afternoon or balmy evening with a drink.

ℹ️ Information

There are several ATMs around town. You can find internet cafes, with wi-fi and computer terminals (₹40 per hour), in Aberdeen Bazaar near the clock tower.

Aberdeen Police Station (📞 03192-232400; MG Rd)

Andaman & Nicobar Tourism (📞 03192-232694; www.andamans.gov.in; Kamaraj Rd; ⏱ 8.30am-1pm & 2-5pm) The main island tourist office has brochures and is the place to book permits for areas around Port Blair. Its website has useful info such as ferry schedules.

GB Pant Hospital (📞 emergency 03192-232102, 03192-233473; GB Pant Rd)

Island Travels (📞 03192-233358; islandtravels@yahoo.com; Aberdeen Bazaar; ⏱ 9am-1pm & 2-6pm Mon-Sat) Reliable travel agency for booking flights. Also has foreign-exchange facilities.

Main Post Office (MG Rd; ⏱ 9am-7pm Mon-Sat)

State Bank of India (MA Rd; ⏱ 9am-noon & 1-3pm Mon-Fri, 10am-noon Sat) Foreign currency can be changed here.

ℹ️ Getting There & Away

BOAT

Most interisland ferries depart from **Phoenix Bay Jetty**. Tickets can be purchased from its **ferry booking office** (⏱ 9am-1pm & 2-4pm Mon-Fri, to noon Sat). Ferries can be pre-booked one to three days in advance; if they are sold out you can chance your luck with a same-day ticket issued an hour before departure from outside the ticket office at the end door. There's a **ferry information office** (📞 03192-245555; Phoenix Bay Jetty; ⏱ 5.30am-6.30pm) outside the ticket office for enquiries.

Ferries to Havelock (₹195, 2½ hours) depart daily at 6.20am, 11am, 1pm and 2pm; with several heading via Neil Island; all book out fast.

Otherwise there are private, pricier ferries. Makruzz (p412) has daily departures to Havelock (₹975 to ₹1700, 1½ hours) at 8.15am and 2pm, which continue to Neil Island (₹1315 to ₹2224, 2½ hours). Tickets are available for the airport or travel agents in town. Coastal Cruise (p412) heads to Neil Island (₹875 to ₹1200) via Havelock (₹875 to ₹1200) at 7.30am.

There are also daily boats to Little Andaman, which also regularly sell out, and several boats a week to Diglipur and Long Island.

New arrivals should make the jetty their first port of call to book tickets.

BUS

Government buses run all day from the **bus stand** at Aberdeen Bazaar to Wandoor (₹20, one hour) and Chiriya Tapu (₹20, one hour). Buses to Diglipur run at 4am (to Aerial Bay) and 7am (₹265, 12 hours), and 9.45am for Mayabunder (₹200, 10 hours) all via Rangat (₹160, six hours) and Baratang (₹190, three hours). More comfortable, but pricier, private buses have 'offices' (a guy with a ticket book) across from the main bus stand.

ⓘ Getting Around

TO & FROM THE AIRPORT

A taxi or autorickshaw from the airport to Aberdeen Bazaar costs around ₹100 for the 4km trip. There are also hourly buses (₹10) between the airport and main bus stand.

AUTORICKSHAW

Aberdeen Bazaar to Phoenix Bay Jetty is about ₹30, and to Haddo Jetty it's around ₹50.

MOTORBIKE

You can hire a scooter from various spots in Port Blair for around ₹400 per day. Try **Saro Tours** (☏ 9933291466; www.rentabikeandaman.com; Marine Rd).

Around Port Blair

There are eco-related volunteering opportunities around Port Blair. See the Volunteering chapter (p46).

Wandoor

Wandoor, a tiny speck of a village 29km southwest of Port Blair, is a good spot to see the interior of the island. It's best known as a jumping-off point for snorkelling at Mahatma Gandhi Marine National Park. Buses run from Port Blair to Wandoor (₹20, one hour).

🏃 Activities

Wandoor has a nice beach, though at the time of research, swimming was prohibited due to crocodiles.

Mahatma Gandhi Marine National Park   SNORKELLING
(permit Indian/foreigner ₹50/500; ⊙ Tue-Sun) Popular with Indian tourists, the half-day snorkelling trips to Mahatma Gandhi Marine National Park are a good option for those wanting to get underwater while in Port Blair. The park comprises 15 islands of mangrove creeks, tropical rainforest and reefs supporting 50 types of coral and plenty of colourful fish. Boats depart 9am from Wandoor Jetty, costing ₹750 in addition to the ₹500 permit which you need to arrange at the tourist office (p415) in Port Blair.

Depending upon the time of year, the marine park's snorkelling sites alternate between Jolly Buoy and Red Skin, allowing the other to regenerate.

🛏 Sleeping

Anugama Resort   RESORT $$$
(☏ 03192-280068;   www.anugamaresort.com; Wandoor; r with fan/AC incl breakfast ₹3000/3500; ✳🛜) Run by an enthusiastic Singaporean diver, Anugama has basic but comfortable cottages in a bucolic setting among forest and mud flats. It's a good spot for outdoor lovers with activities such as snorkelling, bike hire and nature walks exploring mangrove and intertidal zones.

Chiriya Tapu

Chiriya Tapu, 30km south of Port Blair, is a tiny village fringed by beaches and mangroves, and famous for celestial sunsets. It also has Munda Pahar Beach, popular with Indian day-trippers. Hourly buses head from Port Blair (₹20, one hour); the last bus back is at 6pm.

⊙ Sights & Activities

Chiriya Tapu Biological Park   ZOO
(Indian/foreigner ₹20/50; ⊙ 9am-4pm Tue-Sun) A pleasant place to stroll in a forested setting with natural enclosures for indigenous species such as crab-eating macaques, Andaman wild pigs and salt-water crocs.

Diving

Dive companies based in Chiriya Tapu can arrange trips to Cinque and Rutland Islands, both known for their abundance of fish, colourful soft corals and excellent visibility. Cinque also has a blinding white sandbar beach. There's a WWII British minesweeper wreck dive too.

Lacadives   DIVING
(☏ 03192-281013;   www.lacadives.com;   per dive Rutland Island ₹2000, Cinque Island ₹8000; ⊙ Oct-May) Long-established Indian dive company, which can arrange budget diver accommodation. Boats carry up to 10 people.

Infinity Scuba   DIVING
(☑ 03192-281183;   www.infinityscubandamans.
com; 2 dives incl lunch Rutland Island ₹3500,
Cinque Island ₹4000) Set up by Baath, an
ex-Navy commando, Infinity also arranges
popular fishing and live-aboard trips.

🛏 Sleeping & Eating

★**Wildgrass Resort**   RESORT $$$
(☑ 9474204508; www.wildgrassresorts.com; r incl
breakfast ₹4000; ❋) Run by the Infinity Scu-
ba team, Wildgrass offers romantic cottages
with an island ambience and lush jungle
backdrop. It also has an atmospheric bam-
boo restaurant that's good for day-trippers.

Havelock Island

POP 5500

With snow-white beaches, teal shallows, a
coast crammed with beach huts and some
of the best diving in South Asia, Havelock
has a well-deserved reputation as a back-
packer paradise. For many, Havelock *is* the
Andamans, and it's what lures most tourists
across the Bay of Bengal, many of whom are
content to stay here for the whole trip.

🔘 Sights & Activities

Beaches

Radhanagar   BEACH
(Beach 7) One of India's prettiest and most
famous stretches of sand is the critically ac-
claimed Radhanagar. It's a beautiful curve
of sugar fronted by perfectly spiraled waves,
all backed by native forest. It's on the north-
western side of the island, about 12km from
the jetty. Late afternoon is the best time to
visit to avoid the heat and crowds, as well as
for its sunset.

Neils Cove   BEACH
Northwest of Radhanagar is the gorgeous
'lagoon' at Neils Cove, another gem of shel-
tered sand and crystalline water. Swimming
is prohibited at dusk and dawn; take heed of
any warnings regarding crocodiles.

Beach 5   BEACH
On the north-eastern coast of the island, the
palm-ringed Beach 5 has your more classic
tropical vibe, with the bonus of shady patch-
es and fewer sandflies. Swimming is difficult
at low tide when the water becomes shallow.
Most accommodation is out this way.

Kalapathar   BEACH
Hidden away 5km south of Beach 5, you'll
find the low-key Kalapathar, a pristine

beach. You'll have to walk a bit to get away
from package tourists.

Diving & Snorkelling

Havelock is the premier spot for diving in
the Andamans. It's world renowned for its
crystal-clear waters, corals, schools of fish,
turtles and kaleidoscope of colourful marine
life. Diving here is suitable for all levels.

The main dive season is roughly Novem-
ber to April, but trips run year-round.

All companies offer fully equipped boat
dives, and prices vary depending on the loca-
tion, number of participants and duration of
the course. Diving starts from around ₹5000
for a two-tank dive, with options of Discover
Scuba (one hour ₹4500), PADI open-water
(four dives ₹21,700) and advanced (three
dives ₹13,500) courses.

While coral bleaching has been a major
issue since 2010 (mainly due to El Niño
weather patterns), diving remains world-
class. The shallows may not have bright cor-
als, but all the colourful fish are still here,
and for depths beyond 16m, corals remain as
vivid as ever. The Andamans recovered from
a similar bleaching in 1998, and today things
are likewise slowly repairing themselves.

Popular sites are **Dixon's Pinnacle** and
Pilot Reef with colourful soft coral, **South
Button** for macro dives (to see small crit-
ters) and rock formations, **Jackson Bar**
or **Johhny's Gorge** for deeper dives with
schools of snapper, sharks, rays and tur-
tles, and **Minerva's Delight** for a bit of
everything. There's also a **wreck dive** to SS
Incheket, a 1950s cargo carrier. Keep an eye
out for trips further afield such as **Barren
Island**, home to India's only active volcano,
whose ash produces an eerie underwater
spectacle for divers.

Dive companies can arrange **snorkelling**
trips, but it's cheaper to organise a boat
through your guesthouse. Snorkelling gear
is widely available on Havelock but is gen-
erally low quality.

Most boats head to **Elephant Beach**
for snorkelling, which can also be reached
by a 40-minute walk through a muddy el-
ephant logging trail; it's well marked (off
the cross-island road), but turns to bog if it's
been raining. At high tide it's also impossi-
ble to reach – ask locally for more info. Lots
of snorkelling charters, and even jet skis,
come out this way, so be prepared as it can
be a bit of a circus. If you head here around
6am, you'll have the place to yourself.

Prices are standardised, so find a dive op-
erator you feel comfortable with.

Havelock Island

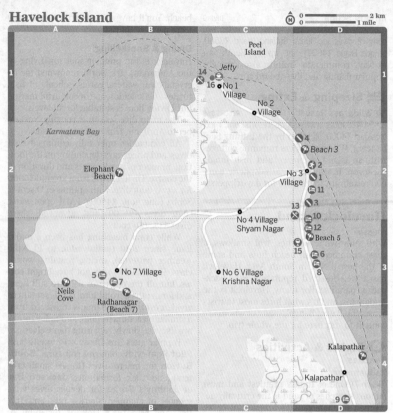

Andaman Bubbles DIVING
(☎03192-282140; www.andamanbubbles.com; No
5 Village) Quality outfit with professional staff.

Barefoot Scuba DIVING
(☎9566088560; www.diveandamans.com; No 3
Village) Popular, long-established company
with budget dive-accommodation packages.

Dive India DIVING
(☎9932082205; www.diveindia.com; btwn No
3 & 5 Village) The original PADI company in
Havelock, and still one of the best.

Ocean Tribe DIVING
(☎03192-210004; www.ocean-tribe.com; No 3 Village) Run by legendary local Karen divers, including Dixon, Johnny and Jackson, all who
have had dive sites named after them.

Other Activities

Most come to Havelock for lazing on the
beach, diving or snorkelling.

Some resorts can organise guided **jungle
treks** for keen walkers or birdwatchers, but
be warned the forest floor turns to glug after
rain. The inside rainforest is a spectacular,
emerald-coloured hinterland cavern, and
the **birdwatching** – especially on the forest
fringes – is rewarding; look out for the blue-
black racket-tailed drongo or golden oriole.

Yoga (per 1½ hours, ₹500) is available during season at Flying Elephant (p419).

Captain Hook's FISHING
(☎9434280543; www.andamansportsfishing.com;
Beach 3; half-/full day for 2 people incl lunch from
₹6000/20,000) Sport fishing is growing in
popularity, with Captain Hook's running
catch-and-release fishing trips where you
can reel in giant trevally, and kayaking trips.

Andaman Kayak Tours KAYAKING
(☎9933269653; www.andamankayaktours.com;
2½hr cruise ₹2500) Tours explore Havelock's
mangroves by sea kayak, and runs memorable

Havelock Island

night trips gliding among bio-luminescence. Minimum two people.

Sleeping

Orient Legend Resort　　　GUESTHOUSE $
(📞03192-282389; Beach 5; hut without bathroom ₹300-500, r with bathroom ₹800-2000, with AC ₹3000) This popular place on Beach 5 covers most budgets, from doghouse A-frame huts and concrete rooms to double-storey cottages.

Coconut Grove　　　GUESTHOUSE $
(📞9474269977; hut ₹400, without bathroom ₹300; ✉) Popular with Israeli travellers, Coconut Grove has an appealing communal vibe with psychedelic-painted huts arranged in a circular outlay.

Sea View Beach Resort　　　BUNGALOW $
(📞943429877; Beach 2; r ₹600-1000) Chilled out beach bungalows, backing on to the Ocean Tribe dive shop, offer the quintessential Havelock experience away from the crowds.

Dreamland Resort　　　GUESTHOUSE $
(📞9474224164; Beach 7; hut without bathroom ₹400) In a prime location, only 50m from Beach 7, Dreamland is an old backpacker favourite now popular with Indian families.

Pellicon Beach Resort　　　BUNGALOW $
(📞9932081673; www.pelliconbeachresort.com; Beach 5; hut from ₹500) Attractive beachside bungalows as well as Nicobari huts with private porches on a peaceful plot of land close to the beach.

Sunrise Beach Resort　　　BUNGALOW $
(📞9474206183; Beach 6; r ₹600-1000, with AC ₹4000) Offers the same thatched goodness as every other resort on Havelock – what sets it apart is its budget A-frame huts with water views. Has a bar too.

★**Emerald Gecko**　　　BUNGALOW $$
(📞9474250821; www.emerald-gecko.com; Beach 5; hut ₹1600-3200) On an island where very little thought goes into design, Emerald Gecko stands miles ahead. Double-storey bungalows look to the water, while pricier rooms have ambient lighting and outdoor bathrooms all lovingly constructed from bamboo rafts drifted ashore from Myanmar. It has one of Havelock's best restaurants (BYO alcohol), friendly staff and free filtered water.

Wild Orchid　　　RESORT $$$
(📞03192-282472; www.wildorchidandaman.com; Beach 5; r incl breakfast from ₹5600; ❄🐾) One of the Andamans' premier resorts, with modern and thoughtfully furnished Andamanese-style cottages, all set around a fabulous tropical garden.

Barefoot at Havelock　　　RESORT $$$
(📞044-24341001; www.barefootindia.com; Beach 7; tented cottage incl breakfast ₹5050, Nicobari cottage ₹8920, with AC ₹11,820; ❄) Luxurious resort boasting beautifully designed timber and bamboo-thatched cottages just back from the famed Radhanagar Beach.

Flying Elephant　　　BUNGALOW, RETREAT $$$
(📞9474250821; www.flying-elephant.in; Kalapathar; r ₹4000) Hidden away on Kalapathar beach, in a pastoral setting among rice paddies and betel palms, this yoga and meditation retreat has elegant bamboo duplexes with outdoor stone-garden bathrooms.

ANDAMAN ISLANDS HAVELOCK ISLAND

Symphony Palms Beach Resort RESORT $$$
(☑ 03192-214315; www.symphonypalmshavelock.
com; Beach 5; r incl breakfast from ₹10,000; ✱)
Only recommended for its seaside luxury
rooms (not the resort across the road), Sym-
phony Palms is like an upmarket version of
Havelock's bungalow resorts. It has a private
beach with sun lounges.

✖ Eating & Drinking

There are *dhabas* (snack bars) near the
jetty or head to the the main bazaar (No 3
Village) for local meals. Alcohol is available
from a **store** (Beach 3; ⊙8am-noon & 3-8pm)
next to the ATM at No 3 Village.

Welcome Restaurant INDIAN, SEAFOOD $
(No 3 Village; mains from ₹150; ⊙7.30am-9pm) In
the market, this eatery does delicious sea-
food curries and prawn rolls with *parathas*.

Rony's INDIAN $
(Beach 5; mains ₹110-250; ⊙7am-11pm) Popular
family-run place serving up seafood curries,
pizzas and other backpacker favs.

Fat Martin's SOUTH INDIAN $
(Beach 5; mains ₹60-120; ⊙7.30am-10pm)
Squeaky-clean open-air cafe with a good se-
lection of chapati rolls and dosas, including
paneer tikka and nutella dosas.

★ Red Snapper SEAFOOD, MULTICUISINE $$
(Wild Orchid; mains ₹250-900; ⊙7.30-10am, noon-
2.30pm & 6-9.30pm) Easily Havelock's best
restaurant and bar, with its atmospheric
polished-bamboo decor and thatched-roof
exuding a romantic island ambience. Pick
from lavish seafood platters, BBQ fish and
handmade pastas, accompanied by delicious
cheese-and-olive naan. The breezy outdoor
deck seating is a good spot for a beer.

Anju-coco Resto INDIAN, CONTINENTAL $$
(Beach 5; mains ₹200-900; ⊙8am-10.30pm) One
of Havelock's best, Anju-coco offers a varied
menu, with standouts being its big break-
fasts and BBQ fish.

Full Moon Cafe MULTICUISINE $$
(Dive India, Beach 5; mains ₹200-450) 🍃 Run by
an Irish-Indian couple, this busy thatched-
roof restaurant shares a site with Dive India on Beach 5. It does excellent seafood,
healthy salads and refreshing cardamom
lime fizzes. Free water refills.

B3 – Barefoot Bar & Restaurant PIZZERIA $$
(Village No 1; mains ₹200-900; ⊙11am-3.30pm &
6-9pm) Modern decor with cult movie post-
ers on the walls, B3 has a Western-heavy
menu, with the best pizzas in Havelock.
Its outside decking makes it a good place
to wait for your ferry. There's no alcohol.
Downstairs has the sophisticated **Dakshin**
(Village No 1; mains ₹80-150; ⊙6-10am & 11.30-
3pm), specialising in South Indian cuisine.

Cicada LIVE MUSIC
(Beach 5) Run by the team from Emerald
Gecko, this live music venue has an appeal-
ing jungle location accessed down a path off
the main road across from Beach 5.

❶ Information

There are two ATMs side by side in No 3 Village.
Satellite internet is insanely slow and pricey at
around ₹300 per hour.
Havelock Tourist Service (Beach 3;
⊙9.30am-8pm) A private operator which can
arrange air tickets, info for government and
private ferries, and sundries for tourists.

❶ Getting There & Away

Government ferries run from Havelock to Port
Blair three times a day (₹378, 2½ hours) at
9am, 2pm and 4pm. You're best to book tickets
from the **jetty** (⊙9.15am-noon & 2-4pm Mon-
Fri, to noon Sat) at least two days in advance
(most hotels can arrange this for a fee). One to
two ferries a day link Havelock with Neil Island
(₹378, one hour 10 minutes), while four boats a
week head to Long Island (₹378, two hours) en
route to Rangat.
  Makruzz (p412) and Coastal Cruise (p412)
have daily services to Port Blair via Neil Island.

❶ Getting Around

A local bus (₹10, 40 minutes) connects the jetty,
villages and Radhanagar on a roughly hourly
circuit until 6pm. You can rent a scooter (per 24
hours from ₹250) or bicycle (per day ₹60).
  An autorickshaw from the jetty to No 3 Village
is ₹50, to No 5 ₹80 and to No 7 ₹500.

Neil Island

Happy to laze in the shadows of its more fa-
mous island neighbour, tranquil Neil is still
the place for that added bit of relaxation. Its
beaches may not be as luxurious as Have-
lock's, but they have ample character and
are a perfect distance apart to explore by
bicycle; cycling through picturesque villag-
es you'll get many friendly hellos. The main
bazaar has a mellow vibe and is a popular
gathering spot in the early evening. In Neil
Island you're about 40km from Port Blair, a
short ferry ride from Havelock and several
universes away from life at home.

◉ Sights & Activitieses

Neil Island's five beaches (numbered one to five) all have their unique charms, though they aren't necessarily great for swimming.

Beach 1   BEACH
(Laxmanpur) Beach 1 is a long sweep of sandy beach and mangrove, a 40-minute walk west of the jetty and village. There's a good sunset viewpoint out this way accessed via Pearl Park Beach Resort (p421). Dugongs are sometime spotted here.

Beach 2   BEACH
On the north side of the island, Beach 2 has the Natural Bridge rock formation, accessible only at low tide by walking around the rocky cove. To get here by bicycle, take the side road that runs through the bazaar, then take a left where the road forks.

Beach 3   BEACH
(RamNagar) Beach 3 is a secluded powdery sand and rocky cove, which is best accessed via Blue Sea restaurant (p422). There's also good snorkelling here.

Beach 4   BEACH
(Bharatpur) The best swimming beach, though its proximity to the jetty is a turn-off, as are rowdy day-trippers who descend upon the beach in motorised boats.

Beach 5   BEACH
(Sitapur) The more rugged Beach 5, 5km from the village on the eastern side of Neil, is a nice place to walk along the sand, with small limestone caves accessible at low tide.

Diving & Snorkelling

Neil Island offers some excellent dive sites, with colourful fish, large schools of Jack, turtles, sharks, rays, and soft and hard corals.

The island's best snorkelling is around the coral reef at the far (western) end of Beach 1 at high tide; if you're extremely lucky you may spot a dugong feeding in the shallows at high tide. Beach 3 also has good snorkelling. Gear costs around ₹150 to hire and available from many guesthouses.

There are two dive operators on Neil Island. Those interested in free diving can contact Sanjay at Gayan Garden (p421).

India Scuba Explorers   DIVING
(☑ 9474238646; www.indiascubaexplorers.com; Beach 1; per 1/2 dives ₹3000/5000) Neil's first dive shop set up by a young husband-wife team is popular for its personalised service.

Dive India   DIVING
(☑ 8001222206; www.diveindia.com/neil.html; per 1/2 dives ₹3000/5000) Established in Havelock, this professional company has recently opened here.

🛏 Sleeping

These days Beach 3 and 5 are the most popular with backpackers. Beach 1 attracts package tourists, but still has excellent choices.

🛏 Beach 1

Sunset Garden Guesthouse   BUNGALOW **$**
(☑ 9933294573; Beach 1; hut ₹250-400) Ideal for those wanting to get away from it all, these bamboo huts are in a secluded spot accessed via a 15-minute walk through rice fields.

Gayan Garden   BUNGALOW **$**
(Beach 1; r ₹300) Bamboo cottages halfway between the bazaar and Beach 1 with a relaxed garden, seafood restaurant and filtered coffee. Offers cooking classes too.

Tango Beach Resort   HOTEL **$**
(☑ 9474212842; www.tangobeachandaman.com; Beach 1; hut ₹500, cottage with fan/AC from ₹1200/4000; ✳) Famous for its sea breeze, this Beach 1 classic is pricier than most, but its sea-facing rooms are still a fine choice.

Pearl Park Beach Resort   BUNGALOW **$$**
(☑ 9434260132; www.andamanpearlpark.com; Beach 1; s/d incl breakfast with fan from ₹1500/1800, with AC from ₹2500/3200; ✳🛜) Neil's original bamboo-bungalow 'resort' now caters more for domestic tourists and is grossly overpriced, but it still has pleasant huts arranged around a flower-filled garden.

Seashell   RESORT **$$$**
(☑ 9933239625; www.seashellneil.com; Beach 1; cottage incl breakfast ₹8590) Upmarket tented cottages leading down to the beach.

🛏 Beach 3

★ Kalapani   BUNGALOW **$**
(☑ 9474274991; Beach 3; hut ₹400, without bathroom ₹200) Run by the delightful Prakash and Bina, laid-back Kalapani has blissfully simple and clean bungalows with quality mattresses. Motorbikes, bicycles and snorkelling gear are available for hire.

Breakwater Beach Resort   BUNGALOW **$**
(☑ 9933292654; www.neilislandaccommodation.in; Beach 3; hut ₹500-1000, without bathroom ₹300) Wins rave reviews for its chilled-out ambience and delicious food.

Beach 5

Sunrise Beach Resort BUNGALOW $
(☑ 9933266900; Beach 5; r without bathroom ₹200-400) Thatched and concrete bungalows a one-minute walk from the beach.

Emerald Gecko BUNGALOW $$
(Beach 5; r ₹1000-3000) Still under construction when we visited, but if it's anything close to its sister guesthouse in Havelock (p419), it'll be a wonderful addition to Neil.

Eating

Moonshine INTERNATIONAL, INDIAN $
(Beach 1; mains ₹90-250) On the road to Beach 1, this backpacker favourite has excellent homemade pastas, fish thalis and cold beer.

Blue Sea SEAFOOD, INDIAN $
(Beach 3; mains from ₹100; ☉ 6am-11pm) Old-school beach shack with sandy floor, dangling beach curios and a blue whale skull centrepiece, serving all the usual dishes. The path here leads to arguably Neil's best beach.

Chand Restaurant INDIAN, CONTINENTAL $
(Bazaar; mains ₹70-200; ☉ 6am-10.30pm) The best place in the market with a good mix of international and Indian dishes, strong filtered coffee and delicious seafood.

ⓘ Information

There's no ATM or moneychanging facilities on Neil, so bring plenty of cash. There's wi-fi access at Pearl Park Beach Resort (p421) on Beach 1 for ₹200 per 24 hours.

ⓘ Getting There & Around

A ferry heads to Port Blair two or three times a day (₹378, two hours). There are also one or two daily ferries to Havelock (₹378, one hour), and three ferries a week to Long Island (₹378, five hours). Makruzz (p412) and Coastal Cruise (p412) also have ferries to/from Port Blair (from ₹875, one hour) and Havelock (from ₹710)

Hiring a bicycle (per day from ₹80) is the best way to get about; roads are flat and distances short. You'll be able to find one in the bazaar or at a guesthouse. An autorickshaw will take you from the jetty to Beach 1 or 3 for ₹70 to ₹100.

Middle & North Andaman

The Andamans aren't just sun and sand. They are also jungle that feels as primeval as the Jurassic, a green tangle of ancient forest that could have been birthed in Mother Nature's subconscious. This wild, antediluvian side of the islands can be seen on a long bus ride up the Andaman Trunk Rd (ATR), crossing tannin-red rivers prowled by saltwater crocodiles on roll-on, roll-off ferries.

But there's a negative side to riding the ATR: the road cuts through the homeland of the Jarawa (p423) and has brought the tribe into incessant contact with the outside world. Modern India and tribal life do not seem able to coexist – every time Jarawa and settlers interact, misunderstandings have led to friction, confusion and, at worst, violent attacks and death. Indian anthropologists and indigenous rights groups such as Survival International have called for the ATR to be closed; its status continues to be under review. At present, vehicles are permitted to travel only in convoys at set times from 6am to 3pm. Photography is strictly prohibited, as is stopping or any other interaction with the Jarawa people who are becoming increasingly reliant on handouts from passing traffic.

The first place of interest north of Port Blair are the limestone caves (☉ Tue-Sun) at Baratang. It's a 45-minute boat trip (₹450) from the jetty, a scenic trip through mangrove forest. A permit is required, organised at the jetty.

Rangat & Around

Rangat is the next main town, a transport hub with not much else going for it. If you do get stuck here, UK Nest has clean budget rooms, while Priya International is a more upmarket choice with handy tourist information on things to do in the area. There's an ATM nearby. The turtle breeding grounds at Dhaninallah Mangrove is the most popular sight, viewed early evening (mid-December to April) from the 1km-long boardwalk, a 45-minute drive from Rangat.

Ferries depart Long Island (₹11) from Yeratta Jetty, 8km from Rangat, at 9am and 3.30pm. Rangat Bay, 5km outside town, has ferries to/from Port Blair (₹378, six hours) and Havelock (₹378, two hours). A daily bus goes to Port Blair (₹145, seven hours) and Diglipur (₹65, four hours).

Long Island

With its friendly island community and lovely slow pace of life, Long Island is perfect for those wanting to take the pace down a few more notches. Other than the odd

ISLAND INDIGENES

The Andaman and Nicobar Islands' indigenous peoples constitute 12% of the population and, in most cases, their numbers are decreasing. The Onge, Sentinelese, Andamanese and Jarawa are all of Negrito ethnicity, and share a strong resemblance to people from Africa. Tragically, numerous groups have become extinct over the past century. In February 2010 the last speaker of the Bo language passed away, bringing an end to a culture and language that originated 65,000 years ago.

The *Land of the Naked People* (2003) by Madhusree Mukerjee provides an interesting anthropological account. It's important to note that these ethnic groups live in areas strictly off limits to foreigners, and people have been arrested for trying to visit these areas.

Jarawa
The 250 remaining Jarawa occupy the 639-sq-km reserve on South and Middle Andaman Islands (p422). In 1953 the chief commissioner requested that an armed sea plane bomb Jarawa settlements, and their territory has been consistently disrupted by the Andaman Trunk Rd, forest clearance and settler and tourist encroachment. In 2012, a video went viral showing an exchange between Jarawa and tourists, whereby a policeman orders them to dance in exchange for food. This resulted in a government inquest that saw to the end of the so-called 'human safari' tours.

Nicobarese
The 30,000 Nicobarese are the only indigenous people whose numbers are not decreasing. The majority have converted to Christianity and been partly assimilated into contemporary Indian society. Living in village units led by a head man, they farm pigs and cultivate coconuts, yams and bananas. The Nicobarese, who probably descended from people of Malaysia and Myanmar, inhabit a number of islands in the Nicobar group, centred on Car Nicobar, the region worst affected by the 2004 tsunami.

Onge
Two-thirds of Little Andaman's Onge Island was taken over by the Forest Department and 'settled' in 1977. The 100 or so remaining members of the Onge tribe live in a 25-sq-km reserve covering Dugong Creek and South Bay. Anthropologists say the Onge population has declined due to demoralisation through loss of territory.

Sentinelese
The Sentinelese, unlike the other tribes on these islands, have consistently repelled outside contact. For years, contact parties arrived on the beaches of North Sentinel Island with gifts of coconuts, bananas, pigs and red plastic buckets, only to be showered with arrows, though some encounters have been a little less hostile. About 150 Sentinelese remain.

Andamanese
As they now number only about 50, it seems impossible the Andamanese can escape extinction. There were around 7000 Andamanese in the mid-19th century, but friendliness to colonisers was their undoing, and by 1971 all but 19 of the population had been swept away by measles, syphilis and influenza epidemics. They have been resettled on Strait Island.

Shompen
Only about 250 Shompen remain in the forests on Great Nicobar. Seminomadic hunter-gatherers who live along the riverbanks, they have resisted integration.

motorcycle, there's no motorised vehicles on the island, and at certain times you may be the only tourist here.

◉ Sights & Activities

Beaches
There's a nice beach close to Blue Planet (p424), reached via the yellow arrows.

Lalaji Bay
BEACH
A 1½-hour trek in the jungle will lead you to the secluded Lalaji Bay, a beautiful white-sand beach with good swimming and snorkelling; follow the red arrows to get here. Hiring a *dunghi* (motorised boat; ₹2500 return for two persons) is also an option. Inconveniently, you need a permit (free) from the Forest Office near the jetty to visit.

Diving & Snorkelling

Blue Planet (p424) has a dive shop (December to March), charging ₹4000 for two dives, and visits Campbell Shoal for its schools of trevally and barracuda.

You can also get a *dunghi* to North Passage Island for snorkelling at the stunning **Merk Bay** (₹3500 for two people) with blinding white sand and translucent waters.

There's excellent offshore **snorkelling** at Lalaji Bay with colourful corals out front from the rest huts. There's also good snorkelling at the 'Blue Planet' beach, directly out from the blue Hindu temple; swim beyond the sea grass to get to the coral. Blue Planet hires snorkelling gear for ₹100.

🛏 Sleeping

⭐ **Blue Planet** GUESTHOUSE **$**
(📞 9474212180; www.blueplanetandamans.com; r from ₹1500, without bathroom ₹500; @) The only place to stay on the island, so fortunately it's a gem, with thatched-bamboo rooms and hammocks set around a lovely Padauk tree. Food is delicious and there's free filtered water. It's a 15-minute walk from the jetty; follow the blue arrow markers. It also has wonderful double-storey bamboo cottages (from ₹3000) at a nearby location.

🛈 Getting There & Away

There are four ferries a week to Havelock, Neil and Port Blair (₹195). From Yeratta, there are two daily boats to Long Island (₹11, one hour)

at 9am and 3.30pm, returning at 7am and 2pm. A bus meets ferries at Yeratta. If you can't get a ferry here from Port Blair, jump on a bus to Rangat to get the ferry from Yeratta.

Diglipur & Around

Those who make it this far north are rewarded with some impressive attractions in the area. It's a giant outdoor adventure playground designed for nature lovers: home to a world-famous turtle nesting site, Andaman's highest peak and a network of caves to go with white-sand beaches and some of the best snorkelling in the Andamans.

However, don't expect much of Diglipur (population 70,000), the second largest town in the Andamans, a sprawling, gritty bazaar town with an ATM and internet access (per hour ₹40). Instead head straight for the tranquil coastal village of **Kalipur**.

Ferries and some buses arrive at **Aerial Bay**, from where it's 11km to Diglipur, and 8km to Kalipur in the other direction.

🏃 Activities

Diglipur has huge tourist potential, and those who hang around will have plenty to discover. In season most come to see the turtles (p425). Get in touch with Pristine Beach Resort (p425), who are involved with the DARTED grassroots tourist initiative to promote Alfred Caves, mud volcanoes and crocodile habitats.

OFF THE BEATEN TRACK

MAYABUNDER & AROUND

In 'upper' Middle Andaman, Mayabunder is most famous for its villages inhabited by Karen, members of a Burmese hill tribe who were relocated here during the British colonial period. It's a low-key destination for travellers looking for an experience away from the crowds.

You can go on a range of day tours, with the highlight being jungle trekking at creepy **Interview Island** (boat hire ₹3000, up to six people), inhabited by a population of 36 wild elephants, descendants of working elephants released after a logging company closed in the 1950s. You'll feel very isolated here. Armed guards accompany you in case of elephant encounters. A permit (₹500) is required, which is best organised by emailing a copy of your arrival permit to Sea'n'Sand guesthouse. Other trips include **turtle nesting** at Dhaninallah Mangrove; **Forty One Caves**, where *hawabills* (swiftlets) make their highly prized edible nests; and snorkelling off **Avis Island** (boat hire ₹1500).

Sea'n'Sand (📞 03192-273454; titusinseansand@yahoo.com; r from ₹750; ❄) is easily the best place to stay with comfortable rooms. Hosts Titus and Elizabeth (and their extended Karen family) are an excellent source for everything Mayabunder. Go the top level for water views. The food here is sensational.

Mayabunder, 71km north of Rangat (₹70, two hours), is linked by daily buses from Port Blair (₹200, 10 hours) and Diglipur (₹55, two hours) and by thrice-weekly ferries. There's an ATM here.

Ross & Smith Islands
BEACH, SNORKELLING

(☉ closed Tue) Like lovely tropical counter-weights, the twin islands of Smith and Ross are connected by a narrow sandbar of dazzling white sand, and are up there with the best in the Andamans for both swimming and snorkelling. No permits are required for Smith Island, which is accessed by boat (₹2500, fits five people) from Aerial Bay. While theoretically you need a permit for Ross Island (₹500), as it's walkable from Smith permits generally aren't checked. Enquire with Pristine Resort for more info.

Ross and Smith are closed Tuesday for beach cleaning; volunteers are welcome (₹250, covering permit, transport and food).

Saddle Peak
TREKKING

(Indian/foreigner ₹25/250) At 732m Saddle Peak is the highest point in the Andamans. You can trek through subtropical forest to the top and back from Kalipur in about six to seven hours; the views from the peaks onto the archipelago are incredible. It's a demanding trek, so bring plenty of water (around 4L). A permit (₹250) is required from the Forest Office at the trailhead, open 6am to 2pm. A local guide (300₹) will make sure you don't get lost, but otherwise follow the red arrows marked on the trees.

Craggy Island
SNORKELLING

A small island off Kalipur, Craggy is a good spot for snorkelling. Strong swimmers can make it across (flippers recommended), otherwise a *dunghi* is available (₹2500 return).

Excelsior Island
SNORKELLING

Recently opened for tourism, Excelsior has beautiful beaches, snorkelling plus resident spotted deer. Permits are required (₹500); boats cost ₹4500 and fit seven people.

🛌 Sleeping & Eating

★ Pristine Beach Resort
GUESTHOUSE $

(☏ 9474286787; www.andamanpristineresorts.com; hut ₹600-1000, r ₹3000-4500; ❋ @) Huddled among the palms between paddy fields and the beach, this relaxing resort has simple bamboo huts, more romantic bamboo 'tree houses' and upmarket rooms. Its attractive restaurant-bar serves up delicious fish Nicobari and cold beer. Alex, the superfriendly owner, is a top source of information. It also rents bicycles/motorcycles (per day ₹100/250) and snorkelling gear (₹100).

TURTLE NESTING IN KALIPUR

Reputedly the only beach in the world where leatherback, hawksbill, olive ridley marine and green turtles all nest along the same coastline, Kalipur is a fantastic place to observe this evening show from mid-December and April. Turtles can be witnessed most nights, and you can assist with collecting eggs, or with the release of hatchlings. Contact Pristine Beach Resort (p425).

The Dhaninallah Mangrove boardwalk north of Rangat is another good spot to see turtles.

Sion
INDIAN $

(Diglipur; mains ₹60-150; ☉ 10am-10pm) If you have time to kill in Diglipur, this rooftop restaurant serving excellent seafood dishes is the place to head.

ℹ Getting There & Around

Diglipur, located about 80km north of Mayabunder, is served by daily buses to Port Blair (₹255, 12 hours) at 5am, 7am and a 10.40pm night bus. There are also buses to Mayabunder (₹55, 2½ hours) and Rangat (₹100, 4½ hours).

Ferries to Port Blair (seat/bunk ₹110/350, nine hours) depart three times a week.

Buses run the 18km journey from Diglipur to Kalipur (₹15, 30 mintues) every 45 minutes; an autorickshaw costs ₹200.

Little Andaman

As far south as you can go in the islands, Little Andaman has an appealing end-of-the-world feel. It's a gorgeous fist of mangroves, jungle and teal, ringed by beaches as fresh as bread out of the oven. It rates as many traveller's favourite spot in the Andamans.

Badly hit by the 2004 tsunami, Little Andaman has slowly rebuilt itself. Located about 120km south of Port Blair, the main settlement here is Hut Bay, a pleasant small town with smiling Bengalis and Tamils.

◎ Sights & Activities

Little Andaman Lighthouse
LIGHTHOUSE

Located 14km east of Hut Bay, Little Andaman lighthouse makes for a worthwhile excursion. Exactly 200 steps spiral up to magnificent views over the coastline and forest. The easiest way to get here is by motorcycle. Otherwise take a sweaty bicycle journey or autorickshaw until the road becomes unpassable; from there, walk for an hour along the blissful stretch of deserted beach.

Beaches

Come prepared for sandflies (p410); crocodiles are also about.

Butler Bay   BEACH

(entry ₹20) Little Andaman's best beach is Butler Bay, a spectacular curve with lifeguards and good surf at the 14km mark.

Netaji Nagar   BEACH

The sprawling and rugged Netaji Nagar, stretching 8km to 12km north of Hut Bay, is where most accommodation is located. The downside is the occasional rubbish that washes ashore from Thailand and Myanmar.

Kalapathar   BEACH

Located before Butler Bay is Kalapathar lagoon, a popular enclosed swimming area with shady patches of sand. Look for the cave in the cliff face that you can scramble through for stunning ocean views. It's accessed via a side road that runs past modern housing constructed after the 2004 tsunami.

Surfing

Intrepid surfing travellers have been whispering about Little Andaman since it first opened to foreigners several years ago. The reef breaks are legendary, but best suited for more experienced surfers. The most accessible is **Jarawa Point**, a left reef break on Butler Bay. Beginners should stick to beach breaks along Km8 to Km11. February to April brings the best waves.

Surfing Little Andaman   SURFING

(☑ 9933269762; www.surfinglittleandaman.com; Hut Bay; board rental half-/full day ₹500/900, 2hr lesson ₹1000) Run by Basque surfer Varuna, here you can hire boards, arrange lessons and get the lowdown on everything about surfing in Little Andaman.

Waterfalls

Inland, the **White Surf** and **Whisper Wave** waterfalls offer a jungle experience for when you're done lazing on the beach. The latter involves a 4km forest trek and a guide is highly recommended. They are pleasant falls and you may be tempted to swim in the rock pools, but beware of crocodiles.

🛏 Sleeping & Eating

There are cheap thali places in town. No guesthouses serve alcohol, but you can stock up from a 'wine shop' in Hut Bay. Accommodation options are across from the beach.

★ Blue View   BUNGALOW $

(☑ 9734480840; www.blueviewresort.net; Km11.5, Netaji Nagar; r without bathroom ₹200-500; ☺ Oct-May) Blue View's simple thatched bungalows are still the pick, mainly for the legendary hospitality of Azad and his lovely wife Papia. Food here is amazing, and surfboards and bicycles/motorbikes (per day ₹50/300) are available for hire.

Aastha Eco Resort   BUNGALOW $

(Km10, Netaji Nagar; r ₹200-400) Set among betel and coconut palms, Aastha has the best rooms on the island with its atmospheric Nicobari huts and comfortable thatched cottages, all with clean bathrooms.

Hawwa Beach Resort   BUNGALOW $

(☑ 9775181290; Km8, Netaji Nagar; s/d ₹300/400) This laid-back, family-run resort has five pink cottages with quality mattresses and spotless attached bathrooms.

Hotel Sea Land   HOTEL $

(☑ 9679534673; Hut Bay; s/d ₹300/500, with AC ₹800) Sea Land offers comfortable, air-con concrete rooms, but lacks atmosphere.

Palm Groove   INDIAN $

(Hut Bay; mains ₹60-135; ☺ 7am-9pm) Attractive heritage-style bungalow where a good selection of biriyanis and thalis can be had in the outdoor garden gazebo.

ℹ Information

There's an ATM in Hut Bay and village at 16Km, but no internet.

ℹ Getting There & Around

Ferries land at Hut Bay Jetty. Buses (₹10, depart hourly) to Netaji Nagar usually coincide with ferry arrivals, but often leaves before you clear immigration, leaving pricey jeeps (per person ₹100) as the other option. An autorickshaw from the jetty to Netaji Nagar is ₹250, or ₹70 to town. Motorbikes and bicycles are popular for getting around, and are available from most lodges; otherwise, shared jeeps (₹20) and buses are handy.

Boats sail to Port Blair daily, alternating between afternoon and evening departures on vessels ranging from big ferries with four-/two-bed rooms (₹230/320, six to 8½ hours) to faster 5½-hour government boats (₹35); all have air-con. The ferry office is closed Sunday. You can get here by helicopter and seaplane (p411).

Understand South India & Kerala

South India & Kerala Today

India's incredibly diverse fabric of cultures, peoples, religions, landscapes and languages is fascinating to observe as you travel around it. South India is no exception. While the south is very much part of the Indian nation, and decisions made in the national capital, Delhi, are as relevant here as everywhere else, there is a sense that the south is somehow different – as some would have it, more progressive and outward-looking than the north, but also more in touch with its Indian soul.

Best on Film

Fire (1996), **Earth** (1998) and **Water** (2005) The Deepa Mehta–directed trilogy on social issues was popular abroad, but controversial in India.

The Lunchbox (2013) A touching, romantic Mumbai (Bombay) tale directed by Ritesh Batra.

Dhobi Ghat (2011) Understated, absorbing story, directed by Kiran Rao, touching on many levels of Mumbai, and Indian, life.

Gandhi (1982) The classic, directed by Richard Attenborough and starring Ben Kingsley.

Best in Print

Midnight's Children Salman Rushdie's allegory about Independence and Partition.

White Tiger Page-turning novel about Indian class injustice, set partly in Bengaluru (Bangalore), by Aravind Adiga.

Shantaram Gregory David Roberts' vivid experiences of his life in India. A travellers' favourite!

A Fine Balance Rohinton Mistry's tragic but heart-warming tale of struggle for survival in Mumbai.

The God of Small Things Magically written novel of passion and caste in Kerala, by Arundhati Roy.

White Mughals Fascinating historical investigation into the Hyderabad of two centuries ago, by William Dalrymple.

The Balance Tilts Southward

In the early decades after Independence in 1947, many South Indians headed north in search of work. Today, the trend is in the opposite direction. Some pundits argue that better and more stable governance in the southern states (despite deep-seated corruption), and a less rigid caste system (allowing greater social mobility) have contributed to the south's upswing. Today, nearly all the states of South India have above-average literacy, employment, life expectancy, income per head, and female-to-male population ratio. The state of Kerala has the country's highest literacy rate and life expectancy, and is the only state with more women than men.

Mumbai (Bombay) has long been India's financial, commercial and industrial powerhouse, as well as its cinema and fashion capital. Chennai (Madras) makes one-third of all India's cars. Goa and, increasingly, Kerala are big tourism success stories. But the biggest story of all is the technology boom, which was sparked by India's economic liberalisation of 1991 and world globalisation. Bengaluru (Bangalore) is India's 'Silicon Valley', and with Hyderabad and Pune forms the 'Deccan Triangle' at the heart of India's IT industry, which generates vast export earnings. These three cities, with their big pool of well-educated, English-speaking, young professionals, also host research and development operations of some 150 top multinational companies. Chennai and Mumbai, along with Delhi, are the other cities making up India's IT big six.

Along with economic progress have come some problems, including the growth of city slums (an estimated 60% of Mumbai's population lives in slums), and dreadful traffic and pollution in the big cities – though new metro systems in Mumbai, Bengaluru, Chennai and Hyderabad are finally bringing transport in these cities into the modern age. Kerala, despite its education and health successes, has high unemployment and India's highest suicide and alcohol-consumption rates; in 2014 it removed liquor licences from some 700 bars in an effort to reduce drinking.

The Political Landscape

Regional parties focused on local issues and local personalities dominate South Indian politics. National parties have to strike alliances with them to gain support in Delhi or a foothold in the regions. Maharashtra shows more support for a national party – the Hindu-nationalist-oriented Bharatiya Janata Party (BJP) – than any state further south, but the BJP has long had to operate in alliance with Shiv Sena, a reactionary local party that opposes migration into Maharashtra by people from other states. Tamil Nadu has had a string of former film stars and scriptwriters from the Tamil movie industry as its chief ministers. The latest, Jayalalithaa Jayaram, received a four-year jail sentence in 2014 for amassing over US$10 million of unaccounted-for wealth, but remains hugely popular.

But the south has certainly sat up and taken notice of national politics since 2014 when, in India's biggest political sea change for decades, Narendra Modi from the western state of Gujarat led the BJP to a stunning general election victory – the first time since 1984 that one party had won an outright majority in parliament. It was a humiliation for the Congress Party – the party of independent India's first prime minister Jawaharlal Nehru, his daughter Indira Gandhi and their descendants – which had ruled India for all but 12 of the 67 years since Independence.

Modi's charisma, derived from his economic reputation as former chief minister of Gujarat state and his appeal to 'ordinary' Indians due to his working-class origins, had much do with the BJP's victory. These factors certainly outweighed accusations (which Modi has always denied) that he did little to stop religious riots in Gujarat in 2002 in which at least 1000 people, mostly Muslims, were killed. He is a masterful political campaigner, making savvy use of digital technology including social media. In office, Modi has set out not only to resurrect India's stuttering economy but also to address social issues such as sanitation, gender equality, poverty and health. Apart from vowing to build millions of toilets, in 2014 he launched the Swachh Bharat Abhiyan (Clean India Mission), which has even seen the PM himself and revered Bollywood and cricket stars publicly clearing rubbish.

Both the World Bank and International Monetary Fund forecast that India's economy was on track to become the world's fastest growing (expected to overtake China in 2016/17), citing renewed investment confidence under the business-friendly Modi as one of the reasons. Another economic achievement came when India broke a Guinness World Record for the most bank accounts opened in one week – 18,096,130 – in a scheme aimed at offering socioeconomic opportunities for the poor, who were often denied banking access in the past.

POPULATION: **367 MILLION**

GDP PER CAPITA: **₹94,900 PER YEAR**

LITERACY RATE: **78%**

GENDER RATIO: **FEMALE/ MALE 964/1000**

AREA: **956,000 SQ KM**

FERTILITY RATE: **BIRTHS PER WOMAN: 1.8**

if India were 100 people

55 would speak one of 21 other official languages
41 would speak Hindi
4 would speak one of 400 other official languages

belief systems
(% of population)

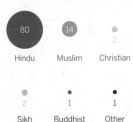

80 Hindu
14 Muslim
2 Christian

2 Sikh
1 Buddhist
1 Other

population per sq km

INDIA   CHINA   USA

≈ 30 people

Dos & Don'ts

Dress modestly Avoid stares by avoiding tight or skimpy clothes, especially at holy places.

Shoes It's polite, often obligatory, to remove shoes before entering places of worship or homes.

Photos Best to ask before photographing people, ceremonies or sacred sites.

Bad vibes Avoid pointing soles of feet towards people or deities, or touching anyone with your feet.

Niceties

Namaste Saying *namaste* with hands together in a prayer gesture is a traditional, respectful Hindu greeting and a universal way to say hello.

Hugs Shaking hands is fine but hugs between strangers are not the norm.

Pure hands Use your right hand for eating and shaking hands; the left hand is the 'toilet' hand.

That head wobble It can mean 'yes', 'maybe' or 'I have no idea'. Go with the flow!

Violence Against Women

In December 2012 a 23-year-old paramedic and her male friend boarded a bus on their way home from the movies in Delhi only to find that it was a fake city bus, where six men awaited them. The men raped the woman so brutally that she died 12 days later. This woman became known in India as Nirbhaya, or 'fearless one', and the event set off massive protests and soul-searching nationwide.

Within weeks, India passed a package of new, but controversial, laws to deter violence against women: rape now carries a seven-year minimum sentence, with the death penalty in cases where the victim dies. But in the years since the murder, new incidents of violence against women have continued to make headlines all too often. Many in India are also now reflecting on other abuses of women (tens of thousands die over dowry disputes alone each year), widespread police and justice-system mishandling of cases, and the larger problems of gender inequality. There is hope that now the issues are out in the open change will follow. Since becoming prime minister, Narendra Modi has been actively trying to change the national psyche regarding gender equality. In his 2014 Independence Day address to the nation, Modi spoke out about rape: 'When your daughter turns 10 or 12 years old, you ask, "Where are you going? When will you return?" Do the parents dare to ask their sons, 'Where are you going? Why are you going? Who are your friends?" After all, the rapist is also someone's son.' In 2015 Modi launched the Beti Bachao Beti Padhao (Save the Daughter, Teach the Daughter) campaign, which aims to work towards gender equality by discouraging female infanticide and encouraging education, among other things. With programs such as this, it's hoped the way society views gender issues will improve. Time, as ever, will tell.

History

South India has always laid claim to its own unique history, largely resulting from its insulation, by distance, from political developments up north. The cradle of Dravidian culture, it has a long and colourful historical tapestry of wrangling dynasties and empires, interwoven with an influx of traders and conquerors arriving by sea, all of which have richly contributed to a remarkable mix of southern traditions that persists to the present day.

Indus Valley Civilisation

India's first major civilisation flourished between about 3000 and 1700 BC in the Indus Valley, much of which lies within present-day Pakistan. Known as the Harappan culture, it appears to have been the culmination of thousands of years of settlement. Some historians attribute its eventual demise to floods or decreased rainfall, which threatened the Harappans' agricultural base. A more enduring theory, with little archaeological proof or evidence from ancient Indian texts to support it, is that an invasion from the northwest by Aryans (peoples speaking languages of the Indo-Iranian branch of the Indo-European language family) put paid to the Harappans. Others say that the arrival of the Aryans was more of a gentle migration that gradually subsumed Harappan culture, rather than an invasion. Some nationalist historians argue that the Aryans (the term comes from a Sanskrit word meaning 'noble') were in fact the original inhabitants of India and that the invasion theory was invented by later, self-serving foreign conquerors. Invasion theorists believe that from around 1500 BC Aryan tribes from Afghanistan and Central Asia began to gradually filter into northwest India, eventually controlling northern India as far south as the Vindhya Range (just north of the Narmada River), and that as a consequence, many of the original inhabitants, the Dravidians, were pushed south.

India: A History by John Keay is an astute and readable account of subcontinental history spanning from the Harappan civilisation to post-Independence India.

To learn more about the ancient Indus Valley civilisation, ramble around Harappa (www.harappa.com), which presents an illustrated yet scholarly overview.

Influences from the North

Aryan culture had a gradual but profound effect on the social order and ethos of South India as well as the north – among other things in

TIMELINE	2600–1700 BC	1500 BC	1500–1200 BC
	The heyday of the Indus Valley civilisation, spanning parts of Rajasthan, Gujarat and the Sindh province in present-day Pakistan, and including cities such as Harappa and Moenjodaro.	The Indo-Aryan civilisation takes root in the fertile plains of the Indo-Gangetic basin. Settlers speak an early form of Sanskrit, from which several Indian vernaculars, including Hindi, later evolve.	The Rig-Veda, the first and longest of Hinduism's canonical texts, the Vedas, is written; three more books follow. Earliest forms of priestly Brahmanic Hinduism emerge.

literature (the four Vedas – a collection of sacred Hindu hymns), religion (gods such as Agni, Varuna, Shiva and Vishnu), language (Sanskrit) and a social structure that organised people into castes, with Brahmins at the top.

Over the centuries other influences flowed from the north, including Buddhism and Jainism. Sravanabelagola in modern-day Karnataka, an auspicious place of pilgrimage to this day, is where, tradition says, the northern ruler Chandragupta Maurya, who had embraced Jainism and renounced his kingdom, arrived with his guru around 300 BC. Jainism was then adopted by the trading community (its tenet of ahimsa, or non-violence, precluded occupations tainted by the taking of life), who spread it through South India.

Emperor Ashoka, a successor of Chandragupta who ruled for 40 years from about 272 BC, was a major force behind Buddhism's inroads into the south. Once a campaigning king, his epiphany came in 260 BC when, overcome by the horrific carnage and suffering caused by his campaign against the powerful Kalinga kingdom of Odisha, he renounced violence and embraced Buddhism. He sent Buddhist missionaries far and wide, and his edicts (carved into rock and incised into specially erected pillars) have been found in Andhra Pradesh and Karnataka. Stupas were also built in South India under Ashoka's patronage, mostly in Andhra Pradesh, although at least one was constructed as far south as Kanchipuram in Tamil Nadu.

The appeal of Jainism and Buddhism was that they rejected the Vedas and condemned the caste system. Buddhism, however, gradually lost favour with its devotees, and was replaced with a new brand of Hinduism, which emphasised devotion to a personal god. This bhakti (surrendering to the gods) order developed in South India around AD 500. Bhakti adherents opposed Jainism and Buddhism, and the movement hastened the decline of both in South India.

Best Buddhist Sites

Ajanta (p96)

Ellora (p93)

Amaravathi (p247)

Nagarjunakonda (p247)

Guntupalli (p249)

Karla & Bhaga Caves (p108)

Aurangabad Caves (p89)

Mauryan Empire & Southern Kingdoms

Chandragupta Maurya was the first in a line of Mauryan kings who ruled what was effectively the first Indian empire. The empire's capital was in present-day Patna in Bihar. Chandragupta's son, Bindusara, who came to the throne around 300 BC, extended the empire as far as Karnataka. He seems to have stopped there possibly because the Mauryan empire was on cordial terms with the southern chieftains of the day.

The identity and customs of these southern chiefdoms have been gleaned from various sources, including archaeological remains and ancient Tamil literature. These literary records describe a land known as the 'abode of the Tamils', within which resided three major ruling families: the Pandyas (centred on Madurai), the Cheras (in what is now Ker-

599–528 BC	563–483 BC	326 BC	321–185 BC
The life of Mahavir, the 24th and last *tirthankar* (enlightened teacher) who established Jainism. Like Buddha, he preaches compassion and a path to enlightenment for all castes.	The life of Siddhartha Gautama. The prince is born in modern-day Nepal and attains enlightenment beneath the Bodhi Tree in Bodhgaya (Bihar), thereby transforming into the Buddha (Awakened One).	Alexander the Great invades India. He defeats King Porus in Punjab to enter the subcontinent, but a rebellion within his army keeps him from advancing beyond Himachal Pradesh's Beas River.	Rule of the Mauryan kings. Founded by Chandragupta Maurya, this pan-Indian empire is ruled from Pataliputra (present-day Patna) and briefly adopts Buddhism during the reign of Emperor Ashoka.

ASHOKA: AN ENLIGHTENED EMPEROR

Apart from the Mughals and then the British many centuries later, no other power controlled more Indian territory than the Mauryan empire. It's therefore fitting that it provided India with one of its most significant historical figures.

Emperor Ashoka's rule was characterised by flourishing art and sculpture, while his reputation as a philosopher-king was enhanced by the rock-hewn edicts he used both to instruct his people and to delineate the enormous span of his territory (they are found from Afghanistan to Nepal to Andhra Pradesh).

Ashoka's reign also represented an undoubted historical high point for Buddhism: he embraced the religion in 260 BC, declaring it the state religion and cutting a radical swath through the spiritual and social body of Hinduism. The emperor also built thousands of stupas and monasteries across the region. Ashoka sent missions abroad, and is revered in Sri Lanka because he sent his son and daughter to carry Buddha's teaching to the island.

The long shadow this emperor of the 3rd century BC still casts over India is evident from the fact that the central motif of the Indian national flag is the Ashoka Chakra, a wheel with 24 spokes. Ashoka's standard (four lions sitting back-to-back atop an abacus decorated with a frieze and the inscription 'truth alone triumphs'), which topped many pillars, is also the seal of modern-day India and its national emblem, chosen to reaffirm the ancient commitment to peace and goodwill.

ala and western Tamil Nadu) and the Cholas (Thanjavur and the Cauvery Valley). The region described in classical Sangam literature (written between 300 BC and AD 300) was still relatively insulated from Sanskrit culture, but the literature indicates that Sanskrit traditions were starting to take root in South India around 200 BC.

A degree of rivalry characterised relations between the main chiefdoms and the numerous minor chiefdoms, and there were occasional clashes with Sri Lankan rulers. Ultimately, the southern powers all suffered at the hands of the Kalabhras, about whom little is known except that they appear to have originated from somewhere north of the Tamil region.

By around 180 BC the Mauryan empire, which had started to disintegrate soon after the death of Emperor Ashoka in 232 BC, had been overtaken by a series of rival kingdoms that were subjected to repeated invasions from the northwest by the Bactrian Greeks and others. The post-Ashokan era did, however, produce at least one line of royalty whose patronage of the arts and ability to maintain a relatively high degree of social cohesion have left an enduring legacy. This was the Satavahanas, who eventually controlled all of modern-day Maharashtra, Madhya

The concepts of zero and infinity are widely believed to have been devised by eminent Indian mathematicians during the reign of the Guptas.

300 BC–AD 300	200 BC–AD 200	1st Century AD	AD 52
Sangam Age, during which Tamil poets produce a body of classical Tamil literature and the Tamil area is dominated by three dynasties, the Pandyas, Cheras and early Cholas.	The Satavahana empire, of Andhra origin, rules over much of the Deccan plateau. Buddhism flourishes and literature, sculpture and philosophy blossom.	The region's overland trade networks connect with ports linked to maritime routes. Trade with Africa, the Gulf, Socotra, Southeast Asia, China and even Rome thrives.	Possible arrival of St Thomas the Apostle on the coast of Kerala. Christianity believed to have been introduced to India with his preaching in Kerala and Tamil Nadu.

Chalukya Sites

Ellora (p93)

Badami (p220)

Pattadakal (p222)

Aihole (p222)

Bhongir (p244)

Pradesh, Chhattisgarh, Karnataka, Telangana and Andhra Pradesh. Under their rule, between about 200 BC and AD 200, the arts blossomed, especially literature, sculpture and philosophy. Buddhism reached a peak in Maharashtra under the Satavahanas, although the greatest of the Buddhist cave temples at Ajanta and Ellora were built later by the Chalukya and Rashtrakuta dynasties. Most of all, the subcontinent enjoyed a period of considerable prosperity. South India may have lacked vast and fertile agricultural plains on the scale of North India, but it compensated by building strategic trade links via the Indian Ocean.

The Chalukyas & Pallavas

Following the suppression of the Tamil chiefdoms by the Kalabhras, South India split into numerous warring kingdoms. The Cholas virtually disappeared and the Cheras on the west coast seem to have prospered through trading, although little is known about them. It wasn't until the late 6th century AD, when the Kalabhras were overthrown, that the political uncertainty in the region ceased. For the next 300 years the history of South India was dominated by the fortunes of the Chalukyas of Badami in northern Karnataka, the Pallavas of Kanchi (Kanchipuram) and the Pandyas of Madurai.

The Badami Chalukyas controlled most of the Deccan at their peak under king Pulakesi II in the early 7th century. A related clan, known as the eastern Chalukyas, ruled Andhra Pradesh from Vengi near Eluru. It's unclear where the Pallavas originated, but it's thought they may have emigrated to Kanchi from Andhra Pradesh. After their successful rout of the Kalabhras, the Pallavas extended their territory as far south as the Cauvery River, and in the 7th and 8th centuries were at the height of their power, building monuments such as the Shore Temple and Arjuna's Penance at Mamallapuram (Mahabalipuram). They engaged in long-running clashes with the Pandyas, who, in the 8th century, allied themselves with the Gangas of Mysore. By the 9th century significant Pallava power had been snuffed out by the Pandyas and the Rashtrakutas, a dynasty based in Gulbarga, Karnataka, who replaced the Chalukyas as the dominant force on the Deccan from the 8th to 10th centuries.

Pallava Architecture in Tamil Nadu

Shore Temple, Mamallapuram (Mahabalipuram) (p347)

Arjuna's Penance, Mamallapuram (p347)

Five Rathas, Mamallapuram (p347)

Kailasanatha Temple, Kanchipuram (p352)

The Chola Empire

As the Pallava dynasty came to an end, a new Chola dynasty was laying the foundations for what would be one of the most significant empires on the subcontinent. From their base at Thanjavur, the Cholas spread north absorbing what was left of the Pallavas' territory, and made inroads southward. Under Rajaraja Chola I (r 985–1014) the Chola kingdom really started to emerge as a great empire. Rajaraja Chola I successfully waged war against the Pandyas in the south, the Gangas of Mysore

319–467	6th–8th Centuries	10th–12th Centuries	1001–1025
The golden era of the North India–based Gupta dynasty, the second of India's great empires after the Mauryas. This era is marked by a creative surge in literature and the arts.	The heyday of the Pallava dynasty, dominating Andhra Pradesh and northern Tamil Nadu from their capital, Kanchipuram.	The Chola empire, based in and around Thanjavur, spreads its influence over much of South India and Southeast Asia, leaving a superb legacy in the arts including sculpture and architecture.	Mahmud of Ghazni (in today's Afghanistan) leads 17 raids into northern India, the first of several invasions by Muslims.

and the Eastern Chalukyas. He also launched a series of naval campaigns that resulted in the capture of the Maldives, the Malabar Coast (coasts of Kerala and Karnataka) and northern Sri Lanka, which became a province of the Chola empire. These conquests gave the Cholas control over critical ports and trading links between India, Southeast Asia, Arabia and East Africa. They were therefore in a position to grab a share of the huge profits involved in selling spices to Europe.

Rajaraja Chola's son, Rajendra Chola I (r 1014–44), continued to expand Chola territory, conquering the remainder of Sri Lanka and campaigning up the east coast as far as Bengal and the Ganges River. Rajendra also launched a campaign in Southeast Asia against the Sumatra-based Srivijaya kingdom, and sent trade missions as far as China. Furthermore, the Chola empire produced a brilliant blossoming of the arts. Their legacy includes three magnificent Shiva temples at Thanjavur and near Kumbakonam. Bronze sculpture reached astonishing heights of aesthetic and technical refinement. Music, dance and literature flourished and developed a distinctly Tamil flavour, enduring in South India long after the Cholas had faded from the picture. The Cholas also took their culture to Southeast Asia, where it lives on in Myanmar (Burma), Thailand, Bali (Indonesia) and Cambodia in dance, religion and mythology.

But the Cholas, weakened by constant campaigning, eventually succumbed to expansionist pressure from the Hoysalas of Halebid (Karnataka) and the Pandyas of Madurai, and by the 13th century they were finally supplanted by the Pandyas. The Hoysalas were themselves eclipsed by the Vijayanagar empire, which arose in the 14th century. The Pandyas prospered and their achievements were much admired by Marco Polo when he visited in 1288 and 1293. But their glory was short-lived, as they were unable to fend off Muslim invaders from the north.

Muslim Expansion & the Vijayanagar Empire

Muslim raiders from the northwest began incursions into northern India in the 11th century and the powerful Delhi sultanate was established in 1206. The sultanate's expansion towards South India began in the 1290s, and by 1323 had reached Madurai.

In 1328 Sultan Mohammed Tughlaq, in pursuit of his dream of conquering the whole of India, moved his capital 1100km south to Daulatabad in Maharashtra, forcing the entire Delhi population to move with him, but had to revert to Delhi after two years because of a water shortage. Though Mohammed Tughlaq controlled a very large part of the subcontinent by 1330, his forces became overstretched and scattered

Chola Bronzes

Government Museum, Chennai (p330)

Royal Palace, Thanjavur (p371)

Puducherry Museum (p359)

HISTORY MUSLIM EXPANSION & THE VIJAYANAGAR EMPIRE

The *Story of India with Michael Wood* is an excellent BBC television series in DVD form with six 50-minute episodes. Also available as a book.

12th–19th Centuries	13th Century	1290s	1336
Africans are brought to the Konkan coast as part of trade with the Persian Gulf; the slaves become servants, dock workers and soldiers, and are known as Siddis or Habshis.	The Pandyas, a Tamil dynasty dating back to the 6th century BC, assume control of Chola territory, expanding into Andhra Pradesh, Kalinga (Odisha) and Sri Lanka from their capital, Madurai.	The Delhi sultanate starts its southward expansion, bringing parts of the Deccan under northern Muslim rule for the first time.	The mighty Vijayanagar empire (Hindu), named after its capital city, is founded. Its ruins can be seen today in the vicinity of Hampi (in modern-day Karnataka).

revolts had begun by 1327. From 1335 his empire started shrinking. Not only did local Muslim rulers in places such as Madurai and Daulatabad declare independence, but the foundations of what was to become one of South India's greatest empires, Vijayanagar, were being laid by Hindu chiefs at Hampi.

The Vijayanagar empire is generally said to have been founded by two brothers who, having been captured and taken to Delhi, converted to Islam and were sent back south to serve as governors for the sultanate. The brothers, however, reconverted to Hinduism and around 1336 set about establishing a kingdom that was eventually to encompass most of Karnataka and Andhra Pradesh, and all of Tamil Nadu and Kerala. Seven centuries later, the centre of this kingdom – the ruins and temples of Hampi – is now one of South India's biggest tourist drawcards.

A History of South India from Prehistoric Times to the Fall of Vijayanagar, by KA Nilakanta Sastri, is arguably the most thorough history of this region; especially recommended if you're heading for Hampi.

The Muslim Bahmani sultanate, initially based at Daulatabad, established its capital at Gulbarga in Karnataka, relocating to Bidar in the 15th century. Its territory eventually included Maharashtra, Telangana and northern Karnataka – and they took pains to protect it.

Not unnaturally, ongoing rivalry characterised the relationship between Vijayanagar and the Bahmani sultanate. Much of the conflict centred on control of fertile agricultural land and trading ports; at one stage the Bahmanis wrested the important port of Goa from their rivals, but the Vijayanagars seized it back in 1378. The Bahmani empire was eventually torn apart by factional fighting and between 1490 and 1528 it broke into five separate sultanates – Bidar, Bijapur, Berar, Ahmadnagar and Golconda. In 1565 the combined forces of the five sultanates laid waste to Vijayanagar's vibrant capital at Hampi, terminating Vijayanagar power.

The Vijayanagar empire is notable for its prosperity, which was the result of a deliberate policy of giving every encouragement to traders from afar, combined with the development of an efficient administrative system and access to important trading links, including west-coast ports. Hampi became quite cosmopolitan, with people from various parts of India as well as from abroad mingling in the bazaars.

Portuguese chronicler Domingo Paez arrived in Vijayanagar during the reign of one of its greatest kings, Krishnadevaraya (r 1509–29), under whom Vijayanagar enjoyed a period of unparalleled prosperity and power. Paez recorded the achievements of the Vijayanagars and described how they had constructed large water tanks and irrigated their fields. He also described how human and animal sacrifices were carried out to propitiate the gods after one of the water tanks had burst repeatedly. He included detail about the fine houses of wealthy merchants and the bazaars full of precious stones (rubies, diamonds, emeralds, pearls), textiles (including silk) and 'every other sort of thing there is on earth and that you may wish to buy'.

1345	1480s	1498	1510
Bahmani sultanate (Muslim) is established in the Deccan following a revolt against the Tughlaqs of Delhi. The capital is set up at Gulbarga, in today's northern Karnataka, later shifting to Bidar.	Bahmani sultanate begins to break up. By 1528 there are five Deccan sultanates: Berar, Ahmadnagar, Bidar, Bijapur and Golconda.	Vasco da Gama, a Portuguese voyager, finds the sea route from Europe to India via East Africa. He arrives in present-day Kerala and engages in trade with the local nobility.	Portuguese forces capture Goa under the command of Alfonso de Albuquerque, whose initial attempt was thwarted by then-ruler Sultan Adil Shah of Bijapur. He succeeds following Shah's death.

ENTER THE PORTUGUESE

On 20 May 1498 Vasco da Gama dropped anchor off the southwest Indian coast near the town of Calicut (now Kozhikode). It had taken him 23 days to sail from the east coast of Africa, guided by a pilot named Ibn Masjid, sent by the ruler of Malindi in Gujarat – the first time Europeans had made the voyage across the Indian Ocean from Africa to India. The Portuguese sought a sea route between Europe and the East so they could trade directly in spices. They also hoped they might find Christians cut off from Europe by the Muslim dominance of the Middle East, including the legendary kingdom of Prester John, a supposedly powerful Christian ruler with whom they could unite against the Muslim rulers of the Middle East. In India they found spices and the Syrian Orthodox community, but not Prester John.

Vasco da Gama sought an audience with the ruler of Calicut, and seems to have been well received. The Portuguese engaged in a limited amount of trading, but became increasingly suspicious that Muslim traders were turning the ruler of Calicut against them. They resolved to leave Calicut, which they did in August 1498. Within a few years other Portuguese expeditions began arriving on India's west coast not just to trade but also to conquer, resulting in an empire of scattered Portuguese possessions around India's coasts which lasted until 1961 when India invaded Goa, Daman and Diu.

Like the Bahmanis, the Vijayanagar kings invested heavily in protecting their territory and trading links. Krishnadevaraya employed Portuguese and Muslim mercenaries to guard the forts and protect his domains. He also fostered good relations with the Portuguese, upon whom he depended for access to trade goods, especially the Arab horses he needed for his cavalry.

Arrival of the Europeans & Christianity

Vasco da Gama's arrival in Kerala in 1498 ushered in a new era of European contact. He was followed by Francisco de Ameida and Alfonso de Albuquerque, who established an eastern Portuguese empire that included Goa (first taken in 1510). Albuquerque waged a constant battle against the local Muslims in Goa, finally defeating them. But perhaps his greatest achievement was in playing off two deadly threats against each other – the Vijayanagar empire (for whom access to Goa's ports was extremely important) and the Bijapur sultanate (which controlled part of Goa).

The Bijapuris and Vijayanagars were sworn enemies, and Albuquerque skilfully exploited this by supplying both sides with Arab horses for their warring cavalries. The horses died in alarming numbers once on Indian soil, so a constant supply had to be imported, keeping Portugal's Goan ports busy and profitable.

The Career and Legend of Vasco da Gama, by Sanjay Subrahmanyam, is one of the better investigations of the person credited with finding the sea route from Europe to India.

1526	1542–45	1560–1812	1600
The Central Asian conqueror Babur becomes the first Mughal emperor after conquering Delhi. Within a century the Mughal empire extends from Afghanistan to Bengal and into the northern Deccan.	St Francis Xavier's first mission to India. He preaches Catholicism in Goa, Tamil Nadu and Sri Lanka, returning in 1548–49 and 1552 in between travels in the Far East.	Portuguese Inquisition in Goa. Trials focus on converted Hindus and Muslims thought to have 'relapsed'. Thousands were tried and several dozen were executed before it was abolished in 1812.	Britain's Queen Elizabeth I grants the first trading charter to the East India Company, with the maiden voyage taking place in 1601 under the command of Sir James Lancaster.

The Portuguese also introduced Catholicism, and the arrival of the Inquisition in 1560 marked the beginning of 200 years of religious suppression in the Portuguese-controlled areas on the west coast of India.

Today the Portuguese influence is most obvious in Goa, with its chalk-white Catholic churches dotting the countryside, Christian festivals and unique cuisine, although the Portuguese also had some influence in Kerala in towns such as Cochin (now Kochi). By the mid-16th century Old Goa had grown into a thriving city said to rival Lisbon in magnificence: now only a ruined shadow of that time, its churches and buildings are still a stunning reminder of Portuguese rule.

In 1580 Spain annexed Portugal and, until Portugal regained its independence in 1640, its interests were subservient to Spain's. After the English defeat of the Spanish Armada in 1588, the sea route to the East lay open to the English and the Dutch. The Dutch were more interested in trade than in religion and empire. Indonesia was their main source of spices, and trade with South India was primarily for pepper and cardamom. So the Dutch East India Company set up a string of trading posts (called factories), which allowed them to maintain a complicated trading structure all the way from the Persian Gulf to Japan. They set up trading posts at Surat (Gujarat) and on the Coromandel Coast of southeast India, and entered into a treaty with the ruler of Calicut (now Kozhikode). In 1660 they captured the Portuguese forts at Cochin and Kodungallor.

The English also set up a trading venture, the British East India Company, to which in 1600 Queen Elizabeth I granted a monopoly on trade east of the Cape of Good Hope. Like the Dutch, the English were initially mainly interested in Indonesian spices. But the Dutch proved too strong there and the English turned instead to India, setting up a trading post at Madras (now Chennai). The Danes traded off and on at Tranquebar (on the Coromandel Coast) from 1616, and the French acquired Pondicherry (now Puducherry) in 1673.

The Mughals & their Aftermath

During the 17th century the Delhi-based Mughal empire made inroads into South India, especially under emperor Aurangzeb (r 1658–1707), gaining the sultanates of Ahmadnagar, Bijapur and Golconda (including Hyderabad) before moving into Tamil Nadu. Among the rivals the Mughals came up against were the Marathas – Hindu warriors originating from near Pune in Maharashtra, who controlled much of the Deccan by 1680, the year their first emperor Shivaji died. Pressing on southward in a series of guerrilla-like raids, the Marathas captured Thanjavur and in the 1690s set up a capital at Gingee near Madras. The Mughal-Maratha wars (1680 to 1707) ended with the Marathas very much on top. By the mid-18th century they controlled a huge swath of territory extending

---

Thousands were burned at the stake during the Goa Inquisition, which lasted more than 200 years. The judgement ceremonies took place outside the Sé Cathedral in Old Goa.

1661	1673	1674	1707
Britain acquires Bombay (Mumbai) from Portugal in the marriage settlement between King Charles II and Catherine of Braganza. The East India Company moves its headquarters to Bombay in 1687.	The French East India Company establishes a post at Pondicherry (now Puducherry), which the French, Dutch and British fight over repeatedly in the following century.	Shivaji establishes the Maratha kingdom in modern Maharashtra, assuming the imperial title Chhatrapati. Within half a century the Marathas dominate much of northern and central India.	Death of Aurangzeb, the last of the Mughal greats. His demise triggers the gradual collapse of the Mughal empire, as anarchy and rebellion erupt across its territory.

from the Punjab and Gujarat in the northwest to Odisha in the east and Karnataka in the south, while Mughal power barely extended beyond the city of Delhi.

In the Deccan and the south the Marathas had plenty of rivals for dominance. One was the Asaf Jahi dynasty (later known as the nizams of Hyderabad), which broke away from the Mughal empire in 1724 to control much of the Deccan, with its capital initially at Aurangabad (Maharashtra) and then, from 1763, at Hyderabad. Another was Mysore, a landlocked kingdom until a cavalry officer, Hyder Ali, assumed power in 1761 and set about acquiring coastal territory. Hyder Ali and his son Tipu Sultan eventually ruled a kingdom that included southern Karnataka and northern Kerala. Tipu conducted trade directly with the Middle East through the west-coast ports he controlled. The other important players were the British East India Company, with a base at Madras, and the French, at Pondicherry. The 18th century saw a constantly shifting succession of alliances and conflicts between these five rivals. The British won out over the French in the three Carnatic Wars fought between 1744 and 1763, and their control over the eastern seaboard denied both Hyderabad and Mysore access to trading ports there.

Down in the far south, the kingdom of Travancore (occupying what is now the southern half of Kerala and a bit of Tamil Nadu) was also trying to consolidate its power by gaining control of strategic trade links. Ruler Martanda Varma (r 1729–58) created his own army and tried to keep the local Syrian Orthodox trading community onside by limiting the activities of European traders. Trade in many goods, with the exception of pepper, became a royal monopoly, especially under Martanda's son Rama Varma (r 1758–98).

The British Take Hold

Initially the British East India Company was supposedly interested only in trade, not conquest. But Mysore's rulers proved something of a vexation. In 1780 Hyder Ali formed an alliance with the Nizam of Hyderabad and the Marathas to attack all three British bases in India (Bombay, Madras and Bengal). It came to nothing but left the British keen to quash the Mysore menace. This time the Marathas and Hyderabad allied with the British against Mysore, now led by Tipu Sultan, whose river-island citadel, Seringapatam (now Srirangapatnam), fell in 1793 after a year-long siege.

Within the East India Company there was a growing body of opinion that only total control of India would really satisfy British trading interests. This was reinforced by fears of a renewed French bid for land in India following Napoleon's Egyptian expedition of 1798–99. The company's governor-general, Lord Richard Wellesley, ordered a new strike against

**Archi-
tecture
of the
Deccan
Sultanates**

Hyderabad (p228)
*Golconda Fort,
Qutb Shahi Tombs,
Charminar, Mecca
Masjid*

Bijapur (p222)
*Citadel, Golgum-
baz, Ibrahim
Rouza, Jama
Masjid*

Bidar (p225) *Fort,
Bahmani Tombs*

Amar Chitra Katha, a popular publisher of comic books about Indian folklore, mythology and history, has several books about Shivaji, including *Shivaji: The Great Maratha, Tales of Shivaji* and *Tanaji, the Maratha Lion*, about Shivaji's close friend and fellow warrior.

1757	1775–1818	1857	1858
The East India Company registers its first military victory on Indian soil. Siraj-ud-Daulah, nawab of Bengal, is defeated by Robert Clive in the Battle of Plassey.	The three Anglo-Maratha Wars (1775–82, 1803–05 and 1817–18) between the East India Company and the Marathas. The third war terminates the Maratha empire and leaves the British in control of most of India.	The First War of Independence against the British. In the absence of a national leader, freedom fighters coerce the Mughal king, Bahadur Shah Zafar, to proclaim himself emperor of India.	British government assumes control over India, with power officially transferred from the East India Company to the Crown – beginning the period known as the British Raj.

MIGHTY SHIVAJI

The name Chhatrapati Shivaji is revered in Maharashtra, with statues of the great warrior astride his horse gracing many towns, and monuments being named (or renamed, as in the case of Mumbai's Victoria Terminus) after him.

Shivaji founded the powerful Maratha kingdom, a Hindu state that controlled much of the Deccan region and beyond from the late 17th to early 19th centuries, and played a big part in the decline of the mighty Delhi-based Mughal empire in the early 18th century. A courageous warrior and charismatic leader, Shivaji was born in 1627 to a prominent Maratha family at Shivneri. As a child he was sent to Pune with his mother, where he was given land and forts and groomed as a future leader. With a very small army, Shivaji seized his first fort at the age of 20 and over the next three decades he continued to expand Maratha power around his base in Pune, holding out against Muslim rivals from the north (the Mughal empire) and the south (the sultanate of Bijapur), and eventually ruling much of the Deccan. He was shrewd enough to play off his enemies (among them Mughal emperor Aurangzeb) against each other, and in a famous incident in 1659 he killed Bijapuri general Afzal Khan in a face-to-face encounter at Pratapgad Fort.

In 1674 Shivaji was crowned Chhatrapati (Emperor or Great Protector) of the Marathas at Raigad Fort. He died six years later. His son and successor, Sambhaji, suffered serious reversals at the hands of the Mughals, but the resilient Marathas bounced back with often guerrilla-style tactics and by the mid-18th century they controlled a large proportion of the subcontinent. Shivaji is an icon to the modern Maharashtrian-nationalist and Hindu-nationalist political party Shiv Sena (Shivaji's Army) which, among other things, opposes immigration into Maharashtra by non-Maharashtrians. For this reason the widespread use of his name is not wholly welcomed by everybody in the state.

Mysore, with the Nizam of Hyderabad as an ally (who was required to disband his French-trained troops in return for British protection). Tipu Sultan, who may have counted on support from the French, was killed when the British stormed Seringapatam in 1799.

Wellesley restored the old ruling family, the Wodeyars, to half of Tipu's kingdom – the rest went to Hyderabad and the East India Company. Thanjavur and Karnataka were also absorbed by the British, who, when the rulers of the day died, pensioned off their successors. By 1818 the Marathas, racked by internal strife, had collapsed and most of India was under British influence. In the south the East India Company had direct control over the Madras Presidency, which stretched from present-day Andhra Pradesh to the southern tip of the subcontinent, and across to northern parts of the Kerala coast. Travancore, Hyderabad and Mysore and other, smaller, chunks of the interior kept their nominal independence as 'princely states', but they were closely watched by their British

In 1839 the British government offered to buy Goa from the Portuguese for half a million pounds.

1869	1869	1885	1891
The birth of Mohandas Karamchand Gandhi in Porbandar (Gujarat) – the man who would later become popularly known as Mahatma Gandhi and affectionately dubbed 'Father of the Nation'.	Opening of the Suez Canal accelerates trade from Europe and makes Bombay India's first port of call; the journey from England shrinks from three months to three weeks. Bombay's economic importance skyrockets.	The Indian National Congress, India's first home-grown political organisation, is set up. It brings educated Indians together and plays a key role in India's enduring freedom struggle.	BR Ambedkar, activist, economist, lawyer and writer, is born to a poor outcaste family. He earns several advanced degrees, becomes a Buddhist and advocates forcefully for Dalit rights.

Residents (de-facto governors). Similarly, much of Maharashtra was part of the Bombay Presidency, but there were a dozen or so small princely states scattered around, including Kolhapur, Sawantwadi, Aundh and Janjira.

The First War of Independence (Indian Uprising)

In 1857 half a century after establishing firm control over India, the British suffered a serious setback. To this day the causes of the Uprising (known at the time as the Indian Mutiny and subsequently labelled by nationalist historians as a War of Independence) are the subject of debate. Key factors included the influx of cheap goods, such as textiles, from Britain that destroyed many livelihoods; the dispossession of territories from many rulers; and taxes imposed on landowners.

The incident that's popularly held to have sparked the Uprising, however, took place at an army barracks in Meerut in Uttar Pradesh on 10 May 1857. A rumour leaked out that a new type of bullet was greased with what Hindus claimed was cow fat, while Muslims maintained that it came from pigs; pigs are considered unclean to Muslims, and cows are sacred to Hindus. Since loading a rifle involved biting the end off the waxed cartridge, these rumours provoked considerable unrest.

In Meerut, the situation was handled with a singular lack of judgement. The commanding officer lined up his soldiers and ordered them to bite off the ends of their issued bullets. Those who refused were immediately marched off to prison. The following morning, the soldiers of the garrison rebelled, shot their officers and marched to Delhi. Of the 74 Indian battalions of the Bengal army, seven (one of them Gurkhas) remained loyal, 20 were disarmed and the other 47 mutinied. The soldiers and peasants rallied around the ageing Mughal emperor in Delhi. They held Delhi for some months and besieged the British Residency in Lucknow for five months before they were finally suppressed. The incident left festering sores on both sides.

Almost immediately the East India Company was wound up, and direct control of the country was assumed by the British government, which announced its support for the existing rulers of the princely states, claiming they would not interfere in local matters as long as the states remained loyal to the British.

The Road to Independence

The desire among many Indians to be free from foreign rule remained. Opposition to the British began to increase at the turn of the 20th century, spearheaded by the Indian National Congress (Congress Party), the

Two fascinating books on princely Hyderabad are John Zubrzycki's *The Last Nizam*, tracing the weird and wonderful story of the Asaf Jahi dynasty from its 18th-century beginnings to the present day, and William Dalrymple's *White Mughals*, focusing on the love affair between British Resident James Achilles Kirkpatrick and local woman Khair-un-Nissa two centuries ago.

David Davidar's novel *The House of Blue Mangoes* weaves the story of three generations of a family at the southern tip of India against the backdrop of the decades leading up to Independence.

HISTORY THE FIRST WAR OF INDEPENDENCE (INDIAN UPRISING)

1919	1940	1942	1947
The massacre, on 13 April, of unarmed Indian protesters at Jallianwala Bagh in Amritsar (Punjab). Gandhi responds with his programme of civil (nonviolent) disobedience against British rule.	The Muslim League adopts its Lahore Resolution, which champions greater Muslim autonomy in India. Campaigns for the creation of a separate Islamic nation follow.	Mahatma Gandhi launches the Quit India campaign, demanding that the British leave India without delay and allow the country to get on with the business of self-governance.	India gains independence on 15 August. Pakistan is formed a day earlier. Partition brings mass cross-border exodus and massacres, as Hindus and Muslims migrate to their respective nations.

nation's oldest political party. The fight for independence gained momentum when, in April 1919, following riots in Amritsar (Punjab), a British army contingent was sent to quell the unrest. Under the direct orders of the officer in charge the army ruthlessly fired into a crowd of unarmed protesters attending a meeting, killing an estimated 1500 people. News of the massacre spread rapidly throughout India, turning huge numbers of otherwise apolitical Indians into Congress supporters. At this time, the Congress movement found a new leader in Mohandas Gandhi, better known as Mahatma Gandhi.

After some three decades of intense campaigning for an independent India, Gandhi's dream finally materialised. However, despite his plea for a united India, the Muslim League's leader, Mohammed Ali Jinnah, was demanding a separate state for India's sizeable Muslim population, and the decision was made to split the country.

The partition of India in 1947 contained all the ingredients for an epic disaster, but the resulting bloodshed was far worse than anticipated. Massive population exchanges took place. Trains full of Muslims, fleeing westward into Pakistan, were held up and slaughtered by Hindu and Sikh mobs. Hindus and Sikhs fleeing to the east suffered the same fate at Muslim hands. By the time the chaos had run its course, more than 10 million people had changed sides and at least 500,000 had been killed.

India and Pakistan became sovereign nations under the British Commonwealth in August 1947, but the violence, migrations and the uncertainty over a few states, especially Kashmir, continued. The Constitution of India was at last adopted in November 1949 and went into effect on 26 January 1950 when, after untold struggle, independent India officially became a republic.

Mahatma Gandhi

One of the great figures of the 20th century, Mohandas Karamchand Gandhi was born on 2 October 1869 in Porbandar, Gujarat. After studying in London (1888–91), he worked as a barrister in South Africa. Here, the young Gandhi became politicised, railing against the racial discrimination he encountered. He soon became the spokesman for South Africa's Indian community, championing equality for all.

Gandhi returned to India in 1915 with the doctrine of ahimsa (nonviolence) central to his political plans, and committed to a simple and disciplined lifestyle. He set up the Sabarmati Ashram in Ahmedabad, which was innovative for its admission of Untouchables (now known as Dalits), the lowest layer of traditional Hindu society.

Within a year, Gandhi had won his first victory, defending farmers in Bihar from exploitation. It's said that this was when he first received the title 'Mahatma' (Great Soul) from an admirer. The passage of the discrim-

A golden oldie, *Gandhi*, directed by Richard Attenborough, is one of the few films to engagingly capture the grand canvas that is India in tracing the country's bumpy road to Independence.

Gandhi in South India

1947–48	1948	17 September 1948	November 1949
First war between India and Pakistan takes place after the (procrastinating) Maharaja of Kashmir signs the Instrument of Accession that cedes his state to India. Pakistan challenges the document's legality.	Mahatma Gandhi is assassinated in New Delhi by Nathuram Godse on 30 January. Godse and his co-conspirator Narayan Apte are later tried, convicted and executed (by hanging).	Asaf Jah VII, the last Nizam of Hyderabad, surrenders to the Indian government. His Muslim dynasty was receiving support from Pakistan but had refused to join either new nation.	The Constitution of India, drafted over two years by a 308-member Constituent Assembly, is adopted. The Assembly included dozens of members from the Scheduled Castes (Dalits).

inatory Rowlatt Acts (which allowed certain political cases to be tried without juries) in 1919 spurred him to further action and he organised a national protest. In the days following this hartal (strike), feelings ran high throughout the country. After the massacre of unarmed protesters in Amritsar (Punjab), a deeply shocked Gandhi immediately called off the movement.

By 1920 Gandhi was a key figure in the Indian National Congress, and he coordinated a national campaign of satyagraha (passive resistance) to British rule, with the effect of raising nationalist feeling while earning the lasting enmity of the British. In early 1930 Gandhi captured the imagination of the country, and the world, when he led a march of several thousand followers from Ahmedabad to Dandi on the coast of Gujarat. On arrival, Gandhi ceremoniously made salt by evaporating sea water, thus publicly defying the much-hated salt tax; not for the first time, he was imprisoned. Released in 1931 to represent the Indian National Congress at the second Round Table Conference in London, he won the hearts of many British people but failed to gain any real concessions from the government.

Disillusioned with politics, he resigned from the Congress Party in 1934. He returned spectacularly to the fray in 1942 with the Quit India campaign, in which he urged the British to leave India immediately. His actions were deemed subversive and he and most of the Congress leadership were imprisoned.

In the frantic Independence bargaining that followed the end of WWII, Gandhi was largely excluded and watched helplessly as plans were made to partition the country – a dire tragedy in his eyes. Gandhi stood almost alone in urging tolerance and the preservation of a single India, and his work on behalf of members of all communities drew resentment from some Hindu hardliners. On his way to a prayer meeting in Delhi on 30 January 1948, he was assassinated by a Hindu zealot.

In 21st-century India, Mahatma Gandhi continues to be an iconic figure and is still widely revered as the 'Father of the Nation'.

Carving up the South

While the chaos of Partition was mostly felt in the north – mainly in Punjab, Kashmir and Bengal – the south faced problems of its own. Though most of the princely states acceded to India peacefully, an exception was Hyderabad. Although only he and about 10% of his subjects were Muslims, the nizam was friendlier with Islamic Pakistan than with India, and favoured the idea of Hyderabad remaining an independent state. Following a Communist-led rebellion against the nizam and attacks on Hindus by a Muslim militia, the Indian army moved in and forcibly took control

Indian Summer, by Alex von Tunzelmann, is a brilliant, detailed account of the road to Independence, with much focus on the personal lives of the main protagonists including the love affair between Jawaharlal Nehru, independent India's first prime minister, and Edwina Mountbatten, wife of the last British viceroy.

The Nehrus and the Gandhis is Tariq Ali's astute portrait-history of these families and the India over which they cast their long shadow.

26 January 1950	1956–60	1961	1965
India becomes a republic. Date commemorates the Purna Swaraj Declaration, or Declaration of Independence, put forth by the Indian National Congress in 1930.	Indian states are reorganised on linguistic lines, giving birth to modern Maharashtra, Andhra Pradesh, Kerala, Mysore (Karnataka) and Madras state (Tamil Nadu).	In a military action codenamed 'Operation Vijay' the Indian government sends armed troops into Goa and – with surprisingly little resistance – ends over four centuries of Portuguese colonial rule in the region.	Skirmishes in Kashmir and the disputed Rann of Kutch in Gujarat flare into the Second India-Pakistan War, said to have involved the biggest tank battles since WWII. The war ends with a UN-mandated ceasefire.

THE KASHMIR CONFLICT

Kashmir is the most enduring symbol of the turbulent partition of India. In the lead-up to Independence, the rulers of India's nominally-independent 'princely states' were asked which country (India or Pakistan) they wished to belong to. Kashmir was a predominantly Muslim-populated state with a Hindu maharaja, Hari Singh, who tried to delay his decision. A ragtag army of Pashtun tribesmen crossed the border from Pakistan into Kashmir, intent on racing to Srinagar and annexing Kashmir for Pakistan. The maharaja panicked and requested armed assistance from India, which arrived only just in time to prevent the fall of Srinagar. The maharaja signed the Instrument of Accession, tying Kashmir to India, in October 1947. The legality of the document was immediately disputed by Pakistan, and the two nations went to war, just two months after Independence.

In 1948 the UN Security Council called for a referendum (which remains a central plank of Pakistani policy) to decide Kashmir's status. A UN-brokered ceasefire in 1949 kept the countries either side of a demarcation line, later to become known as the Line of Control (LOC), with little else resolved. Two-thirds of Kashmir fell on the Indian side of the LOC, but neither side accepts this as the official border. Since the LOC was drawn, incursions across it have occurred with dangerous regularity and at least 40,000 people have died in violence in the Indian-controlled part of Kashmir. Many of the terrorist attacks that have hit tourist spots in India have a Kashmir link.

of Hyderabad state in 1948. Many thousands of Muslims were massacred by Hindus during and after this so-called 'police action'.

In the 1950s, the princely states and British-delineated provinces were dismantled and South India was reorganised into states along linguistic lines. Mysore state was extended in 1956 into the Kannada-speaking state of Greater Mysore, which was renamed Karnataka in 1972.

Malayalam-speaking Kerala was created in 1956 from Travancore (except for its Tamil-speaking far south), Cochin (now Kochi) and Malabar (formerly part of the Madras Presidency). The maharajas in both Travancore and Cochin were especially attentive to the provision of basic services and education, and their legacy today is India's most literate state. Kerala also blazed a trail in post-Independence India by becoming the first state in the world to freely elect a communist government in 1957.

The state of Andhra Pradesh was created in 1956 by combining the Telugu-speaking Andhra state (the northern parts of the old Madras Presidency) with Telugu-speaking areas of the old Hyderabad state. In 2014 the latter were separated off as the new state of Telangana, after years of complaints that they were neglected and exploited within Andhra Pradesh.

In 1997 KR Narayanan became India's president, the first member of the lowest Hindu caste (the Dalits; formerly known as Untouchables) to hold the position.

1966	1971	1984	1991
Indira Gandhi, daughter of independent India's first prime minister, Jawaharlal Nehru, becomes prime minister of India. She has so far been India's only female prime minister.	East Pakistan seeks independence from West Pakistan. India gets involved, sparking the Third India-Pakistan War. West Pakistan surrenders, losing sovereignty of East Pakistan, which becomes Bangladesh.	Prime Minister Indira Gandhi is assassinated by two of her Sikh bodyguards after her highly controversial decision to have Indian troops storm Amritsar's Golden Temple, the Sikhs' holiest shrine.	Former prime minister Rajiv Gandhi, son of Indira Gandhi, is assassinated by a suicide bomber believed to be from Sri Lanka's Tamil Tigers, at Sriperumbudur near Chennai (formerly Madras).

Tamil Nadu was the name given in 1969 to the former Madras state, which since 1956 had comprised the Tamil-speaking areas of the old Madras Presidency plus the southernmost areas of the former Travancore kingdom (also Tamil-speaking).

The creation of Maharashtra was one of the most contested issues of the language-based demarcation of states. After Independence, western Maharashtra and Gujarat were joined to form Bombay state, to which Marathi-speaking parts of Hyderabad and Madhya Pradesh states were added in 1956. In 1960, after agitation by both Marathis and Gujaratis, Bombay state was divided into the existing states of Maharashtra and Gujarat.

The French relinquished Pondicherry in 1954 – 140 years after reclaiming it from the British. It's a Union Territory (controlled by the government in Delhi), though a largely self-governing one. Lakshadweep was granted Union Territory status in 1956, as were the Andaman and Nicobar Islands.

Throughout most of this carve-up, the tiny enclave of Goa was still under the rule of the Portuguese. Although a rumbling Independence movement had existed in Goa since the early 20th century, the Indian government was reluctant to intervene and take Goa by force, hoping the Portuguese would leave of their own volition. The Portuguese refused, so in December 1961 Indian troops crossed the border and liberated the state with surprisingly little resistance. It became a Union Territory of India, but after splitting from Daman and Diu (Gujarat) in 1987, it was officially recognised as the 25th state of the Indian Union.

The princely ruling family of Mysore, the Wodeyars, were so popular with their subjects that the maharaja became the first governor of the post-Independence state of Mysore.

HISTORY CARVING UP THE SOUTH

2004	2008	May 2014	June 2014
A tsunami batters coastal parts of eastern and South India as well as the Andaman and Nicobar Islands, killing over 10,000 people and leaving hundreds of thousands homeless.	On 26 November a series of coordinated bombing and shooting attacks on landmark Mumbai sites begins; the terrorist attacks last three days and kill at least 163 people.	Narendra Modi, born into a Gujarati grocery family, becomes prime minister after achieving a landslide victory for the Hindu-nationalist-oriented Bharatiya Janata Party (BJP), routing the Congress Party.	The northern part of Andhra Pradesh splits off to become India's 29th state, Telangana, following years of agitation and allegations of neglect and unfair treatment.

The Way of Life

Spirituality is the common thread in the richly diverse tapestry that is India. It, along with family, lies at the heart of society, and the two intertwine in ceremonies to celebrate life's milestones. Despite the rising number of nuclear families – primarily in the more cosmopolitan cities such as Mumbai, Bengaluru and Delhi – the extended family remains a cornerstone in both urban and rural India, with males – usually the breadwinners – considered the head of the household.

Marriage, Birth & Death

The Wonder That Was India by AL Basham gives descriptions of Indian civilisations, major religions and social customs – a good thematic approach to weave the disparate strands together.

Different religions practice different traditions, but for all communities, marriage, birth and death are important and marked with traditional ceremonies according to the faith. Hindus are in the majority in India. Around 15% of the population is Muslim (though, at 180 million, Indian Muslims roughly equal the population of Pakistan).

Marriage is an exceptionally auspicious event for Indians – for most Indians, the idea of being unmarried by their mid-30s is unpalatable. Although 'love marriages' have spiralled upwards in recent times (mainly in urban hubs), most Indian marriages are still arranged, be the family Hindu, Muslim, Sikh or Buddhist. Discreet enquiries are made within the community. If a suitable match is not found, the help of professional matchmakers may be sought, or advertisements may be placed in newspapers and/or on the internet. In Hindu families, the horoscopes of both potential partners are checked and, if propitious, there's a meeting between the two families.

Dowry, although illegal, is still a key issue in more than a few arranged marriages (mostly in conservative communities), with some families plunging into debt to raise the required cash and merchandise (from cars and computers to refrigerators and televisions). Health workers claim that India's high rate of abortion of female foetuses (sex identification medical tests are banned in India, but they still clandestinely occur in some clinics) is predominantly due to the financial burden of providing a daughter's dowry. Muslim grooms have to pay what is called a *mehr* to the bride.

The Hindu wedding ceremony is officiated over by a priest and the marriage is formalised when the couple walk around a sacred fire seven times. Muslim ceremonies involve the reading of the Quran, and traditionally the husband and wife view each other via mirrors. Despite the existence of nuclear families, it's still the norm for a wife to live with her husband's family once married and assume the household duties outlined by her mother-in-law. Not surprisingly, the mother–daughter-in-law relationship can be a tricky one, as portrayed in various Indian TV soap operas.

Divorce and remarriage is becoming more common (primarily in bigger cities), but divorce is still not granted by courts as a matter of routine and is not looked upon very favourably by society. Among the higher castes, in more traditional areas, widows are traditionally expected not to remarry and are expected to wear white and live pious, celibate lives. It is still legal for Muslim males in India to obtain oral divorce according to sharia law (by uttering the word *talaq* meaning 'divorce' three times).

The birth of a child is another momentous occasion, with its own set of special ceremonies which take place at various auspicious times during the early years of childhood. For Hindus these include the casting of the child's first horoscope, name-giving, feeding the first solid food, and the first hair cutting.

Hindus cremate their dead, and funeral ceremonies are designed to purify and console both the living and the deceased. An important aspect of the proceedings is the *sharadda,* paying respect to one's ancestors by offering water and rice cakes. It's an observance that's repeated at each anniversary of the death. After the cremation, the ashes are collected and, 13 days after the death (when blood relatives are deemed ritually pure), a member of the family usually scatters them in a holy river such as the Ganges or in the ocean. Sikhs similarly wash then cremate their dead. Muslims also prepare their dead carefully, but bury them, while the minority Zoroastrian Parsi community place their dead in 'Towers of Silence' (stone towers) to be devoured by birds.

Matchmaking has, inevitably, gone online, with popular sites including www.shaadi.com, www.bharatmatrimony.com and, in a sign of the times, www.second-shaadi.com – for those seeking a partner again.

The Caste System

Although the Indian constitution does not recognise the caste system, caste still wields powerful influence, especially in rural India, where the caste you are born into largely determines your social standing in the community. It can also influence your vocational and marriage prospects. Castes are further divided into thousands of *jati,* groups of 'families' or social communities, which are sometimes but not always linked to occupation. Conservative Hindus will only marry someone of the same *jati,* and you'll often see caste as a criteria in matrimonial adverts, 'Mahar seeks Mahar', etc. In some traditional areas, young men and women who fall in love outside their caste have been murdered.

According to tradition, caste is the basic social structure of Hindu society. Living a righteous life and fulfilling your dharma (moral duty) raises your chances of being reborn into a higher caste and thus into better circumstances. Hindus are born into one of four varnas (castes): Brahmin (priests and scholars), Kshatriya (soldiers and administrators), Vaishya (merchants) and Shudra (labourers). The Brahmins were said to have emerged from the mouth of Lord Brahma at the moment of creation, Kshatriyas were said to have come from his arms, Vaishyas from his thighs and Shudras from his feet. Beneath the four main castes are the

INDIAN ATTIRE

Widely worn by Indian women, the elegant sari comes in a single piece (between 5m and 9m long and 1m wide) and is ingeniously tucked and pleated into place without the need for pins or buttons. Worn with the sari is the choli (tight-fitting blouse) and a drawstring petticoat. The *palloo* is the part of the sari draped over the shoulder. Also commonly worn is the *salwar kameez,* a traditional dresslike tunic and trouser combination accompanied by a dupatta (long scarf). Saris and *salwar kameez* come in a fantastic range of fabrics, colours and designs.

Traditional attire for men includes the dhoti, and in the south, the *lungi* and the *mundu*. The dhoti is a loose, long loincloth pulled up between the legs. The *lungi* is more like a sarong, with its end usually sewn up like a tube. The *mundu* is like a lungi but is always white. A kurta is a long tunic or shirt worn mainly by men, usually with no collar. Kurta pyjama is a cotton shirt and trousers set worn for relaxing or sleeping. *Churidar* are close-fitting trousers often worn under a kurta. A *sherwani* is a long coat-like men's garment, which originated as a fusion of the *salwar kameez* with the British frock coat.

There are regional and religious variations in costume – for example, you may see Muslim women wearing the all-enveloping burka.

RANGOLIS

Rangolis, the striking and breathtakingly intricate chalk, rice-paste or coloured powder designs (also called *kolams*) that adorn thresholds, especially in South India, are both auspicious and symbolic. *Rangolis* are traditionally drawn at sunrise and are sometimes made of rice-flour paste, which may be eaten by little creatures – symbolising a reverence for even the smallest living things. Deities are deemed to be attracted to a beautiful *rangoli*, which may also signal to sadhus (ascetics) that they will be offered food at a particular house. Some people believe that *rangolis* protect against the evil eye.

Dalits (formerly known as Untouchables), who hold menial jobs such as sweepers and latrine cleaners. Many of India's complex codes of ritual purity were devised to prevent physical contact between people of higher castes and Dalits. A less rigid system exists in Islamic communities in India, with society divided into *ashraf* (high born), *ajlaf* (low born) and *arzal* (equivalent to the Dalits).

The word 'pariah' is derived from the name of a Tamil Dalit group, the Paraiyars. Some Dalit leaders, such as the renowned Dr BR Ambedkar (1891–1956), sought to change their status by adopting another faith; in his case it was Buddhism. At the bottom of the social heap are the Denotified Tribes. They were known as the Criminal Tribes until 1952, when a reforming law officially recognised 198 tribes and castes. Many are nomadic or seminomadic tribes, forced by the wider community to eke out a living on society's fringes.

To improve the Dalits' position, the government reserves considerable numbers of public-sector jobs, parliamentary seats and university places for them. Today these quotas account for almost 25% of government jobs and university (student) positions. The situation varies regionally, as different political leaders chase caste vote-banks by promising to include them in reservations. The reservation system, while generally regarded in a favourable light, has also been criticised for unfairly blocking tertiary and employment opportunities for those who would have otherwise got positions on merit. On the other hand, there are still regular examples of discrimination against Dalits in daily life, for example, higher castes denying them entry into certain temples.

Based on Rabindranath Tagore's novel, *Chokher Bali* (directed by Rituparno Ghosh) is a poignant film about a young widow living in early-20th-century Bengal who challenges the 'rules of widowhood' – something unthinkable in that era.

Pilgrimage

Devout Hindus are expected to go on a *yatra* (pilgrimage) at least once a year. Pilgrimages are undertaken to implore the gods or goddesses to grant a wish, to take the ashes of a cremated relative to a holy river, or to gain spiritual merit. India has thousands of holy sites to which pilgrims travel; the elderly often make Varanasi their final one, as it's believed that dying in this sacred city releases a person from the cycle of rebirth. Sufi shrines in India attract thousands of Muslims to commemorate holy days, such as the birthday of a sufi saint, and many Muslims also make the hajj to Mecca in Saudi Arabia.

Sati: A Study of Widow Burning in India by Sakuntala Narasimhan explores the history of *sati* (a widow's suicide on her husband's funeral pyre; now banned) on the subcontinent.

Most festivals in India have religious roots and are thus a magnet for throngs of pilgrims. Remember that most festivals are spiritual occasions, even those that have a carnivalesque sheen. Also be aware that there are deaths at festivals every year because of stampedes, so be cautious in crowds.

Women in India

According to the most recent census, in 2011, India's 586 million women accounted for some 48.5% of the total population, with an estimated 68% of those working (mostly as labourers) in the agricultural sector.

Women in India are entitled to vote and own property. While the percentage of women in politics has risen over the past decade, they're still notably underrepresented in the national parliament, accounting for 11% of parliamentary members.

Although the professions are male dominated, women are steadily making inroads, especially in urban centres. Kerala was India's first state to break societal norms by recruiting female police officers in 1938. It was also the first state to establish an all-female police station (1973). For village women it's much more difficult to get ahead, but groups such as the Self-Employed Women's Association (SEWA) in Gujarat have shown what's possible, organising socially disadvantaged women into unions and offering microfinance loans.

In low-income families, especially, girls can be regarded as a serious financial liability because at marriage a dowry must often be supplied.

For the urban middle-class woman, life is much more comfortable, but pressures still exist. Broadly speaking, she is far more likely to receive a tertiary education, but once married is still usually expected to 'fit in' with her in-laws and be a homemaker above all else. Like her village counterpart, if she fails to live up to expectations – even if it's just not being able to produce a grandson – the consequences can sometimes be dire, as demonstrated by the extreme practice of 'bride burning', wherein a wife is doused with flammable liquid and set alight. In 2013, the National Crime Records Bureau (NCRB) figures reported 8083 incidences, almost one every hour.

Although the constitution allows for divorcees (and widows) to remarry, relatively few reportedly do so, simply because divorcees are traditionally considered outcasts from society, most evidently so beyond big cities. Divorce rates in India are among the world's lowest, though they are steadily rising. Most divorces take place in urban centres and are deemed less socially unacceptable among those occupying the upper echelons of society.

In October 2006, following women's civil rights campaigns, the Indian parliament passed a landmark bill (on top of existing legislation) which gives women who are suffering domestic violence increased protection and rights. Prior to this legislation, although women could lodge police complaints against abusive spouses, they weren't automatically entitled to a share of the marital property or to ongoing financial support. Critics

THE WAY OF LIFE WOMEN IN INDIA

If you want to learn more about India's caste system, these two books are a good start: *Interrogating Caste* by Dipankar Gupta and *Translating Caste* edited by Tapan Basu.

Read more about India's tribal communities at www.tribal.nic.in, a site maintained by the Indian government's Ministry of Tribal Affairs.

ADIVASIS

India's Adivasis (tribal communities; Adivasi translates to 'original inhabitant' in Sanskrit) have origins that precede the Vedic Aryans and the Dravidians of the south. These groups range from the Gondi of the central plains to the animist tribes of the Northeast States. Today, they constitute less than 10% of the population and are comprised of more than 400 different tribal groups. The literacy rate for Adivasis is significantly below the national average.

Historically, contact between Adivasis and Hindu villagers on the plains rarely led to friction as there was little or no competition for resources and land. However, in recent decades an increasing number of Adivasis have been dispossessed of their ancestral land and turned into impoverished labourers. Although they still have political representation thanks to a parliamentary quota system, the dispossession and exploitation of Adivasis have reportedly sometimes been with the connivance of officialdom – an accusation the government denies. Whatever the arguments, unless more is done, the Adivasis' future is an uncertain one.

Read more about Adivasis in *Archaeology and History: Early Settlements in the Andaman Islands* by Zarine Cooper, *The Tribals of India* by Sunil Janah and *Tribes of India: The Struggle for Survival* by Christoph von Fürer-Haimendorf.

claim that many women, especially those outside India's larger cities, are still reluctant to seek legal protection because of the social stigma involved. And despite legal reforms, conviction rates remain low enough for perpetrators to feel a sense of impunity.

India remains an extremely prudish and conservative society, and despite the highly sexualised images of women churned out in Bollywood movies (although kissing is still rarely seen on screen), it's considered by many traditionally minded people that a woman is somehow wanton if she so much as goes out after dark.

India has the world's second largest diaspora – over 25 million people – with Indian banks holding upwards of US$70 billion in Non-Resident Indian (NRI) accounts.

According to India's National Crime Records Bureau (NCRB), reported incidences of rape have gone up over 50% in the last 10 years, but it's believed that only a small percentage of sexual assaults are reported, largely due to family pressure and/or shame, especially if the perpetrator is known to the family (which is true in many cases).

Following the highly publicised gang-rape and murder of a 23-year-old Indian physiotherapy student in Delhi in December 2012, tens of thousands of people protested in the capital, and beyond, demanding swift government action to address the country's escalating gender-based violence. It took a further year before legal amendments were made to existing laws to address the problem of sexual violence, including stiffer punishments such as life imprisonment and the death penalty (but there is still limited recognition of marital rape, and government permission is necessary before security forces can be prosecuted for criminal offences). Despite the action taken, more shocking cases are horrifyingly regular occurrences. The NCRB reported that in 2013, 309,546 crimes were against women. Of these, 33,707 were rape and 70,739 were molestation. The conviction rate for rape was 27.1% in 2013. It's doubtless that sexual violence is a pervasive social problem in India. For information on safety for female visitors, see Women & Solo Travellers, p492.

Sport

Cricket has long been engraved on the nation's heart, with the first recorded match in 1721, and India's first test match victory in 1952 in Chennai against England. It's not only a national sporting obsession, but a matter of enormous patriotism, especially evident whenever India plays against Pakistan. Matches between these South Asian neighbours – which have had rocky relations since Independence – attract especially passionate support, and the players of both sides are under immense pressure to do their respective countries proud. The most celebrated Indian cricketer of recent years is Sachin Tendulkar – fondly dubbed the 'Little Master' – who, in 2012, became the world's only player to score 100 international centuries, retiring on a high the following year. Cricket – especially the

HIJRAS

India's most visible nonheterosexual group is the hijras, a caste of transvestites and eunuchs who dress in women's clothing. Some are gay, some are hermaphrodites and some were unfortunate enough to be kidnapped and castrated. Hijras have long had a place in Indian culture, and in 2014 the Indian Supreme Court recognised hijras as a third gender and as a class entitled to reservation in education and jobs. Conversely, in 2013, homosexuality was ruled to be unlawful (having been legal since 2009).

Hijras work mainly as uninvited entertainers at weddings and celebrations of the birth of male children, and possibly as prostitutes. In 2014, Padmini Prakash became India's first transgender daily television news show anchor, indicating a new level of acceptance.

Read more about hijras in The Invisibles by Zia Jaffrey and Ardhanarishvara the Androgyne by Dr Alka Pande.

Twenty20 format (www.cricket20.com) – is big business in India, attracting lucrative sponsorship deals and celebrity status for its players. The sport has not been without its murky side though, with Indian cricketers among those embroiled in match-fixing scandals over past years. International games are played at various centres – see Indian newspapers or check online for details about matches that coincide with your visit. Keep your finger on the cricketing pulse at www.espncricinfo.com (rated most highly by many cricket aficionados) and www.cricbuzz.com.

The launch of the Indian Super League (ISL; www.indiansuperleague.com) in 2013 has achieved its aim of promoting football as a big-time, big-money sport. With games attracting huge crowds and international players, such as the legendary Juventus footballer Alessandro del Piero (who was signed for the Delhi Dynamos in 2014) or Marco Materazzi (of World Cup headbutt fame) as trainer of Chennai, the ISL has become an international talking point. The first week of the ISL in 2014 had 170.6m viewers in the first week – the figures for the first phase of the Indian Premier League cricket was 184m, which gives a sense of football's growth in popularity. The I-League is the longer-running domestic league, but it has never attracted such media attention or funding.

The country is also known for its historical links to horse polo, which intermittently thrived on the subcontinent (especially among nobility) until Independence, after which patronage steeply declined due to dwindling funds. Today there's a renewed interest in polo thanks to beefed-up sponsorship and, although it still remains an elite sport, it's attracting more attention from the country's burgeoning upper middle class. The origins of polo are not completely clear. Believed to have its roots in Persia and China around 2000 years ago, on the subcontinent it's thought to have first been played in Baltistan (in present-day Pakistan). Some say that Emperor Akbar (who reigned in India from 1556 to 1605) first introduced rules to the game, but that polo, as it's played today, was largely influenced by a British cavalry regiment stationed in India during the 1870s. A set of international rules was implemented after WWI. The world's oldest surviving polo club, established in 1862, is in Kolkata (Calcutta Polo Club; www.calcuttapolo.com). Polo takes place during the cooler winter months in major cities, including Delhi, Jaipur, Mumbai, Hyderabad and Kolkata. It is also occasionally played in Ladakh and Manipur.

Although officially the national sport, field hockey no longer enjoys the same fervent following it once did, though currently India's national men's/women's hockey world rankings are 9/13 respectively. During its golden era, between 1928 and 1956, India won six consecutive Olympic gold medals in hockey; it later bagged two further Olympic gold medals, one in 1964 and the other in 1980. Recent initiatives to ignite renewed interest in the game have had mixed results. Tap into India's hockey scene at Indian Hockey (www.indianhockey.com) and Indian Field Hockey (www.bharatiyahockey.org).

Kabaddi is another popular competitive sport in the region. Two teams occupy two sides of a court. A raider runs into the opposing side, taking a breath and try to tag one or more members of the opposite team. The raider chants '*kabaddi*' repeatedly to show that they have not taken a breath, returning to the home half before exhaling.

Other sports gaining ground in India include tennis (the country's star performers are Sania Mirza, Leander Paes and Mahesh Bhupathi – to delve deeper, click www.aitatennis.com) and horse racing, which is reasonably popular in the larger cities such as Mumbai, Delhi, Kolkata and Bengaluru.

If you're interested in catching a sports match during your time in India, consult local newspapers (or ask at a tourist office) for current details about dates and venues.

THE WAY OF LIFE SPORT

Cricket lovers are likely to be bowled over by *The Illustrated History of Indian Cricket* by Boria Majumdar and *The States of Indian Cricket* by Ramachandra Guha.

Several of the Indian Super League teams are co-owned by Bollywood superstars, for example, Pune by Hrithik Roshan, and Chennai by Abhishek Bachchan.

Spiritual India

From elaborate city shrines to simple village temples, spirituality suffuses almost every facet of life in India. The nation's major faith, Hinduism, is practised by around 80% of the population and is one of the world's oldest extant religions, with roots extending beyond 1000 BC. Buddhism, Jainism and Zoroastrianism are also among the oldest religions, dating back to the 6th century BC. The mind-stirring sight of sacred architecture, and soul-warming sound of bhajans and *qawwali*, are bound to burn bright in your memory long after you've left India.

Hinduism

The Hindu pantheon is said to have a staggering 330 million deities; those worshipped are a matter of personal choice or tradition.

Hinduism has no founder or central authority and it isn't a proselytising religion. Essentially, Hindus believe in Brahman, who is eternal, uncreated and infinite. Everything that exists emanates from Brahman and will ultimately return to it. The multitude of gods and goddesses are merely manifestations – knowable aspects of this formless phenomenon.

Hindus believe that earthly life is cyclical: you are born again and again (a process known as 'samsara'), the quality of these rebirths being dependent upon your karma (conduct or action) in previous lives. Living a righteous life and fulfilling your dharma (moral code of behaviour; social duty) will enhance your chances of being born into a higher caste and better circumstances. Alternatively, if enough bad karma has accumulated, rebirth may take animal form. But it's only as a human that you can gain sufficient self-knowledge to escape the cycle of reincarnation and achieve moksha (liberation).

Gods & Goddesses

All Hindu deities are regarded as a manifestation of Brahman, who is often described as having three main representations, the Trimurti: Brahma, Vishnu and Shiva.

Brahman

The One; the ultimate reality. Brahman is formless, eternal and the source of all existence. Brahman is *nirguna* (without attributes), as opposed to all the other gods and goddesses, which are manifestations of Brahman and therefore *saguna* (with attributes).

Brahma

Only during the creation of the universe does Brahma play an active role. At other times he is in meditation. His consort is Saraswati, the goddess of learning, and his vehicle is a swan. He is sometimes shown sitting on a lotus that rises from Vishnu's navel, symbolising the interdependence of the gods. Brahma is generally depicted with four (crowned and bearded) heads, each turned towards a point of the compass.

Vishnu

The preserver or sustainer, Vishnu is associated with 'right action'. He protects and sustains all that is good in the world. He is usually depicted with four arms, holding a lotus, a conch shell (it can be blown like a trumpet so symbolises the cosmic vibration from which existence emanates), a discus and a mace. His consort is Lakshmi, the goddess of wealth, and his vehicle is Garuda, the man-bird creature. The Ganges is said to flow from his feet.

Shiva

Shiva is the destroyer – to deliver salvation – without whom creation couldn't occur. Shiva's creative role is phallically symbolised by his representation as the frequently worshipped lingam. With 1008 names, Shiva takes many forms, including Nataraja, lord of the *tandava* (cosmic victory dance), who paces out the creation and destruction of the cosmos.

Sometimes Shiva has snakes draped around his neck and is shown holding a trident (representative of the Trimurti) as a weapon while riding Nandi, his bull. Nandi symbolises power and potency, justice and moral order. Shiva's consort, Parvati, is capable of taking many forms.

Other Prominent Deities

Elephant-headed Ganesh is the god of good fortune, remover of obstacles, and patron of scribes (the broken tusk he holds was used to write sections of the Mahabharata). His animal vehicle is Mooshak (a ratlike creature). How Ganesh came to have an elephant's head is a story with several variations. One legend says that Ganesh was born to Parvati in the absence of his father Shiva, and so grew up not knowing him. One day, as Ganesh stood guard while his mother bathed, Shiva returned and asked to be let into Parvati's presence. Ganesh, who didn't recognise Shiva, refused. Enraged, Shiva lopped off Ganesh's head, only to later discover, much to his horror, that he had slaughtered his own son. He vowed to replace Ganesh's head with that of the first creature he came across, which happened to be an elephant.

Another prominent deity, Krishna is an incarnation of Vishnu sent to earth to fight for good and combat evil. His dalliances with the *gopis* (milkmaids) and his love for Radha have inspired countless paintings and songs. Depicted with blue-hued skin, Krishna is often seen playing the flute.

Hanuman is the hero of the Ramayana and loyal ally of Rama. He embodies the concept of bhakti (devotion). He's the king of the monkeys, but is capable of taking on other forms.

Among Shaivites (followers of the Shiva movement), Shakti, the universe's divine feminine creative force, is worshipped in her own right. The concept of *shakti* is embodied in the ancient goddess Devi (divine mother), who is also manifested as Durga and Amman, and in a fiercer, evil-destroying incarnation, Kali. Other widely worshipped goddesses include Lakshmi, the goddess of wealth, and Saraswati, the goddess of learning.

One of Shiva's sons, Murugan, is a popular deity in South India, especially in Tamil Nadu. He is sometimes identified with another of Shiva's sons, Skanda, who enjoys a strong following in North India. Murugan's main role is that of protector, and he is depicted as young and victorious.

Another son of Shiva who is identified with the role of protector is Ayyappan, whose temple at Sabarimala in Kerala attracts between 40 and 60 million pilgrims a year. It's said that he was born from the union of Shiva and Vishnu, both male. Vishnu is said to have assumed female form (as Mohini) to give birth. Ayyappan is often depicted riding on a tiger and accompanied by leopards, symbols of his victory over dark forces. Today the Ayyappan following has become something of a men's movement, with devotees required to avoid alcohol, drugs, cigarettes and general misbehaviour before making the pilgrimage.

Shiva is sometimes characterised as the lord of yoga, a Himalaya-dwelling ascetic with matted hair, an ash-smeared body and a third eye symbolising wisdom.

For an insight into the depth, breadth and quirks of Tamils' Hindu beliefs, as well as absorbing travel description, read Michael Wood's *A South Indian Journey*.

OM

One of Hinduism's most venerated symbols is 'Om'. Pronounced 'aum', it's a highly propitious mantra (sacred word or syllable). The 'three' shape symbolises the creation, maintenance and destruction of the universe (and thus the holy Trimurti). The inverted *chandra* (crescent or half moon) represents the discursive mind and the *bindu* (dot) within it, Brahman.

Buddhists believe that, if intoned often enough with complete concentration, it will lead to a state of blissful emptiness.

Sacred Texts

Hindu sacred texts fall into two categories: those believed to be the word of god (*shruti,* meaning 'heard') and those produced by people (smriti, meaning 'remembered'). The Vedas are regarded as *shruti* knowledge and are considered the authoritative basis for Hinduism. The oldest of the Vedic texts, the Rig-Veda, was compiled over 3000 years ago. Within its 1028 verses are prayers for prosperity and longevity, as well as an explanation of the universe's origins. The Upanishads, the last parts of the Vedas, reflect on the mystery of death and emphasise the oneness of the universe. The oldest of the Vedic texts were written in Vedic Sanskrit (related to Old Persian). Later texts were composed in classical Sanskrit, but many have been translated into the vernacular.

The smriti texts comprise a collection of literature spanning centuries and include expositions on the proper performance of domestic ceremonies, as well as the proper pursuit of government, economics and religious law. Among its well-known works are the Ramayana and Mahabharata, as well as the Puranas, which expand on the epics and promote the notion of the Trimurti. Unlike the Vedas, reading the Puranas is not restricted to initiated higher-caste males.

Did you know that blood-drinking Kali is another form of milk-giving Gauri? *Myth = Mithya: A Handbook of Hindu Mythology*, by Devdutt Pattanaik, sheds light on this and other fascinating Hindu folklore.

The Mahabharata

Thought to have been composed around 1000 BC, the Mahabharata focuses on the exploits of Krishna. By about 500 BC the Mahabharata had evolved into a far more complex creation with substantial additions, including the Bhagavad Gita (where Krishna proffers advice to Arjuna before a battle).

The story centres on conflict between the heroic gods (Pandavas) and the demons (Kauravas). Overseeing events is Krishna, who has taken on human form. Krishna acts as charioteer for the Pandava hero Arjuna, who eventually triumphs in a great battle against the Kauravas.

The Ramayana

Composed around the 3rd or 2nd century BC, the Ramayana is believed to be largely the work of one person, the poet Valmiki. Like the Mahabharata, it centres on conflict between the gods and the demons.

The story goes that Dasharatha, the childless king of Ayodhya, called upon the gods to provide him with a son. His wife duly gave birth to a boy. But this child, named Rama, was in fact an incarnation of Vishnu, who had assumed human form to overthrow the demon king of Lanka (now Sri Lanka), Ravana.

As an adult, Rama, who won the hand of the princess Sita in a competition, was chosen by his father to inherit his kingdom. At the last minute Rama's stepmother intervened and demanded her son, Barathan, take Rama's place. Rama, Sita and Rama's brother, Lakshmana, were exiled and went off to the forests, where Rama and Lakshmana battled demons and dark forces. Ravana's sister attempted to seduce Rama but she was rejected and, in revenge, Ravana captured Sita and spirited her away to his palace in Lanka.

Rama, assisted by an army of monkeys led by the loyal monkey god Hanuman, eventually found the palace, killed Ravana and rescued Sita. All returned victorious to Ayodhya, where Rama was welcomed by Barathan and crowned king.

Naturally Sacred

Animals, particularly snakes and cows, have long been worshipped on the subcontinent. For Hindus, the cow represents fertility and nurturing, while snakes (especially cobras) are associated with fertility and welfare. Naga stones (snake stones) serve the dual purpose of protecting humans from snakes and appeasing snake gods.

Plants can also have sacred associations, such as the banyan tree, which symbolises the Trimurti, while mango trees are symbolic of love – Shiva is believed to have married Parvati under one. Meanwhile, the lotus flower is said to have emerged from the primeval waters and is connected to the mythical centre of the earth through its stem. Often found in the most polluted of waters, the lotus has the remarkable ability to blossom above murky depths. The centre of the lotus corresponds to the centre of the universe, the navel of the earth: all is held together by the stem and the eternal waters. The fragile yet resolute lotus is an embodiment of beauty and strength and a reminder to Hindus of how their own lives should be. So revered has the lotus become that today it's India's national flower.

Worship

Worship and ritual play a paramount role in Hinduism. In Hindu homes you'll often find a dedicated worship area, where members of the family pray to the deities of their choice. Beyond the home, Hindus worship at temples. *Puja* is a focal point of worship and ranges from silent prayer to elaborate ceremonies. Devotees leave the temple with a handful of *prasad* (temple-blessed food) which is shared among others. Other forms of worship include *aarti* (the auspicious lighting of lamps or candles) and the playing of bhajans (devotional songs).

Islam

Islam is India's largest minority religion, followed by approximately 13.4% of the population. It's believed that Islam was introduced to northern India by Muslim rulers (parts of the north first came under Muslim rule in the 12th century) and to the south by Arab traders.

Islam was founded in Arabia by the Prophet Mohammed in the 7th century AD. The Arabic term *islam* means to surrender, and believers (Muslims) undertake to surrender to the will of Allah (God), which is revealed in the scriptures, the Quran. In this monotheistic religion, God's word is conveyed through prophets (messengers), of whom Mohammed was the most recent.

Unravelling the basic tenets of Hinduism are two books both called *Hinduism: An Introduction* – one is by Shakunthala Jagannathan, the other by Dharam Vir Singh.

Two recommended publications containing English translations of holy Hindu texts are *The Bhagavad Gita*, by S Radhakrishnan, and *The Valmiki Ramayana*, by Romesh Dutt.

SPIRITUAL INDIA ISLAM

THE SACRED SEVEN

The number seven has special significance in Hinduism. There are seven sacred Indian cities, which are all major pilgrimage centres: Varanasi, associated with Shiva; Haridwar, where the Ganges enters the plains from the Himalaya; Ayodhya, birthplace of Rama; Dwarka, with the legendary capital of Krishna thought to be off the Gujarat coast; Mathura, birthplace of Krishna; Kanchipuram, site of the historic Shiva temples; and Ujjain, venue of the Kumbh Mela every 12 years.

There are also seven sacred rivers: the Ganges (Ganga), Saraswati (thought to be underground), Yamuna, Indus, Narmada, Godavari and Cauvery.

RELIGIOUS ETIQUETTE

Whenever visiting a sacred site, dress and behave respectfully – don't wear shorts or sleeveless tops (this applies to men and women) – and refrain from smoking. Loud and intrusive behaviour isn't appreciated, and neither are public displays of affection or kidding around.

Before entering a holy place, remove your shoes (tip the shoe-minder a few rupees when retrieving them) and check if photography is allowed. You're permitted to wear socks in most places of worship – often necessary during warmer months, when floors can be uncomfortably hot.

Religious etiquette advises against touching locals on the head, or directing the soles of your feet at a person, religious shrine or image of a deity. Protocol also advises against touching someone with your feet or touching a carving of a deity.

Head cover (for women and sometimes men) is required at some places of worship – especially gurdwaras (Sikh temples) and mosques – so carry a scarf just to be on the safe side. There are some sites that don't admit women and some that deny entry to non-adherents of their faith – enquire in advance. Women may be required to sit apart from men. Jain temples request the removal of leather items you may be wearing or carrying and may also request that menstruating women not enter. When walking around any Buddhist sacred site (chortens, stupas, temples, gompas) go clockwise. Don't touch them with your left hand. Turn prayer wheels clockwise, with your right hand.

Taking photos inside a shrine, at a funeral, at a religious ceremony or of people taking a holy dip can be offensive – ask first. Flash photography may be prohibited in certain areas of a shrine, or may not be permitted at all.

Following Mohammed's death, a succession dispute split the movement, and the legacy today is the Sunnis and the Shiites. Most Muslims in India are Sunnis. The Sunnis emphasise the 'well-trodden' path or the orthodox way. Shiites believe that only imams (exemplary leaders) can reveal the true meaning of the Quran.

All Muslims, however, share a belief in the Five Pillars of Islam: the shahada (declaration of faith: 'There is no God but Allah; Mohammed is his prophet'); prayer (ideally five times a day); the zakat (tax), in the form of a charitable donation; fasting (during Ramadan) for all except the sick, young children, pregnant women, the elderly and those undertaking arduous journeys; and the hajj (pilgrimage) to Mecca, which every Muslim aspires to do at least once.

Muslims form around a quarter of the population of Kerala and over 10% in Maharashtra and Karnataka.

Sikhism

To grasp the intricacies of Sikhism read Volume One (1469–1839) or Volume Two (1839–2004) of *A History of the Sikhs*, by Khushwant Singh.

Sikhism, founded in Punjab by Guru Nanak in the 15th century, began as a reaction against the caste system and Brahmin domination of ritual. Sikhs believe in one god and although they reject the worship of idols, some keep pictures of the 10 gurus as a point of focus. The Sikhs' holy book, the Guru Granth Sahib, contains the teachings of the 10 Sikh gurus, among others. Like Hindus and Buddhists, Sikhs believe in rebirth and karma. In Sikhism, there's no ascetic or monastic tradition ending the cycles of rebirth. Almost 2% of India's citizens are Sikhs, with most living in Punjab.

Born in present-day Pakistan, Guru Nanak (1469–1539) was largely dissatisfied with both Muslim and Hindu religious practices. He believed in family life and the value of hard work – he married, had two sons and worked as a farmer when not travelling around, preaching and singing self-composed *kirtan* (Sikh devotional songs) with his Muslim musician,

Mardana. He is said to have performed miracles and he encouraged meditation on God's name as a prime path to enlightenment.

Nanak believed in equality centuries before it became socially fashionable and campaigned against the caste system. He was a practical guru – 'a person who makes an honest living and shares earnings with others recognises the way to God'. He appointed his most talented disciple to be his successor, not one of his sons.

His *kirtan* are still sung in gurdwaras (Sikh temples) today and his picture is kept in millions of homes on and beyond the subcontinent. Members of the Khalsa (the body of initiated Sikhs) adopt five symbols known as the Five Kakars (or Five Ks), which help identify them:

➡ *kesh* – uncut hair, covered with a *keski* (turban), which some regard as the kakar instead of the hair

➡ *kanga* – wooden comb

➡ *kaccha* or *kachhera* – cotton undershorts

➡ *kara* – steel bracelet

➡ *kirpan* – small sword

A sadhu is someone who has surrendered all material possessions in pursuit of spirituality through meditation, the study of sacred texts, self-mortification and pilgrimage. Explore further in *Sadhus: India's Mystic Holy Men*, by Dolf Hartsuiker.

Buddhism

About 0.8% of India's population is Buddhist. Bodhgaya, in the state of Bihar, is one of Buddhism's most sacred sites, drawing pilgrims from right across the world.

Buddhism arose in the 6th century BC as a reaction against the strictures of Brahminical Hinduism. The Buddha (Awakened One) is believed to have lived from about 563 to 483 BC. Formerly a prince (Siddhartha Gautama), the Buddha, at the age of 29, embarked on a quest for emancipation from the world of suffering. He achieved nirvana (the state of full awareness) at Bodhgaya, aged 35. Critical of the caste system and the unthinking worship of gods, the Buddha urged his disciples to seek truth within their own experiences.

The Buddha taught that existence is based on Four Noble Truths: that life is rooted in suffering, that suffering is caused by craving, that one can find release from suffering by eliminating craving, and that the way to eliminate craving is by following the Noble Eightfold Path. This path consists of right understanding, right intention, right speech, right action, right livelihood, right effort, right awareness and right concentration. By successfully complying with these one can attain nirvana.

Buddhism was spread widely around India by the Mauryan emperor Ashoka in the 3rd century BC, and Buddhist communities were quite influential in Andhra Pradesh between the 3rd century BC and 5th century AD; missionaries from Andhra helped establish monasteries and temples in countries such as Thailand. But Buddhism had ceased to play a major role in India by the 12th century AD. It saw a revival in the 1950s among intellectuals and Dalits, who were disillusioned with the caste system. About three-quarters of Indian Buddhists today live in Maharashtra. The number of followers has been further increased with the influx of Tibetan refugees into India. Both the current Dalai Lama and the lama (monk) widely accepted as the 17th Karmapa reside in northern state of Himachal Pradesh. There are several Tibetan refugee communities in South India, the biggest being Bylakuppe in Karnataka.

Set in Kerala against the backdrop of caste conflict and India's struggle for independence, *The House of Blue Mangoes*, by David Davidar, spans three generations of a Christian family.

Jainism

Jainism arose in the 6th century BC as a reaction against the caste restraints and rituals of Hinduism. It was founded by Mahavira, a contemporary of the Buddha.

Jains believe that liberation can be attained by achieving complete purity of the soul. Purity means shedding all *karman,* matter generated by one's actions that binds itself to the soul. By following various austerities (eg fasting and meditation) one can shed *karman* and purify the soul. Right conduct is essential, and fundamental to this is ahimsa (nonviolence) in thought and deed towards any living thing.

The religious disciplines of followers are less severe than for monks (some Jain monks go naked). The slightly less ascetic maintain a bare minimum of possessions which include a broom to sweep the path before them to avoid stepping on any living creature, and a piece of cloth tied over their mouth to prevent the accidental inhalation of insects.

The Zoroastrian funerary ritual involves the 'Towers of Silence' where the corpse is laid out and exposed to vultures that pick the bones clean.

Today, around 0.4% of India's population is Jain, with the majority living in Gujarat, Rajasthan and Mumbai. One notable Jain holy site in South India is Sravanabelagola in Karnataka.

Christianity

There are various theories circulating about Christ's link to the Indian subcontinent. Some, for instance, believe that Jesus spent his 'lost years' in India, while others say that Christianity came to South India with St Thomas the Apostle in AD 52. However, many scholars attest it's more likely Christianity is traced to around the 4th century with a Syrian merchant, Thomas Cana, who set out for Kerala with around 400 families. India's Christian community today stands at about 2.3% of the population, with the bulk residing in South India.

Catholicism established a strong presence in South India in the wake of Vasco da Gama's visit in 1498, and orders that have been active – not always welcomed – in the region include the Dominicans, Franciscans and Jesuits. Protestant missionaries are believed to have begun arriving – with a conversion agenda – from around the 18th century.

Zoroastrianism

Zoroastrianism, founded by Zoroaster (Zarathustra), had its inception in Persia in the 6th century BC and is based on the concept of dualism, whereby good and evil are locked in a continuous battle. Zoroastrianism isn't quite monotheistic: good and evil entities coexist, although believers are urged to honour only the good. On the day of judgement the errant soul is not called to account for every misdemeanour – but a pleasant afterlife does depend on one's deeds, words and thoughts during earthly existence.

Zoroastrianism was eclipsed in Persia by the rise of Islam in the 7th century. Over the following centuries some followers emigrated to India, where they became known as Parsis. Historically, Parsis settled in Gujarat and became farmers; during British rule they moved into commerce, forming a prosperous community in Mumbai.

There are now believed to be only 40,000 to 45,000 Parsis left in India, with most residing in Mumbai.

Tribal Religions

Tribal religions have merged with Hinduism and other mainstream religions so that very few are now clearly identifiable. It's believed that some basic tenets of Hinduism may have originated in ancient tribal culture.

Village and tribal people in South India have their own belief systems, which are much less accessible or obvious than the temples, rituals and other outward manifestations of the mainstream religions. The village deity may be represented by a stone pillar in a field, a platform under a tree or an iron spear stuck in the ground. Village deities are generally seen as less remote and more concerned with the immediate happiness and prosperity of the community; in most cases they are female. There are also many beliefs about ancestral spirits, including those who died violently.

Delicious India

India's culinary terrain – with its especially impressive patchwork of vegetarian cuisine – is a feast for all the senses, using fresh local ingredients, be they fragrant spices or desert vegetables. You can delight in everything from sensational street food to work-of-art thalis, from creative contemporary masterpieces to family-run stalls that have served up one speciality for over 50 years. Indeed, it's the sheer diversity of what's on offer that makes eating your way through India so deliciously rewarding.

A Culinary Carnival

India's culinary story is an ancient one, and the food you'll find here today reflects a mass of regional and global influences.

Land of Spices

Christopher Columbus was actually searching for the black pepper of Kerala's Malabar Coast when he stumbled upon America. This Indian region still grows the finest quality of the world's favourite spice, and it's integral to most savoury Indian dishes.

Turmeric is the essence of the majority of Indian curries, but coriander seeds are the most widely used spice and lend flavour and body to just about every savoury dish. Indian 'wet' dishes – commonly known as curries in the West – usually begin with the crackle of cumin seeds in hot oil. Tamarind is sometimes known as the 'Indian date' and is a popular souring agent in the south. The green cardamom of Kerala's Western Ghats is regarded as the world's best, and you'll find it in savouries, desserts and warming chai (tea). Saffron, the dried stigmas of crocus flowers grown in Kashmir, is so light it takes more than 1500 hand-plucked flowers to yield just one gram.

Spotlighting rice, *Finest Rice Recipes* by Sabina Sehgal Saikia shows just how versatile this humble grain is, with classy creations such as rice-crusted crab cakes.

Rice Paradise

Rice is a staple throughout India and especially so in the south. Long-grain white-rice varieties are the most popular, served hot with just about any 'wet' cooked dish. From Assam's sticky rice in the far northeast to Kerala's red grains in the extreme south, you'll find countless regional varieties that locals will claim to be the best in India, though this honour is usually conceded to basmati, a fragrant long-grain variety which is widely exported around the world. Rice is usually served after you have finished with the rotis (breads), usually accompanied by curd to enrich the mix.

Pongal, the major harvest festival of the south, is closely associated with the dish of the same name, made with the season's first rice plus jaggery, nuts, raisins and spices.

Flippin' Fantastic Bread

Although rice is the mainstay of the south, traditional breads are also eaten. Roti, the generic term for Indian-style bread, is a name used interchangeably with chapati to describe the most common variety, the irresistible unleavened round bread made with whole-wheat flour and cooked on a *tawa* (hotplate). It may be smothered with ghee (clarified butter) or oil. In some places, rotis are bigger and thicker than chapatis and possibly cooked in a tandoor. Paratha is a layered pan-fried flat

SOUTHERN BELLES

Savoury dosas (also spelt *dosai*), a family of large, crispy, papery, rice-flour crêpes, usually served with a bowl of hot *sambar* (soupy lentil dish) and another bowl of cooling coconut *chatni* (chutney), are a South Indian breakfast speciality that can be eaten at any time of day. The most popular is the *masala* dosa (stuffed with spiced potatoes), but there are also other fantastic dosa varieties – the *rava* dosa (batter made with semolina), the Mysore dosa (like *masala* dosa but with more vegetables and chilli in the filling), and the *pessarettu* dosa(batter made with mung-bean dhal) from Andhra Pradesh.

The humble *idli*, a traditional South Indian snack, is low-cal and nutritious, providing a welcome alternative to oil, spice and chilli. *Idlis* are spongy, round, white fermented rice cakes that you dip in *sambar* and coconut *chatni*. *Dahi idli* is an *idli* dunked in very lightly spiced yoghurt – brilliant for tender tummies. Other super southern snacks include *vadas* (doughnut-shaped deep-fried lentil savouries) and *appams* or *uttappams* (thick, savoury rice pancakes with finely chopped onions, green chillies, coriander and coconut).

bread, that may also be stuffed, and makes for a hearty and popular breakfast. Naan is a larger, thicker bread, baked in a tandoor and usually eaten with meaty sauces or kebabs. *Puri* is an unleavened bread that puffs up when deep fried and is served with accompaniments such as *bhajia* (vegetable fritters).

Dhal-icious!

The whole of India is united in its love for dhal (curried lentils or pulses). You may encounter up to 60 different pulses: the most common are *channa* (chickpeas); tiny yellow or green ovals called *moong* (mung beans); salmon-coloured *masoor* (red lentils); the ochre-coloured southern favourite, *tuvar* (yellow lentils; also known as *arhar*); *rajma* (kidney beans); *urad* (black gram or lentils); and *lobhia* (black-eyed peas).

Meaty Matters

Although India probably has more vegetarians than the rest of the world combined, it still has an extensive repertoire of carnivorous fare. Chicken, lamb and mutton (sometimes actually goat) are the mainstays; religious taboos make beef forbidden to devout Hindus and pork to Muslims.

The meaty Chettinadu cuisine from Tamil Nadu is beautifully spiced without being too fiery. In some southern restaurants you'll come across meat-dominated Mughlai cuisine, which includes rich curries, kebabs, koftas and biryanis – the last is a particular speciality of Hyderabad. This spicy cuisine traces its history back to the (Islamic) Mughal empire that once reigned supreme over much of India. Tandoori meat dishes are another North Indian favourite also found in the south. The name is derived from the clay oven, or tandoor, in which the marinated meat is cooked.

Deep-Sea Delights

India has around 7500km of coastline, so it's no surprise that seafood is an important ingredient, especially on the west coast, from Mumbai down to Kerala. Kerala is the biggest fishing state, while Goa boasts particularly succulent prawns and fiery fish curries, and the fishing communities of the Konkan Coast – sandwiched between Mumbai and Goa – are renowned for their seafood and other recipes. The far-flung Andaman Islands also won't disappoint seafood lovers with the fresh catch featuring on all menus.

The fiery cuisine of the Karnatakan coastal city of Mangalore is famed for its flavour-packed seafood dishes. Mangalorean cuisine is diverse, distinct and characterised by its liberal use of chilli and fresh coconut.

Fish is a staple of non-vegetarian Marathi food; Maharashtra's signature fish dish is *bombil* (Bombay duck; a misnomer for this slimy, pikelike fish), which is eaten fresh or sun-dried.

The Fruits (& Vegetables) of Mother Nature

A visit to any South Indian market will reveal a vast and vibrant assortment of fresh fruit and vegetables, overflowing from large baskets or stacked in neat pyramids. The south is especially well known for its abundance of tropical fruits such as pineapples and papaya. Mangos abound during the summer months (especially April and May), with India boasting more than 500 varieties, the pick of the luscious bunch being the sweet Alphonso. You'll find fruit inventively fashioned into a *chatni* (chutney) or pickle, and also flavouring lassi, *kulfi* and other sweet treats.

Naturally in a region with so many vegetarians, *sabzi* (vegetables) make up a predominant part of the diet. Vegetables can be cooked *sukhi* (dry) or *tari* (in a sauce) and within these two categories they can be fried, roasted, curried, baked, mashed and stuffed into dosas, or dipped in chickpea-flour batter to make a deep-fried *pakora* (fritter). Potatoes are ubiquitous and popularly cooked with various masalas (spice mixes), with other vegetables, or mashed and fried for the street snack *aloo tikki* (mashed-potato patties).

Onions are fried with other vegetables, ground into a paste for cooking with meats, or served raw as relishes. Heads of cauliflower are usually cooked dry on their own, with potatoes to make *aloo gobi* (potato-and-cauliflower curry), or with other vegetables such as carrots and beans. Fresh green peas turn up stir-fried with other vegetables in pilaus and biryanis. *Baigan* (eggplant/aubergine) can be curried or sliced and deep-fried. Also popular is *saag* (a generic term for leafy greens), which can include mustard, spinach and fenugreek. Something a little more unusual is the bumpy-skinned *karela* (bitter gourd) which, like the delectable *bhindi* (okra), is commonly prepared dry with spices.

Pickles, Chutneys & Relishes

Pickles, chutneys and relishes are accompaniments that add zing to meals. A relish can be anything from a tiny pickled onion to a delicately crafted fusion of fruit, nuts and spices. One of the most popular side dishes is yoghurt-based raita, which makes a tongue-cooling counter to spicy food. *Chatnis* can come in any number of varieties (sweet or savoury) and can be made from many different vegetables, fruits, herbs and spices. Proceed with caution before polishing off that pickled speck sitting on your thali: it may quite possibly be the hottest thing you have ever tasted.

Sweet at Heart

India has a colourful kaleidoscope of often sticky and squishy *mithai* (Indian sweets), most of them sinfully sugary. The main categories are

In coastal areas, especially Goa and Kerala, it's hard to beat the beach shacks for a fresh, inexpensive seafood meal – from fried mussels, prawns and calamari to steamed fish, crab and lobster.

Ghee is the Hindi word for 'fat'. It's made by melting butter and removing the water and milk solids – ghee is the clear butter fat that remains. It's better for high-heat cooking than butter and keeps for longer.

PAAN

Meals are often rounded off with *paan*, a fragrant mixture of betel nut (also called areca nut), lime paste, spices and condiments wrapped in an edible, silky *paan* leaf. Peddled by *paan*-wallahs, who are usually strategically positioned outside busy restaurants, *paan* is eaten as a digestive and mouth-freshener. The betel nut is mildly narcotic and some aficionados eat *paan* the same way heavy smokers consume cigarettes – over the years these people's teeth can become rotted red and black. Usually the gloopy red juice is spat out, which is not always particularly sightly.

There are two basic types of *paan: mitha* (sweet) and *saadha* (with tobacco). A parcel of *mitha paan* is a splendid way to finish a meal. Pop the whole parcel in your mouth and chew slowly, allowing the juices to oooooooooze.

FEASTING INDIAN-STYLE

Most people in India eat with their right hand. In the south, they use as much of the hand as is necessary, while elsewhere they use the tips of the fingers. The left hand is reserved for unsanitary actions such as removing shoes. You can use your left hand for holding drinks and serving yourself from a communal bowl, but it shouldn't be used for bringing food to your mouth. Before and after a meal, it's good manners to wash your hands.

Once your meal is served, mix the food with your fingers. If you are having dhal and *sabzi* (vegetables), only mix the dhal into your rice and have the *sabzi* in small scoops with each mouthful. If you are having fish or meat curry, mix the gravy into your rice. Scoop up lumps of the mix and, with your knuckles facing the dish, use your thumb to shovel the food into your mouth.

barfi (a fudgelike, milk-based sweet), soft *halwa* (made with vegetables, cereals, lentils, nuts or fruit), *ladoos* (sweet balls made with gram flour and semolina), and those made from *chhana* (unpressed paneer), such as *rasgullas*. There are also simpler – but equally scrumptious – offerings such as crunchy *jalebis* that you'll see all over the country.

Payasam (called *kheer* in the north) is one of the most popular end-of-meal desserts. It's a creamy pudding with a light, delicate flavour, that can be made from rice, sago, vermicelli noodles or *moong* dhal, usually with some combination of jaggery (or molasses), ghee, coconut, spices, milk, cashews or almonds, and dried fruit. Other favourite desserts include hot *gulab jamun* and refreshing *kulfi*.

Each year, an estimated 14 tonnes of pure silver is converted into the edible foil that decorates many Indian sweets, especially during the Diwali festival.

Technically speaking, there's no such thing as an Indian 'curry' – the word, an anglicised derivative of the Tamil word *kari* (sauce), was used by the British as a term for any spiced dish.

Vegetarians & Vegans

South India is king when it comes to vegetarian fare. There's little understanding of veganism (the term 'pure vegetarian' means without eggs), and animal products such as milk, butter, ghee and curd are included in most Indian dishes. If you are vegan your first problem is likely to be getting the cook to understand your requirements, though big hotels and larger cities are getting better at catering to vegans.

For further information, surf the web – try Indian Vegan (www.indian-vegan.com) and Vegan World Network (www.vegansworldnetwork.org).

Dakshin: Vegetarian Cuisine from South India, by Chandra Padmanabhan, is an easy-to-read and beautifully illustrated book of southern recipes.

Where to Fill Up?

You can eat well in South India everywhere from ramshackle *dhabas* (simple streetside eateries) to otherworldly five-star hotels. Most mid-range restaurants serve one of two basic genres: South Indian (which usually means the vegetarian food of Tamil Nadu and Karnataka) and North Indian (which largely comprises Punjabi/Mughlai fare). You'll also find the cuisines of neighbouring regions and states. Indians frequently migrate in search of work and these restaurants cater to the large communities seeking the familiar tastes of home.

Not to be confused with burger joints and pizzerias, restaurants in the south advertising 'fast food' are some of India's best. They serve the whole gamut of tiffin (snack) items and often have separate sweet counters. Many upmarket hotels have outstanding restaurants, usually with pan-Indian menus so you can explore various regional cuisines. Meanwhile, the independent restaurant dining scene keeps mushrooming in India's larger cities, with every kind of cuisine available, from Mexican and Mediterranean to Japanese and Italian.

The Anger of Aubergines: Stories of Women and Food, by Bulbul Sharm, is an amusing culinary analysis of social relationships interspersed with enticing recipes.

Dhabas are oases to millions of truck drivers, bus passengers and sundry travellers going anywhere by road. The original *dhabas* dot the North Indian landscape, but you'll find versions of them throughout the country. The rough-and-ready but satisfying food served in these happy-go-lucky shacks has become a genre of its own known as '*dhaba* food'.

Street Food

Whatever the time of day, street food vendors are frying, boiling, roasting, peeling, simmering, mixing, juicing or baking different types of food and drink to lure peckish passers-by. Small operations usually have one special that they serve all day, while other vendors have different dishes for breakfast, lunch and dinner. The fare varies as you venture between neighbourhoods, towns and regions; it can be as simple as puffed rice or peanuts roasted in hot sand, or as complex as the riot of different flavours known as *chaat* (savoury snack). *Idli sambar* (rice patties served with delectable sauce and chutney) is a favourite in Chennai; Mumbai is famed for its *bhelpuri* (fried rounds of dough with puffed rice, lentils, lemon juice, onion, herbs and chutney); *mirchi bhajji* (chilli fritters stuffed with tamarind, sesame and spices) are a delicacy in Hyderabad; while samosas (deep-fried pastry triangles filled with spiced vegetables) and *golgappa/panipuri/gup chup* (puffed spheres of bread with a spicy filling) are found all over India.

Railway Snack Attack

One of the thrills of travelling by rail in India is the culinary circus that greets you at almost every station. Roving vendors accost arriving trains, yelling and scampering up and down the carriages; fruit, *namkin* (savoury nibbles), omelettes, nuts and sweets are offered through the grills on the windows; and platform cooks try to lure you from the train with the sizzle of spicy goodies such as samosas. Frequent rail travellers know which station is famous for which food item: Lonavla station in Maharashtra is known for *chikki* (rock-hard, toffeelike confectionery),

101 Kerala Delicacies, by G Padma Vijay, is a detailed recipe book of vegetarian and non-vegetarian dishes from this coast-hugging state.

DELICIOUS INDIA WHERE TO FILL UP?

For India-wide restaurant reviews and recommendations, check out the excellent Zomato (zomato.com).

STREET FOOD: TIPS

Tucking into street eats is a highlight of travelling in India, but to avoid tummy troubles:

➡ Give yourself a few days to adjust to the local cuisine, especially if you're unaccustomed to spicy food.

➡ If locals are avoiding a particular vendor, you should too. Also note the profile of the customers – any place popular with families will probably be your safest bet.

➡ Check how and where the vendor is cleaning the utensils, and how and where the food is covered. If the vendor is cooking in oil, have a peek to check it's clean. If the pots or surfaces are dirty, there are food scraps about or too many buzzing flies, don't be shy to make a hasty retreat.

➡ Don't be put off when you order some deep-fried snack and the cook throws it back into the wok. It's common practice to partly cook the snacks first and then finish them off once they've been ordered. Frying them hot again kills germs.

➡ Unless a place is reputable (and busy), it's best to avoid eating meat from the street.

➡ The hygiene standard at juice stalls varies, so exercise caution. Have the vendor press the juice in front of you and steer clear of anything stored in a jug or served in a glass (unless you're confident with the washing standards).

➡ Don't be tempted by glistening pre-sliced melon and other fruit, which keeps its luscious veneer with regular dousing of (often dubious) water.

Hyderabad's stations for their biryanis, and Tirupati for its *ladoos* (ball-shaped sweets made from gram flour, semolina and other ingredients).

Daily Dining Habits

Three main meals a day is the norm in India. Breakfast is usually fairly light, often *idlis* and *sambar* in the south. Lunch can be substantial (perhaps a thali) or light, especially for time-strapped office workers. Dinner is usually the main meal of the day. It's generally comprised of a few different preparations – several curried vegetable dishes (maybe also meat) and dhal, accompanied by rice and/or chapatis. Dishes are served all at once rather than as courses. Desserts are optional and most prevalent during festivals or other special occasions. Fruit may wrap up a meal. In many Indian homes dinner can be a rather late affair (post 9pm) depending on personal preference and the season (eg late dinners during the warmer months). Restaurants usually spring to life after 9pm in the cities, but in smaller towns they're busy earlier.

Spiritual Sustenance

For many in India, food is considered just as critical for fine-tuning the spirit as it is for sustaining the body. Broadly speaking, Hindus traditionally avoid foods that are thought to inhibit physical and spiritual development, although there are few hard-and-fast rules. The taboo on eating beef (the cow is holy to Hindus) is the most rigid restriction. Jains avoid foods such as garlic and onions, which, apart from harming insects in their extraction from the ground, are thought to heat the blood and arouse sexual desire. You may come across vegetarian restaurants that make it a point to advertise the absence of onion and garlic in their dishes for this reason. Devout Hindus may also avoid garlic and onions. These items are also banned from many ashrams.

Some foods, such as dairy products, are considered innately pure and are eaten to cleanse the body, mind and spirit. Ayurveda, the ancient science of life, health and longevity, also influences food customs.

Pork is taboo for Muslims and stimulants such as alcohol are avoided by the most devout. Halal is the term for all permitted foods, and haram for those prohibited. Fasting is considered an opportunity to earn the

Got the munchies? Grab *Street Foods of India*, by Vimla and Deb Kumar Mukerji, which has recipes of much-loved Indian snacks, from samosas and *bhelpuri* to *jalebis* and *kulfi*.

Dakshin Bhog, by Santhi Balaraman, offers a yummy jumble of southern stars, from iconic dosas and *idlis* to *kootan choru* (vegetable rice).

THE GREAT SOUTH INDIAN THALI

In South India the thali is a favourite lunchtime meal and is often called just a 'meal' rather than thali. Inexpensive, satiating, wholesome and incredibly tasty, this is Indian food at its simple best. The name 'thali' refers to the stainless steel plate on which the meal is served: whereas in North India the plate usually has indentations for the various side dishes, in the south a thali is traditionally served on a flat steel plate that may be covered with a fresh banana leaf, or on a banana leaf itself.

In a restaurant, when the steel plate is placed in front of you, you may like to follow local custom and pour some water on the leaf then spread it around with your right hand. Soon enough a waiter with a large pot of rice will come along and heap mounds of it onto your plate, followed by servings of dhal, *sambar* (soupy lentils), *rasam* (dhal-based broth flavoured with tamarind), vegetable dishes, chutneys, pickles and *dahi* (curd/yoghurt). Using the fingers of your right hand, start by mixing the various side dishes with the rice, kneading and scraping it into mouth-sized balls, then scoop it into your mouth using your thumb to push the food in. It is considered poor form to stick your hand right into your mouth or to lick your fingers. Observing fellow diners will help get your thali technique just right. If it's all getting a bit messy, there should be a finger bowl of water on the table. Waiters will continue to fill your plate until you wave your hand over one or all of the offerings to indicate you have had enough.

approval of Allah, to wipe the sin-slate clean and to understand the suffering of the poor.

Buddhists and Jains subscribe to the philosophy of ahimsa (nonviolence) and are mostly vegetarian. Jainism's central tenet is ultra-vegetarianism, and rigid restrictions are in place to avoid injury to any living creature – Jains abstain from eating vegetables that grow underground because of the potential to harm insects during cultivation and harvesting.

India's Sikh, Christian and Parsi communities have little or no restrictions on what they can eat.

Cooking Courses

You might find yourself so inspired by Indian food that you want to take home a little Indian kitchen know-how, via a cooking course. They are offered in Goa and Kerala, with the best in Palolem, Anjuna and Siolim in Goa, and at homestays in Kumily (Periyar) and Kochi in Kerala. Some courses are professionally run, others are informal. Most require at least a few days' advance notice.

Drinks, Anyone?

Gujarat, Nagaland and Mizoram, all in the north, are India's only dry states but there are drinking laws in place all over the country, and each state may have regular dry days when the sale of alcohol from liquor shops is banned. Kerala, where alcohol consumption was twice the national average, removed liquor licences from some 700 bars in 2014, restricting them to beer and wine sales (four- and five-star hotels can still sell liquor). On Gandhi's birthday (2 October), you'll find it hard to get an alcoholic drink anywhere. To avoid paying high taxes, head for Goa, where booze is much cheaper and the drinking culture less restricted.

You'll find excellent watering holes in most big cities, especially Mumbai and Bengaluru (the craft beer capital of India), which are usually at their liveliest on weekends. The more upmarket bars serve an impressive selection of domestic and imported drinks as well as draught beer. Many bars turn into music-thumping nightclubs after 8pm although there are quiet lounge-bars to be found in most large cities. In smaller towns the bar scene can be a seedy, male-dominated affair – not the kind of place thirsty female travellers would want to venture into alone.

Wine-drinking is steadily on the rise, despite the domestic wine-producing industry still being relatively new. The favourable climate and soil conditions in certain areas – such as parts of Maharashtra and Karnataka – have spawned some commendable Indian wineries such as those of the Grover and Sula Vineyards.

Stringent licensing laws discourage drinking in some restaurants but places that depend on the tourist rupee may covertly serve you beer in teapots and disguised glasses – but don't assume anything, at the risk of causing offence.

Very few vegetarian restaurants serve alcohol.

Nonalcoholic Beverages

Chai (tea), the much-loved drink of the masses, is made with copious amounts of milk and sugar. A glass of steaming, frothy chai is the perfect antidote to the vicissitudes of life on the Indian road; the disembodied voice droning '*garam* chai, *garam* chai' (hot tea, hot tea) is likely to become one of the most familiar and welcome sounds of your trip. Masala chai adds cardamom, ginger and other spices.

While chai is the traditional choice of most of the nation, South Indians have long shared their loyalty with coffee. The popular South Indian filter coffee is a combination of boiled milk, sugar and a strong decoction

---

DELICIOUS INDIA COOKING COURSES

Food that is first offered to the gods at temples then shared among devotees is known as *prasad*.

Complete Indian Cooking, by Mridula Baljekar, Rafi Fernandez, Shehzad Husain and Manisha Kanani, contains a host of southern favourites including chicken with green mango, masala mashed potatoes and Goan prawn curry.

The subcontinent's wine industry is an ever-evolving one – take a cyber-sip of Indian wine at www.indianwine. com.

made from freshly ground coffee beans, often with a bit of chicory added. In the cities you'll also find plenty of branches of slick modern coffee-house chains such as Café Coffee Day and Barista, serving standard international cappuccinos, lattes, Americanos and the like.

Masala soda is the quintessentially Indian soft drink. It's a freshly opened bottle of fizzy soda, pepped up with lime, spices, salt and sugar. You can also plump for a plain lime soda, which is soda with fresh lime, served sweet (with sugar) or salted as you prefer. Also refreshing is *jal jeera,* made of lime juice, cumin, mint and rock salt. Sweet and savoury *lassi,* a yoghurt-based drink, is popular nationwide and is another wonderfully cooling beverage.

Falooda is a rose-flavoured drink made with milk, cream, nuts and strands of vermicelli, while *badam* milk (served hot or cold) is flavoured with almonds and saffron.

Homegrown Brews

An estimated three-quarters of India's drinking population quaffs 'country liquor' such as the notorious arak (liquor distilled from coconut-palm sap, potatoes or rice) of the south. This is widely known as the poor-man's drink and millions are addicted to the stuff. Each year, many people are blinded or even killed by the methyl alcohol in illegal arak.

An interesting local drink is a clear spirit with a heady pungent flavour called *mahua,* distilled from the flower of the *mahua* tree. It's brewed in makeshift village stalls all over central India during March and April, when the trees bloom. *Mahua* is safe to drink as long as it comes from a trustworthy source. There have been cases of people being blinded after drinking *mahua* adulterated with methyl alcohol.

Toddy, the sap from the palm tree, is drunk in coastal areas, especially Kerala, while feni is the primo Indian spirit, and the preserve of laid-back Goa. Coconut feni is light and rather unexceptional but the more popular cashew feni – made from the fruit of the cashew tree – is worth a try.

Containing handy tips, including how to best store spices, Monisha Bharadwaj's *The Indian Spice Kitchen* is a slick cookbook with more than 200 traditional recipes.

The *Penguin Food Guide to India*, by Charmaine O'Brien, is engrossing and evocative.

Menu Decoder

achar	pickle
aloo	potato; also *alu*
aloo tikki	mashed-potato patty
appam	South Indian rice pancake
arak	liquor distilled from coconut milk, potatoes or rice
baigan	eggplant/aubergine; also known as *brinjal*
barfi	fudgelike sweet made from milk
bebinca	Goan 16-layer cake
besan	chickpea flour
betel	nut of the betel tree; also called areca nut
bhajia	vegetable fritters
bhang lassi	blend of lassi and bhang (a derivative of marijuana)
bhelpuri	thin fried rounds of dough with puffed rice, lentils, lemon juice, onion, herbs and chutney
bhindi	okra
biryani	fragrant spiced steamed rice with meat or vegetables
bonda	mashed-potato patty
chaat	savoury snack, may be seasoned with *chaat* masala
chach	buttermilk beverage

chai	tea
channa	spiced chickpeas
chapati	round unleavened Indian-style bread; also known as roti
chawal	rice
cheiku	small, sweet brown fruit
dahi	curd/yoghurt
dhal	spiced lentil dish
dhal makhani	black lentils and red kidney beans with cream and butter
dhansak	Parsi dish; meat, usually chicken or lamb, with curried lentils, pumpkin or gourd and rice
dosa	large South Indian savoury crepe
falooda	rose-flavoured drink made with milk, cream, nuts and vermicelli
faluda	long chickpea-flour noodles
feni	Goan liquor distilled from cashew fruit or coconut palm toddy
ghee	clarified butter
gobi	cauliflower
gulab jamun	deep-fried balls of dough soaked in rose-flavoured syrup
halwa	soft sweet made with vegetables, lentils, nuts or fruit
idli	South Indian spongy, round fermented rice cake
imli	tamarind
jaggery	hard brown, sugarlikesweetener made from palm sap
jalebi	orange-coloured coils of deep-fried batter dunked in sugar syrup; served hot
karela	bitter gourd
keema	spiced minced meat
kheer	creamy rice pudding
khichdi	blend of lightly spiced rice and lentils; also *khichri*
kofta	minced vegetables or meat; often ball-shaped
korma	currylike braised dish
kulcha	soft leavened Indian-style bread
kulfi	flavoured (often with pistachio) firm-textured ice cream
ladoo	sweet ball made with gram flour and semolina; also *ladu*
lassi	yoghurt-and-iced-water drink
malai kofta	paneer cooked in a creamy sauce of cashews and tomato
masala dosa	large South Indian savoury crepe (dosa) stuffed with spiced potatoes
mattar paneer	unfermented cheese and pea curry
methi	fenugreek
mishti doi	Bengali sweet; curd sweetened with jaggery
mithai	Indian sweets
momo	savoury Tibetan dumpling
naan	tandoor-cooked flat bread
namak	salt
namkin	savoury nibbles
noon chai	salt tea (Kashmir)
pakora	bite-sized vegetable pieces in batter
palak paneer	unfermented cheese chunks in a puréed spinach gravy

paneer	soft, unfermented cheese made from milk curd
pani	water
pappadam	thin, crispy lentil or chickpea-flour circle-shaped wafer; also pappad
paratha/ parantha	flaky flatbread (thicker than chapati); often stuffed
phulka	a chapati that puffs up on an open flame
pilau	rice cooked in spiced stock; also *pulau*, *pilao* or *pilaf*
pudina	mint
puri	flat savoury dough that puffs up when deep-fried; also *poori*
raita	mildly spiced yoghurt, often containing shredded cucumber or diced pineapple
rasam	dhal-based broth flavoured with tamarind
rasgulla	cream-cheese balls flavoured with rose-water
rogan josh	rich, spicy lamb curry
saag	leafy greens
sabzi	vegetables
sambar	South Indian soupy lentil dish with cubed vegetables
samosa	deep-fried pastry triangles filled with spiced vegetables
sonf	aniseed; used as a digestive and mouth-freshener; also *saunf*
tandoor	clay oven
tawa	flat hotplate/iron griddle
thali	all-you-can-eat meal; stainless steel (sometimes silver) compartmentalised plate
thukpa	Tibetan noodle soup
tiffin	snack; also refers to meal container often made of stainless steel
tikka	spiced, often marinated, chunks of chicken, paneer etc
toddy	alcoholic drink, tapped from palm trees
tsampa	Tibetan staple of roast-barley flour
upma	*rava* (semolina) cooked with onions, spices, chili peppers and coconut
uttapam	thick savoury South Indian rice pancake with finely chopped onions, green chillies, coriander and coconut
vada	South Indian doughnut-shaped deep-fried lentil savoury
vindaloo	Goan dish; fiery curry in a marinade of vinegar and garlic

The Great Indian Bazaar

India's bazaars and shops sell a staggering range of goodies: from woodwork to silks, chunky tribal jewellery to finely embroidered shawls, sparkling gemstones to rustic village handicrafts. The array of arts and handicrafts is vast, with every region – sometimes every village – maintaining its own traditions, some of them ancient. Be prepared to encounter – and bring home – some spectacular items. India's shopping opportunities are as inspiring and multifarious as the country itself.

Bronze Figures, Stone Carving & Terracotta

In southern India and parts of the Himalaya, small bronze images of deities are created by the age-old lost-wax process. A wax figure is made, a mould is formed around it, then the wax is melted, poured out and replaced with molten metal; the mould is then broken open to reveal the figure inside. Figures of Shiva as Nataraja, the cosmic dancer (a sculptural tradition going back to medieval Chola times in Tamil Nadu) are the most popular, but you can also find images of numerous other deities from the Hindu pantheon, and images of the Buddha and Tantric deities, finished off with finely polished and painted faces. Don't confuse bronze (a copper-tin alloy) with brass (a cheaper copper-zinc alloy).

In Mamallapuram (Mahabalipuram) in Tamil Nadu, craftspeople using local granite and soapstone have revived the ancient artistry of the Pallava sculptors; souvenirs range from tiny stone elephants to enormous deity statues weighing half a tonne. Tamil Nadu is also known for bronzeware from Thanjavur and Trichy (Tiruchirappalli).

A number of places produce attractive terracotta items, ranging from vases and decorative flowerpots to images of deities and children's toys.

Outside temples across India you can buy small clay or plaster effigies of Hindu deities.

> State government handicraft emporiums usually have numerous branches, reasonable fixed prices and a good selections of local crafts. Try Tamil Nadu's Poompuhar (http://tn-poompuhar.org); Lepakshi (www.lepakshihandi-crafts.gov.in) in Andhra Pradesh and Telangana; Kairali and SMSM Institute in Kerala; and Karnataka's Cauvery Handicrafts Emporium (www.cauveryhandi-crafts.net).

Carpets, Carpets, Carpets!

Carpet-making is a living craft in India, with workshops throughout the country producing fine wool and silkwork, though most of the finest carpets are made in the north of the country, especially in Kashmir, Ladakh, Himachal Pradesh, Sikkim and West Bengal. Most Tibetan refugee settlements have cooperative carpet workshops. Antique carpets usually aren't antique – unless you buy from an internationally reputable dealer; stick to 'new' carpets.

Coarsely woven woollen *numdas* (or *namdas*) from Kashmir and Rajasthan are much cheaper than knotted carpets. Various regions manufacture flat-weave *dhurries* (kilimlike cotton rugs); Warangal in Telangana is one of the main centres in the south.

THE ART OF HAGGLING

Government emporiums, fair-trade cooperatives, department stores and modern shopping centres almost always charge fixed prices. Almost anywhere else you need to bargain. Shopkeepers in tourist hubs are accustomed to travellers who have lots of money and little time to spend it, so you can often expect to be charged double or triple the going rate. Souvenir shops are generally the most notorious.

The first 'rule' to haggling is to never show too much interest in the item you've got your heart set upon. Second, resist purchasing the first thing that takes your fancy. Wander around several shops and price items, but don't make it too obvious: if you return to the first shop, the vendor will know it's because they are the cheapest (resulting in less haggling leeway).

Decide how much you would be happy paying, and then express a casual interest in buying. If you have absolutely no idea of the going rate, a common approach is to start by slashing the price by half. The vendor will, most likely, look aghast, but you can now work up and down respectively in small increments until you reach a mutually agreeable price. You'll find that many shopkeepers lower their so-called 'final price' if you head out of the store saying you'll 'think about it'.

Haggling is a way of life in India and is usually taken in good spirit. It should never turn ugly. Always keep in mind how much a rupee is worth in your home currency, and how much you'd pay for the item back home, to put things in perspective. If you're not sure of the 'right' price for an item, think about how much it is worth to you. If a vendor seems to be charging an unreasonably high price, look elsewhere.

Children have been employed as carpet weavers in the subcontinent for centuries. The carpets produced by Tibetan refugee cooperatives are almost always made by adults; government emporiums and charitable cooperatives are usually the best places to buy.

Costs & Shipping

The price of a carpet is determined by the number and the size of the hand-tied knots, the range of dyes and colours, the intricacy of the design and the material. Silk carpets cost more and look more luxurious, but wool carpets usually last longer. Expect to pay upwards of US$250 for a good quality, 90cm by 1.5m wool carpet, and around US$2000 for a similar-sized carpet in silk.

Many places can ship carpets home for you – although it may be safest to send things independently to avoid scams. Shipping to Europe for a 90cm by 1.5m carpet should cost around ₹4000. You can also carry carpets as check-in baggage on a plane (allow 5kg to 10kg of your baggage allowance for a 90cm by 1.5m carpet, and check that your airline allows oversized baggage).

Be cautious when buying items that include international delivery, and avoid being led to shops by smooth-talking touts, but don't worry about too much else – except your luggage space!

Jewellery

Virtually every town in India has at least one bangle shop with an extraordinary range, from colourful plastic and glass bracelets to brass and silver. Hyderabad is a centre for the making and selling of bangles made from lac, a resinous insect secretion, that are encrusted with colourful beads or stones.

Heavy folk-art silver jewellery can be bought in various parts of the country, as can chunky Tibetan jewellery made from silver (or white metal) and semiprecious stones. Many Tibetan pieces feature Buddhist motifs and text in Tibetan script, including the famous mantra *om mani padme hum* (hail to the jewel in the lotus). There's a huge industry in

India, Nepal and China making artificially aged Tibetan souvenirs. For creative types, loose beads of agate, turquoise, carnelian and silver are widely available.

Pearls are produced by most Indian seaside states, and they're a particular speciality of Hyderabad. You'll find them at most state emporiums across the country. Prices vary depending on the colour and shape: you pay more for pure white pearls or rare colours such as black, and perfectly round pearls are generally more expensive than misshapen or elongated pearls. A single strand of seeded pearls can cost as little as ₹500, but better-quality pearls start at around ₹1000.

Beware of scams involving buying jewels and reselling them overseas.

Leatherwork

As cows are sacred in India, leatherwork is made from buffalo, camels, goats or some other animal skin. Most large cities offer a smart range of modern leather footwear at very reasonable prices, some stitched with zillions of sparkly sequins – marvellous partywear! Jootis (traditional, often pointy-toed, slip-in shoes) from the northern states of Punjab and Rajasthan can be found in a number of South Indian shops.

Chappals, those wonderful (often curly-toed) leather sandals, are sold throughout India but are particularly good in the Maharashtrian cities of Kolhapur, Pune and Matheran.

Metalware

You'll find copper and brassware throughout India. Candle holders, trays, bowls, tankards and ashtrays are particularly popular buys.

In all Indian towns you can find *kadhai* (Indian woks, also known as *balti*) and other cookware for incredibly low prices. Beaten-brass pots are particularly attractive, while steel storage vessels, copper-bottomed cooking pans and steel thali trays are also popular souvenirs. Be sure to have your name engraved on them (free of charge)!

Bidri, a method of damascening where gunmetal (a zinc alloy) is inlaid with silver or other wire then rubbed with a dark paste containing soil from Bidar, Karnataka, is used to make jewellery, boxes and ornaments, especially in Bidar itself and Hyderabad.

Many Tibetan religious objects are created by inlaying silver in copper: prayer wheels, ceremonial horns and traditional document cases are all inexpensive buys.

The people of Bastar in Chhattisgarh use an iron-smelting technique similar to one discovered 35,000 years ago to create abstract sculptures of spindly animal and human figures. These are often also made into functional items such as lamp stands and coat racks, and can be found in tribal-crafts shops around India.

Musical Instruments

Quality Indian musical instruments are mostly available in the larger cities; prices vary according to the quality and sound of the instrument.

Decent tabla sets – a pair of hand drums comprising a wooden tabla (tuned treble drum) and a metal *dugi* or *bayan* (bass drum) – cost upwards of ₹5000. Cheaper sets are generally heavier and often sound inferior.

Sitars range in price from ₹5000 to ₹20,000 (possibly even more). The sound of each sitar will vary with the wood that is used and the shape of the gourd, so try a few. Note that some cheaper sitars can warp in colder or hotter climates. On any sitar, make sure that the strings ring clearly and check the gourd carefully for any damage.

THE GREAT INDIAN BAZAAR LEATHERWORK

Throughout South India you can find finely crafted gold and silver rings, anklets, earrings, toe rings, necklaces and bangles, and pieces can often be crafted to order.

Top Musical Instrument Shops

BX Furtado & Sons, Mumbai (Bombay; p77)

Sri Sharada Grand Musical Works, Mysore (Mysuru; p195)

Spare string sets, sitar plectrums and a screw-in 'amplifier' gourd are sensible additions.

Other popular instruments include the *shehnai* (Indian flute), the *sarod* (like an Indian lute), the harmonium and the *esraj* (similar to an upright violin). Conventional violins are great value – prices start at ₹3500.

Paintings

Reproductions of Indian miniature paintings are widely available, but the quality varies: the cheaper ones have less detail and are made with inferior materials. A bigger range of quality miniatures is generally found in northern India than in the south, but state-run craft emporiums and antique shops are always worth a browse.

In regions such as Kerala and Tamil Nadu, you'll come across miniature paintings on leaf skeletons that portray domestic life, rural scenes and deities. Tamil Nadu's Tanjore (or Thanjavur) paintings typically depict Hindu deities in bright colours with decoration of gold foil and glass beads, or occasionally gemstones. They may be done on canvas, wood or glass. Much of today's output is a somewhat kitschified version of a venerable tradition that goes back to the 17th century, but it's worth keeping an eye open for authentic old works in antique shops.

In Andhra Pradesh, *cheriyal* paintings, in bright, primary colours, were originally made as scrolls for travelling storytellers. The ancient textile-painting art of *kalamkari* is also practised in Andhra Pradesh (where Sri Kalahasti is the best place to see artists at work and buy their art), and at Chennai's Kalakshetra Foundation. It involves priming cotton cloth with resin and cow's milk, then drawing and painting deities or legendary or historic events with a pointed bamboo stick *(kalam)* dipped in fermented jaggery and water; the dyes are made from cow dung, ground seeds, plants and flowers. *Kalamkari* from Machilipatnam in Andhra Pradesh employs block-printing in combination with freehand drawing.

Tibetan craft shops often sell *thangkas* (rectangular Tibetan paintings on cloth) depicting Tantric Buddhist deities and ceremonial mandalas. Some re-create the glory of the murals in India's medieval gompas (Tibetan Buddhist monasteries); others are simpler. Bank on paying at least ₹4000 for a decent-quality *thangka* of A3 size, and a lot more (up to around ₹30,000) for large intricate *thangkas*.

India's bazaars are the heart and soul of its commercial life but they are not always markets in the sense you might expect: the name Bazar often refers to a street lined with shops and/or stalls rather than a separate area set aside for trading.

PUTTING YOUR MONEY WHERE IT COUNTS

Overall, a comparatively small proportion of the money brought to India by tourism reaches people in rural areas. Travellers can make a greater contribution by shopping at community cooperatives, set up to protect and promote traditional cottage industries, and provide education, training and a sustainable livelihood at the grassroots level. Many of these projects focus on low-caste women, tribal people, refugees and others living on society's fringes.

The quality of products sold at cooperatives is high and the prices are usually fixed, which means you won't have to haggle. A share of the sales money is channelled directly into social projects such as schools, health care, training and other advocacy programs for socially disadvantaged groups. Shopping at the national network of Khadi & Village Industries Commission emporiums, or the shops of Tribes India (www.tribesindia.com), the profits of which help support tribal artisans, will also contribute to rural communities.

Wherever you travel, keep your eyes peeled for fair-trade cooperatives.

GANDHI'S CLOTH

More than 80 years ago Mahatma Gandhi urged Indians to support the freedom movement by ditching their foreign-made clothing and turning to *khadi* – homespun cloth. *Khadi* became a symbol of Indian independence, and the fabric is still closely associated with politics. The government-run, nonprofit group Khadi & Village Industries Commission (www.kvic.org.in) serves to promote *khadi,* which is usually cotton, but can also be silk or wool.

Khadi outlets are simple, no-nonsense places where you can pick up genuine Indian clothing such as kurta pyjamas, headscarves, saris and, at some branches, assorted handicrafts – you'll find them all over India. Prices are reasonable and are often discounted in the period around Gandhi's birthday (2 October). A number of outlets also have a tailoring service.

India has a sizeable contemporary art scene, and major cities such as Chennai (Madras), Bengaluru (Bangalore) and Hyderabad have a number of independent galleries and shops selling work by local artists.

Textiles

Textile production is India's major industry and around 40% takes place at a village level, where it's known as *khadi* (homespun cloth, usually cotton) – hence the government-backed *khadi* emporiums around the country. These inexpensive superstores sell all sorts of items made from *khadi,* including the popular Nehru jackets and kurta pyjamas (long shirt and loose-fitting trousers), with sales benefiting rural communities. *Khadi* has recently become increasingly chic, with India's designers referencing the fabrics in their collections.

You'll find a truly amazing variety of weaving and embroidery techniques around India. In tourist centres such as Goa, Rajasthan and Himachal Pradesh, patterned textiles are made into popular items such as shoulder bags, wall hangings, cushion covers, bedspreads, clothes and much more; items from Adivasi (tribal) peoples of Telangana, Gujarat and Rajasthan often have small pieces of mirrored glass eye-catchingly embroidered on to them.

Shawls

Indian shawls are famously warm and lightweight – they're often better than the best down jackets. It's worth buying one to use as a blanket on cold night journeys. Shawls are made from all sorts of wool, and many are embroidered with intricate designs. The best-known varieties all come from northern regions but some of them make their way to outlets in the south, including Kashmiri *pashmina* shawls (made from the downy hair of the Pashmina goat) and subtly embroidered and mirrored lambswool shawls from Gujarat's Kachchh (Kutch) region. Authentic *pashmina* shawls cost several thousand rupees, though many '*pashminas*' are actually made from a *pashmina*-silk blend, which are cheaper at around ₹1200 but still often beautiful.

Saris

Saris are a very popular souvenir, especially given that they can be easily adapted to other purposes (from cushion covers to skirts). Real silk saris are the most expensive, and the silk usually needs to be washed

Many Indian tailor's shops can run up new items for you in the same day, and if you just want a copy of a favourite garment that you already have, they can do that too. Madurai's **Pudhu Mandapa** (p381) is a 16th-century temple pavilion filled with finely sculpted stone pillars and also with dozens of tailors busy treadling away at sewing machines for just this purpose.

before it becomes soft. The 'silk capital' of India is Kanchipuram in Tamil Nadu (Kanchipuram silk is also widely available in Chennai), but you can also find fine silk saris (and cheaper scarves) in other centres including Mysore. You'll pay upwards of ₹3000 for a quality embroidered silk sari.

Aurangabad, in Maharashtra, is the traditional centre for the production of Himroo shawls, sheets and saris, made from a blend of cotton, silk and silver thread. Silk and gold-thread saris produced at Paithan (near Aurangabad) are some of India's finest – prices range from around ₹7000 to a mind-blowing ₹300,000. Another region famous for sari production is Madhya Pradesh for its cotton Maheshwari saris (from Maheshwar) and silk Chanderi saris (from Chanderi).

Patan in Gujarat is the centre for the ancient and laborious craft of Patola-making. Every thread in these fine silk saris is individually hand-dyed before weaving, and patterned borders are woven with real gold.

Appliqué & Block Print

Appliqué, where decorative motifs are sewn on to a larger cloth, is an ancient art in India, with most states producing their own version, often featuring abstract or anthropomorphic patterns. The traditional lampshades and *pandals* (tents) used in weddings and festivals are usually produced using this technique.

Block-printed and woven textiles are produced, and sold by fabric shops, all over India: each region has its own speciality. Block-printing involves stamping the design on the fabric with carved wooden blocks – a laborious but highly skilled process that produces some beautiful results. The India-wide retail chain stores Fabindia (www.fabindia.com) and Anokhi (www.anokhi.com) strive to preserve traditional patterns and fabrics, transforming them into home-decor items and Indian- and Western-style fashions.

Woodcarving

Woodcarving is an ancient art form throughout India. Sandalwood carvings of Hindu deities are one of Karnataka's specialities, but you'll pay a king's ransom for the real thing – a 10cm-high Ganesh costs around ₹3000 in sandalwood, compared to roughly ₹300 in *kadamb* wood. However, the sandalwood will release fragrance for years. Beautiful deity figures and decorative inlaid boxes and furniture are carved from rosewood in Andhra Pradesh, Karnataka and Kerala.

Buddhist woodcarvings are a speciality of Tibetan refugee areas; they include wall plaques of the eight lucky signs, carved dragons and reproductions of *chaam* masks used for ritual dances.

Other Great Finds

It's little surprise that Indian spices are snapped up by tourists. Virtually all towns have shops and bazaars selling locally made spices at great prices. Karnataka, Kerala, Uttar Pradesh, Rajasthan and Tamil Nadu produce most of the spices that go into garam masala (the 'hot mix' used to flavour Indian dishes), while the Northeast States and Sikkim are known for black cardamom and cinnamon bark. Note that some countries, such as Australia, have stringent rules regarding the import of animal and plant products. Check with your country's embassy for details.

Attar (essential oil, mostly made from flowers) shops can be found around the country. Mysore in Karnataka is famous for its sandalwood oil, while Mumbai is a major centre for the trade of traditional fragrances, including valuable *oud,* made from a rare mould that grows on the bark of the agarwood tree. Tamil Nadu, Ooty and Kodaikanal produce aromatic and medicinal oils from herbs, flowers and eucalyptus.

Indian incense is exported worldwide, with Bengaluru and Mysore, both in Karnataka, being major producers. Incenses, as well as other products such as clothing, essential oils and perfumed candles, from Auroville in Tamil Nadu and Puducherry's Sri Aurobindo Ashram are also appealing and easy to come by locally.

A speciality of Goa is feni (liquor distilled from coconut milk or cashews): a head-spinning spirit that often comes in decorative bottles.

Quality Indian tea is sold in parts of South India, such as Munnar in Kerala and the Ooty area in Tamil Nadu's Western Ghats. There are also top tea retailers in urban hubs.

Fine-quality handmade paper – often fashioned into cards, boxes and notebooks – is worth seeking out. Puducherry (Pondicherry) and Mumbai are good places to start.

Indian cities have some pretty good bookshops, with books at very competitive prices, including leather-bound titles. Higginbothams in Chennai, in business since 1844, is India's oldest bookshop and is still going strong. Asian Educational Services publishes old (17th- to early-20th-century) and out-of-stock titles, in original typeface.

Indian Textiles, by John Gillow and Nicholas Barnard, explores the cultural background of India's many beautiful textile techniques, including weaving, block-printing, painting, tie-dye and embroidery, and looks in detail at the products of the different regions.

THE GREAT INDIAN BAZAAR OTHER GREAT FINDS

The Arts

Over the millennia India's many ethnic groups have spawned a rich artistic heritage, and today you'll experience art both lofty and humble around every corner: from intricately painted trucks on dusty roads to harmonic chanting from an ancient temple. The wealth of creative expression is a highlight of travelling here, and today's artists fuse ancient and modern influences to create works of art, dance, literature and music that are as evocative as they are beautiful.

Dance

Indian Classical Dance, by Leela Venkataraman and Avinash Pasricha, is a lavishly illustrated book covering various Indian dance forms, including *bharatanatyam*, Kuchipudi and Kathakali.

The ancient Indian art of dance is traditionally linked to mythology and classical literature. Dance can be divided into two main forms: classical and folk.

Classical

Classical dance is based on well-defined traditional disciplines. The following are some popular styles:

➡ *Bharatanatyam*, which originated in Tamil Nadu, has been embraced throughout India. Noted for its graceful movements, it was traditionally performed by solo women, but now often includes male dancers and/or group performances. Songs, poems, prayers and Carnatic music are part of a performance.

➡ *Kathak* has Hindu and Islamic influences and is prevalent in northern India.

➡ Kathakali, with its roots in Kerala, is a type of classical dance-drama with drum and vocal accompaniment, based on the Hindu epics.

➡ Kuchipudi is a 17th-century dance-drama that originated in the Andhra Pradesh village from which it takes its name. The story centres on the envious wife of Krishna.

➡ *Mohiniyattam*, the 'dance of the enchantress', is a graceful Keralan form performed by solo women.

Folk

Most big cities have venues staging regular classical dance or music performances, but Chennai (Madras) and Mumbai (Bombay) have the most frequent performances (almost nightly). Kochi is the best place to catch Kathakali performances.

Indian folk dance is widespread and varied, ranging from the theatrical dummy-horse dances of Karnataka and Tamil Nadu to Punjab's high-spirited bhangra dance. Northern Kerala's *theyyam* rituals feature wild drumming and frenzied dancing by participants embodying deities or heroes, with headdresses sometimes several metres high.

Pioneers of modern dance forms in India include Uday Shankar (older brother of the late sitar master, Ravi), who once partnered the Russian ballerina Anna Pavlova. The dance you'll most commonly see, though, is in films. Dance has featured in Indian movies since the dawn of 'talkies' and often combines traditional, folk, modern and contemporary choreography.

Music

Indian classical music traces its roots back to Vedic times, when religious poems chanted by priests were first collated in the Rig-Veda. Over the millennia classical music has been shaped by many influences, and the legacy today is Carnatic (characteristic of South India) and Hindustani (the classical style of North India) music. With common origins, they share a number of features. Composition and improvisation are both based on the raga (the melodic shape of the music) and the *tala* (the rhythmic metre characterised by the number of beats); *tintal,* for example, has a *tala* of 16 beats. The audience follows the *tala* by clapping at the appropriate beat, which in *tintal* is at beats one, five and 13. The ninth beat is the *khali* (empty section), which is indicated by a wave of the hand.

Both Carnatic and Hindustani music are performed by small ensembles, generally comprising three to six musicians, and both have many instruments in common. The most obvious difference is Carnatic's greater use of voice. Hindustani has been more heavily influenced by Persian musical conventions (a result of Mughal rule); Carnatic music, as it developed in South India, cleaves more closely to theory.

One of the best-known Indian instruments is the sitar (a large stringed instrument), with which the soloist plays the raga. Other stringed instruments include the sarod (which is plucked) and the sarangi (played with a bow). Also popular is the tabla (twin drums), which provides the *tala*. The drone, which runs on two basic notes, is provided by the oboelike *shehnai* or the stringed *tampura* (also spelt *tamboura*). The hand-pumped keyboard harmonium is used as a secondary melody instrument for vocal music.

Indian regional folk music is widespread and varied. Wandering musicians, magicians, snake charmers and storytellers often use song to entertain their audiences; the storyteller usually sings the tales from the great epics.

You may also possibly come across *qawwali* (Sufi devotional singing), performed in mosques or at musical concerts.

A completely different genre altogether, *filmi* (music from films) includes modern, slower-paced love serenades along with hyperactive dance songs.

Painting

South India's earliest art was painted on cave walls and reached its supreme expression around 1500 years ago when artists covered the walls and ceilings of the Ajanta Caves (p96), in Maharashtra, with scenes from the Buddha's past lives. The figures are endowed with an unusual freedom and grace. Later, painters also decorated the walls of temples and palaces, though little of this mural art has survived from before the time of the Vijayanagar empire (14th to 16th centuries), which left fine frescoes at Hampi's Virupaksha Temple (p212).

The Indo-Persian painting style, coupling geometric design with flowing form, developed in Islamic royal courts, with some indigenous influences. Persian influence blossomed when artisans fled to India

Get arty with *Indian Art*, by Roy C Craven, *Contemporary Indian Art: Other Realities*, edited by Yashodhara Dalmia, and *Indian Miniature Painting*, by Dr Daljeet and Professor PC Jain.

For a peep into the contemporary art scene, check out the Mumbai-based online auction house Saffronart (www.saffronart.com).

THE ARTS PAINTING

CLASSICAL DANCE & MUSIC FESTIVALS

➡ **Mumbai Sanskruti** (p45) January

➡ **Thyagaraja Aradhana** (p373) Thiruvaiyuru (Tamil Nadu), January

➡ **Natyanjali Dance Festival** (p368) Chidambaram, February/Mach

➡ **Elephanta Festival** (p45) Mumbai, March

➡ **Ellora Ajanta Aurangabad Festival** (p85) Aurangabad, November

➡ **Chennai Festival of Music & Dance** (p333) December/January

➡ **Mamallapuram Dance Festival** (p349) December/January

MEHNDI

Mehndi is the traditional art of painting a woman's hands (and sometimes feet) with intricate henna designs for auspicious ceremonies, such as marriage. If quality henna is used, the design, which is orange-brown, can last up to one month.

In touristy areas, *mehndi*-wallahs are adept at applying henna tattoo 'bands' on the arms, legs and lower back. If you get *mehndi* applied, allow at least a few hours for the design process and required drying time (during drying you can't use your hennaed hands).

It's wise to request the artist to do a 'test' spot on your arm before proceeding: some dyes contain chemicals that can cause allergies. (Avoid 'black henna', which is mixed with some chemicals that may be harmful.)

following the 1507 Uzbek attack on Herat (in present-day Afghanistan), and with trade and gift-swapping between Shiraz, a Persian centre for miniature production, and Indian provincial sultans. The most celebrated Indo-Persian art developed at the Mughal court in northern India from the mid-16th century, particularly under emperor Akbar (r 1556–1605), who recruited artists from far and wide. The Mughal style, often in colourful miniature form, largely depicts court life, architecture, battle and hunting scenes, as well as detailed portraits.

Miniature painting also flourished in the Deccan sultanates of the 16th and 17th centuries. The landscapes and floral backgrounds here reflect Persian influence, though Deccani in subject matter, while the elongated figures draw on Vijayanagar traditions. Colours are rich, with much use of gold and white.

Temple mural painting, on multifarious historical and mythological themes, continued to flourish in the south: there are fine Nayak-era frescoes at Thanjavur, Kumbakonam and Chidambaram. Superb Hindu-myth murals were painted at Kochi's Mattancherry Palace (p301) in the 16th century.

A unique local style known as Tanjore painting took root in Thanjavur from the 17th century, typically depicting Krishna and other Hindu deities in bright colours with rounded bodies and big eyes, against a background of thrones, curtains and arches which, along with the deities' clothing, are picked out in gold leaf studded with gemstones or glass beads. This tradition lives on today in a somewhat debased, kitsch form.

Kerala's Ravi Varma (1848–1906) popularised oil painting with colourful, European-style treatments of scenes from Indian mythology and literature, including depictions of Hindu goddesses modelled from South Indian women, and has had a huge influence on subsequent religious art and movie posters.

The Madras Movement, whose cooperative base you can visit at Cholamandal Artists' Village (p346) near Chennai, pioneered modern art in South India in the 1960s. In the 21st century, paintings by modern and contemporary Indian artists have been selling at record numbers (and prices) around the world. Delhi and Mumbai are India's contemporary-art centres, but there are worthwhile galleries in most large cities (check local papers for exhibition listings).

> The prolific writer and artist Rabindranath Tagore won the Nobel Prize in Literature in 1913 for *Gitanjali*. For a taste of Tagore's work, read *Selected Short Stories*.

> **Film Festivals**
>
> *Mumbai Film Festival (p45), October*
>
> *International Film Festival of India (p123), Panaji, Goa, November*

Cinema

India's film industry was born in the late 19th century – the first major Indian-made motion picture, *Panorama of Calcutta*, was screened in 1899. India's first real feature film, *Raja Harishchandra*, was made during the silent era in 1913 and it's ultimately from this film that Indian cinema traces its vibrant lineage.

Today, India's film industry is the biggest in the world. Mumbai, the Hindi-language film capital, aka 'Bollywood', is the biggest name, but India's other major film-producing cities – Chennai (Kollywood), Hyderabad (Tollywood) and Bengaluru (Sandalwood) – also have a huge output. Big-budget films are often partly or entirely shot abroad, with some countries vigorously wooing Indian production companies because of the spin-off tourism these films can generate.

Broadly speaking, there are two categories of Indian films. Most prominent is the mainstream 'masala' movie, named for its 'spice mix' of elements for every member of the family: romance, action, slapstick humour and moral themes. Three hours and still running, these often tear-jerking blockbusters are packed with dramatic twists interspersed with numerous song-and-dance performances. There's no explicit sex in Indian films made for the local market, and even kissing is rare. Instead, there is heaps of intense flirting and loaded innuendos, and heroines are often seen in skimpy or body-hugging attire.

The second Indian film genre is art house, also called parallel cinema, which adopts Indian 'reality' as its base and aims to be socially and politically relevant. Usually made on infinitely smaller budgets than their commercial cousins, these films are the ones that win kudos at global film festivals. The late Bengali director Satyajit Ray, most famous for his 1950s work, is the father of Indian art films.

Literature

India has a long tradition of Sanskrit literature, and works in the vernacular languages have also contributed to a particularly rich legacy. In fact, it's claimed there are as many literary traditions in India as there are written languages. The Tamil poetic works known as the Sangams, written between the 3rd century BC and 3rd century AD, are the earliest known South Indian literature.

Bengal is traditionally credited with producing some of India's finest literature, and Rabindranath Tagore (1861–1941) was the first Indian writer to really to propel India's cultural richness onto the world literary stage, through the fiction, plays and poetry he wrote in Bengali.

One of the earliest Indian authors to receive an international audience was RK Narayan, who wrote in English in the 1930s and whose deceptively simple writing about life in a fictional South Indian town called Malgudi is subtly hilarious. Keralan Kamala Das (aka Kamala Suraiyya) wrote poetry and memoirs in English; her frank approach to love and sexuality broke ground for women writers in the 1960s and '70s.

India has an ever-growing list of internationally acclaimed contemporary authors. Winners of the prestigious Man Booker Prize have included Chennai-bred Aravind Adiga (2008), for his debut novel *The White Tiger,* set between Bengaluru and northern India, and Kiran Desai (2006) for *The Inheritance of Loss.* Desai's mother Anita Desai has thrice made the Booker shortlist, as has Rohinton Mistry, a Mumbai-bred Parsi, with three novels all set in Mumbai. In 1997 Keralan Arundhati Roy won the Booker for *The God of Small Things,* set in a small Keralan town, while Mumbai-born Salman Rushdie took this coveted award in 1981 for *Midnight's Children.*

Around 2000 feature films are produced annually in India. Apart from hundreds of millions of local Bolly-, Tolly- and Kollywood buffs, there are also millions of Non-Resident Indian (NRI) fans, who have played a significant role in catapulting Indian cinema onto the international stage.

The top-earning Bollywood stars, all raking in over US$15 million a year for films and endorsements according to www.filmibeat.com, are Shahrukh Khan, Salman Khan, Amitabh Bachchan and Akshay Kumar.

Architectural Splendour

From looming temple gateways adorned with a rainbow of delicately carved deities to whitewashed cubelike village houses, South India has a fascinatingly rich architectural heritage. Traditional buildings, such as temples, often have a superb sense of placement within the local environment, whether perched on a boulder-strewn hill or standing on a lakeshore. British bungalows with corrugated-iron roofs and wide verandahs are a feature of many hill stations, but more memorable are the attempts to meld European and Indian architecture, such as the breathtaking Maharaja's Palace in Mysore.

Sacred Creations

Discover more about India's diverse temple architecture (in addition to other temple-related information) at Temple Net (www.templenet.com).

Throughout India, most early large-scale architecture was not built but excavated. Buddhist, Hindu and Jain temples, shrines and monasteries were carved out of solid rock or developed from existing caves at various times between the 3rd century BC and 10th century AD. The outstanding rock-cut architecture in the south includes awe-inspiring Ajanta (p96) and Ellora (p93) in Maharashtra, Mamallapuram (p347) in Tamil Nadu, Mumbai's Elephanta Caves (p59), Karnataka's Badami cave temples (p220), and the Andhra Pradesh Buddhist complex Guntupalli (p249).

It was during the Gupta period in North India (4th to 6th century AD) that the first free-standing temples were built, to enshrine Hindu deities. The Badami Chalukyas of Karnataka took up the idea at Aihole (p222) and Pattadakal (p222) between the 4th and 8th centuries, as did the Pallavas of Tamil Nadu at Kanchipuram (p352) and Mamallapuram (p347) in the 8th century. Towers called *vimanas* on some temples were equivalent to the *sikhara* towers of North Indian temples. The great 11th- and 12th-century Chola temples at Thanjavur and near Kumbakonam, with enormous *vimanas* rising above their central shrines, represent the apogee of early southern temple architecture. In many later southern temples, tall, sculpture-encrusted entrance towers called *gopurams* replaced the *vimana* as the main architectural feature. Madurai's Meenakshi Amman Temple (p381), with its 12 tall *gopurams,* is reckoned by many to be the peak of South Indian temple architecture. Also typical of what has become known as the Dravidian temple style is the *mandapa,* a pavilion of often richly carved columns that serves as a meeting hall or approach to the central shrine.

The basic elements of mosque layout are similar worldwide. A large hall is dedicated to communal prayer and within the hall is the mihrab, a niche indicating the direction of Mecca. Outside the prayer hall is often a courtyard with a pool or fountain for ritual pre-prayer ablutions. The faithful are called to prayer from minarets.

The Hoysala empire based in southern Karnataka in the 12th and 13th centuries developed a distinctive style of temples covered in elaborate, detailed carving, with relatively low *vimanas,* as seen at Belur, Halebid and Somnathpur. The 14th-to-16th-century Vijayanagar empire took the *gopuram* and *mandapa* to some of their finest levels not only at the capital, Hampi in Karnataka, but also at Vellore and Trichy's Sri Ranganathaswamy Temple (p375).

Muslim rule over much of northern India from the late 12th century, extending later to the Deccan, saw typical Islamic forms such as domes, arches and minaret towers coming to dominate monumental architecture. The 15th-century Bahmani Tombs (p225) at Bidar are among the earliest major Islamic monuments on the Deccan. They were followed by the great 16th- and 17th-century Qutb Shahi monuments (Tolichowki; p233) of Hyderabad and Golconda (magnificent big-domed royal tombs, a huge mosque and a unique mosque-cum-landmark, the Charminar) and Bijapur's wonderful 17th-century mausoleum, the Golgumbaz (p222) – the latter completed just a few years after Mughal architecture in northern India achieved its peak of perfection in the Taj Mahal.

Holy Squares & Purifying Waters

For Hindus, the square is a perfect shape, and southern temples often take the form of several square (or rectangular) compounds of diminishing size nested one inside another. Complex rules govern the location, design and building of a temple, based on numerology, astrology, astronomy and religious principles. Essentially, a temple represents a map of the universe. At the centre is the *garbhagriha* (inner sanctum), symbolic of the 'womb-cave' from which the universe is believed to have emerged. This provides a residence for the deity to which the temple is dedicated.

Temple tanks are another focal point of temple activity, used for ritual bathing and certain ceremonies, as well as adding aesthetic appeal. These often-vast reservoirs of water, sometimes fed by rain, sometimes by rivers (via complicated channelling systems), serve both sacred and secular purposes. The waters of some tanks are believed to have healing properties (physical and/or spiritual). Devotees (as well as travellers) may be required to wash their feet in a tank before entering a place of worship.

Forts & Palaces

The frequent wars between old Indian kingdoms and empires, as well as the later involvement of colonial powers, naturally led to the construction of some highly imposing fortresses. A typical South Indian fort is situated on a hill or rocky outcrop, with a ring or rings of moated battlements protecting the inner citadel. It usually has a town nestled at its base, which would have developed after the fortifications were built. Gingee (Senji; p358) in Tamil Nadu is a particularly good example. Vellore Fort, also in Tamil Nadu, is one of India's best-known moated forts, while Bidar (p225) and Bijapur in Karnataka and Golconda (Hyderabad) are home to great metropolitan forts.

Daulatabad (p92) in Maharashtra is another magnificent structure, with 5km of walls surrounding a hilltop fortress that is reached by passageways filled with ingenious defences, including spike-studded doors and false tunnels, which in times of war led either to a pit of boiling oil or to a crocodile-filled moat! Maharashtra's many other impressive forts include several built or used by the 17th-century Maratha hero Shivaji, including Raigad (p103) and Pratapgad (p116) forts. The 16th-century Janjira fort (p102), off the Maharashtrian coast, was built by descendants of African slaves and will blow you away with its 12m walls rising straight from the sea, brooding gateway and mighty bastions. Like Goa's almost as impressively situated 17th-century Fort Aguada, it was never conquered.

Few old palaces remain in South India, as conquerors often targeted these for destruction. The remains of the Vijayanagar royal complex at Hampi indicate local engineers weren't averse to using the sound structural techniques and fashions (such as domes and arches) of their Muslim adversaries, the Bahmanis. The remarkable palace of the Travancore maharajas at Padmanabhapuram (Tamil Nadu; p390) dates back to the 16th century and is Asia's largest wooden palace complex.

Masterpieces of Traditional Indian Architecture, by Satish Grover, and *Introduction to Indian Architecture*, by Bindia Thapar, Surat Kumar Manto and Suparna Bhalla, offer interesting insights into temple and other architecture.

You can get a good idea of the scarcely believable wealth of Hyderabad's former rulers, the nizams, from their **Chowmahalla** (p229) and **Falaknuma** (p236) palaces, the latter now a luxury hotel.

Indo-Saracenic, a conflation of assorted European, Islamic and Hindu architectural styles that blossomed all over India in the late 19th century, produced not just grandiose functional edifices such as Mumbai's Victoria (Chhatrapati Shivaji) Terminus (p47) railway station but also numerous flamboyant Indian royal palaces. The opulent diamond of the south is Mysore's marvellous Maharaja's Palace (p187), its interior a kaleidoscope of stained glass, mirrors and mosaic floors.

Tamil Nadu's Chettinadu region contains at least 10,000 mansions, some of them genuinely palatial, built by a community of traders who got very rich in the 19th century. Many are now abandoned, but some are maintained or restored and open to visitors; a few are fascinating hotels.

Wildlife & Landscape

The wildlife of South India is a fascinating melange of animals whose ancestors roamed Europe, Asia and the ancient southern supercontinent Gondwana, in a great mix of habitats from steamy mangrove forests and jungles to expansive plains and flower-filled hill-country meadows. The South Asian subcontinent is an ancient block of earth crust that arrived with a wealth of unique plants and animals when it collided with the Eurasian Plate an estimated 40 million years ago, after a journey of around 100 million years from Gondwana.

Wildlife

India is celebrated for its big, bold, eminent species: tigers, elephants, rhinos, leopards, bears and monkeys. But there is much, much more, including a mesmerising collection of colourful birds.

Signature Species

It's fortunate that Asian elephants – a thoroughly different species from the larger African elephant – are revered in Hindu custom and were able to be domesticated and put to work. Otherwise they may well have been hunted to extinction long ago, as they were in neighbouring China. Indian wild elephant numbers were estimated to be about 27,700 in 2007. Numbers are reckoned to have increased since then despite poaching and habitat destruction. These 3000kg animals migrate long distances in search of food and require huge parks, running into predictable conflict when herds attempt to follow ancestral paths that are now occupied by villages and farms. Be mindful that the purchase of ivory souvenirs supports the poaching of these magnificent creatures, and many countries have strict customs guidelines preventing the importation of ivory products.

The tiger is fixed in the subcontinent's subconscious as the mythological mount of the powerful, demon-slaying goddess Durga, while prowling the west's imagination of India as Mowgli's jungle nemesis. This awesome, iconic animal is endangered but its numbers seem to be on the rise and it can be seen, if you're lucky, at tiger reserves around the country.

India is also home to 15 other species of cat. Leopards are quite widespread in different types of forest and in several parks and sanctuaries in the south – but elusive to spot, nevertheless. In recent decades some leopards have increasingly been found close to some of India's ever-expanding towns and cities, where they prey on dogs, cats and rodents (with the occasional human fatality too).

Adaptation the Key to Success

Easily the most abundant forms of wildlife you'll see in India are deer (nine species), antelope (six species), goats and sheep (10 species), and primates (15 species). The ones you'll most likely see in the parks and reserves of the south include the chital (spotted deer), sambar (a large deer), nilgai or bluebull (a large antelope), the elegant grey (hanuman) langur with its characteristic black face and ears, and the bonnet

India harbours some of the richest biodiversity in the world. There are around 400 species of mammals, 1250 of birds, 500 of reptiles, 340 of amphibians and 3000 of fish – nearly 7% of the earth's animal species on just 2.5% of its land, also inhabited by 18% of the planet's human population.

India's national animal is the tiger, its national bird is the peacock and its national flower is the lotus.

macaque which often loiters around temples and tourist sites. Also fairly often seen are the gaur (Indian bison) and wild boar; you can also hope to see the occasional sloth bear, with its long white snout, or giant squirrel.

Endangered Species

Despite its amazing biodiversity, India faces a growing challenge from its exploding human population. Wildlife is severely threatened by poaching and habitat loss. The 2013 Red List of the International Union for Conservation of Nature listed 973 threatened species in India, including 325 plants, 95 mammals, 80 birds, 52 reptiles, 74 amphibians, 213 fish and 134 invertebrates. Of these, 132 species are in the most at-risk category, 'critically endangered', and 310 are in the next-most imperilled group, 'endangered'.

Even the massively resourced National Tiger Conservation Authority faces an uphill battle every day. Even though the number of tiger reserves is growing, the total amount of territory roamed by tigers is shrinking. And every good news story seems to be followed by another story of poaching gangs or tiger or leopard attacks on villagers. The Wildlife Protection Society of India documented nearly 1000 tigers and nearly 4000 leopards killed by poachers between 1994 and 2013, and warns that total numbers may be far higher.

Critically endangered animals found in South India include the great Indian bustard, a large, heavy bird of which perhaps only 250 survive in isolated pockets of South and North India; the Anamalai flying frog (living only in Anamalai Tiger Reserve); the Malabar large-spotted civet (less than 250 in the Western Ghats); and four species of vulture. The story of India's vultures is perhaps the most devastating of all – especially that of the white-rumped vulture, which in the 1980s numbered around 80 million and was the world's most abundant vulture. Today white-rumped vultures number no more than several thousand – a near-annihilation blamed on the veterinary chemical diclofenac, which causes kidney failure in birds that eat the carcasses of cattle that have been treated with it. The absence of vultures has led to a rise in the number of disease-spreading feral dogs, feeding on carcasses that would formerly have been picked clean by the birds.

India has 238 species of snake, of which about 50 are poisonous. Of the various species of cobra, the king cobra is the world's largest venomous snake, attaining a length of 5m!

PROJECT TIGER

When naturalist Jim Corbett first raised the alarm in the 1930s, no one believed that tigers would ever be threatened. At the time it was believed there were 40,000 tigers in India, although no one had ever counted them. Then came Independence, which put guns into the hands of villagers who pushed into formerly off-limits hunting reserves seeking highly profitable tiger skins. By the time an official census was conducted in 1972, there were only an estimated 1800 tigers left and international outcry prompted Indira Gandhi to set up Project Tiger. The project has since established 47 tiger reserves totalling 67,676 sq km (including buffer zones) that not only protect this top predator but all animals that live in the same habitats. After an initial round of successes, neglect, corruption and relentless poaching – spurred by the international skin trade and demand for tiger parts in Chinese traditional medicine – saw tiger numbers down to just 1411 in 2006, the first year a relatively reliable counting system based on camera traps was used. That year, Project Tiger was transformed into the National Tiger Conservation Authority (http://projecttiger.nic.in, www.tigernet.nic.in), a statutory body with a bigger budget, more staff on the ground, and more teeth to fight poaching and the trade in tiger parts. Tiger numbers rose to 1706 in the 2010 census and 2226 in the 2014 census – encouraging statistics, but tigers continue to be poached and their habitat outside tiger reserves is shrinking. India's tigers account for around 70% of the total world tiger population.

Species of South India on the 'endangered' list include the tiger; elephant; dhole (wild dog; around 2500 surviving); the lion-tailed macaque, with its splendid silvery-white mane (3000 to 3500 remaining); and the Nilgiri tahr, a wild sheep of the Nilgiri hills.

Birds

With over 1250 highly varied species (925 of which breed here), India is a birdwatcher's dream. Wherever critical habitat has been preserved in the midst of dense human activity you might see phenomenal numbers of birds in one location. Winter can be a particularly good time, as wetlands host northern migrants arriving to kick back in the subtropical warmth of the Indian peninsula. Bird sanctuaries are generally the best places to head for intensive birdwatching, but many other protected areas also have vast avian variety.

Plants

India was once almost entirely covered in forest; now its total forest cover is estimated at around 20% – but the country still boasts over 45,000 documented plant species, over 4000 of them endemic.

Nearly all of India's lowland forests are types of tropical forest, with native sal forests forming the mainstay of the timber industry. Some of these tropical forests are true rainforest, staying green year-round, such as in the Western Ghats and in the northeast states, but most forests are deciduous, losing their canopies during the hot, dry months of April and May.

High-value trees such as Indian rosewood, Malabar kino and teak have been virtually cleared from the Western Ghats, and sandalwood is endangered across India due to illegal logging for the incense and woodcarving industries. A bigger threat on forested lands is firewood harvesting, often carried out by landless peasants squatting on government land.

Several Indian trees have significant religious value, including the huge silk-cotton tree, with its spiny bark and large red flowers under which Pitamaha (Brahma), the creator of the world, sat after his labours. Two well-known figs, the banyan and peepal, grow to immense size by dangling roots from their branches and fusing into massive jungles of trunks and stems. It is said that the Buddha achieved enlightenment while sitting under a peepal (also known as the Bodhi tree).

Parks, Sanctuaries & Reserves

Before 1972 India had only five national parks. That year, the Wildlife Protection Act was introduced to set aside national parks and stem the abuse of wildlife. The act was followed by a string of similar pieces of legislation with bold ambitions but often too few teeth with which to enforce them.

India now has over 100 national parks and 500 wildlife sanctuaries, covering around 5% of its territory. There are also 47 tiger reserves and 18 biosphere reserves (designed to protect ecosystems and biodiversity while permitting human activities), often overlapping with other protected areas. Many contiguous parks, reserves and sanctuaries in the highly biodiverse Western Ghats provide valuable migration corridors for wildlife.

One consequence of creating protected areas has been that about 1.6 million Adivasis (tribal people) and other forest-dwellers have had to leave their traditional lands. Many were resettled into villages and forced to abandon their age-old ways of life. The Forest Rights Act of 2006 forbids the displacement of forest-dwellers from national parks (except in

Online Resources

Wildlife, conservation and environment awareness-raising at www.sanctuaryasia.com

Wildlife Trust of India news at www.wti.org.in

Top birdwatching information at www.birding.in

Around 2000 plant species are described in ayurveda (traditional Indian herbal medicine) texts.

WILDLIFE & LANDSCAPE PARKS, SANCTUARIES & RESERVES

TOP PARKS FOR...

Tigers

Maharashtra's **Tadoba-Andhari Tiger Reserve** (p101) and **Pench Tiger Reserve** (www.penchnationalpark.com; Indian/foreigner ₹1250/2450, jeep ₹200, guide ₹300; ⊙16 Oct-30 Jun, closed Wed evenings) in Madhya Pradesh (easily accessed from Nagpur) are among India's top spots for tiger sightings. Chances are slimmer, but not negligible, in Karnataka's **Nagarhole** (p199) and **Bandipur** (p197) national parks, and Kerala's **Periyar Wildlife Sanctuary** (p290).

Elephants

The best parks for elephant spotting in South India include **Nagarhole National Park** (p199), **Wayanad Wildlife Sanctuary** (p317) (Kerala), and **Mudumalai Tiger Reserve** (p406) (Tamil Nadu).

Birds

Kerala's **Kumarakom Bird Sanctuary** (p289) and Tamil Nadu's **Vedanthangal Bird Sanctuary** (p352) are top spots for migratory water birds between November and February. **Thattekkad Bird Sanctuary** (p297) in Kerala is home to 320 mainly forest species.

Other Wildlife

➡ **Parambikulam Wildlife Sanctuary** (p298)

➡ **Neyyar Wildlife Sanctuary** (p270)

➡ **Mudumalai Tiger Reserve** (p406)

➡ **Daroji Sloth Bear Sanctuary** (p219)

so-called 'critical wildlife habitat'), and should protect the four million or so people who still live in them.

Visiting Protected Areas

Many parks, sanctuaries and reserves encourage visitors and your visit adds momentum to efforts to protect India's natural resources. The experience of watching an elephant, sloth bear or even, if you're lucky, a leopard or tiger, in the wild will stay with you for a lifetime. The best parks and reserves take a bit of reaching, but usually have a range of accommodation – from comfortable lodges to tree huts – inside or just outside the park. In some parks, guided hikes and 4WD safaris are available, while others may offer only cursory minibus tours. Independent operators offer 4WD safaris or guided treks on some parks' fringes, which can be just as wildlife-rich as the park itself. Unguided hiking within parks is generally not allowed for safety reasons.

The monsoon months (June to August in most places) are generally the least favourable for visits, and during holiday periods parks and their accommodation can overflow with visitors. A few parks close during the ultradry and hot couple of premonsoon months, though this can be the best time to view wildlife, as the cover is thinner and animals seek out scarce waterholes.

The contiguous Bandipur, Nagarhole, Wayanad and Mudumalai protected areas in the Western Ghats are home to 570 tigers according to the 2014 tiger census – the largest single tiger population in India.

The Lie of the Land

The Himalaya, the world's highest mountains, form an almost impregnable barrier separating India from its northern neighbours (India's highest peak, Khangchendzonga, reaches 8598m). The Himalaya were formed when the Indian subcontinent, after a 100-million-year northward drift from Gondwana, slammed slowly into the Eurasian continent, buckling the ancient sea floor upward.

South of the Himalaya, the floodplains of the Indus and Ganges Rivers form the fertile heartland of North India. To their south, the elevated Deccan plateau forms the core of India's triangular southern peninsula. The Deccan is bounded by the hills of the Western and Eastern Ghats. The Western Ghats, stretching from north of Mumbai almost to India's southern tip, drop sharply down to a narrow coastal lowland, forming a luxuriant slope of rainforest. Their highest peak is Anamudi (2695m) in Kerala. With many endemic species, they are a world biodiversity hot spot and 39 areas of the Western Ghats were inscribed on the World Heritage list in 2012 for their natural values. The lower Eastern Ghats stretch from West Bengal to south-central Tamil Nadu, and are cut by the four major rivers of peninsular India, flowing west to east across the Deccan: the Mahanadi, Godavari, Krishna and Cauvery.

Offshore are a series of island groups, politically part of India but geographically linked to the land masses of Southeast Asia and islands of the Indian Ocean. The 572 Andaman and Nicobar Islands, far out in the Andaman Sea, are the peaks of a submerged mountain range extending almost 1000km between Myanmar (Burma) and Sumatra. The coral atolls of Lakshadweep, 300km west of Kerala, are a northerly extension of the Maldives islands.

Environmental Issues

With a population expected to reach 1.3 billion in 2016, ever-expanding industrial and urban centres, and growth in chemical-intensive farming, India's environment is under tremendous pressure. An estimated 65% of the land is degraded in some way. Many current problems are a direct result of the Green Revolution of the 1960s, when chemical fertilisers and pesticides enabled huge growth in agricultural output, at enormous cost to the environment.

Despite numerous environmental laws, corruption has exacerbated environmental degradation – exemplified by flagrant flouting of laws by companies involved in hydroelectricity and mining. Usually, the people most affected are low-caste rural farmers and Adivasis (tribal people).

Agricultural production has been reduced by soil degradation from overfarming, rising soil salinity, loss of tree cover and poor irrigation. The human cost is heart-rending, and India constantly grapples with the dilemma of how to develop economically without destroying what's left of its environment. Narendra Modi, elected prime minister in 2014, has offered mixed signals about his priorities. On one hand, Modi has made it his personal mission to clean the appallingly polluted Ganges River by 2019, has launched the much-publicised Swachh Bharat campaign to reduce trash pollution nationwide, and supports large-scale solar-power generation. But his government has also pledged to increase domestic coal mining and double coal use, adding significantly to India's greenhouse gas emissions.

As anywhere, tourists tread a fine line between providing an incentive for change and making the problem worse. Many of Goa's environmental problems, for example, are the direct result of irresponsible development for tourism.

Climate Change

Changing climate patterns, linked to global carbon emissions, have been creating dangerous extremes of weather in India. While India's per capita carbon emissions still rank far behind those of the West and China, its sheer size of population makes it the world's third-largest carbon-dioxide emitter.

Get the inside track on Indian environmental issues at Down to Earth (www.downtoearth.org.in), an online magazine that delves into stories overlooked by mainstream media.

Air pollution in many Indian cities has been measured at more than double the maximum safe level recommended by the World Health Organization.

It has been estimated that by 2030 India will see a 30% increase in the severity of its floods and droughts. Islands in the Lakshadweep group, as well as the low-lying Ganges delta, are being inundated by rising sea levels.

Deforestation

Since Independence, over 50,000 sq km of India's forests have been cleared for logging and farming, or destroyed by urban expansion, mining, industrialisation and river dams. The number of mangrove forests has halved since the early 1990s, reducing the nursery grounds for the fish that stock the Indian Ocean and Bay of Bengal.

India's first Five Year Plan in 1951 recognised the importance of forests for soil conservation, and various policies have been introduced to increase forest cover. Almost all have been flouted by officials or criminals and by ordinary people clearing forests for firewood and grazing.

Water Resources

Arguably the biggest threat to public health in India is inadequate access to clean drinking water and proper sanitation. With the population continuing to grow, agricultural, industrial and domestic water usage are all expected to spiral. Sewage treatment facilities can handle only about a quarter of waste water produced. Many cities dump untreated sewage and partially cremated bodies directly into rivers, while open defecation is a simple fact of life, practised by over 600 million people according to a 2010 UN report.

Rivers are also affected by run-off, industrial pollution and sewage contamination. At least 70% of the freshwater sources in India are now polluted in some way.

Since 1947 an estimated 35 million people in India have been displaced by major dams, mostly built to provide hydro-electricity for the nation. Valleys across India are being sacrificed to create new power plants, and displaced people rarely receive adequate compensation.

Survival Guide

Scams

India has a deserved reputation for scams. Of course, most can be easily avoided with a little common sense and an appropriate amount of caution. Scams tend to be more of a problem in the big cities of arrival (such as Delhi or Mumbai), or very touristy spots (such as Rajasthan), though in Goa and Kerala they are rare. Chat with fellow travellers to keep abreast of the latest cons. Look at the India branch of Lonely Planet's Thorn Tree Travel Forum (www.lonelyplanet.com/thorntree), where travellers post warnings about problems they have encountered on the road.

Contaminated Food & Drink

➡ The late 1990s saw a scam in North India where travellers died after consuming food laced with dangerous bacteria from restaurants linked to dodgy medical clinics; we've heard no recent reports but the scam could resurface. In unrelated incidents, some clinics have also given more treatment than necessary to procure larger payments.

➡ Most bottled water is legit, but ensure the seal is intact and the bottom of the bottle hasn't been tampered with. While in transit, try to carry packed food. If you eat at bus or train stations, buy cooked food only from fast-moving places.

Credit-Card Con

Be careful when paying for souvenirs with a credit card. While government shops are usually legitimate, private souvenir shops have been known to run off extra copies of the credit-card imprint slip and use them for phoney transactions later. Ask the trader to process the transaction in front of you. Memorising the CVV/CVC2 number and scratching it off the card is also a good idea, to avoid misuse. In some restaurants, waiters will ask you for your PIN with the intention of taking your credit card to the machine – never give your PIN to anyone, and ask to use the machine in person.

Druggings

Occasionally, tourists (especially solo travellers) are drugged and robbed during train or bus journeys. A spiked drink is the most commonly used method for sending them off to sleep – chocolates, chai from a co-conspiring vendor and 'homemade' Indian food are also known to be used. Use your instincts, and if you're unsure, politely decline drinks or food offered by strangers.

Gem Scams

This classic scam involves charming con artists who promise foolproof 'get rich quick' schemes. Travellers are asked to carry or mail gems home and then sell them to the trader's (nonexistent) overseas representatives at a profit. Without exception, the goods – if they arrive at all – are worth a fraction of what you paid, and the 'representatives' never materialise.

KEEPING SAFE

➡ A good travel-insurance policy is essential.

➡ Email copies of your passport identity page, visa and airline tickets to yourself, and keep copies on you.

➡ Keep your money and passport in a concealed money belt or a secure place under your shirt.

➡ Store at least US$100 separately from your main stash.

➡ Don't publicly display large wads of cash when paying for services or checking into hotels.

➡ If you can't lock your hotel room securely from the inside, stay somewhere else.

Don't believe hard-luck stories about an inability to obtain an export licence, or the testimonials they show you from other travellers – they are fake. Travellers have reported this con happening in Agra, Delhi, and Jaisalmer among other places, but it's particularly prevalent in Jaipur. Carpets, curios and *pashminas* are other favourites for this con.

Overpricing

Always agree on prices beforehand while availing services that don't have regulated tariffs. This particularly applies to friendly neighbourhood guides, snack bars at places of touristy interest, and autorickshaws and taxis without meters.

Photography

Use your instincts (better still, ask for permission) while photographing people. The common argument – sometimes voiced after you've snapped your photos – is you're going to sell them to glossy international magazines, so it's only fair that you pay a fee.

Theft

Theft is a risk in India, as anywhere else. Keep luggage locked and chained on buses and trains. Remember that snatchings often occur when a train is pulling out of the station, as it's too late for you to give chase.

Touts & Commission Agents

→ Touts come in many avatars and operate in mysterious ways. Cabbies and autorickshaw drivers will often try to coerce you to stay at a budget hotel of their choice, only to collect a commission (included within your room tariff) from the receptionists afterward.

→ Wherever possible, arrange hotel bookings (if only for

OTHER TOP SCAMS

→ Gunk (dirt, paint, poo) suddenly appears on your shoes, only for a shoe cleaner to magically appear and offer to clean it off – for a price.

→ Some shops are selling overpriced SIM cards and not activating them; it's best to buy your SIM from an official shop (Airtel, Vodafone etc) and check it works before leaving the area (activation can take 24 hours).

→ Shops and restaurants 'borrow' the name of their more successful and popular competitor.

→ Touts claim to be 'government-approved' guides or agents, and sting you for large sums of cash. Enquire at the local tourist office about licensed guides and ask to see identification from guides themselves.

→ Artificial 'tourist offices' that are actually dodgy travel agencies whose aim is to sell you overpriced tours, tickets and tourist services.

the first night), and request a hotel pick-up. You'll often hear stories about hotels of your choice being 'full' or 'closed' – check things out yourself. Reconfirm and double-check your booking the day before you arrive.

→ Be very sceptical of phrases like 'my brother's shop' and 'special deal at my friend's place'. Many fraudsters operate in collusion with souvenir stalls, so be careful while making expensive purchases in private stores.

→ Avoid friendly people and 'officials' in train and bus stations who offer unsolicited help, then guide you to a commission-paying travel agent. Look confident, and if anyone asks if this is your first trip to India, say you've been here several times, even if you haven't. Telling touts that you have already prepaid your transfer/tour/onward journey may help dissuade them.

Transport Scams

→ Upon arriving at train stations and airports, if you haven't prearranged pick-up, book transport from government-approved booths. All major airports now have radio cab, prepaid taxi and

airport shuttle bus counters in the arrival lounge. Never go with a loitering cabbie who offers you a cheap ride into town, especially at night.

→ While booking multiday sightseeing tours, stick to itineraries offered by tourism departments, or those that come recommended either in this guidebook or by friends who've personally used them. Be extremely wary of anyone in Delhi offering houseboat tours to Kashmir – we've received many complaints over the years about dodgy deals.

→ When buying a bus, train or plane ticket anywhere other than the registered office of the transport company, make sure you're getting the ticket class you paid for. Use official online booking facilities where possible.

→ Some tricksters pose as Indian Railways officials and insist you pay to have your e-ticket validated on the platform; ignore them.

→ Train station touts (even in uniform or with 'official' badges) may tell you that your intended train is cancelled/flooded/broken down or that your ticket is invalid. Do not respond to any 'official' approaches at train stations.

Women & Solo Travellers

There are extra considerations for women and solo travellers when visiting India – from cost to safety. As with anywhere else in the world, it pays to be prepared.

Women Travellers

Although Bollywood might suggest otherwise, India remains a conservative society. Female travellers should be aware that their behaviour and attire choice are likely to be under constant scrutiny.

Unwanted Attention

Unwanted attention from men is a common problem.

➡ Be prepared to be stared at; it's something you'll simply have to live with, so don't allow it to get the better of you.

➡ Refrain from returning male stares; this can be considered encouragement.

➡ Dark glasses, phones, books or electronic tablets are useful props for averting unwanted conversations.

Clothing

Avoiding culturally inappropriate clothing will help avert undesirable attention.

➡ Steer clear of sleeveless tops, shorts, short skirts (ankle-length skirts are recommended) and anything else that's skimpy, see-through or tight-fitting.

➡ Wearing Indian-style clothes is viewed favourably.

➡ Draping a dupatta (long scarf) over T-shirts is another good way to avoid stares – it's shorthand for modesty, and also handy if you visit a shrine that requires your head to be covered.

➡ Wearing a salwar kameez (traditional dresslike tunic and trousers) will help you blend in; a smart alternative is a kurta (long shirt) worn over jeans or trousers.

➡ Avoid going out in public wearing a choli (sari blouse) or a sari petticoat (which some foreign women mistake for a skirt); it's like strutting around half-dressed.

➡ Aside from at pools, many Indian women wear long shorts and a T-shirt when swimming in public view; it's wise to wear a sarong from the beach to your hotel.

Health & Hygiene

➡ Sanitary pads are widely available but tampons are usually restricted to pharmacies in big cities and tourist towns (even then, the choice may be limited). Carry additional stocks for travel off the beaten track.

Sexual Harassment

Many female travellers have reported some form of sexual harassment while in India, such as lewd comments, invasion of privacy and even groping. Serious sexual assaults do happen but are rare; follow similar safety precautions as you would at home.

➡ Women travellers have experienced provocative gestures, jeering, getting 'accidentally' bumped into on the street and being followed.

➡ Incidents are common at exuberant (and crowded) public events such as the Holi festival. If a crowd is gathering, make yourself scarce or find a safer place overlooking the event so that you're away from wandering hands.

➡ Women travelling with a male partner will receive far less hassle.

Staying Safe

The following tips will help you avoid uncomfortable or dangerous situations during your journey:

➡ Always be aware of your surroundings. If it feels wrong, trust your instincts. Tread with care. Don't be scared, but don't be reckless either.

➡ If travelling after 9pm, use a recommended, registered taxi service.

➡ Don't organise your travel in such a way that means you're hanging out at bus/train stations or arriving late at night. Arrive in towns before dark.

➡ Keep conversations with unknown men short – getting involved in an inane conversation with someone you barely know can be misinterpreted as a sign of sexual interest.

→ Some women wear a pseudo wedding ring, or announce early on in the conversation that they're married or engaged (regardless of the reality).

→ If you feel that a guy is encroaching on your space, he probably is. A firm request to keep away usually does the trick, especially if your tone is loud and curt enough to draw the attention of passers-by.

→ The silent treatment can also be very effective.

→ Follow local women's cues and instead of shaking hands say *namaste* – the traditional, respectful Hindu greeting.

→ Avoid wearing expensive-looking jewellery and carrying flashy accessories.

→ Check the reputation of any teacher or therapist before going to a solo session (get recommendations from travellers). Some women have reported being molested by masseurs and other therapists. If you feel uneasy at any time, leave.

→ Female filmgoers may attract less attention and lessen the chances of harassment by going to the cinema with a companion.

→ Lone women may want to invest in a good-quality hotel in a better neighbourhood.

→ At hotels keep your door locked, as staff (particularly at budget and midrange places) can knock and walk in without waiting for your permission.

→ Avoid wandering alone in isolated areas even during daylight. Steer clear of gallis (narrow lanes) and deserted roads.

→ When on rickshaws alone, call/text someone, or pretend to, to indicate someone knows where you are.

→ Act confidently in public; to avoid looking lost (and thus more vulnerable) consult maps at your hotel (or at a restaurant) rather than on the street.

Taxis & Public Transport

Being female has some advantages; women can usually queue-jump for buses and trains without consequence and on trains there are special ladies-only carriages. There are also women-only waiting rooms at some stations.

→ Solo women should prearrange an airport pick-up from their hotel, especially if their flight is scheduled to arrive after dark.

→ Delhi and some other cities have licensed prepaid radio cab services such as Easycabs – they're more expensive than the regular prepaid taxis, but promote themselves as being safe, with drivers who have been vetted as part of their recruitment.

→ If you do catch a regular prepaid taxi, make a point of writing down the registration and driver's name – in front of the driver – and giving it to one of the airport police.

→ Avoid taking taxis alone late at night and never agree to have more than one man (the driver) in the car – ignore claims that this is 'just my brother' etc.

→ Solo women have reported less hassle by choosing more expensive classes on trains.

→ If you're travelling overnight in a three-tier carriage, try to get the uppermost berth, which will give you more privacy (and distance from potential gropers).

→ On public transport, don't hesitate to return any errant limbs, put an item of luggage between you and others, be vocal (attracting public attention, thus shaming the pest), or simply find a new spot.

Solo Travellers

One of the joys of travelling solo in India is that you're more likely to be 'adopted' by families, especially if you're commuting together on a long rail journey. It's a great opportunity to make friends and get a deeper understanding of local culture. If you're keen to hook up with fellow travellers, tourist hubs such as Goa, Rajasthan, Kerala, Manali, McLeod Ganj, Leh, Agra and Varanasi are some popular places to do so. You may also be able to find travel companions on Lonely Planet's **Thorn Tree Travel Forum** (www.lonelyplanet. com/thorntree).

Cost

The most significant issue facing solo travellers is cost.

→ Single-room accommodation rates are sometimes not much lower than double rates.

→ Some midrange and top-end places don't even offer a single tariff.

→ It's always worth trying to negotiate a lower rate for single occupancy.

Safety

Most solo travellers experience no major problems in India but, like anywhere else, it's wise to stay on your toes in unfamiliar surroundings.

→ Some less honourable souls (locals and travellers alike) view lone tourists as an easy target for theft and sexual assault.

→ Single men wandering around isolated areas have been mugged, even during the day.

Transport

→ You'll save money if you find others to share taxis and autorickshaws, as well as when hiring a car for longer trips.

→ Solo bus travellers may be able to get the 'co-pilot' (near the driver) seat on buses, which not only has a good view out front, but is also handy if you've got a big bag.

Directory A–Z

Accommodation

Accommodation in South India ranges from backpacker hostels with concrete floors and cold 'bucket' showers to opulent heritage hotels.

Categories

As a general rule, budget ($) covers everything from basic hostels, hotels and guesthouses in urban areas to traditional homestays in villages. Midrange hotels ($$) tend to have larger, cleaner rooms, usually with air-conditioning, and are more likely to have restaurants. Top-end places ($$$) stretch from luxury chain hotels to gorgeous heritage palaces and resorts.

Costs

Costs vary widely: highest in large cities, especially Mumbai (Bombay), and lowest in small cities and rural areas. Costs are also highly seasonal – hotel prices can drop by 20% to 50% outside peak season. Most establishments raise tariffs annually, so the prices may have risen by the time you read this.

BOOK YOUR STAY ONLINE

For more accommodation reviews by Lonely Planet authors, check out www.lonelyplanet.com/india/hotels. You'll find independent reviews, as well as recommendations on the best places to stay. Best of all, you can book online.

Reservations

➡ It's a good idea to book ahead, online or by phone, especially when travelling to more popular destinations. Some hotels require a credit-card deposit at the time of booking.

➡ Some budget options won't take reservations as they don't know when people are going to check out; call ahead or just turn up around check-in time.

➡ Other places may want a deposit at check-in – ask for a receipt and be wary of any request to sign a blank impression of your credit card. If the hotel insists, pay cash and get a receipt.

➡ Verify the check-out time when you check in – some hotels have a fixed check-out time (usually 10am or noon), while others offer 24-hour check-out (you have the room for 24 hours from the time you check in). Sometimes you can request to check in early and the hotel will oblige if the room is empty.

Seasons

➡ High season usually coincides with the best weather for the area's sights and activities – normally spring in the hills (April to June), and the cooler months in the lowlands (around November to February).

➡ In areas popular with tourists, there's an additional peak period over Christmas and New Year; make reservations well in advance.

➡ At other times you may find big discounts; if the hotel seems quiet, ask for one.

➡ Some hotels in places like Goa close during the monsoon period.

➡ Many temple towns have additional peak seasons around major festivals and pilgrimages.

Taxes & Service Charges

➡ State governments slap a variety of taxes on hotel accommodation (except at the cheaper hotels), and these are added to the cost of your room.

➡ Taxes vary from state to state and rates can vary according to room price, with higher taxes for more expensive rooms.

➡ Some upmarket hotels and restaurants also add a 'service charge' (usually around 10%).

➡ Rates we quote include taxes unless noted.

Accommodation Types

BUDGET & MIDRANGE HOTELS

➡ Sometimes you'll get lucky and find these in atmospheric old houses or heritage buildings, but the majority of budget and midrange hotels are modern-style concrete blocks with varying degrees of comfort. Some are charming, clean and good value; others less so.

➡ Room quality can vary considerably within a hotel so try to inspect a few rooms first. Many places have a range of prices for rooms of different quality. Avoid carpeted rooms at cheaper hotels unless you like the smell of mouldy socks.

➡ Shared bathrooms (often with squat toilets) are usually only found at the cheapest lodgings.

➡ Most rooms have ceiling fans and better rooms have mosquito-screened windows, though cheaper rooms may lack windows altogether.

➡ If you're mostly staying in budget places, bring your own sheet or sleeping-bag liner. Sheets and bedcovers at cheap hotels can be stained, well worn and in need of a wash. You may also have to provide your own towel, toilet paper and soap.

➡ Insect repellent and a torch (flashlight) are recommended for budget hotels.

➡ Noise can be irksome (especially in urban hubs); pack good-quality earplugs and request a room that doesn't face a busy road.

➡ It's wise to keep your door locked, as some staff (particularly in budget hotels) may knock and walk in without awaiting your permission.

➡ Blackouts are common (especially during the monsoon), so double-check that the hotel has a backup generator if you're paying for electric 'extras' such as air-conditioners, TVs and wi-fi.

➡ Some hotels lock their doors at night. Members of staff might sleep in the lobby but waking them up can be a challenge. Let the hotel know in advance if you'll be arriving late at night, or leaving early in the morning.

➡ Away from tourist areas, cheaper hotels may not take foreigners because they don't have the necessary foreigner-registration forms.

CAMPING

➡ There are very few public campgrounds. The only places you're likely to find yourself sleeping in a tent are a few coastal resort hotels or lodges in and around wildlife sanctuaries, where the tents will usually be permanently sited and often as large and comfortable as hotel rooms, with bathrooms too.

GOVERNMENT-RUN ACCOMMODATION

➡ The Indian and state governments maintain networks of guesthouses for travelling officials and public workers, known variously as rest houses, dak bungalows, circuit houses, PWD (Public Works Department) bungalows and forest rest houses. These places may accept travellers if no government employees need the rooms, but permission is sometimes required from local officials.

➡ Most state governments run chains of budget and midrange hotels aimed primarily at domestic tourists. They include a few lovely heritage properties, but most are in the functional-but-bland category. Details are normally available from state tourism offices.

HOMESTAYS/B&BS FOR PAYING GUESTS

➡ Available in some areas only, these family-run guesthouses will appeal to those seeking a small-scale, uncommercial setting with home-cooked meals.

➡ Standards range from mud-and-stone village huts with hole-in-the-floor toilets to comfortable middle-class homes in cities.

➡ Very popular in Kerala, where Fort Cochin is the homestay capital of India, with Alappuzha (Alleppey) and Kumily close behind.

➡ Contact local tourist offices for lists of participating families.

HOSTELS

➡ Goa and Kerala have an expanding number of genuine backpacker hostels with clean dorms, free wi-fi and lockers, and communal kitchens and lounges. There are half a dozen independent places

SLEEPING PRICE RANGES

Here are a sample of accommodation costs. Lonely Planet price indicators refer to the cost of a double room with private bathroom, in high season, unless otherwise noted.

Category	Kerala	Karnataka	Goa
$	less than ₹1200	less than ₹800	less than ₹1200
$$	₹1200-3500	₹800-2500	₹1200-5000
$$$	more than ₹3500	more than ₹2500	more than ₹5000

PRACTICALITIES

➡ **Newspapers & Magazines** Major English-language dailies include the *Hindustan Times, Times of India, Indian Express, Hindu, Deccan Chronicle, Deccan Herald* and *Economic Times*. Regional English-language and local-vernacular publications are found nationwide. Incisive current-affairs magazines include *Frontline, India Today, The Week, Open, Tehelka* and *Outlook*.

➡ **Radio** Government-controlled All India Radio (AIR), India's national broadcaster, has over 220 stations broadcasting local and international news. Private FM channels broadcast music, current affairs, talkback and more.

➡ **Television** The national (government) TV broadcaster is Doordarshan. More people watch satellite and cable TV; English-language channels include BBC, CNN, Star World, HBO, National Geographic and Discovery.

➡ **Weights & Measures** Officially India is metric. Numerical terms you're likely to hear are lakhs (one lakh = 100,000) and crores (one crore = 10 million).

in Goa, and **Vedanta Wake Up!** (www.vedantawakeup.com) has opened several places in Kerala.

➡ A few hostels are run by the YWCA, YMCA or Salvation Army. Sometimes called guesthouses, these usually have clean, comfy rooms (some with air-con) as well as (or instead of) dorms, and offer a decent standard of accommodation at high-budget or low-midrange prices.

➡ Basic but cheap dorms are available at a few locally run youth hostels (popular mainly with Indian students) and budget hotels, where they may be mixed and in, in less touristy places, full of drunken males.

RAILWAY RETIRING ROOMS

➡ Most large train stations (listed at www.irctctourism.com) have basic rooms for travellers holding an ongoing train ticket or Indrail Pass. Some are grim, others are surprisingly pleasant, but can suffer from the noise of passengers and trains.

➡ They're useful for early-morning train departures and there's usually a choice of dormitories or private rooms (24-hour check-out) depending on the class you're travelling in.

➡ Some smaller stations may only have waiting rooms, with different rooms for passengers travelling in different classes.

TEMPLES & PILGRIMS' REST HOUSES

➡ Accommodation is available at some ashrams (spiritual retreats), gurdwaras (Sikh temples) and *dharamsalas* (pilgrims' guesthouses) for a donation or a nominal fee. Vegetarian meals are usually available at the refectories.

➡ These places have been established for genuine pilgrims so please exercise judgment about the appropriateness of staying.

➡ Always abide by any protocols. Smoking and drinking within the premises are a complete no-no.

TOP-END & HERITAGE HOTELS

➡ South India has plenty of top-end properties, from modern luxury chain hotels to glorious palaces, luxury beach resorts and lodges in and around national parks and wildlife sanctuaries.

➡ Heritage hotels give you the chance to stay in former (or sometimes still current) palaces, mansions and other abodes of Indian royalty and aristocracy.

Customs Regulations

➡ You're supposed to declare any amount of cash over US$5000, or total amount of currency over US$10,000 on arrival.

➡ Indian rupees shouldn't be taken out of India; however, this is rarely policed.

➡ Officials very occasionally ask tourists to enter expensive items such as video cameras and laptop computers on a 'Tourist Baggage Re-export' form to ensure they're taken out of India at the time of departure.

Electricity

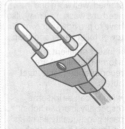

230V/50Hz

230V/50Hz

Embassies & Consulates

Most foreign diplomatic missions are based in Delhi, but several nations operate consulates in other Indian cities.

Australian Delhi (☏011-41399900; www.india.high-commission.gov.au; 1/50G Shantipath, Chanakyapuri); Chennai (☏044-45921300; 9th fl, Express Chambers, Express Avenue Estate, White's Rd, Royapettah); Mumbai (10th fl, A Wing, Crescenzo Bldg, G Block, Plot C 38-39, Bandra Kurla Complex)

Canadian Delhi (☏011-41782000; www.canadainternational.gc.ca/india-inde; 7/8 Shantipath, Chanakyapuri); Mumbai (21st fl, Tower 2, Indiabulls Finance Centre, Senapati Bapat Marg, Elphinstone Rd West)

Dutch Delhi (☏011-24197600; http://india.nlembassy.org; 6/50F Shantipath, Chanakyapuri); Mumbai (☏022-22194200; Forbes Bldg, Charanjit Rai Marg, Fort)

French Delhi (☏011-24196100; http://ambafrance-in.org; 2/50E Shantipath, Chanak-yapuri); Mumbai (☏022-56694000; Wockhardt Towers, East Wing, 5th fl, Bandra Kurla Complex, Bandra East); Puducherry (☏0413-2231000; 2 Marine St)

German Delhi (☏011-44199199; www.new-delhi.diplo.de; 6/50G Shantipath, Chanakyapuri); Chennai (☏044-24301600; 9 Boat Club Rd, RA Puram); Mumbai (☏022-22832422; 10th fl, Hoechst House, Nariman Point)

Irish (☏011-49403200; www.irelandinindia.com; C17 Malcha Marg, Chanakyapuri, Delhi)

Israeli Delhi (☏011-30414500; www.delhi.mfa.gov.il; 3 Aurangzeb Rd); Mumbai (☏022-61600500; Marathon Futurex, 1301, A Wing, N M Joshi Marg, Lower Parel)

Malaysian (☏011-26111291/97; www.kln.gov.my/web/ind_new-delhi/home; 50M Satya Marg, Chanakyapuri, Delhi)

Myanmar (☏011-24678822; www.myanmedelhi.com; 3/50F Nyaya Marg, Delhi)

Nepali (☏011-23476200; www.nepalembassy.in; Mandi House, Barakhamba Rd, Delhi)

New Zealand Delhi (☏011-46883170; www.nzembassy.com/india; Sir Edmund Hillary Marg, Chanakyapuri); Chennai (☏044-28112472; Rane Holdings Ltd, Maithri, 132 Cathedral Rd, Gopalapuram); Mumbai (☏022-61316666; Level 2, Maker Maxity, 3 North Ave, Bandra Kurla Complex)

Singaporean Delhi (☏011-46000915; www.mfa.gov.sg/newdelhi; E6 Chandragupta Marg, Chanakyapuri); Chennai (☏044-28158207; 17A North Boag Rd, T Nagar); Mumbai (☏022-22043205; Maker Chambers IV, 10th fl, 222 Jamnalal Bajaj Rd, Nariman Point)

Sri Lankan Delhi (☏011-23010202; www.slhcindia.org; 27 Kautilya Marg, Chanakyapuri); Chennai (☏044-28241896; www.sldhcchennai.org; 56 Sterling Rd, Nungambakkam); Mumbai (☏022-22045861; Mulla House, 34 Homi Modi St, Fort)

UK Delhi (☏011-24192100; Shantipath); Chennai (☏044-42192151; 20 Anderson Rd); Mumbai (☏022-66502222; Naman Chambers, C/32 G Block Bandra Kurla Complex, Bandra East)

US Delhi (☏011-24198000; www.newdelhi.usembassy.gov; Shantipath); Chennai (☏044-28574000; 220 Anna Salai, Gemini Circle); Mumbai (☏022-26724000; C49, G Block, Bandra Kurla Complex,)

Food

See Delicious India (p459) for information about food in South India.

Gay & Lesbian Travellers

➡ Homosexuality was made illegal in India in 2013, having only been decriminalised since 2009. Gay and lesbian visitors should be discreet in this conservative country. Public displays of affection are frowned upon for both homosexual and heterosexual couples.

➡ Despite the ban, there are gay scenes (and Gay Pride marches) in a number of cities including Mumbai (Bombay; p72), Chennai

EATING PRICE RANGES

The following price ranges refer to a standard main course.

$ less than ₹100

$$ ₹100–300

$$$ more than ₹300

(Madras), Bengaluru (Bangalore) and Hyderabad, as well as a holiday gay scene in Goa.

Websites & Publications

Gay Bombay (www.gaybombay. org) Lists gay events as well as offering advice and support.

Gaylaxy (www.gaylaxymag.com) Probably India's best gay e-zine, including news, blogs, articles, reviews and fashion.

Gaysi Zine (www.gaysifamily. com) A thoughtful monthly magazine and website featuring gay writing and issues.

Indian Dost (www.indiandost. com/gay.php) News and information including contact groups in India.

Indja Pink (www.indjapink.co.in) India's first 'gay travel boutique', founded by a well-known Indian fashion designer.

Orinam (www.orinam.net) This Chennai-based site offers advice and support, and lists gay events. The Twitter feed @ chennaipride is useful too.

Queer Azaadi Mumbai (www. queerazaadi.wordpress.com) Mumbai's queer-pride blog, with news.

Queer Ink (www.queer-ink.com) Online bookshop specialising in gay- and lesbian-interest books from the subcontinent.

Support Groups

Chennai Dost (www.chennai-dost.blogspot.com) Community space for stories and information; organises events, including parties, exhibitions, campaigns, film festivals and Chennai Rainbow Pride (June).

Humsafar Trust (022-26673800; www.humsafar.org; Old BMC Bldg, 1st fl, Nehru Rd, Vakola, Santa Cruz East) Gay and transgender support groups and advocacy. The drop-in centre hosts workshops and has a library – pick up a copy of LGBT magazine *Bombay Dost*.

Queer Campus Hyderabad (www.facebook.com/qcampushyd) Student-focused group holds weekly meetings and monthly events including carnival days and film festivals.

Wajood Society (www.wajoodsociety.com) Hyderabad queer-support group, involved in organising events such as Queer Pride (February).

Insurance

→ Comprehensive travel insurance to cover theft, loss and medical problems (as well as air evacuation) is strongly recommended.

→ Some policies specifically exclude potentially dangerous activities such as scuba diving, skiing, motorcycling, paragliding and even trekking: read the fine print.

→ Some trekking agents may only accept customers who have cover for emergency helicopter evacuation.

→ If you plan to hire a motorcycle in India, make sure the rental policy includes at least third-party insurance.

→ Check in advance whether your insurance policy will pay doctors and hospitals directly or reimburse you later (keep all documentation for your claim).

→ It's crucial to get a police report in India if you've had anything stolen; insurance companies may refuse to reimburse you without one.

→ Worldwide travel insurance is available at www.lonelyplanet.com/travel-insurance. You can buy, extend and claim online anytime – even if you're already on the road.

Internet Access

→ Internet cafes are widespread and connections are usually reasonably fast, except in more remote areas.

→ Wi-fi access is available in many places to stay, and some cafes in larger cities. Access is often free but not always – bizarrely enough, the hotels that charge for wi-fi are usually the expensive ones that are already charging you plenty for your room.

→ Wi-fi signals everywhere are subject to temporary outages because of power cuts and the vagaries of servers.

Practicalities

→ Internet cafe charges fall anywhere between ₹15 and ₹100 per hour, often with a 15- to 30-minute minimum.

→ Bandwidth load tends to be lowest in the early morning and early afternoon.

→ Some internet cafes may ask to see your passport.

Security

→ Using online banking or sending credit-card details or other personal data on any nonsecure system is unwise. If you have no choice but to do this, it's wise to change all passwords (email, netbanking, credit-card secure code etc) afterwards.

Laptops

→ The simplest way to connect to the internet, when away from a wi-fi connection, is to use your smartphone as a personal wi-fi hot-spot (use a local SIM to avoid roaming charges).

→ Alternatively, companies that offer prepaid wireless 2G/3G modem sticks (dongles) include Reliance, Airtel, Tata Docomo and Vodafone. To organise a connection you have to submit your proof of identity and address in India, and activation can take up to 24 hours. A nonrefundable activation fee (around ₹2000) has to be paid, which includes the price of the dongle and around 10GB of data. A 20GB recharge costs around ₹1000.

→ Make sure the areas you will be travelling to are covered by your service provider.

→ Consider purchasing a fuse-protected universal AC adaptor to protect your circuit board from power surges.

→ Plug adaptors are widely available throughout India.

Legal Matters

If you're in a sticky legal situation, contact your embassy as quickly as possible. However, be aware that all your embassy may be able to do is monitor your treatment in custody and arrange a lawyer. In the Indian justice system, the burden of proof can often be on the accused and stints in prison before trial are not unheard of.

Antisocial Behaviour

→ Smoking in public places is illegal throughout India but this is very rarely enforced; fines are ₹200, though there are proposals to raise this to ₹20,000.

→ People can smoke inside their homes and in most open spaces such as streets (heed any signs stating otherwise).

→ Some Indian cities have banned spitting and littering, but this is also variably enforced.

Drugs

→ Indian law does not distinguish between 'hard' and 'soft' drugs; possession of any illegal drug is regarded as a criminal offence, which will result in a custodial sentence.

→ Sentences may be up to a year for possession of a small amount for personal use, to a minimum of 10 years if it's deemed the purpose was for sale or distribution. There's also usually a hefty fine on top of any sentence.

→ Cases can take months, even several years, to appear before a court, while the accused may have to wait in prison.

PROHIBITED EXPORTS

To protect India's cultural heritage, the export of certain antiques is prohibited, especially those which are verifiably more than 100 years old. Reputable antique dealers know the laws and can make arrangements for an export-clearance certificate for old items that are OK to export. Detailed information on prohibited items can be found on the government webpage www.asi.nic.in/pdf_data/8.pdf. The rules may seem stringent but the loss of ancient artworks and sculptures due to the international trade in antiques has been alarming. Look for quality reproductions instead.

The Indian Wildlife Protection Act bans any form of wildlife trade. Don't buy any product that endangers threatened species and habitats – doing so can result in heavy fines and even imprisonment. This includes ivory, shahtoosh shawls (made from the down of the rare chiru, the Tibetan antelope) and anything made from the fur, skin, horns or shell of any endangered species. Products made from certain rare plants are also banned.

→ Be aware that travellers have been targeted in sting operations in Goa and other backpacker enclaves.

→ Marijuana grows wild in various parts of India, but consuming it is still an offence, except in towns where bhang is legally sold for religious rituals.

→ Police are getting particularly tough on foreigners who use drugs, so you should take this risk very seriously.

→ Pharmaceutical drugs that are restricted in other countries may be available in India over the counter or via prescription. Be aware that taking these without professional guidance can be dangerous.

Police

→ You should always carry your passport; police are entitled to ask you for identification at any time.

→ If you're arrested for an alleged offence and asked to pay a bribe, note that this is illegal in India. However, many travellers deal with an on-the-spot fine by just

paying up to avoid trumped-up charges.

→ Corruption is rife so the less you have to do with local police the better; try to avoid all potentially risky situations.

Maps

Maps available inside India are of variable quality. Most state-government tourist offices stock basic local maps. Following are some of the better map series, which should be available at good bookshops:

Eicher (http://maps.eicherworld.com)

Nelles (www.nelles-verlag.de)

Survey of India (www.surveyofindia.gov.in) Many maps are downloadable free from the website.

TTK (www.ttkmaps.com)

Money

The Indian rupee (₹) is divided into 100 paise, but only 50-paise coins are legal tender and these are rarely seen. Coins come in denominations of ₹1, ₹2, ₹5 and ₹10 (the ₹1s and ₹2s look almost identical); notes come in ₹5, ₹10, ₹20, ₹50, ₹100, ₹500 and ₹1000 (this last is handy for paying large bills but can pose problems when getting change for small services). The Indian rupee is linked to a basket of currencies and has been subject to fluctuations in recent years.

See Need to Know (p15) for exchange rates and information on costs.

ATMs

➡ ATMs are found in most urban centres.

➡ Visa, MasterCard, Cirrus, Maestro and Plus are the most commonly accepted cards.

➡ ATMs at Axis Bank, Citibank, HDFC, HSBC, ICICI and State Bank of India recognise foreign cards. Other banks' ATMs may accept major cards (Visa, MasterCard etc).

➡ Most ATMs have a limit of ₹10,000 to ₹15,000 per withdrawal. Citibank ATMs generally allow you to withdraw up to ₹40,000 in one transaction, which reduces transaction charges.

➡ Before your trip, check whether your card can reliably access banking networks in India and ask for details of charges.

➡ Notify your bank that you'll be using your card in India to avoid having it blocked; take along your bank's phone number just in case.

➡ Away from major towns, always carry cash and possibly also travellers cheques as backup.

Black Market

➡ Black-market money changers exist but legal moneychangers are so common that there's no reason to use illegal services.

➡ If someone approaches you on the street and offers to change money, you're probably being set up for a scam.

Cash

➡ Major currencies such as US dollars, pounds sterling and euros are easy to change throughout India, although some bank branches insist on travellers cheques only.

➡ Some banks also accept other currencies such as Australian and Canadian dollars, and Swiss francs.

➡ Private money changers deal with a wider range of currencies than banks, but Pakistani, Nepali and Bangladeshi currency can be harder to change away from the border.

➡ When travelling off the beaten track, always carry an adequate stock of rupees.

➡ Whenever changing money, check every note. Don't accept any filthy, ripped or disintegrating notes, as these may be difficult to use.

➡ It can be tough getting change in India so keep a stock of smaller currency; ₹10, ₹20 and ₹50 notes are helpful.

➡ Officially you cannot take rupees out of India, but this is laxly enforced. You can change any leftover rupees back into foreign currency, most easily at the airport (some banks have a ₹1000 minimum). You may have to present encashment certificates or credit-card/ATM receipts, and show your passport and airline ticket.

Credit Cards

➡ Credit cards are accepted at many shops, upmarket restaurants and midrange and top-end hotels, and they can usually be used to pay for flights and train tickets.

➡ Cash advances on major credit cards are possible at some banks.

➡ MasterCard and Visa are the most widely accepted.

➡ Always keep the emergency lost-and-stolen numbers for your credit cards in a safe place, separate from your cards, and report any loss or theft immediately.

Encashment Certificates

➡ Indian law states that all foreign currency must be changed at official money changers or banks.

➡ For every (official) foreign-exchange transaction, you'll receive an encashment certificate (receipt), which will allow you to change rupees back into foreign currency when departing India.

➡ Encashment certificates should cover the amount of rupees you intend to change back to foreign currency.

➡ Printed receipts from ATMs are also accepted as evidence of an international transaction at most banks.

International Transfers

➡ If you run out of money, someone back home can wire you cash via money changers affiliated with **Moneygram** (www.moneygram.com) or **Western Union** (www.westernunion.com). A fee is added to the transaction.

➡ To collect cash, bring your passport and the name and reference number of the person who sent the funds.

Money Changers

➡ Private money changers are usually open for longer hours than banks, and are found almost everywhere (many also double as internet cafes and travel agents).

➡ Upmarket hotels may also change money, but their rates are usually not as competitive.

Tipping, Baksheesh & Bargaining

➡ In tourist restaurants or hotels, a service fee is often

added to your bill so tipping is optional. Otherwise, a tip is appreciated.

➡ Hotel bellboys and train/airport porters appreciate anything around ₹50; hotel staff should be given similar gratuities for services above and beyond the call of duty.

➡ It's not mandatory to tip taxi or rickshaw drivers, but it's good to tip drivers who are honest about the fare.

➡ If you hire a car with driver, a tip of 10% is recommended for good service.

➡ Baksheesh can loosely be defined as a 'tip'; it covers everything from alms for beggars to bribes.

➡ Many Indians implore tourists not to hand out sweets, pens or money to children, as it encourages them to beg. To make a lasting difference, donate to a reputable school or charitable organisation.

➡ Except in fixed-price shops (such as government and fair-trade emporiums), bargaining is the norm.

Travellers Cheques

➡ American Express (Amex) and Thomas Cook are the most widely accepted brands.

➡ Euro, pounds sterling and US dollars are the safest currencies, especially in smaller towns.

➡ Keep a record of the cheques' serial numbers separate from your cheques, along with the proof-of-purchase slips, encashment vouchers and photocopied passport details.

➡ If you lose your cheques, contact the Amex or Thomas Cook office in Delhi. To replace lost travellers cheques, you need the proof-of-purchase slip and the numbers of the missing cheques, and possibly a photocopy of the police report and a passport photo.

Opening Hours

➡ Official business hours are from 10am to 5pm Monday to Friday but many offices open later and close earlier, and take an official lunch hour from around 1pm.

➡ Some midrange and top-end restaurants do not open till lunchtime.

➡ Foreign-exchange offices may open longer than banks and operate daily.

➡ Minor post offices open shorter hours than major ones Monday to Saturday, and not at all on Sunday.

➡ Some establishments with six-day weeks close on the second and fourth Saturdays of the month.

Typical Opening Hours

Business	Opening hours
airline offices	9.30am-5.30pm Mon-Sat
banks	10am-4pm Mon-Fri, to 1pm Sat
government offices	9.30am-1pm & 2-5.30pm Mon-Fri, closed 2nd and 4th Sat in some places
major post offices	9am-8pm Mon-Sat, 10am-4pm Sun
museums	10am-5pm Tue-Sun
restaurants	8am or 9am to 10pm or 11pm
sights	10am-5pm or dawn-dusk
shops	10am-8pm, some closed Sun

Photography

For useful tips and techniques on travel photography, read Lonely Planet's guide to *Travel Photography*.

➡ Memory cards for digital cameras are available from photographic shops in most large cities and towns. However, quality is variable – some don't carry the advertised amount of data.

➡ Expect to pay upwards of ₹200 for a 4GB card.

➡ To be safe, regularly back up your memory cards. If your camera isn't wi-fi-enabled, take a memory-card reader with you. Alternatively some internet cafes will write your pictures to CD.

➡ Some photographic shops make prints from digital photographs.

Restrictions

➡ India is touchy about anyone taking photographs of military installations – this can include train stations, bridges, airports, military sites and sensitive border regions.

➡ Photography from the air is mostly OK, unless you're taking off from (or landing in) airports actively shared by defence forces.

➡ Many places of worship – such as monasteries, temples and mosques – prohibit photography. Taking photos inside shrines or at funerals or religious ceremonies, or of people publicly bathing (including rivers) can be offensive – ask first.

➡ Flash photography may be prohibited in certain areas of shrines or historical monuments.

➡ Exercise sensitivity when photographing people, especially women – some may find it offensive, so obtain permission in advance.

➡ It is not uncommon for people in touristic areas to demand a posing fee in return for being photographed. Exercise your discretion in these situations. In any case, ask first to avoid misunderstandings later.

Post

India has the biggest postal network on earth, with over 155,000 post offices. Mail and poste-restante services are generally good, although the speed of delivery will depend on the efficiency of any given office. Airmail is faster and more reliable than sea mail, although it's best to use courier services (such as DHL and TNT) to send and receive items of value; expect to pay around ₹3000 per kilogram to Europe, Australia or the USA. Smaller private couriers are often cheaper, but goods may be repacked into large packages to cut costs and things sometimes go missing.

Poste Restante

➡ India still has a poste-restante system by which you can have mail sent to you at post offices.

➡ Ask senders to address letters to you with your surname in capital letters and underlined, followed by Poste Restante, GPO (main post office), and the city or town in question.

➡ To claim mail you'll need to show your passport.

➡ Letters sent via poste restante are generally held for around one to two months before being returned.

➡ Many 'lost' letters are simply misfiled under given/first names, so check under both your names and ask senders to provide a return address.

➡ It's best to have any parcels sent to you by registered post.

Sending Mail
LETTERS

➡ Posting airmail letters to anywhere overseas costs ₹25 (aerogrammes cost ₹15).

➡ International postcards cost around ₹12.

➡ For postcards, stick on the stamps *before* writing on them, as post offices can give you as many as four stamps per card.

➡ Sending a letter overseas by registered post costs an extra ₹50.

PARCELS

➡ Posting parcels can either be relatively straightforward or involve multiple counters and lots of queuing; get to the post office in the morning.

➡ All parcels sent through the government postal service must be packed up in white linen and the seams sealed with wax; agents near

post offices usually offer this service for a small fee.

➡ An unregistered airmail package up to 250g in weight costs around ₹400 to ₹850 to any country, plus ₹50 to ₹150 per additional 250g (up to a maximum of 2000g; different charges apply for higher weights).

➡ Parcel post has a maximum of 20kg to 30kg depending on the destination.

➡ Airmail takes one to three weeks, sea mail two to four months and Surface Air-Lifted (SAL) – a curious hybrid where parcels travel by both air and sea – around one month.

➡ Express mail service (EMS; delivery within three days) costs around 30% more than the normal airmail price.

➡ Customs declaration forms, available from the post office, must be stitched or pasted to the parcel. No duty is payable by the recipient for gifts under the value of ₹1000.

➡ Carry a permanent marker to write on the parcel any information requested by the desk.

➡ You can send printed matter via surface mail 'Bulk Bag' for ₹350 (maximum 5kg, plus ₹100 for each additional kilogram). The parcel has to be packed with an opening so it can be checked by customs – tailors can do this in such a way that nothing falls out.

➡ **India Post** (www.indiapost.gov.in) has an online calculator for domestic and international postal tariffs.

Public Holidays

There are three official national public holidays – Republic and Independence Days and Gandhi's birthday (Gandhi Jayanti) – plus a lot of other holidays celebrated nationally or locally, many

---

WARNING: BHANG LASSI

Although it's rarely printed in menus, some restaurants in popular tourist centres will clandestinely whip up bhang lassi, a yoghurt and iced-water beverage laced with cannabis (occasionally other narcotics). Commonly dubbed 'special lassi', this often-potent concoction can cause varying degrees of ecstasy, drawn-out delirium, hallucination, nausea and paranoia. Some travellers have been ill for several days, robbed, or hurt in accidents after drinking this fickle brew. A few towns have legal (controlled) bhang outlets.

of them marking important days in various religions and falling on variable dates. The most important are the 18 'gazetted holidays' (listed below) which are observed by central-government offices throughout India. On these days most businesses (offices, shops etc), banks and tourist sites close, but transport is usually unaffected. It's wise to make transport and hotel reservations well in advance if you intend visiting during major festivals.

Republic Day 26 January

Holi February/March

Ramnavami March/April

Mahavir Jayanti March/April

Good Friday March/April

Dr BR Ambedkar's Birthday 14 April

Buddha Jayanti May

Eid al-Fitr June/July

Independence Day 15 August

Janmastami August/September

Eid al-Adha September

Dussehra September/October

Gandhi Jayanti 2 October

Muharram October

Diwali October/November

Guru Nanak Jayanti November

Eid-Milad-un-Nabi December

Christmas Day 25 December

Safe Travel

Travellers to India's major cities may fall prey to petty and opportunistic crime but most problems can be avoided with a bit of common sense and an appropriate amount of caution. Have a look at the India branch of Lonely Planet's Thorn Tree travel forum (www.lonelyplanet.com/thorntree), where travellers often post timely warnings about problems they've encountered on the road. See also Women & Solo Travellers (p492) and Scams (p490), and always check your government's travel advisory warnings.

GOVERNMENT TRAVEL ADVICE

The following government websites offer travel advice and information on current hot spots.

Australian Department of Foreign Affairs (www.smarttraveller.gov.au)

British Foreign Office (www.gov.uk/fco)

Canadian Department of Foreign Affairs (www.voyage.gc.ca)

German Foreign Office (www.auswaeriges-amt.de)

Japan Ministry of Foreign Affairs (www.mofa.go.jp)

Netherlands Ministry of Foreign Affairs (www.government.nl)

New Zealand Ministry of Foreign Affairs & Trade (www.safetravel.govt.nz)

US State Department (http://travel.state.gov)

Political Violence

India has a number of (sometimes armed) dissident groups championing various causes, who have employed the same tried and tested techniques of rebel groups everywhere: assassinations and bomb attacks on government infrastructure, public transport, religious centres, tourist sites and markets. Certain areas, mostly in the north of the country, are prone to insurgent violence: read the latest government travel advisories for recent reports on where is considered unsafe.

International terrorism is as much of a risk in Europe or the USA, so this is no reason not to go to India, but it makes sense to check the local security situation carefully before travelling (especially in high-risk areas).

Strikes and political protests can sometimes close the roads (as well as banks, shops etc) for days on end in any region.

Telephone

Calling Booths

➡ There are few payphones in South India (apart from in airports), but private STD/ISD/PCO call booths do the same job, offering inexpensive local, interstate and international calls at lower prices than calls made from hotel rooms.

➡ These booths are found around the country. A digital meter displays how much the call is costing and usually provides a printed receipt when the call is finished.

➡ Costs vary depending on the operator and destination but can be from ₹1 per minute for local calls and between ₹5 and ₹10 for international calls.

➡ Some booths also offer a 'call-back' service: you ring home, provide the phone number of the booth and wait for people at home to call you back, for a fee of around ₹20 on top of the cost of the preliminary call.

Directory Information

Useful online resources include the **Yellow Pages** (www.yellowpages.co.in) and **Justdial** (www.justdial.com).

Mobile Phones

➡ Indian mobile phone numbers usually have 10 digits, mostly beginning with 9 (but sometimes 7 or 8).

→ There's roaming coverage for international GSM phones in most cities and large towns.

→ To avoid expensive roaming costs (often highest for incoming calls), get hooked up to the local mobile-phone network by applying for a local prepaid SIM card.

→ Mobiles bought in some countries may be locked to a particular network; you'll have to get the phone unlocked, or buy a local phone (available from ₹2000) to use an Indian SIM card.

GETTING CONNECTED

→ Getting connected is inexpensive and fairly straightforward in many areas. It's easiest to obtain a local SIM card in large cities and tourist centres. Tamil Nadu, Telangana and Andhra Pradesh are states where it is particularly difficult.

→ Foreigners must supply between one and five passport photos, and photocopies of their passport identity and visa pages. Often mobile shops can arrange all this for you, or you can ask your hotel to help you.

→ You must also supply a residential address, which can be the address of your hotel. Usually the phone company will call your hotel (warn the hotel a call will come through) any time up to 24 hours after your application to verify that you are staying there.

→ It's a good idea to obtain the SIM card somewhere where you're staying for a day or two so that you can return to the vendor if there's any problem. Only obtain your SIM card from a reputable branded phone store to avoid scams.

→ SIMs are sold as regular size, but most places have machines to cut them

down to the required size if necessary.

→ Another option is to get a friendly local to obtain a connection in their name.

→ Prepaid mobile-phone kits (SIM card and phone number, plus an allocation of calls) are available in most towns for about ₹200 from a phone shop, local STD/ISD/PCO booth or grocery store.

→ You must then purchase more credit, sold as direct credit. You pay the vendor and the credit is deposited straight into your account, minus some taxes and a service charge.

CHARGES & COVERAGE

→ Calls made within the state or city where you bought the SIM card cost less than ₹1 a minute. You can call internationally for less than ₹10 a minute.

→ SMS messaging is even cheaper. International outgoing messages cost ₹5. Incoming calls and messages are free.

→ Unreliable signals and problems with international texting (messages or replies not coming through or being delayed) are not uncommon.

→ The leading service providers are Airtel, Vodafone, Reliance, Idea and BSNL. Coverage varies from region to region; Airtel has among the widest coverage.

→ As the mobile-phone industry continues to develop, rates, coverage and suppliers are all likely to evolve.

Phone Codes

→ Calling India from abroad, dial your country's international access code, then ☑91 (India's country code), then the area code (without the initial zero), then the local number. For mobile phones, the area code and initial zero are not required.

→ Calling internationally from India, dial ☑00 (the international access code),

then the country code of the country you're calling, then the area code (without the initial zero) and the local number.

→ Indian land phone numbers have an area code followed by up to eight digits.

→ Toll-free numbers begin with ☑1800.

→ To make interstate calls to a mobile phone, add ☑0 before the 10-digit number.

→ To call a land phone from a mobile phone, you always have to add the area code (with the initial zero).

→ To access an international operator, dial ☑000 127. The operator can place a call to anywhere in the world and allow you to make collect calls.

→ Home Country Direct service, which gives you access to the international operator in your home country, exists for the US (☑000 117) and the UK (☑000 4417).

Time

India uses the 12-hour clock, and the local standard time is known as Indian Standard Time (IST). IST is 5½ hours ahead of GMT/UTC. The floating half-hour was added to maximise daylight hours over such a vast country.

Toilets

→ Public toilets are most easily found in major cities and tourist sites; the cleanest are usually at modern restaurants, shopping complexes and cinemas.

→ Beyond urban centres, toilets are often of the squat variety and locals may use the 'hand-and-water' technique, which involves performing ablutions with a small jug of water and the left hand. It's always a good idea to carry toilet paper and hand sanitiser, just in case.

Tourist Information

In addition to Government of India tourist offices (also known as 'India Tourism'), each state maintains its own network of tourist offices. These vary in their efficiency and usefulness – some are run by enthusiastic souls who go out of their way to help, others are little more than a means of drumming up business for State Tourism Development Corporation tours.

The first stop for information should be the Government of India tourism website, **Incredible India** (www.incredibleindia.org); for details of India Tourism's regional offices around the country, click on the 'Help Desk' tab at the top of the homepage. Official state tourism websites often also contain helpful information.

Travellers with Disabilities

India's crowded public transport, crush of humanity and variable infrastructure can test even the hardiest able-bodied traveller. If you have a physical disability or are vision-impaired, these can pose even more of a challenge. If your mobility is considerably restricted, you may like to ease the stress by travelling with an able-bodied companion.

Accessibility Some restaurants and offices have ramps but most tend to have at least one step. Staircases are often steep; lifts frequently stop at mezzanines between floors.

Accommodation Wheelchair-friendly hotels are almost exclusively top end. Make pre-trip enquiries and book ground-floor rooms at hotels that lack adequate facilities.

Footpaths Where pavements exist, they can be riddled with holes, littered with debris and packed with pedestrians. If using crutches, bring along spare rubber caps.

Transport Hiring a car with driver will make moving around a lot easier; if you use a wheelchair, make sure the car-hire company can provide an appropriate vehicle to carry it.

For further advice pertaining to your specific requirements, consult your doctor before heading to India.

The following organisations may be able to proffer further information.

Access-Able Travel Source (www.access-able.com)

Accessible Journeys (www.disabilitytravel.com)

Global Access News (www.globalaccessnews.com)

Mobility International USA (MIUSA; www.miusa.org)

Visas

Visa on Arrival

Citizens of Australia, Brazil, Cambodia, Cook Islands, Djibouti, Fiji, Finland, Germany, Guyana, Indonesia, Israel, Japan, Jordan, Kenya, Kiribati, Laos, Luxembourg, Marshall Islands, Mauritius, Mexico, Micronesia, Myanmar, Nauru, New Zealand, Niue Island, Norway, Oman, Palau, Palestine, Papua New Guinea, Philippines, Republic of Korea, Russia, Samoa, Singapore, Solomon Islands,Thailand, Tonga, Tuvalu, UAE, Ukraine, USA, Vanuatu and Vietnam are currently granted a 30-day single-entry visa on arrival (VOA) at Bengaluru (Bangalore), Chennai (Madras), Kochi (Cochin), Delhi, Goa, Hyderabad, Kolkata (Calcutta), Mumbai (Bombay) and Thiruvananthapuram (Trivandrum) airports.

However, to participate in the scheme, you need to apply online at https://indianvisaonline.gov.in for an Electronic Travel Authority (ETA), a minimum of four days and maximum 30 days before you are due to travel. The fee is US$60, and you have to upload a photograph as well as a copy of your passport. Some travellers have reported being asked

---

GET TO KNOW YOUR BATHROOM

➡ Most Indian midrange hotels and all top-end ones have sit-down toilets with toilet paper and soap supplied. In ultracheap hotels, and in places off the tourist trail, squat toilets (sometimes described as 'Indian style', as opposed to 'Western style') are the norm and toilet paper is rarely provided.

➡ Terminology for hotel bathrooms varies. 'Attached bath' or 'private bath' means the room has its own en suite bathroom. 'Common bath' or 'shared bath' means communal bathroom facilities.

➡ Not all rooms have hot water. 'Running', '24-hour' or 'constant' hot water means it is available round-the-clock (not always the case in reality). 'Bucket' hot water is only available in buckets (sometimes for a small charge).

➡ Many places use wall-mounted electric geysers (water heaters) that need to be switched on up to an hour before use. The geyser's switch can sometimes be located outside the bathroom.

➡ The hotel rooms we have listed have private bathrooms unless otherwise indicated.

for documentation showing their hotel confirmation at the airport, though this is not specified on the VOA website.

The VOA is valid from the date of arrival; your passport must be valid for at least six months from the date of arrival.

It's intended that the scheme will be rolled out to 180 nations, including the UK and China, so check online for any updates.

Other Visas

If you want to stay longer than 30 days, or are not covered by the VOA scheme, you must get a visa before arriving in India (apart from Nepali or Bhutanese citizens, who do not need visas). Visas are available from Indian missions worldwide, though in many countries, applications are processed by a separate private company. In some countries, including the UK, you must apply in person at the designated office as well as filing an application online.

➡ Your passport must be valid for at least six months from the date of your visa application (or from the date of issue of your visa or its date of expiry, depending on which arm of Indian bureaucracy is dealing with it), with at least two blank pages.

➡ Most people are issued with a standard six-month tourist visa, which for most nationalities permits multiple entry.

➡ Tourist visas are valid from the date of issue, not the date you arrive in India.

➡ Student and business visas have strict conditions (consult the Indian embassy for details).

➡ Five- and 10-year tourist visas are available to US citizens under a bilateral arrangement, and five-year visas are available to some European and Latin American nationalities applying in Australia; however, you can still only stay in India for up to 180 days continuously.

➡ Currently visa applicants are required to submit two passport photographs with their application; these must be in colour and must be 5.08cm by 5.08 cm (2in by 2in; larger than regular passport photos).

➡ An onward travel ticket is a requirement for some visas, but this isn't always enforced (check in advance).

➡ Additional restrictions apply to travellers from Bangladesh and Pakistan, as well as certain Eastern European, African and Central Asian countries. Check any special conditions for your nationality with the Indian embassy in your country.

➡ Visas are priced in the local currency and may have an added service fee.

➡ Extended visas are possible for people of Indian origin (excluding those in Pakistan and Bangladesh) who hold a non-Indian passport and live abroad.

➡ For visas lasting more than six months, you're supposed to register at the **Foreigners' Regional Registration Office** (FRRO; ☏011-26711443; frrodil@nic.in; Level 2, East Block 8, Sector 1, Rama Krishna (RK) Puram, Delhi; ⏱9.30am-3pm Mon-Fri) in Delhi within 14 days of arriving in India; enquire about these special

conditions when you apply for your visa.

Re-entry Requirements

Most tourists are permitted to transit freely between India and its neighbouring countries. However, citizens of China, Pakistan, Iraq, Iran, Afghanistan, Bangladesh and Sudan are barred from re-entry into India within two months of their last exit.

Visa Extensions

India has traditionally been very stringent with visa extensions. At the time of writing, the government was granting extensions only in circumstances such as medical emergencies or theft of passport just before the expiry of an applicant's visa.

If you do need to extend your visa due to any such exigency, you should contact the Foreigners' Regional Registration Office in Delhi. This is also the place to come for a replacement visa, and if you need your lost/stolen passport replaced (required before you can leave the country). Regional FRROs are even less likely to grant an extension.

Assuming you meet the stringent criteria, the FRRO is permitted to issue an extension of 14 days (free for nationals of most countries). You must bring your confirmed air ticket, one passport photo (take two, just in case), and a photocopy of your passport identity and visa pages. Note that this system is designed to get you out of the country promptly with the correct official stamps, not to give you two extra weeks of travel and leisure.

Transport

GETTING THERE & AWAY

South India is most easily reached from other countries via its major international airports at Mumbai (Bombay), Chennai (Madras), Bengaluru (Bangalore) and Hyderabad. There are seasonal charter flights to Goa from some European countries (including Russia). The south can also be reached overland from elsewhere in India. Flights, tours and other tickets can be booked online at www. lonelyplanet.com/bookings.

Entering India

Entering India by air or land is relatively straightforward, with standard immigration and customs procedures. A frustrating law barring re-entry into India within two months of departure has been done away with (except for citizens of some Asian countries), thus allowing travellers to make side trips to nearby countries and return.

Passport

➡ To enter India you need a valid passport, a visa and an onward/return ticket.

➡ Your passport must be valid for at least six months from the date of your visa application (or from the date of issue of your visa or its date of expiry, depending on which arm of Indian bureaucracy is dealing with it). In any case it's always recommendable for your passport to be valid till well after you plan to leave India.

➡ If your passport is lost or stolen, immediately contact your country's representative.

➡ Keep photocopies of your airline ticket and the identity and visa pages of your passport in case of emergency. Better yet, scan or photograph them and email copies to yourself.

➡ Check with your local Indian embassy for any special conditions that may exist for your nationality.

Air

Airports & Airlines

As India is a big country, it makes sense to fly into the airport that's nearest to the area you'll be visiting. South India has four main gateways for international flights (see the following list), but there are also some direct international flights to other centres including Goa, Kochi (Cochin), Thiruvananthapuram (Trivandrum), Trichy (Tiruchirappalli) and Madurai.

India's national carrier is **Air India** (☏1800 1801407; www.airindia.com). Air travel in India has had a relatively decent safety record in recent years.

CLIMATE CHANGE & TRAVEL

Every form of transport that relies on carbon-based fuel generates CO_2, the main cause of human-induced climate change. Modern travel is dependent on aeroplanes, which might use less fuel per kilometre per person than most cars but travel much greater distances. The altitude at which aircraft emit gases (including CO_2) and particles also contributes to their climate change impact. Many websites offer 'carbon calculators' that allow people to estimate the carbon emissions generated by their journey and, for those who wish to do so, to offset the impact of the greenhouse gases emitted with contributions to portfolios of climate-friendly initiatives throughout the world. Lonely Planet offsets the carbon footprint of all staff and author travel.

Bengaluru (Bangalore; BLR; ☎1800 4254425; www.bengaluruairport.com; Kempegowda International Airport)

Chennai (Madras; MAA; ☎044-22560551; www.aai.aero/chennai; Chennai International Airport)

Hyderabad (HYD; ☎040-66546370; http://hyderabad.aero; Rajiv Gandhi International Airport)

Mumbai (Bombay; BOM; ☎022-66851010; www.csia.in; Chhatrapati Shivaji International Airport)

Land
Border Crossings

➡ It is possible to travel overland between India and Bangladesh, Bhutan, Nepal, Pakistan and Myanmar (though the border is only open occasionally and this route is not recommended). For more on these routes, consult the 'Europe to India overland' section on www.seat61.com/India.htm.

➡ You *must* have a valid Indian visa in advance, as no visas are available at the border.

➡ Drivers will need their vehicle's registration papers, liability insurance and an international drivers' permit in addition to their domestic licence. You'll also need a *Carnet de passage en douane*, which acts as a temporary waiver of import duty on the vehicle.

➡ To find out the latest paperwork requirements and other important driving information, contact your local automobile association.

Sea

After a 28-year hiatus, a ferry service between southern India and Sri Lanka began again in 2011, linking Thoothikudi (Tuticorin) in Tamil Nadu with Colombo. However, it was suspended after five months. A new service be-

tween the same ports, or on the old route between Rameswaram and Talaimannar, may start; check locally or online to see if there has been any progress.

Tours

Many international companies offer tours to South India, from straightforward sightseeing trips to adventure tours and activity-based holidays. Some good places to start your tour hunt:

Dragoman (www.dragoman.com) One of several reputable overland tour companies offering trips on customised vehicles.

Exodus (www.exodus.co.uk) A wide array of specialist trips, including tours with a holistic, wildlife and adventure focus.

India Wildlife Tours (www.india-wildlife-tours.com) All sorts of wildlife tours, plus jeep/horse/camel safaris and bird-watching.

Indian Encounter (www.indianencounters.com) Special-interest tours include wildlife spotting, river-rafting and ayurvedic treatments.

Intrepid Travel (www.intrepidtravel.com) Endless possibilities, from wildlife tours to sacred rambles.

Shanti Travel (www.shanti-travel.com/en) A range of tours including family and adventure tours, run by a Franco-Indian team.

World Expeditions (www.worldexpeditions.com) An array of options that includes trekking and cycling tours.

GETTING AROUND

Air
Airlines in South India

➡ India has a competitive domestic airline industry, but in a crowded marketplace some players have suffered

huge financial losses and run into trouble, and at the time of writing the future of SpiceJet was uncertain. Well-established carriers include Air India, IndiGo and Jet Airways.

➡ Airline seats can be booked cheaply over the internet or through travel agencies. Apart from airline sites, bookings can be made through reliable ticketing portals such as **Cleartrip** (www.cleartrip.com), **Make My Trip** (www.makemytrip.com) and **Yatra** (www.yatra.com).

➡ Fares can fluctuate dramatically according to demand. Booking as far ahead as possible is always a good idea.

➡ Security norms require you to produce your ticket and passport when entering an airport. If you don't have a copy of your ticket with you, airline counters can issue you one for a small fee.

➡ Security at airports is generally stringent. At smaller airports, all hold baggage must be x-rayed prior to check-in (major airports now have in-line baggage screening facilities). Every item of cabin baggage needs a label, which must be stamped as part of the security check (don't forget to collect tags at the check-in counter).

➡ Keeping peak-hour congestion in mind, the recommended check-in time for domestic flights is two hours before departure – the deadline is 45 minutes. The usual economy-class baggage allowance is 20kg, but it can be 15kg or 10kg on some flights.

At the time of writing, the following airlines were operating between various destinations in India.

Air Costa (☎1800-42500666; www.aircosta.in) Serves several southeastern airports including Bengaluru, Chennai and Hyderabad.

Air India (☏1800 1801407; www.airindia.com) India's national carrier operates many domestic and international flights.

AirAsia (☏1860-5008000; www.airasia.com) Serves Chennai, Kochi, Bengaluru, Hyderabad, with flights to Kuala Lumpur too.

GoAir (☏020-25662111; www.goair.in) Reliable low-cost carrier servicing Goa, Cochin, Jaipur, Delhi and Bagdogra, among other destinations.

IndiGo (☏099-10383838; www.goindigo.in) Reliable and popular, with myriad flights across India and to select overseas destinations.

Jet Airways (☏1800-225522; www.jetairways.com) Operates flights across India and to select overseas destinations.

SpiceJet (☏0987-1803333; www.spicejet.com) Destinations include Bengaluru, Varanasi, Srinagar, Colombo (Sri Lanka) and Kathmandu (Nepal).

Bicycle

Bicycles sent by sea can take a few weeks to clear customs in India, so it's better to fly them in. It may actually be cheaper, and less hassle, to hire or buy one in India. Read up on bicycle touring before you travel: Stephen Lord's *Adventure Cycle-Touring Handbook* is a good place to start. The **Cycling Federation of India** (☏011-23753528; www.cyclingfederationofindia.org) can provide local information.

Hire

➡ Tourist centres and traveller hang-outs are the easiest spots to find bicycles for hire.

➡ Prices vary between about ₹40 and ₹100 per day for a roadworthy, Indian-made bicycle; mountain bikes, where available, are usually upwards of ₹400 per day.

➡ Hire places may require a cash security deposit.

Practicalities

➡ Mountain bikes with off-road tyres give the best protection against India's rugged roads.

➡ Roadside cycle mechanics abound but you should carry spare tyres, brake cables, lubricating oil, a chain repair kit and plenty of puncture patches.

➡ Bikes can often be carried free, or for a small fee, on the roof of buses – handy for uphill stretches.

➡ Contact your airline for information about transporting your bike and customs formalities in your home country.

Purchase

➡ Reputable brands of mountain bikes such as Hero and Atlas generally start at around ₹7000.

➡ Reselling is usually fairly easy – ask at local cycle or hire shops or advertise on travel noticeboards. If you purchased a new bike and it's still in reasonable condition, you should be able to recoup around 50% of what you paid.

On the Road

➡ Vehicles drive on the left in India but otherwise road rules are virtually nonexistent.

➡ Cities and national highways can be hazardous places to cycle so, where possible, stick to back roads.

➡ Be conservative about the distance you expect to cover: an experienced cyclist can manage around 60km to 100km a day on the plains, 40km to 60km on all-weather mountain roads and 40km or less on dirt roads.

Boat

➡ Scheduled ferries connect Chennai, Visakhapatnam and Kolkata with Port Blair in the Andaman Islands.

➡ Cruise packages sail from Kochi (Kerala) to the Lakshadweep islands.

➡ Numerous shorter ferry services run across or along rivers, from coracles to proper passenger ferries, and there are various boat cruises – notably the many options for sailing Kerala's beautiful backwaters (p288).

Bus

➡ Buses go almost everywhere and tend to be the cheapest way to travel. Services are generally fast and frequent.

➡ Roads in hilly terrain can be perilous; buses may be driven with abandon, and accidents are a risk.

➡ Avoid night buses unless there's no alternative: driving conditions are more hazardous and drivers may be inebriated or suffering from lack of sleep.

RIDING THE RAILS WITH YOUR BIKE

For long hauls, transporting your bike or motorbike by train can be a convenient option. Buy your train ticket for the journey, then take your bike to the station parcel office with your passport, registration papers, driver's licence and insurance documents. Packing-wallahs will wrap your bike in protective sacking for around ₹200 to ₹500 and you must fill out various forms and pay a shipping fee, plus an insurance fee of 1% of the declared value of the bike. Bring the same paperwork to collect your bike from the goods office at the other end.

→ All buses make snack and toilet stops.

Classes

→ State-owned and private bus companies both offer several types of bus, graded as 'ordinary', 'semi-deluxe', 'deluxe' or 'super-deluxe' or some variation on that theme. The exact degrees of comfort of the various categories offered can vary from place to place.

→ In general, ordinary buses tend to be ageing rattletraps while the deluxe grades range from less decrepit versions of ordinary buses to flashy air-con Volvo buses with reclining ('push-back') two-by-two seating.

→ Buses run by state governments are usually the more reliable option (if there's a breakdown, another bus will be sent to pick up passengers), and many state governments now operate super-deluxe buses on some routes.

→ Private buses are either more expensive (but more comfortable) than government buses, or cheaper but with kamikaze drivers and conductors who cram in passengers to maximise takings.

→ Travel agencies in many tourist towns offer relatively expensive private two-by-two buses, which tend to leave and terminate at convenient central stops.

→ Take earplugs to muffle the often deafening music or movies played in some long-distance buses.

→ Try to sit near the front to minimise the bumpy effect of potholes. Never sit directly above the wheels.

Costs

→ The cheapest buses are 'ordinary' government buses, but prices vary from state to state.

→ Add around 50% to the ordinary fare for deluxe services, double the fare for air-con, and triple or quadruple the fare for a two-by-two super-deluxe service.

Luggage

→ Luggage is stored in compartments underneath the bus (sometimes for a small fee) or carried on the roof.

→ Arrive well before departure time – some buses cover roof-stored bags with a canvas sheet, making last-minute additions inconvenient/impossible.

→ If your bags go on the roof, make sure they're securely locked, and tied to the metal baggage rack: unsecured bags can fall off on rough roads.

→ Theft is a (minor) risk: watch your bags at snack and toilet stops. Never leave daypacks or valuables unattended inside the bus.

Reservations

→ Most deluxe buses can be booked in advance – government buses usually a month, sometimes two months, ahead – at bus stations or local travel agencies.

→ Online bookings are now possible in select states such as Karnataka or at excellent portals **Cleartrip** (www.cleartrip.com), **Make My Trip** (www.makemytrip.com) and **Redbus** (☑1800-30010101; www.redbus.in).

→ Reservations are rarely possible on 'ordinary' buses; to secure seats when there's a big crowd pushing to board, send a travelling companion ahead to claim some, or pass a book or article of clothing through an open window on to an empty seat. This last 'reservation' method rarely fails.

→ If you board a bus midway through its journey, you may have to stand until a seat becomes free.

→ Many buses only depart when full – passengers might suddenly leave yours to join one that looks nearer to departing.

→ Many bus stations have a separate women's queue (not always obvious when signs are in Hindi and men join the melee).

→ Women have an unspoken right to elbow their way to the front of any bus queue in India, so don't be shy, ladies!

Car

Few people bother with self-drive car hire – not only because of the hair-raising driving conditions, but also because hiring a car with a driver is wonderfully affordable in India, particularly if several people share the cost. Seatbelts are either nonexistent or of variable quality. **Hertz** (www.hertz.com) is one of the few international companies with representatives in India.

Hiring a Car & Driver

→ Most towns have taxi stands or car-hire companies where you can arrange short or long tours. You can also make arrangements through many hotels.

→ Not all hire cars are licensed to travel beyond their home state. Those that are will pay extra state taxes, which are added to the hire charge.

→ Ask for a driver who speaks some English and knows the region you intend visiting, and try to see the car and meet the driver before paying anything.

→ A wide range of vehicles now ply as taxis. From a proletarian Tata Indica hatchback to a comfy jeep-type Toyota Innova, there's a model to suit most budgets.

→ To help avoid misunderstandings, it's important to set the ground rules from day one; politely but firmly let the driver know that you're boss.

Costs

➡ Car-hire costs depend on the distance, vehicle and terrain (driving on mountain roads uses more petrol, hence the higher cost).

➡ Hire charges for multiday trips cover the driver's meals and accommodation. Drivers should make their own sleeping and eating arrangements.

➡ One-way trips often cost the same as return ones (to cover the petrol and driver charges for getting back).

➡ Some taxi unions set minimum daily rates or maximum daily time or kilometre limits – if you go over the maximum, you have to pay extra.

➡ To avoid potential misunderstandings, get *in writing* what you've been promised (quotes should include petrol, sightseeing stops, all your chosen destinations, and meals and accommodation for the driver).

➡ If a driver requests money for petrol en route, get receipts for reimbursement later. If you're travelling by the kilometre, check the odometer reading before you set out so as to avoid confusions while paying up.

➡ For day trips in and around a single city, expect to pay ₹1000/1200 or more for a car without/with air-con and with an eight-hour, 80km limit (extra if you go over).

➡ For multiday trips, operators usually peg a 250km or 300km minimum distance per day and charge around ₹8/10 per kilometre for a non-AC/AC car. If you overshoot, you pay extra.

➡ A tip to the driver is customary at the end of your journey; somewhere between 7% and 10% is fair.

Hitching

For a negotiable fee, truck drivers supplement the bus service in some remote areas. However, as drivers rarely speak English, you may have difficulty explaining where you wish to go, and working out a fair price to pay. Be aware that truck drivers have a reputation for driving under the influence of alcohol. As anywhere, women are strongly advised against hitching alone or even in pairs. Always use your instincts.

Hitching is never entirely safe, and we don't recommend it. Travellers who hitch should understand that they are taking a small but potentially serious risk.

Local Transport

➡ Buses, cycle-rickshaws, autorickshaws, taxis, boats, suburban trains and, in a few places, metro systems, provide transport around South India's cities.

➡ For any transport without a meter or fixed fare, agree on the price *before* you start your journey and make sure that it covers your luggage and every passenger.

➡ Even where meters exist, drivers may refuse to use them, demanding an elevated fare. Try to insist on the meter; if that fails, find another vehicle. Or just bargain hard.

➡ Taxi and autorickshaw fares usually increase at night (by up to 100%) and some drivers charge a few rupees extra for luggage.

➡ Carry plenty of small-denomination banknotes for taxi and rickshaw fares as drivers rarely have change.

➡ In some places, taxi/autorickshaw drivers are involved in the commission racket, receiving kickbacks from shops and hotels.

Autorickshaw, Tempo & Vikram

➡ Similar to the tuk-tuks of Southeast Asia, the Indian autorickshaw is a three-wheeled motorised contraption with a tin or canvas roof and sides, with room for two or three passengers (although you'll often see more squeezed in) and limited luggage.

➡ They are also referred to as autos, scooters and riks, and are cheaper than taxis.

➡ Some train and bus stations have pre-paid autorickshaw stands, with fixed fares depending on distance.

➡ Travelling by auto is great fun but, thanks to the open windows, can be noisy and hot (or severely cold!).

➡ Tempos and *vikrams* (large tempos) are outsized autorickshaws with room for more passengers, shuttling on fixed routes for a fixed fare.

Boat

Various kinds of local boats offer transport across and down rivers in South India, from big car ferries to wooden canoes and wicker coracles. Most of the larger boats carry bicycles and motorcycles for a fee.

Bus

Urban buses range from fume-belching, human-stuffed mechanical monsters to sanitised AC vehicles with comfortable seating and smoother ride quality. Buses are cheap, but autorickshaws and taxis are usually quicker.

Cycle-Rickshaw

➡ A cycle-rickshaw is a pedal cycle with two rear wheels, supporting a bench seat for passengers. Most have a canopy that can be raised in wet weather, or lowered to provide extra space for luggage.

➡ Fares must be agreed in advance – speak to locals to get an idea of a fair price for the distance involved.

Metro & Train

New metro systems are starting to transform urban

transport in the biggest cities. Metros in Bengaluru (Bangalore) and Mumbai (Bombay) are already open, and the Chennai (Madras), Hyderabad and Kochi (Cochin) metros were expected to start operating in late 2015 or 2016. They will become increasingly useful as their networks expand over the coming years.

Mumbai, Hyderabad and Chennai, among other cities, also have useful suburban trains leaving from ordinary train stations.

Taxi

Most towns have taxis, and these are usually metered; however, getting drivers to use the meter can be a hassle. To avoid fare-setting hassles, use prepaid taxis where possible.

➡ Most major Indian airports and train stations, and some bus stations, have prepaid-taxi and/or radio-cab booths. Here, you can book a taxi for a fixed price (which will include baggage) and thus avoid fare shenanigans and commission scams. Hold onto your receipt until you reach your destination, as proof of payment.

➡ Radio cabs (which can usually be booked by phone from anywhere in the city) cost marginally more than prepaid taxis, but are air-conditioned and driven by the company's chauffeurs. They are fitted with electronic fare meters and, usually, GPS units so that the company can monitor the vehicle's movement.

Motorcycle

Despite traffic challenges, India is an amazing country for long-distance motorcycle touring. However, it can be quite an undertaking; there are some popular motorcycle tours for those who don't want the rigmarole of going it alone.

Weather is an important factor and you should check for the best times to visit different areas.

Driving Licence

To hire a motorcycle in India, technically you're required to have a valid international drivers' permit in addition to your domestic licence. In tourist areas, some places may rent out a motorcycle without asking for these documents, but you won't be covered by insurance in the event of an accident, and may also face a fine.

Hire

➡ The classic way to motorcycle around India is on a Royal Enfield, built in India to either vintage or modern specs. As well as making a satisfying chugging sound, these bikes are fully manual, making them easy to repair (parts can be found almost everywhere in India).

➡ On the other hand, Enfields are often less reliable than many of the newer, Japanese-designed bikes.

➡ Plenty of places rent out motorcycles for local trips and longer tours. Local rental is particularly popular in Goa, typically for ₹300 to ₹500 per day for a motorbike and

₹200 to ₹300 for scooters. Japanese- and Indian-made bikes in the 100cc-to-150cc range are cheaper than the big 350cc-to-500cc Enfields.

➡ As security, you'll usually need to leave a large cash deposit (ensure you get a receipt that stipulates the refundable amount), or your passport or air ticket. We strongly advise not leaving these documents, in particular your passport, which you need for hotel check-ins and if asked for by the police.

➡ For three weeks' hire, a 500cc Enfield costs from around ₹22,000, and a 350cc from about ₹15,000. The price normally includes excellent advice and an invaluable crash course in Enfield mechanics and repairs.

➡ Helmets are available for ₹500 to ₹2000; extras (panniers, luggage racks, protection bars, rear-view mirrors, lockable fuel caps, petrol filters, extra tools) are also easy to come by.

➡ A useful website for Enfield models is www.royalenfield. com. In Mumbai, **Allibhai Premji Tyrewalla** (☏022-23099313; www.premjis. com; 205 Dr D Bhadkamkar/ Lamington Rd) sells new and secondhand motorcycles with a buy-back option.

Purchase

➡ For longer tours, purchasing a motorcycle may sound like a great idea. It does, however, involve reams of complicated paperwork, and in many situations, procuring a motorcycle might not be feasible at all.

➡ Secondhand bikes are widely available (and paperwork is simpler than for a new machine). To find one, check travellers' noticeboards and ask motorcycle mechanics and other bikers.

➡ A well-looked-after secondhand 350cc Enfield

TAXI METERS

Getting a metered ride is only half the battle. Meters are often outdated, so fares are calculated using a combination of the meter reading and a complicated 'fare adjustment card'. Predictably, this system is open to abuse. To get a rough estimate of fares in advance, try the portal www.taxiautofare.com.

costs ₹50,000 to ₹100,000. The 500cc model ranges between ₹85,000 to ₹135,000.

OWNERSHIP PAPERS

➡ The paperwork associated with owning a motorcycle is complicated and time-consuming, so it's wise to seek advice from the agent selling the bike.

➡ Registration papers are signed by the local registration authority when the bike is first sold; you need these when you buy a secondhand bike.

➡ Foreign nationals cannot change the name on the registration but you must fill out forms for change of ownership and transfer of insurance.

➡ Registration must be renewed every 15 years (for around ₹5000); make absolutely sure that it states the 'roadworthiness' of the vehicle, and that there are no outstanding debts or criminal proceedings associated with the bike.

Insurance

➡ Only hire a bike that has at least third-party insurance – if you hit someone and you don't have insurance, the consequences can be very costly. Reputable companies will include third-party cover in their rentals.

➡ You must also arrange insurance if you buy a motorcycle (usually you can organise this through the person selling the bike).

➡ The minimum level of cover is third-party insurance, available for around ₹800 to ₹1500 per year. This will cover repair and medical costs for any other vehicles, people or property you might hit, but won't cover your own machine. Comprehensive insurance (recommended) costs ₹1200 to ₹3500 per year.

Fuel, Spare Parts & Extras

➡ Petrol and engine oil are widely available in the plains, but petrol stations are fewer in the hills. If travelling to remote regions, ask about fuel availability beforehand and carry enough extra fuel.

➡ In remote regions it's also important to carry basic spares (valves, fuel lines, piston rings etc). Parts for Indian and Japanese machines are widely available in cities and larger towns.

➡ Get your machine serviced regularly (particularly older ones). Indian roads and engine vibration work things loose quite quickly.

➡ Check the engine and gearbox oil level at least every 500km, and clean the oil filter every few thousand kilometres.

➡ The chances are you'll make at least a couple of visits to a puncture-wallah – start with new tyres and carry spanners to remove your own wheels.

➡ It's a good idea to bring your own protective equipment (jackets, gloves etc).

Road Conditions

➡ Given the varied road conditions, India can be challenging for novice riders.

➡ Hazards range from cows and chickens crossing the carriageway to broken-down trucks, unruly traffic, pedestrians on the road, and ubiquitous potholes and unmarked speed humps.

➡ Rural roads sometimes have grain crops strewn across them to be threshed by passing vehicles – a serious sliding hazard for motorcyclists.

➡ Try not to cover too much territory in one day and never ride in the dark – many vehicles drive without lights, and dynamo-powered motorcycle headlamps are useless at low revs while negotiating around potholes.

➡ On busy national highways, expect to average 40km/h to 50km/h without stops; on winding back roads and dirt tracks this can drop to 10km/h.

Organised Motorcycle Tours

Dozens of companies offer organised motorcycle tours around India with a support vehicle, mechanic and guide. Here are some reputable outfits that can arrange South India trips:

Blazing Trails (www.blazing trailstours.com)

Classic Bike Adventure (www.classic-bike-india.com; Assagao) This well-established Goan company organises motorbike tours on Enfields through the Himalayas, Nepal, South India and Goa.

H-C Travel (www.hctravel.com)

Kerala Bike Tours (www.keralabiketours.com; Kochi) Based in Ravipuram, Kochi.

Lalli Singh Tours (www.lallisingh.com)

Moto Discovery (www.motodiscovery.com)

Wheel of India (www.wheelofindia.com)

Tours

Tours are available all over South India, run by local companies, state government tourism enterprises and others. Some excellent small-group city tours on foot and/or motorised transport really help you get under the skin of some cities. Food tours are a great option for getting to know local cuisines.

At tourist sites you'll often be approached by would-be guides. Good ones can certainly make a place more interesting; if you're thinking of taking one, ask for their official authorisation and sort out the fee beforehand.

Train

Travelling by train is a quintessential Indian experience. Trains offer a smoother ride than buses and are especially recommended for long journeys that include overnight travel. India's rail network is one of the largest and busiest in the world and Indian Railways is the largest utility employer on earth, with roughly 1.5 million workers and around 6900 train stations scattered across the country.

The easiest way of sourcing updated railway information is to use relevant internet sites such as **Indian Railways** (www.indianrail.gov. in) or the excellent **India Rail Info** (www.indiarailinfo.com), with added offline browsing support, or the user-friendly eRail.in. There's also the comprehensive *Trains at a Glance* (₹45), available at many station book-stands and better bookshops/newsstands, but it's published annually so it's not as up to date as websites.

Booking Tickets in India

➜ You can book tickets through a travel agency or hotel (for a commission) or in person at a train station. At many stations you can book for any train in the country.

➜ You can also book online through portals such as

Cleartrip (www.cleartrip. com), **Make My Trip** (www. makemytrip.com) and **Yatra** (www.yatra.com), or **IRCTC** (www.irctc.co.in), the e-ticketing division of Indian Railways.

➜ Online booking has its share of glitches, though: travellers have reported problems with registering on some portals and using certain overseas credit cards.

➜ Staff at booking offices in big stations usually speak English; at smaller stations, the stationmaster and deputy usually speak English.

➜ See Booking Trains (p26) for more information.

AT THE STATION

Get a reservation slip from the information window, fill in the name of the departure station, destination station, the class you want and the name and number of the train. Join the queue for the ticket window where your ticket will be printed. If there isn't a separate women's queue, women can go to the front of the regular queue.

TOURIST RESERVATION BUREAU

Larger cities and major tourist centres have an International Tourist Bureau, which allows you to book train tickets in relative calm; check www.indianrail.gov.in for a list.

Reservations

➜ Bookings open up to 60 days before departure and you must make a reservation for chair-car, sleeper, 1AC, 2AC and 3AC carriages. No reservations are required for unreserved general (2nd-class) compartments; you have to grab seats here the moment the train pulls in.

➜ Trains are always busy so it's wise to book as far in advance as possible, especially for overnight journeys.

➜ If the train you want is sold out, enquire about other options.

➜ Trains can be delayed at any stage of the journey; to avoid stress, factor some leeway into your plans.

➜ Reserved tickets show your carriage number and seat or berth number. Carriage numbers are written on the side of the train and a list of names and berths is posted on the side of each reserved carriage.

➜ Refunds are available on almost any ticket, even after departure, with a penalty – rules are complicated, check when you book.

➜ Be mindful of potential drugging and theft.

TOURIST QUOTA

A special (albeit small) tourist quota is set aside for foreign tourists and Non-Resident Indians on many trains. These seats can only be booked at dedicated reservation offices in major cities, and passports (with visas) of all passengers must be shown. Tickets can be paid for in rupees (some offices may ask to see foreign-exchange certificates – ATM receipts will suffice).

TATKAL TICKETS

Indian Railways holds back a small number of tickets on key trains and releases them at 10am one day before the train is due to depart. A charge of ₹10 to ₹400 is

EXPRESS TRAIN FARES (₹)

Distance (km)	1AC	2AC	3AC	Chair Car (CC)	Sleeper	Second (II)
100	1047	613	428	205	120	47
200	1047	613	428	278	120	72
300	1047	613	428	370	177	101
500	1711	996	688	545	261	150
1000	2895	1683	1156	916	439	253
2000	4592	2644	1788	1433	692	410

added to each ticket price. 1AC tickets are excluded from the scheme.

RESERVATION AGAINST CANCELLATION (RAC)

Even when a train is fully booked, Indian Railways sells a handful of seats in each class as 'Reservation Against Cancellation' (RAC). This means that if you have an RAC ticket and someone cancels before the departure date, you may get his or her seat (or berth). You'll have to check the reservation list at the station on the day of travel to see if you've been allocated a confirmed seat/ berth. Even if no one cancels, you can still board the train as an RAC ticket holder and travel without a seat.

WAITLIST (WL)

If the RAC quota is maxed out as well, you can get a waitlisted ticket. If there are enough cancellations, you may eventually move up the order to land a confirmed berth, or at least an RAC ticket. Check your booking status at http://www.indian-rail.gov.in/pnr_Enq.html by entering your ticket's PNR

FARE FINDER

••
Go to www.indiarailinfo.com or eRail.in and type in your starting point and destination. You'll promptly get a list of every train (with the name, number, arrival/departure times and journey details) plying the route, as well as fares for each available class. These sites will also tell you ticket availability.

number. You can't board the train on a waitlisted ticket, but a refund is available; ask the ticket office about your chances.

Costs

➡ Fares are calculated by distance, class of accommodation and type of train. There is also a reservation fee of ₹15 to ₹60 depending on class. See Booking Trains (p26) for information on classes.

➡ Express trains are the mainstay of intercity services; Superfast and Sampark Kranti trains go a bit faster and cost slightly more.

➡ Quickest are Rajdhani Express, Duronto Express and Shatabdi Express trains, which include meals in the fare. Rajdhani and Duronto fares are about one-third higher than ordinary Express fares. Shatabdis are daytime seat-only trains: ordinary chair-class fares are similar to 3AC on ordinary Express trains.

➡ Most air-conditioned carriages have a catering service (meals are brought to your seat). In unreserved classes, it's a good idea to carry snacks.

➡ Male/female seniors (those over 60/58) get 40/50% off all fares in all classes on all types of trains. Children below the age of six travel free, those aged between six and 12 are charged half price, up to 300km.

Health

Hygiene is generally poor in most regions so food and water-borne illnesses are fairly common. A number of insect-borne diseases are present, particularly in tropical areas. Medical care is basic in various areas (especially beyond the larger cities) so it's essential to be well prepared.

Pre-existing medical conditions and accidental injury (especially traffic accidents) account for most that are life-threatening. Becoming ill in some way, however, is common. Fortunately, most travellers' illnesses can be prevented with some common-sense behaviour or treated with a well-stocked travellers' medical kit – however, never hesitate to consult a doctor while on the road, as self-diagnosis can be hazardous.

The following information is a general guide only and certainly does not replace the advice of a doctor trained in travel medicine.

BEFORE YOU GO

You can buy many medications over the counter in India without a doctor's prescription, but it can be difficult to find some of the newer drugs, particularly the latest antidepressant drugs, blood-pressure medications and contraceptive pills. Bring the following:

➡ medications in their original, labelled containers

➡ a signed, dated letter from your doctor describing your medical conditions and medications, including generic names

➡ a doctor's letter documenting the necessity of any syringes you bring

➡ if you have a heart condition, a copy of your ECG taken just prior to travelling

➡ any regular medication (double your ordinary needs)

Insurance

Don't travel without health insurance. Emergency evacuation is expensive. Consider the following when buying insurance:

➡ You may require extra cover for adventure activities such as rock climbing.

➡ In India, doctors usually require immediate payment in cash. Your insurance plan may make payments directly to providers or it will reimburse you later for overseas health expenditures. If you do have to claim later, make sure you keep all relevant documentation.

➡ Some policies ask that you telephone back (reverse charges) to a centre in your home country where an immediate assessment of your problem will be made.

Vaccinations

Specialised travel-medicine clinics are your best source of up-to-date information; they stock all available vaccines and can give specific recommendations for your trip. Most vaccines don't give immunity until at least two weeks after they're given, so visit a doctor well before de-

parture. Ask your doctor for an International Certificate of Vaccination (sometimes known as the 'yellow booklet'), which will list all the vaccinations you've received.

Medical checklist

Recommended items for a personal medical kit:

➡ Antifungal cream, eg clotrimazole

➡ Antibacterial cream, eg mupirocin

➡ Antibiotic for skin infections, eg amoxicillin/ clavulanate or cephalexin

➡ Antihistamine – there are many options, eg cetirizine for daytime and promethazine for night

➡ Antiseptic, eg Betadine

➡ Antispasmodic for stomach cramps, eg Buscopam

➡ Contraceptive

➡ Decongestant, eg pseudoephedrine

➡ DEET-based insect repellent

➡ Diarrhoea medication – consider an oral rehydration solution (eg Gastrolyte), diarrhoea 'stopper' (eg loperamide) and antinausea medication (eg prochlorperazine). Antibiotics for diarrhoea include ciprofloxacin; for bacterial diarrhoea azithromycin; for giardia or amoebic dysentery tinidazole

➡ First-aid items such as elastoplasts, bandages, gauze, thermometer (but not mercury), sterile needles and syringes, and tweezers

➡ Ibuprofen or another anti-inflammatory

➡ Iodine tablets (unless you're pregnant or have a thyroid problem) to purify water

➡ Migraine medication if you suffer from migraines

➡ Paracetamol

➡ Pyrethrin to impregnate clothing and mosquito nets

➡ Steroid cream for allergic or itchy rashes, eg 1% to 2% hydrocortisone

➡ High-factor sunscreen

➡ Throat lozenges

➡ Thrush (vaginal yeast infection) treatment, eg clotrimazole pessaries or Diflucan tablet

➡ Ural or equivalent if prone to urine infections

Websites

There is lots of travel-health advice on the internet; www.lonelyplanet.com is a good place to start. Other options:

Centers for Disease Control and Prevention (CDC; www.cdc.gov) Travel health advice.

MD Travel Health (www.mdtravelhealth.com) Travel-health recommendations for every country, updated daily.

World Health Organization (WHO; www.who.int/ith) Its helpful book *International Travel & Health* is revised annually and is available online.

Further Reading

Lonely Planet's *Healthy Travel – Asia & India* is pocket sized with useful information, including pre-trip planning, first aid, immunisation

---

REQUIRED & RECOMMENDED VACCINATIONS

The only vaccine required by international regulations is **yellow fever**. Proof of vaccination will only be required if you have visited a country in the yellow-fever zone within the six days prior to entering India. If you are travelling to India from Africa or South America, you should check to see if you require proof of vaccination.

The World Health Organization (WHO) recommends the following vaccinations for travellers to India (as well as being up to date with measles, mumps and rubella vaccinations):

Adult diphtheria & tetanus Single booster recommended if none in the previous 10 years. Side effects include sore arm and fever.

Hepatitis A Provides almost 100% protection for up to a year; a booster after 12 months provides at least another 20 years' protection. Mild side effects such as headache and sore arm occur in 5% to 10% of people.

Hepatitis B Now considered routine for most travellers. Given as three shots over six months. A rapid schedule is also available, as is a combined vaccination with Hepatitis A. Side effects are mild and uncommon, usually headache and sore arm. In 95% of people lifetime protection results.

Polio Only one booster is required as an adult for lifetime protection. Inactivated polio vaccine is safe during pregnancy.

Typhoid Recommended for all travellers to India, even those only visiting urban areas. The vaccine offers around 70% protection, lasts for two to three years and comes as a single shot. Tablets are also available, but the injection is usually recommended as it has fewer side effects. Sore arm and fever may occur.

Varicella If you haven't had chickenpox, discuss this vaccination with your doctor.

These immunisations are recommended for long-term travellers (more than one month) or those at special risk (seek further advice from your doctor):

Japanese B Encephalitis Three injections in all. Booster recommended after two years. Sore arm and headache are the most common side effects. In rare cases, an allergic reaction comprising hives and swelling can occur up to 10 days after any of the three doses.

Meningitis Single injection. There are two types of vaccination: the quadravalent vaccine gives two to three years' protection; meningitis group C vaccine gives around 10 years' protection. Recommended for long-term backpackers aged under 25.

Rabies Three injections in all. A booster after one year will then provide 10 years' protection. Side effects are rare – occasionally headache and sore arm.

Tuberculosis (TB) Adult long-term travellers are usually recommended to have a TB skin test before and after travel, rather than vaccination. Only one vaccine given in a lifetime.

information, and what to do if you get sick on the road. Other good references include *Travellers' Health* by Dr Richard Dawood and *Travelling Well* by Dr Deborah Mills – check out the website (www.travellingwell.com.au) too.

IN INDIA

Availability of Health Care

Medical care is hugely variable in India. Some cities now have clinics catering specifically to travellers and expatriates; these clinics are usually more expensive than local medical facilities, and offer a higher standard of care. Additionally, they know the local system, including reputable local hospitals and specialists. They may also liaise with insurance companies should you require evacuation. It is usually difficult to find reliable medical care in rural areas.

Self-treatment may be appropriate if your problem is minor (eg traveller's diarrhoea), you are carrying the relevant medication, and you cannot attend a recommended clinic. If you suspect a serious disease, especially malaria, travel to the nearest quality facility.

Before buying medication over the counter, check the use-by date, and ensure the packet is sealed and properly stored (eg not exposed to the sunshine).

Infectious Diseases

Malaria

This is a potentially deadly disease. Before you travel, seek expert advice according to your itinerary (rural areas are especially risky) and on medication and side effects.

Malaria is caused by a parasite transmitted by the bite of an infected mosquito. The most important symptom of malaria is fever, but general symptoms, such as headache, diarrhoea, cough or chills, may also occur. Diagnosis can only be properly made by taking a blood sample.

Two strategies should be combined to prevent malaria: mosquito avoidance and antimalarial medications. Most people who catch malaria are taking inadequate or no antimalarial medication.

Travellers are advised to prevent mosquito bites by taking these steps:

➡ Use a DEET-based insect repellent on exposed skin. Wash this off at night – as long as you are sleeping under a mosquito net. Natural repellents such as citronella can be effective, but must be applied more frequently than products containing DEET.

➡ Sleep under a mosquito net impregnated with pyrethrin.

➡ Choose accommodation with proper screens and fans (if not air-conditioned).

➡ Impregnate clothing with pyrethrin in high-risk areas.

➡ Wear long sleeves and trousers in light colours.

➡ Use mosquito coils.

➡ Spray your room with insect repellent before going out for your evening meal.

There are a variety of medications available:

Chloroquine & Paludrine combination Limited effectiveness in many parts of South Asia. Common side effects include nausea (40% of people) and mouth ulcers.

Doxycycline (daily tablet) A broad-spectrum antibiotic that helps prevent a variety of tropical diseases, including leptospirosis, tick-borne disease and typhus. Potential side effects include photosensitivity (a tendency to sunburn), thrush (in women), indigestion, heartburn, nausea and interference with the contraceptive pill. More serious side effects include ulceration of the oesophagus – take your tablet with a meal and a large glass of water, and never lie down within half an hour of taking it. It must be taken for four weeks after leaving the risk area.

Lariam (mefloquine) This weekly tablet suits many people. Serious side effects are rare but include depression, anxiety, psychosis and seizures. Anyone with a history of depression, anxiety, other psychological disorders or epilepsy should not take Lariam. It is considered safe in the second and third trimesters of pregnancy. Tablets must be taken for four weeks after leaving the risk area.

Malarone A combination of atovaquone and proguanil. Side effects are uncommon and mild, most commonly nausea and headache. It is the best tablet for scuba divers and for those on short trips to high-risk areas. It must be taken for one week after leaving the risk area.

Other diseases

Avian Flu 'Bird flu' or Influenza A (H5N1) is a subtype of the type A influenza virus. Contact with dead or sick birds is the principal source of infection and bird-to-human transmission does not easily occur. Symptoms include high fever and flu-like symptoms with rapid deterioration, leading to respiratory failure and death in many cases. Immediate medical care should be sought if bird flu is suspected. Check www. who.int/en/or www.avianinflu-enza.com.au.

Dengue Fever This mosquito-borne disease is becomingly increasingly problematic, especially in the cities. As there is no vaccine available it can only be prevented by avoiding mosquito bites at all times. Symptoms include high fever, severe headache and body ache and sometimes a rash and diarrhoea. Treatment is rest and paracetamol – do not take aspirin or ibuprofen as it increases the likelihood of haemorrhaging. Make sure you see a doctor to be diagnosed and monitored.

Hepatitis A This food- and water-borne virus infects the liver, causing jaundice (yellow skin and eyes), nausea and lethargy. There is no specific treatment for hepatitis A; just allow time for the liver to heal. All travellers to India should be vaccinated against hepatitis A.

Hepatitis B This sexually transmitted disease is spread by body fluids and can be prevented by vaccination. The long-term consequences can include liver cancer and cirrhosis.

Hepatitis E Transmitted through contaminated food and water, hepatitis E has similar symptoms to hepatitis A, but is far less common. It is a severe problem in pregnant women and can result in the death of both mother and baby. There is no commercially available vaccine, and prevention is by following safe eating and drinking guidelines.

HIV Spread via contaminated body fluids. Avoid unsafe sex, unsterile needles (including in medical facilities) and procedures such as tattoos. The growth rate of HIV in India is one of the highest in the world.

Influenza Present year-round in the tropics, influenza (flu) symptoms include fever, muscle aches, a runny nose, cough and sore throat. It can be severe in people over the age of 65 or in those with medical conditions such as heart disease or diabetes – vaccination is recommended for these individuals. There is no specific treatment, just rest and paracetamol.

Japanese B Encephalitis This viral disease is transmitted by mosquitoes and is rare in travellers. Most cases occur in rural areas and vaccination is recommended for travellers spending more than one month outside of cities. There is no treatment, and it may result in permanent brain damage or death. Ask your doctor for further details.

Rabies This fatal disease is spread by the bite or possibly even the lick of an infected animal – most commonly a dog or monkey. You should seek medical advice immediately after any animal bite and commence postexposure treatment. Having pretravel vaccination means the postbite treatment is greatly simplified. If an animal bites you, gently wash the wound with soap and water, and apply iodine-based antiseptic. If you are not prevaccinated you will need to receive rabies immunoglobulin as soon as possible, and this is very difficult to obtain in much of India.

Tuberculosis While TB is rare in travellers, those who have significant contact with the local population (such as medical and aid workers and long-term travellers) should take precautions. Vaccination is usually only given to children under the age of five, but adults at risk are recommended to have pre- and post-travel TB testing. The main symptoms are fever, cough, weight loss, night sweats and fatigue.

Typhoid This bacterial infection is also spread via food and water. It gives a high and progressive fever and headache, and may be accompanied by a dry cough and stomach pain. It is diagnosed by blood tests and treated with antibiotics. Vaccination is recommended for all travellers who are spending more than a week in India. Be aware that vaccination is not 100% effective, so you must still be careful with what you eat and drink.

Travellers' Diarrhoea

This is by far the most common problem affecting travellers in India – between 30% and 70% of people will suffer from it within two weeks of starting their trip. It's usually caused by a bacteria, and thus responds promptly to treatment with antibiotics.

Travellers' diarrhoea is defined as the passage of more than three watery bowel actions within 24 hours, plus at least one other symptom, such as fever, cramps, nausea, vomiting or feeling generally unwell.

Treatment consists of staying well hydrated; rehydration solutions like Gastrolyte are the best for this. Antibiotics such as ciprofloxacin or azithromycin should kill the bacteria quickly. Seek medical attention quickly if you do not respond to an appropriate antibiotic.

Loperamide is just a 'stopper' and doesn't get to the cause of the problem. It can be helpful, though (eg if you have to go on a long bus ride). Don't take loperamide if you have a fever or blood in your stools.

Amoebic Dysentery Amoebic dysentery is very rare in travellers but is quite often misdiagnosed by poor-quality labs. Symptoms are similar to bacterial diarrhoea: fever, bloody diarrhoea and generally feeling unwell. You should always seek reliable medical care if you have blood in your diarrhoea. Treatment involves two drugs: tinidazole or metronidazole to kill the parasite in your gut and then a second drug to kill the cysts. If left untreated complications such as liver or gut abscesses can occur.

Giardiasis Giardia is a parasite that is relatively common in travellers. Symptoms include nausea, bloating, excess gas, fatigue and intermittent diarrhoea. The parasite will eventually go away if left untreated but this can take months; the best advice is to seek medical treatment. The treatment of choice is tinidazole, with metronidazole being a second-line option.

Environmental Hazards

Air Pollution

Air pollution, particularly vehicle pollution, is an increasing problem in most of India's urban hubs. If you have severe respiratory problems, speak with your doctor before travelling to India.

Diving & Surfing

Divers and surfers should seek specialised advice before they travel to ensure their medical kit contains treatment for coral cuts and tropical ear infections. Divers should ensure their insurance covers them for decompression illness – get specialised dive insurance through an organisation such as Divers Alert Network (www.danasiapacific.org). Certain medical conditions are incompatible with diving; check with your doctor.

Food

Dining out brings with it the possibility of contracting diarrhoea. Ways to help avoid food-related illness:

➡ eat only freshly cooked food

➡ avoid shellfish and buffets

➡ peel fruit

➡ cook vegetables

➡ soak salads in iodine water for at least 20 minutes

➡ eat in busy restaurants with a high turnover of customers

Heat

Many parts of India, especially down south, are hot and humid throughout the year. For most visitors it takes around two weeks to comfortably adapt to the hot climate. Swelling of the feet and ankles is common, as are muscle cramps caused by excessive sweating. Prevent these by avoiding dehydration and excessive activity in the heat. Don't eat salt tablets (they aggravate the gut); drinking rehydration solution or eating salty food helps. Treat cramps by resting, rehydrating with double-strength rehydration solution and gently stretching.

Dehydration is the main contributor to heat exhaustion. Recovery is usually rapid and it is common to feel weak for some days afterwards. Symptoms include:

➡ feeling weak

➡ headache

➡ irritability

➡ nausea or vomiting

➡ sweaty skin

➡ a fast, weak pulse

➡ normal or slightly elevated body temperature.

Treatment:

➡ get out of the heat

➡ fan the sufferer

➡ apply cool, wet cloths to the skin

➡ lay the sufferer flat with their legs raised

➡ rehydrate with water containing one-quarter teaspoon of salt per litre.

Heat stroke is a serious medical emergency. Symptoms include:

➡ weakness

➡ nausea

➡ a hot dry body

➡ temperature of over 41°C

➡ dizziness

➡ confusion

➡ loss of coordination

➡ seizures

➡ eventual collapse.

Treatment:

➡ get out of the heat

➡ fan the sufferer

➡ apply wet cloths to the skin or ice to the body, especially to the groin and armpits.

Prickly heat is a common skin rash in the tropics, caused by sweat trapped under the skin. Treat it by moving out of the heat for a few hours and by having cool showers. Creams and ointments clog the skin so they should be avoided. Locally bought prickly-heat powder can be helpful.

Altitude Sickness

If you are going to altitudes above 3000m, Acute Mountain Sickness (AMS) is an issue. The biggest risk factor is going too high too quickly – follow a conservative acclimatisation schedule found in good trekking guides, and *never* go to a higher altitude when you have any symptoms that could be altitude related. There is no way to

---

DRINKING WATER

➡ Never drink tap water.

➡ Bottled water is generally safe – check the seal is intact at purchase.

➡ Avoid ice unless you know it has been made hygienically.

➡ Be careful of fresh juices served at street stalls in particular – they may have been watered down or may be served in unhygienic jugs/glasses.

➡ Boiling water is the most efficient method of purifying it.

➡ The best chemical purifier is iodine. It should not be used by pregnant women or those with thyroid problems.

➡ Water filters should also filter out most viruses. Ensure your filter has a chemical barrier such as iodine and a small pore size (less than four microns).

predict who will get altitude sickness and it is quite often the younger, fitter members of a group who succumb.

Symptoms usually develop during the first 24 hours at altitude but may be delayed up to three weeks. Mild symptoms include:

→ headache
→ lethargy
→ dizziness
→ difficulty sleeping
→ loss of appetite.

AMS may become more severe without warning and can be fatal. Severe symptoms include:

→ breathlessness
→ a dry, irritative cough (which may progress to the production of pink, frothy sputum)
→ severe headache
→ lack of coordination and balance
→ confusion
→ irrational behaviour
→ vomiting
→ drowsiness
→ unconsciousness.

Treat mild symptoms by resting at the same altitude until recovery, which usually takes a day or two. Paracetamol or aspirin can be taken for headaches. If symptoms persist or become worse, immediate descent is necessary; even 500m can help. Drug treatments should never be used to avoid descent or to enable further ascent.

The drugs acetazolamide and dexamethasone are recommended by some doctors for the prevention of AMS; however, their use is controversial. They can reduce the symptoms, but they may also mask warning signs; severe and fatal AMS has occurred in people taking these drugs.

To prevent acute mountain sickness:

→ ascend slowly – have frequent rest days, spending

CARBON-MONOXIDE POISONING

Some mountain areas rely on charcoal burners for warmth, but these should be avoided due to the risk of fatal carbon-monoxide poisoning. The thick, mattress-like blankets used in many mountain areas are amazingly warm once you get beneath the covers. If you're still cold, improvise a hot-water bottle by filling your drinking-water bottle with boiled water and covering it with a sock.

two to three nights at each rise of 1000m

→ sleep at a lower altitude than the greatest height reached during the day, if possible. Above 3000m, don't increase sleeping altitude by more than 300m daily
→ drink extra fluids
→ eat light, high-carbohydrate meals
→ avoid alcohol and sedatives

Insect Bites & Stings

Bedbugs Don't carry disease but their bites can be very itchy. They usually live in furniture and walls and then migrate to the bed at night. You can treat the itch with an antihistamine.

Lice Most commonly appear on the head and pubic areas. You may need numerous applications of an antilice shampoo such as pyrethrin. Pubic lice are usually contracted from sexual contact.

Ticks Contracted walking in rural areas. Ticks are commonly found behind the ears, on the belly and in armpits. If you have had a tick bite and have a rash at the site of the bite or elsewhere, fever or muscle aches, you should see a doctor. Doxycycline prevents tick-borne diseases.

Leeches Found in humid rainforest areas. They do not transmit any disease but their bites are often intensely itchy for weeks and can easily become infected. Apply an iodine-based antiseptic to any leech bite to help prevent infection.

Bee and wasp stings Anyone with a serious bee or wasp allergy should carry an injection of adrenalin (eg an Epipen). For others pain is the main problem –

apply ice to the sting and take painkillers.

Skin Problems

Fungal rashes There are two common fungal rashes that affect travellers. The first occurs in moist areas, such as the groin, armpits and between the toes. It starts as a red patch that slowly spreads and is usually itchy. Treatment involves keeping the skin dry, avoiding chafing and using an antifungal cream such as clotrimazole or Lamisil. The second, *Tinea versicolor*, causes light-coloured patches, most commonly on the back, chest and shoulders. Consult a doctor.

Cuts and scratches These become easily infected in humid climates. Immediately wash all wounds in clean water and apply antiseptic. If you develop signs of infection (increasing pain and redness), see a doctor.

Women's Health

For gynaecological health issues, seek out a female doctor.

Birth control Bring adequate supplies of your own form of contraception.

Sanitary products Pads, rarely tampons, are readily available.

Thrush Heat, humidity and antibiotics can all contribute to thrush. Treatment is with antifungal creams and pessaries such as clotrimazole. A practical alternative is a single tablet of fluconazole (Diflucan).

Urinary-tract infections These can be precipitated by dehydration or long bus journeys without toilet stops; bring suitable antibiotics.

Language

The number of languages spoken in India helps explain why English is still widely spoken here, and why it's still in official use. Another 22 languages are recognised in the constitution, and more than 1600 other languages are spoken throughout the country.

While Hindi is the predominant language in the north, it bears little relation to the Dravidian languages of India's south and few people in the south speak Hindi. The native languages of the southern regions covered in this book (and in this chapter) are Tamil, Kannada, Konkani, Malayalam, Marathi and Telugu. Most of them belong to the Dravidian language family, although they have been influenced to varying degrees by Hindi and Sanskrit. As the predominant languages in specific geographic areas, they have in effect been used to determine the regional boundaries for the southern states.

Many educated Indians speak English as virtually their first language and for a large number of Indians it's often their second tongue, so you'll also find it very easy to get by in South India with English.

Pronunciation

The pronunciation systems of all languages covered in this chapter include a number of 'retroflex' consonants (pronounced with the tongue bent backwards), and all languages except for Tamil also have 'aspirated' consonants (pronounced with a puff of air). Our simplified pronunciation guides don't dis-linguish the retroflex consonants from their nonretroflex counterparts. The aspirated sounds are indicated with an apostrophe (') after the consonant. If you read our coloured pronunciation guides as if they were English, you'll be understood. The stressed syllables are indicated with italics for languages that have noticeable word stress; for others, all syllables should be equally stressed.

TAMIL

Tamil is the official language in the South Indian state of Tamil Nadu (as well as a national language in Sri Lanka, Malaysia and Singapore). It is one of the major Dravidian languages of South India, with records of its existence going back more than 2000 years. Tamil has about 62 million speakers in India.

A pronunciation tip: aw is pronounced as in 'law' and ow as in 'how'.

Basics

Hello.	வணக்கம்.	va·*nak*·kam
Goodbye.	போய் வருகிறேன்.	*po*·i va·*ru*·ki·reyn
Yes./No.	ஆமாம்./இல்லை.	aa·maam/*il*·lai
Excuse me.	தயவு செய்து.	ta·ya·*vu* sei·*du*
Sorry.	மன்னிக்கவும்.	*man*·nik·ka·vum
Please.	தயவு செய்து.	ta·ya·*vu* chey·*tu*
Thank you.	நன்றி.	*nan*·dri

How are you?
நீங்கள் நலமா?   neeng·kal na·*la*·maa

Fine, thanks. And you?
நலம், நன்றி.   na·*lam nan*·dri
நீங்கள்?   neeng·kal

What's your name?
உங்கள் பெயர் என்ன?   ung·kal pe·*yar* en·na

My name is ...
என் பெயர் ...   en pe·*yar* ...

WANT MORE?

For in-depth language information and handy phrases, check out Lonely Planet's *India Phrasebook*. You'll find it at **shop.lonelyplanet.com**, or you can buy Lonely Planet's iPhone phrasebooks at the Apple App Store.

Do you speak English?

நீங்கள் ஆங்கிலம் பேசுவீர்களா?		*neeng*·kal aang·ki·lam *pey*·chu·veer·ka·la

I don't understand.

எனக்கு வீளங்கவில்லை.		e·*nak*·ku vi·*lang*·ka·vil·*lai*

Accommodation

Where's a ... nearby?	அருகே ஒரு ... எங்கே உள்ளது?	a·ru·*ke* o·*ru* ... eng·ke ul·la·tu
guesthouse	விருந்தினர் இல்லம	vi·*run*·ti·nar il·lam
hotel	ஹோட்டல	*hot*·tal

Do you have a ... room?	உங்களிடம் ஓர் ... அறை உள்ளதா?	*ung*·ka·li·tam awr ... a·*rai* ul·la·taa
single	தன	ta·*ni*
double	இரட்டை	i·rat·*tai*

How much is it per ...?	ஓர் ... என்னவிலை?	awr ... en·na·vi·*lai*
night	இரவுக்கு	i·ra·*vuk*·ku
person	ஒருவருக்கு	o·ru·va·*ruk*·ku

bathroom	குளியலறை	ku·li·*ya*·la·rai
bed	படுக்கை	pa·*tuk*·kai
window	சன்னல	*chan*·nal

Directions

Where's the ...?

... எங்கே இருக்கிறது? ... eng·*key* i·*ruk*·ki·ra·tu

What's the address?

வீலாசம் என்ன? vi·*laa*·cham en·na

Can you show me (on the map)?

எனக்கு (வரைபடத்தில்) காட்ட முடியுமா? e·*nak*·ku (va·*rai*·pa·*tat*·til) *kaat*·ta mu·ti·yu·*maa*

How far is it?

எவ்வளவு தூரத்தில் இருக்கிறது? ev·va·la·vu too·*rat*·til i·*ruk*·ki·ra·tu

It's ...	அது இருப்பது ...	a·*tu* i·*rup*·pa·tu ...
behind ...	... க்குப் பின்னால	... kup *pin*·naal
in front of ...	... க்கு முன்னால	... ku *mun*·naal
near (to ...)	(... க்கு) அருகே	(... ku) a·ru·*key*
on the corner	ஓரத்தில	aw·*rat*·til
straight ahead	நேரடியாக முன்புறம்	*ney*·ra·di·*yaa*·ha *mun*·pu·ram

Turn ...	... புறத்தில் திருபுக.	pu·*rat*·til *ti*·rum·pu·ka
left	இடது	i·ta·*tu*
right	வலது	va·la·*tu*

Eating & Drinking

Can you recommend a ...?	நீங்கள் ஒரு ... பரிந்துரைக்க முடியுமா?	*neeng*·kal o·*ru* ... pa·rin·tu·*raik*·ka mu·ti·*yu*·maa
bar	பார்	paar
dish	உணவு வகை	u·na·*vu* va·*kai*
place to eat	உணவகம்	u·na·va·*ham*

I'd like (a/the) ..., please.	எனக்கு தயவு செய்து ... கொடுங்கள்.	e·*nak*·ku ta·ya·vu *chey*·tu ... ko·*tung*·kal
bill	வீலைச்சீட்டு	vi·*laich*·cheet·tu
menu	உணவுப்– பட்டியல்	u·na·*vup*· pat·ti·yal
that dish	அந்த உணவு வகை	an·ta u·na·*vu* va·*hai*

(cup of) coffee/tea ...	(கப்) காப்பி/ தேனீர் ...	(kap) *kaap*·pi/ *tey*·neer ...
with milk	பாலுடன்	paa·lu·*tan*
without sugar	சர்க்கரை இல்லாமல	*chark*·ka·rai· il·*laa*·mal

a bottle/ glass of ... wine	ஒரு பாட்டில்/ கிளாஸ ... வைன்	o·*ru* *paat*·til/ ki·*laas* ... vain
red	சிவப்பு	chi·*vap*·pu
white	வெள்ளை	*vel*·lai

Do you have vegetarian food?

உங்களிடம சைவ உணவு உள்ளதா? *ung*·ka·li·tam *chai*·va u·na·*vu* ul·la·taa

I'm allergic to (nuts).

எனக்கு (பருப்பு வகை) உணவு சேராது. e·*nak*·ku (pa·*rup*·pu va·*kai*) u·na·*vu* *chey*·raa·tu

beer	பீர்	peer
breakfast	காலை உணவு	kaa·*lai* u·na·*vu*
dinner	இரவு உணவு	i·ra·*vu* u·na·*vu*
drink	பானம்	paa·*nam*
fish	மீன்	meen
food	உணவு	u·na·*vu*
fruit	பழம்	pa·*zam*
juice	சாறு	chaa·*ru*
lunch	மதிய உணவு	ma·*ti*·ya u·na·*vu*
meat	இறைச்சி	i·*raich*·chi

milk	பால்	paal
soft drink	குளிர் பானம்	ku·*lir* paa·*nam*
vegetable	காய்கறி	*kai*·ka·ri
water	தண்ணீர்	*tan*·neyr

Emergencies

Help!	உதவ!	u·ta·vi
Go away!	போய் வீடு!	pow·i vi·tu

Call a doctor!
ஐ அழைக்கவும் / ஒரு மருத்துவர்! — i a·*zai*·ka·vum / o·*ru* ma·*rut*·tu·var

Call the police!
ஐ அழைக்கவும் / போலீஸ்! — i a·*zai*·ka·vum / pow·*lees*

I'm lost.
நான் வழி தவறி போய்விட்டேன். — naan va·*zi* ta·va·ri pow·i·*vit*·teyn

I have to use the phone.
நான் தொலைபேசியை பயன்படுத்த வேண்டும். — naan to·lai·pey·*chi*·yai pa·*yan*·pa·*tut*·ta veyn·*tum*

Where are the toilets?
கழிவறைகள் எங்கே? — ka·*zi*·va·rai·kal *eng*·key

Shopping & Services

Where's the market?
எங்கே சந்தை இருக்கிறது? — *eng*·key chan·tai i·*ruk*·ki·ra·tu

Can I look at it?
நான் இதைப் பார்க்கலாமா? — naan i·*taip* *paark*·ka·laa·maa

How much is it?
இது என்ன வீலை? — i·*tu* en·na vi·*lai*

That's too expensive.
அது அதிக வீலையாக இருக்கிறது. — a·*tu* a·*ti*·ka vi·*lai*·yaa·ka i·*ruk*·ki·ra·tu

There's a mistake in the bill.
இந்த வீலைச்சீட்டில் ஒரு தவறு இருக்கிறது. — *in*·ta vi·*laich*·cheet·til o·*ru* ta·va·ru i·*ruk*·ki·ra·tu

bank	வங்கி	vang·ki
internet	இணையம்	i·nai·*yam*
post office	தபால் நிலையம்	ta·*paal* ni·*lai*·yam
tourist office	சுற்றுப்பயண அலுவலகம்	chut·*rup*·pa·ya·na a·lu·va·la·*kam*

Numbers

1	ஒன்று	on·*dru*
2	இரண்டு	i·*ran*·tu
3	மூன்று	*moon*·dru
4	நான்கு	naan·*ku*
5	ஐந்து	ain·*tu*
6	ஆறு	aa·ru
7	ஏழு	ey·zu
8	எட்டு	et·*tu*
9	ஒன்பது	on·pa·*tu*
10	பத்து	pat·*tu*
20	இருபது	i·*ru*·pa·*tu*
30	முப்பது	mup·pa·*tu*
40	நாற்பது	naar·pa·*tu*
50	ஐம்பது	aim·pa·*tu*
60	அறுபது	a·*ru*·pa·*tu*
70	எழுபது	e·zu·pa·*tu*
80	எண்பது	en·pa·*tu*
90	தொன்னூறு	ton·noo·*ru*
100	நூறு	noo·ru
1000	ஓராயிரம்	aw·raa·yi·ram

Time & Dates

What time is it?
மணி என்ன? — ma·*ni* en·na

It's (two) o'clock.
மணி (இரண்டு). — ma·*ni* (i·ran·tu)

Half past (two).
(இரண்டு) முப்பது. — (i·*ran*·tu) mup·pa·*tu*

morning	காலை	kaa·*lai*
evening	மாலை	maa·*lai*
yesterday	நேற்று	*neyt*·tru
today	இன்று	in·*dru*
tomorrow	நாளை	naa·lai

Monday	திங்கள்	*ting*·kal
Tuesday	செவ்வாய்	chev·*vai*
Wednesday	புதன்	pu·*tan*
Thursday	வீயாழன்	vi·*yaa*·zan
Friday	வெள்ளி	vel·*li*
Saturday	சனி	cha·*ni*
Sunday	ஞாயிறு	*nyaa*·yi·ru

Transport

Is this the ... to (New Delhi)?
இது தானா (புது–டில்லிக்குப்) புறப்படும் ...? — i·*tu* taa·*naa* (pu·*tu*–til·lik·*kup*) pu·*rap*·pa·tum ...

bus	பஸ்	pas
plane	வீமானம்	vi·*maa*·nam
train	இரயில்	i·ra·*yil*

One ... ticket (to Madurai), please.	(மதுரைக்கு) தயவு செய்து ... டிக்கட் கொடுங்கள்.	(ma·tu·raik·ku) ta·ya·vu chey·tu ... tik·kat ko·tung·kal
one-way	ஒரு வழிப்பயணம்	o·ru va·zip·pa·ya·na
return	இரு வழிப்பயணம்	i·ru va·zip·pa·ya·na

What time's the first/last bus?
எத்தனை மணிக்கு முதல்/இறுதி பஸ் வரும்?
et·ta·nai ma·nik·ku mu·tal/i·ru·ti pas va·rum

How long does the trip take?
பயணம் எவ்வளவு நேரம் எடுக்கும்?
pa·ya·nam ev·va·la·vu ney·ram e·tuk·kum

How long will it be delayed?
எவ்வளவு நேரம் அது தாமதப்படும்?
ev·va·la·vu ney·ram a·tu taa·ma·tap·pa·tum

Please tell me when we get to (Ooty).
(ஊட்டிக்குப்) போனவுடன் தயவு செய்து எனக்குக கூறுங்கள்.
(oot·tik·kup) paw·na·vu·tan ta·ya·vu chey·tu e·nak·kuk koo·rung·kal

Please take me to (this address).
தயவு செய்து என்னை இந்த (வீலாசத்துக்குக) கொண்டு செல்லுங்கள்.
ta·ya·vu chey·tu en·nai in·ta (vi·laa·chat·tuk·kuk) kon·tu chel·lung·kal

Please stop/wait here.
தயவு செய்து இங்கே நிறுத்துங்கள்/ காத்திருங்கள்.
ta·ya·vu chey·tu ing·key ni·rut·tung·kal/ kaat·ti·rung·kal

I'd like to hire a car (with a driver).
நான் ஒரு மோட்டார் வண்டி (ஓர் ஓட்டுநருடன்) வாடகைக்கு எடுக்க விரும்புகிறேன்.
naan o·ru mowt·taar van·ti (awr aw·tu·na·ru·tan) vaa·ta·haik·ku e·tuk·ka vi·rum·pu·ki·reyn

Is this the road to (Mamallapuram)?
இது தான் (மாமல்லபுரத்துக்கு) செல்லும் சாலையா?
i·tu taan (maa·mal·la·pu·rat·tuk·ku) chel·lum chaa·lai·yaa

airport	வீமான நிலையம்	vi·maa·na ni·lai·yam
bicycle	சைக்கிள்	chaik·kil
boat	படகு	pa·ta·ku
bus stop	பஸ் நிறுத்தும்	pas ni·rut·tum
economy class	சிக்கன வகுப்பு	chik·ka·na va·kup·pu
first class	முதல் வகுப்பு	mu·tal va·kup·pu
motorcycle	மோட்டார் சைக்கிள்	mowt·taar chaik·kil
train station	நிலையம்	ni·lai·yam

KANNADA

Kannada is the official language of the state of Karnataka. It has 38 million speakers.

The symbol oh is pronounced as the 'o' in 'note' and ow as in 'how'.

Basics

Hello.	ನಮಸ್ಕಾರ.	na·mas·kaa·ra
Goodbye.	ಸಿಗೋಣ.	si·goh·na
Yes./No.	ಹೌದು./ಇಲ್ಲ.	how·du/il·la
Please.	ದಯವಿಟ್ಟು.	da·ya·vit·tu
Thank you.	ಥ್ಯಾಂಕ್ಯೂ.	t'ank·yoo
Excuse me.	ಸ್ವಲ್ಪ ದಾರಿ ಬಿಡಿ.	sval·pa daa·ri bi·di
Sorry.	ಕ್ಷಮಿಸಿ.	ksha·mi·si

What's your name?
ನಿಮ್ಮ ಹೆಸರೇನು?
nim·ma he·sa·rey·nu

My name is ...
ನನ್ನ ಹೆಸರು ...
nan·na he·sa·ru ...

Do you speak English?
ನೀವು ಇಂಗ್ಲೀಷ್ ಮಾತಾಡುತ್ತೀರಾ?
nee·vu ing·lee·shu maa·taa·dut·tee·ra

I don't understand.
ನನಗೆ ಅರ್ಥವಾಗುವುದಿಲ್ಲ.
na·na·ge ar·t'a·aa·gu·vu·dil·la

How much is it?
ಎಷ್ಟು ಇದು?
esh·tu i·du

Where are the toilets?
ಟಾಯ್ಲೆಟ್ಟುಗಳು ಎಲ್ಲಿ?
taay·let·tu·ga·lu el·li

Emergencies

Help!	ಸಹಾಯ ಮಾಡಿ!	sa·haa·ya maa·di
Go away!	ದೂರ ಹೋಗಿ!	doo·ra hoh·gi

Call ...!	... ಕಾಲ್ ಮಾಡಿ!	... kaal maa·di
a doctor	ಡಾಕ್ಟರಿಗೆ	daak·ta·ri·ge
the police	ಪೋಲೀಸಿಗೆ	poh·lee·si·ge

I have to use the phone.
ನಾನು ಫೋನು ಬಳಸಬೇಕು.
naa·nu foh·nu ba·la·sa·bey·ku

I'm lost.
ನಾನು ಕಳೆದುಹೋಗಿರುವೆ.
naa·nu ka·le·du·hoh·gi·ru·ve

Numbers

1	ಒಂದು	on·du
2	ಎರಡು	e·ra·du
3	ಮೂರು	moo·ru
4	ನಾಲ್ಕು	naa·ku
5	ಐದು	ai·du
6	ಆರು	aa·ru

7	ಎಳು	ey·lu
8	ಎಂಟು	en·tu
9	ಒಂಬತ್ತು	om·bat·tu
10	ಹತ್ತು	hat·tu
20	ಇಪ್ಪತ್ತು	ip·pat·tu
30	ಮೂವತ್ತು	moo·vat·tu
40	ನಲವತ್ತು	na·la·vat·tu
50	ಐವತ್ತು	ai·vat·tu
60	ಅರವತ್ತು	a·ra·vat·tu
70	ಎಪ್ಪತ್ತು	ep·pat·tu
80	ಎಂಬತ್ತು	em·bat·tu
90	ತೊಂಬತ್ತು	tom·bat·tu
100	ನೂರು	noo·ru
1000	ಗಾವಿರ	saa·vi·ra

KONKANI

Konkani is the official language of the state of Goa. It has 2.5 million speakers. The Devanagari script (also used to write Hindi and Marathi) is the official writing system for Konkani in Goa. However, many Konkani speakers in Karnataka use the Kannada script, as given in this section.

Pronounce eu as the 'u' in 'nurse', oh as the 'o' in 'note' and ts as in 'hats'.

Basics

Hello.	ಹಲ್ಲೋ.	hal·lo
Goodbye.	ಮೆಳ್ಯಾಂ.	mel·yaang
Yes./No.	ವ್ಹಯ್./ನಾಂ.	weu·i/naang
Please.	ಉಪ್ಕಾರ್ ಕರ್ನ್.	up·kaar keurn
Thank you.	ದೇವ್ ಬರೆಂ ಕರುಂ.	day·u bo·reng ko·roong
Excuse me.	ಉಪ್ಕಾರ್ ಕರ್ನ್.	up·kaar keurn
Sorry.	ಚೂಕ್ ಝಾಲಿ, ಮಾಫ್ ಕರ್.	ts'ook zaa·li maaf keur

What's your name?
ತುಜೆಂ ನಾಂವ್ ಕಿತೆಂ?   tu·jeng naang·ung ki·teng

My name is ...
ಮ್ಹಜೆಂ ನಾಂವ್ ...   m'eu·jeng naang·ung ...

Do you speak English?
ಇಂಗ್ಲಿಶ್ ಉಲೈತಾಯ್ಗೀ?   ing·leesh u·leuy·taay·gee

Do you understand?
ಸಮ್ಜಾಲೆಂಗೀ?   som·zaa·leng·gee

I understand.
ಸಮ್ಜಾಲೆಂ.   som·zaa·leng

I don't understand.
ನಾಂ, ಸಮ್ಜೊಂಕ್–ನಾಂ.   naang som·zonk·naang

How much is it?
ತಾಕಾ ಕಿತ್ಲೆ ಪೈಶೆ?   taa·kaa kit·le peuy·she

Where are the toilets?
ಟೊಯ್ಲೆಟ್ ಕೈಂಚೆರ್ ಆಸಾತ್?   toy·let k'eu·ing·ts'eur aa·saat

Emergencies

Help!	ಮ್ಹಾಕಾ ಕುಮಕ್ ಕರ್!	m'aa·kaa ku·meuk keur
Go away!	ವೆಸ್!	weuts'
Call ...!	... ಆಪೈ!	... aa·pai
a doctor	ದಾಕ್ಟೆರಾಕ್	daak·te·raak
the police	ಪೊಲಿಸಾಂಕ್	po·li·saank

I have to use the phone.
ಮ್ಹಾಕಾ ಫೊನಾಚಿ ಗರ್ಜ್ ಆಸಾ.   m'aa·kaa fo·na·chi g'eurz aa·saa

I'm lost.
ಮ್ಹಜೀ ವಾಟ್ ಚುಕ್ಲ್ಯಾ   m'eu·ji waat ts'uk·lyaa

Could you help me, please?
ಮ್ಹಾಕಾ ಇಲ್ಲ್ಯೊಚೊ ಉಪ್ಕಾರ್ ಕರ್ಶಿಗೀ?   m'aa·kaa il·lo·ts'o up·kaar keur·shi·gee

Numbers

1	ಏಕ್	ayk
2	ದೋನ್	dohn
3	ತೀನ್	teen
4	ಚಾರ್	chaar
5	ಪಾಂಚ್	paants'
6	ಸೊ	so
7	ಸಾತ್	saat
8	ಆಟ್	aat'
9	ನೋವ್	nohw
10	ಧಾ	d'aa
20	ವೀಸ್	wees
30	ತೀಸ್	tees
40	ಚಾಳೀಸ್	ts'aa·lees
50	ಪನ್ನಾಸ್	pon·naas
60	ಸಾಟ್	saat'
70	ಸತ್ತರ್	seut·teur
80	ಐಂಶಿಂ	euyng·shing
90	ನೊವ್ಪೋದ್	no·wod
100	ಶೆಂಭರ್	shem·bor
1000	ಹಜ್ಜಾರ್	ha·zaar

MALAYALAM

Malayalam is the official language of the state of Kerala. It has around 33 million speakers.

Note that zh is pronounced as the 's' in 'measure'.

Basics

Hello.	ഹലോ.	ha·*lo*
Goodbye.	ഗുഡ് ബൈ.	good bai
Yes.	അതെ.	a·*t'e*
No.	അല്ല.	al·*la*
Please.	ദയവായി.	da·ya·va·*yi*
Thank you.	നന്ദി.	nan·*n'i*
Excuse me.	ക്ഷമിക്കണം.	ksha·mi·ka·*nam*
Sorry.	ക്ഷമിക്കുക.	ksha·mi·ku·*ka*

Do you speak English?
നിങ്ങൾ ഇംഗ്ലീഷ് ning·*al* in·*glish*
സംസാരിക്കുമോ? sam·*saa*·ri·ku·*mo*

I don't understand.
എനിക്ക് മനസ്സിലാകില്ല. e·ni·*ku* ma·na·*si*·la·ki·la

What's your name?
താങ്കളുടെ പേര് t'ang·a·lu·*te* pey·ru
എന്താണ്? en·*t'aa*·nu

My name is ...
എന്റെ പേര് ... en·*te* pey·ru ...

How much is it?
എത്രയാണ് ഇതിന്? et'·ra·yaa·nu i·*t'i*·nu

Where are the toilets?
എവിടെയാണ് കക്കൂസ്? e·vi·de·yaa·*nu* ka·koo·*su*

Emergencies

Help!	സഹായിക്കൂ!	sa·ha·yi·*koo*
Go away!	ഇവിടുന്ന് പോകൂ!	i·vi·du·*nu* po·*koo*

Call ...!	... വിളിക്കൂ!	... vi·li·*koo*
a doctor	ഒരു ഡോക്ടറെ	o·ru dok·ta·*re*
the police	പൊലീസിനെ	po·li·si·*ne*

I have to use the phone.
എനിക്ക് ഈ ഫോൺ e·ni·*ku* ee fon
ഒന്നു വേണമായിരുന്നു. o·*nu* vey·na·maa·yi·ru·nu

I'm lost.
എനിക്ക് വഴി e·ni·*ku* va·zhi
അറിഞ്ഞുകൂട. a·ri·*nyu*·koo·da

Numbers

1	ഒന്ന്	*on*·na
2	രണ്ട്	*ran*·d'a
3	മൂന്ന്	*moo*·na
4	നാല്	*naa*·la
5	അഞ്ച്	*an*·ja
6	ആറ്	*aa*·ra
7	ഏഴ്	e·zha
8	എട്ട്	e·*t'a*
9	ഒമ്പത്	*on*·pa·t'a
10	പത്ത്	pa·*t'a*
20	ഇരുപത്	i·*ru*·pa·t'a
30	മുപ്പത്	*mu*·p'a·t'a
40	നാൽപത്	naal·*pa*·t'a
50	അമ്പത്	an·ba·*t'a*
60	അറുപത്	a·*ru*·pa·t'a
70	എഴുപത്	e·zhu·pa·*t'a*
80	എൺപത്	en·pa·*t'a*
90	തൊണ്ണൂറ്	t'on·*noo*·ra
100	നൂറ്	*n'oo*·ra
1000	ആയിരം	*aa*·ye·ram

MARATHI

Marathi is the official language of the state of Maharashtra. It is spoken by an estimated 71 million people. Marathi is written in the Devanagari script (also used for Hindi).

Keep in mind that oh is pronounced as the 'o' in 'note'.

Basics

Hello.	नमस्कार.	na·mas·*kaar*
Goodbye.	बाय.	bai
Yes.	होय.	hoy
No.	नाही.	naa·*hee*
Please.	कृपया.	kri·pa·*yaa*
Thank you.	धन्यवाद.	d'an·ya·*vaad*
Excuse me.	क्षमस्व.	ksha·mas·*va*
Sorry.	खेद आहे.	k'ed aa·*he*

What's your name?
आपले नांव ? aa·pa·*le* naa·*nav*

My name is ...
माझे नांव ... maa·*j'e* naa·*nav* ...

Do you speak English?
आपण इंग्रजी बोलता का? aa·*pan* ing·re·jee bol·*taa* kaa

I don't understand.
मला समजत नाही. ma·*laa* sam·*jat* naa·*hee*

How much is it?
याची काय किंमत आहे ? yaa·*chee* kaay ki·*mat* aa·he

Where are the toilets?
शौचालय कुठे आहे ? shoh·chaa·*lai* ku·t'e aa·he

Emergencies

Help!	मदत !	ma·*dat*
Go away!	दूर जा !	door jaa

Call ...!	कॉल करा ...!	kaal ka·raa ...
a doctor	डॉक्टरांना	dok·ta·raan·naa
the police	पोलिसांना	po·li·saa·naa

I have to use the phone.
मला फोन वापरायचा आहे. — ma·laa fon vaa·pa·raa·ya·chaa aa·he

I'm lost.
मी हरवले आहे. — mee ha·ra·va·le aa·he

Numbers

1	एक	ek
2	दोन	don
3	तीन	teen
4	चार	chaar
5	पाच	paach
6	सहा	sa·haa
7	सात	saat
8	आठ	aat'
9	नऊ	na·oo
10	दहा	da·haa
20	वीस	vees
30	तीस	tees
40	चाळीस	chaa·lees
50	पन्नास	pan·naas
60	साठ	saat'
70	सत्तर	sat·tar
80	ऐंशी	ain·shee
90	नव्वद	nav·vad
100	शंभर	sham·b'ar
1000	एक हजार	ek ha·jaar

TELUGU

Telugu is the official language of the states of Telengana and Andhra Pradesh. It has 70 million speakers.

Remember to pronounce oh as the 'o' in 'note'.

Basics

Hello.	నమస్కారం.	na·mas·kaa·ram
Goodbye.	వెళ్ళొస్తాను.	vel·loh·staa·nu
Yes./No.	అవును./కాదు.	a·vu·nu/kaa·du
Please.	దయచేసి.	da·ya·chay·si
Thank you.	ధన్యవాదాలు.	d'an·ya·vaa·daa·lu
Excuse me.	ఏమండి.	ay·an·di
Sorry.	క్షమించండి.	ksha·min·chan·di

What's your name?
మీపేరెంటి? — mee pay·rayn·ti

My name is ...
నా పేరు ... — naa pay·ru ...

Do you speak English?
మీరు ఇంగ్లీషు మాట్లాడుతారా? — mee·ru ing·lee·shu maat·laa·du·taa·raa

I don't understand.
అర్థం కాదు. — ar·t'am kaa·du

How much is it?
అది ఎంత? — a·di en·ta

Where are the toilets?
బాత్రూములు ఎక్కడ ఉన్నాయి? — baat·room·lu ek·ka·da un·naa·yi

Emergencies

| Help! | సహాయం కావాలి! | sa·haa·yam kaa·vaa·li |
| Go away! | వెళ్ళిపో! | vel·li·poh |

Call ...!	... పిలవండి!	... pi·la·van·di
a doctor	డాక్టర్ని	daak·tar·ni
the police	పోలీసుల్ని	poh·lee·sul·ni

I have to use the phone.
నేను ఫోను వాడుకోవాలి. — nay·nu p'oh·nu vaa·du·koh·vaa·li

I'm lost.
నేను దారి తప్పి పోయాను. — nay·nu daa·ri tap·pi poh·yaa·nu

Numbers

1	ఒకటి	oh·ka·ti
2	రెండు	ren·du
3	మూడు	moo·du
4	నాలుగు	naa·lu·gu
5	ఐదు	ai·du
6	ఆరు	aa·ru
7	ఏడు	ay·du
8	ఎనిమిది	e·ni·mi·di
9	తొమ్మిది	tohm·mi·di
10	పది	pa·di
20	ఇరవై	i·ra·vai
30	ముప్పై	mup·p'ai
40	నలబై	na·la·b'ai
50	యాభై	yaa·b'ai
60	అరవై	a·ra·vai
70	డెబ్బై	deb·b'ai
80	ఎనబై	e·na·b'ai
90	తొంబై	tohm·b'ai
100	వంద	van·da
1000	వెయ్యి	vey·yi

GLOSSARY

Adivasi – tribal person

Agni – major deity in the *Vedas*; mediator between men and the gods; also fire

ahimsa – discipline of non-violence

air-cooler – noisy water-filled cooling fan

Ananta – serpent on whose coils *Vishnu* reclined

apsara – heavenly nymph

Aryan – Sanskrit for 'noble'; those who migrated from Persia and settled in northern India

Ashoka – ruler in the 3rd century BC; responsible for spreading Buddhism throughout South India

ashram – spiritual community or retreat

autorickshaw – noisy, three-wheeled, motorised contraption for transporting passengers, livestock etc for short distances; found throughout the country, they are cheaper than taxis

avatar – incarnation, usually of a deity

ayurveda – the ancient and complex science of Indian herbal medicine and healing

azad – free (Urdu), as in Azad Jammu & Kashmir

baba – religious master or father; term of respect

bagh – garden

baksheesh – tip, donation (alms) or bribe

banyan – Indian fig tree; spiritual to many Indians

Bhagavad Gita – Hindu Song of the Divine One; *Krishna*'s lessons to *Arjuna*, the main thrust of which was to emphasise the philosophy of *bhakti*; it's part of the *Mahabharata*

bhajan – devotional song

bhakti – surrendering to the gods; faith

bhang – dried leaves and flowering shoots of the marijuana plant

bhavan – house, building; also spelt *bhawan*

BJP – Bharatiya Janata Party; political party

bodhisattva – literally 'one whose essence is perfected wisdom'; in Early Buddhism, bodhisattva refers only to the Buddha during the period between his conceiving the intention to strive for Buddhahood and the moment he attained it; in *Mahayana* Buddhism, it is one who renounces nirvana in order to help others attain it

Bollywood – India's answer to Hollywood; the film industry of Mumbai (Bombay)

Brahma – Hindu god; worshipped as the creator in the *Trimurti*

Brahmin – member of the priest/scholar caste, the highest Hindu caste

Buddha – Awakened One; the originator of Buddhism; also regarded by Hindus as the ninth incarnation of *Vishnu*

cantonment – administrative and military area of a Raj-era town

Carnatic music – classical music of South India

caste – a Hindu's hereditary station (social standing) in life; there are four castes: the *Brahmins*, the *Kshatriyas*, the *Vaishyas* and the *Shudras*; the Brahmins occupy the top spot

chaitya – Sanskrit form of 'cetiya', meaning shrine or object of worship; has come to mean temple, and more specifically, a hall divided into a central nave and two side aisles by a line of columns, with a votive *stupa* at the end

chappals – sandals or leather thonglike footwear; flip-flops

charas – resin of the marijuana plant; also referred to as 'hashish'

chital – spotted deer

choli – sari blouse

chowk – town square, intersection or marketplace

dagoba – see *stupa*

Dalit – preferred term for India's *Untouchable* caste

dargah – shrine or place of burial of a Muslim saint

darshan – offering or audience with someone; auspicious viewing of a deity

Deccan – meaning 'South', this refers to the central South Indian plateau

Devi – *Shiva*'s wife; goddess

dhaba – basic restaurant or snack bar; especially popular with truck drivers

dharamsala – pilgrims' rest house

dharma – for Hindus, the moral code of behaviour or social duty; for Buddhists, following the law of nature, or path, as taught by the Buddha

dhobi – person who washes clothes; commonly referred to as *dhobi-wallah*

dhobi ghat – place where clothes are washed by the *dhobi*

dhoti – like a *lungi*, but the ankle-length cloth is then pulled up between the legs; worn by men

dhurrie – rug

dowry – money and/or goods given by a bride's parents to their son-in-law's family; it's illegal but still exists in many arranged marriages

Dravidian – general term for the cultures and languages of the deep south of India, including Tamil, Malayalam, Telugu and Kannada

dupatta – long scarf for women often worn with the *salwar kameez*

durbar – royal court; also a government

Durga – the Inaccessible; a form of *Shiva*'s wife, *Devi*, a beautiful, fierce goddess riding a tiger/lion

filmi – slang term describing anything to do with Indian movies

Ganesh – Hindu god of good fortune and remover of obstacles; popular elephant-headed son of *Shiva* and *Parvati*, he is also known as Ganpati; his vehicle is a ratlike creature

Ganga – Hindu goddess representing the sacred Ganges River; said to flow from *Vishnu*'s toe

Garuda – man-bird vehicle of *Vishnu*

gaur – Indian bison

ghat – steps or landing on a river, range of hills, or road up hills

giri – hill

gopuram – soaring pyramidal gateway tower of *Dravidian* temples

gurdwara – Sikh temple

guru – holy teacher; in Sanskrit literally *goe* (darkness) and *roe* (to dispel)

Hanuman – Hindu monkey god, prominent in the *Ramayana*, and a follower of *Rama*

Indo-Saracenic – style of colonial architecture that integrated Western designs with Islamic, Hindu and Jain influences

Indra – significant and prestigious Vedic god; god of rain, thunder, lightning and war

Jagannath – Lord of the Universe; a form of *Krishna*

ji – honorific that can be added to the end of almost anything as a form of respect; thus 'Babaji', 'Gandhiji'

Kailasa – sacred Himalayan mountain; home of *Shiva*

kalamkari – designs painted on cloth using vegetable dyes

Kali – the ominous-looking evil-destroying form of *Devi*; commonly depicted with dark skin, dripping with blood, and wearing a necklace of skulls

kameez – woman's shirtlike tunic

Kannada – state language of Karnataka

karma – Hindu, Buddhist and Sikh principle of retributive justice for past deeds

khadi – homespun cloth; Mahatma Gandhi encouraged people to spin this rather than buy English cloth

Khan – Muslim honorific title

kolam – elaborate chalk, rice-paste or coloured powder design; also known as *rangoli*

Konkani – state language of Goa

Krishna – *Vishnu*'s eighth incarnation, often coloured blue; he revealed the *Bhagavad Gita* to *Arjuna*

Kshatriya – Hindu caste of soldiers or administrators; second in the caste hierarchy

kurta – long shirt with either short collar or no collar

lakh – 100,000

Lakshmana – half-brother and aide of *Rama* in the *Ramayana*

Lakshmi – *Vishnu*'s consort, Hindu goddess of wealth; she sprang forth from the ocean holding a lotus

lama – Tibetan Buddhist priest or monk

lingam – phallic symbol; auspicious symbol of *Shiva*; plural 'linga'

lungi – worn by men, this loose, coloured garment (similar to a sarong) is pleated at the waist to fit the wearer

maha – prefix meaning 'great'

Mahabharata – Great Hindu Vedic epic poem of the Bharata dynasty; containing approximately 10,000 verses describing the battle between the Pandavas and the Kauravas

mahal – house or palace

maharaja – literally 'great king'; princely ruler

mahatma – literally 'great soul'

Mahavir – last *tirthankar*

mahout – elephant rider or master

maidan – open (often grassed) area; parade ground

Malayalam – state language of Kerala

mandapa – pillared pavilion; a temple forechamber

mandir – temple

Maratha – central Indian people who controlled much of India at various times and fought the *Mughals* and *Rajputs*

marg – road

masjid – mosque

mehndi – henna; ornate henna designs on women's hands (and often feet), traditionally for certain festivals or ceremonies (eg marriage)

mela – fair or festival

moksha – liberation from samsara

mudra – ritual hand movements used in Hindu religious dancing; gesture of Buddha figure

Mughal – Muslim dynasty of subcontinental emperors from Babur to Aurangzeb

Naga – mythical serpentlike beings capable of changing into human form

namaste – traditional Hindu greeting (hello or goodbye), often accompanied by a respectful small bow with the hands together at the chest or head level

Nandi – bull, vehicle of *Shiva*

Narasimha – man-lion incarnation of *Vishnu*

Narayan – incarnation of *Vishnu* the creator

Nataraja – *Shiva* as the cosmic dancer

nizam – hereditary title of the rulers of Hyderabad

NRI – Non-Resident Indian

Om – sacred invocation representing the essence of the divine principle; for Buddhists, if repeated often enough with complete concentration, it leads to a state of emptiness

Parsi – adherent of the Zoroastrian faith

Partition – formal division of British India in 1947 into two separate countries, India and Pakistan

Parvati – a form of *Devi*

PCO – Public Call Office from where to make local, interstate and international phone calls

Pongal – Tamil harvest festival

pradesh – state

prasad – temple-blessed food offering

puja – literally 'respect'; offering or prayers

Puranas – set of 18 encyclopaedic Sanskrit stories, written in verse, relating to the three gods, dating from the 5th century AD

Radha – favourite mistress of *Krishna* when he lived as a cowherd

raga – any of several conventional patterns of melody and rhythm that form the basis for freely interpreted compositions

raj – rule or sovereignty; British Raj (sometimes just Raj) refers to British rule

raja – king; sometimes *rana*

Rajput – Hindu warrior caste, former rulers of northwestern India

Rama – seventh incarnation of *Vishnu*

Ramadan – the Islamic holy month of sunrise-to-sunset fasting (no eating, drinking or smoking); also referred to as Ramazan

Ramayana – the story of *Rama* and *Sita* and their conflict with *Ravana* is one of India's best-known epics

rana – king; sometimes *raja*

rangoli – see *kolam*

rani – female ruler or wife of a king

rathas – rock-cut *Dravidian* temples

rickshaw – small, two- or three-wheeled passenger vehicle

sadhu – ascetic, holy person; one who is trying to achieve enlightenment; often addressed as *swamiji* or *babaji*

sagar – lake, reservoir

sahib – respectful title applied to a gentleman

salwar – trousers usually worn with a *kameez*

salwar kameez – traditional dresslike tunic and trouser combination for women

sambar – deer

Sangam – ancient academy of Tamil literature; means literally 'the meeting of two hearts'

sangha – community of monks and nuns

Saraswati – wife of *Brahma*; goddess of learning; sits on a white swan

Sati – wife of *Shiva*; became a *sati* ('honourable woman') by immolating herself; although banned more than a century ago, the act of *sati* is still (very) occasionally performed

satyagraha – nonviolent protest involving a hunger strike, popularised by Mahatma Gandhi; from Sanskrit, literally meaning 'insistence on truth'

Scheduled Castes – official term used for the *Untouchables* or *Dalits*

shahadah – Muslim declaration of faith ('There is no God but Allah; Mohammed is his prophet')

Shaivite – follower of *Shiva*

Shakti – creative energies perceived as female deities; devotees follow Shaktism

Shiv Sena – Hindu nationalist political party

Shiva – the Destroyer; also the Creator, in which form he is worshipped as a lingam

Shivaji – great Maratha leader of the 17th century

shola – virgin forest

Shudra – caste of labourers

sikhara – Hindu temple-spire or temple

Sita – the Hindu goddess of agriculture; more commonly associated with the *Ramayana*

sitar – Indian stringed instrument

Sivaganga – water tank in temple dedicated to *Shiva*

stupa – Buddhist religious monument composed of a solid hemisphere topped by a spire, containing relics of the Buddha; also known as a *dagoba* or pagoda

Sufi – Muslim mystic

Surya – the sun; a major deity in the *Vedas*

swami – title of respect meaning 'lord of the self'; given to initiated Hindu monks

tabla – twin drums

Tamil – language of Tamil Nadu; people of *Dravidian* origin

tandava – *Shiva's* cosmic victory dance

tank – reservoir; pool or large receptacle of holy water found at some temples

tempo – noisy three-wheeler public-transport vehicle; bigger than an *autorickshaw*

tilak – auspicious forehead mark of devout Hindu men

tirthankars – the 24 great Jain teachers

tonga – two-wheeled horse or pony carriage

Trimurti – triple form; the Hindu triad of *Brahma*, *Shiva* and *Vishnu*

Untouchable – lowest caste or 'casteless', for whom the most menial tasks are reserved; the name derives from the belief that higher castes risk defilement if they touch one; now known as *Dalit*

Vaishya – member of the Hindu caste of merchants

Vedas – Hindu sacred books; collection of hymns composed in preclassical Sanskrit during the second millennium BC and divided into four books: Rig-Veda, Yajur-Veda, Sama-Veda and Atharva-Veda

vihara – Buddhist monastery, generally with central court or hall off which open residential cells, usually with a Buddha shrine at one end

vikram – *tempo* or a larger version of the standard *tempo*

vimana – principal part of Hindu temple; a tower over the sanctum

vipassana – the insight meditation technique of *Theravada* Buddhism in which mind and body are closely examined as changing phenomena

Vishnu – part of the *Trimurti*; Vishnu is the Preserver and Restorer who so far has nine *avatars*: the fish Matsya, the tortoise Kurma, the wild boar Naraha, *Narasimha*, Vamana, Parasurama, *Rama*, *Krishna* and *Buddha*

wallah – man; added onto almost anything, eg *dhobi*-wallah, chai-wallah, taxi-wallah

yali – mythical lion creature

yatra – pilgrimage

zenana – area of a home where women are secluded; women's quarters

Behind the Scenes

SEND US YOUR FEEDBACK

We love to hear from travellers – your comments keep us on our toes and help make our books better. Our well-travelled team reads every word on what you loved or loathed about this book. Although we cannot reply individually to postal submissions, we always guarantee that your feedback goes straight to the appropriate authors, in time for the next edition. Each person who sends us information is thanked in the next edition – the most useful submissions are rewarded with a selection of digital PDF chapters.

Visit **lonelyplanet.com/contact** to submit your updates and suggestions or to ask for help. Our award-winning website also features inspirational travel stories, news and discussions.

Note: We may edit, reproduce and incorporate your comments in Lonely Planet products such as guidebooks, websites and digital products, so let us know if you don't want your comments reproduced or your name acknowledged. For a copy of our privacy policy visit lonelyplanet.com/privacy.

OUR READERS

Many thanks to the travellers who used the last edition and wrote to us with helpful hints, useful advice and interesting anecdotes:

Anna Goetzke, Beatriz Castier, Bill Jenkins, Charlot Morgan, Coen van Hasselt, Gregory Buie, James Bayne, Joel Travelstead, Jérôme Leveque, Petra O'Neill, Rosanne Onrust

AUTHOR THANKS

John Noble

Thanks to everybody in South India who answered my questions, pointed me in the right direction and helped with the logistics of a fabulous trip, especially Jonty Rajagopalan and Ashish and Rucha Gupta. Thanks also to Abigail Blasi, whose work I drew on extensively for the front- and back-end chapters, DE Joe Bindloss, and all the rest of the fantastic India team, especially Isabella Noble with whom it was wonderful to share so much of this project.

Abigail Blasi

Thank you Joe Bindloss and Sarina Singh, CE and CA supreme, and to my wonderful co-authors. Thanks in Delhi to Sarah Fotheringham, to Nicolas Thompson and Danish Abbas, to Dilliwala Mayank Austen Soofi, to Rajinder and Surinder Budhraja, to Nirinjan and Jyoti Desai, my Delhi family, and to Luca for holding the fort.

Paul Harding

Thanks to Hannah and Layla for accompanying me to Goa and putting up with my absence while in Kerala. Cheers to Joe for entrusting me with such a great part of India. In India, thanks to all who offered advice and company but especially to all the friends in Goa and Kerala that I met up with again – you all know who you are!

Trent Holden

Thanks first up to Joe Bindloss for giving me the opportunity to work again on India – a seriously dream gig. As well as to my co-authors, especially Sarina for all the help and tips along the way. A shout out to all the good folk I met along the road and shared a beer with. But as always my biggest thanks goes to my beautiful girlfriend Kate, and my family and friends who I all miss back home in Melbourne.

Isabella Noble

Cheers to everyone who helped out in Tamil Nadu, Ashish and Rucha Gupta for endless hospitality, Bernard Dragon and Rom Whitaker, and Junaid Sait for saving the day when I forgot to book Ooty accommodation. Special thanks to fellow authors Abi and Sarina for girl support, and to Andrew for Pondy fun and keeping me sane in Trichy. At home, huge thanks to Jacky and Paps for the laughs and advice. Mostly, to Susan Forsyth, for being there always.

Iain Stewart

It was great to hang with Laksh in Bandra and have a virtual beer with Paul Harding by the sea. Thanks to the good folk at the MTDC all over the state, particularly Mr Shaker and Mrs Singh in Mumbai. I'm also very grateful to Aditya in Nagpur and Tadoba, Maria in Matheran and the merry musicians of Kolhapur.

ACKNOWLEDGMENTS

Climate map data adapted from Peel MC, Finlayson BL & McMahon TA (2007) 'Updated World Map of the Köppen-Geiger Climate Classification', *Hydrology and Earth System Sciences, 11, 163344*.

Illustration pp190-1 by Michael Weldon.

Cover photograph: Marigold flowers, Andhra Pradesh/Tim Gainey/Alamy.

BEHIND THE SCENES

THIS BOOK

This 8th edition of Lonely Planet's *South India & Kerala* guidebook was researched and written by John Noble, Abigail Blasi, Paul Harding, Trent Holden, Isabella Noble and Iain Stewart.

This guidebook was produced by the following:

Destination Editor
Joe Bindloss

Product Editors Kate Mathews, Alison Ridgway

Book Designer
Jessica Rose

Assisting Editors Nigel Chin, Samantha Forge, Paul Harding, Gabrielle Innes, Kate James, Elizabeth Jones, Katie O'Connell, Lauren O'Connell, Charlotte Orr, Kathryn Rowan, Tracy Whitmey

Cover Researcher
Naomi Parker

Thanks to Lonely Planet Cartography, Ellie Simpson, Tony Wheeler

Index

Map Legend

Sights

- Beach
- Bird Sanctuary
- Buddhist
- Castle/Palace
- Christian
- Confucian
- Hindu
- Islamic
- Jain
- Jewish
- Monument
- Museum/Gallery/Historic Building
- Ruin
- Shinto
- Sikh
- Taoist
- Winery/Vineyard
- Zoo/Wildlife Sanctuary
- Other Sight

Activities, Courses & Tours

- Bodysurfing
- Diving
- Canoeing/Kayaking
- Course/Tour
- Sento Hot Baths/Onsen
- Skiing
- Snorkelling
- Surfing
- Swimming/Pool
- Walking
- Windsurfing
- Other Activity

Sleeping

- Sleeping
- Camping

Eating

- Eating

Drinking & Nightlife

- Drinking & Nightlife
- Cafe

Entertainment

- Entertainment

Shopping

- Shopping

Information

- Bank
- Embassy/Consulate
- Hospital/Medical
- Internet
- Police
- Post Office
- Telephone
- Toilet
- Tourist Information
- Other Information

Geographic

- Beach
- Hut/Shelter
- Lighthouse
- Lookout
- Mountain/Volcano
- Oasis
- Park
- Pass
- Picnic Area
- Waterfall

Population

- Capital (National)
- Capital (State/Province)
- City/Large Town
- Town/Village

Transport

- Airport
- Border crossing
- Bus
- Cable car/Funicular
- Cycling
- Ferry
- Metro station
- Monorail
- Parking
- Petrol station
- Subway station
- Taxi
- Train station/Railway
- Tram
- Underground station
- Other Transport

Note: Not all symbols displayed above appear on the maps in this book

Routes

- Tollway
- Freeway
- Primary
- Secondary
- Tertiary
- Lane
- Unsealed road
- Road under construction
- Plaza/Mall
- Steps
- Tunnel
- Pedestrian overpass
- Walking Tour
- Walking Tour detour
- Path/Walking Trail

Boundaries

- International
- State/Province
- Disputed
- Regional/Suburb
- Marine Park
- Cliff
- Wall

Hydrography

- River, Creek
- Intermittent River
- Canal
- Water
- Dry/Salt/Intermittent Lake
- Reef

Areas

- Airport/Runway
- Beach/Desert
- Cemetery (Christian)
- Cemetery (Other)
- Glacier
- Mudflat
- Park/Forest
- Sight (Building)
- Sportsground
- Swamp/Mangrove

Isabella Noble

Tamil Nadu & Chennai Isabella's first experience of South India was a masala dosa at Shimla's Indian Coffee House. She has been travelling to India for over five years, but loves the ever-so-slightly more laid-back pace of the friendly South. This time she got lost in Valparai's tea plantations, checked out Chennai's countless bars, then got stuck in the Nilgiris thanks to landslide. Between trips, Isabella lives in London with a wardrobe of Indian shawls. She tweets @isabellamnoble.

Read more about Isabella at:
http://auth.lonelyplanet.com/profiles/isabellanoble

Iain Stewart

Mumbai (Bombay), Maharashtra Iain grew up in Leicester, a very Indian town transplanted to the Midlands, UK (complete with its own curry mile). He first visited India in 1991 and explored the sights at totally the wrong time of year with temperatures approaching 50°C in parts. For this trip he wised up and travelled post-monsoon: bar-hopping in Mumbai, meandering down the Konkan coast and having several near-misses with tigers in Tadoba.

OUR STORY

A beat-up old car, a few dollars in the pocket and a sense of adventure. In 1972 that's all Tony and Maureen Wheeler needed for the trip of a lifetime – across Europe and Asia overland to Australia. It took several months, and at the end – broke but inspired – they sat at their kitchen table writing and stapling together their first travel guide, *Across Asia on the Cheap*. Within a week they'd sold 1500 copies. Lonely Planet was born.

Today, Lonely Planet has offices in Franklin, London, Melbourne, Oakland, Beijing and Delhi, with more than 600 staff and writers. We share Tony's belief that 'a great guidebook should do three things: inform, educate and amuse'.

OUR WRITERS

John Noble

Coordinating Author, Telangana & Andhra Pradesh John, from England, has written about six different Indian states and 20-odd other countries for Lonely Planet. He first experienced South India in the 1980s when Chennai's Triplicane High Rd was clogged with bullock carts, and families milked their buffaloes beside it. Autorickshaws have replaced bullock carts now, but he loves returning to South India because, in a nutshell, there's never a dull moment there! As a long-time fan of William Dalrymple's *White Mughals*, John's biggest thrill of this trip was getting the chance to explore fascinating Hyderabad in depth. He wrote the Plan Your Trip and Understand sections and the Directory and Transport chapters. He tweets @john_a_noble and Instagrams as johnnoble11.

Read more about John at:
http://auth.lonelyplanet.com/profiles/ewoodrover

Abigail Blasi

Abigail fell in love with India on her first visit in 1994, and since then she's explored and written on India from north to south and back again. She's covered plenty of other places for Lonely Planet too, from Mauritania and Mali to Rome and Lisbon. Abigail wrote the Booking Trains, Scams, Women & Solo Travellers and Health chapters.

Paul Harding

Goa, Kerala Paul first landed in India in the mid-90s and has returned regularly over the years, usually writing about it. He still has a soft spot for the south, where the pace of life is slower, the food tastier and the beer (usually) colder. For this edition he was fortunate enough to return to Goa and Kerala where he researched beaches and backwaters, homestays and bamboo huts, seafood curries and chicken xacutis.

Trent Holden

Karnataka & Bengaluru, Andaman Islands On his third time co-authoring the *India* book, Trent was assigned with the not-so-shabby task of testing out Bengaluru's microbreweries, searching for tigers in Bandipur NP and checking out Hampi's ruins before hitting the beaches in Gokarna. He then returned to the Andaman Islands for more sun, surf and sand. A freelance travel writer based in London, Trent also covers destinations such as Nepal, Zimbabwe and Japan. In between travels he writes about food and music. You can catch him on Twitter @hombreholden.

OVER PAGE MORE WRITERS

Published by Lonely Planet Publications Pty Ltd
ABN 36 005 607 983
8th edition – October 2015
ISBN 978 1 74321 677 4
© Lonely Planet 2015   Photographs © as indicated 2015
10 9 8 7 6 5 4 3 2 1
Printed in Singapore

Although the authors and Lonely Planet have taken all reasonable care in preparing this book, we make no warranty about the accuracy or completeness of its content and, to the maximum extent permitted, disclaim all liability arising from its use.